Handbook of
FINANCIAL ECONOMETRICS

VOLUME 1

HANDBOOKS IN FINANCE

Series Editor

WILLIAM T. ZIEMBA

Handbook of
FINANCIAL ECONOMETRICS
Tools and Techniques

VOLUME 1

Edited by

YACINE AÏT-SAHALIA
Bendheim Center for Finance
Princeton University
Princeton, NJ

LARS PETER HANSEN
Department of Economics
The University of Chicago
Chicago, IL

ELSEVIER

Amsterdam • Boston • Heidelberg • London
New York • Oxford • Paris • San Diego
San Francisco • Singapore • Sydney • Tokyo
North-Holland is an imprint of Elsevier

N·H

North-Holland is an imprint of Elsevier
The Boulevard, Langford Lane, Kidlington, Oxford OX5 1GB, UK
Radarweg 29, PO Box 211, 1000 AE Amsterdam, The Netherlands

British Library Cataloguing in Publication Data
A catalogue record for this book is available from the British Library

Library of Congress Cataloging-in-Publication Data
Application submitted

ISBN: 978-0-444-50897-3

For information on all North-Holland publications
visit our website at *www.elsevierdirect.com*

Typeset by: diacriTech, India

Printed and bound in the United Kingdom
Transferred to Digital Printing, 2011

INTRODUCTION TO THE SERIES

Advisory Editors

Kenneth J. Arrow, Stanford University; George C. Constantinides, University of Chicago; B. Espen Eckbo, Dartmouth College; Harry M. Markowitz, University of California, San Diego; Robert C. Merton, Harvard University; Stewart C. Myers, Massachusetts Institute of Technology; Paul A. Samuelson, Massachusetts Institute of Technology; and William F. Sharpe, Stanford University.

The *Handbooks in Finance* are intended to be a definitive source for comprehensive and accessible information. Each volume in the series presents an accurate, self-contained survey of a subfield of finance, suitable for use by finance and economics professors and lecturers, professional researchers, and graduate students and as a teaching supplement. The goal is to have a broad group of outstanding volumes in various areas of finance.

William T. Ziemba
University of British Columbia

CONTENTS

CONTENTS

LIST OF CONTRIBUTORS

Yacine Aït-Sahalia
Department of Economics, Princeton University, Princeton, NJ

Torben G. Andersen
Department of Finance, Kellogg School of Management, Northwestern University, Evanston, IL; NBER, Cambridge, MA; and CREATES, Aarhus, Denmark

Federico M. Bandi
Carey Business School, Johns Hopkins University, Baltimore, MD

Bo M. Bibby
Institute of Mathematics and Physics, the Royal Veterinary and Agricultural University, Frederiksberg, Denmark

Tim Bollersley
Department of Economics, Duke University, Durham, NC; NBER, Cambridge, MA; and CREATES, Aarhus, Denmark

Michael W. Brandt
The Fuqua School of Business, Duke University, Durham, NC

Stephanie E. Curcuru
Board of Governors of the Federal Reserve System, Washington, DC

Francis X. Diebold
Department of Economics, University of Pennsylvania, Philadelphia, PA; and NBER, Cambridge, MA

Robert F. Engle
Stern School of Business, New York University, New York, NY

A. Ronald Gallant
The Fuqua School of Business, Duke University, Durham, NC

Rene Garcia
Département de Sciences Économiques, Université de Montréal CIREQ, Montréal, QC, Canada

Eric Ghysels
Department of Economics, University of North Carolina, Chapel Hill, NC

Christian Gourieroux
Department of Economics, University of Toronto, Toronto, ON, Canada

Lars Peter Hansen
Department of Economics, University of Chicago, Chicago, IL

John Heaton
Booth School of Business, University of Chicago, Chicago, IL

Martin Jacobsen
Department of Mathematical Sciences, University of Copenhagen, Denmark

Jean Jacod
Institut de Mathématiques de Jussieu, Université P. et M. Curie (Paris-6), Paris, France

Ravi Jagannathan
Department of Finance, Kellogg School of Management, Northwestern University, Evanston, IL

Joann Jasiak
Department of Economics, York University, Toronto, ON, Canada

Michael Johannes
Graduate School of Business, Columbia University, New York, NY

Martin Lettau
Haas School of Business, University of California at Berkeley, Berkeley, CA

Andrew Lo
Sloan School of Management, Massachusetts Institute of Technology, Cambridge, MA; and NBER, Cambridge, MA

Sidney C. Ludvigson
Department of Economics, New York University, New York, NY

Deborah Lucas
Kellogg School of Management, Northwestern University, Evanston, IL

Damien Moore
Congressional Budget Office, Washington, DC

Per A. Mykland
Department of Statistics, University of Chicago, Chicago, IL

Peter C. B. Phillips
Cowles Foundation for Research in Economics, Yale University, New Haven, CT

Monika Piazzesi
Department of Economics, Stanford University, Stanford, CA

Nicholas Polson
Booth School of Business, University of Chicago, Chicago, IL

Eric Renault
Department of Economics, University of North Carolina, Chapel Hill, NC

Jeffrey R. Russell
Booth School of Business, University of Chicago, Chicago, IL

Jose A. Scheinkman
Department of Economics, Princeton University, Princeton, NJ

Georgios Skoulakis
Department of Finance, R. H. Smith School of Business, University of Maryland, College Park, MD

Michael Sørensen
Department of Mathematical Sciences, University of Copenhagen, Denmark

George Tauchen
Department of Economics, Duke University, Durham, NC

Jiang Wang
Sloan School of Management, Massachusetts Institute of Technology, Cambridge, MA; NBER, Cambridge, MA

Zhenyu Wang
Federal Reserve Bank of New York, New York, NY

CHAPTER 1

Operator Methods for Continuous-Time Markov Processes

Yacine Aït-Sahalia*, Lars Peter Hansen,** *and* **José A. Scheinkman***

*Department of Economics, Princeton University, Princeton, NJ

**Department of Economics, The University of Chicago, Chicago, IL

Contents

Abstract

This chapter surveys relevant tools, based on operator methods, to describe the evolution in time of continuous-time stochastic process, over different time horizons. Applications include modeling the long-run stationary distribution of the process, modeling the short or intermediate run transition dynamics of the process, estimating parametric models via maximum-likelihood, implications of the spectral decomposition of the generator, and various observable implications and tests of the characteristics of the process.

Keywords: Markov process; Infinitesimal Generator; Spectral decomposition; Transition density; Maximum-Likelihood; Stationary density; Long-run.

1. INTRODUCTION

Our chapter surveys a set of mathematical and statistical tools that are valuable in understanding and characterizing nonlinear Markov processes. Such processes are used extensively as building blocks in economics and finance. In these literatures, typically the local evolution or short-run transition is specified. We concentrate on the continuous limit in which case it is the instantaneous transition that is specified. In understanding the implications of such a modeling approach we show how to infer the intermediate and long-run properties from the short-run dynamics. To accomplish this, we describe operator methods and their use in conjunction with continuous-time stochastic process models.

Operator methods begin with a local characterization of the Markov process dynamics. This local specification takes the form of an *infinitesimal generator*. The infinitesimal generator is itself an operator mapping test functions into other functions. From the infinitesimal generator, we construct a family (semigroup) of conditional expectation operators. The operators exploit the time-invariant Markov structure. Each operator in this family is indexed by the forecast horizon, the interval of time between the information set used for prediction and the object that is being predicted. Operator methods allow us to ascertain global, and in particular, long-run implications from the local or infinitesimal evolution. These global implications are reflected in (a) the implied stationary distribution, (b) the analysis of the eigenfunctions of the generator that dominate in the long run, and (c) the construction of likelihood expansions and other estimating equations.

The methods we describe in this chapter are designed to show how global and long-run implications follow from local characterizations of the time series evolution. This connection between local and global properties is particularly challenging for nonlinear time series models. Despite this complexity, the Markov structure makes characterizations of the dynamic evolution tractable. In addition to facilitating the study of a given Markov process, operator methods provide characterizations of the observable implications of potentially rich families of such processes. These methods can be incorporated into statistical estimation and testing. Although many Markov processes used in practice are formally misspecificied, operator methods are useful in exploring the specific nature and consequences of this misspecification.

Section 2 describes the underlying mathematical methods and notation. Section 3 studies Markov models through their implied stationary distributions. Section 4 develops some operator methods used to characterize transition dynamics including long-run behavior of Markov process. Section 5 provides approximations to transition densities that are designed to support econometric estimation. Section 6 describes the properties of some parameter estimators. Finally, Section 7 investigates alternative ways to characterize the observable implications of various Markov models, and to test those implications.

2. ALTERNATIVE WAYS TO MODEL A CONTINUOUS-TIME MARKOV PROCESS

There are several different but essentially equivalent ways to parameterize continuous time Markov processes, each leading naturally to a distinct estimation strategy. In this section, we briefly describe five possible parametrizations.

2.1. Transition Functions

In what follows, $(\Omega, \mathcal{F}, Pr)$ will denote a probability space, S a locally compact metric space with a countable basis, $\mathcal{S}$ a σ-field of Borelians in S, I an interval of the real line, and for each $t \in I$, $X_t : (\Omega, \mathcal{F}, Pr) \to (S, \mathcal{S})$ a measurable function. We will refer to $(S, \mathcal{S})$ as the state space and to X as a stochastic process.

Definition 1 $P : (S \times \mathcal{S}) \to [0, 1)$ *is a transition probability if, for each* $x \in S$, $P(x, \cdot)$ *is a probability measure in* $\mathcal{S}$, *and for each* $B \in \mathcal{S}$, $P(\cdot, B)$ *is measurable.*

Definition 2 *A transition function is a family* $P_{s,t}$, $(s, t) \in I^2$, $s < t$ *that satisfies for each* $s < t < u$ *the Chapman–Kolmogorov equation:*

$$P_{s,u}(x, B) = \int P_{t,u}(y, B) P_{s,t}(x, dy).$$

A transition function is time homogeneous if $P_{s,t} = P_{s',t'}$ *whenever* $t - s = t' - s'$. *In this case we write* P_{t-s} *instead of* $P_{s,t}$.

Definition 3 *Let $\mathcal{F}_t \subset \mathcal{F}$ be an increasing family of σ-algebras, and X a stochastic process that is adapted to $\mathcal{F}_t$. X is Markov with transition function $P_{s,t}$ if for each nonnegative Borel measurable $\phi : S \to \mathbb{R}$ and each $(s,t) \in I^2$, $s < t$,*

$$E[\phi(X_t)|\mathcal{F}_s] = \int \phi(y) P_{s,t}(X_s, \mathrm{d}y).$$

The following standard result (for example, Revuz and Yor, 1991; Chapter 3, Theorem 1.5) allows one to parameterize Markov processes using transition functions.

Theorem 1 *Given a transition function $P_{s,t}$ on $(S, \mathcal{S})$ and a probability measure Q_0 on $(S, \mathcal{S})$, there exists a unique probability measure Pr on $\left(S^{[0,\infty)}, \mathcal{S}^{[0,\infty)}\right)$, such that the coordinate process X is Markov with respect to $\sigma(X_u, u \le t)$, with transition function $P_{s,t}$ and the distribution of X_0 given by Q_0.*

We will interchangeably call transition function the measure $P_{s,t}$ or its conditional density p (subject to regularity conditions which guarantee its existence):

$$P_{s,t}(x, \mathrm{d}y) = p(y, t|x, s)\mathrm{d}y.$$

In the time homogenous case, we write $\Delta = t - s$ and $p(y|x, \Delta)$. In the remainder of this chapter, unless explicitly stated, we will treat only the case of time homogeneity.

2.2. Semigroup of Conditional Expectations

Let P_t be a homogeneous transition function and L be a vector space of real-valued functions such that for each $\phi \in L$, $\int \phi(y) P_t(x, \mathrm{d}y) \in L$. For each t define the conditional expectation operator

$$\mathcal{T}_t\phi(x) = \int \phi(y) P_t(x, \mathrm{d}y). \tag{2.1}$$

The Chapman–Kolmogorov equation guarantees that the linear operators $\mathcal{T}_t$ satisfy:

$$\mathcal{T}_{t+s} = \mathcal{T}_t \mathcal{T}_s. \tag{2.2}$$

This suggests another parameterization for Markov processes. Let $(L, \|\cdot\|)$ be a Banach space.

Definition 4 *A one-parameter family of linear operators in L, $\{\mathcal{T}_t : t \ge 0\}$ is called a semigroup if (a) $\mathcal{T}_0 = I$ and (b) $\mathcal{T}_{t+s} = \mathcal{T}_t\mathcal{T}_s$ for all $s, t \ge 0$. $\{\mathcal{T}_t : t \ge 0\}$ is a strongly continuous contraction semigroup if, in addition, (c) $\lim_{t \downarrow 0} \mathcal{T}_t\phi = \phi$, and (d) $||\mathcal{T}_t|| \le 1$.*

If a semigroup represents conditional expectations, then it must be positive, that is, if $\phi \ge 0$ then $\mathcal{T}_t\phi \ge 0$.

Two useful examples of Banach spaces L to use in this context are as follows:

Example 1 *Let S be a locally compact and separable state space. Let $L = C_0$ be the space of continuous functions $\phi : S \to \mathbb{R}$, that vanish at infinity. For $\phi \in C_0$ define:*

$$\|\phi\|_\infty = \sup_{x \in S} |\phi(x)|.$$

A strongly continuous contraction positive semigroup on C_0 is called a Feller semigroup.

Example 2 *Let Q be a measure on a locally compact subset S of $\mathbb{R}^m$. Let $L^2(Q)$ be the space of all Borel measurable functions $\phi : S \to \mathbb{R}$ that are square integrable with respect to the measure Q endowed with the norm:*

$$\|\phi\|_2 = \left(\int \phi^2 \mathrm{d}Q \right)^{\frac{1}{2}}.$$

In general, the semigroup of conditional expectations determine the finite-dimensional distributions of the Markov process (see e.g. Ethier and Kurtz, 1986; Proposition 1.6 of Chapter 4.) There are also many results (e.g. Revuz and Yor, 1991; Proposition 2.2 of Chapter 3) concerning whether given a contraction semigroup one can construct a homogeneous transition function such that Eq. (2.1) is satisfied.

2.3. Infinitesimal Generators

Definition 5 *The infinitesimal generator of a semigroup $\mathcal{T}_t$ on a Banach space L is the (possibly unbounded) linear operator $\mathcal{A}$ defined by:*

$$\mathcal{A}\phi = \lim_{t \downarrow 0} \frac{\mathcal{T}_t \phi - \phi}{t}.$$

The domain $D(\mathcal{A})$ is the subspace of L for which this limit exists.

If $\mathcal{T}_t$ is a strongly continuous contraction semigroup then $D(\mathcal{A})$ is dense. In addition $\mathcal{A}$ is closed, that is if $\phi_n \in D(\mathcal{A})$ converges to ϕ and $\mathcal{A}\phi_n$ converges to ψ then $\phi \in D(\mathcal{A})$ and $\mathcal{A}\phi = \psi$. If $\mathcal{T}_t$ is a strongly continuous contraction semigroup, we can reconstruct $\mathcal{T}_t$ using its infinitesimal generator $\mathcal{A}$ (e.g. Ethier and Kurtz, 1986; Proposition 2.7 of Chapter 2). This suggests using $\mathcal{A}$ to parameterize the Markov process. The Hille–Yosida theorem (e.g. Ethier and Kurtz, 1986; Theorem 2.6 of Chapter 1) gives necessary and sufficient conditions for a linear operator to be the generator of a strongly continuous, positive contraction semigroup. Necessary and sufficient conditions to ensure that the semigroup can be interpreted as a semigroup of conditional expectations are also known (e.g. Ethier and Kurtz, 1986; Theorem 2.2 of Chapter 4).

As described in Example 1, a possible domain for a semigroup is the space C_0 of continuous functions vanishing at infinity on a locally compact state space endowed with the sup-norm. A process is called a multivariate diffusion if its generator $\mathcal{A}_d$ is an extension of the second-order differential operator:

$$\mu \cdot \frac{\partial \phi}{\partial x} + \frac{1}{2}\text{trace}\left(\nu \frac{\partial^2 \phi}{\partial x \partial x'}\right) \tag{2.3}$$

where the domain of this second-order differential operator is restricted to the space of twice continuously differentiable functions with a compact support. The $\mathbb{R}^m$-valued function μ is called the drift of the process and the positive semidefinite matrix-valued function ν is the diffusion matrix. The generator for a Markov jump process is:

$$\mathcal{A}_p \phi = \lambda(\mathcal{J}\phi - \phi)$$

on the entire space C_0, where λ is a nonnegative function of the Markov state used to model the jump intensity and $\mathcal{J}$ is the expectation operator for a conditional distribution that assigns probability zero to staying put.

Markov processes may have more complex generators. Revuz and Yor (1991) show that for a certain class of Markov processes the generator can be depicted in the following manner.[1] Consider a positive conditional Radon measure $R(dy|x)$ on the product space X excluding the point $\{x\}$[2]

$$\int_{X-\{x\}} \frac{|x-y|^2}{1+|x-y|^2} R(dy|x) < \infty.$$

The generator is then an extension of the following operator defined for twice differentiable functions with compact support:

$$\begin{aligned} \mathcal{A}\phi(x) = \mu(x) \cdot \frac{\partial \phi(x)}{\partial x} &+ \int \left[\phi(y) - \phi(x) - \frac{y-x}{1+|y-x|^2} \cdot \frac{\partial \phi(x)}{\partial x}\right] R(dy|x) \\ &+ \frac{1}{2}\text{trace}\left(\nu(x) \frac{\partial^2 \phi}{\partial x \partial x'}\right). \end{aligned} \tag{2.4}$$

The measure $R(dy|x)$ may be infinite to allow for an infinite number of arbitrarily small jumps in an interval near the current state x. With this representation, $\mathcal{A}$ is the generator of a pure jump process when $R(dy|x)$ is finite for all x,

$$\mu(x) \cdot \frac{\partial \phi(x)}{\partial x} = \frac{y-x}{1+|y-x|^2} \cdot \frac{\partial \phi(x)}{\partial x} R(dy|x),$$

and $\nu = 0$.

[1] See Theorem 1.13 of Chapter 7.

[2] A Radon measure is a Borel measure that assigns finite measure to every compact subset of the state space and strictly positive measure to nonempty open sets.

When the measure $R(dy|x)$ is finite for all x, the Poisson intensity parameter is:

$$\lambda(x) = \int R(dy|x),$$

which governs the frequency of the jumps. The probability distribution conditioned on the state x and a jump occurring is: $R(dy|x)/\int R(dy|x)$. This conditional distribution can be used to construct the conditional expectation operator $\mathcal{J}$ via:

$$\mathcal{J}\phi = \frac{\int \phi(y)R(dy|x)}{\int R(dy|x)}.$$

The generator may also include a level term $-\iota(x)\phi(x)$. This level term is added to allow for the so-called killing probabilities, the probability that the Markov process is terminated at some future date. The term ι is nonnegative and gives the probabilistic instantaneous termination rate.

It is typically difficult to completely characterize $D(\mathcal{A})$ and instead one parameterizes the generator on a subset of its domain that is "big enough." As the generator is not necessarily continuous, one cannot simply parameterize the generator in a dense subset of its domain. Instead one uses a *core*, that is a subspace $N \subset D(\mathcal{A})$ such that $(N, \mathcal{A}N)$ is dense in the graph of $\mathcal{A}$.

2.4. Quadratic Forms

Suppose $L = L^2(Q)$ where we have the natural inner product

$$< \phi, \psi >= \int \phi(x)\psi(x)dQ.$$

If $\phi \in \mathcal{D}(\mathcal{A})$ and $\psi \in L^2(Q)$ then we may define the (quadratic) form

$$f_2(\phi, \psi) = - < \mathcal{A}\phi, \psi > .$$

This leads to another way of parameterizing Markov processes. Instead of writing down a generator one starts with a quadratic form. As in the case of a generator it is typically not easy to fully characterize the domain of the form. For this reason one starts by defining a form on a smaller space and showing that it can be extended to a closed form in a subset of $L^2(Q)$. When the Markov process can be initialized to be stationary, the measure Q is typically this stationary distribution. More generally, Q does not have to be a finite measure.

This approach to Markov processes was pioneered by Beurling and Deny (1958) and Fukushima (1971) for symmetric Markov processes. In this case both the operator $\mathcal{A}$ and the form f are symmetric. A stationary, symmetric Markov process is *time-reversible*.

If time were reversed, the transition operators would remain the same. On the other hand, multivariate standard Brownian motion is a symmetric (nonstationary) Markov process that is not time reversible. The literature on modeling Markov processes with forms has been extended to the nonsymmetric case by Ma and Rockner (1991). In the case of a symmetric diffusion, the form is given by:

$$f_2(\phi, \psi) = \frac{1}{2}\int (\nabla\phi)^* \nu(\nabla\psi) \mathrm{d}Q,$$

where $*$ is used to denote transposition, ∇ is used to denote the (weak) gradient[3], and the measure Q is assumed to be absolutely continuous with respect to the Lebesgue measure. The matrix ν can be interpreted as the diffusion coefficient. When Q is a probability measure, it is a stationary distribution. For standard Brownian motion, Q is the Lebesgue measure and ν is the identity matrix.

2.5. Stochastic Differential Equations

Another way to generate (homogeneous) Markov processes is to consider solutions to time autonomous stochastic differential equations. Here we start with an n-dimensional Brownian motion on a probability space $(\Omega, \mathcal{F}, Pr)$, and consider $\{\mathcal{F}_t : t \geq 0\}$, the (augmented) filtration generated by the Brownian motion. The process X_t is assumed to satisfy the stochastic differential equation

$$\mathrm{d}X_t = \mu(X_t)\mathrm{d}t + \sigma(X_t)\mathrm{d}W_t, \tag{2.5}$$

X_0 given.

Several theorems exist that guarantee that the solution to Eq. (2.5) exists, is unique, and is a Markov diffusion. In this case the coefficients of (2.5) are related to those of the second-order differential operator (2.3) via the formula $\nu = \sigma\sigma'$.

2.6. Extensions

We consider two extensions or adaptations of Markov process models, each with an explicit motivation from finance.

2.6.1. Time Deformation

Models with random time changes are common in finance. There are at least two ways to motivate such models. One formulation due to Bochner (1960) and Clark (1973) posits a distinction between calendar time and economic time. The random time changes are used to alter the flow of information in a random way. Alternatively, an econometrician might confront a data set with random sample times. Operator methods give a tractable way of modeling randomness of these types.

[3]That is, $\int \nabla\phi\psi = \int \phi\psi'$ for every ψ continuously differentiable and with a compact support.

A model of random time changes requires that we specify two objects. An underlying Markov process $\{X_t : t \geq 0\}$ that is not subject to distortions in the time scale. For our purposes, this process is modeled using a generator $\mathcal{A}$. In addition, we introduce a process $\{\tau_t\}$ for the time scale. This process is increasing and can be specified in continuous time as $\{\tau_t : t \geq 0\}$. The process of interest is:

$$Z_t = X_{\tau_t}. \tag{2.6}$$

Clark (1973) refers to $\{\tau_t\}$ as the *directing process* and the process $\{X_t\}$ is *subordinated* to the directing process in the construction of $\{Z_t\}$. For applications with random sampling, we let $\{\tau_j : j = 1, 2, \ldots\}$ to be a sequence of sampling dates with observations $\{Z_j : j = 1, 2, \ldots\}$. In what follows we consider two related constructions of the constructed process $\{Z_t : t \geq 0\}$.

Our first example is in which the time distortion is smooth, with τ_t expressible as a simple integral over time.

Example 3 *Following Ethier and Kurtz (1986), consider a process specified recursively in terms of two objects: a generator $\mathcal{A}$ of a Markov process $\{X_t\}$ and a nonnegative continuous function ζ used to distort calendar time. The process that interests us satisfies the equation:*

$$Z_t = X_{\int_0^t \zeta(Z_s)ds}.$$

In this construction, we think of

$$\tau_t = \int_0^t \zeta(Z_s)\, ds$$

as the random distortion in the time of the process we observe. Using the time distortion we may write:

$$Z_t = X_{\tau_t},$$

as in (2.6).

This construction allows for dependence between the directing process and the underlying process $\{X_t\}$. By construction the directing process has increments that depend on Z_t. Ethier and Kurtz (1986) show that under some additional regularity conditions, the continuous-time process $\{Z_t\}$ is itself Markovian with generator $\zeta\mathcal{A}$ (see Theorem 1.4 on page 309). Since the time derivative of τ_t is $\zeta(Z_t)$, this scaling of the generator is to be expected. In the case of a Markov diffusion process, the drift μ and the diffusion matrix ν are both scaled by the function ζ of the Markov state. In the case of a Markov jump process, ζ alters the jump frequency by scaling the intensity parameter.

Our next example results in a discrete-time process.

Example 4 *Consider next a specification suggested by Duffie and Glynn (2004). Following Clark (1973), they use a Poisson specification of the directing process. In contrast to Clark (1973), suppose the Poisson intensity parameter is state dependent. Thus consider an underlying continuous time process* $\{(X_t, Y_t)\}$ *where* Y_t *is a process that jumps by one unit where the jump times are dictated by an intensity function* $\lambda(X_t)$. *Let*

$$\tau_j = \inf\{t : Y_t \geq j\},$$

and construct the observed process as:

$$Z_t = X_{\tau_j}.$$

There is an alternative construction of this process that leads naturally to the computation of the one period conditional expectation operator. First, construct a continuous time process as in Example 3 by setting $\zeta = \frac{1}{\lambda}$. We then know that the resulting process $\{\check{Z}_t\}$ has generator $\check{\mathcal{A}} \doteq \zeta\mathcal{A} = \frac{1}{\lambda}\mathcal{A}$. In addition to this smooth time distortion, suppose we sample the process using a Poisson scheme with a unit intensity. Notice that:

$$E\left[\int_0^\infty \exp(-t)\psi(\check{Z}_t)dt|\check{Z}_0 = z\right] = \left(\int_0^\infty \exp\left[\left(\check{\mathcal{A}} - \mathcal{I}\right)t\right]dt\right)\psi(z) = (\mathcal{I} - \check{\mathcal{A}})^{-1}\psi(z),$$

where $\mathcal{I}$ is the identity operator. Thus, $(\mathcal{I} - \check{\mathcal{A}})^{-1}$ is a conditional expectation operator that we may use to represent the discrete time process of Duffie and Glynn.

2.6.2. Semigroup Pricing

Rogers (1997), Lewis (1998), Darolles and Laurent (2000), Linetsky (2004), Boyarchenko and Levendorskii (2007), and Hansen and Scheinkman (2009) develop semigroup theory for Markov pricing. In their framework, a semigroup is a family of operators that assigns prices today to payoffs that are functions of the Markov state in the future. Like semigroups for Markov processes, the Markov pricing semigroup has a generator.

Darolles and Laurent (2000) apply semigroup theory and associated eigenfunction expansions to approximate asset payoffs and prices under the familiar *risk neutral probability distribution*. Although risk neutral probabilities give a convenient way to link pricing operators to conditional expectation operators, this device abstracts from the role of interest rate variations as a source of price fluctuations. Including a state-dependent instantaneous risk-free rate alters pricing in the medium and long term in a nontrivial way. The inclusion of a interest rate adds a level term to the generator. That is, the generator $\mathcal{B}$ for a pricing semigroup can be depicted as:

$$\mathcal{B}\phi = \mathcal{A} - \iota\phi.$$

where $\mathcal{A}$ has the form given in representation (2.4) and ι is the instantaneous risk-free rate.

As we mentioned earlier, a level term is present in the generator depiction given in Revuz and Yor (1991) (Theorem 1.13 of Chapter 7). For pricing problems, since ι is an interest rate it can sometimes be negative. Rogers (1997) suggests convenient parameterizations of pricing semigroups for interest rate and exchange rate models. Linetsky (2004) and Boyarchenko and Levendorskii (2007) characterize the spectral or eigenfunction structure for some specific models, and use these methods to approximate prices of various fixed income securities and derivative claims on these securities.

3. PARAMETRIZATIONS OF THE STATIONARY DISTRIBUTION: CALIBRATING THE LONG RUN

Over a century ago, Pearson (1894) sought to fit flexible models of densities using tractable estimation methods. This led to a method-of-moments approach, an approach that was subsequently criticized by Fisher (1921) on the grounds of statistical efficiency. Fisher (1921) showed that Pearson's estimation method was inefficient relative to maximum likelihood estimation. Nevertheless there has remained a considerable interest in Pearson's family of densities. Wong (1964) provided a diffusion interpretation for members of the Pearson family by producing low-order polynomial models of the drift and diffusion coefficient with stationary densities in the Pearson family. He used operator methods to produce expansions of the transition densities for the processes and hence to characterize the implied dynamics. Wong (1964) is an important precursor to the work that we describe in this and subsequent sections. We begin by generalizing his use of stationary densities to motivate continuous-time models, and we revisit the Fisher (1921) criticism of method-of-moments estimation.

We investigate this approach because modeling in economics and finance often begins with an idea of a target density obtained from empirical observations. Examples are the literature on city sizes, income distribution, and the behavior of exchange rates in the presence of bands. In much of this literature, one guesses transition dynamics that might work and then checks this guess. Mathematically speaking, this is an inverse problem and is often amenable to formal analysis. As we will see, the *inverse* mapping from stationary densities to the implied transitions or local dynamics can be solved after we specify certain features of the infinitesimal evolution. Wong's analysis (Wong, 1964) is a good illustration in which this inverse mapping is transparent. We describe extensions of Wong's approach that exploit the mapping between the infinitesimal coefficients (μ, σ^2) and the stationary distributions for diffusions.

3.1. Wong's Polynomial Models

To match the Pearson family of densities, Wong (1964) studied the solutions to the stochastic differential equation:

$$dX_t = \varrho_1(X_t)dt + \varrho_2(X_t)^{\frac{1}{2}}dW_t$$

where $\{X_t\}$ is a scalar diffusion process and $\{W_t\}$ is a scalar Brownian motion. The polynomial ϱ_1 used to model the drift coefficient is first order and the polynomial ϱ_2 used to model the diffusion coefficient is no more than second order. Using arguments we sketch in the following section, the stationary density q for this process satisfies the differential equation:

$$(\ln q)' = \frac{2\varrho_1 - \varrho_2'}{\varrho_2} \tag{3.1}$$

where $'$ denotes differentiation with respect to the state. The logarithmic derivative of the density is the ratio of a first-order to a second-order polynomial as required by Pearson (1894). When the density is restricted to the nonnegative real numbers, we may add a boundary condition that requires the process to reflect at zero.

Wong (1964) identified the diffusion coefficient ϱ_2 up to scale as the denominator of $(\ln q)'$ expressed as the ratio of polynomials in reduced form. Given ϱ_2 the polynomial ϱ_1 can be constructed from the pair $((\ln q)', \varrho_2)$ using formula (3.1). In Section 3.2, we will discuss generalizations of this identification scheme.

Wong (1964) went on to characterize and interpret the stochastic processes whose densities reside in the Pearson class. Many of the resulting processes have been used in economics and finance.

Example 5 *When ϱ_1 has a negative slope and ϱ_2 is a positive constant, the implied density is normal and the resulting process is the familiar* Ornstein–Uhlenbeck *process. This process has been used to model interest rates and volatility. Vasicek (1977) features this process in his construction of an equilibrium model of the real term structure of interest rates.*

Example 6 *When ϱ_1 has a negative slope and ϱ_2 is linear with a positive slope, the implied density is gamma and the resulting process is the* Feller *square-root process. Sometimes zero is an attracting barrier, and to obtain the gamma distribution requires the process to reflect at zero. Cox et al. (1985) feature the Feller square root process in their model of the term structure of interest rates.*

Example 7 *When ϱ_1 has a negative slope and ϱ_2 is proportional to x^2, the stationary density has algebraic tails. This specification is used as a model of volatility and as a model of size distribution. In particular, Nelson (1990) derives this model as the continuous-time limit of the volatility evolution for a GARCH(1,1) model. Nelson (1990) uses the fat (algebraic) tail of the stationary distribution to capture volatility clustering over time.*

Example 8 *A limiting case of this example also gives a version of Zipf's law. (See Rapoport, 1978; for a nice historical discussion.) Consider a density of the form:* $q \propto x^{-2}$ *defined on* (y, ∞) *for* $y > 0$*. Notice that the probability of being greater than some value x is proportional to* x^{-1}*. This density satisfies the differential equation:*

$$\frac{\mathrm{d} \ln q(x)}{\mathrm{d}x} = -\frac{2}{x}.$$

Zipf's law fits remarkably well the distribution of city sizes. For example, see Auerbach (1913) and Eaton and Eckstein (1997).

Restrict $\varrho_2(x) \propto x^2$*. In the context of cities this means that the variance of growth rates is independent of city sizes, which is a reasonable approximation for the data in Japan 1965–1985 and France 1911–1990 discussed in Eaton and Eckstein (1997). (See also Gabaix, 1999.) Formula (3.1) implies that*

$$(\ln q)' + (\ln \varrho_2)' = \frac{2\varrho_1}{\varrho_2} = 0.$$

Thus the drift is zero and the process is a stationary local martingale. The boundary y is an attracting barrier, which we assume to be reflexive. We will have more to say about this process after we develop spectral tools used in a more refined study of the dynamics.

The density $q \propto x^{-2}$ *has a mode at the left boundary y. For the corresponding diffusion model, y is a reflecting barrier. Zipf's law is typically a statement about the density for large x, however. Thus we could let the left boundary be at zero (instead of* $y > 0$*) and set* ϱ_1 *to a positive constant. The implied density behaves like a constant multiple of* x^{-2} *in the right tail, but the zero boundary will not be attainable. The resulting density has an interior mode at one-half times the constant value of* ϱ_1*. This density remains within the Pearson family.*

Example 9 *When* ϱ_1 *is a negative constant and* ϱ_2 *is a positive constant, the stationary density is exponential and the process is a Brownian motion with a negative drift and a reflecting barrier at zero. This process is related to the one used to produce Zipf's law. Consider the density of the logarithm of x. The Zipf's law implied stationary distribution of* $\ln x$ *is exponential translated by* $\ln y$*. When the diffusion coefficient is constant, say* α^2*, the drift of* $\ln x$ *is* $-\frac{\alpha^2}{2}$*.*

The Wong (1964) analysis is very nice because it provides a rather complete characterization of the transition dynamics of the alternative processes investigated. Subsequently, we will describe some of the *spectral* or *eigenfunction* characterizations of dynamic evolution used by Wong (1964) and others. It is the ability to characterize the transition dynamics fully that has made the processes studied by Wong (1964) valuable building blocks for models in economics and finance. Nevertheless, it is often convenient to move outside this family of models.

Within the Pearson class, $(\ln q)'$ can only have one interior zero. Thus stationary densities must have at most one interior mode. To build diffusion processes with multimodal densities, Cobb et al. (1983) consider models in which ϱ_1 or ϱ_2 can be higher-order polynomials. Since Zipf's law is arguably about tail properties of a density, nonlinear drift specifications (specifications of ϱ_1) are compatible with this law. Chan et al. (1992) consider models of short-term interest rates in which the drift remains linear, but the diffusion coefficient is some power of x other than linear or quadratic. They treat the volatility elasticity as a free parameter to be estimated and a focal point of their investigation. Aït-Sahalia (1996b) compares the constant volatility elasticity model to other volatility specifications, also allowing for a nonlinear drift. Conley et al. (1997) study the constant volatility elasticity model but allowing for drift nonlinearity. Jones (2003) uses constant volatility elasticity models to extend Nelson's (Nelson, 1990) model of the dynamic evolution of volatility.

3.2. Stationary Distributions

To generalize the approach of Wong (1964), we study how to go from the infinitesimal generator to the stationary distribution. Given a generator $\mathcal{A}$ of a Feller process, we can deduce an integral equation for the stationary distribution. This formula is given by:

$$\lim_{\tau \downarrow 0} \int \frac{\mathcal{T}_\tau \phi - \phi}{\tau} \mathrm{d}Q = \int \mathcal{A}\phi \mathrm{d}Q = 0, \tag{3.2}$$

for *test functions* ϕ in the domain of the generator. (In fact the collection of functions used to check this condition can be reduced to a smaller collection of functions called the *core* of the generator. See Ethier and Kurtz, 1986; for a discussion.)

Integral equation (3.2) gives rise to the differential equation used by Wong (1964) [see (3.1)] and others. Consider test functions ϕ that are twice continuously differentiable and have zero derivatives at the boundaries of the scalar state space. Write the integral equation

$$\int \left(\mu\phi' + \frac{1}{2}\sigma^2\phi'' \right) q = 0.$$

Using integration by parts once, we see that

$$\int \left[\mu q - \frac{1}{2}(\sigma^2 q)' \right] \phi' = 0.$$

Given the flexibility of our choice of ϕ', it follows that

$$\mu q - \frac{1}{2}(\sigma^2 q)' = 0. \tag{3.3}$$

From this equation, we may solve for μ as a function of (q, σ^2) or for q'/q as a function of (μ, σ^2). Alternatively, integrating as in Aït-Sahalia (1996a), we may solve for σ^2 as a function of (μ, q).

Equation (3.3) has a multivariate counterpart used in our treatment of Markov diffusion processes using quadratic forms. Suppose that there is an m-dimensional Markov state, an m-dimensional drift vector μ that is consistent with a given smooth stationary density q and a diffusion matrix $\nu = [\nu_{ij}]$ has component j given by:

$$\mu_j q = \frac{1}{2} \sum_{i=1}^{m} \frac{\partial(\nu_{ij} q)}{\partial y_i}.$$

This choice of μ is not unique, however. As discussed by Chen et al. (2008), it is the unique *symmetric* solution where symmetry is defined in terms of quadratic forms. We will have more to say about this parameterization subsequently.

3.3. Fitting the Stationary Distribution

In applied research in macroeconomics and international economics, motivation for parameter choice and model selection is sometimes based on whether they produce reasonable steady-state implications. An analysis like that envisioned by Wong (1964) is germane to this estimation problem. A Wong (1964)-type approach goes beyond the fascination of macroeconomists with deterministic steady states and considers the entire steady state distribution under uncertainty. Although Wong (1964) produced diffusion models that imply prespecified densities, it is also straightforward to infer or estimate densities from parameterized diffusion models.

We now consider the problem of fitting an identified model of a generator to the stationary distribution. By calibrating to the implied stationary density and ignoring information about transitions, we may gain some robustness to model misspecification. Of course, we will also lose statistical efficiency and may also fail to identify features of the dynamic evolution. From a statistical standpoint, the entire joint distribution of the data should be informative for making inferences about parameters. A misspecified model may, however, continue to imply correct marginal distributions. Knowledge of this implication is valuable information to a model-builder even if the joint distributions are misspecified.

Initially we allow jump processes, diffusion processes, and mixtures, although we will subsequently specialize our discussion to diffusion models. Hansen and Scheinkman (1995) use Eq. (3.2) to produce estimating equations. Their idea is to parameterize the generator and use the empirical distribution of the data to estimate unknown parameters. That is, consider a family of generators $\mathcal{A}_b$ parameterized by b. Given time series data $\{x_t\}$ and a family of test functions,

$$E\left[\mathcal{A}_\beta \phi(x_t)\right] = 0, \tag{3.4}$$

for a finite set of test functions where β is the parameter vector for the Markov model used to generate the data. This can be posed as a generalized-method-of-moments (GMM) estimation problem of the form studied by Hansen (1982).

Two questions arise in applying this approach. Can the parameter β in fact be identified? Can such an estimator be efficient? To answer the first question in the affirmative often requires that we limit the parameterization. We may address Fisher's (Fisher, 1921) concerns about statistical efficiency by looking over a rich (infinite-dimensional) family of test functions using characterizations provided in Hansen (1985). Even if we assume a finite dimensional parametrization, statistical efficiency is still not attained because this method ignores information on transition densities. Nevertheless, we may consider a more limited notion of efficiency because our aim is to fit only the stationary distribution.

In some analyses of Markov process models of stationary densities, it is sometimes natural to think of the data as being draws from independent stochastic processes with the same stationary density. This is the case for many applications of Zipf's law. This view is also taken by Cobb et al. (1983). We now consider the case in which data were obtained from a single stochastic process. The analysis is greatly simplified by assuming a continuous-time record of the Markov process between date zero and T. We use a central limit approximation as the horizon T becomes large. From Bhattacharya (1982) or Hansen and Scheinkman (1995) we know that

$$\frac{1}{\sqrt{T}} \int_0^T \mathcal{A}_\beta \phi \Rightarrow \text{Normal}(0, -2 < \mathcal{A}_\beta \phi | \phi >), \tag{3.5}$$

where $\Rightarrow$ denotes convergence in distribution, and

$$< \mathcal{A}_\beta \phi | \phi > \doteq \int \phi \left(\mathcal{A}_\beta \phi \right) \mathrm{d}Q,$$

for ϕ in the $L^2(Q)$ domain of $\mathcal{A}_\beta$. This central limit approximation is a refinement of (3.4) and uses an explicit martingale approximation. It avoids having to first demonstrate mixing properties.

Using this continuous-time martingale approximation, we may revisit Fisher's (Fisher, 1921) critique of Pearson (1894). Consider the special case of a scalar stationary diffusion. Fisher (1921) noted that Pearson's (Pearson, 1894) estimation method was inefficient, because his moment conditions differed from those implicit in maximum likelihood estimation. Pearson (1894) shunned such methods because they were harder to implement in practice. Of course computational costs have been dramatically reduced since the time of this discussion. What is interesting is that when the data come from (a finite interval of) a single realization of a scalar diffusion, then the analysis of efficiency is altered. As shown by Conley et al. (1997), instead of using the score vector for building moment conditions the score vector could be used as test functions in relation (3.4).

To use this approach in practice, we need a simple way to compute the requisite derivatives. The score vector for a scalar parameterization is:

$$\phi = \frac{\mathrm{d}\ln q_b}{\mathrm{d}b}(\beta).$$

Recall that what enters the moment conditions are test function first and second derivatives (with respect to the state). That is, we must know ϕ' and ϕ'', but not ϕ. Thus we need not ever compute $\ln q$ as a function of b. Instead we may use the formula:

$$\ln q_b{}' = \frac{2\mu_b}{\sigma_b^2} - \ln \sigma_b^{2\prime}$$

to compute derivatives with respect to the unknown parameters. Even though the score depends on the true parameter, it suffices to use test functions that are depicted in terms of b instead of β. Asymptotic efficiency will be preserved.

While formally the efficient test function construction uses an assumption of a continuous-time record, the resulting estimator will remain "approximately" efficient when discrete-time samples are used to approximate the estimation equations. For a formal characterization of statistical efficiency of estimators constructed using only information about the stationary distribution for a discrete-time Markov process see Kessler et al. (2001); but in this case the implementation is typically more complicated.[4] Finally, Aït-Sahalia and Mykland (2008) compare estimators of the type proposed by Hansen and Scheinkman (1995) and Conley et al. (1997) to maximum likelihood counterparts. They find that such an approach can produce credible estimators of the drift coefficient for a given diffusion coefficient.

While statistical efficiency presumes a correct specification, any misspecification that leaves intact the parameterized model of the stationary density will remain consistent under ergodicity and some mild regularity assumptions. Checking whether a model fits the stationary density for some set of parameters is an interesting question in its own right. One possible approach is to add test functions aimed at specific features of the stationary distribution to obtain an additional set of over-identifying restrictions. Following Bierens (1990), such a method could be refined using an ever enlarging collection of test functions as the sample size is increased, but the practical impact of this observation seems limited.

An alternative comprehensive comparison of a parametric density estimator can be made to a nonparametric estimator to obtain a specification test. Consider the following comparison criterion:

$$\int (q_b - q)^2 q\omega \tag{3.6}$$

[4]For an earlier and closely related discussion that focuses on sampled diffusions, see Kessler (2000) and for additional discussion, see Bibby et al. (2010).

where q is the true density of the data and ω a weighting function.[5] Instead of constructing a small number of test functions that feature specific aspects of the distribution, a researcher specifies the weighting function ω that dictates which ranges of data receive more emphasis in the statistical test. By design, objective (3.6) is zero only when q_b and q coincide for some admissible value of b. As before, a parameterization of q_b can be inferred from a parameterization of the generator $\mathcal{A}$. The implied model of the stationary density is parameterized correctly when the objective is zero for some choice of b. Aït-Sahalia (1996b) uses this to devise a statistical test for misspecification of the stationary density.

Following Aït-Sahalia (1996b), the density q can be estimated consistently from discrete-time data using nonparametric methods. The parameter b can be estimated using the method previously described or by minimizing the sample-counterpart to (3.6). Aït-Sahalia (1996b) derives the limiting distribution of the resulting test statistic and applies this method to test models of the short-term interest rate process.[6] One challenge facing such nonparametric tests is producing accurate small sample distributions. The convergence to the asymptotic distribution obtained by assuming stationarity of the process can be slow when the data are highly persistent, as is the case with US interest rates. (See Pritsker, 1998; Conley et al., 1999.)

3.4. Nonparametric Methods for Inferring Drift or Diffusion Coefficients

Recall that for a scalar diffusion, the drift coefficient can be inferred from a stationary density, the diffusion coefficient and their derivatives. Alternatively the diffusion coefficient can be deduced from the density and the drift coefficient. These functional relationships give rise to nonparametric estimation methods for the drift coefficient or the diffusion coefficient. In this section, we describe how to use local parametrizations of the drift or the diffusion coefficient to obtain nonparametric estimates. The parameterizations become localized by their use of test functions or kernels familiar from the literature on nonparametric estimation. The local approaches for constructing estimators of μ or σ^2 estimate nonparametrically one piece (μ or σ^2) given an estimate of the other piece.

In the framework of test functions, these estimation methods can be viewed as follows. In the case of a scalar diffusion,

$$\int \left(\mu\phi' + \frac{1}{2}\sigma^2\phi'' \right) q = 0. \tag{3.7}$$

Construct a test function ϕ such that ϕ' is zero everywhere except in the vicinity of some prespecified point y. The function ϕ' can be thought of as a kernel and its localization

[5]Distance measures other than this L^2 weighted norm can be used, such as an entropy measure.

[6]See Section 6.4 and Aït-Sahalia (1996b) for an analogous test based on transition densities.

can be governed by the choice of a bandwidth. As in Banon (1978), suppose that the diffusion coefficient is known. We can construct a locally constant estimator of μ that is very close to Banon's (Banon, 1978) estimator by solving the sample counterpart to (3.7) under the possibly false assumption that μ is constant. The local specification of ϕ' limits the range over which constancy of μ is a good approximation, and the method produces a local estimator of μ at the point y. This method is easily extended to other local parametrizations of the drift. Conley et al. (1997) introduce a local linear estimator using two local test functions to identify the level and the slope of the linear approximation. Using logic closely related to that of Florens-Zmirou (1984), these local estimators sometimes can presumably be justified when the integrability of q is replaced by a weaker recurrence assumption.

Suppose that a linear function is in the domain of the generator. Then

$$\int \mu q = 0. \tag{3.8}$$

We may now localize the parameterization of the diffusion coefficient by localizing the choice of ϕ''. The specific construction of ϕ' from ϕ'' is not essential because moment condition (3.8) is satisfied. For instance, when ϕ'' is scaled appropriately to be a density function, we may choose ϕ' to be its corresponding distribution function. Applying integration by parts to (3.7), we obtain

$$\int_l^r \mu(x)\phi'(x)q(x)\mathrm{d}x = \int_l^r \left[\int_x^r \mu q\right]\phi''(x)\mathrm{d}x,$$

provided that the localization function ϕ'' has support in the interior of the state space (l, r). By localizing the parameterization of the diffusion coefficient at x, the limiting version of (3.7) is:

$$\int_x^r \mu q + \frac{\sigma^2(x)q(x)}{2} = 0.$$

Using (3.8), we then obtain the diffusion recovery formula derived in Aït-Sahalia (1996a).

$$\sigma^2(x) = \frac{2}{q(x)}\int_l^x \mu(u)q(u)\mathrm{d}u. \tag{3.9}$$

For a given estimator of μ, an estimator of σ^2 can be based directly on recovery formula (3.9) as in Aït-Sahalia (1996a) or using a locally constant estimator obtained by solving the sample counterpart to (3.7). Not surprisingly, the two approaches turn out to be very similar.

The local approaches for constructing estimators of μ or σ^2 require knowledge of estimates of the other piece. Suppose we parameterize μ as in Aït-Sahalia (1996a) to be affine in the state variable, $\mu(x) = -\kappa(x - \alpha)$, and a linear function is in the domain of the generator, then

$$\mathcal{A}(x - \alpha) = -\kappa(x - \alpha).$$

This says that $x - \alpha$ is an eigenfunction of $\mathcal{A}$, with eigenvalue $-\kappa$. We shall have more to say about eigenfunctions and eigenvalues in Section 4. The conditional expectation operator for any interval t must have the same eigenfunction and an eigenvalue given via the exponential formula:

$$\mathcal{T}_t x = E\left[X_t | X_0\right] = \alpha + e^{-\kappa t}\left(X_0 - \alpha\right). \tag{3.10}$$

This conditional moment condition applies for any $t > 0$. As a consequence, (α, κ) can be recovered by estimating a first-order scalar autoregression via least squares for data sampled at any interval $t = \Delta$. Following Aït-Sahalia (1996a), the implied drift estimator may be plugged into formula (3.9) to produce a semiparameteric estimator of $\sigma^2(x)$. Since (3.10) does not require that the time interval be small, this estimator of $\sigma^2(x)$ can be computed from data sampled at any time interval Δ, not just small ones.

As an alternative, Conley et al. (1997) produce a semiparameteric estimator by adopting a constant volatility elasticity specification of the diffusion coefficient, while letting the drift be nonparametric. The volatility elasticity is identified using an additional set of moment conditions derived in Section 6.4 applicable for some subordinated diffusion models. Subordinated Markov processes will be developed in Section 6.7.

We will have more to say about observable implications including nonparametric identification in Section 6.

4. TRANSITION DYNAMICS AND SPECTRAL DECOMPOSITION

We use quadratic forms and eigenfunctions to produce decompositions of both the stationary distribution and the dynamic evolution of the process. These decompositions show what features of the time series dominate in the long run and, more generally, give decompositions of the transient dynamics. Although the stationary density gives one notion of the *long run*, transition distributions are essential to understanding the full dynamic implications of nonlinear Markov models. Moreover, stationary distributions are typically not sufficient to identify all of the parameters of interest. We follow Wong (1964) by characterizing transition dynamics using a *spectral decomposition*. This decomposition is analogous to the spectral or principal component decomposition of a symmetric matrix. As we are interested in nonlinear dynamics, we develop a functional counterpart to principal component analysis.

4.1. Quadratic Forms and Implied Generators

Previously, we demonstrated that a scalar diffusion can be constructed using a density q and a diffusion coefficient σ^2. By using quadratic forms described in Section 2, we may extend this construction to a broader class of Markov process models. The form construction allows us to define a nonlinear version of principal components.

Let Q be a Radon measure on the state space X. For the time being this measure need not be finite, although we will subsequently add this restriction. When Q is finite, after normalization it will be the stationary distribution of the corresponding Markov process. We consider two positive semidefinite quadratic forms on the space of functions $L^2(Q)$. One is given by the usual inner product:

$$f_1(\phi, \psi) \doteq <\phi, \psi> = \int \phi\psi \mathrm{d}Q.$$

This form is *symmetric* $[f_1(\phi, \psi) = f_1(\psi, \phi)]$ and *positive semidefinite* $(f_1(\phi, \phi) \geq 0)$.

The second form is constructed from two objects: (a) a state dependent positive semidefinite matrix ν and (b) a symmetric, positive Radon measure R on the product space $X \times X$ excluding the diagonal $D \doteq \{(x, x) : x \in X\}$ with

$$\int_{X\times X-D} \frac{|x-y|^2}{1+|x-y|^2} R(\mathrm{d}x, \mathrm{d}y) < \infty.$$

It is given by:

$$f_2(\phi, \psi) \doteq \frac{1}{2}\int (\nabla\phi)^* \nu(\nabla\psi)\mathrm{d}Q + \frac{1}{2}\int [\phi(y) - \phi(x)][\psi(y) - \psi(x)]R(\mathrm{d}x, \mathrm{d}y)$$

where $*$ is used to denote transposition.[7] The form f_2 is well-defined at least on the space C_K^2 of twice continuously differentiable functions with compact support. Under additional regularity conditions, the form f_2 is closable, that is, it has a closed extension in $L^2(Q)$.[8] However, even this extension has a limited domain. Like f_1, the form f_2 is also symmetric and positive semidefinite. Notice that f_2 is the sum of two forms. As we will see, the first is associated with a diffusion process and the second with a jump process.[9]

4.1.1. Implied Generator

We may now follow the approach of Beurling and Deny (1958) and Fukushima (1971) by constructing a Markov process associated with the form f_1 and the closed extension

[7] We may use weak gradients in the construction of f_2.

[8] For instance, if Q has density q, and q and ν are continuously differentiable, then the form f_2 is closable.

[9] In fact there exist generalizations of this representation in which ν is replaced by a matrix-valued measure, and an additional term $\int \phi(x)\psi(x)\mathrm{d}k(x)$ is introduced where k is a *killing* measure. See Beurling and Deny (1958) and Fukushima et al. (1994).

of f_2. In what follows we will sketch only part of this construction. We describe how to go from the forms f_1 and f_2 to an implied generator. The generator $\mathcal{A}$ is the symmetric solution to:

$$f_2(\phi, \psi) = -f_1[(\mathcal{A}\phi), \psi] = -\int (\mathcal{A}\phi)\psi \mathrm{d}Q. \tag{4.1}$$

Since f_2 is a positive semidefinite form, $\mathcal{A}$ is a negative semidefinite operator.

We explore this construction for each of the two components of f_2 separately. Suppose initially that R is identically zero and write $\mathcal{A}_{\mathrm{d}}$ for the corresponding generator. Then

$$f_2(\phi, \psi) \doteq \frac{1}{2}\int (\nabla\phi)^* \nu (\nabla\psi) q \tag{4.2}$$

where q is the density of Q. Applying an integration-by-parts argument to (4.2) shows that $\mathcal{A}_{\mathrm{d}}$ can be depicted as a second-order differential operator on the space C_K^2 of twice continuously differentiable functions with compact support:

$$\mathcal{A}_{\mathrm{d}}\phi = \frac{1}{2}\sum_{i,j} \nu_{ij}\frac{\partial^2\phi}{\partial y_i \partial y_j} + \frac{1}{2q}\sum_{i,j}\frac{\partial(q\nu_{ij})}{\partial y_i}\frac{\partial\phi}{\partial y_j}$$

provided that both q and ν are continuously differentiable.[10] In this formula, we set ν_{ij} to be the (i,j) element of the matrix ν. Moreover, the implicit drift is

$$\mu_j = \frac{1}{2q}\sum_{i=1}^{m}\frac{\partial(\nu_{ij}q)}{\partial y_i}. \tag{4.3}$$

This gives us a multivariate extension to the idea of parameterizing a Markov diffusion process in terms of a density q and the diffusion matrix ν, with the drift being implicit.

Next suppose that ν is identically zero, and again assume that Q has a density q. Write:

$$\begin{aligned} f_2(\phi, \psi) &= \frac{1}{2}\int [\phi(y) - \phi(x)]\,[\psi(y) - \psi(x)]\, R(\mathrm{d}x, \mathrm{d}y) \\ &= -\frac{1}{2}\int [\phi(y) - \phi(x)]\,\psi(x)\frac{R(\mathrm{d}x, \mathrm{d}y)}{q(x)}q(x)\mathrm{d}x + \frac{1}{2}\int [\phi(y) - \phi(x)]\,\psi(y) R(\mathrm{d}x, \mathrm{d}y) \\ &= -\int [\phi(y) - \phi(x)]\,\psi(x)\frac{R(\mathrm{d}x, \mathrm{d}y)}{q(x)}q(x)\mathrm{d}x \end{aligned}$$

[10] The continuous differentiability restriction can be weakened by introducing weak derivatives.

where we used the symmetry of R. The joint measure $R(dx, dy)/q(x)$ implies a conditional measure $R(dy|x)$ from which we define:

$$\mathcal{A}_p\phi \doteq \int [\phi(y) - \phi(x)]\, R(dy|x).$$

We have just shown how to go from the forms to the generator of Markov processes. There is one technical complication that we sidestepped. In general, there may be several closed extensions of f_2 depending on boundary restrictions. The smallest of these closed extensions always generates a semigroup of contractions. This semigroup will correspond to a semigroup of conditional expectations provided that the associated operator $\mathcal{A}$ *conserves probabilities*. When this happens all closed extensions that lead to a Markov process produce exactly the same process constructed with the aid of the minimal extension (e.g. Chen et al., 2008; Proposition 4.6 and references therein).[11]

Fukushima et al. (1994) provide sufficient conditions for conservation of probabilities. An implication of the sufficient conditions of Fukushima et al. (1994) is that if $|\nu_{ij}(x)| \leq c|x|^{2+2\delta}$ and q has a 2δ moment, probabilities are conserved. (See also Chen et al., 2008.) Another set of sufficient conditions can be obtained by observing that a recurrent semigroup conserves probabilities (Fukushima et al., 1994; Lemma 1.6.5). Hasminskii (1960) and Stroock and Varadhan (1979) suggest using Liapounov functions to demonstrate recurrence.

4.1.2. Symmetrization

There are typically nonsymmetric solutions to (4.1). Given a generator $\mathcal{A}$, let $\mathcal{A}^*$ denote its adjoint. Define a symmetrized generator as:

$$\mathcal{A}^s = \frac{\mathcal{A} + \mathcal{A}^*}{2}.$$

Then $\mathcal{A}^s$ can be recovered from the forms f_1 and f_2 using the algorithm suggested previously. The symmetrized version of the generator is identified by the forms, while the generator itself is not.

We consider a third form using one-half the difference between $\mathcal{A}$ and $\mathcal{A}^*$. Define:

$$f_3(\phi, \psi) = \int \left(\frac{\mathcal{A} - \mathcal{A}^*}{2}\phi\right)\psi \, dQ.$$

This form is clearly antisymmetric. That is

$$f_3(\phi, \psi) = -f_3(\psi, \phi)$$

[11]When the smallest closed extension fails to conserve probabilities, we may still build an associated Markov process, provided that we allow the process to be *killed* in finite time when it hits a boundary. Other boundary protocols are also possible and lead to the study of alternative closed extensions.

for all ϕ and ψ in the common domain of $\mathcal{A}$ and its adjoint. We may recover a version of $\frac{\mathcal{A}+\mathcal{A}^*}{2}$ from (f_1, f_2) and $\frac{\mathcal{A}-\mathcal{A}^*}{2}$ from (f_1, f_3). Taken together we may construct $\mathcal{A}$. Thus to study nonsymmetric Markov processes via forms, we are led to introduce a third form, which is antisymmetric. See Ma and Rockner (1991) for an exposition of nonsymmetric forms and their resulting semigroups.

In what follows we specialize our discussion to the case of multivariate diffusions. When the dimension of the state space is greater than one, there are typically also nonsymmetric solutions to (4.1). Forms do not determine uniquely operators without additional restrictions such as symmetry. These nonsymmetric solutions are also generators of diffusion processes. While the diffusion matrix is the same for the operator and its adjoint, the drift vectors differ. Let μ denote the drift for a possibly nonsymmetric solution, μ^s denote the drift for the symmetric solution given by (4.3), and let μ^* denote the drift for the adjoint of the nonsymmetric solution. Then

$$\mu^s = \frac{\mu^* + \mu}{2}.$$

The form pair (f_1, f_2) identifies μ^s but not necessarily μ.

The form f_3 can be depicted as:

$$f_3(\phi, \psi) = \frac{1}{2} \int \left[(\mu - \mu^*) \cdot (\nabla\phi)\right] \psi q$$

at least for functions that are twice continuously differentiable and have compact support. For such functions we may use integration by parts to show that in fact:

$$f_3(\phi, \psi) = -f_3(\psi, \phi).$$

Moreover, when q is a density, we may extend f_3 to include constant functions via

$$f_3(\phi, 1) = \frac{1}{2} \int (\mu - \mu^*) \cdot (\nabla\phi) q = 0.$$

4.2. Principal Components

Given two quadratic forms, we define the functional versions of principal components.

Definition 6 *Nonlinear principal components are functions ψ_j, $j = 1, 2 \ldots$ that solve:*

$$\max_{\phi} f_1(\phi, \phi)$$

subject to

$$f_2(\phi, \phi) = 1$$
$$f_1(\phi, \psi_s) = 0, s = 0, \ldots, j-1$$

where ψ_0 is initialized to be the constant function one.

This definition follows Chen et al. (2008) and is a direct extension of that used by Salinelli (1998) for i.i.d. data. In the case of a diffusion specification, form f_2 is given by (4.2) and induces a quadratic smoothness penalty. Principal components maximize variation subject to a smoothness constraint and orthogonality. These components are a nonlinear counterpart to the more familiar principal component analysis of covariance matrices advocated by Pearson (1901). In the functional version, the state dependent, positive definite matrix ν is used to measure smoothness. Salinelli (1998) advocated this version of principal component analysis for $\nu = I$ to summarize the properties of i.i.d. data. As argued by Chen et al. (2008) they are equally valuable in the analysis of time series data. The principal components, when they exist, will be orthogonal under either form. That is:

$$f_1(\psi_j, \psi_k) = f_2(\psi_j, \psi_k) = 0$$

provided that $j \neq k$.

These principal components coincide with the principal components from the canonical analysis used by Darolles et al. (2004) under symmetry, but otherwise they differ. In addition to maximizing variation under smoothness restrictions (subject to orthogonality), they maximize autocorrelation and they maximize the long run variance as measured by the spectral density at frequency zero. See Chen et al. (2008) for an elaboration.

This form approach and the resulting principal component construction is equally applicable to i.i.d. data and to time series data. In the i.i.d. case, the matrix ν is used to measure function smoothness. Of course in the i.i.d. case there is no connection between the properties of ν and the data generator. The Markov diffusion model provides this link.

The smoothness penalty is special to diffusion processes. For jump processes, the form f_2 is built using the measure R, which still can be used to define principal components. These principal components will continue to maximize autocorrelation and long run variance subject to orthogonality constraints.

4.2.1. Existence

It turns out that principal components do not always exist. Existence is straightforward when the state space is compact, the density q is bounded above and bounded away from zero, and the diffusion matrix is uniformly nonsingular on the state space. These restrictions are too severe for many applications. Chen et al. (2008) treat cases where these conditions fail.

Suppose the state space is not compact. When the density q has thin tails, the notion of approximation is weaker. Approximation errors are permitted to be larger in the tails. This turns out to be one mechanism for the existence of principal components. Alternatively, ν might increase in the tails of the distribution of q limiting the admissible functions. This can also be exploited to establish the existence of principal components.

Chen et al. (2008) exhibit sufficient conditions for existence that require a trade-off between growth in ν and tail thinness of the density q. Consider the (lower) radial bounds,

$$\nu(x) \geq c(1+|x|^2)^{\beta} I$$
$$q(x) \geq \exp[-2\vartheta(|x|)].$$

Principal components exist when $0 \leq \beta \leq 1$ and $r^{\beta}\vartheta'(r) \to \infty$ as r gets large. Similarly, they also exist when $\vartheta(r) = \frac{\gamma}{2}\ln(1+r^2)+c^*$, and $1 < \beta < \gamma - \frac{m}{2} + 1$. The first set of sufficient conditions is applicable when the density q has an exponentially thin tail; the second is useful when q has an algebraic tail.

We now consider some special results for the case $m = 1$. We let the state space be (l, r), where either boundary can be infinite. Again q denotes the stationary density and $\sigma > 0$ the volatility coefficient (that is, $\sigma^2 = \nu$.) Suppose that

$$\int_l^r \left| \int_{x_o}^x \frac{1}{q(y)\sigma^2(y)} \mathrm{d}y \right| q(x)\mathrm{d}x < \infty \tag{4.4}$$

where x_o is an interior point in the state space. Then principal components are known to exist. For a proof see, e.g. Hansen et al. (1998), page 13, where this proposition is stated using the *scale function*

$$s(x) \doteq \int_{x_o}^x \frac{1}{q(y)\sigma^2(y)} \mathrm{d}y,$$

and it is observed that (4.4) admits entrance boundaries, in addition to attracting boundaries.

When assumption (4.4) is not satisfied, at least one of the boundaries is natural. Recall that the boundary $l(r)$ is natural if $s(l) = -\infty$ ($s(r) = +\infty$ resp.) and,

$$\int_l^{x_0} s(x)q(x)\mathrm{d}x = -\infty \left(\int_{x_0}^r s(x)q(x)\mathrm{d}x = +\infty \text{ resp.} \right)$$

Hansen et al. (1998) show that in this case principal components exist whenever

$$\limsup_{x \to r} \frac{\mu}{\sigma} - \frac{\sigma'}{2} = \limsup_{x \to r} \frac{\sigma q'}{2q} + \frac{\sigma'}{2} = -\infty$$
$$\liminf_{x \to l} \frac{\mu}{\sigma} - \frac{\sigma'}{2} = \liminf_{x \to l} \frac{\sigma q'}{2q} + \frac{\sigma'}{2} = +\infty. \tag{4.5}$$

We can think of the left-hand side of (4.5) as a local measure of *pull* towards the center of the distribution. If one boundary, say l, is reflexive and r is natural, then a principal component decomposition exists provided that the lim inf in (4.5) is $+\infty$.

4.2.2. Spectral Decomposition

Principal components, when they exist, can be used to construct the semigroup of conditional expectation operators as in Wong (1964). A principal component decomposition is analogous to the spectral decomposition of a symmetric matrix. Each principal component is an eigenfunction of all of the conditional expectation operators and hence behaves like a first-order scalar autoregression (with conditionally heteroskedastic innovations). See Darolles et al., 2001; for an elaboration. Thus, principal components constructed from the stationary distribution must satisfy an extensive family of conditional moment restrictions.

Both the generator and the semigroup of conditional expectations operators have *spectral* (principal component) decompositions. The generator has spectral decomposition:

$$\mathcal{A}\phi = \sum_{j=0}^{\infty} -\delta_j f_1(\psi_j, \phi)\psi_j,$$

where each $\delta_j > 0$ and, ψ_j is a principal component (normalized to have a unit second moment) and an eigenvector associated with the eigenvalue $-\delta_j$, that is,

$$\mathcal{A}\psi_j = -\delta_j \psi_j.$$

The corresponding decomposition for the semigroup uses an exponential formula:

$$\mathcal{T}_\Delta \phi = \sum_{j=0}^{\infty} \exp(-\Delta\delta_j) f_1(\psi_j, \phi)\psi_j. \tag{4.6}$$

This spectral decomposition shows that the principal components of the semigroup are ordered in importance by which dominate in the long run.

Associated with (4.6) for a diffusion is an expansion of the transition density. Write:

$$p(y|x, t) = \sum_{j=0}^{\infty} \exp(-t\delta_j)\psi_j(y)\psi_j(x)q(y) \tag{4.7}$$

where q is the stationary density. Notice that we have constructed $p(y|x, t)$ so that

$$\mathcal{T}_t\phi(x) = \int \phi(y)p(y|x, t)dy.$$

The basis functions used in this density expansion depend on the underlying model. Recall that an *Ornstein-Uhlenbeck* process has a stationary distribution that is normal (see Example 5). Decomposition (4.6) is a Hermite expansion when the stationary distribution has mean zero and variance one. The eigenfunctions are the orthonormal polynomials with respect to a standard normal distribution.

4.2.3. Dependence

Spectral decomposition does not require the existence of principal components. We have seen how to construct Markov processes with self adjoint generators using forms. A more general version of the spectral decomposition of generators is applicable to the resulting semigroup and generator that generalizes formula (4.6), see Rudin (1973), Hansen and Scheinkman (1995), and Schaumburg (2005). This decomposition is applicable generally for scalar diffusions even when a stationary density fails to exist, for a wide class of Markov processes defined via symmetric forms. The measure q used in constructing the forms and defining a sense of approximation need not be integrable.

The existence of a principal component decomposition typically requires that the underlying Markov process be only weakly dependent. For a weakly dependent process, autocorrelations of test functions decay exponentially. It is possible, however, to build models of Markov processes that are strongly dependent. For such processes, the autocorrelations of some test functions decay at a slower than exponential rate. Operator methods give a convenient way to characterize when a process is strongly dependent.

In our study of strongly dependent, but stationary, Markov processes, we follow Chen et al. (2008) using two measures of mixing. Both of these measures have been used extensively in the stochastic process literature. The first measure, ρ-mixing uses the $L^2(Q)$ formulation. Let

$$U \doteq \{\phi \in L^2(Q) : \int \phi \mathrm{d}Q = 0, \int \phi^2 \mathrm{d}Q = 1\}.$$

The concept of ρ-mixing studies the maximal correlation of two functions of the Markov state in different time periods.

Definition 7 *The ρ-mixing coefficients of a Markov process are given by:*

$$\rho_t = \sup_{\psi,\phi \in U} \int \psi\,(T_t \phi)\,\mathrm{d}Q.$$

The process $\{X_t\}$ is ρ-mixing or weakly dependent if $\lim_{t \to \infty} \rho_t = 0$.

When the ρ-mixing coefficients of a Markov process decline to zero, they do so exponentially. When a Markov process has a principal component decomposition, it is ρ-mixing with exponential decay. In fact, ρ-mixing requires something weaker.

As argued by Banon (1978) and Hansen and Scheinkman (1995), ρ-mixing is guaranteed by a *gap* in the spectrum of the negative semidefinite operator $\mathcal{A}$ to the left of zero. Although not always symmetric, the operator $\mathcal{A}$ is negative semidefinite:

$$\int \phi(\mathcal{A}\phi)\mathrm{d}Q \leq 0$$

on the $L^2(Q)$ domain of $\mathcal{A}$. This negative-semidefinite property follows from the restriction that $\mathcal{T}_t$ is a weak contraction on $L^2(Q)$ for each t. A spectral gap is present when we can strengthen this restriction as follows:

$$\sup_{\phi \in U \bigcap D(\mathcal{A})} < \phi, \mathcal{A}\phi > \; < \; 0. \tag{4.8}$$

When this condition is satisfied $\mathcal{T}_t$ is a strong contraction on the subspace U for each t, and the ρ-mixing coefficients decay exponentially.

In the case of a scalar diffusion, Hansen and Scheinkman (1995) show that this inequality is satisfied provided that

$$\begin{aligned} \limsup_{x \to r} \frac{\mu}{\sigma} - \frac{\sigma'}{2} &= \limsup_{x \to r} \frac{\sigma q'}{2q} + \frac{\sigma'}{2} < 0 \\ \liminf_{x \to \ell} \frac{\mu}{\sigma} - \frac{\sigma'}{2} &= \liminf_{x \to \ell} \frac{\sigma q'}{2q} + \frac{\sigma'}{2} > 0. \end{aligned} \tag{4.9}$$

where r is the right boundary and ℓ is the left boundary of the state space. This restriction is a weakening of restriction (4.5), which guaranteed the existence of principal components. Condition (4.9) guarantees that there is sufficient pull from each boundary towards the center of the distribution to imply ρ-mixing. When one of these two limits is zero, the ρ-mixing coefficients may be identically equal to one. In this case the Markov process is strongly dependent.[12]

Since the ρ-mixing coefficients for a Markov process either decay exponentially or are equal to one, we need a different notion of mixing to obtain a more refined analysis of strong dependence. This leads us to consider the β-mixing coefficients:

Definition 8 *The β-mixing coefficients for a Markov process are given by:*

$$\beta_t = \int \sup_{0 \leq \phi \leq 1} |\mathcal{T}_t\phi - \int \phi \mathrm{d}Q| \mathrm{d}Q.$$

[12] Recall that the term in the left-hand side of (4.9) can be interpreted as the drift of a corresponding diffusion with a unit diffusion coefficient obtained by transforming the scale. As a consequence, condition (4.9) can also be related to Veretennikov's drift restriction for a diffusion to be strongly dependent (Veretennikov, 1997).

The process $\{X_t\}$ *is* β*-mixing if* $\lim_{t\to\infty}\beta_t = 0$; *is* β*-mixing with an exponential decay rate if* $\beta_t \leq \gamma\exp(-\delta t)$ *for some* $\delta, \gamma > 0$.

At least for scalar diffusions, Chen et al. (2008) show that the exponential decay of the ρ-mixing coefficients is essentially equivalent to the exponential decay of the β-mixing coefficients. When the ρ-mixing coefficients are identically one, however, the β-mixing coefficients will still decay to zero, but at a rate slower than exponential. Thus, the decay properties of the β-mixing coefficients provides a more sensitive characterization of strong dependence.

4.3. Applications

4.3.1. Zipf's Law

Recall Zipf's law discussed in Section 3.1. Zipf suggested a generalization of his law in which there was a free parameter that related rank to size. Consider a family of stationary densities that satisfy a power law of the form: $q_\xi \propto x^{-(2+\xi)}$ defined on (y, ∞) where $y > 0$ and $\xi \geq 0$. Then the rank-size relation becomes $\text{size}(\text{rank})^{\frac{1}{1+\xi}} = \text{constant}$. This family of densities is of interest to economists, because of power-law distributions that seem to describe income distribution and city sizes. With $\sigma^2(x) = \alpha^2 x^2$, the corresponding drift is, using Eq. (3.3),

$$\mu = -\frac{\xi\alpha^2 x}{2}$$

Notice that $\mu(y) < 0$, so that $y > 0$ is an attainable boundary. We make this barrier reflexive to deliver the requisite stationary density.

To study temporal dependence, we consider the pull measure:

$$\frac{\mu}{\sigma} - \frac{\sigma'}{2} = -\frac{\alpha(1+\xi)}{2},$$

which is negative and independent of the state. The negative pull at the right boundary in conjunction with the reflexive left boundary guarantees that the process has a spectral gap, and thus it is weakly dependent even in the case where $\xi = 0$. Because the pull measure is constant, it fails to satisfy restriction (4.5). The full principal component decomposition we described in Section 4.2 fails to exists because the boundary pull is insufficient.

4.3.2. Stationarity and Volatility

Nonlinearity in a Markov diffusion coefficient changes the appropriate notion of mean reversion. Stationarity can be induced by how volatility changes as a function of the Markov state and may have little to do with the usual notion of mean reversion as measured by the drift of the diffusion process. This phenomenon is most directly seen in scalar diffusion models in which the drift is zero, but the process itself is stationary. Conley et al. (1997) generalize this notion by arguing that for stationary processes with an infinite right boundary, the stationarity is volatility induced when:

$$\int_x^\infty \frac{\mu(y)}{\sigma^2(y)} dy > -\infty \tag{4.10}$$

for some x in the interior of the state space. This requirement is sufficient for $+\infty$ not to be attracting. For the process to be stationary, the diffusion coefficient must grow sufficiently fast as a function of the state. In effect $1/\sigma^2$ needs to be integrable. The high volatility in large states is enough to guarantee that the process eventually escapes from those states. Reversion to the center of the distribution is induced by this high volatility and not by the pull from the drift. An example is Zipf's with drift $\mu = 0$. Conley et al. (1997) give examples for models with a constant volatility elasticity.

Jones (2003) uses a stochastic volatility model of equity in which the *volatility of volatility* ensures that the volatility process is stationary. Consider a process for volatility that has a linear drift $\mu(x) = \alpha - \kappa x$ and constant volatility elasticity: $\sigma^2(x) \propto x^{2\gamma}$. Jones estimates that κ is essentially zero for data he considers on equity volatility. Even with a zero value of κ the pull measure $\mu/\sigma - \sigma'/2$ diverges to $-\infty$ at the right boundary provided that γ is greater than one. Jones (2003) in fact estimates a value for γ that exceeds one. The pull measure also diverges at the left boundary to $+\infty$. The process is ρ-mixing and it has a simple spectral decomposition. Stationarity is volatility induced when $\kappa = 0$ because relation (4.10) is satisfied provided that γ exceeds one. The state-dependence in the volatility (of volatility) is sufficient to pull the process to the center of its distribution even though the pull coming from the drift alone is in the wrong direction at the right boundary.

Using parameter estimates from Jones (2003), we display the first five principal components for the volatility process in Fig. 1.1. For the principal component extraction, we use the two weighting functions described previously. For the quadratic form in function levels we weight by the stationary density implied by these parameter values. The quadratic form in the derivatives is weighted by the stationary density times the diffusion coefficient. As can be seen from Fig. 1.1, this function converges to a constant in the right tail of the stationary distribution.

While they are nonlinear, the principal components evaluated at the underlying stochastic process each behave like a scalar autoregression with heteroskedastic innovations. As expected the higher-order principal components oscillate more as measured by zero crossings.[13] The higher-order principal components are less smooth as measured

[13]The intuition comes from the Sturm–Liouville theory of second-order differential equations.

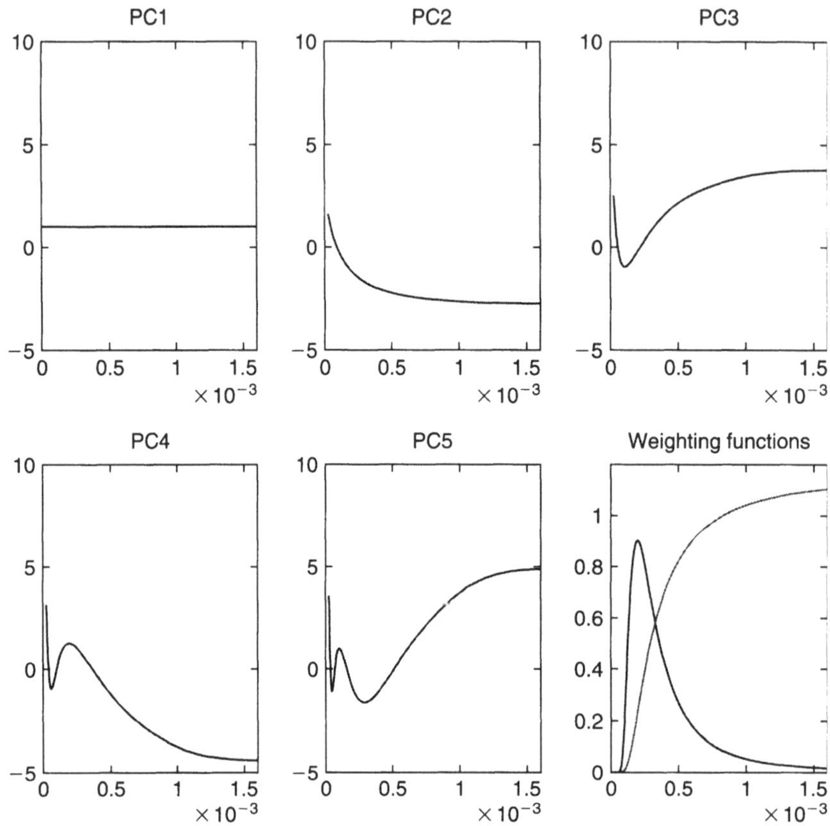

Figure 1.1 The first five principal components for a volatility model estimated by Jones. The weighting functions are the density and the density scaled by the diffusion coefficient. The parameter values are $\kappa = 0$, $\alpha = 0.58 \times 10^{-6}$, and $\sigma^2 = 6.1252x^{2.66}$. Except for κ, the parameter values are taken from the fourth column of Table 1 in Jones (2003). Although the posterior mean for κ is different from zero, it is small relative to its posterior standard deviation.

by the quadratic form in the derivatives. Given the weighting used in the quadratic form for the derivatives, the principal components are flat in the tails.

4.3.3. Approximating Variance Processes

Meddahi (2001) and Andersen et al. (2004) use a nonlinear principal component decomposition to study models of volatility. Recall that each principal component behaves as a univariate (heteroskedastic) autoregression and the components are mutually orthogonal. These features of principal components make them attractive for forecasting conditional variances and time-averages of conditional variances. Simple formulas exist for predicting the time-average of a univariate autoregression, and Andersen et al. (2004) are able to apply those formulas in conjunction with a finite number of the most important principal components to obtain operational prediction formulas.

4.3.4. Imitating Long Memory Processes

Linear characterizations of time series typically define long memory in terms of the behavior of the spectral density function (the Fourier transform of the autocovariance function). When the spectral density diverges to infinity at zero, there is strong linear dependence. The degree of fractional integration is defined using the rate at which this spectral density diverges. As we have seen, stationary Markov processes can be strongly dependent as characterized by the behavior of the implied mixing coefficients.

The spectral density function at frequency zero is typically the variance used in a central limit approximation. From Bhattacharya (1982) and Hansen and Scheinkman (1995) and formula (3.5), we know that the asymptotic variance for the central limit approximation for $\frac{1}{\sqrt{T}}\int_0^T \mathcal{A}\phi(x_t)$ is:

$$2f_2(\phi,\phi) = -2\int \phi(\mathcal{A}\phi)\mathrm{d}Q = \int (\nabla\phi)^* \nu(\nabla\phi)q$$

where the second right-hand side expression is the formula for diffusion processes. The formula for jump processes is different. Thus, the long-run variance for the process $\{\mathcal{A}\phi(x_t)\}$ is given by the form $2f_2$ applied to the test function ϕ. This long-run variance is also the spectral density at frequency zero.

This long-run variance is not always finite, however. Using this long-run variance, we may define weak dependence as:

$$\sup_{\phi\in D(\mathcal{A}), \int \mathcal{A}(\phi)^2\mathrm{d}Q=1} f_2(\phi,\phi) < \infty.$$

This is in effect the inverse counterpart to (4.8) and is equivalent to the restriction that the ρ-mixing coefficients have exponential decay. This criterion also suggests how we might construct strongly dependent diffusion processes with a divergent spectral density. Find a pair (ν, Q) and a test function ϕ such that for

$$\psi \doteq \mu \cdot \frac{\partial\phi}{\partial x} + \frac{1}{2}\mathrm{trace}\left(\nu\frac{\partial^2\phi}{\partial x\partial x'}\right)$$

we have $\int |\psi|^2 q < \infty$, $\int \psi q = 0$, and $\int \left(\frac{\partial\phi}{\partial x}\right)^* \nu \left(\frac{\partial\phi}{\partial x}\right) = \infty$.

Such a process gives an alternative way to produce long-range dependence to the self-similar fractional Brownian motion model of Mandelbrot and Ness (1968). Although these diffusions are not self-similar, they have the mathematical advantage of being semimartingales.

We illustrate a family of scalar diffusion models that are strongly dependent. It is often argued that strong dependence is a feature of volatility models. One important source of evidence for strong dependence is a spectral density matrix that diverges at frequency zero. We now display one construction of a nonlinear diffusion model that is strongly dependent. This example is taken from Chen et al. (2008).

Consider a scalar process with a zero mean and a diffusion coefficient $\sigma^2(x) = (1 + x^2)^\gamma$ for $1/2 < \gamma < 1$. The candidate stationary density is proportional to $1/\sigma^2$. In fact this process is stationary, but its ρ-mixing coefficients are unity. In particular, the pull measure is zero at both boundaries. Form a new process by taking a time invariant transformation of the original process. That is, let

$$\psi = \frac{\sigma^2}{2}\phi''$$

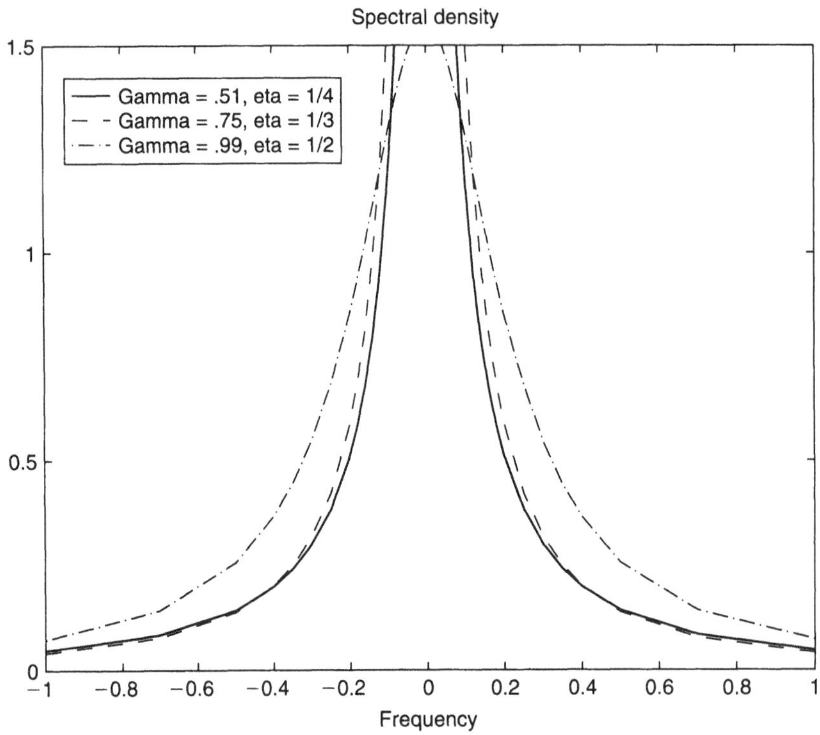

Figure 1.2 Spectral density functions for different pairs (γ, η). Spectral densities are rescaled to integrate to one.

where ϕ is such that $\phi'(x) = (1 + x^2)^{-\eta/2}$. Restrict η to satisfy: $\gamma - 1/2 \leq \eta \leq 1/2$. Then ψ has mean zero and finite variance when integrated against the stationary density.[14] Its long-run variance, however, is infinite. Notice that

$$\int \sigma^2 (\phi')^2 q = \infty$$

because $\eta \leq 1/2$. The divergence of the spectral density function near frequency zero is illustrated in Fig. 1.2. The rate of divergence of this spectral density function at frequency zero is shown in Fig. 1.3 using logarithmic scaling.

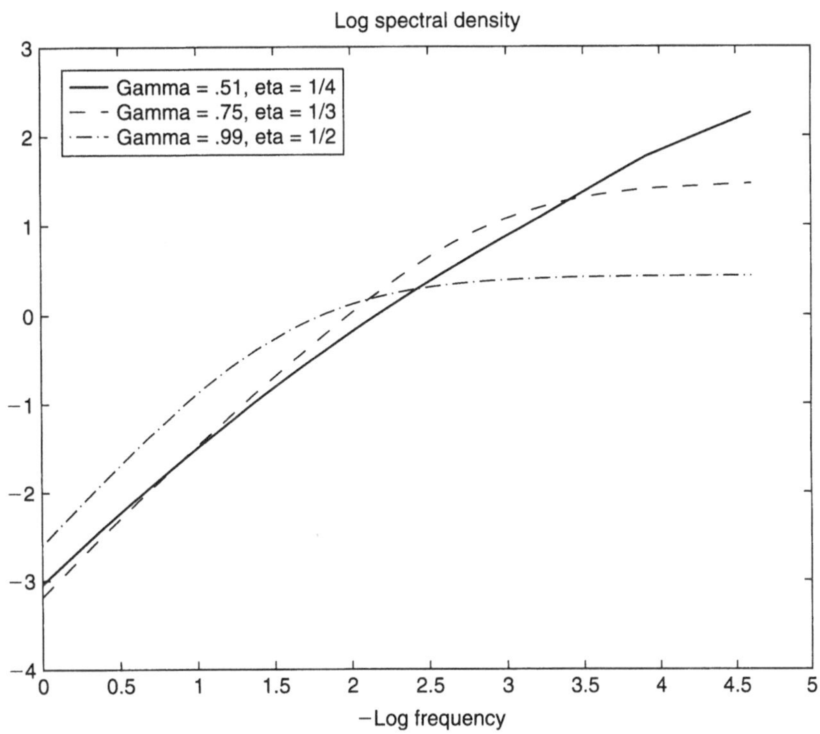

Figure 1.3 Spectral density functions for different pairs (γ, η) plotted on a log−log scale. Spectral densities are rescaled to integrate to one.

[14]The function ϕ will not typically be in the $L^2(Q)$ domain of the generator.

5. HERMITE AND RELATED EXPANSIONS OF A TRANSITION DENSITY

We now consider two methods to approximate the transition density of diffusions. These methods often lead to *closed form* expressions for the density; and as a consequence, these expansions are readily usable for parametric estimation. First, we consider the univariate Hermite expansions of Aït-Sahalia (2002b); by making a judicious change of variable, these expansions use polynomial basis functions that are common across all models. This commonality makes them particularly attractive to use in likelihood approximation. Second, in the multivariate case, we consider the local expansions of Aït-Sahalia (2008), which rely on expansions in both the time and state dimensions. Prior to our study of transition densities, we discuss an exponential expansion for approximating conditional expectations over small time intervals.[15] This will be used as input into some of the subsequent calculations.

5.1. Exponential Expansion

When diffusion coefficients are smooth, a power series expansion can be used for a subset of functions in the domain of the generator. By a power series we mean:

$$\mathcal{T}_\Delta \phi \approx \sum_{k=0}^{K} \frac{\Delta^k \mathcal{A}^k \phi}{k!}, \tag{5.1}$$

which converges in K. Schaumburg (2005) provides a justification for this formula for a specific collection of functions. Consider a function ϕ in the image of $\mathcal{T}_t$, that is a function that satisfies $\phi = \mathcal{T}_t \psi$ for some $\psi \in L^2(Q)$. Then under an additional arguably weak regularity condition (see Assumption 2A in Schaumburg, 2005), the power series converges for $\Delta \le t$.

To illustrate this result, suppose there exists a spectral decomposition of the form given in (4.6) for ψ and hence for ϕ. Then

$$\phi = \sum_{j=0}^{\infty} \exp(-\delta_j t) f_1(\psi_j, \psi)\psi_j.$$

Notice that

$$f_1(\psi_j, \psi) = f_1(\phi, \psi_j) \exp(\delta_j t).$$

This suggests that ψ could be constructed by "inverting" the conditional expectation operator. For this construction to work, however,

$$\sum_{j=0}^{\infty} f_1(\phi, \psi_j)^2 \exp(2\delta_j t) < \infty \tag{5.2}$$

[15]Although the spectral depiction 4.6 of the exponential formula is applicable to all functions that are square integrable with respect to Q, it can be difficult to compute.

which illustrates the strength of Schaumburg's (Schaumburg, 2005) restriction that ϕ be in the image of $\mathcal{T}_t$. See Carrasco et al. (2007) for an extensive discussion of such restrictions for conditional expectation operators used in a variety of econometric applications.

When restriction (5.2) is satisfied, we can establish the approximation. Write

$$\sum_{k=0}^{K} \frac{\Delta^k \mathcal{A}^k \phi}{k!} - \exp(\mathcal{A})\,\phi = \sum_{j=0}^{\infty} \left[\sum_{k=0}^{K} \frac{(-\Delta\delta_k)^k}{k!} - \exp\big(-\Delta\delta_j\big) \right] f_1(\psi_j, \phi)\psi_j$$

$$= \sum_{j=0}^{\infty} \left[\sum_{k=0}^{K} \frac{(-\Delta\delta_k)^k}{k!} - \exp\big(-\Delta\delta_j\big) \right] \exp\big(-\delta_j t\big) f_1(\psi_j, \psi)\psi_j.$$

The discounting of the *coefficients* $f_1(\psi_k, \psi)$ by $\exp(-\delta_k t)$ is used to limit the magnitude of the approximation error. Notice that

$$\exp\big(-t\delta_j\big) \left| \sum_{k=0}^{K} \frac{(-\Delta\delta_j)^k}{k!} - \exp\big(-\Delta\delta_j\big) \right| \le \exp\big(-\Delta\delta_j\big) \left[\sum_{k=0}^{K} \frac{(\Delta\delta_j)^k}{k!} + \exp\big(-\Delta\delta_j\big) \right] \le 2.$$

This bound together with the pointwise (in $\Delta\delta_k$) of the power series expansion of the exponential can be used in conjunction with the Dominated Convergence Theorem to show that the approximation error converges to zero in the norm on $L^2(Q)$.

Schaumburg (2005) establishes this approximation without requiring the simple spectral decomposition we used here. The remaining challenge in using this approach is to characterize more explicitly the set of functions that are in the image of $\mathcal{T}_t$. For instance, in Wong's models (Wong, 1964) with polynomial eigenfunctions, it can be shown that polynomials are in the image of $\mathcal{T}_t$, but it remains an interesting challenge to establish this property for more general classes of diffusion models.

Kessler (1997) and Stanton (1997) suggest using this expansion method to construct conditional moment restrictions to be used in estimation. In what follows we will see how this expansion can be applied as input into the approximation of transition densities.

5.2. Hermite Expansion of the Transition Function

We have already noted that a spectral decomposition of the semigroup for an *Ornstein-Uhlenbeck* process with a standard normal stationary distribution is a Hermite expansion. In problems of estimation it is often convenient to use a common expansion for alternative models, and Hermite expansion is a leading example. In what follows, we follow Aït-Sahalia (1999) and Aït-Sahalia (2002b) and describe Hermite series expansions for scalar diffusions. These expansions lead to *closed form* expressions that can be applied to scalar diffusions with sufficient regularity.

It is clearly special and limiting to have a stationary distribution that is standard normal. To make the standard normal distribution useful for approximation, we transform the state and rescale the change in the state over an interval of time Δ. To understand the construction, the following analogy may be helpful. Consider a standardized sum of random variables to which the Central Limit Theorem (CLT) apply. Often, one is willing to approximate the actual sample size by infinity and use the $\mathcal{N}(0, 1)$ limiting distribution for the properly standardized transformation of the data. If not, higher order terms of the limiting distribution (for example the classical Edgeworth expansion based on Hermite polynomials) can be calculated to improve the accuracy of the approximation.

Consider now approximating the transition density of a diffusion and think of the sampling interval Δ as playing the role of the sample size n in the CLT. For a small Δ, the conditional distribution is closer to being normal because of the contribution from the Brownian increment. If we properly standardize the data, then we can find out the limiting distribution of the standardized data as Δ tends to 0 (by analogy with what happens in the CLT when sample size tends to ∞). Properly standardizing the data in the CLT means subtracting the population mean summing and dividing by the square root of the sample size. For this application, it involves transforming the original diffusion X into another one, called Z below. In both cases, the appropriate standardization makes $\mathcal{N}(0, 1)$ the leading term of the approximation. This $\mathcal{N}(0, 1)$ approximation is then refined by including higher order terms based on Hermite polynomials, which are orthogonal with respect to the leading $\mathcal{N}(0, 1)$ term.

5.2.1. Change of Variable and Rescaling

A property of a diffusion is that over small increments of time, first differences divided by $\sqrt{\Delta}$ are approximately normal. The normal approximation becomes better as the interval Δ becomes small, but the variance may be state dependent. Thus prior to shrinking Δ to zero, we transform the state to make the limiting approximation a standard normal. The transformation is:

$$Y_t \equiv \gamma(X_t) = \int^{X_t} \frac{du}{\sigma(u)} \tag{5.3}$$

where the lower endpoint of integration is some interior point in the state space. The constructed process $\{Y_t\}$ has a unit diffusion coefficient, so as to eliminate heteroskedasticity, and a drift:

$$\mu_y(y) = \frac{\mu\left[\gamma^{-1}(y)\right]}{\sigma\left[\gamma^{-1}(y)\right]} - \frac{1}{2}\frac{d\sigma}{dx}\left[\gamma^{-1}(y)\right]. \tag{5.4}$$

The stationary density q_y for the transformed process is typically not normal, but it satisfies:

$$q_y(y) \propto \exp\left[2\int^{y} \mu_y(u)du\right].$$

While it is possible for the transformed state to have finite upper or lower bounds, we focus on the case in which the implied state space is $\mathbb{R}$. The stationary density will have exponentially thin tails provided that the drift μ_y is negative (positive) for large positive (negative) y and bounded away from zero in the tails. Thus, polynomials have finite second moments after this transformation has been applied, provided that there is some pull towards the origin in the implied drift. As discussed in Section 4.2.3, these conditions on the pull measure imply weak dependence of the diffusion process.

If the drift of the process $\{Y_t\}$ was zero, then it would be a standard Brownian motion. The first difference in $\{Y_t\}$ would have a standard normal density only after dividing by the square root of the sampling interval Δ. More generally, let p_y denote the transition function of the process $\{Y_t\}$. Without this scaling, the first difference of $\{Y_t\}$ will converge to a degenerate measure with a unit probability mass (a Dirac mass) at zero. To obtain the Hermite refinement of a standard normal approximation, we form

$$Z_\Delta \doteq \Delta^{-1/2}\left(Y_\Delta - Y_0\right)$$

and condition on $Y_0 = y_0 = \gamma(x_0)$. Let p_z denote the conditional distribution of Z_Δ where Δ denotes the time interval used in the approximation.

Since Z_Δ is a known transformation of X, we can recover the transition density of X from the density of Z_Δ using the familiar Jacobian formula:

$$p(x|x_0, \Delta) = \frac{p_Y[\gamma(x)|\gamma(x_0), \Delta]}{\sigma(x)} = \frac{p_z\left(\Delta^{-1/2}\left[\gamma(x) - \gamma(x_0)\right] |\gamma(x_0), \Delta\right)}{\sigma(x)\Delta^{1/2}}. \tag{5.5}$$

So this leaves us with the need to approximate the density function p_z.

5.2.2. Coefficients of the Expansion

Let h_j denote the Hermite polynomials, the orthogonal polynomials with respect to the standard normal density. They can be computed as:

$$h_j(z) \doteq \exp\left(\frac{z^2}{2}\right)\frac{\mathrm{d}^j}{\mathrm{d}z^j}\left[\exp\left(\frac{-z^2}{2}\right)\right], \quad j \geq 0.$$

The Hermite expansion is

$$p_z(z|y_0, \Delta) = \frac{\exp(-z^2/2)}{\sqrt{2\pi}}\sum_{j=0}^{\infty}\eta_j(\Delta, y_0)h_j(z) \tag{5.6}$$

with coefficients given by:

$$\begin{aligned}
\eta_j(\Delta, y_0) &= \left(\frac{1}{j!}\right)\int_{-\infty}^{+\infty} h_j(z)\, p_z(z|y_0, \Delta)\mathrm{d}z \\
&= \left(\frac{1}{j!}\right)E\left(h_j\left[\Delta^{-1/2}\left(Y_\Delta - Y_0\right)\right]|Y_0 = y_0\right) \\
&= (1/j!)\,\mathcal{T}_\Delta h_j\left(\Delta^{-1/2}(Y_\Delta - y_0)\right).
\end{aligned} \tag{5.7}$$

A Hermite approximation to p_z uses a finite number of terms in expansion (5.6). A corresponding approximation for p_x follows from (5.5).

As the coefficients η_j are specific conditional moments of the process $\{Y_t\}$, they can be computed using numerical methods such as Monte Carlo integration. An attractive alternative proposed in Aït-Sahalia (2002b) is to use an exponential expansion of the form (5.1). With (5.7) in mind, let $\phi(y)$ be a polynomial (which also depends on y_0, but y_0 is held fixed here). Given growth and smoothness of the drift and diffusion coefficients, polynomials and their iterates obtained by repeated application of the generator $\mathcal{A}$ are in $D(\mathcal{A})$ under regularity assumptions on the boundary behavior of the process. This guarantees that Taylor series:

$$\sum_{k=0}^{K} \frac{\Delta^k \mathcal{A}^k \phi}{k!}$$

is well defined and a viable approximation to $\mathcal{T}_\Delta$.

Using this method, Aït-Sahalia (1999) gives the formulae corresponding to popular models in finance, and Aït-Sahalia (2002b) uses this approach to approximate numerically a parametric likelihood function for scalar diffusion estimation. Jensen and Poulsen (2002) show that this Hermite approximation works very well in practice and that it dominates other methods for the benchmark examples they consider.

5.3. Local Expansions of the Log-Transition Function

In the univariate Hermite expansion described in Section 5.2, we first deduced the Hermite expansion in terms of polynomials in $y - y_0$ for a given Δ. Once the Hermite coefficients $\eta_j(\Delta, y_0)$ are replaced by their Taylor series approximation in Δ, the corresponding approximation expansion becomes local in Δ. In addition to using a finite number of Hermite polynomials, we limited our use to a finite number of Δ terms in the Taylor expansion used to approximate the coefficients.[16] Following Aït-Sahalia (2008), we will use a similar strategy except that we will deduce directly a small Δ expansion first. In contrast to the Hermite expansion, this expansion applies directly to the logarithm of the transition density and permits the diffusion to be multivariate. After deducing the Δ expansion, we will explore an approximation based on the discrepancy between the state to which the diffusion moves to and from the current state. Formally we will deduce this as a small discrepancy approximation. Taken together, this joint expansion provides an operational way to approximate (logarithms) of transition densities for multivariate diffusions. Extensions to multivariate jump-diffusions are considered in Yu (2003).

[16]Different ways of gathering the terms are available as in the Central Limit Theorem, where both the Edgeworth and Gram-Charlier expansions are based on a Hermite expansion.

5.3.1. Expansion in Δ

Aït-Sahalia (2008) shows that an expansion at order K in Δ for $\ell(x|x_0,\Delta) \doteq \ln p(x|x_0,\Delta)$ can be obtained in the form:

$$\ell_K(x|x_0,\Delta) \approx C_{-1}(x|x_0)\Delta^{-1} + \tilde{C}(x|x_0)\ln\Delta + \sum_{k=0}^{K} C_k(x|x_0)\frac{\Delta^k}{k!}$$

The derivative with respect to Δ of the approximating function is therefore:

$$\frac{\partial \ell_K}{\partial \Delta}(x|x_0,\Delta) \approx -C_{-1}(x|x_0)\Delta^{-2} + \tilde{C}(x|x_0)\Delta^{-1} + \sum_{k=1}^{K} C_k(x|x_0)\frac{\Delta^{k-1}}{(k-1)!}.$$

Before computing the coefficients of the expansion, reconsider Example 9.

Example 10 *Consider a Brownian motion process with a constant drift (see Example 9). The transition density is known to be normal with mean $x_0 + \Delta\mu$ and variance $\Delta\sigma^2$. The log density is:*

$$\ell(x|x_0,\Delta) = \frac{1}{2}\left[-\ln 2\pi - \ln\sigma^2 - \ln\Delta - \frac{(x - x_0 - \mu\Delta)^2}{\Delta\sigma^2}\right].$$

We may compute directly the coefficients of the small Δ expansion:

$$C_{-1}(x|x_0) = -\frac{(x-x_0)^2}{2\sigma^2}$$

$$\tilde{C}(x|x_0) = -\frac{1}{2}$$

$$C_0(x|x_0) = -\ln\sigma + \frac{(x-x_0)\mu}{\sigma^2} - \frac{1}{2}\ln 2\pi$$

$$C_1(x|x_0) = -\frac{\mu^2}{2\sigma^2}$$

More generally, these coefficients can be computed using the Kolmogorov forward and backward equations. In particular, the forward equation is typically stated in terms of the densities, but it has a log-density counterpart:

$$\begin{aligned}\frac{\partial \ell}{\partial \Delta}(x|x_0,\Delta) &= C^*(x) + \sum_{i=1}^{m}\mu_i(x)\frac{\partial \ell}{\partial x_i}(x|x_0,\Delta) + \sum_{i=1}^{m}\sum_{j=1}^{m}\frac{\partial \nu_{ij}(x)}{\partial x_i}\frac{\partial \ell}{\partial x_j}(x|x_0,\Delta)\\ &+ \frac{1}{2}\sum_{i=1}^{m}\sum_{j=1}^{m}\nu_{ij}(x)\frac{\partial^2 \ell}{\partial x_i \partial x_j}(x|x_0,\Delta) \qquad (5.8)\\ &+ \frac{1}{2}\sum_{i=1}^{m}\sum_{j=1}^{m}\frac{\partial \ell}{\partial x_i}(x|x_0,\Delta)\nu_{ij}(x)\frac{\partial \ell}{\partial x_j}(x|x_0,\Delta).\end{aligned}$$

where

$$C^*(x) \doteq -\sum_{i=1}^{m} \frac{\partial \mu_i(x)}{\partial x_i} + \frac{1}{2}\sum_{i=1}^{m}\sum_{j=1}^{m} \frac{\partial^2 \nu_{ij}(x)}{\partial x_i \partial x_j}$$

This differential equation is linear in the second derivative of ℓ with respect to x but quadratic in the first derivative.

5.3.2. Leading Term

The leading term in this expansion must solve:

$$-C_{-1}(x|x_0) = \frac{1}{2}\left[\frac{\partial C_{-1}(x|x_0)}{\partial x}\right]' \nu(x) \left[\frac{\partial C_{-1}(x|x_0)}{\partial x}\right]. \tag{5.9}$$

This follows because the lowest power in Δ on the left-hand side of (5.8) is -2. Only the last term on the right-hand side contributes to this. We consider the solution that has a strict maximum at $x = x_0$.

Example 11 *Suppose that $\nu(x) = I$. Aït-Sahalia (2008) discusses when the state can be transformed so that this restriction is satisfied. The differential equation (5.9) then has as a solution:*

$$C_{-1}(x|x_0) = -\frac{|x - x_0|^2}{2}.$$

This suggests a transition density approximation of the form:

$$\exp\left(-\frac{|x - x_0|^2}{2\Delta}\right)$$

over an interval Δ. In turn this suggests a normal approximation as the leading term. Because the leading term will not even approximately integrate to one, we will need to explore other terms of the expansion. In this example, by adding the expression

$$-\frac{m}{2}\ln\Delta - \frac{m}{2}\ln 2\pi$$

to the leading term ensures that the resulting approximation is a log density. In fact it is the log density of a multivariate normal with mean x_0 and covariance matrix ΔI.

Consider next a quadratic (in $x - x_0$) approximation to the solution to Eq. (5.9) determining $C_{-1}(x|x_0)$. The linear term is necessarily zero when the matrix ν is nonsingular. Write the second-order expansion as:

$$C_{-1}(x|x_0) \approx -\frac{1}{2}(x - x_0)' V (x - x_0).$$

Equation (5.9) implies the Riccati equation,

$$V = V\nu(x_0)V$$

with the solution of interest being:

$$V = \nu^{-1}(x_0).$$

As a consequence the leading term in the expansion is:

$$-\frac{1}{2\Delta}(x - x_0)'\nu(x_0)^{-1}(x - x_0)$$

implying an approximate density:

$$\exp\left[-\frac{1}{2\Delta}(x - x_0)'\nu(x_0)^{-1}(x - x_0)\right]$$

when we localize in both the interval Δ and $x - x_0$. Adding

$$-\frac{m}{2}(\ln \Delta + \ln 2\pi) - \frac{1}{2}\ln \det \nu(x_0)$$

scales the implied density approximation to integrate to one. The resulting density is normal with mean x_0 and covariance matrix $\Delta\nu(x_0)$.

We will have more to say about the $x - x_0$ component of the expansion subsequently.

5.3.3. Next Two Terms

We now consider the implications of (5.8) for the next two terms in the small Δ expansion. Adding a constant term in x does not alter the differential equation. Thus, we do not expect that the coefficients will be fully determined from this equation alone.

To avoid higher-order terms in $\ln \Delta$, we look for solutions in which $\tilde{C}(x|x_0)$ is independent of x. Using the previous discussion as motivation, we set

$$\tilde{C}(x|x_0) = -\frac{m}{2}.$$

In addition, we initialize $C_0(x_0|x_0) = -\frac{1}{2}\ln \det \nu(x_0) - \frac{m}{2}\ln(2\pi)$.

From the forward Eq. (5.8), we also have the restriction:

$$\begin{aligned}\tilde{C}(x|x_0) &= \sum_{i=1}^{m} \mu_i(x)\frac{\partial C_{-1}}{\partial x_i}(x|x_0) + \sum_{i=1}^{m}\sum_{j=1}^{m} \frac{\partial \nu_{ij}(x)}{\partial x_i}\frac{\partial C_{-1}}{\partial x_j}(x|x_0) \\ &+ \frac{1}{2}\sum_{i=1}^{m}\sum_{j=1}^{m} \nu_{ij}(x)\frac{\partial^2 C_{-1}}{\partial x_i \partial x_j}(x|x_0) \\ &+ \sum_{i=1}^{m}\sum_{j=1}^{m} \frac{\partial C_{-1}}{\partial x_i}(x|x_0)\nu_{ij}(x)\frac{\partial C_0}{\partial x_j}(x|x_0)\end{aligned} \tag{5.10}$$

After substituting the solutions for C_{-1} and $\tilde{C}$, this becomes a first-order partial differential equation in $C_0(x|x_0)$.

Recall that in Example 11, we set $\nu = I$. In this example, differential equation (5.10) simplifies and is satisfied provided that:

$$\sum_{i=1}^{m} \frac{\partial C_0}{\partial x_i}(x|x_0)(x_i - x_{0i}) = -\sum_{i=1}^{m} \mu_i(x)(x_i - x_{0i}).$$

Integrating along a line segment between x_0 and x we obtain:

$$C_0(x|x_0) = -\sum_{i=1}^{m} (x_i - x_{0i}) \int_0^1 \mu_i\left[x + u\left(x_0 - x_0\right)\right] du$$

since $\ln \det I = 0$.

5.3.4. Remaining Terms

There is a recursive structure to the remaining coefficients. The left-hand side of (5.8) entails the derivative with respect to Δ, whereas the right-hand side does not,

$$\begin{aligned} C_{k+1}(x|x_0) = {} & C_k^*(x) + \sum_{i=1}^{m} \mu_i(x) \frac{\partial C_k}{\partial x_i}(x|x_0) + \sum_{i=1}^{m}\sum_{j=1}^{m} \frac{\partial \nu_{ij}(x)}{\partial x_i} \frac{\partial C_k}{\partial x_j}(x|x_0) \\ & + \frac{1}{2}\sum_{i=1}^{m}\sum_{j=1}^{m} \nu_{ij}(x) \frac{\partial^2 C_k}{\partial x_i \partial x_j}(x|x_0) \\ & + \frac{1}{2}\sum_{i=1}^{m}\sum_{j=1}^{m}\sum_{r=-1}^{k} \frac{\partial C_r}{\partial x_i}(x|x_0)\nu_{ij}(x) \frac{\partial C_{k-r}}{\partial x_j}(x|x_0). \end{aligned} \tag{5.11}$$

where $C_0^* = C^*$ and $C_j^* = 0$ for $j \geq 1$. Notice that the right-hand side has a term in

$$\frac{\partial C_{k+1}}{\partial x_j}(x|x_0)$$

obtained when $r = -1$. The remaining terms are computed as simple functions of derivatives of lower order coefficients. Thus we are again left with a differential equation to solve, but it is an equation that is linear in this derivative and not quadratic as in partial differential equation (5.9) for $C_{-1}(x|x_0)$. We are interested in solutions for which $C_{k+1}(x_0|x_0) = 0$.

5.3.5. Expansions in Powers of $x - x_0$

Typically one cannot solve the differential equation (5.11). Instead, we can compute the coefficients of an expansion in powers of $x - x_0$ that is guaranteed to be accurate for x

close to x_0. After constructing an expansion to a given order of each coefficient $C_j(x|x_0)$, the result is a joint expansion in Δ and $x - x_0$.

Like the expansion in Δ, a polynomial expansion of $C_j(x|x_0)$ can be computed explicitly in powers of $x - x_0$: see Aït-Sahalia (2008) for details, and the order at which to expand the coefficient C_j. These Taylor expansions of $C_j(x|x_0)$ may be computed by solving systems of linear equations with one exception, which fortunately also has an explicit expansion in $x - x_0$. Consider the Eq. (5.9) determining $C_{-1}(x|x_0)$. As we have previously argued the first nonzero term in the expansion is quadratic:

$$C_{-1}(x|x_0) = -\frac{1}{2}(x - x_0)'\nu(x_0)^{-1}(x - x_0),$$

obtained by solving a Riccati equation. The higher-order terms $(x - x_0)$ for C_{-1} can be calculated by solving linear equations, however.

In conclusion, combining expansions in Δ and $x - x_0$, as described in Aït-Sahalia (2008), provides a sequence of local approximations to the function $\ln p(x|x_0, \Delta)$. These expansions can be computed conveniently for a multivariate diffusion process by evaluating derivatives of the drift and diffusion coefficients and solving a Riccati equation for one term and linear equations for the remaining terms.

6. OBSERVABLE IMPLICATIONS AND TESTS

We have seen in Sections 4 and 5 how to characterize transition densities of Markov processes. In this section we explore the inverse problem. Suppose from data we can infer information about transitions, could these data have come from special classes of continuous-time Markov processes? What are the observable implications of the special types of Markov processes?

6.1. Local Characterization

By its very nature the generator gives a local counterpart to conditional moment restrictions. It gives us a formal sense in which:

$$\frac{E\phi(x_{t+\Delta}|x_t) - \phi(x_t)}{\Delta} \approx \mathcal{A}\phi(x_t).$$

Thus estimation of the left-hand side allows for the approximation of $\mathcal{A}$. By looking at appropriately chosen families of test functions, we can learn about $\mathcal{A}$ provided discretization errors are small.

First, we consider the identification scheme advocated by Johannes (2004). Consider first linear test functions parameterized as $\phi(x) = a \cdot (x - x^*)$ for some $a \in \mathbb{R}^m$ and some x^*. Then

$$\mathcal{A}\phi(x) = a \cdot \mu(x) + a \cdot \left[\int (y - x^*)R(dy|x) - (x - x^*)\right].$$

Evaluating this at $x = x^*$ gives:

$$\mathcal{A}\phi(x^*) = a \cdot \mu(x^*) + a \cdot \int (y - x^*) R(\mathrm{d}y | x^*).$$

By letting a be each of the coordinate vectors we identify:

$$\mu(x^*) + \int (y - x^*) R(\mathrm{d}y | x^*).$$

Using an entirely similar argument for quadratic functions of the form $(x - x^*)' V (x - x^*)$ for symmetric matrices V, we may infer

$$\nu(x^*) + \int (y - x^*)(y - x^*)' R(\mathrm{d}y | x^*).$$

More generally, higher-order polynomials centered around x^* will reveal higher-order moments of the conditional jump distribution scaled by the jump intensity. The drift and diffusion will only contribute to the first two conditional moments. Johannes (2004) used this observation to infer the importance of jump components in interest rates.

Polynomials will sometimes not be in the domain of the generator. Other collections of localized test functions can be employed in making these approximations. For instance, $a \cdot (x - x^*)$ might be replaced by $\phi(x) = a \cdot (x - x^*)\psi(|x - x^*|^2)$ where ψ is a symmetric twice continuously differentiable function that is one at zero and has compact support. Notice that the derivative of this test function at $x = x^*$ is a. In the absence of jumps,

$$\mathcal{A}\phi(x^*) = a \cdot \mu(x^*).$$

Similarly, when $\phi(x) = (x - x^*)' V (x - x^*)\psi(|x - x^*|^2)$,

$$\mathcal{A}\phi(x^*) = \mathrm{trace}[\nu(x^*) V]$$

which can be used to identify ν.

Given that the diffusion component is a local operator, localization of first- and second-order polynomials continues to permit the identification of the drift and the diffusion coefficients. When the jump component is present, we must add corrections that depend more specifically on the function ψ used in localization. The corrections will cease to be conditional moments of the jump distribution scaled by the jump intensity parameter λ.

Finally, in the absence of jump components we may also use a localization that is not smooth. For instance, the infinitesimal parameters can be recovered using the familiar formulas:

$$\mu(x^*) = \lim_{\Delta \to 0} \frac{1}{\Delta} \int_{|y - x^*| < \varepsilon} (y - x^*) P_\Delta(x^*, \mathrm{d}y)$$

$$\nu(x^*) = \lim_{\Delta \to 0} \frac{1}{\Delta} \int_{|y - x^*| < \varepsilon} (y - x^*)(y - x^*)' P_\Delta(x^*, \mathrm{d}y)$$

where P_Δ is the transition distribution for the diffusion process. Florens-Zmirou (1984), Stanton (1997), Fan and Zhang (2003), Bandi (2002), Bandi and Phillips (2003), and others consider estimation of diffusion based on these local conditional moment restrictions. See also Bandi and Phillips (2010) for a discussion.

6.2. Total Positivity and Testing for Jumps

The local characterizations are justified by taking a limit as $\Delta \to 0$. We now examine what can be said if the process is only observed at a finite observation interval Δ but arbitrarily large sample sizes. Let $\mathbb{R}$ be the state space for a Markov process, and consider a family of probability distributions indexed by the time interval Δ: $P_\Delta(\cdot|x)$. Could this family of densities have come from a scalar diffusion process, i.e., a scalar Markov process with continuous sample paths, or must a more general process be considered? Aït-Sahalia (2002c) develops statistical tests based on the *total positivity* restrictions on transition densities (see Karlin and McGregor, 1959a).

While total positivity has a more general representation and probabilistic interpretation, it implies

$$P_\Delta(x, B)\, P_\Delta(\tilde{x}, \tilde{B}) - P_\Delta(\tilde{x}, B)\, P_\Delta(x, \tilde{B}) > 0 \tag{6.1}$$

whenever, $x < \tilde{x}$ and $B < \tilde{B}$ (where $B < \tilde{B}$ is interpreted to mean that every element of B is less than every element of $\tilde{B}$). Since this must hold for any choice of $\tilde{x}$ and $\tilde{B}$, there is a local (in the state) counterpart that we express using the logarithm of the density:

$$\frac{\partial^2}{\partial x \partial y} \ell(y|x, \Delta) > 0 \tag{6.2}$$

for all x and y and interval Δ. This cross derivative restriction for each choice of x, y, and Δ is a necessary condition for transition distributions to be those implied by a scalar diffusion.

A partial converse is also available. Suppose that the family of distribution functions of a Markov process on $\mathbb{R}$ satisfies (6.1) for any positive Δ, then under a side condition, there exists a realization of the process such that almost all sample paths are continuous.

The following example shows how criterion (6.2) can be used to eliminate some transition densities as coming from a model of a scalar diffusion.

Example 12 *Suppose that $\ell(y|x, \Delta)$ depends on the composite state (y, x) only through $y - x$. Then criterion (6.2) is equivalent to requiring that ℓ be concave in $y - x$. It can be shown that the only admissible solution is*

$$\ell(y|x, \Delta) = -\frac{1}{2}\ln(2\pi\beta^2\Delta) - \frac{(y - x - \alpha\Delta)^2}{2\beta^2\Delta}$$

where α and β are free parameters. That is the transition density is an arithmetic Brownian motion.

As an alternative, consider the generalized Cauchy density

$$\ell(y|x,\Delta) = -\ln \pi + \ln \alpha(\Delta) - \ln\left[\alpha(\Delta)^2 + (y-x)^2\right]$$

where $\alpha(\Delta)$ is positive. Criterion (6.2) fails for large $y-x$.

Aït-Sahalia (2002c) contains other examples. More generally, total positivity implies restrictions on processes defined on state spaces other than $\mathbb{R}$. Consider a continuous-time, stationary, Markov chain that can only take countable discrete values, say, $\{\ldots,-1,0,1,\ldots\}$. In a discrete state space, the appropriate notion of continuity of the chain's sample paths is the following intuitive one: the chain never jumps by more than one state at a time, either up or down. It turns out that the restriction on the chain's transition probabilities analogous to (6.1) characterizes precisely this form of continuity: total positivity across all intervals restricts the process to be a so-called birth-and-death process (see Karlin and McGregor, 1959b). In this sense, a birth-and-death process is the discrete-state analog to a scalar diffusion. See Aït-Sahalia (2002c) for further discussion and implications for derivative pricing methods, such as binomial trees.

For a fixed Δ, total positivity is a necessary restriction on the transition distribution but not a sufficient one. Given a candidate transition distribution over an interval Δ, we did not construct a diffusion with that transition distribution. Frydman and Singer (1979) study the analogous question for a finite state birth and death process. In their study, they show that to embed a single transition matrix (over an interval Δ) satisfying total positivity in a continuous-time Markov process it is sometimes necessary that the continuous-time process be time-inhomogeneous. They show that the total positivity function is a weaker restriction than embeddability for a continuous-time process that is restricted to be time-homogeneous.

6.3. Principal Component Approach

We now explore an alternative approach to the embeddability question in the context of scalar diffusions: when does there exist a (time-homogeneous) scalar diffusion process that is consistent with a given discrete-time transition distribution? We follow Hansen et al. (1998) by answering this question using a principal component decomposition. As we have seen, the existence of this decomposition is restrictive.

First, consider a scalar diffusion with stationary density q and diffusion coefficient σ^2. As we have seen there is a corresponding form constructed with these objects. Each principal component satisfies the eigenvalue relation:

$$\frac{1}{2}\int \phi' \psi_j' \sigma^2 q = \delta_j \int \phi \psi_j q.$$

for any ϕ that is twice continuously differentiable for which ϕ' has compact support. An integration-by-parts argument implies that

$$\psi_j'(x)\sigma^2(x)q(x) = -2\delta_j \int^x \psi_j q \tag{6.3}$$

because ϕ' can be localized at the point x.

To achieve identification, we must construct σ^2 from a discrete-time transition operator. The density q and the principal components ψ_j and associated eigenvalues δ_j are identifiable from discrete-time data. The principle components are identifiable because they maximize autocorrelation. Moreover, they satisfy the discrete-time conditional moment restriction:[17]

$$E\left[\phi_j(X_{t+\Delta})|X_t\right] = \exp(-\Delta\delta_j)\phi_j(X_t).$$

We can think of (6.3) as a set of restrictions that can be used to infer σ^2. While σ^2 can be identified from one of these equations (except for the constant eigenfunction equation), over-identification comes from the fact that the same σ^2 must work for all eigenfunctions.[18] As σ^2 is restricted to be positive, there is a testable implication for even a single choice of j in (6.3) provided the constant eigenfunction is not used. Unfortunately, statistical testing is likely to be more challenging for testing eigenfunction restrictions than for testing total positivity.

6.4. Testing the Specification of Transitions

The generator of a semigroup commutes with the family of conditional expectation operator that it generates:

$$\mathcal{A}\mathcal{T}_\Delta\phi = \mathcal{T}_\Delta\mathcal{A}\phi \tag{6.4}$$

for any ϕ in the domain of the generator and any Δ. This follows from the semigroup property (2.2) and the construction of the generator as the time derivative of the semigroup (at $t = 0$). As emphasized by Hansen and Scheinkman (1995), this gives rise to a set of testable restrictions beyond stationarity that we now explore.

[17] An alternative parametric identification and inference approach is suggested by Kessler and Sorensen (1999). They use the fact that principal components satisfy this conditional moment restriction to build estimating equations for parameterized diffusions. See Bibby et al. (2010) for further discussion.

[18] There is a close relation between recovery formula (6.3) and formula (3.9) that we described previously. Suppose that a linear function is in the domain of the generator, the drift is linear. Then the drift coefficient is an eigenfunction and the corresponding value of δ is the negative of the derivative of this function. With these substitutions, the two recovery formulas coincide. Demoura (1998) suggests a similar identification by looking across two distinct eigenfunctions and their first two derivatives to identify the pair (μ, σ^2). In contrast, recovery formula (6.3) avoids using second derivatives and instead uses a single eigenfunction in conjunction with the stationary density.

From an abstract perspective, given a candidate generator $\hat{\mathcal{A}}$ (not necessarily $\mathcal{A}$) and a conditional expectation operator $\mathcal{T}_\Delta$ suppose

$$\hat{\mathcal{A}}\mathcal{T}_\Delta\phi = \mathcal{T}_\Delta\hat{\mathcal{A}}\phi \tag{6.5}$$

for any ϕ among a rich collection of test functions (formally a core of the generator). In what way does this restrict the candidate $\hat{\mathcal{A}}$? How might we actually test this implication?

If the candidate generator $\hat{\mathcal{A}}$ commutes with $\mathcal{A}$, then $\hat{\mathcal{A}}$ cannot be distinguished from $\mathcal{A}$ based on (6.4). In particular, when $\hat{\mathcal{A}}$ is a scalar multiple of $\mathcal{A}$, they commute and hence cannot be distinguished. Thus, the most one can hope for from (6.5) is the identification of the generator up to scale. As illustrated by Hansen and Scheinkman (1995), without further restrictions, the identification problem can be more severe than this. On the other hand, Hansen and Scheinkman (1995) show that stationary scalar diffusions can be identified up to scale by (2.2) and the information encoded in the stationary distribution.

Stationary scalar diffusions are examples of processes that are reversible. More generally, stationary Markov processes modeled via symmetric forms are reversible. Such models are identifiable from discrete time data sampled at any fixed interval Δ.[19] Thus, the commuting restriction does not encode all of the identifying information contained in the transition distribution.

For reversible Markov process models, there is an equivalent statement of restriction (6.5):

$$E\left(\left[\hat{\mathcal{A}}\phi(x_{t+1})\right]\psi(x_t)\right) = E\left(\phi(x_{t+1})\left[\hat{\mathcal{A}}\psi(x_t)\right]\right) \tag{6.6}$$

for ϕ and ψ in the domain of $\hat{\mathcal{A}}$. The restriction can be tested via statistical methods by focusing on a limited number of test functions, or it can be made comprehensive by adapting the approach of Bierens (1990). This type of moment condition is extended in Conley et al. (1997).[20] Instead of analyzing the forward and backward evolution of the product of two functions, $\phi(x_{t+1})$ and $\psi(x_t)$, the evolution of a more general function $\varphi(x_{t+1}, x_t)$ is used. In what follows we describe a different approach.

For stationary diffusions, there is an equivalent statement of restriction (6.5) that is deduced in Aït-Sahalia (1996b). In contrast to (6.6) reversibility is not required. We may deduce this directly from the Kolmogorov forward and backward equations as in Aït-Sahalia (1996b). Alternatively (and essentially equivalently) we may localize the test function ϕ in (6.5). Let $\hat{\mathcal{A}}$ be a candidate generator of a diffusion with drift $\hat{\mu}$ and

[19]See Proposition 5 in Hansen and Scheinkman (1995).
[20]See their Appendix E for a justification.

diffusion matrix $\hat{\nu}$. After localization, the left-hand side of (6.5) becomes:

$$\sum_i \hat{\mu}_i(x)\frac{\partial}{\partial x_i}p(y|x,\Delta)+\frac{1}{2}\sum_{i,j}\hat{\nu}_{ij}(x)\frac{\partial^2}{\partial x_i\partial x_j}p(y|x,\Delta).$$

Prior to localizing the right-hand side of (6.5), we apply integration by parts to a test function with compact support in the interior of the state space and write:

$$\mathcal{T}_\Delta\hat{\mathcal{A}}\phi(x)=-\int\left[\sum_i\frac{\partial}{\partial y_i}\hat{\mu}_i(y)p(y|x,\Delta)\right]\phi(y)dy+\frac{1}{2}\int\left[\sum_{i,j}\frac{\partial^2}{\partial y_i y_j}\hat{\nu}_{ij}(y)p(y|x,\Delta)\right]\phi(y)dy$$

By localizing the test function around a given value of y, it follows from (6.5) that

$$\begin{aligned}&\sum_i \hat{\mu}_i(x)\frac{\partial}{\partial x_i}p(y|x,\Delta)+\frac{1}{2}\sum_{i,j}\hat{\nu}_{ij}(x)\frac{\partial^2}{\partial x_i\partial x_j}p(y|x,\Delta)\\&=-\sum_i\frac{\partial}{\partial y_i}\left[\hat{\mu}_i(y)p(y|x,\Delta)\right]+\frac{1}{2}\sum_{i,j}\frac{\partial^2}{\partial y_i y_j}\left[\hat{\nu}_{ij}(y)p(y|x,\Delta)\right].\end{aligned}\tag{6.7}$$

Aït-Sahalia (1996b) calls the difference $K(y|x,\Delta)$ between the left-hand and right-hand side as the *transition discrepancy*.[21]

Indeed, the left-hand side of the inequality is the contribution of the Kolmogorov forward equation

$$\frac{\partial p(y,t|x,s)}{\partial t}=-\sum_i\frac{\partial}{\partial y_i}\left[\hat{\mu}_i(y)p(y,t|x,s)\right]+\frac{1}{2}\sum_{i,j}\frac{\partial^2}{\partial y_i y_j}\left[\hat{\nu}_{ij}(y)p(y,t|x,s)\right]\tag{6.8}$$

and the right-hand side is the contribution from the backward equation:

$$-\frac{\partial p(y,t|x,s)}{\partial s}=\sum_i\hat{\mu}_i(x)\frac{\partial}{\partial x_i}p(y,t|x,s)+\frac{1}{2}\sum_{i,j}\hat{\nu}_{ij}(x)\frac{\partial^2}{\partial x_i\partial x_j}p\left(y,t|x,s\right).\tag{6.9}$$

These two equations cannot be used as such because their left-hand side contains the derivative of the transition density with respect to time. Time derivatives cannot be estimated without observations on how the process changes over small intervals of time. But we can work around this problem by getting rid of the time derivatives as follows.

[21] Although the above discussion focuses on diffusions, the Kolmogorov equations have natural extensions for more general Markov processes (such as processes with jumps) and the corresponding transition discrepancy can be defined (see Aït-Sahalia, 1996b).

Under time-homogeneity, $p(y, t|x, s) = p(y, t - s|x, 0) \equiv p(y|x, t - s)$ as discussed in Section 2.1 and therefore: $\partial p/\partial t = -\partial p/\partial s$. Combining the two Eqs. (6.8)–(6.9) then yields the transition discrepancy, namely the fact that the sum of the left-hand sides of (6.8) and (6.9) must be zero.

Restrictions (6.6) or (6.7) could in principle be used to identify a scalar diffusion nonparametrically up to a free scale parameter on the drift and diffusion coefficients. They are also of value in estimating and testing parameterized diffusions processes (again up to free scale parameter). Restriction (6.6) avoids having to estimate second derivatives of transition densities, but it is applicable only to reversible processes and requires a specific selection of test functions.[22] Restriction (6.7) gives rise to a comprehensive test in Aït-Sahalia (1996b) formalized by choosing a weighting function to use in conjunction with the discrepancy measure. Indeed, if we parametrize the diffusion process, then K (with μ and σ^2 replaced by their assumed parametric form $\mu(\cdot, \theta)$ and $\sigma^2(\cdot, \theta)$, respectively) must be zero at the true parameter value under the null of correct parametric specification. Given nonparametric estimates of the transition function, $K = 0$ provides a testable implication. The statistically efficient choices of test functions or weighting functions have not been formally analyzed to date.

6.5. Testing Markovianity

The specification analysis described earlier assumes that the process is Markovian. Can this be tested? A continuous time Markov process sampled with an interval Δ is a discrete-time Markov process. One common approach to test a discrete-time Markov process is to include additional lags of the state vector into the state evolution equation and test for their statistical significance. Following Aït-Sahalia (2002a), we consider an alternative approach based on the Chapman–Kolmogorov equation given in Definition 2.

Under time-homogeneity, an implication of the Chapman–Kolmogorov equation is that $\mathcal{T}_{2\Delta} = (\mathcal{T}_\Delta)^2$ as required by the semigroup property. Stated in terms of transition densities, the Markov hypothesis can be tested in the form H_0 against H_1, where

$$\begin{cases} H_0 : p(y|x, 2\Delta) - r(y|x, 2\Delta) = 0 & \text{for all } (x, y) \in S^2 \\ H_1 : p(y|x, 2\Delta) - r(y|x, 2\Delta) \neq 0 & \text{for some } (x, y) \in S^2 \end{cases}$$

with

$$r(y|x, 2\Delta) \doteq \int_{z \in S} p(y|z, \Delta) p(z|x, \Delta) dz. \tag{6.10}$$

Both $p(y|x, \Delta)$ and $p(y|x, 2\Delta)$ can be estimated from data sampled at interval Δ. The successive pairs of observed data (X_0, X_Δ), $(X_\Delta, X_{2\Delta})$, $(X_{2\Delta}, X_{3\Delta})$, etc., can be used to

[22] Hansen and Scheinkman (1995) derive a more general counterpart based on the generator of the reverse-time process.

estimate the density $p(y|x, \Delta)$ and hence the function r given by (6.10). Meanwhile, the successive pairs $(x_0, x_{2\Delta})$, $(x_\Delta, x_{3\Delta})$, ..., can be used to estimate directly the density $p(y|x, 2\Delta)$. In other words, the test compares a *direct* estimator of the 2Δ-interval conditional density, with the *indirect* estimator of the 2Δ-interval conditional density based on formula (6.10). If the process is actually Markovian, then the two estimates should be close (for some distance measure) in a sense made precise by the use of the statistical distribution of these estimators.

More generally, we could study the $j\Delta$ transitions where j is an integer greater than or equal to 2. For larger j, there are more options for comparison. A test could be based on constructing a $j\Delta$ period transition from shorter ones including $(\Delta, (j-1)\Delta)$, $(2\Delta, (j-2)\Delta), \ldots$. It is not necessary to check all of these configurations as many will be redundant. In general, a vector of *transition equalities* can be tested in a single pass in a GMM framework with as many moment conditions as transition intervals.

6.6. Testing Symmetry

The symmetry of the transition distribution implied by our use of forms to build Markov processes is restrictive. This restriction has motivated the construction of tests of symmetry and as we have seen more general formulations that allow for asymmetry. In one important special case symmetry is not limiting: scalar diffusions on the real line. In higher dimensions, however, symmetry is restrictive even for diffusions. When a Markov process is stationary, the symmetry implied by the forms implies that the process is time reversible when initialized at the stationary distribution. Reversible Markov processes are identifiable from discrete-time data, even without parametric restrictions. There is no aliasing problem for these processes. See Hansen and Scheinkman (1995) for a discussion.

Florens et al. (1998) propose a test for reversibility as a necessary condition to embed a stationary, reversible continuous-time process in a discrete time process sampled at regular intervals. Their idea is the following. A reversible process should display positive autocorrelation in the following sense. For any test function ϕ,

$$E\phi(X_t)\phi(X_{t+s}) \geq 0$$

for any interval s. (See the Theorem in Florens et al., 1998 on page 75.) To build a statistical test, use a vector of such functions, which we denote by Φ. Form the symmetrized autocovariance matrix:

$$\frac{1}{2}\left[E\Phi(X_t)\Phi(X_{t+1})' + E\Phi(X_{t+1})\Phi(X_t)'\right]. \tag{6.11}$$

While this matrix has real eigenvalues by construction, the eigenvalues should all be positive if the discretely sampled process can be embedded in a continuous-time, reversible

Markov process. Because all linear combinations of test functions in Φ should show positive persistence, eigenfunctions should also display positive persistence. Thus, eigenvalues must be positive. Florens et al. (1998) suggest building a test based on the smallest eigenvalue of the sample analog to (6.11).

An alternative approach to testing reversibility is given by Darolles et al. (2004). It is based on nonlinear canonical analysis of the joint density of adjacent observations, say (X_t, X_{t+1}). With limitations on the temporal dependence, canonical analysis produces principal component pairs of functions say $\phi(X_t)$ and $\psi(X_{t+1})$ that maximize correlation under orthogonality constraints. This becomes a nonlinear analysis because the functions ϕ and ψ can be nonlinear in the Markov state. These principal components can be used to construct an orthogonal decomposition of the joint density. Dauxois and Nkiet (1998) use canonical analysis as a test of independence between two random vectors, and Darolles et al. (2004) use it to produce a test of reversibility. Their statistical tests are based on the restrictions that reversibility imposes on the canonical analysis. Under reversibility, the two functions (ϕ, ψ) in each orthogonal pair should coincide.

6.7. Random Time Changes

As we remarked in Section 2.6.1, models with random time changes are common in finance. There are at least two ways to motivate such models. One formulation due to Bochner (1960) and Clark (1973) posits a distinction between calendar time and economic time. The random time changes are used to alter the flow of information in a random way. Alternatively an econometrician might confront a data set with random sample times, a situation we will return to in Section 7.3.

A model of random time changes requires that we specify two objects. An underlying Markov process $\{X_t : t \geq 0\}$ that is not subject to distortions in the time scale. For our purposes, this process is modeled using a generator $\mathcal{A}$. In addition, we introduce a process $\{\tau_t\}$ for a continuous-time specification, or as $\{\tau_j : j = 1, 2, ...\}$ for discrete time observations. The discrete time process of interest is:

$$Z_j = X_{\tau_j}.$$

In Section 2.6.1, we describe a specification due to Duffie and Glynn (2004) and showed that the one-step ahead conditional expectation operator for the resulting $\{Z_j : j = 1, 2, ...\}$ is:

$$(\mathcal{I} - \zeta\mathcal{A})^{-1}$$

where $\mathcal{A}$ is a generator, ζ distorts the time clock of the process $\{X_t : t \geq 0\}$, and $\check{\mathcal{A}} = \zeta\mathcal{A}$. As Duffie and Glynn (2004) show, we can avoid computing the operator inverse for test functions ψ of the form:

$$\psi = \phi - \check{\mathcal{A}}\phi$$

for some ϕ in the domain of the generator $\check{\mathcal{A}}$. For this convenient but flexible choice of ψ,

$$E[\psi(Z_{j+1})|Z_j] = \left(\mathcal{I} - \check{\mathcal{A}}\right)^{-1} \psi(Z_j) = \phi(Z_j),$$

or

$$E[\phi(Z_{j+1}) - \check{\mathcal{A}}\phi(Z_{j+1}) - \phi(Z_j)|Z_j] = 0. \tag{6.12}$$

This implies an extensive array of conditional moment restrictions to be used in estimation and testing.[23]

Models with random time distortions present special challenges for identification and estimation. Without observations on the directing process or sampling times, nonparametric identification of even reversible processes breaks down. If the directing process $\{\tau_j\}$ is independent of the underlying process $\{X_t\}$, then the most we can hope for is its identification of $\mathcal{A}$ up to scale. It will not be possible to distinguish an original process from one that moves through time say twice as fast. Hansen and Scheinkman (1995) establish that scalar diffusions can be identified up to a free constant scale parameter without data on observation times. Identification is even more challenging when the sampling or directing process is dependent on the underlying process. As we have seen in examples 3 and 4, the generator of the original process is scaled by a scalar function of the underlying Markov state in the characterization of the generator for a process with a distorted time scale. Thus without data on the process $\{\tau_j\}$, we are left not being able to distinguish $\mathcal{A}$ from $\zeta^*\mathcal{A}$ for some positive function ζ^* of the Markov state. The free scale factor is a function not a constant. Finite-dimensional parameterizations, when appropriate, will simplify or in some cases even solve this identification problem.

Consider next the case in which $\{\tau_j\}$ is directly interpreted as a set of sample times and not some unobserved distortion in the time scale. These sampling times provide important identifying information about the possibly dependent sampling scheme and about the underlying process $\{X_t\}$. Direct or indirect (through say trading volume) data on the directing process will be useful in inferring the underlying process. We will have more to say about this question in Section 7.3.

7. THE PROPERTIES OF PARAMETER ESTIMATORS

7.1. Maximum Likelihood Estimation

A direct consequence of the expansion approach described in Sections 5.2 and 5.3 is the practical feasibility of maximum likelihood estimators for discretely sampled diffusions.

[23]This is a particular case of Duffie and Glynn (2004), who deduce a more general class of conditional moment restrictions by allowing for test functions that depend on Z_j's at adjacent integers.

A fixed interval sample of a time-homogenous continuous-time Markov process is a Markov process in discrete time. Given that the Markov state vector is observed and the unknown parameters are identified, properties of the ML estimator follow from what is known about ML estimation of discrete-time Markov processes.[24] There is an extensive literature applicable to discrete-time stationary Markov processes starting with the work of Billingsley (1961). The asymptotic covariance matrix for the ML estimator is the inverse of the score covariance or *information* matrix where the score at date t is $\partial \ln p(X_{t+\Delta}|X_t, \Delta, \theta)/\partial\theta$ where $\ln p(\cdot|x, \Delta, \theta)$ is the logarithm of the conditional density over an interval of time Δ and a parameter value θ.

When the underlying Markov process is nonstationary, the score process inherits this nonstationarity. The rate of convergence and the limiting distribution of the maximum likelihood estimator depends upon growth properties of the score process (e.g., see Hall and Heyde, 1980; Chapter 6.2). A nondegenerate limiting distribution can be obtained when the score process behaves in a sufficiently regular fashion. The limiting distribution can be deduced by showing that general results pertaining to time series asymptotics (see e.g., Jeganathan, 1995) can be applied to the present context. One first establishes that the likelihood ratio has the locally asymptotically quadratic (LAQ) structure, then within that class separates between the locally asymptotically mixed Normal (LAMN), locally asymptotically Normal (LAN), and locally asymptotically Brownian functional (LABF) structures. As we have seen, when the data generating process is stationary and ergodic, the estimation is typically in the LAN class. The LAMN class can be used to justify many of the standard inference methods given the ability to estimate the covariance matrix pertinent for the conditional normal approximating distribution. Rules for inference are special for the LABF case. These structures are familiar from the linear time series literature on unit roots and co-integration. Details for the case of a nonlinear Markov process can be found in Aït-Sahalia (2002b).

Example 13 *As an example of the types of results that can be derived, consider the Ornstein-Uhlenbeck specification,* $dX_t = -\kappa X_t dt + \sigma dW_t$, *where* $\theta = (\kappa, \sigma^2)$. *The discrete-time process obtained by sampling at a fixed interval* Δ *is a Gaussian first-order autoregressive process with autoregressive parameter* $\exp(-\kappa\Delta)$ *and innovation variance* $\frac{\sigma^2}{2\kappa}\left(1 - e^{-2\kappa\Delta}\right)$. *White (1958) and Anderson (1959) originally characterized the limiting distribution for the discrete-time autoregressive parameter when the Markov process is not stationary. Alternatively, by specializing the general theory of the limiting behavior of the ML estimation to this model, one obtains the following asymptotic distribution for the the ML estimator of the continuous-time parameterization (see Corollary 2 in Aït-Sahalia, 2002b):*

[24] Identification of a *multivariate* continuous-time Markov process from discrete-time can be problematic when the process is not reversible. It is well known that an *aliasing problem* can be present. For example, see Phillips (1973) and Hansen and Sargent (1983).

- *If $\kappa > 0$ (LAN, stationary case):*

$$\sqrt{N}\left(\begin{pmatrix}\hat{\kappa}_N\\ \hat{\sigma}_N^2\end{pmatrix} - \begin{pmatrix}\kappa\\ \sigma^2\end{pmatrix}\right)$$
$$\Rightarrow \mathcal{N}\left(\begin{pmatrix}0\\0\end{pmatrix}, \begin{pmatrix}\frac{e^{2\kappa\Delta}-1}{\Delta^2} & \frac{\sigma^2(e^{2\kappa\Delta}-1-2\kappa\Delta)}{\kappa\Delta^2}\\ \frac{\sigma^2(e^{2\kappa\Delta}-1-2\kappa\Delta)}{\kappa\Delta^2} & \frac{\sigma^4\left((e^{2\kappa\Delta}-1)^2+2\kappa^2\Delta^2(e^{2\kappa\Delta}+1)+4\kappa\Delta(e^{2\kappa\Delta}-1)\right)}{\kappa^2\Delta^2(e^{2\kappa\Delta}-1)}\end{pmatrix}\right)$$

- *If $\kappa < 0$ (LAMN, explosive case), assume $X_0 = 0$, then:*

$$\frac{e^{-(N+1)\kappa\Delta}\Delta}{e^{-2\kappa\Delta}-1}\left(\hat{\kappa}_N-\kappa\right) \Rightarrow G^{-1/2}\times\mathcal{N}(0,1)$$
$$\sqrt{N}\left(\hat{\sigma}_N^2-\sigma^2\right) \Rightarrow \mathcal{N}\left(0,2\sigma^4\right)$$

where G has a $\chi^2[1]$ distribution independent of the $\mathcal{N}(0,1)$. $G^{-1/2} \times \mathcal{N}(0,1)$ is a Cauchy distribution.

- *If $\kappa = 0$ (LABF, unit root case), assume $X_0 = 0$, then:*

$$N\hat{\kappa}_N \Rightarrow \left(1-W_1^2\right)\left(2\Delta\int_0^1 W_t^2\,dt\right)^{-1}$$
$$\sqrt{N}\left(\hat{\sigma}_N^2-\sigma^2\right) \Rightarrow \mathcal{N}\left(0,2\sigma^4\right)$$

where N is the sample size, $\{W_t : t \geq 0\}$ is a standard Brownian motion, and $\Rightarrow$ denotes convergence in distribution.

7.2. Estimating the Diffusion Coefficient in the Presence of Jumps

Suppose now that jumps are in fact present, in addition to the usual Brownian noise, as in

$$dX_t = \mu dt + \sigma dW_t + dU_t,$$

where $\{U_t\}$ is a pure jump Lévy process with jump measure υ and independent of the Brownian motion $\{W_t\}$. By restricting $\{U_t\}$ to be a pure Lévy process, we eliminate state dependence. In terms of the setup in Section 2, we let the conditional measure $R(dy|x) = \upsilon(du)$ for $u = y - x$. When υ is a finite measure the jump process is referred to as a compound Poisson process. Other Lévy processes allow $\upsilon([-\varepsilon, +\varepsilon]) = \infty$ for any $\varepsilon > 0$, so that the process exhibits an infinite number of small jumps in any finite time interval. Typical examples are members of the class of symmetric stable processes of index $0 < \alpha < 2$ and rate $\xi > 0$, for which $\upsilon(dy) = \alpha\xi^\alpha dy/|y|^{1+\alpha}$. The Cauchy process corresponds to $\alpha = 1$, while the limit $\alpha \to 2$ (from below) produces a Gaussian distribution. Following

Aït-Sahalia (2003), we assess the effect of jumps on the estimation of the Brownian variance parameter σ^2.

When the Lévy measure is finite, the tiny jumps ought to be harder to distinguish from Brownian noise. Surprisingly, using maximum likelihood, it is possible to identify σ^2 with the same degree of precision as if there were no jumps. Specifically, when the Brownian motion is contaminated by jumps, with a known measure, the asymptotic variance AVAR of the maximum likelihood estimator ML for the diffusion coefficient estimator satisfies

$$\mathrm{AVAR}_{\mathrm{ML}}\left(\sigma^2\right) = 2\sigma^4\Delta + o(\Delta) \tag{7.1}$$

so that in the limit when the sample interval shrinks to zero ($\Delta \to 0$), the MLE of σ^2 has the same asymptotic distribution as if no jumps were present. This result holds not only for the specific examples considered in Aït-Sahalia (2003) but for all Lévy processes that stay at a finite distance from the limiting case $\alpha = 2$ (see Aït-Sahalia and Jacod, 2009).

This result also states that the presence of the jumps imposes no cost on our ability to estimate σ^2. From (7.1), the leading term in the asymptotic variance expansion is the asymptotic variance that applies when jumps are absent. In contrast, suppose we contaminated the Brownian motion with another independent Brownian motion with known variance ς^2. In that case, we could still estimate σ^2, but the asymptotic variance of the MLE would be $2\left(\sigma^2 + \varsigma\right)^2 \Delta$.

Aït-Sahalia (2003) also studies the ability of method-of-moments to reproduce the efficiency of ML, considering, in particular, absolute moments of order r and shows that the optimal choice of moment functions involves noninteger values of r which are less than one.

7.3. Maximum Likelihood Estimation with Random Sampling Times

Transaction-level data in finance are not only discretely sampled in time, they are also sampled at random time intervals. Aït-Sahalia and Mykland (2003a) study the impact of including or discarding observations on the sampling intervals in that situation. Sampling intervals $\{\Delta_j : j = 1, 2, \ldots\}$ are random where $\Delta_j = \tau_j - \tau_{j-1}$ is drawn conditionally upon $X_{\tau_{j-1}}$ from a known distribution. By letting Δ_j be drawn conditionally on $X_{\tau_{j-1}}$, one can capture effects such as an increase in trading activity following a large price movement say at τ_{j-1}. This model is closely related to the models developed in Section 2.6.1 except that the models described previously allow movements in X_t, for $\tau_{j-1} < t < \tau_j$, to influence the τ_j.

Aït-Sahalia and Mykland (2003a) study three likelihood-based estimators of $\theta = (\kappa, \sigma)$ in the model

$$\mathrm{d}X_t = \mu(X_t; \kappa)\mathrm{d}t + \sigma \mathrm{d}W_t.$$

The three estimators are as follows:

- FIML: Full information maximum likelihood using the bivariate observations (X_{τ_j}, Δ_j);
- IOML: Partial information maximum likelihood estimator using only the state observations X_{τ_j}, with the sampling intervals *integrated out*;
- PFML: Pseudo maximum likelihood estimator *pretending* that the sampling intervals are *fixed* at $\Delta_j = \bar{\Delta}$.

These estimators are designed so that each one of them is subject to a specific subset of the different effects they wish to measure. FIML is asymptotically efficient, making the best possible use of the joint data (X_{τ_j}, Δ_j). The extent to which FIML with these data is less efficient than the corresponding FIML when the full sample path is observable is the *cost of discreteness*. IOML is the asymptotically optimal choice if one recognizes that the sampling intervals are random Δ_j but does not observe them. The extra efficiency loss relative to FIML is the *cost of discreteness*. PFML corresponds to doing as if the sampling intervals were all identical (pretending that $\Delta_j = \bar{\Delta}$) when in fact they are random. The extent by which PFML underperforms FIML is the *cost of ignoring the randomness*.

All three estimators rely on maximizing a version of the likelihood function of the observations, i.e., some functional of the transition density p: $p(X_{\tau_j}|X_{\tau_{j-1}}, \Delta_j, \theta)$ for FIML; $\tilde{p}(X_{\tau_j}|X_{\tau_{j-1}}, \theta) = E_{\Delta_j}\left[p(X_{\tau_j}|X_{\tau_{j-1}}, \Delta_j, \theta)\right]$, that is the over the law of $\Delta_j|X_{\tau_j}$ for IOML; and $p(X_{\tau_j}|X_{\tau_{j-1}}, \bar{\Delta}, \theta)$ for PFML (which is like FIML except that $\bar{\Delta}$ is used in place of the actual Δ_j). Under stationarity, $T^{1/2}(\hat{\theta} - \bar{\theta}) \rightarrow N(0, \Omega)$. For FIML and IOML, $\bar{\theta} = \theta_0$, where $\theta_0 = (\kappa_0, \sigma_0)$ is the true parameter value, but PFML is asymptotically biased.

Aït-Sahalia and Mykland (2003a) derive Taylor expansions of the asymptotic variance and bias of these estimators. A random variable from the common distribution of the sampling intervals is

$$\Delta = \varepsilon \Delta_0, \tag{7.2}$$

where ε is deterministic and Δ_0 has a given finite distribution conditional on X_0. They compute Taylor expansions in ε of the expectations of interest, around $\varepsilon = 0$ (the limiting case were the full continuous-time sample path is observable), leading to results of the form:

$$\Omega = \Omega^{(0)} + \varepsilon\, \Omega^{(1)} + \varepsilon^2\, \Omega^{(2)} + O\left(\varepsilon^3\right) \tag{7.3}$$

$$\bar{\theta} - \theta_0 = \varepsilon\, b^{(1)} + \varepsilon^2\, b^{(2)} + O\left(\varepsilon^3\right) \tag{7.4}$$

where the higher order terms in ε correct the leading term for the discreteness of the sampling. Differences between estimation methods and data use the matrices $\Omega^{(i)}$ and $b^{(i)}$, $i = 0, 1, \ldots$.[25]

These characterizations are based on a modification of the infinitesimal generator. Consider first test functions that depend on the elapsed time interval and, as we considered previously, on an initial state:

$$f(X_t, X_0, t)$$

A well-known extension of the infinitesimal generator is:

$$\mu(x;\kappa_0)\frac{\partial f(x, x_0, t)}{\partial x} + \frac{\sigma_0^2}{2}\frac{\partial^2 f(x, x_0, t)}{\partial y^2} + \frac{\partial f(x, x_0, t)}{\partial t},$$

which now includes a simple derivative with respect to time.

To analyze sampling under (7.2), Aït-Sahalia and Mykland (2003a) use a related construction. Consider a test function of the form:

$$f(Y_1, Y_0, \Delta, \bar{\theta}, \varepsilon)$$

where $Y_j \doteq X_{\Delta_j}$. While it is possible to condition on the random Δ and Y_0 in taking a small ϵ approximation, Δ and in the case of the PFML estimator, $\bar{\theta}$ depend implicitly on ϵ. This gives rise to a related but different extension of the infinitesimal generator:

$$\begin{aligned}\mathcal{G}f(y, y_0, \delta, \theta, \varepsilon) = \delta_0\left[\mu(y;\kappa_0)\frac{\partial f(y, y_0, \delta, \theta, \varepsilon)}{\partial y} + \frac{\sigma_0^2}{2}\frac{\partial^2 f(y, y_0, \delta, \theta, \varepsilon)}{\partial y^2} + \frac{\partial f(y, y_0, \delta, \theta, \varepsilon)}{\partial \delta}\right] \\ + \frac{\partial f(y, y_0, \delta, \theta, \varepsilon)}{\partial \theta}\frac{\partial \bar{\theta}}{\partial \varepsilon} + \frac{\partial f(y, y_0, \delta, \theta, \varepsilon)}{\partial \varepsilon}.\end{aligned}$$

In this depiction, δ_0 is used to denote the realized value of Δ_0 and y_0 the realized value of Y_0. The scaling by δ_0 is needed because of the time distortion induced by sampling. It is reminiscent of the scaling deduced in Section 2.6.1. The additional terms are included because of the dependence of the test function on ε directly and indirectly through $\bar{\theta}$.[26] The corresponding Taylor approximation for the conditional expectation is:

$$E\left[f(Y_1, Y_0, \Delta, \bar{\theta}, \varepsilon)|Y_0 = y_0, \Delta = \varepsilon\delta_0\right] \approx \sum_{j=0}^{J}\frac{\varepsilon^j}{j!}\mathcal{G}^j f(y, y_0, \delta, \bar{\theta}, \varepsilon)|_{y=y_0,\delta=0,\theta=\theta_0,\varepsilon=0}.$$

[25] These objects depend implicitly on the underlying parameter value, but we suppress this dependence for notational convenience.
[26] Aït-Sahalia and Mykland (2003a) refer to this new operator as a *generalized infinitesimal generator*.

The two Eqs. (7.3)–(7.4) are used to analyze the effects of a given sampling scheme on parameter estimation. The cost of discreteness is measured by the coefficient at the first order i in ε for which the FIML variance differs from its continuous-time limit $\Omega^{(0)}$. It is also the error that one would make if one were to use continuous-time asymptotics ($\Omega^{(0)}$) instead of the full Ω when the data are in fact discretely sampled.

The cost of ignoring sampling times is quantified by examining the first order i in ε at which the coefficient $\Omega^{(i)}$ for IOML differs from the corresponding coefficient $\Omega^{(i)}$ for FIML. The cost is measured by how much bigger the IOML coefficient at that order is than the FIML coefficient. For this example, the cost of randomness is at least as great, and often substantially greater than the cost of discreteness.

Because the PFML estimator is asymptotically biased, its asymptotic mean-square error is dominated by the square of the bias. Its performance under an asymptotic mean-square error loss function will always be worse than an estimator that is asymptotically unbiased. Expansion (7.4) can be use to quantify the squared bias.

The main conclusion is that the loss from not observing, or not using, the sampling intervals, will be at least as great, and often substantially greater, than the loss because the data are discrete rather than continuous. Although correcting for the latter effect has been the main focus of the literature in recent years, these results suggest that empirical researchers using randomly spaced data should pay as much attention, if not more, to sampling randomness as they do to sampling discreteness. Introducing unknown parameters in the sampling distribution for Δ_j will alter the quantitative comparison, but we know from the related results in the Section 6.7 that full identification of the diffusion can fail without some knowledge of the sampling distribution.

Aït-Sahalia and Mykland (2003b) extend this approach by developing a theory of approximation for a broad class of estimators of a diffusion

$$dX_t = \mu(X_t; \kappa)dt + \sigma(X_t; \gamma)dW_t$$

where κ and γ are unknown parameters. As is the case in general (e.g. see Hansen, 1982), many estimators for the parameters of a continuous time Markov process can be viewed as belonging to the class of generalized methods of moments estimators for (κ, γ). Aït-Sahalia and Mykland (2003b) construct small δ expansions of for the asymptotic variances and, when applicable, the biases of these estimators. Applications of this approach include the study of Euler approximation and the study of the moment conditions deduced by Hansen and Scheinkman (1995) when they are used in constructing the estimators of diffusion parameters when data are sampled at random intervals.

8. CONCLUSIONS

Markov models are designed to be convenient models of nonlinear stochastic processes. We show how operator methods can contribute to useful characterizations of dynamic evolution and approximations of a likelihood function. We described these various characterizations and some of the resulting estimation strategies and tests based on their observable implications.

ACKNOWLEDGMENTS

We received very helpful remarks from Eric Renault and two referees. This material is based upon work supported by the National Science Foundation including work under Award Numbers SES0519372, SES0350770, and SES0718407.

REFERENCES

Aït-Sahalia, Y. (1996a). Nonparametric pricing of interest rate derivative securities. *Econometrica 64*, 527–560.

Aït-Sahalia, Y. (1996b). Testing continuous-time models of the spot interest rate. *Review of Financial Studies 9*, 385–426.

Aït-Sahalia, Y. (1999). Transition densities for interest rate and other nonlinear diffusions. *Journal of Finance 54*, 1361 1395.

Aït-Sahalia, Y. (2008). Closed-form likelihood expansions for multivariate diffusions. *Annals of Statistics 36*, 906–937.

Aït-Sahalia, Y. (2002a). Empirical option pricing and the Markov property. Technical report, Princeton University.

Aït-Sahalia, Y. (2002b). Maximum-likelihood estimation of discretely-sampled diffusions: A closed-form approximation approach. *Econometrica 70*, 223–262.

Aït-Sahalia, Y. (2002c). Telling from discrete data whether the underlying continuous-time model is a diffusion. *Journal of Finance 57*, 2075–2112.

Aït-Sahalia, Y. (2003). Disentangling diffusion from jumps. *Journal of Financial Economics 74*(3), 487–528.

Aït-Sahalia, Y. and J. Jacod (2009). Testing for jumps in a discretely observed process. *Annals of Statistics 37*(1), 184–222.

Aït-Sahalia, Y. and P. A. Mykland (2003a). The effects of random and discrete sampling when estimating continuous-time diffusions. *Econometrica 71*, 483–549.

Aït-Sahalia, Y. and P. A. Mykland (2003b). Estimators of diffusions with randomly spaced discrete observations: A general theory. *Annals of Statistics 32*(5), 2186–2222.

Aït-Sahalia, Y. and P. A. Mykland (2008). An analysis of Hansen-Scheinkman estimators for randomly sampled diffusions. *Journal of Econometrics 144*, 1–26.

Andersen, T. G., T. Bollerslev, and N. Meddahi (2004). Analytic evaluation of volatility forecasts. *International Economic Review 45*(4), 1079–1110.

Anderson, T. W. (1959). On asymptotic distributions of estimates of parameters of stochastic difference equations. *Annals of Mathematical Statistics 30*, 676–687.

Auerbach, F. (1913). Das gbesetz der bevolkerungskonzentration. *Petermanns Geographische Mitteilungen 59*, 74–76.

Bandi, F. and P. C. B. Phillips (2003). Fully nonparametric estimation of scalar diffusion models. *Econometrica 71*, 241–283.

Bandi, F. M. (2002). Short-term interest rate dynamics: A spatial approach. *Journal of Financial Economics 65*, 73–110.

Bandi, F. M. and P. C. B. Phillips (2010). Nonstationary continuous-time processes. In L.P. Hansen and Y. Aït-Sahalia (Eds.), *Handbook in Financial Econometrics*. Elsevier. Forthcoming.

Banon, G. (1978). Nonparametric identification for diffusion processes. *SIAM Journal of Control and Optimization 16*, 380–395.

Beurling, A. and J. Deny (1958). Espaces de Dirichlet i, le cas elementaire. *Acta Mathematica 99*, 203–224.

Bhattacharya, R. N. (1982). On the functional central limit theorem and the law of the iterated logarithm for Markov processes. *Zeitschrift fur Wahrsheinlichkeitstheorie und verwandte Gebiete 60*, 185–201.

Bibby, B. M., M. Jacobsen, and M. Sorensen (2010). Estimating functions for discretely sampled diffusion-type models. In L. P. Hansen and Y. Aït-Sahalia (Eds.), *Handbook in Financial Econometrics*. Elsevier. Forthcoming.

Bierens, H. J. (1990). A consistent conditional moment test of functional form. *Econometrica 58*, 1443–1458.

Billingsley, P. (1961). *Statistical Inferences for Markov Processes*. Chicago: University of Chicago Press.

Bochner, S. (1960). *Harmonic Analysis and the Theory of Probability*. Berkley: University of California Press.

Boyarchenko, N. and S. Levendorskii (2007). The eigenfunction expansion method in multifactor quadratic term structure models. *Mathematical Finance 17*, 503–540.

Carrasco, M., J.-P. Florens, and E. Renault (2007). Linear inverse problems in structural econometrics estimation based on spectral decomposition and regularization. In J. J. Heckman and E. E. Leamer (Eds.), *Handbook of Econometrics* (1st ed.), Volume 6, Chapter 77. Elsevier.

Chan, K. C., G. A. Karolyi, F. A. Longstaff, and A. B. Sanders (1992). An empirical comparison of alternative models of the short-term interest rate. *Journal of Finance 48*, 1209–1227.

Chen, X., L. P. Hansen, and M. Carrasco (2008). Nonlinearity and temporal dependence. manuscript.

Chen, X., L. P. Hansen, and J. A. Scheinkman (2008). Principal components and the long-run implications of multivariate diffusions. manuscript.

Clark, P. (1973). A subordinated stochastic process model with finite variance for speculative prices. *Econometrica 41*, 135–155.

Cobb, L., P. Koppstein, and N. Y. Chan (1983). Estimation and moment recursions for multimodal distributions of the exponential family. *Journal of the American Statistical Association 78*, 124–130.

Conley, T., L. P. Hansen, and W. F. Liu (1999). Bootstrapping the long run. *Macroeconomic Dynamics 1*, 279–311.

Conley, T. G., L. P. Hansen, E. G. J. Luttmer, and J. A. Scheinkman (1997). Short-term interest rates as subordinated diffusions. *Review of Financial Studies 10*, 525–577.

Cox, J. C., J. E. Ingersoll, and S. A. Ross (1985). A theory of the term structure of interest rates. *Econometrica 53*, 385–408.

Darolles, S., J. P. Florens, and C. Gourieroux (2004). Kernel based nonlinear canonical analysis and time reversibility. *Journal of Econometrics 119*(2), 232–353.

Darolles, S., J. P. Florens, and C. Gourieroux (2001). Factor arma representation of a Markov process. *Economic Letters 71*, 165–171.

Darolles, S. and J. P. Laurent (2000). Approximating payoffs and pricing formulas. *Journal of Economic Dynamics and Control 24*, 1721–1746.

Dauxois, J. and G. M. Nkiet (1998). Nonlinear canonical analysis and independence tests. *Annals of Statistics 26*, 1254–1278.

Demoura, S. G. (1998). The nonparametric estimation of the expected value operator. manuscript.

Duffie, D. and P. Glynn (2004). Estimation of continuous-time Markov processes sampled at random time intervals. *Econometrica 72*(6), 1773–1808.

Eaton, J. and Z. Eckstein (1997). Cities and growth: Theory and evidence from France and Japan. *Regional Science and Urban Economics 27*, 443–474.

Ethier, S. N. and T. G. Kurtz (1986). *Markov Processes: Characterization and Convergence*. New York: John Wiley and Sons.

Fan, J. and C. Zhang (2003). A re-examination of Stanton's diffusion estimations with applications to financial market validation. *Journal of the American Statistical Association 98*, 118–134.

Fisher, R. A. (1921). On the mathematical foundation of theoretical statistics. *Philosophical Transactions of the Royal Society 222*, 309–368.

Florens, J. P., E. Renault, and N. Touzi (1998). Testing for embeddability by stationary reversible continuous-time Markov processes. *Econometric Theory 14*, 744–769.

Florens-Zmirou, D. (1984). Theorem de limte central pour une diffusion et pour sa discretisee. *Comptes Rendus de l'Acadhmie des sciences Paris, Series I, 299*(9), 995–998.

Frydman, H. and B. Singer (1979). Total positivity and the embedding problem for Markov chains. *Mathematical Proceedings of Cambridge Philosophical Society 86*, 339–344.

Fukushima, M. (1971). Dirichlet spaces and strong Markov processes. *Transactions of the American Mathematics Society 162*, 185–224.

Fukushima, M., Y. Oshima, and M. Takeda (1994). *Dirichlet Forms and Symmetric Markov Processes*. Berlin: Walter de Gruyter.

Gabaix, Z. (1999). Zipf's law for cities: An explanation. *Quarterly Journal of Economics 111*, 738–767.

Hall, P. and C. C. Heyde (1980). *Martingale Limit Theory and Its Application*. Boston: Academic Press.

Hansen, L. P. (1982). Large sample properties of generalized method of moments estimators. *Econometrica 50*, 1029–1054.

Hansen, L. P. (1985). A method for calculating bounds on asymptotic covariance matrices of generalized method of moments estimators. *Journal of Econometrics 30*, 203–238.

Hansen, L. P. and T. J. Sargent (1983). The dimensionality of the aliasing problem in models with rational spectral densities. *Econometrica 51*, 377–387.

Hansen, L. P. and J. Scheinkman (2009). Long-term risk: An operator approach. *Econometrica* 77(1), 177–324.

Hansen, L. P., J. Scheinkman, and N. Touzi (1998). Spectral methods for identifying scalar diffusion processes. *Journal of Econometrics 86*, 1–32.

Hansen, L. P. and J. A. Scheinkman (1995). Back to the future: Generating moment implications for continuous-time Markov processes. *Econometrica 63*, 767–804.

Hasminskii, R. Z. (1960). Ergodic properties of recurrent diffusion processes and stabilization of the solution of the Cauchy problem for parabolic equations. *Theory, Probability and Applications 5*, 179–196.

Jeganathan, P. (1995). Some aspects of asymptotic theory with applications to time series models. *Econometric Theory 11*, 818–887.

Jensen, B. and R. Poulsen (2002). Transition densities of diffusion processes: Numerical comparison of approximation techniques. *Journal of Derivatives 9*, 18–32.

Johannes, M. (2004). The statistical and economic role of jumps in continuous-time interest rate models. *Journal of Finance 59*(1), 227–260.

Jones, C. S. (2003). The dynamics of stochastic volatility: Evidence from the underlying and options market. *Journal of Econometrics 116*, 181–224.

Karlin, S. and J. McGregor (1959a). Coincidence probabilities. *Pacific Journal of Mathematics 9*, 1141–1164.

Karlin, S. and J. McGregor (1959b). Coincidence properties of birth and death processes. *Pacific Journal of Mathematics 9*, 1109–1140.

Kessler, M. (1997). Estimation of an ergodic diffusion from discrete observations. *Scandinavian Journal of Statistics 24*, 211–229.

Kessler, M. (2000). Simple and explicit estimating functions for a discretely observed diffusion process. *Scandinavian Journal of Statistics 27*(1), 65–82.

Kessler, M., A. Schick, and W. Wefelmeyer (2001). The information in the marginal law of a Markov chain. *Bernoulli* 7(2), 243–266.

Kessler, M. and M. Sorensen (1999). Estimation equations based on eigenfunctions for discretely observed diffusion processes. *Bernoulli 5*, 299–314.

Lewis, A. L. (1998). Applications of eigenfunction expansions in continuous-time finance. *Mathematical Finance 8*(4), 349–383.

Linetsky, V. (2004). Lookback options and diffusion hitting times: A spectral approach. *Finance and Stochastics 8*, 373–398.

Ma, Z. M. and M. Rockner (1991). *Introduction to the Theory of (Non-Symmetric) Dirichlet Forms.* Berlin: Springer-Verlag.

Mandelbrot, B. B. and J. W. V. Ness (1968). Fractional Brownian motions, fractional noises and applications. *SIAM Review 10*, 422–437.

Meddahi, N. (2001). An eigenfunction approach for modeling volatility modeling. CIRANO working paper 2001s-70.

Nelson, D. B. (1990). Arch models as diffusion approximations. *Journal of Econometrics 45*, 7–38.

Pearson, K. (1894). On the dissection of asymmetric frequency curves. *Philosophical Transactions of the Royal Society of London: Series A 185*, 71–110.

Pearson, K. (1901). On lines and planes of closest fit to systems of points in space. *Philosophical Magazine 2*, 559–572.

Phillips, P. C. B. (1973). The problem of identification in finite parameter continuous time models. *Journal of Econometrics 1*, 351–362.

Pritsker, M. (1998). Nonparametric density estimation and tests of continuous-time interest rate models. *Review of Financial Studies 11*, 449–489.

Rapoport, A. (1978). Rank-size relations. In W. H. Kruskal and J. M. Tanur (Eds.), *International Encyclopedia of Statistics*, pp. 847–854. New York: The Free Press.

Revuz, D. and M. Yor (1991). *Continuous Martingales and Brownian Motion* (2nd ed.). Berlin: Springer-Verlag.

Rogers, L. C. G. (1997). The potential approach to the term structure of interest rates and foreign exchange rates. *Mathematical Finance* 7(2), 157–164.

Rudin, W. (1973). *Functional Analysis*. New York: McGraw-Hill, Inc.

Salinelli, E. (1998). Nonlinear principal components I: Absolutely continuous variables. *Annals of Statistics 26*, 596–616.

Schaumburg, E. (2005). Estimation of Markov processes with levy type generators. Kellogg School of Management, Northwestern University.

Stanton, R. (1997). A nonparametric model of term structure dynamics and the market price of interest rate risk. *Journal of Finance 52*, 1973–2002.

Stroock, D. W. and S. R. S. Varadhan (1979). *Multidimensional Diffusion Processes*. Berlin: Springer-Verlag.

Vasicek, O. (1977). An equilibrium characterization of the term structure. *Journal of Financial Economics 5*, 177–188.

Veretennikov, A. Y. (1997). On polynomial bounds for stochastic differetial equations. *Stochastic Processes and their Applications 70*, 115–127.

White, J. S. (1958). The limiting distribution of the serial correlation coefficient in the explosive case. *Annals of Mathematical Statistics 29*, 1188–1197.

Wong, E. (1964). The construction of a class of stationary Markoff processes. In R. Bellman (Ed.), *Sixteenth Symposium in Applied Mathematics - Stochastic Processes in Mathematical Physics and Engineering*, pp. 264–276. Providence, RI: American Mathematical Society.

Yu, J. (2003). *Closed-Form Likelihood Estimation of Jump-Diffusions with an Application to the Realignment Risk Premium of the Chinese Yuan*. Ph.D. thesis, Princeton University.

CHAPTER 2

Parametric and Nonparametric Volatility Measurement

Torben G. Andersen*, Tim Bollerslev,** *and* **Francis X. Diebold*****

*Department of Finance, Kellogg School of Management, Northwestern University, Evanston, IL
**Department of Economics, Duke University, Durham, NC
***Department of Economics, University of Pennsylvania, Philadelphia, PA

Contents

Abstract

Volatility has been one of the most active areas of research in empirical finance and time series econometrics during the past decade. This chapter provides a unified continuous-time, frictionless, no-arbitrage framework for systematically categorizing the various volatility concepts, measurement procedures, and modeling procedures. We define three different volatility concepts: (i) the notional volatility corresponding to the sample-path return variability over a fixed time interval, (ii) the expected volatility over a fixed time interval, and (iii) the instantaneous volatility corresponding to the strength of the volatility process at a point in time. The parametric procedures rely on explicit functional form assumptions regarding the expected and/or instantaneous volatility. In the discrete-time ARCH class of models, the expectations are formulated in terms of directly observable variables, while the discrete- and continuous-time stochastic volatility models involve latent state variable(s). The nonparametric procedures are generally free from such functional form assumptions and hence afford estimates of notional volatility that are flexible yet consistent (as the sampling frequency of the underlying returns increases). The nonparametric procedures include ARCH filters and smoothers designed to measure the volatility over infinitesimally short horizons, as well as the recently-popularized realized volatility measures for (nontrivial) fixed-length time intervals.

Keywords: realized volatility; stochastic volatility; quadratic return variation; ARCH filters; GARCH

1. INTRODUCTION

Since Engle's (1982) seminal paper on ARCH models, the econometrics literature has focused considerable attention on time-varying volatility and the development of new tools for volatility measurement, modeling, and forecasting.[1] These advances have, in large part, been motivated by the empirical observation that *financial asset return volatility* is time-varying in a persistent fashion, across assets, asset classes, time periods, and countries.[2] Asset return volatility, moreover, is central to finance, whether in asset pricing, portfolio allocation, or risk management, and standard financial econometric methods and models take on a very different, *conditional*, flavor when volatility is properly recognized to be time-varying.

The combination of powerful methodological advances and important applications within empirical finance produced explosive growth in the financial econometrics of volatility dynamics, with the econometrics and finance literatures cross-fertilizing each other furiously. Initial developments were tightly parametric, but the recent literature has moved in less parametric, and even fully nonparametric directions. Here, we review and provide a unified framework for interpreting both the parametric and nonparametric approaches.

In Section 2, we define three different volatility concepts: (i) the notional volatility corresponding to the ex-post sample-path return variability over a fixed time interval, (ii) the ex-ante expected volatility over a fixed time interval, and (iii) the instantaneous volatility corresponding to the strength of the volatility process at a point in time.

In Section 3, we survey parametric approaches to volatility modeling, which are based on explicit functional form assumptions regarding the expected and/or instantaneous volatility. In the discrete-time ARCH class of models, the expectations are formulated in terms of directly observable variables, while the discrete- and continuous-time stochastic volatility (SV) models both involve latent state variable(s).

In Section 4, we survey nonparametric approaches to volatility modeling, which are generally free from such functional form assumptions and hence afford estimates of notional volatility that are flexible yet consistent (as the sampling frequency of the underlying returns increases). The nonparametric approaches include ARCH filters and

[1]We use the terms volatility and variation interchangeably throughout, with the exact meaning specifically defined in the relevant context.
[2]See, for example, Bollerslev et al. (1992).

smoothers designed to measure the volatility over infinitesimally short horizons, as well as the recently-popularized realized volatility measures for (nontrivial) fixed-length time intervals.

We conclude in Section 5 by highlighting promising directions for future research.

2. VOLATILITY DEFINITIONS

Here, we introduce a unified framework for defining and classifying different notions of return volatility in a continuous-time no-arbitrage setting. We begin by outlining the minimal set of regularity conditions invoked on the price processes and establish the notation used for the decomposition of returns into an expected, or mean, return and an innovation component. The resulting characterization of the price process is central to the development of our different volatility measures, and we rely on the concepts and notation introduced in this section throughout the chapter.

2.1. Continuous-Time No-Arbitrage Price Processes

Measurement of return volatility requires determination of the component of a given price increment that represents a return innovation as opposed to an expected price movement. In a discrete-time setting, this identification may only be achieved through a direct specification of the conditional mean return, for example through an asset pricing model, as economic principles impose few binding constraints on the price process. However, within a frictionless continuous-time framework, the no-arbitrage requirement quite generally guarantees that, instantaneously, the return innovation is an order of magnitude larger than the mean return. This result is not only critical to the characterization of arbitrage-free continuous-time price processes but it also has important implications for the approach one may use for measurement and modeling of volatility over short return horizons.

We take as given a univariate risky logarithmic price process $p(t)$ defined on a complete probability space $(\Omega, \mathscr{F}, \mathrm{P})$. The price process evolves in continuous time over the interval $[0, T]$, where T is a (finite) integer. The associated natural filtration is denoted $(\mathscr{F}_t)_{t\epsilon[0,T]} \subseteq \mathscr{F}$, where the information set, $\mathscr{F}_t$, contains the full history (up to time t) of the realized values of the asset price and other relevant (possibly latent) state variables, and is otherwise assumed to satisfy the usual conditions. It is sometimes useful to consider the information set generated by the asset price history alone. We refer to this coarser filtration, consisting of the initial conditions and the history of the asset prices only, by $(F_t)_{t\epsilon[0,T]} \subseteq F \equiv F_T$ so that by definition, $F_t \subseteq \mathscr{F}_t$. Finally, we assume there is an asset guaranteeing an instantaneously risk-free rate of interest although we shall not refer to this rate explicitly. Many more risky assets may, of course, be available, but we explicitly retain a univariate focus for notational simplicity. The extension to the multivariate setting is conceptually straightforward as discussed in specific instances below.

The continuously compounded return over the time interval $[t-h, t]$ is then

$$r(t,h) = p(t) - p(t-h), \quad 0 \leq h \leq t \leq T. \tag{2.1}$$

We also adopt the following short-hand notation for the cumulative return up to time t, i.e., the return over the $[0, t]$ time interval:

$$r(t) \equiv r(t,t) = p(t) - p(0), \quad 0 \leq t \leq T. \tag{2.2}$$

These definitions imply a simple relation between the period-by-period and the cumulative returns that we use repeatedly in the sequel:

$$r(t,h) = r(t) - r(t-h), \quad 0 \leq h \leq t \leq T. \tag{2.3}$$

A maintained assumption throughout is that – almost surely (P) (henceforth denoted ($a.s.$)) – the asset price process remains strictly positive and finite so that $p(t)$ and $r(t)$ are well defined over [0,T] ($a.s.$). It follows that $r(t)$ has only countably (although possibly infinitely) many jump points over $[0, T]$, and we adopt the convention of equating functions that have identical left and right limits everywhere. We also assume that the price and return processes are squared integrable.

Defining $r(t-) \equiv \lim_{\tau \to t, \tau < t} r(\tau)$ and $r(t+) \equiv \lim_{\tau \to t, \tau > t} r(\tau)$ uniquely determines the right-continuous, left-limit (càdlàg) version of the process, for which $r(t) = r(t+)$ ($a.s.$), and the left-continuous, right-limit (càglàd) version, for which $r(t) = r(t-)$ ($a.s.$), for all t in $[0, T]$. In the following, we assume without loss of generality that we are working with the càdlàg version of the various return processes.

The jumps in the cumulative price and return process are then

$$\Delta r(t) \equiv r(t) - r(t-), \quad 0 \leq t \leq T. \tag{2.4}$$

Obviously, at continuity points for $r(t)$, we have $\Delta r(t) = 0$. Moreover, given the at most countably infinite number of jumps, we generically have

$$P(\Delta r(t) \neq 0) = 0, \tag{2.5}$$

for an arbitrarily chosen t in $[0, T]$. This does not imply that jumps necessarily are rare, since as already noted, Eq. (2.5) is consistent with there being a (countably) infinite number of jumps over any discrete interval – a phenomenon referred to as an explosion. Jump processes that do not explode are termed *regular*. For regular processes, the anticipated jump frequency is conveniently characterized by the instantaneous jump intensity, i.e., the probability of a jump over the next instant of time, and expressed in units that reflect the expected (and finite) number of jumps per unit time interval.

Henceforth, we invoke the standard assumptions of no arbitrage and finite-expected returns. Within our frictionless setting, these conditions imply that the log-price process must constitute a (special) semimartingale (see Back, 1991; Harrison and Kreps, 1978). This, in turn, affords the following unique canonical return decomposition (e.g., Protter, 1992).

Proposition 1 *Return Decomposition*

Any arbitrage-free logarithmic price process subject to the regularity conditions outlined above may be uniquely represented as

$$r(t) \equiv p(t) - p(0) = \mu(t) + M(t) = \mu(t) + M^c(t) + M^J(t), \tag{2.6}$$

where $\mu(t)$ is a predictable and finite-variation process, $M(t)$ is a local martingale that may be further decomposed into $M^c(t)$, a continuous sample path, infinite-variation local martingale component, and $M^J(t)$, a compensated jump martingale. We may normalize the initial conditions such that all components may be assumed to have initial conditions normalized such that $\mu(0) \equiv M(0) \equiv M^c(0) \equiv M^J(0) \equiv 0$, which implies that $r(t) \equiv p(t)$.

Proposition 1 provides a unique decomposition of the instantaneous return into an expected return component and an (martingale) innovation. Over discrete intervals, the relation becomes slightly more complex. Letting the expected returns over $[t-h, t]$ be denoted by $m(t, h)$, Eq. (2.6) implies

$$m(t,h) \equiv E[r(t,h)|\mathcal{F}_{t-h}] = E[\mu(t,h)|\mathcal{F}_{t-h}], \quad 0 < h \leq t \leq T, \tag{2.7}$$

where

$$\mu(t,h) \equiv \mu(t) - \mu(t-h), \quad 0 < h \leq t \leq T, \tag{2.8}$$

and the return innovation takes the form

$$r(t,h) - m(t,h) = (\mu(t,h) - m(t,h)) + M(t,h), \quad 0 < h \leq t \leq T. \tag{2.9}$$

The first term on the right-hand side of (2.9) signifies that the expected return process, even though it is (locally) predictable, may evolve stochastically over the $[t-h, t]$ interval.[3] If $\mu(t, h)$ is predetermined (measurable with respect to $\mathcal{F}_{t-h}$), and thus known at time $t-h$, then the discrete-time return innovation reduces to $M(t,h) \equiv$

[3] In other words, even though the conditional mean is *locally* predictable, all return components in the special semimartingale decomposition are generally stochastic: not only volatility but also the jump intensity, the jump size distribution and the conditional mean process may evolve randomly over a finite interval.

$M(t) - M(t-h)$. However, any shift in the expected return process during the interval will generally render the initial term on the right-hand side of (2.9) nonzero and thus contribute to the return innovation over $[t-h, t]$.

Although the discrete-time return innovation incorporates two distinct terms, the martingale component, $M(t,h)$, is generally the dominant contributor to the return variation over short intervals, i.e., for h small. To discuss the intuition behind this result, which we formalize in the following section, it is convenient to decompose the expected return process into a purely continuous, predictable finite-variation part, $\mu^c(t)$, and a purely predictable jump part, $\mu^J(t)$. Because the continuous component, $\mu^c(t)$, is of finite variation, it is locally an order of magnitude smaller than the corresponding contribution from the continuous component of the innovation term, $M^c(t)$. The reason is – loosely speaking – that an asset earning, say a positive expected return over the risk-free rate must have innovations that are an order of magnitude larger than the expected return over infinitesimal intervals. Otherwise, a sustained long position (infinitely, many periods over any interval) in the risky asset will tend to be perfectly diversified due to a law of large numbers, as the martingale part is uncorrelated. Thus, the risk-return relation becomes unbalanced. Only if the innovations are large, preventing the law of large numbers from becoming operative, will this not constitute a violation of the no-arbitrage condition (see Maheswaran and Sims, 1993, for further discussion related to the implications of the classical Harrison and Kreps, 1978, equivalent martingale assumption). The presence of a nontrivial $M^J(t)$ component may similarly serve to eliminate arbitrage and retain a balanced risk-return trade-off relationship.

Analogous considerations apply to the jump component for the expected return process, $\mu^J(t)$, if this factor is present. There cannot be a predictable jump in the mean – i.e., a perfectly anticipated jump in terms of both time and size – unless it is accompanied by large jump innovation risk as well so that $Pr(\Delta M(t) \neq 0) > 0$. Again, intuitively, if there was a known, say, positive jump, then this induces arbitrage (by going long the asset) unless there is offsetting (jump) innovation risk.[4] Most of the continuous-time asset pricing literature ignores predictable jumps, even if they are logically consistent with the framework. One reason may be that their existence is fragile in the following sense. A fully anticipated jump must be associated with release of new (price relevant) information at a given point in time. However, if there is any uncertainty about the timing of the announcement so that it is only known to occur within a given minute, or even a few seconds, then the timing of the jump is more aptly modeled by a continuous hazard

[4] This point is perhaps most readily understood by analogy to a discrete-time setting. When there is a predictable jump at time t, the instant from $t-$ to t is effectively equivalent to a trading period, say from $t-1$ to t, within a discrete-time model. In that setting, no asset can earn a positive (or negative) excess return relative to the risk-free rate over $(t-1, t]$ without bearing genuine risk as this would otherwise imply a trivial arbitrage opportunity. The argument ruling out a predictable price jump without an associated positive probability of a jump innovation is entirely analogous.

function where the jump probability at each point in time is zero, and the predictable jump event is thus eliminated. In addition, even if there were predictable jumps associated with scheduled news releases, the size of the predictable component of the jump is likely much smaller than the size of the associated jump innovation so that the descriptive power lost by ignoring the possibility of predictable jumps is minimal. Thus, rather than modifying the standard setup to allow for the presence of predictable (but empirically negligible) jumps, we follow the tradition in the literature and assume away such jumps.

Although we will not discuss specific model classes at length until later sections, it is useful to briefly consider a simple example to illustrate the somewhat abstract definitions given in the current section.

Example 1 *Stochastic Volatility Jump Diffusion with Nonzero Mean Jumps*

Consider the following continuous-time jump diffusion expressed in stochastic differential equation (SDE) form,

$$\mathrm{d}p(t) = (\mu + \beta\sigma^2(t))\mathrm{d}t + \sigma(t)\mathrm{d}W(t) + \kappa(t)\mathrm{d}q(t), \quad 0 \le t \le T,$$

where $\sigma(t)$ is a strictly positive continuous sample path process (a.s.), $W(t)$ denotes a standard Brownian motion, $q(t)$ is a counting process with $\mathrm{d}q(t) = 1$ corresponding to a jump at time t, and $\mathrm{d}q(t) = 0$ otherwise, while the $\kappa(t)$ process gives the sizes of the jumps and is only defined for jump times t for which $\mathrm{d}q(t) = 1$. We assume that the jump size distribution has a constant mean of μ_κ and variance of σ_κ^2. Finally, the jump intensity is assumed constant (and finite) at a rate λ per unit time. In the notation of Proposition 1, we then have the return components,

$$\mu(t) = \mu^c(t) = \mu \cdot t + \beta \int_0^t \sigma^2(s)\mathrm{d}s + \lambda \cdot \mu_\kappa \cdot t,$$

$$M^c(t) = \int_0^t \sigma(s)\mathrm{d}W(s),$$

$$M^J(t) = \Sigma_{0 \le s \le t}\, \kappa(s)\mathrm{d}q(s) - \lambda \cdot \mu_\kappa \cdot t,$$

where by definition, the last summation consists of all the jumps that occurred over the $[0, T]$ time interval. Notice that the last term of the mean representation captures the expected contribution coming from the jumps, while the corresponding term is subtracted from the jump innovation process to provide a unique (compensated) jump martingale representation for M^J.

A final comment is in order. We purposely express the price changes and associated returns in Proposition 1 over a discrete time interval. The concept of an instantaneous return used in the formulation of continuous-time models, as in Example 1 given above, is mere short-hand notation that is formally defined only through the corresponding integral representation, such as Eq. (2.6). Although this is a technical point, it has an important empirical analogy: real-time price data are not available at every instant, and due to pertinent microstructure features, prices are invariably constrained to lie on a discrete grid, both in the price and time dimension. Hence, there is no real-world counterpart to the notion of a continuous sample path martingale with infinite variation over arbitrarily small time intervals (say, less than a second). It is only feasible to measure return (and volatility) realizations over discrete time intervals. Moreover, sensible measures can typically only be constructed over much longer horizons than given by the minimal interval length for which consecutive trade prices or quotes are recorded. We return to this point later. For now, we simply note that our main conceptualization of volatility in the next section conforms directly with the focus on realizations measured over nontrivial discrete time intervals rather than vanishing, or instantaneous interval lengths.

2.2. Notional, Expected, and Instantaneous Volatility

This section introduces three different volatility concepts, each of which serves to formalize the process of measuring and modeling the strength of the return variation within our frictionless arbitrage-free setting. Two distinct features importantly differentiate the construction of the different measures. First, given a set of actual return observations, how is the *realized* volatility computed? Here, the emphasis is explicitly on *ex-post* measurement of the volatility. Second, decision making often requires forecasts of future return volatility. The focus is then on *ex-ante* expected volatility. The latter concept naturally calls for a model that may be used to map the current information set into a volatility *forecast*. In contrast, the (ex-post) realized volatility may be computed (or approximated) without reference to any specific model, thus rendering the task of volatility measurement essentially a nonparametric procedure.

It is natural first to concentrate on the behavior of the martingale component in the return decomposition (2.6). However, a prerequisite for observing the $M(t)$ process is that we have access to a continuous record of price data. Such data are simply not available, and even for extremely liquid markets, microstructure effects (discrete price grids, bid-ask bounce effects, etc.) prevent us from ever getting really close to a true continuous sample-path realization. Consequently, we focus on measures that represent the (average) volatility over a discrete time interval rather than the instantaneous (point-in-time) volatility.[5] This, in turn, suggests a natural and general notion of volatility based

[5] Of course, by choosing the interval very small, one may, in principle, approximate the notion of point-in-time volatility, as discussed further below.

on the quadratic variation process for the local martingale component in the unique semimartingale return decomposition.

Specifically, let $X(t)$ denote any (special) semimartingale. The unique *quadratic variation process*, $[X, X]_t$, $t\epsilon[0, T]$, associated with $X(t)$ is formally defined as

$$[X, X]_t \equiv X(t)^2 - 2\int_0^t X(s-)\mathrm{d}X(s), \quad 0 < t \leq T, \tag{2.10}$$

where the stochastic integral of the adapted càglàd process, $X(s-)$, with respect to the càdlàg semimartingale, $X(s)$, is well-defined (e.g., Protter, 1992). It follows directly that the quadratic variation, $[X, X]$, is an increasing stochastic process. Also, jumps in the sample path of the quadratic variation process necessarily occur concurrent with the jumps in the underlying semimartingale process, $\Delta[X, X] = (\Delta X)^2$.

Importantly, if M is a locally square integrable martingale, then the associated $(M^2 - [M, M])$ process is a local martingale,

$$E[M(t,h)^2 - ([M, M]_t - [M, M]_{t-h})|\mathscr{F}_{t-h}] = 0, \quad 0 < h \leq t \leq T. \tag{2.11}$$

This relation, along with the following well-known result, provides the key to the interpretation of the quadratic variation process as one of our volatility measures.

Proposition 2 *Theory of Quadratic Variation*[6]

Let a sequence of partitions of $[0, T]$, (τ_m), *be given by* $0 = \tau_{m,0} \leq \tau_{m,1} \leq \tau_{m,2} \leq \cdots \leq \tau_{m,m} = T$ *such that* $\sup_{j\geq 0}(\tau_{m,j+1} - \tau_{m,j}) \rightarrow 0$ *for* $m \rightarrow \infty$. *Then, for* $t\epsilon[0, T]$,

$$\lim_{m\rightarrow\infty} \left\{\Sigma_{j\geq 1}(X(t \wedge \tau_{m,j}) - X(t \wedge \tau_{m,j-1}))^2\right\} \rightarrow [X, X]_t,$$

where $t \wedge \tau \equiv \min(t, \tau)$, *and the convergence is uniform in probability.*

Intuitively, the proposition says that the quadratic variation process represents the (cumulative) realized sample-path variability of $X(t)$ over the $[0, t]$ time interval. This observation, together with the martingale property of the quadratic variation process in (2.11), immediately points to the following theoretical notion of return variability.

Definition 1 *Notional Volatility*

The Notional Volatility *over* $[t - h, t]$, $0 < h \leq t \leq T$, *is*

$$\upsilon^2(t, h) \equiv [M, M]_t - [M, M]_{t-h} = [M^c, M^c]_t - [M^c, M^c]_{t-h} + \Sigma_{t-h<s\leq t}\Delta M^2(s). \tag{2.12}$$

[6] The theory of quadratic variation generalizes to situations in which the "stopping times" or partitions of $[0, T]$ are random and independent of $X(t)$, and satisfy, with probability one for $m \rightarrow \infty$, $\tau_{m,0} \rightarrow 0$ $\sup_{j\geq 1}\tau_{m,j} \rightarrow T$, and $\sup_{j\geq 0}(\tau_{m,j+1} - \tau_{m,j}) \rightarrow 0$.; see, e.g., Chung and Williams (1983).

This same volatility was first highlighted in a series of papers by Andersen et al. (2001b, 2003a) and Barndorff-Nielsen and Shephard (2002a,b). The latter authors term the corresponding concept actual volatility.

Under the maintained assumption of no predictable jumps in the return process and noting that the quadratic variation of any finite-variation process, such as $\mu^c(t)$, is zero, we also have

$$\upsilon^2(t,h) \equiv [r,r]_t - [r,r]_{t-h} = [M^c,M^c]_t - [M^c,M^c]_{t-h} + \Sigma_{t-h<s\leq t}\Delta r^2(s). \tag{2.13}$$

Consequently, the notional volatility equals (the increment to) the quadratic variation for the return series. Equation (2.13) and Proposition 2 also suggest that (ex-post) it is possible to approximate the notional volatility arbitrarily well through the accumulation of ever finely sampled high-frequency squared return, and that this approach remains consistent independent of the expected return process. We shall return to a much more detailed analysis of this idea in our discussion of nonparametric ex-post volatility measures in Section 4.

Similarly, from (2.13) and Proposition 2, it is evident that the notional volatility, $\upsilon^2(t,h)$, directly captures the sample path variability of the log-price process over the $[t-h,t]$ time interval. In particular, the notional volatility explicitly incorporates the effect of (realized) jumps in the price process: jumps contribute to the realized return variability and forecasts of volatility must account for the potential occurrence of such jumps. It also follows, from the properties of the quadratic variation process, that

$$E[\upsilon^2(t,h)|\mathscr{F}_{t-h}] = E[M(t,h)^2|\mathscr{F}_{t-h}] = E[M^2(t)|\mathscr{F}_{t-h}] - M^2(t-h), \quad 0 < h \leq t \leq T. \tag{2.14}$$

Hence, the *expected notional volatility* represents the expected future (cumulative) squared return innovation. As argued in Section 2.1, this component is typically the dominant determinant of the expected return volatility.

For illustration, consider again the example introduced in Section 2.1. More complicated specifications and issues related to longer horizon returns are considered in Section 3.

Example 2 *Stochastic Volatility Jump Diffusion with Nonzero Mean Jumps (Revisited)*
The log-price process evolves according to

$$dp(t) = (\mu + \beta\sigma^2(t))dt + \sigma(t)dW(t) + \kappa(t)dq(t), \quad 0 \leq t \leq T.$$

The notional volatility is then

$$\upsilon^2(t,h) = \int_{t-h}^{t} \sigma^2(s)ds + \Sigma_{t-h<s\leq t}\,\kappa^2(s),$$

where again the last sum is to be interpreted as consisting of all the nonzero squared jumps that occurred over the $[t-h, t]$ *time interval. The expected notional volatility involves taking the conditional expectation of this expression. Without an explicit model for the volatility process, this cannot be given in closed form. However, for small h, the (expected) notional volatility is typically very close to the value attained if volatility is constant. In particular, to a first-order approximation,*

$$E[\upsilon^2(t,h)|\mathcal{F}_{t-h}] \approx \sigma^2(t-h)\cdot h + \lambda \cdot h \cdot (\mu_\kappa^2 + \sigma_\kappa^2) = [\sigma^2(t-h) + \lambda(\mu_\kappa^2 + \sigma_\kappa^2)]\cdot h,$$

while

$$m(t,h) \approx [\mu + \beta \cdot \sigma^2(t-h) + \lambda \cdot \mu_\kappa]\cdot h.$$

Thus, the expected notional volatility is of order h, the expected return is of order h (and the variation of the mean return of order h^2*), whereas the martingale (return innovation) is of the order* $h^{1/2}$*, and hence an order of magnitude larger for small h.*

It is obvious that, when volatility is stochastic, the ex-post (realized) notional volatility will not correspond to the ex-ante expected volatility. More importantly, Eq. (2.14) implies that even the ex-ante expected notional volatility generally is *not* identical to the usual notion of return volatility as an *ex-ante* characterization of future return variability over a discrete holding period. The fact that the latter quantity is highly relevant for financial decision making motivates the standard discrete-time expected volatility concept as defined below.

Definition 2 *Expected Volatility*
The expected volatility *over* $[t-h, t], 0 < h \leq t \leq T$*, is defined by*

$$\begin{aligned}\zeta^2(t,h) &\equiv E[\{r(t,h) - E(\mu(t,h)|\mathcal{F}_{t-h})\}^2|\mathcal{F}_{t-h}] \\ &= E[\{r(t,h) - m(t,h)\}^2|\mathcal{F}_{t-h}].\end{aligned} \tag{2.15}$$

If the $\mu(t,h)$ process is not measurable with respect to $\mathcal{F}_{t-h}$, the expected volatility will typically differ from the expected notional volatility in Eq. (2.14).[7] Specifically, the future return variability in Eq. (2.15) reflects both genuine return innovations, as in Eq. (2.14), and intraperiod innovations to the conditional mean process. Trivially, of course, for models with an assumed constant mean return, or for one-period-ahead discrete-time volatility forecasts with given conditional mean representation, the two concepts coincide.

[7] Note that (t,h) refers to the $[t-h, t]$ time interval. So that while the notional volatility, $\upsilon^2(t,h)$, is only measurable with respect to $\mathcal{F}_t$, the expected volatility, $\zeta^2(t,h)$, is by definition $\mathcal{F}_{t-h}$-measurable.

Of course, for a continuous-time model, any volatility forecast over a discrete time interval invariably entails multiperiod considerations (typically a continuum). In particular, following Andersen et al. (2001b), the expected volatility may generally be expressed as

$$\begin{aligned}\zeta^2(t,h) &= E[(r(t,h) - m(t,h))^2 | \mathscr{F}_{t-h}] \\ &= E[\upsilon^2(t,h)|\mathscr{F}_{t-h}] + \mathrm{Var}[\mu(t,h)|\mathscr{F}_{t-h}] + 2 \cdot \mathrm{Cov}[M(t,h), \mu(t,h)|\mathscr{F}_{t-h}].\end{aligned} \tag{2.16}$$

The expected volatility therefore involves the expected notional volatility (quadratic variation) as well as two terms induced by future within-forecast-period variation in the conditional mean. The random variation in the mean component is a direct source of future return variation, and any covariation between the return and conditional mean innovations will further impact the return variability. However, under standard conditions and moderate forecast horizons, the dominant factor is indisputably the expected notional volatility, as the innovations to the mean return process generally will be very small relative to the cumulative return innovations. Importantly, this does not rule out asymmetric effects from current return innovations to future return volatility, as in the so-called leverage and volatility feedback effects discussed further below, which work exclusively or primarily through the notional volatility process.

Continuous-time models often portray the volatility process as perpetually evolving. From this perspective, the focus on volatility measurement over a fixed interval length, h, is ultimately arbitrary. A more natural theoretical concept is provided by the expected instantaneous volatility, measured as the current strength of the volatility process expressed per unit of time,

$$\lim_{h\to 0} \zeta^2(t+h,h)/h = \lim_{h\to 0} [E\{([M,M]_{t+h} - [M,M]_t)/h\}|\mathscr{F}_t]. \tag{2.17}$$

This is especially true when the underlying logarithmic price path is continuous, i.e., $M^J(t) \equiv 0$, in which case the (scaled) notional and expected instantaneous volatilities coincide,

$$\begin{aligned}\lim_{h\to 0} \zeta^2(t+h,h)/h &= \lim_{h\to 0} [E\{([M^c,M^c]_{t+h} - [M^c,M^c]_t)/h\}|\mathscr{F}_t] \\ &= \lim_{h\to 0} \{([M^c,M^c]_{t+h} - [M^c,M^c]_t)/h\} = \lim_{h\to 0} \upsilon^2(t+h,h)/h.\end{aligned} \tag{2.18}$$

Inspired by these relations, we adopt the following definition of instantaneous volatility.[8]

[8] The definition adapted here implies that σ_t^2 is a càdlàg process. An alternative càglàd definition is sometimes used in the literature.

Definition 3 *Instantaneous Volatility*

The instantaneous volatility *at time* $t, 0 \leq t \leq T$, *is*

$$\sigma_t^2 \equiv \lim_{h \to 0} [E\{([M^c, M^c]_{t+h} - [M^c, M^c]_t)/h\} | \mathscr{F}_t]. \tag{2.19}$$

This definition is consistent with the terminology commonly used in the literature on continuous-time parametric SV models.[9] Barndorff-Nielsen and Shephard (2002a,b), in a slightly different setting, refer to the corresponding concept as Spot Volatility.

The continuous-time models in the theoretical asset and derivatives pricing literature frequently assume that the sample paths are continuous, with the corresponding diffusion processes given in the form of SDEs (as in the Example 2 given above), rather than through (abstract) integral representations for continuous sample path semimartingales along the lines of Proposition 1. This does not involve any loss of generality, as illustrated by the following well-known result (e.g., Karatzas and Shreve, 1991; Protter, 1992).

Proposition 3 *Martingale Representation Theorem*

For any univariate, square-integrable, continuous sample path, logarithmic price process, which is not locally riskless, there exists a representation such that for all $0 \leq t \leq T$, *a.s.*(P),

$$r(t,h) = \mu(t,h) + M(t,h) = \int_{t-h}^{t} \mu(s)\mathrm{d}s + \int_{t-h}^{t} \sigma(s)\mathrm{d}W(s), \tag{2.20}$$

where $\mu(s)$ *is an integrable, predictable, and finite-variation stochastic process,* $\sigma(s)$ *is a strictly positive càdlàg stochastic process satisfying*

$$P\left[\int_{t-h}^{t} \sigma^2(s)\mathrm{d}s < \infty\right] = 1,$$

and $W(s)$ *is a standard Brownian motion.*

The integral representation in (2.20) is equivalent to the standard (short-hand) sde specification for the logarithmic price process,

$$\mathrm{d}p(t) = \mu(t)\mathrm{d}t + \sigma(t)\mathrm{d}W(t), \quad 0 \leq t \leq T. \tag{2.21}$$

Hence, within the class of continuous sample path semimartingale (diffusion) models, there are no consequential restrictions involved in stating the model directly through a SDE. In accordance with Definition 3, the volatility coefficient process in this formulation, $\{\sigma_t^2\}_{t\in[0,T]}$, is usually termed the *instantaneous volatility*, and we have the following

[9]A definition of instantaneous volatility similar to Eq. (2.17) is suggested by Comte and Renault (1998) in their discussion of alternative inference procedures for a continuous-time long-memory volatility model.

direct link between these alternative volatility representations,

$$\sigma_t^2 = \lim_{h \to 0} \sigma^2(t+h) = \lim_{h \to 0} \left(\int_t^{t+h} \sigma^2(s) \mathrm{d}s / h \right). \tag{2.22}$$

It is also immediately evident that in this situation, the notional volatility (or the increment to the quadratic variation process) equals the so-called *Integrated Volatility*,

$$\upsilon^2(t,h) = [M,M]_t - [M,M]_{t-h} = \int_{t-h}^{t} \sigma^2(s) \mathrm{d}s. \tag{2.23}$$

The integrated volatility plays a key role in the SV option pricing literature. Hull and White (1987) document that option prices follow Black–Scholes with the simple modification that the constant volatility is replaced by the expected quadratic return variation over the time to expiry for pure diffusive models without asymmetries between return and volatility innovations.[10] For further discussion of derivatives pricing models and related empirical procedures, see, e.g., Bates (1996b), Garcia et al. (2001), and Garcia et al. (2010).

To further appreciate the different volatility concepts, it is instructive to consider an illustrative example.

Illustration 1 *Continuous-Time GARCH Model*

The three panels in Fig. 2.1 show the time series of artificially simulated logarithmic prices, $p(t)$, one-period returns, $r(t,1)$, and corresponding instantaneous volatilities, $\sigma(t)$, for $t = 1, 2, \ldots, 2{,}500$.[11] *Comparing the middle and bottom panel, it is evident that the instantaneous volatility from the model directly dictates the strength of the observed return variation. However, even though the instantaneous volatility is a natural theoretical concept, and we refer to it frequently below, practical volatility measurement invariably takes place over discrete time intervals. The notational h-period volatility was introduced with exactly this consideration in mind. Of course, the difference between the notional and instantaneous volatility will depend upon the persistency of the underlying process and the value of h. In particular, the two volatility concepts formally coincide in the limit*

[10] More generally, the concept of model-free implied volatility, constructed from the cross-section of out-of-the-money options over different strikes but at the identical maturity, see, e.g., Britten-Jones and Neuberger (2000) and Carr and Madan (1998), allows for extraction of a nonparametric measure of the expected notional volatility under the risk-neutral (pricing or martingale) measure. We discuss these developments briefly later on.

[11] The data are generated by the continuous-time GARCH model defined in Eq. (4.4) below, $\mathrm{d}p(t) = \sigma(t)\mathrm{d}W(t)$ and $\mathrm{d}\sigma^2(t) = (\omega - \theta\sigma^2(t))\mathrm{d}t + (2\alpha)^{1/2}\sigma^2(t)\mathrm{d}V(t)$, where $\theta = 0.01005$, $\omega = 0.01005$, and $\alpha = 0.01095$, corresponding to a one-period discrete-time weak-form GARCH(1,1) model with $\alpha_1 = 0.09$, $\beta_1 = 0.9$, and unconditional variance equal to unity (see Andersen and Bollerslev, 1998a, for further details).

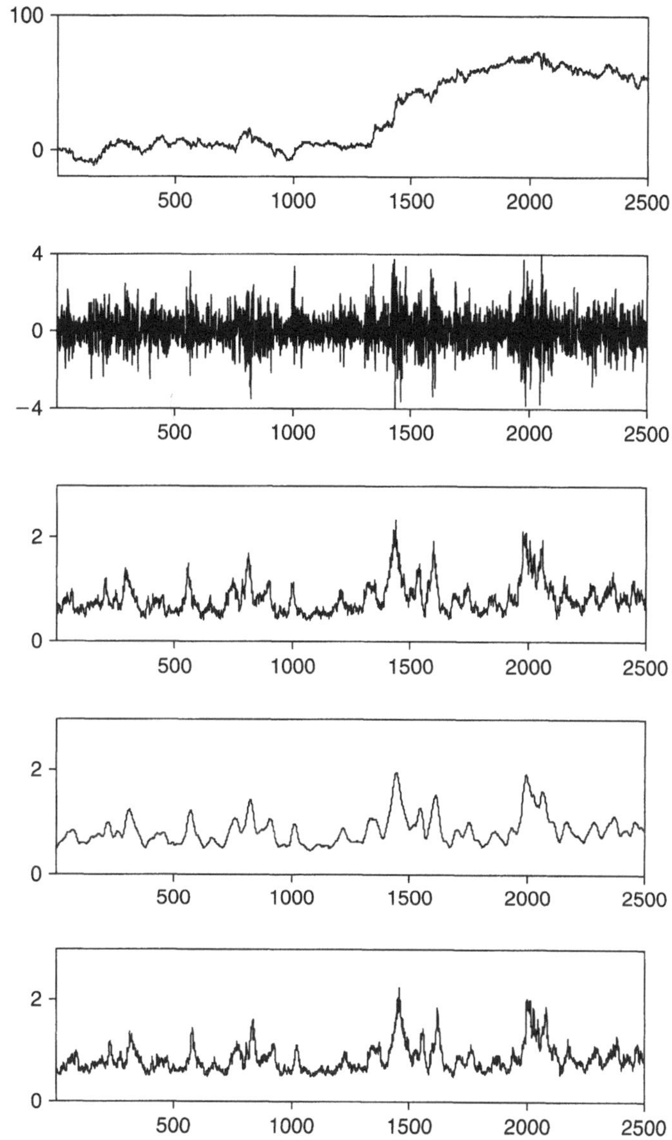

Figure 2.1 The first three panels in the figure plot simulated logarithmic prices, $p(t)$, one-period returns, $r(t, 1)$, and instantaneous volatilities, $\sigma_t = \sigma(t)$, for $t = 1, 2, \ldots, 2500$. The fourth and fifth panel depict the corresponding scaled h-period notional volatilities, $\upsilon(t, h)\sqrt{h}$, and scaled expected volatilities, $\zeta(t, h)\sqrt{h}$, for $h = 22$. The prices and volatilities are generated by a continuous-time GARCH model defined by $\mathrm{d}p(t) = \sigma(t)\mathrm{d}W(t)$ and $\mathrm{d}\sigma^2(t) = (\omega - \theta\sigma^2(t))\mathrm{d}t + (2\alpha)^{1/2}\sigma^2(t)\mathrm{d}V(t)$. The parameters in the continuous-time model are calibrated to match a one-period weak-form GARCH(1,1) model with $\alpha_1 = 0.09$, $\beta_1 = 0.9$ and unconditional variance equal to unity; see the discussion in Sections 3.1.1 and 4.1, along with Andersen and Bollerslev (1998a), for further details.

for $h \rightarrow 0$, but for large values of h, the two measures are clearly different, and in the limit for $h \rightarrow \infty$, the per period notional volatility, $\upsilon^2(t,h)/h$, will generally be constant (provided that it exist). To illustrate, the fourth panel in the figure plots the scaled notional volatility, $\upsilon(t,h)\sqrt{h}$, from the same model corresponding to a "month," or $h = 22$. This series is obviously much smoother than the instantaneous volatility. Finally, the fifth panel in the figure shows the "monthly" expected volatility,[12] where for comparison purposes with the other plots, we have scaled by the forecast horizon, i.e., $\zeta(t,22)/\sqrt{22}$. Because $\mu(t,h)$ is constant (and equal to zero), the expected volatility equals the expected notional volatility, which explains the apparent similarities in the two shapes. Also, since the underlying volatility process is quite persistent, the (scaled) expected volatility appears fairly similar to the previously depicted instantaneous volatility, even for $h = 22$. Nonetheless, the three volatility measures shown in the figure obviously differ and speak importantly to different aspects of the underlying data-generating process.

In the next section, we further stress the general relationship between the various volatility concepts for alternative parametric volatility models and nonparametric volatility measurements. Specific characterization of the volatility estimates and measurements are postponed to the following sections, where we present a more detailed study for each major class of models.

2.3. Volatility Modeling and Measurement

The approaches for empirically quantifying volatility naturally falls into two separate categories, namely procedures based on estimation of parametric models and more direct nonparametric measurements. Within the parametric volatility classification, alternative models exploit different assumptions regarding the expected volatility, $\zeta^2(t,h)$, through distinct functional forms and the nature of the variables in the information set, $\mathcal{F}_{t-h}$. In contrast, the data-driven or nonparametric volatility measurements typically quantify the notional volatility, $\upsilon^2(t,h)$, directly. Both set of procedures differ importantly in terms of the choice of time interval for which the volatility measure applies, e.g., a discrete interval, $h > 0$, or a point-in-time (instantaneous) measure, obtained as the limiting case for $h \rightarrow 0$.

Within the discrete-time parametric models, the most significant distinction concerns the character of the variables in the information set, $\mathcal{F}_{t-h}$, which in turn governs the type of estimation and inference techniques that are required for their practical implementation. In the ARCH class of models, the expected volatility, $\zeta^2(t,h)$, is parameterized as a function of past returns only, or F_{t-h}, although other observable variables could easily be included in $\mathcal{F}_{t-h}$. In contrast, the parameterized expectations in the SV class of

[12] The expected volatility in the continuous-time GARCH model is formally given by $\zeta^2(t,h) = h(\omega/\theta) + \theta^{-1}[\sigma^2(t) - (\omega/\theta)]$ $[1 - \exp(-h\theta)]$.

models explicitly rely on latent state variables. As we move to continuous-time parametric representations of either model, the assumption that all past returns are observable implies that the distinction between the two classes of models effectively vanishes, as the latent volatility state variables may be extracted without error from the frictionless, continuous-time price record. The following definition formalizes these categorizations.

Definition 4 *Parametric Volatility Models*
Discrete-time parametric volatility models *explicitly parameterize the expected volatility,* $\zeta^2(t,h), h > 0$, *as a nontrivial function of the time* $t-h$ *information set,* $\mathcal{F}_{t-h}$. *In the ARCH class of models,* $\mathcal{F}_{t-h}$ *depends on past returns and other directly observable variables only. In the SV class of models,* $\mathcal{F}_{t-h}$ *explicitly incorporates past returns as well as* latent *state variables.* Continuous-time volatility models *provide an explicit parameterization of the instantaneous volatility,* σ_t^2, *as a (nontrivial) function of the* $\mathcal{F}_t$ *information set, with additional volatility dynamics possibly introduced through time variation in the process governing jumps in the price path.*

In addition to these three separate model classes, so-called implied volatility approaches also figure prominently in the literature. The implied volatilities are typically based on a parametric model for the returns, as defined above, along with an *asset pricing model* and an augmented information set consisting of options prices and/or term structure variables. Intuitively, if the number of available derivatives prices at time $t-h$ pertaining to the price of the asset at time t included in the augmented information set, $\mathcal{F}_{t-h}$, exceeds the number of latent state variables in the parametric model for the returns, it is possible to back out a value for $\zeta^2(t,h)$ by inverting the theoretical asset pricing model; see, e.g., Bates (1996b), Renault (1997), and Chapters 9 and 12 in this volume for a discussion of the extensive literature on options implied volatilities and related procedures.[13,14]

In contrast to the parametric procedures categorized above, the nonparametric volatility measurements are generally void of any specific functional form assumptions about the stochastic process(es) governing the local martingale, $M(t)$, as well as the predictable

[13] Most prominent among these procedures are, of course, the Black–Scholes option implied volatilities based on the assumption of an underlying continuous-time random walk model first analyzed empirically by Latané and Rendleman (1976). More detailed empirical analyses of Black–Scholes-implied volatilities along with generalizations to allow for more realistic price dynamics have been the subject of an enormous literature, an incomplete list of which includes Bakshi et al. (1997), Canina and Figlewski (1993), Chernov and Ghysels (2000), Christensen and Prabhala (1998), Day and Lewis (1992), Duan (1995), Dumas et al. (1998), Fleming (1998), Heston (1993), Heston and Nandi (2000), Hull and White (1987), and Wiggins (1992). The so-called model-free implied volatilities computed from option prices without the use of a particular pricing model have recently been proposed by Britten-Jones and Neuberger (2002), Carr and Madan (1998), and Demeterfi et al. (1999), and analyzed empirically by Bollerslev and Zhou (2006), Bollerslev et al. (2005), Carr and Wu (2006, 2009), Garcia et al. (2001), and Jiang and Tian (2005).

[14] The 30-day VIX-implied volatility index of the Chicago Board Options Exchange (CBOE), for which there is an active futures market, are based on S&P500 index options along with the model-free-implied volatility formula of Britten-Jones and Neuberger (2002); see Carr and Wu (2009) for further discussion. A similar construct underlies the VXN index for the NASDAQ-100 and the new VDAX for the DAX index on the Deutsche Termin Börse (DTB). Earlier versions of these indexes were based on weighted averages of Black–Scholes-implied volatilities; see Fleming et al. (1995) and Whaley (1993) for further discussion of these historically first volatility indexes.

and finite-variation process, $\mu(t)$, in the unique return decomposition. These procedures also differ importantly from the parametric models in their focus on providing measures of the notional volatility, $\upsilon^2(t,h)$, rather than the expected volatility, $\zeta^2(t,h)$. In addition, the nonparametric procedures generally restrict the measurements to be functions of the coarser filtration, F_t, generated by the return on the asset only. In parallel to the parametric measures, the nonparametric procedures may be further differentiated depending upon whether they let $h \to 0$ and thus provide measures of instantaneous volatility, or whether they explicitly operate with a strictly positive $h > 0$ resulting in realized volatility measures over a discrete nontrivial time interval.

Definition 5 *Nonparametric Volatility Measurement*
Nonparametric volatility measurement *utilizes the* ex-post *returns, or F_τ, in extracting measures of the notional volatility.* ARCH filters and smoothers *are designed to measure the instantaneous volatility, σ_t^2. The filters only use information up to time $\tau = t$, while the smoothers are based on $\tau > t$.* Realized volatility *measures directly quantify the notional volatility, $\upsilon^2(t,h)$, over (nontrivial) fixed-length time intervals, $h > 0$.*

Within the class of instantaneous volatility measures, the ARCH filters first formally developed by Nelson (1992) (see also the collection of papers in Rossi, 1996) rely exclusively on the past return record, typically through a weighted rolling regression, while the smoothers, or two-sided filters, from Nelson (1996b) exploit (ex-post) future prices. Realized volatility approaches may similarly be categorized according to whether the measurement of $\upsilon^2(t,h)$ exploits only price observations within the interval $[t-h, t]$ itself or filtering/smoothing techniques are used to also incorporate return observations outside of $[t-h, t]$. An important advantage of exploiting only interval-specific information is it produces asymptotically unbiased measures, and therefore approximately serially uncorrelated measurement errors, under quite general conditions. A potential drawback is that useful information from adjacent intervals is ignored. Consistency of both ARCH filters and smoothers and realized volatility procedures generally require the length of the underlying sampling interval for the returns within $[t-h, t]$ approaches zero (even for the ARCH filters and smoothers where h itself is shrinking). We next turn to a more detailed discussion of these different procedures for modeling and measuring volatility within the context of the general setup in Section 2.1.

3. PARAMETRIC METHODS

Parametric volatility models and their implementation constitute one of the cornerstones of modern empirical asset pricing, and a large econometrics and statistics literature has been devoted to the development and theoretical foundation of differently parameterized volatility models. A thorough review of this literature is beyond the scope of this chapter; see, e.g., the existing surveys by Andersen et al. (2006a), Bollerslev et al. (1992),

Bollerslev et al. (1994), Ghysels et al. (1996), and Shephard (1996). Instead, we shall merely highlight the most important ideas as they relate specifically to the volatility measurement for the different model classes.

3.1. Continuous-Time Models

Much of the theoretical asset pricing literature is cast in continuous time. Within this tradition, the sample path of the price process is also commonly assumed to be continuous. This approach is convenient because the representation in Proposition 1 then ensures that, locally, the mean and variance are of the same order. Consequently, the framework effectively involves a dynamic mean–variance trade-off, which typically allows for a tractable analysis of asset pricing and portfolio choice problems. On the other hand, we usually do not observe a record of continuously evolving asset prices, and all but the very simplest specifications tend to imply intractable conditional return distributions for the corresponding discretely observed returns. This issue has historically inhibited empirical work on estimation and inference for realistic continuous-time asset price processes, although a burst of research activity in this area over the last few years has allowed important headway to be made. As a result, the parametric approach to continuous-time modeling is beginning to have a practical impact on return volatility modeling. We will not discuss estimation and inference techniques for this class of model in any detail, however, but rather outline the conceptual issues that distinguish this approach from the discrete-time modeling approach discussed above and the nonparametric volatility measurement discussed subsequently. Other chapters in this handbook offer extensive coverage of parametric and semi(non)parametric estimation techniques for diffusion processes (e.g., Aït-Sahalia et al., 2010; Bandi and Phillips, 2010; Bibby et al., 2010; Gallant and Tauchen, 2010; Jacod, 2010; Johannes and Polson, 2010)

The continuous-time parametric models are directly compatible with the no-arbitrage framework outlined in Section 2, so the specific volatility concepts carry over without modification. However, the specifications of the models traditionally adapted in the literature differ from the general semimartingale representation, and instead rely (implicitly) on Proposition 3 in expressing the models (in short-hand format) as SDEs driven by underlying Brownian motions and, in the case of discontinuities, Poisson jump processes.

3.1.1. Continuous Sample Path Diffusions

The number of alternative continuous-time specifications for asset returns used in the literature is much too large for a comprehensive review to be included here. For illustrative purposes, we simply consider the relevant volatility concepts implied by a few standard formulations.

The simplest possible case is provided by the time-invariant diffusion,

$$\mathrm{d}p(t) = \mu \mathrm{d}t + \sigma \mathrm{d}W(t), \quad 0 \leq t \leq T, \tag{3.1}$$

which underlies the Black–Scholes option pricing formula. Obviously, this process has a deterministic mean return so the expected return volatility trivially equals the expected notional volatility. Moreover, because the volatility is also constant, the expected notional volatility is identical to the notional volatility. Formally, we thus have for the Black–Scholes setting,

$$\varsigma^2(t,h) = E[(r(t,h) - m(t,h))^2|\mathcal{F}_{t-h}] = \upsilon^2(t,h) = \int_{t-h}^{t} \sigma^2(s)\mathrm{d}s = \sigma^2 \cdot h.$$

As discussed further in Section 4.1 below, this model is also straightforward to estimate from discretely sampled data by, e.g., maximum likelihood, as the returns are i.i.d. and normally distributed. Of course, the model is overwhelmingly rejected for moderately frequently sampled data (say, daily, weekly, or monthly), as it fails to accommodate the well-documented strong intertemporal volatility dependencies.

For some price series (notably real commodity prices and exchange rates), it is often sensible to postulate a stationary logarithmic price process. Popular models for such series – inspired by the interest rate literature – include the Ornstein–Uhlenbeck (OU) processes and the square-root, or Cox, Ingersoll and Ross (1985) (CIR), processes. These models take the general form

$$\mathrm{d}p(t) = \phi(\mu - p(t))\mathrm{d}t + \sigma(t)\mathrm{d}W(t), \quad 0 \le t \le T. \tag{3.2}$$

The drift specification ensures mean reversion in the process, given appropriate regularity conditions and a well-behaved diffusion (volatility) coefficient process. Letting $\sigma(s) \equiv \sigma$ results in the standard OU model, while having $\sigma(s) \equiv \sigma p^{\gamma}(s)$ produces a constant elasticity of variance (CEV) model, with the CIR model as a special case for $\gamma = 1/2$. The CEV class of models was first proposed in the asset pricing literature by Cox and Ross (1976), and further popularized for interest rates by Chan et al. (1992). The attraction of the specific OU and CIR formulations stems primarily from the tractable distributions for discretely observed data, and from the accompanying closed-form solutions for many related asset and derivatives pricing problems. Explicit solutions for the expected volatility and the expected notional volatility may be derived from existing results in the literature. One immediate observation is that these two volatility concepts now differ as the return innovations will impact the mean process randomly over the forecast horizon. Nonetheless, the expected notional volatility will remain the dominant component in empirically realistic situations.

Example 3 *Ornstein–Uhlenbeck (OU) Processes*

To illustrate, consider the simple OU process,

$$\mathrm{d}p(t) = -\phi p(t)\mathrm{d}t + \sigma \mathrm{d}W(t), \tag{3.3}$$

where for simplicity, we fix $\mu \equiv 0$. *Also, for simplicity and without loss of generality, consider the return* $r(h,h) \equiv r(h)$ *over the* $[0,h]$ *time interval, or* $t-h=0$. *The associated martingale component,* $M(h) = \sigma \int_0^h \mathrm{d}W(s) = \sigma \cdot W(h)$, *then implies that the notional volatility equals* $\upsilon^2(h,h) = \sigma^2 \cdot h$. *Furthermore, the explicit solution to the OU SDE takes the form*

$$\begin{aligned} r(h) &= p(0)(\exp(-\phi h) - 1) + \sigma \int_0^h \exp(-\phi(h-s))\mathrm{d}W(s) \\ &= \{p(0)(\exp(-\phi h) - 1) + \sigma \int_0^h [\exp(-\phi(h-s)) - 1]\mathrm{d}W(s)\} + \sigma \int_0^h \mathrm{d}W(s) \\ &= \mu(h) + M(h). \end{aligned} \tag{3.4}$$

Notice, the predictable component, corresponding to the first parenthesis in the second equation, only depends on the martingale innovation process through a weighted average of past realizations, as the current realization of $W(h)$ *receives zero weight from* $[\exp(-\phi(h-s)) - 1]$ *at time* $s = h$. *Moreover, by (conditional) normality of the OU process, the expected volatility,* $\zeta^2(h,h) = E[(r(h) - m(h))^2 | \mathscr{F}_0]$, *may be expressed as*

$$\begin{aligned} \zeta^2(h,h) &= [(1 - \exp(-2\phi h))/(2\phi)]\sigma^2 \approx \sigma^2 \cdot h - \phi h^2\sigma^2 + (2/3) \cdot \sigma^2\phi^2 h^3 \\ &= E[\upsilon^2(h,h)|\mathscr{F}_0] - \phi h^2\sigma^2 + (2/3) \cdot \sigma^2\phi^2 h^3. \end{aligned}$$

Since $\phi > 0$, *the expected volatility is thus locally smaller than the expected notional volatility. This occurs because of the mean-reverting drift coefficient. Large return innovations will tend to be partially undone over the forecast horizon. However, to first order in* h, *expected volatility equals expected notional volatility, confirming the crucial role of the latter concept.*[15] *Further, in reference to Eq. (2.16) in Section 2, it is possible to show that*

$$\begin{aligned} \mathrm{Var}[\mu(h)|\mathscr{F}_0] &= [h + \{1 - \exp(-2\phi h)/(2\phi)\} - 2\{1 - \exp(-\phi h)/\phi\}] \cdot \sigma^2 \\ &\approx (\phi^2/3)h^3\sigma^2, \end{aligned}$$

and

$$\mathrm{Cov}[M(h), \mu(h)|\mathscr{F}_0] = [\{1 - \exp(-\phi h)/\phi\} - h] \cdot \sigma^2 \approx -(\phi/2)h^2\sigma^2 + (\phi^2/6)h^3\sigma^2.$$

[15] A simple numerical example illustrates the orders of magnitude. The OU process is typically estimated, or calibrated, to capture slowly evolving long-run swings in the logarithmic price process (or interest rate) away from the unconditional mean. Such movements induce a relatively small degree of predictability in the short-term asset returns, but long-term mean reversion, as manifest by a small mean reversion parameter for data calibrated to an annual frequency, say $\phi = 0.1$. At the daily frequency, or $h = 1/250$, clearly $\phi \cdot h^2 \approx 0$ so that the difference between the expected volatility and the notional volatility is negligible. Even at the quarterly frequency, or $h = 1/4$, the deviation is a modest 2.5%. Of course, this number is somewhat sensitive to the assumed strength of the mean reversion.

Obviously, the contribution of the variation in the drift process is generally (locally) negligible, so that the main contribution to the expected volatility (beyond the notional volatility) stems from the covariance between return innovations and the future path of the mean process. The negative correlation between these components lowers the overall expected volatility (albeit the effect typically is small).[16]

Unfortunately, the entire class of one-factor models covered by Eq. (3.2) falter dramatically when confronted with actual price or return data. In order to obtain more satisfactory empirical fits, the literature has moved towards multi-factor parametric formulations. A natural approach is to let the volatility process be governed by an independent source of random variation, leading to a (genuine) continuous-time SV model. An influential specification is given by the square-root volatility model popularized by Heston (1993) corresponding to $\delta = 1/2$ in the CEV diffusion,

$$d\sigma^2(t) = (\omega - \theta\sigma^2(t))dt + \varsigma(\sigma^2(t))^2 dV(t), \quad 0 \leq t \leq T, \tag{3.5}$$

where the standard Brownian motion process, $V(t)$, may be correlated with the $W(t)$ proccss driving the returns, thus introducing an asymmetric return-volatility relation into the asset price dynamics. This model is particularly attractive as it allows for closed-form solutions for option prices. An extensive analysis of multivariate square-root (or affine) processes in modeling term-structure dynamics is provided in Dai and Singleton (2000) (see also Piazzesi, 2010 in this handbook).

Alternatively, the diffusive volatility may be assumed proportional to $\sigma^2(t)$ as in the continuous-time GARCH model of Nelson (1990a),

$$d\sigma^2(t) = (\omega - \theta\sigma^2(t))dt + \varsigma\sigma^2(t)dV(t), \quad 0 \leq t \leq T. \tag{3.6}$$

We will return to a more detailed discussion of this specific model in Section 4.1 below on ARCH filters and smoothers. This is also the model used in generating the different volatility sample paths depicted in Fig. 2.1.

Another popular choice is to represent the logarithmic volatility process by an OU diffusion process. As discussed further in Section 3.2.2 below, this formulation corresponds to an (approximate) discrete-time lognormal stochastic autoregressive volatility (SARV)(1) model. In either case, the relation between the expected volatility and the expected notional volatility may be found from the general formula in Eq. (2.16). If the two Wiener innovation processes are correlated, all three terms become operative,

[16] Although these calculations are specific to the OU process, the orders of magnitude are indicative of the relative importance of the components governing the expected volatility. In fact, the OU process displays a very strong covariance between the return innovations and the expected returns process, suggesting that this example, if anything, overstates the typical contribution of the terms beyond the (expected) notional volatility in determining the expected volatility for many asset classes.

although the expected notional volatility (expected quadratic variation) continues to dominate empirically.

The SV diffusions above are considerably harder to estimate from discretely observed data than the classical one-factor models of the OU or CIR variety. Intuitively, because of the latent information structure, any inference procedure must either rely on a (potentially noisy) proxy for the latent volatility or integrate out the latent stochastic variable(s) from the model. However, recent progress has made relatively efficient inference possible through a variety of simulation-based procedures such as Efficient Method of Moments (EMM) or Markov Chain Monte Carlo (MCMC) methods. More detailed discussions of these procedures are available in other chapters in the handbook.

Also, optimal measurements of the latent instantaneous volatility process may, in principle, be obtained by standard nonlinear filtering and smoothing procedures (e.g., Kitagawa, 1987), although the direct implementation of these procedures in the present context typically involves prohibitively expensive high-dimensional integration. Important advances to circumvent these problems allowing for the practical numerical calculation and extraction of latent volatility measurements include the particle filters in Pitt and Shephard (1999) and the reprojection approach advocated by Gallant and Tauchen (1998). Again, we refer to other chapters in this handbook for a more detailed treatment of these procedures. We will, however, return to a discussion of specialized continuous-time filtering methods in Section 4.1 below.

Meanwhile, the mounting empirical evidence obtained from the estimation of the continuous-time SV models discussed immediately above clearly suggest that while the models do provide major improvements over the traditional one-factor models in which $\sigma(t)$ is assumed to depend directly $p(t)$ only, the models continue to be decidedly rejected (see, e.g., Andersen et al., 2002; Andersen and Lund, 1997; Bollerslev and Zhou, 2002; Eraker, 2004; Eraker et al., 2003; Gallant and Tauchen, 1997).

These failures have prompted a number of authors to add additional parametrically specified diffusion factors (e.g., Chernov et al., 2003). In light of the general representation in Eq. (2.20) in Proposition 3, it is evident that such multifactor models simply provide an alternative way of specifying the return dynamics that ultimately may be reduced to a single-factor representation for the univariate process. The advantage is that the system may be defined through a sum of different factors, each following a simple dynamic process rather than a single factor with a more complex specification. For example, one may approximate (apparent) long-range dependencies in the volatility process through a sum of multiple distinct AR(1) factors (e.g., Gallant et al., 1999).[17]

[17] As shown by Chen et al. (2003), nonlinear functions of a continuous-time Markovian process may exhibit long-memory type dependencies in the form of an unbounded spectrum at frequency zero. Alternative diffusive long-memory type formulations have also been considered by Comte and Renault (1996, 1998).

The ability to produce a simple parametric representation is extremely convenient, if not critical, for economic interpretation and implementation of tractable estimation strategies through standard (simulation based) likelihood and method of moments techniques. To illustrate, consider the general k-factor model,

$$r(t) \equiv p(t) - p(0) = \int_{t-h}^{t} \mu(s)\mathrm{d}s + \sum_{j=1,\ldots,k} \int_{t-h}^{t} \sigma_j(s)\mathrm{d}W_j(s),$$

where the $\sigma_j(t)$ refer to the jth volatility factor and $W(t) = (W_1(t), \ldots, W_k(t))$ denotes a k-dimensional vector process of independent standard Brownian motions. The notional volatility then follows straightforwardly as the sum of the integrated constituent components,

$$\upsilon^2(t,h) = \int_{t-h}^{t} \sigma^2(s)\mathrm{d}s = \int_{t-h}^{t} \left\{ \sum_{j=1,\ldots,k} \sigma_j^2(s) \right\} \mathrm{d}s = \sum_{j=1,\ldots,k} \int_{t-h}^{t} \sigma_j^2(s)\mathrm{d}s.$$

As such, none of the general principles change, but the requisite calculations for, say, the different terms in Eq. (2.16) may certainly become more involved.

It is arguably premature to judge the empirical performance of the parametric multifactor continuous sample path (pure diffusion) volatility models for asset returns, as this work truly is in its infancy. It is clear, nonetheless, that such models serve as alternatives as well as complements for the parametric jump-diffusion models that we turn to next.

3.1.2. Jump Diffusions and Lévy-Driven Processes

At the highest sampling frequencies, there is compelling evidence of the existence of jumps in asset price processes. Specifically, the arrival of important news such as macroeconomic announcements (at the aggregate level) or earnings reports (at the firm level) typically induce a discrete jump associated with an immediate revaluation of the asset; see, e.g., Andersen and Bollerslev (1998b), Andersen et al. (2003b), and Johannes (2004) for direct parametric modeling of jumps along with an analysis of their economic import. Likewise, much evidence from the implied volatility literature – which extracts information about market expectations concerning the future return distribution directly from option prices – point toward the importance of incorporating discrete jump probabilities into the analysis of the return dynamics; see, e.g., Bates (1996a) and Bakshi et al. (1997) for earlier work along these lines.

In the same way that the Brownian motion constitutes the basic building block of continuous-time martingales, the standard Poisson jump process serves as the basic building block for pure (compensated) jump martingales (e.g., Merton, 1982). Thus, one may accommodate the relevant jump features in an arbitrage-free continuous-time logarithmic price process by adding a Poisson jump component with appropriate time variation in the jump intensity and/or in the jump distribution (as in Example 1 and 2 in Section 2 above). In line with this reasoning, let $q(t)$ denote a Poisson point process, with $\mathrm{d}q(t) = 1$ indicating a jump at time t, and $\mathrm{d}q(t) = 0$ otherwise, and (possibly time-varying) jump intensity denoted $\lambda(t)$.[18] Also, let the random jump size be denoted by $\kappa(t)$, where the process is only defined for $\mathrm{d}q(t) = 1$. We then have the general representation

$$\begin{aligned} r(t,h) &= \mu(t,h) + M(t,h) \\ &= \int_{t-h}^{t} \mu(s)\mathrm{d}s + \int_{t-h}^{t} \sigma(s)\mathrm{d}W(s) + \Sigma_{t-h\leq s\leq t}\, \kappa(s)\cdot \mathrm{d}q(s). \end{aligned} \tag{3.7}$$

The associated notional volatility process explicitly incorporates the jumps,

$$\begin{aligned} \upsilon^2(t,h) &\equiv [M,M]_t - [M,M]_{t-h} = [M^c,M^c]_t - [M^c,M^c]_{t-h} + \Sigma_{t-h\leq s\leq t}\, \Delta M^2(s) \\ &= \int_{t-h}^{t} \sigma^2(s)\mathrm{d}s + \Sigma_{t-h\leq s\leq t}\, \kappa^2(s)\cdot \mathrm{d}q(s). \end{aligned} \tag{3.8}$$

The computation of the corresponding expressions for the expected notional volatility and the expected volatility will depend on the specific parametric formulation.

To illustrate, consider the simple jump diffusion in Merton (1976) with constant mean and diffusion volatility coefficients as well as i.i.d. jumps; i.e., $\sigma(t) \equiv \sigma, \lambda(t) \equiv \lambda$. Also, denote the mean and the variance of the jump distribution by μ_κ and σ_κ^2, respectively. The notional volatility is now a stochastic variable, reflecting the random occurrence of jumps. Moreover, only if the mean jump size is zero, $\mu_\kappa = 0$, the expected notional volatility will coincide with the expected volatility (the latter does not contain the squared mean term, μ_κ^2, below),

$$E[\upsilon^2(t,h)|\mathcal{F}_{t-h}] = \sigma^2\cdot h + E[\Sigma_{t-h\leq s\leq t}\Delta M^2(s)|\mathcal{F}_{t-h}] = \sigma^2\cdot h + \lambda\cdot h\cdot(\mu_\kappa^2 + \sigma_\kappa^2).$$

Also, considering the corresponding normalized expected volatility for $h \to \infty$, it follows from Eq. (2.16) that

$$\lim_{h\to 0} \zeta^2(t,h)/h = \sigma^2 + \lambda\cdot(\mu_\kappa^2 + \sigma_\kappa^2),$$

[18]Formally, $P[q(t) - q(t-h) = 0] = 1 - \int_0^h \lambda(t-h+s)\mathrm{d}s + o(h)$, $P[q(t) - q(t-h) = 1] = \int_0^h \lambda(t-h+s)\mathrm{d}s + o(h)$, and $P[q(t) - q(t-h) \geq 2] = o(h)$.

which differs from the instantaneous volatility associated with the continuous martingale component, as defined in Eq. (2.19), and here restricted to be constant, $\sigma^2(t) \equiv \sigma^2$.

In this context, it is also important to recognize that the assumption on $\sigma(t)$, and the corresponding continuous sample path martingale representation in Proposition 3, does not rule out jumps in the $\sigma(t)$ process. However, the presence of jumps in either $\sigma(t)$ and/or $r(t,h)$ invalidates the standard consistency arguments underlying the nonparametric ARCH filters and smoothers discussed in Section 4.1 below,[19] while the so-called realized volatility measures in Section 4.2 generally remains consistent for the notional volatility, even in the presence of jumps.

As for the multifactor parametric diffusion representations, the empirical evidence on jump diffusion models for asset returns is still inconclusive. Early work estimated (overly) simple representations in line with the time-invariant jump diffusion discussed above (e.g., Akgiray and Booth, 1986; Ball and Torous, 1985; Jarrow and Rosenfeld, 1984; Press, 1967), but these models are clearly at odds with the data. More realistic models have recently been explored by, e.g., Andersen et al. (2002), Duffie et al. (2000), Eraker (2004), Eraker et al. (2003), and Pan (2002). Although these formulations improve dramatically on the fit of traditional univariate diffusion and standard SV representations, a general consensus about the relative performance of the various alternative specifications remains elusive at this (early) point.

Another recent proposal is to retain the continuous sample path strategy for the asset returns, but model the volatility process as a non-Gaussian OU process driven by pure upward Lévy jumps (e.g., Barndorff-Nielsen and Shephard, 2001). A primary motivation for this approach is to retain analytic tractability of the temporal aggregation process involved in the construction of volatility forecasts within a reasonably descriptive continuous-time setting.[20] Technically, the jumps in the volatility process introduces no new conceptual theoretical issues, as the Lévy processes are semimartingales, and as such the general apparatus for diffusion processes discussed above applies directly. Lévy-driven long-memory type formulations have also been proposed by Anh et al. (2002) and Brockwell and Marquardt (2005). The empirical implementation of these approaches are still in their infancy, but the preliminary results are intriguing.

3.2. Discrete-Time Models

Even if trading and pricing are naturally thought of as evolving in continuous time within the frictionless no-arbitrage setting outlined in Section 2, it is often more convenient to work directly with parametric models for the associated discrete-time returns. Such an approach is naturally motivated by situations in which prices are only observed

[19]As discussed further below, the consistence of the ARCH filters may still be established on a case-by-case basis for certain jump processes.
[20]Although the markets are formally incomplete in this situation, a corresponding analytical option pricing formula based on the minimal-entropy martingale measure have been developed by Nicolato and Venardos (2003).

at regular fixed time intervals (daily closing prices, end-of-the-month prices). Alternatively, if trading is only feasible at given discrete points in time, the relevant return distribution is fully described by the conditional discrete-time dynamics. Either perspective allows us to embed the discrete-time ARCH and SV models in our basic continuous-time setting. Hence, for the remainder of this section, we assume that prices are only observed (and trades only possible) at discrete and equally spaced points in time, $t = 0, h, 2 \cdot h, \ldots, T-h, T$, where by assumption T is proportional to h.

The discrete-time models, at a minimum, assume that the correct specification of the one-step-ahead conditional mean and variances is known up to a low-dimensional parameter vector. That is, the models (parsimoniously) parameterize the first two conditional return moments,[21]

$$m(t,h) = E[r(t,h)|\mathcal{F}_{t-h}] = E[\mu(t,h)|\mathcal{F}_{t-h}] = \mu(t,h) \tag{3.9}$$

$$\varsigma^2(t,h) = E[(r(t,h) - m(t,h))^2|\mathcal{F}_{t-h}], \tag{3.10}$$

where $m(t,h)$ and $\mu(t,h)$ coincide because the one-step-ahead conditional mean is predictable. Of course, in contrast to the continuous sample path diffusion models corresponding to $h \to 0$, which may be defined completely through the instantaneous drift and volatility coefficients, the first two conditional moments of the one-period returns do not fully characterize the dynamic return distribution.

The restriction of only observing prices at equidistant points in time is readily interpreted, within the continuous-time setting, as a pure jump process with known jump times but random jump sizes. In the notation of the previous section,

$$\Delta M(t) = r(t,h) - \mu(t,h) = r(t,h) - m(t,h), \quad t = h, \ldots, T. \tag{3.11}$$

As such, it follows directly from the definition of the notional volatility over $[t-h,t]$ that

$$\upsilon^2(t,h) = [M,M]_t - [M,M]_{t-h} = \Delta M^2(t). \tag{3.12}$$

Moreover, the expected notional volatility over $[t-h,t]$ simply equals the conditional one-period-ahead variance as specified by the model,

$$\varsigma^2(t,h) = E[\upsilon^2(t,h)|\mathcal{F}_{t-h}] = E[\Delta M^2(t)|\mathcal{F}_{t-h}]. \tag{3.13}$$

[21] The information set, $\mathcal{F}_{t-h}$, is (implicitly) restricted to the corresponding discrete-time realizations of the process along with any other discrete-time (possibly latent) state variables.

This same result is generally not true for multiperiod forecasts, or volatilities over longer horizons, $[t - k \cdot h, t]$ where $k > 1$. In this situation, any variation in the conditional mean process within the forecast horizon will contribute to the return variation, so the expected notional volatility typically is not equal to the expected volatility. However, as discussed further below, the contribution from the variation in the conditional mean will usually only be of second-order importance unless the forecast horizon is very long.

To more explicitly clarify the relationship between the notional volatility and total return variability within the multiperiod setting, recall the generic return decomposition for a discrete-time pure-jump process in Proposition 1,

$$r(t) = \mu(t) + M^J(t), \quad t = 0, h, 2 \cdot h, \ldots, T - h, T, \tag{3.14}$$

where

$$\mu(t) = \Sigma_{\tau=1,\ldots,t/h} E\big(r(\tau \cdot h, h)|\mathscr{F}_{(\tau-1)\cdot h}\big) = \Sigma_{\tau=1,\ldots,t/h}\, \mu(\tau \cdot h, h), \tag{3.15}$$

$$M^J(t) = \Sigma_{\tau=1,\ldots,t/h} \Delta M(\tau) = \Sigma_{\tau=1,\ldots,t/h} (r(\tau \cdot h, h) - \mu(\tau \cdot h, h)) \tag{3.16}$$

Now, for any integer $k > 0$,

$$\mu(t, k \cdot h) = \mu(t) - \mu(t - k \cdot h) = \Sigma_{\tau=1,\ldots,k}\, \mu(t - (k - \tau) \cdot h, h).$$

This $\mu(t, k \cdot h)$ term represents the cumulative conditional one-period-ahead expected returns and not the conditional multistep-ahead expected return. Specifically, for $k > 1$, the term $\mu(t, k \cdot h)$ is generally not equal to $E(r(t, k \cdot h)|\mathscr{F}_{t-k\cdot h}) = m(t, k \cdot h)$, even though

$$E[\mu(t, k \cdot h)|\mathscr{F}_{t-k\cdot h}] = m(t, k \cdot h). \tag{3.17}$$

Hence, we obtain the decomposition of the k-period-expected volatility over $[t - k \cdot h, t]$,

$$\begin{aligned}
\zeta^2(t, k \cdot h) &= E[(r(t, k \cdot h) - m(t, k \cdot h))^2|\mathscr{F}_{t-k\cdot h}] \\
&= E[M^2(t, k \cdot h) + (\mu(t, k \cdot h) - m(t, k \cdot h))^2 + 2 \cdot M(t, k \cdot h) \cdot \mu(t, k \cdot h)|\mathscr{F}_{t-k\cdot h}] \\
&= E([M, M]_t - [M, M]_{t-k\cdot h}|\mathscr{F}_{t-k\cdot h}) + \mathrm{Var}[\mu(t, k \cdot h)|\mathscr{F}_{t-k\cdot h}] \\
&\quad + 2 \cdot \mathrm{Cov}[M(t, k \cdot h), \mu(t, k \cdot h)|\mathscr{F}_{t-k\cdot h}].
\end{aligned} \tag{3.18}$$

Trivially, as noted above, for the one-period-ahead forecasts, or $k = 1$, there cannot be any within-period variability in the conditional mean process, so the last two terms in (3.18) vanish, and the expected volatility equals the expected notional volatility. However, for multiple-period forecasts, the stochastic evolution of the conditional mean within the interval contributes to the overall return variability, both through the variation in the conditional mean itself and through the covariance between the return innovations and future (within forecast horizon) changes in the conditional mean return. However, the period-by-period conditional mean is generally much smaller than the volatility, and the shifts in the conditional mean are smaller yet. Hence, the expected notional volatility, or expected quadratic variation, remains the dominant component for the multiperiod return variability in empirically realistic situations.[22]

Further, notice that the so-called *Leverage Effect* (e.g., Black, 1976) impacts only the expected notional volatility (expected quadratic variation) and none of the other terms. The hypothesis stipulates a (negative) correlation between the return innovations, ΔM, and the size of future return innovations, $(\Delta M)^2$, essentially predicting a left-skewed distribution for the return innovations. With no impact on the conditional mean, only the quadratic variation process is affected. The closely related *volatility feedback effect* (e.g., Campbell and Hentschel, 1992) has an impact through the covariance term, but it remains limited by the size of the shifts in the conditional mean. Again, the hypothesis essentially implies a leftward skew in the return innovation distribution. Intuitively, given a positive volatility risk premium, large negative return innovations are magnified, whereas large positive return innovations are dampened due to the increase in the expected future return required to compensate for a positive and persistent shock to future volatility. Hence, technically, the volatility feedback not only tends to raise the expected volatility directly but it also induces a negative correlation between the return innovations and the future expected mean returns.

Returning to the basic discrete-time setup, the conditional moments in Eqs. (3.9) and (3.10) allow for relatively easy and consistent statistical inference concerning the unknown parameters by a standard generalized method of moments (GMM) estimator (Hansen, 1982), or for SV and latent state variable(s), a Simulated Method of Moments (SMM) type estimator (Duffie and Singleton, 1993). Of course, simple method-of-moments estimators with ill-chosen moment conditions may behave poorly, both asymptotically and in finite samples (Andersen et al., 1999), and much of the literature on discrete-time volatility models has been concerned with the development of more efficient estimation procedures under auxiliary assumptions. In particular, assuming that the standardized innovations, $(r(t,h) - \mu(t,h))/\zeta(t,h)$, belong to a specific parametric family of distributions, maximum likelihood estimation (MLE) and corresponding

[22] Of course, the exact terms involved in the multiple-period volatility forecasts will depend upon the specific functional form and the underlying distributional assumptions. Their practical computation may not be trivial, or even feasible in closed form, necessitating the use of numerical simulation techniques (see, e.g., Geweke, 1989). We shall not be concerned with these more computationally oriented aspects of the problem in this chapter.

Gaussian quasi-MLE (QMLE) procedures (Bollerslev and Wooldridge, 1992) are both conceptually straightforward to implement for the ARCH class of models, while more complicated procedures are generally required for discrete-time SV models.

Next, we briefly review some of the popular discrete-time parametric volatility models. The key distinguishing features for each class of models consist of the functional form for the conditional moments in Eqs. (3.9) and (3.10), the variables in the information set $\mathscr{F}_{t-h}$, along with any additional distributional assumptions. The performance of the different models, such as the fit to the data and precision of forecasts, as well as the ease of computing parameter estimates and the various terms in the volatility forecast expressions, depends importantly on these features.

3.2.1. ARCH Models

The ARCH class of models was first introduced in the seminal paper by Engle (1982). It has since enjoyed unprecedented empirical success along with a myriad of extensions and further theoretical developments. Indeed, most of our empirical knowledge to date concerning the temporal dependencies in financial market volatility have arguably been gleaned from estimation and inference with ARCH type models. Several surveys of this burgeoning literature already exist (an incomplete list of which includes, Andersen and Bollerslev, 1998c; Andersen et al., 2006a; Bollerslev et al., 1992, 1994; Diebold and Lopez, 1995; Engle and Kroner, 1995; Engle, 2004; Engle and Patton, 2001), and we will not attempt yet another comprehensive review. However, it is useful to briefly summarize the key developments and model formulations within the current framework.

The ARCH class of models differ from the discrete-time SV models discussed below, in that the parameterized conditional expectations in Eqs. (3.9) and (3.10) depend exclusively on directly observable variables. This assumption greatly facilitates statistical inference vis-a-vis SV models, and the widespread empirical use of ARCH style models, in part, stems from the ease with which traditional (quasi-) maximum likelihood–based procedures may be implemented.

Any time series model in which the conditional variance depends nontrivially on the time $t-h$ observable information set is now commonly referred to as an ARCH model. This terminology is explained by the particular parametric formulation first adapted by Engle (1982). Specifically, in the so-called ARCH(p) model, $\zeta^2(t,h)$ is parameterized as an autoregressive distributed lag of p-squared innovations,

$$\zeta^2(t,h) = \omega + \sum_{j=1,\ldots,p} \alpha_j \cdot (r(t-j\cdot h,h) - \mu(t-j\cdot h,h))^2 \equiv \omega + \alpha(L,h)(r(t,h) - \mu(t,h))^2, \tag{3.19}$$

where $\omega > 0$ and $\alpha_j \geq 0$ to ensure positivity of $\zeta^2(t,h)$ (a.s.), and the $\alpha(L,h)$ lag polynomial is defined by $\alpha_1 L^h + \alpha_2 L^{2h} + \cdots + \alpha_p L^{ph}$. Meanwhile, a more parsimonious characterization of the intertemporal volatility dependencies is often obtained by the generalized ARCH, or GARCH(p, q), model (Bollerslev, 1986),

$$\begin{aligned}\varsigma^2(t,h) &= \omega + \sum_{j=1,\ldots,p} \alpha_j \cdot (r(t-j\cdot h,h) - \mu(t-j\cdot h,h))^2 + \sum_{i=1,\ldots,q} \beta_i \cdot \varsigma^2(t-j\cdot h,h) \\ &= \omega + \alpha(L,h)(r(t,h)-\mu(t,h))^2 + \beta(L,h)\varsigma^2(t,h). \end{aligned} \tag{3.20}$$

For the popular GARCH(1,1) model, the parameter restrictions $\omega > 0$, $\alpha_1 \geq 0$, and $\beta_1 \geq 0$ obviously guarantees positivity of $\varsigma^2(t,h)$. Corresponding conditions for the general case are presented in Nelson and Cao (1992). Rearranging the terms, the GARCH(p, q) model is readily interpreted as an ARMA model for $[r(t,h) - \mu(t,h)]^2$ in which the autoregressive and moving average polynomials are given by $[\alpha(L,h) + \beta(L,h)]$ and $[1 - \beta(L,h)]$, respectively.[23] Hence, provided that all the roots of the characteristic equation, $\alpha(x,h) + \beta(x,h) = 1$, have norm greater than one, the model is covariance stationary, and the unconditional h-period (one-period) variance equals $E[\varsigma^2(t,h)] = \omega(1 - \alpha(1,h) + \beta(1,h))^{-1}$. Weaker conditions for strict stationarity have been derived by Nelson (1990b) and Bougerol and Picard (1992), while higher order moment conditions have been developed by Ling and McAleer (2002) among others.

The leverage effect, briefly discussed earlier, stipulates a negative correlation between current return innovations and future expected conditional variances. The GJR–GARCH model (Glosten et al., 1993), in which the α_j coefficients in $\alpha(L,h)$ in Eq. (3.20) depend on the sign of the corresponding return innovations, $r(t-j\cdot h,h) - \mu(t-j\cdot h,h)$, was specifically designed to accommodate such asymmetries. A similar motivation underlies the EGARCH model in Nelson (1991). Defining the standardized innovations,

$$z(t,h) \equiv (r(t,h) - \mu(t,h))/\varsigma(t,h), \tag{3.21}$$

the EGARCH(p, q) model takes the form

$$\begin{aligned}\log[\varsigma^2(t,h)] &= \omega + \alpha(L,h)\,\{\theta \cdot z(t,h) + \gamma \cdot [|z(t,h)| - E(|z(t,h)|)]\} \\ &\quad + \beta(L,h)\log[\varsigma^2(t,h)], \end{aligned} \tag{3.22}$$

where as before $\alpha(L,h)$ and $\beta(L,h)$ denote pth- and qth- order lag polynomials, respectively. Obviously, for $\theta < 0$, the model predicts a negative relation between current returns and future conditional variances. The logtransform complicates the calculation of (unbiased) multistep conditional variance forecasts but conveniently avoids having to impose nonnegativity constraints on the parameters. The EGARCH model also requires a specific distributional assumption for $z(t,h)$.

[23] Note that the assumption of a finite second-order moment in the ARMA representation corresponds to finite fourth-order unconditional moments of the returns.

Alternatively, as discussed above, asymmetries in the return-volatility relationship may also be attributed to the so-called volatility feedback effect. This feature is captured by the ARCH-in-Mean type formulation (Engle et al., 1987), in which the functional form for the conditional mean, $\mu(t,h)$, depends explicitly on the conditional variance of the process, $\zeta^2(t,h)$. Which of these competing specifications is best able to capture the empirically observed asymmetry in equity return volatility has been the subject of several empirical studies (e.g., Bekaert and Wu, 2000; Campbell and Hentschel, 1992).

Another important empirical finding concerns the strong degree of volatility persistence estimated with most daily and weekly financial rates of return. This is manifested by the autoregressive polynomials describing the variance dynamics in the GARCH(p,q) formulations, $1-\alpha(x,h)-\beta(x,h)$, and the EGARCH formulations, $1-\beta(x,h)$, having (their largest) roots very close to unity. The IGARCH model of Engle and Bollerslev (1986) directly imposes this condition; i.e., $\alpha(1,h)+\beta(1,h)=1$. However, the imposition of a unit root in the conditional variance arguably exaggerates the true dynamic dependencies, and several alternative long-memory, or fractionally integrated, ARCH type formulations have recently been estimated and analyzed more formally in the literature (e.g., Baillie et al., 1996; Bollerslev and Mikkelsen, 1996; Ding et al., 1993; Giraitis et al., 2000, 2004, 2005; Robinson, 1991, 2001; Zumbach, 2004). Possible explanations for the apparent long-memory dependencies based on the aggregation of multiple volatility components and/or stochastic regime-switching models have been explored by Andersen and Bollerslev (1997), Diebold and Inoue (2001), and Liu (2000) among others (see also the related component model in Engle and Lee, 1999). This remains a very active area of current research.

Our focus in this chapter has been almost exclusively univariate. Nonetheless, most interesting questions in asset pricing finance and risk management call for a multivariate framework involving not just conditional variances but also time-varying conditional covariances. From a conceptual view point, the extension of the univariate ARCH class of models to a multivariate setting presents few new issues. However, conditions to ensure that the parameterized conditional covariance matrices are positive definite (a.s.) and involve only a manageable (small) number of parameters are both important considerations from a practical perspective. In the diagonal GARCH model of Bollerslev et al. (1988), the conditional variances and covariances are parameterized as univariate GARCH(p,q) processes; i.e., the ijth element in the conditional covariance matrix depends on a distributed lag of past values of the same element and the cross products of the corresponding innovations. The related BEKK GARCH formulation (Engle and Kroner, 1995) guarantees that the covariance matrices are positive definite. The constant conditional correlation model in Bollerslev (1990) is empirically among the most frequently applied multivariate ARCH models. This model has recently been extended to incorporate parsimoneously parameterized time-varying conditional correlations by Engle (2002) and Tse and Tsui (2002). Other multivariate formulations allowing for relatively easy implementation in large dimensions include the R-GARCH model in Gallant and Tauchen (2000), the flexible GARCH model of Ledoit et al. (2003), the regime-switching dynamic correlation model of Pelletier (2006), the sequential conditional correlation model of Palandri (2006), and the matrix EGARCH model of Kawakatsu (2006).

Meanwhile, most industry applications entailing large-scale covariance matrix measurements rely on J.P. Morgan's RiskMetrics (Morgan, 1997). The RiskMetrics procedure is based on exponential smoothing, and as such corresponds directly to a diagonal IGARCH(1,1) model in which all the intercepts in the conditional covariance matrix are fixed at zero and identical values of α and $\beta \equiv 1 - \alpha$ are used across all assets. The use of the same smoothing parameter ($\beta = 0.94$ with daily data) obviously facilitates the implementation and automatically guarantees that the covariance matrix measurements are positive definite. Nonetheless, when viewed as a data-generating process as opposed to a filter, the RiskMetrics procedure is formally degenerate (Nelson, 1990b).

One major theoretical drawback to the GARCH class of models concerns their lack of closed-form aggregation. This is true both intertemporally and cross-sectionally. For example, if daily asset returns follow a univariate GARCH(p, q) model, the corresponding weekly returns are not GARCH(p, q). Similarly, if a collection of asset returns follow a multivariate GARCH(p, q) model, (nontrivial) portfolio returns are not GARCH(p, q). The Weak GARCH class of models was explicitly introduced by Drost and Nijman (1993) and Nijman and Sentana (1996) to address this issue. In a weak GARCH model, $\zeta^2(t, h)$ has the interpretation of a parameterized linear projection for the squared innovation. In contrast to the conditional expectations underlying the standard ARCH formulations, the linear projections are closed under temporal (and in the multivariate case cross-sectional) aggregation. However, the linear projections do not easily translate into the volatility concepts in Section 2 and, as emphasized by Meddahi and Renault (1996, 2004), asset pricing relationships are based on conditional expectations as opposed to linear projections. Thus, even though the difference between the linear projections and the true conditional expectations may be numerically small in empirical realistic situations, this limits the applicability and the formal interpretation of the weak GARCH class of models. The discrete-time square-root SARV (SR-SARV) models provide an alternative formulation that circumvent these problems. We next turn to a discussion of this and other discrete-time SV models.

3.2.2. Stochastic Volatility Models

The SV models differ from the ARCH class of models in that the information set, $\mathscr{F}_{t-h}$, underlying the conditional expectations in Eqs. (3.9) and (3.10) is not directly measurable with respect to the time $t - h$ observable filtration. This is typically the result of the inclusion of two separate stochastic innovations: one innovation term relating the conditional mean of the process to the actually observed return and a second innovation relating the *latent* volatility process to its conditional mean. This type of formulation is typically motivated by the mixture-of-distributions hypothesis (MDH) and the idea of a latent information arrival process. The MDH was originally put forth by Clark (1973) as a way of conceptualizing the distributional characteristics of speculative returns, and the basic hypothesis has subsequently been extended and analyzed empirically by Epps and Epps (1976), Taylor (1982), Tauchen and Pitts (1983), Andersen (1996), Andersen and Bollerslev (1997), Ané and Geman (2000), among many others, to allow for more realistic temporal dependencies in the underlying latent information arrival process(es). We shall return to a discussion of these ideas in Section 4.2 below. The actual parameterizations of the most popular discrete-time SV models are often rationalized through the discretization of specific continuous-time SV models. We do not provide an exhaustive review of the pertinent discrete-time SV class of models here but simply refer to the excellent surveys offered in Taylor (1994), Shephard (1996), and Ghysels et al. (1996).

In parallel to the GARCH and EGARCH class of models discussed above, most of the parametric SV models used in the literature are based on an autoregressive formulation for a continuous function of the (now) latent volatility process,

$$f[\zeta^2(t,h)] = \omega + \beta(L,h) f[\zeta^2(t,h)] + u(t,h), \tag{3.23}$$

where $\beta(L,h)$ denotes a pth-order distributed lag polynomial, and $u(t,h)$ is a martingale difference sequence; i.e., $E[u(t,h)|\mathscr{F}_{t-h}] = 0$. This class of models is commonly referred to as a SARV(p), model. Intuitively, it is the innovation term, $u(t,h)$, which distinguishes the SV from the ARCH class of models.[24] Of course, analogous to the GARCH class of models discussed above, for the SARV(p) model in (3.23) to be well defined, $\zeta^2(t,h)$ must be positive (a.s.). Depending on the functional form for $f(\cdot)$, this restricts the admissible parameters in $\beta(L,h)$ and/or the support of $u(t,h)$. Most of the models estimated in the literature have included only a single lag in the $\beta(L,h)$ polynomial. Conditions to ensure ergodicity and stationarity for the general SARV(1) model are presented in Andersen (1994). The two leading cases are given by the lognormal stochastic autoregressive volatility model in which $f(x) \equiv \log(x)$ and $u(t,h)$ is assumed to be Gaussian, and the square-root,[25] or SR-SARV, model corresponding to $f(x) \equiv x$.

The lognormal SV model was first analyzed by Taylor (1982) and subsequently popularized in influential papers by Harvey et al. (1994) and Jacquier et al. (1994). The logarithmic volatility model arises naturally from the standard return formulation, $r(t,h) = \mu(t,h) + \zeta(t,h) \cdot z(t,h)$, in which $z(t,h)$ is an i.i.d. mean zero, unit variance,

[24] Formal conditions under which the $u(t,h)$ term in the autoregressive formulation cannot be integrated out of the conditional expectations in (3.9) and (3.10), resulting in a genuine SV model, are presented in Andersen (1992).

[25] This terminology derives from Andersen (1994), who parameterizes an AR(1) model for $f^{-1}[\zeta(t,h)]$. Similarly, the lognormal SV model is sometimes referred to as an exponential SARV model.

white noise process. Rearranging the terms, squaring both sides, and taking logarithms, it follows that

$$y(t,h) \equiv \log[r(t,h) - \mu(t,h)]^2 = \log[\zeta^2(t,h)] + \log[z(t,h)^2]. \tag{3.24}$$

Assuming the mean to be known, this may be interpreted as the measurement equation in a state space representation of the model, with corresponding transition equation defined by the parametric model for $\log[\zeta^2(t,h)]$. In particular, for the lognormal SARV(1) model,

$$\log[\zeta^2(t,h)] = \omega + \beta \cdot \log[\zeta^2(t-h,h)] + u(t,h). \tag{3.25}$$

In this situation, filtered and smoothed measurements of the latent $\log[\zeta^2(t,h)]$ volatility process are readily available by linear Kalman filtering which, as pointed out by Nelson (1988) and Harvey et al. (1994), in turn allows for relatively easy to compute Gaussian QMLE parameter estimates. Of course, the innovations in the measurement equation will generally not be Gaussian, so the Kalman may result in poor measurements of the latent volatility state variable and correspondingly highly inefficient parameter estimates.[26]

The lognormal SARV(1) formulation may also be justified as a discrete-time approximation to the OU diffusion for the logarithmic instantaneous volatility,

$$\mathrm{d}\log(\sigma^2(t)) = -\beta(\log(\sigma^2(t)) - \alpha)\mathrm{d}t + \psi \mathrm{d}V(t), \tag{3.26}$$

referred to in Section 3.1.1 above. In particular, by a standard Euler scheme, the discrete-time version of the model in (3.26) takes the form

$$\log[\zeta^2(t,h)] = \log[\zeta^2(t-h,h)] - h \cdot \beta \cdot \{\log[\zeta^2(t-h,h) - \alpha] \\ + h^{1/2} \cdot \psi \cdot [V(t,h) - V(t-h,h)].$$

The actual parameterization is, of course, different from the model in Eq. (3.25), but the structure corresponds exactly to that of the lognormal SARV(1) model. Interestingly, the continuous-time OU process in Eq. (3.26) also has the interpretation of being the diffusion limit of the discrete-time EGARCH model, in the sense that a sequence of appropriately parameterized EGARCH(1,1) models (as discussed in Section 4.1 below) converges weakly to this model as the length of the sampling interval, h, approaches zero.

Although the latent logarithmic volatility in (3.25) takes the form of an AR(1) model, this translates into an ARMA(1,1) correlation structure for the demeaned logarithmic returns in (3.24), $y(t,h)$. Moreover, following Taylor (1986) and Harvey (1998), this same approximate correlation structure is present for any positive power transform of

[26] This motivates the extension of the QMLE procedure for the lognormal SV model to a non-Gaussian state space in Kim et al. (1998).

the squared returns; i.e., $\exp[y(t,h)]^c$ where $c > 0$. Hence, the shape of the autocorrelogram for the squared returns from the log-normal SARV(1) model mimics that of the empirically popular GARCH(1,1) model.

The second leading class of SV models is given by the SR-SARV(p) model. Following Meddahi and Renault (2004), the SR-SARV(p) model for $\zeta^2(t,h)$ is naturally defined by the marginalization of a p-dimensional latent VAR(1) process. As emphasized by Meddahi and Renault (1996, 2004), this class of models has the advantage of being closed under temporal (and in the multivariate setting cross sectional) aggregation. To appreciate this result, suppose that the true underlying continuous-time volatility is determined by the CEV diffusion,

$$d\sigma^2(t) = (\omega - \theta \cdot \sigma^2(t))dt + \sqrt{2} \cdot \alpha \cdot (\sigma^2(t))^\delta dV(t), \tag{3.27}$$

where $\delta \geq 1/2$ to ensure that the process for $\sigma^2(t)$ is stationary and nonnegative. Since $\zeta^2(t,h)$ is an affine function of $\sigma^2(t)$, it follows that for $\delta \leq 1$, the *exact* discretization of the process must adhere to the basic SR-SARV(1) model structure,

$$\zeta^2(t,h) = \omega + \beta \cdot \zeta^2(t-h,h) + u(t,h), \tag{3.28}$$

where $E[u(t,h)|\mathscr{F}_{t-h}] = 0$. Of course, the h-period time interval is arbitrary so that the expected volatility for the temporally aggregated process, $\zeta^2(t \cdot k, h \cdot k)$, where $k > 1$ and $t = 0, 1, 2 \ldots$, must be governed the same AR(1) model structure. As discussed further in Section 4.1 below, the CEV model in (3.27) with $\delta = 1$ may also be interpreted as the diffusion limit of the GARCH(1,1) model.

The discrete-time AR(1) formulations in (3.25) and (3.28) are, of course, somewhat restrictive. In parallel to the developments within the parametric ARCH class of models discussed above, long-memory, or fractionally integrated SV models, better suited at capturing the apparent long-run dependencies in the volatility, have been estimated by Breidt et al. (1998) and Harvey (1998).

Direct extensions of the univariate discrete-time SV models discussed above to a multivariate setting was first explored by King et al. (1994), while earlier work by Diebold and Nerlove (1989) used a related univariate latent ARCH factor structure in parameterizing time-varying conditional covariances. More flexible large-dimensional systems have recently been proposed by Chib et al. (2006).

The SV diffusions (both univariate and multivariate) discussed above are considerably harder to estimate from discretely observed data than the classical one-factor models of the OU or CIR variety, as the inference in essence involve the same complications that plague the estimation of continuous-time SV models. Intuitively, because of the latent information structure, any inference procedure must either rely on a (potentially noisy) proxy for the latent volatility or integrate out the latent stochastic variable(s) from the model. Again, we refer to other chapters in the handbook for a more detailed discussion of the different procedures designed for doing so,[27] as well as the aforementioned surveys by Ghysels et al. (1996) and Shephard (1996). Importantly, from the perspective of volatility measurements, as a by-product of the estimation, many of these procedures result in (approximately optimal) filtered and/or smoothed measurements of the functional latent volatility process, $f[\varsigma^2(t,h)]$, conditional on the underlying parametric model and the observable information.

4. NONPARAMETRIC METHODS

The data-driven, or nonparametric volatility measurements afford direct empirical appraisals of the notional volatility, $\upsilon^2(t,h)$, without any specific functional form assumptions. The most obvious such measure is, of course, given by the ex-post squared return spanning the $[t-h,t]$ time interval. However, even though the (demeaned) squared return generally provides an unbiased estimator for $\upsilon^2(t,h)$, it is also a very noisy estimate. The nonparametric measurements more generally achieve consistency by measuring the volatility as (weighted) sample averages of increasingly finer sampled squared (or absolute) returns over (and possible outside) the $[t-h,t]$ interval. This immediately raises important issues of efficiency, rates of convergence, and the (asymptotic) distributions for the measurement errors associated with different weighting schemes. At a more fundamental level, however, the nonparametric procedures differ importantly in their assumptions about the length of the time interval h. The instantaneous volatility filters, or ARCH filters and smoothers, discussed next, are based on the assumption of ever more observations over ever finer time intervals (a double limit theory), while the realized volatility measures build on the idea of an increasing number of observations over fixed length time intervals (a single limit theory).[28]

4.1. ARCH Filters and Smoothers

Parametric ARCH models were designed to parsimoneously model the expected volatility as an explicit function of discretely observed returns; i.e., a parameterized conditional expectation, $\varsigma^2(t,h) = E[(r(t,h) - m(t,h))^2 | F_{t-h}]$, where $h > 0$ and F_{t-h} denotes the information set generated by the past returns $r(t-h,h), r(t-2h,h), \ldots$ However, as observed by Nelson (1992), these same discrete-time parametric models may alternatively

[27] In addition to the general inference procedures, some noteworthy procedures explicitly developed for the estimation of discrete-time SV models include the Bayesian MCMC method in Jacquier et al. (1994, 2004) and Kim et al. (1998), the simulated maximum likelihood technique of Danielsson (1994), the Monte Carlo maximum likelihood approach of Sandmann and Koopman (1998), and the direct MLE through recursive numerical integration in Fridman and Harris (1998).

[28] Of course, the discrete-time parametric ARCH and SV models discussed in Section 3.1 may also be given the interpretation of fixed length interval filters for extracting $\upsilon^2(t,h)$, $h > 0$. However, these type of filters are difficult to characterize and formally justify outside the realm of a specific parametric framework.

be given a nonparametric interpretation as filters designed to extract information about the (latent) instantaneous volatility. In particular, assuming that the sample path of the price and the corresponding instantaneous volatility processes are both continuous, then, although formally misspecified at all discrete sampling frequencies, $h > 0$, an appropriately parameterized sequence of ARCH models, or expected (scaled) volatilities $\zeta^2(t,h)/h$, will consistently (for $h \to \infty$) estimate the instantaneous volatility, σ_t^2, at each point in time.

To grasp the intuition behind this powerful result, consider the simple continuous-time random walk model in Eq. (3.1), previously studied by Merton (1980) in this context,

$$\mathrm{d}p(t) = \mu \mathrm{d}t + \sigma \mathrm{d}W(t), \quad 0 \le t \le T.$$

Suppose that observations are only available at $n+1$ equally spaced points over the $[t-h, t]$ time interval, where $0 \le h < t \le T$; i.e., $t-h, t-h+(h/n), \ldots, t-h+(n-1)\cdot(h/n), t$. By the definition of the process, the corresponding sequence of $i = 1, 2, \ldots, n$, discrete (h/n)-period returns,

$$r(t-h+i\cdot(h/n), h/n) \equiv p(t-h+i\cdot(h/n)) - p(t-h+(i-1)\cdot(h/n)),$$

is then i.i.d. normally distributed with mean $\mu\cdot(h/n)$ and variance $\sigma^2\cdot(h/n)$. Hence, the MLE of the drift is simply given by the sample mean of the (scaled) returns,

$$\hat{\mu}_n \equiv n^{-1}\cdot\Sigma_{i=1,\ldots,n}\,(h/n)^{-1}\cdot r(t-h+i\cdot(h/n), h/n) \equiv r(t,h)/h.$$

It follows immediately that

$$E(\hat{\mu}_n) = \mu.$$

This fixed-interval, or in-fill asymptotic, estimator for the drift only depends on h and not n. The sampling frequency is irrelevant, only the span of the data matters. Thus, although $\hat{\mu}_n$ is an unbiased estimator for μ, it is not consistent as $n \to \infty$.

Consider now the (unadjusted) estimator for σ^2 defined by the sum of the (scaled) squared returns,

$$\begin{aligned}\hat{\sigma}_n^2 &\equiv n^{-1}\cdot\Sigma_{i=1,\ldots,n}\,(h/n)^{-1}\cdot r(t-h+i\cdot(h/n),(h/n)^2\\ &= h^{-1}\cdot\Sigma_{i=1,\ldots,n}\,r(t-h+i\cdot(h/n),h/n)^2.\end{aligned}$$

Because

$$E[r(t-h+i\cdot(h/n),h/n)^2] = \sigma^2\cdot(h/n)+\mu^2\cdot(h/n)^2,$$

it follows readily that

$$E(\hat{\sigma}_n^2) = \sigma^2 + \mu^2\cdot(h/n).$$

Hence, the drift induces only a second-order bias, or $O(n^{-1})$ term, in the estimation of σ^2 for $n \to \infty$. Moreover, this estimator for the diffusion coefficient is consistent as $n \to \infty$. To see this, note that

$$E[r(t-h+i\cdot(h/n),h/n)^3] = 3\cdot\mu\cdot\sigma^2\cdot(h/n)^2+\mu^3\cdot(h/n)^3,$$

$$E[r(t-h+i\cdot(h/n),h/n)^4] = 3\cdot\sigma^4\cdot(h/n)^2+6\cdot\mu^2\cdot\sigma^2\cdot(h/n)^3+\mu^4\cdot(h/n)^4,$$

which along with the second moment given above, and the fact that the returns are i.i.d., implies that

$$\mathrm{Var}(\hat{\sigma}_n^2) = 2\cdot\sigma^4\cdot n^{-1}+4\cdot\mu^2\cdot\sigma^2\cdot n^{-2}\cdot h.$$

Hence by a standard law of large numbers,

$$\mathrm{plim}_{n\to\infty}\,\hat{\sigma}_n^2 = \sigma^2.$$

The consistency result for the sample variance estimator for the time-invariant diffusion hinges on the true volatility being constant over $[t-h,t]$. Increasing the number of (scaled) squared return observations over the interval then produces an increasing number of unbiased and uncorrelated measures of σ^2, and simply averaging these yields a consistent estimator.

This basic idea may, given appropriate regularity conditions, be extended to the general class of continuous sample path diffusions considered in Proposition 3 and Eq. (2.21),

$$\mathrm{d}p(t) = \mu(t)\mathrm{d}t+\sigma(t)\mathrm{d}W(t), \quad 0\le t\le T,$$

under the additional assumption that the sample path for the $\sigma(t)$ process also is continuous. The main difference between this general model and the time-invariant diffusion $\sigma(t)\equiv\sigma$ analyzed in detail above, is that the length of the sampling interval, h, now also must shrink to zero as the sampling intensity within the interval, n, increases.

At an intuitive level, by the assumed sample path continuity, the temporal variation in $\sigma^2(t)$ is readily bounded by restricting the length of the time interval, h, over which the variation is measured,

$$\forall\xi>0,\exists h>0: \quad \sup_{t-h\le\tau\le t}|\sigma^2(\tau)-\sigma^2(t)|<\xi, \quad \text{(a.s)}.$$

Using this result and refining the arguments above, it is possible to show that the analogous time t (unadjusted) sample variance estimator,

$$\hat{\sigma}_{n,h}(t) \equiv n^{-1}\cdot\Sigma_{i=1,\ldots,n}\,(h/n)^{-1}\cdot r(t-h+i\cdot(h/n),h/n)^2, \tag{4.1}$$

consistently estimates the instantaneous volatility, provided that $h \to 0$ and $n \to \infty$ at the proper rates,

$$\text{plim}_{n\to\infty,h\to 0}\ \hat{\sigma}^2_{n,h}(t) = \sigma^2(t),$$

where the convergence is pointwise in probability.

The trade-off between the length of the sampling interval, $h \to 0$, and the number of observations, $n \to \infty$, is analogous to the usual bias-variance trade-off encountered in nonparametric kernel estimation. Similarly, the sample variance estimator in Eq. (4.1) corresponds to a flat kernel scheme and the efficiency of this estimator may generally be improved by using a weighted one- or two-sided average of squared returns. That is the motivation behind the ARCH filters and smoothers developed in a series of papers by Nelson (1992, 1996a,b), Nelson and Foster (1994, 1995), and Nelson and Schwartz (1992) [see also the discussion in Drost and Werker (1996); Duan (1997); Fornari and Mele (2001), and Mele and Fornari (2000)].[29]

To illustrate, consider the GARCH(1,1) filter for the $(1/n)$-period returns defined in Nelson (1992),

$$\begin{aligned}\hat{\sigma}^2_n(t) &= \omega_n + \alpha_n \cdot r(t, 1/n)^2 + \beta_n \cdot \hat{\sigma}^2_n(t - 1/n)\\ &= \omega_n \cdot (1 - \beta_n)^{-1} + \Sigma_{i=0,\ldots,\infty}\, \alpha_n \cdot \beta^i_n \cdot r(t - i/n, 1/n)^2,\end{aligned} \tag{4.2}$$

where

$$\omega_n = \omega/n, \quad \alpha_n = \alpha \cdot (1/n)^{1/2}, \quad \beta_n = 1 - \alpha \cdot (1/n)^{1/2} - \theta/n,$$

and where $\omega > 0, \alpha > 0, \theta > 0$, corresponding to $p = q = 1$, $\varsigma^2(t, 1/n) \equiv \hat{\sigma}^2_n(t)$, and $\mu(t, 1/n) \equiv 0$ in Eqs. (3.9–3.10) above. This filter again achieves consistency as $n \to \infty$ for $\sigma^2(t)$,

$$\text{plim}_{n\to\infty}\ \hat{\sigma}^2_n(t) = \sigma^2(t),$$

and, as before, the convergence is pointwise in probability. Note, these arguments explicitly rule out jumps, or discontinuities, in either the drift or diffusion coefficients[30] so that the sample path for the instantaneous volatility process, $\sigma^2(t)$, is continuous and coincides with that of the expected (scaled) instantaneous volatility, $\lim_{h\to 0}$ $\upsilon^2(t, h)/h$.

[29] For earlier work on nonparametric diffusion estimation based on stronger assumptions and different asymptotic arguments; see, e.g., Banon (1978), Dohnal (1987), Genon-Catalot et al. (1992), and Florens-Zmirou (1993).

[30] The consistency of ARCH filters may still be established on a case-by-case basis for certain jump processes. For instance, the Lévy-driven OU SV model of Barndorff-Nielsen and Shephard (2001) permits an ARMA(1,1) representation so that the GARCH(1,1) filter remains consistent for this particular jump model; see Meddahi and Renault (2004) for further discussion along these lines.

Heuristically, the GARCH(1,1) filter works analogously to the sample variance estimator in Eq. (4.1) by using an (infinite weighted) average of increasingly finer sampled squared returns ever closer to time t. However, the continuous record, or in-fill, asymptotics of ever more observations per interval, $n \to \infty$, over ever smaller time intervals, $h \to \infty$, is here achieved by a single asymptotic device dictating both the return sampling frequency and the simultaneous down-weighting of the more distant squared return observations, $r(t - i/n, 1/n)^2$, for large values of i. Note that the parameter configuration in (4.2) underlying this result implies that

$$\lim_{n \to \infty} (\alpha_n + \beta_n) = \lim_{n \to \infty} (1 - \theta/n) = 1$$

so that the sequence of GARCH(1,1) filters approaches an IGARCH model, as discussed in Section 3.2.1, in the limit.

Besides providing a consistent volatility filter, such sequences of GARCH models have other interesting and useful properties. For example, if the standardized returns,

$$z(t, 1/n) \equiv n^{1/2} \cdot r(t, 1/n)/\hat{\sigma}_n(t - 1/n), \tag{4.3}$$

are i.i.d. normally distributed then, as shown by Nelson (1990a), the sequence of GARCH(1,1) models defined implicitly by (4.2) converges weakly to the continuous-time GARCH model previously defined in Eq. (3.6),[31]

$$\begin{aligned} dp(t) &= \sigma^2(t) dW(t), \\ d\sigma^2(t) &= (\omega - \theta \cdot \sigma^2(t))dt + (2 \cdot \alpha)^{1/2} \sigma^2(t) dV(t), \end{aligned} \tag{4.4}$$

where the two Wiener processes are uncorrelated, $\text{Corr}(dW(t), dV(t)) = 0$. Of course, it remains true, that when interpreted as a filter, the sequence of GARCH(1,1) models in (4.2) underlying this diffusion limit consistently extracts the instantaneous volatility, $\sigma^2(t)$, for *any* continuous sample path diffusion.

Many other appropriately parameterized ARCH models share this important property. Specifically, consider the sequence of EGARCH(0,1) models defined by

$$\begin{aligned} \log\left(\hat{\sigma}_n^2(t)\right) &= \omega_n + \beta_n \cdot \log\left(\hat{\sigma}_n^2(t - 1/n)\right) + \theta_n \cdot z(t, 1/n) + \gamma_n \cdot [|z(t, 1/n)| - (2/\pi)^{1/2}] \\ \omega_n &= \alpha \cdot \beta/n, \beta_n = 1 - \beta/n, \quad \theta_n = \rho \cdot \psi \cdot (1/n)^{1/2}, \\ \gamma_n &= \psi \cdot (1 - \rho^2) \cdot (1 - (2/\pi))^{-1/2} \cdot (1/n)^{1/2}, \end{aligned} \tag{4.5}$$

where $\beta > 0$, $\psi > 0$, and the standardized innovations are defined as in Eq. (4.3). Interpreted as a sequence of filters, this similarly provides consistent estimates (as $n \to \infty$) of

[31] This particular CEV diffusion process for the instantaneous volatility has also previously been analyzed by Wong (1964).

the instantaneous volatility at each point in time for any continuous sample path diffusion of the general form in Eq. (2.21). In parallel to the consistent GARCH(1,1) filter,

$$\lim_{n\to\infty} \beta_n = 1$$

so that the root in the autoregressive polynomial dictating the exponential decay in the weights associated with the past absolute standardized returns approaches unity. Under the additional assumption of i.i.d. normally distributed standardized returns, the sequence of EGARCH(0,1) models defined by Eq. (4.5) converges weakly to the OU diffusion for $\log(\sigma^2(t))$,

$$\begin{aligned} \mathrm{d}p(t) &= \sigma(t)\mathrm{d}W(t) \\ \mathrm{d}\log(\sigma^2(t)) &= -\beta\,[\log(\sigma^2(t)) - \alpha]\mathrm{d}t + \psi\mathrm{d}V(t), \end{aligned} \tag{4.6}$$

where the instantaneous correlation between the two Wiener processes is determined by the leverage parameter ρ; i.e., $\mathrm{Corr}(\mathrm{d}W(t), \mathrm{d}V(t)) = \rho\mathrm{d}t$.

Because many candidate ARCH models may serve as consistent filters for the instantaneous volatility, this naturally raises the question of efficiency. The asymptotic distribution theory for the filter errors developed by Nelson and Foster (1994) and Nelson (1996a) allows for a formal analysis of this issue. Intuitively, in the diffusion limit (with continuous sample paths), the process is completely characterized by the first two conditional moments, and the optimal ARCH filter matches both of these. These results for continuous-time SDEs carry over to the design of optimal ARCH filters for the type of SDEs used in the formulation of the discrete-time SV models discussed in Section 3.2.2. In this situation, if the conditional distribution of the innovations are sufficiently fat-tailed, estimating $\sigma^2(t)$ by squaring a distributed lag of past absolute returns, as originally proposed by Taylor (1986) and Schwert (1989), may be more efficient than using a distributed lag of past squared returns. A detailed discussion of these results is beyond the scope of this chapter. However, it is worth noting that the comparisons in Nelson and Foster (1994) related to the diffusion in Eq. (4.6) show that asymptotically (for $n \to \infty$) the efficiency loss in extracting $\log(\sigma^2(t))$ based on the lognormal SARV(1) model in Eq. (3.26) coupled with the (suboptimal) linear Kalman filter can be substantial relative to the (asymptotically) optimal ARCH filter [which essentially looks like the EGARCH filter defined in Eq. (4.5)]. Of course, this still entails an efficiency loss relative to the optimal nonlinear extraction filter (e.g., Kitagawa, 1987), but as noted above, the numerical integration involved in the implementation of such filters is computationally much more demanding than the simple recursions underlying the filtered volatility estimates from ARCH models.

The ARCH filters explicitly restrict the information set used in the extraction of $\sigma^2(t)$ to past and current returns only; i.e., F_t. Asymptotic (for $n \to \infty$) optimal ARCH smoothers involving both lagged and future returns have been developed by Nelson (1996b). The basic idea behind the construction of optimal ARCH smoothers exploit principles similar to those involved in the extension of the Kalman filter to a Kalman smoother (e.g., Anderson and Moore, 1979). It is noteworthy that in contrast to the optimal ARCH filters, the resulting optimal ARCH smoothers do not necessarily match the first two conditional moments of the true distribution. An alternative asymptotic distribution theory for analyzing smoothed volatility measurements is provided by the rolling regression approach in Foster and Nelson (1996). We return to a discussion of some of these results in the following section.

4.2. Realized Volatility

The use of historical, ex-post sample variances computed from higher frequency return data as lower frequency volatility measures has many precedents within the empirical finance literature. For example, Poterba and Summers (1986), French et al. (1987), Pagan and Schwert (1990), and Schwert (1989) rely on monthly sample variances computed from daily returns, Dybvig (1993) uses the cumulative sample variance obtained from daily Treasury yields as a diagnostic, noting its link to the square-bracket process from the theory of semimartingales, while Schwert (1990), Hsieh (1991), and Taylor and Xu (1997) exploit intraday data to produce daily sample return variance measures.[32] In spite of the intuitive appeal of using sample variance estimators over fixed horizons as simple non-parametric volatility measures, they appear hard to justify theoretically if volatility truly is time varying. However, by connecting the sample variances, termed *realized volatility* in financial economics, to the theory of quadratic variation, it is possible to more formally justify and assess the properties of such measures. Moreover, this approach to volatility measurement has inspired promising and ongoing new research into volatility modeling based on general distributional assumptions. The formal definition is straightforward.

Definition 6 *Realized Volatility*

The realized volatility *over* $[t-h, t]$, *for* $0 < h \le t \le T$, *is defined by*

$$v^2(t, h; n) \equiv \Sigma_{i=1,\ldots,n}\, r(t - h + (i/n) \cdot h, h/n)^2. \tag{4.7}$$

The realized volatility is simply the second (uncentered) sample moment of the return process over a fixed interval of length h, scaled by the number of observations n (corresponding to the sampling frequency $1/n$) so that it provides a volatility measure calibrated to the h-period measurement interval. Although the definition is stated in terms of equally

[32] The work of the Olsen & Associates group in Zürich, Switzerland, as highlighted in the book by Dacorogna et al. (2001), has also been extremely influential in promoting the use of high-frequency intraday price date for more effectively measuring and modeling financial market volatility.

spaced observations, most results discussed below carry over to situations in which the realized volatility is based on the sum of unevenly but increasingly finely sampled squared returns.

The realized volatility measure is closely related to, but different from, the theoretical volatility concepts introduced in Section 2. For example, if the mean return is zero, $\mu(t) \equiv 0$, the realized volatility represents the ex-post sample variance computed from n discretely sampled (h/n)-period returns over $[t-h, t]$. In this case, the realized volatility is (ex-ante) unbiased for the expected volatility, $\varsigma^2(t,h)$. Formally, we have the following slight extension of Eq. (2.14) (see, e.g., Protter, 1992, Corollary 3 of Theorem 27, Chapter 2).

Proposition 4 *Realized Volatility as an Unbiased Volatility Estimator*

If the return process is square-integrable and $\mu(t) \equiv 0$, then for any value of $n \geq 1$ and $h > 0$,

$$\varsigma^2(t,h) = E[\upsilon^2(t,h)|\mathscr{F}_{t-h}] = E[M^2(t,h)|\mathscr{F}_{t-h}] = E[\upsilon^2(t,h;n)|\mathscr{F}_{t-h}]. \tag{4.8}$$

As such, the *ex-post* realized volatility is an unbiased estimator of *ex-ante* expected volatility. Of course, the zero mean assumption is highly restrictive but, as we discuss later, the result remains *approximately* true for a stochastically evolving mean return process over relevant horizons under weak auxiliary conditions, as long as the underlying returns are sampled at sufficiently high frequencies.

Another link to our previous discussion is provided by the theory of rolling sample variance estimators within the continuous sample path (diffusion) setting, as formally developed by Foster and Nelson (1996).[33] This theory implies that the realized volatility based on increasingly many return observations over finer and finer time intervals is consistent for the corresponding instantaneous volatility. That is, for $h \to 0$ and $n \to \infty$ (at proper rates),

$$\text{plim}_{n\to\infty,h\to 0}\ \upsilon^2(t,h;n)/h = \text{plim}_{h\to 0}\ \upsilon^2(t,h)/h = \sigma^2(t).$$

Although this result is of theoretical interest, it is less robust and less useful in practice. One constraint is that the theory excludes jumps in both the return and volatility processes. More importantly, from a practical perspective, the result hinges on the length of the time interval going to zero and the number of observations going to infinity (over the vanishing interval) simultaneously. This construction is hard to mimic in any relevant sense. Market microstructure features invariably limit the number of (effectively) uncorrelated return observations, so even for highly liquid markets, it is not possible to measure returns (or volatilities) instantaneously. We discuss these practical issues in more detail below.

[33] See also the related simulation-based evidence in Andreou and Ghysels (2002).

The rolling regression procedures and associated ARCH filters and smoothers for the instantaneous volatilities are also usually based on long (weighted) averages of the returns. Adjacent instantaneous volatility measures will therefore involve overlapping return observations. This renders formal statistical analysis of the time-series properties of any such derived volatility series complex. The realized volatility approach explicitly seeks to avoid such difficulties by fixing $h > 0$ and interpreting $\upsilon^2(t, h; n)$ as a measure of the overall volatility for the $[t - h, t]$ time interval. We turn now toward a general discussion of this approach.

The theoretical properties of realized volatility have been discussed from different perspectives in a number of recent studies including Andersen and Bollerslev (1998a), Andersen et al. (2001b, 2003a), and Barndorff-Nielsen and Shephard (2001, 2002a,b). A simple yet fundamental result follows directly by combining the theory of quadratic variation in Proposition 2 with the Definitions 1 and 6.

Proposition 5 *Consistency of Realized Volatility*

The realized volatility *provides a consistent nonparametric measure of the notional volatility,*

$$\text{plim}_{n\to\infty}\, \upsilon^2(t, h; n) = \upsilon^2(t, h), \quad 0 < h \leq t \leq T, \tag{4.9}$$

where the convergence is uniform in probability.

The notional volatility plays a crucial role in the return dynamics. From the relation between expected notional volatility and expected volatility in Eq. (2.16), the ex-ante expected notional volatility is also the critical determinant of expected volatility. Any empirical measures of (ex-ante expected) notional volatility based on (2.16) will necessarily depend on the assumed parametric model structure. Proposition 5 implies that, in the limit for increasingly finely sampled returns, or $n \to \infty$, realized volatility is a consistent (nonparametric) estimator of the (realized) notional volatility over any fixed-length time interval, $h > 0$.

Illustration 2 *Continuous-Time GARCH Model (Revisited)*

The first panel in Fig. 2.2 plots the simulated sample path for the one-period notional volatility, $\upsilon(t, h), t = 1, 2, \ldots, 2500,$ *for the same continuous-time GARCH model depicted in Fig. 2.1. To illustrate the consistence of the realized volatility (as* $n \to \infty$*) for the notional volatility, the last four panels in Fig. 2.2 plot the time series of realized volatilities,* $\upsilon(t, h; n)$*, for n equal to* $1, 3, 24,$ *and* 288*, respectively. The squared returns (*$n = 1$*) shown in the second panel obviously provide very noise measures of the notional volatilities. While it is possible to pick out the general shape, the plot is extremely erratic, and it would be hard to accurately assess the true value of* $\upsilon(t, h)$ *on a period-by-period basis. Squaring and summing three within period returns, as in the third panel, clearly helps in reducing the noise. Moving one step further in constructing the realized volatilities from* $n = 24$ *returns, corresponding to an hourly sampling frequency in a 24-h market,*

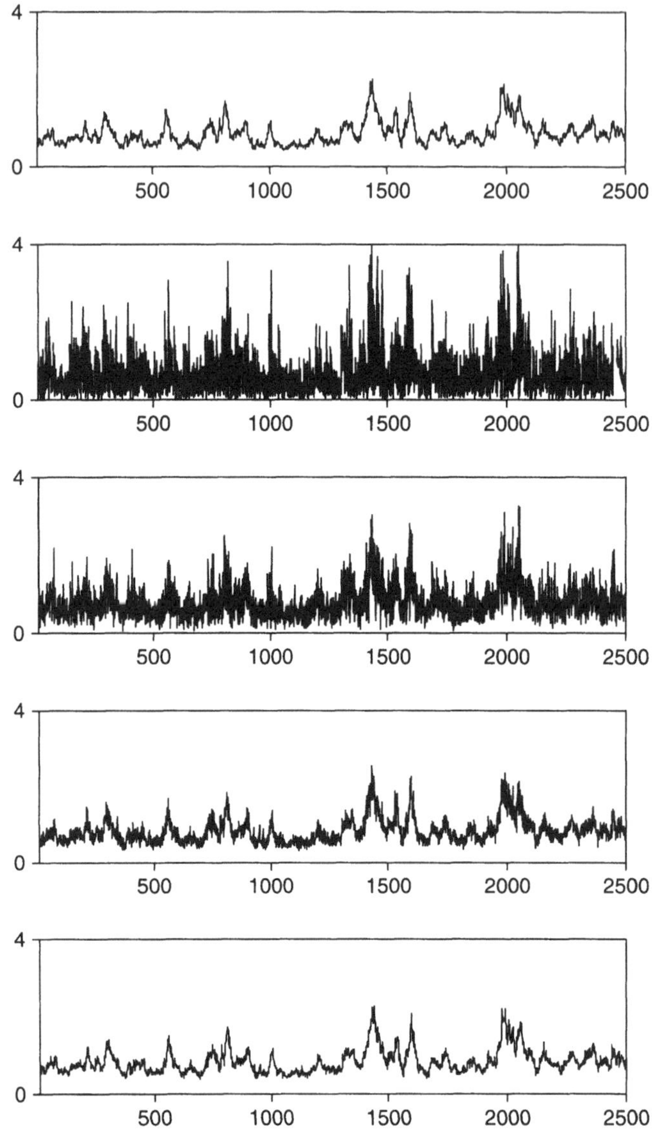

Figure 2.2 The first panel in the figure plots the one-period notional volatility, $\upsilon(t, 1)$, $t = 1, 2, \ldots, 2500$, from the same continuous-time GARCH model depicted in Fig. 2.1. The remaining four panels show the corresponding realized volatilities, $\upsilon(t, 1, n)$, for n equal to 1, 3, 24, and 288, respectively.

or 20-min returns, in a market operating eight hours a day, results in further dramatic improvements. Finally, the final panel for $n = 288$, or five-minute returns in a twenty-four hour market, is almost indistinguishable from the time series of notional volatilities in the top panel.

It is natural to combine the unbiasedness property of realized volatility in Proposition 4 and the consistency result in Proposition 5 to think of ex-post realized volatility measures, in general, as approximately unbiased estimators, and the ex-ante expected values of the realized volatility measures as consistent estimators for the ex-ante expected notional volatility. That is, subject to a uniform integrability condition, as formally discussed in Andersen et al. (2003a),[34]

$$\text{plim}_{n\to\infty} E[\upsilon^2(t,h;n)|\mathscr{F}_{t-h}] = E[\upsilon^2(t,h)|\mathscr{F}_{t-h}], \quad 0 < h \leq t \leq T. \tag{4.10}$$

Importantly, as explained in more detail below, this result and the ability to compute conditional expectations of the notional volatility from the realized volatility in turn allow for the construction of easy-to-implement reduced form volatility forecasting models.

Still, the above consistency results leaves important considerations regarding the size of potential error terms and any finite-sample biases unanswered. We discuss the issue of the measurement errors involved in using realized volatilities for volatility measurement and modeling in more detail below. Meanwhile, it is instructive first to consider a decomposition of the realized volatility measure into the separate terms associated with the potential sources of error and bias. For that purpose, we apply the canonical decomposition to each return component of the realized volatility definition in Eq. (4.7) and simplify notation, so for $i = 1, \ldots, n$,

$$\begin{aligned} r(t-h+(i/n)\cdot h, h/n) &= \mu(t-h+(i/n)\cdot h, h/n) + M(t-h+(i/n)\cdot h, h/n) \\ &\equiv \mu_i + M_i. \end{aligned} \tag{4.11}$$

In the frictionless arbitrage-free setting, the return on a risky asset over time intervals of length (h/n) has a martingale innovation of order $(h/n)^{1/2}$, while the corresponding mean component is at most of order (h/n). In particular, exploiting the notation introduced in Eq. (4.11), we have

$$\begin{aligned} \upsilon^2(t,h;n) &= \Sigma_{i=1,\ldots,n}\left[\mu_i^2 + 2\cdot\mu_i M_i + M_i^2\right] \\ &= \upsilon^2(t,h) + O_p(n^{-1}) + O_p(n^{-1/2}) + \left[\Sigma_{i=1,\ldots,n} M_i^2 - \upsilon^2(t,h)\right]. \end{aligned} \tag{4.12}$$

It is apparent that the realized volatility may differ from the notional volatility for two distinct reasons. First, the second and third terms on the right-hand side of the last

[34] The assumption of a bounded return process provides a simple sufficient condition for this convergence in mean; see, e.g., Hoffmann-Jørgensen (1994), sections 3.22–3.25. For example, one may imagine a bound on the return that prevents a small investment in the asset from ever producing a return that exceeds a (large) multiple of the expected value of all resources available in the worldwide economy. Nonetheless, this result is not true for all admittable price processes covered by Proposition 1; see, e.g., Barndorff-Nielsen and Shephard (2002b) for a counter example.

equation in (4.12) reflect the mean returns, which only truly vanishes in the limit for $n \to \infty$. However, the expected return over short intervals (large n) are necessarily small, so the contribution from these terms will be empirically negligible. This conclusion is only reinforced by noting that the component of the largest order, $O_p(n^{-1/2})$, represents a covariance term that is limited by the size of the innovations to the expected return over the (h/n) time interval, which typically will be very small. Second, the last term on the right-hand side of (4.12) has the interpretation of a measurement error term, as Proposition 4 shows that the cumulative-squared martingale innovations provide unbiased estimators for the corresponding notional volatility (quadratic variation). Hence, this term has a zero expected value. Nonetheless, for any given value of n, it induces a measurement error that is unrelated to the mean return. This component is the source of empirically relevant deviations between realized volatility and (realized) notional volatility.

The actual size and exact distribution of the errors obviously depend on the particular return process and must be analyzed on a case-by-case basis. Barndorff-Nielsen and Shephard (2002a) provide specific evidence for the OU specification with a background-driving Lévy process. Similarly, Meddahi (2002) presents explicit expressions for the different terms in Eq. (4.12) for the class of eigenfunction SV models and goes on to numerically compare the size of the unconditional variance of the measurement error to the unconditional variance of the notional (integrated) volatility for some of the continuous-time diffusions of the general form in Eq. (2.20) that have been estimated in the existing literature.

The preceding discussion implies that realized volatility is approximately (apart from minor biases induced by the mean component) unbiased for the corresponding notional volatility. Importantly, it also follows from the local martingale property in (2.11) and the decomposition in (4.12), that the associated measurement errors are approximately uncorrelated, i.e.,

$$E[(\upsilon^2(t+j,h;n) - \upsilon^2(t+j,h)) \cdot (\upsilon^2(t,h;n) - \upsilon^2(t,h))] = O_p(n^{-1}), \qquad (4.13)$$

where $j \neq 0$. Again, the $O(n^{-1})$ term is identically equal to zero in the case of constant mean returns and is otherwise likely to be small in empirically realistic situations. This confirms that realized volatilities provide meaningful and theoretically well-founded volatility measurements. Moreover, they constitute natural and convenient inputs into modeling and inference procedures concerning the expected notional volatility and, by extension, the expected return volatility.[35]

[35] This result also underlies the simple GMM estimation procedure for parametric continuous-time SV models in Barndorff-Nielsen and Shephard (2002a) and Bollerslev and Zhou (2002) based on matching sample moments of realized volatility with corresponding model implied moments for notional (integrated) volatility.

It is worth reiterating that the fixed h, large n asymptotics, or realized volatility asymptotics, underlying the results discussed above, is pivotal in practice. In particular, in spite of the theoretical desirability of letting interval size, h, shrink indefinitely as an increasing number of high-frequency return observations is used within each (vanishing) interval (as in the ARCH filters and smoothers discussed in Section 4.1), this idea is difficult (impossible) to mimic in practice. The number of data points, n, that adhere (approximately) to the underlying no-arbitrage semimartingale property over short time intervals is severely limited by various market microstructure frictions. This invariably puts an effective (asset and/or market specific) lower bound on the highest sampling frequency that is applicable in empirical work, say $1/n > 1/N$. We return to this important practical consideration below.

In summary, the realized volatility approach exploiting intraday return observations allow for directly observable return volatility measures that are consistent, approximately unbiased, and have uncorrelated measurement errors. It is natural to exploit these properties by building a time series model directly for the observed realized volatility measures through standard ARMA style modeling. Importantly, such procedures sidestep the complex task of providing an appropriate model for the intraday volatility patterns while still exploiting the inherent information in the high-frequency data for lower frequency volatility movements. Of course, the use of nonparametric volatility measurements invariably entails a loss in statistical efficiency relative to the use of a fully (and by assumption correctly) specified parametric volatility model. We comment further on this issue, and the practical merits of reduced form realized volatility modeling below.

The imposition of additional restrictions on the return process allows for important additional insight into the size and asymptotic distribution of the realized volatility errors. In particular, consider the class of continuous sample path diffusions, characterized by the sde,

$$dp(t) = \mu(t)dt + \sigma(t)dW(t), \quad 0 \leq t \leq T, \tag{4.14}$$

where $\mu(t)$ is predictable and of finite variation (c.f., Proposition 3 and the corresponding SDE in Eq. (2.21)). Extending the infeasible distributional implications of Jacod (1994) and Jacod and Protter (1998), the results of Barndorff-Nielsen and Shephard (2002a, 2004a) provide the following feasible mixed-Gaussian asymptotic (for $n \to \infty$) approximation to the distribution of the measurement errors.

Proposition 6 *Asymptotic Mixed Normality of Realized Volatility*

The realized volatility errors *for the continuous sample path diffusion in Eq. (4.14) is distributed as*

$$[\upsilon^2(t,h;n) - \upsilon^2(t,h)] \cdot [2/3 \cdot \upsilon^{[4]}(t,h;n)]^{-1/2} \to N(0,1), \tag{4.15}$$

for $n \rightarrow \infty$, where

$$\upsilon^{[4]}(t,h;n) \equiv \Sigma_{i=1,\ldots,n}\, r(t-h+i\cdot(h/n),h/n)^4. \tag{4.16}$$

Importantly, as shown in Barndorff-Nielsen and Shephard (2006b), this proposition remain valid in the presence of leverage effects, or correlations between the $\sigma(t)$ volatility process and the Brownian motion, $W(t)$, dictating the price innovations.[36] Thus, this results considerably strengthens the aforementioned convergence of realized volatility to notional volatility (in probability) by providing the asymptotic distribution of the corresponding errors. Formally, the variance of the realized volatility errors is given by $2/3 \cdot \int_{t-h}^{t} \sigma^4(\tau)d\tau$, which is consistently estimated by $2/3 \cdot \upsilon^{[4]}(t,h;n)$ as defined in Eq. (4.16). Hence, the magnitude of the errors depends upon the level of the (latent) volatility. This result represents a fundamental extension of the corresponding expression for the variance of the (uncentered) sample variance for the continuous-time random walk model discussed in Section 4.1 above, $2 \cdot \sigma^4 \cdot h^2 \cdot n^{-1} + O(n^{-1})$. Of course, the general expression for the variance of the realized volatility errors, or $\upsilon^{[4]}(t,h;n)$, is straightforward to calculate in practice.

The more powerful distributional result in Proposition 6, compared to the weak convergence in Proposition 4, comes at the cost of the stronger assumption on the underlying log-price process. Although the additional conditions, most notably the absence of jumps in the price path, likely are violated empirically at the highest sampling frequencies, the asymptotic distribution should nonetheless serve as a useful theoretical benchmark for assessing the properties of the realized volatility measures and further assist in guiding empirical procedures.

In this regard, Barndorff-Nielsen and Shephard (2005) find that an improved finite-sample (finite n) approximation may be obtained by the log-linearization,

$$[\log(\upsilon^2(t,h;n)) - \log(\upsilon^2(t,h)) + 1/2 \cdot s(t,h;n)^2] \cdot s(t,h;n)^{-1} \sim N(0,1), \tag{4.17}$$

where

$$s(t,h;n)^2 \equiv \max\left\{2/3\, \upsilon^{[4]}(t,h;n) \cdot \upsilon^2(t,h;n)^{-2},\ 2/n\right\}. \tag{4.18}$$

The upper bound of $2/n$ in Eq. (4.18) arises from imposing the theoretical lower bound for $n \rightarrow \infty$ on the first ratio. This approximation seems to work well, even for moderately sized n (say $n \geq 10$), in a (stylized) simulation setting. The improvement is related to the logarithm delivering a variance-stabilizing transformation. In that sense, the improved finite-sample distribution obtained by Eqs. (4.17) and (4.18) is directly in line with

[36] This is also corroborated by the related finite-sample (finite n) simulation evidence reported in Andersen et al. (2005).

the evidence for the parametric discrete-time SV models discussed in Section 3.1.1, for which the innovation process for the formulations involving the logarithmic volatility typically exhibits much reduced (conditional) heteroskedasticity.[37]

The above results speak to the precision in extracting information about the (realized) notional volatility from the realized volatility measures. Realizations of the notional volatility are, of course, of direct interest as indicators of return variability. However, they also provide an indication of the character of the underlying return distribution itself. In particular, it follows under appropriate conditions that the returns, $r(t, h)$, conditional on the notional volatility (and the mean return) over the $[t - h, t]$ return interval will be Gaussian.

Proposition 7 *Normal Mixture Distribution*

The discrete-time returns $r(t, h)$ over $[t - h, t], 0 < h \leq t \leq T$, for the continuous sample path diffusion in Eq. (4.14) is distributed as a normal mixture,

$$r(t, h)|\sigma\{\mu(t, h), \upsilon^2(t, h)\} \sim N(\mu(t, h), \upsilon^2(t, h)), \tag{4.19}$$

provided that the Brownian Motion, $W(t)$, is independent of $\mu(p(t), \sigma(t))$ and $\sigma(t)$.

Of course, the (ex-ante) mean return and the notional volatility is not directly observable. However, integrating out $\sigma\{\mu(t, h), \upsilon^2(t, h)\}$, the proposition implies that the return distribution conditional on time $t - h$ information should be governed by a normal mixture distribution.[38] This is directly in line with the implications of the MDH pioneered by Clark (1973) which, as discussed in Section 3.2.2, has motivated the formulation of some of the most widely used empirical discrete-time SV models.

The consistency of the realized volatility for the notional volatility in Proposition 4 along with the approximate log-normality of the realized volatility distribution and the normal mixture distribution in Proposition 7 suggest a simple alternative empirical return-volatility modeling strategy. Assume that the demeaned returns standardized by the realized volatilities, $[r(t, h) - \mu(t, h)] \cdot \upsilon^2(t, h; n)^{-1}$, are (approximately) Gaussian, coupled with a simple reduced form (approximately) Gaussian time series model for the logarithmic realized volatilities, $\log[\upsilon^2(t, h; n)]$. Effectively, this modeling strategy relies exclusively on forecasts for the distribution of the future notional volatilities through the observed realized volatilities, and as such is in principle straightforward to implement in practice.[39] Moreover, leverage effects, or asymmetries, in the notional volatility are

[37] This is also consistent with the empirical evidence in Andersen et al. (2001a,b) suggesting that the unconditional distribution of realized volatility is approximately log-normal.

[38] As discussed further below, the presence of jumps in the price process will generally render the corresponding distribution of the (standardized) returns nonnormal. This may be exploited in the formulation of tests for (the importance of) jumps, as in, e.g., Drost et al. (1998), Aït-Sahalia (2002, 2004), Andersen et al. (2007b), and Andersen et al. (2009).

[39] Of course, the realized volatility invariably differs from the true notional volatility for finite n. However, the measurement errors are (approximately) serially uncorrelated, and therefore, effectively averaged out in any reduced form time-series model for $\upsilon^2(t, h; n)$.

easily incorporated by allowing the time series model for $\log[\upsilon^2(t,h;n)]$ to depend (nontrivially) on the level of the (past) returns. This empirical modeling framework has been pursued successfully by Andersen et al. (2003a), who report impressive forecast performance from the estimation of simple standard time series models for the realized volatilities.[40] Related empirical work by Fleming et al. (2003) also suggests that important improvement can be obtained by using this realized volatility modeling approach in lieu of more standard parametric volatility modeling procedures in practical portfolio allocation decisions.[41]

As mentioned repeatedly, the realized volatility approach of holding $h > 0$ fixed is motivated by the fact that it is undesirable, and due to the presence of market microstructure frictions indeed practically infeasible, to sample returns infinitely often ($n \to \infty$) over infinitesimally short time intervals ($h \to 0$). To more directly illustrate these issues, suppose that the observed logarithmic price process, say $p^o(t)$, is equal to the true (latent) semimartingale price process that would obtain in the absence of any frictions, $p(t)$, plus a "noise" term, $u(t)$, coming from the use of discrete price grids, bid-ask spreads, and other pertinent market microstructure frictions; see, e.g., Hasbrouck (1996) and Stoll (2000). In this situation, the continuously compounded observed return over the $[t-(i/n)h, t-((i-1)/n)h]$ time interval, $i = 1, 2, \ldots, n$, is then given by,

$$\begin{aligned} r^o(t-((i-1)/n)\cdot h, h/n) &= p^o(t-((i-1)/n)\cdot h) - p^o(t-(i/n)\cdot h) \\ &= r(t-((i-1)/n)\cdot h, h/n) \\ &\quad + u(t-((i-1)/n)\cdot h) - u(t-(i/n)\cdot h). \end{aligned} \tag{4.20}$$

Hence, the realized volatility constructed from the summation of these n-squared returns within $[t-h,t]$ will typically not provide a consistent estimate of the increment to the quadratic variation of the true latent return process, or the notional volatility $\upsilon^2(t,h) \equiv [r,r]_t - [r,r]_{t-h}$. Indeed, assuming that the variance of the $u(t-((i-1)/n)h)$ process does not depend upon the value of n and is $O(1)$, the realized volatility estimator constructed from the observed returns, $r^o(t-((i-1)/n)\cdot h, h/n)$, will generally diverge for $n \to \infty$. This directly motivates choosing n sufficiently large so as to render the asymptotic results discussed above reliable, yet not too large so as not to overwhelm the estimate by the variation stemming from the noise component. The realized volatility signature plots of Andersen et al. (2000a), in which the sample means of $\upsilon^2(t,h;n)$, $t = 1, 2, \ldots, T$,

[40] These empirical results have been further corroborated by the corresponding theoretical implications for specific continuous-time SV models derived in Andersen et al. (2004).

[41] Many other empirical studies highlighting the potential benefits of the realized volatility framework in volatility forecasting, asset and option pricing, risk management, and other practical financial decision making have emerged over the past few years; see, e.g., Andersen et al. (2005), Areal and Taylor (2002), Bandi et al. (2006), Bollerslev and Zhang (2003), Corsi (2003), Deo et al. (2006), Engle and Gallo (2006), Koopman et al. (2005), Maheu and McCurdy (2002), Martens (2002), and Thomakos and Wang (2003). For a survey of some of these methods, see also Andersen et al. (2006b).

for a large value of T, are plotted against different values of n, provides a simple informal tool for gauging this trade-off and identifying the highest possible sampling frequency at which the impact of the noise appears negligible. More advanced techniques for directly determining the optimal, in a mean-square error sense, value of n has also been developed by Aït-Sahalia et al. (2005), and Bandi and Russell (2006a, 2008). For many actively traded assets, this often implies a value of n equivalent to about five minutes. Although the resulting measurement errors in the realized volatilities invariably depend upon the true underlying model and the exact form of the frictions, it is nonetheless evident that in most empirically realistic situations, the errors are often nontrivial.[42]

This in turn has inspired the development of several modified realized volatility measures designed to circumvent the impact of the microstructure frictions in estimating the notional volatility. In particular, suppose that the $u(t)$ noise process is i.i.d. It follows then readily from Eq. (4.20) that the discretely observed returns will inherent an MA(1) error structure. Motivated by this, early work along these lines relied on different MA (and AR) filters to mitigate the impact of the noise component; e.g., Andersen et al. (2001a), Areal and Taylor (2002), Bollen and Inder (2002), Corsi et al. (2001), among many others. Similarly, Zhou (1996) first proposed a kernel-based estimator, adding twice the first-order autocovariance to the realized variance as a way to account for the spurious first-order serial correlation induced by the i.i.d. noise component. More sophisticated kernel-based estimators, allowing for a wider variety of dependent noise processes, have been developed by Barndorff-Nielsen et al. (2008) and Hansen and Lunde (2006).[43] Alternatively, Zhang et al. (2005) suggested the use of subsampling schemes to correct for the bias induced by the noise component. Intuitively, under fairly general assumptions about the noise process, the bias in the realized volatility will grow at rate n. Thus, by properly combining realized volatilities for different sampling frequencies, it becomes possible to annihilate this first-order bias through a Jackknife-type estimator. As shown in Barndorff-Nielsen et al. (2008), this two-scale estimator may be expressed as a kernel-type estimator. Refined multiscale estimators have also been developed by Aït-Sahalia et al. (2006). Comprehensive surveys of this rapidly growing literature and the many different methods proposed therein can be found in Aït-Sahalia (2007), Bandi and Russell (2006b), Barndorff-Nielsen and Shephard (2006b), and McAleer and Medeiros (2006).

[42] Model-specific calculations and simulations by Andersen and Bollerslev (1998a), Andersen et al. (1999), Andersen et al. (2004, 2005), Andreou and Ghysels (2002), Bai et al. (2004), Barndorff-Nielsen and Shephard (2005), Barucci and Renò (2002), and Zumbach et al. (2002), among others, illustrate the effects of finite n (and h) in a variety of different settings.

[43] These estimators have a parallel in the so-called Heteroskedasticity and Autocorrelation Consistent (HAC) estimators used for estimating long-run covariance matrices (e.g., Newey and West, 1987, and Andrews, 1991). Importantly, however, the realized kernel-based estimators are not scaled by the sample size, which make their asymptotic properties very different. This also mirrors (in many ways) earlier developments related to the estimation of Capital Asset Pricing Model (CAPM) beta's in the presence of asynchronous trading effects by Scholes and Williams (1977), and the adjustment to the sample variance in French et al. (1987) obtained by including the cross-product between successive returns.

Meanwhile, the desire to guard against the potentially distorting impact of high-frequency real-world frictions has also inspired the use of alternative robust variation measures. One such measure, dating back to the work of Garman and Klass (1980) and Parkinson (1980), is the range; i.e., the difference between the maximum and the minimum price over some nontrivial $[t-h, t]$ time interval. As argued in Alizadeh et al. (2002) and Brandt and Diebold (2006), range-based volatility measures that involve only two as opposed to a large number of intrainterval price observations are less susceptible to both bid-ask bounce and asynchronous trading effects.[44] However, this desirable robustness feature must be weighed against the fact that formal statistical analysis of range-based estimators generally require specific distributional assumptions conveniently avoided by the realized volatility measures, as well as other power-based variation measures.

There is a long history in statistics of relying on absolute returns rather than squared returns as more robust (to outliers) measure of the ex-post variation; e.g., Davidian and Carroll (1987).[45] These results have a direct analog for the continuous sample path diffusion in Eq. (4.14). In particular, returning to the general frictionless arbitrage-free setting, the following definitions of *notional* and *realized power variation*, adapted from Barndorff-Nielsen and Shephard (2003), directly parallel the notional and realized volatility concepts discussed earlier.

Definition 7 *Power Variation Measures*

The notional sth order power variation *and the* realized sth order power variation, $s > 0$, *for the diffusion in Eq. (4.14) over* $[t-h, t], 0 < h \leq t \leq T$, *are defined, respectively, as*

$$\upsilon^{[s]}(t,h) \equiv \int_{t-h}^{t} \sigma^{s}(\tau)d\tau \tag{4.21}$$

and

$$\upsilon^{[s]}(t,h;n) \equiv \mu_s^{-1}(h/n)^{1-s/2}\ \Sigma_{i=1,\ldots,n}\ |r(t-h+i\cdot(h/n),h/n)|^{s}, \tag{4.22}$$

where $\mu_s = E(|Z|^s)$, *and* Z *denotes a standard normal distribution.*

It is apparent that, for $s=2$, the definitions correspond directly to the previously discussed notional and realized volatility concepts; i.e., $\upsilon^{[2]}(t,h) \equiv \upsilon^2(t,h)$ and $\upsilon^{[2]}(t,h;n) \equiv \upsilon^2(t,h;n)$, respectively. However, other values of s may allow for more robust measurements. In particular, extending the distributional results for the (standard)

[44] More formal statistical properties of realized range-based estimator and comparisons with other realized volatility estimators are discussed in Christensen and Podolskij (2007), Martens and van Dijk (2007), and Dobrev (2007).

[45] Also, as noted in Section 4.1 above, the optimal ARCH filters for discrete-time SV models may entail a distributed lag of past absolute returns as opposed to the squared returns (Nelson and Foster, 1994).

realized volatility in Proposition 5 to the generalized power variation measures defined above, the following proposition follows directly from Barndorff-Nielsen and Shephard (2003).

Proposition 8 *Asymptotic Mixed Normality of Realized Power Variation*
The realized sth order power variation errors, $s \geq 1/2$, *for the continuous sample path diffusion in Eq. (4.11) is distributed as*

$$\mu_s \cdot \omega_s^{-1/2}(h/n)^{s/2-1} \cdot [\upsilon^{[s]}(t,h;n) - \upsilon^{[s]}(t,h)]\upsilon^{[2s]}(t,h;n)^{-1/2} \to N(0,1), \qquad (4.23)$$

for $n \to \infty$, *where* $\mu_s = E(|Z|^s), \omega_s = \mathrm{Var}(|Z|^s)$, *and* Z *denotes a standard normal distribution.*

The special case corresponding to $s = 1$ is naturally termed *absolute variation.* The realized absolute variation is, of course, simply constructed by the (scaled) summation of the n absolute returns, $|r(t-h+i\cdot(h/n), h/n)|, i = 1, 2, \ldots, n$, within the $[t-h, t]$ time interval. From Proposition 8, the asymptotic (for $n \to \infty$) distribution of the corresponding measurement error for the notional absolute variation thus satisfies

$$(\pi/2-1)^{-1/2} \cdot (h/n)^{-1/2} \cdot [\upsilon^{[1]}(t,h;n) - \upsilon^{[1]}(t,h)]\upsilon^2(t,h;n)^{-1/2} \to N(0,1).$$

This provides a formal theoretical basis for gauging the empirical results in Andersen and Bollerslev (1998b) among others based on $\upsilon^{[1]}(t,h;n)$. Similarly, these distributional results may be helpful in better understanding the so-called Taylor Effect (e.g., Granger and Ding, 1995), according to which the autocorrelations of power transforms of the absolute returns are maximized (empirically) for values of s close to unity.

Meanwhile, the most desirable feature of the power variation measures arguable relates to their robustness to jumps for appropriate choice of s. In particular, consider the jump-diffusion model discussed earlier in Section 3.1.2 expressed in short-hand sde form,

$$\mathrm{d}p(t) = \mu(t)\mathrm{d}t + \sigma(t)\mathrm{d}W(t) + \kappa(t)\mathrm{d}q(t), \quad 0 \leq t \leq T, \qquad (4.24)$$

where $q(t)$ denote a Poisson point process, with $\mathrm{d}q(t) = 1$ indicating a jump at time t, and $\mathrm{d}q(t) = 0$ otherwise, and the random jump size is determined by the $\kappa(t)$ process (which is only defined for $\mathrm{d}q(t) = 1$). From the discussion in Section 3.1.2 and Eq. (3.8) along with Proposition 5, the realized volatility is then consistent for the integrated volatility plus the squared jumps,

$$\mathrm{plim}_{n\to\infty}\upsilon^2(t,h;n) = \upsilon^2(t,h) = \int_{t-h}^{t} \sigma^2(\tau)\mathrm{d}\tau + \Sigma_{t-h\leq\tau\leq t}\kappa^2(\tau)\cdot\mathrm{d}q(\tau), \quad 0 < h \leq t \leq T. \qquad (4.25)$$

One may further show (e.g., Aït-Sahalia, 2004; Barndorff-Nielsen and Shephard, 2003) that even in the presence of jumps, but for $s < 2$, the sth-order realized power variation is unaffected by jumps and remains consistent for the notional sth-order power variation, as defined above,

$$\text{plim}_{n\to\infty} \upsilon^{[s]}(t,h;n) = \upsilon^{[s]}(t,h) \equiv \int_{t-h}^{t} \sigma^s(\tau)d\tau, \quad 0 < h \leq t \leq T. \tag{4.26}$$

Hence, by summing high-frequency absolute returns raised to powers less than two, it is possible to mitigate the impact of the discontinuous jump component in the volatility measurement. Related realized power variation measures have also recently been explored empirically in a series of paper by Ghysels et al. (2004, 2006) in the form of so-called MIDAS, or mixed-data-sample, regressions.

More general so-called multipower variation measures have also recently been analyzed in the literature, with the following definition adapted from Barndorff-Nielsen and Shephard (2006a).

Definition 8 *Multipower Variation Measures*
The realized multipower variation of order $\{s1, s2, \ldots, sj\}$ *over* $[t-h, t]$, *for* $0 < h \leq t \leq T$, *is defined by*

$$\upsilon^{[s1,s2,\ldots,sj]}(t,h;n) \equiv \mu_{s1}^{-1} \cdot \ldots \cdot \mu_{sj}^{-1} \cdot (h/n)^{1-sm/2} \Sigma_{i=-j,\ldots,n} |r(t-h+i\cdot(h/n), h/n)|^{s1} \cdot \\ |r(t-h+(i-1)\cdot(h/n), h/n)|^{s2} \cdot \ldots \cdot |r(t-h+(i-j+1)\cdot(h/n), h/n)|^{sj}, \tag{4.27}$$

where $s1 \geq 0, \ldots, sj \geq 0$, $sm \equiv s1 + \cdots + sj$, $\mu_s = E(|Z|^s)$, *and* Z *denotes a standard normal distribution.*

This definition obviously includes the standard realized volatility,

$$\upsilon^{[2,0,\ldots,0]}(t,h;n) = \upsilon^2(t,h;n),$$

and the sth-order power variation measure,

$$\upsilon^{[s,0,\ldots,0]}(t,h;n) = \upsilon^{[s]}(t,h;n),$$

as special cases. However, in contrast to the realized volatility and power variation measures, which are based on the summation of power transforms of the absolute returns, the more general multipower variation measures are constructed by the summation of the product of *sequential* transformed absolute returns. Just like the power variation measures may be rendered robust to jumps by considering $s < 2$, the realized multipower variation measures may similarly be insulated from the impact of jumps by appropriately choosing the different orders of the power transforms. The following proposition, due Barndorff-Nielsen and Shephard (2006a) and Barndorff-Nielsen et al. (2006), formally justifies this idea.

Proposition 9 *Consistency of Realized Multipower Variation*
The realized multipower variation *for the jump-diffusion in Eq. (4.24) provides a consistent estimate for the corresponding* integrated variation,

$$\text{plim}_{n\to\infty}\, \upsilon^{[s1,s2,\ldots,sj]}(t,h;n) = \int_{t-h}^{t} \sigma^{sm}(\tau)\mathrm{d}\tau, \quad 0 < h \leq t \leq T, \tag{4.28}$$

where $\text{sm} \equiv s1 + \cdots + sj$*, and* $s1 < 2, \ldots, sj < 2$

Thus, the sum of the powers in the multipower variation measure directly dictates the specific limiting integrated variation measure. In particular, the so-called bipower variation measure, constructed by the summation of adjacent absolute returns, consistently (for $n \to \infty$) estimates conventional integrated volatility,

$$\text{plim}_{n\to\infty}\, \upsilon^{[1,1]}(t,h;n) = \int_{t-h}^{t} \sigma^{2}(\tau)\mathrm{d}\tau. \tag{4.29}$$

Combining this result with the consistency of the realized volatility in Eq. (4.25), the difference between the two measures affords a relatively simple-to-implement consistent estimate of the squared jumps that occurred over the $[t-h, t]$ time interval,

$$\text{plim}_{n\to\infty}\, [\upsilon^{2}(t,h;n) - \upsilon^{[1,1]}(t,h;n)] = \Sigma_{t-h\leq\tau\leq t}\, \kappa^{2}(\tau)\cdot \mathrm{d}q(\tau). \tag{4.30}$$

Moreover, Barndorff-Nielsen and Shephard (2006a) have shown that for the continuous sample path diffusion in Eq. (4.14), or $q(t) \equiv 0$ in Eq. (4.24),

$$(h/n)^{-1/2}\cdot[\upsilon^{2}(t,h;n) - \upsilon^{[1,1]}(t,h;n)]\cdot\left[\left(\mu_1^{-4}+2\mu_1^{-2}-5\right)\cdot\upsilon^{[1,1,1,1]}(t,h;n)\right]^{-1/2} \to N(0,1), \tag{4.31}$$

for $n \to \infty$. This, therefore, allows for the construction of high-frequency-based nonparametric tests for the existence jumps. Further, theoretical refinements and actual empirical applications involving this test have recently been pursued by Andersen et al. (2007a) and Huang and Tauchen (2005), among others.

Research in the realized volatility area has evolved rapidly over the past few years, and it is still too early to draw firm conclusions or consensus opinion about the preferred procedures. However, the theoretical and empirical results reported to date have been very promising. Recent research into multivariate extensions of the different variation measures and propositions discussed above should also help in further establishing a firm theoretical foundation for corresponding new realized covariation measures, CAPM betas, and factor loadings. The formulation of feasible co-jump measures and test statistics present another theoretically challenging set of problems. Of course, as discussed repeatedly, the development of reliable empirical procedures for dealing with the inherent market microstructure frictions at the highest possible sampling frequencies, both univariate and multivariate, and across different assets and market mechanisms, remains of the utmost importance from a practical perspective.

5. DIRECTIONS FOR FUTURE RESEARCH

In the last 10 years, there has been a movement toward the use of newly available high-frequency asset return data, and away from restrictive and hard-to-estimate parametric models toward flexible and computationally simple nonparametric approaches. Those trends will continue. Two related directions for future research are apparent: (i) continued development of methods for exploiting the volatility information in high-frequency data, and (ii) volatility modeling and forecasting in the high-dimensional multivariate environments of practical financial economic relevance. The realized volatility concept tackles both: it incorporates the highly useful information in high-frequency data while dispensing with the need to actually model the high-frequency data, and it requires only the most trivial of computations, thereby bringing within reach the elusive goal of accurate and high-dimensional volatility measurement, modeling, and forecasting. We look forward to realization of that goal in the foreseeable future.

ACKNOWLEDGMENTS

We acknowledge an anonymous referee, Lars Hansen, Nour Meddahi, and Neil Shephard for providing us with exceptionally helpful comments on the initial draft of the chapter. The work of Andersen and Bollerslev is supported by a grant from the NSF to NBER and CREATES funded by the Danish Research Foundation, and Diebold's work is funded by a grant from the NSF to the University of Pennsylvania.

REFERENCES

Anh, V.V., C.C. Heyde and N.N. Leonenko (2002), "Dynamic Models of Long-Memory Processes Driven by Lévy Noise," *Journal of Applied Probability*, 39, 730–747.

Aït-Sahalia, Y. (2002), "Telling from Discrete Data Whether the Underlying Continuous-Time Model is a Diffusion," *Journal of Finance*, 57, 2075–2121.

Aït-Sahalia, Y. (2004), "Disentangling Volatility from Jumps," *Journal of Financial Economics*, 74, 487–528.

Aït-Sahalia (2007), "Estimating Continuous-Time Models with Discretely Sampled Data," in R. Blundell, P. Torsten and W.K. Newey (eds.), *Advances in Economics and Econometrics, Ninth World Congress*, 261–327. Cambridge, UK: Cambridge University Press.

Aït-Sahalia, Y., P.A. Mykland and L. Zhang (2005), "How Often to Sample a Continuous-Time Process in the Presence of Market Microstructure Noise," *Review of Financial Studies*, 18, 351–416.

Aït-Sahalia, Y., P.A. Mykland and L. Zhang (2006), "Ultra High Frequency Volatility Estimation with Dependent Microstructure Noise," Manuscript, Department of Economics, Princeton University.

Aït-Sahalia, Y., L.P. Hansen and J. Scheinkman (2010), "Operator Methods for Continuous-Time Markov Processes," in Y. Aït-Sahalia and L.P. Hansen (eds.), *Handbook of Financial Econometrics*. Amsterdam: North-Holland.

Akgiray, V. and G. Booth (1986), "Stock Price Processes with Discontinuous Time Paths: An Empirical Investigation," *The Financial Review*, 21, 163–184.

Alizadeh, S., M.W. Brandt and F.X. Diebold (2002), "Range-Based Estimation of Stochastic Volatility Models," *Journal of Finance*, 57, 1047–1092.

Andersen, T.G. (1992), "Volatility," Manuscript, Kellogg Graduate School of Management, Northwestern University.

Andersen, T.G. (1994), "Stochastic Autoregressive Volatility: A Framework for Volatility Modeling," *Mathematical Finance*, 4, 75–102.

Andersen, T.G. (1996), "Return Volatility and Trading Volume: An Information Flow Interpretation of Stochastic Volatility," *Journal of Finance*, 51, 169–204.

Andersen, T.G., L. Benzoni and J. Lund (2002), "An Empirical Investigation of Continuous Time Equity Return Models," *Journal of Finance*, 57, 1239–1284.

Andersen, T.G. and T. Bollerslev (1997), "Heterogeneous Information Arrivals and Return Volatility Dynamics: Uncovering the Long-Run in High Frequency Returns," *Journal of Finance*, 52, 975–1005.

Andersen, T.G. and T. Bollerslev (1998a), "Answering the Skeptics: Yes, Standard Volatility Models Do Provide Accurate Forecasts," *International Economic Review*, 39, 885–905.

Andersen, T.G. and T. Bollerslev (1998b), "Deutschemark-Dollar Volatility: Intraday Activity Patterns, Macroeconomic Announcements, and Longer Run Dependencies," *Journal of Finance*, 53, 219–265.

Andersen, T.G. and T. Bollerslev (1998c), "ARCH and GARCH Models," in S. Kotz, C.B. Read and D.L. Banks (eds.), *Encyclopedia of Statistical Sciences, Vol. II* (6–16). New York: John Wiley and Sons.

Andersen, T.G., T. Bollerslev, P. Christoffersen and F.X. Diebold (2006a), "Volatility and Correlation Forecasting," in G. Elliott, C.W.J. Granger and A. Timmermann (eds.), *Handbook of Economic Forecasting*, Chapter 15, 777–878. Amsterdam: North-Holland.

Andersen, T.G., T. Bollerslev, P. Christoffersen and F.X. Diebold (2006b), "Practical Volatility and Correlation Modeling for Financial Market Risk Management," pp. 512–548 (with discussion); M. Carey and R. Stulz (eds.), *Risks of Financial Institutions*. Chicago: University of Chicago Press and National Bureau of Economic Research.

Andersen, T.G., T. Bollerslev and F.X. Diebold (2007a), "Roughing It Up: Including Jump Components in the Measurement, Modeling and Forecasting of Return Volatility," *Review of Economics and Statistics*, 89, 701–720.

Andersen, T.G., T. Bollerslev, F.X. Diebold and P. Labys (2000a), "Great Realizations," *Risk*, 13, 105–108.

Andersen, T.G., T. Bollerslev, F.X. Diebold and P. Labys (2000b), "Exchange Rate Returns Standardized by Realized Volatility are (Nearly) Gaussian," *Multinational Finance Journal*, 4, 159–179.

Andersen, T.G., T. Bollerslev, F.X. Diebold and H. Ebens (2001a), "The Distribution of Realized Stock Return Volatility," *Journal of Financial Economics*, 61, 43–76.

Andersen, T.G., T. Bollerslev, F.X. Diebold and P. Labys (2001b), "The Distribution of Realized Exchange Rate Volatility," *Journal of the American Statistical Association*, 96, 42–55.

Andersen, T.G., T. Bollerslev, F.X. Diebold and P. Labys (2003a), "Modeling and Forecasting Realized Volatility," *Econometrica*, 71, 579–625.

Andersen, T.G., T. Bollerslev, F.X. Diebold and C. Vega (2003b), "Micro Effects of Macro Announcements: Real-Time Price Discovery in Foreign Exchange," *American Economic Review*, 93, 38–62.

Andersen, T.G., T. Bollerslev, F.X. Diebold and G. Wu (2005), "A Framework for Exploring the Macroeconomic Determinants of Systematic Risk," *American Economic Review*, 95, 398–404.

Andersen, T.G., T. Bollerslev and D.P. Dobrev (2007b), "No-Arbitrage Semi-Martingale Restrictions for Continuous-Time Volatility Models subject to Leverage Effects, Jumps and i.i.d. Noise: Theory and Testable Distributional Implications," *Journal of Econometrics*, 138, 125–180.

Andersen, T.G., T. Bollerslev, P.H. Frederiksen and M.Ø. Nielsen (2009), "Continuous-Time Models, Realized Volatilities, and Testable Distributional Implications for Daily Stock Returns," *Journal of Applied Econometrics*, in press.

Andersen, T.G., T. Bollerslev and S. Lange (1999), "Forecasting Financial Market Volatility: Sample Frequency vis-a-vis Forecast Horizon," *Journal of Empirical Finance*, 6, 457–477.

Andersen, T.G., T. Bollerslev and N. Meddahi (2004), "Analytic Evaluation of Volatility Forecasts," *International Economic Review*, 45, 1079–1110.

Andersen, T.G., T. Bollerslev and N. Meddahi (2005), "Correcting the Errors: Volatility Forecast Evaluation Using High-Frequency Data and Realized Volatilities," *Econometrica*, 73, 279–296.

Andersen, T.G., H.J. Chung and B.E. Sørensen (1999), "Efficient Method of Moments Estimation of a Stochastic Volatility Model: A Monte Carlo Study," *Journal of Econometrics*, 91, 61–87.

Andersen, T.G., and J. Lund (1997), "Estimating Continuous-Time Stochastic Volatility Models of the Short Term Interest Rate," *Journal of Econometrics*, 77, 343–377.

Anderson, B.D.O. and J.B. Moore (1979), *Optimal Filtering*. Englewood Cliffs, NJ: Princeton Hall.

Andreou, E. and E. Ghysels (2002), "Rolling Sample Volatility Estimators: Some New Theoretical, Simulation and Empirical Results," *Journal of Business and Economic Statistics*, 20, 363–376.

Andrews, D.W.K. (1991), "Heteroskedasticity and Autocorrelation Consistent Covariance Matrix Estimation," *Econometrica*, 59, 817–858.

Ané, T. and H. Geman (2000), "Order Flow, Transaction Clock, and Normality of Asset Returns," *Journal of Finance*, 55, 2259–2284.

Areal, N.M.P.C. and S.J. Taylor (2002), "The Realized Volatility of FTSE-100 Futures Prices," *Journal of Futures Markets*, 22, 627–648.

Back, K. (1991), "Asset Prices for General Processes," *Journal of Mathematical Economics*, 20, 371–395.

Bai, X., J.R. Russell and G.C. Tiao (2004), "Effects on Non-Normality and Dependence on the Precision of Variance Estimates using High-Frequency Data," Manuscript, Graduate School of Business, University of Chicago.

Baillie, R.T., T. Bollerslev and H.O. Mikkelsen (1996), "Fractionally Integrated Generalized Autoregressive Conditional Heteroskedasticity," *Journal of Econometrics*, 74, 3–30.

Bakshi, G., C. Cao and Z. Chen (1997), "Empirical Performance of Alternative Option Pricing Models," *Journal of Finance*, 52, 2003–2049.

Ball, C.A. and W.N. Torous (1985), "On Jumps in Common Stock Prices and Their Impact on Call Option Pricing," *Journal of Finance*, 40, 155–173.

Bandi, F. and P.C.B. Phillips (2010), "Nonstationary Continuous-Time Processes," in Y. Aït-Sahalia and L.P. Hansen (eds.), *Handbook of Financial Econometrics*. Amsterdam: North-Holland.

Bandi, F. and J.R. Russell (2006a), "Separating Microstructure Noise from Volatility," *Journal of Financial Economics*, 79, 655–692.

Bandi, F. and J.R. Russell (2006b), "Volatility," in J.R. Birge and V. Linetsky (eds.), *Handbook of Financial Engineering*. Amsterdam: North-Holland, inpress.

Bandi, F. and J.R. Russell (2008), "Microstructure Noise, Realized Volatility, and Optimal Sampling," *Review of Economic Studies*, 75, 339–369.

Bandi, F., J.R. Russell and Y. Zhou (2006), "Using High-Frequency Data in Dynamic Portfolio Choice," *Econometric Reviews*, inpress.

Banon, G. (1978), "Nonparametric Identification for Diffusion Processes," *SIAM Journal of Optimization and Control*, 16, 380–395.

Barndorff-Nielsen, O.E. and N. Shephard (2001), "Non-Gaussian Ornstein-Uhlenbeck-Based Models and Some of Their Uses in Financial Economics," *Journal of the Royal Statistical Society, Series B*, 63, 167–241.

Barndorff-Nielsen, O.E. and N. Shephard (2002a), "Econometric Analysis of Realised Volatility and its Use in Estimating Stochastic Volatility Models," *Journal of the Royal Statistical Society, Series B*, 64, 253–280.

Barndorff-Nielsen, O.E. and N. Shephard (2002b), "Estimating Quadratic Variation Using Realised Variance," *Journal of Applied Econometrics*, 17, 457–477.

Barndorff-Nielsen, O.E. and N. Shephard (2003), "Realized Power Variation and Stochastic Volatility Models," *Bernoulli*, 9, 243–265.

Barndorff-Nielsen, O.E. and N. Shephard (2004a), "Econometric Analysis of Realised Covariation: High-Frequency Covariance, Regression and Correlation in Financial Econometrics," *Econometrica*, 72, 885–925.

Barndorff-Nielsen, O.E. and N. Shephard (2004b), "Power and Bipower Variation with Stochastic Volatility and Jumps," *Journal of Financial Econometrics*, 2, 1–37.

Barndorff-Nielsen, O.E. and N. Shephard (2005), "How Accurate is the Asymptotic Approximation to the Distribution of Realized Volatility?" in D.W.F. Andrews, J.L. Powell, P.A. Ruud and J.H. Stock (eds.), *Identification and Inference for Econometric Models. A Festschrift in Honour of T.J. Rotenberg*. Cambridge, UK: Cambridge University Press.

Barndorff-Nielsen, O.E. and N. Shephard (2006a), "Econometrics of Testing for Jumps in Financial Economics Using Bipower Variation," *Journal of Financial Econometrics*, 4, 1–30.

Barndorff-Nielsen, O.E. and N. Shephard (2006b), "Variation, Jumps and High-Frequency Data in Financial Econometrics," in R. Blundell, P. Torsten and W.K. Newey (eds.), *Advances in Economics and Econometrics, Ninth World Congress*. Cambridge, UK: Cambridge University Press.

Barndorff-Nielsen, O.E., S.E. Graversen, J. Jacod and N. Shephard (2006), "Limit Theorems for Realised Bipower Variation in Econometrics," *Econometric Theory*, 22, 677–719.

Barndorff-Nielsen, O.E., P.R. Hansen, A. Lunde and N. Shephard (2008), "Designing Realised Kernels to Measure the Ex-Post Variation of Equity Prices in the Presence of Noise," *Econometrica*, 76, 1481–1536.

Barucci, E. and R. Renò (2002), "On Measuring Volatility and the GARCH Forecasting Performance," *Journal of International Financial Markets, Institutions & Money*, 12, 183–200.

Bates, D. (1996a), "Jumps and Stochastic Volatility: Exchange Rate Processes Implicit in Deutschemark Options," *Review of Financial Studies*, 9, 69–107.

Bates (1996b), "Testing Option Pricing Models," in G.S. Maddala (ed.), *Handbook of Statistics Vol. 14, Statistical Methods in Finance*, 567–611. Amsterdam: North-Holland.

Bekaert, G. and G. Wu (2000), "Asymmetric Volatility and Risk in Equity Markets," *Review of Financial Studies*, 13, 1–42.

Bibby, B.M., M. Jacobsen and M. Sørensen (2010), "Estimating Functions for Discretely Sampled Diffusion-Type Models," in Y. Aït-Sahalia and L.P. Hansen (eds.), *Handbook of Financial Econometrics*. Amsterdam: North-Holland.

Black, F. (1976), "Studies of Stock Market Volatility Changes," *Proceedings of the American Statistical Association, Business and Economic Statistics Section*, 177–181.

Bollen, B. and B. Inder (2002), "Estimating Daily Volatility in Financial Markets Utilizing Intraday Data," *Journal of Empirical Finance*, 9, 551–562.

Bollerslev, T. (1986), "Generalized Autoregressive Conditional Heteroskedasticity," *Journal of Econometrics*, 31, 307–327.

Bollerslev, T. (1990), "Modeling the Coherence in Short-Run Nominal Exchange Rates: A Multivariate Generalized ARCH Approach," *Review of Economic and Statistics*, 72, 498–505.

Bollerslev, T., R.Y. Chou and K.F. Kroner (1992), "ARCH Modeling in Finance: A Selective Review of the Theory and Empirical Evidence," *Journal of Econometrics*, 52, 5–59.

Bollerslev, T., R.F. Engle and D.B. Nelson (1994), "ARCH Models," in R.F. Engle and D. McFadden (eds.), *Handbook of Econometrics, Volume IV*, 2959–3038. Amsterdam: North-Holland.

Bollerslev, T., R.F. Engle and J.M. Wooldridge (1988), "A Capital Asset Pricing Model with Time Varying Covariances," *Journal of Political Economy*, 96, 116–131.

Bollerslev, T., M. Gibson and H. Zhou (2005), "Dynamic Estimation of Volatility Risk Premia and Investor Risk Aversion from Option-Implied and Realized Volatilities," Manuscript, Department of Economics, Duke University.

Bollerslev, T. and H.O. Mikkelsen (1996), "Modeling and Pricing Long Memory in Stock Market Volatility," *Journal of Econometrics*, 73, 151–184.

Bollerslev, T. and J.M. Wooldridge (1992), "Quasi-Maximum Likelihood Estimation and Inference in Dynamic Models with Time Varying Covariances," *Econometric Reviews*, 11, 143–172.

Bollerslev, T. and B.Y.B. Zhang (2003), "Measuring and Modeling Systematic Risk in Factor Pricing Models Using High-Frequency Data," *Journal of Empirical Finance*, 10, 533–558.

Bollerslev, T. and H. Zhou (2002), "Estimating Stochastic Volatility Diffusion Using Conditional Moments of Integrated Volatility," *Journal of Econometrics*, 109, 33–65.

Bollerslev, T. and H. Zhou (2006), "Volatility Puzzles: A Simple Framework for Gauging Return-Volatility Regressions," *Journal of Econometrics*, 131, 123–150.

Bougerol, P. and N. Picard (1992), "Stationarity of GARCH Processes and Some Non-Negative Time Series," *Journal of Econometrics*, 52, 115–128.

Brandt, M.W. and F.X. Diebold (2006), "A No-Arbitrage Approach to Range-Based Estimation of Return Covariances and Correlations," *Journal of Business*, 79, 61–73.

Breidt, F.J., N. Crato and P. de Lima (1998), "On the Detection and Estimation of Long Memory in Stochastic Volatility," *Journal of Econometrics*, 73, 325–334.

Britten-Jones, M. and A. Neuberger (2000), "Option Prices, Implied Price Processes, and Stochastic Volatility," *Journal of Finance*, 55, 839–866.

Brockwell, P. and T. Marquardt (2005), "Lévy-Driven and Fractional Integrated ARMA Processes with Continuous Time Parameters," *Statistica Sinica*, 15, 477–494.

Campbell, J.Y. and L. Hentschel (1992), "No News is Good News: An Asymmetric Model of Changing Volatility in Stock Returns," *Journal of Financial Economics*, 31, 281–318.

Canina, L. and S. Figlewski (1993), "The Information Content of Implied Volatility," *Review of Financial Studies*, 6, 659–681.

Carr, P. and D. Madan (1998), "Towards a Theory of Volatility Trading," in R. Jarrow (ed.), *Volatility: New Estimation Techniques for Pricing Derivatives*, 417–428. London: Risk Books.

Carr, P. and L. Wu (2006), "A Tale of Two Indices," *Journal of Derivatives*, Spring, 13–29.

Carr, P. and L. Wu (2009), "Variance Risk Premia," *Review of Financial Studies*, 22, 1311–1342.

Chan, K.C., G.A. Karolyi, F.A. Longstaff and A. Sanders (1992), "An Empirical Comparison of Alternative Models of the Short-Term Interest Rate," *Journal of Finance*, 47, 1209–1227.

Chen, X., L.P. Hansen and M. Carrasco (2003), "Nonlinearity and Temporal Dependence," Manuscript, Department of Economics, University of Chicago.

Chernov, M., A.R. Gallant, E. Ghysels and G.E. Tauchen (2003), "Alternative Models for Stock Price Dynamics," *Journal of Econometrics*, 116, 225–257.

Chernov, M. and E. Ghysels (2000), "A Study Towards a Unified Approach to the Joint Estimation of Objective and Risk Neutral Measures for the Purpose of Options Valuation," *Journal of Financial Economics*, 57, 407–458.

Chib, S., F. Nardari and N. Shephard (2006), "Analysis of High Dimensional Multivariate Stochastic Volatility Models," *Journal of Econometrics*, 134, 341–371.

Christensen, K. and M. Podolskij (2007), "Realized Range-Based Estimation of Integrated Variance," *Journal of Econometrics*, 141, 323–349.

Christensen, B.J. and N.R. Prabhala (1998), "The Relation Between Implied and Realized Volatility," *Journal of Financial Economics*, 37, 125–150.

Chung, K.L. and R.J. Williams (1983), *Introduction to Stochastic Integration*. Boston: Birkhäuser, Inc.

Clark, P.K. (1973), "A Subordinated Stochastic Process Model with Finite Variance for Speculative Prices," *Econometrica*, 41, 135–155.

Comte, F. and E. Renault (1996), "Long Memory Continuous Time Models," *Journal of Econometrics*, 73, 101–149.

Comte, F. and E. Renault (1998), "Long Memory in Continuous Time Stochastic Volatility Models," *Mathematical Finance*, 8, 291–323.

Corsi, F. (2003), "A Simple Long-Memory Model of Realized Volatility," Manuscript, University of Southern Switzerland.

Corsi, F., G. Zumbach, U. Müller and M.M. Dacorogna (2001), "Consistent High-Precision Volatility from High-Frequency Data," *Economic Notes*, 30, 183–204.

Cox, J.C., J.E. Ingersoll, Jr. and S.A. Ross (1985), "A Theory of the Term Structure of Interest Rates," *Econometrica*, 53, 385–407.

Cox, J.C. and S.A. Ross (1976), "The Valuation of Options for Alternative Stochastic Processes," *Journal of Financial Economics*, 7, 229–263.

Dacorogna, M.M., R. Gencay, U. Müller, R.B. Olsen and O.V. Pictet (2001). *An Introduction to High-Frequency Finance*. San Diego, CA: Academic Press.

Dai, Q. and K.J. Singleton (2000), "Specification Analysis of Affine Term Structure Models," *Journal of Finance*, 55, 1943–1978.

Danielsson, J. (1994), "Stochastic Volatility in Asset Prices: Estimation with Simulated Maximum Likelihood," *Journal of Econometrics*, 61, 375–400.

Davidian, M. and R.J. Carroll (1987), "Variance Function Estimation," *Journal of the American Statistical Association*, 82, 1079–1091.

Day, T.E. and C.M. Lewis (1992), "Stock Market Volatility and the Information Content of Stock Index Options," *Journal of Econometrics*, 52, 267–287.

Demeterfi, K., E. Derman, M. Kamal and J. Zou (1999), "A Guide to Volatility and Variance Swaps," *Journal of Derivatives*, 6, 9–32.

Deo, R., C. Hurvich and Y. Lu (2006), "Forecasting Realized Volatility Using a Long-Memory Stochastic Volatility Model: Estimation, Prediction and Seasonal Adjustment," *Journal of Econometrics*, 131, 29–58.

Diebold, F.X. and A. Inoue (2001), "Long Memory and Structural Change," *Journal of Econometrics*, 105, 131–159.

Diebold, F.X. and J.A. Lopez (1995), "Modeling Volatility Dynamics," in K.V. Hoover (ed.), *Macroeconometrics: Developments, Tensions and Prospects*, 427–472. Boston: Kluwer Academic Press.

Diebold, F.X. and M. Nerlove (1989), "The Dynamics of Exchange Rate Volatility: A Multivariate Latent Factor ARCH Model," *Journal of Applied Econometrics*, 4, 1–22.

Ding, Z., C.W.J. Granger and R.F. Engle (1993), "A Long Memory Property of Stock Market Returns and a New Model," *Journal of Empirical Finance*, 1, 83–106.

Dohnal, G. (1987), "On Estimating the Diffusion Coefficient," *Journal of Applied Probability*, 24, 105–114.

Dobrev, D.P. (2007), "Capturing Volatility from Large Price Moves: Generalized Range Theory and Applications," Manuscript, Department of Finance, Kellogg School, Northwestern University.

Drost, F.C. and T.E. Nijman (1993), "Temporal Aggregation of GARCH Processes," *Econometrica*, 61, 909–927.

Drost, F.C., T.E. Nijman and B.J.M. Werker (1998), "Estimation and Testing in Models Containing Both Jumps and Conditional Heteroskedasticity," *Journal of Business and Economic Statistics*, 16, 237–243.

Drost, F.C. and B.J.M. Werker (1996), "Closing the GARCH Gap: Continuous Time GARCH Modeling," *Journal of Econometrics*, 74, 31–58.

Duan, J.C. (1995), "The GARCH Option Pricing Model," *Mathematical Finance*, 5, 13–32.

Duan, J.C. (1997), "Augmented GARCH(p,q) Process and Its Diffusion Limit," *Journal of Econometrics*, 79, 97–127.

Duffie, D. and K.J. Singleton (1993), "Simulated Moments Estimation of Markov Models of Asset Prices," *Econometrica*, 61, 929–952.

Duffie, D., J. Pan and K. Singleton (2000), "Transform Analysis and Asset Pricing for Affine Jump Diffusions," *Econometrica*, 68, 1343–1376.

Dumas, B., J. Fleming and R.E. Whaley (1998), "Implied Volatility Functions: Empirical Tests," *Journal of Finance*, 53, 2059–2106.

Dybvig, P.H. (1993), "Exploration of Interest Rate Data," Manuscript, Department of Finance, Olin School of Business, Washington University.

Engle, R.F. (1982), "Autoregressive Conditional Heteroskedasticity with Estimates of the Variance of U.K. Inflation," *Econometrica*, 50, 987–1008.

Engle, R.F. (1995). *ARCH: Selected Readings*. Oxford, UK: Oxford University Press.

Engle, R.F. (2002), "Dynamic Conditional Correlations: A Simple Class of Multivariate GARCH Models," *Journal of Business and Economic Statistics*, 20, 339–350.

Engle, R.F. (2004), "Risk and Volatility: Econometric Models and Financial Practice," *American Economic Review*, 94, 405–420.

Engle, R.F. and T. Bollerslev (1986), "Modeling the Persistence of Conditional Variances," *Econometric Reviews*, 5, 1–50.

Engle, R.F. and G.M. Gallo (2006), "A Multiple Indicators Model for Volatility Using Intra-Daily Data," *Journal of Econometrics*, 131, 3–27.

Engle, R.F. and K. Kroner (1995), "Multivariate Simultaneous Generalized ARCH," *Econometric Theory*, 11, 122–150.

Engle, R.F. and G.G.J. Lee (1999), "A Permanent and Transitory Component Model of Stock Return Volatility," in R.F. Engle and H. White (eds.), *Cointegration, Causality, and Forecasting: A Festschrift in Honor of Clive W.J. Granger*, 475–497. Oxford, UK: Oxford University Press.

Engle, R.F., D.M. Lilien and R.P. Robins (1987), "Estimating Time-Varying Risk Premia in the Term Structure: The ARCH-M Model," *Econometrica*, 58, 525–542.

Engle, R.F. and A.J. Patton (2001), "What Good is a Volatility Model?" *Quantitative Finance*, 1, 237–245.

Epps, T.W. and M.L. Epps (1976), "The Stochastic Dependence of Security Prices Changes and Transaction Volumes: Implications for the Mixture-of-Distributions Hypothesis," *Econometrica*, 44, 305–321.

Eraker, B. (2004), "Do Stock Prices and Volatility Jump? Reconciling Evidence from Spot and Option Prices," *Journal of Finance*, 59, 1367–1403.

Eraker, B., M. Johannes and N. Polson (2003), "The Impact of Jumps in Equity Index Volatility and Returns," *Journal of Finance*, 58, 1269–1300.

Fleming, J. (1998), "The Quality of Market Volatility Forecasts Implied by S&P100 Index Options Prices," *Journal of Empirical Finance*, 5, 317–345.

Fleming, J., C. Kirby and B. Ostdiek (2003), "The Economic Value of Volatility Timing Using Realized Volatility," *Journal of Financial Economics*, 67, 473–509.

Fleming, J., B. Ostdiek and R.E. Whaley (1995), "Predicting Stock Market Volatility: A New Measure," *Journal of Futures Market*, 15, 265–302.

Florens-Zmirou, D. (1993), "On Estimating the Diffusion Coefficient from Discrete Observations," *Journal of Applied Probability*, 30, 790–804.

Fornari, F. and A. Mele (2001), "Recovering the Probability Density Function of Asset Prices Using GARCH as Diffusion Approximations," *Journal of Empirical Finance*, 8, 83–109.

Foster, D. and D.B. Nelson (1996), "Continuous Record Asymptotics for Rolling Sample Estimators," *Econometrica*, 64, 139–174.

French, K.R., G.W. Schwert and R.F. Stambaugh (1987), "Expected Stock Returns and Volatility," *Journal of Financial Economics*, 19, 3–29.

Fridman, M. and L. Harris (1998), "A Maximum Likelihood Approach for Non-Gaussian Stochastic Volatility Models," *Journal of Business and Economic Statistics*, 16, 284–291.

Gallant, A.R., C.T. Hsu and G.E. Tauchen (1999), "Using Daily Range Data to Calibrate Volatility Diffusions and Extract the Forward Integrated Variance," *Review of Economics and Statistics*, 81, 617–631.

Gallant, A.R. and G.E. Tauchen (1997), "Estimation of Continuous-Time Models for Stock Returns and Interest Rates," *Macroeconomic Dynamics*, 1, 135–168.

Gallant, A.R. and G.E. Tauchen (1998), "Reprojecting Partially Observed Systems with Applications to Interest Rate Diffusions," *Journal of the American Statistical Association*, 93, 10–24.

Gallant, A.R. and G.E. Tauchen (2000), "SNP, A Program for Nonparametric Time Series Analysis: A Users Guide," available at ftp.econ.duke.edu, folder pub/arg/snp.

Gallant, A.R. and G.E. Tauchen (2010), "Simulated Score Methods and Indirect Inference for Continuous-Time Models," in Y. Aït-Sahalia and L.P. Hansen (eds.), *Handbook of Financial Econometrics*. Amsterdam: North-Holland.

Garcia, R., M.A. Lewis and E. Renault (2001), "Estimation of Objective and Risk-Neutral Distributions Based on Moments of Integrated Volatility," Manuscript, Department of Economics, University of Montreal and CIRANO.

Garcia, R., E. Ghysels and E. Renault (2010), "The Econometrics of Option Pricing," in Y. Aït-Sahalia and L.P. Hansen (eds.), *Handbook of Financial Econometrics*. Amsterdam: North-Holland.

Garman, M.B. and M.J. Klass (1980), "On the Estimation of Security Price Volatilities from Historical Data," *Journal of Business*, 53, 67–78.

Genon-Catalot, V., C. Laredo and D. Picard (1992), "Non-parametric Estimation of the Diffusion Coefficient by Wavelets Methods," *Scandinavian Journal of Statistics*, 19, 317–335.

Geweke, J. (1989), "Exact Predictive Densities for Linear Models with ARCH Disturbances," *Journal of Econometrics*, 40, 63–86.

Ghysels, E., A. Harvey and E. Renault (1996), "Stochastic Volatility," in G.S. Maddala (ed.), *Handbook of Statistics Vol. 14, Statistical Methods in Finance*, 119–191. Amsterdam: North-Holland.

Ghysels, E., P. Santa-Clara and R. Valkanov (2004), "The MIDAS Touch: Mixed Data Sampling Regressions," Manuscript, Department of Economics, University of North Carolina.

Ghysels, E., P. Santa-Clara and R. Valkanov (2006), "Predicting Volatility: How to Get the Most out of Returns Data Sampled at Different Frequencies," *Journal of Econometrics*, 131, 59–95.

Giraitis, L., P. Kokoszka and R. Leipus (2000), "Stationary ARCH Models: Dependence Structure and Central Limit Theorem," *Econometric Theory*, 16, 3–22.

Giraitis, L., R. Leipus, P.M. Robinson and D. Surgailis (2004), "LARCH, Leverage and Long Memory," *Journal of Financial Econometrics*, 2, 177–210.

Giraitis, L., R. Leipus and D. Surgailis (2005), "Recent Advances in ARCH Modeling," in A. Kirman and G. Teyssiere (eds.), *Long-Memory in Economics*, 3–38. Berlin: Springer Verlag.

Glosten, L.R., R. Jagannathan and D. Runkle (1993), "On the Relation Between the Expected Value and the Volatility of the Nominal Excess Return on Stocks," *Journal of Finance*, 48, 1779–1801.

Granger, C.W.J. and Z. Ding (1995), "Some Properties of Absolute Returns, an Alternative Measure of Risk," *Annals d'Economie et de Statistique*, 40, 67–91.

Hansen, L.P. (1982), "Large Sample Properties of Generalized Method of Moments Estimators," *Econometrica*, 50, 1029–1054.

Hansen, P.R. and A. Lunde (2006), "Realized Variance and Market Microstructure Noise," *Journal of Business and Economic Statistics*, 24, 127–161.

Harrison, J.M. and D. Kreps (1978), "Martingales and Arbitrage in Multiperiod Securities Markets," *Journal of Economic Theory*, 20, 381–408.

Harvey, A.C. (1998), "Long Memory in Stochastic Volatility," in J. Knight and J. Satchell (eds.), *Forecasting Volatility in Financial Markets*, 307–320. London, UK: Butterworth-Heinemann.

Harvey, A.C., E. Ruiz and N. Shephard (1994), "Multivariate Stochastic Variance Models," *Review of Economic Studies*, 61, 247–264.

Hasbrouck, J. (1996), "Modeling Market Microstructure Time Series," in G.S. Maddala and C.R. Rao (eds.), *Handbook of Statistics, Vol. 14*, 647–692. Amsterdam: North-Holland.

Heston, S.L. (1993), "A Closed Form Solution for Options with Stochastic Volatility, with Applications to Bond and Currency Options," *Review of Financial Studies*, 6, 327–343.

Heston, S.L. and S. Nandi (2000), "A Closed-Form GARCH Option Valuation Model," *Review of Financial Studies*, 13, 585–625.

Hoffmann-Jørgensen, J. (1994), *Probability with a View Toward Statistics*, Volume 1. Chapman and Hall Probability Series, New York: Chapman & Hall.

Huang, X. and G. Tauchen (2005), "The Relative Contribution of Jumps to Total Price Variation," *Journal of Financial Econometrics*, 3, 456–499.

Hull, J. and A. White (1987), "The Pricing of Options on Assets with Stochastic Volatilities," *Journal of Finance*, 42, 281–300.

Hsieh, D.A. (1991), "Chaos and Nonlinear Dynamics: Application to Financial Markets," *Journal of Finance*, 46, 1839–1877.

Morgan, J.P. (1997), *RiskMetrics, Technical Documents*, (Fourth Edition). New York.

Jacod, J. (1994), "Limit of Random Measures Associated with the Increments of a Brownian Semimartingale," Manuscript, Laboratoire de Probabilitiés, Université Pierre et Marie Curie, Paris.

Jacod, J. (2010), "Inference for Stochastic Processes," in Y. Aït-Sahalia and L.P. Hansen (eds.), *Handbook of Financial Econometrics*. Amsterdam: North-Holland.

Jacod, J. and P. Protter (1998), "Asymptotic Error Distributions for the Euler Method for Stochastic Differential Equations," *Annals of Probability*, 26, 267–307.

Jacquier, E., N.G. Polson and P.E. Rossi (1994), "Bayesian Analysis of Stochastic Volatility Models," *Journal of Business and Economic Statistics*, 12, 371–389.

Jacquier, E., N.G. Polson and P.E. Rossi (2004), "Bayesian Analysis of Stochastic Volatility Models with Fat Tails and Leverage Effect," *Journal of Econometrics*, 122, 185–212.

Jarrow, R. and E. Rosenfeld (1984), "Jump Risk and the Intertemporal Asset Pricing Model," *Journal of Business*, 57, 337–351.

Jiang, G. and Y. Tian (2005), "Model-Free Implied Volatility and Its Information Content," *Review of Financial Studies*, 18, 1305–1342.

Johannes, M.S. (2004), "The Statistical and Economic Role of Jumps in Continuous-Time Interest Rate Models," *Journal of Finance*, 59, 227–260.

Johannes, M. and N. Polson (2010), "MCMC Methods for Continuous-Time Financial Econometrics," in Y. Aït-Sahalia and L.P. Hansen (eds.), *Handbook of Financial Econometrics*. Amsterdam: North-Holland.

Karatzas, I. and S.E. Shreve (1991), *Brownian Motion and Stochastic Calculus* (Second Edition). New York: Springer-Verlag.
Kawakatsu, H. (2006), "Matrix Exponential GARCH," *Journal of Econometrics*, 134, 95–128.
Kim, S., N. Shephard and S. Chib (1998), "Stochastic Volatility: Likelihood Inference and Comparisons with ARCH Models," *Review of Economic Studies*, 65, 361–393.
King, M., E. Sentana and S. Wadhwani (1994), "Volatility and Links Between National Stock Markets," *Econometrica*, 62, 901–933.
Kitagawa, G. (1987), "Non-Gaussian State Space Modeling of Nonstationary Time Series," *Journal of the American Statistical Association*, 82, 1032–1063.
Koopman, S.J., B. Jungbacker and E. Hol (2005), "Forecasting Daily Variability of the S&P500 Stock Index Using Historical, Realised and Implied Volatility Measures," *Journal of Empirical Finance*, 12, 445–475.
Latané, H. and R.J. Rendleman (1976), "Standard Deviations of Stock Price Ratios Implied in Option Prices," *Journal of Finance*, 31, 369–381.
Ledoit, O., P. Santa-Clara and M. Wolf (2003), "Flexible Multivariate GARCH Modeling with an Application to International Stock Markets," *Review of Economics and Statistics*, 85, 735–747.
Ling, S. and M. McAleer (2002), "Necessary and Sufficient Moment Conditions for the GARCH(r,s) and Asymmetric Power GARCH(r,s) Models," *Econometric Theory*, 18, 722–729.
Liu, M. (2000), "Modeling Long Memory in Stock Market Volatility," *Journal of Econometrics*, 99, 139–171.
Maheu, J.M. and T.H. McCurdy (2002), "Nonlinear Features of Realized FX Volatility," *Review of Economics and Statistics*, 84, 668–681.
Maheswaran, S. and C.A. Sims (1993), "Empirical Implications of Arbitrage-Free Asset Markets," in P.C.B. Phillips (ed.), *Models, Methods and Applications of Econometrics*, 301–316. Oxford: Basil Blackwell.
Martens, M. (2002), "Measuring and Forecasting S&P500 Index-Futures Volatility Using High-Frequency Data," *Journal of Futures Markets*, 22, 497–518.
Martens, M. and D. van Dijk (2007), "Measuring Volatility with the Realized Range," *Journal of Econometrics*, 138, 112–133.
McAleer, M. and M.C. Medeiros (2006), "Realized Volatility: A Review," Manuscript, Department of Economics, Pontifical Catholic University of Rio de Janeiro, Brazil.
Meddahi, N. (2002), "A Theoretical Comparison Between Integrated and Realized Volatilities," *Journal of Applied Econometrics*, 17, 479–508.
Meddahi, N. and E. Renault (1996), "Aggregation and Marginalization of GARCH and Stochastic Volatility Models," Manuscript, Department of Economics, University of Montreal and CIRANO.
Meddahi, N. and E. Renault (2004), "Temporal Aggregation of Volatility Models," *Journal of Econometrics*, 119, 355–379.
Mele, A. and F. Fornari (2000), *Stochastic Volatility in Financial Markets: Crossing the Bridge to Continuous Time*. Boston: Kluwer Academic Publishers.
Merton, R.C. (1976), "Option Pricing when Underlying Stock Returns Are Discontinuous," *Journal of Financial Economics*, 3, 125–144.
Merton, R.C. (1980), "On Estimating the Expected Return on the Market: An Exploratory Investigation," *Journal of Financial Economics*, 8, 323–361.

Merton, R.C. (1982), "On the Mathematics and Economics Assumptions of Continuous-Time Models," in W.F. Sharpe and C.M. Cootner (eds.), *Financial Economics: Essays in Honor of Paul Cootner*. Englewood Cliffs, NJ: Prentice-Hall Inc.

Nelson, D.B. (1988), "The Time Series Behavior of Stock Market Volatility and Returns," Unpublished Ph.D. Dissertation, Department of Economics, MIT.

Nelson, D.B. (1990a), "ARCH Models as Diffusion Approximations," *Journal of Econometrics*, 45, 7–39.

Nelson, D.B. (1990b), "Stationarity and Persistence in the GARCH(1,1) Model," *Econometric Theory*, 6, 318–334.

Nelson, D.B. (1991), "Conditional Heteroskedasticity in Asset Returns: A New Approach," *Econometrica*, 59, 347–370.

Nelson, D.B. (1992), "Filtering and Forecasting with Misspecified ARCH Models I: Getting the Right Variance with the Wrong Model," *Journal of Econometrics*, 52, 61–90.

Nelson, D.B. (1996a), "Asymptotic Filtering Theory for Multivariate ARCH Models," *Journal of Econometrics*, 71, 1–47.

Nelson, D.B. (1996b), "Asymptotically Optimal Smoothing with ARCH Models," *Econometrica*, 64, 561–573.

Nelson, D.B. and C.Q. Cao (1992), "Inequality Constraints in the Univariate GARCH Model," *Journal of Business and Economic Statistics*, 10, 229–235.

Nelson, D.B. and D. Foster (1994), "Asymptotic Filtering Theory for Univariate ARCH Models," *Econometrica*, 62, 561–573.

Nelson, D.B. and D. Foster (1995), "Filtering and Forecasting with Misspecified ARCH Models II: Making the Right Forecast with the Wrong Model," *Journal of Econometrics*, 67, 303–335.

Nelson, D.B. and B. Schwartz (1992), "Filtering with ARCH Models: A Monte Carlo Investigation," *Proceedings of the American Statistical Association, Business and Economic Statistics Section*, 1–6.

Newey, W.K. and K.D. West (1987), "A Simple Positive Semi-Definite, Heteroskedasticity and Autocorrelation Consistent Covariance Matrix," *Econometrica*, 55, 703–708.

Nicolato, E. and E. Venardos (2003), "Option Pricing in Stochastic Volatility Models of the Ornstein-Uhlenbeck type," *Mathematical Finance*, 13, 445–466.

Nijman, T.H. and E. Sentana (1996), "Marginalization and Contemporaneous Aggregation of Multivariate GARCH Processes," *Journal of Econometrics*, 71, 71–86.

Pagan, A. and G.W. Schwert (1990), "Alternative Models for Conditional Stock Volatility," *Journal of Econometrics*, 45, 267–290.

Palandri, A. (2006), "Sequential Conditional Correlations: Inference and Evaluation," Manuscript, Department of Economics, Duke University.

Pan, J. (2002), "The Jump-Risk Premia Implicit in Options: Evidence from an Integrated Time-Series Study," *Journal of Financial Economics*, 63, 3–50.

Parkinson, M. (1980), "The Extreme Value Method for Estimating the Variance of the Rate of Return," *Journal of Business*, 53, 61–65.

Pelletier, D. (2006), "Regime Switching for Dynamic Correlations," *Journal of Econometrics*, 131, 445–473.

Piazzesi, M. (2010), "Affine Term Structure Models," in Y. Aït-Sahalia and L.P. Hansen (eds.), *Handbook of Financial Econometrics*. Amsterdam: North-Holland.

Pitt, M.K. and N. Shephard (1999), "Filtering via Simulation: Auxiliary Particle Filter," *Journal of the American Statistical Association*, 94, 590–599.

Poterba, J. and L. Summers (1986), "The Persistence of Volatility and Stock Market Fluctuations," *American Economic Review*, 76, 1124–1141.

Press, J.S. (1967), "A Compound Events Model for Security Prices," *Journal of Business*, 40, 317–335.

Protter, P. (1992), *Stochastic Integration and Differential Equations: A New Approach* (Second Edition). New York: Springer-Verlag.

Renault, E. (1997), "Econometric Models of Option Pricing Errors," in D.M. Kreps and K.F. Wallis (eds.) *Advances in Economics and Econometrics: Theory and Applications*, 223–278. Cambridge, UK: Cambridge University Press.

Robinson, P.M. (1991), "Testing for Strong Serial Correlation and Dynamic Conditional Heteroskedasticity in Multiple Regression," *Journal of Econometrics*, 47, 67–84.

Robinson, P.M. (2001), "The Memory of Stochastic Volatility Models," *Journal of Econometrics*, 101, 195–218.

Rossi, P.E. (1996), *Modelling Stock Market Volatility: Bridging the Gap to Continuous Time*. San Diego, CA: Academic Press.

Sandmann, G. and S.J. Koopman (1998), "Estimation of Stochastic Volatility Models via Monte Carlo Maximum Likelihood," *Journal of Econometrics*, 87, 271–301.

Scholes, M. and J. Williams (1977), "Estimating Beta from Non-Synchronous Data," *Journal of Financial Economics*, 5, 309–327.

Schwert, G.W. (1989), "Why Does Stock Market Volatility Change Over Time?," *Journal of Finance*, 44, 1115–1153.

Schwert, G.W. (1990), "Stock Volatility and the Crash of '87," *Review of Financial Studies*, 3, 77–102.

Shephard, N. (1996), "Statistical Aspects of ARCH and Stochastic Volatility Models," in D.R. Cox, D.V. Hinkley and O.E. Barndorff-Nielsen (eds.), *Time Series Models in Econometrics, Finance and Other Fields*, 1–67. London: Chapman & Hall.

Stoll, H.R. (2000), "Frictions," *Journal of Finance*, 55, 1479–1514.

Tauchen, G.E. and M. Pitts (1983), "The Price Variability-Volume Relationship on Speculative Markets," *Econometrica*, 51, 485–505.

Taylor, S.J. (1982), "Financial Returns Modeled by the Product of two Stochastic Processes - a Study of the Daily Sugar Prices 1961–75," in O.D. Anderson (ed.), *Time Series Analysis: Theory and Practice*, 203–226. Amsterdam: North-Holland.

Taylor, S.J. (1986), *Modeling Financial Time Series*. Chichester, UK: John Wiley and Sons.

Taylor, S.J. (1994), "Modeling Stochastic Volatility: A Review and Comparative Study," *Mathematical Finance*, 4, 183–204.

Taylor, S.J. and X. Xu (1997), "The Incremental Volatility Information in One Million Foreign Exchange Quotations, *Journal of Empirical Finance*, 4, 317–340.

Thomakos, D.D. and T. Wang (2003), "Realized Volatility in the Futures Markets," *Journal of Empirical Finance*, 10, 321–353.

Tse, Y.K. and A.K.C. Tsui (2002), "A Multivariate GARCH Model with Time-Varying Correlations," *Journal of Business and Economic Statistics*, 20, 351–362.

Whaley, R.E. (1993), "Derivatives on Market Volatility: Hedging Tools Long Overdue," *Journal of Derivatives*, 1, 71–84.

Wiggins, J.B. (1992), "Estimating the Volatility of S&P500 Futures Prices Using the Extreme Value Method," *Journal of Futures Market*, 12, 265–273.

Wong, E. (1964), "The Construction of a Class of Stationary Markoff Processes," in R. Bellman (ed.), *Sixteenth Symposium in Applied Mathematics – Stochastic Processes in Mathematical Physics and Engineering*, 264–276. Providence, RI: American Mathematical Society.

Zhang, L., P.A. Mykland and Y. Aït-Sahalia (2005), "A Tale of Two Time Scales: Determining Integrated Volatility with Noisy High-frequency Data," *Journal of the American Statistical Association*, 100, 1394–1411.

Zhou, B. (1996), "High-Frequency Data and Volatility in Foreign Exchange Rates," *Journal of Business and Economic Statistics*, 14, 45–52.

Zumbach, G. (2004), "Volatility Processes and Volatility Forecasts with Long Memory," *Quantitative Finance*, 4, 70–86.

Zumbach, G., F. Corsi and A. Trapletti (2002), "Efficient Estimation of Volatility using High Frequency Data," Manuscript, Olsen & Associates, Zürich, Switzerland.

CHAPTER 3

Nonstationary Continuous-Time Processes

Federico M. Bandi* *and* **Peter C. B. Phillips****
*Carey Business School, Johns Hopkins University, Baltimore, MD
**Cowles Foundation for Research in Economics, Yale University, New Haven, CT

Contents

Abstract

We survey local nonparametric methods applied to the estimation of scalar and multidimensional continuous-time Markov processes (with continuous and discontinuous sample paths). In doing so, particular emphasis is placed on recently proposed identification methods and asymptotic approaches which do not necessitate strict stationarity but hinge only on recurrence, possibly of the nonstationary kind.

Keywords: continuous-time Markov processes; kernel estimation; recurrence; nonparametric stochastic volatility

1. INTRODUCTION

A large body of recent asset pricing theory is written in continuous time, for which Merton (1990) and Duffie (1996) are classic references. Notwithstanding the evident benefit of continuous-time tools for modeling purposes and recent advances in the econometric treatment of continuous-time models,[1] the use of stochastic processes with continuous (in time) sample paths still poses important challenges when it comes to the econometric estimation and empirical implementation of modern asset pricing models. *The Econometrics of Financial Markets* (Campbell et al., 1997), *Financial Econometrics: Problems, Models and Methods* (Gourieroux and Jasiak, 2001), and *Analysis of Financial Time Series* (Tsay, 2005) are recent textbooks on the general topic of financial econometrics and outline some of the relevant issues.

Perhaps the most basic econometric problem arises because, although the relevant series are often specified as processes that evolve continuously in time, observations of the process occur only at discrete points in time. The discrete nature of the data has forced researchers to design estimation methodologies that are capable of circumventing the so-called "aliasing problem" and that can uniquely identify the fine grain structure of the underlying process from a sample of observations located along the continuous sample path rather than from a continuous record of the process over that path. (Readers are referred to the chapters by Aït-Sahalia et al., 2010; Gallant and Tauchen, 2010; Jacod, 2010; Johannes and Polson, 2010, in this handbook for a treatment of these issues.) Such methodologies generally, but not exclusively (cf., Hansen and Sargent, 1983; McCrorie, 2009; Phillips, 1973), rely on stationarity. The reason is clear. Should the underlying process be endowed with a stationary probability density, then the information extracted from the discrete data can fruitfully be used to identify the probability measure and thereby, hopefully, characterize the continuous dynamics of the system. In this way, stationarity can be a powerful aid to identification and estimation.

Despite the advantages of assuming the existence of a time-invariant probability distribution, it appears that for many empirical applications in continuous-time asset pricing it would be more appropriate to allow for martingale and other forms of nonstationary behavior, while not ruling out stationarity either. In such cases, an additional layer of complication in estimation comes from the necessity of achieving identification without resorting to the restrictions that are provided by the existence of a stationary probability density for the process of interest.

This chapter discusses techniques that have been recently introduced to identify potentially nonstationary, time-homogeneous, continuous-time Markov processes. The focus will be on classes of processes that are widely used in continuous-time asset pricing,

[1] In his survey on continuous-time methods in finance appeared in the Papers and Proceedings of the Sixtieth Annual Meeting of the American Finance Association, Sundaresan (2000) writes, "Perhaps the most significant development in the continuous-time field during the last decade has been the innovations in econometric theory and in the estimation techniques for models in continuous time."

namely scalar and multivariate diffusion processes as well as jump-diffusion processes. Such processes, irrespective of their stationarity properties, have infinitesimal conditional moment definitions. Their infinitesimal moments are known to fully characterize the temporal evolution of the corresponding system and, in consequence, readily lend themselves to estimation for the purpose of the identification of the system's dynamics. Consider a standard scalar diffusion (i.e., the solution to (3.1) below), but a similar argument holds for more involved continuous-time Markov processes of the type reviewed in this chapter. Its transition density (which is, in general, not known in closed form) is fully determined by the two functions that are commonly known as the drift, $\mu(.)$, and the diffusion, $\sigma^2(.)$. The drift represents the conditional expected rate of change of the process for infinitesimal time changes, i.e.,

$$\mu(a) = \lim_{t\to 0} \frac{1}{t}\mathbf{E}[X_t - X_0 | X_0 = a] = \lim_{t\to 0} \frac{1}{t}\mathbf{E}^a[X_t - a], \tag{1.1}$$

whereas the diffusion gives the conditional rate of change of volatility for infinitesimal variations in time, i.e.,

$$\sigma^2(a) = \lim_{t\to 0} \frac{1}{t}\mathbf{E}\left[(X_t - X_0)^2 | X_0 = a\right] = \lim_{t\to 0} \frac{1}{t}\mathbf{E}^a\left[(X_t - a)^2\right]. \tag{1.2}$$

Formulae (1.1) and (1.2) are suggestive in that one could hope to identify the functions of interests, which are defined as conditional expectations over infinitesimal time distances, using sample analogs to conditional expectations as in standard nonparametric inference for conditional moments in discrete time. For example, it is natural to estimate the drift at a by differencing the data and then averaging the first differences $X_{t+\Delta} - X_t$ corresponding to observations X_t in the spatial neighborhood of the generic level a. Provided the level a is visited an infinite number of times over time so that an infinite number of differences can be averaged asymptotically, we would expect the procedure to be consistent in the limit (i.e., the sample average converges, in probability at least, to the conditional moment). Interestingly, the underlying process (and, under some conditions, the sampled process) visits the level a an infinite number of times provided recurrence is satisfied. Recurrence implies return of the sample path of the underlying process to any spatial set of nonzero Lebesgue measure with probability one and is known to be a milder assumption than stationarity. (Section 2 provides a definition and additional discussions.)

Some recent papers have pursued the econometric implications of these observations and designed spatial estimation methods for various classes of continuous-time, time-homogeneous, recurrent Markov processes. The methods are easy to implement and have some natural appeal because they are based on commonly used nonparametric (and semiparametric) estimation procedures for conditional moments in more conventional stationary, discrete-time frameworks. However, they have the additional attraction that their statistical properties apply even though stationarity of the underlying continuous-time model is never assumed. These methods have been introduced in research by Bandi and Phillips (2003), Bandi and Nguyen (2003), and Bandi and Moloche (2004), which develops Nadaraya–Watson (NW) kernel estimation procedures for recurrent scalar diffusions, scalar jump-diffusions, and multivariate diffusions, respectively, and have subsequently been extended in a variety of directions.

Specifically, following work by Brugière (1991, 1993), Florens-Zmirou (1993), and Jacod (1997) in nonparametric volatility estimation for diffusions, this literature lays theoretical foundations for using well-understood and conventional nonparametric and semiparametric methods in the estimation of all the infinitesimal moment functionals driving the evolution of continuous-time Markov processes (with or without discontinuities in the sample path). The literature explores conditions (like recurrence) under which consistency and weak convergence results can be obtained in the (potential) absence of a stationary distribution for the process, and it provides results that can be evaluated in a manner that is closely related to conventional interpretations of nonparametric estimates for stationary discrete-time series. Although the findings that emerge from this literature contain the stationary case as a subcase, their more general form reflects the fact that a stationary density of the underlying process may not exist, which leads to important issues of interpretation. We discuss these issues and indicate avenues for future research both in the estimation of potentially nonstationary continuous-time processes (which are, as said, the core subject of our review) and in the estimation of potentially nonstationary (recurrent) discrete-time series.

This chapter is organized as follows. Section 2 provides some intuition for the methodology, introduces the notion of recurrence, and discusses the asymptotic features of our adopted sampling scheme. In particular, consistency is shown to hinge on the joint implementation of "infill" and "long span" asymptotics. The latter is crucial in exploiting the recurrence properties of the process under investigation. The former is vital in replicating the infinitesimal features of the functions of interest. Both conditions are necessary for the identification of continuous-time Markov processes under minimal assumptions on their dynamic properties and parametric form. Accordingly, the discussion in this chapter focuses on estimation procedures which impose mild assumptions on the stochastic nature of the underlying process but require the presence, at least in the limit, of "frequent" observations[2] to achieve consistent estimation. In this regard, our review can be viewed as complementary to those by Aït-Sahalia et al. (2010), Phillips and Yu (2009), and Johannes and Polson (2010). The former two papers discuss functional and parametric estimation methods for diffusions that do not require infill asymptotics

[2] The appropriateness of this asymptotic approximation is an empirical issue which depends on the application. However, it is known to be a realistic approximation in fields, such as finance, where data sets are often characterized by a large number of observations sampled at relatively high frequencies. Importantly, the highest frequency we consider here is generally the daily frequency (see Subsections 3.6 and 4.3 for exceptions). Although higher (intra-daily) frequencies would pose additional theoretical and empirical complications induced by the presence of market microstructure noise contaminations (see, e.g., Bandi and Phillips, 2007, for discussions), it is well known that daily data are good approximations to very frequent observations for estimators relying on very frequent observations (see, e.g., the simulation study of Jiang and Knight, 1999).

but rely on stationarity and mixing for identification and estimation. The latter reviews Bayesian simulation procedures that are sufficiently flexible to deal with nonstationarities but impose a tight parametric structure on the process of interest. This review is also complementary to recent survey articles on selected nonparametric methods in continuous-time asset pricing (Cai and Hong, 2003; Fan, 2005).

Sections 3, 4, and 5 specialize the analysis to the estimation of recurrent scalar diffusions, recurrent jump-diffusions, and recurrent multivariate diffusions, respectively. Some emphasis is also placed on stochastic volatility modeling (with and without discontinuities in the volatility's sample path) which, in light of the latent nature of volatility, poses additional challenges and is the subject of much research currently under way.

This chapter is largely self-contained, and its discussion is kept at a fairly intuitive level. Nonetheless, some basic notions of stochastic process theory and functional estimation in discrete-time econometrics will help the reader. Karatzas and Shreve (1991), Protter (1995), and Revuz and Yor (1998) are standard references for the former and, while not providing all the background material for the present chapter, are strongly recommended references. Thorough discussions of functional methods for discrete-time series are contained in Härdle (1990), Fan and Yao (2003), Pagan and Ullah (1999), and Li and Racine (2006). A concise and highly accessible introduction to nonparametric techniques is Härdle and Linton (1994). Chapter 12 of the book by Campbell et al. (1997) also provides accessible discussions of kernel regression methods similar to those used here.

2. INTUITION AND CONDITIONS[3]

As noted in the Introduction, the existence of conditional moments for interesting classes of continuous-time Markov models provides a mechanism for inference based on the construction of sample analogs (i.e., weighted averages) to infinitesimal conditional expectations. To fix ideas, consider a simple example in discrete time. Suppose the observations $X_1, X_2, \ldots, X_n$ are generated by a time-homogeneous Markov process X. One might be interested in estimating the conditional moment functional

$$M(a) = \mathbf{E}^a[f(X_1, a)], \tag{2.1}$$

where $X_0 = a$ is a generic initial condition and f is some integrable function. A crude (but intuitively appealing) sample analog estimator for $M(a)$ is

$$\widehat{M}_{(n)}(a) = \frac{\sum_{i=1}^{n} \mathbf{1}_{X_i=a} f(X_{i+1}, X_i)}{\sum_{i=1}^{n} \mathbf{1}_{X_i=a}}, \tag{2.2}$$

[3]Parts of this section are based on the discussion of the paper "On the functional estimation of jump-diffusion models" (Bandi and Nguyen, 2003) given by Darrell Duffie at the 2001 Winter Meetings of the Econometric Society (New Orleans, January 9, 2001).

where $\mathbf{1}_A$ is the indicator function of the set A. Formula (2.2) implies identification of the conditional expectation (at $X_0 = a$) of the function $f(X_1, X_0)$ [as in the definition of $M(a)$] through a (weighted) sample average of functions of the observations $[f(X_{i+1}, X_i)]$ taken at values X_i which are equal to a. Simple intuitive arguments based on the law of large numbers suggest that the level a ought to be visited an infinite number of times to achieve consistency. In consequence, it appears that the condition $\#\{i : X_i = a\} = \sum_{i=1}^{n} \mathbf{1}_{X_i=a} \to \infty$ as $n \to \infty$[4] is, in general, necessary to obtain asymptotic convergence of $\widehat{M}_{(n)}(a)$ to $M(a)$.

We now turn to a similar example in the context of a continuous-time Markov process X not necessarily endowed with a continuous sample path (one such case will be covered in Section 4 below). Suppose we are interested in estimating the infinitesimal conditional moment

$$M(a) = \lim_{t\to 0} \frac{1}{t}\mathbf{E}[f(X_t, X_0)|X_0 = a] = \lim_{t\to 0} \frac{1}{t}\mathbf{E}^a[f(X_t, a)]. \tag{2.3}$$

Note that if X is a scalar diffusion and $f(y, a)$ is equal to either $(y - a)$ or $(y - a)^2$, then $M(a)$ coincides with either the drift in Eq. (1.1) or the diffusion function in Eq. (1.2), respectively. Then, coherently with (2.2) above and the earlier discussion, one could estimate (2.3) using

$$\widehat{M}^{(1)}_{(n,\Delta,\varepsilon)}(a) = \frac{\sum_{i=1}^{n} \mathbf{1}_{X_i\in(a-\varepsilon,a+\varepsilon)} f(X_{i+\Delta}, X_i)/\Delta}{\sum_{i=1}^{n} \mathbf{1}_{X_i\in(a-\varepsilon,a+\varepsilon)}}, \tag{2.4}$$

where Δ is the time distance between discretely observed observations and ε is a bandwidth parameter according to which an interval around a on the sample path of the process is determined. Asymptotically, we send Δ to 0 to replicate the limit operation in the definition of $M(a)$ (i.e., $\lim_{t\to 0}$). Furthermore, (i) we let the bandwidth ε vanish so as to obtain averages of functions $f(X_{i+\Delta}, X_i)$ such that X_i is in a close neighborhood of a and (ii) we let n grow to infinity to guarantee that the number of observations X_i in the actual vicinity of a [i.e., $\#\{i : X_i \in (a - \varepsilon, a + \varepsilon)\} = \sum_{i=1}^{n} \mathbf{1}_{X_i\in(a-\varepsilon,a+\varepsilon)}$] diverges to infinity for identification. Again, we expect $\widehat{M}^{(1)}_{(n,\Delta,\varepsilon)}(a)$ to converge to $M(a)$ as $n \to \infty$, $\Delta \to 0$, and $\varepsilon \to 0$.[5]

Clearly, the function $\sum_{i=1}^{n} \mathbf{1}_{X\in(a-\varepsilon,a+\varepsilon)}$ counts the number of observations inside the window $(a - \varepsilon, a + \varepsilon)$ and weighs them equally. It seems plausible, however, that observations that are closer to a contain more useful information than more distant ones. In consequence, it might be worth replacing the so-called indicator kernel, i.e., $\mathbf{1}_{X\in(a-\varepsilon,a+\varepsilon)}$, with a function that is centered at a and converges monotonically to 0 as $|X| \to \infty$. Such a function would give a higher weight to observations that are closer

[4] We are purposely nonspecific about the mode of divergence at this point. We will be clear about it in what follows.

[5] Naturally, any notion of consistency (and convergence in distribution) requires appropriate (limiting) relations among n, Δ, and ε. In what follows, we will make these conditions explicit for all estimators.

to a, thereby increasing efficiency. This is typically achieved using smooth kernels $\mathbf{K}(.)$ satisfying $\int \mathbf{K}(u)du = 1$ (see, e.g., Härdle and Linton, 1994 and the assumptions below). The ubiquitous second-order Gaussian kernel is an example. Hence, we may write

$$\widehat{M}^{(2)}_{(n,\Delta,\varepsilon)}(a) = \frac{\sum_{i=1}^{n} \mathbf{K}\left(\frac{X_i - a}{\varepsilon}\right) f(X_{i+\Delta}, X_i)/\Delta}{\sum_{i=1}^{n} \mathbf{K}\left(\frac{X_i - a}{\varepsilon}\right)}, \tag{2.5}$$

which is simply a version of (2.4). As earlier, we expect $\widehat{M}^{(2)}_{(n,\Delta,\varepsilon)}(a)$ to be consistent for $M(a)$ as $n \to \infty$, $\Delta \to 0$, and $\varepsilon \to 0$ at appropriate rates.

We now summarize the features of the asymptotic requirements which appear to be necessary for consistency. In general, we will need to assume that the distance between observations Δ vanishes in the limit (i.e., infill asymptotics) while the time span (T, say) diverges to infinity (i.e., long span asymptotics) along with the number of observations n. As briefly mentioned in the introduction and illustrated above in the context of simple examples, the former assumption (i.e., $\Delta \to 0$) is important to replicate the infinitesimal features of the theoretical quantities. The latter (i.e., $T, n \to \infty$) is crucial to guarantee that the number of visits that the sampled process makes in the neighborhood of a generic point a diverges to infinity in the limit (i.e., $\sum_{i=1}^{n} \mathbf{1}_{X_i \in (a-\varepsilon, a+\varepsilon)} \to \infty$ or $\sum_{i=1}^{n} \mathbf{K}\left(\frac{X_i - a}{\varepsilon}\right) \to \infty$), provided the same happens for the path of the underlying process. Of course, the additional assumption $\varepsilon \to 0$ permits proper (asymptotic) conditioning at a.

Coherently with our discussion, the following sampling scheme has been adopted by the recent literature on the functional estimation of continuous-time Markov processes and will be used throughout this chapter. We will assume that we observe the process of interest X_t at points $\{t = t_1, t_2, \ldots, t_n\}$ in the time interval $[0, T]$ with $T > 0$. Also, the data will be taken to be equispaced. Thus,

$$\left\{X_{\Delta_{n,T}}, X_{2\Delta_{n,T}}, X_{3\Delta_{n,T}}, \ldots, X_{n\Delta_{n,T}}\right\} \tag{2.6}$$

will be n observations at

$$\left\{t_1 = \Delta_{n,T}, t_2 = 2\Delta_{n,T}, t_3 = 3\Delta_{n,T}, \ldots, t_n = n\Delta_{n,T}\right\}, \tag{2.7}$$

where $\Delta_{n,T} = T/n$. In the limit, we will let $n \to \infty$, $T \to \infty$, and $\Delta_{n,T} = T/n \to 0$. In a few instances, T will be fixed at $\overline{T}$. In the sequel, we will be explicit about the limiting behavior of the time span T.

Based on our discussion, it appears that the only requirements that we have to impose on the dynamic properties of the processes of interest for identification are those that guarantee divergence of the number of visits in the spatial vicinity of points in the range of the process. This is a typical feature of recurrent processes. Specifically, the sample path of a recurrent process returns to sets of nonzero Lebesgue measure an infinite number of times over time with probability one. We now rigorously state the definitions of recurrence used in this review (the interested reader is referred to the classical treatment in Meyn and Tweedie, 1993, for additional discussions).

Definition 1 (Null and Positive Harris Recurrence): *Let A be a measurable set of the range $\mathfrak{D}$ of the process of interest. Define the first hitting time of A as $\tau_A = \inf\{t \geq 0 : X_t \in A\}$.*

The process X_t is called null Harris recurrent if there is a $\sigma-$finite measure $m^*(\mathrm{d}x)$ such that $m^*(A) > 0$ implies $P^a[\tau_A < \infty] = 1$ for every $a \in \mathfrak{D}/\overline{A}$, where $\overline{A}$ is the closure of the set A.

It is called positive Harris recurrent (ergodic) if there is a $\sigma-$finite measure $m^*(\mathrm{d}x)$ such that $m^*(A) > 0$ implies $\mathbf{E}^a[\tau_A] < \infty$ for every $a \in \mathfrak{D}/\overline{A}$.

Define the occupation time measure of the set A of positive Lebesgue measure as

$$\eta_A^T = \int_0^T \mathbf{1}_{\{X_s \in A\}} \mathrm{d}s. \tag{2.8}$$

The quantity η_A^T gives the amount of time spent by the process at A between 0 and T. Under both notions of recurrence, we obtain $\mathbf{P}^a[\lim_{T\to\infty} \eta_A^T = \infty] = 1$ for $\forall a \in \mathfrak{D}/\overline{A}$. Specifically, starting from a level a not belonging to the generic set A, the process X_t visits A an infinite number of times as $T \to \infty$, almost surely. This property is of course crucial for (pointwise) identification.

Null and positive recurrence are milder assumptions than stationarity. Stationary processes are recurrent, but recurrent processes do not have to be stationary. In particular, recurrent processes do not have to be endowed with a stationary probability measure. Null recurrent processes, in fact, do not possess a time-invariant probability measure. Nonetheless, null Harris recurrence implies the existence of a unique invariant measure $m(\mathrm{d}x)$ ($= m^*(\mathrm{d}x)$ in the Definition). Assume $X^{(x)}$ is the unique strong solution of the process with initial condition $X_0^{(x)} = x \in \mathfrak{D}$. The invariant measure is such that

$$m(A) = \int_{\mathfrak{D}} P\left(X_t^{(x)} \in A\right) m(\mathrm{d}x) \quad \forall A \subset \mathfrak{B}(\mathfrak{D}), \tag{2.9}$$

for every $0 \leq t < \infty$ (see, e.g., Azéma et al., 1967; Karatzas and Shreve, 1991, Exercise 6.18, p. 362).[6] If the invariant measure is finite on $\mathfrak{D}$ (i.e., $m(\mathfrak{D}) < \infty$), then the process is positive recurrent (ergodic) and has a time-invariant stationary probability measure (distribution) to which it converges, at least in the limit. Such measure is given by $f(\mathrm{d}x) = \frac{m(\mathrm{d}x)}{m(\mathfrak{D})}$. A positive-recurrent process that is started in its stationary distribution remains in the stationary distribution and, as a consequence, is strictly stationary. Examples will be provided in the sequel. For now it suffices to say that Brownian motion in one (cf., Example 1 in Section 3) and two dimensions are classical examples of null recurrent processes. Classical Vasicek (Ornstein–Uhlenbeck) and CIR processes (cf., Cox et al.,

[6] Alternatively, one could write

$$m = P_t m \qquad \forall t \geq 0,$$

where $(P_t)_{t\geq 0}$ is the semigroup of the process X_t (cf., Aït-Sahalia et al., 2010, in this volume; Ethier and Kurtz, 1986).

1985; Vasicek, 1977) are strictly stationary or positive recurrent depending on whether they are initiated at their stationary measures or not (cf., Example 5 in Section 3).

To conclude, the estimators reviewed in this chapter are nonparametric or semiparametric in nature and either follow the general form of (2.5) above or are constructed based on it. Null recurrence is all that we require to guarantee consistency of the estimates for the infinitesimal moments of interest. Importantly, positive recurrence and stationarity, which are clearly more stringent assumptions than null recurrence, will be shown to only yield an increase in the rates of convergence of the estimators to the corresponding moments.

We now turn to a detailed analysis of the specific processes mentioned in the introduction, namely scalar diffusion processes (SDPs), scalar jump-diffusion processes (SJDPs), and multivariate diffusion processes (MDPs). A separate section will be devoted to each of these. In what follows we will not review the definitions of recurrence that were laid out earlier but simply list conditions under which the processes display either ergodic or null recurrent behavior.

The following, rather standard, Assumption (1) will be imposed on the kernel function $\mathbf{K}(.)$ throughout the present chapter.

(1) *The kernel* $\mathbf{K}(.)$ *is a continuously differentiable, symmetric, and nonnegative function on the real line so that*

$$\int \mathbf{K}(s)ds = 1, \quad \mathbf{K}_1 = \int s^2\mathbf{K}(s)ds < \infty \tag{2.10}$$

and

$$\mathbf{K}_2 = \int \mathbf{K}^2(s)ds < \infty, \int |\mathbf{K}'(s)|ds < \infty. \tag{2.11}$$

3. SCALAR DIFFUSION PROCESSES

In this section, we model a generic time series as the solution X_t to the stochastic differential equation

$$dX_t = \mu(X_t)dt + \sigma(X_t)dB_t, \tag{3.1}$$

where B_t is a standard Brownian motion defined on the filtered probability space $(\Omega, \Im^B, (\Im_t^B)_{t\geq 0}, P)$. The initial condition $X_0 = \overline{X}$ belongs to L^2 and is taken to be independent of $\{B_t : t \geq 0\}$. Define the left-continuous filtration

$$\overline{\Im}_t := \sigma(\overline{X}) \vee \Im_t^B = \sigma(\overline{X}, B_s; 0 \leq s \leq t) \qquad 0 \leq t < \infty, \tag{3.2}$$

and the collection of null sets

$$\aleph := \{N \subseteq \Omega; \exists G \in \overline{\Im}_\infty \text{ with } N \subseteq G \text{ and } P(G) = 0\}. \tag{3.3}$$

Create the augmented filtration

$$\widetilde{\mathfrak{I}}_t^X := \sigma(\overline{\mathfrak{I}}_t \cup \aleph) \qquad 0 \le t < \infty, \tag{3.4}$$

and impose Assumptions 2 through 4 (5) below, to assure the existence and pathwise uniqueness of a null recurrent (positive recurrent) and $\{\widetilde{\mathfrak{I}}_t^X\}$-adapted solution to (3.1).

(2) *$\mu(.)$ and $\sigma(.)$ are time-homogeneous, $\mathfrak{B}$-measurable functions on $\mathfrak{D} = (l, u)$ with $-\infty \le l < u \le \infty$ where $\mathfrak{B}$ is the σ-field generated by Borel sets on $\mathfrak{D}$. Both functions satisfy local Lipschitz and growth conditions. Thus, for every compact subset J of the range of the process, there exist constants C_1 and C_2 such that, for all x and y in J,*

$$|\mu(x) - \mu(y)| + |\sigma(x) - \sigma(y)| \le C_1|x - y|, \tag{3.5}$$

and

$$|\mu(x)| + |\sigma(x)| \le C_2\{1 + |x|\}. \tag{3.6}$$

(3) *$\sigma^2(.) > 0$ on $\mathfrak{D}$.*

(4) *(Null recurrence) Define the second-order elliptic operator*[7]

$$\mathfrak{L}\varphi(.) = \varphi'(.)\mu(.) + \frac{1}{2}\varphi''(.)\sigma^2(.). \tag{3.7}$$

There is a function $\varphi(.) : \mathfrak{R}\backslash\{0\} \to \mathfrak{R}$ of class C^2 in the domain of the operator that satisfies

$$\mathfrak{L}\varphi(.) \le 0 \qquad \text{on} \qquad \mathfrak{R}\backslash\{0\} \tag{3.8}$$

and is such that $\Psi(r) := \min_{|x|=r} \varphi(.)$ is strictly increasing with $\lim_{r\to\infty} \Psi(r) = \infty$ (cf., Karatzas and Shreve, 1991, Exercise 7.13, part (i), p. 370).

(5) *(Positive recurrence) There is a function $\varphi(.) : \mathfrak{R}\backslash\{0\} \to \mathfrak{R}$ of class C^2 in the domain of the operator that satisfies*

$$\mathfrak{L}\varphi(.) \le -1 \qquad \text{on} \qquad \mathfrak{R}\backslash\{0\} \tag{3.9}$$

and is such that $\Psi(r) := \min_{|x|=r} \varphi(.)$ is strictly increasing with $\lim_{r\to\infty} \Psi(r) = \infty$ (cf., Karatzas and Shreve, 1991, Exercise 7.13, part (iii), p. 371).

Under Assumptions 2 through 4 (5), the stochastic differential equation (3.1) yields a strong solution X_t which is unique, null recurrent (positive recurrent), and continuous in $t \in [0, T]$. In particular, the process X_t satisfies

$$X_t = \overline{X} + \int_0^t \mu(X_s)\mathrm{d}s + \int_0^t \sigma(X_s)\mathrm{d}B_s \tag{3.10}$$

[7] The operator $\mathfrak{L}$ is generally called the infinitesimal generator of the SDP X_t. We refer the interested reader to Aït-Sahalia et al. (2010), in the present volume, and Hansen and Scheinkman (1995) for a discussion of estimation methods for strictly stationary diffusions based on the properties of the infinitesimal generator.

almost surely, with $\int_0^t \mathbf{E}\left(X_s^2\right) ds < \infty$, and is a semimartingale. The dynamics of X_t are determined by the functions $\mu(.)$ and $\sigma(.)$. These functions are the object of econometric interest.

Assumptions 4 and 5 are vital in determining recurrent behavior for X_t. As pointed out earlier, null recurrence is a sufficient condition for the existence of σ-finite invariant measure $m(\mathrm{d}x)$. Such a measure is unique up to multiplication by a constant and, in the case of SDPs, is known to be equal (up to a proportionality factor) to the so-called *speed measure*, i.e.,

$$m(\mathrm{d}x) = \frac{2\mathrm{d}x}{S'(x)\sigma^2(x)} \qquad \forall x \in \mathfrak{D} \subseteq \mathfrak{R}, \tag{3.11}$$

where $S'(x)$ is the first derivative of the *scale function*, namely

$$S(x) = \int_c^x \exp\left\{\int_c^y \left[-\frac{2\mu(s)}{\sigma^2(s)}\right] \mathrm{d}s\right\} \mathrm{d}y, \tag{3.12}$$

where $c \in \mathfrak{D}$. Under Assumption 5, the SDP is positive recurrent (i.e., $m(\mathfrak{D}) < \infty$) and admits a time-invariant probability measure. In particular, the normalized speed measure, i.e., $m(\mathrm{d}x)/m(\mathfrak{D})$, is the limiting stationary probability measure of X_t implying

$$\lim_{t\to\infty} P^x(X_t < z) = \frac{m((l, z))}{m(\mathfrak{D})} \qquad \forall x, z \in \mathfrak{D} \subseteq \mathfrak{R}, \tag{3.13}$$

(see, e.g., Karatzas and Shreve, 1991; Pollack and Siegmund, 1985, Exercise 5.40, p. 353). More explicitly, we can write the stationary probability density of the process as

$$\begin{aligned} f(x) &= \frac{m(x)}{m(\mathfrak{D})} = \frac{1}{m(\mathfrak{D})} \frac{\exp\left\{\int_c^x \left[\frac{2\mu(s)}{\sigma^2(s)}\right] \mathrm{d}s\right\}}{\sigma^2(x)} \\ &= \left(\int_{\mathfrak{D}} \frac{\exp\left\{\int_c^x \left[\frac{2\mu(s)}{\sigma^2(s)}\right] \mathrm{d}s\right\}}{\sigma^2(x)} \mathrm{d}x\right)^{-1} \frac{\exp\left\{\int_c^x \left[\frac{2\mu(s)}{\sigma^2(s)}\right] \mathrm{d}s\right\}}{\sigma^2(x)}. \end{aligned} \tag{3.14}$$

We now provide some examples.

Example 1 (Natural scale diffusions): *For general scalar diffusions, if the scale function $S(x)$ is such that $\lim_{x\to l+} S(x) = -\infty$ and $\lim_{x\to u-} S(x) = \infty$, then the process is recurrent, that is it satisfies $\mathfrak{L}\varphi(.) \leq 0$, where φ is defined in (4) above (cf., Khasminskii, 1980). Apparently, the solution to $\mathrm{d}X_t = \sigma(X_t)\mathrm{d}B_t$, with $\sigma(.)$ continuous and strictly positive, is Harris recurrent over $\mathfrak{R}$ with scale function $S(x) = x - c$ and invariant measure $m(\mathrm{d}x) = \frac{2\mathrm{d}x}{\sigma^2(x)}$. Chen et al. (1999), e.g., discuss the mixing properties of the natural scale diffusion with $\sigma^2(x) = (1 + x^2)^\gamma$ for $\frac{1}{2} < \gamma < 1$ (see also Aït-Sahalia et al., 2010, in this volume). If $0 \leq \gamma \leq \frac{1}{2}$, the process is* *null recurrent on $\Re$. For values of γ strictly larger than $\frac{1}{2}$, the process is positive recurrent. This is a case of "volatility-induced" reversion to the mean (Conley et al., 1997). Trivially, standard Brownian motion (i.e., $\gamma = 0$) is null recurrent.*

Example 2 (Brownian motion with drift): *Assume X_t is the solution to $\mathrm{d}X_t = \mu \mathrm{d}t + \sigma \mathrm{d}B_t$ with $\sigma > 0$. The scale function and the speed measure are $S(x) = \frac{1-e^{-\alpha(x-c)}}{\alpha}$ and $m(\mathrm{d}x) = \frac{2e^{\alpha x}}{\sigma^2}\mathrm{d}x$, where $\alpha = \frac{2\mu}{\sigma^2}$, respectively. If $\mu > 0$, then $\lim_{x\to\infty} S(x) = \frac{1-e^{\alpha c}}{2\alpha}$ and $\lim_{x\to-\infty} S(x) = -\infty$. The process is not recurrent and $P[\inf_{0\le t<\infty} X_t > -\infty] = 1$. If $\mu < 0$, then $\lim_{x\to\infty} S(x) = \infty$ and $\lim_{x\to-\infty} S(x) = \frac{1-e^{\alpha c}}{2\alpha}$. The process is not recurrent and $P[\sup_{0\le t<\infty} X_t < \infty] = 1$. In the former case, X_t has an attracting boundary at ∞(i.e., $P[\lim_{t\to\infty} X_t = \infty] = 1$). In the latter case, X_t has an attracting boundary at $-\infty$(i.e., $P[\lim_{t\to\infty} X_t = -\infty] = 1$). In both cases, it is easy to show that the boundary is unattainable, i.e., it cannot be reached in finite time with positive probability (cf., Karatzas and Shreve, 1991; Karlin and Taylor, 1981).*

Example 3 (Geometric Brownian motion): *Assume X_t is the solution to $\mathrm{d}X_t = \mu X_t \mathrm{d}t + \sigma X_t \mathrm{d}B_t$, with $\mu, \sigma > 0$ and $\overline{X} > 0$. Then, $S(x) = c^{\alpha}\left[\frac{x^{-\alpha+1}}{-\alpha+1} - \frac{c^{-\alpha+1}}{-\alpha+1}\right]$, where $\alpha = \frac{2\mu}{\sigma^2}$ provided $\alpha < 1$ or $\alpha > 1$. The process is not recurrent for these choices of α. Specifically, if $\alpha < 1$, then $\lim_{x\to 0} S(x) = \frac{-c}{-\alpha+1}$ and $\lim_{x\to\infty} S(x) = \infty$ implying $P[\sup_{0\le t<\infty} X_t < \infty] = 1 = P[\lim_{t\to\infty} X_t = 0]$. If $\alpha > 1$, then $\lim_{x\to\infty} S(x) = \frac{-c}{-\alpha+1}$ and $\lim_{x\to 0} S(x) = -\infty$ implying $P[\inf_{0\le t<\infty} X_t > 0] = 1 = P[\lim_{t\to\infty} X_t = \infty]$. If $\alpha = 1$, then $S(x) = c[\log x - c]$ which implies $\lim_{x\to 0} S(x) = -\infty$ and $\lim_{x\to\infty} S(x) = \infty$, giving recurrence. In addition $m(\mathrm{d}x) = \frac{2\mathrm{d}x}{c\sigma^2 x}$ and is not integrable. Therefore, geometric Brownian motion is null recurrent when $2\mu = \sigma^2$.*

Of course, the same implications could have been derived by noticing that monotone transformations, such as exponentiation, preserve recurrence. By Ito's lemma, $\mathrm{d}\log(X_t) = \theta \mathrm{d}t + \sigma \mathrm{d}B_t$, where $\theta = \mu - \frac{1}{2}\sigma^2$, thereby yielding Example 2, again, for the log transformation. Using Example 2, one could readily obtain that $\log(X_t)$ (X_t) is not recurrent and has an unattainable, attracting boundary at $\infty(\infty)$ if $\theta > 0$ (or if $2\mu > \sigma^2$). Similarly, $\log(X_t)$ (X_t) is not recurrent and has an unattainable, attracting boundary at $-\infty$ (0) if $\theta < 0$ (or if $2\mu < \sigma^2$). If $\theta = 0$ (or if $2\mu = \sigma^2$), $\log(X_t)$ and X_t are null recurrent.

Example 4 (Bessel process): *Assume $\mathrm{d}X_t = \frac{\mathrm{d}-1}{2X_s}dt + \mathrm{d}B_t$ with $d \ge 2$ and $\overline{X} > 0$. If $d > 2$, we obtain $S(x) = c^{d-1}\left[\frac{c^{2-d}-x^{2-d}}{d-2}\right]$ giving $\lim_{x\to\infty} S(x) = \frac{c}{d-2}$ and $\lim_{x\to 0} S(x) = -\infty$. In consequence, the process is not recurrent and $P[\lim_{t\to\infty} X_t = \infty] = 1$. If $d = 2$, then $S(x) = c[\log x - \log c]$ implying recurrence. Furthermore, the speed measure (i.e., $m(\mathrm{d}x) = \frac{2x\mathrm{d}x}{c}$) is not integrable between 0 and ∞ giving null recurrence.*

Example 5 (Affine models): *Assume both the drift and the infinitesimal variance are linear functions of the state (i.e., $\mu(x) = c_0 + c_1 x$ and $\sigma^2(x) = c_2 + c_3 x$ with $c_2, c_3 \ge 0$). The* *well-known Vasicek (Ornestein-Uhlenbeck) and CIR processes belong to this general class and are obtained by setting c_3 and c_2 equal to zero, respectively (cf., Cox et al., 1985; Vasicek, 1977). Under standard assumptions on the parameters (see Piazzesi, 2010, in this volume, for a discussion of scalar and multivariate affine models and related estimation procedures), affine diffusions are strongly ergodic (positive recurrent). Should c_0 and c_1 be equal to zero and $\sigma^2(x) = c_2 + c_3|x|$ with $c_2 > 0$ and $c_3 \geq 0$, then the invariant measure would not be integrable over $\Re$ and the resulting process would be null recurrent (cf., Example 1).*

Before describing the estimation strategy, we wish to discuss descriptive tools that have been recently introduced to characterize recurrent SDPs. These tools rely on the notion of local time (Protter, 1995, and Revuz and Yor, 1998, are classical references). Local time is a random quantity which measures the amount of time that the process spends in the vicinity of a point. As a consequence, it might be interpreted as a spatial density and might be used to analyze the locational features of a possibly nonstationary process (for which it is defined, of course) in just the same way as a stationary probability density may be used to study stationary processes (Phillips, 2001, 2004). The next subsection defines local time and introduces a simple estimation strategy to identify it based on a discrete sample of observations. We will also discuss the role that estimated local time can play as a descriptive statistic for recurrent SDPs and its importance in designing robust (to deviations from stationarity) identification procedures for processes whose dynamics are driven by (3.1) (Bandi, 2002). The terms "local time," "spatial density," and "sojourn time" will be used interchangeably in what follows.

3.1. Generalized Density Estimation for SDPs

The local time of a continuous semimartingale is defined as the random quantity $L_X(t, a)$ satisfying

$$L_X(t,a) = \lim_{\varepsilon \to 0} \frac{1}{\varepsilon} \int_0^t \mathbf{1}_{[a,\, a+\varepsilon[}(X_s) d[X]_s \ \forall a, t, \tag{3.15}$$

where $[X]_t$ is the quadratic variation process of the underlying continuous semimartingale at t. Formula (3.15) clarifies the sense in which $L_X(t, a)$ measures time in information units or, more rigorously, in units of the quadratic variation process. Interestingly, one could write

$$[X]_t = \int_{-\infty}^{\infty} L_X(t,a) da, \tag{3.16}$$

thus expressing the quadratic variation process in terms of contributions coming from fluctuations in the process that occur in the vicinity of different spatial points $a \in (-\infty, \infty)$. Equation (3.16) is a spatial decomposition of variation. Readers familiar with stationary time series analysis will recognize the similarity of (3.16) to the decomposition of the variance σ_X^2 of a process X in terms of its spectral density at different frequencies, i.e.,

$$\sigma_X^2 = \int_{-\pi}^{\pi} f_{xx}(w)\mathrm{d}w, \tag{3.17}$$

where $f_{xx}(w)$ is the spectral density of X.

We can specialize the analysis to the case of SDPs and consider a rescaled version of the standard notion of sojourn time defined as

$$\overline{L}_X(t,a) = \frac{L_X(t,a)}{\sigma^2(a)}. \tag{3.18}$$

Because, for an SDP as in (3.10), $\mathrm{d}[X]_s = \sigma^2(X_s)\mathrm{d}s$, then formula (3.18) can be interpreted as representing time in real-time units rather than in units of the nondecreasing quadratic variation process. In other words, $\overline{L}_X(t,a)$ records the amount of calendar time spent by the process in the neighborhood of a and can be defined as "chronological local time" (Bosq, 1998; Phillips and Park, 1998). Such a notion has an interesting interpretation. Consider the occupation measure that was introduced in Section 2. As pointed out earlier, the quantity η_A^T represents the amount of time spent by the process in a certain spatial set of nonzero Lebesgue measure. Chronological local time is nothing but the density of the occupation measure of the process. Put differently, chronological local time is a version of the Radon–Nikodym derivative of the occupation measure with respect to the Lebesgue measure and is an occupation density (Geman and Horowitz, 1980). In fact, we can write

$$\eta_A^T = \int_0^T \mathbf{1}_{\{X_s \in A\}}\mathrm{d}s = \int_A \overline{L}_X(T,a)\mathrm{d}a, \qquad \forall A \subset \mathfrak{B}(\mathfrak{D}), \tag{3.19}$$

and, by linearity and monotone convergence,

$$\int_0^T \Phi(X_s)\mathrm{d}s = \int \Phi(a)\overline{L}_X(T,a)\mathrm{d}a, \tag{3.20}$$

where Φ is a Borel measurable, nonnegative function (Bosq, 1998, *inter alia*). Equation (3.20) is typically called the "occupation time formula" and may be regarded as the analog of a more classical expectation (i.e., the integral with respect to a time-invariant probability measure) in the analysis of times series which are not necessarily endowed with a time-invariant probability measure.

From an applied standpoint, the notion of chronological local time is relevant for at least three mutually reinforcing reasons. First, chronological local time has an appealing interpretation in terms of calendar time spent by the process in the vicinity of values in its range. Second, chronological local time arises naturally as the limiting process to which density-like kernel estimators converge, provided the underlying process is a scalar semimartingale and suitable conditions on the relevant bandwidth are met. Third, as shown in the next subsection, this is the notion of local time which will play a crucial role in understanding the limiting distributions of kernel estimates of the infinitesimal moments $\mu(.)$ and $\sigma^2(.)$. In what follows, we will use the convention of referring to it simply as "local time."

The first two reasons together suggest the usefulness of local time as a new method for the descriptive analysis of data that might not be stationary so that the techniques may be used in situations where estimated probability density functions do not make theoretical sense. Consistent with this logic, recent work has proposed nonparametric estimates of the local time process and has interpreted them in terms of generalized densities to be used as new descriptive tools for studying the spatial characteristics of time series which might be nonstationary. The original intuition is due to Phillips (2001, 2004) in the context of nonstationary discrete-time series embeddable in Brownian motion (namely discrete time series of the unit-root type). In continuous-time finance models, local time was first used as a descriptive tool for possibly nonstationary (recurrent) SDPs of the form analyzed here by Bandi (2002).

As pointed out earlier, a natural way to identify local time is to use density-like kernel estimators. Based on the same sampling scheme as in Section 2 with $T = \overline{T}$, we define an estimate of $\overline{L}_X(\overline{T}, a)$ as

$$\widehat{\overline{L}}_X(\overline{T}, a) = \frac{\Delta_{n,\overline{T}}}{h_{n,\overline{T}}} \sum_{i=1}^{n} \mathbf{K}\left(\frac{X_{i\Delta_{n,\overline{T}}} - a}{h_{n,\overline{T}}}\right), \tag{3.21}$$

where $h_{n,\overline{T}}$ is bandwidth sequence depending on n and $\mathbf{K}(.)$ is a conventional kernel function satisfying the assumptions in Section 2. Theorems 1 and 2 below show consistency of the local time estimator for its theoretical counterpart and provide a limiting distribution.

Theorem 1 *Assume X_t is the solution to (3.1). If $h_{n,\overline{T}} \to 0$ as $n \to \infty$ for a fixed time span T $(= \overline{T})$ in such a way that $\frac{1}{h_{n,\overline{T}}}(\Delta_{n,\overline{T}} \log(1/\Delta_{n,\overline{T}}))^{1/2} = o(1)$, then*

$$\widehat{\overline{L}}_X(\overline{T}, a) \overset{a.s.}{\to} \overline{L}_X(\overline{T}, a) \qquad \forall a \in \mathfrak{D}. \tag{3.22}$$

Proof See Florens-Zmirou (1993). For a proof that allows for more general kernel functions than the indicator kernel used in Florens-Zmirou (1993) and uses different statistical tools, such as the occupation time formula in (3.20), see Bandi and Phillips (2003). Park (2006) studies uniform L^1-consistency.

We now turn to the asymptotic distribution. Here, and in what follows, the notation **MN** denotes the mixed Gaussian density.

Theorem 2 *Assume X_t is the solution to (3.1). If $h_{n,\overline{T}} \to 0$ as $n \to \infty$ for a fixed time span T $(= \overline{T})$ in such a way that $\frac{1}{h_{n,\overline{T}}^{3/2}}(\Delta_{n,\overline{T}} \log(1/\Delta_{n,\overline{T}}))^{1/2} = o(1)$, then*

$$\frac{1}{\sqrt{h_{n,\overline{T}}}}\left(\widehat{\overline{L}}_X(\overline{T},a) - \overline{L}_X(\overline{T},a)\right) \Rightarrow \mathbf{MN}\left(0, 8\mathbf{k}\frac{1}{\sigma^2(a)}\overline{L}_X(\overline{T},a)\right) \quad \forall a \in \mathfrak{D}, \tag{3.23}$$

where $\mathbf{k} = \int_0^\infty \int_0^\infty \min(s,q)\mathbf{K}(s)\mathbf{K}(q)dsdq$.

Proof See Bandi (2002) for a proof in the case of an underlying SDP that is assumed to be the unique and strong solution to a stochastic differential equation like (3.1), in agreement with the statement of the theorem. See Phillips (2001, 2004) for a proof in the case of the estimated local time of linear, nonstationary, discrete-time series embeddable in Brownian motion.

Theorem 1 justifies estimating the calendar time that an SDP spends in the local vicinity of a point by using a density-like kernel estimator. Theorem 2 enables us to construct asymptotic confidence intervals that closely resemble conventional intervals for probability densities obtained from kernel estimates (Bandi, 2002; Phillips, 2004). The (estimated) asymptotic 95% confidence interval of $\overline{L}_X(\overline{T},a)$ is, in fact, given by

$$\widehat{\overline{L}}_X(\overline{T},a) \pm 1.96\left(8\mathbf{k}\frac{h_{n,\overline{T}}}{\widehat{\sigma}^2(a)}\widehat{\overline{L}}_X(\overline{T},a)\right)^{1/2}. \tag{3.24}$$

It is worth recalling here that the limiting process $\overline{L}_X(\overline{T},a)$ is random. As opposed to standard probability densities, spatial densities have a time dimension that can be fruitfully explored by changing the span of data used in the implementation of (3.21). In other words, $\widehat{\overline{L}}_X(\overline{T}_1,a)$ and $\widehat{\overline{L}}_X(\overline{T}_2,a)$ measure the time spent by the SDP of interest at a in the time intervals $[0,\overline{T}_1]$ and $[0,\overline{T}_2]$, respectively, and can be used as robust (to deviations from stationarity) descriptive statistics to summarize the spatial evolution of the SDP over time.

Some additional observations are in order. Given the interpretation of local time, the following result should come as no surprise.

Theorem 3 *Assume X_t the solution to (3.1) and $m(\mathfrak{D}) < \infty$ (as implied by Assumption 5). If $h_{n,T} \to 0$ as $n, T \to \infty$ in such a way that $\frac{1}{h_{n,T}}(\Delta_{n,T} \log(1/\Delta_{n,T}))^{1/2} = o(1)$, then*

$$\frac{\widehat{\overline{L}}_X(T,a)}{T} \xrightarrow{a.s.} f(a) = \frac{m(a)}{m(\mathfrak{D})} \quad \forall a \in \mathfrak{D}. \tag{3.25}$$

Proof See Bandi and Phillips (2003) and Moloche (2004a). The interested reader is also referred to Moloche (2004a) for a discussion of the limiting properties of the expected local time process. An asymptotic theory for estimates of the expected local time is given in Park (2006).

This result simply tells us that the standardized local time estimator of a strictly stationary (or positive recurrent) SDP converges pointwise to the stationary density of the process with probability one. Loosely speaking, if we divide the estimated time spent by the process at a between 0 and T by T, by appealing to the conventional frequentist notion of probability, we expect the ratio to converge to the probability mass at a when letting T diverge to infinity. Equivalently, we can say that the local time of a stationary, or positive recurrent, process diverges to infinity linearly with T (see also Bosq, 1997; Bosq and Davydov, 1998). Naturally, we expect nonstationary, but recurrent, processes to have local times which diverge at speeds that are slower than T. Such speeds are generally not quantifiable. Nonetheless, Brownian motion is known to have a local time that diverges at speed $\sqrt{T}$. The following result can be easily proved for a standard Brownian motion (see Bandi and Phillips, 2003, and, for a more general method of proof, Moloche, 2004a):

$$\frac{\widehat{L}_B(T,a)}{\sqrt{T}} = \frac{\sqrt{T}L_B\left(1, \frac{a}{\sqrt{T}}\right)}{\sqrt{T}} + o_{a.s.}(1) \overset{a.s.}{\to} L_B(1,0). \tag{3.26}$$

We will come back to a discussion of the divergence rates of local time when describing the estimation procedures for drift and diffusion function. For the time being, it suffices to stress that the class of SDPs that we are studying, namely the class of recurrent SDPs, has local times that diverge to infinity with probability one when the time span does so. The reason is easy to explain. Local time measures the time spent by the process at a point between 0 and T, say. Scalar recurrent processes visit every point an infinite number of times as T goes to infinity with probability one. Necessarily, therefore, the local time of a recurrent process diverges to infinity almost surely as T diverges to infinity.

We complete this subsection by pointing out that functions of spatial densities can be used as descriptive tools for possibly nonstationary SDPs just like functions of probability densities are used as descriptive statistics in the context of stationary time series (Phillips, 2001, 2004). For example, Phillips (2004) defines a new kind of hazard function for discrete-time nonstationary time series as

$$\overline{H}_X(T,a) = \frac{\overline{L}_X(T,a)}{\int_a^\infty \overline{L}_X(T,s)ds}, \tag{3.27}$$

where, as usual, $\overline{L}_X(T,a)$ is the standard sojourn time. Such a function can be interpreted as the spatial counterpart of conventional hazard functions (see, e.g., Prakasa-Rao, 1983; Silverman, 1986), where probability densities replace local times, and might be used to quantify hazards of certain financial time series such as inflation rates or interest rates. When applied to interest rates (as done in Bandi, 2002), for instance, formula (3.27) gives the conditional risk over the period $[0, T]$ of an interest rate level of a, given that interest rates are at least as large as a. An asymptotic theory for kernel estimates of spatial hazard rates is available to assist statistical inference.

Theorem 4 *Assume X_t is the solution to (3.1). If $h_{n,\overline{T}} \to 0$ as $n \to \infty$ for a fixed time span T $(= \overline{T})$ in such a way that $\frac{1}{h_{n,\overline{T}}}(\Delta_{n,\overline{T}} \log(1/\Delta_{n,T}))^{1/2} = o(1)$, then*

$$\widehat{H}_X(\overline{T}, a) = \frac{\widehat{\overline{L}}_X(\overline{T}, a)}{\int_a^{\infty} \widehat{\overline{L}}_X(\overline{T}, s) ds} \xrightarrow{a.s.} \overline{H}_X(\overline{T}, a) \quad \forall a \in \mathfrak{D}. \tag{3.28}$$

Furthermore, if $h_{n,\overline{T}} \to 0$ as $n \to \infty$ for a fixed time span T $(= \overline{T})$ and

$$\frac{1}{h^{3/2}_{n,\overline{T}}}(\Delta_{n,\overline{T}} \log(1/\Delta_{n,T}))^{1/2} = o(1), \tag{3.29}$$

then

$$\frac{1}{\sqrt{h_{n,\overline{T}}}}\left(\widehat{\overline{H}}_X(\overline{T}, a) - \overline{H}_X(\overline{T}, a)\right) \Rightarrow \mathbf{MN}\left(0, \frac{8\mathbf{k}(\overline{H}_X(\overline{T}, a))^2}{\sigma^2(a)\overline{L}_X(\overline{T}, a)}\right) \quad \forall a \in \mathfrak{D}, \tag{3.30}$$

where $\mathbf{k} = \int_0^\infty \int_0^\infty \min(s, q)\mathbf{K}(s)\mathbf{K}(q) ds dq$.

Proof See Bandi (2002) for a proof in the case of an underlying SDP that is assumed to be the unique and strong solution to a stochastic differential equation like (3.1), consistent with the statement of the theorem. See Phillips (2001, 2004) for a proof in the case of the estimated local time of linear, nonstationary, discrete-time series embeddable in Brownian motion.

For an introduction to descriptive methods for nonstationary discrete-time series using local time and related notions, the reader is referred to Phillips (2001, 2004). Estimated spatial densities and spatial hazard rates have been used by Bandi (2002) in studying the temporal dynamics of a nonparametric continuous-time specification [as in (3.1) above] for the short-term interest rate process. We refer the interested reader to that paper for a discussion about empirical implementation of the methodology in the case of SDPs. Park (2006) provides an estimation theory for functionals of spatial densities and spatial distributions while introducing novel (spatial) notions of value-at-risk and stochastic dominance, among other concepts. We now turn to the estimation of the infinitesimal conditional moments $\mu(.)$ and $\sigma^2(.)$.

3.2. NW Kernel Estimation of the Infinitesimal Moments of an SDP

It is well known that the transition density of the unique solution to (3.1) is completely characterized by the functions $\mu(.)$ and $\sigma^2(.)$. In other words, understanding the temporal evolution of a general SDP amounts to identifying the drift and the diffusion function. As discussed in Section 2, such functions have (infinitesimal) conditional moment definitions, i.e.,

$$\mathbf{E}^a[X_t - a] = t\mu(a) + o(t) \tag{3.31}$$

$$\mathbf{E}^a[(X_t - a)^2] = t\sigma^2(a) + o(t), \tag{3.32}$$

as $t \downarrow 0$, or

$$\mu(a) = \lim_{t \to 0} \frac{1}{t} \mathbf{E}^a[X_t - a], \tag{3.33}$$

$$\sigma^2(a) = \lim_{t \to 0} \frac{1}{t} \mathbf{E}^a\left[(X_t - a)^2\right], \tag{3.34}$$

where a is a generic initial condition and $\mathbf{E}^a$ is, as earlier in the introduction, the expectation operator associated with the process started at a. Loosely speaking, (3.31) and (3.32) can be interpreted as representing the "instantaneous" conditional mean and the "instantaneous" conditional variance of the process when $X_0 = a$.

Our previous, informal arguments, combined with the definitions of $\mu(.)$ and $\sigma^2(.)$ in (3.31) and (3.32) above, suggest that standard functional techniques for conditional expectations based on local averages may be natural tools to estimate the two functions driving the evolution of a general SDP. This is the intuition in Bandi and Phillips (2003) where sample analogs to infinitesimal conditional expectations are used to estimate *both* the drift and the diffusive volatility. Consider the same sampling scheme as in Section 2 (i.e., $n, T \to \infty$ with $\Delta_{n,T} = \frac{T}{n} \to 0$). Define

$$\widehat{\mu}_{(n,T)}(a) = \frac{1}{\Delta_{n,T}} \frac{\sum_{i=1}^{n-1} \mathbf{K}\left(\frac{X_{i\Delta_{n,T}} - a}{h_{n,T}}\right)\left(X_{(i+1)\Delta_{n,T}} - X_{i\Delta_{n,T}}\right)}{\sum_{i=1}^{n} \mathbf{K}\left(\frac{X_{i\Delta_{n,T}} - a}{h_{n,T}}\right)}, \tag{3.35}$$

$$\widehat{\sigma}^2_{(n,T)}(a) = \frac{1}{\Delta_{n,T}} \frac{\sum_{i=1}^{n-1} \mathbf{K}\left(\frac{X_{i\Delta_{n,T}} - a}{h_{n,T}}\right)\left(X_{(i+1)\Delta_{n,T}} - X_{i\Delta_{n,T}}\right)^2}{\sum_{i=1}^{n} \mathbf{K}\left(\frac{X_{i\Delta_{n,T}} - a}{h_{n,T}}\right)}, \tag{3.36}$$

where $\mathbf{K}(.)$ is a kernel function satisfying the assumptions in Section 2. Formulae (3.35) and (3.36) can be interpreted as the NW kernel estimates corresponding to (3.33) and (3.34) above, and they belong to the more general class of functional estimates suggested in Bandi and Phillips (2003). We now consider some aspects of the asymptotic theory in that paper. We begin with (3.35).

Theorem 5 *Assume X_t is the solution to (3.1). Also, assume $h_{n,T}$ is such that*

$$\frac{\overline{L}_X(T,a)}{h_{n,T}} (\Delta_{n,T} \log(1/\Delta_{n,T}))^{1/2} = o_{a.s.}(1) \tag{3.37}$$

and $h_{n,T}\overline{L}_X(T,a) \overset{a.s.}{\to} \infty$ *as* $n, T \to \infty$ *with* $\frac{T}{n} \to 0$. *Then,*

$$\widehat{\mu}_{(n,T)}(a) \overset{a.s.}{\to} \mu(a). \tag{3.38}$$

Furthermore, if $h^5_{n,T}\overline{L}_X(T,a) = O_{a.s.}(1)$, *then*

$$\sqrt{h_{n,T}\widehat{\overline{L}}_X(T,a)}\left\{\widehat{\mu}_{(n,T)}(a) - \mu(a) - \Gamma_\mu(a)\right\} \Rightarrow \mathbf{N}\left(0, \mathbf{K}_2\sigma^2(a)\right), \tag{3.39}$$

where

$$\Gamma_\mu(a) = h^2_{n,T}\mathbf{K}_1\left[\mu'(a)\frac{m'(a)}{m(a)} + \frac{1}{2}\mu''(a)\right], \tag{3.40}$$

and $m(a)$ *is the speed function of the process* X *at* a, *i.e.,* $m(a) = \frac{2}{S'(a)\sigma^2(a)}$.

Proof See Bandi and Phillips (2003).

We now turn to (3.36).

Theorem 6 *Assume* X_t *is the solution to (3.1). Also, assume* $h_{n,T}$ *is such that*

$$\frac{\overline{L}_X(T,a)}{h_{n,T}}(\Delta_{n,T}\log(1/\Delta_{n,T}))^{1/2} = o_{a.s.}(1) \tag{3.41}$$

as $n, T \to \infty$ *with* $\frac{T}{n} \to 0$. *Then,*

$$\widehat{\sigma}^2_{(n,T)}(a) \overset{a.s.}{\to} \sigma^2(a). \tag{3.42}$$

Furthermore, if $\frac{h^5_{n,T}\overline{L}_X(T,a)}{\Delta_{n,T}} = O_{a.s.}(1)$, *then*

$$\sqrt{\frac{h_{n,T}\widehat{\overline{L}}_X(T,a)}{\Delta_{n,T}}}\left\{\widehat{\sigma}^2_{(n,T)}(a) - \sigma^2(a) - \Gamma_{\sigma^2}(a)\right\} \Rightarrow \mathbf{N}\left(0, 2\mathbf{K}_2\sigma^4(a)\right),^{8} \tag{3.43}$$

where

$$\Gamma_{\sigma^2}(a) = h^2_{n,T}\mathbf{K}_1\left[\left(\sigma^2(a)\right)'\frac{m'(a)}{m(a)} + \frac{1}{2}\left(\sigma^2(a)\right)''\right], \tag{3.44}$$

and $m(a)$ *is the speed function of the process* X *at* a, *i.e.,* $m(a) = \frac{2}{S'(a)\sigma^2(a)}$.

Proof See Bandi and Phillips (2003).

[8] The proportionality factor reported in Bandi and Phillips (2003), i.e., 4 rather than 2, is of course a typo (see, e.g., the related findings in Bandi and Phillips, 2007; Bandi and Moloche, 2004).

Under appropriate conditions on the bandwidths, the estimators converge to the true functions with probability one. The asymptotic distributions are normal and centered at the relevant functions, provided the bandwidth sequences converge to zero sufficiently fast. If this is not the case, nonrandom bias terms affect the limiting distributions. The diffusion estimator converges to its theoretical counterpart at a faster rate $\left(\sqrt{\frac{h_{n,T}\widehat{\overline{L}}_X(T,a)}{\Delta_{n,T}}}\right)$ than the drift estimator $\left(\sqrt{h_{n,T}\widehat{\overline{L}}_X(T,a)}\right)$. We will now be more specific about the drift case, but similar arguments apply to the diffusion function. A discussion of the difference between the two cases will follow.

When dealing with the drift, local time plays the same role which is played by the number of observations in the more standard estimation of conditional moments in discrete time. What matters to identify the drift at a point a is not the rate of divergence of the number of data points n but the rate of divergence of the number of calendar time units spent by the process in the vicinity of the level a (cf., Section 2). Not surprisingly, therefore, the standard condition $nh_n \to \infty$ (or $Th_T \to \infty$) is replaced in our case by $h_{n,T}\overline{L}_X(T,a) \overset{a.s.}{\to} \infty$ as $n, T \to \infty$ with $\frac{T}{n} \to 0$. Equivalently, the pointwise condition that needs to be imposed on the bandwidth to prevent the insurgence of a bias term in the limit is $h^5_{n,T}\overline{L}_X(T,a) \overset{a.s.}{\to} 0$ as opposed to the more conventional condition $h^5_n n \to 0$ (or $h^5_T T \to 0$). In other words, the smoothing parameter has to converge to zero slowly enough as to guarantee that $h_{n,T}\overline{L}_X(T,a) \overset{a.s.}{\to} \infty$ (rather than $nh_n \to \infty$) but sufficiently fast as to satisfy $h^5_{n,T}\overline{L}_X(T,a) \overset{a.s.}{\to} 0$ (rather than $h^5_n n \to 0$).

Correspondingly, the rate of convergence of the estimator is random and equal to $\sqrt{h_{n,T}\widehat{\overline{L}}_X(T,a)}$ rather than $\sqrt{nh_n}$. Let us now consider the asymptotic variance and bias. These are given by

$$\frac{\left(\int_{-\infty}^{\infty}\mathbf{K}^2(s)\mathrm{d}s\right)\sigma^2(a)}{h_{n,T}\widehat{\overline{L}}_X(T,a)} \tag{3.45}$$

and

$$h^2_{n,T}\left(\int_{-\infty}^{\infty}s^2\mathbf{K}(s)\mathrm{d}s\right)\left[\mu'(a)\frac{m'(a)}{m(a)}+\frac{1}{2}\mu''(a)\right], \tag{3.46}$$

respectively. Their interpretation is clear when considering well-known findings about the asymptotic bias and variance of the standard NW estimator of conditional moments in discrete time (see, for instance, formula (3.60) and Theorem 5 in Pagan and Ullah, 1999). In particular, the spatial density estimate $\widehat{\overline{L}}_X(T,a)$ and the ratio between the derivative of the speed function and the speed function itself play the same role as that played by the term $Tf(a)$, where $f(a)$ is the stationary density at a, and the ratio between the derivative of the density function and the density function itself in conventional nonparametric time-series analysis under stationarity. The features of the theory we discuss in this review are a reflection of the mildness of the assumptions imposed on the underlying process. As pointed out earlier, recurrence is all that is required.

This said, the theory is specializable to the positive recurrent and stationary cases. The following theorems mirror more conventional results in the functional estimation of conditional expectations for stationary, discrete-time series and are immediate after noticing that, under conditions laid out earlier,

$$\frac{\widehat{\overline{L}}_X(T,a)}{T} \overset{a.s.}{\rightarrow} f(a) \tag{3.47}$$

and[9]

$$\frac{m'(a)}{m(a)} = \frac{f'(a)}{f(a)} = \left(\log f(a)\right)' = \frac{2\mu(a) - \left(\sigma^2(a)\right)'}{\sigma^2(a)} \tag{3.48}$$

under positive recurrence or stationarity (cf., the discussion in the previous subsection).

Theorem 7 *Assume X_t is the solution to (3.1) and $m(\mathfrak{D}) < \infty$ (as implied by Assumption 5). Furthermore, assume $h_{n,T} \rightarrow 0$ as $n, T \rightarrow \infty$ with $\Delta_{n,T} \rightarrow 0$ so that $\frac{T}{h_{n,T}}(\Delta_{n,T}\log(1/\Delta_{n,T}))^{1/2} = o(1)$ and $h_{n,T}T \rightarrow \infty$. Then,*

$$\widehat{\mu}_{(n,T)}(a) \overset{a.s.}{\rightarrow} \mu(a). \tag{3.49}$$

Additionally,

$$\sqrt{h_{n,T}T}\left\{\widehat{\mu}_{(n,T)}(a) - \mu(a) - \Gamma_\mu(a)\right\} \Rightarrow \mathbf{N}\left(0, \mathbf{K}_2\frac{\sigma^2(a)}{f(a)}\right), \tag{3.50}$$

if $h_{n,T} = O(T^{-1/5})$, where

$$\Gamma_\mu(a) = h_{n,T}^2\mathbf{K}_1\left[\mu'(a)\frac{f'(a)}{f(a)} + \frac{1}{2}\mu''(a)\right], \tag{3.51}$$

and $f(a)$ is the stationary density function of the process at a.

Proof See Bandi and Phillips (2003).

[9]The last equality in (3.48) can be proved by solving the equation

$$\int_{\mathfrak{D}} \mathfrak{L}\varphi(x)f(x)dx = 0$$

for a function $\varphi(.)$ in the domain of the infinitesimal generator $\mathfrak{L}$ (cf., Aït-Sahalia et al., 2010, in this volume). Such an equation holds by stationarity (cf., Hansen and Scheinkman, 1995).

Theorem 8 *Assume X_t is the solution to (3.1) and $m(\mathfrak{D}) < \infty$ as implied by Assumption 5). Furthermore, assume $h_{n,T} \to 0$ as $n, T \to \infty$ with $\Delta_{n,T} \to 0$ so that $\frac{T}{h_{n,T}}(\Delta_{n,T} \log(1/\Delta_{n,T}))^{1/2} = o(1)$. Then,*

$$\widehat{\sigma}^2_{(n,T)}(a) \overset{a.s.}{\to} \sigma^2(a). \tag{3.52}$$

Additionally,

$$\sqrt{nh_{n,T}}\left\{\widehat{\sigma}^2_{(n,T)}(a) - \sigma^2(a) - \Gamma_{\sigma^2}(a)\right\} \Rightarrow \mathbf{N}\left(0, 2\mathbf{K}_2 \frac{\sigma^4(a)}{f(a)}\right), \tag{3.53}$$

if $h_{n,T} = O(n^{-1/5})$, where

$$\Gamma_{\sigma^2}(a) = h^2_{n,T}\mathbf{K}_1\left[\left(\sigma^2(a)\right)' \frac{f'(a)}{f(a)} + \frac{1}{2}\left(\sigma^2(a)\right)''\right], \tag{3.54}$$

and $f(a)$ is the stationary density function of the process at a.

Proof See Bandi and Phillips (2003).

It was noted earlier that the rate of convergence of the drift estimator is $\sqrt{h_{n,T}\widehat{\overline{L}}_X(T,a)}$. This rate clarifies the sense in which identification of the infinitesimal first moment of an SDP requires an enlarging span of data (see, e.g., Geman, 1979). In effect, should T be fixed, then $\overline{L}_X(T,a)$ would be bounded in probability and the drift estimator would diverge at the rate $\sqrt{h_{n,T}}$ (Bandi, 2002). On the contrary, $\overline{L}_X(T,a)$ diverges to infinity as $T \to \infty$ by the assumption of recurrence, thereby ensuring that $\sqrt{h_{n,T}\widehat{\overline{L}}_X(T,a)} \overset{a.s.}{\to} \infty$, provided the bandwidth $h_{n,T}$ converges to zero slowly enough. The intuition why an enlarging span of data for drift estimation is needed was put forward in Section 2, but it is worth repeating here for clarity. To achieve consistency of the drift estimator at a certain spatial level, say a, we need the process to visit that level an infinite number of times over time. In this case, we can take averages of first differences between observations on the continuous path of the process occurring in the local neighborhood of a (as suggested in Section 2) and hope to apply an appropriate law of large number. Recurrence guarantees that every level will be visited an infinite number of times over time provided $T \to \infty$. A diverging local time at a as $T \to \infty$ is simply the manifestation of the fact that, with probability one, the level a is crossed an infinite number of times, as the time span grows indefinitely.

Importantly, the diffusion function can be identified over a fixed span of data as shown by Florens-Zmirou (1993), Brugière (1991, 1993), and Jacod (1997) in important early work. In other words, one can use (3.36) above and fix $T = \overline{T}$ to derive limiting results.

Theorem 9 *Assume X_t is the solution to (3.1). Given $n \to \infty$, $T = \overline{T}$, and $h_{n,\overline{T}} \to 0$ as $n \to \infty$ so that $\frac{1}{h_{n,\overline{T}}}(\Delta_{n,\overline{T}} \log(1/\Delta_{n,\overline{T}}))^{1/2} = o(1)$, the estimator (3.36) converges to the true function with probability one.*

If $nh^4_{n,\overline{T}} \to 0$, then the asymptotic distribution of (3.36) is driven by a "martingale" effect and has the form

$$\sqrt{nh_{n,\overline{T}}}\left\{\widehat{\sigma}^2_{(n,\overline{T})}(a) - \sigma^2(a)\right\} \Rightarrow \mathbf{MN}\left(0, \frac{2\mathbf{K}_2\sigma^4(a)}{\overline{L}_X(\overline{T},a)/\overline{T}}\right). \tag{3.55}$$

If $nh^4_{n,\overline{T}} \to \infty$, then the asymptotic distribution of (3.36) is driven by a "bias" effect and has the form

$$\frac{1}{h^{3/2}_{n,\overline{T}}}\left\{\widehat{\sigma}^2_{(n,\overline{T})}(a) - \sigma^2(a)\right\} \Rightarrow \mathbf{MN}\left(0, 16\varphi^{\text{ind}}\frac{\left(\sigma'(a)\right)^2}{\overline{L}_X(\overline{T},a)}\right), \tag{3.56}$$

where $\varphi^{\text{ind}} = 2\int_0^\infty \int_0^\infty ab\mathbf{K}(a)\mathbf{K}(b)\min(a,b)dadb$.

Proof Florens-Zmirou (1993) was the first to use the estimator (3.36) above to identify the diffusion function. The kernel used in Florens-Zmirou (1993) is a discontinuous indicator kernel, and the consistency proof is based on mean-squared deviations (see also Jacod, 1997, for a interesting refinement of this approach). The asymptotic distribution (3.55) is provided in Florens-Zmirou (1993) with $2\mathbf{K}_2 = 1$ due to the nature of the kernel used. Jiang and Knight (1997) modify the Florens-Zmirou estimator and define it using a continuous kernel. Their consistency proof follows Florens-Zmirou (1993) and is also in mean-squared. The statement of the theorem above is based on Bandi and Phillips (2003). The treatment in Bandi and Phillips (2003) highlights the potential for a random bias term (i.e., in Eq. (3.56) above) which might dominate the asymptotic distribution should the bandwidth sequence not converge to zero at a fast enough pace.

We now turn to a brief discussion of bandwidth selection.

3.2.1. The Choice of Bandwidth

Optimal bandwidth selection is technically very demanding in these models and represents an open field of research, no rigorous treatment being available at present, at least to the knowledge of the authors. Based on Theorem 5, in the drift case, one can write

$$h^{\text{drift}}_{n,T} = c^{\text{drift}}_{n,T}\frac{1}{\log \widehat{\overline{L}}_X(T,a)}\widehat{\overline{L}}_X(T,a)^{-1/5}, \tag{3.57}$$

where $\widehat{\overline{L}}_X(T,a)$ is the estimated local time at a and $c^{\text{drift}}_{n,T}$ is a constant of proportionality. Such an expression derives from the fact that the asymptotic mean-squared-error (MSE) at a generic level a is of order

$$O_{a.s.}\left(\left(h_{n,T}^{\text{drift}}\right)^4\right)+O_{a.s.}\left(\frac{1}{h_{n,T}^{\text{drift}}\widehat{\overline{L}}_X(T,a)}\right), \tag{3.58}$$

and the best rate is obtained by taking $h_{n,T}^{\text{drift}} \propto \widehat{\overline{L}}_X(T,a)^{-1/5}$ in which case the limiting MSE is of order $\widehat{\overline{L}}_X(T,a)^{-4/5}$. Premultiplication by $\frac{1}{\log \widehat{\overline{L}}_X(T,a)}$ is, of course, somewhat adhoc but useful to achieve a close-to-optimal rate of convergence and undersmooth slightly, thereby eliminating the influence of the nonrandom bias term from the asymptotic distribution of the drift estimates.

As for the diffusion function, Theorem 6, and a similar argument to that above, suggests the expression

$$h_{n,T}^{\text{diff}}=c_{n,T}^{\text{diff}}\frac{1}{\log\left(\widehat{\overline{L}}_X(T,a)/\Delta_{n,T}\right)}\left(\widehat{\overline{L}}_X(T,a)/\Delta_{n,T}\right)^{-1/5} \tag{3.59}$$

and, in consequence, the approximation

$$h_{n,T}^{\text{diff}}\approx c_{n,T}^{\text{diff}}\frac{1}{\log n}n^{-1/5}, \tag{3.60}$$

for a T diverging to infinity sufficiently slowly (or for the case of local time diverging at speed T, i.e., the stationary case). When T is fixed, as in Theorem 9, the previous condition becomes

$$h_{n,T}^{\text{diff}}=c_{n,T}^{\text{diff}}\frac{1}{\log n}n^{-1/4}. \tag{3.61}$$

Again, both (3.59) and (3.61) imply close-to-optimal rates, namely rates that almost maximize the speed of convergence of the proposed estimators to the functions of interest while preventing the insurgence of a (deterministic or random) bias term in the limit.

Some observations are in order. First, Eq. (3.57) suggests that there is explicit scope for local adaptation of the drift bandwidth sequence to the number of visits to the point at which estimation is performed. In fact, it appears that the optimal bandwidth for the drift should be smaller at levels that are often visited.[10] In light of the approximation (3.60) and the result in (3.61) such an effect is more pronounced in the drift case than in the diffusion case. Second, Theorems 5 and 6 suggest that the optimal drift bandwidth is

[10] Bias reduction is the standard justification for suggesting variable bandwidths whose magnitude is inversely related to the estimated density function (cf., Pagan and Ullah, 1999, p. 31).

generally larger than the optimal diffusion bandwidth. Both observations are of course reflections of the fact that the local dynamics of an SDP contain more information about the diffusion function than about the drift, thereby rendering consistent estimation of the infinitesimal second moment possible over a fixed span of data.

Unfortunately, despite being widely used in empirical work, standard automatic technologies (as discussed in Pagan and Ullah, 1999, among others) to select the constants $c_{n,T}^{\text{drift}}, c_{n,T}^{\text{diff}}$, and $c_{n,\overline{T}}^{\text{diff}}$, such as least squares cross-validation, have not been justified in the case of SDPs. Nonetheless, contrary to drift estimation, conventional cross-validation procedures appear to perform reasonably well when dealing with diffusion function estimation (cf., Bandi and Nguyen, 1999). Future work should usefully focus on the development of convincing criteria for determining the constants $c_{n,T}^{\text{drift}}, c_{n,T}^{\text{diff}}$, and $c_{n,\overline{T}}^{\text{diff}}$ in (3.57), (3.59), (3.60), and (3.61) above and for selecting a preliminary smoothing sequence to define $\widehat{\overline{L}}_X(T,a)$, a fundamental quantity in the theory we are reviewing.

3.3. Extensions in Kernel Estimation for SDPs

3.3.1. Double-Smoothing

The estimators (3.35) and (3.36) belong to the general class of estimators suggested by Bandi and Phillips (2003). Consistently with the discussion in Bandi and Phillips (2003), one could envisage a more involved two-step procedure with further smoothing. First, one could define sample analogs to the values that drift and diffusion take on at the sampled points, i.e.,

$$\widetilde{\mu}_{(n,T)}(X_{i\Delta_{n,T}}) = \frac{1}{\Delta_{n,T}} \frac{\sum_{j=1}^{n-1} \mathbf{K}\left(\frac{X_{j\Delta_{n,T}}-X_{i\Delta_{n,T}}}{h_{n,T}}\right)\left(X_{(j+1)\Delta_{n,T}} - X_{j\Delta_{n,T}}\right)}{\sum_{j=1}^{n} \mathbf{K}\left(\frac{X_{j\Delta_{n,T}}-X_{i\Delta_{n,T}}}{h_{n,T}}\right)}, \tag{3.62}$$

$$\widetilde{\sigma}^2_{(n,T)}(X_{i\Delta_{n,T}}) = \frac{1}{\Delta_{n,T}} \frac{\sum_{j=1}^{n-1} \mathbf{K}\left(\frac{X_{j\Delta_{n,T}}-X_{i\Delta_{n,T}}}{h_{n,T}}\right)\left(X_{(j+1)\Delta_{n,T}} - X_{j\Delta_{n,T}}\right)^2}{\sum_{j=1}^{n} \mathbf{K}\left(\frac{X_{j\Delta_{n,T}}-X_{i\Delta_{n,T}}}{h_{n,T}}\right)}. \tag{3.63}$$

Second, estimated drift and diffusion values at the sampled points could be averaged using weights based on smooth kernels to recover the theoretical functions at levels that the sampled process does not visit, i.e.,

$$\overline{\mu}_{(n,T)}(a) = \frac{\sum_{i=1}^{n} \overline{\mathbf{K}}\left(\frac{X_{i\Delta_{n,T}}-a}{\varepsilon_{n,T}}\right)\widetilde{\mu}_{(n,T)}\left(X_{i\Delta_{n,T}}\right)}{\sum_{i=1}^{n} \overline{\mathbf{K}}\left(\frac{X_{i\Delta_{n,T}}-a}{\varepsilon_{n,T}}\right)}, \tag{3.64}$$

$$\overline{\sigma}^2_{(n,T)}(a) = \frac{\sum_{i=1}^{n} \overline{\mathbf{K}}\left(\frac{X_{i\Delta_{n,T}}-a}{\varepsilon_{n,T}}\right)\widetilde{\sigma}^2_{(n,T)}\left(X_{i\Delta_{n,T}}\right)}{\sum_{i=1}^{n} \overline{\mathbf{K}}\left(\frac{X_{i\Delta_{n,T}}-a}{\varepsilon_{n,T}}\right)}, \tag{3.65}$$

with $\overline{\mathbf{K}}(.)$ possibly different from $\mathbf{K}(.)$ and $h_{n,T}$ possibly different from $\varepsilon_{n,T}$. Both $\overline{\mathbf{K}}(.)$ and $\mathbf{K}(.)$ satisfy the assumptions in Section 2.[11]

Asymptotically, the doubly smoothed estimates (3.64) and (3.65) offer additional flexibility over their simple counterparts in (3.35) and (3.36) above. In effect, they can improve the asymptotic trade-off between bias and variance effects, thereby delivering smaller limiting MSEs than simple smoothing. As usual, let us focus on the drift while keeping in mind that the intuition extends to the diffusion function.

If $h_{n,T}$ satisfies the conditions in Theorem 5 and $\varepsilon_{n,T}/h_{n,T} \to \phi$, then the limiting bias and variance of the drift estimator (3.64) at a generic point a are, from Bandi and Phillips (2003),

$$\frac{\theta_\phi \sigma^2(a)}{h_{n,T}\widehat{\overline{L}}_X(T,a)}, \tag{3.66}$$

with

$$\theta_\phi = \int\int\int \overline{\mathbf{K}}(a)\overline{\mathbf{K}}(e)\mathbf{K}(z-\phi e)\mathbf{K}(z-\phi a)\mathrm{d}z\mathrm{d}e\mathrm{d}a, \tag{3.67}$$

and

$$h_{n,T}^2 \mathbf{K}^\phi \left[\mu'(a)\frac{m'(a)}{m(a)} + \frac{1}{2}\mu''(a)\right], \tag{3.68}$$

with

$$\mathbf{K}^\phi = \int s^2 \mathbf{K}(s)\mathrm{d}s + \phi \int s^2 \overline{\mathbf{K}}(s)\mathrm{d}s. \tag{3.69}$$

Clearly, if $\varepsilon_{n,T}/h_{n,T} \to \phi = 0$, then double-smoothing coincides asymptotically with single-smoothing by a straightforward comparison of (3.66) and (3.68) with (3.45) and (3.46) above, respectively. Nonetheless, because θ_ϕ is a decreasing function of ϕ and $\mathbf{K}^\phi$ is an increasing function of it, there is scope for using convoluted kernels to achieve asymptotic MSEs which are optimized at values ϕ that are strictly larger than zero.

In finite samples, the extra level of smoothing that is implied by the use of convoluted kernels might be particularly beneficial, especially in the drift case. The intuition is as follows. We stressed earlier that the optimal smoothing parameter for the drift is generally

[11] An interesting, alternative approach is studied in Renò (2008) where the preliminary spot variance estimates $\widetilde{\sigma}^2_{(n,T)}$ at times $i\Delta_{n,T}$ are Fourier estimates as in Malliavin and Mancino (2002).

larger than the corresponding choice for diffusion estimation. Nonetheless, there appears to be a fundamental difficulty in choosing the optimal drift bandwidth as a function of the estimated local time (as implied by Eq. (3.57)) and, consequently, as a function of the recurrence properties of the underlying Markov process. The use of convoluted kernels may achieve, in finite samples, the level of smoothing for the drift that weighted averages based on simple kernels would guarantee with relatively more appropriate (larger) choices of the bandwidth (Bandi and Nguyen, 1999).

3.3.2. Local Linear and Polynomial Estimation

It is immediate to see that the estimators (3.35) and (3.36) can be written as

$$\widehat{\mu}_{n,T}(a) = \arg\min_{\theta^{\mu}} \sum_{i=1}^{n-1} \mathbf{K}\left(\frac{X_{i\Delta_{n,T}} - a}{h_{n,T}}\right)\left\{\frac{1}{\Delta_{n,T}}\left(X_{(i+1)\Delta_{n,T}} - X_{i\Delta_{n,T}}\right) - \theta^{\mu}\right\}^2 \tag{3.70}$$

and

$$\widehat{\sigma}^2_{n,T}(a) = \arg\min_{\theta^{\sigma^2}} \sum_{i=1}^{n-1} \mathbf{K}\left(\frac{X_{i\Delta_{n,T}} - a}{h_{n,T}}\right)\left\{\frac{1}{\Delta_{n,T}}\left(X_{(i+1)\Delta_{n,T}} - X_{i\Delta_{n,T}}\right)^2 - \theta^{\sigma^2}\right\}^2, \tag{3.71}$$

respectively. Specifically, as always, the NW estimates of drift and diffusion function fit a constant line to data in vicinity of the level a. Alternatively, one might fit a polynomial locally and minimize the criteria

$$\sum_{i=1}^{n-1} \mathbf{K}\left(\frac{X_{i\Delta_{n,T}} - a}{h_{n,T}}\right)\left\{\frac{1}{\Delta_{n,T}}\left(X_{(i+1)\Delta_{n,T}} - X_{i\Delta_{n,T}}\right) - \sum_{s=0}^{r} \theta^{\mu}_{s}\left(X_{i\Delta_{n,T}} - a\right)^s\right\}^2 \tag{3.72}$$

and

$$\sum_{i=1}^{n-1} \mathbf{K}\left(\frac{X_{i\Delta_{n,T}} - a}{h_{n,T}}\right)\left\{\frac{1}{\Delta_{n,T}}\left(X_{(i+1)\Delta_{n,T}} - X_{i\Delta_{n,T}}\right)^2 - \sum_{s=0}^{r} \theta^{\sigma^2}_{s}\left(X_{i\Delta_{n,T}} - a\right)^s\right\}^2 \tag{3.73}$$

with respect to $\boldsymbol{\theta}^{\mu} = (\theta^{\mu}_0, \theta^{\mu}_1, \ldots, \theta^{\mu}_r)^{\top}$ and $\boldsymbol{\theta}^{\sigma^2} = (\theta^{\sigma^2}_0, \theta^{\sigma^2}_1, \ldots, \theta^{\sigma^2}_r)^{\top}$ for all levels a. A simple argument based on Taylor expansions around a suggests that the proper estimates of $\mu(a)$ and $\sigma^2(a)$ are now the first components ($\widehat{\theta}^{\mu}_0$ and $\widehat{\theta}^{\sigma^2}_0$) of the estimated vectors $\widehat{\boldsymbol{\theta}}^{\mu}$ and $\widehat{\boldsymbol{\theta}}^{\sigma^2}$. The remaining components are estimates of the (standardized) derivatives of the functions of interest (provided these derivatives exist, of course).

In the case of recurrent SDPs of the kind analyzed in this review, this approach was suggested by Moloche (2004a) following classical work by Fan (1992, 1993) and Fan and Gijbels (1996) in nonparametric regression analysis for discrete-time series (see also

Pagan and Ullah, 1999, p. 93, for discussions). In the stationary SDP case, local polynomial methods are used by Fan and Zhang (2003).[12] Importantly, the estimated vectors $\widehat{\boldsymbol{\theta}}^{\mu}$ and $\widehat{\boldsymbol{\theta}}^{\sigma^2}$ can be expressed in the form of regression estimates because the criteria (3.72) and (3.73) may be readily interpreted in terms of classical weighted least-squares problems. As always, we are explicitly only about the drift case but similar observations apply to the diffusion function. Write

$$\mathbf{X}_{n,T}(a) = \begin{bmatrix} 1 & (X_{\Delta_{n,T}} - a) & \dots & (X_{\Delta_{n,T}} - a)^r \\ \dots & \dots & \dots & \dots \\ 1 & (X_{(n-1)\Delta_{n,T}} - a) & \dots & (X_{(n-1)\Delta_{n,T}} - a)^r \end{bmatrix}, \tag{3.74}$$

$$\mathbf{y}_{n,T} = \begin{bmatrix} \frac{1}{\Delta_{n,T}}(X_{2\Delta_{n,T}} - X_{\Delta_{n,T}}) \\ \dots \\ \frac{1}{\Delta_{n,T}}(X_{n\Delta_{n,T}} - X_{(n-1)\Delta_{n,T}}) \end{bmatrix}, \tag{3.75}$$

and

$$\mathbf{W}_{n,T}(a) = diag\left(\frac{\Delta_{n,T}}{h_{n,T}}\mathbf{K}\left(\frac{X_{\Delta_{n,T}} - a}{h_{n,T}}\right), \dots, \frac{\Delta_{n,T}}{h_{n,T}}\mathbf{K}\left(\frac{X_{(n-1)\Delta_{n,T}} - a}{h_{n,T}}\right)\right). \tag{3.76}$$

The pointwise drift estimator $\widehat{\theta}_0^{\mu}$ is the first component of the $(r+1)$-vector

$$\widehat{\boldsymbol{\theta}}^{\mu} = (\mathbf{X}_{n,T}^{\top}(a)\mathbf{W}_{n,T}(a)\mathbf{X}_{n,T}(a))^{-1}\mathbf{X}_{n,T}^{\top}(a)\mathbf{W}_{n,T}(a)\mathbf{y}_{n,T}. \tag{3.77}$$

[12] In particular, Fan and Zhang (2003) apply local polynomial methods to Stanton's kth-order approximations to drift and diffusion function (Stanton, 1997). Write

$$\begin{aligned}\mathbf{E}_t\{f(X_{t+\Delta}, t+\Delta)\} &= f(X_t, t) + \mathfrak{L}f(X_t, t)\Delta + \frac{1}{2}\mathfrak{L}^2 f(X_t, t)\Delta^2 + \dots + \\ &+ \frac{1}{k!}\mathfrak{L}^k f(X_t, t)\Delta^k + O(\Delta^{k+1}),\end{aligned}$$

where $\mathfrak{L}$ is the infinitesimal generator in Eq. (3.7). Given discrete observations sampled at multiples of Δ (and weights $c_{k,j}$ with $j = 1, \dots, k$), we can write

$$\begin{aligned}\frac{1}{\Delta}\sum_{j=1}^{k} c_{k,j}\mathbf{E}_t\left\{f(X_{t+j\Delta}, t+j\Delta) - f(X_t, t)\right\} &= \left\{\sum_{j=1}^{k} jc_{k,j}\right\}\mathfrak{L}f(X_t, t) + \left\{\sum_{j=1}^{k} j^2 c_{k,j}\right\}\frac{\mathfrak{L}^2 f(X_t, t)}{2}\Delta \\ &+ \dots + \left\{\sum_{j=1}^{k} j^{k+1} c_{k,j}\right\}\frac{\mathfrak{L}^{k+1} f(X_t, t)}{(k+1)!}\Delta^k + O(\Delta^{k+1}).\end{aligned}$$

Now consider the drift case, i.e., $f(X_t, t) = X_t$. Clearly, $\mathfrak{L}f(X_t, t) = \mu(X_t)$. Thus, if the weights $c_{k,j}$ are chosen so that $\sum_{j=1}^{k} jc_{k,j} = 1$ and $\sum_{j=1}^{k} j^p c_{k,j} = 0$ for all $2 \le p \le k$, then it follows that

$$\frac{1}{\Delta}\sum_{j=1}^{k} c_{k,j}\mathbf{E}_t\left\{X_{t+j\Delta} - X_t\right\} = \mu(X_t) + O(\Delta^k).$$

NW kernel estimates can now be applied to data sampled at different frequencies (controlled by j) and can be appropriately weighed to estimate $\mu(.)$ (Stanton, 1997). Clearly, the case $k = 1$ corresponds to Eq. (3.33) above. Fan and Zhang (2003) use local polynomial estimates to show that a large k can be beneficial in terms of asymptotic bias but may translate into an exponentially growing limiting variance.

Moloche (2004a) shows that under the same conditions on the bandwidth as in Theorem 5 and provided that the same sampling scheme as in Section 2 is adopted, the estimate $\widehat{\theta}_0^{\mu}$ converges to the true function with probability one and is (mixed) normally distributed in the limit. The local linear case ($r = 1$) is particularly relevant. The drift estimator can be conveniently expressed as a weighted NW kernel estimator

$$\widehat{\mu}^{ll}_{(n,T)}(a) = \frac{1}{\Delta_{n,T}} \frac{\sum_{i=1}^{n-1} \mathbf{w}_i^{ll}(a, h_{n,T})\mathbf{K}\left(\frac{X_{i\Delta_{n,T}}-a}{h_{n,T}}\right)(X_{(i+1)\Delta_{n,T}} - X_{i\Delta_{n,T}})}{\sum_{i=1}^{n-1} \mathbf{w}_i^{ll}(a, h_{n,T})\mathbf{K}\left(\frac{X_{i\Delta_{n,T}}-a}{h_{n,T}}\right)} \tag{3.78}$$

with $\mathbf{w}_i^{ll} = \Xi_{n,2} - (X_{i\Delta_{n,T}} - a)\Xi_{n,1}$, where $\Xi_{n,k} = \frac{1}{h_{n,T}} \sum_{i=1}^{n-1}(X_{i\Delta_{n,T}} - a)^k \mathbf{K}(\frac{X_{i\Delta_{n,T}}-a}{h_{n,T}})$ with $k = 1, 2$. Its asymptotic variance and bias have the form

$$\frac{\mathbf{K}_2\sigma^2(a)}{h_{n,T}\widehat{\overline{L}}_X(T,a)}, \tag{3.79}$$

and

$$h^2_{n,T}\mathbf{K}_1 \frac{1}{2}\mu''(a). \tag{3.80}$$

Expressions (3.79) and (3.80) should now be compared to the corresponding quantities for the NW kernel estimates discussed earlier, namely (3.45) and (3.46) above. The comparison is standard, and we refer the interested reader to the original work by Fan (1992) and the review of Pagan (1999, pp. 104–106) for details. Here, we simply stress that the variances are the same, but the biases are different. In particular, the bias of the local linear estimator does not depend on the ratio $\frac{m'(.)}{m(.)}$ and on the first derivative of μ at a and is "design adaptive" in the sense of Fan (1992). Similar expressions hold for the diffusion function estimator $\widehat{\theta}_0^{\sigma^2}$ (Moloche, 2004a).

3.3.3. Finite Sample Refinements

Local linear methods have favorable bias properties but may not guarantee positivity when positivity is required, as is the case for diffusion function estimation. To this extent, Xu (2008) suggests a *reweighted* NW diffusion estimator which is asymptotically equivalent (in terms of MSE properties) to the local linear estimator while retaining the nonnegativity features of the classical local constant (or NW) kernel estimator. Write

$$\widehat{\sigma}^{2(rNW)}_{(n,T)}(a) = \frac{1}{\Delta_{n,T}} \frac{\sum_{i=1}^{n-1} \mathbf{w}_i^{rNW}(a, h_{n,T})\mathbf{K}\left(\frac{X_{i\Delta_{n,T}}-a}{h_{n,T}}\right)\left(X_{(i+1)\Delta_{n,T}} - X_{i\Delta_{n,T}}\right)^2}{\sum_{i=1}^{n-1} \mathbf{w}_i^{rNW}\left(a, h_{n,T}\right)\mathbf{K}\left(\frac{X_{i\Delta_{n,T}}-a}{h_{n,T}}\right)}, \tag{3.81}$$

where the weights $\{\mathbf{w}_i^{rNW}(a, h_{n,T})\}$ are such that $\mathbf{w}_i \geq 0$, $\sum_{i=1}^{n-1} \mathbf{w}_i = 1$, and solve

$$\left\{\mathbf{w}_i^{rNW}(a, h_{n,T})\right\} = \max_{\{\mathbf{w}_i\}} \sum_{i=1}^{n-1} \log((n-1)\mathbf{w}_i), \tag{3.82}$$

under

$$\frac{1}{h_{n,T}} \sum_{i=1}^{n-1} \mathbf{w}_i (X_{i\Delta_{n,T}} - a)\mathbf{K}\left(\frac{X_{i\Delta_{n,T}} - a}{h_{n,T}}\right) = 0. \tag{3.83}$$

As emphasized by Xu (2008), the restriction in Eq. (3.83) is motivated by local linear estimation. It is, in fact, easily satisfied by $\mathbf{w}_i^{ll}$. Just like in local linear estimation, this is the restriction which yields a "design adaptive" bias component

$$h_{n,T}^2 \mathbf{K}_1 \frac{1}{2}\left(\sigma^2(a)\right)'' \tag{3.84}$$

and the same asymptotic variance as earlier. The positivity of the weights, of course, guarantees positivity of the final local estimates. For further discussions about the form of the weights and their derivation, we refer to Xu (2008). In particular, Xu (2008) discusses the interpretation of the criterion in terms of empirical likelihood. Inference for SDPs based on empirical likelihood is studied, e.g., in Chen et al. (2008) and Xu (2007), and we do not expand on it here.

Although for the data routinely used in continuous-time econometrics, the assumption of a limiting, vanishing distance between discretely sampled observations ($\Delta_{n,T} \to 0$) represents an empirically valid asymptotic design, finite sample adjustments might sometimes be important. Nicolau (2003) studies the finite-sample bias properties of the NW diffusion estimator [in Eq. (3.36)] for a fixed distance between adjacent observations. He shows that if $\Delta_{n,T} = \Delta$ fixed, $T \to \infty$, $h_{n,T} \to 0$, and $nh_{n,T} \to \infty$ as $n \to \infty$,

$$\widehat{\sigma}^2_{(n,T)}(a) \xrightarrow{p} \sigma^2(a) + \mu^2(a)\Delta + \Pi(a)\Delta + O(\Delta^2), \tag{3.85}$$

with

$$\Pi(a) = \sigma^2(a)\mu'(a) + \mu(a)\sigma(a)\sigma'(a) + \frac{1}{2}\sigma^2(a)\left(\sigma'(a)\right)^2 + \frac{1}{2}\sigma^3(a)\sigma''(a). \tag{3.86}$$

Hence, of course, the estimator is biased for a fixed Δ. However, the first bias component ($\mu^2(a)\Delta$) may be eliminated asymptotically using a (feasible) bias correction. One could, for instance, compute $\widehat{\sigma}^2_{(n,T)}(a)$ by averaging terms $(X_{(i+1)\Delta_{n,T}} - X_{i\Delta_{n,T}} - \widehat{\mu}_{(n,T)}(a)\Delta_{n,T})^2$, where $\widehat{\mu}_{(n,T)}(a)$ is the drift estimator in Eq. (3.35) rather than the traditional terms $(X_{(i+1)\Delta_{n,T}} - X_{i\Delta_{n,T}})^2$. Although the asymptotic distribution of the resulting estimator for an increasing sampling frequency ($\Delta_{n,T} = \Delta \to 0$) is of course identical to that laid out in Theorem 6, the finite sample adjustment might be useful. In effect, it might work particularly well at levels a corresponding to large (in absolute terms) drift values (in regions where the degree of drift-induced mean-reversion is substantial). Renò (2006) provides further discussions.

3.4. Using Nonparametric Information to Estimate and Test Parametric Models for SDPs

It is natural to use the information contained in the nonparametric estimates to design more accurate parametric models and test parametric assumptions. Bandi and Phillips (2007) discuss a simple (semi-)parametric procedure to estimate potentially nonstationary diffusions which overcomes the usual inference problems posed by the unavailability of a closed-form expression for the transition density of the underlying process and does not require simulations. They consider a parametric class $(\boldsymbol{\theta}^{\mu}, \boldsymbol{\theta}^{\sigma}) = \boldsymbol{\theta} \in \Theta$ for the underlying SDP and compute the parameters of interest as

$$\begin{aligned} \widehat{\boldsymbol{\theta}}^{\mu}_{n,T} &:= \underset{\boldsymbol{\theta}^{\mu} \in \Theta^{\mu} \subset \Theta}{\arg\min}\ Q^{\mu}_{n,T} \\ &= \underset{\boldsymbol{\theta}^{\mu} \in \Theta^{\mu} \subset \Theta}{\arg\min}\ \frac{\overline{T}}{n} \sum_{i=1}^{n} \left(\widehat{\mu}_{(n,T)} \left(X_{i\Delta_{n,\overline{T}}} \right) - \mu \left(X_{i\Delta_{n,\overline{T}}}, \boldsymbol{\theta}^{\mu} \right) \right)^2, \end{aligned} \tag{3.87}$$

and

$$\begin{aligned} \widehat{\boldsymbol{\theta}}^{\sigma^2}_{n,T} &:= \underset{\boldsymbol{\theta}^{\sigma^2} \in \Theta^{\sigma^2} \subset \Theta}{\arg\min}\ Q^{\sigma^2}_{n,T} \\ &= \underset{\boldsymbol{\theta}^{\sigma^2} \in \Theta^{\sigma^2} \subset \Theta}{\arg\min}\ \frac{\overline{T}}{n} \sum_{i=1}^{n} \left(\widehat{\sigma}^2_{(n,T)} \left(X_{i\Delta_{n,\overline{T}}} \right) - \sigma^2 \left(X_{i\Delta_{n,\overline{T}}}, \boldsymbol{\theta}^{\sigma^2} \right) \right)^2, \end{aligned} \tag{3.88}$$

where $\widehat{\mu}_{(n,T)}(X_{i\Delta_{n,\overline{T}}})$ and $\widehat{\sigma}^2_{(n,T)}(X_{i\Delta_{n,\overline{T}}})$ are functional estimates (defined over an enlarging span of data for consistency – see Subsection 3.2) of the NW type [cf., (3.35) and (3.36) above] at the ith observation. The parameter values are chosen so that the average squared distance between the nonparametric curves at the sampled points and the adopted parametric specification is minimized. The asymptotic distributions of the parameter estimates are (variance mixtures of) normals and can be readily interpreted on the basis of well-known results for conventional nonlinear least-squares problems. Nonetheless, the integrals that appear in the limiting variances are not integrals with respect to probability measures (i.e., expectations) but integrals with respect to local times [i.e., occupation integrals, cf., (3.20)] due to the generality of the approach in the present context. By virtue of the averaging, the rates of convergence of the parameter estimates are faster than the rates of convergence of the functional estimators used to define (3.87) and (3.88) above. This is, of course, a typical result in semiparametric problems (see, e.g., Andrews, 1989).

Apparently, the above criteria can be used to test alternative parametric assumptions about the functions of interest. Consider the drift case. Assume one wishes to test the hypotheses $H_0 : \mu_0(x) = \mu(x, \boldsymbol{\theta}^{\mu})$ against $H_1 : \mu_0(x) \neq \mu(x, \boldsymbol{\theta}^{\mu})$. Provided a consistent (under the null) parametric estimate of $\boldsymbol{\theta}^{\mu}$, say $\widetilde{\boldsymbol{\theta}}^{\mu}_{n,T}$, is obtained (the value $\widehat{\boldsymbol{\theta}}^{\mu}_{n,T}$ which minimizes (3.87) is, of course, a viable option) and the distribution of $\widehat{Q}^{\mu}_{n,T}(\widetilde{\boldsymbol{\theta}}^{\mu}_{n,T})$ is derived under the null, standard methods can be used to construct a consistent test. The use of nonparametric information to test parametric models based on the minimization of average squared errors like (3.87) and (3.88) above has a long history in hypothesis testing about density functions. Important early references in discrete-time are Bickel and Rosenblatt (1973) and Rosenblatt (1975). More recently, Aït-Sahalia (1996) has applied the idea to the study of stationary scalar diffusion models for the short-term interest rate process. Corradi and White (1999) focus on the infinitesimal second moment over a fixed span of data and can, therefore, allow for transient dynamics. Relying on the informational content of the transition density of the process, Hong and Li (2003) provide specification tests for both the drift and the diffusion of a stationary diffusion process. Empirical distribution function-based tests for stationary scalar and multivariate diffusion processes are proposed in Corradi and Swanson (2005).

To the authors' knowledge, little work exists on parametric inference for null-recurrent diffusions. In addition to Bandi and Phillips (2007), a recent contribution is the work by Höpfner and Kutoyants (2001) who discuss a method of inference for the parameter θ in the SDP

$$\mathrm{d}X_t = \theta \frac{X_t}{1 + X_t^2}\mathrm{d}t + \sigma \mathrm{d}B_t, \tag{3.89}$$

where $\theta \in \Theta = \left(-\frac{\sigma^2}{2}, \frac{\sigma^2}{2}\right)$. As they show, θ is the parameter determining the speed of divergence of additive integrable functionals of the process (in the sense discussed in Section 5, Theorem 11) and Θ is the maximal open interval over which the process is null recurrent. Given knowledge of the diffusion function σ and availability of a continuum of observations, parametric estimation is conducted by maximum likelihood through arguments based on measure changes.

3.5. Time-Inhomogeneous SDPs

Allowing for time-dependence in the infinitesimal first and second moment may be empirically useful. However, although time-inhomogeneous diffusions have received some emphasis in the mathematical finance literature (see, e.g., Black et al., 1990; Heath et al., 1992; and the references therein), little work exists on their inference. Rewrite Eq. (3.1) as

$$\mathrm{d}X_t = \mu(X_t, t)\mathrm{d}t + \sigma(X_t, t)\mathrm{d}B_t. \tag{3.90}$$

The drift and diffusion function now depend on the state as well as on time. Fan et al. (2003) parametrize them as functions of X_t with time-varying parameters before localizing in time. Assume, as they do, that $\mu(X_t, t) = \alpha_0(t) + \alpha_1(t)X_t$. Given discretely sampled observations X_{t_i} for $i = 1, \ldots, n$ with $\Delta_i = t_{i+1} - t_i$, a natural local least-squares criterion minimizes

$$\frac{1}{h}\sum_{i=1}^{n-1} \mathbf{K}\left(\frac{t_i - \widetilde{t}}{h}\right)\left\{\frac{X_{t_{i+1}} - X_{t_i}}{\Delta_i} - \left(\theta_0 + \theta_1 X_{t_i}\right)\right\} \tag{3.91}$$

with respect to θ_0 and θ_1. Clearly, both estimates depend on $\widetilde{t}$, thereby giving $\widehat{\theta}_0 = \widehat{\alpha}_0(\widetilde{t})$ and $\widehat{\theta}_1 = \widehat{\alpha}_1(\widetilde{t})$. An analogous procedure can be applied to diffusion estimation under a similar parametrization. Fan et al. (2003), for instance, assume a constant elasticity-of-variance diffusion with time-varying parameters and write $\sigma(X_t, t) = \beta_0(t)X^{\beta_1(t)}$. Noting that the ratio

$$Y_{t_i} = \frac{X_{t_{i+1}} - X_{t_i} - \left(\widehat{\alpha}_0(t_i) + \widehat{\alpha}_1(t_i)X_{t_i}\right)\Delta_i}{\sqrt{\Delta_i}} \approx \beta_0(t)X_{t_i}^{\beta_1(t)}\varepsilon_{t_i} \tag{3.92}$$

is approximately (conditionally) Gaussian, they optimize (for all $\widetilde{t}$) the local pseudo log-likelihood

$$-\frac{1}{2h}\sum_{i=1}^{n-1} \mathbf{K}\left(\frac{t_i - \widetilde{t}}{h}\right)\left\{\left(\log(\vartheta_0^2 X_{t_i}^{2\vartheta_1}\right) + \frac{Y_{t_i}^2}{\vartheta_0^2 X_{t_i}^{2\vartheta_1}}\right\} \tag{3.93}$$

to obtain $\widehat{\vartheta}_0 = \widehat{\beta}_0(\widetilde{t})$ and $\widehat{\vartheta}_1 = \widehat{\beta}_1(\widetilde{t})$. Alternatively, writing

$$\log(Y_{t_i}^2) \approx \log(\beta_0^2(t_i)) + \beta_1(t_i)\log(X_{t_i}^2) + \log(\varepsilon_{t_i}^2), \tag{3.94}$$

a similar (local) least-squares procedure as in Eq. (3.91) may be applied to the diffusion estimator. Although notions of consistency for the resulting estimates under suitable sampling schemes have not been established yet, the methods are of course suggestive of the usefulness of kernel-based approaches to capture time-varying dynamics in parameters.

A fundamental class of models allowing for stochastic time-variation in the infinitesimal second moment is the family of stochastic volatility models. Consider Eq. (3.90) and write $\sigma(X_t, t) = \sigma(t)$. Assume the dynamics of $\sigma(t)$ are driven by an homogeneous stochastic differential equation and are recurrent. The next section provides a concise application of the ideas laid out in this section to stochastic volatility modeling in continuous time. For interesting, recent work focused on testing the null hypothesis $H_0 : \sigma^2(X_t, t) = \sigma^2(X_t)$ against the alternative $H_A : \sigma^2(X_t, t) =$ SDP not measurable with respect to the filtration generated by X_t, we refer the reader to Corradi and Distaso (2007). In what follows, we work under Corradi and Distaso's alternative hypothesis.

3.6. An Empirical Application: Stochastic Volatility

The recent literature on volatility estimation by virtue of high-frequency (intra-daily) asset price data has provided a set of tools to identify daily variance without the need for filtering using low-frequency asset returns. These high-frequency variance estimates may be put to work to understand variance dynamics from a new perspective. Using (i) intra-daily asset price data to generate *spot* variance estimates and (ii) NW kernel estimates of the spot variance drift and diffusion (as suggested by Bandi and Phillips, 2003), Bandi and Renò (2008) and Kanaya and Kristensen (2008) discuss a nonparametric theory of (continuous-time) stochastic volatility estimation (see also Comte et al., 2007, for an alternative approach). The preliminary spot variance estimates in Kanaya and Kristensen (2008) are local (in time) averages of realized variance estimates as suggested in Kristensen (2009). In Bandi and Renò (2008), they are local (in time) averages of a family of robust (to market microstructure noise or jumps in returns) integrated variance estimates (for which an asymptotic theory of inference is provided in Bandi and Renò, 2008). Both Bandi and Renò (2008) and Kanaya and Kristensen (2008) discuss conditions (to be added to those in Theorems 5 and 6) under which the estimation error introduced by the preliminary spot variance estimates is asymptotically negligible.

To briefly illustrate the methods in the SDP case, we follow Bandi and Renò (2008) in this review. Specifically, we estimate the spot variance of the S&P 500 index returns for all days between January 2, 1998, and March 31, 2006, by applying the two-scale estimator of Zhang et al. (2005) to intra-daily SPY returns (see Bandi and Renò, 2008, for details).[13] Figure 3.1a represents the sojourn time of the spot variance estimates along with its asymptotic confidence bands (cf., Theorem 2). Spot variance is expressed (on the horizontal axis, for instance) in daily terms and is multiplied by 10,000 for consistency with S&P 500 returns expressed in percentage terms. The sojourn time has a peak around 1 (corresponding to a volatility of annual S&P 500 returns equal to 15%). More generally, the stochastic variance process makes most of its visit at levels between approximately 0.3 and 1.5, namely for a volatility of annual market returns between approximately 8.5% and 19.5%. In this range, we expect the drift and diffusion estimates (in Fig. 3.1b and c to be more precisely estimated as implied by pointwise asymptotic confidence bands whose width is inversely related to the number of visit to each spatial point. The drift is largely positive over the relevant variance range. The diffusion is a monotonically increasing and nonlinear function of the variance level. We do not dwell on these two functions here. We simply point out that the magnitude of the estimated drift in this subsection may be largely induced by the presence of positive jumps in the variance process affecting the infinitesimal first moment's estimates [see Eq. (4.40) below].

[13] SPY is the ticker symbol for the Standard and Poor's depository receipts (also known as Spiders). SPYs are shares in a trust which owns stocks in the same proportion as that found in the S&P 500 index. Importantly, they trade like a stock at approximately one-tenth of the level of the index. Thus, because changes in SPY value reflect changes in market value, SPY volatility reflects market volatility.

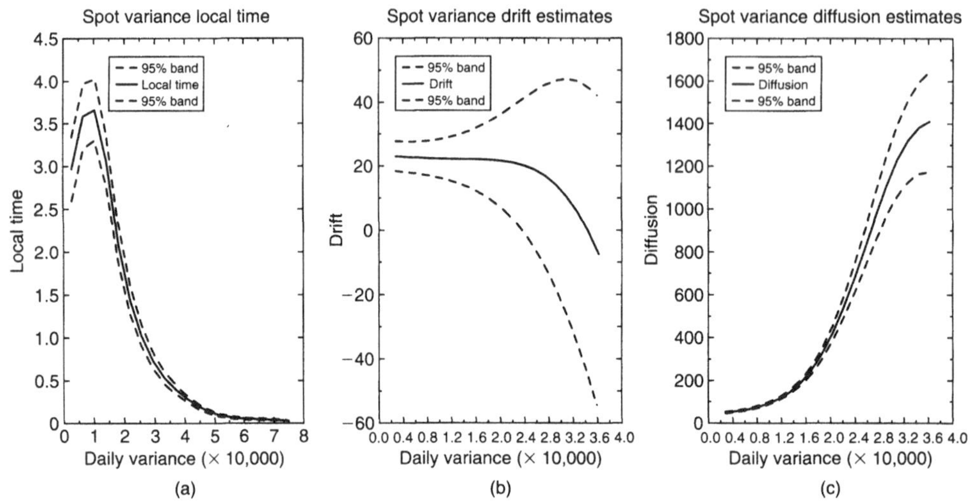

Figure 3.1 Local time, drift, and diffusion estimates of an SDP for stochastic volatility.

Similarly, the magnitude of the diffusion estimates might be induced by infinitesimal second moment estimates which, in the presence of variance jumps, comprise genuinely diffusive volatility as well as the second moment of the discontinuous variance component [see Eq. (4.41) below]. Consistent with these observations and the analysis in Bandi and Renò (2008), in Subsection 4.3 we will discuss a functional jump-diffusion model with exponential jump sizes for the market spot variance. This specification will represent a considerably superior modeling alternative to the SDP discussed here.

4. SCALAR JUMP-DIFFUSION PROCESSES

Throughout this section, we model a time-series X_t as the solution of a stochastic differential equation with infrequent Poisson jumps. The jumps occur with conditional intensity $\lambda(.)$ (i.e., $\lambda(a)dt$ is the infinitesimal probability of a jump at the level a). The impact of a jump is given by the function $g(., y)$ whose arguments are the level of the process and a generic random variable y which we assume to be endowed with the stationary probability measure $\Gamma(.)$. Specifically,

$$\Delta X_t = X_t - X_{t-} = \int_Y g(X_{t-}, y) N(\mathrm{d}t, \mathrm{d}y) = \mathrm{d}J_t, \tag{4.1}$$

where

$$N_t^{\Phi} = \sum_{j=1} \mathbf{1}_{[\tau_j \le t, y_{\tau_j} \in \Phi]} \tag{4.2}$$

is, given a set Φ, a Poisson counting measure with stationary and independent increments (see, e.g., Protter, 1995). Write

$$\begin{aligned} dX_t &= \left[\mu(X_{t-}) - \lambda(X_{t-}) \int_Y g(X_{t-}, y)\Gamma(dy) \right] dt + \sigma(X_{t-})dB_t + dJ_t \\ &= [\mu(X_{t-}) - \lambda(X_{t-})\mathbf{E}_Y[g(X_{t-}, y)]]\, dt + \sigma(X_{t-})dB_t + dJ_t, \end{aligned} \tag{4.3}$$

where the standard Brownian motion $\{B_t : t \geq 0\}$ and the jump process $\{J_t : t \geq 0\}$ are assumed to be independent. The initial condition $X_0 = \overline{X}$ belongs to L^2 and is taken to be independent of both B_t and J_t.

The functions $\mu(.)$ and $\sigma(.)$ have a similar interpretation as in scalar diffusion models (cf., Section 3). Nonetheless, because of the presence of a discontinuous jump-component $dJ_t = \Delta X_t$, the sample path of X_t fails to be continuous in the state space as in the case of standard SDPs despite being right continuous with left limits (*càdlàg*).

Conditions 6 through 9 (or 6 through 10) below are imposed on the model (Bandi and Nguyen, 2003).

(6) *The functions $\mu(.)$, $\sigma(.)$, $g(., y)$, and $\lambda(.)$ are time-homogeneous and $\mathfrak{B}$-measurable on $\mathfrak{D} = (l, u)$ with $-\infty \leq l < u \leq \infty$, where $\mathfrak{B}$ is the σ-field generated by Borel sets on $\mathfrak{D}$. They satisfy local Lipschitz and growth conditions. Thus, for every compact subset J of the domain of the process, there exist constants C_1 and C_2 so that, for all x and z in J,*

$$|\mu(x) - \mu(z)| + |\sigma(x) - \sigma(z)| + \lambda(x) \int_Y |g(x, y) - g(z, y)|\Gamma(dy) \leq C_1|x - z|, \tag{4.4}$$

and

$$|\mu(x)| + |\sigma(x)| + \lambda(x) \int_Y |g(x, y)|\Gamma(dy) \leq C_2\{1 + |x|\}. \tag{4.5}$$

(7) *For a given $\alpha > 2$, there exists a constant C_3 such that*

$$\lambda(x) \int_Y |g(x, y)|^{\alpha}\Gamma(dy) \leq C_3\{1 + |x|^{\alpha}\}. \tag{4.6}$$

(8) *$\lambda(.) > 0$ and $\sigma^2(.) > 0$ on $\mathfrak{D}$.*

(9) *(Null recurrence) Define the second-order elliptic operator $\mathfrak{L}$ and the integro-differential operator $\mathfrak{A}$ of the continuous and discontinuous portions of the solution to (4.3) above as*

$$\mathfrak{L}\varphi(.) = \varphi'(.)\mu(.) + \frac{1}{2}\varphi''(.)\sigma^2(.) \tag{4.7}$$

and

$$\mathfrak{A}\varphi(.) = \lambda(.) \int_Y \left[\varphi(. + g(., y)) - \varphi(.) - \varphi'(.)g(., y)\right] \Gamma(dy), \tag{4.8}$$

respectively. Assume Φ is a Borel measurable and bounded function on the closure $\overline{A}$. The exterior Dirichlet problem, i.e.,

$$(\mathfrak{L}+\mathfrak{A})e = 0 \quad a.e. \quad in\ \mathfrak{D}\setminus\overline{A} \tag{4.9}$$

$$e = \Phi \quad a.e. \quad in\ \overline{A} \tag{4.10}$$

admits a unique bounded solution e (see, e.g., Menaldi and Robin, 1999).

(10) *(Positive recurrence) Assume f is a Borel measurable and bounded function on $\mathfrak{D}\setminus\overline{A}$. The exterior Dirichlet problem, i.e.,*

$$-(\mathfrak{L}+\mathfrak{A})e = f \quad a.e. \quad in\ \mathfrak{D}\setminus\overline{A} \tag{4.11}$$

$$e = 0 \quad a.e. \quad in\ \overline{A} \tag{4.12}$$

admits a unique bounded solution e (see, e.g., Menaldi and Robin, 1999).

Under Assumptions 6 through 9 (10), the SJDP (4.3) has a strong solution which is unique and null recurrent (positive recurrent). In particular, the càdlàg process X_t satisfies

$$X_t = \overline{X} + \int_0^t \mu(X_{s-})\mathrm{d}s + \int_0^t \sigma(X_{s-})\mathrm{d}B_s + \int_{0+}^t\int_Y g(X_{s-},y)\overline{\nu}(\mathrm{d}s,\mathrm{d}y) \tag{4.13}$$

where

$$\overline{\nu}(\mathrm{d}s,\mathrm{d}y) = N(\mathrm{d}s,\mathrm{d}y) - \nu(X_{s-},\mathrm{d}y)\mathrm{d}s \tag{4.14}$$

$$= N(\mathrm{d}s,\mathrm{d}y) - \lambda(X_{s-})\Gamma(\mathrm{d}y)\mathrm{d}s \tag{4.15}$$

is a compensated random measure, and the notation $\int_{0+}^t = \int_{(0,t]}$ denotes the integral over the half open interval. It is noted that

$$\int_{0+}^t\int_Y g(X_{s-},y)\overline{\nu}(\mathrm{d}s,\mathrm{d}y) \tag{4.16}$$

represents the conditional variation between $0+$ and t in the path of the process due to discontinuous jumps of random size y (with impact $g(.,y)$) net of its expected conditional magnitude at $0+$. The model is defined as "compensated" by virtue of the presence of the term $\lambda(X_t)\mathbf{E}_Y[g(X_t,y)]$ denoting the conditional mean of the jump part. Its presence ensures that the jump component is a martingale, thereby making the solution to Eq. (4.3) a semimartingale. The semimartingale property, which is trivially satisfied by standard SDPs of the types analyzed earlier, makes SJDPs of the kind reviewed here attractive for modeling purposes in continuous-time finance. As is well known, in the case of price processes, this property implies the existence of an equivalent martingale measure under which the process is a (local) martingale and absence of arbitrage in the spaces that preclude doubling strategies (Duffie, 1996).

Given Assumptions 6 through 8, the infinitesimal conditional moments of the changes in the solution to (4.3) above can be written in terms of the functions $\mu(.),\sigma(.),g(.,.)$, and $\lambda(.)$ (Gikhman and Skorohod, 1972), i.e.,

$$M^1(a) = \lim_{t\to 0} \frac{1}{t}\mathbf{E}^a[X_t - a] = \mu(a), \tag{4.17}$$

$$M^2(a) = \lim_{t\to 0} \frac{1}{t}\mathbf{E}[(X_t - a)^2] = \sigma^2(a) + \lambda(a)\mathbf{E}_Y[g^2(a, y)], \tag{4.18}$$

$$M^k(a) = \lim_{t\to 0} \frac{1}{t}\mathbf{E}[(X_t - a)^k] = \lambda(a)\mathbf{E}_Y[g^k(a, y)] \ \forall k > 2, \tag{4.19}$$

for a generic $a \in \mathfrak{D}$. Specifically, formulae (4.17) through (4.19) suggest that the conditional infinitesimal moments of order higher than two contain important information about the intensity of the jumps and the distribution of the jump component. These moments are of course zero in the case of SDPs. Similarly to the case of SDPs, however, the first and second infinitesimal moments may be used to identify the drift and the diffusive volatility (given the estimated features of the jumps). These observations led Johannes (2004) to suggest nonparametric estimates of the infinitesimal moments and a procedure to extract the parameters and functions of interest from the estimated moments. We will be more accurate in the sequel. For now it suffices to point out that the $M^k(.)$s (for $k \geq 1$) will be our object of econometric interest.

We now turn to generalized density estimation for processes that are possibly nonstationary solutions to stochastic differential equations with infrequent jumps such as (4.3) above.

4.1. Generalized Density Estimation for SJDPs

The theory of local times for càdlàg semimartingales is well established in the stochastic process literature. We refer the reader to Protter (1995) for a thorough treatment. Here, consonant with our discussion in Section 3, we review some basic notions that will serve the purpose of illustrating the role that estimated local time may play as a descriptive tool for recurrent SJDPs. Assume X_t is a càdlàg semimartingale, then its sojourn time at T and a can be written as

$$L_X(T, a) = \lim_{\varepsilon\to 0} \frac{1}{\varepsilon} \int_0^T \mathbf{1}_{[a,a+\varepsilon[}(X_s)d[X]_s^c, \tag{4.20}$$

where $[X]_t^c$ is the continuous part of the quadratic variation process of X_t, namely the nondecreasing process defined as

$$[X]_t^c = [X]_t - \sum_{0<s\leq t} (\Delta X_s)^2 - X_0^2 \tag{4.21}$$

$$= [X]_t - \sum_{0\leq s\leq t} (\Delta X_s)^2 \tag{4.22}$$

with

$$[X]_0^c = 0 \tag{4.23}$$

(see, e.g., Yor, 1978). The interpretation is standard. Formula (4.20) represents the amount of time, in information units, that the càdlàg semimartingale spends in an arbitrarily small right neighborhood of a between time 0 and time T. Differently put, local time is an occupation density relative to the random clock $\mathrm{d}[X]_s^c$.

A corresponding notion in calendar units can be easily obtained after noticing that $\mathrm{d}[X]_t^c = \sigma^2(X_{t-})\mathrm{d}t$ in the presence of a process whose dynamics are driven by (4.3) above. In fact,

$$\overline{L}_X(T,a) = \frac{1}{\sigma^2(a)} L_X(T,a) \tag{4.24}$$

is the chronological counterpart to (4.20) for SJDPs of the type analyzed here. As in the case of standard SDPs, the chronological sojourn time (4.24) can be interpreted as a version of the Radon–Nikodym derivative of the occupation measure with respect to the Lebesgue measure, i.e.,

$$\eta_A^T = \int_0^T \mathbf{1}_{\{X_s \in A\}} \mathrm{d}s = \int_A \overline{L}_X(T,a)\mathrm{d}a, \quad \forall A \subset \mathfrak{B}(\mathfrak{D}), \tag{4.25}$$

and, as pointed out above, is an occupation density. Additionally, formula (4.25) readily leads to

$$[X]_t^c = \int_{-\infty}^{\infty} L_X(t,a)\mathrm{d}a, \tag{4.26}$$

which can be interpreted as a decomposition of variance [cf., (3.16)], coherently with our remarks in Section 3.

We now turn to estimation. As earlier when dealing with SDPs, there is a natural way to identify (4.24) using a sample of observations generated from (4.3), namely we can perform density-like kernel estimation as in (3.21). We proceed under the same sampling scheme as in Section 2.

Theorem 10 *Assume X_t is the solution to (4.3). If $h_{n,\overline{T}} \to 0$ as $n \to \infty$ with $T = \overline{T}$ in such a way as to guarantee that $\frac{1}{h_{n,\overline{T}}}(\Delta_{n,\overline{T}} \log(1/\Delta_{n,\overline{T}})^{1/2} = o(1)$, then*

$$\widehat{\overline{L}}_X(\overline{T},a) = \frac{\Delta_{n,\overline{T}}}{h_{n,\overline{T}}} \sum_{i=1}^{n} \mathbf{K}\left(\frac{X_{i\Delta_{n,\overline{T}}} - a}{h_{n,\overline{T}}}\right) \stackrel{a.s.}{\to} \overline{L}_X(\overline{T},a) \quad \forall a \in \mathfrak{D}. \tag{4.27}$$

Proof See Bandi and Nguyen (2003).

Coherently with Theorem 1 in Section 3, Theorem 10 justifies using density-like kernel estimates as descriptive tools for SJDPs even in the presence of processes which might not possess a time-invariant stationary distribution. All we need to do is modify their interpretation because, in general, they cannot be regarded as estimates of the stationary density of the process and recognize instead the role played by local time in characterizing the locational features of the process.

We conclude this subsection with two observations. First, recurrence implies divergence of the local time process as $T \to \infty$, just as when dealing with standard SDPs. In general, the rate of divergence cannot be quantified, although we expect positive recurrent and stationary processes to have local times that diverge at the fastest rate T. As in the case of the estimation of the infinitesimal moments of an SDP, the divergence properties of the local time factor affect the convergence properties of the infinitesimal moment estimators of (4.3) above, as shown in the next subsection. Second, functions of spatial densities, such as spatial hazard rates, can be readily defined as in Section 3. The intuition is immediate and follows from our discussion in the previous section. We do not dwell on it here.

4.2. NW Kernel Estimation of the Infinitesimal Moments of an SJDP

As pointed out earlier, identification of a recurrent solution to (4.3) above essentially entails estimation of four quantities: the drift $\mu(.)$, the diffusive variance $\sigma^2(.)$, the intensity of a jump $\lambda(.)$, and the distribution of the jump component. Importantly, such quantities can be identified from the estimated infinitesimal moments, as we show below by virtue of two examples.

To this extent, we first turn to infinitesimal moment estimation by virtue of NW kernel estimates. Assume the same sampling mechanism as in Section 2 is adopted and write

$$\widehat{M}^k_{(n,T)}(a) = \frac{1}{\Delta_{n,T}} \frac{\sum_{i=1}^{n-1} \mathbf{K}\left(\frac{X_{i\Delta_{n,T}}-a}{h_{n,T}}\right)\left(X_{(i+1)\Delta_{n,T}} - X_{i\Delta_{n,T}}\right)^k}{\sum_{i=1}^{n} \mathbf{K}\left(\frac{X_{i\Delta_{n,T}}-a}{h_{n,T}}\right)}, \tag{4.28}$$

$\forall k \geq 1$, where $\mathbf{K}(.)$ is a kernel function satisfying the assumptions in Section 2. The limiting properties of $\widehat{M}^k_{(n,T)}(a)$ are laid out in Theorem 11.

Theorem 11 *Assume X_t is the solution to (4.3). If $n \to \infty$, $T \to \infty$, $\frac{T}{n} \to 0$, and $h_{n,T} \to 0$ so that $\frac{\overline{L}_X(T,a)}{h_{n,T}}(\Delta_{n,T}\log(1/\Delta_{n,T}))^{1/2} = o_{a.s.}(1)$ and $h_{n,T}\overline{L}_X(T,a) \stackrel{a.s.}{\to} \infty$, then*

$$\widehat{M}^k_{(n,T)}(a) \stackrel{a.s.}{\to} M^k(a) \quad \forall k \geq 1. \tag{4.29}$$

Furthermore, if $h^5_{n,T}\overline{L}_X(T,a) = O_{a.s.}(1)$, then

$$\sqrt{h_{n,T}\widehat{\overline{L}}_X(T,a)}\left(\widehat{M}^k_{(n,T)}(a) - M^k(a) - \Gamma_{M^k}(a)\right) \Rightarrow \mathbf{N}\left(0, \mathbf{K}_2 M^{2k}(a)\right), \tag{4.30}$$

$\forall k \geq 1$, *where*

$$\Gamma_{M^k}(a) = h_{n,T}^2 \mathbf{K}_1 \left(\left(M^k(a) \right)' \frac{m'(a)}{m(a)} + \frac{1}{2} \left(M^k(a) \right)'' \right) \quad \forall k \geq 1, \tag{4.31}$$

and $m(\mathrm{d}x) = m(x)\mathrm{d}x$ *is the invariant measure of the process.*

Proof See Bandi and Nguyen (2003).

By virtue of our discussion in the case of SDPs, the implications of Theorem 11 should be clear. Here, we focus on the main differences between the case with discontinuities and the case without discontinuities examined in the previous section. Contrary to diffusion estimation, all the infinitesimal moment estimators converge at the same rate, namely $\sqrt{h_{n,T}\widehat{\overline{L}}_X(T,a)}$. The intuition is as follows. The family of estimators in (4.28) above hinges on averages of terms of probability order $\sqrt{dt}$ for every $k \geq 1$. In the case of standard SDPs, the drift estimator (3.35) is an average of terms of order $\sqrt{\mathrm{d}t}$, whereas the diffusion estimator (3.36) averages terms of order $\mathrm{d}t$, leading to a faster rate of convergence. Apparently, no infinitesimal moment can be identified over a fixed span of data in the presence of an underlying SJDP. If T were fixed, then $\widehat{\overline{L}}_X(T,a)$ would be bounded in probability and $\sqrt{h_{n,T}}$ would not be a proper convergence rate. Again, the intuition is simple. In jump-diffusion models like (4.3) above, the function $\mu(.)$ has the same interpretation as in the standard setup without jumps. As a consequence, an enlarging span of data is expected to be necessary for the consistency of $\widehat{M}^1_{(n,T)}(.)$. As for the higher moments, formulae (4.18) and (4.19) illustrate their dependence on the characteristics of the discontinuous jump component. A fixed span of data cannot possibly contain sufficient information for the identification of the features of infrequent Poisson jumps because the number of jumps of this type on any fixed time span is finite with probability one.

We now turn to the identification of the functions and parameters of interest by virtue of two examples.

Example 6 *Assume* $g(x,y) = y$, *where* y *is normally distributed with mean* 0 *and variance* σ_y^2. *In other words,* $\mathrm{d}J_t = y\mathrm{d}N_t$, *with* $y \sim N(0, \sigma_y^2)$. *Then, we can rewrite (4.17), (4.18), and (4.19) with* $k = 1, 2, 4,$ *and* 6 *as*

$$M^1(a) = \mu(a), \tag{4.32}$$

$$M^2(a) = \sigma^2(a) + \lambda(a)\sigma_y^2, \tag{4.33}$$

$$M^4(a) = 3\lambda(a)\left(\sigma_y^2\right)^2, \tag{4.34}$$

$$M^6(a) = 15\lambda(a)\left(\sigma_y^2\right)^3, \tag{4.35}$$

$\forall a \in \mathfrak{D}$. Given (4.32) through (4.35), Johannes (2004) suggested the following identification scheme:

$$\left(\widehat{\sigma}_Y^2\right)_{(n,T)} = \frac{1}{n}\sum_{i-1}^{n} \frac{\widehat{M}^6_{(n,T)}(X_{i\Delta_{n,T}})}{5\widehat{M}^4_{(n,T)}(X_{i\Delta_{n,T}})}, \tag{4.36}$$

$$\widehat{\lambda}_{(n,T)}(a) = \frac{\widehat{M}^4_{(n,T)}(a)}{3\left(\widehat{\sigma}_Y^4\right)_{(n,T)}}, \tag{4.37}$$

$$\widehat{\sigma}^2_{(n,T)}(a) = \widehat{M}^2_{(n,T)}(a) - \widehat{\lambda}_{(n,T)}(a)\left(\widehat{\sigma}_Y^2\right)_{(n,T)}, \tag{4.38}$$

$$\widehat{\mu}_{(n,T)}(a) = \widehat{M}^1_{(n,T)}(a). \tag{4.39}$$

This simple scheme was successfully applied to the analysis of the continuous-time dynamics of the short end of the term structure of interest rates (Johannes, 2004). For an interesting, alternative approach to identification in this class of discontinuous processes, we refer the reader to Mancini and Renò (2006).

Example 7 *Assume $g(x, y) = y$, where y is exponentially distributed with mean β. In other words, $\mathrm{d}J_t = y\mathrm{d}N_t$, with $y \sim \exp(\beta)$. Also, assume the process X_t is not compensated, thereby implying that the first infinitesimal moment also contains a component equal to the first conditional moment of the jump part. We can thus rewrite (4.17), (4.18), and (4.19) with $k = 1$, 2, 3, and 4 as*

$$M^1(a) = \mu(a) + \lambda(a)\beta, \tag{4.40}$$

$$M^2(a) = \sigma^2(a) + 2\lambda(a)\beta^2, \tag{4.41}$$

$$M^3(a) = 6\lambda(a)\beta^3, \tag{4.42}$$

$$M^4(a) = 24\lambda(a)\beta^4, \tag{4.43}$$

$\forall a \in \mathfrak{D}$. Given (4.40) through (4.43), Bandi and Renò (2008) suggested the following identification scheme:

$$\widehat{\beta}_{(n,T)} = \frac{1}{n}\sum_{i=1}^{n} \frac{\widehat{M}^4_{(n,T)}(X_{i\Delta_{n,T}})}{4\widehat{M}^3_{(n,T)}(X_{i\Delta_{n,T}})}, \tag{4.44}$$

$$\widehat{\lambda}_{(n,T)}(a) = \frac{\widehat{M}^4_{(n,T)}(a)}{24\widehat{\beta}^4_{(n,T)}}, \tag{4.45}$$

$$\widehat{\sigma}^2_{(n,T)}(a) = \widehat{M}^2_{(n,T)}(a) - 2\widehat{\lambda}_{(n,T)}(a)\widehat{\beta}^2_{(n,T)}, \tag{4.46}$$

$$\widehat{\mu}_{(n,T)}(a) = \widehat{M}^1_{(n,T)}(a) - \widehat{\lambda}_{(n,T)}(a)\widehat{\beta}_{(n,T)}. \tag{4.47}$$

Given preliminary spot variance estimates (as in Subsection 3.6 above, for instance), Bandi and Renò (2008) apply this scheme to the analysis of the continuous-time dynamics of the spot variance process. We will follow their treatment in the empirical application below.

Some observations are in order. First, reasonable parametric assumptions on the jump component are necessary for identification. Although the identification methods in the examples above have been shown to be empirically successful in a variety of contexts in continuous-time finance, more involved (and potentially more efficient) methodologies making use of alternative moments may have been suggested instead. This said, any sensible identification scheme entails averages of nonparametric estimates for the purpose of the estimation of the model's parameters [cf., (4.36) and (4.44) above]. Hence, although the estimates of the functions of interest [namely $\mu(.)$, $\sigma^2(.)$, and $\lambda(.)$] converge at the nonparametric rate $\sqrt{h_{n,T}\widehat{\overline{L}}_X(T,a)}$ (by a simple application of the delta method), the parameter estimates $\widehat{\sigma}_y^2$ and $\widehat{\beta}$ converge at a faster rate. Differently put, although causing a loss in terms of generality of the model, the important (for identification) imposition of parametric assumptions is, not surprisingly, beneficial for estimation (Bandi and Renò, 2008). Second, the methodology is flexible. Alternative parametric assumptions could have been imposed. Obviously, the functions $\mu(.)$, $\sigma^2(.)$, and $\lambda(.)$ are left fairly unrestricted, thereby allowing for nonlinearities which, as shown below, might prove useful in continuous-time finance modeling.

4.3. An Empirical Application: Stochastic Volatility

The estimation scheme in Eq. (4.44) through (4.47) has been applied by Bandi and Renò (2008) to identify the features of exponential jumps in spot variance while allowing drift, diffusive variance, and intensity of the jumps to be nonlinear functions of the state. Here, we consider two-scale estimates of spot market variance relying on SPY data (for the period between January 2, 1998, and March 31, 2006), as in Subsection 3.6. In addition to drift and diffusive variance, Fig. 3.2 reports the probability of the exponential jumps (expressed in terms of the number of annual jumps per variance level) and the (constant) expected jump size.[14] For all plots, we display the parametric estimates (dotted lines) reported in Eraker et al. (2003) for a model with linear drift ($\mu(a) = c_0 + c_1 a$), square-root volatility ($\sigma^2(a) = c_3 a$), and constant jump intensity ($\lambda(a) = c_4$) – cf., Eraker et al., 2003, Table III. As indicated in Subsection 3.6, allowing for jumps reduces the magnitude of the estimated drift and diffusion vis-à-vis the SDP case reported earlier. The functional drift implies a bit more mean-reversion than the parametric model. The nonparametric diffusive function suggests more variability associated with the continuous component of the process than in the parametric specification of Eraker et al. (2003).

[14] The form of the corresponding asymptotic bands is derived in Bandi and Renò, 2008.

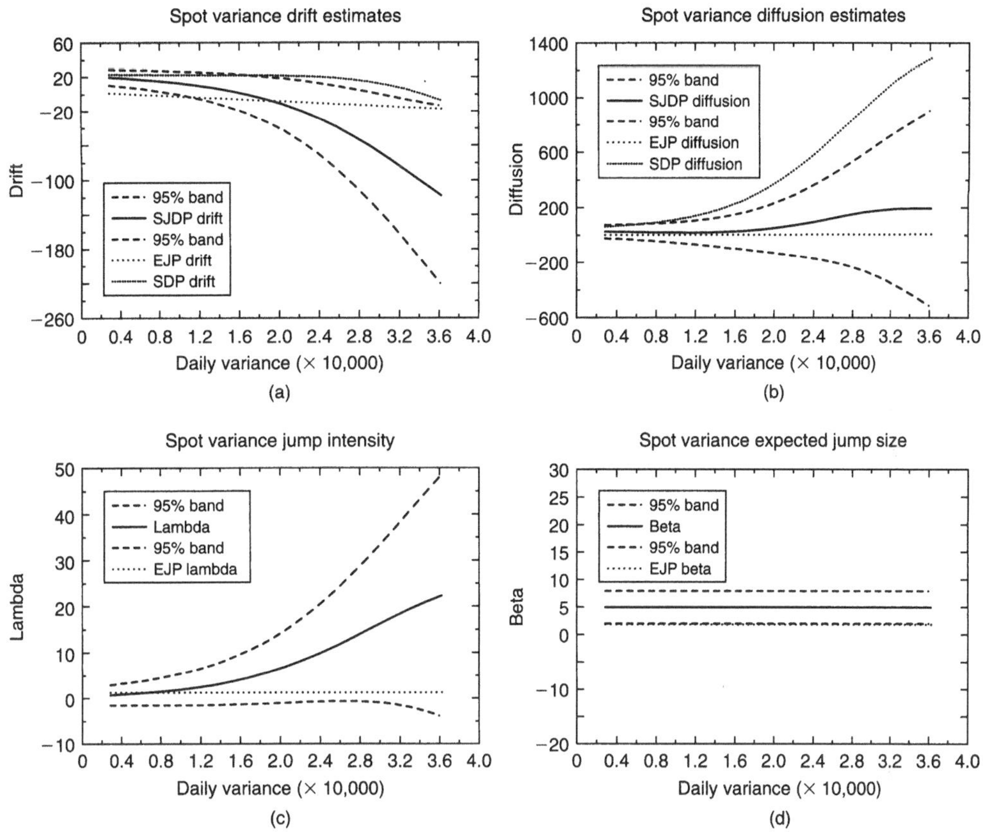

Figure 3.2 Drift, diffusion, jump intensity, and expected jump size estimates of an SJDP for stochastic volatility.

Although this difference may be visually small and is statistically insignificant, model diagnostics reported in Bandi and Renò (2008) indicate that it is important. In the more informative, empirical range of the process (as highlighted by the local time estimates in Fig. 3.1a), the average annual number of jumps is about 1, which is consistent with the parametric model. The expected jump size is about 5 with the parametric estimate (about 1.8) within the 95% asymptotic bands. Importantly, the obtained value for the expected jump size may be influenced by spot variance estimates (constructed using the two-scale estimator) which are affected by the presence of jumps in the market return process. The use of spot variance estimates robust to discontinuities in market returns would yield an expected jump size of about 2 and roughly unchanged jump intensities (Bandi and Renò, 2008). These values would therefore lend some support to the variance jump sizes and the frequency of jumps obtained by Eraker et al. (2003) by virtue of (i) a fully parametric model allowing for jumps in returns and (ii) a more classical volatility-filtering method relying on MCMC methods (for a discussion of MCMC methods in finance, see Johannes and Polson, 2010, in this volume).

5. MULTIVARIATE DIFFUSION PROCESSES

In this section, we focus on a vector process X_t expressed as the d-dimensional solution of the multivariate stochastic differential equation

$$\mathrm{d}X_t = \boldsymbol{\mu}(X_t)\,\mathrm{d}t + \boldsymbol{\sigma}(X_t)\,\mathrm{d}\mathbf{B}_s, \tag{5.1}$$

where $\mathbf{B} = \left\{\mathbf{B}_t, \Im_t^B; 0 \le t < \infty\right\}$ is an m-dimensional standard Brownian motion, $\boldsymbol{\mu}(.) = \{\mu_i(.)\}_{1\le i\le d}$ is a $d \times 1$ Borel measurable vector, $\boldsymbol{\sigma}(.) = \left\{\sigma_{ij}(.)\right\}_{\substack{1\le i\le d\\1\le j\le m}}$ is a $d \times m$ Borel measurable matrix, and $X_0 = \overline{X} \in \mathfrak{D} \subseteq \mathfrak{R}^d$ is a given initial condition taken to be independent of $\Im_\infty^B$ and with finite second moment, i.e., $\mathbf{E}||\overline{X}|| < \infty$. Define the left-continuous filtration

$$\overline{\Im}_t := \sigma(\overline{X}) \vee \Im_t^B = \sigma(\overline{X}, \mathbf{B}_s; 0 \le s \le t) \quad 0 \le t < \infty \tag{5.2}$$

and the collection of null sets

$$\aleph := \{N \subseteq \Omega; \exists G \in \overline{\Im}_\infty \text{ with } N \subseteq G \text{ and } P(G) = 0\}. \tag{5.3}$$

Now create the augmented filtration

$$\widetilde{\Im}_t^X := \sigma(\overline{\Im}_t \cup \aleph) \quad 0 \le t < \infty. \tag{5.4}$$

Assumptions 11 through 12 (11 and 13) below are imposed on (5.1) to guarantee the existence of a unique and null recurrent (positive recurrent) solution to (5.1).

(11) *$\boldsymbol{\mu}(.)$ and $\boldsymbol{\sigma}(.)$ are time-homogeneous, $\mathfrak{B}$-measurable functions on $\mathfrak{D} \subseteq \mathfrak{R}^d$ where $\mathfrak{B}$ is the σ-field generated by Borel sets on $\mathfrak{D}$. Both functions satisfy local Lipschitz and linear growth conditions. Thus, for every compact subset J of the range of the process, there exist constants C_1 and C_2 such that, for all x and y in J,*

$$||\boldsymbol{\mu}(x) - \boldsymbol{\mu}(y)|| + ||\boldsymbol{\sigma}(x) - \boldsymbol{\sigma}(y)|| \le C_1||x - y|| \tag{5.5}$$

and

$$||\boldsymbol{\mu}(x)|| + ||\boldsymbol{\sigma}(x)|| \le C_2\{1 + ||x||\}, \tag{5.6}$$

where $||\sigma|| = \sum_{i=1}^d \sum_{j=1}^m \sigma_{ij}^2$ and $||\mu|| = \sum_{i=1}^d \mu_i^2$.

(12) *(Null recurrence) Define the positive definite matrix* $\mathbf{s}(x) = \boldsymbol{\sigma}(x)\boldsymbol{\sigma}(x)^{\top}$ *so that* $s_{ik}(x) = \sum_{g=1}^{m} \sigma_{ig}(x)\sigma_{gk}(x)\ \forall x \subset \mathfrak{D} \subseteq \mathfrak{R}^d$ *and assume that every open and bounded set* $A \in \mathfrak{D}$ *satisfies*

$$\min_{x \in \overline{A}} s_{ii}(x) > 0, \tag{5.7}$$

for some $1 \leq i \leq d$. *Write the second-order elliptic operator*

$$\mathfrak{L}\varphi(.) = \sum_{i=1}^{d} \mu_i(.)\frac{\partial\varphi(.)}{\partial x_i} + \frac{1}{2}\sum_{i=1}^{d}\sum_{k=1}^{d} s_{ik}(.)\frac{\partial\varphi(.)}{\partial x_i \partial x_k}. \tag{5.8}$$

There is a function $\varphi(.) : \mathfrak{R}^d \backslash \{0\} \rightarrow \mathfrak{R}$ *of class* C^2 *in the domain of the operator which satisfies*

$$\mathfrak{L}\varphi(.) \leq 0 \quad \text{on} \quad \mathfrak{R}^d \backslash \{0\} \tag{5.9}$$

and is so that $\Psi(r) := \min_{||x||=r} \varphi(.)$ *is strictly increasing with* $\lim_{r\to\infty} \Psi(r) = \infty$ *(Karatzas and Shreve, 1991, Exercise 7.13, part (i), p. 370).*

(13) *(Positive recurrence) There is a function* $\varphi(.) : \mathfrak{R}^d \backslash \{0\} \rightarrow \mathfrak{R}$ *of class* C^2 *in the domain of the operator which satisfies*

$$\mathfrak{L}\varphi(.) \leq -1 \quad \text{on} \quad \mathfrak{R}^d \backslash \{0\} \tag{5.10}$$

and is so that $\Psi(r) := \min_{||x||=r} \varphi(.)$ *is strictly increasing with* $\lim_{r\to\infty} \Psi(r) = \infty$ *(Karatzas and Shreve, 1991, Exercise 7.13, part (iii), p. 371).*

Under Assumptions 11 through 12 (11 and 13), the stochastic differential equation (5.1) has a strong solution X_t which is unique and null recurrent (positive recurrent). Specifically, the process X_t satisfies

$$X_t = \overline{X} + \int_0^t \boldsymbol{\mu}(X_s)\,\mathrm{d}s + \int_0^t \boldsymbol{\sigma}(X_s)\,\mathrm{d}\mathbf{B}_s \tag{5.11}$$

and is square integrable, i.e., $\mathbf{E}||X_t||^2 < \infty \quad \forall t$. Equivalently, we can write each coordinate X_t^j as

$$X_t^j = \overline{X}^j + \int_0^t \mu_j(X_s)\,\mathrm{d}s + \sum_{g=1}^{m}\int_0^t \sigma_{jg}(X_s)\,\mathrm{d}B_s^g, \quad 0 \leq t < \infty, 1 \leq j \leq d. \tag{5.12}$$

In agreement with the scalar model in Section 3, the dynamics of X_t are driven by Brownian shocks and determined by the functional forms of the matrices $\boldsymbol{\mu}(.)$ and $\mathbf{s}(.)$

(recall from Assumption 12 above that $\mathbf{s}(x) = \boldsymbol{\sigma}(x)\boldsymbol{\sigma}(x)^{\top}$). Such matrices will be the object of econometric interest in the present section. As in the scalar case, they both have straightforward representations in terms of infinitesimal conditional moments. In particular,

$$\mathbf{E}^a\left[X_t^i - a_i\right] = t\mu_i(a) + o(t) \tag{5.13}$$

$$\mathbf{E}^a\left[\left(X_t^i - a_i\right)\left(X_t^j - a_j\right)\right] = ts_{ij}(a) + o(t) \tag{5.14}$$

as $t \downarrow 0$ (see, e.g., Karatzas and Shreve, 1991).

The notions of recurrence implied by Assumptions 12 and 13 are standard (cf., Section 2). Namely, the multidimensional process X_t is Harris recurrent if there is a σ−finite measure $m(dx)$ so that $m(A) > 0$ implies $\lim_{T\to\infty} \eta_A^T = \infty$ with probability one $\forall A \subset \mathfrak{B}(\mathfrak{D})$, where $\eta_A^T = \int_0^T \mathbf{1}_{\{X_s \in A\}} ds$ is, as earlier, the occupation measure of A. The following result gives us the (implicit) rate at which η_A^T diverges to infinity and a weak convergence result for η_A^T.

Theorem 12 *Assume X_t is the solution to (5.1) above.*[15] *Consider a nonnegative function $\delta(.)$. If there exists a constant $\alpha \subset [0, 1]$ and a slowly varying function at infinity $L(T)$ such that*

$$\lim_{T\to\infty} \mathbf{E}^a\left[\int_0^\infty e^{-\frac{s}{T}}\delta(X_s)ds\right]/(T^\alpha L(T)) = C_X > 0 \quad \forall a \in \mathfrak{D}, \tag{5.15}$$

then

$$\lim_{T\to\infty} P^a\left\{\frac{1}{C_X(T^\alpha L(T))}\int_0^T \delta(X_s)ds < x\right\} = G_\alpha(x), \tag{5.16}$$

where

$$G_\alpha(x) = \frac{1}{\pi\alpha}\int_0^x \sum_{j=1}^\infty \frac{(-1)^{j-1}}{j!}\sin(\pi\alpha j)\,\Gamma(\alpha j + 1)y^{j-1}dy, \tag{5.17}$$

$\Gamma(.)$ is the Gamma function, $C_X = C_X^* \int_{-\infty}^\infty \delta(x)m(dx)$, $m(dx)$ is the invariant measure, and C_X^* is a process-specific constant.

Proof See Darling and Kac (1957) for the original statement of the theorem. Bingham (1971) contains a functional version of the same finding. Several papers discuss limit results for slowly increasing occupation times associated with null-recurrent Markov processes, see Höpfner and Löcherbach (2001) for a complete, recent survey of the literature on

[15] The theorem, in its form stated here, applies to more general continuous-time Markov processes than MDPs (Darling and Kac, 1957).

the subject. The interested reader is referred to Khasminskii (2001) and Khasminskii and Yin (2000) for a detailed treatment of the one-dimensional null-recurrent diffusion case.

We can rewrite (5.16) as follows:

$$\frac{\int_0^T \delta(X_s)\mathrm{d}s}{C_X u(T)} \Rightarrow g_\alpha, \tag{5.18}$$

where g_α is the Mittag–Leffler density with parameter α, [16] i.e.,

$$g_\alpha(x) = \frac{1}{\pi\alpha}\sum_{j=1}^{\infty}\frac{(-1)^{j-1}}{j!}\sin(\pi\alpha j)\Gamma(\alpha j+1)x^{j-1}, \tag{5.19}$$

and $u(T) = T^\alpha L(T)$. Theorem 12 shows that additive functionals of the process ($\int_0^T \delta(X_s)\mathrm{d}s$) converge weakly to a random variable endowed with the Mittag–Leffler density g_α when standardized appropriately (by $u(T)$). The rate of divergence to infinity of the standardizing factor (and, as a consequence, the rate of divergence to infinity of the continuous averages) depends on the statistical features of the process through the constant α. Clearly, α defines the nature of the Mittag–Leffler density as well.

Some observations are in order. First, the theorem readily applies to the occupation measures because we can take $\delta(.) = \mathbf{1}_A$ (the characteristic function of the generic set A) giving $\int_0^T \delta(X_s)\mathrm{d}s = \eta_A^T\ \forall A \subset \mathfrak{B}(\mathfrak{D})$. Second, it extends to a large class of continuous-time Harris recurrent Markov processes, provided assumption (5.15) is satisfied (Darling and Kac, 1957). In general, we can apply it to SDPs and SDJPs of the type analyzed in the present review. Importantly, its implications appear to be particularly interesting when studying processes for which a standard notion of local time cannot be defined, as is the case with multivariate diffusions, for example. We do not dwell on this idea here (and refer the reader to Bandi and Moloche, 2004), but the meaning of the statement will become clear in the next subsection.

We now briefly consider some interesting special cases. We noticed earlier that the characteristics of the underlying recurrent process affect the weak convergence result through the constant α which modifies both the rate of divergence of the occupation measure and the resulting limiting distribution. This constant is known only for a few processes. Specifically, if X_t is Brownian motion on the plane, then $\alpha = 0$ and the Mittag–Leffler distribution coincides with the exponential distribution, i.e.,

$$\frac{\int_0^T \delta(X_s)\mathrm{d}s}{C_X \log T} \Rightarrow \mathrm{e}^{-x} \quad x \geq 0. \tag{5.20}$$

[16] We abuse notation somewhat to signify convergence to a limiting random variable endowed with the Mittag–Leffler density.

If X_t is a scalar Brownian motion, then $\alpha = \frac{1}{2}$ and the Mittag–Leffler density is equal to the truncated normal, i.e.,

$$\frac{\int_0^T \delta(X_s)\mathrm{d}s}{C_X\sqrt{T}} \Rightarrow \frac{2}{\sqrt{2\pi}}\mathrm{e}^{-x^2/2} \quad x \geq 0, \tag{5.21}$$

implying, importantly, that the dimensionality of the system has, in general, an impact on the rate of divergence of continuous averages of the process. It is noted, in fact, that we go from a $\sqrt{T}$-rate to a $\log T$-rate when moving from the scalar Brownian case to its bivariate counterpart. Importantly, the dimensionality of the process does not influence the rate of divergence of the continuous averages (or the rate of divergence of the occupation measures) if stationarity is satisfied. Under stationarity, $\alpha = 1$ and

$$\frac{\int_0^T \delta(X_s)\mathrm{d}s}{T} \xrightarrow{p} \int_{-\infty}^{\infty} \delta(x) f(\mathrm{d}x), \tag{5.22}$$

where $f(\mathrm{d}x) = f(x)\mathrm{d}x$ is the stationary probability measure of X_t, which is a form of the classical ergodic theorem. We will return to Theorem 12 and its implications in the sequel. We now consider generalized density estimation for multivariate solutions to (5.1).

5.1. Generalized Density Estimation for MDPs

Just as it is natural to estimate multivariate density functions using multidimensional extensions of kernel estimates for scalar densities (see, e.g., Pagan and Ullah, 1999), it might appear natural to estimate the local time of a vector process using a multivariate counterpart of the standard estimator from Section 3, i.e.,

$$\widehat{\mathbb{L}}_{(n,T)}(\overline{T}, a) = \frac{\Delta_{n,\overline{T}}}{\mathbf{h}_{n,\overline{T}}} \sum_{i=1}^{n} \left(\prod_{j=1}^{d} \mathbf{K}\left(\frac{X^j_{i\Delta_{n,\overline{T}}} - a_j}{h_{n,\overline{T}}} \right) \right), \tag{5.23}$$

where $\mathbf{h}_{n,\overline{T}} = h^d_{n,\overline{T}}$ and $a = (a_1, a_2, \ldots, a_d) \in \mathfrak{R}^d$.[17] As it happens, local time is not generally defined for multidimensional semimartingales (see Brugière, 1991, among others). In consequence, we cannot build a notion of (spatial) density for multivariate, potentially nonstationary, continuous-time processes based on local time as suggested in Section 3 for SDPs and in Section 4 for SJDPs. Consistently, over a fixed span of data $\overline{T}$, the quantity $\widehat{\mathbb{L}}_{(n,\overline{T})}(\overline{T}, a)$ cannot be interpreted as a multivariate sojourn time estimator despite

[17] Solely for notational simplicity, to focus on the main ideas, we assume here that all bandwidths are the same (i.e., $h_{n,\overline{T},j} = h_{n,\overline{T}}$ for all j) in which case $\mathbf{h}_{n,\overline{T}} = \prod_{j=1}^{d} h_{n,\overline{T},j} = h^d_{n,\overline{T}}$. It is of course straightforward to extend the framework and allow for process-specific smoothing parameters. We refer the reader to Bandi and Moloche (2004) for discussions.

being a local time estimator for $d = 1$. Nonetheless, its asymptotic features as $n \to \infty$ for a fixed $T = \overline{T}$ can still be characterized. Using a multivariate indicator kernel (but we expect the results not to change in the presence of a continuous kernel function), Brugière (1993) shows that

$$\frac{1}{\mathbf{h}_{n,\overline{T}} \log\left(1/\mathbf{h}^2_{n,\overline{T}}\right)} \widehat{\mathbb{L}}_{(n,\overline{T})}(\overline{T}, a) \tag{5.24}$$

converges weakly (as $n \to \infty$) to an exponentially distributed random variable when the dimension of the system d is equal to two. Furthermore, the quantity

$$\frac{1}{\mathbf{h}_{n,\overline{T}}} \widehat{\mathbb{L}}_{(n,\overline{T})}(\overline{T}, a) \tag{5.25}$$

converges weakly to

$$\int_0^\infty \mathbf{1}_{\{\sigma(0)\mathbf{B}_s < 1\}} ds \tag{5.26}$$

when $d \geq 3$.

Interestingly, although preventing us from constructing appealing descriptive statistics for multidimensional (potentially nonstationary) semimartingales based on (5.23), the nonexistence of a notion of local time is not prohibitive when it comes to dealing with the estimation of the infinitesimal moments of (5.1). This result might at first appear surprising because the local time estimates are known to play a fundamental role in the scalar limit theory for recurrent SDPs and SJDPs. On the other hand, it is well know that simple matrix functionals of multivariate processes, such as the functional $\int_0^t \mathbf{B}(s) \mathbf{B}(s)^\top ds$ of the vector Brownian motion $\mathbf{B}$, are well defined and sample functions converge weakly to them, even though these functionals may not have a representation in terms of local time, as they do from the occupation time formula in the scalar case.

Coherently, we now discuss a finding that is important in building an estimation theory for recurrent, multivariate diffusions without resorting to a notion of local time. The following result, which heavily hinges on Theorem 12 above, characterizes the behavior of $\widehat{\mathbb{L}}_{(n,T)}(T, a)$ over an enlarging span of observations, namely as $T \to \infty$ (with $n \to \infty$). In the next subsection, we will show that the asymptotic behavior of $\widehat{\mathbb{L}}_{(n,T)}(T, a)$ as $T, n \to \infty$ is crucial in interpreting the limit theory of kernel estimates of the infinitesimal moments of the solution to (5.1). We continue to use the sampling scheme that was laid out in Section 2.

Theorem 13 *Assume X_t is the solution to (5.1). If the vanishing bandwidth $h_{n,T}$ satisfies*

$$\frac{(\Delta_{n,T} \log(1/\Delta_{n,T}))^{1/2}}{\mathbf{h}_{n,T}} = o(1), \tag{5.27}$$

as $n, T \to \infty$ *with* $\Delta_{n,T} \to 0$, *then*

$$\frac{\widehat{\widehat{\mathbb{L}}}_{(n,T)}(T,a)}{C_X u(T)} \Rightarrow m(a)\, g_\alpha \quad \forall a \in \mathfrak{D} \subseteq \Re^d \tag{5.28}$$

for some function $u(T) = T^{\alpha}L(T)$, *with* $0 \leq \alpha \leq 1$ *and* $L(T)$ *slowly varying, where* g_α *is the Mittag–Leffler random variable with the same parameter* α, *and* $m(\mathrm{d}x) = m(x)\mathrm{d}x$ *is the invariant measure of the process.* C_X *is a process-specific constant.*

Proof See Bandi and Moloche (2004).

Theorem 13 links the divergence properties of $\widehat{\widehat{\mathbb{L}}}_{(n,T)}(T,a)$ to those of the occupation time measure η_A^T. This result is hardly surprising, being that $\widehat{\widehat{\mathbb{L}}}_{(n,T)}(T,a)$ is an estimate of the time spent by the process in the vicinity of the spatial point a, even though the dimensionality of the system prevents us from interpreting it as a consistent estimate of the local time of the process at a.

Two observations are in order. First, Theorem 13 applies to SDPs of the type analyzed in Section 3. Previously, we pointed out that the local time estimates of stationary processes and standard scalar Brownian motion diverge at rate T and $\sqrt{T}$, respectively. The same result can be deduced from Theorem 13 as a subcase of the more general theory laid out in this section. Second, in the presence of stationary processes of any dimension, $\widehat{\widehat{\mathbb{L}}}_{(n,T)}(T,a)$ represents a well-defined density estimator. In fact, if $\alpha = 1$, then $g_\alpha = 1$ and $C_X = \frac{1}{m(\mathfrak{D})}$. Thus,

$$\frac{\widehat{\widehat{\mathbb{L}}}_{(n,T)}(T,a)}{T} = \frac{1}{n\mathbf{h}_{n,T}} \sum_{i=1}^{n} \left(\prod_{j=1}^{d} \mathbf{K}\left(\frac{X^j_{i\Delta_{n,T}} - a_j}{h_{n,T}} \right) \right) \tag{5.29}$$

converges to $\frac{m(a)}{m(\mathfrak{D})} = f(a)$, which is a standard finding in multivariate density estimation for both discrete and continuous-time stationary processes (see, e.g., Prakasa-Rao, 1983; Silverman, 1986).[18] We now turn to the estimation of the infinitesimal moments.

5.2. NW Kernel Estimation of the Infinitesimal Moments of an MDP

Following our discussion in the previous sections, it is natural to estimate the matrices $\boldsymbol{\mu}(.)$ and $\mathbf{s}(.) = \boldsymbol{\sigma}(.)\boldsymbol{\sigma}(.)^{\top}$ using nonparametric kernel estimates of the NW type, i.e.,

$$\widehat{\boldsymbol{\mu}}_{(n,T)}(a) = \frac{\frac{1}{\Delta_{n,T}} \sum_{i=1}^{n-1} \mathbf{K}_i^a \left(X_{(i+1)\Delta_{n,T}} - X_{i\Delta_{n,T}} \right)}{\sum_{i=1}^{n} \mathbf{K}_i^a} \tag{5.30}$$

[18] For invariant density estimation in the case of multidimensional diffusions, we refer the reader to Bianchi (2007) and Dalalyan and Reiss (2006).

and

$$\widehat{\mathbf{s}}_{(n,T)}(a) = \frac{\frac{1}{\Delta_{n,T}} \sum_{i=1}^{n-1} \mathbf{K}_i^a \left(X_{(i+1)\Delta_{n,T}} - X_{i\Delta_{n,T}}\right) \left(X_{(i+1)\Delta_{n,T}} - X_{i\Delta_{n,T}}\right)^{\mathrm{T}}}{\sum_{i=1}^{n} \mathbf{K}_i^a}, \tag{5.31}$$

where

$$\mathbf{K}_i^a = \prod_{j=1}^{d} \mathbf{K}\left(\frac{X_{i\Delta_{n,T}}^j - a_j}{h_{n,T}}\right). \tag{5.32}$$

As pointed out earlier, the nonexistence of local time for multivariate solutions to (5.1) above does not represent an impossible obstacle when deriving an estimation theory based on (5.30) and (5.31). The intuition relies on the following observations: any limit results for (5.30) and (5.31) in the $d \geq 1$ case should collapse in the findings that we illustrated in Section 3, i.e., (3.39) and (3.43), when reducing the dimensionality of the system to $d = 1$. Let us focus on the drift for illustration purposes. Based on (3.39), our best guess of a weak convergence result for (5.30) is

$$\sqrt{\mathbf{h}_{n,T}\widehat{\overline{\mathbb{L}}}_{(n,T)}(T,a)}\left\{\widehat{\boldsymbol{\mu}}_{(n,T)}(a) - \boldsymbol{\mu}(a)\right\} \Rightarrow \mathbf{N}\left(0, \mathbf{K}_2^d \mathbf{s}(a)\right), \tag{5.33}$$

where $\mathbf{h}_{n,T} = h_{n,T}^d$. First, (5.33) reduces to (3.39) when $d = 1$, thereby satisfying our requirement. Second, the impossibility of interpreting $\widehat{\overline{\mathbb{L}}}_{(n,T)}(T,a)$ as a local time estimator for $d > 1$ does not have an impact on the credibility of the intuition leading to (5.33). In fact, as shown earlier, $\widehat{\overline{\mathbb{L}}}_{(n,T)}(T,a)$ converges (as $n, T \to \infty$ and if standardized appropriately) to a well-defined random variable for dimensions higher than one while also being a local time estimator when $d = 1$. The following theorem confirms our intuition. As usual, we adopt the same sampling scheme as in Section 2.

Theorem 14 *Assume X_t is the solution to (5.1). Also, assume the vanishing sequence $h_{n,T}$ satisfies*

$$\frac{(\Delta_{n,T}\log(1/\Delta_{n,T}))^{1/2}u(T)}{\mathbf{h}_{n,T}} = o(1) \tag{5.34}$$

and

$$\mathbf{h}_{n,T}u(T) \to \infty, \tag{5.35}$$

as $n, T \to \infty$ with $\Delta_{n,T} \to 0$, for some function $u(T) = T^{\alpha}L(T)$ with $L(T)$ slowly varying and a process-specific parameter α so that $0 \leq \alpha \leq 1$. Then,

$$\widehat{\boldsymbol{\mu}}_{(n,T)}(a) \overset{a.s.}{\to} \boldsymbol{\mu}(a) \quad \forall a \in \mathfrak{D} \subseteq \mathfrak{R}^d. \tag{5.36}$$

Furthermore, if $h_{n,T} = O\left(u(T)^{-\frac{1}{d+4}}\right)$, *then*

$$\sqrt{\mathbf{h}_{n,T}\widehat{\overline{\mathbb{L}}}_{(n,T)}(T,a)}\left(\widehat{\boldsymbol{\mu}}_{(n,T)}(a) - \boldsymbol{\mu}(a) - \boldsymbol{\Gamma}_{\boldsymbol{\mu}}(a)\right)$$

$$\Rightarrow \quad (\mathbf{s}(a))^{1/2}\mathbf{N}\left(0, \mathbf{K}_2^d\mathbf{I}\right) \quad \forall a \in \mathfrak{D} \subseteq \mathfrak{R}^d, \tag{5.37}$$

where

$$\boldsymbol{\Gamma}_{\boldsymbol{\mu}}(a) = (bias_1, bias_2, \ldots, bias_d)(a), \tag{5.38}$$

$$bias_i(a) = h_{n,T}^2\mathbf{K}_1\left(\sum_{k=1}^{d}\frac{\partial\mu_i(a)}{\partial a_k}\frac{\frac{\partial m(a)}{\partial a_k}}{m(a)} + \frac{1}{2}\sum_{k=1}^{d}\frac{\partial^2\mu_i(a)}{\partial a_k\partial a_k}\right) \quad i = 1, \ldots, \mathrm{d}, \tag{5.39}$$

and $m(\mathrm{d}x) = m(x)\mathrm{d}x$ *is the invariant measure of the process.*

Proof See Bandi and Moloche (2004).

All our comments in the scalar case apply to the multivariate setup examined here up to some minor modifications. We will therefore not be as detailed as in Section 3. Nonetheless, it should be noted that the asymptotic bias is $O(h_{n,T}^2)$, as in the scalar case, whereas the asymptotic variance is of order $\widehat{\overline{\mathbb{L}}}_{(n,T)}(T,a)^{-1}h_{n,T}^{-d}$ rather than $\widehat{\overline{\mathbb{L}}}_{(n,T)}(T,a)^{-1}h_{n,T}$. In the standard estimation of conditional first moments in the discrete-time, stationary framework, the limiting bias is $O(h_{n,T}^2)$, whereas the limiting variance is $n^{-1}h_{n,T}^{-d}$ rather than $(nh_{n,T})^{-1}$. In other words, the variance increases with the dimensionality of the system. This effect is commonly known as *the curse of dimensionality* (see, e.g., Silverman, 1986). Importantly, here we have a curse of dimensionality which mirrors the classical result in conventional nonparametric estimation of conditional moments in discrete time and manifests itself through the factor h^{-d}, as well as an additional curse of dimensionality operating via the quantity $\widehat{\overline{\mathbb{L}}}_{(n,T)}(T,a)$. The latter effect is a genuine by-product of the generality of this theory and, in particular, is due to robustness to deviations from stationarity. In fact, should the system be stationary (or positive recurrent), then $\widehat{\overline{\mathbb{L}}}_{(n,T)}(T,a)$ would diverge at speed T (cf., the previous subsection) regardless of the number of equations and the order of the variance term would simply be $T^{-1}h_{n,T}^{-d}$. Hence, we would be in the presence of a rather ordinary dimensionality problem because only the power d would be affected by the number of equations in the system. By contrast, consider the null recurrent situation. We pointed out earlier that scalar Brownian motion and Brownian motion on the plane imply divergence rates for $\widehat{\overline{\mathbb{L}}}_{(n,T)}(T,a)$ that are equal to $\sqrt{T}$ and $\log T$, respectively (see the previous subsection). This result has broader implications. We expect the dimensionality of the system to have a negative influence on the rate of divergence of the factor $\widehat{\overline{\mathbb{L}}}_{(n,T)}(T,a)$ for null recurrent processes that are more general than Brownian motion, thereby reinforcing the conventional effect that comes into play through the term $h_{n,T}^d$ and leading to a slower rate of convergence of the nonparametric estimates to the theoretical vector $\boldsymbol{\mu}(.)$. The optimal bandwidth sequence, i.e.,

$$h_{n,T} \propto \widehat{\overline{\mathbb{L}}}_{(n,T)}^{-\frac{1}{d+4}}(T,a) \tag{5.40}$$

accounts for both effects or for *the two curses of dimensionality*, in the terminology of Bandi and Moloche (2004).

We now turn to diffusion estimation. The symbol $\otimes$ in the statement of Theorem 15 denotes the standard Kronecker product. When applied to a generic matrix A, the operator *vec* stacks the columns of A. The operator *vech* selects the nonredundant elements of *vec*.

Theorem 15 *Assume X_t is the solution to (5.1). Also, assume the vanishing sequence $h_{n,T}$ satisfies*

$$\frac{(\Delta_{n,T}\log(1/\Delta_{n,T}))^{1/2}u(T)}{\mathbf{h}_{n,T}} = o(1), \tag{5.41}$$

as $n, T \to \infty$ with $\Delta_{n,T} \to 0$, for some function $u(T) = T^{\alpha}L(T)$ with $L(T)$ slowly varying and a process-specific parameter α so that $0 \leq \alpha \leq 1$. Then,

$$\widehat{\mathbf{s}}_{(n,T)}(a) \stackrel{a.s.}{\to} \mathbf{s}(a) \quad \forall a \in \mathfrak{D} \subseteq \mathfrak{R}^d. \tag{5.42}$$

Furthermore, if $h_{n,T}^2\sqrt{\frac{\mathbf{h}_{n,T}u(T)}{\Delta_{n,T}}} = O(1)$, then

$$\sqrt{\frac{\mathbf{h}_{n,T}\widehat{\overline{\mathbb{L}}}_{(n,T)}(T,a)}{\Delta_{n,T}}}\left(\text{vech}\widehat{\mathbf{s}}_{(n,T)}(a) - \text{vech}\mathbf{s}(a) - \boldsymbol{\Gamma}_{\sigma^2}(a)\right)$$
$$\Rightarrow \quad (\Xi(a))^{1/2}\mathbf{N}\left(0, \mathbf{K}_2^d\mathbf{I}\right), \quad \forall a \in \mathfrak{D} \subseteq \mathfrak{R}^d, \tag{5.43}$$

where

$$\boldsymbol{\Gamma}_{\sigma^2}(a) = (bias_{1,1}, bias_{2,1}, \ldots, bias_{d,d})(a), \tag{5.44}$$

$$bias_{i,j}(a) = h_{n,T}^2\mathbf{K}_1\left(\sum_{k=1}^{d}\frac{\partial s_{i,j}(a)}{\partial a_k}\frac{\frac{\partial m(a)}{\partial a_k}}{m(a)} + \frac{1}{2}\sum_{k=1}^{d}\frac{\partial^2 s_{i,j}(a)}{\partial a_k \partial a_k}\right) \quad i,j = (1,1),\ldots,(d,d), \tag{5.45}$$

$$\Xi(a) = L_D\left(2\mathbf{s}(a) \otimes \mathbf{s}(a)\right)L_D^{\top}, \tag{5.46}$$

$$L_D = (D^{\top}D)^{-1}D^{\top}, \tag{5.47}$$

D is the standard duplication matrix, i.e., the unique $d^2 \times (d(d+1))/2$ matrix so that L_D eliminates redundant elements, viz.,

$$\text{vechs}(a) = L_D\text{vecs}(a) = \begin{bmatrix} s_{1,1} \\ s_{2,1} \\ s_{2,2} \\ s_{3,1} \\ \dots \\ s_{d,d} \end{bmatrix}, \tag{5.48}$$

and $m(\mathrm{d}x) = m(x)\mathrm{d}x$ *is the invariant measure of the process.*

Proof See Bandi and Moloche (2004).

Our comments in the scalar diffusion case (cf., Section 3) and in the multivariate drift case should suffice to interpret the results in Theorem 15 above. Here, we simply note that, as in the scalar case, the local properties of the process contain sufficient information to identify the diffusion matrix, i.e., $\mathbf{s}(a)$ can be estimated consistently over a fixed span of data $T = \overline{T}$. The interested reader is referred to the work by Brugière (cf., Brugière, 1991, 1993) for a thorough treatment in the fixed T case. In particular, Brugière (1991) discusses weak consistency of (5.31) for the matrix of interest, whereas Brugière (1993) proves the asymptotic normality of the diffusion matrix estimator. The kernel used in both papers is the discontinuous indicator kernel. Extending the results in Brugière to the use of continuous kernels should be immediate. Genon-Catalot and Jacod (1993) offer interesting, related methods.

In recent work, Jeffrey et al. (2004) propose and study a multivariate nonparametric volatility estimator in the context of the successful HJM term-structure model (Heath et al., 1992). An alternative approach to functional multivariate volatility estimation for the purpose of fixed income pricing is contained in Knight et al. (2006). We refer the reader to both papers for multidimensional kernel methods for diffusions tailored to flexible continuous-time pricing issues. The consistency and limiting distribution of derivative prices obtained by virtue of parametric, semiparametric, and nonparametric estimators for diffusions is studied in Kristensen (2008).

6. CONCLUDING REMARKS

In surveying the tools that have been recently introduced to describe and study the formulation and estimation of classes of continuous-time Markov models, this chapter illustrates the important role that is played by *local nonparametric* methods along with the assumption of *recurrence*. Our focus has been on estimation procedures which are general both in terms of model specification and in terms of statistical assumptions needed for identification. Local nonparametric methods achieve the former by being robust (at the cost of an efficiency loss) to model mispecifications. Recurrence is a promising avenue to achieve the latter.

Similar arguments in favor of minimal conditions on the underlying statistical structure of the process of interest may, however, be put forward when dealing with parametric models and discrete-time series. Sometimes empirical researchers may be a lot more comfortable avoiding restrictions like stationarity or arbitrary mixing conditions on the processes they are modeling. In the same circumstances, it might also seem inappropriate to impose explicit nonstationary behavior (often of the random walk or $\frac{1}{2}$-null recurrent type) in the specification. Indeed, many practical situations arise where neither stationarity nor nonstationarity can be safely ruled out in advance, and in such situations, the assumption of recurrence appears to be a suitable alternative condition that permits a wide range of plausible sample behaviors and includes both stationary and nonstationary processes. Interestingly, statistical inference can often be carried out in recurrent models using limiting laws defined in terms of random norming (the averaged kernel in the definition of the estimated local time being an example, cf., (3.39) and (3.43) for instance). Such random norming captures the divergence features of time series with various degrees of recurrence and allows the user to be agnostic about the recurrence features of the processes of interest. The practical advantage of this fact is apparent. Although standard asymptotic theory treats stationary and nonstationary models differently in deriving implications for statistical inference, reliance on recurrence permits one to consider both cases as subcases of a more general theory of inference. Additionally, even when the existence of a stationary density appears to be an unquestionable feature of the data and/or is dictated by economic theory, the dynamic structure of Markov processes renders conventional forms of mixing not crucial to derive limiting results and, consequently, vital tools for statistical analysis.

Having made these points, we should add the qualification that the use of recurrence as an identifying condition is still in its infancy in the econometrics literature. Harris recurrence is the identifying assumption in Yakowitz (1989), but the treatment in that paper only focuses on the discrete-time ergodic case.[19] More recently, kernel density estimation for real-valued positive Harris recurrent Markov chains is discussed in Athreya and Atuncar (1998). Karlsen and Tjøstheim (2001) provide a theory of inference for nonparametric (auto-)regressions of β-null recurrent discrete-time Markov chains. As was discussed earlier, should the rate of divergence of the occupation density of the process be known in closed form, then the optimal bandwidth choice would depend on it. However, this is not the case in general, and suitable data-driven methods should deliver bandwidths capable of capturing the recurrence properties of the covariates. This is the proposal formulated in recent work by Guerre (2004). Karlsen et al. (2007) and Schienle (2008) focus on the functional estimation of cointegrating relations between β-null recurrent

[19] In his 1989 paper, Yakowitz conjectured that "...in the Markov case the mixing assumptions are not essential. ...Even in the absence of a stationary distribution, under conditions general enough to include unbounded random walks and ARMA processes, [nonlinear] regression estimation is possible. We require only stationarity of the transition law, not of the process."

discrete-time Markov chains. Moloche (2004b) tackles the nonparametric estimation of (potentially cointegrating) regressions between (either null or positive) Harris recurrent discrete-time Markov processes. An alternative approach based on Skorohod embedding and nonlinear transformations of the embedded process was initiated by Phillips and Park (1998). They study nonparametric kernel estimation of nonstationary time series embeddable in Brownian motion. Wang and Phillips (2008, 2009), and the references therein, expand on that approach and make it applicable more generally, including cases of fractional limit processes.

The methods reviewed in this chapter, along with the recent treatments mentioned above, have helped to lay some foundations for econometric inference with continuous- and discrete-time series under mild assumptions on their parametric form and statistical evolution. The field is a new one, however, and as this chapter has suggested, much more needs to be done.

ACKNOWLEDGMENTS

We thank Darrell Duffie, Jianqing Fan, Benoit Perron, Mark Watson, the Editor Lars Peter Hansen, and two anonynous referees for useful suggestions. We are grateful to Seoyeon (Suzanne) Lee for research assistance on a previous draft. In attempting to survey what is an extremely vast field relating to inference for continuous-time Markov processes, we adopt the perspective of focusing on (local) nonparametric methods and mild assumptions regarding specification and conditions needed for identification. We sought to keep this survey updated from its original completed form in 2001 and apologize for any relevant omissions given the intervening time gap. Bandi acknowledges financial support from the IBM Corporation Faculty Research Fund at the University of Chicago. Phillips thanks the NSF for support under grant nos. SES 00-92509 and SS 06-47086.

REFERENCES

Aït-Sahalia, Y. (1996). Testing Continuous-Time Models of the Spot Interest Rate. *Review of Financial Studies* 2, 385–426.

Aït-Sahalia, Y., L.P. Hansen, and J. Scheinkman (2010). Operator Methods for Continuous-Time Markov Processes. In Y. Aït-Sahalia and L.P. Hansen (Eds.), *Handbook of Financial Econometrics*. Amsterdam: North-Holland.

Andrews, D.W.K. (1989). Asymptotics for Semiparametric Econometric Models: III. Testing and Examples. Cowles Foundation Discussion Paper N. 910, Yale University.

Athreya, K.B., and G.S. Atuncar (1998). Kernel Estimation for Real-Valued Markov Chains. *Sankhyā* 60, 1–17.

Azéma, J., M. Kaplan-Duflo, and D. Revuz (1967). Mesure Invariante Sur Les Classes Récurrentes des Processus de Markov. *Zeitschrift für Wahrscheinlichkeitstheorie und Verwandte Gebiete* 8, 157–181.

Bandi, F.M. (2002). Short-Term Interest Rate Dynamics: A Spatial Approach. *Journal of Financial Economics* 65, 73–110.

Bandi, F.M., and G. Moloche (2004). On the Functional Estimation of Multivariate Diffusion Processes. Working Paper.

Bandi, F.M., and T. Nguyen (1999). Fully Nonparametric Estimators for Diffusions: A Small Sample Analysis. Working Paper.

Bandi, F.M., and T. Nguyen (2003). On the Functional Estimation of Jump-Diffusion Models. *Journal of Econometrics* 116, 293–328.

Bandi, F.M., and P.C.B. Phillips (2003). Fully Nonparametric Estimation of Scalar Diffusion Models. *Econometrica* 71, 241–283.

Bandi, F.M., and P.C.B. Phillips (2007). A Simple Approach to the Parametric Estimation of Potentially Nonstationary Diffusions. *Journal of Econometrics* 137, 354–395.

Bandi, F.M., and R. Renò (2008). Nonparametric Stochastic Volatility. Working Paper.

Bandi, F.M., and J.R. Russell (2007). Volatility. In J. Birge and V. Linetski (Eds.), *Handbook of Financial Engineering*. Amsterdam: Elsevier, 183–222.

Bianchi, A. (2007). Invariant Density Estimation for Multidimensional Diffusions. In G. Aletti, M. Burger, A. Micheletti, and D. Morale (Eds.), *Math Everywhere*. Berlin and Heidelberg: Springer, 39–50.

Bickel, P.J., and M. Rosenblatt (1973). On Some Global Measures of The Deviations of Density Function Estimates. *Annals of Statistics* 1, 1071–1095.

Bingham, N.H. (1971). Limit Theorems for Occupation Times of Markov Processes. *Zeitschrift für Wahrscheinlichkeitstheorie und Verwandte Gebiete*, 17, 1–22.

Black, F., E. Derman, and W. Toy (1990). A One-Factor Model of Interest Rates and its Applications to Treasury Bond Options. *Financial Analysts Journal* 46, 33–39.

Bosq, D. (1997). Temps Local et Estimation Sans Biais de la Densité en Temps Continu. *C.R. Acad. Sci.*, T. 325, 1, 527–530.

Bosq, D. (1998). *Nonparametric Statistics for Stochastic Processes*. New York: Springer-Verlag.

Bosq, D., and Y. Davydov (1998). Local Time and Density Estimation in Continuous Time. *Publ. IRMA Univ. Lille 1, Vol. 44, III.*

Brugière, P. (1991). Estimation de la Variance d'un Processus de Diffusion dans le Cas Multidimensionnel. *C. R. Acad. Sci.*, T. 312, 1, 999–1005.

Brugière, P. (1993). Théorém de Limite Centrale Pour un Estimateur Non Paramétrique de la Variance d'un Processus de Diffusion Multidimensionnelle. *Ann. Inst. Henri Poincaré* 29, 357–389.

Cai, Z., and Y. Hong (2003). Nonparametric Methods in Continuous-Time Finance: A Selective Review. In M.G. Akritas and D.N. Politis (Eds.), *Recent Advances and Trends in Nonparametric Statistics*. Amsterdam: Elsevier, 283–302.

Campbell, J.Y., A. Lo, and A.C. MacKinlay (1997). *The Econometrics of Financial Markets*. Princeton, NJ: Princeton University Press.

Chen, S.X., J. Gao, and C.Y. Tang (2008). A Test for Model Specification of Diffusion Processes. *Annals of Statistics*, 36, 167–198.

Chen, X., L.P. Hansen, and M. Carrasco (1999). Nonlinearity and Temporal Dependence. Working Paper.

Comte, F., V. Genon-Catalot, and Y. Rozenholc (2007). Nonparametric Estimation for a Stochastic Volatility Model. Working Paper.

Conley, T., L.P. Hansen, E. Luttmer, and J. Scheinkman (1997). Short-Term Interest Rates as Subordinated Diffusions. *Review of Financial Studies* 10, 525–577.

Corradi, V., and W. Distaso (2007). Diagnostic Tests for Volatility Models. Working Paper.

Corradi, V., and N.R. Swanson (2005). Bootstrap Specification Tests for Diffusion Processes. *Journal of Econometrics* 124, 117–148.

Corradi, V., and H. White (1999). Specification Tests for the Variance of a Diffusion. *Journal of Time Series Analysis* 20, 253–270.

Cox, J.C., J.E. Ingersoll, and S.A. Ross (1985). A Theory of the Term Structure of Interest Rates. *Econometrica* 53, 385–408.

Dalalyan, A., and M. Reiss (2006). Asymptotic Statistical Equivalence for Ergodic Diffusions: The Multidimensional Case. *Probability Theory and Related Fields* 137, 25–47.

Darling, D.A., and M. Kac (1957). On Occupation Times for Markoff Processes. *Transactions of the American Mathematical Society* 84, 444–458.

Duffie, D. (1996). *Dynamic Asset Pricing Theory*. Princeton, NJ: Princeton University Press.

Eraker, B., M. Johannes, and N. Polson (2003). The Impact of Jumps in Volatility and Returns. *Journal of Finance,* 53, 1269–1300.

Ethier, S.N., and T.G. Kurtz (1986). *Markov Processes: Characterization and Convergence*. New York: John Wiley & Sons.

Fan, J. (1992). Design-Adaptive Nonparametric Regression. *Journal of the American Statistical Association* 87, 998–1004.

Fan, J. (1993). Local Linear Regression Smoothers and their Minimax Efficiencies. *Annals of Statistics* 21, 196–216.

Fan, J. (2005). A Selective Overview of Nonparametric Methods in Financial Econometrics. *Statistical Science* 20, 317–357.

Fan, J., and I. Gijbels (1996). *Local Polynomial Modelling and Its Applications.* London: Chapman and Hall.

Fan, J., J. Jiang, C. Zhang, and Z. Zhou (2003). Time-Dependent Diffusion Models for Term Structure Dynamics. *Statistica Sinica* 13, 965–992.

Fan, J., and Q. Yao (2003). *Nonlinear Time Series: Parametric and Nonparametric Methods.* New York: Springer-Verlag.

Fan, J., and C. Zhang (2003). A Re-Examination of Diffusion Estimators with Applications to Financial Model Validation. *Journal of the American Statistical Association* 98, 118–134.

Florens-Zmirou, D. (1993). On Estimating the Diffusion Coefficient from Discrete Observations. *Journal of Applied Probability* 30, 790–804.

Gallant, R., and G. Tauchen (2010). Simulated Methods and Indirect Inference for Continuous-Time Models. In Y. Aït-Sahalia and L.P. Hansen (Eds.), *Handbook of Financial Econometrics.* Amsterdam: North-Holland, inpress.

Geman, S.A. (1979). On a Common Sense Estimator for the Drift of a Diffusion. Working Paper.

Geman, D., and J. Horowitz (1980). Occupation Densities. *Annals of Probability* 8, 1–67.

Genon-Catalot, V., and J. Jacod (1993). On the Estimation of the Diffusion Coefficient for Multi-Dimensional Diffusion Processes. *Ann. Inst. H. Poincaré Probab. Statist.* 29, 119–151.

Guerre, E. (2004). Design-Adaptive Point-Wise Nonparametric Regression Estimation for Recurrent Markov Time Series. Working Paper.

Gikhman, I.I., and A.V. Skorohod (1972). *Stochastic Differential Equations.* Berlin: Springer-Verlag.

Gourieroux, C., and J. Jasiak (2001). *Financial Econometrics: Problems, Models and Methods.* Princeton, NJ: Princeton University Press.

Hansen, L.P., and T.J. Sargent (1983). The Dimensionality of the Aliasing Problem in Models with Rational Spectral Densities. *Econometrica* 50, 377–387.

Hansen, L.P., and J.A. Scheinkman (1995). Back to the Future: Generating Moment Implications for Continuous-Time Markov Processes. *Econometrica* 63, 767–804.

Härdle, W. (1990). *Applied Nonparametric Regression.* Cambridge: Cambridge University Press.

Härdle, W., and O. Linton (1994). Applied Nonparametric Methods. In D. McFadden and R.F. Engle (Eds.), *Handbook of Econometrics,* Vol. IV. Amsterdam: Elsevier, 2295–2339.

Heath, D., R. Jarrow, and A. Morton (1992). Bond Pricing and the Term Structure of Interest Rates: A New Methodology for Contingent Claims Valuation. *Econometrica* 60, 77–105.

Hong, Y., and H. Li (2003). Nonparametric Specification Testing for Continuous-time Models with Application to Spot Interest Rates. *Review of Financial Studies* 18, 37–84.

Höpfner, R., and Y. Kutoyants (2001). On a Problem of Statistical Inference in Null Recurrent Diffusions. Preprint N. 7, Fachbereich Mathematik, Universität Mainz.

Höpfner, R., and E. Löcherbach (2001). Limit Theorems for Null-Recurrent Markov Processes. Preprint N. 22, Fachbereich Mathematik, Universität Mainz.

Jacod, J. (1997). Nonparametric Kernel Estimation of the Diffusion Coefficient of a Diffusion. Prépublication No. 405. du Laboratoire de Probabilités de l'Université Paris VI.

Jacod, J. (2010). Inference for Stochastic Processes. In Y. Aït-Sahalia and L.P. Hansen (Eds.), *Handbook of Financial Econometrics.* Amsterdam: North-Holland, inpress.

Jeffrey, A., D. Kristensen, O. Linton, T. Nguyen, and P.C.B. Phillips (2004). Nonparametric Estimation of a Multifactor Heath-Jarrow-Morton Model: An Integrated Approach. *Journal of Financial Econometrics* 2, 251–289.

Jiang, G.J., and J. Knight (1997). A Nonparametric Approach to the Estimation of Diffusion Processes, with An Application to a Short-Term Interest Rate Model. *Econometric Theory* 13, 615–645.

Jiang, G.J., and J. Knight (1999). Finite Sample Comparison of Alternative Estimators of Itô Diffusion Processes: A Monte-Carlo Study. *Journal of Computational Finance* 2, 5–38.

Johannes, M. (2004). The Statistical and Economic Role of Jumps in Continuous-Time Interest Rate Models. *Journal of Finance* 59, 227–260.

Johannes, M., and N. Polson (2010). Numerical Bayesian Methods for Estimating Continuous-Time Models. In Y. Aït-Sahalia and L.P. Hansen (Eds.), *Handbook of Financial Econometrics.* Amsterdam: North-Holland, inpress.

Kanaya, S., and D. Kristensen (2008). Estimation of Stochastic Volatility Models by Nonparametric Filtering. Working Paper.

Karatzas, I., and S.E. Shreve (1991). *Brownian Motion and Stochastic Calculus.* New York: Springer-Verlag.

Karlin, S., and H.M. Taylor (1981). *A Second Course in Stochastic Processes.* New York and London: Academic Press.

Karlsen, H.A., T. Myklebust, and D. Tjøstheim (2007). Nonparametric Estimation in a Nonlinear Cointegrating Type Model. *Annals of Statistics* 35, 252–299.

Karlsen, H.A., and D. Tjøstheim (2001). Nonparametric Estimation in Null Recurrent Time Series. *Annals of Statistics* 29, 372–416.

Khasminskii, R.Z. (1980). *Stochastic Stability of Differential Equations.* Rockville, MD: Sijthoff & Noordhoff.

Khasminskii, R.Z. (2001). Limit Distributions of Some Integral Functionals for Null-Recurrent Diffusions. *Stochastic Processes and their Applications* 92, 1–9.

Khasminskii, R.Z., and G. Yin (2000). Asymptotic Behavior of Parabolic Equations Arising from One-Dimensional Null-Recurrent Diffusions. *Journal of Differential Equations* 161, 154–173.

Knight, J., F. LI, and M. Yuan (2006). A semiparametric Two-Factor Term Structure Model. *Journal of Financial Econometrics* 4, 204–237.

Kristensen, D. (2008). Estimation of Partial Differential Equations with Applications in Finance. *Journal of Econometrics* 144, 392–408.

Kristensen, D. (2009). Nonparametric Filtering of the Realized Spot Volatility: A Kernel-Based Approach. *Econometric Theory*, inpress.

Li, Q., and J.S. Racine. (2006). *Nonparametric Econometrics: Theory and Practice.* Princeton, NJ: Princeton University Press.

Mancini, C., and R. Renò (2006). Threshold Estimation of Jump-Diffusion Models and Interest Rate Modeling. Working Paper.

Malliavin, P., and M. Mancino (2002). Fourier Series Method for Measurement of Multivariate Volatilities. *Finance and Stochastics* 6, 49–61.

McCrorie, J.R. (2009). Estimating Continuous-Time Models on the Basis of Discrete Data via an Exact Discrete Analog. *Econometric Theory*, inpress.

Menaldi, J.L., and M. Robin (1999). Invariant Measure for Diffusions with Jumps. *Applied Mathematics and Optimization* 40, 105–140.

Meyn, S.P., and R.L. Tweedie (1993). *Markov Chains and Stochastic Stability*. London and New York: Springer-Verlag.

Merton, R.C. (1990). *Continuous-Time Finance.* Oxford: Blackwell.

Moloche, G. (2004a). Local Nonparametric Estimation of Scalar Diffusions. Working Paper.

Moloche, G. (2004b). Kernel Regression for Non-Stationary Harris Recurrent Processes. Working Paper.

Nicolau, J. (2003). Bias-Reduction in Nonparametric Diffusion Coefficient Estimation. *Econometric Theory* 19, 754–777.

Pagan, A., and A. Ullah (1999). *Nonparametric Statistics.* Cambridge and New York: Cambridge University Press.

Park, J. (2006). The Spatial Analysis of Time Series. Working Paper.

Phillips, P.C.B. (1973). The Problem of Identification in Finite Parameter Continuous-Time Models. *Journal of Econometrics* 4, 351–362.

Phillips, P.C.B. (2001). Descriptive Econometrics for Nonstationary Time Series with Empirical Illustrations. *Journal of Applied Econometrics* 16, 389–413.

Phillips, P.C.B. (2004). Econometric Analysis of Fisher's Equation. In J. Geanakoplos and W.C. Brainard (Eds.), *Essays in Memory of Irving Fisher.* Cowles Foundation for Economic Research, Yale University, 1–35.

Phillips, P.C.B., and J. Park (1998). Nonstationary Density Estimation and Kernel Autoregression. Cowles Foundation Discussion Paper, No. 1181, Yale University.

Phillips, P.C.B., and J. Yu (2009). Maximum Likelihood and Gaussian Estimation of Continuous-Time Models in Finance. In Andersen T.G., Davis, R.A., Kreiss J.P. and T. Mikosch (Eds.), *Handbook of Financial Time Series.* Berlin and Heidelberg: Springer, 497– 530.

Piazzesi, M. (2010). Affine Term-Structure Models. In Y. Aït-Sahalia and L.P. Hansen (Eds.), *Handbook of Financial Econometrics*. Amsterdam: North-Holland, inpress.
Pollack, M., and D. Siegmund (1985). A Diffusion Process and its Applications to Detecting a Change in the Drift of Brownian Motion. *Biometrika* 72, 267–280.
Prakasa-Rao, B.L.S. (1983). *Nonparametric Functional Estimation*. Orlando, FL: Academic Press.
Protter, P. (1995). *Stochastic Integration and Differential Equations*. Heidelberg: Springer-Verlag.
Renò, R. (2006). Nonparametric Estimation of Stochastic Volatility Models. *Economic Letters* 90, 390–395.
Renò, R. (2008). Nonparametric Estimation of the Diffusion Coefficient of Stochastic Volatility Models. *Econometric Theory*, 24, 1174–1206.
Revuz, D., and M. Yor (1998). *Continuous Martingales and Brownian Motion*. Berlin, Heidelberg, and New York: Springer-Verlag.
Rosenblatt, M. (1975). Quadratic Measure of Deviation of Two-Dimensional Density Estimates and a Test of Independence. *Annals of Statistics* 3, 1–14.
Schienle, M. (2008). Nonparametric Nonstationary Regression. Doctoral Thesis, Mannheim University.
Silverman, B. (1986). *Density Estimation for Statistics and Data Analysis*. Bristol; UK: Chapman and Hall.
Stanton, R. (1997). A Nonparametric Model of Term Structure Dynamics and the Market Price of Interest Rate Risk. *Journal of Finance* 52, 1973–2002.
Sundaresan, S.M. (2000). Continuous-Time Methods in Finance: A Review and an Assessment. *Journal of Finance* 55, 1569–1622.
Tsay, R.S. (2005). *Analysis of Financial Time Series*. New York: John Wiley & Sons.
Vasicek, O. (1977). An Equilibrium Characterization of the Term Structure. *Journal of Financial Economics* 5, 177–188.
Wang, Q., and P.C.B. Phillips (2008). Structural Nonparametric Cointegrating Regression. Working Paper.
Wang, Q., and P.C.B. Phillips (2009). Asymptotic Theory for Local Time Density Estimation and Nonparametric Cointegrating Regression. *Econometric Theory* 25, 710–738.
Xu, K.-L. (2007). Empirical Likelihood-Based Inference for Nonlinear Diffusions. Econometric Theory, inpress.
Xu, K.-L. (2008). Re-Weighted Functional Estimation of Diffusion Models. *Econometric Theory*, inpress.
Yakowitz, S. (1989). Nonparametric Density and Regression Estimation for Markov Sequences Without Mixing Assumptions. *Journal of Multivariate Analysis* 30, 124–136.
Yor, M. (1978). Sur la Continuité des Temps Locaux Associés à Certaines Semi-Martingales. *Astérisque* 52–53, 219–221.
Zhang, L., P. Mykland, and Y. Aït-Sahalia (2005). A Tale of Two Time Scales: Determining Integrated Volatility with Noisy High-Frequency Data. *Journal of the American Statistical Association* 100, 1394–1411.

CHAPTER 4

Estimating Functions for Discretely Sampled Diffusion-Type Models

Bo Martin Bibby*, Martin Jacobsen, and Michael Sørensen****

*Institute of Mathematics and Physics, The Royal Veterinary and Agricultural University, Frederiksberg, Denmark
**Department of Mathematical Sciences, University of Copenhagen, Copenhagen, Denmark

Contents

Abstract

We shall demonstrate that estimating functions can be found not only for ordinary diffusions, but also for stochastic volatility models and diffusions with jumps. For stochastic volatility models the estimating functions will be constructed in such a way that asymptotic properties of the estimator can easily be established. The main advantage of the estimating functions discussed in this chapter is that they usually require less computation than the alternative methods listed above and in several cases actually provide explicit estimators. It is therefore a particularly useful approach when quick estimators are needed. These simple estimators have a rather high efficiency when the estimating function is well-chosen. The hall-mark of the estimating functions approach is the use of a given collection of relations between observations at different time points to construct an optimal estimator, i.e. the most efficient estimator possible on the basis of these relations. In a high-frequency sampling asymptotic scenario optimal martingale estimating functions are in fact efficient for diffusion models.

Keywords: martingale estimating functions; prediction-based estimating functions; small-delta optimality; stochastic differential equations; stochastic volatility models

1. INTRODUCTION

Estimating functions provide a general framework for finding estimators and studying their properties in many different kinds of statistical models, including stochastic process models. An estimating function is a function of the data as well as of the parameter to be estimated. An estimator is obtained by equating the estimating function to zero and solving the resulting estimating equation with respect to the parameter. The idea of using estimating equations is an old one and goes back at least to Karl Pearson's introduction of the method of moments. The term *estimating function* may have been coined by Kimball (1946). In the econometric literature, the method was introduced by Hansen (1982) and is known as the generalized method of moments (GMM).

The estimating function approach has turned out to be very useful in obtaining, improving, and studying estimators for discretely sampled parametric diffusion-type models, where the likelihood function is usually not explicitly known. Estimating functions are often constructed by combining relationships (dependent on the unknown parameter) between an observation and one or more of the previous observations that are informative about the parameters. Estimators obtained by maximization or minimization of a differentiable objective function are zero points for the estimating function obtained by differentiating the objective function. In particular, the estimating function corresponding to the likelihood function is the score function (the derivative of the log-likelihood function).

There are a number of approaches that render likelihood inference and Bayesian inference feasible for ordinary diffusion models; for likelihood inference, see Pedersen (1995), Poulsen (1999), Aït-Sahalia (2002), Durham and Gallant (2002), Beskos et al. (2006) Aït-Sahalia (2008) and Aït-Sahalia et al. (2010), and for Markov chain Monte Carlo methods, see Elerian et al. (2001), Eraker (2001), Roberts and Stramer (2001), and Johannes and Polson (2010). Markov chain Monte Carlo methods can also be used for more general diffusion-type models such as stochastic volatility models, but the usual asymptotic results for the maximum likelihood estimator (and Bayesian estimators) have not yet been established for stochastic volatility models. An approximate likelihood function for stochastic volatility models with tractable asymptotics was proposed by Sørensen (2003). Another useful approach to inference for general diffusion-type models is indirect inference, see Gallant and Tauchen (1996) and Gallant and Tauchen (2010).

In this chapter, we shall, only to a very limited extent, be concerned with estimators obtained by maximizing or minimizing objective functions. The focus of the chapter is on estimating functions constructed directly by combining functions of observations at one or more time points. A review covering more broadly statistical methods for stochastic differential equation models can be found in Sørensen (2004). We shall demonstrate that estimating functions can be found not only for ordinary diffusions but also for stochastic volatility models and diffusions with jumps. For stochastic volatility models, the estimating functions will be constructed in such a way that asymptotic properties of the estimator can easily be established. The main advantage of the estimating functions discussed in this chapter is that they usually require less computation than the alternative methods listed above and in several cases actually provide explicit estimators. It is, therefore, a particularly useful approach when quick estimators are needed. These simple estimators have a rather high efficiency when the estimating function is well chosen. The hallmark of the estimating function approach is the use of a given collection of relations between observations at different time points to construct an optimal estimator, i.e. the most efficient estimator possible on the basis of these relations. In a high-frequency sampling asymptotic scenario, optimal martingale estimating functions are in fact efficient for diffusion models.

Let us give a few examples of estimating functions for a diffusion model given by the stochastic differential equation

$$dX_t = b(X_t;\theta)dt + \sigma(X_t;\theta)dW_t,$$

where W is a Wiener process and θ is a parameter to be estimated. To simplify the exposition, let us assume here that X and θ are one dimensional and that the data are observations of X at the time points $1, 2, \ldots, n$. Hansen and Scheinkman (1995) proposed the following simple and broadly applicable estimating function. For any twice continuously differentiable function h, an estimating function can be defined by

$$G_n(\theta) = \sum_{i=1}^{n}\left(b(X_i;\theta)h'(X_i) + \frac{1}{2}\sigma^2(X_i;\theta)h''(X_i)\right).$$

One advantage of this estimating function is that it is an explicit function of θ. The estimator obtained by solving the estimating equation $G_n(\theta) = 0$ is consistent under weak conditions. Hansen and Scheinkman (1995) also introduced an easily implementable estimating function where each term depends on a pair of consecutive observations that will be presented in Section 3.5. Another type of estimating function introduced by Bibby and Sørensen (1995) is

$$G_n(\theta) = \sum_{i=1}^{n} \frac{\partial_\theta b(X_{i-1};\theta)}{\sigma^2(X_{i-1};\theta)}[X_i - E_\theta(X_i|X_{i-1})],$$

which is an approximation to the optimal estimating function based on the relationship given by the function $h(x, y; \theta) = y - F(x; \theta)$ with $F(x; \theta) = \mathrm{E}_\theta(X_2 | X_1 = x)$. It can also be obtained by compensating a discretization of the continuous-time score function. This estimating function is a martingale, which simplifies the asymptotic theory. A disadvantage is that for most models, there is not an explicit expression for the conditional expectation $F(x; \theta)$, which must in such cases be determined numerically. For models with mean reversion, there is an explicit expression for $F(x; \theta)$. Let us finish this list of examples with an explicit martingale estimating function. For the diffusion on the interval $(-\pi/2, \pi/2)$ with $b(x; \theta) = -\theta \tan(x)$ and $\sigma(x; \theta) = 1$,

$$G_n(\theta) = \sum_{i=1}^{n} \sin(X_{i-1}) \left[\sin(X_i) - \mathrm{e}^{-\left(\theta + \frac{1}{2}\right)} \sin(X_{i-1}) \right],$$

(Kessler and Sørensen (1999)) is an approximation to the optimal estimating function based on the relationship given by the function $h(x, y; \theta) = \sin(y) - \mathrm{e}^{-\left(\theta + \frac{1}{2}\right)} \sin(x)$. Note that in this example, the estimating equation $G_n(\theta) = 0$ has an explicit solution. The three examples given here will be treated more fully later in this chapter.

The general theory for estimating functions for time series models is presented in Section 2. The emphasis is on martingale estimating functions, for which the limit theory is relatively simple and which play an central role for diffusion models. Various types of estimating functions for diffusion models are presented in Section 3. First, a collection of useful limit results for ergodic diffusion processes is given and the maximum likelihood estimator is briefly considered. Then a general class of martingale estimating functions is presented and discussed. Martingale estimating functions obtained by simulation are treated, and a thorough discussion is given of how to construct explicit estimating functions, whether martingales or not. A martingale estimating functions for diffusion with jumps is considered, and finally prediction-based estimating functions that can be used for non-Markovian diffusion-type models are treated. Stochastic volatility models are discussed in particular. In Section 4, optimal martingale estimating functions for diffusion models are found. In practice, considerable computational simplifications can often be obtained by using a suitable approximation to the optimal estimating function. This aspect is discussed in Section 4.2. A global optimality criterion for estimating functions for diffusion models, called small Δ-optimality, is the subject of Section 4.4. This criterion is particularly suitable at high sampling frequencies, where it is equivalent to efficiency.

2. ESTIMATING FUNCTIONS

Suppose as a model for the data $X_1, X_2, \ldots, X_n$ that they are observations from a stochastic process model indexed by a p-dimensional parameter $\theta \in \Theta$. We are particularly interested in the case, where the model is a continuous-time model observed at discrete time points that need not be equidistant. An *estimating function* is a p-dimensional function of the parameter θ and the data: $G_n(\theta; X_1, X_2, \ldots, X_n)$. Usually, we suppress the dependence on the observations in the notation and write $G_n(\theta)$. We get an estimator by solving the equation

$$G_n(\theta) = 0.$$

It is possible that there are several solutions or no solution at all. An estimator obtained from an estimating functions is usually called a GMM estimator in the econometric literature. General results on consistency and asymptotic normality of GMM estimators were given by Hansen (1982). Reviews of asymptotic theory for estimating functions with a particular view to diffusion models can be found in Sørensen (1999) and Jacod and Sørensen (2009).

Here, we only very briefly outline the main asymptotic results. An estimating function is called *unbiased* if $E_\theta(G_n(\theta)) = 0$. We will assume that the unbiasedness condition is satisfied either exactly (i.e., for all n) or asymptotically as $n \to \infty$, which ensures consistency of the estimator as $n \to \infty$ under weak regularity conditions. Consider an estimating function of the form

$$G_n(\theta) = \sum_{i=r}^{n} g(X_{i-r+1}, \ldots, X_i; \theta), \tag{2.1}$$

where the function g is p-dimensional, and where r is a fixed integer smaller than n. We will suppose that for all values of θ, the process $\{X_i\}$ is stationary and that $Q_\theta(g(\theta)) = 0$ and $Q_\theta(g_i(\theta)^2) < \infty$, where Q_θ denotes the joint distribution of $(X_1, \ldots, X_r)$, and $Q_\theta(f)$ is the expectation of $f(X_1, \ldots, X_r)$ for a function $f : \mathbb{R}^r \mapsto \mathbb{R}$. Suppose that a central limit theorem

$$\frac{1}{\sqrt{n}} \sum_{i=r}^{n} g(X_{i-r+1}, \ldots, X_i; \theta) \xrightarrow{\mathcal{D}} N(0, V(\theta)) \tag{2.2}$$

holds for some $p \times p$-matrix $V(\theta)$. If $G_n(\theta)$ is a P_θ-martingale, this follows from the central limit theorem for martingales. Under weak regularity conditions, an estimator $\hat{\theta}_n$ exists that solves the estimating equation $G_n(\hat{\theta}_n) = 0$, with a probability tending to one as $n \to \infty$, and is consistent and asymptotically normal:

$$\sqrt{n}\left(\hat{\theta}_n - \theta_0\right) \xrightarrow{\mathcal{D}} N\left(0, S(\theta_0)^{-1} V(\theta_0)(S(\theta_0)^{-1})^T\right), \tag{2.3}$$

as $n \to \infty$, where θ_0 denotes the true parameter value, and

$$S(\theta) = \left\{Q_\theta\left(\partial_{\theta_j} g_i(\theta)\right)\right\}. \tag{2.4}$$

Here, and later, ∂_{θ_j} denotes the partial derivative with respect to θ_j.

Suppose we have a class $\mathcal{G}_n$ of unbiased estimating functions. How do we choose the best member in $\mathcal{G}_n$? This is the question studied in the theory of optimal estimating functions, which has been developed in parallel, but with little interaction, in the econometrics and in the statistics literature. A comprehensive treatment of both literatures and their relations is outside the scope of this chapter, so here just a few references will be given. In the statistics literature, the theory dates back to the papers by Godambe (1960) and Durbin (1960); however, the basic idea was in a sense already used in Fisher (1935). The theory was extended to stochastic processes by Godambe (1985), Godambe and Heyde (1987), Heyde (1988), and several others; see the references in Heyde (1997). In the econometrics literature, the foundation was laid by Hansen (1982), who followed Sagan (1958) by using selection matrices. This study treats a very general class of models including time series models. Important extensions to the theory were made by Hansen (1985), Chamberlain (1987), Newey and West (1987), and Newey (1990); see also the discussion and references in Hall (2005). Particular attention is given to the time series setting in Hansen (1985), Hansen (1993), West (2001), and Kuersteiner (2002). Explorations of nonparametric implementations were made by Newey (2004) and others. A discussion of links between the econometrics and statistics literature can be found in Hansen (2001).

Ideally, we would base the statistical inference on the likelihood function $L_n(\theta)$ and hence use as our estimating function the score function $U_n(\theta) = \partial_\theta \log L_n(\theta)$. The optimal estimating function G_n^* in $\mathcal{G}_n$ is the one that is closest to $U_n(\theta)$ in a mean square sense. Under weak regularity conditions, it is also characterized as the estimating function in $\mathcal{G}_n$ for which the asymptotic variance in (2.3) is as small as possible. If an estimating function G_n^* in $\mathcal{G}_n$ satisfies that

$$S_{G_n}(\theta)^{-1} E_\theta\Big(G_n(\theta) G_n^*(\theta)^T\Big) = S_{G_n^*}(\theta)^{-1} E_\theta\Big(G_n^*(\theta) G_n^*(\theta)^T\Big) \tag{2.5}$$

for all $\theta \in \Theta$ and for all $G_n \in \mathcal{G}_n$, then it is *optimal in* $\mathcal{G}_n$. Here, $S_{G_n}(\theta)$ denotes the $p \times p$-matrix

$$S_{G_n}(\theta) = E_\theta(\partial_{\theta^T} G_n(\theta)) = \begin{pmatrix} E_\theta(\partial_{\theta_1} G_n(\theta)_1) & \cdots & E_\theta(\partial_{\theta_p} G_n(\theta)_1) \\ \vdots & & \vdots \\ E_\theta(\partial_{\theta_1} G_n(\theta)_p) & \cdots & E_\theta(\partial_{\theta_p} G_n(\theta)_p) \end{pmatrix}. \tag{2.6}$$

We denote the transpose of a vector or a matrix a by a^T. Vectors are column vectors.

2.1. Martingale Estimating Functions

Estimating functions that are martingales have particularly nice properties and a relatively simple asymptotic theory based on the well-developed martingale limit theory, see, e.g., Hall and Heyde (1980). A martingale estimating function is an estimating functions G_n satisfying that

$$\mathrm{E}_\theta(G_n(\theta)|\mathcal{F}_{n-1}) = G_{n-1}(\theta), \quad n = 1, 2, \ldots,$$

where $\mathcal{F}_{n-1}$ is the σ-field generated by the observations $X_1, \ldots, X_{n-1}$ ($G_0 = 0$ and $\mathcal{F}_0$ is the trivial σ-field). In other words, the stochastic process $\{G_n(\theta) : n = 1, 2, \ldots\}$ is a martingale under the model given by the parameter value θ. As will be discussed in Section 3.2, the score function is usually a martingale estimating function (for more details, see, e.g., Barndorff-Nielsen and Sørensen (1994)). When a more easily calculated alternative is needed, it is natural to approximate the score function by a simpler martingale estimating function.

Here, we briefly discuss an optimality criterion that is particular to martingale estimating functions. Suppose the estimating function $G_n(\theta)$ satisfies the conditions of the central limit theorem for martingales, and let $\hat{\theta}_n$ be a solution of the equation $G_n(\theta) = 0$. Then, under standard regularity conditions, the inverse of the random matrix

$$I_{G_n}(\theta) = \overline{G}_n(\theta)^T \langle G(\theta)\rangle_n^{-1} \overline{G}_n(\theta)$$

estimates the covariance matrix of the asymptotic distribution of the estimator $\hat{\theta}_n$; for details, see Heyde (1997). Here, $\overline{G}_n(\theta)$ is the predictable version (also called the compensator) of $\partial_{\theta^T} G_n(\theta)$ given by

$$\overline{G}_n(\theta) = \sum_{i=1}^{n} \mathrm{E}_\theta\big(\partial_{\theta^T} H_i(\theta)|\mathcal{F}_{i-1}\big),$$

where $H_i = G_i - G_{i-1}$. The quadratic cocharacteristic of two martingales, G and $\tilde{G}$, both with finite variance, is defined by

$$\langle G, \tilde{G}\rangle_n = \sum_{i=1}^{n} \mathrm{E}\Big(H_i \tilde{H}_i^T | \mathcal{F}_{i-1}\Big), \tag{2.7}$$

where $\tilde{H}_i = \tilde{G}_i - \tilde{G}_{i-1}$, and the quadratic characteristic of a martingale G_n is $\langle G\rangle_n = \langle G, G\rangle_n$. If $\mathcal{G}_n$ is a class of martingale estimating functions with finite variance, an estimating function G_n^* in $\mathcal{G}_n$ is called *Heyde-optimal* in $\mathcal{G}_n$ if

$$I_{G_n^*}(\theta) \geq I_{G_n}(\theta) \tag{2.8}$$

for all $\theta \in \Theta$, for all $G_n \in \mathcal{G}_n$, and for all $n \in \mathbb{N}$. The following useful result is similar to (2.5).

Theorem 1 (Heyde, 1988). *If* $G_n^* \in \mathcal{G}_n$ *satisfies*

$$\overline{G}_n(\theta)^{-1}\langle G(\theta), G^*(\theta)\rangle_n = \overline{G}_n^*(\theta)^{-1}\langle G^*(\theta)\rangle_n \tag{2.9}$$

for all $\theta \in \Theta$, $G_n \in \mathcal{G}_n$, *and* $n \in \mathbb{N}$, *then it is is Heyde-optimal in* $\mathcal{G}_n$. *When* $\mathcal{G}_n$ *is closed under addition, then any Heyde-optimal estimating function* G_n^* *satisfies (2.9). Moreover, if* $\overline{G}_n^*(\theta)^{-1}\langle G^*(\theta)\rangle_n$ *is nonrandom, then* G_n^* *satisfies the optimality condition (2.5) too.*

See Lemmas 4.2 and 4.3 in Hansen (1985) for essentially the same result, except that Hansen uses martingale approximation methods to study a general class of estimating equations constructed from stationary ergodic processes. Often, condition (2.9) can be verified by showing that $\langle G(\theta), G^*(\theta)\rangle_n = -\overline{G}_n(\theta)$ for all $G_n \in \mathcal{G}_n$, implying that (2.5) holds too.

Example 1 *Consider the situation that a number of functions,* $h_{ij}(x_1, \ldots, x_i; \theta), j = 1, \ldots, N$, $i = 1, \ldots n$, *are available, which satisfy that*

$$\mathrm{E}_\theta(h_{ij}(X_1, \ldots, X_i; \theta)|\mathcal{F}_{i-1}) = 0$$

for $j = 1, \ldots, N, i = 1, \ldots n$. *These relationships (dependent on* θ*) between an observation* X_i *and the previous observations* $X_1, \ldots, X_{i-1}$ *(or a subset of them) can be used to estimate* θ. *Specifically,*

$$G_n(\theta) = \sum_{i=1}^{n} a_i(X_1, \ldots, X_{i-1}; \theta) h_i(X_1, \ldots, X_i; \theta) \tag{2.10}$$

is a p-dimensional unbiased martingale estimating function. Here, h_i *denotes the* N*-dimensional vector* $(h_{i1}, \ldots, h_{iN})^T$, *and* $a_i(x_1, \ldots, x_{i-1}; \theta)$ *is a function from* $\mathbb{R}^{i-1} \times \Theta$ *into the set of* $p \times N$*-matrices that is differentiable with respect to* θ.

Let $\mathcal{G}_n$ *be the class of martingale estimating functions of the form (2.10) that have finite variance. To find the matrices* a_i *that combine the* N *relations in an optimal way, note that*

$$\overline{G}_n(\theta) = \sum_{i=1}^{n} a_i(X_1, \ldots, X_{i-1}; \theta) \mathrm{E}_\theta(\partial_{\theta^T} h_i(X_1, \ldots, X_i; \theta)|\mathcal{F}_{i-1})$$

and

$$\langle G(\theta), G^*(\theta)\rangle_n = \sum_{i=1}^{n} a_i(X_1, \ldots, X_{i-1}; \theta) V_{h_i}(X_1, \ldots, X_{i-1}; \theta) a_i^*(X_1, \ldots, X_{i-1}; \theta)^T,$$

where

$$G_n^*(\theta) = \sum_{i=1}^{n} a_i^*(X_1, \ldots, X_{i-1}; \theta) h_i(X_1, \ldots, X_i; \theta), \tag{2.11}$$

and

$$V_{h_i}(X_1,\ldots,X_{i-1};\theta) = \mathrm{E}_\theta\Big(h_i(X_1,\ldots,X_i;\theta)h_i(X_1,\ldots,X_i;\theta)^T|\mathcal{F}_{i-1}\Big)$$

is the conditional covariance matrix of the random vector $h_i(X_1,\ldots,X_i;\theta)$ *given* $(X_1,\ldots,X_{i-1})$. *The optimality condition (2.9) is satisfied for*

$$a_i^*(X_1,\ldots,X_{i-1};\theta) = -\mathrm{E}_\theta(\partial_{\theta^T}h_i(X_1,\ldots,X_i;\theta)|\mathcal{F}_{i-1})^T V_{h_i}(X_1,\ldots,X_{i-1};\theta)^{-1}, \tag{2.12}$$

so with this choice, the estimating function $G_n^*(\theta)$ *is Heyde-optimal by Theorem 1. Since* $\overline{G}_n^*(\theta)^{-1}\langle G^*(\theta)\rangle_n = -I_p$, *the estimating function* $G_n^*(\theta)$ *satisfies the optimality condition (2.5) too.*

Let $p_i(x;\theta|x_1,\ldots,x_{i-1})$ *denote the conditional density of* X_i *given that* $(X_1,\ldots,X_{i-1}) = (x_1,\ldots,x_{i-1})$. *Then the likelihood function for* θ *based on the data* $(X_1,\ldots,X_n)$ *is*

$$L_n(\theta) = \prod_{i=1}^n p_i(X_i;\theta|X_1,\ldots,X_{i-1})$$

(with p_1 *denoting the unconditional density of* X_1*). If we assume that all* p_i*s are differentiable with respect to* θ, *the score function is*

$$U_n(\theta) = \sum_{i=1}^n \partial_\theta \log p_i(X_i;\theta|X_1,\ldots,X_{i-1}). \tag{2.13}$$

We can now see in exactly what sense the optimal estimating function (2.11) approximates the score function. Let us fix $i, x_1,\ldots,x_{i-1}$ *and* θ. *We let* $\mathbf{x}_{i-1}$ *denote the vector* $(x_1,\ldots,x_{i-1})$ *and consider the* L_2*-space* $\mathcal{K}_i(\mathbf{x}_{i-1},\theta)$ *of functions* $f:\mathbb{R}\mapsto\mathbb{R}$, *for which*

$$\int f(x)^2 p_i(x;\theta|\mathbf{x}_{i-1})\mathrm{d}x < \infty.$$

We equip $\mathcal{K}_i(\mathbf{x}_{i-1},\theta)$ *with the usual inner product*

$$\langle f,g\rangle = \int f(x)g(x)p_i(x;\theta|\mathbf{x}_{i-1})\mathrm{d}x,$$

and let $\mathcal{H}_i(\mathbf{x}_{i-1},\theta)$ *denote the* N*-dimensional subspace of* $\mathcal{K}_i(\mathbf{x}_{i-1},\theta)$ *spanned by the functions* $x\mapsto h_{ij}(\mathbf{x}_{i-1},x;\theta), j=1,\ldots,N$. *That the functions are linearly independent in* $\mathcal{K}_i(\mathbf{x}_{i-1},\theta)$ *follows from the earlier assumption that the covariance matrix* $V_{h_i}(\mathbf{x}_{i-1};\theta)$ *is regular.*

Now, assume that $\partial_{\theta_j}\log p_i(\cdot\,|\,\mathbf{x}_{i-1};\theta)\in\mathcal{K}_i(\mathbf{x}_{i-1},\theta)$ *for* $j=1,\ldots,p$, *let* g_{ij}^* *denote the orthogonal projection with respect to* $\langle\cdot,\cdot\rangle$ *of* $\partial_{\theta_j}\log p_i$ *onto* $\mathcal{H}_i(\mathbf{x}_{i-1},\theta)$, *and define a* *p-dimensional function by* $g_i^* = (g_{i1}, \ldots, g_{ip})^T$. *Then*

$$g_i^*(\mathbf{x}_{i-1}, x; \theta) = a_i^*(\mathbf{x}_{i-1}; \theta) h_i(\mathbf{x}_{i-1}, x; \theta), \tag{2.14}$$

where a_i^* *is the matrix defined by (2.12). To see this, note that* g^* *must have the form (2.14) with* a_i^* *satisfying the normal equations*

$$\langle \partial_{\theta_j} \log p_i - g_j^*, \, h_{ik} \rangle = 0,$$

$j = 1, \ldots, p$ *and* $k = 1, \ldots, N$. *These equations can also be expressed in the form*

$$B_i = a_i^* V_{h_i},$$

where B_i *is the* $p \times p$*-matrix whose* (j, k)*th element is* $\langle \partial_{\theta_j} \log p_i, \, h_{ik} \rangle$. *If we can interchange differentiation and integration so that*

$$\int \partial_{\theta_j} [h_{ik}(\mathbf{x}_{i-1}, x; \theta) p(\mathbf{x}_{i-1}, x; \theta)] \mathrm{d}x = \partial_{\theta_j} \int h_{ik}(\mathbf{x}_{i-1}, x; \theta) p(\mathbf{x}_{i-1}, x; \theta) \mathrm{d}x = 0,$$

it follows that

$$B_i = - \int \partial_{\theta^T} h_i(\mathbf{x}_{i-1}, x; \theta) p(\mathbf{x}_{i-1}, x; \theta) \mathrm{d}x,$$

which proves (2.14).

The result (2.14) was first shown by Kessler (1996) in the case of a Markov process. The proof in the general case, given here for the first time, is essentially the same as that for a Markov process. It is important to note that if for all i the functions h_{ij} *are chosen such that as* $N \to \infty$, *the subspace* $\mathcal{H}_i(\mathbf{x}_{i-1}, \theta)$ *converges to a subspace of* $\mathcal{K}_i(\mathbf{x}_{i-1}, \theta)$ *containing the functions* $\partial_{\theta_j} \log p_i$, $j = 1, \ldots, p$, *then the optimal estimating function will approach the score function, and it is possible to obtain a sequence of estimators that is asymptotically fully efficient.*

3. ESTIMATING FUNCTIONS FOR DIFFUSION-TYPE PROCESSES

Suppose a d-dimensional continuous-time process X has been observed at discrete time points: $X_{t_0}, X_{t_1}, \ldots, X_{t_n}$, $t_0 = 0 < t_1 < \cdots < t_n$. As a model for these data, we assume that X is a d-dimensional diffusion, i.e., that X solves the stochastic differential equation

$$\mathrm{d}X_t = b(X_t; \theta)\mathrm{d}t + \sigma(X_t; \theta)\mathrm{d}W_t, \tag{3.1}$$

with b a d-dimensional vector, σ a $d \times d$-matrix, and W a d-dimensional standard Wiener process. We assume that the drift b and the diffusion coefficient σ are known apart from the parameter θ, which varies in a subset Θ of $\mathbb{R}^p$. These functions are assumed to be smooth enough to ensure the existence of a unique weak solution for all θ in Θ. The *state space* of X, i.e., the set of possible values of the process, is assumed not to depend on θ. The statistical problem considered here is to draw inference about the parameter θ based on the observations. We consider only the case where the sampling times are not random. The effect of random sampling times can be considerable, see Aït-Sahalia and Mykland (2003).

3.1. Limit Results for Diffusion Processes

In this section, we review asymptotic results for ergodic diffusion processes. We shall first consider *one-dimensional diffusion models*, i.e., solutions to stochastic differential equations of the form (3.1), where W is a standard Wiener process. Estimation of the parameter θ will not be discussed in this section, but the parameter is included in the notation for consistency with the rest of the section. The *state space* of X is an interval from ℓ to r, where ℓ could possibly be $-\infty$ and r might be ∞.

First, we give a condition ensuring that the solution X of (3.1) is ergodic. The *scale measure* of X is a measure on the state space (ℓ, r) with the density

$$s(x;\theta) = \exp\left(-2\int_{x^{\#}}^{x} \frac{b(y;\theta)}{v(y;\theta)}\mathrm{d}y\right) \tag{3.2}$$

with respect to the Lebesgue measure. Here, $x^{\#}$ is an arbitrary point in (ℓ, r), so the scale measure is only defined up to a multiplicative constant, which does not matter in the following. Since we shall often need the squared diffusion coefficient, we define

$$v(x;\theta) = \sigma^2(x;\theta). \tag{3.3}$$

Condition 1 *The following holds for all $\theta \in \Theta$:*

$$\int_{x^{\#}}^{r} s(x;\theta)\mathrm{d}x = \int_{\ell}^{x^{\#}} s(x;\theta)\mathrm{d}x = \infty$$

and

$$\int_{\ell}^{r} [s(x;\theta)v(x;\theta)]^{-1}\mathrm{d}x = A(\theta) < \infty.$$

Under Condition 1, the process X is *ergodic* with an *invariant probability measure* that has density

$$\mu_\theta(x) = [A(\theta)s(x;\theta)v(x;\theta)]^{-1}, \quad x \in (\ell, r), \tag{3.4}$$

with respect to the Lebesgue measure on (ℓ, r). We will assume that $X_0 \sim \mu_\theta$ so that X is a stationary process with $X_t \sim \mu_\theta$ for all $t \geq 0$. The distribution of (X_t, X_{t+s}) $t > 0, s > 0$ has density

$$Q_\theta^s(x, y) = \mu_\theta(x)p(s, x, y; \theta), \tag{3.5}$$

where $y \mapsto p(s, x, y; \theta)$ is the *transition density*, i.e., the conditional density of X_{t+s} given that $X_t = x$. For a function $f : (\ell, r)^2 \mapsto \mathbb{R}$, we use the notation

$$Q_\theta^s(f) = \int\limits_{(\ell,r)^2} f(x, y)p(s, x, y; \theta)\mu_\theta(x)\mathrm{d}y\mathrm{d}x$$

(provided, of course, that the integral exists). Similarly, we define

$$\mu_\theta(f) = \int\limits_\ell^r f(x)\mu_\theta(x)\mathrm{d}x$$

for a function $f : (\ell, r) \mapsto \mathbb{R}$.

Suppose Condition 1 holds, that $f : (\ell, r) \mapsto \mathbb{R}$ satisfies $\mu_\theta(|f|) < \infty$, and that $g : (\ell, r)^2 \mapsto \mathbb{R}$ satisfies $Q_\theta^\Delta(|g|) < \infty$ for a $\Delta > 0$. Then

$$\frac{1}{n}\sum_{i=1}^n f(X_{i\Delta}) \xrightarrow{a.s.} \mu_\theta(f) \tag{3.6}$$

and

$$\frac{1}{n}\sum_{i=1}^n g(X_{(i-1)\Delta}, X_{i\Delta}) \xrightarrow{a.s.} Q_\theta^\Delta(g) \tag{3.7}$$

as $n \to \infty$, see Billingsley (1961b). The result (3.6) is obviously a particular case of (3.7).

If we assume that the sum $\sum_{i=1}^n g(X_{(i-1)\Delta}, X_{i\Delta})$ is a martingale with finite variance, i.e., that

$$\int\limits_\ell^r g(x, y)p(\Delta, x, y; \theta)\mathrm{d}y = 0 \quad \text{for all } x \in (\ell, r)$$

and that $Q_\theta^\Delta(g^2) < \infty$, then under Condition 1,

$$\frac{1}{\sqrt{n}}\sum_{i=1}^n g(X_{(i-1)\Delta}, X_{i\Delta}) \xrightarrow{\mathcal{D}} N(0, V(\theta)) \tag{3.8}$$

as $n \to \infty$, where $V(\theta) = Q_\theta^\Delta(g^2)$; see Billingsley (1961a). The central limit theorem (3.8) holds in the multidimensional case $g : (\ell, r)^2 \mapsto \mathbb{R}^p$ too, provided that each coordinate of $\sum_{i=1}^n g(X_{(i-1)\Delta}, X_{i\Delta})$ is a martingale with finite variance. In the multidimensional case, $V(\theta) = Q_\theta^\Delta\left(gg^T\right)$. Here, and later, T denotes transposition and vectors are column vectors.

In cases where $\sum_{i=1}^n g(X_{(i-1)\Delta}, X_{i\Delta})$ is not a martingale, stronger conditions on the diffusion are needed to ensure the central limit result (3.8). Often, it is assumed that the process X is geometrically α-mixing, i.e., α-mixing with mixing coefficients that tend to zero exponentially fast. Sufficient conditions for geometrical α-mixing were given by Veretennikov (1987), Doukhan (1994), Hansen and Scheinkman (1995), Kusuoka and Yoshida (2000), and Genon-Catalot et al. (2000); see also Aït-Sahalia et al. (2010). Suppose the diffusion is stationary and geometrically α-mixing. Then (3.8) holds in the multidimensional case with

$$V(\theta) = Q_\theta^\Delta(gg^T) + \sum_{k=1}^{\infty}\Big[E_\theta\Big(g(X_\Delta, X_0)g(X_{(k+1)\Delta}, X_{k\Delta})^T\Big) + E_\theta\Big(g(X_{(k+1)\Delta}, X_{k\Delta})g(X_\Delta, X_0)^T\Big)\Big], \tag{3.9}$$

provided that $V(\theta)$ is strictly positive definite, and that $Q_\theta^\Delta\left(g_i(\theta)^{2+\epsilon}\right) < \infty, i = 1, \ldots, p$, for some $\epsilon > 0$, see, e.g., Doukhan (1994). Here g_i denotes the ith coordinate of g.

Finally, we consider briefly the case where X is a *multivariate diffusion*, i.e., when X is the d-dimensional process that solves (3.1) with b now a d-dimensional vector, σ a $d \times d$-matrix, and W a d-dimensional standard Wiener process. We assume that X moves freely on an open, connected set $D \subseteq \mathbb{R}^d$ (that does not depend on θ), $C(x;\theta) = \sigma(x;\theta)\sigma(x;\theta)^T$ is strictly positive definite for all $x \in D$, $\theta \in \Theta$, and X is ergodic for all θ with an invariant density $\mu_\theta(x)$. Under these assumptions, the above results (3.6), (3.7), and (3.8) hold in the multivariate case too for martingales, and more generally when X is geometrically α-mixing. The problem is that the conditions ensuring ergodicity are not as simple as those for one-dimensional diffusions. A rich theory including conditions for exponential ergodicity was presented in Meyn and Tweedie (1993). An application of these results to one-dimensional diffusions can be found in Chen et al. (2008).

3.2. Maximum Likelihood Estimation

The diffusion process X is a Markov process, so the likelihood function (conditional on X_0) is

$$L_n(\theta) = \prod_{i=1}^{n} p(t_i - t_{i-1}, X_{t_{i-1}}, X_{t_i}; \theta), \tag{3.10}$$

where $y \mapsto p(s, x, y; \theta)$ is the transition density. Under weak regularity conditions, the maximum likelihood estimator is efficient, i.e., it has the smallest asymptotic variance among all estimators. The transition density is only rarely explicitly known, but there are a number of numerical approaches that render likelihood inference feasible for diffusion models. Pedersen (1995) proposed a method for obtaining an approximation to the likelihood function by rather extensive simulation. Pedersen's method was very considerably improved by Durham and Gallant (2002), whose method is computationally much more efficient. Poulsen (1999) obtained an approximation to the transition density by numerically solving a partial differential equation, while Aït-Sahalia (2002) and Aït-Sahalia (2008) proposed to approximate the transition density by means of a Hermite expansion, see also Aït-Sahalia et al. (2010). A Gaussian approximation to the likelihood function obtained by local linearization of the stochastic differential equation was proposed by Ozaki (1985). Bayesian estimators with the same asymptotic properties as the maximum likelihood estimator can be obtained by Markov chain Monte Carlo methods, see Elerian et al. (2001), Eraker (2001), Roberts and Stramer (2001), and Johannes and Polson (2010). Finally, exact and computationally efficient likelihood-based estimation methods were presented by Beskos et al. (2006). These various approaches to maximum likelihood estimation will not be considered further in this chapter.

The vector $U_n(\theta)$ of partial derivatives of the log-likelihood function $\log L_n(\theta)$ with respect to the coordinates of θ is called the *score function* (or score vector). The maximum likelihood estimator solves the estimating equation $U_n(\theta) = 0$. The score function based on the observations $X_{t_0}, X_{t_1}, \ldots, X_{t_n}$ is

$$U_n(\theta) = \sum_{i=1}^{n} \partial_\theta \log p(\Delta_i, X_{t_{i-1}}, X_{t_i}; \theta), \tag{3.11}$$

where $\Delta_i = t_i - t_{i-1}$. The score function is a martingale estimating function, which is easily seen provided that the following interchange of differentiation and integration is allowed:

$$E_\theta\big(\partial_\theta \log p(\Delta_i, X_{t_{i-1}}, X_{t_i}; \theta) \big| X_{t_1}, \ldots, X_{t_{i-1}}\big) = E_\theta\left(\frac{\partial_\theta p(\Delta_i, X_{t_{i-1}}, X_{t_i}; \theta)}{p(\Delta_i, X_{t_{i-1}}, X_{t_i}; \theta)} \,\middle|\, X_{t_{i-1}} \right)$$

$$= \int_\ell^r \frac{\partial_\theta p(\Delta_i, X_{t_{i-1}}, y; \theta)}{p(\Delta_i, X_{t_{i-1}}, y; \theta)} p(\Delta_i, X_{t_{i-1}}, y, \theta) \mathrm{d}y = \partial_\theta \underbrace{\int_\ell^r p(\Delta_i, X_{t_{i-1}}, y; \theta) \mathrm{d}y}_{=1} = 0.$$

A wide spectrum of estimators based on estimating functions other than the score function have been proposed and are useful alternatives to the maximum likelihood estimator in situation where simpler estimators that require less computation are needed. Some of these alternatives are not much less efficient than the maximum likelihood estimator, and in some cases, they are even fully efficient. Another advantage of these alternative approaches is that the estimators are often more robust to model misspecification than the maximum likelihood estimator because typically the estimating functions do not involve the full model specification. For instance, the martingale estimating functions considered below depends only on the conditional moments of certain functions of the observations. In the following sections, some of these alternative estimating functions will be reviewed and discussed.

3.3. Martingale Estimating Functions for Diffusion Models

The score function is a martingale estimating function of the form

$$G_n(\theta) = \sum_{i=1}^{n} g(\Delta_i, X_{t_{i-1}}, X_{t_i}; \theta). \tag{3.12}$$

It is therefore natural to approximate the score function by martingale estimating functions of the general form (3.12) with

$$g(\Delta, x, y; \theta) = \sum_{j=1}^{N} a_j(\Delta, x; \theta) h_j(\Delta, x, y; \theta), \tag{3.13}$$

where $h_j(\Delta, x, y; \theta), j = 1, \ldots, N$ are given real-valued functions satisfying that

$$\int_{\ell}^{r} h_j(\Delta, x, y; \theta) p(\Delta, x, y; \theta) dy = 0$$

for all $\Delta > 0$, $x \in (\ell, r)$, and $\theta \in \Theta$. Each of the functions h_j could separately be used to define an estimating function of the form (3.12), but more efficient estimators are obtained by combining them in an optimal way. The p-dimensional functions a_j in (3.13) determine how much weight is given in the estimation procedure to each of the relationships defined by the h_js. These functions, which we will refer to as the *weights*, can be chosen in an optimal way using the theory of optimal estimating functions. This is quite straightforward, see Section 2. The choice of the functions h_j, on the other hand, is an art rather than a science. The ability to tailor these functions to a given model or to particular parameters of interest is a considerable strength of the estimating functions methodology. It is, on the other hand, also a source of weakness since it is not always clear how best to choose the h_js. However, for diffusion models, the global small Δ-optimality criterion presented in Section 4.4 gives some guidance to the choice of the functions h_j. In what follows and in Section 3.5, we shall present some standard ways of choosing these functions that usually work in practice. Note that the weights a_j are usually called *instruments* in the econometric literature.

Martingale estimating functions have turned out to be very useful in obtaining estimators for discretely sampled diffusion-type models; see, for instance, Bibby and Sørensen (1995), Bibby and Sørensen (1996), Sørensen (1997), Kessler and Sørensen (1999), Kessler (2000), Bibby and Sørensen (2001), Jacobsen (2001a), and Sørensen (2007). Applications to financial data can be found in Bibby and Sørensen (1997), and Larsen and Sørensen (2007).

A simple type of estimating function is the *linear estimating function* obtained for $N = 1$ and

$$h_1(\Delta, x, y; \theta) = y - F(\Delta, x; \theta),$$

where

$$F(\Delta, x; \theta) = \mathrm{E}_\theta(X_\Delta | X_0 = x) = \int_\ell^r y p(\Delta, x, y; \theta) \mathrm{d}y. \tag{3.14}$$

In some models, the conditional expectation $F(\Delta, x; \theta)$ and the conditional variance $\phi(\Delta, x; \theta) = \mathrm{Var}_\theta(X_\Delta | X_0 = x)$ are known, but in most cases, they are not and must be determined by simulations, which can usually be done easily; see the following subsection. Linear martingale estimating functions for diffusion models were studied by Bibby and Sørensen (1995), where they were derived as an approximation to the continuous-time likelihood function. An advantage of this type of estimating functions is that the estimators are very robust to model misspecification. If only the first moment F of the transition distribution is correctly specified, the estimator is consistent.

When the diffusion coefficient (the volatility) σ depends on a parameter, the linear estimating function are too simple to be useful, whereas the *quadratic estimating functions* are a natural, generally applicable choice. They are obtained for $N = 2$ and, when the diffusion is one dimensional,

$$\begin{aligned} h_1(\Delta, x, y; \theta) &= y - F(\Delta, x; \theta) \\ h_2(\Delta, x, y; \theta) &= (y - F(\Delta, x; \theta))^2 - \phi(\Delta, x, \theta), \end{aligned}$$

where

$$\phi(\Delta, x; \theta) = \mathrm{Var}_\theta(X_\Delta | X_0 = x) = \int_\ell^r [y - F(\Delta, x; \theta)]^2 p(\Delta, x, y; \theta) \mathrm{d}y. \tag{3.15}$$

The version for multivariate diffusions is defined in an analogous way. An argument for using this type of estimating function goes as follows. When Δ is small, the transition density $p(\Delta, x, y; \theta)$ is well approximated by a Gaussian density function with expectation $F(\Delta, x; \theta)$ and variance $\phi(\Delta, x; \theta)$. By inserting this Gaussian density in the expression for the likelihood function (3.10), an approximate likelihood function is obtained, and the corresponding approximate score function is

$$\begin{aligned} \sum_{i=1}^n \Bigg\{ & \frac{\partial_\theta F(\Delta_i, X_{t_{i-1}}; \theta)}{\phi(\Delta_i, X_{t_{i-1}}; \theta)} [X_{t_i} - F(\Delta_i, X_{t_{i-1}}; \theta)] \\ & + \frac{\partial_\theta \phi(\Delta_i, X_{t_{i-1}}; \theta)}{2\phi^2(\Delta_i, X_{t_{i-1}}; \theta) \Delta_i} [(X_{t_i} - F(\Delta_i, X_{t_{i-1}}; \theta))^2 - \phi(\Delta_i, X_{t_{i-1}}; \theta)] \Bigg\}. \end{aligned} \tag{3.16}$$

Quadratic martingale estimating functions for diffusion models were considered in Bibby and Sørensen (1996). Estimators obtained from this type of estimating functions are also rather robust to model misspecification. If the first and the second conditional moments, F and ϕ, are correctly specified, the estimator is consistent.

Example 2 *For a* mean-reverting diffusion model *given by*

$$dX_t = -\beta(X_t - \alpha)dt + \sigma(X_t)dW_t, \tag{3.17}$$

where $\beta > 0$,

$$F(t, x; \alpha, \beta) = xe^{-\beta t} + \alpha(1 - e^{-\beta t}) \tag{3.18}$$

under weak conditions on σ*. This can be seen by noting that for fixed* x, α*, and* β*, the function* $f(t) = F(t, x; \alpha, \beta)$ *solves the ordinary differential equation* $f' = -\beta(f - \alpha)$*. Thus, linear estimating functions can be easily calculated.*

If we make the further assumption that $\sigma(x) = \tau\sqrt{x}\,(\tau > 0)$*, we obtain the model proposed by Cox et al. (1985) for interest rates (the spot rate). In the rest of the chapter, we will refer to this model as the CIR model or the CIR process. It was originally introduced by Feller (1951) in a biological context, and it is often referred to as the square root process. For the CIR model, the function* ϕ *and hence quadratic estimating functions can be found explicitly:*

$$\phi(x; \alpha, \beta, \tau) = \frac{\tau^2}{\beta}\left(\left(\frac{1}{2}\alpha - x\right)e^{-2\beta} - (\alpha - x)e^{-\beta} + \frac{1}{2}\alpha\right).$$

Another model, where ϕ *can be found explicitly is the mean-reverting model with* $\sigma = \sqrt{\beta + x^2}$*. For this model (with* $\alpha = 0$*),*

$$\phi(x; \beta) = x^2 e^{-2\beta}(e - 1) + \frac{\beta}{2\beta - 1}(1 - e^{1-2\beta}).$$

A natural generalization of the quadratic martingale estimating functions is obtained by choosing h_js of the form

$$h_j(\Delta, x, y; \theta) = f_j(y; \theta) - \pi_\Delta^\theta(f_j(\theta))(x) \tag{3.19}$$

for suitably chosen functions f_j and with the transition operator π_Δ^θ defined by

$$\pi_s^\theta(f)(x) = \int_D f(y)p(s, x, y; \theta)dy = E_\theta(f(X_s)|X_0 = x), \tag{3.20}$$

where D denotes the state space. We refer to the functions $f_j, j = 1, \ldots, N$ as the *base* of the estimating function. Almost all martingale estimating functions proposed in the literature are of this form. An example is the higher order *polynomial martingale estimating functions* for one-dimensional diffusions considered by Pedersen (1994a) and Kessler (1996). These are obtained by choosing the base as $f_j(y) = y^j, j = 1, \ldots, N$. However, there is no reason to believe that polynomial estimating functions are in general the best possible way to approximate the true score function when the transition distribution is far from Gaussian, and it may be useful to choose a base that is tailored to a particular diffusion model. An example are the estimating functions based on eigenfunctions of the generator of the diffusion that were proposed by Kessler and Sørensen (1999). These estimating functions and other examples will be discussed in Section 3.5.

3.4. Constructing Estimating Functions by Simulation

In many cases, the conditional moments needed in a martingale estimating function are not explicitly available and must be calculated numerically, for instance by means of simulations. In this section, we briefly consider the effect on the variance of the estimator caused by simulation. Suppose that we need the conditional expectation of $f(X_{t+\Delta})$ given that $X_t = x$ for a particular value θ of the parameter. As usual, it is assumed that X solves (3.1). Then we can use one of the approximation schemes in Kloeden and Platen (1999) with a step size δ much smaller than Δ to generate an approximation $Y(\delta, \theta, x)$ to X starting at x. A simple example is the Euler scheme

$$Y_{i\delta} = Y_{(i-1)\delta} + b(Y_{(i-1)\delta}; \theta)\delta + \sigma(Y_{(i-1)\delta}; \theta) Z_i, \quad Y_0 = x,$$

where the Z_is are independent and $Z_i \sim N(0, \delta)$. By generating N independent simulations $Y^{(j)}(\delta, \theta, x), j = 1, \ldots, N$, we can approximate the conditional expectation of $f(X_{t+\Delta})$ given that $X_t = x$ by

$$\frac{1}{N} \sum_{j=1}^{N} f\left(Y_\Delta^{(j)}(\delta, \theta, x)\right).$$

The discretization error is indicated by δ. We can avoid the discretization error by simulating the diffusion X exactly by the methods in Beskos and Roberts (2005) and Beskos et al. (2006). Under strong boundedness conditions, this algorithm is relatively simple, whereas it is considerably more involved for general diffusions.

This procedure is closely related to the simulated method of moments, see Duffie and Singleton (1993) and Clement (1997). General results on asymptotic properties of simulated estimating functions were given by Pakes and Pollard (1989). The asymptotic properties of the estimators obtained when the conditional moments are approximated by simulation of diffusion models were investigated by Kessler and Paredes (2002), who considered approximations to martingale estimating functions of the form

$$G_n(\theta) = \sum_{i=1}^{n} \left[f(X_{i\Delta}, X_{(i-1)\Delta}; \theta) - F(X_{(i-1)\Delta}; \theta) \right], \tag{3.21}$$

where $F(x;\theta)$ is the conditional expectation of $f(X_\Delta, x;\theta)$ given $X_0 = x$ when the parameter value is θ. Let $\hat{\theta}_n^{N,\delta}$ denote the estimator obtained from the approximate martingale estimating function

$$G_n^{N,\delta}(\theta) = \sum_{i=1}^{n} \left[f(X_{i\Delta}, X_{(i-1)\Delta};\theta) - \frac{1}{N}\sum_{j=1}^{N} f\left(Y_\Delta^{(j)}(\delta,\theta,X_{(i-1)\Delta}), X_{(i-1)\Delta};\theta\right)\right]. \tag{3.22}$$

If an exact simulation method is used, there is no discretization error, so only the usual Monte Carlo effect of a finite value of N will increase the asymptotic variance of the estimator. Under usual regularity conditions

$$\sqrt{n}\left(\hat{\theta}_n^{N,\delta} - \theta_0\right) \xrightarrow{\mathcal{D}} N(0, (1+1/N)\Sigma), \tag{3.23}$$

as $n \to \infty$, where θ_0 is the true parameter value and Σ denotes the asymptotic covariance matrix for the estimator obtained from the estimating function (3.21); see (2.3).

To consider simulation schemes with a discretization error, suppose that $Y(\delta,\theta,x)$ satisfies that there exists a $\delta > 0$ such that

$$\left|E_\theta(g(X_\Delta(x), x;\theta)) - E(g(Y_\Delta(\delta,\theta,x), x;\theta))\right| \le R(x;\theta)\delta^\beta \tag{3.24}$$

for all $x \in \mathbb{R}$ and $\theta \in \Theta$, and for δ sufficiently small. Here, $g(y,x;\theta) = f(y,x;\theta) - F(x;\theta)$, $X_t(x)$ is a solution of (3.1) with $X_0(x) = x$, and $R(x;\theta)$ is of polynomial growth in x uniformly for θ in compact sets. According to Kessler and Paredes (2002), condition (3.24) is satisfied by the order β weak schemes based on Ito–Taylor expansions given in chapter 14 of Kloeden and Platen (1999). Under (3.24) and a number of further regularity conditions, Kessler and Paredes (2002) showed that if δ goes to zero sufficiently fast that $\sqrt{n}\delta^\beta \to 0$ as $n \to \infty$, then the result (3.23) is still valid. Thus by choosing δ sufficiently small, the asymptotic variance of the estimators obtained with simulated moments is only inflated by the factor $(1+1/N)$ compared to the estimator obtained by using exact conditional moments, and obviously, we can make this factor as close to one as we like by choosing N sufficiently large. However, Kessler and Paredes (2002) also gives a warning against using a simulation method with a too large discretization error. When $0 < \lim_{n\to\infty} \sqrt{n}\delta^\beta < \infty$,

$$\sqrt{n}\left(\hat{\theta}_n^{N,\delta} - \theta_0\right) \xrightarrow{\mathcal{D}} N(m(\theta_0), (1+1/N)\Sigma),$$

and when $\sqrt{n}\delta^\beta \to \infty$,

$$\delta^{-\beta}\left(\hat{\theta}_n^{N,\delta} - \theta_0\right) \to m(\theta_0)$$

in probability, where the p-dimensional vector $m(\theta_0)$ depends on f and is generally different from zero. Thus, the estimator can be badly misbehaved if a value of δ is used that is too large.

3.5. Explicit Estimating Functions

In this section, we focus on estimating functions for which explicit analytic expressions are available. These are particularly useful because the problem of finding the resulting estimators then amounts to solving p explicitly given equations, and although typically the solution must be obtained numerically, that will not create practical problems if the dimension of the parameter is not too large – in particular no simulations are required for the calculations.

We start the discussion of explicit estimating functions by considering first *martingale estimating functions* of the form (3.12), (3.13), and (3.19), i.e.,

$$G_n(\theta) = \sum_{i=1}^{n} a(\Delta_i, X_{t_{i-1}}, \theta) \left(f\left(X_{t_i}; \theta\right) - \pi_{\Delta}^{\theta}(f(\theta))(X_{t_{i-1}}) \right) \tag{3.25}$$

with $f = (f_j)_{1 \le j \le N}$ a (column) vector of given functions, the *base*, and $a = (a_{kj})_{1 \le k \le p, 1 \le j \le N}$ a $p \times N$-matrix of given functions, the *weights*. The transition operator, π_{Δ}^{θ}, is defined by (3.20). We shall call $G_n(\theta)$ explicit if all the f_j and a_{kj} are given in explicit form *and* the conditional expectations $\pi_{\Delta}^{\theta}(f(\theta))(x)$ can be determined explicitly. In this section, the weight matrix a can be chosen in any way we please, so we shall not be concerned with the explicit determination of a. In the next section, we shall discuss how to determine a in an optimal or approximately optimal way. Then, we shall also discuss when an explicit expression for the optimal a is available.

By far, the simplest case in which $\pi_{\Delta}^{\theta}(f(\theta))(x)$ can be found explicitly is when the base consists of eigenfunctions for the generator of the diffusion as proposed by Kessler and Sørensen (1999) for one-dimensional diffusions. The differential operator

$$L_\theta = b(x; \theta) \frac{\mathrm{d}}{\mathrm{d}x} + \frac{1}{2} \sigma^2(x; \theta) \frac{\mathrm{d}^2}{\mathrm{d}x^2} \tag{3.26}$$

is called the *generator* of the diffusion process given by (3.1). Generators of Markov processes are treated more fully in Aït-Sahalia et al. (2010). A twice differentiable function $\phi(x; \theta)$ is called an *eigenfunction* for the generator L_θ if

$$L_\theta \phi(x; \theta) = -\lambda(\theta) \phi(x; \theta), \tag{3.27}$$

where the real number $\lambda(\theta) \ge 0$ is called the *eigenvalue* corresponding to $\phi(x; \theta)$. Under weak regularity conditions, see, e.g., Kessler and Sørensen (1999),

$$\pi_{\Delta}^{\theta}(\phi(\theta))(x) = \mathrm{E}_\theta(\phi(X_\Delta; \theta) | X_0 = x) = \mathrm{e}^{-\lambda(\theta)\Delta} \phi(x; \theta). \tag{3.28}$$

We can therefore define a martingale estimating function by (3.12) and (3.13) with

$$h_j(\Delta, x, y; \theta) = \phi_j(y; \theta) - e^{-\lambda_j(\theta)\Delta}\phi_j(x; \theta), \tag{3.29}$$

where $\phi_1(\cdot;\theta), \ldots, \phi_N(\cdot;\theta)$ are eigenfunctions for L_θ with eigenvalues $\lambda_1(\theta), \ldots, \lambda_N(\theta)$.

An important class of one-dimensional diffusions for which explicit eigenfunctions are available is the class of *Pearson diffusions*. This is the class of diffusions with linear drift and quadratic squared diffusion coefficient, i.e., $b(x) = -\beta(x - \alpha)$ and $\sigma^2(x) = ax^2 + bx + c$. Because in this case, the generator (3.26) maps polynomials into polynomials, it is easy to find explicit polynomial eigenfunctions. This class of diffusions was introduced by Wong (1964). The class of stationary distributions equals the Pearson class of distributions introduced in Pearson (1895). If X is a Pearson diffusion, an explicit eigenfunction is also available for the diffusion $F(X)$, where F is a twice differentiable, invertible mapping. Explicit estimating functions for the Pearson diffusions and their transformations (and for more complex models build using these processes) have recently been studied by Forman and Sørensen (2008). In the following examples, the observed process is either a Pearson diffusion or a transformation of a Pearson diffusion.

Example 3 *For the Cox-Ingersoll-Ross model, the eigenfunctions are the Laguerre polynomials, and we obtain polynomial estimating functions, some of which were discussed in Example 2.*

Example 4 *The class of diffusions, which solve the equation*

$$dX_t = -\theta \tan(X_t)dt + dW_t, \quad X_0 = x_0$$

is more interesting because here the eigenfunctions are not polynomials, and we get estimating functions that we have not seen before. For $\theta \geq \frac{1}{2}$, the process X is an ergodic diffusion on the interval $(-\pi/2, \pi/2)$, which can be thought of as an Ornstein–Uhlenbeck process on a finite interval. The eigenfunctions are $\phi_i(x;\theta) = C_i^\theta(\sin(x))$, $i = 0, 1, \ldots$, with eigenvalues $i(\theta + i/2)$, $i = 0, 1, \ldots$, where C_i^θ is the Gegenbauer polynomial of order i. This model was studied in more detail in Kessler and Sørensen (1999). An asymmetric version was introduced in Larsen and Sørensen (2007).

Example 5 *In Larsen and Sørensen (2007), the following model is proposed for the random variation of an* exchange rate in a target zone *between realignments. Let X denote the logarithm of the exchange rate. Then*

$$dX_t = -\beta[X_t - (m + \gamma Z)]dt + \sigma\sqrt{Z^2 - (X_t - m)^2}\,dW_t, \tag{3.30}$$

where $\beta > 0$ and $\gamma \in (-1, 1)$. This is a diffusion on the interval $(m - Z, m + Z)$ with mean reversion around $m + \gamma Z$. Here, m denotes the central parity and $Z = \log(1 + z)$ with z denoting the largest deviation from m that is allowed. The quantities m and z are known fixed quantities.

When $\beta(1-\gamma) \geq \sigma^2$ and $\beta(1+\gamma) \geq \sigma^2$, X an ergodic diffusion, for which the stationary distribution is the beta-distribution on $(m-Z, m+Z)$ with parameters $\beta(1-\gamma)\sigma^{-2}$ and $\beta(1+\gamma)\sigma^{-2}$. For $\gamma = 0$, the target zone model proposed by De Jong et al. (2001) is obtained. The purpose of introducing the parameter γ is to allow an asymmetric stationary distribution, which is usually needed to fit observations of exchange rates in a target zone, see Larsen and Sørensen (2007). The eigenfunctions for the generator of the diffusion (3.30) are the Jacobi polynomials

$$\phi_i(x;\beta,\gamma,\sigma) = \sum_{j=1}^{i} 2^{-j} \binom{\beta(1-\gamma)\sigma^{-2}+i-1}{i-j} \binom{2\beta\sigma^{-2}-2+i+j}{j} [(x-m)/Z-1]^j$$

with eigenvalues $\lambda_i = i\left[\beta + \frac{1}{2}\sigma^2(i-1)\right]$, $i = 1, 2, \ldots$.

Although it is quite natural to search for eigenfunctions for the generator of a one-dimensional diffusion, it is less natural in higher dimensions (e.g., the eigenvalues need no longer be real). Instead, one may use invariant subspaces and do the following. Let X be a general d-dimensional diffusion satisfying (3.1) with b a d-dimensional vector and σ a $d \times d$-matrix. For a d-dimensional diffusion, the generator is defined by

$$L_\theta f(x) = \sum_{k=1}^{d} b_k(x;\theta)\partial_{x_k} f(x) + \frac{1}{2} \sum_{k,\ell=1}^{d} C_{k\ell}(x;\theta)\partial^2_{x_k x_\ell} f(x),$$

where f is a real twice differentiable function defined on the d-dimensional state space of X and $C = \sigma\sigma^T$ with σ^T denoting the transpose of σ. Suppose that for every θ, $\mathcal{L}_\theta$ is a finite-dimensional vector space of twice differentiable real-valued functions f^* such that $L_\theta f^* \in \mathcal{L}_\theta$ for all $f^* \in \mathcal{L}_\theta$ (the simplest case is, of course, when $\mathcal{L}_\theta$ is a one-dimensional eigenspace). If $(f_j)_{1\leq j\leq N}$ is a basis for $\mathcal{L}_\theta$, we may write

$$L_\theta f = \Psi_\theta f, \tag{3.31}$$

where Ψ_θ is an $N \times N$-matrix of constants and f is the column vector $(f_j)_{1\leq j\leq N}$. The basis f will typically depend on θ, but that dependence is suppressed in the notation. By $L_\theta f$ we mean that L_θ is applied to each coordinate of f, i.e., $L_\theta f$ is the column vector $(L_\theta f_j)_{1\leq j\leq N}$. Then by Itô's formula

$$\pi_t^\theta f(x) = f(x) + \int_0^t \Psi_\theta\left(\pi_s^\theta f\right)(x)\,ds \quad (x \in D) \tag{3.32}$$

provided all $f_j(X_s)$ are integrable, $E_\theta\left(\left|f_j(X_s)\right| \,\middle|\, X_0 = x\right) < \infty$, for all x, and provided each of the local martingales

$$M_t^{f_j} = \sum_{k=1}^{d} \int_0^t \partial_{x_k} f_j(X_s) \sum_{\ell=1}^{d} \sigma_{k\ell}(X_s)\, dW_{\ell,s}$$

is a true martingale conditionally on $X_0 = x$. In that case, (3.32) gives $\partial_t \pi_t^\theta f = \Psi_\theta \pi_t^\theta f$ with the boundary condition $\pi_0^\theta f = f$ so that

$$\pi_t^\theta f(x) = \mathrm{e}^{t\Psi_\theta} f(x) \quad (x \in D) \tag{3.33}$$

with the matrix exponential function defined through its series expansion,

$$\mathrm{e}^{t\Psi_\theta} = \sum_{m=0}^{\infty} \frac{t^m}{m!} \Psi_\theta^m.$$

It is perhaps debatable whether (3.33) is an explicit expression, but at least, if N is not too large, a more compact expression may be found.

Note that (3.18) in Example 2 (where the diffusion is one-dimensional) may be deduced as a special case of (3.33) with $\mathcal{L}_\theta = \mathcal{L}$ equal to the space of polynomials of degree less than or equal to one. We have $N = 2$ and can use $f_1(x) = 1$ and $f_2(x) = x$ as basis for $\mathcal{L}$. Then $L_\theta f_1 = 0$, $L_\theta f_2 = \alpha\beta f_1 - \beta f_2$ so that

$$\Psi_\theta = \begin{pmatrix} 0 & 0 \\ \alpha\beta & -\beta \end{pmatrix}.$$

A straightforward calculation gives

$$\mathrm{e}^{t\Psi_\theta} = \begin{pmatrix} 1 & 0 \\ \alpha\left(1 - \mathrm{e}^{-t\beta}\right) & \mathrm{e}^{-t\beta} \end{pmatrix},$$

and by multiplying from the right with the vector $(1, x)^T$, formula (3.18) is recovered.

The integrability conditions from above may be verified as follows. If X has an invariant density μ_θ, and *all* f_j*s are* μ_θ*-integrable*, then since

$$\int_D \mu_\theta(\mathrm{d}x)\, \mathrm{E}_\theta\left(\left|f_j(X_s)\right| \,\middle|\, X_0 = x\right) = \mu_\theta\left(\left|f_j\right|\right) < \infty,$$

it follows (at least for μ_θ-almost all x) that $f_j(X_s)$ is integrable. Similarly, if *all functions*

$$\eta_\ell(x) = \left(\sum_k \partial_{x_k} f_j(x) \sigma_{k\ell}(x)\right)^2 \quad (1 \le \ell \le d)$$

are μ_θ*-integrable*, it can be verified that for μ_θ almost all x, M^{f_j} is a true martingale when conditioning on $X_0 = x$.

A particularly nice case of the setup above arises when $\mathcal{L}_\theta = \mathcal{L}$ is the space of polynomials of degree less than or equal to r for some $r \in \mathbb{N}$. Then the invariance, $L_\theta \mathcal{L} \subseteq \mathcal{L}$, holds for *all* r, provided each $b_k(x;\theta)$ is a polynomial in x of degree less than or equal to one and each $C_{k\ell}(x;\theta)$ is a polynomial in x of degree less than or equal to two. These conditions are, for instance, satisfied by the *affine term structure models*, see Duffie and Kan (1996), where the $C_{k\ell}$ are of degree ≤ 1. Thus, with these conditions on b and C satisfied, the conditional moments

$$\pi_t\left(\prod_{k=1}^{d} x_k^{p_k}\right) = \mathrm{E}\left(\prod_{k=1}^{d} X_t^{p_k} \,\middle|\, X_0 = x\right)$$

with all $p_k \in \mathbb{N}_0$ may be found from (3.33) provided they exist and the relevant local martingales are true martingales.

Note that since $L_\theta \mathbf{1} = 0$, where $\mathbf{1} = (1, \ldots, 1)^T$, the constant functions may always be included in $\mathcal{L}$, and it is not really required that the basis f satisfy the linear relationship (3.31) – it is sufficient that there is a vector $\mathbf{c}$ of constant functions such that $L_\theta f = \mathbf{c} + \Psi_\theta f$.

We now turn to some estimating functions of the form (3.12) that are *not martingale estimating functions* but can be found in explicit form. Consider first *simple* estimating functions, where the function g appearing in (3.12) is of the form

$$g(\Delta, x, y; \theta) = h(x;\theta)$$

(or $= h(y;\theta)$). We assume in the following that the diffusion X is ergodic with invariant density μ_θ. The unbiasedness property, $\mathrm{E}_\theta(G_n(\theta)) = 0$, is satisfied if $\mu_\theta(h(\theta)) = 0$. Note that here it holds exactly only when X_0 has distribution μ_θ. Otherwise, it holds only asymptotically (as $n \to \infty$). This is in contrast to (3.25), where exact unbiasedness holds regardless of the distribution of X_0.

A simple example is

$$h(x;\theta) = \partial_\theta \log \mu_\theta(x), \tag{3.34}$$

which was proposed by Kessler (2000). This estimating function corresponds to assuming that all observations are independent with density μ_θ. The unbiasedness condition is satisfied under usual conditions allowing the interchange of differentiation and integration. A somewhat complex modification of this simple estimating function was shown by Kessler et al. (2001) to be efficient in the sense of semiparametric models. The semiparametric model for X considered in the study by Kessler et al. (2001) was that the process is Markovian with only the invariant measures $\{\mu_\theta | \theta \in \Theta\}$ specified parametrically. The modified version of the estimating function was derived by Kessler and Sørensen (2005) in a completely different way.

The unbiasedness property holds for all h of the form

$$h(x;\theta) = L_\theta f(x) \tag{3.35}$$

provided each coordinate f_j and $L_\theta f_j$ belong to $L^2(\mu_\theta)$ and that $\lim_{x\to r} f'(x)\sigma^2(x;\theta)\mu_\theta(x) = \lim_{x\to \ell} f'(x)\sigma^2(x;\theta)\mu_\theta(x)$. This is the basic property of the invariant measure expressed in terms of the generator, a fact noted and used to construct estimating functions by Hansen and Scheinkman (1995), see also Kessler (2000), Baddeley (2000), and Aït-Sahalia et al. (2010). A simple choice for f in (3.35) is a polynomial, but better results can often be obtained by choosing an f that is related to the model at hand. Conley et al. (1997) proposed the model-based choice $f = \partial_\theta \log \mu_\theta$ such that

$$h(x;\theta) = L_\theta \partial_\theta \log \mu_\theta(x). \tag{3.36}$$

They proved, under the simplifying assumption that a continuous record of the process is available, that an efficient estimator is obtained. Using approximations to the score function for continuous-time observation of the diffusion X, Sørensen (2001) independently derived the choice (3.36), and Jacobsen (2001a) showed that for parameters appearing in the drift, the resulting estimator is *small Δ-optimal*, a concept that is the subject of the Section 4.4. The latter result was recently rediscovered by Aït-Sahalia and Mykland (2008), who obtain similar results for estimating functions given by (3.37) below.

Example 6 *An example of successful use of a simple estimating function is given by Kessler (2000), who considered estimation of the drift parameter in the one-dimensional Ornstein–Uhlenbeck model*

$$dX_t = -\theta X_t dt + dW_t$$

where $\theta > 0$ to make X ergodic. Kessler used (3.35) with $f(x) = x^2$ so that $h(x;\theta) = -2\theta x^2 + 1$ resulting in the estimator

$$\hat{\theta} = \frac{n}{2\sum_{i=1}^{n} X_{(i-1)\Delta}^2},$$

which he showed is the most efficient of all estimators that can be obtained using estimating functions of the form (3.35). Since the invariant probability measure is the $N(0, 2\theta)$-distribution, Kessler's choice is equivalent to using (3.36), which is known to give a small Δ-optimal estimator. Thus, this result is not surprising. The estimator is, however, better than could be expected. Kessler showed that the estimator performs remarkably well with an asymptotic efficiency relative to the (complicated) maximum-likelihood estimator that is always greater than or equal to 95.6%, no matter what Δ is.

That simple estimating functions can also be very bad is illustrated by Kessler (2000) using the example

$$dX_t = -\theta X_t dt + \sqrt{\theta + X_t^2}\, dW_t$$

where the estimator based on (3.35) with $f(x) = x^2$ behaves terribly for all values of Δ. For the second model, this choice of f is not equivalent to (3.36) and is not small Δ-optimal.

One might consider it a major weakness that (3.35) depends on the argument x only. In fact, Hansen and Scheinkman (1995) proved that only parameters on which the invariant density μ_θ depends can be estimated by (3.35). The same is obviously true of (3.34). Hence, the importance of the class of *explicit, transition dependent estimating functions* introduced and studied thoroughly by Hansen and Scheinkman (1995), viz. each coordinate g_j is of the form

$$g_{j,\Delta}(x, y; \theta) = h_j(y) L_\theta f_j(x) - f_j(x) \hat{L}_\theta h_j(y). \tag{3.37}$$

Both here and in (3.35), the functions f and h are allowed to depend on θ and Δ – mostly, however, we think of cases where they do not. The general form of (3.37) requires an explanation: when X_0 has distribution μ_θ, the process X is stationary (for that value of θ), and for any finite $T > 0$, the fragment $(X_{T-t})_{0 \le t \le T}$ has the same distribution as $(\hat{X}_t)_{0 \le t \le T}$, where $\hat{X}$ is another diffusion, stationary with $\hat{X}_0$ having distribution μ_θ. This new diffusion, the *time reversal of* X, has generator

$$\hat{L}_\theta f(x) = \sum_{k=1}^{d} \hat{b}_k(x; \theta) \partial_{x_k} f(x) + \frac{1}{2} \sum_{k,\ell=1}^{d} C_{k\ell}(x; \theta) \partial^2_{x_k x_\ell} f(x),$$

where

$$\hat{b}_k(x; \theta) = -b_k(x; \theta) + \frac{1}{\mu_\theta(x)} \sum_{\ell=1}^{d} \partial_{x_\ell} (\mu_\theta C_{kl})(x; \theta),$$

see, e.g., Hansen and Scheinkman (1995). It is the dual generator $\hat{L}_\theta$ that appears in (3.37). As Hansen and Scheinkman (1995) make clear along with Conley et al. (1997), an important motivation for estimating functions given by (3.35) and (3.37) is that they also work when the observed process is a subordinated diffusion, so the estimation is robust to temporally dependent forms of sampling. Thus, the models for the observed process can be non-Markovian.

We call X *reversible* if $\hat{X}$ and X are the same diffusion, i.e., X is reversible if and only if $\hat{b}(x; \theta) = b(x; \theta)$ for all x. For $d = 1$, X is always reversible – the equation $\hat{b} \equiv b$ when solved for μ_θ immediately gives the expression (3.4). For $d \ge 2$, it is the exception rather than the rule that X be reversible, and that makes (3.37) an explicit estimating function only if μ_θ is known explicitly which, again in contrast to the one-dimensional case, hardly ever happens. Thus in practice, the class (3.37) of estimating functions will be relevant mostly for reversible diffusion models, in particular always when $d = 1$. For reversible models, it seems natural to enlarge the class (3.37) by considering functions g of the form

$$g_{i,\Delta}(x, y; \theta) = \sum_{q=1}^{r} \left[h_{iq}(y) L_\theta f_{iq}(x) - f_{iq}(x) L_\theta h_{iq}(y) \right]. \tag{3.38}$$

Much more generally, Conley et al. (1997) showed that a large class of functions g can be used, which is not restricted to be multiplicatively separable.

3.6. A Diffusion with Jumps

In this section, we consider a simple example where the stochastic process $\{X_t\}$ is a Markov process, but not a standard diffusion process. The process is, in fact, a diffusion with jumps. It is well known that if the price, P_t, of a stock is described by the Black–Scholes model (geometric Brownian motion), that is,

$$dP_t = \alpha^\diamond P_t dt + \sigma P_t dW_t,$$

then the logarithm of the price is a Brownian motion with drift, more precisely $X_t = \log P_t$ solves the stochastic differential equation

$$dX_t = \alpha dt + \sigma dW_t, \tag{3.39}$$

where $\alpha = \alpha^\diamond + \frac{1}{2}\sigma^2$. This follows from Itô's formula.

Suppose now that we want to allow jumps in the price process (and therefore also in the log-price process X). One of the simplest ways to achieve this is by adding a compound Poisson process term to the log-price process, that is to modify (3.39) in the following way,

$$dX_t = \alpha dt + \sigma dW_t + dZ_t, \tag{3.40}$$

where

$$Z_t = \sum_{j=0}^{N_t} Y_j,$$

and $\{N_t\}$ is a Poisson process with intensity λ. The stochastic process $\{N_t\}$ is thus a counting process with independent increments and N_t, the number of jumps in the time interval $[0, t]$, is Poisson distributed with parameter λt. The jump sizes $Y_j, j = 1, 2, \ldots$, are assumed to be i.i.d. normal with mean μ and variance τ^2. Furthermore, we assume that $\{W_t\}, \{N_t\}$, and $\{Y_j\}$ are independent and that $N_0 = Y_0 = 0$ so that $Z_0 = 0$. This is a simplified version of the kind of jump-diffusion models studied in Andersen et al. (2002). The solution to (3.40) is given by

$$X_t = \alpha t + \sigma W_t + Z_t, \quad t \geq 0.$$

For simplicity, we consider observations $X_1, X_2, \ldots, X_n$. The parameter vector is in this case five dimensional, $\theta = (\alpha, \sigma^2, \lambda, \mu, \tau^2)^T$. We will derive an optimal martingale estimating function based on the functions

$$h(x, y; \theta) = \begin{pmatrix} y - F(x; \theta) \\ (y - F(x; \theta))^2 - \phi(x; \theta) \\ e^y - \kappa(x; \theta) \end{pmatrix},$$

where

$$F(x; \theta) = E_\theta(X_i | X_{i-1} = x) = x + \alpha + \lambda\mu,$$

$$\phi(x; \theta) = \mathrm{Var}_\theta(X_i | X_{i-1} = x) = \sigma^2 + \lambda(\mu^2 + \tau^2),$$

$$\kappa(x; \theta) = E_\theta\left(e^{X_i} | X_{i-1} = x\right) = \exp\left(x + \alpha + \frac{1}{2}\sigma^2 + \lambda\left(e^{\mu+\frac{1}{2}\tau^2} - 1\right)\right).$$

To find an expression for the optimal martingale estimating function based on h, we need the following quantities, see (2.12). The conditional covariance matrix for h is given by

$$V_h(x; \theta) = E_\theta\left(h(X_{i-1}, X_i; \theta) h(X_{i-1}, X_i; \theta)^T \middle| X_{i-1} = x \right) = \begin{pmatrix} \phi(x; \theta) & \eta(x; \theta) & \nu(x; \theta) \\ \eta(x; \theta) & \psi(x; \theta) & \rho(x; \theta) \\ \nu(x; \theta) & \rho(x; \theta) & \zeta(x; \theta) \end{pmatrix},$$

where

$$\eta(x; \theta) = E_\theta((X_i - F(X_{i-1}; \theta))^3 | X_{i-1} = x) = \lambda\mu(\mu^2 + 3\tau^2),$$

$$\begin{aligned} \psi(x; \theta) &= E_\theta((X_i - F(X_{i-1}; \theta))^4 | X_{i-1} = x) - \phi(x; \theta)^2 \\ &= 2\sigma^4 + \lambda\left[4\sigma^2(\mu^2 + \tau^2) + (2\lambda + 1)\mu^4 + (2\lambda + 3)\tau^2(\tau^2 + 2\mu^2)\right], \end{aligned}$$

$$\begin{aligned} \nu(x; \theta) &= E_\theta\left((X_i - F(X_{i-1}; \theta))(e^{X_i} - \kappa(X_{i-1}; \theta)) | X_{i-1} = x\right) \\ &= \left(\sigma^2 - \lambda\mu + \lambda(\mu + \tau^2)e^{\mu+\frac{1}{2}\tau^2}\right)\kappa(x; \theta), \end{aligned}$$

$$\begin{aligned} \rho(x; \theta) &= E_\theta\left((X_i - F(X_{i-1}; \theta))^2 - \phi(X_{i-1}; \theta))(e^{X_i} - \kappa(X_{i-1}; \theta)) | X_{i-1} = x\right) \\ &= \left(\sigma^2 + \lambda\left(\tau^2 + (\mu + \tau^2)^2\right)e^{\mu+\frac{1}{2}\tau^2}\right)\kappa(x; \theta) + \frac{(\nu(x; \theta) + F(x; \theta)\kappa(x; \theta))^2}{\kappa(x; \theta)} \\ &\quad - 2F(x; \theta)\nu(x; \theta) - F(x; \theta)^2\kappa(x; \theta) - \phi(x; \theta)\kappa(x; \theta), \end{aligned}$$

$$\begin{aligned} \zeta(x; \theta) &= \mathrm{Var}_\theta\left(e^{X_i} | X_{i-1} = x\right) \\ &= e^{2x+2\alpha+\sigma^2-\lambda}\left(\exp\left(\sigma^2 + \lambda e^{2\mu+2\tau^2}\right) - \exp\left(2\lambda e^{\mu+\frac{1}{2}\tau^2} - \lambda\right)\right). \end{aligned}$$

Table 4.1 Empirical mean and standard error of 500 simulated estimates of the parameters in (3.40)

Parameter	Mean	Standard error
α	-0.0009	0.0070
σ	0.0945	0.0180
λ	0.0155	0.0209
μ	0.9604	0.5126
τ	0.2217	0.3156

The true parameter values are $\alpha = 0.0001, \sigma = 0.1, \lambda = 0.01$, $\mu = 1$, and $\tau = 0.1$.

Furthermore,

$$-\mathrm{E}_\theta(\partial_\theta h(X_{i-1}, X_i; \theta)|X_{i-1} = x) = \begin{pmatrix} 1 & 0 & \kappa(x;\theta) \\ 0 & 1 & \frac{1}{2}\kappa(x;\theta) \\ \mu & \mu^2+\tau^2 & \left(e^{\mu+\frac{1}{2}\tau^2}-1\right)\kappa(x;\theta) \\ \lambda & 2\lambda\mu & \lambda e^{\mu+\frac{1}{2}\tau^2}\kappa(x;\theta) \\ 0 & \lambda & \frac{1}{2}\lambda e^{\mu+\frac{1}{2}\tau^2}\kappa(x;\theta) \end{pmatrix}.$$

Hence, an explicit expression for the optimal martingale estimating function is obtained, though the corresponding estimating equations have to be solved numerically. Note that if we do not use all the three functions defining h, fewer than the required five estimating equations are obtained.

Table 4.1 summarizes the result of a simulation study. The empirical mean and standard error of 500 independent estimates of the five parameters are given. Each estimate is obtained from a simulated data set with 500 simulated $n = 500$ and $X_0 = 0$. The true parameter values in the simulation study are $\alpha = 0.0001, \sigma = 0.1, \lambda = 0.01, \mu = 1$, and $\tau = 0.1$.

From Table 4.1, we see that the means of the parameter estimates are quite close to the true values. It is also clear from the standard errors that, for this particular choice of parameter values, the parameters associated with the jump size (μ and τ) are harder to estimate than the other parameters. This is not surprising as there are rather few jumps in each data set because the jump intensity λ is small.

3.7. Non-Markovian Models

An important type of a non-Markovian model that is widely used in finance is the *stochastic volatility model*

$$\begin{aligned} dY_t &= \sqrt{v_t}dW_t \\ dv_t &= b(v_t;\theta)dt + c(v_t;\theta)dB_t, \end{aligned} \tag{3.41}$$

where W and B are independent standard Wiener processes. We assume that v is an ergodic, positive diffusion with invariant probability measure μ_θ, and that $v_0 \sim \mu_\theta$ and is independent of B and W. The process Y is, for instance, used as a model for the logarithm of the price of a stock. The returns $X_i = Y_{\Delta i} - Y_{\Delta(i-1)}$ are observations from a stationary non-Markovian process. More complex stochastic volatility models have been proposed in the literature. In particular, it is well-established that to model equity prices, it is important to allow the Wiener processes W and B to be correlated (the leverage effect), see, e.g., Andersen et al. (2002). For simplicity of exposition, we will here only consider the most basic type.

A number of approaches are available for inference about the parameters in stochastic volatility models. One is indirect inference or the efficient method of moments, see Gourieroux et al. (1993), Gallant and Tauchen (1996), and Gallant and Tauchen (2010). Likelihood based methods for stochastic volatility models have been proposed by Kim et al. (1998), Sørensen (2003), and Durham (2003), and simulation-based Bayesian methods using Markov chain Monte Carlo have been developed by Elerian et al. (2001) and Eraker (2001), see also Johannes and Polson (2010). Estimating functions for stochastic volatility models were proposed by Genon-Catalot et al. (1999) and Genon-Catalot et al. (2000). Here, we concentrate on the prediction-based estimating functions introduced by Sørensen (2000) that are widely applicable to non-Markovian diffusion models. Example are estimation for integrals of diffusions in Ditlevsen and Sørensen (2004) and sums of diffusions in Forman and Sørensen (2008).

We consider the general situation that the model for the data $X_1, \ldots, X_n$ is a class of stationary non-Markovian processes parametrized by the parameter $\theta \in \Theta \subseteq \mathbb{R}^p$. For Markovian models, we used martingale estimating functions to approximate the score function, which is a martingale. For non-Markovian models, the score function is a martingale too, so it must be expected that it is best approximated by a martingale estimating function. However, the conditional expectations appearing in martingale estimating functions are too complicated to be calculated in practice, so it is desirable to approximate them as well as possible by other predictors. This is the idea behind the prediction-based estimating functions.

Assume that $f_j, j = 1, \ldots, N$ are one-dimensional functions defined on the state space of X such that $E_\theta(f_j(X_1)^2) < \infty$ for all $\theta \in \Theta$. A martingale estimating function could have been based on the difference between $f_j(X_i)$ and the conditional moment $E_\theta\big(f_j(X_i)|X_1, \ldots, X_{i-1}\big)$. We shall now introduce an estimating function with a similar structure, where the intractable conditional expectation is replaced by a simpler expression that can be interpreted as an approximation to the conditional expectation. For each j, we predict $f_j(X_i)$ by predictors of the form

$$\pi_j^{(i-1)} = \alpha_{j0} + \alpha_{j1} h_{j1}(X_{i-1}, \ldots, X_{i-s}) + \cdots + \alpha_{jq} h_{jq}(X_{i-1}, \ldots, X_{i-s}), \tag{3.42}$$

where $h_{jk}, k = 1, \ldots q$ are given functions from $\mathbb{R}^s$ into $\mathbb{R}$ satisfying that $E_\theta(h_{jk}(X_1, \ldots, X_s)^2) < \infty$. Note that the predictor depends only on observations s time steps back in time. This is essential and simplifies the asymptotic theory for the estimators enormously. The minimum mean square error unbiased predictor of $f_j(X_i)$ of the form (3.42) is given by

$$\breve{\pi}_j^{(i-1)}(\theta) = \breve{\alpha}_{j0}(\theta) + \breve{\alpha}_j(\theta)^T Z_j^{(i-1)}, \tag{3.43}$$

where $Z_j^{(i-1)} = \left(Z_{j1}^{(i-1)}, \ldots, Z_{jq}^{(i-1)}\right)^T$ with $Z_{jk}^{(i-1)} = h_{jk}(X_{i-1}, \ldots, X_{i-s}), k = 1, \ldots q$,

$$\breve{\alpha}_j(\theta) = (\breve{\alpha}_{j1}(\theta), \ldots, \breve{\alpha}_{jq}(\theta))^T = C_j(\theta)^{-1} b_j(\theta), \tag{3.44}$$

and

$$\breve{\alpha}_{j0}(\theta) = E_\theta\big(f_j(X_1)\big) - \breve{\alpha}_j(\theta)^T E_\theta\left(Z_j^{(s)}\right). \tag{3.45}$$

As earlier, T denotes transposition. In formula (3.44), $C_j(\theta)$ denotes the covariance matrix of $Z_j^{(s)}$, while

$$b_j(\theta) = \left(\mathrm{Cov}_\theta\left(Z_{j1}^{(s)}, f_j(X_{s+1})\right), \ldots, \mathrm{Cov}_\theta\left(Z_{jq}^{(s)}, f_j(X_{s+1})\right)\right)^T. \tag{3.46}$$

Thus the minimum mean square error unbiased predictor can be calculated whenever we can find the covariances in $C_j(\theta)$ and $b_j(\theta)$. When these moments cannot be found explicitly, they are usually easy to obtain by simulation. A simple and natural choice of $Z_j^{(i-1)}$ is $Z_j^{(i-1)} = (f_j(X_{i-1}), \ldots, f_j(X_{i-q}))^T$, in which case the coefficients $\breve{\alpha}_{j0}, \ldots, \breve{\alpha}_{jq}$ can easily be found by means of the Durbin-Levinson algorithm, see Brockwell and Davis (1991).

The minimum mean square error unbiased predictor of $f_j(X_i)$ is the projection in the L_2-space of functions of $X_i, X_{i-1}, \ldots, X_{i-s}$ with finite variance onto the linear subspace of functions on the form (3.42). Therefore, $\breve{\pi}_j^{(i-1)}(\theta)$ satisfies the normal equation

$$E_\theta\left(\pi_j^{(i-1)}\left[f_j(X_i) - \breve{\pi}_j^{(i-1)}(\theta)\right]\right) = 0 \tag{3.47}$$

for all $\pi_j^{(i-1)}$ of the form (3.42). This implies (3.44). The fact that $\breve{\pi}_j^{(i-1)}(\theta)$ is a projection also shows that it can be interpreted as an approximation to the conditional expectation of $f_j(X_i)$ given $X_1, \ldots, X_{i-1}$ because this conditional expectation is the projection of $f_j(X_i)$ onto the linear space of all functions of $X_1, \ldots, X_{i-1}$ with finite variance.

Now, we can introduce estimating functions with weights similar to those appearing in martingale estimating functions that can be used to improve the efficiency of the estimators. The normal equation (3.47) show that

$$G_n(\theta) = \sum_{i=s+1}^{n} \sum_{j=1}^{N} \Pi_j^{(i-1)}(\theta) \left\{ f_j(X_i) - \breve{\pi}_j^{(i-1)}(\theta) \right\}, \tag{3.48}$$

is an unbiased estimating function, i.e., $E_\theta(G_n(\theta)) = 0$, whenever $\Pi_j^{(i-1)}(\theta) = \left(\pi_{1,j}^{(i-1)}(\theta), \ldots, \pi_{p,j}^{(i-1)}(\theta)\right)^T$, where the coordinates are of the form (3.42). Thus, we can expect (3.48) to produce a consistent estimator. An estimating function of the type (3.48) is called a *prediction-based estimating function.*

Note the computational advantage of prediction-based estimating functions in comparison to nonexplicit martingale estimating functions. Here, we need only unconditional moments that are relatively easy to compute by simulation, whereas for martingale estimating functions, moments conditional on all data points are needed, which involve much more computation. Note also that since $\breve{\pi}_j^{(i-1)}(\theta)$ depends exclusively on the first- and second-order moments of the random vector $\left(f_j(X_i), Z_{j1}^{(i-1)}, \ldots, Z_{jq}^{(i-1)}\right)$, only parameters appearing in these moments for at least one j can be estimated using (3.48). This is intuitively obvious and indeed follows from Condition 2 given later in this section. Of course, one would usually choose the functions f_j and h_{jk} in such a way that it is possible to estimate all parameters of interest.

Example 7 *For the stochastic volatility model (3.41), the returns $X_i = Y_{\Delta i} - Y_{\Delta(i-1)}$ satisfy that*

$$X_i = \int_{(i-1)\Delta}^{i\Delta} \sqrt{v_t} \mathrm{d}W_t \tag{3.49}$$

so that

$$X_i = \sqrt{S_i} Z_i, \tag{3.50}$$

where

$$S_i = \int_{(i-1)\Delta}^{i\Delta} v_t \mathrm{d}t \tag{3.51}$$

and where the Z_is are independent, identically standard normal distributed random variables, that are independent of $\{S_i\}$. It is easy to see from (3.50) that the returns are uncorrelated (which is a stylized feature of empirical returns; for data with correlated returns, a stochastic volatility model of the type (3.41) can obviously not be used). Therefore, the function $f(x) = x$ cannot be used to define a prediction-based estimating function. A simple alternative with $N = 1$ is $f(x) = x^2$, *and* $h_k(x_q, \ldots, x_1) = x_{q-k+1}^2$, $k = 1, \ldots, q$. *Here* $s = q$. *In this way, we obtain the estimating function*

$$G_n(\theta) = \sum_{i=q+1}^{n} \Pi^{(i-1)}(\theta)\left\{X_i^2 - \breve{\alpha}_0(\theta) - \breve{\alpha}_1(\theta)X_{i-1}^2 - \cdots - \breve{\alpha}_q(\theta)X_{i-q}^2\right\}, \tag{3.52}$$

where the quantities $\breve{\alpha}_k(\theta)$, $k = 0, \ldots, q$ *are given by*

$$\breve{\alpha}_0(\theta) = \mathrm{E}_\theta\big(X_1^2\big)\big\{1 - \big(\breve{\alpha}_1(\theta) + \cdots + \breve{\alpha}_q(\theta)\big)\big\}$$

and (3.44) with $C(\theta)$ *equal to the covariance matrix of the stochastic vector* $\big(X_q^2, \ldots, X_1^2\big)$, *and* $b(\theta)^T = \big(\mathrm{Cov}_\theta\big(X_{q+1}^2, X_q^2\big), \ldots, \mathrm{Cov}_\theta\big(X_{q+1}^2, X_1^2\big)\big)$.

To ensure that the quantities $C(\theta)$ *and* $b(\theta)$ *are well-defined, we must assume that* $\mathrm{E}_\theta(X_1^4) < \infty$. *This is the case provided that the second moment of the volatility process* v *exists. Let us briefly discuss how to calculate the covariances. It follows from (3.50) that*

$$\begin{aligned}
\mathrm{E}_\theta\big(X_i^2\big) &= \mathrm{E}_\theta(S_1)\\
\mathrm{Var}_\theta\big(X_i^2\big) &= 3\mathrm{Var}_\theta(S_1) + 2\mathrm{E}_\theta(S_1)^2\\
\mathrm{Cov}_\theta\big(X_i^2, X_{i+j}^2\big) &= \mathrm{Cov}_\theta(S_1, S_{1+j}).
\end{aligned}$$

Define $\xi(\theta) = E_\theta(v_t)$, $\omega(\theta) = \mathrm{Var}_\theta(v_t)$, *and* $r(u;\theta) = \mathrm{Cov}_\theta(v_t, v_{t+u})/\omega(\theta)$. *Using (3.51), it is not difficult to see that*

$$\mathrm{E}_\theta\big(X_n^2\big) = \Delta\xi(\theta) \tag{3.53}$$

$$\begin{aligned}
\mathrm{Var}_\theta\big(X_n^2\big) &= 6\omega(\theta)R^*(\Delta;\theta) + 2\Delta^2\xi(\theta)^2\\
\mathrm{Cov}_\theta\big(X_n^2, X_{n+i}^2\big) &= \omega(\theta)\left[R^*(\Delta(i+1);\theta) - 2R^*(\Delta i;\theta) + R^*(\Delta(i-1);\theta)\right],
\end{aligned} \tag{3.54}$$

where

$$R^*(t;\theta) = \int_0^t \int_0^s r(u;\theta)\mathrm{d}u\mathrm{d}s;$$

see Barndorff-Nielsen and Shephard (2001). For numerical calculations, it is perhaps more useful that

$$\mathrm{Cov}_\theta\big(X_n^2, X_{n+i}^2\big) = \omega(\theta) \int_{(i-1)\Delta}^{i\Delta} \int_s^{s+\Delta} r(u;\theta)\mathrm{d}u\mathrm{d}s, \tag{3.55}$$

which follows by easy calculations. Thus, all that is needed to compute the minimal mean squared error predictor in (3.52) are the first- and second-order moments of the volatility process. For general diffusion models, the autocorrelation function is rarely explicitly known and must be determined numerically. Flexible classes of processes for which an explicit expression is available can be found in Barndorff-Nielsen et al. (1998), Barndorff-Nielsen and Shephard (2001), and Bibby et al. (2005). In particular, $r(u;\theta) = e^{-\beta u}$ *when* $b(v;\theta) = -\beta(v-\alpha)$ *under weak regularity conditions on* $c(v;\theta)$*. The models discussed in these studies can also fit data where the volatility is the sum of a slowly and a quickly moving component as found for instance by Alizadeh et al. (2002).*

To discuss the asymptotic properties of an estimator obtained from a prediction-based estimating function of the general type (3.48), we first give it a more compact form. Write the ℓth coordinate of the vector $\Pi_j^{(i-1)}(\theta)$ as

$$\pi_{\ell,j}^{(i-1)}(\theta) = \sum_{k=0}^{q} \alpha_{\ell jk}(\theta) Z_{jk}^{(i-1)},$$

with $Z_{j0}^{(i-1)} = 1$. Then (3.48) can be written in the form

$$G_n(\theta) = A(\theta) \sum_{i=s+1}^{n} Z^{(i-1)}\left(F(X_i) - \breve{\pi}^{(i-1)}(\theta)\right), \tag{3.56}$$

where

$$A(\theta) = \begin{pmatrix} \alpha_{110}(\theta) & \cdots & \alpha_{11q}(\theta) & \cdots & \cdots & \alpha_{1N0}(\theta) & \cdots & \alpha_{1Nq}(\theta) \\ \vdots & & \vdots & & & \vdots & & \vdots \\ \alpha_{p10}(\theta) & \cdots & \alpha_{p1q}(\theta) & \cdots & \cdots & \alpha_{pN0}(\theta) & \cdots & \alpha_{pNq}(\theta) \end{pmatrix}, \tag{3.57}$$

$F(x) = (f_1(x), \ldots, f_N(x))^T$, $\breve{\pi}^{(i-1)}(\theta) = \left(\breve{\pi}_1^{(i-1)}(\theta), \ldots, \breve{\pi}_N^{(i-1)}(\theta)\right)^T$, and $Z^{(i-1)}$ is the $N(q+1) \times N$-matrix given by

$$Z^{(i-1)} = \begin{pmatrix} Z_{10}^{(i-1)} & 0 & \cdots & 0 \\ \vdots & \vdots & & \vdots \\ Z_{1q}^{(i-1)} & 0 & \cdots & 0 \\ 0 & Z_{20}^{(i-1)} & \cdots & 0 \\ \vdots & \vdots & & \vdots \\ 0 & Z_{2q}^{(i-1)} & \cdots & 0 \\ \vdots & \vdots & & \vdots \\ 0 & 0 & \cdots & Z_{N0}^{(i-1)} \\ \vdots & \vdots & & \vdots \\ 0 & 0 & \cdots & Z_{Nq}^{(i-1)} \end{pmatrix}. \tag{3.58}$$

The following condition implies the existence of a $\sqrt{n}$-consistent and asymptotically normal estimator. As usual, θ_0 denotes the true parameter value.

Condition 2

1. *The process X is stationary and geometrically α-mixing.*
2. $\mathrm{E}_{\theta_0}\left(\left|Z_{jk}^{(s)} f_j(X_{s+1})\right|^{2+\delta}\right) < \infty$ *and* $\mathrm{E}_{\theta_0}\left(\left|Z_{jk}^{(s)} Z_{j\ell}^{(s)}\right|^{2+\delta}\right) < \infty, j = 1, \ldots, N,\ k,\ \ell = 0, \ldots q.$
3. *The matrix* $A(\theta)$ *and the vector* $\breve{a}(\theta)$ *given by*

$$\breve{\alpha}(\theta) = (\breve{\alpha}_{10}(\theta), \breve{\alpha}_{11}(\theta), \ldots, \breve{\alpha}_{1q}(\theta), \ldots, \breve{\alpha}_{N0}(\theta), \ldots \breve{\alpha}_{Nq}(\theta))^T, \tag{3.59}$$

where $\breve{\alpha}_{jk}$ *is given by* (3.44) and (3.45), *are twice continuously differentiable with respect to* θ.
4. *The matrix* $A(\theta_0)D(\theta_0)\partial_{\theta^T}\breve{a}(\theta_0)$ *has rank p. The matrix* $D(\theta_0)$ *is given by*

$$D(\theta) = \mathrm{E}_\theta\left(Z^{(i-1)}(Z^{(i-1)})^T\right). \tag{3.60}$$

Under Condition 2 (1)–(2) the covariance matrix of $\sum_{i=s+1}^n H^{(i)}(\theta)/\sqrt{n-s}$,

$$\overline{M}_n(\theta) = \mathrm{E}_\theta\left(H^{(s+1)}(\theta)H^{(s+1)}(\theta)^T\right) + \sum_{k=1}^{n-s-1} \frac{(n-s-k)}{(n-s)} \left\{\mathrm{E}_\theta\left(H^{(s+1)}(\theta)H^{(s+1+k)}(\theta)^T\right) + \mathrm{E}_\theta\left(H^{(s+1+k)}(\theta)H^{(s+1)}(\theta)^T\right)\right\}, \tag{3.61}$$

where $H^{(i)}(\theta) = Z^{(i-1)}\left(F(X_i) - \breve{\pi}^{(i-1)}(\theta)\right)$, satisfies that

$$\overline{M}_n(\theta_0) \rightarrow M(\theta_0),$$

and a central limit theorem holds for $G_n(\theta_0)$, provided that $M(\theta_0)$ is strictly positive definite; see, e.g., theorem 1 in section 1.5 of Doukhan (1994). The rest of Condition 2 implies that with a probability tending to one as $n \rightarrow \infty$, the estimating equation $G_n(\theta) = 0$ defines a $\sqrt{n}$-consistent estimator $\hat{\theta}_n$ satisfying that

$$\sqrt{n}(\hat{\theta}_n - \theta_0) \xrightarrow{\mathcal{D}} N\left(0, S(\theta_0)^{-1}A(\theta_0)M(\theta_0)A(\theta_0)^T(S(\theta_0)^{-1})^T\right), \tag{3.62}$$

where

$$S(\theta_0) = -\mathrm{E}_{\theta_0}\left(A(\theta_0)Z^{(i-1)}(Z^{(i-1)})^T\partial_{\theta^T}\breve{\alpha}(\theta_0)\right) = -A(\theta_0)D(\theta_0)\partial_{\theta^T}\breve{\alpha}(\theta_0).$$

We conclude this subsection by finding the optimal choice of the weights $\Pi_j^{(i-1)}(\theta)$, $j = 1, \ldots, N$ for a class of prediction-based estimating functions of the general type

(3.48). Consider the compact representation (3.56). We are free to choose the matrix $A(\theta)$ in an optimal way, whereas the $N(q+1)$-dimensional vectors $Z^{(i-1)}\big(F(X_i) - \breve{\pi}^{(i-1)}(\theta)\big)$ are fixed by our earlier choice of the functions f_j and h_{jk}. The matrix $A(\theta)$ must have rank p in order that we can estimate all p parameters. The $p \times p$ matrix (2.6) is given by

$$S_{G_n}(\theta) = -(n-q)A(\theta)D(\theta)\partial_{\theta^T}\breve{\alpha}(\theta),$$

and if we denote the optimal choice of the matrix $A(\theta)$ by $A_n^*(\theta)$, then

$$\mathrm{E}_\theta\Big(G_n(\theta)G_n^*(\theta)^T\Big) = (n-q)A(\theta)\overline{M}_n(\theta)A_n^*(\theta)^T,$$

where $\overline{M}_n(\theta)$ is given by (3.61). Under weak regularity conditions, the matrix $\overline{M}_n(\theta)$ is invertible, see Sørensen (2000), in which case the optimality criterion (2.5) is satisfied for

$$A_n^*(\theta) = \partial_\theta\breve{\alpha}(\theta)^T D(\theta)\overline{M}_n(\theta)^{-1}. \tag{3.63}$$

An estimator with the same asymptotic variance is obtained if $A_n^*(\theta)$ is replaced by $A_n^*(\tilde{\theta}_n)$, where $\tilde{\theta}_n$ is some consistent preliminary estimator. This modification is highly recommended because the calculation of $A_n^*(\theta)$ usually requires a considerable amount of simulation so that a dramatic reduction of computing time can be achieved by calculating it at only one parameter value. The preliminary estimator $\tilde{\theta}_n$ can, for instance, be obtained from (3.56) with $A(\theta)$ equal to some simple matrix that does not depend on θ.

If we know $C_j(\theta)$, $b_j(\theta)$, $\mathrm{E}_\theta\big(Z_j^{(q)}\big)$, $\mathrm{E}_\theta(f_j(X_1))$, $j = 1,\ldots,N$, their derivatives with respect to θ, and the moments appearing in (3.61), we can calculate the optimal prediction-based estimating function. Note that only moments and derivatives of moments are needed. Note also that $C_j(\theta)$, $b_j(\theta)$, $E_\theta\big(Z_j^{(q)}\big)$, and $E_\theta(f_j(X_1))$ were needed earlier to find the predictor $\breve{\pi}_j^{(i-1)}(\theta)$, so the only new requirements to compute the optimal estimating function are the derivatives and the moments in (3.61). Many models are sufficiently mixing that there exist $K > 0$ and $\lambda > 0$ such that the absolute values of all entries in the expectation matrices in the kth term in the sum in (3.61) are dominated by $Ke^{-\lambda(k-q)}$ when $k > q$. Therefore, the sum in (3.61) can in practice often be truncated so that only a few moments need to be calculated.

Example 8 *To find the optimal estimating function of the form (3.52) for the stochastic volatility model (3.41), we must assume that* $\mathrm{E}_\theta\big(X_i^8\big) < \infty$, *and apart from the quantities mentioned above, we need to find* $\mathrm{E}_\theta\big(X_i^2X_j^2X_1^2\big)$ *and* $\mathrm{E}_\theta\big(X_i^2X_j^2X_k^2X_1^2\big)$ *for* $i \geq j \geq k$. *We can essentially find these moments by integrating the moments* $\mathrm{E}_\theta(v_sv_tv_u)$ *and* $\mathrm{E}_\theta(v_sv_tv_uv_z)$ *of the volatility process as functions of* s, t, u, *and* z *over suitable sets. For details, see Sørensen (2000).*

The moments of the volatility process must, in general, be found by simulation, but can in some cases be found explicitly. This is, for instance, the case for the Pearson diffusions discussed in Section 3.5, see Forman and Sørensen (2008). An example is the CIR process

$$dv_t = -\theta(v_t - \alpha)dt + \sigma\sqrt{v_t}dB_t, \tag{3.64}$$

for which we obtain the stochastic volatility model proposed by Hull and White (1988) and Heston (1993).

Another example of a stochastic volatility model, for which the necessary moments can be found explicitly, is when $v_t = \exp(U_t)$, *where* U *is a stationary Ornstein–Uhlenbeck process,*

$$dU_t = -\theta(U_t - \alpha)dt + \sigma dB_t$$

with $\theta > 0$ *(Wiggins, 1987; Chesney and Scott, 1989; Melino and Turnbull, 1990). This model can be obtained as a limit of the EGARCH(1,1) model, see Nelson (1990). Here,*

$$E_\theta(v_s v_t v_u v_z) = E_{\theta,\alpha,\sigma}\{\exp(U_s + U_t + U_u + U_z)\},$$

which is the Laplace transform of a Gaussian distribution, and hence is explicitly known.

4. OPTIMAL ESTIMATING FUNCTIONS FOR DIFFUSION MODELS

We now again focus on diffusion models where X is supposed to be the solution to a stochastic differential equation (3.1). To simplify matters, we assume that X is one dimensional, except in Section 4.4, where a d-dimensional diffusion is considered.

4.1. Optimal Linear Combinations of Relationships between Consecutive Observations

Consider a class of estimating functions of the form (3.12) and (3.13), i.e.,

$$G_n(\theta) = \sum_{i=1}^{n} a(\Delta_i, X_{t_{i-1}}, \theta)h(\Delta, X_{t_{i-1}}, X_{t_i}; \theta), \tag{4.1}$$

where $h = (h_1, \ldots, h_N)^T$ is a column vector of N given functions satisfying that

$$\int_\ell^r h_j(\Delta, x, y; \theta)p(\Delta, x, y; \theta)dy = 0 \tag{4.2}$$

for all $\Delta > 0, x \in (\ell, r)$, and $\theta \in \Theta$, while the weight matrix a, a $p \times N$-matrix, can vary freely. The functions h_j define relationships (dependent on θ) between an observation X_i and the previous observation X_{i-1} that can be used to estimate θ. We shall now find the weight matrix a^* for which we obtain optimal combination of these relationships.

The class of estimating functions considered here is a particular case of the general type studied in Example 1, so by (2.12), the optimal estimating function is

$$G_n^*(\theta) = \sum_{i=1}^{n} a^*(\Delta_i, X_{t_{i-1}}; \theta) h(\Delta_i, X_{t_{i-1}}, X_{t_i}; \theta), \tag{4.3}$$

where

$$a^*(\Delta, x; \theta) = -\int_{\ell}^{r} \partial_\theta h(\Delta, x, y; \theta)^T p(\Delta, x, y; \theta) \mathrm{d}y V_h(\Delta, x; \theta)^{-1}, \tag{4.4}$$

with

$$V_h(\Delta, x; \theta) = \int_{\ell}^{r} h(\Delta, x, y; \theta) h(\Delta, x, y; \theta)^T p(\Delta, x, y; \theta) \mathrm{d}y. \tag{4.5}$$

Here, it is assumed that $V_h(\Delta, x; \theta)$ is invertible, or equivalently, that the functions $h_j, j = 1, \ldots N$ are linearly independent.

When the functions h are of the form (3.19) with π_Δ^θ defined by (3.20), the optimal estimating function is given by (4.3) with

$$a^*(\Delta, x; \theta) = B(\Delta, x; \theta) V(\Delta, x; \theta)^{-1}, \tag{4.6}$$

where

$$B(\Delta, x; \theta)_{ij} = -\int_{\ell}^{r} \partial_{\theta_i} f_j(y; \theta) p(\Delta, x, y; \theta) \mathrm{d}y + \partial_{\theta_i} \pi_\Delta^\theta (f_j(\theta))(x), \tag{4.7}$$

$i = 1, \ldots, p, j = 1, \ldots, N$, and

$$V(\Delta, x; \theta)_{ij} = \int_{\ell}^{r} f_i(y; \theta) f_j(y; \theta) p(\Delta, x, y; \theta) \mathrm{d}y - \pi_\Delta^\theta (f_i(\theta))(x) \pi_\Delta^\theta (f_j(\theta))(x), \tag{4.8}$$

$i, j = 1, \ldots, N$.

Particularly important examples are the linear and quadratic estimating functions. The optimal linear estimating function for a one-dimensional diffusion is

$$\sum_{i=1}^{n} \frac{\partial_\theta F(\Delta_i, X_{t_{i-1}}; \theta)}{\phi(\Delta_i, X_{t_{i-1}}; \theta)} [X_{t_i} - F(\Delta_i, X_{t_{i-1}}; \theta)], \tag{4.9}$$

where F and ϕ are given by (3.14) and (3.15). In the expression for the optimal linear estimating function, the derivative of F appears. If F is determined by simulation, it is necessary to be careful to ensure that the derivative is correctly calculated. Pedersen

(1994a) proposed a procedure for determining $\partial_\theta F(\Delta, x; \theta)$ by simulation based on results in Friedman (1975). However, it is often easier to use an approximation to the optimal estimating function, see the following section.

If the first and second moment of the transition distribution are both correctly specified, the estimator obtained from (4.9) is efficient in the nonparametric model that assumes X is a Markov process but specifies only the first two moments, see Wefelmeyer (1996) and Wefelmeyer (1997). Moreover, the estimator is consistent whenever the first moment is correctly specified. This is an interesting robustness property of the estimating function. For models with linear drift, the first conditional moment does not depend on the diffusion coefficient. For models with nonlinear drift, the same is true to order Δ_i. Continuous-time processes with the same first and second conditional moments as a diffusion model can be obtained for other types of driving processes, e.g., more general compensated Lévy processes. From a robustness point of view, the functions h_j appearing in (4.1) should, more generally, be chosen in such a way that (4.2) is expected to hold under relevant deviations from the diffusion model to preserve consistency. To preserve efficiency, it is necessary that the conditional moments appearing in (4.4) are robust to model misspecification too, which in general is not easy to achieve.

The optimal quadratic estimating function depends on the third and fourth moments of the transition distribution. For a one-dimensional diffusion, it is given by

$$\sum_{i=1}^{n}\Big\{\alpha^*(\Delta_i, X_{t_{i-1}}; \theta)[X_{t_i} - F(\Delta_i, X_{t_{i-1}}; \theta)] \\ + \beta^*(\Delta_i, X_{t_{i-1}}; \theta)[(X_{t_i} - F(\Delta_i, X_{t_{i-1}}; \theta))^2 - \phi(\Delta_i, X_{t_{i-1}}; \theta)]\Big\}, \tag{4.10}$$

with

$$\alpha^*(x;\theta) = \frac{\partial_\theta \phi(x;\theta)\eta(x;\theta) - \partial_\theta F(x;\theta)\psi(x;\theta)}{\phi(x;\theta)\psi(x;\theta) - \eta(x;\theta)^2}$$

and

$$\beta^*(x;\theta) = \frac{\partial_\theta F(x;\theta)\eta(x;\theta) - \partial_\theta \phi(x;\theta)\phi(x;\theta)}{\phi(x;\theta)\psi(x;\theta) - \eta(x;\theta)^2},$$

where the Δs have been omitted,

$$\eta(x;\theta) = E_\theta([X_\Delta - F(x;\theta)]^3 | X_0 = x)$$

and

$$\psi(x;\theta) = E_\theta([X_\Delta - F(x;\theta)]^4 | X_0 = x) - \phi(x;\theta)^2.$$

If the first four moments of the transition distribution are correctly specified, the estimator is efficient in the nonparametric model that assumes a Markov process but specifies only the first four moments, see Wefelmeyer (1996, 1997).

Example 9 *For a* mean-reverting diffusion model *given by (3.17) with $\beta > 0$, the first conditional moment F is given by (3.18). Hence, the optimal linear estimating function is*

$$G_n^*(\alpha,\beta) = \begin{pmatrix} \sum_{i=1}^{n} \dfrac{1-e^{-\beta}}{\phi(X_{i-1};\alpha,\beta)} \left[X_i - X_{i-1}e^{-\beta} - \alpha(1-e^{-\beta})\right] \\ \sum_{i=1}^{n} \dfrac{e^{-\beta}(\alpha - X_{i-1})}{\phi(X_{i-1};\alpha,\beta)} \left[X_i - X_{i-1}e^{-\beta} - \alpha(1-e^{-\beta})\right] \end{pmatrix},$$

where for simplicity of exposition, we have taken $\Delta_i = 1$. There is in general no explicit expression for the function ϕ that must be found by simulation or be approximated, see Sections 3.4 and 4.2. The following simpler estimating function gives us exactly the same estimators:

$$\tilde{G}_n^*(\alpha,\beta) = \begin{pmatrix} \sum_{i=1}^{n} \dfrac{1}{\phi(X_{i-1};\alpha,\beta)} \left[X_i - X_{i-1}e^{-\beta} - \alpha(1-e^{-\beta})\right] \\ \sum_{i=1}^{n} \dfrac{X_{i-1}}{\phi(X_{i-1};\alpha,\beta)} \left[X_i - X_{i-1}e^{-\beta} - \alpha(1-e^{-\beta})\right] \end{pmatrix}.$$

This is because $\tilde{G}_n^*(\alpha,\beta) = M(\alpha,\beta)\, G_n^*(\alpha,\beta)$, where the matrix

$$M(\alpha,\beta) = \begin{pmatrix} \dfrac{1}{1-e^{-\beta}} & 0 \\ \dfrac{\alpha}{1-e^{-\beta}} & -e^{-\beta} \end{pmatrix}$$

is invertible. Quite generally, if $G(\theta)$ is an estimating function and if $M(\theta)$ is an invertible matrix, then the estimating function $M(\theta)G(\theta)$ defines the same estimators as $G(\theta)$. Moreover, if $G(\theta)$ is optimal, then so is $M(\theta)G(\theta)$. We say that the two estimating functions are equivalent. Usually, we use the simplest possible version of the estimating function.

For the CIR model where $\sigma(x) = \tau\sqrt{x}$, the functions ϕ, η, and ψ, and hence the optimal quadratic estimating function can be found explicitly:

$$\phi(x;\alpha,\beta,\tau) = \frac{\tau^2}{\beta}\left(\left(\frac{1}{2}\alpha - x\right)e^{-2\beta} - (\alpha - x)e^{-\beta} + \frac{1}{2}\alpha\right)$$

$$\eta(x;\alpha,\beta,\tau) = \frac{\tau^4}{2\beta^2}\left(\alpha - 3(\alpha - x)e^{-\beta} + 3(\alpha - 2x)e^{-2\beta} - (\alpha - 3x)e^{-3\beta}\right)$$

$$\psi(x;\alpha,\beta,\tau) = \frac{3\tau^6}{4\beta^3}\left(\left(\alpha - 4x\right)e^{-4\beta} - 4(\alpha - 3x)e^{-3\beta} + 6(\alpha - 2x)e^{-2\beta} - 4(\alpha - x)e^{-\beta} + \alpha\right) + 2\phi(x;\alpha,\beta,\tau)^2.$$

In view of Example 3 and results given in the following, it is not surprising that the conditional moments can be found explicitly for the CIR model.

The optimal estimating function takes a particularly simple form in the case where the base $f_1, \ldots, f_N$ of the class of estimating functions consists of eigenfunctions of the generator, see (3.26) and the discussion below that formula. For such a base, the optimal estimating function is given by (4.6) with

$$B(\Delta, x; \theta)_{ij} = -\int \partial_{\theta_i}\varphi_j(y;\theta)p(\Delta, x, y;\theta)\mathrm{d}y + \partial_{\theta_i}[\mathrm{e}^{-\lambda_j(\theta)\Delta}\varphi_j(x;\theta)],$$

$i = 1, \ldots, p, j = 1, \ldots, N$ and

$$C(\Delta, x; \theta)_{ij} = \int \varphi_i(y;\theta)\varphi_j(y;\theta)p(\Delta, x, y;\theta)\mathrm{d}y - \mathrm{e}^{-[\lambda_i(\theta)+\lambda_j(\theta)]\Delta}\varphi_i(x;\theta)\varphi_j(x;\theta),$$

$i, j = 1, \ldots, N$. These expressions are relatively easy to determine by simulation because the differentiation is inside the integral. As mentioned earlier, numerical determination of quantities like $\partial_\theta F$ in (4.9) requires care, but this problem disappears in the case of an eigenfunction base.

For many models where eigenfunctions can be found, they are of the form

$$\varphi_i(y;\theta) = \sum_{j=0}^{i} a_{i,j}(\theta)\kappa(y)^j, \tag{4.11}$$

where κ is a real function defined on the state space and independent of θ. This is the case for the Pearson diffusions and transformations of Pearson diffusions, see Wong (1964) and Forman and Sørensen (2008). In this situation, the optimal estimating function is explicit. To see this, note that

$$C_{i,j}(x,\theta) = \sum_{r=0}^{i}\sum_{s=0}^{j} a_{i,r}(\theta)a_{j,s}(\theta)\int \kappa(y)^{r+s}p(\Delta, x, y;\theta)\mathrm{d}y - \mathrm{e}^{-[\lambda_i(\theta)+\lambda_j(\theta)]\Delta}\ \varphi_i(x;\theta)\varphi_j(x;\theta)$$

and

$$B_i(x,\theta) = -\sum_{j=0}^{i} \partial_\theta a_{i,j}(\theta)\int \kappa(y)^i p(\Delta, x, y;\theta)\mathrm{d}y + \partial_\theta(\mathrm{e}^{-\lambda_j(\theta)\Delta}\varphi_i)(x;\theta).$$

Hence, if we can find the moments $\int \kappa(y)^i p(\Delta, x, y;\theta)\mathrm{d}y$ for $1 \leq i \leq 2N$, we have found the optimal estimating function based on the first N eigenfunctions. But this is easy because by integrating both sides of (4.11) with respect to $p(\Delta, x, y;\theta)$ for $i = 1, \ldots, 2N$, we obtain the following system of linear equations

$$e^{-\lambda_i(\theta)}\varphi_i(x;\theta) = \sum_{j=0}^{i} a_{i,j}(\theta) \int \kappa(y)^j p(\Delta, x, y; \theta)\mathrm{d}y \tag{4.12}$$

for $i = 1, \ldots, 2N$.

Example 10 *For the model considered in Example 4, the eigenfunctions are* $\phi_i(x;\theta) = C_i^{\theta}(\sin(x))$, $i = 0, 1, \ldots,$ *with eigenvalues* $i(\theta + i/2)$, $i = 0, 1, \ldots,$ *where* C_i^{θ} *is the Gegenbauer polynomial of order* i. *The optimal estimating function based on any set of eigenfunctions can thus be found explicitly using (4.12). The optimal estimating function based on the first nontrivial eigenfunction,* $\sin(x)$, *is*

$$G_n^*(\theta) = \sum_{i=1}^{n} \frac{\sin(X_{t_{i-1}})[\sin(X_{t_i}) - e^{-(\theta+\frac{1}{2})\Delta}\sin(X_{t_{i-1}})]}{\frac{1}{2}(e^{2(\theta+1)\Delta} - 1)/(\theta+1) - (e^{\Delta} - 1)\sin^2(X_{t_{i-1}})}.$$

When Δ *is small, the optimal estimating function can be approximated by*

$$\tilde{G}_n(\theta) = \sum_{i=1}^{n} \sin(X_{t_{i-1}})[\sin(X_{t_i}) - e^{-(\theta+\frac{1}{2})\Delta}\sin(X_{t_{i-1}})],$$

which yields the explicit estimator

$$\tilde{\theta}_n = -\Delta^{-1}\log\left(\frac{\sum_{i=1}^{n}\sin(X_{t_{i-1}})\sin(X_{t_i})}{\sum_{i=1}^{n}\sin^2(X_{t_{i-1}})}\right) - 1/2,$$

provided the numerator is positive. In a simulation study with $\Delta \leq 0.5$, *this estimator was almost as efficient as the optimal estimator based on* G^*, *see Kessler and Sørensen (1999).*

Statistical inference based on an optimal estimating function with an eigenfunction base is *invariant* under twice continuously differentiable transformations of data, see Kessler and Sørensen (1999). After such a transformation, the data are, by Itô's formula, still observations from a certain diffusion process, and the eigenfunctions transform in exactly the way needed to keep the optimal estimating function invariant. Inference based on polynomial estimating functions is not invariant under transformations of the data. As mentioned above, the optimal estimating functions with eigenfunction base have clear computational advantages over other estimating functions. The problem is that it is not always possible to find eigenfunctions for the generator of a given diffusion model. However, the class of Pearson diffusions and transformations of Pearson diffusions provide a very flexible class of diffusion models for which explicit optimal estimating functions of this type are available, see Forman and Sørensen (2008). For models where eigenfunctions cannot be found, the polynomial estimating functions, in particular the quadratic, provide a very useful alternative.

A further justification for estimating functions based on eigenfunctions is that the eigenvalue problem (3.27) is a Sturm–Liouville problem. By a classical result of this theory, we have, for an ergodic diffusion with invariant probability μ_θ, a series expansion in terms of the eigenfunctions $(\phi_i)_{i\geq 0}$ of any function f satisfying that $\mu_\theta(f^2) < \infty$ (see Coddington and Levinson, 1955), i.e.,

$$f(y) = \sum_{i=0}^{\infty} c_i \phi_i(y), \tag{4.13}$$

where (c_i) is a sequence of real numbers and the series converges with respect to the norm given by $\|f\|_\theta = \mu_\theta(f^2)^{\frac{1}{2}}$. Thus for a fixed x, $\sum_{j=0}^{k} \alpha_j(x;\theta)\,\phi_j(y;\theta)$ can be seen as a truncated series of the form (4.13). The estimating function given by (3.29) is obtained when one compensates the sum to obtain a martingale. The transition density can usually be expanded in the form (4.13), which mainly depends on the eigenfunctions with the smallest eigenvalues. In fact, the weights c_i decrease exponentially with the eigenvalues. If the score function can be expanded similarly, there is reason to expect rather efficient estimators. Suppose that the union $\cup_{k=1}^{\infty} V_k$, where V_k is the space spanned by $\{\phi_1(\cdot\,;\theta),\ldots,\phi_k(\cdot\,;\theta)\}$, is dense in the space $L_2(p(\Delta,x,y;\theta)\mathrm{d}y)$ for every x. Then there exists a sequence N_n such that the estimator $\hat{\theta}_{n,N_n}$ is efficient. Here $\hat{\theta}_{n,N}$ is the optimal estimator based on N eigenfunctions and n observations. For details, see Kessler (1996). In particular, in the case of a bounded state interval, where it is well known that the sequence $\phi_1(\cdot\,;\theta),\phi_2(\cdot\,;\theta),\ldots$ is complete in $L_2(\mu_\theta)$, the union $\cup_{k=1}^{\infty} V_k$ is dense in $L_2(p(\Delta,x,y;\theta)\mathrm{d}y)$, so in this case, there generally exists a sequence N_n such that the estimator $\hat{\theta}_{n,N_n}$ is efficient. In the case of an unbounded state interval, the sequence $\phi_1(.;\theta),\phi_2(.;\theta),\ldots$ is also complete in $L_2(\mu_\theta)$ when the set of eigenfunctions is discrete, but to deduce denseness of $\cup_{k=1}^{\infty} V_k$ in $L_2(p(\Delta,x,y;\theta)\mathrm{d}y)$, additional conditions are needed. The efficiency of $\hat{\theta}_{n,N}$ obviously increases with increasing N, but so does the computational complexity. It is conjectured that for many models, $\cup_{k=1}^{\infty} V_k$ is dense in $L_2(p(\Delta,x,y;\theta)\mathrm{d}y)$ so that the efficiency is high, provided that N is sufficiently large, and a compromise between efficiency and computational feasibility must be found. Recently, Sørensen (2007) has shown that in a high-frequency asymptotics, efficient estimators are obtained with optimal estimating functions as soon as $N \geq 2$.

Example 11 *For the target zone model in Example 5, the eigenfunctions are the Jacobi polynomials with eigenvalues* $\lambda_i = i[\beta + \frac{1}{2}\sigma^2(i-1)]$, $i = 1,2,\ldots$. *Therefore, it is easy to apply (4.12) to obtain explicit expressions for the optimal estimating function based on any fixed number of eigenfunctions. In Larsen and Sørensen (2007), the asymptotic variances of the estimators obtained from several combinations of eigenfunctions were calculated for certain parameter values. It turned out that in no case was the efficiency much above that obtained when using the optimal estimating function based on the first two eigenfunctions* ϕ_1 *and* ϕ_2. *In view of the results on efficiency discussed above, it is reasonable to assume that, for the parameter values considered in* *the paper, this estimating function is close to fully efficient, at least when the sampling frequency is sufficiently high. In the study, weekly data were considered.*

4.2. Approximately Optimal Estimating Functions

For models where the optimal weight matrix $a^*(\Delta, x; \theta)$ is not explicit and must be calculated by means of simulations, it is often preferable to use a good explicit approximation to $a^*(\Delta, x; \theta)$ instead. This will usually save a lot of computer time and make the estimation procedure more numerically robust.

To make such an approximation, the following result is useful. As in the previous section, we focus here on one-dimensional diffusions, but a similar result holds for multivariate diffusions. Suppose f is a $2(k+1)$ times continuously differentiable function. Then under weak conditions on f and the diffusion model

$$\mathrm{E}_\theta(f(X_{t+s})|X_t) = \sum_{i=0}^{k} \frac{s^i}{i!} L_\theta^i f(X_t) + O(s^{k+1}), \tag{4.14}$$

where L_θ is the generator (3.26), and L_θ^i denotes i-fold application of the generator. Note that (4.14) is an expansion result, so the corresponding power series does not necessarily converge. For a fixed k, the sum is a good approximation to the conditional expectation when s is small. The remainder term depends on k, θ, and X_t. The following explicit sufficient condition for (4.14) to hold for ergodic diffusions was given in Jacobsen (2001a). Let Φ_θ be the class of real functions φ defined on the state space (ℓ, r) that are twice continuously differentiable and satisfy that

$$\int_\ell^r \varphi^2(x)\mu_\theta(x)dx < \infty$$

$$\int_\ell^r (L_\theta\varphi(x))^2\mu_\theta(x)dx < \infty$$

$$\int_\ell^r \varphi'(x)^2\sigma^2(x;\theta)\mu_\theta(x)dx < \infty,$$

where, as usual, $\mu_\theta(x)$ denotes the invariant probability measure (3.4). If $L_\theta^i f \in \Phi_\theta, i = 1, \ldots, k$, then (4.14) holds. Under this condition, the expansion can be derived by iterated application of Ito's formula. Schaumburg (2005) gave rather high-level sufficient conditions that can be hard to verify.

By applying (4.14) to $f(x) = x$ and $f(x) = x^2$, it follows that

$$\begin{aligned} E_\theta(X_\Delta|X_0 = x) = x + \Delta b(x;\theta) + \frac{1}{2}\Delta^2\{b(x;\theta)\partial_x b(x;\theta) \\ + \frac{1}{2}v(x;\theta)\partial_x^2 b(x;\theta)\} + O(\Delta^3) \end{aligned} \tag{4.15}$$

and

$$\mathrm{Var}_\theta(X_\Delta | X_0 = x) = \Delta v(x;\theta) + \Delta^2 \left[\frac{1}{2} b(x;\theta)\partial_x v(x;\theta) + v(x;\theta)\{\partial_x b(x;\theta) + \frac{1}{4}\partial_x^2 v(x;\theta)\}\right] + O(\Delta^3), \tag{4.16}$$

where $v(x;\theta) = \sigma^2(x;\theta)$.

If we insert the approximations

$$\partial_\theta F(t,x;\theta) \doteq t\partial_\theta b(x;\theta) \quad \text{and} \quad \phi(t,x;\theta) \doteq tv(x;\theta) \tag{4.17}$$

in the expression for the optimal linear estimating function (4.9), we obtain the approximately optimal estimating function

$$\sum_{i=1}^{n} \frac{\partial_\theta b(X_{t_{i-1}};\theta)}{v(X_{t_{i-1}};\theta)} [X_{t_i} - F(\Delta_i, X_{t_{i-1}};\theta)], \tag{4.18}$$

which is usually considerably easier to calculate than (4.9). When t is small, the approximation (4.17) is good, but the approximately optimal estimating function (4.18) works surprisingly well for large values of Δ_i too. By means of the formulae (4.15) and (4.16), Bibby and Sørensen (1995) showed that in the case of equidistant sampling times (i.e., for $\Delta_i = \Delta$), the asymptotic variance of the estimators based on the optimal estimating function (4.9) and the approximation (4.18) coincide up to and including terms of order $O(\Delta^2)$. The term of order $O(\Delta)$ is equal to the similar term for the maximum likelihood estimator found by Dacunha-Castelle and Florens-Zmirou (1986). Numerical calculations in Bibby and Sørensen (1995) indicate that for the CIR model, the efficiencies of the two estimators are similar even for large values of Δ.

To simplify the optimal quadratic estimating function, we supplement (4.17) by the Gaussian approximations

$$\eta(t,x;\theta) \doteq 0 \quad \text{and} \quad \psi(t,x;\theta) \doteq 2\phi(t,x;\theta)^2 \tag{4.19}$$

that are also good for small Δ-values. By inserting these approximations into (4.10), we obtain the approximately optimal quadratic estimating function

$$\sum_{i=1}^{n} \left\{ \frac{\partial_\theta b(X_{t_{i-1}};\theta)}{v(X_{t_{i-1}};\theta)} [X_{t_i} - F(\Delta_i, X_{t_{i-1}};\theta)] + \frac{\partial_\theta v(X_{t_{i-1}};\theta)}{2v^2(X_{t_{i-1}};\theta)\Delta_i} \left[(X_{t_i} - F(\Delta_i, X_{t_{i-1}};\theta))^2 - \phi(\Delta_i, X_{t_{i-1}};\theta) \right] \right\}, \tag{4.20}$$

which is a very considerable computational improvement over (4.10). This is not least because in (4.20), there are only derivatives of known functions, while (4.10) contains derivatives of functions that must often be determined by simulation. The approximately optimal quadratic estimating function (4.20) can be obtained from the score corresponding to the Gaussian pseudo-likelihood (3.16), by using the approximations (4.17) in the weights.

Example 12 *For the CIR model given by (3.17) with $\sigma(x) = \tau\sqrt{x}$, we obtain the approximately optimal quadratic estimating function*

$$\begin{pmatrix} \sum_{i=1}^{n} \frac{1}{X_{i-1}}\left[X_i - X_{i-1}e^{-\beta} - \alpha\left(1 - e^{-\beta}\right)\right] \\ \sum_{i=1}^{n}\left[X_i - X_{i-1}e^{-\beta} - \alpha\left(1 - e^{-\beta}\right)\right] \\ \sum_{i=1}^{n} \frac{1}{X_{i-1}}\left[\left(X_i - X_{i-1}e^{-\beta} - \alpha\left(1 - e^{-\beta}\right)\right)^2 - \frac{\tau^2}{\beta}\left(\left(\frac{\alpha}{2} - X_{i-1}\right)e^{-2\beta} - (\alpha - X_{i-1})e^{-\beta} + \frac{\alpha}{2}\right)\right] \end{pmatrix}.$$

As earlier, we have assumed that $t_i = i$ and given the simplest possible version of the estimating function, which is obtained by multiplying the estimating function obtained from (4.20) by the matrix

$$\begin{Bmatrix} \tau^2/\beta & 0 & 0 \\ \alpha\tau^2/\beta & -\tau^2 & 0 \\ 0 & 0 & \tau^3 \end{Bmatrix}.$$

We find the following explicit estimators of the parameters

$$\tilde{\alpha}_n = \frac{1}{n}\sum_{i=1}^{n} X_i + \frac{e^{-\tilde{\beta}_n}}{n\left(1 - e^{-\tilde{\beta}_n}\right)}(X_n - X_0)$$

$$e^{-\tilde{\beta}_n} = \frac{n\sum_{i=1}^{n} X_i/X_{i-1} - \left(\sum_{i=1}^{n} X_i\right)\left(\sum_{i=1}^{n} X_{i-1}^{-1}\right)}{n^2 - \left(\sum_{i=1}^{n} X_{i-1}\right)\left(\sum_{i=1}^{n} X_{i-1}^{-1}\right)}$$

$$\tilde{\tau}_n^2 = \frac{\sum_{i=1}^{n} X_{i-1}^{-1}\left(X_i - X_{i-1}e^{-\tilde{\beta}_n} - \tilde{\alpha}_n\left(1 - e^{-\tilde{\beta}_n}\right)\right)^2}{\sum_{i=1}^{n} X_{i-1}^{-1}\left(\left(\frac{1}{2}\tilde{\alpha}_n - X_{i-1}\right)e^{-2\tilde{\beta}_n} - (\tilde{\alpha}_n - X_{i-1})e^{-\tilde{\beta}_n} + \frac{1}{2}\tilde{\alpha}_n\right)/\tilde{\beta}_n},$$

which exist provided that the expression for $e^{-\tilde{\beta}_n}$ is strictly positive, an event that happens with a probability tending to one as $n \to \infty$. A simulation study and an investigation of the asymptotic variance of the estimators $\tilde{\alpha}_n$ and $\tilde{\beta}_n$ in Bibby and Sørensen (1995) indicate that these estimators are quite efficient; see also the simulation study in Overbeck and Rydén (1997). Note that the level α is essentially estimated by the average of the observations. In practice, it is easier to use the average as this causes no lost of asymptotic efficiency.

The expansion (4.14) can be used to simplify the expressions for the optimal weights in many other estimating functions. This will save computer time and improve the numerical performance of the estimation procedure. The approximation will not affect the consistency of the estimators, and if Δ_i is not too large, it will just lead to a minor loss of efficiency. The magnitude of this loss of efficiency can be calculated by means of (4.14) or in the case of the quadratic estimating function by means of (4.15) and (4.16).

It is tempting to go on and approximate the functions F and ϕ still appearing in (4.18) and (4.20) by $F(t, x; \theta) \doteq x + tb(x; \theta)$ and $\phi(t, x; \theta) \doteq tv(x; \theta)$. This certainly leads to a very simple estimation procedure that has often been used, but it is important to note that there is a dangerous pitfall here. First, if F and ϕ are replaced by approximations, the martingale property is destroyed so that stronger conditions on the process are needed to ensure asymptotic normality, see the discussion in Section 3.1. This is usually a minor problem. What is much worse is that the estimating function becomes biased, which implies that the estimator becomes inconsistent, at least under the kind of asymptotics considered so far. For consistency of the estimators to hold for an estimating function of the form (3.12), it is important that the estimating function is unbiased, i.e., that $Q_\theta^\Delta(g(\Delta, \theta)) = 0$ so that as $n \to \infty$,

$$\frac{1}{n}\sum_{i=1}^{n} g(\Delta, X_{\Delta(i-1)}, X_{\Delta i}; \theta) \to 0.$$

For biased estimating functions,

$$\hat{\theta}_n \to \bar{\theta}$$

in probability under P_{θ_0} as $n \to \infty$, where $\bar{\theta}$ is the solution to the equation

$$Q_{\theta_0}^\Delta(g(\Delta, \bar{\theta})) = 0, \tag{4.21}$$

which we assume to be unique. As usual, θ_0 is the true parameter value.

Example 13 *For a general mean-reverting process (3.17), the approximate linear estimating function where the conditional expectation is replaced by the first-order expansion is (for equidistant observation, $t_i = \Delta i$)*

$$\begin{pmatrix} \sum_{i=1}^{n} \frac{1}{v(X_{\Delta(i-1)})}\left[X_{\Delta i} - X_{\Delta(i-1)} + \Delta\beta(X_{\Delta(i-1)} - \alpha)\right] \\ \sum_{i=1}^{n} \frac{X_{\Delta(i-1)}}{v(X_{\Delta(i-1)})}\left[X_{\Delta i} - X_{\Delta(i-1)} + \Delta\beta(X_{\Delta(i-1)} - \alpha)\right] \end{pmatrix}. \tag{4.22}$$

For the CIR process, the weights are $X_{\Delta(i-1)}^{-1}$ and 1, and it is not difficult to find the explicit estimators obtained from (4.22) for this model:

$$\hat{\alpha}_n = \frac{1}{n}\sum_{i=1}^{n} X_{\Delta(i-1)} + \frac{1}{\hat{\beta}_n \Delta n}(X_{\Delta n} - X_0)$$

$$\hat{\beta}_n = \frac{\frac{1}{n}(X_{\Delta n} - X_0)\sum_{i=1}^{n} X_{\Delta(i-1)}^{-1} - \sum_{i=1}^{n} X_{\Delta(i-1)}^{-1}(X_{\Delta i} - X_{\Delta(i-1)})}{\Delta\left[n - \left(\sum_{i=1}^{n} X_{\Delta(i-1)}\right)\left(\sum_{i=1}^{n} X_{\Delta(i-1)}^{-1}\right)/n\right]}.$$

The asymptotic bias of these estimators as $n \to \infty$ can easily be found using the ergodic theorem and the fact that the invariant probability measure for the CIR model is a gamma distribution. However, a result for general mean-reverting processes can be obtained by solving the Eq. (4.21) for the estimating function (4.22). The solutions are

$$\overline{\alpha} = \alpha_0 \quad \textit{and} \quad \overline{\beta}\Delta = 1 - e^{-\beta_0 \Delta} \leq 1.$$

Thus, the estimator of α is in fact consistent. Contrary to this, the estimator of the reversion parameter β is reasonable only when $\beta_0\Delta$ is considerably smaller than one. Note that $\overline{\beta} \leq \Delta^{-1}$, so the estimator will always converge to a limit smaller than the sampling frequency. When $\beta_0\Delta$ is large, the behavior of the estimator is bizarre, see Bibby and Sørensen (1995). Without prior knowledge of the value of β_0, it is thus a very dangerous estimator, which has unfortunately frequently been applied in the literature.

Using (4.15), it is easy to see that in general the bias of

$$\sum_{i=1}^{n} \frac{\partial_\theta b(X_{\Delta(i-1)};\theta)}{v(X_{\Delta(i-1)};\theta)}\left[X_{\Delta i} - X_{\Delta(i-1)} - \Delta b(X_{\Delta(i-1)};\theta)\right]$$

is of order Δ^2 when the observation time points are equidistant. One would therefore expect that in an asymptotic scenario, where Δ goes to zero as $n \to \infty$, the estimator is consistent. This is in fact true. Dorogovcev (1976), Prakasa Rao (1983), Prakasa Rao (1988), Florens-Zmirou (1989), and Yoshida (1990) proved that the estimator is consistent provided that $\Delta \to 0$ and $n\Delta \to \infty$ as $n \to \infty$. Moreover, the estimator is asymptotically normal if it is further assumed that $n\Delta^2 \to 0$. A general result comprising also more accurate approximations of F and ϕ in (4.20) was given by Kessler (1997). By choosing the approximations in a suitable way, Kessler obtained estimators that are asymptotically normal provided just that $n\Delta^k \to 0$ for a $k \in \mathbb{N}$ that depends on the order of the approximation. As similar, result for general martingale estimating functions can be found in Sørensen (2007).

4.3. Simple Diffusion Models for Interest Rates

In this section, we consider monthly observations of U.S. one-month treasury bill yields from June 1964 to December 1989. These data were also analyzed by Chan et al. (1992). The rates have been annualized and converted into continuously compounded yields. In Fig. 4.1, the yields are plotted against time.

We use two different diffusion process models to describe the data. One is the model introduced in Chan et al. (1992), which we refer to as the CKLS-model. If X_t denotes the yield at time t, then the CKLS-model is given by the stochastic differential equation,

$$dX_t = \kappa(\theta - X_t)dt + \sigma X_t^{\gamma} dW_t, \tag{4.23}$$

where, as usual, W denotes a standard Wiener process. The second model is given by the stochastic differential equation

$$dX_t = \left(aX_t^{2\gamma-1} + bX_t\right)dt + \sigma X_t^{\gamma}\, dW_t \tag{4.24}$$

where $a, b \in \mathbb{R}$, $\gamma \neq 1$, and $\sigma > 0$. For $\gamma = \frac{1}{2}$, this is the stochastic differential equation for the CIR-process, see Example 2. The generalization (4.24) is arrived at by considering all powers $\widetilde{X}^{\rho}$ of a CIR process with $\rho \neq 0$. More precisely, if X solves (4.24), then the

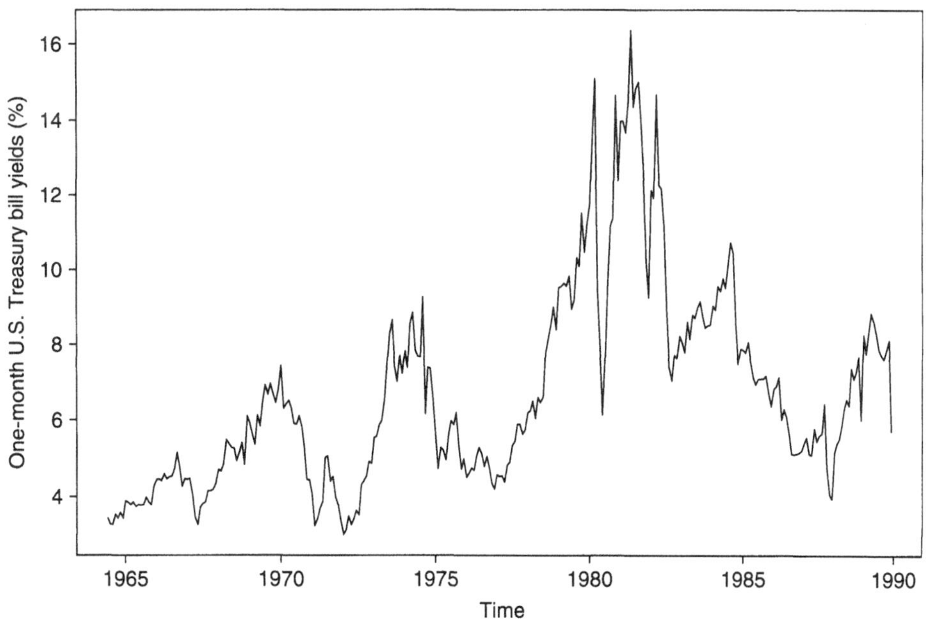

Figure 4.1 The one-month treasury bill yields plotted against time.

associated CIR process is $\widetilde{X} = X^{2-2\gamma}$ solving

$$d\widetilde{X}_t = (\widetilde{a} + \widetilde{b}\widetilde{X}_t)dt + \widetilde{\sigma}\sqrt{\widetilde{X}_t}dW_t, \tag{4.25}$$

where

$$\widetilde{b} = (2-2\gamma)\,b, \quad \widetilde{\sigma}^2 = (2-2\gamma)^2\sigma^2, \quad \widetilde{a} - \frac{1}{2}\widetilde{\sigma}^2 = (2-2\gamma)\left(a - \frac{1}{2}\sigma^2\right). \tag{4.26}$$

This also explains why $\gamma = 1$ is not allowed in (4.24). The process (4.24) was introduced in Jacobsen (2002), where it was called the *generalized Cox-Ingersoll-Ross model* (or generalized CIR process). Because of the connection to the CIR process, the generalized CIR process is much simpler to handle mathematically than the more standard CKLS model (4.23). In particular, for (4.24), it is easy to find martingale estimating functions of the form (3.25) (although the base will now depend on the parameter γ). The generalized CIR model (GCIR model) will be considered again in Example 14. In (4.24), the parameter space has dimension $p = 4$. We shall want X to be strictly positive and ergodic, which happens if and only if the associated CIR process $\widetilde{X}$ is strictly positive and ergodic, i.e., when $\widetilde{b} < 0$ and $2\widetilde{a} \geq \widetilde{\sigma}^2$, or equivalently, when either $\gamma < 1, b < 0, 2a \geq \sigma^2$ or $\gamma > 1, b > 0, 2a \leq \sigma^2$. Since the invariant distribution for $\widetilde{X}$ is a Γ-distribution, the invariant distribution for X is that of a Γ-distributed random variable raised to the power $(2-2\gamma)^{-1}$. Because a Γ-distribution has finite moments of all orders $m \in \mathbb{N}$, we have $E_\theta(X_0^{(2\gamma-2)m}) < \infty$ for all $m \in \mathbb{N}$ when $X_0 \sim \mu_\theta$, and $\pi_\Delta^\theta x^{(2\gamma-2)m} < \infty$ for all $\Delta > 0$, $m \in \mathbb{N}$, and all $x > 0$. Furthermore, since the conditional moments for a CIR process are known, for the generalized CIR process all $\pi_\Delta^\theta x^{(2\gamma-2)m}$ are known explicitly. The generalized CIR-model (GCIR-model) will be considered again in Example 14.

The observations are denoted as $X_\Delta, X_{2\Delta}, \ldots, X_{n\Delta}$, where n is 307 and $\Delta = 1/12$. For both models, the parameters are estimated using the approximation to the optimal quadratic martingale estimating function given by (4.20). For the CKLS model, the conditional expectation can be found explicitly, while the conditional variance is found using simulations. In case of the GCIR model, both the conditional mean and the conditional variance are determined by simulations. In Tables 4.2 and 4.3, the estimates for the parameter in the two models are given based on both the whole time series and for the period June 1964 to September 1979 ($n = 184$). The reason for considering the latter period separately is that between October 1979 and October 1982, the U.S. Federal Bank employed a monetary rather than an interest rate–targeting policy resulting in a quite different stochastic regime.

For a more detailed analysis of these data based on the CKLS model, see Christensen et al. (2001). Note from Table 4.3 that the estimate of the parameter γ in the GCIR model is quite close to 1. In Fig. 4.2, a Q-Q plot of uniform residuals corresponding to both models and both time periods are given. We see that the two models fit the data

Table 4.2 Estimates for the parameters in the CKLS model based on two periods

	1964–1989	1964–1979
θ	0.0735	0.0676
κ	0.3309	0.3376
σ	1.0119	0.6311
γ	1.3833	1.2755

Table 4.3 Estimates for the parameters in the GCIR model based on two periods

	1964–1989	1964–1979
α	1.4093	0.7571
β	−1.2110	−0.5491
σ	0.3905	0.2987
γ	0.9997	0.9997

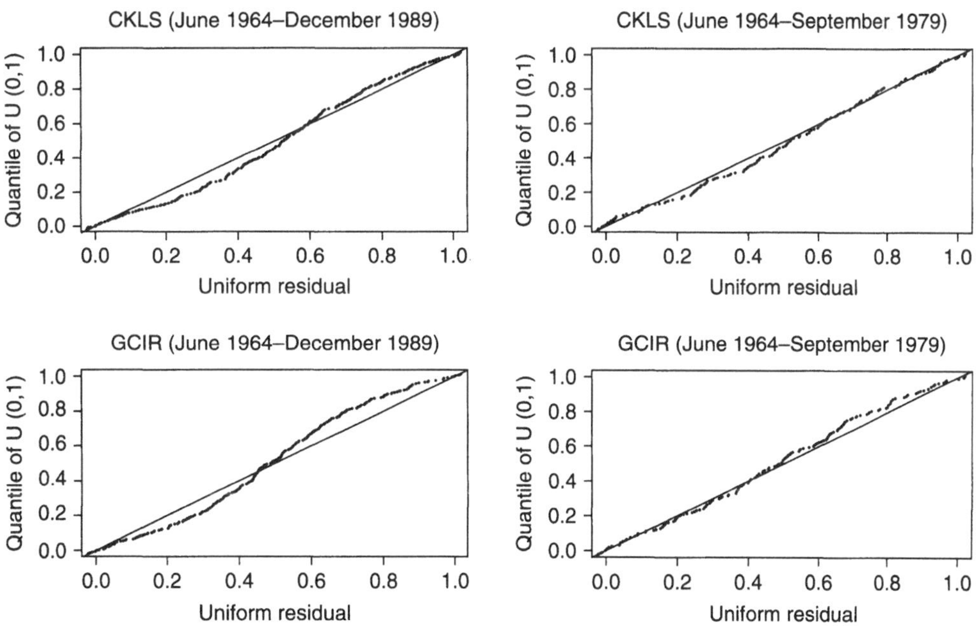

Figure 4.2 Q-Q-plots of uniform residuals corresponding to the CKLS model and the GCIR model based on observations in two periods. The points should follow the identity line for a perfect fit.

equally well. We may also note that the models clearly fit the data from June 1964 to September 1979 better than the whole data set. Model diagnostics based on uniform residuals was introduced and discussed by Pedersen (1994b).

Let us complete the discussion here by pointing out that simple diffusion models have been found to give a less satisfactory fit to short-term interest rate data than stochastic volatility models, see, e.g., Durham (2003), where interesting alternative models are given.

4.4. Small Δ-optimality

We shall here discuss an optimality criterion for unbiased estimating functions for diffusion models, called small Δ-optimality, which was introduced by Jacobsen (2001a) and explored further in the case of martingale estimating functions of the form (3.25) in Jacobsen (2001b). The same idea was later applied in Aït-Sahalia and Mykland (2004) and Aït-Sahalia and Mykland (2008). Recently, Sørensen (2007) has shown that for martingale estimating functions, small Δ-optimality is equivalent to rate optimality and efficiency in a high-frequency asymptotics.

Throughout this section, we shall assume that the observation times are equidistant, i.e., $t_i = i\Delta,\ 0 \le i \le n$, where Δ is fixed. That an estimating function is small Δ-optimal implies that for $\Delta > 0$ small, the resulting estimator is nearly efficient. Furthermore, as will be demonstrated, it is easy to find explicitly given estimating functions that are small Δ-optimal.

To illustrate the main idea, consider a martingale estimating function as in (3.12). The covariance matrix of the asymptotic distribution of $\hat{\theta}_n$ is (with θ denoting the true parameter value)

$$\mathrm{Var}_{\Delta,\theta}\big(g,\hat{\theta}\big) = S(\theta)^{-1}\,V(\theta)\,\big(S^{-1}(\theta)\big)^{T}, \tag{4.27}$$

where the matrices $S(\theta) = \big(S_{ij}(\theta)\big)_{i\le i,j\le p}$ and $V(\theta) = \big(V_{ij}(\theta)\big)_{i\le i,j\le p}$ are given by

$$S_{ij}(\theta) = \mathrm{E}_\theta\big(\partial_{\theta_j} g_i(\Delta, X_0, X_\Delta;\theta)\big), \quad V_{ij}(\theta) = \mathrm{E}_\theta\big(g_i(\Delta, X_0, X_\Delta;\theta) g_j(\Delta, X_0, X_\Delta;\theta)\big), \tag{4.28}$$

see (2.3). Now allow $\Delta > 0$ to vary freely and consider the covariance matrix $\mathrm{Var}_{\Delta,\theta}(g,\hat{\theta})$ as a function of Δ. The optimal martingale estimating function with base f (c.f. (3.25)) comes about by minimizing $\mathrm{Var}_{\Delta,\theta}(g,\hat{\theta})$ for a *given* $\Delta > 0$ when the weights vary (minimizing in the partial order on the space of covariance matrices). Different choices of f lead to different optimal martingale estimating functions of different quality. Each of them is *locally optimal* in the sense that the resulting estimator is the best within the subclass of estimators given by the chosen base f, but estimators from subclasses given by other choices of f may do better.

By contrast, for the discussion of small Δ-optimality, we consider $\mathrm{Var}_{\Delta,\theta}(g,\hat{\theta})$ given by (4.27) for $\Delta \to 0$ and show that in the limit, a universal lower bound for the asymptotic covariance can be obtained. This implies that for small values of Δ (high-frequency data), the estimator obtained from a small Δ-optimal estimating function is in practice (almost) as good as the maximum likelihood estimator. Thus, small Δ-optimality is a *global optimality* criterion. Although small Δ-optimality refers explicitly to the limit $\Delta \to 0$, for any given fixed $\Delta > 0$, the estimator obtained is still $\sqrt{n}$-consistent and asymptotically Gaussian as the sample size goes to infinity. There is no guarantee that it is optimal in the sense discussed in Section 2 (relative to the base f), but for Δ not too large, it should still behave well, as has been verified in several examples.

The martingale estimating functions we shall use for the discussion here are of the form (3.12) with the ith coordinate of g given by

$$g_i\big(\Delta, x, y; \theta\big) = \sum_{j=1}^{N} a_{ij}(x;\theta)\left(f_j(y) - \pi_\Delta^\theta(f_j)(x)\right) \quad \big(1 \le i \le p\big). \tag{4.29}$$

It is assumed that neither the base functions f_j nor the weights a_{ij} depend on Δ. The f_j may depend on θ, but for the time, we ignore such a dependence. We also make the following vital assumption.

Condition 3 *The functions $f_j(x)$ are twice differentiable. Also, the base f has full affine rank N on the state space D, i.e., the identity*

$$\sum_{j=1}^{N} c_j f_j(x) + \gamma = 0 \quad (x \in D)$$

for some constants c_j, γ implies that $c_1 = \cdots = c_N = \gamma = 0$. The functions $a_{ij}(x;\theta)$ satisfy that for any θ, the p N-dimensional functions $x \to (a_{i1}(x;\theta), \ldots, a_{iN}(x;\theta))$ forming the rows of $a(x;\theta)$ are linearly independent on D.

As $\Delta \to 0$, neighboring observations $\big(X_{(i-1)\Delta}, X_{i\Delta}\big)$ will, since X is continuous, get very close together. It is therefore not surprising that it is the limit

$$g_{i,0}(x, y; \theta) = \lim_{\Delta \to 0} g_i(\Delta, x, y; \theta) = \sum_{j=1}^{N} a_{ij}(x,\theta)\left(f_j(y) - f_j(x)\right) \tag{4.30}$$

and its behavior close to the diagonal $y = x$ that determines the structure of $\mathrm{Var}_{\Delta,\theta}(g,\hat{\theta})$ as $\Delta \to 0$. More specifically, using Itô–Taylor expansions of the random variables that determine the matrices $V(\theta)$ and $S(\theta)$ in the expression for $\mathrm{Var}_{\Delta,\theta}(g,\hat{\theta})$, see (4.27) and

(4.28), subject to integrability conditions, we obtain an expansion of the form

$$\mathrm{Var}_{\Delta,\theta}(g,\hat{\theta}) = \frac{1}{\Delta}\nu_{-1,\theta}(g,\hat{\theta}) + \nu_{0,\theta}(g,\hat{\theta}) + o(1) \tag{4.31}$$

as $\Delta \to 0$ (Jacobsen (2001a), section 6). The expressions for the coefficient matrices $\nu_{-1,\theta}$ and $\nu_{0,\theta}$ depend in an essential way on the structure of the model, and we shall distinguish between three cases (i), (ii), and (iii) (where to achieve the structure in (iii), it may be necessary first to reparametrize the model). For each case, we list conditions under which the relevant coefficients are minimized, i.e., conditions under which small Δ-optimality is achieved. For the cases (i) and (ii), we also give the universal lower bounds on $\nu_{-1,\theta}$ [case (i)] and $\nu_{0,\theta}$ [case(ii)]. In this section, X is a general d-dimensional diffusion satisfying (3.1) with b a d-dimensional vector and σ a $d \times d$-matrix. As previously, $C = \sigma\sigma^T$ with σ^T denoting the transpose of σ.

(i) $C(x;\theta) = C(x)$ *does not depend on* θ. In this case, the main term in (4.31) is always present and small Δ-optimality is achieved by minimizing globally (over all g) the quantity $\nu_{-1,\theta}(g,\hat{\theta})$. A sufficient condition for a given g to be small Δ-optimal is that

$$\partial_y g_0(x,x;\theta) = \dot{b}^T(x;\theta)C^{-1}(x). \tag{4.32}$$

Here, $\partial_y g_0(x,x;\theta)$ evaluates $\partial_y g_0(x,y;\theta) = \left(\partial_{y_k} g_{i,0}(x,y;\theta)\right) \in \mathbb{R}^{p\times d}$ along the diagonal $y = x$, and $\dot{b}(x;\theta) \in \mathbb{R}^{d\times p}$ with $\left(\dot{b}(x;\theta)\right)_{ki} = \partial_{\theta_i} b_k(x;\theta)$. If (4.32) holds, $\nu_{-1,\theta}(g,\hat{\theta})$ attains its lower bound

$$\left[E_\theta\left(\dot{b}^T(X_0;\theta)C^{-1}(X_0)\,\dot{b}(X_0;\theta)\right)\right]^{-1}.$$

(ii) $C(x;\theta)$ *depends on all parameters* $\theta_1,\ldots,\theta_p$. Then the main term in (4.31) vanishes provided $\partial_y g_0(x,x;\theta) \equiv 0$, and small Δ-optimality is achieved by minimizing $\nu_{0,\theta}(g,\hat{\theta})$. A sufficient condition for g to be small Δ-optimal is that

$$\partial_y g_0(x,x;\theta) = 0, \quad \partial^2_{yy} g_0(x,x;\theta) = \dot{C}^T(x;\theta)\left(C^{\otimes 2}(x;\theta)\right)^{-1}, \tag{4.33}$$

where $\partial^2_{yy} g_0(x,x;\theta) \in \mathbb{R}^{p\times d^2}$ evaluates the second derivatives $\partial^2_{y_k y_\ell} g_{i,0}(x,y;\theta)$ along the diagonal $y = x$, $\dot{C}(x;\theta) \in \mathbb{R}^{d^2\times p}$ with $(\dot{C}(x;\theta))_{k\ell,i} = \partial_{\theta_i} C_{k\ell}(x;\theta)$, and $C^{\otimes 2} \in \mathbb{R}^{d^2\times d^2}$ is given by $(C^{\otimes 2})_{k\ell,k'\ell'} = C_{kk'}C_{\ell\ell'}$. If (4.33) holds, $\nu_{0,\theta}(g,\hat{\theta})$ attains its lower bound

$$2\left[E_\theta\left(\dot{C}^T(X_0;\theta)\left(C^{\otimes 2}(X_0;\theta)\right)^{-1}\dot{C}(X_0;\theta)\right)\right]^{-1}.$$

(iii) *C_θ depends on the parameters $\theta_1, \ldots, \theta_{p'}$ but not on $\theta_{p'+1}, \ldots, \theta_p$ for some p' with* $1 \leq p' < p$. Here, parts of the main term in (4.31) can be made to disappear so that

$$v_{-1,\theta}\big(g, \hat{\theta}\big) = \begin{pmatrix} \mathbf{0}_{p' \times p'} & \mathbf{0}_{p' \times (p-p')} \\ \mathbf{0}_{(p-p') \times p'} & v_{22,-1,\theta}\big(g, \hat{\theta}\big) \end{pmatrix}.$$

Here, $\mathbf{0}_{r \times s}$ denotes the $r \times s$-matrix with all entries equal to zero. Furthermore, the matrix $v_{22,-1,\theta}\big(g, \hat{\theta}\big) \in \mathbb{R}^{(p-p') \times (p-p')}$ can be minimized, and small Δ-optimality is achieved by, in addition, minimizing the upper left $p' \times p'$-block $v_{11,0,\theta}\big(g, \hat{\theta}\big)$ of $v_{0,\theta}\big(g, \hat{\theta}\big)$. A sufficient condition for small Δ-optimality is that

$$\partial_y g_0(x, x; \theta) = \begin{pmatrix} \mathbf{0}_{p' \times d} \\ \dot{b}_2^T(x; \theta) C^{-1}(x; \theta) \end{pmatrix}, \tag{4.34}$$

$$\partial^2_{yy} g_{1,0}(x, x; \theta) = \dot{C}_1^T(x; \theta) \left(C^{\otimes 2}(x; \theta)\right)^{-1}, \tag{4.35}$$

where $\dot{b}_2 \in \mathbb{R}^{d \times (p-p')}$ comprises the last $p - p'$ columns of $\dot{b}$, $g_{1,0}$ the first p' coordinates of g_0, and $\dot{C}_1 \in \mathbb{R}^{d^2 \times p'}$ the first p' columns of $\dot{C}$.

The complicated case (3) may best be understood as follows: for $\theta_1, \ldots, \theta_{p'}$ fixed, (4.34) requires in particular that the last $p - p'$ coordinates of g be small Δ-optimal for estimating $\theta_{p'+1}, \ldots, \theta_p$, see case (i); and for $\theta_{p'+1}, \ldots, \theta_p$ fixed, (4.34) and (4.35) require that the first p' coordinates of g be small Δ-optimal for estimating $\theta_1, \ldots, \theta_{p'}$, see case (ii).

As mentioned above, to check for small Δ-optimality, more is required than just checking (4.32), (4.33) or (4.34), (4.35), viz., it must be verified that various matrices involving expectations of quantities related to $\dot{b}$, $\dot{C}$, $\partial_y g_0$, and $\partial^2_{yy} g_0$ are nonsingular, see theorem 2 in Jacobsen (2001a).

We used the special structure (4.29) above to get directly an expression for the limit $g_{i,0}(x, y; \theta)$ in (4.30). For a general martingale estimating function, the existence of a nontrivial (in particular nonzero) limit must be assumed, and to find it in concrete cases, it may be necessary to renormalize g, i.e., replace $g(\Delta, x, y; \theta)$ by $K_\Delta(\theta) g(\Delta, x, y; \theta)$ for some nonsingular $p \times p$-matrix $K_\Delta(\theta)$ not depending on x or y. As discussed earlier, such a renormalization does not affect the solutions to the estimating equations. Small Δ-optimality can be discussed also for any family of unbiased estimating functions defined by a class of functions $(g_\Delta)_{\Delta > 0}$. For details, see Jacobsen (2001a), section 6.

It is important to comment further on the qualitatively different forms that the expansion (4.31) takes under small Δ-optimality in the three cases (i), (ii), and (iii). Obviously, a major gain in estimation accuracy is obtained for Δ small, if the leading term v_{-1} can be dispensed with, and the reason why this is possible in case (ii), partly in case (iii), and never in case (i) is best understood by considering complete observation of X in continuous time on a finite time interval – as $\Delta \to 0$, we are getting close to continuous-time observation. So let $T > 0$ be fixed and denote by $P_{\theta,T}$ the distribution of $(X_t)_{0\le t\le T}$ when X is stationary and the true parameter value is θ. In case (i), when θ varies, only the drift $b(x;\theta)$ changes, and for $\theta \neq \theta'$, the measures $P_{\theta,T}$ and $P_{\theta',T}$ will typically be equivalent with a Radon–Nikodym derivative given by Girsanov's theorem. By contrast, in case (ii) where also $C(x;\theta)$ changes with θ, it may well happen that $P_{\theta,T}$ and $P_{\theta',T}$ are singular for $\theta \neq \theta'$, i.e., it is (in principle) possible to read off the exact value of θ from the observed sample path of X. Of course, for the discrete time observations $(X_{i\Delta})_{0\le i\le n}$, perfect information about θ is not available, but through small Δ-optimality, it is possible to increase the information about θ per observation $X_{i\Delta}$ from $O(\Delta)$ in case (i) to $O(1)$ in case (ii). Note that for the general martingale estimating functions, even in case (ii), the leading term v_{-1} will be present unless one is careful, and the result will then be an estimator that as $\Delta \to 0$ is infinitely worse than a small Δ-optimal estimator.

We shall now again return to the specific martingale estimating functions emanating from (4.29) and discuss when and how, for a given base $f = (f_j)_{1\le j\le N}$ satisfying Condition 3, the weights a may be chosen so as to achieve small Δ-optimality. In particular, this will reveal a critical value

$$\dim(d) := d + \left(d + \binom{d}{2}\right) = d(d+3)/2$$

for the dimension N of the base. The value $\dim(d)$ comes about naturally by fixing a base f of dimension d and then supplementing this with the functions $f_j f_{j'}$ for $1 \le j \le j' \le d$. The discussion splits into the same three cases as before, but for illustration, we just consider case (i). From (4.30),

$$\partial_y g_0(x,x;\theta) = a(x;\theta)\partial_x f(x),$$

which is required to equal $\dot{b}^T(x;\theta)C^{-1}(x)$, see (4.32). Solving for $a(x;\theta)$ is clearly possible if $N = d$ provided the $d \times d$-matrix $\partial_x f(x)$ with jkth element $\partial_{x_k} f_j(x)$ is nonsingular, and possible also if $N > d$ provided $\partial_x f(x)$ has full rank d. In cases (ii) and (iii), similar linear equation systems are obtained (but now involving d first derivatives of g_0 and all the different second derivatives, i.e., $\dim(d)$ derivatives in all), resulting in the following shortened version of theorem 2 of Jacobsen (2002). In the theorem, we use the following notation: if $M \in \mathbb{R}^{r\times d^2}$ is a matrix with entries $M_{q,k\ell}$ for $1 \le q \le r$ and $1 \le k,\ell \le d$ that are symmetric in k and ℓ, we write $MR \in \mathbb{R}^{r\times \rho(d)}$ for the matrix with entries $M_{q,k\ell}$ for $1 \le q \le r$ and $1 \le k \le \ell \le d$ obtained by multiplying M by the reduction matrix

$R \in \mathbb{R}^{d^2 \times \rho(d)}$ with entries $R_{k'\ell',k\ell} = 1$ if $k' = k$ and $\ell' = \ell$ and $R_{k'\ell',k\ell} = 0$ otherwise $(1 \le k', \ell' \le d$ and $1 \le k \le \ell \le d)$. Here, $\rho(d)$ is the number of choices for (k, ℓ) such that $1 \le k \le \ell \le d$, i.e., $\rho(d) = d + \binom{d}{2} = \dim(d) - d$.

Theorem 2 *Consider martingale estimating functions of the form*

$$G_n(\theta) = \sum_{i=1}^{n} a^*(X_{(i-1)\Delta}, \theta)\left(f(X_{i\Delta};\theta) - \pi_\Delta^\theta(f(\theta))(X_{(i-1)\Delta})\right), \tag{4.36}$$

where the base $f = (f_j)_{1 \le j \le N}$ is of full affine rank N, and where the matrix-valued function $a^*(x, \theta)$ is chosen differently in the following three cases.

(i) *Suppose that $N = d$, that for μ_θ-a.a. x, the matrix $\partial_x f(x) \in \mathbb{R}^{d \times d}$ is nonsingular, and that the p d-variate functions of x forming the columns of $\dot{b}(x;\theta)$ are linearly independent. Then the rows of*

$$a^*(x;\theta) = \dot{b}^T(x;\theta)C^{-1}(x)\left(\partial_x f(x)\right)^{-1} \tag{4.37}$$

are linearly independent as required by Condition 3, and the estimating function (4.36) satisfies the small Δ-optimality condition (4.32).

(ii) *Suppose that $N = \dim(d)$, that for μ_θ-a.a. x, the matrix*

$$Q(x) = \left(\partial_x f(x) \quad \partial_{xx}^2 f(x)R\right) \in \mathbb{R}^{\dim(d)\times\dim(d)} \tag{4.38}$$

is nonsingular and that the p d^2-variate functions of x forming the columns of $\dot{C}(x;\theta)$ are linearly independent. Then the rows of

$$a^*(x;\theta) = \left(\mathbf{0}_{p\times d} \quad \dot{C}^T(x;\theta)\left(C^{\otimes 2}(x;\theta)\right)^{-1}R\right)(Q(x))^{-1} \tag{4.39}$$

are linearly independent, and the estimating function (4.36) satisfies the small Δ-optimality condition (4.33).

(iii) *Suppose that $N = \dim(d)$, that for μ_θ-a.a. x, the matrix $Q(x)$ given by (4.38) is nonsingular, that the $p - p'$ d-variate functions forming the columns of $\dot{b}_{2,\theta}$ are linearly independent and the p' d^2-variate functions forming the columns of $\dot{C}_{1,\theta}$ are linearly independent. Then the rows of*

$$a^*(x;\theta) = \begin{pmatrix} \mathbf{0}_{p'\times d} & \dot{C}_1^T(x;\theta)\left(C^{\otimes 2}(x;\theta)\right)^{-1}R \\ \dot{b}_2^T(x;\theta)C^{-1}(x;\theta) & \mathbf{0}_{(p-p')\times\rho(d)} \end{pmatrix}(Q(x))^{-1} \tag{4.40}$$

are linearly independent, and the estimating function (4.36) satisfies the small Δ-optimality conditions (4.34) and (4.35).

For models with a special structure, the critical value $\dim(d)$ for the dimension of the base f may be lowered. This is, for instance, the case when $X = (X_1, \ldots, X_c)$ with $X_1, \ldots, X_c$ independent diffusions of dimensions $d_1, \ldots, d_c$, where $\sum_{m=1}^{c} d_m = d$. In this situation, small Δ-optimality can be achieved using a base of dimension $\sum_{m=1}^{c} \dim(d_m)$. In general, however, $\dim(d)$ is the critical dimension, even for the optimal martingale estimating function determined by a given base for any given $\Delta > 0$ to be small Δ-optimal (Jacobsen, 2002, theorem 2.3). Thus, it may well happen if $d = 1$ for a model belonging to case (ii), that the optimal martingale estimating function determined by a base of dimension 1, will result in an estimator that behaves disastrously for high-frequency data.

In case (iii) of Theorem 2, one may find a host of small Δ-optimal martingale estimating functions other than that specified by (4.40), in fact the entry $\mathbf{0}_{(p-p')\times\rho(d)}$ may be replaced by an arbitrary matrix depending on x and θ (subject to Condition 3 and smoothness and integrability requirements). Another useful recipe (adopted in Example 14 below) for finding small Δ-optimal estimating functions in case (iii), is to fix a base f° of dimension d, augment it to a base f of dimension $\dim(d)$ by adding the products $f_j^\circ f_{j'}^\circ$ for $1 \leq j \leq j' \leq d$, and then defining the first p' rows of $a^*(x;\theta)$ by

$$\left(\mathbf{0}_{p'\times d} \quad \dot{C}_1^T(x;\theta)\left(C^{\otimes 2}(x;\theta)\right)^{-1} R\right)(Q(x))^{-1}$$

and the last $p - p'$ rows by

$$\dot{b}_2^T(x;\theta)\, C^{-1}(x;\theta)\left(\partial_x f(x)\right)^{-1}.$$

Sørensen (2007) showed that martingale estimating functions that are optimal in the sense of Section 2 are, under regularity conditions, also small Δ-optimal.

Although it is easy to obtain small Δ-optimality for martingale estimating functions, it is not known what happens in general with the classes of simple and explicit, transition-dependent estimating functions also discussed above, see (3.35) and (3.38). It is known (Jacobsen, 2001a) that for $d = 1$ and if $C = \sigma^2$ does not depend on θ, then the simple estimating function with h given by (3.35) is small Δ-optimal provided that f satisfies that $\partial_x f(x) = K_\theta \dot{b}_\theta^T(x)/\sigma^2(x)$ for some nonsingular matrix K_θ not depending on x. This is the case for Kessler's estimating function in the Ornstein–Uhlenbeck model, see Example 6, and more generally, as follows easily using (3.4), also for the estimating function proposed by Conley et al. (1997), which is obtained for $f = \partial_\theta \log \mu_\theta$. However, if either $d \geq 2$ or the model is of type (ii) or (iii), it seems virtually impossible to achieve small Δ-optimality. For the much wider class (3.38), nothing much is known, but it does appear difficult to obtain small Δ-optimality for models belonging to case (ii).

We shall conclude this section by showing how small Δ-optimality works for the one-dimensional diffusion model with four parameters discussed in Section 4.3. The model was introduced by Jacobsen (2002) and the simulation study below is from Jacobsen (2001b).

Example 14 *Consider the problem of estimating the four-dimensional parameter vector θ in the generalized CIR process from discrete observations. The generalized CIR process is the solution of the one-dimensional ($d = 1$) stochastic differential equation (4.24). It is clear that the model (4.24) belongs to case (iii) with $p = 4$, $p' = 2$. We need a base of dimension $\dim(1) = 2$ and shall simply use $f = \left(f_j\right)_{1\leq j\leq 2}$ given by*

$$f_1(x) = x^{2-2\gamma} \quad \text{and} \quad f_2(x) = x^{4-4\gamma}, \tag{4.41}$$

which trivially satisfies Condition 3. This corresponds to choosing $f^\circ(x) = x^{2-2\gamma}$ (see page 260 for the general use of f°). By the methods described above, one may then show that the martingale estimating function given by

$$g(\Delta, x, y; \theta) = \begin{pmatrix} -2\log x & x^{2\gamma-2}\log x \\ -2 & x^{2\gamma-2} \\ x^{2\gamma-2} & 0 \\ 1 & 0 \end{pmatrix} \begin{pmatrix} y^{2-2\gamma} - \pi_\Delta^\theta x^{2-2\gamma} \\ y^{4-4\gamma} - \pi_\Delta^\theta x^{4-4\gamma} \end{pmatrix} \tag{4.42}$$

is small Δ-optimal. Here, the conditional expectations are given by the expressions

$$\pi_\Delta^\theta x^{2-2\gamma} = e^{\tilde{b}\Delta}\left(x^{2-2\gamma} - \tilde{\xi}_1\right) + \tilde{\xi}_1,$$

$$\pi_\Delta^\theta x^{4-4\gamma} = e^{2\tilde{b}\Delta}\left(x^{4-4\gamma} - \tilde{\xi}_2 - 2(\tilde{\xi}_2/\tilde{\xi}_1)\left(x^{2-2\gamma} - \tilde{\xi}_1\right)\right) + 2(\tilde{\xi}_2/\tilde{\xi}_1)e^{\tilde{b}\Delta}\left(x^{2-2\gamma} - \tilde{\xi}_1\right) + \tilde{\xi}_2$$

where $\tilde{\xi}_1 = E_\theta\left(X_0^{2-2\gamma}\right) = -\tilde{a}/\tilde{b}$ and $\tilde{\xi}_2 = E_\theta\left(X_0^{4-4\gamma}\right) = \tilde{a}/(2\tilde{b}^2)\left(2\tilde{a} + \tilde{\sigma}^2\right)$ with $\tilde{a}, \tilde{b}, \tilde{\sigma}^2$ as in (4.26); see Section 4.3.

The results of a simulation study using this small Δ-optimal estimating function are given in Table 4.4. Note that in agreement with the theory, the estimators of a and b deteriorate for Δ small, while the estimators of γ and σ^2 perform well throughout.

Table 4.4 The result of a simulation study using the estimating function given by (4.42) with the parameter values $a = 1, b = -1, \gamma = \frac{1}{2}$, and $\sigma^2 = 1$

Δ	Success		Mean	Standard deviation	Smallest	Largest
0.01	50/50	a	1.77	0.864	0.737	4.51
		b	−1.88	0.872	−4.84	−0.612
		γ	0.493	0.054	0.396	0.641
		σ^2	1.00	0.073	0.806	1.17
0.1	50/50	a	1.04	0.207	0.685	1.62
		b	−1.08	0.262	−2.01	−0.662
		γ	0.494	0.050	0.393	0.571
		σ^2	1.00	0.086	0.786	1.18
0.5	45/50	a	1.22	0.335	0.597	1.92
		b	−1.22	0.308	−1.93	−0.674
		γ	0.545	0.081	0.361	0.680
		σ^2	0.995	0.087	0.730	1.24

Simulations were done for the indicated values of Δ based on $n + 1 = 501$ observations. For each value of Δ, 50 data sets were simulated. The column labeled "success" indicates the proportion of data sets for which estimates for all four parameters were obtained. The mean value and the standard deviation of these estimates are given in the table. The columns labeled "smallest" and "largest" indicate the range of the estimates obtained.

ACKNOWLEDGMENTS

The research of Michael Sørensen was supported by the Danish Center for Accounting and Finance funded by the Danish Social Science Research Council and by the Center for Research in Econometric Analysis of Time Series funded by the Danish National Research Foundation. Martin Jacobsen's research was supported by the Danish Natural Science Research Council, grant 272-06-0442. The data were put at our disposal by the Danish Center for Accounting and Finance. Very helpful and insightful comments by Per Mykland and the editors that have improved the exposition considerably are gratefully acknowledged.

REFERENCES

Aït-Sahalia, Y. (2002). "Maximum likelihood estimation of discretely sampled diffusions: A closed-form approximation approach." *Econometrica*, 70:223–262.

Aït-Sahalia, Y. (2008). "Closed-form likelihood expansions for multivariate diffusions." *Annals of Statistics*, 36:906–937.

Aït-Sahalia, Y.; Hansen, L. P. & Scheinkman, J. (2010). "Operator methods for continuous-time Markov models." In Aït-Sahalia, Y. & Hansen, L. P., editors, *Handbook of Financial Econometrics*. Elsevier. Forthcoming.

Aït-Sahalia, Y. & Mykland, P. A. (2003). "The effect of random and discrete sampling when estimating continuous-time diffusions." *Econometrica*, 71:483–549.

Aït-Sahalia, Y. & Mykland, P. A. (2004). "Estimators of diffusions with randomly spaced discrete observations: A general theory." *Annals of Statistics*, 32:2186–2222.

Aït-Sahalia, Y. & Mykland, P. A. (2008). "An analysis of Hansen-Scheinkman moment estimators for discretely and randomly sampled diffusions." *Journal of Econometrics*, 144:1–26.

Alizadeh, S.; Brandt, M. W. & Diebold, F. X. (2002). "Range-based estimation of stochastic volatility models." *Journal of Finance*, 57:1047–1091.

Andersen, T. G.; Benzoni, L. & Lund, J. (2002). "An empirical investigation of continuous-time models for equity returns." *Journal of Finance*, 57:1239–1284.

Baddeley, A. J. (2000). "Time-invariance estimating equations." *Bernoulli*, 6:783–808.

Barndorff-Nielsen, O. E.; Jensen, J. L. & Sørensen, M. (1998). "Some stationary processes in discrete and continuous time." *Advances in Applied Probability*, 30:989–1007.

Barndorff-Nielsen, O. E. & Shephard, N. (2001). "Non-gaussian ornstein-uhlenbeck-based models and some of their uses in financial econometrics (with discussion)." *Journal of the Royal Statistical Society B*, 63:167–241.

Barndorff-Nielsen, O. E. & Sørensen, M. (1994). "A review of some aspects of asymptotic likelihood theory for stochastic processes." *International Statistical Review*, 62:133–165.

Beskos, A.; Papaspiliopoulos, O. & Roberts, G. O. (2006). "Retrospective exact simulation of diffusion sample paths with applications." *Bernoulli*, 12:1077–1098.

Beskos, A.; Papaspiliopoulos, O.; Roberts, G. O. & Fearnhead, P. (2006). "Exact and computationally efficient likelihood-based estimation for discretely observed diffusion processes." *Journal of the Royal Statistical Society B*, 68:333–382.

Beskos, A. & Roberts, G. O. (2005). "Exact simulation of diffusions." *Annals of Applied Probability*, 15:2422–2444.

Bibby, B. M.; Skovgaard, I. M. & Sørensen, M. (2005). "Diffusion-type models with given marginals and autocorrelation function." *Bernoulli*, 11:191–220.

Bibby, B. M. & Sørensen, M. (1995). "Martingale estimation functions for discretely observed diffusion processes." *Bernoulli*, 1:17–39.

Bibby, B. M. & Sørensen, M. (1996). "On estimation for discretely observed diffusions: A Review." *Theory of Stochastic Processes*, 2:49–56.

Bibby, B. M. & Sørensen, M. (1997). "A hyperbolic diffusion model for stock prices." *Finance and Stochastics*, 1:25–41.

Bibby, B. M. & Sørensen, M. (2001). "Simplified estimating functions for diffusion models with a high-dimensional parameter." *Scandinavian Journal of Statistical*, 28(1):99–112.

Billingsley, P. (1961a). "The Lindeberg-Lévy theorem for martingales." *Proceedings of the American Mathematical Society*, 12:788–792.

Billingsley, P. (1961b). *Statistical Inference for Markov Processes*. The University of Chicago Press, Chicago.

Brockwell, P. J. & Davis, R. A. (1991). *Time Series: Theory and Methods*. Springer, New York.

Chamberlain, G. (1987). "Asymptotic efficiency in estimation with conditional moment restrictions." *Journal of Econometrics*, 34:305–334.

Chan, K. C.; Karolyi, G. A.; Longstaff, F. A. & Sanders, A. B. (1992). "An empirical comparison of alternative models of the short-term interest rate." *Journal of Finance*, 47:1209–1227.

Chen, X.; Hansen, L. P. & Carrasco, M. (2008). "Nonlinearity and temporal dependence." Working paper, University of Chicago.

Chesney, M. & Scott, L. (1989). "Pricing European currency options: A comparison of the modified Black-Scholes model and a random variance model." *Journal of Financial Quantitative Analysis*, 24:267–289.

Christensen, B. J.; Poulsen, R. & Sørensen, M. (2001). "Optimal inference for diffusion processes with applications to the short rate of interest." Working Paper No. 102, Centre for Analytical Finance, University of Aarhus.

Clement, E. (1997). "Estimation of diffusion processes by simulated moment methods." *Scandinavian Journal of Statistical*, 24:353–369.

Coddington, E. A. & Levinson, N. (1955). *Theory of Ordinary Differential Equations*. McGraw-Hill, New York.

Conley, T. G.; Hansen, L. P.; Luttmer, E. G. J. & Scheinkman, J. A. (1997). "Short-term interest rates as subordinated diffusions." *Review of Financial Studies*, 10:525–577.

Cox, J. C.; Ingersoll, Jr., J. E. & Ross, S. A. (1985). "A theory of the term structure of interest rates." *Econometrica*, 53(2):385–407.

Dacunha-Castelle, D. & Florens-Zmirou, D. (1986). "Estimation of the coefficients of a diffusion from discrete observations." *Stochastics*, 19:263–284.

De Jong, F.; Drost, F. C. & Werker, B. J. M. (2001). "A jump-diffusion model for exchange rates in a target zone." *Statistica Neerlandica*, 55:270–300.

Ditlevsen, S. & Sørensen, M. (2004). "Inference for observations of integrated diffusion processes." *Scandinavian Journal of Statistical*, 31:417–429.

Dorogovcev, A. J. (1976). "The consistency of an estimate of a parameter of a stochastic differential equation." *Theory Probability and Mathematical Statistical*, 10:73–82.

Doukhan, P. (1994). *Mixing, Properties and Examples*. Springer, New York. Lecture Notes in Statistics 85.

Duffie, D. & Singleton, K. (1993). "Simulated moments estimation of Markov models of asset prices." *Econometrica*, 61:929–952.

Duffie, D. J. & Kan, R. (1996). "A yield factor model of interest rates." *Mathematical Finance*, 6:379–406.

Durbin, J. (1960). "Estimation of parameters in time-series regression models." *Journal of the Royal Statistical Society Series B*, 22:139–153.

Durham, G. B. (2003). "Likelihood-based specification analysis of continuous-time models of the short-term interest rate." *Journal of Financial Economics*, 70:463–487.

Durham, G. B. & Gallant, A. R. (2002). "Numerical techniques for maximum likelihood estimation of continuous-time diffusion processes." *Journal of Business and Economic Statistics*, 20:297–338.

Elerian, O.; Chib, S. & Shephard, N. (2001). "Likelihood inference for discretely observed nonlinear diffusions." *Econometrica*, 69:959–993.

Eraker, B. (2001). "MCMC analysis of diffusion models with application to finance." *Journal of Business and Economic Statistics*, 19:177–191.

Feller, W. (1951). "Diffusion processes in genetics." In Neyman, J., editor, *Proceedings of the Second Berkeley Symposium on Mathematical Statistics and Probability*, pages 227–246. University of California Press.

Fisher, R. A. (1935). "The logic of inductive inference." *Journal of Royal Statistical Society*, 98:39–54.

Florens-Zmirou, D. (1989). "Approximate discrete-time schemes for statistics of diffusion processes." *Statistics*, 20:547–557.

Forman, J. L. & Sørensen, M. (2008). "The Pearson diffusions: A class of statistically tractable diffusion processes." *Scandinavian Journal of Statistical*, 35:438–465.

Friedman, A. (1975). *Stochastic Differential Equations and Applications, Vol. 1*. Academic Press, New York.

Gallant, A. R. & Tauchen, G. (1996). "Which moments to match?." *Econometric Theory*, 12: 657–681.

Gallant, A. R. & Tauchen, G. (2010). "Simulated score methods and indirect inference for continuous-time models." In Aït-Sahalia, Y. & Hansen, L. P., editors, *Handbook of Financial Econometrics*. Elsevier. Forthcoming.

Genon-Catalot, V.; Jeantheau, T. & Larédo, C. (1999). "Parameter estimation for discretely observed stochastic volatility models." *Bernoulli*, 5:855–872.

Genon-Catalot, V.; Jeantheau, T. & Larédo, C. (2000). "Stochastic volatility models as hidden Markov models and statistical applications." *Bernoulli*, 6:1051–1079.

Godambe, V. P. (1960). "An optimum property of regular maximum likelihood estimation." *Annals of Mathematical Statistics*, 31:1208–1212.

Godambe, V. P. (1985). "The foundations of finite sample estimation in stochastic processes." *Biometrika*, 72:419–428.

Godambe, V. P. & Heyde, C. C. (1987). "Quasi likelihood and optimal estimation." *International Statistical Review*, 55:231–244.

Gourieroux, C.; Monfort, A. & Renault, E. (1993). "Indirect inference." *Journal of Applied Econometrics*, 8:S85–S118.

Hall, A. R. (2005). *Generalized Method of Moments*. Oxford University Press, New York.

Hall, P. & Heyde, C. C. (1980). *Martingale Limit Theory and its Applications*. Academic Press, New York.

Hansen, L. P. (1982). "Large sample properties of generalized method of moments estimators." *Econometrica*, 50:1029–1054.

Hansen, L. P. (1985). "A method for calculating bounds on the asymptotic covariance matrices of generalized method of moments estimators." *Journal of Econometrics*, 30:203–238.

Hansen, L. P. (1993). "Semiparametric efficiency bounds for linear time-series models." In Phillips, P. C. B., editor, *Models, Methods and Applications of Econometrics: Esseys in Honor of A. R. Bergstrom*, pages 253–271. Blackwell, Cambridge, MA.

Hansen, L. P. (2001). "Method of moments." In *International Encyclopedia of the Social and Behavior Sciences*. Elsevier, New York.

Hansen, L. P. & Scheinkman, J. A. (1995). "Back to the future: generating moment implications for continuous-time Markov processes." *Econometrica*, 63:767–804.

Heston, S. L. (1993). "A closed-form solution for options with stochastic volatility with applications to bond and currency options." *Review of Financial Studies*, 6:327–343.

Heyde, C. C. (1988). "Fixed sample and asymptotic optimality for classes of estimating functions." *Contemporary Mathematics*, 80:241–247.

Heyde, C. C. (1997). *Quasi-Likelihood and Its Application*. Springer-Verlag, New York.

Hull, J. & White, A. (1988). "An analysis of the bias in option pricing caused by a stochastic volatility." *Advances in Futures and Options Research*, 3:29–61.

Jacobsen, M. (2001a). "Discretely observed diffusions; classes of estimating functions and small Δ-optimality." *Scandinavian Journal of Statistical*, 28:123–150.

Jacobsen, M. (2001b). "Small Δ-optimal martingale estimating functions for discretely observed diffusions: A simulation study." Preprint No. 2, Department of Theoretical Statistics, University of Copenhagen.

Jacobsen, M. (2002). "Optimality and small Δ-optimality of martingale estimating functions." *Bernoulli*, 8:643–668.

Jacod, J. & Sørensen, M. (2009). "Asymptotic statistical theory for stochastic processes: A review." Preprint, Department of Mathematical Sciences, University of Copenhagen. In preparation.

Johannes, M. & Polson, N. (2010). "MCMC methods for financial econometrics." In Aït-Sahalia, Y. & Hansen, L. P., editors, *Handbook of Financial Econometrics*. Elsevier. Forthcoming.

Kessler, M. (1996). *Estimation paramétrique des coefficients d'une diffusion ergodique à partir d'observations discrètes*. PhD thesis, Laboratoire de Probabilités, Université Paris VI.

Kessler, M. (1997). "Estimation of an ergodic diffusion from discrete observations." *Scandinavian Journal of Statistical*, 24:211–229.

Kessler, M. (2000). "Simple and explicit estimating functions for a discretely observed diffusion process." *Scandinavian Journal of Statistical*, 27:65–82.

Kessler, M. & Paredes, S. (2002). "Computational aspects related to martingale estimating functions for a discretely observed diffusion." *Scandinavian Journal of Statistical*, 29:425–440.

Kessler, M.; Schick, A. & Wefelmeyer, W. (2001). "The information in the marginal law of a Markov chain." *Bernoulli*, 7:243–266.

Kessler, M. & Sørensen, M. (1999). "Estimating equations based on eigenfunctions for a discretely observed diffusion process." *Bernoulli*, 5:299–314.

Kessler, M. & Sørensen, M. (2005). "On time-reversibility and estimating functions for Markov processes." *Statistical Inference for Stochastic Processes*, 8:95–107.

Kim, S.; Shephard, N. & Chib, S. (1998). "Stochastic volatility: Likelihood inference and comparison with ARCH models." *Review of Economic Studies*, 65:361–393.

Kimball, B. F. (1946). "Sufficient statistical estimation functions for the parameters of the distribution of maximum values." *Annals of Mathematical Statistics*, 17:299–309.

Kloeden, P. E. & Platen, E. (1999). *Numerical Solution of Stochastic Differential Equations*. 3rd revised printing. Springer-Verlag, New York.

Kuersteiner, G. (2002). "Efficient instrumental variables estimation for autoregressive models with conditional heteroscedasticity." *Econometric Theory*, 18:547–583.

Kusuoka, S. & Yoshida, N. (2000). "Malliavin calculus, geometric mixing, and expansion of diffusion functionals." *Probability Theory and Related Fields*, 116:457–484.

Larsen, K. S. & Sørensen, M. (2007). "A diffusion model for exchange rates in a target zone." *Mathematical Finance*, 17:285–306.

Melino, A. & Turnbull, S. M. (1990). "Pricing foreign currency options with stochastic volatility." *Journal of Econometrics*, 45:239–265.

Meyn, S. P. & Tweedie, R. L. (1993). "Stability of Markovian processes III: Foster-Lyapunov criteria for continuous time processes." *Advances in Applied Probability*, 25:518–548.

Nelson, D. B. (1990). "ARCH models as diffusion approximations." *Journal of Econometrics*, 45:7–38.

Newey, W. K. (1990). "Efficient instrumental variables estimation of nonlinear models." *Econometrica*, 58:809–837.

Newey, W. K. (2004). "Efficient semiparametric estimation via moment restrictions." *Econometrica*, 72:1877–1897.

Newey, W. K. & West, K. D. (1987). "Hypothesis testing with efficient method of moments estimation." *International Economic Review*, 28:777–787.

Overbeck, L. & Rydén, T. (1997). "Estimation in the Cox-Ingersoll-Ross model." *Econometric Theory*, 13:430–461.

Ozaki, T. (1985). "Non-linear time series models and dynamical systems." In Hannan, E. J.; Krishnaiah, P. R. & Rao, M. M., editors, *Handbook of Statistics, Vol. 5*, pages 25–83. Elsevier Science Publishers.

Pakes, A. & Pollard, D. (1989). "The asymptotics of simulation estimators." *Econometrica*, 57: 1027–1058.

Pearson, K. (1895). "Contributions to the mathematical theory of evolution II. Skew variation in homogeneous material." *Philosophical Transactions of the Royal Society of London. A*, 186:343–414.

Pedersen, A. R. (1994a). "Quasi-likelihood inference for discretely observed diffusion processes." Research Report No. 295, Department of Theoretical Statistics, Institute of Mathematics, University of Aarhus.

Pedersen, A. R. (1994b). "Uniform residuals for discretely observed diffusion processes." Research Report No. 292, Department of Theoretical Statistics, University of Aarhus.

Pedersen, A. R. (1995). "A new approach to maximum likelihood estimation for stochastic differential equations based on discrete observations." *Scandinavian Journal of Statistical*, 22:55–71.

Poulsen, R. (1999). "Approximate maximum likelihood estimation of discretely observed diffusion processes." Working Paper 29, Centre for Analytical Finance, Aarhus.

Prakasa Rao, B. L. S. (1983). "Asymptotic theory for non-linear least squares estimator for diffusion processes." *Math. Operationsforsch. u. Statist., Ser. Statist.*, 14:195–209.

Prakasa Rao, B. L. S. (1988). "Statistical inference from sampled data for stochastic processes." *Contemporary Mathematics*, 80:249–284.

Roberts, G. O. & Stramer, O. (2001). "On inference for partially observed nonlinear diffusion models using Metropolis-Hastings algorithms." *Biometrika*, 88:603–621.

Sagan, J. D. (1958). "The estimation of economic relationsships using instrumental variables." *Econometrica*, 26:393–415.

Schaumburg, E. (2005). "Estimation of Markov processes with Levy type generators." Working paper, Kellogg School of Management, Northwestern University.

Sørensen, H. (2001). "Discretely observed diffusions: Approximation of the continuous-time score function." *Scandinavian Journal of Statistical*, 28:113–121.

Sørensen, H. (2003). "Simulated likelihood approximations for stochastic volatility models." *Scandinavian Journal Statistical*, 30:257–276.

Sørensen, H. (2004). "Parametric inference for diffusion processes observed at discrete points in time: a survey." *International Statistical Review*, 72:337–354.

Sørensen, M. (1997). "Estimating functions for discretely observed diffusions: A Review." In Basawa, I. V.; Godambe, V. P. & Taylor, R. L., editors, *Selected Proceedings of the Symposium on Estimating Functions*, pages 305–325. Institute of Mathematical Statistics, Hayward. IMS Lecture Notes – Monograph Series, Vol. 32.

Sørensen, M. (1999). "On asymptotics of estimating functions." *Brazilian Journal of Probability and Statistics*, 13:111–136.

Sørensen, M. (2000). "Prediction-based estimating functions." *Econometrics Journal*, 3:123–147.

Sørensen, M. (2007). "Efficient estimation for ergodic diffusions sampled at high frequency." Working paper, Department of Mathematical Sciences, University of Copenhagen. Submitted.

Veretennikov, A. Y. (1987). "Bounds for the mixing rate in the theory of stochastic equations." *Theory of Probability and its Applications*, 32:273–281.

Wefelmeyer, W. (1996). "Quasi-likelihood models and optimal inference." *Annals of Statistics*, 24:405–422.

Wefelmeyer, W. (1997). "Quasi-likelihood regression models for Markov chains." In Basawa, I. V.; Godambe, V. P. & Taylor, R. L., editors, *Selected Proceedings of the Symposium on Estimating Functions*, pages 149–173. Institute of Mathematical Statistics, Hayward. IMS Lecture Notes – Monograph Series, Vol. 32.

West, K. D. (2001). "On optimal instrumental variables estimation of stationary time series models." *International Economic Review*, 42:1043–1050.

Wiggins, J. B. (1987). "Option values under stochastic volatility: Theory and empirical estimates." *Journal of Financial Economics*, 19:351–372.

Wong, E. (1964). "The construction of a class of stationary markoff processes." In Bellman, R., editor, *Stochastic Processes in Mathematical Physics and Engineering*, pages 264–276. American Mathematical Society, Rhode Island.

Yoshida, N. (1990). "Asymptotic behaviour of M-estimator and related random field for diffusion process." *Annals of the Institute of Statistical Mathematics*, 42:221–251.

CHAPTER 5

Portfolio Choice Problems

Michael W. Brandt
Fuqua School of Business, Duke University, Durham, NC

Contents

Abstract

This chapter is devoted to the econometric treatment of portfolio choice problems. The goal is to describe, discuss, and illustrate through examples the different econometric approaches proposed in the literature for relating the theoretical formulation and solution of a portfolio choice problem to the data. In focusing on the econometrics of the portfolio choice problem, this chapter is at best a cursory overview of the broad portfolio choice literature. In particular, much of the discussion is focused on the single period portfolio choice problem with standard preferences, normally distributed returns, and frictionless markets. There are many recent advances in the portfolio choice literature, some cited below but many regrettably omitted, that relax one or more of these simplifying assumptions. The econometric techniques discussed in this chapter can be applied to these more realistic formulations. The chapter is divided into three parts. Section 2 reviews the theory of portfolio choice in discrete and continuous time. It also discusses a number of modeling issues and extensions that arise in formulating the problem. Section 3 presents the two traditional econometric approaches to portfolio choice problems: plug-in estimation and Bayesian decision theory. In Section 4, I then describe a more recently developed econometric approach for drawing inferences about optimal portfolio weights without modeling return distributions.

Keywords: portfolio choice; discrete time; continuous time; plug-in estimation; Bayesian decision theory; optimal portfolio weights

1. INTRODUCTION

After years of relative neglect in academic circles, portfolio choice problems are again at the forefront of financial research. The economic theory underlying an investor's optimal portfolio choice, pioneered by Markowitz (1952), Merton (1969, 1971), Samuelson (1969), and Fama (1970), is by now well understood. The renewed interest in portfolio choice problems follows the relatively recent empirical evidence of time-varying return distributions (e.g., predictability and conditional heteroskedasticity) and is fueled by realistic issues including model and parameter uncertainty, learning, background risks, and frictions. The general focus of the current academic research is to identify key aspects of real-world portfolio choice problems and to understand qualitatively as well as quantitatively their role in the optimal investment decisions of individuals and institutions.

Whether for academic researchers studying the portfolio choice implications of return predictability, for example, or for practitioners whose livelihood depends on the outcome of their investment decisions, a critical step in solving realistic portfolio choice problems is to relate the theoretical formulation of the problem and its solution to the data. There are a number of ways to accomplish this task, ranging from calibration with only vague regard for the data to decision theoretic approaches which explicitly incorporate the specification of the return model and the associated statistical inferences in the investor's decision process. Surprisingly, given the practical importance of portfolio choice problems, no single econometric approach has emerged yet as clear favorite. Because each approach has its advantages and disadvantages, an approach favored in one context is often less attractive in another.

This chapter is devoted to the econometric treatment of portfolio choice problems. The goal is to describe, discuss, and illustrate through examples the different econometric approaches proposed in the literature for relating the theoretical formulation and solution of a portfolio choice problem to the data. The chapter is intended for academic researchers who seek an introduction to the empirical implementation of portfolio choice problems as well as for practitioners as a review of the academic literature on the topic. In focusing on the econometrics of the portfolio choice problem, this chapter is at best a cursory overview of the broad portfolio choice literature. In particular, much of the discussion is focused on the single period portfolio choice problem with standard preferences, normally distributed returns, and frictionless markets. There are many recent advances in the portfolio choice literature, some cited below but many regrettably omitted, that relax one or more of these simplifying assumptions. The econometric techniques discussed in this chapter can be applied to these more realistic formulations.

The chapter is divided into three parts. Section 2 reviews the theory of portfolio choice in discrete and continuous time. It also discusses a number of modeling issues and extensions that arise in formulating the problem. Section 3 presents the two traditional econometric approaches to portfolio choice problems: plug-in estimation and Bayesian decision theory. In Section 4, I then describe a more recently developed econometric approach for drawing inferences about optimal portfolio weights without modeling return distributions.

2. THEORETICAL PROBLEM

2.1. Markowitz Paradigm

The mean–variance paradigm of Markowitz (1952) is by far the most common formulation of portfolio choice problems. Consider N risky assets with random return vector R_{t+1} and a riskfree asset with known return R_t^f. Define the *excess* returns $r_{t+1} = R_{t+1} - R_t^f$ and denote their conditional means (or risk premia) and covariance matrix by μ_t and Σ_t, respectively. Assume, for now, that the excess returns are i.i.d. with constant moments.

Suppose the investor can only allocate wealth to the N risky securities. In the absence of a risk-free asset, the mean–variance problem is to choose the vector of portfolio weights x, which represent the investor's relative allocations of wealth to each of the N risky assets, to minimize the variance of the resulting portfolio return $R_{p,t+1} = x'R_{t+1}$ for a predetermined target expected return of the portfolio $R_t^f + \overline{\mu}$:

$$\min_x \text{var}[R_{p,t+1}] = x'\Sigma x, \tag{2.1}$$

subject to

$$\text{E}[R_{p,t+1}] = x'(R^f + \mu) = (R^f + \overline{\mu}) \quad \text{and} \quad \sum_{i=1}^{N} x_i = 1. \tag{2.2}$$

The first constraint fixes the expected return of the portfolio to its target, and the second constraint ensures that all wealth is invested in the risky assets. Setting up the Lagrangian and solving the corresponding first-order conditions (FOCs), the optimal portfolio weights are as follows:

$$x^\star = \Lambda_1 + \Lambda_2 \overline{\mu} \tag{2.3}$$

with

$$\Lambda_1 = \frac{1}{D}\left[B(\Sigma^{-1}\iota) - A(\Sigma^{-1}\mu)\right] \quad \text{and} \quad \Lambda_2 = \frac{1}{D}\left[C(\Sigma^{-1}\mu) - A(\Sigma^{-1}\iota)\right], \tag{2.4}$$

where ι denotes an appropriately sized vector of ones and where $A = \iota'\Sigma^{-1}\mu$, $B = \mu'\Sigma^{-1}\mu$, $C = \iota'\Sigma^{-1}\iota$, and $D = BC - A^2$. The minimized portfolio variance is equal to $x^{\star\prime}\Sigma x^\star$.

The Markowitz paradigm yields two important economic insights. First, it illustrates the effect of diversification. Imperfectly correlated assets can be combined into portfolios

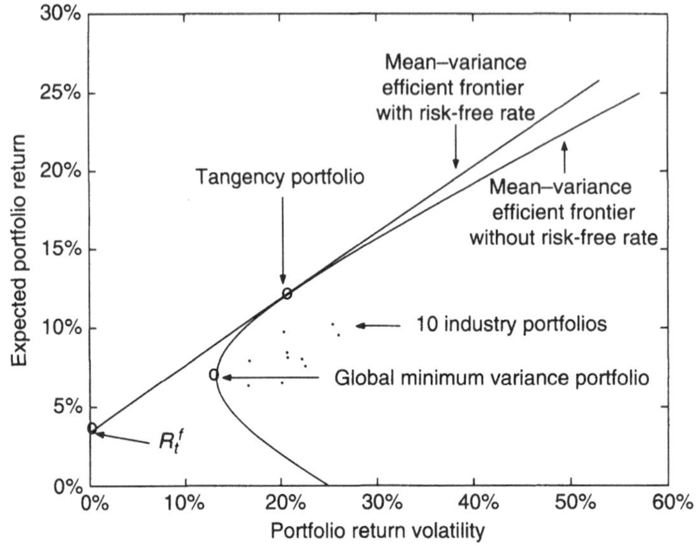

Figure 5.1 Mean–variance frontiers with and without risk-free asset generated by historical moments of monthly returns on 10 industry-sorted portfolios. Expected return and volatility are annualized.

with preferred expected return-risk characteristics. Second, the Markowitz paradigm shows that, once a portfolio is fully diversified, higher expected returns can only be achieved through more extreme allocations (notice $x^\star$ is linear in $\overline{\mu}$) and therefore by taking on more risk.

Figure 5.1 illustrates graphically these two economic insights. The figure plots as hyperbola the mean–variance frontier generated by the historical moments of monthly returns on 10 industry-sorted portfolios. Each point on the frontier gives along the horizonal axis the minimized portfolio return volatility (annualized) for a predetermined expected portfolio return (also annualized) along the vertical axis. The dots inside the hyperbola represent the 10 individual industry portfolios from which the frontier is constructed. The fact that these dots lie well inside the frontier illustrates the effect of diversification. The individual industry portfolios can be combined to generate returns with the same or lower volatility and the same or higher expected return. The figure also illustrates the fundamental trade-off between expected return and risk. Starting with the least volatile portfolio at the left tip of the hyperbola (the global minimum variance portfolio), higher expected returns can only be achieved at the cost of greater volatility.

If the investor can also allocate wealth to the risk-free asset, in the form of unlimited risk-free borrowing and lending at the risk-free rate R_t^f, any portfolio on the mean–variance frontier generated by the risky assets (the hyperbola) can be combined with the risk-free asset on the vertical axis to generate an expected return-risk profile that lies on a straight line from the risk-free rate (no risky investments) through the frontier portfolio (fully invested in risky asset) and beyond (leveraged risky investments). The optimal combination of the risky frontier portfolios with risk-free borrowing and lending is the one that maximizes the Sharpe ratio of the overall portfolio, defined as $\mathrm{E}[r_{p,t+1}]/\mathrm{std}[r_{p,t+1}]$ and represented graphically by the slope of the line from the risk-free asset through the risky frontier portfolio. The highest obtainable Sharpe ratio is achieved by the upper tangency on the hyperbola shown in Fig. 5.1. This tangency therefore represents the mean–variance frontier with risk-free borrowing and lending. The critical feature of this mean–variance frontier with risk-free borrowing and lending is that every investor combines the risk-free asset with the *same* portfolio of risky assets – the tangency portfolio in Fig. 5.1.

In the presence of a risk-free asset, the investor allocates fractions x of wealth to the risky assets and the remainder $(1 - \iota' x)$ to the risk-free asset. The portfolio return is therefore $R_{p,t+1} = x' R_{t+1} + (1 - \iota' x) R_t^f = x' r_{t+1} + R_t^f$ and the mean–variance problem can be expressed in terms of excess returns:

$$\min_x \mathrm{var}[r_p] = x' \Sigma x \quad \text{subject to} \quad \mathrm{E}[r_p] = x' \mu = \overline{\mu}. \tag{2.5}$$

The solution to this problem is much simpler than in the case without a risk-free asset:

$$x^\star = \underbrace{\frac{\overline{\mu}}{\mu' \Sigma^{-1} \mu}}_{\lambda} \times \Sigma^{-1} \mu, \tag{2.6}$$

where λ is a constant that scales proportionately all elements of $\Sigma^{-1}\mu$ to achieve the desired portfolio risk premium $\overline{\mu}$. From this expression, the weights of the tangency portfolio can be found simply by noting that the weights of the tangency portfolio must sum to one, because it lies on the mean–variance frontier of the risky assets. For the tangency portfolio:

$$\lambda_{\mathrm{tgc}} = \frac{1}{\iota' \Sigma^{-1} \mu} \quad \text{and} \quad \overline{\mu}_{\mathrm{tgc}} = \frac{\mu' \Sigma^{-1} \mu}{\iota' \Sigma^{-1} \mu}. \tag{2.7}$$

The formulations (2.1) and (2.2) or (2.5) of the mean–variance problem generate a mapping from a predetermined portfolio risk premium $\overline{\mu}$ to the minimum-variance portfolio weights $x^\star$ and resulting portfolio return volatility $\sqrt{x^{\star\prime} \Sigma x^\star}$. The choice of the desired risk premium, however, depends inherently on the investor's tolerance for risk. To incorporate the investor's optimal trade-off between expected return and risk, the mean–variance problem can be formulated alternatively as the following expected utility maximization:

$$\max_x \mathrm{E}[r_{p,t+1}] - \frac{\gamma}{2} \mathrm{var}[r_{p,t+1}], \tag{2.8}$$

where γ measures the investor's level of relative risk aversion. The solution to this maximization problem is given by Eq. (2.6) with $\lambda = 1/\gamma$, which explicitly links the optimal allocation to the tangency portfolio to the investor's tolerance for risk.

The obvious appeal of the Markowitz paradigm is that it captures the two fundamental aspects of portfolio choice – diversification and the trade-off between expected return and risk – in an analytically tractable and easily extendable framework. This has made it the de-facto standard in the finance profession. Nevertheless, there are several common objections to the Markowitz paradigm. First, the mean–variance problem only represents an expected utility maximization for the special case of quadratic utility, which is a problematic preference specification because it is not monotonically increasing in wealth. For all other utility functions, the mean–variance problem can at best be interpreted as a second-order approximation of expected utility maximization. Second, but related, the mean–variance problem ignores any preferences toward higher-order return moments, in particular toward return skewness and kurtosis. In the context of interpreting the mean–variance problem as a second-order approximation, the third and higher-order terms may be economically nonnegligible. Third, the mean–variance problem is inherently a myopic single-period problem, whereas we think of most investment problems as involving longer horizons with intermediate portfolio rebalancing. Each criticism has prompted numerous extensions of the mean–variance paradigm.[1] However, the most straightforward way to address all these issues, and particularly the third, is to formulate the problem explicitly as an intertemporal expected utility maximization.

2.2. Intertemporal Expected Utility Maximization

2.2.1. Discrete Time Formulation

Consider the portfolio choice at time t of an investor who maximizes the expected utility of wealth at some future date $t+\tau$ by trading in N risky assets and a risk-free asset at times $t, t+1, \ldots, t+\tau-1$. The investor's problem is

$$V(\tau, W_t, z_t) = \max_{\{x_s\}_{s=t}^{t+\tau-1}} \mathrm{E}_t\big[u(W_{t+\tau})\big], \tag{2.9}$$

subject to the budget constraint:

$$W_{s+1} = W_s\big(x_s{}' r_{s+1} + R_s^f\big) \tag{2.10}$$

and having positive wealth each period, $W_s \geq 0$. The function $u(\cdot)$ measures the investor's utility of terminal wealth $W_{t+\tau}$, and the subscript on the expectation denotes that

[1]The majority of extensions deal with incorporating higher-order moments. For example, in Brandt et al. (2005), we propose a fourth-order approximation of expected utility maximization that captures preferences toward skewness and kurtosis. While the optimal portfolio weights cannot be solved for analytically, we provide a simple and efficient numerical procedure. Other work on incorporating higher-order moments include Kraus and Litzenberger (1976), Kane (1982), Simaan (1993), de Athayde and Flores (2004), and Harvey et al. (2004).

the expectation is taken conditional on the information set z_t available at time t. For concreteness, think of z_t as a $K < \infty$ dimensional vector of state variables and assume that $y_t \equiv [r_t, z_t]$ evolves as a first-order Markov process with transition density $f(y_t|y_{t-1})$.[2]

The case $\tau = 1$ corresponds to a static single-period optimization. In general, however, the portfolio choice is a more complicated dynamic multiperiod problem. In choosing at date t the optimal portfolio weights x_t conditional on having wealth W_t and information z_t, the investor takes into account that at every future date s the portfolio weights will be optimally revised conditional on the then available wealth W_s and information z_s.

The function $V(\tau, W_t, z_t)$ denotes the investor's expectation at time t, conditional on the information z_t, of the utility of terminal wealth $W_{t+\tau}$ generated by the current wealth W_t and the sequence of *optimal* portfolio weights $\{x_s^\star\}_{s=t}^{t+\tau-1}$ over the next τ periods. $V(\cdot)$ is called the value function because it represents the value, in units of expected utils, of the portfolio choice problem to the investor. Think of the value function as measuring the quality of the investment opportunities available to the investor. If the current information suggests that investment opportunities are good, meaning, for example, that the sequence of optimal portfolio choices is expected to generate an above average return with below average risk, the current value of the portfolio choice problem to the investor is high. If investment opportunities are poor, the value of the problem is low.

The dynamic nature of the multiperiod portfolio choice is best illustrated by expressing the problem (2.9) as a single-period problem with state-dependent utility $V(\tau - 1, W_{t+1}, z_{t+1})$ of next period's wealth W_{t+1} and information z_{t+1}:

$$\begin{aligned} V(\tau, W_t, z_t) &= \max_{\{x_s\}_{s=t}^{t+\tau-1}} \mathrm{E}_t\big[u\big(W_{t+\tau}\big)\big] \\ &= \max_{x_t} \mathrm{E}_t\left[\max_{\{x_s\}_{s=t+1}^{t+\tau-1}} \mathrm{E}_{t+1}\big[u\big(W_{t+\tau}\big)\big]\right] \\ &= \max_{x_t} \mathrm{E}_t\big[V\big(\tau - 1, W_t\big(x_t{}'r_{t+1} + R_t^f\big), z_{t+1}\big)\big], \end{aligned} \tag{2.11}$$

subject to the terminal condition $V(0, W_{t+\tau}, z_{t+\tau}) = u(W_{t+\tau})$. The second equality follows from the law of iterated expectations and the principle of optimality. The third equality uses the definition of the value function as well as the budget constraint. It is important to recognize that the expectation in the third line is taken over the *joint* distribution of next period's returns r_{t+1} and information z_{t+1}, conditional on the current information z_t.

[2]The first-order assumption is innocuous because z_t can contain lagged values.

Equation (2.11) is the so-called Bellman equation and is the basis for any recursive solution of the dynamic portfolio choice problem. The FOCs for an optimum at each date t are[3]

$$\mathrm{E}_t\Big[V_2\big(\tau-1, W_t\big(x_t' r_{t+1} + R_t^f\big), z_{t+1}\big) r_{t+1}\Big] = 0, \tag{2.12}$$

where $V_i(\cdot)$ denotes the partial derivative with respect to the ith argument of the value function. These FOCs make up a system of nonlinear equations involving possibly high-order integrals and can in general be solved for x_t only numerically.

CRRA Utility Example For illustrative purposes, consider the case of constant relative risk aversion (CRRA) utility $u(W_{t+\tau}) = W_{t+\tau}{}^{1-\gamma}/(1-\gamma)$, where γ denotes the coefficient of relative risk aversion. The Bellman equation then simplifies to:

$$\begin{aligned}
V(\tau, W_t, z_t) &= \max_{x_t} \mathrm{E}_t\left[\max_{\{x_s\}_{s=t+1}^{t+\tau-1}} \mathrm{E}_{t+1}\left[\frac{W_{t+\tau}{}^{1-\gamma}}{1-\gamma}\right]\right] \\
&= \max_{x_t} \mathrm{E}_t\left[\max_{\{x_s\}_{s=t+1}^{t+\tau-1}} \mathrm{E}_{t+1}\left[\frac{\big(W_t \prod_{s=t}^{t+\tau-1}\big(x_s' r_{s+1} + R_s^f\big)\big)^{1-\gamma}}{1-\gamma}\right]\right] \\
&= \max_{x_t} \mathrm{E}_t\Bigg[\underbrace{\frac{\big(W_t\big(x_t' r_{t+1} + R_t^f\big)\big)^{1-\gamma}}{1-\gamma}}_{u(W_{t+1})} \underbrace{\max_{\{x_s\}_{s=t+1}^{t+\tau-1}} \mathrm{E}_{t+1}\Big[\Big(\prod_{s=t+1}^{t+\tau-1}\big(x_s' r_{s+1} + R_s^f\big)\Big)^{1-\gamma}\Big]}_{\psi(\tau-1, z_{t+1})}\Bigg]
\end{aligned} \tag{2.13}$$

In words, with CRRA utility the value function next period, $V(\tau-1, W_{t+1}, z_{t+1})$, is equal to the product of the utility of wealth $u(W_{t+1})$ and a function $\psi(\tau-1, z_{t+1})$ of the horizon $\tau-1$ and the state variables z_t. Furthermore, as the utility function is homothetic in wealth we can, without loss of generality, normalize $W_t = 1$. It follows that the value function depends only on the horizon and state variables, and that the Bellman equation is

$$\frac{1}{1-\gamma}\psi(\tau, z_t) = \max_{x_t} \mathrm{E}_t\left[\frac{\big(x_t' r_{t+1} + R_t^f\big)^{1-\gamma}}{1-\gamma}\psi\big(\tau-1, z_{t+1}\big)\right]. \tag{2.14}$$

The corresponding FOCs are

$$\mathrm{E}_t\Big[\big(x_t' r_{t+1} + R_t^f\big)^{-\gamma}\psi\big(\tau-1, z_{t+1}\big) r_{t+1}\Big] = 0, \tag{2.15}$$

which, despite being simpler than in the general case, can still only be solved numerically.

[3]As long as the utility function is concave, the second-order conditions are satisfied.

The Bellman equation for CRRA utility illustrates how the dynamic and myopic portfolio choices can differ. If the excess returns r_{t+1} are contemporaneously independent of the innovations to the state variables z_{t+1}, the optimal τ and one-period portfolio choices at date t are identical because the conditional expectation in the Bellman equation factors into a product of two conditional expectations. The first expectation is of the utility of next period's wealth $u(W_{t+1})$, and the second is of the function of the state variables $\psi(\tau - 1, z_{t+1})$. Because the latter expectation does not depend on the portfolio weights, the FOCs of the multiperiod problem are the same as those of the single-period problem. If, in contrast, the excess returns are not independent of the innovations to the state variables, the conditional expectation does not factor, the FOCs are not the same, and, as a result, the dynamic portfolio choice may be substantially different from the myopic portfolio choice. The differences between the two policies are called *hedging demands* because by deviating from the single-period portfolio choice the investor tries to hedge against changes in the investment opportunities.

More concretely, consider as data generating process $f(y_t|y_{t-1})$ the following restricted and homoscedastic vector auto-regression (VAR) for the excess market return and dividend yield (in logs):[4]

$$\begin{bmatrix} \ln(1 + r_{t+1}) \\ \ln \mathrm{d}p_{t+1} \end{bmatrix} = \beta_0 + \beta_1 \ln \mathrm{d}p_t + \varepsilon_{t+1}, \tag{2.16}$$

where $\mathrm{d}p_{t+1}$ denotes the dividend-to-price ratio and $\varepsilon_{t+1} \overset{\text{i.i.d.}}{\sim} \mathrm{MVN}[0, \Sigma]$. Table 5.1 presents ordinary least squares (OLS) estimates of this return model for quarterly real data on the value weighted CRSP index and 90-day Treasury bill rates from April 1952

Table 5.1 OLS estimates of the VAR using quarterly real data on the value weighted CRSP index and 90-day Treasury bill rates from April 1952 through December 1996

Dependent variable	Intercept	$\ln \mathrm{d}p_t$	$\mathrm{var}[\varepsilon_{t+1}]$ ($\times 10^{-3}$)	
$\ln(1 + r_{t+1})$	0.2049	0.0568		
	(0.0839)	(0.0249)	6.225	−6.044
$\ln \mathrm{d}p_{t+1}$	−0.1694	0.9514	−6.044	6.316
	(0.0845)	(0.0251)		

Standard errors in parentheses.

[4]This data generating process is motivated by the evidence of return predictability by the dividend yield (e.g., Campbell and Shiller, 1988; Fama and French, 1988) and has been used extensively in the portfolio choice literature (e.g., Barberis, 2000; Campbell and Viceira, 1999; Kandel and Stambaugh, 1996).

through December 1996.[5] The equation-by-equation adjusted R^2s are 2.3 and 89.3%, reflecting the facts that is it quite difficult to forecast excess returns and that the dividend yield is highly persistent and predictable.

Taking these estimates of the data generating process as the truth, the FOCs (2.15) can be solved numerically using a variety of dynamic programming methods (see Judd, 1998, for a review of numerical methods for dynamic programming). Figure 5.2 presents the solution to the single-period (one-quarter) problem. Plot A shows the optimal fraction of wealth invested in stocks $x_t^\star$ as a function of the dividend yield. Plot B shows the corresponding annualized certainty equivalent rate of return $R_t^{ce}(\tau)$, defined as the risk-free rate that makes the investor indifferent between holding the optimal portfolio and earning the certainty equivalent rate over the next τ periods.[6] The solid, dashed-dotted, and dotted lines are for relative risk aversion γ of 2, 5, and 10, respectively.

At least three features of the solution to the single-period problem are noteworthy. First, both the optimal allocation to stocks and the certainty equivalent rate increase with the dividend yield, which is consistent with the fact that the equity risk premium increases with the dividend yield. Second, the extent to which the investor tries to time the market decreases with risk aversion. The intuition is simple. When the risk premium increases, stocks become more attractive (higher expected return for the same

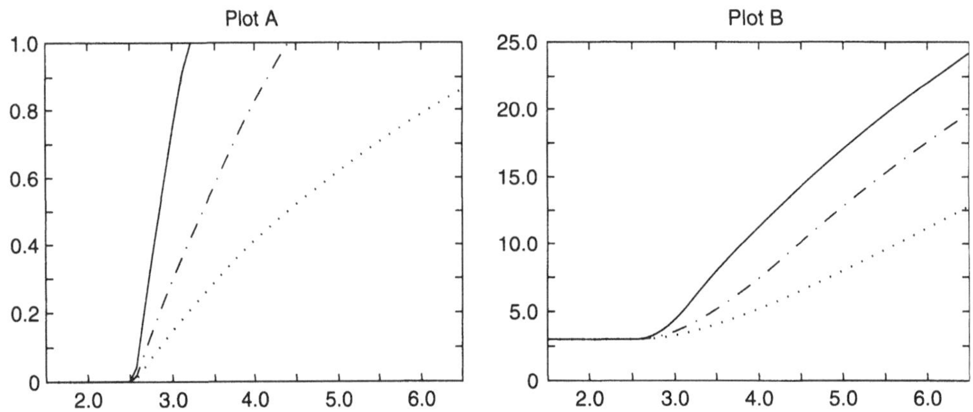

Figure 5.2 Plot A shows the optimal fraction of wealth invested in stocks as a function of the dividend yield for a CRRA investor with one-quarter horizon and relative risk aversion of 2 (solid line), 5 (dashed-dotted line), and 10 (dotted line). Plot B shows the corresponding annualize certainty equivalent rates of return (in percent).

[5] Note that the evidence of return predictability by the dividend yield has significantly weakened over the past 7 years (1997–2003) (e.g., Ang and Bekaert, 2007; Goyal and Welch, 2003). I ignore this most recent sample period for illustrative purposes and to reflect the literature on portfolio choice under return predictability by the dividend yield (e.g., Barberis, 2000; Campbell and Viceira, 1999; Kandel and Stambaugh, 1996). However, keep in mind that the results do not necessarily reflect the current data.

[6] For CRRA utility, the certainty equivalent rate is defined by $\left[R_t^{ce}(\tau)W_t\right]^{1-\gamma}/(1-\gamma) = V(\tau, W_t, z_t)$.

level of risk), and consequently the investor allocates more wealth to stocks. As the stock allocation increases, the mean of the portfolio return increases linearly while the variance increases quadratically and hence at some point increases faster than the mean. Ignoring higher-order moments, the optimal allocation sets the expected utility gain from a marginal increase in the portfolio mean to equal the expected utility loss from the associated increase in the portfolio variance. The willingness to trade off expected return for risk at the margin depends on the investor's risk aversion. Third, the benefits from market timing also decrease with risk aversion. This is because a more risk averse investor allocates less wealth to stocks and therefore has a lower expected portfolio return and because, even for the same expected portfolio return, a more risk averse investor requires a smaller incentive to abstain from risky investments.

Figure 5.3 presents the solution to the multiperiod portfolio choice for horizons τ ranging from one quarter to 10 years for an investor with $\gamma = 5$ (corresponding to the dashed-dotted lines in Fig. 5.2). Rather than plotting the entire policy fuction for each horizon, plot A shows only the allocations for current dividend yields of 2.9% (25th percentile, dotted line), 3.5% (median, dashed-dotted line), and 4.1% (75th percentile, solid line). Plot B shows the expected utility *gain*, measured by the increase in the annualized certainty equivalent rates (in percent), from implementing the dynamic multiperiod portfolio policy as opposed to making a sequence of myopic single-period portfolio choices.

It is clear from plot A that the optimal portfolio choice depends on the investor's horizon. At the median dividend yield, for example, the optimal allocation is 58% stocks for a one-quarter horizon (one period), 66% stocks for a 1-year horizon (four periods),

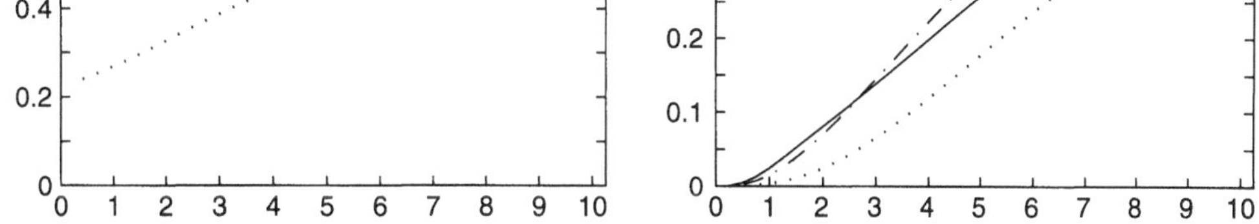

Figure 5.3 Plot A shows the optimal fraction of wealth invested in stocks as a function of the investment horizon for a CRRA investor with relative risk aversion of five conditional on the current dividend yield being equal to 2.9 (dotted line), 3.5 (dashed-dotted line), and 4.1 (solid line) percent. Plot B shows the corresponding increase in the annualized certainty equivalent rates of return from investing optimally as opposed to myopically (in percent).

96% stocks for a 5-year horizon (20 periods), and 100% stocks for all horizons longer than 6 years (24 periods). The differences between the single-period allocations (23, 58, and 87% stocks at the 25th, 50th, and 75th percentiles of the dividend yield, respectively) and the corresponding multiperiod allocations represent the investor's hedging demands. Plot B shows that these hedging demands can lead to substantial increases in expected utility. At the median dividend yield, the increase in the certainty equivalent rate is 2 basis points per year for the 1-year problem, 30 basis points per year for the 5-year problem, and 57 basis points per year for the 10-year problem. Although these gains are small relative to the level of the certainty equivalent rate (5.2% at the median dividend yield), they are large when we ask "how much wealth is the investor willing to give up today to invest optimally, as opposed to myopically, for the remainder of the horizon?" The answer is less than 0.1% for a 1-year investor, but 1.5% for a 5-year investor and 5.9% for a 10-year investor.

Although it is not the most realistic data generating process, the homoscedastic VAR has pedagogical value. First, it demonstrates that in a multiperiod context the optimal portfolio choice can be substantially different from a sequence of single-period portfolio choices, both in terms of allocations and expected utilities. Second, it illustrates the mechanism by which hedging demands arise. The expected return increases with the dividend yield and the higher-order moments are constant. A high (low) dividend yield therefore implies a relatively high (low) value of the portfolio choice problem. In a multiperiod context, this link between the dividend yield and the value of the problem means that the investor faces not only the uncertainty inherent in returns but also uncertainty about whether in the future the dividend yield will be higher, lower, or the same and whether, as a result, the investment opportunities will improve, deteriorate, or remain the same, respectively. Analogous to diversifying cross-sectionally the return risk, the investor wants to smooth intertemporally this risk regarding future investment opportunities. Because the VAR estimates imply a large negative correlation between the stock returns and innovations to the dividend yield, the investment opportunities risk can be smoothed quite effectively by *over-investing* in stocks, relative to the myopic allocation. By over-investing, the investor realizes a greater gain when the return is positive and a greater loss when it is negative. A positive return tends to be associated with a drop in the dividend yield and an expected utility loss due to deteriorated investment opportunities in the future. Likewise, a negative return tends to be associated with a rise in the dividend yield and an expected utility gain due to improved investment opportunities. Thus, the financial gain (loss) from over-investing partially offsets the expected utility loss (gain) associated with the drop (rise) in the dividend yield (hence, the name "hedging demands").

2.2.2. Continuous-Time Formulation

The intertemporal portfolio choice problem can alternatively be expressed in continuous time. The main advantage of the continuous-time formulation is its analytical tractability.

As Merton (1975) and the continuous-time finance literature that followed demonstrates, stochastic calculus allows us to solve in closed-form portfolio choice problems in continuous-time that are analytically intractable in discrete time.[7]

The objective function in the continuous-time formulation is the same as in Eq. (2.9), except that the maximization is over a continuum of portfolio choices x_s, with $t \leq s < t + \tau$, because the portfolio is rebalanced at every instant in time. Assuming that the risky asset prices p_t and the vector of state variables evolve jointly as correlated Itô vector processes:

$$\begin{aligned} \frac{\mathrm{d}p_t}{p_t} - r\mathrm{d}t &= \mu^p(z_t, t)\mathrm{d}t + D^p(z_t, t)\mathrm{d}B_t^p \\ \mathrm{d}z_t &= \mu^z(z_t, t)\mathrm{d}t + D^z(z_t, t)\mathrm{d}B_t^z, \end{aligned} \tag{2.17}$$

the budget constraint is

$$\frac{\mathrm{d}W_t}{W_t} = \left(x_t{}'\mu_t^p + r\right)\mathrm{d}t + x_t{}'D_t^p\mathrm{d}B_t^p, \tag{2.18}$$

Using the abbreviated notation $f_t = f(z_t, t)$, μ_t^p and μ_t^z are N- and K-dimensional conditional mean vectors, D_t^p and D_t^z are $N \times N$ and $K \times K$ conditional diffusion matrices that imply covariance matrices $\Sigma_t^p = D_t^p D_t^{p\prime}$ and $\Sigma_t^z = D_t^z D_t^{z\prime}$, and B_t^p and B_t^z are N- and K-dimensional vector Brownian motion processes with $N \times K$ correlation matrix ρ_t. Finally, r denotes here the instantaneous riskfree rate (assumed constant for notational convenience).

The continuous time Bellman equation is (Merton, 1969):

$$\begin{aligned} 0 = \max_{x_t}\Big[& V_1(\cdot) + W_t\left(x_t{}'\mu_t^p + r\right) V_2(\cdot) + \mu_t^{z\prime}\, V_3(\cdot) + \frac{1}{2} W_t^2\, x_t{}'\Sigma_t^p x_t\, V_{22}(\cdot) \\ & + W_t x_t{}'\, D_t^p \rho_t{}'\, D_t^{z\prime}\, V_{23}(\cdot) + \frac{1}{2}\mathrm{tr}\big[\Sigma_t^z\, V_{33}(\cdot)\big]\Big], \end{aligned} \tag{2.19}$$

subject to the terminal condition $V(0, W_{t+\tau}, z_{t+\tau}) = u(W_{t+\tau})$.

As one might expect, Eq. (2.19) is simply the limit, as $\Delta t \to 0$, of the discrete time Bellman equation (2.11). To fully appreciate this link between the discrete and continuous time formulations, rearrange Eq. (2.11) as:

$$0 = \max_{x_t} \mathrm{E}_t\big[V(\tau - 1, W_{t+1}, z_{t+1}) - V(\tau, W_t, z_t)\big] \tag{2.20}$$

and take the limit of $\Delta t \to 0$:

$$0 = \max_{x_t} \mathrm{E}_t\big[\mathrm{d}V(\tau, W_t, z_t)\big]. \tag{2.21}$$

[7]See Shimko (1999) for an introduction to stochastic calculus. Mathematically more rigorous treatments of the material can be found in Karatzas and Shreve (1991) and Steele (2001).

Then, apply Itô's lemma to the value function to derive:

$$dV(\cdot) = V_1(\cdot)dt + V_2(\cdot)dW_t + V_3(\cdot)dz_t + V_{22}(\cdot)dW_t^2 + V_{23}(\cdot)dW_t dz_t + V_{33}(\cdot)dz_t^2. \tag{2.22}$$

Finally, take the expectation of Eq. (2.22), which picks up the drifts of $dW_t, dz_t, dW_t^2, dW_t dz_t$, and dz_t^2 (the second-order processes must be derived through Itô's lemma), plug it into Eq. (2.21), and cancel out the common term dt. The result is Eq. (2.19).

The continuous-time FOCs are

$$\mu_t^p V_2(\cdot) + W_t x_t' \Sigma_t^p V_{22}(\cdot) + D_t^p \rho_t' D^{z\prime} V_{23} = 0, \tag{2.23}$$

which we can solve for the optimal portfolio weights:

$$x_t^\star = \underbrace{-\frac{V_2(\cdot)}{W_t V_{22}(\cdot)} \left(\Sigma_t^p\right)^{-1} \mu_t^p}_{\text{myopic demand}} \underbrace{- \frac{V_2(\cdot)}{W_t V_{22}(\cdot)} \frac{V_{23}(\cdot)}{V_2(\cdot)} (\Sigma_t^p)^{-1} D_t^p \rho_t' D_t^{z\prime}}_{\text{hedging demand}}. \tag{2.24}$$

This analytical solution illustrates more clearly the difference between the dynamic and myopic portfolio choice. The optimal portfolio weights $x_t^\star$ are the sum of two terms, the first being the myopically optimal portfolio weights and the second representing the difference between the dynamic and myopic solutions. Specifically, the first term depends on the ratio of the first to second moments of excess returns and on the inverse of the investor's relative risk aversion $\gamma_t \equiv -W_t V_{22}(\cdot)/V_2(\cdot)$. It corresponds to holding a fraction $1/\gamma_t$ in the tangency portfolio of the instantaneous mean–variance frontier. The second term depends on the *projection* of the state variable innovations dB_t^z onto the return innovations dB_t^p, which is given by $\left(\Sigma_t^p\right)^{-1} D_t^p \rho_t' D_t^{z\prime}$, on the inverse of the investor's relative risk aversion, and on the sensitivity of the investor's marginal utility to the state variables $V_{23}(\cdot)/V_2(\cdot)$. The projection delivers the weights of K portfolios that are *maximally correlated* with the state variable innovations and the derivatives of marginal utility with respect to the state variables measure how important each of these state variables is to the investor. Intuitively, the investor takes positions in each of the maximally correlated portfolios to partially hedge against undesirable innovations in the state variables. The maximally correlated portfolios are therefore called *hedging portfolios*, and the second term in the optimal portfolio weights is labeled the hedging demand. It is important to note that both the myopic and hedging demands are scaled equally by relative risk aversion and that the trade-off between holding a myopically optimal portfolio and intertemporal hedging is determined by the derivatives of marginal utility with respect to the state variables.

CRRA Utility Example Continued To illustrate the tractability of the continuous-time formulation, consider again the CRRA utility example. *Conjecture* that the value function has the separable form:

$$V(\tau, W_t, z_t) = \frac{W_t^{1-\gamma}}{1-\gamma}\,\psi(\tau, z_t), \tag{2.25}$$

which implies that the optimal portfolio weights are

$$x_t^\star = \frac{1}{\gamma}\left(\Sigma_t^p\right)^{-1}\mu_t^p + \frac{1}{\gamma}\frac{\psi_2(\cdot)}{\psi(\cdot)}\left(\Sigma_t^p\right)^{-1}D_t^p\rho_t' D_t^{z\prime}. \tag{2.26}$$

This solution is sensible given the well-known properties of CRRA utility. Both the tangency and hedging portfolio weights are scaled by a constant $1/\gamma$ and the relative importance of intertemporal hedging, given by $\psi_2(\cdot)/\psi(\cdot)$, is independent of wealth.

Plugging the derivatives of the value function (2.25) and the optimal portfolio weights (2.26) into the Bellman equation (2.19), yields the nonlinear differential equation:

$$\begin{aligned} 0 = {}& \psi_1(\cdot) + (1-\gamma)\left(x_t^{\star\prime}\mu_t^p + r\right)\psi(\cdot) + \mu_t^{z\prime}\,\psi_2(\cdot) - \frac{1}{2}\gamma(1-\gamma)\,x_t^{\star\prime}\Sigma_t^p x_t^\star\psi(\cdot) \\ & + (1-\gamma)x_t^{\star\prime}\,D_t^p\rho_t'\,D_t^z\,\psi_2(\cdot) + \frac{1}{2}\mathrm{tr}\left[\Sigma_t^z\,\psi_{22}(\cdot)\right]. \end{aligned} \tag{2.27}$$

The fact that this equation, which implicitly defines the function $\psi(\tau, z_t)$, does not depend on the investor's wealth W_t confirms the conjecture of the separable value function.

Continuous Time Portfolio Policies in Discrete Time Because the continuous-time Bellman equation is the limit of its discrete-time counterpart, it is tempting to think that the *solutions* to the two problems share the same limiting property. Unfortunately, this presumption is wrong. The reason is that the continuous time portfolio policies are often *inadmissible* in discrete time because they cannot guarantee nonnegative wealth unless the portfolio is rebalanced at every instant.

Consider a simpler example of logarithmic preferences (CRRA utility with $\gamma = 1$) and i.i.d. log-normal stock returns with annualized risk premium of 5.7% and volatility of 16.1% (consistent with the VAR in the previous section). In the continuous-time formulation, the optimal stock allocation is $x_t^\star = 0.057/0.161^2 = 2.20$, which means that the investor borrows 120% of wealth to invest a total of 220% in stocks. Technically, such levered position is inadmissable over *any* discrete time interval, irrespective of how short it is. The reason is that under log-normality the gross return on stocks over any finite interval can be arbitrarily close to zero, implying a positive probability that the investor cannot repay the loan next period. This constitutes a possible violation of the no-bankruptcy constraint $W_s \geq 0$ and, with CRRA utility, can lead to infinite disutility. The continuous-time solution is therefore inadmissable in discrete time, and the optimal discrete-time allocation is $x_t^\star \leq 1$.

Whether this inadmissability is important enough to abandon the analytical convenience of the continuous-time formulation is up to the researcher to decide. On the one hand, the probability of bankruptcy is often very small. In the log utility example, for instance, the probability of realizing a sufficiently negative stock return over the period of one quarter is only 1.3×10^{-9}. On the other hand, in reality an investor always faces some risk of loosing all, or almost all wealth invested in risky securities due to an extremely rare but severe event, such as a stock market crash, the collapse of the financial system, or investor fraud.[8]

2.3. When is it Optimal to Invest Myopically?

Armed with the discrete and continuous-time formulations of the portfolio choice problem, we can be more explicit about when it is optimal to invest myopically. The myopic portfolio choice is an important special case for practitioners and academics alike. There are, to my knowledge, few financial institutions that implement multi-period investment strategies involving hedging demands.[9] Furthermore, until recently the empirically oriented academic literature on portfolio choice was focused almost exclusively on single-period problems, in particular, the mean–variance paradigm of Markowitz (1952) discussed in Section 2.1.

In addition to the obvious case of having a single-period horizon, it is optimal to invest myopically under each of the following three assumptions:

2.3.1. Constant Investment Opportuntities

Hedging demands only arise when the investment opportunities vary stochastically through time. With constant investment opportunities, the value function does not depend on the state variables, so that z_t drops out of the discrete time FOCs (2.12) and $V_{23}(\cdot) = 0$ in the continuous-time solution (2.24). The obvious case of constant investment opportunities is i.i.d. returns. However, the investment opportunities can be constant even when the conditional moments of returns are stochastic. For example, Nielsen and Vassalou (2006) show that in the context of the diffusion model (2.17), the investment opportunities are constant as long as the instantaneous riskfree rate and the Sharpe ratio of the optimal portfolio of an investor with logarithmic preferences are

[8]Guided by this rare events argument, there are at least two ways to formally bridge the gap between the discrete and continuous-time solutions. We can either introduce the rare events through jumps in the continuous-time formulation (e.g., Longstaff et al., 2003) or allow the investor to purchase insurance against the rare events through put options or other derivatives in the discrete-time formulation.

[9]A common justification from practitioners is that the expected utility loss from errors that could creep into the solution of a complicated dynamic optimization problem outweighs the expected utility gain from investing optimally as opposed to myopically. Recall that in the dividend yield predictability case the gain for CRRA utility is only a few basis points per year.

constant. The conditional means, variances, and covariances of the individual assets that make up this log-optimal portfolio can vary stochastically.

2.3.2. Stochastic but Unhedgable Investment Opportunities

Even with stochastically varying investment opportunities, hedging demands only arise when the investor can use the available assets to hedge against changes in future investment opportunities. If the variation is completely independent of the returns, the optimal portfolio is again myopic. In discrete time, independence of the state variables and returns implies that the expectation in the Bellman equation can be decomposed into an expectation with respect to the portfolio returns and an expectation with respect to the state variables. The FOCs then turn out to be the same as in the single-period problem. In continuous time, a correlation $\rho_t = 0$ between the return and state variable innovations eliminates the hedging demands term in the optimal portfolio weights.

2.3.3. Logarithmic Utility

Finally, the portfolio choice reduces to a myopic problem when the investor has logarithmic preferences $u(W) = \ln(W)$. The reason is that with logarithmic preferences the utility of terminal wealth is simply the sum of the utilities of single-period portfolio returns:

$$\ln(W_{t+\tau}) = \ln\left(W_t \prod_{s=t}^{t+\tau-1} \left(x_s' r_{s+1} + R_s^f\right)\right) = \ln W_t + \sum_{s=t}^{t+\tau-1} \ln\left(x_s' r_{s+1} + R_s^f\right). \tag{2.28}$$

The portfolio weights that maximize the expectation of the sum are the same as the ones that maximize the expectations of each element of the sum, which are, by definition, the sequence of single-period portfolio weights. Therefore, the portfolio choice is myopic.

2.4. Modeling Issues and Extensions

2.4.1. Preferences

The most critical ingredient to any portfolio choice problem is the objective function. Historically, the academic literature has focused mostly on time-separable expected utility with hyperbolic absolute risk aversion (HARA), which includes as special cases logarithmic utility, power or constant relative risk aversion (CRRA) utility, negative exponential or constant absolute risk aversion (CARA) utility, and quadratic utility. The reason for this popularity is the fact that HARA is a necessary and sufficient condition to obtain asset demand functions expressed in currency units, not percent of wealth, that are linear in wealth (Merton, 1969). In particular, the portfolio choice expressed in currency units is proportional to wealth with CRRA utility and independent of wealth with CARA utility. Alternatively, the corresponding portfolio choice expressed in percent of wealth is independent of wealth with CRRA utility and inversely proportional to wealth with CARA utility.

In the HARA class, power or CRRA preferences are by far the most popular because the value function turns out to be homogeneous in wealth (see the examples mentioned earlier). However, CRRA preferences are not without faults. One critique that is particularly relevant in the portfolio choice context is that with CRRA the elasticity of intertemporal substitution is directly tied to the level of relative risk aversion (one is the reciprocal of the other), which creates an unnatural link between two very different aspects of the investor's preferences – the willingness to substitute consumption intertemporally versus the willingness to take on risk. Epstein and Zin (1989) and Weil (1989) propose a generalization of CRRA preferences based on recursive utility that severs this link between intertemporal substitution and risk aversion. Campbell and Viceira (1999) and Schroder and Skiadas (1999) consider these generalized CRRA preferences in portfolio choice problems.

A number of stylized facts of actual investment decisions and professional investment advice are difficult to reconcile with HARA or even Epstein–Zin–Weil preferences. The most prominent empirical anomaly is the strong dependence of observed and recommended asset allocations on the investment horizon.[10] There have been a number of attempts to explain this horizon puzzle using preferences in which utility is defined with respect to a nonzero and potentially time-varying lower bound on wealth or consumption, including a constant subsistence level (Jagannathan and Kocherlakota, 1996; Samuelson, 1989), consumption racheting (Dybvig, 1995), and habit formation (Lax, 2002; Schroder and Skiadas, 2002).

Experiments by psychologists, sociologists, and behavioral economists have uncovered a variety of more fundamental behavioral anomalies. For example, the way experimental subjects make decisions under uncertainty tends to systematically violate the axioms of expected utility theory (e.g., Camerer, 1995). To capture these behavioral anomalies in an optimizing framework, several nonexpected utility preference formulations have been proposed, including loss aversion and prospect theory (Kahneman and Tversky, 1979), anticipated or rank-dependent utility (Quiggin, 1982), ambiguity aversion (Gilboa and Schmeidler, 1989), and disappointment aversion (Gul, 1991). These nonexpected utility preferences have been applied to portfolio choice problems by Benartzi and Thaler (1995), Shefrin and Statman (2000), Aït-Sahalia and Brandt (2001), Liu (2002), Ang et al. (2005), and Gomes (2005), among others.

Finally, there are numerous applications of more practitioner-oriented objective functions, such as minimizing the probability of a short-fall (Kataoka, 1963; Roy, 1952; Telser, 1956), maximizing expected utility with either absolute or relative portfolio insurance (Black and Jones, 1987; Grossman and Vila, 1989; Perold and Sharpe, 1988), maximizing expected utility subject to beating a stochastic benchmark (Browne, 1999; Tepla, 2001),

[10] E.g., see Bodie and Crane (1997), Canner et al. (1997), and Ameriks and Zeldes (2004).

and maximizing expected utility subject to maintaining a critical value at risk (VaR) (Alexander and Baptista, 2002; Basak and Shapiro, 2001; Cuoco et al., 2007).

2.4.2. Intermediate Consumption

Both the discrete- and continuous-time formulations of the portfolio choice problem can be amended to accommodate intermediate consumption. Simply add to the utility of terminal wealth (interpreted then as the utility of bequests to future generations) the utility of the life-time consumption stream (typically assumed to be time-separable and geometrically discounted), and replace in the budget constraint the current wealth W_t with the current wealth net of consumption $(1 - c_t) W_t$, where c_t denotes the fraction of wealth consumed. The investor's problem with intermediate consumption then is to choose at each date t the optimal consumption c_t as well as the asset allocation x_t.

For example, the discrete-time problem with time-separable CRRA utility of consumption and without bequests is

$$V(\tau, W_t, z_t) = \max_{\{x_s, c_s\}_{s=t}^{t+\tau-1}} \mathrm{E}_t\left[\sum_{s=t}^{t+\tau} \beta^{s-t} \frac{(c_t W_t)^{1-\gamma}}{1-\gamma}\right], \tag{2.29}$$

subject to the budget constraint:

$$W_{s+1} = (1 - c_s) W_s \left(x_s' r_{s+1} + R_s^f\right), \tag{2.30}$$

the no-bankruptcy constraint $W_s \geq 0$, and the terminal condition $c_{t+\tau} = 1$. Following a few steps analogous to the case without intermediate consumption, the Bellman equation can in this case be written as:

$$\frac{1}{1-\gamma}\psi(\tau, z_t) = \max_{x_t, c_t}\left[\frac{c_t^{1-\gamma}}{1-\gamma} + \beta\,\mathrm{E}_t\left[\frac{\left((1-c_t)\left(x_t' r_{t+1} + R_t^f\right)\right)^{1-\gamma}}{1-\gamma}\psi(\tau - 1, z_{t+1})\right]\right], \tag{2.31}$$

where $\psi(\tau, z_t)$ is again a function of the horizon and state variables that is in general different from the case without intermediate consumption.

Although the Bellman equation with intermediate consumption is more involved than without, in the case of CRRA utility the problem is actually easier to handle numerically because the value function can be solved for explicitly from the envelope condition $\partial V(\tau, W, z)/\partial W = \partial u(cW)/\partial(cW)$. Specifically, $\psi(\tau, z) = c(\tau, z)^{-\gamma}$ for $\gamma > 0$ and $\gamma \neq 1$ or $\psi(\tau, z) = 1$ for $\gamma = 1$. This explicit form of the value function implies that in a backward-recursive dynamic programming solution to the policy functions $x(\tau, z)$ and $c(\tau, z)$, the value function at date $t + 1$, which enters the FOCs at date t, is automatically provided by the consumption policy at date $t + 1$ obtained in the previous recursion. Furthermore, with CRRA utility the portfolio and consumption choices turn out to be sequential. Because the value function is homothetic in wealth and the consumption choice c_t only scales the investable wealth $(1 - c_t)W_t$, the FOCs for the portfolio weights x_t are independent of c_t. Therefore, the investor first makes the portfolio choice ignoring consumption and then makes the consumption choice given the optimal portfolio weights.

As Wachter (2002) demonstrates, the economic implication of introducing intermediate consumption in a CRRA framework is to shorten the effective horizon of the investor. Although the myopic portfolio choice is the same with and without intermediate consumption, the hedging demands are quite different in the two cases. In particular, Wachter shows that the hedging demands with intermediate consumption are a weighted sum of the hedging demands of a sequence of terminal wealth problems, analogous to the price of a coupon-bearing bond being a weighted sum of the prices of a sequence of zero-coupon bonds.

2.4.3. Complete Markets

A financial market is said to be complete when all future outcomes (states) are spanned by the payoffs of traded assets. In a complete market, state-contingent claims or so-called Arrow–Debreu securities that pay off one unit of consumption in a particular state and zero in all other states can be constructed for every state. These state-contingent claims can then be used by investors to place bets on a particular state or set of states.

Markets can be either statically or dynamically complete. For a market to be statically complete, there must be as many traded assets as there are states, such that investors can form state-contingent claims as buy-and-hold portfolios of these assets. Real asset markets, in which there is a continuum of states and only a finite number of traded assets, are at best dynamically complete. In a dynamically complete market, investors can construct a continuum of state-contingent claims by *dynamically* trading in the finite set of base assets. Dynamic completion underlies, for example, the famous Black and Scholes (1973) model and the extensive literature on derivatives pricing that followed.[11]

The assumption of complete markets simplifies not only the pricing of derivatives but, as Cox and Huang (1989, 1991) demonstrate, also the dynamic portfolio choice. Rather than solve for a dynamic trading strategy in a set of base assets, Cox and Huang solve for the optimal buy-and-hold portfolio of the state-contingent claims. The intuition is that any dynamic trading strategy in the base assets generates a particular terminal payoff distribution that can be replicated by some buy-and-hold portfolio of state-contingent claims. Conversely, any state-contingent claim can be replicated by a dynamic trading

[11] Dynamic completion arises usually in a continuous time setting, but Cox et al. (1979) illustrate that continuous trading is not a critical assumption. They construct an $(N+1)$ state discrete time economy as a sequence of N binomial economies and show that this statically incomplete economy can be dynamically completed by trading in only two assets.

strategy in the base assets. It follows that the terminal payoff distribution generated by the optimal dynamic trading strategy in the base assets is *identical* to that of the optimal static buy-and-hold portfolio of state-contingent claims. Once this static problem is solved (which is obviously much easier than solving the dynamic optimization), the optimal dynamic trading strategy in the base assets can be recovered by adding up the replicating trading strategies of each state-contingent claim position in the buy-and-hold portfolio.

The Cox and Huang (1989, 1991) approach to portfolio choice relies on the existence of a state price density or equivalent Martingale measure (see Harrison and Kreps, 1979) and is therefore often referred to as the "Martingale approach" to portfolio choice. Cox and Huang solve the continuous time HARA problem with intermediate consumption and confirm that the results are identical to the dynamic programming solution of Merton (1969). Recent applications of the Martingale approach to portfolio choice problems with frictionless markets and the usual utility functions include Wachter (2002), who specializes Cox and Huang's solution to CRRA utility and a return process similar to the VAR mentioned earlier, Detemple et al. (2003), who show how to recover the optimal trading strategy in the base assets as opposed to the Arrow–Debreu securities for a more general return processes using simulations, and Aït-Sahalia and Brandt (2007), who incorporate the information in option-implied state prices in the portfolio choice problem.

Although originally intended for solving portfolio choice problems in complete markets, the main success of the Martingale approach has been in the context of problems with incompleteness due to portfolio constraints, transaction costs, and other frictions, which are notoriously difficult to solve using dynamic programming techniques. He and Pearson (1991) explain how to deal with market incompleteness in the Martingale approach. Cvitanic (2001) surveys the extensive literature that applies the Martingale approach to portfolio choice problems with different forms of frictions. Another popular use of the Martingale approach is in the context of less standard preferences (see the references in Section 2.4.1).

2.4.4. Infinite or Random Horizon

Solving an infinite horizon problem is often easier than solving an otherwise identical finite horizon problem because the infinite horizon assumption eliminates the dependence of the Bellman equation on time. An infinite horizon problem only needs to be solved for a steady-state policy, whereas a finite horizon problem must be solved for a different policy each period. For example, Campbell and Viceira (1999) and Campbell et al. (2003) are able to derive approximate analytical solutions to the infinite horizon portfolio choice of an investor with recursive Epstein–Zin–Weil utility, intermediate consumption, and mean-reverting expected returns. The same problem with a finite horizon can only be solved numerically, which is difficult (in particular in the multi-asset case considered by Campbell et al.) and the results are not as transparent as an analytical solution.

Intuitively, one would expect the sequence of solutions to a finite horizon problem to converge to that of the corresponding infinite horizon problem as the horizon increases.[12] In the case of CRRA utility and empirically sensible return processes, this convergence appears to be quite fast. Brandt (1999), Barberis (2000), and Wachter (2002) document that 10- to 15-year CRRA portfolio policies are very similar to their infinite horizon counterparts. This rapid convergence suggests that the solution to the infinite horizon problem can, in many cases, be confidently used to study the properties of long- but finite-horizon portfolio choice in general (e.g., Campbell and Viceira, 1999, 2002).

Having a known finite or an infinite horizon are pedagogical extremes. In reality, an investor rarely knows the terminal date of an investment, which introduces another source of uncertainty. In the case of intermediate consumption, the effect of horizon uncertainty can be substantial because the investor risks either running out of wealth before the terminal date or leaving behind accidental bequests (e.g., Barro and Friedman, 1977; Hakansson, 1969). An alternative motivation for a random terminal date is to set a finite *expected horizon* in an infinite horizon problem to sharpen the approximation of a long-horizon portfolio choice by its easier-to-solve infinite horizon counterpart (e.g., Viceira, 2001).

2.4.5. Frictions and Background Risks

Arguably the two most realistic features of an investor's problem are frictions, such as transaction costs and taxation, and background risks, which refers to any risks other than those directly associated with the risky securities. Frictions are particularly difficult to incorporate because they generally introduce path dependencies in the solution to the portfolio choice problem. For example, with proportional transaction costs, the costs incurred by rebalancing depend on both the desired allocations for the next period and the current allocation inherited from the previous period. In the case of capital gains taxes, the basis for calculating the tax liability generated by selling an asset depends on the price at which the asset was originally bought. Unfortunately, in the usual backward recursive solution of the dynamic program, the previous investment decisions are unknown.

Because of its practical relevance, the work on incorporating frictions, transaction costs and taxation in particular, into portfolio choice problems is extensive and ongoing. Recent papers on transaction costs include Davis and Norman (1990), Duffie and Sun (1990), Akian et al. (1996), Balduzzi and Lynch (1999), Leland (2001), Liu (2004), and Lynch and Tan (2009). The implications of capital gains taxation are considered in a single-period context by Elton and Gruber (1978) and Balcer and Judd (1987) and in a multiperiod context by Dammon et al. (2001a,b), Garlappi et al. (2001), Leland (2001),

[12]Merton (1969) proves this intuition for the continuous time portfolio choice with CRRA utility. Kim and Omberg (1996) provide counter-examples with HARA utility for which the investment problem becomes ill-defined at sufficiently long horizons (so-called nirvana solutions).

Dammon et al. (2004), DeMiguel and Uppal (2005), Gallmeyer et al. (2006), and Huang (2008), among others.

In principle, background risks encompass all risks faced by an investor other than those directly associated with the risky securities. The two most common sources of background risk considered in the academic literature are uncertain labor or entrepreneurial income and both the investment in and consumption of housing. Recent work on incorporating uncertain labor or entrepreneurial income include Heaton and Lucas (1997), Koo (1998), Chan and Viceira (2000), Heaton and Lucas (2000), Viceira (2001), and Gomes and Michaelides (2003). The role of housing in portfolio choice problems is studied by Grossman and Laroque (1991), Flavin and Yamashita (2002), Cocco (2000, 2005), Campbell and Cocco (2003), Hu (2005), and Yao and Zhang (2005), among others. The main challenge in incorporating background risks is to specify a realistic model for the joint distribution of these risks with asset returns at different horizons and over the investor's life-cycle.

3. TRADITIONAL ECONOMETRIC APPROACHES

The traditional role of econometrics in portfolio choice problems is to specify the data generating process $f(y_t|y_{t-1})$. As straightforward as this seems, there are two different econometric approaches to portfolio choice problems: *plug-in estimation* and *decision theory*. In the plug-in estimation approach, the econometrician draws inferences about some investor's optimal portfolio weights to make descriptive statements, while in the decision theory approach, the econometrician takes on the role of the investor and draws inferences about the return distribution to choose portfolio weights that are optimal with respect to these inferences.

3.1. Plug-In Estimation

The majority of the portfolio choice literature, and much of what practitioners do, falls under the heading of plug-in estimation or calibration, where the econometrician estimates or otherwise specifies the parameters of the data generating process and then plugs these parameter values into an analytical or numerical solution to the investor's optimization problem. Depending on whether the econometrician treats the parameters as estimates or simply assumes them to be the truth, the resulting portfolio weights are estimated or calibrated. Estimated portfolio weights inherit the estimation error of the parameter estimates and therefore are almost certainly different from the true optimal portfolio weights in finite samples.

3.1.1. Theory

Single-Period Portfolio Choice Consider first a single-period portfolio choice problem. The solution of the investor's expected utility maximization maps the preference parameters ϕ (e.g., the risk aversion coefficient γ for CRRA utility), the state vector z_t, and the parameters of the data generating process θ into the optimal portfolio weights x_t:

$$x_t^\star = x(\phi, z_t, \theta), \tag{3.1}$$

where ϕ is specified ex-ante and z_t is observed. Given data $Y_T \equiv \{y_t\}_{t=0}^T$, we can typically obtain unbiased or at least consistent estimates $\hat{\theta}$ of the parameters θ. Plugging these estimate into Eq. (3.1) yields estimates of the optimal portfolio weights $\hat{x}_t^\star = x(\phi, z_t, \hat{\theta})$.

Assuming $\hat{\theta}$ is consistent with asymptotic distribution $\sqrt{T}(\hat{\theta} - \theta) \overset{T\to\infty}{\sim} \mathrm{N}[0, V_\theta]$ and the mapping $x(\cdot)$ is sufficiently well-behaved in θ, the asymptotic distribution of the estimator $\hat{x}_t^\star$ can be computed using the delta method:

$$\sqrt{T}\big(\hat{x}_t^\star - x_t^\star\big) \overset{T\to\infty}{\sim} \mathrm{N}\big[0, x_3(\cdot)\, V_\theta x_3(\cdot)'\big]. \tag{3.2}$$

To be more concrete, consider the mean–variance problem (2.8). Assuming i.i.d. excess returns with constant risk premia μ and covariance matrix Σ, the optimal portfolio weights are $x^\star = (1/\gamma)\, \Sigma^{-1}\mu$. Given excess return data $\{r_{t+1}\}_{t=1}^T$, the moments μ and Σ can be estimated using the following sample analog:

$$\hat{\mu} = \frac{1}{T}\sum_{t=1}^{T} r_{t+1} \quad \text{and} \quad \hat{\Sigma} = \frac{1}{T-N-2}\sum_{t=1}^{T}(r_{t+1} - \hat{\mu})(r_{t+1} - \hat{\mu})' \tag{3.3}$$

(notice the unusual degrees of freedom of $\hat{\Sigma}$). Plugging these estimates into the expression for the optimal portfolio weights gives the plug-in estimates $\hat{x}^\star = (1/\gamma)\, \hat{\Sigma}^{-1}\hat{\mu}$.

Under the assumption of normality, this estimator is unbiased:

$$\mathrm{E}[\hat{x}^\star] = \frac{1}{\gamma}\, \mathrm{E}[\hat{\Sigma}^{-1}]\, \mathrm{E}[\hat{\mu}] = \frac{1}{\gamma}\, \Sigma^{-1}\mu, \tag{3.4}$$

where the first equality follows from the standard independence of $\hat{\mu}$ and $\hat{\Sigma}$, and the second equality is due to the unbiasedness of $\hat{\mu}$ and $\hat{\Sigma}^{-1}$.[13] Without normality or with the more standard $1/T$ or $1/(T-1)$ normalization for the sample covariance matrix, the plug-estimator is generally biased but nonetheless consistent with plim $\hat{x}^\star = x^\star$.

The second moments of the plug-in estimator can be derived by expanding the estimator around the true risk premia and return covariance matrix. With multiple risky assets, this expansion is algebraicly tedious because of the nonlinearities from the inverse

[13] The unbiasedness of $\hat{\mu}$ is standard. For the unbiasedness of $\hat{\Sigma}^{-1}$, recall that with normality, the matrix $\hat{S} = \sum_{t=1}^T (r_{t+1} - \hat{\mu})(r_{t+1} - \hat{\mu})'$ has a Wishart distribution (the multivariate extension of a chi-squared distribution) with a mean of $(T-1)\Sigma$. Its inverse $\hat{S}^{-1}$ therefore has an inverse Wishart distribution, which has a mean of $(T-N-2)\Sigma^{-1}$ (see Marx and Hocking, 1977). This implies that $\hat{\Sigma}^{-1}$ is an unbiased estimator of Σ^{-1} and explains the unusual degrees of freedom.

of the covariance matrix (see Jobson and Korkie, 1980). To illustrate the technique, consider therefore a single risky asset. Expanding $\hat{x}^\star = (1/\gamma)\hat{\mu}/\hat{\sigma}^2$ around both μ and σ^2 yields:

$$\hat{x}^\star = \frac{1}{\gamma}\frac{1}{\sigma^2}(\mu - \hat{\mu}) - \frac{1}{\gamma}\frac{\mu}{\sigma^4}(\sigma^2 - \hat{\sigma}^2). \tag{3.5}$$

Take variances and rearrange:

$$\text{var}\left[\hat{x}^\star\right] = \frac{1}{\gamma^2}\left(\frac{\mu}{\sigma^2}\right)^2\left(\frac{\text{var}[\hat{\mu}]}{\mu^2} + \frac{\text{var}[\hat{\sigma}^2]}{\sigma^4}\right). \tag{3.6}$$

This expression shows that the imprecision of the plug-in estimator is scaled by the magnitude of the optimal portfolio weight $x^\star = (1/\gamma)\mu/\sigma^2$ and depends on both the imprecision of the risk premia and volatility estimates, each scaled by their respective magnitudes.

To get a quantitative sense for the estimation error, evaluate Eq. (3.6) for some realistic values for μ, σ, var$[\hat{\mu}]$, and var$[\hat{\sigma}^2]$. Suppose, for example, we have 10 years of monthly data on a stock with $\mu = 6\%$ and $\sigma = 15\%$. With i.i.d. data, the standard error of the sample mean is std$[\hat{\mu}] = \sigma/\sqrt{T} = 1.4\%$. Second moments are generally thought of as being more precisely estimated than first moments. Consistent with this intuition, the standard error of the sample variance under i.i.d. normality is std$[\hat{\sigma}^2] = \sqrt{2}\sigma^2/\sqrt{T} = 0.3\%$. Putting together the pieces, the standard error of the plug-in estimator $\hat{x}^\star$ for a reasonable risk aversion of $\gamma = 5$ is equal to 14%, which is large relative to the magnitude of the true $x^\star = 53.3\%$. This example illustrates a more general point: portfolio weights tend to be very imprecisely estimated because the inputs to the estimator are difficult to pin down.

It is tempting to conclude from this example that, at least for the asymptotics, uncertainty about second moments is swamped by uncertainty about first moments. As Cho (2007) illustrates, however, this conclusion hinges critically on the assumption of i.i.d. normality. In particular, the precision of the sample variance depends on the kurtosis of the data. The fatter are the tails, the more difficult it is to estimate second moments because outliers greatly affect the estimates. This means that conditional heteroskedasticity, in particular, can considerably inflate the asymptotic variance of the unconditional sample variance. Returning to the example, suppose that, instead of i.i.d. normality, the conditional variance h_t of returns follows a standard GARCH(1,1) process:

$$h_t = \omega + \alpha\epsilon_{t-1}^2 + \beta h_{t-1}. \tag{3.7}$$

In this case, the variance of the unconditional sample variance is

$$\text{var}\left[\hat{\sigma}^2\right] = \frac{2\sigma^4}{T}\left(1 + \frac{\kappa}{2}\right)\left(1 + \frac{2\rho}{1-\alpha-\beta}\right), \tag{3.8}$$

where κ denotes the unconditional excess kurtosis of returns and ρ denotes the first-order autocorrelation of the squared return innovations. Both κ and ρ can be computed from the GARCH parameters α and β. With reasonable GARCH parameter values of $\alpha = 0.0175$ and $\beta = 0.9811$, the variance of the sample variance is inflated by a factor of 233.3. As a result, the standard error of $\hat{x}^\star$ is 105.8%, as compared to 14% under i.i.d. normality. Although this example is admittedly extreme (as volatility is close to being nonstationary), it illustrates the point that both return moments, as well as high-order moments for other preferences, can contribute to the asymptotic imprecision of plug-in portfolio weight estimates.

Returning to the computationally more involved case of multiple risky assets, Britten-Jones (1999) derives a convenient way to draw asymptotic inferences about mean–variance optimal portfolio weights. He shows that the plug-in estimates of the tangency portfolio:

$$\hat{x}^\star_{\text{tgc}} = \frac{\hat{\Sigma}^{-1}\hat{\mu}}{\iota'\hat{\Sigma}^{-1}\hat{\mu}} \tag{3.9}$$

can be computed from OLS estimates of the slope coefficients b of regressing a vector of ones on the matrix of excess returns (without intercept):

$$1 = b\, r_{t+1} + u_{t+1}, \tag{3.10}$$

where $\hat{x}^\star_{\text{tgc}} = \hat{b}/(\iota'\hat{b})$. We can therefore use standard OLS distribution theory for $\hat{b}$ to draw inferences about $x^\star_{\text{tgc}}$. For example, testing whether the weight of the tangency portfolio on a particular asset equals zero is equivalent to testing whether the corresponding element of b is zero, which corresponds to a standard t test. Similarly, testing whether an element of $x^\star_{\text{tgc}}$ equals a constant c is equivalent to testing whether the corresponding element of b equals $c(\iota' b)$, which is a linear restriction that can be tested using a joint F test.

Multiperiod Portfolio Choice The discussion mentioned earlier applies directly to both analytical and approximate solutions of multiperiod portfolio choice problems, in which the optimal portfolio weights at time t are functions of the preference parameters ϕ, the state vector z_t, the parameters of the data generating process θ, and perhaps the investment horizon $T - t$. In the case of a recursive numerical solution, however, the portfolio weights at time t depend explicitly on the value function at time $t + 1$, which in turn depends on the sequence of optimal portfolio weights at times $\{t + 1, t + 2, \ldots, T - 1\}$. Therefore, the portfolio weight estimates at time t not only reflect the imprecision of the parameter estimates but also the imprecision of the estimated portfolio weights for future periods (which themselves reflect the imprecision of the parameter estimates). To capture this recursive dependence of the estimates, express the mapping from the parameters to the optimal portfolio weights as a set of recursive functions:

$$\begin{aligned} x^{\star}_{t+\tau-1} &= x(1, \phi, z_{t+\tau-1}, \theta) \\ x^{\star}_{t+\tau-2} &= x\left(2, \phi, z_{t+\tau-2}, \theta, x^{\star}_{t+\tau-1}\right) \\ x^{\star}_{t+\tau-3} &= x\left(3, \phi, z_{t+\tau-3}, \theta, \left\{x^{\star}_{t+\tau-1}, x^{\star}_{t+\tau-2}\right\}\right) \\ &\dots \\ x^{\star}_{t} &= x\left(\tau, \phi, z_{t}, \theta, \left\{x^{\star}_{t+\tau-1}, \dots, x^{\star}_{t+1}\right\}\right). \end{aligned} \tag{3.11}$$

To compute the asymptotic standard errors of the estimates $\hat{x}^{\star}_t$ we also need to account for the estimation error in the preceding portfolio estimates $\{\hat{x}^{\star}_s\}_{s=t+1}^{T-1}$. This is accomplished by including in the derivatives $x_4(\cdot)$ in Eq. (3.2), also the terms:

$$\sum_{s=t+1}^{T-1} \frac{\partial x\left(t, \phi, z_t, \theta, \left\{x^{\star}_s\right\}_{s=t+1}^{T-1}\right)}{\partial x^{\star}_s} \frac{\partial x^{\star}_s}{\partial \theta}. \tag{3.12}$$

Intuitively, the longer the investment horizon, the more imprecise are the estimates of the optimal portfolio weights, because the estimation error in the sequence of optimal portfolio weights accumulates through the recursive nature of the solution.

Bayesian Estimation There is nothing inherently frequentist about the plug-in estimation. Inferences about optimal portfolio weights can be drawn equally well from a Bayesian perspective. Starting with a posterior distribution of the parameters $p(\theta|Y_T)$, use the mapping (3.1) or (3.11) to compute the posterior distribution of the portfolio weights $p(x^{\star}_t|Y_T)$ and then draw inferences about $x^{\star}_t$ using the moments of this posterior distribution.

Consider again the mean–variance problem. Assuming normally distributed returns and uninformative priors, the posterior of μ conditional on Σ^{-1}, $p(\mu|\Sigma^{-1}, Y_T)$, is Gaussian with mean $\hat{\mu}$ and covariance matrix Σ/T. The marginal posterior of Σ^{-1}, $p(\Sigma^{-1}|Y_T)$, is a Wishard distribution with mean $\overline{\Sigma}^{-1} = (T-N)\hat{S}^{-1}$ and $T-N$ degrees of freedom.[14] It follows that the posterior of the optimal portfolio weights $x^{\star} = (1/\gamma)\Sigma^{-1}\mu$, which can be computed from $p(\mu, \Sigma^{-1}|Y_T) \equiv p(\mu|\Sigma^{-1}, Y_T)\, p(\Sigma^{-1}|Y_T)$, has a mean of $(1/\gamma)\overline{\Sigma}^{-1}\hat{\mu}$.[15] As is often the case with uninformative priors, the posterior means, which are the Bayesian estimates for quadratic loss, coincide with frequentist estimates (except for the difference in degrees of freedom).

[14] See Box and Tiao (1973) for a review of Bayesian statistics.

[15] Although the posterior of $x = (1/\gamma)\Sigma^{-1}\mu$ is not particularly tractable, its mean can be easily computed using the law of iterated expectations $\mathrm{E}[\Sigma^{-1}\mu] = \mathrm{E}\big[\mathrm{E}[\Sigma^{-1}\mu|\Sigma]\big] = \mathrm{E}\big[\Sigma^{-1}\mathrm{E}[\mu|\Sigma]\big] = \mathrm{E}[\Sigma^{-1}]\hat{\mu} = \overline{\Sigma}^{-1}\hat{\mu}$.

Economic Loss How severe is the statistical error of the plug-in estimates in an economic sense? One way to answer this question is to measure the economic loss from using the plug-in estimates as opposed to the truly optimal portfolio weights. An intuitive measure of this economic loss is the difference in certainty equivalents. In the mean–variance problem (2.8), for example, the certainty equivalent of the true portfolio weights $x^\star$ is

$$\mathrm{CE} = x^{\star\prime}\mu - \frac{\gamma}{2}x^{\star\prime}\Sigma x^\star \tag{3.13}$$

and the certainty equivalent of the plug-in estimates $\hat{x}^\star$ is

$$\hat{\mathrm{CE}} = \hat{x}^{\star\prime}\mu - \frac{\gamma}{2}\hat{x}^{\star\prime}\Sigma\hat{x}^\star. \tag{3.14}$$

The certainty equivalent loss is defined as the expected difference between the two:

$$\mathrm{CE\ loss} = \mathrm{CE} - \mathrm{E}\big[\hat{\mathrm{CE}}\big], \tag{3.15}$$

where the expectation is taken with respect to the statistical error of the plug-in estimates (the certainty equivalents already capture the return uncertainty). Cho (2007) shows that this certainty equivalent loss can be approximated by:

$$\mathrm{CE} - \mathrm{E}\big[\hat{\mathrm{CE}}\big] \simeq \frac{\gamma}{2} \times \mathrm{tr}\big[\mathrm{cov}[\hat{x}^\star]\Sigma\big]. \tag{3.16}$$

The certainty equivalent loss depends on the level of risk aversion, the covariance matrix of the plug-in estimates, and the return covariance matrix. Intuitively, the consistency of the plug-in estimator implies that on average the two portfolio policies generate the same mean return, so the first terms of the certainty equivalents cancel out. The statistical error of the plug-in estimates introduces additional uncertainty in the portfolio return, referred to as *parameter uncertainty*, which is penalized by the utility function the same way as the uncertainty inherent in the optimal portfolio returns.

For the mean–variance example with a single risky asset above:

$$\mathrm{CE\ loss} \simeq \frac{\gamma}{2} \times \mathrm{var}[\hat{x}^\star]\sigma^2. \tag{3.17}$$

Plugging in the numbers from the example, the certainty equivalent of the optimal portfolio is $\mathrm{CE} = 0.533 \times 0.06 - 2.5 \times 0.533^2 \times 0.15^2 = 1.6\%$ (the investor is indifferent between the risky portfolio returns and a certain return equal to the risk-free rate plus 1.6%) and the (asymptotic) certainty equivalent loss due to statistical error under normality is $\mathrm{CE\ loss} = 2.5 \times 0.14^2 \times 0.15^2 = 0.11\%$. Notice that, although the standard error of the plug-in portfolio weights is the magnitude as the portfolio weight itself, the certainty equivalent loss is an order of magnitude smaller. This illustrates the point made in a more general context by Cochrane (1989), that for standard preferences first-order deviations from optimal decision rules tend to have only second-order utility consequences.

Given an expression for the economic loss due to parameter uncertainty, we can search for variants of the plug-in estimator that perform better in terms of their potential economic losses. This task is taken on by Kan and Zhou (2007), who consider estimators of the form $\hat{w}^{\star} = c \times \hat{\Sigma}^{-1}\hat{\mu}$ and solve for an "optimal" constant c. Optimality here is defined as the resulting estimator being admissible, which means that no other value of c generates a smaller economic loss for some values of the true μ and Σ. Their analysis can naturally be extended to estimators that have different functional forms.

3.1.2. Finite Sample Properties

Although asymptotic results are useful to characterize the statistical uncertainty of plug-in estimates, the real issue, especially for someone considering to use plug-in estimates in real-life applications, is finite-sample performance. Unfortunately, there is a long line of research documenting the shortcomings of plug-in estimates, especially in the context of large-scale mean–variance problems (e.g., Best and Grauer, 1991; Chopra and Ziemba, 1993; Jobson and Korkie, 1980, 1981; Michaud, 1989). The general conclusions from these papers is that plug-in estimates are extremely imprecise and that, even in relatively large samples, the asymptotic approximations above are quite unreliable. Moreover, the precision of plug-in estimates deteriorates drastically with the number of assets held in the portfolio. Intuitively, this is because, as the number of assets increases, the number of unique elements of the return covariance matrix increases at a *quadratic* rate. For instance, in the realistic case of 500 assets the covariance matrix involves more than 125,000 unique elements, which means that for a post-war sample of about 700 monthly returns we have less than three degrees of freedom per parameter ($500 \times 600 = 350{,}000$ observations and 125,000 parameters). I first illustrate the poor finite-sample properties of plug-in estimates through a simulation experiment and then discuss a variety of ways of dealing with this problem in practice.

Jobson–Korkie Experiment Jobson and Korkie (1980) were among the first to document the finite-sample properties of plug-in estimates. The following simulation experiment replicates their main finding. Consider 10 industry-sorted portfolios. To address the question of how reliable plug-in estimates of mean–variance efficient portfolio weights are for a given sample size, take the historical sample moments of the portfolios to be the truth and simulate independent sets of 250 hypothetical return samples of different sample sizes from a normal distribution with the true moments. For each hypothetical sample, compute again plug-in estimates of the mean–variance frontier and then evaluate how close these estimates come to the true frontier. Figures 5.4 and 5.5 illustrate the results graphically, for the unconstrained and constrained (nonnegative weights) case,

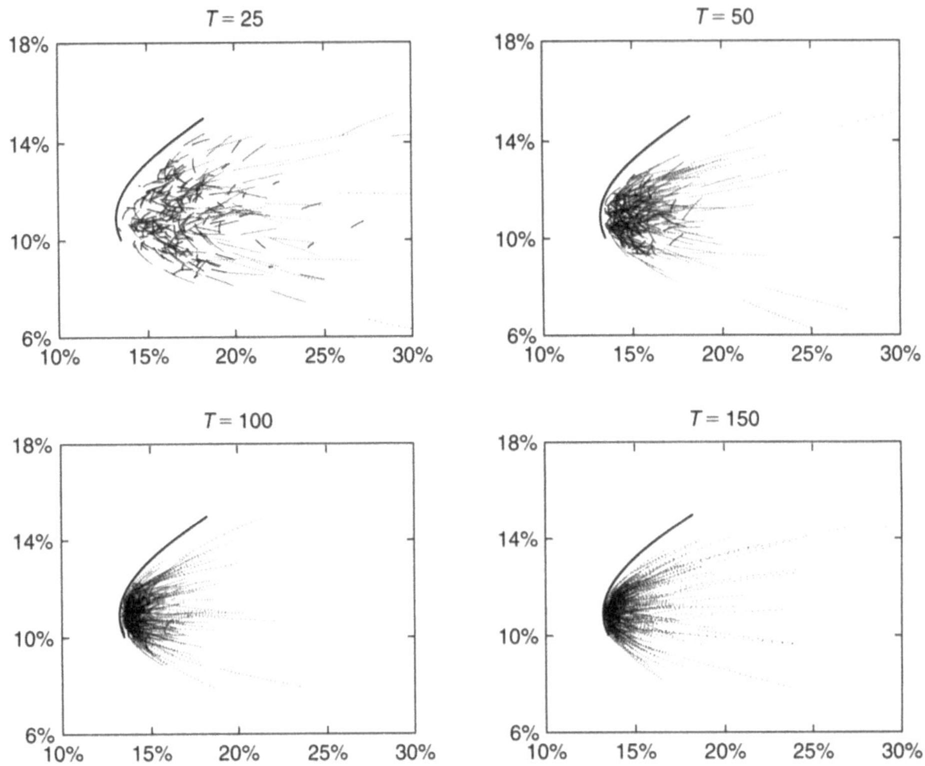

Figure 5.4 The solid line in each plot is the unconstrained mean–variance frontier for 10 industry portfolios, taking sample moments as the truth. The dotted lines show the mean–variance trade-off, evaluated using the true moments, of 250 independent plug-in estimates for 25, 50, 100, and 150 simulated returns.

respectively. Each figure shows as solid line the true mean–variance frontier and as dotted lines the mean–variance trade-off, evaluated using the true moments, of the 250 plug-in estimates for samples of 25, 50, 100, and 150 monthly returns.

The results of this experiment are striking. The mean–variance trade-off achieved by the plug-in estimates are extremely volatile and on average considerably inferior to the true mean–variance frontier. Furthermore, increasing the sample size, for example from 50 to 150, does not substantially reduce the sampling variability of the plug-in estimates. Comparing the constrained and unconstrained results, it is clear that constraints help reduce the sampling error, but clearly not to a point where one can trust the plug-in estimates, even for a sample as large as 150 months (more than 10 years of data).

To get a sense for the economic loss due to the statistical error, Fig. 5.6 shows histograms of the Sharpe ratio, again evaluated using the true moments, of the estimated unconstrained and constrained tangency portfolios for 25 and 150 observations. As a

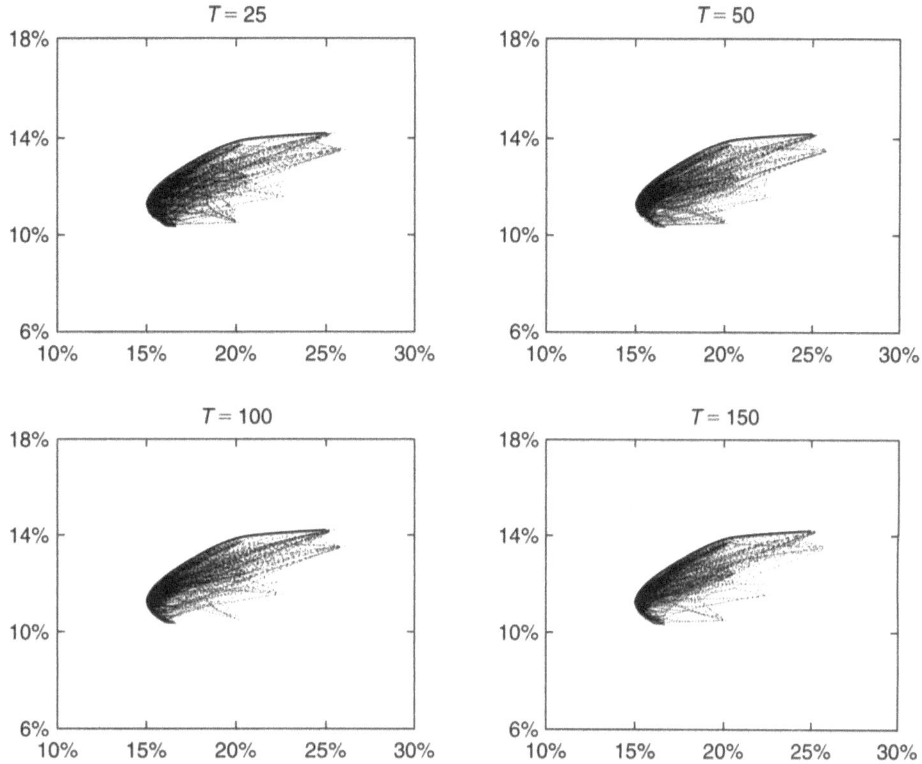

Figure 5.5 The solid line in each plot is the constrained (nonnegative portfolio weights) mean–variance frontier for 10 industry portfolios, taking sample moments as the truth. The dotted lines show the mean–variance trade-off, evaluated using the true moments, of 250 independent plug-in estimates for 25, 50, 100, and 150 simulated returns.

reference, the figure also shows as vertical lines the Sharpe ratios of the true tangency portfolio (0.61 and 0.52 for the unconstrained and constrained problems, respectively). The results in this figure are as dramatic as in the previous two figures. The Sharpe ratios of the plug-in estimates are very volatile and on average considerably lower than the truth. For example, even with 150 observations, the unconstrained Sharpe ratios have an average of 0.42 with 25th and 75th percentiles of 0.37 and 0.48, respectively. In stark contrast to the asymptotic results discussed earlier, the economic loss due to statistical error in finite samples is substantial.

In addition to being very imprecise, plug-in estimates tend to exhibit extreme portfolio weights, which, at least superficially, contradicts the notion diversification (more on this point below). For example, in the unconstrained case, the plug-in estimate of the tangency portfolio based on the historical sample moments allocates 82% to the nondurables industry and −48% to the manufacturing industry. Furthermore, the extreme portfolio

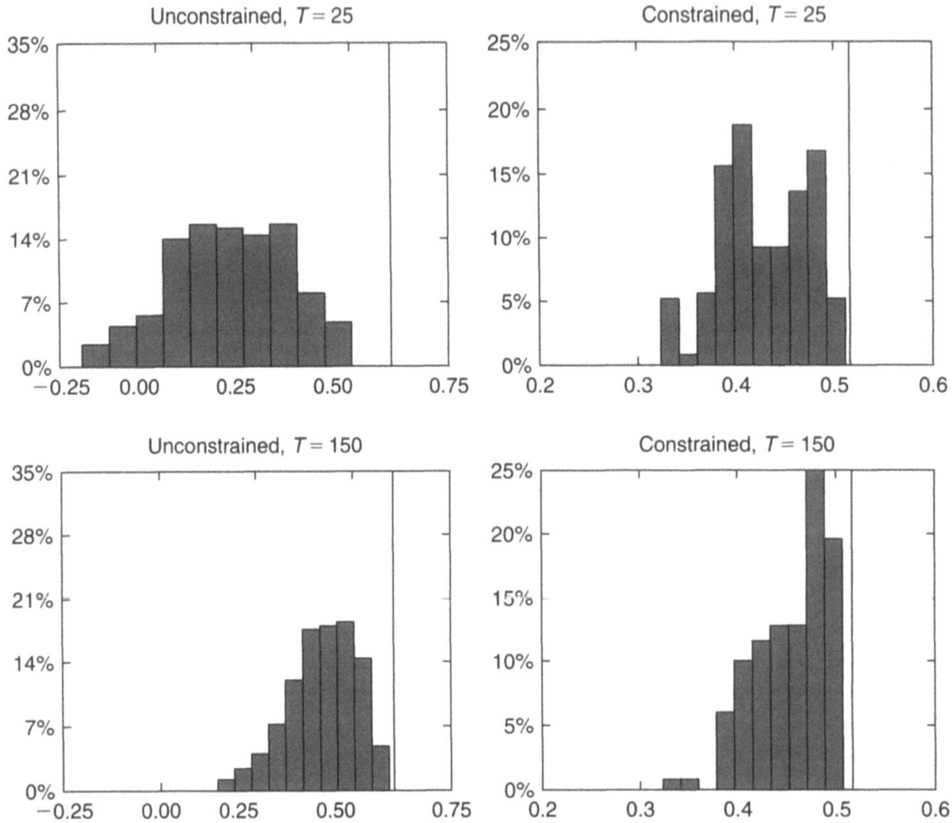

Figure 5.6 The vertical line in each plot represents the Sharpe ratio of the true unconstrained or constrained (nonnegative portfolio weights) tangency portfolios for 10 industry portfolios, taking sample moments as the truth. The histograms correspond to the Sharpe ratios, evaluated using the true moments, of 250 independent plug-in estimates for 25 or 150 simulated returns.

weights tend to be relatively unstable. Small changes in the inputs (the risk premia and covariance matrix) result in large changes in the plug-in estimates. Both of these issues have significant practical implications. Extreme positions are difficult to implement and instability causes unwarranted turnover, tax liabilities, and transaction costs. Michaud (1989) argues that extreme and unstable portfolio weights are inherent to mean–variance optimizers because they tend to assign large positive (negative) weights to securities with large positive (negative) estimation errors in the risk premium and/or large negative (positive) estimation errors in the volatility. Mean–variance optimizers therefore act as statistical "error maximizers."

Motivated by the poor finite-sample property of plug-in estimates, there exists by now an extensive literature suggesting different, but to some extent complementary, ways of improving on plug-in estimates for practical applications. These approaches include (i) shrinkage estimation, (ii) the use of factor models, and (iii) imposing portfolio constraints. I discuss each of these approaches in turn.

Shrinkage Estimation The idea of shrinkage estimation is attributed to James and Stein (1961), who noted that for $N \geq 3$ independent normal random variables, the vector of sample means $\overline{\mu}$ is dominated in terms of joint mean-squared error by a convex combination of the sample means and a common constant μ_0 (see also Efron and Morris, 1977), resulting in the estimator:

$$\mu_s = \delta\mu_0 + (1 - \delta)\overline{\mu}, \tag{3.18}$$

for $0 < \delta < 1$. The James–Stein estimator "shrinks" the sample means toward a common value, which is often chosen to be the grand mean across all variables. The estimator thereby reduces the extreme estimation errors that may occur in the cross-section of individual means, resulting in a lower overall variance of the estimators that more than compensates for the introduction of small biases. The optimal trade-off between bias and variance is achieved by an optimal shrinkage factor $\delta^{\star}$, given for mean-squared error loss by:

$$\delta^{\star} = \min\left[1, \frac{(N-2)/T}{(\overline{\mu} - \mu_0)'\Sigma^{-1}(\overline{\mu} - \mu_0)}\right]. \tag{3.19}$$

Intuitively, the optimal shrinkage factor increases in the number of means N, decreases in the sample size T (which determines the precision of the sample means), and decreases in the dispersion of the sample means $\overline{\mu}$ from the shrinkage target μ_0.

Shrinkage estimation for risk premia has been applied to portfolio choice problems by Jobson et al. (1979), Jobson and Korkie (1981), Frost and Savarino (1986), and Jorion (1986), among others. Jorion shows theoretically and in a simulation study that the optimality of the shrinkage estimator in the mean-squared error loss context considered by James and Stein (1961) carries over to estimating risk premia in the portfolio choice context. Plug-in portfolio weight estimates constructed with shrunk sample means dominate, in terms of expected utility, plug-in estimates constructed with the usual sample means.

To illustrate the potential benefits of shrinkage estimation, consider again the mean–variance example with 10 industry portfolios. Table 5.2 reports the average Sharpe ratios, evaluated using the true moments, of the 250 plug-in estimates of the unconstrained tangency portfolios for different sample sizes with and without shrinkage. To isolate the effect of statistical error in sample means, the table shows results for both a known and unknown covariance matrix. The improvement from using shrinkage is considerable. For example, with 50 observations, the average Sharpe ratio without shrinkage is 0.24

Table 5.2 Average Sharpe ratios, evaluated using the true moments, of plug-in estimates with and without shrinkage of the unconstrained tangency portfolio for 10 industry portfolios with known and unknown covariance matrix

		Known Σ		Unknown Σ	
T	Truth	Sample means	Shrinkage	Sample means	Shrinkage
25	0.624	0.190	0.428	0.169	0.270
50	0.624	0.236	0.446	0.223	0.371
100	0.624	0.313	0.477	0.298	0.443
150	0.624	0.362	0.495	0.348	0.473
250	0.624	0.418	0.512	0.411	0.501

The results are based on 250 simulated samples of size T.

or 0.22, depending on whether the covariance matrix is know or unknown, compared to the Sharpe ratio of the true tangency portfolio of 0.62. With shrinkage, in contrast, the average Sharpe ratio is 0.45 with known covariance matrix (87% improvement) and 0.37 with unknown covariance matrix (63% improvement). The average shrinkage factor with a known covariance matrix ranges from 0.78 for $T = 25$–0.71 for $T = 250$. This means that the individual sample means are shrunk about two-thirds toward a common mean across all portfolios. The reason for why shrinkage estimation is in relative terms less effective with an unknown covariance matrix is that the optimal shrinkage factor in Eq. (3.19) is evaluated with a noisy estimate of the covariance matrix, which, due to the nonlinearity of optimal shrinkage factor, results in a less shrinkage overall. In particular, the average shrinkage factor with an unknown covariance matrix is 0.51 for $T = 25$, 0.72 for $T = 100$, and 0.69 for $T = 250$.

Shrinkage estimation can also be applied to covariance matrices. In the portfolio choice context, Frost and Savarino (1986) and Ledoit and Wolf (2003, 2004) propose return covariance matrix estimators that are convex combinations of the usual sample covariance matrix $\hat{\Sigma}$ and a shrinkage target S (or its estimate $\hat{S}$):

$$\hat{\Sigma}_s = \delta\hat{S} + (1 - \delta)\hat{\Sigma}. \tag{3.20}$$

Sensible shrinkage targets include an identity matrix, the covariance matrix corresponding to a single- or multifactor model, or a covariance matrix with equal correlations.

Ledoit and Wolf (2003) derive the following approximate expression for the optimal shrinkage factor assuming mean-squared error loss:

$$\delta^* \simeq \frac{1}{T}\frac{A - B}{C}, \tag{3.21}$$

with

$$A = \sum_{i=1}^{N}\sum_{j=1}^{N} \text{asy var}\left[\sqrt{T}\hat{\sigma}_{i,j}\right]$$

$$B = \sum_{i=1}^{N}\sum_{j=1}^{N} \text{asy cov}\left[\sqrt{T}\hat{\sigma}_{i,j}, \sqrt{T}\hat{s}_{i,j}\right] \tag{3.22}$$

$$C = \sum_{i=1}^{N}\sum_{j=1}^{N} \left(\sigma_{i,j} - s_{i,j}\right)^2.$$

The optimal shrinkage factor reflects the usual bias versus variance trade-off. It decreases in the sample size T, increases in the imprecision of $\hat{\Sigma}$ (through A), decreases in the covariance of the errors in estimates of $\hat{\Sigma}$ and $\hat{S}$ (through B), and decreases in the bias of S (through C). Ledoit and Wolf (2003) also describe how to consistently estimate the asymptotic second moments needed to evaluate the optimal shrinkage factor in practice. Finally, they show that, besides reducing sampling error, shrinkage to a positive definite target guarantees that the resulting estimate is also positive definite, even when the sample covariance matrix itself is singular (when $N > T$). This makes shrinkage a particularly practical statistical tool for constructing large-scale equity portfolios.

The idea of shrinkage estimation can in principle also be applied directly to the plug-in estimates of the optimal portfolio weights, resulting in an estimator of the form:

$$\hat{w}_s^\star = \delta w_0 + (1-\delta)\hat{w}^\star, \tag{3.23}$$

for some sensible shrinkage target w_0. There are several potential advantages of shrinking the plug-in estimates, compared to shrinking their inputs. First, it may be easier to specify ex-ante sensible shrinkage targets, such as equal weights $1/N$ or observed relative market capitalization weights in a benchmark portfolio. Second, shrinking the plug-in estimates may be more effective because it explicitly links first and second moments. It is possible, for example, to shrink both first and second moments toward zero, thinking that the statistical error has been reduced, but leave the plug-in portfolio weights unchanged. Third, shrinkage of the plug-in estimates can be more naturally combined with an economic loss function. Specifically, the optimal shrinkage factor could be chosen to maximize the expected utility from using the shrunk plug-in estimates, as opposed to minimize its mean-squared error. Whether any of these advantages are materialized in practice remains to be seen.

Any form of shrinkage estimation involves seemingly ad-hoc choices of the shrinkage target and the degree of shrinkage (or equivalently the loss function which determines the optimal degree of shrinkage). Both of these issues are naturally resolved in a Bayesian framework, where the location of the prior beliefs can be interpreted as the shrinkage target and the variability of the prior beliefs relative to the information contained in the data automatically determines how much the estimates are shrunk toward the prior. I will return to the Bayesian interpretation of shrinkage and the choice of priors in Section 3.2.

Factor Models The second approach to reducing the statistical error of the plug-in estimates is to impose a factor structure for the covariation among assets to reduce the number of free parameters of the covariance matrix. Sharpe (1963) first proposed using the covariance matrix implied by a single-factor market model in the mean–variance problem:

$$r_{i,t} = \alpha_i + \beta_i r_{m,t} + \varepsilon_{i,t}, \tag{3.24}$$

where the residuals $\varepsilon_{i,t}$ are assumed to be uncorrelated across assets. Stacking the N market betas β_i into a vector β, the covariance matrix implied by this single-factor model is

$$\Sigma = \sigma_m^2 \beta\beta' + \Sigma_\epsilon, \tag{3.25}$$

where Σ_ϵ is a diagonal residual covariance matrix with non-zero elements $\sigma_{\varepsilon,i}^2 = \text{var}[\varepsilon_{i,t}]$. The advantage of this approach is that it reduces the dimensionality of the portfolio problem to $3N + 1$ terms $\left(\{\alpha_i, \beta_i, \sigma_{\varepsilon,i}^2\}_{i=1}^N \text{ and } \sigma_m^2\right)$. The drawback, in exchange, is that a single factor may not capture all of the covariation among assets, leading not only to a biased but potentially systematically biased estimate of the return covariance matrix.

The obvious way to overcome this drawback is to increase the number of factors capturing the covariation among assets. In a more general K-factor model:

$$r_{i,t} = \alpha_i + \beta_i' f_t + \varepsilon_{i,t}, \tag{3.26}$$

where β_i is now a vector of factor loadings, f_t is a vector a factor realizations (which still need to be specified), and the residuals $\varepsilon_{i,t}$ are again assumed to be uncorrelated across asset. The implied return covariance matrix is

$$\Sigma = B\Sigma_f B' + \Sigma_\varepsilon, \tag{3.27}$$

where B denotes the $N \times K$ matrix of stacked factor loadings, Σ_f is the covariance matrix of the factors, and Σ_ε is a diagonal residual covariance matrix. If the factors are correlated, the portfolio problem is reduced to $K(K+1)/2 + N(K+2)$ terms. If the factors are uncorrelated, which is a common assumption implying that Σ_f is also diagonal, the problem is further reduced to $K + N(K+2)$ terms. To illustrate the degree of dimension reduction achieved by multifactor models, consider again the case of 500 assets. With five factors, there are 3515 coefficients to estimate if the factors are correlated, as opposed to 125,000 in the case without factors. This translates into a more than 33-fold increase in the degrees of freedom (from less than 3 to more than 99).

The practical difficulty with implementing a multifactor model is the choice of common factors. There are essentially three ways to approach this problem. First, the choice of factors can be based on economic theory. Examples include using the market or aggregate wealth portfolio, as implied by the CAPM, which results in the approach of Sharpe (1963), or using multiple intertemporal hedge portfolios that are maximally correlated with changes in the aggregate investment opportunity set, as implied by Merton's (1973) ICAPM. Second, the choice of factors can be based on empirical work, including, for example, macroeconomic factors (e.g., Chen et al., 1986), industry factors, firm characteristic-based factors (e.g., Fama and French, 1993), and combinations thereof (e.g., BARRA's equity risk models). Third, the factors can be extracted directly from returns using a statistical procedure such as factor analysis or principal components analysis (e.g., Connor and Korajczyk, 1988). Moving from theoretical factors, to empirical factors, to statistical factors, we capture, by construction, increasingly more of the covariation among assets. In exchange, the factors become more difficult to interpret, which raises concerns about data mining.

Chan et al. (1999) study the performance of different factor model specifications in a realistic rolling-sample portfolio choice problem. Their results show that factor models clearly improve the performance of the plug-in estimates. However, no clear favorite specification emerges, both in terms of the number and the choice of factors. A simple CAPM-based single-factor model performs only marginally worse than a high-dimensional model with industry and characteristic-based factors.

Portfolio Constraints The third approach to reducing the statistical error inherent in plug-in estimation is to impose constraints on the portfolio weights. It is clear from comparing the results in Figs. 5.4 and 5.5 that imposing portfolio constraints helps. Frost and Savarino (1988) confirm this impression more scientifically by demonstrating that portfolio constraints truncate the extreme portfolio weights and thereby improve the performance of the estimates. Their results suggest that, consistent with Michaud's (1989) view of optimizers as error maximizers, the extreme portfolio weights that being truncated are associated with estimation error.

There are numerous ways of constraining portfolio weights. The most popular constraints considered in the academic literature are constraints that limit short-selling and constraints that limit the amount of borrowing to invest in risky assets. Although these constraints are obviously also very relevant in practice, realistic investment problems are subject to a host of other constraints, such as constraints on the maximum position in a single security, on the maximum exposure to a given industry or economic sector, on the liquidity of a security, or on the risk characteristics of a security. In addition, it is common practice to perform an initial screening of the universe of all securities to obtain a smaller and more manageable set of securities. These initial screens can be based on firm characteristics, including accounting and risk measures, liquidity measures, transaction cost measures, or even return forecasts.

Although portfolio constraints are an integral part of the investment process in practice, Green and Hollifield (1992) argue that, from a theoretical perspective, extreme portfolio weights do not necessarily imply that a portfolio is undiversified. The intuition of their argument is as follows. Suppose returns are generated by a single-factor model and therefore contain both of systematic and idiosyncratic risk. The aim is to minimize both sources of risk through diversification. Instead of using a mean–variance optimizer, consider an equivalent but more transparent two-step procedure in which we first diversify away idiosyncratic risk and then diversify away systematic risk. In the first step, sort stocks based on their factor loading and form equal-weighted portfolios with high factor loadings and with low factor loadings. With a large number of stocks, each of these portfolios will be well diversified and therefore only exposed to systematic risk. In the second step, take partially offsetting positions in the systematic risk portfolios to eliminate, as much as possible given the adding-up constraint on the overall portfolio weights, the systematic risk exposure. Although the outcome is a portfolio that is well diversified in terms of both idiosyncratic and systematic risk, Green and Hollifield show that the second step can involve extreme long-short positions. The implication of this argument is that, contrary to popular belief and common practice, portfolio constraints may actually hurt the performance of plug-in estimates.

Relating Shrinkage Estimation, Factor Models, and Portfolio Constraints The argument of Green and Hollifield (1992) creates tension between economic theory and the empirical fact that imposing portfolio constraints indeed improves the performance of plug-in estimates in practice. This tension is resolved by Jagannathan and Ma (2003), who show that certain constraints on the portfolio weights can be interpreted as a form of shrinkage estimation. Because shrinkage improves the finite-sample properties of plug-in estimates, it is no longer puzzling that constraints also help, even if they are not theoretically justified. As with all forms of shrinkage estimation, constrained plug-in estimates are somewhat biased but much less variable than unconstrained plug-in estimates.

Specifically, for the problem of finding a global minimum variance portfolio (in Fig. 5.1) subject to short-sale constraints $x_t \geq 0$ and position limits $x_t \leq \bar{x}$, the constrained portfolio weights x_t^+ are mathematically equivalent to the unconstrained portfolio weights for the adjusted covariance matrix:

$$\tilde{\Sigma} = \Sigma + (\delta\iota' + \iota\delta') - (\lambda\iota' + \iota'\lambda), \tag{3.28}$$

where λ is the vector a Lagrange multipliers for the short-sale constraints and δ is the vector of Lagrange multipliers for the position limits. Each Lagrange multiplier takes on a positive value whenever the corresponding constraint is binding and is equal to zero otherwise. To understand better how Eq. (3.28) amounts to shrinkage, suppose the position limit constraints are not binding but the short-sale constraint is binding for stock i, so that $\delta = 0$ and $\lambda_i > 0$. The variance of stock i is reduced to $\tilde{\sigma}_{i,i} = \sigma_{i,i} - 2\lambda_i$ and all covariance are reduced to $\tilde{\sigma}_{i,j} = \sigma_{i,j} - \lambda_i - \lambda_j$. As stocks with negative weights in minimum variance portfolios tend to have large positive covariances with other stocks, short-sale constraints effectively shrink these positive covariances toward zero. Analogously, suppose the short-sale constraints are not binding but the position limit constraint is binding for stock i, so that $\lambda = 0$ and $\delta_i > 0$. In that case, the variance of stock i is increased to $\tilde{\sigma}_{i,i} = \sigma_{i,i} + 2\delta_i$ and the covariances are all increased to $\tilde{\sigma}_{i,j} = \sigma_{i,j} + \delta_i + \delta_j$. Since stocks with large positive weights in minimum variance portfolios tend to have large negative covariances with other stocks, position limit constraints effectively shrink these negative covariances toward zero.

A similar result holds for the constrained mean–variance problem. The constrained mean–variance efficient portfolio weights x_t^+ are mathematically equivalent to the unconstrained portfolio weights for the adjusted mean vector:

$$\tilde{\mu} = \mu + \frac{1}{\lambda_0}\lambda - \frac{1}{\lambda_0}\delta \tag{3.29}$$

and adjusted target return:

$$\tilde{\overline{\mu}} = \overline{\mu} + \frac{1}{\lambda_0}\delta'\overline{x}, \tag{3.30}$$

where $\lambda_0 > 0$ is the Lagrange multiplier for the expected return constraint $x_t'\mu = \overline{\mu}$, which is always binding. If the position limit constraints are not binding but the short-sale constraint is binding for stock i, the expected return on stock i is increased to $\tilde{\mu}_i = \mu_i + \lambda_i/\lambda_0$. Since stocks with negative weights in mean–variance efficient portfolios tend to have negative expected returns, the short-sale constraints shrink the expected return toward zero. Analogously, if the short-sale constrains are not binding but the position limit constraint is binding for stock i, the expected return on stock i is decreased to $\tilde{\mu}_i = \mu_i - \delta_i/\lambda_0$. Since stocks with large positive weights tend to have large positive expected returns, position limit constraints also shrink the expected return toward zero.

3.2. Decision Theory

In the second traditional econometric approach, decision theory, the econometrician takes on the role of the investor by choosing portfolio weights that are optimal with respect to his or her subjective belief about the true return distribution.[16]

[16]An alternative way of dealing with parameter uncertainty is "robust control," where instead of improving on the statistical side of the problem, the decision maker adjusts the optimization problem. For example, in the max-min approach pioneered by Hansen and Sargent (1995), the decision maker maximizes expected utility evaluated under a worst-case return distribution (for a set of candidate distribution). See Maenhout (2004, 2006) for applications of robust control to portfolio choice problems.

In the presence of statistical uncertainty about the parameters or even about the parameterization of the data generating process, this subjective return distribution may be quite different from the results of plugging point estimates in the data generating process. As a result, the econometrician's optimal portfolio weights can also be quite different from the plug-in estimates described earlier.

3.2.1. Parameter Uncertainty

Consider, for illustrative purposes, a single-period or myopic portfolio choice with i.i.d. returns. We can write the expected utility maximization more explicitly as:

$$\max_{x_t} \int u\big(x_t' r_{t+1} + R^f\big) p(r_{t+1}|\theta) \mathrm{d}r_{t+1}, \tag{3.31}$$

where $p(r_{t+1}|\theta)$ denotes the true return distribution parameterized by θ. Until now, it was implicitly assumed that this problem is well posed, in the sense that the investor has all information required to solve it. However, suppose instead that the investor knows the parametric form of the return distribution but not the true parameter values, which, of course, is far more realistic. In that case, the problem cannot be solved as it is because the investor does not know for which parameter values θ to maximize the expected utility.

There are at least three ways for the investor to proceed. First, the investor can naively use estimates of the parameters in place of the true parameter values, analogous to the plug-in estimation approach (except now it is the investor who needs to make a decision, not an econometrician drawing inferences, relying on point estimates). The resulting portfolio weights are optimal only if the estimates happen to coincide with the true values, a zero-probability event in finite samples, and suboptimal otherwise. Second, the investor can consider the parameter values that correspond to the *worst case* outcome under some prespecified set of possible parameter values, leading to extremely conservative portfolio weights that are robust, as opposed to optimal, with respect to the uncertainty about the parameters (a decision theoretic approach called robust control). Third, the investor can eliminate the dependence of the optimization problem on the unknown parameters by replacing the true return distribution with a subjective distribution that depends only on the data the investor observes and on personal ex-ante beliefs the investor may have had about the unknown parameters before examining the data. The resulting portfolio weights are optimal with respect to this subjective return distribution but suboptimal with respect to the true return distribution. However, this suboptimality is irrelevant, in some sense, because the truth is never revealed anyway. To the extent that the subjective return distribution incorporates all of the available information (as oppose to just a point estimate or worst case outcome), this third approach is the most appealing to many.

Zellner and Chetty (1965), Klein and Bawa (1976), and Brown (1978) were among the first to advocate using subjective return distributions in portfolio choice problems. Given the data Y_T and a prior belief about of the parameters $p_0(\theta)$, the posterior distribution of the parameters is given by Bayes' theorem as:

$$p(\theta|Y_T) = \frac{p(Y_T|\theta)\, p_0(\theta)}{p(Y_T)} \propto p(Y_T|\theta)\, p_0(\theta), \tag{3.32}$$

where the distribution of the data conditional on the parameters can also be interpreted as the likelihood function $\mathcal{L}(\theta|Y_T)$. This posterior distribution can then be used to *integrate out* the unknown parameters from the return distribution to obtain the investor's *subjective* (since it involves subjective priors) return distribution:

$$p\big(r_{t+1}|Y_T\big) = \int p\big(r_{t+1}|\theta\big)p\big(\theta|Y_T\big)\mathrm{d}\theta. \tag{3.33}$$

Finally, we simply replace the true return distribution in the expected utility maximization with this subjective return distribution and solve for the optimal portfolio weights.

Formally, the investor solves the problem:

$$\max_{x_t} \int u\big(x_t' r_{t+1} + R^f\big)p\big(r_{t+1}|Y_T\big)\mathrm{d}r_{t+1}, \tag{3.34}$$

which can we can rewrite, using the construction of the posterior, as:

$$\max_{x_t} \int \left[\int u\big(x_t' r_{t+1} + R^f\big)p\big(r_{t+1}|\theta\big)\mathrm{d}r_{t+1}\right]p\big(\theta|Y_T\big)\mathrm{d}\theta. \tag{3.35}$$

Comparing Eqs. (3.31) and (3.35), it is now clear how the investor overcomes the issue of not knowing the true parameter values. Rather than solving the optimization problem for a single choice of parameter values, the investor effectively solves an *average* problem over all possible set of parameter values, where the expected utility of any given set of parameter values, the expression in brackets above, is weighted by the investor's subjective probability of these parameter values corresponding to the truth.

Uninformative Priors The choice of prior is critical in this Bayesian approach. Priors are either informative or uninformative. Uninformative priors contain little if any information about the parameters and lead to results that are comparable, but not identical in finite samples, to plug-in estimates. Consider the simplest possible example of a single i.i.d. normal return with constant mean μ and volatility σ. Assume initially that the volatility is known. Given a standard uninformative prior for the mean, $p(\mu) \propto c$, the posterior distribution of the mean is

$$p(\mu|\sigma, Y_T) = \mathrm{N}\big[\hat{\mu}, \sigma^2/T\big], \tag{3.36}$$

where $\hat{\mu}$ is the usual sample mean. This posterior distribution of the mean then implies the following predictive return distribution:

$$p(r_{T+1}|\sigma, Y_T) = \int p(r_{T+1}|\mu,\sigma)p(\mu|\sigma, Y_T)\mathrm{d}\mu = \mathrm{N}\big[\hat{\mu}, \sigma^2 + \sigma^2/T\big]. \quad (3.37)$$

Comparing this predictive return distribution to the plug-in estimate $\mathrm{N}[\hat{\mu}, \sigma^2]$ illustrates one of the effects of parameter uncertainty. In the Bayesian portfolio choice problem, the variance of returns is inflated because, intuitively, returns differ from the sample mean for two reasons. Returns have a known variance around the unknown true mean of σ^2, and the sample mean is a noisy estimate of the true mean with a variance of σ^2/T. The posterior variance of returns is therefore $\sigma^2 + \sigma^2/T$.

Relaxing the assumption of a known volatility, an uninformative prior of the form $p(\mu, \ln\sigma) = c$ leads to the joint posterior distribution of the parameters:

$$p(\mu,\sigma|Y_T) \propto \frac{1}{\sigma^{N+1}}\exp\left\{-\frac{N(\mu-\hat{\mu})^2}{2\sigma^2} - \frac{(N-1)\hat{\sigma}^2}{2\sigma^2}\right\}, \quad (3.38)$$

which, in turn, implies the following predictive return distribution:

$$p(r_{T+1}|Y_T) = \iint p(r_{T+1}|\mu,\sigma)p(\mu,\sigma|Y_T)\mathrm{d}\mu\,\mathrm{d}\sigma = t\big[\hat{\mu}, \hat{\sigma}^2 + \hat{\sigma}^2/T, N-1\big], \quad (3.39)$$

where $t[m, s^2, v]$ denotes a Student-t distribution with mean m, variance s^2, and v degrees of freedom. The mean of the predictive distribution is again the sample mean and the variance is analogous to the case with a known volatility, except with sample estimates. The only difference between the posteriors (3.37) and (3.39) is the distributional form. Specifically, since the t distribution has fatter tails than the normal distribution, especially for small degrees of freedom, parameter uncertainty about the volatility causes the tails of the posterior return distribution to fatten, relative to the case with a known volatility. Intuitively, the predictive return distribution turns into a mixture of normal distributions, each with a different volatility, as the uncertainty about the volatility is averaged out.

Although the aforementioned discussion is fairly simplistic, in that it only deals with a single risky asset and i.i.d. returns, the basic intuition extends directly to cases with multiple assets and with more complicated return models. In general, uncertainty about unconditional and/or conditional first moments tends to increase the posterior variance of returns, and uncertainty about unconditional and/or conditional second moments tends to fatten the tails of the predictive return distribution.

Equations (3.37) and (3.39) illustrate that there are differences between the Bayesian portfolio choice and plug-in estimates. However, it is important to acknowledge that, at least in this simple i.i.d. example, these differences are in practice a small-sample phenomenon. For example, suppose the volatility is known to be 18%. With only 12 observations, the posterior volatility of returns in Eq. (3.37) is equal to $\sqrt{(1 + 1/12)} \times 18\% = 18.75\%$. Parameter uncertainty increase the return volatility by 4%. With a more realistic sample size of 120 observations, however, the posterior volatility of returns is $\sqrt{1 + 1/120} \times 18\% = 18.07\%$, an increase of a negligible 0.4%. Similarly, in the case with an unknown volatility. The 5% critical value of the t distribution with 11 degrees of freedom (for $T = 12$) equals 2.18, considerably larger than 1.96 under normality. However, with 119 degrees of freedom, the critical value is 1.97, which means that the predictive distribution is virtually Gaussian (and in fact identical to its plug-in counterpart).

Guided by the long-held belief that returns unpredictable, the initial papers on parameter uncertainty were formulated in the context of i.i.d. normal returns. Following the relatively recent evidence of return predictability, Kandel and Stambaugh (1996) and Barberis (2000) reexamine the role of parameter uncertainty when returns are predictable by the dividend yield in the context of the VAR model (2.16). In particular, Barberis (2000) documents that, even in moderate size sample, parameter uncertainty can lead to substantial differences in the optimal allocation to stocks in a long-horizon portfolio choice problem. The intuition for this result is the following. As the horizon increases, the variance of returns around the true conditional mean increases linearly, because returns are conditionally uncorrelated. The variance of the estimated conditional mean around the true conditional mean, however, increases more than linearly, because the estimation error is the same in every future time period (ignoring the important issue of learning). As a result, the contribution of parameter uncertainty to the posterior variance of returns increases in relative terms as the return horizon increases.

Informative Priors Most applications of Bayesian statistics in finance employ uninformative priors, with the reasoning that empirical results with uninformative priors are most comparable to results obtained through classical statistics and therefore are easier to relate to the literature. In the context of an investor's portfolio choice problem, however, the main advantage of the Bayesian approach is the ability to incorporate subjective information through informative priors. Because portfolio choice problems are by nature subjective decision problems, not objective inference problems, there is no need to facilitate comparison.

The difficulty with using informative priors lies in maintaining analytic tractability of the posterior distributions. For this reason, the literature deals almost exclusively with so-called conjugate priors, for which the conditional posteriors are members of the same distributional class as the priors. For example, the most common conjugate prior problem involves a Gaussian likelihood function, a Gaussian prior for first moments, and an inverse gamma (or inverse Wishard in the multivariate case) prior for second moments. With this particular combination, the conditional posteriors of the first and second moments are once again Gaussian and inverse gamma, respectively. Conjugate priors are particularly convenient in problems that involve updating of previously formed posteriors with new data. In such problems, the old posterior becomes the new prior, which is then combined with the likelihood function evaluated at the new data. With conjugate priors, the updated posterior has the same distributional form as the old posterior.

To illustrate the role of informative priors and the similarities to classical shrinkage estimation, consider again the case of a single risky asset with i.i.d. normal returns and a known volatility. Assume that the investor has a normally distributed prior belief about μ centered at a prior mean of $\overline{\mu}$ with a variance of τ^2:

$$p(\mu) = \mathrm{N}[\overline{\mu}, \tau^2]. \tag{3.40}$$

Because of the conjugate structure, combining this prior with the likelihood function yields the posterior distribution:

$$p(\mu|\sigma, Y_T) = \mathrm{N}\left[\frac{\tau^2}{\tau^2 + \sigma^2/T}\hat{\mu} + \frac{\sigma^2/T}{\tau^2 + \sigma^2/T}\overline{\mu}, \frac{(\sigma^2/T)\tau^2}{\sigma^2/T + \tau^2}\right]. \tag{3.41}$$

The posterior mean is simply a relative precision weighted average of the sample and prior means. The smaller the prior uncertainty τ, the more weight is placed on the prior mean $\overline{\mu}$ and, conversely, the larger T or the smaller σ, both of which imply that the sample mean is more precisely estimated, the more weight is placed on the sample mean $\hat{\mu}$. Intuitively, the posterior mean shrinks the sample mean toward the prior mean, with the shrinkage factor depending on the relative precisions of the sample and prior means. The posterior variance is lower than the variance of the sample mean by a factor of $\tau^2/(\sigma^2/T + \tau^2)$, reflecting the fact that information is added through the informative prior. Finally, given the posterior of the mean, the predictive return distribution is obtained analogous to Eq. (3.37):

$$\begin{aligned} p(r_{T+1}|\sigma, Y_T) &= \int p(r_{T+1}|\mu, \sigma)p(\mu|\sigma, Y_T)\mathrm{d}\mu \\ &= \mathrm{N}\Bigg[\underbrace{\frac{\tau^2}{\tau^2 + \sigma^2/T}\hat{\mu} + \frac{\sigma^2/T}{\tau^2 + \sigma^2/T}\overline{\mu}}_{\mathrm{E}[\mu|\sigma, \mathcal{Y}_T]}, \sigma^2 + \underbrace{\frac{(\sigma^2/T)\tau^2}{\sigma^2/T + \tau^2}}_{\mathrm{var}[\mu|\sigma, \mathcal{Y}_T]}\Bigg]. \end{aligned} \tag{3.42}$$

There are many ways of coming up with a subjective guess for the prior mean $\overline{\mu}$. One approach considered in the statistics literature is to take a preliminary look at the data and simply estimate the prior by maximum likelihood. Frost and Savarino (1986) apply this so-called empirical Bayes approach to the mean–variance problem. Imposing a prior belief of equal means across assets and estimating this grand mean from the data, the resulting posterior mean is remarkably similar to the James–Stein shrinkage estimator.

3.2.2. Incorporating Economic Views and Models

Arguably a more intuitive and certainly a more popular way of specifying a prior in the portfolio choice context is to rely on the theoretical implications of an economic model. The most famous example of this approach is Black and Litterman (1992), who use as prior the risk premia implied by mean–variance preferences and market equilibrium. Before elaborating on their model and two other examples of incorporating economic models, I describe a more general framework for combining two sources of information about expected returns, through Bayes theorem, into a single predictive return distribution.

Mixed Estimation Mixed estimation was first developed by Theil and Goldberger (1961) as a way to update the Bayesian inferences drawn from old data with the information contained in a set of new data. It applies more generally, however, to the problem of combining information from two data sources into a single posterior distribution. The following description of mixed estimation is tailored to a return forecasting problem and follows closely the econometric framework underlying the Black–Litterman model (GSAM Quantitative Strategies Group, 2000). A very similar setup is described by Scowcroft and Sefton (2003).

Assume excess returns are i.i.d. normal:

$$r_{t+1} \sim \text{MVN}[\mu, \Sigma]. \tag{3.43}$$

The investor starts with a set of benchmark beliefs about the risk premia:

$$p(\mu) = \text{MVN}[\overline{\mu}, \Lambda]. \tag{3.44}$$

which can be based on theoretical predictions, previous empirical analysis, or dated forecasts. In addition to these benchmark beliefs, the investor has a set of new views or forecasts v about a subset of $K \leq N$ linear combinations of returns $P\,r_{t+1}$, where P is a $K \times N$ matrix selecting and combining returns into portfolios for which the investor is able to express views. The new views are assumed to be unbiased but imprecise, with distribution:

$$p(v|\mu) = \text{MVN}[P\mu, \Omega]. \tag{3.45}$$

Besides the benchmark beliefs, the estimator requires three inputs: the portfolio selection matrix P, the portfolio return forecasts v, and the forecast error covariance matrix Ω.

To demonstrate the flexibility of this specification, suppose there are three assets. The investor somehow forecasts the risk premium of the first two assets to be 5% and 15%, but, for whatever reason, is unable or unwilling to express a view on the risk premium of the third asset. This scenario corresponds to:

$$P = \begin{bmatrix} 1 & 0 & 0 \\ 0 & 1 & 0 \end{bmatrix} \quad \text{and} \quad v = \begin{bmatrix} 0.05 \\ 0.15 \end{bmatrix}. \tag{3.46}$$

If instead of expressing views on the levels of the risk premia, the investor can only forecast the difference between the risk premia to be 10%, the matrices are

$$P = \begin{bmatrix} 1 & -1 & 0 \end{bmatrix} \quad \text{and} \quad v = \begin{bmatrix} -0.10 \end{bmatrix}. \tag{3.47}$$

Once the views have been formalized, the investor also needs to specify their accuracy and correlations through the choice of Ω. In the first scenario, for instance, the investor might be highly confident in the forecast of the first risk premium, with a 1% forecasts error volatility, but less certain about the forecast of the second risk premium, with a 10% forecast error volatility. Assuming further that the two forecasts are obtained independently, the covariance matrix of the forecast errors is

$$\Omega = \begin{bmatrix} 0.01^2 & 0 \\ 0 & 0.10^2 \end{bmatrix}. \tag{3.48}$$

The off-diagonal elements of Ω capture correlations between the forecasts. Specifically, high confidence in the forecast of $\mu_1 - \mu_2$ is intuitively equivalent to very low confidence in the forecasts of μ_1 and μ_2, but with a high correlation between the two forecast errors.

Combining Eqs (3.45) and (3.45) using Bayes' theorem:

$$\begin{aligned} p(\mu|v) &\propto p(v|\mu)\, p(\mu) \\ &= \text{MVN}\big[\text{E}[\mu|v], \text{var}[\mu, v]\big], \end{aligned} \tag{3.49}$$

where the posterior moments of μ are given by:

$$\begin{aligned} \text{E}[\mu|v] &= \big[\Lambda^{-1} + P'\Omega P\big]^{-1}\big[\Lambda^{-1}\overline{\mu} + P'\Omega^{-1}v\big] \\ \text{var}[\mu|v] &= \big[\Lambda^{-1} + P'\Omega P\big]^{-1}. \end{aligned} \tag{3.50}$$

Finally, assuming Σ is known, the predictive return distribution is given by:

$$p(r_{T+1}|v) = \text{MVN}\Big[\text{E}[\mu|v], \big[\Sigma^{-1} + \text{var}[\mu|v]^{-1}\big]^{-1}\Big]. \tag{3.51}$$

Alternatively, if Σ is unknown, the predictive return distribution with conjugate prior for the covariance matrix is multivariate t with the same first and second moments, analogous to the univariate case in Eq. (3.39).

As in the more general case of informative priors, the posterior mean is simply a relative precision weighted average of the benchmark means $\overline{\mu}$ and the forecasts v (a form of shrinkage). The advantage of this particular mixed estimation setup is the ability to input forecasts of subsets and linear combinations of the risk premia. This is particularly relevant in real-life applications where forecasting the returns on every security in the investable universe (e.g., AMEX, NASDAQ, and NYSE) is practically impossible.

Black–Litterman Model The Black and Litterman (1992) model is an application of this mixed estimation approach using economically motivated benchmark beliefs $p(\mu)$ and proprietary forecasts ν (obtained through empirical studies, security analysis, or other forecasting techniques). The benchmark beliefs are obtained by inferring the risk premia that would induce a mean–variance investor to hold all assets in proportion to their observed market capitalizations. Since such risk premia clear the market by setting the supply of shares equal to demand at the current price, they are labeled equilibrium risk premia.

More specifically, the equilibrium risk premia are calculated by reversing the inputs and outputs of the mean–variance optimization problem. In the mean–variance problem (2.8), the inputs are the mean vector μ and covariance matrix Σ. The output is the vector of optimal portfolio weights $x^{\star} = (1/\gamma)\Sigma^{-1}\mu$. Now suppose that the market as a whole acts as a mean–variance optimizer, then, in equilibrium, the risk premia and covariance matrix must be such that the corresponding optimal portfolio weights equal the observed market capitalization weights, denoted $x^{\star}_{\text{mkt}}$. Assuming a known covariance matrix, the relationship between the market capitalization weights and the equilibrium risk premia μ_{equil} is therefore given by $x^{\star}_{\text{mkt}} = (1/\gamma)\Sigma^{-1}\mu_{\text{equil}}$. Solving for the equilibrium risk premia:

$$\mu_{\text{equil}} = \gamma \Sigma\, x^{\star}_{\text{mkt}}. \tag{3.52}$$

The inputs to this calculation are the market capitalization weights, return covariance matrix, and aggregate risk aversion γ. The output is a vector of implied equilibrium risk premia.

Black and Litterman (1992) center the benchmark beliefs at these equilibrium risk premia and assume a precision matrix Λ proportional to the return covariance matrix Σ:

$$p(\mu) = \text{MVN}[\mu_{\text{equil}}, \lambda \Sigma]. \tag{3.53}$$

The constant λ measures the strength of the investor's belief in equilibrium. For instance, a value of $\lambda = 1/T$ places the benchmark beliefs on equal footing with sample means. Combining the benchmark beliefs with proprietary views ν results in a posterior distribution for the risk premia with the following moments:

$$\begin{aligned} \text{E}[\mu|\nu] &= \left[(\lambda\Sigma)^{-1} + P'\Omega^{-1}P\right]^{-1}\left[(\lambda\Sigma)^{-1}\mu_{\text{equil}} + P'\Omega^{-1}\nu\right] \\ &= \left[(\lambda\Sigma)^{-1} + P'\Omega^{-1}P\right]^{-1}\left[\frac{\gamma}{\lambda}x^{\star}_{\text{mkt}} + P'\Omega^{-1}\nu\right] \\ \text{var}[\mu|\nu] &= \left[(\lambda\Sigma)^{-1} + P'\Omega^{-1}P\right]^{-1}, \end{aligned} \tag{3.54}$$

where the second line for the posterior mean, which follows from substituting Eq. (3.52) into the first line, makes clear the dependence of the mixed estimator on the observed market capitalization weights.

The idea of implied equilibrium risk premia is best illustrated through an example. Table 5.3 presents descriptive statistics for the returns on six size and book-to-market sorted stock portfolios. Table 5.4 shows in the third column the corresponding market capitalization weights for December 2003 and in the next four columns the equilibrium risk premia implied by the covariance matrix from Table 5.3 and relative risk aversion ranging from $\gamma = 1$ to $\gamma = 7.5$. For comparison, the last column repeats the sample risk premia from Table 5.3.

The results in the second table illustrate two important features of the implied equilibrium risk premia. First, the levels of the risk premia depend on the level of risk aversion, which therefore needs to be calibrated before using the results in the mixed estimator. One way to calibrate γ is to set the implied Sharpe ratio of the market portfolio to a sensible level. For instance, with $\gamma = 5$ the annualized Sharpe ratio of the market portfolio is 0.78, which is reasonable though still on the high side of historical experience for the market index. The second striking result in the table is that the implied equilibrium

Table 5.3 Descriptive statistics of six portfolios of all AMEX, NASDAQ, and NYSE stocks sorted by their market capitalization and book-to-market ratio

Size	Book to market	Risk premia (%)	Volatility (%)	Correlations				
Small	Low	5.61	24.56	1				
Small	Medium	12.75	17.01	0.926	1			
Small	High	14.36	16.46	0.859	0.966	1		
Big	Low	9.72	17.07	0.784	0.763	0.711	1	
Big	Medium	10.59	15.05	0.643	0.768	0.763	0.847	1
Big	High	10.44	13.89	0.555	0.698	0.735	0.753	0.913

Monthly data from January 1983 through December 2003.

Table 5.4 Equilibrium risk premia implied by market capitalization weights of six portfolios of all AMEX, NASDAQ, and NYSE stocks sorted by their market capitalization and book-to-market ratio on December 2003 and mean–variance preferences with different levels of risk aversion

Size	Book to market	Market weight (%)	Equilibrium risk premia (%)				Historical risk premia (%)
			$\gamma = 1$	$\gamma = 2.5$	$\gamma = 5$	$\gamma = 7.5$	
Small	Low	2.89	3.07	7.69	15.37	23.06	5.61
Small	Medium	3.89	2.21	5.52	11.03	16.55	12.75
Small	High	2.21	2.04	5.11	10.22	15.33	14.36
Big	Low	59.07	2.62	6.55	13.10	19.64	9.72
Big	Medium	23.26	2.18	5.44	10.88	16.32	10.59
Big	High	8.60	1.97	4.91	9.83	14.74	10.44

risk premia are quite different from the empirical risk premia, in particular for the small and low book-to-market portfolio. In fact, the two sets of risk premia are *negatively* correlated in the cross-section (a correlation coefficient of -0.83). A mixed estimator that places equal weights on the equilibrium risk premia and the sample risk premia, which corresponds to using $\lambda = 1/T$ and historical moments for v, therefore generates return forecasts that are substantially less variable in the cross-section than either the equilibrium risk premia or the sample risk premia.

Return Forecasting with a Belief in No Predictability Another interesting example of incorporating economic views is the problem of forecasting returns with an prior belief in no predictability, studied by Kandel and Stambaugh (1996) as well as Connor (1997). Consider the regression:[17]

$$r_{t+1} = a + b\,z_t + \varepsilon_{t+1}, \tag{3.55}$$

where $\varepsilon_{t+1} \sim \mathrm{N}\left[0, \sigma_\varepsilon^2\right]$ and z_t are assumed exogenous with zero mean and a variance of σ_z^2. Using a standard OLS approach, the one-period ahead return forecast is given by $\hat{a} + \hat{b}\,z_T$, with $\hat{b}_{\text{ols}} = \hat{\sigma}_{z,r}/\hat{\sigma}_z^2$. Unfortunately, this forecast tends to be very noisy because the regression usually has an R^2 around 1% and a t-statistic of the slope coefficient close to two. The potential for large estimation error renders the forecast practically useless, particularly when the forecast is used as an input to an error maximizing portfolio optimizer.

Kandel and Stambaugh (1996) and Connor (1997) recommend imposing an informative prior centered on the case of no predictability, which implies that the slope coefficient should be zero. Specifically, using the prior $p(b) = \mathrm{N}\left[0, \sigma_b^2\right]$ in a standard Bayesian regression setup yields a posterior of the slope coefficient with a mean of:

$$\hat{b}_{\text{Bayes}} = \left[\frac{T\hat{\sigma}_z^2/\hat{\sigma}_\varepsilon^2}{\left(T\hat{\sigma}_z^2/\hat{\sigma}_\varepsilon^2\right) + \left(1/\sigma_b^2\right)}\right]\hat{b}_{\text{ols}}. \tag{3.56}$$

As expected, the OLS estimate is shrunk toward the prior mean of zero, with a shrinkage factor that depends on the relative precisions of the OLS estimate and the prior mean. The critical ingredient of this approach is obviously the prior variance σ_b^2.

Because it is difficult to specify a sensible value for this prior variance ex-ante, especially without knowing σ_r^2 and σ_z^2, Connor (1997) reformulates the problem in a more intuitive and practical way. Define:

$$\rho = \mathrm{E}\left[\frac{R^2}{1-R^2}\right], \tag{3.57}$$

[17] Although often associated in the literature, no predictability does not necessarily corresponding to market efficiency. In particular, returns can well be predictable in an efficient market with time-varying preferences or fundamental uncertainty.

Table 5.5 Shrinkage factor for the slope coefficient of a univariate return forecast regression with belief in market efficiency for different sample sizes and expected degrees of return predictability

$\rho \simeq E[R^2]$ (%)	$T = 24$	$T = 48$	$T = 60$	$T = 120$
0.50	0.11	0.19	0.23	0.38
0.75	0.15	0.26	0.31	0.47
1.00	0.19	0.32	0.38	0.55
2.00	0.32	0.49	0.55	0.71
3.00	0.42	0.59	0.64	0.78

which, for the low values of R^2 we observe in practice, is approximately equal to the expected degree of predictability $\mathrm{E}[R^2]$. Equation (3.56) can then be rewritten as:

$$\hat{b}_{\text{Bayes}} = \left[\frac{T}{T + (1/\rho)}\right]\hat{b}_{\text{ols}}, \tag{3.58}$$

where the degree of shrinkage toward zero depends only on the sample size T and on the expected degree of predictability ρ.

The appealing feature of the alternative formulation (3.58) is that the shrinkage factor applies generically to any returns forecasting regression with a prior belief in no predictability (or a regression slope of zero). Table 5.5 evaluates the shrinkage factor for different sample sizes and expected degrees of predictability. The extend of shrinkage toward zero is striking. With a realistic expected R^2 of 1% and a sample size between 5 and 10 years, the OLS estimate is shrunk roughly half-way toward zero (62% for $T = 60$ and 45% for $T = 120$).

Connor (1997) further shows that in the case of a multivariate return forecast regression $r_{t+1} = b'z_t + \varepsilon_{t+1}$, the shrinkage factor applied to each slope coefficient is also given by Eq. (3.58), except that the expected degree of return predictability ρ is replaced by a "marginal" counterpart ρ_i. This marginal expected degree of return predictability simply measures the marginal contribution of variable i to the expected regression R^2. For example, suppose the expected R^2 of a regression with three predictors is 1% and $T = 60$. If each variable contributes equally to the overall predictability, $\rho_i = 0.33\%$ and each slope coefficient is shrunk about 84% toward zero. In contrast, if the first variable accounts for 2/3 of the overall predictability, its slope coefficient is only shrunk 71% toward zero.

Cross-Sectional Portfolio Choice with a Belief in an Asset Pricing Model The third example of incorporation economic beliefs, this time originating from an equilibrium asset pricing model, is formulated by Pastor (2000). Suppose returns are generated by a single-factor model:

$$r_{i,t+1} = \alpha_i + \beta_i\, r_{m,t+1} + \varepsilon_{i,t+1} \tag{3.59}$$

with uncorrelated residuals $\varepsilon_{i,t+1} \sim \mathrm{N}[0, \sigma_\varepsilon^2]$. The theoretical prediction of the CAPM is that differences in expected returns in the cross-section are fully captured by differences in market betas and that $\alpha_i = 0$, for all stocks i. Therefore, an investor's ex-ante belief in the CAPM can be captured through an informative prior for the stacked intercepts α:

$$p(\alpha) = \mathrm{MVN}[0, \sigma_\alpha I]. \tag{3.60}$$

This prior is centered at zero, the theoretical prediction of the CAPM, with a dispersion σ_α measuring the strength of the investor's belief in the equilibrium model.

Combining the informative prior (3.60) with uninformative priors for the market betas and residual variances, the resulting posterior distribution has the following means:

$$\begin{aligned} \mathrm{E}[\alpha | Y_T] &= (1 - \delta)\hat{\alpha}_{\mathrm{ols}} \\ \mathrm{E}[\beta | Y_T] &= \hat{\beta}_{\mathrm{ols}} + \xi \end{aligned} \tag{3.61}$$

Intuitively, the intercepts are shrunk toward zero with the shrinkage factor δ depending, as usual, on T, σ_m^2, σ_ε^2, and σ_α^2. However, the problem is somewhat more complicated because, as the intercepts are shrunk toward zero, the market betas also change by ξ to better fit the cross-sectional differences in expected returns. Pastor (2000) provides expressions for δ and ξ and also considers the case of multifactor asset pricing models. Further extensions and applications are pursued by Pastor and Stambaugh (2000, 2002) and Avramov (2004).

3.2.3. Model Uncertainty

The idea of dealing with parameter uncertainty by averaging the return distribution over plausible parameter values can be naturally extended to dealing with model uncertainty by averaging over plausible model specifications. Define a model M_j as being a particular specification of the conditional return distribution and consider a finite set of J models containing the true model $M \in \{M_1, M_2, \ldots, M_J\}$. For any model j, the return distribution is $p(r_{t+1} | M_j, \theta_j)$, where the parameter vector θ_j can have different dimensions across models. Analogous to parameter uncertainty, the problem of model uncertainty is that the investor does not know which of the models to use in the portfolio choice problem.

Assume the investor can express a prior belief about each model j being the true data generator, $p(M_j)$, as well as a prior belief about the parameters of each model, $p(\theta_j | M_j)$. Combining these priors and the likelihood function, $p(Y_T | M_j, \theta_j)$, Bayes' theorem implies for each model the following posterior model probability:

$$p(M_j | Y_T) = \frac{p(Y_T | M_j)\, p(M_j)}{\sum_{j=1}^{J} p(Y_T | M_j)\, p(M_j)}, \tag{3.62}$$

where

$$p(Y_T | M_j) = \int p(Y_T | M_j, \theta_j)\, p(\theta_j | M_k) \mathrm{d}\theta_j \tag{3.63}$$

denotes the marginal likelihood of model j after integrating out the parameters θ_j.

The posterior model probabilities serve a number of purposes. First, they help to characterize the degree of model uncertainty. For instance, suppose there are five plausible models. Model uncertainty is obviously more prevalent when each model has a posterior probability of 20%, than when one model dominates with a posterior probability of 90%. Second, the posterior model probabilities can be used to select a model with highest posterior probability, or to eliminate models with negligible probabilities from the set of all models, thereby reducing the inherently high dimensionality of model uncertainty. Third, the posterior model probabilities can be used to construct a predictive return distribution by averaging across all models according to their posterior probabilities. This so-called model averaging approach is particularly useful when the degree of model uncertainty is too high for the investor to confidently single out a model as being the true data generator. Model averaging is analogous to averaging the return distribution over all parameter values according to the posterior distribution of the parameters [as in Eq. (3.35)].

Formally, we construct the following posterior probability weighted average return distribution:

$$p(r_{T+1}|Y_T) = \sum_{j=1}^{J} p(r_{T+1}|Y_T, M_j)\, p(M_j|Y_T), \tag{3.64}$$

where

$$p(r_{T+1}|Y_T, M_j) = \int p(r_{t+1}|M_j, \theta_j)\, p(\theta_j, Y_T, M_j) \mathrm{d}\theta_j \tag{3.65}$$

denotes the marginal return distribution after integrating out the parameters θ_j. An extremely convenient property of this averaged predictive return distribution is that, due to the linearity of the average, all noncentral moments are also model-averaged:

$$\mathrm{E}\left[r_{T+1}^q | Y_T\right] = \sum_{j=1}^{J} \mathrm{E}\left[r_{T+1}^q | Y_T, M_j\right] p(M_j|Y_T), \tag{3.66}$$

for any order q. Equation (3.66) can be used to construct (subjective) mean–variance efficient portfolio weights using as inputs the posterior return moments implied by each model as well as the posterior model probabilities.

Although intuitive and theoretically elegant, the practical implementation of model averaging is less straightforward, both from a computational and conceptual perspective. There are at least two computational issues. First, the marginal distributions (3.63) and (3.65) are typically analytically intractable and need to be evaluated numerically. Second, even in the context of linear regression models, which are most common in practice, the model space with K regressors contains 2^K permutations, for which the marginal distributions have to be evaluated (numerically). With 15 regressors, a relatively modest number, there are over 32,000 models to consider. Both of these issues can be overcome, with some effort, using the Markov chain Monte Carlo (MCMC) approach of George and McCulloch (1993).

The conceptual difficulties lie in the choice of the model set and the choice of the model priors, which are intimately related issues. By having to specify ex-ante the list of all plausible models, the investor explicitly rules out all nonincluded models (by essentially setting the prior probabilities of those models to zero). Given the existing disagreement about return modeling in the literature, it is hard to imagine that any model can be ruled out ex-ante with certainty. As for the form of the priors, an obvious choice is an uninformative prior assigning equal probabilities to all models. However, such uniform prior may actually be surprisingly informative about certain subsets of models. For example, consider a linear forecasting regression framework with K regressors. Only one of the 2^K models does not include any forecasters and is therefore consistent with the notion of market efficiency. The remaining models all exhibit some violation of market efficiency. With equal priors of $1/2^K$ for each model, the implied prior odds against market efficiency are an overwhelming $(2^K - 1)$ to one. An economically more intuitive prior might assign a probability of $1/2$ to the no-predictability case and distribute the remaining probability of $1/2$ evenly across all other model. Unfortunately, even this approach does not fully resolve the issue. Suppose that two-thirds of the K predictors are (highly correlated) price-scaled variables (e.g., dividend yield, earnings yield, book-to-market) and one-third are (highly correlated) interest rate variables (e.g., short rate, long rate). In that case, an evenly distributed prior across all models with predictability assigns odds of 3:2 in favor of predictability due to price-scaled variables as opposed to interest rate variables. The point of this example is to illustrate that the choice of model priors is a tricky issue that requires careful economic reasoning.

There have been a number of recent applications of model averaging to portfolio choice. Specifically, Avramov (2002) and Cremers (2002) both consider model uncertainty in linear return forecasting models. Tu and Zhou (2004) considers uncertainty about the shape of the return distribution in cross-sectional applications, and Nigmatullin (2003) introduces model uncertainty in the nonparametric approach of Aït-Sahalia and Brandt (2001) (discussed further below). The fundamental conclusion of all of these papers is that model uncertainty contributes considerably to the subjective uncertainty faced by an investor. For example, Avramov (2002) demonstrates that the contribution of model uncertainty to the posterior variance of returns is as large or even larger than the contribution of parameter uncertainty discussed earlier. It is clear from this recent literature that model uncertainty is an important econometric aspect of portfolio choice.

4. ALTERNATIVE ECONOMETRIC APPROACH

The traditional econometric approach is fundamentally a two-step procedure. In the first step, the econometrician or investor models and draws inferences about the data generating process (either through plug-in estimation or by forming a subjective belief) to ultimately, in the second step, solve for the optimal portfolio weights. The majority of my own research on portfolio choice has focused on ways to skip the first step of modeling returns and directly draw inferences about the optimal portfolio weights from the data.

Besides the obvious fact that the optimal portfolio weights are the ultimate object of interest, there are at least three other benefits from focusing directly on the portfolio weights. First, the return modeling step is without doubt the Achilles' heel of the traditional econometric approach. There is vast disagreement even among finance academicians on how to best model returns, and the documented empirical relationships between economic state variables (forecasters) and return moments are usually quite tenuous. Combined, this leads to substantial risk of severe model mispecification and estimation error, which are subsequently accentuated by the portfolio optimizer in the second step of the procedure. The intuition underlying my research is that optimal portfolio weights are easier to model and estimate than conditional return distributions. A second but related benefit of focusing on the portfolio weights is dimension reduction. Consider once again an unconditional mean–variance problem with 500 assets. The return modeling step involves more than 125,000 parameters, but the end-result of the two-step procedure are only 500 optimal portfolio weights. Focusing directly on the optimal portfolio weights therefore reduced considerably the room for model mispecification and estimation error. Third, drawing inferences about optimal portfolio weights lends itself naturally to using an expected utility-based loss function in a classical setting, as opposed to the obviously inconsistent practice of using standard squared error loss to estimate the return model in the first step and then switching to an expected utility function to solve for the optimal portfolio weights in the second step.

4.1. Parametric Portfolio Weights

The simplest way to directly estimate optimal portfolio weights is to parameterize the portfolio weights as functions of observable quantities (economic state variables and/or firm characteristics) and then solve for the parameters that maximize expected utility. This idea is developed in the context of single and multiperiod market timing problems by Brandt and Santa-Clara (2006) and in the context of a large cross-sectional portfolio choice problem by Brandt et al. (2009). Since the implementations in these two papers are somewhat different, yet complimentary, I explain each in turn.

4.1.1. Conditional Portfolio Choice by Augmenting the Asset Space

In Brandt and Santa-Clara (2006), we solve a market timing problem with parameterized portfolio weights of the form $x_t = \theta z_t$. We demonstrate that solving a conditional problem with parameterized portfolio weights is mathematically equivalent to solving an unconditional problem with an augmented asset space that includes naively managed zero-investment portfolios with excess returns of the form z_t times the excess return of each basis asset. This makes implementing our approach to dynamic portfolio choice no more difficult than implementing the standard Markowitz problem.

Consider first a single-period mean–variance problem. Assuming that the optimal portfolio weights are linear functions of K state variables z_t (which generally include a constant):

$$x_t = \theta z_t, \tag{4.1}$$

where θ is a $N \times K$ matrix of coefficients, the investor's conditional optimization problem is

$$\max_{\theta} \mathrm{E}_t\left[(\theta z_t)' r_{t+1}\right] - \frac{\gamma}{2} \operatorname{var}_t\left[(\theta z_t)' r_{t+1}\right]. \tag{4.2}$$

We use the following result from linear algebra:

$$(\theta z_t)' r_{t+1} = z_t' \theta' r_{t+1} = \operatorname{vec}(\theta)'(z_t \otimes r_{t+1}), \tag{4.3}$$

where $\operatorname{vec}(\theta)$ stacks the columns of θ and $\otimes$ denotes a Kronecker product, and define:

$$\begin{aligned} \tilde{x} &= \operatorname{vec}(\theta) \\ \tilde{r}_{t+1} &= z_t \otimes r_{t+1}. \end{aligned} \tag{4.4}$$

The investor's conditional problem can then be written as:

$$\max_{\tilde{x}} \mathrm{E}_t\left[\tilde{x}' \tilde{r}_{t+1}\right] - \frac{\gamma}{2} \operatorname{var}_t\left[\tilde{x}' \tilde{r}_{t+1}\right]. \tag{4.5}$$

Since the same $\tilde{x}$ maximizes the conditional mean–variance tradeoff at all dates t (hence no time-subscript), it also maximizes the unconditional mean–variance tradeoff:

$$\max_{\tilde{x}} \mathrm{E}\left[\tilde{x}' \tilde{r}_{t+1}\right] - \frac{\gamma}{2} \operatorname{var}\left[\tilde{x}' \tilde{r}_{t+1}\right], \tag{4.6}$$

which corresponds simply to the problem of finding the unconditional mean–variance optimal portfolio weights $\tilde{x}$ for the expanded set of $N \times K$ assets with returns $\tilde{r}_{t+1}$. The expanded set of assets can be interpreted as managed portfolios, each of which invests in a single basis asset an amount proportional to the value of one of the state variables. We therefore label these expanded set of assets "conditional portfolios." Given the solution to the unconditional mean–variance problem:

$$\tilde{x}^{\star} = \frac{1}{\gamma} \operatorname{var}[\tilde{r}_{t+1}]^{-1} \mathrm{E}[r_{t+1}], \tag{4.7}$$

we recover the conditional weight invested in each of the basis assets at any time t by simply adding up the corresponding products of elements of $\tilde{x}^{\star}$ and z_t in Eq. (4.1).

The idea of augmenting the asset space with naively managed portfolios extends to the multiperiod case. For example, consider a two-period mean–variance problem:

$$\max \mathrm{E}_t\left[r_{p,t\rightarrow t+2}\right] - \frac{\gamma}{2} \operatorname{var}_t\left[r_{p,t\rightarrow t+2}\right], \tag{4.8}$$

where $r_{p,t\rightarrow t+2}$ denotes the excess portfolio return of a two-period investment strategy:

$$\begin{aligned} r_{p,t\rightarrow t+2} &= \left(R_t^f + x_t' r_{t+1}\right)\left(R_{t+1}^f + x_{t+1}' r_{t+2}\right) - R_t^f R_{t+1}^f \\ &= x_t'\left(R_{t+1}^f r_{t+1}\right) + x_{t+1}'\left(R_t^f r_{t+2}\right) + \left(x_t' r_{t+1}\right)\left(x_{t+1}' r_{t+2}\right). \end{aligned} \tag{4.9}$$

The first line of this equation shows that $r_{p,t\rightarrow t+2}$ is a two-period excess return. The investor borrows a dollar at date t and allocates it to the risky and risk-free assets according to the first-period portfolio weights x_t. At $t+1$, the one-dollar investment results in $\left(R_t^f + x_t^{\top} r_{t+1}\right)$ dollars, which the investor then allocates again to the risky and risk-free assets according to the second-period portfolio weights x_{t+1}. Finally, at $t+2$, the investor has $\left(R_t^f + x_t^{\top} r_{t+1}\right)\left(R_{t+1}^f + x_{t+1}^{\top} r_{t+2}\right)$ dollars but pays $R_t^f R_{t+1}^f$ dollars for the principal and interest of the one-dollar loan. The second line of the equation decomposes the two-period excess return into three terms. The first two terms have a natural interpretation as the excess return of investing in the risk-free rate in the first (second) period and in the risky asset in the second (first) period. The third term captures the effect of compounding. Comparing the first two terms to the third, the latter is two orders of magnitude smaller than the former. The return $\left(x_t^{\top} r_{t+1}\right)\left(x_{t+1}^{\top} r_{t+2}\right)$ is a product of two single-period excess returns, which means that its units are of the order of 1/100th of a percent per year. The returns on the first two portfolios, in contrast, are products of a gross return $\left(R_t^f\right.$ or $\left.R_{t+1}^f\right)$ and an excess return $\left(r_{t+1}\right.$ or $\left.r_{t+2}\right)$, so their units are likely to be percent per year. Given that the compounding term is orders of magnitude smaller, we suggest to ignore it.

Without the compounding term, the two-period problem involves simply a choice between two intertemporal portfolios, one that holds the risky asset in the first period only and the other that holds the risky asset in the second period only. Using these two intertemporal portfolios, which we label "timing portfolios," we can solve the dynamic problem as a static mean–variance optimization. The solution is

$$\tilde{x}^{\star} = \frac{1}{\gamma} \operatorname{var}[\tilde{r}_{t\rightarrow t+2}]^{-1}\, \mathrm{E}[\tilde{r}_{t\rightarrow t+2}], \tag{4.10}$$

with $\tilde{r}_{t\rightarrow t+2} = \left[R_{t+1}^f r_{t+1}, R_t^f r_{t+2}\right]$. The first N elements of $\tilde{x}$, corresponding to $R_{t+1}^f r_{t+1}$, represents the fraction of wealth invested in the risky assets in the first period, and the remaining elements, corresponding to $R_t^f r_{t+2}$, are for the risky assets in the second period.

In a general H-period problem, we proceed in exactly the same way. We construct a set of timing portfolios:

$$\tilde{r}_{t\rightarrow t+H} = \left\{ \prod_{\substack{i=0 \\ i\neq j}}^{H-1} R^f_{t+i} r_{t+j+1} \right\}_{j=0}^{H-1}, \tag{4.11}$$

where each term represents a portfolio that invests in risky assets in period $t+j$ and in the risk-free rate in all other periods $t+i$, with $i \neq j$, and obtain the mean–variance solution:

$$\tilde{x}^{\star} = \frac{1}{\gamma} \mathrm{var}[\tilde{r}_{t\rightarrow t+H}]^{-1} \, \mathrm{E}[\tilde{r}_{t\rightarrow t+H}] \tag{4.12}$$

In addition, we can naturally combine the ideas of conditional and timing portfolios. For this, we simply replace the risky returns r_{t+j+1} in Eq. (4.11) with the conditional portfolio returns $z_{t+j} \otimes r_{t+j+1}$. The resulting optimal portfolio weights then provide the optimal allocations to the conditional portfolios at each date $t+j$.

The critical property of the solutions (4.7) and (4.12) is that they depend only on the unconditional moments of the expanded set of assets and therefore do not require any assumptions about the conditional joint distribution of the returns and state variables (besides that the unconditional moments exist). In particular, the solutions do not require any assumptions about how the conditional moments of returns depend on the state variables or how the state variables evolve through time. Furthermore, the state variables can predict time-variation in the first, second, and, if we consider more general utility functions, even higher-order moments of returns. Notice also that the assumption and the optimal portfolio weights are linear functions of the state variables is innocuous because z_t can include non-linear transformations of a set of more basic state variables y_t. The linear portfolio weights can be interpreted as more general portfolio weight functions $x_t = g(y_t)$ for any $g(\cdot)$ that can be spanned by a polynomial expansion in the more basic state variables y_t.

The obvious appeal of our approach is its simplicity and the fact that all of the statistical techniques designed for the static mean–variance problem can be applied directly to the single- and multiperiod market timing problems. Naturally, this simplicity comes with drawbacks that are discussed and evaluated carefully in Brandt and Santa-Clara (2006). We also demonstrate in the chapter how our parametric portfolio weights relate to the more traditional approach of modeling returns and state variables with a VAR in logs (equation (2.16)). Finally, we provide an extensive empirical application.

4.1.2. Large-Scale Portfolio Choice with Parametric Weights

Our approach in Brandt et al. (2009) is similar, in that we parameterize the optimal portfolio weights, but is geared toward large-scale cross-sectional applications. Suppose that at each date t there are large number of N_t stocks in the investable universe. Each stock i has an excess return of $r_{i,t+1}$ from date t to $t+1$ and a vector of characteristics $y_{i,t}$ observed at date t. For example, the characteristics could be the market beta of the stock, the market capitalization of the stock, the book-to-market ratio of the stock, and the lagged 12-month return on the stock. The investor's problem is to choose the portfolio weights $x_{i,t}$ to maximize the expected utility of the portfolio return $r_{p,t+1} = \sum_{i=1}^{N_t} x_{i,t} r_{i,t+1}$.

We parameterize the optimal portfolio weights as a function of the characteristics:

$$x_{i,t} = \overline{x}_{i,t} + \frac{1}{N_t} \theta' \hat{y}_{i,t} \tag{4.13}$$

where $\overline{x}_{i,t}$ is the weight of stock i in a benchmark portfolio, θ is a vector of coefficients to be estimated, and $\hat{y}_{i,t}$ are the characteristics of stock i standardized cross-sectionally to have a zero mean and unit standard deviation across all stocks at date t. This particular parameterization captures the idea of active portfolio management relative to a performance benchmark. The intercept is the weight in the benchmark portfolio and the term $\theta'\hat{y}_{i,t}$ represents the deviations of the optimal portfolio from the benchmark. The characteristics are standardized for two reasons. First, the cross-sectional distribution of $\hat{y}_{i,t}$ is stationary through time, while that of $y_{i,t}$ can be nonstationary (depending on the characteristic). Second, the standardization implies that the cross-sectional average of $\theta'\hat{y}_{i,t}$ is zero, which means that the deviations of the optimal portfolio weights from the benchmark weights sum to zero, and that the optimal portfolio weights always sum to one. Finally, the term $1/N_t$ is a normalization that allows the portfolio weight function to be applied to an arbitrary number of stocks. Without this normalization, doubling the number of stocks without otherwise changing the cross-sectional distribution of the characteristics results in twice as aggressive allocations, although the investment opportunities are fundamentally unchanged.

The most important aspect of our parameterization is that the coefficients θ do not vary across assets or through time. Constant coefficients across assets implies that the portfolio policy only cares about the characteristics of the stocks, not the stocks themselves. The underlying economic idea is that the characteristics fully describe the stock for investment purposes. Constant coefficients through time means that the coefficients that maximize the investor's conditional expected utility at a given date are the same for all dates and therefore also maximize the investor's unconditional expected utility. This allows us to estimate θ by maximizing the sample analogue of the unconditional expected utility:

$$\begin{aligned} \max_{\theta} \frac{1}{T} \sum_{t=0}^{T-1} u(r_{p,t+1}) &= \frac{1}{T} \sum_{t=0}^{T-1} u\left(\sum_{i=1}^{N_t} x_{i,t} r_{i,t+1} \right) \\ &= \frac{1}{T} \sum_{t=0}^{T-1} u\left(\sum_{i=1}^{N_t} \left(\overline{x}_{i,t} + \frac{1}{N_t} \theta' \hat{y}_{i,t} \right) r_{i,t+1} \right), \end{aligned} \tag{4.14}$$

for some prespecified utility function (e.g., mean–variance, quadratic, or CRRA utility).

Our approach has several practical advantages. First, it allows us to optimize a portfolio with a very large number of stocks, as long as the dimensionality of the parameter vector is kept reasonably low. Second, but related, the optimal portfolio weights are less prone to error maximization and over-fitting because we optimize the entire portfolio by choosing only a few parameters. The optimized portfolio weights tend to be far less extreme than the portfolio weights resulting from a more standard plug-in approach. Third, our approach implicitly takes into account the dependence of expected returns, variances, covariances, and higher-order moments on the stock characteristics, to the extent that cross-sectional differences in these moments affect the expected utility of the portfolio returns.

We develop several extensions of our parametric portfolio weights approach in Brandt et al. (2009), including parameterizations that restrict the optimal portfolio weights to be nonnegative and nonlinear parameterizations that allow for interactions between characteristics (e.g., small stocks with high momentum). We also show how the idea of cross-sectionally parameterizing the optimal portfolio weights can be combined naturally with the idea of parametric market timing described earlier. In particular, to allow the impact of the characteristics on the optimal portfolio weights to vary through time as a function of the macroeconomic predictors z_t, we suggest the parameterization:

$$x_{i,t} = \overline{x}_{i,t} + \frac{1}{N_t}\theta'\left(z_t \otimes \hat{y}_{i,t}\right) \tag{4.15}$$

where $\otimes$ again denotes the Kronecker product of two vectors. As in the pure market timing case, the optimization problem can then be rewritten as a cross-sectionally parameterized portfolio choice for an augmented asset space with naively managed portfolios.

4.1.3. Nonparametric Portfolio Weights

Although parameterized portfolio weights overcome the dependence on return models, they still suffer from potential mispecification of the portfolio weight function. In Brandt (1999), I develop a nonparametric approach for estimating the optimal portfolio weights without explicitly modeling returns or portfolio weights, which can be used as a mis-pecification check. The idea of my nonparametric approach is to estimate the optimal portfolio weights from sample analogues of the FOCs or Euler equations (2.12). These Euler equations involve conditional expectations that cannot be conditioned down to unconditional expectations, because the portfolio weights solving the Euler equations are generally different across economic states and dates. Instead, I replace the conditional expectations with nonparametric regressions and then solve for the portfolio weights that satisfy the resulting sample analogs of the conditional Euler equations.

Consider a single-period portfolio choice. The optimal portfolio weights x_t are characterized by the conditional Euler equations $\mathrm{E}_t\left[u'\left(x_t{}'r_{t+1} + R_t^f\right)r_{t+1}\right] = 0$. Suppose the returns are i.i.d. so that the optimal portfolio weights are the same across all states. In that case, we can take unconditional expectations of the conditional Euler equations to obtain a set of unconditional Euler equations that characterize the optimal unconditional portfolio weights $x_t \equiv x$. Replacing these unconditional expectations with sample averages in the spirit of method of moments estimation yields the estimator:

$$\hat{x} = \left\{ x : \frac{1}{T} \sum_{t=1}^{T} u'\left(x' r_{t+1} + R_t^f\right) r_{t+1} = 0 \right\}. \tag{4.16}$$

The same logic applies to a time-varying return distribution, except that the Euler equations cannot be conditioned down because the optimal portfolio weights depend on the macroeconomic state variables z_t (and/or firm characteristics $y_{i,t}$). Instead, we can directly replace the conditional expectations with sample analogs, where the sample analog of a conditional expectation is a locally weighted (in state-space) sample average. For a given state realization $z_t = z$, the resulting estimator of the optimal portfolio weights is

$$\hat{x}(z) = \left\{ x : \frac{1}{Th_T^K} \sum_{t=1}^{T} \omega\left(\frac{z_t - z}{h_T}\right) u'\left(x' r_{t+1} + R_t^f\right) r_{t+1} = 0 \right\}, \tag{4.17}$$

Where $\omega(\cdot)$ is a kernel function that weights marginal utility realizations according to how similar the associated z_t is to the value z on which the expectations are conditioned, and h_T denotes a sequence of kernel bandwidths that tends to zero as T increases.[18] (The factor Th_T^K assures that the weighted average is not degenerate.) Applying Eq. (4.17) to all values of z, one value at a time, recovers state-by-state the optimal portfolio weights.

To better understand this estimator, we can interpret it in a more standard nonparametric regression framework. For any portfolio weights x, the weighted average represents a kernel regression of the marginal utility realizations on the state variables. With optimal bandwidths, this kernel regression is consistent, in that:

$$\frac{1}{Th_T^K} \sum_{t=1}^{T} \omega\left(\frac{z_t - z}{h_T}\right) u'\left(x' r_{t+1} + R_t^f\right) r_{t+1} \overset{T\to\infty}{\longrightarrow} \mathrm{E}\left[u'\left(x' r_{t+1} + R_t^f\right) r_{t+1} \middle| z_t = z\right]. \tag{4.18}$$

It follows that the portfolios weights that set to zero the nonparametric regressions converge to the portfolio weights that set to zero the corresponding conditional expectations.

[18]The kernel function must satisfy $\omega(u) = \prod_{i=1}^{K} k(u_i)$ with $\int k(u)du = 1$, $\int uk(u)du = 0$, and $\int u^2 k(u)du < \infty$. A common choice is a K-variate standard normal density with $k(u) = \exp\{-1/2u^2\}/\sqrt{2\pi}$. See Härdle (1990) or Altman (1992) for a more detailed discussion of kernel functions.

The estimator is developed in greater detail and for a more general multiperiod portfolio choice problem with intermediate consumption in Brandt (1999). I also discuss the optimal bandwidth choice, derive the asymptotics of the estimator (with optimal bandwidths, it is consistent and asymptotically Gaussian with a convergence rate of $\sqrt{Th_T^K}$), and examine its finite sample properties through Monte Carlo experiments. In Brandt (2003), I locally parameterize the portfolio weights to further improve the finite sample properties (in the spirit of the local polynomial regression approach of Fan, 1993).

Kernel regressions are not the only way to nonparametrically estimate optimal portfolio weights from conditional Euler equations. Another way is to flexibly parameterize the portfolio weights with polynomial expansions, condition down the Euler equations, and estimate the polynomial coefficients using a standard method of moments approach. Yet another way is to flexibly parameterize the conditional expectations and construct sample analogs of the conditional Euler equations through polynomial regressions. Irrespective of the method, however, all of these estimators are limited in practice by some form of the "curse of dimensionality." For kernel regressions, the curse of dimensionality refers to the fact that the rate of convergence of the estimator to its asymptotic distribution deteriorates exponentially with the number of regressors. For polynomial expansion methods, the number of terms in an expansion of fixed order increases exponentially. Realistically, the curse of dimensionality means that we cannot reliably implement nonparametric estimators with more than two predictors (given the usual quarterly or monthly postwar data).

In Aït-Sahalia and Brandt (2001), we propose an intuitive way to overcome the curse of dimensionality in a portfolio choice context. Borrowing from the idea of index regressions (Powell et al., 1989), we collapse the vector of state variables z_t into a single linear index $z_t'\beta$ and then implement the kernel regression approach described earlier with this univariate index. The index coefficients β are chosen such that the expected utility loss relative to the original problem is minimized. (Empirically, the expected utility loss turns out to be negligible in most cases). We interpret the relative magnitude and statistical significance of each index coefficient as a measure of how important the corresponding state variable is to the investor's portfolio choice. We then use this interpretation to single out the one or two most important predictors for a range of different preferences.

ACKNOWLEDGMENTS

I thank Pedro Santa-Clara, Luis Viceira, and an anonymous referee for their comments and suggestions.

REFERENCES

Aït-Sahalia, Y., and M.W. Brandt, 2001, Variable selection for portfolio choice, *Journal of Finance* 56, 1297–1351.

Aït-Sahalia, Y., and M.W. Brandt, 2007, Portfolio and consumption choice with option-implied state prices, working paper, Princeton University.

Akian, M., J.L. Menaldi, and A. Sulem, 1996, On an investment-consumption model with transaction costs, *SIAM Journal of Control and Optimization* 34, 329–364.

Alexander, G., and A. Baptista, 2002, Economic implications of using a mean-VaR model for portfolio selection: A comparison with mean-variance analysis, *Journal of Economic Dynamics and Control* 26, 1159–1193.

Altman, N.S., 1992, An introduction to kernel and nearest-neighbor nonparametric regression, *American Statistician* 46, 175–185.

Ameriks, J., and S.P. Zeldes, 2004, How do household portfolio shares vary with age? working paper, Columbia University.

Ang, A., and G. Bekaert, 2007, Stock return predictability: Is it there? *Review of Financial Studies* 20, 651–707.

Ang, A., G. Bekaert, and J. Liu, 2005, Why stocks may disappoint, *Journal of Financial Economics* 76(3), pages 471–508.

Avramov, D., 2002, Stock return predictability and model uncertainty, *Journal of Financial Economics* 64, 423–458.

Avramov, D., 2004, Stock return predictability and asset pricing models, *Review of Financial Studies* 17, 699–738.

Balcer, Y., and K. Judd, 1987, Effects of capital gains taxation on life-cylce investment and portfolio management, *Journal of Finance* 42, 743–761.

Balduzzi, P., and A. Lynch, 1999, Transaction costs and predictability: Some utility cost calculations, *Journal of Financial Economics* 52, 47–58.

Barberis, N., 2000, Investing for the long run when returns are predictable, *Journal of Finance* 55, 225–264.

Barro, R.J., and J.W. Friedman, 1977, On uncertain lifetimes, *Journal of Political Economy* 85, 843–849.

Basak, S., and A. Shapiro, 2001, Value-at-risk based risk management: Optimal policies and asset prices, *Review of Financial Studies* 14, 371–405.

Benartzi, S., and R.H. Thaler, 1995, Myopic loss aversion and the equity premium puzzle, *Quarterly Journal of Economics* 110, 73–92.

Best, M.J., and R. Grauer, 1991, On the sensitivity of mean-variance efficient portfolios to changes in asset means: Some analytical and computational results, *Review of Financial Studies* 4, 315–342.

Black, F., and M.S. Scholes, 1973, The pricing of options and corporate liabilities, *Journal of Political Economy* 81, 637–654.

Black, F., and R. Jones, 1987, Simplifying portfolio insurance, *Journal of Portfolio Management* 14, 48–51.

Black, F., and R. Litterman, 1992, Global portfolio optimization, *Financial Analysts Journal* 48, 28–43.

Bodie, Z., and D.B. Crane, 1997, Personal investing: Advice, theory, and evidence, *Financial Analyst Journal* 53, 13–23.

Box, G.E.P., and G.C. Tiao, 1973, *Bayesian Inference in Statistical Analysis* (John Wiley and Sons: New York, NY).

Brandt, M.W., 1999, Estimating portfolio and consumption choice: A conditional euler equations approach, *Journal of Finance* 54, 1609–1646.

Brandt, M.W., 2003, Hedging demands in hedging contingent claims, *Review of Economics and Statistics* 85, 119–140.

Brandt, M.W., A. Goyal, P. Santa-Clara, and J.R. Stroud, 2005, A simulation approach to dynamic portfolio choice with an application to learning about return predictability, *Review of Financial Studies* 18, 831–873.

Brandt, M.W., and P. Santa-Clara, 2006, Dynamic portfolio selection by augmenting the asset space, *Journal of Finance* 61, 2187–2217.

Brandt, M.W., P. Santa-Clara, and R. Valkanov, 2009, Parametric portfolio policies: Exploiting characteristics in the cross section of equity returns, *Review of Financial Studies* forthcoming.

Britten-Jones, M., 1999, The sampling error in estimates of mean-variance efficient portfolio weights, *Journal of Finance* 54, 655–671.

Brown, S., 1978, The portfolio choice problem: Comparison of certainty equivalent and optimal Bayes portfolios, *Communications in Statistics: Simulation and Computation* B7, 321–334.

Browne, S., 1999, Beating a moving target: Optimal portfolio strategies for outperforming a stochastic benchmark, *Finance and Stochastics* 3, 275–294.

Camerer, C.F., 1995, Individual decision making, in J.H. Kagel, and A.E. Roth, ed.: *Handbook of Experimental Economics*. pp. 587–703 (Princeton University Press: Princeton, NJ).

Campbell, J.Y., and J.F. Cocco, 2003, Household risk managament and optimal mortgage choice, *Quarterly Journal of Economics* 118, 1449–1494.

Campbell, J.Y., and L.M. Viceira, 1999, Consumption and portfolio decisions when expected returns are time varying, *Quarterly Journal of Economics* 114, 433–495.

Campbell, J.Y., and L.M. Viceira, 2002, *Strategic Asset Allocation: Portfolio Choice for Long-Term Investors* (Oxford University Press: New York, NY).

Campbell, J.Y., and R.J. Shiller, 1988, The dividend price ratio and expectations of future dividends and discount factors, *Review of Financial Studies* 1, 195–228.

Campbell, J.Y., Y.L. Chan, and L.M. Viceira, 2003, A multivariate model of strategic asset allocation, *Journal of Financial Economics* 67, 41–80.

Canner, N., N.G. Mankiw, and D.N. Weil, 1997, An asset allocation puzzle, *American Economic Review* 87, 181–191.

Chan, L., J. Karceski, and J. Lakonishok, 1999, On portfolio optimization: Forecasting covariances and choosing the risk model, *Review of Financial Studies* 12, 937–974.

Chan, Y.L., and L.M. Viceira, 2000, Asset allocation with endogenous labor income: The case of incomplete markets, working paper, Hong Kong University of Science and Technology.

Chen, N.F., R. Roll, and S.A. Ross, 1986, Economic forces and the stock market, *Journal of Business* 59, 383–403.

Cho, D., 2007, Uncertainty in second moments: Implications for portfolio allocation, working paper, SUNY at Buffalo.

Chopra, V.K., and W.T. Ziemba, 1993, The effects of errors in the means, variances, and covariances, *Journal of Portfolio Management* 19, 6–11.

Cocco, J.F., 2000, Hedging house price risk with incomplete markets, working paper, London Business School.
Cocco, J.F., 2005, Portfolio choice in the presence of housing, *Review of Financial Studies* 18, 535–567.
Cochrane, J.H., 1989, The sensitivity of tests of the intertemporal allocation of consumption to near-rational alternatives, *American Economic Review* 79, 319–337.
Connor, G., 1997, Sensible return forecasting for portfolio management, *Financial Analyst Journal* 53, 44–51.
Connor, G., and R. Korajczyk, 1988, Risk and return in an equilibrium APT: Application of a new test methodology, *Journal of Financial Economics* 21, 255–290.
Cox, J.C., and C.F. Huang, 1989, Optimum consumption and portfolio policies when asset prices follow a diffusion process, *Journal of Economic Theory* 49, 33–83.
Cox, J.C., and C.F. Huang, 1991, A variational problem occurring in financial economics, *Journal of Mathematical Economics* 20, 465–487.
Cox, J.C., S.A. Ross, and M. Rubinstein, 1979, Option pricing: A simplified approach, *Journal of Financial Economics* 7, 229–263.
Cremers, M., 2002, Stock return predictability: A Bayesian model selection perspective, *Review of Financial Studies* 15, 1223–1249.
Cuoco, D., H. He, and S. Issaenko, 2007, Optimal dynamic trading strategies with risk limits, *Operations Research* forthcoming.
Cvitanic, J., 2001, Theory of portfolio optimization in markets with frictions, in *Handbook of Mathematical Finance* (Cambridge University Press: Cambridge), Chapter 17.
Dammon, R., C. Spatt, and H. Zhang, 2001a, Diversification and capital gains taxes with multiple risky assets, working paper, Carnegie Mellon University.
Dammon, R., C. Spatt, and H. Zhang, 2001b, Optimal consumption and investment with capital gains taxes, *Review of Financial Studies* 14, 583–616.
Dammon, R., C. Spatt, and H. Zhang, 2004, Optimal asset location and allocation with taxable and tax-deferred investing, *Journal of Finance* 59, 999–1037.
Davis, M., and A. Norman, 1990, Portfolio selection with transaction costs, *Mathematics of Operations Research* 15, 676–713.
de Athayde, G.M., and R.G. Flores, 2004, A general solution to three-moments portfolio choice, *Journal of Economics Dynamics and Control* 28, 1335–1352.
DeMiguel, A.V., and R. Uppal, 2005, Portfolio investment with the exact tax basis via nonlinear programming, *Management Science* 51, 277–290.
Detemple, J., R. Garcia, and M. Rindisbacher, 2003, Monte Carlo method for optimal portfolios, *Journal of Finance* 58, 401–446.
Duffie, D., and T. Sun, 1990, Transaction costs and portfolio choice in a discrete-continuous time setting, *Journal of Economic Dynamics and Control* 14, 35–51.
Dybvig, P.H., 1995, Duesenberry's racheting of consumption: Optimal dynamic allocation and investment given intolerance for any decline in standard of living, *Review of Economic Studies* 62, 287–313.
Efron, B.F., and C.N. Morris, 1977, Stein's paradox in statistics, *Scientific American* 236, 119–127.
Elton, E.J., and M.J. Gruber, 1978, Taxes and portfolio composition, *Journal of Finance* 41, 751–762.

Epstein, L., and S. Zin, 1989, Substitution, risk aversion, and the temporal behavior of consumption and asset returns: A theoretical framework, *Econometrica* 57, 937–969.

Fama, E., and K. French, 1993, Common risk factors in the returns on stocks and bonds, *Journal of Financial Economics* 33, 3–56.

Fama, E.F., 1970, Multiperiod consumption-investment decisions, *American Economic Review* 60, 163–174.

Fama, E.F., and K.R. French, 1988, Dividend yields and expected stock returns, *Journal of Financial Economics* 22, 3–25.

Fan, J., 1993, Local linear regression smoothers and their minimax efficiencies, *Annals of Statistics* 21, 196–216.

Flavin, M., and T. Yamashita, 2002, Owner-occupied housing and the composition of the household portfolio over the life-cylce, *American Economic Review* 92, 345–362.

Frost, P.A., and J.E. Savarino, 1986, An empirical Bayes approach to efficient portfolio selection, *Journal of Financial and Quantitative Analysis* 21, 293–305.

Frost, P.A., and J.E. Savarino, 1988, For better performance: Constrain portfolio weights, *Journal of Portfolio Management* 15, 29–34.

Gallmeyer, M., R. Kaniel, and S. Tompaidis, 2006, Tax management strategies with multiple risky assets, *Journal of Financial Economcis* 80, 277–290.

Garlappi, L., L.V. Naik, and J. Slive, 2001, Portfolio selection with multiple assets and capital gains taxes, working paper, University of British Columbia.

George, E.I., and R.E. McCulloch, 1993, Variable selection via Gibbs sampling, *Journal of the American Statistical Association* 88, 881–889.

Gilboa, I., and D. Schmeidler, 1989, Maxmin expected utility with non-unique prior, *Journal of Mathematical Economics* 18, 141–153.

Gomes, F., 2005, Portfolio choice and trading volume with loss-averse investors, *Journal of Business* 78, 675–706.

Gomes, F., and A. Michaelides, 2003, Portfolio choice with internal habit formation: A life-cycle model with uninsurable labor income risk, *Review or Economic Dynamics* 6, 729–766.

Goyal, A., and I. Welch, 2003, Predicting the equity premium with dividend ratios, *Management Science* 49, 639–654.

Green, R., and B. Hollifield, 1992, When will mean-variance efficient portfolios be well-diversified? *Journal of Finance* 47, 1785–1809.

Grossman, S., and G. Laroque, 1991, Asset pricing and optimal portfolio choice in the presence of illiquid durable consumption goods, *Econometrica* 58, 25–51.

Grossman, S.J., and J. Vila, 1989, Portfolio insurance in complete markets: A note, *Journal of Business* 62, 473–476.

GSAM Quantitative Strategies Group, 2000, An introduction to the Black-Litterman asset allocation model, working paper, Goldman Sachs Asset Management.

Gul, F., 1991, A theory of dissapointment aversion, *Econometrica* 59, 667–686.

Härdle, W., 1990, *Applied Nonparametric Regression* (Cambridge University Press: New York, NY).

Hakansson, N.H., 1969, Optimal investment and consumption strategies under risk, an uncertain lifetime, and insurance, *International Economic Review* 10, 443–466.

Hansen, L.P., and T. Sargent, 1995, Discounted linear exponential quadratic gaussian control, *IEEE Transactions on Automatic Control* 40, 968–971.

Harrison, M.J., and D.M. Kreps, 1979, Martingales and arbitrage in multiperiod securities markets, *Journal of Economic Theory* 2, 381–408.

Harvey, C.R., J.C. Liechty, M.W. Liechty, and P. Müller, 2004, Portfolio selection with higher moments, working paper, Duke University.

He, H., and N.D. Pearson, 1991, Consumption and portfolio policies with incomplete markets and short-sale constraints: The infinite dimensional case, *Journal of Economic Theory* 54, 259–304.

Heaton, J., and D.J. Lucas, 1997, Market frictions, savings behavior, and portfolio choice, *Macroeconomic Dynamics* 1, 76–101.

Heaton, J., and D.J. Lucas, 2000, Portfolio choice and asset prices: The importance of entrepeneurial risk, *Journal of Finance* 55, 1163–1198.

Hu, X., 2005, Portfolio choice for homeowners, *Journal of Urban Economics* 58, 114–136.

Huang, J., 2008, Taxable and tax-deferred investing: A tax-arbitrage approach, *Review of Financial Studies* 21, 2173–2207.

Jagannathan, R., and N. Kocherlakota, 1996, Why should older people invest less in stocks than younger people? *FRB of Minneapolis Quarterly Review* 20, 11–23.

Jagannathan, R., and T. Ma, 2003, Risk reduction in large portfolios: Why imposing the wrong constraints helps, *Journal of Finance* 58, 1651–1683.

James, W., and C. Stein, 1961, Estimation with quadratic loss, *Proceedings of the Fourth Berkeley Symposium on Mathematics and Statistics* pp. 361–379.

Jobson, J.D., and B. Korkie, 1980, Estimation of Markowitz efficient portfolios, *Journal of the American Statistical Association* 75, 544–554.

Jobson, J.D., and B. Korkie, 1981, Putting Markowitz theory to work, *Journal of Portfolio Management* 7, 70–74.

Jobson, J.D., B. Korkie, and V. Ratti, 1979, Improved estimation for Markowitz portfolios using James-Stein type estimators, *Proceedings of the American Statistical Association, Business and Economic Statistics Section* pp. 279–284.

Jorion, P., 1986, Bayes-Stein estimation for portfolio analysis, *Journal of Financial and Quantitative Analysis* 21, 279–292.

Judd, K.L., 1998, *Numerical Methods in Economics* (MIT Press: Cambridge, MA).

Kahneman, D., and A. Tversky, 1979, Prospect theory: An analysis of decision under risk, *Econometrica* 47, 263–291.

Kan, R., and G. Zhou, 2007, Optimal portfolio choice with parameter uncertainty, *Journal of Financial and Quantitative Analysis* 42, 621–656.

Kandel, S., and R.F. Stambaugh, 1996, On the predictability of stock returns: An asset-allocation perspective, *Journal of Finance* 51, 385–424.

Kane, A., 1982, Skewness preferences and portfolio choice, *Journal of Financial and Quantitative Analysis* 17, 15–25.

Karatzas, I., and S.E. Shreve, 1991, *Brownian Motion and Stochastic Calculus* (Springer Verlag: New York, NY).

Kataoka, A., 1963, A stochastic programming model, *Econometrica* 31, 181–196.

Kim, T.S., and E. Omberg, 1996, Dynamic nonmyopic portfolio behavior, *Review of Financial Studies* 9, 141–161.

Klein, R.W., and V.S. Bawa, 1976, The effect of estimation risk on optimal portfolio choice, *Journal of Financial Economics* 3, 215–231.

Koo, H.K., 1998, Consumptyion and portfolio selection with labor income: A continuous time approach, *Mathematical Finance* 8, 49–65.
Kraus, A., and R.H. Litzenberger, 1976, Skewness preferences and the valuation of risky assets, *Journal of Finance* 31, 1085–1100.
Lax, Y., 2002, Habit formation and lifetime portfolio selection, working paper, Goldman Sachs Asset Management.
Ledoit, O., and M. Wolf, 2003, Improved estimation of the covariance matrix of returns with an application to portfolio selection, *Journal of Empirical Finance* 10, 603–621.
Ledoit, O., and M. Wolf, 2004, Honey, I shrunk the sample covariance matrix, *Journal of Portfolio Management* pp. 110–119.
Leland, H., 2001, Optimal portfolio implementation with transaction costs and capital gains taxes, working paper, Unversity of California, Berkeley.
Liu, H., 2004, Optimal consumption and investment with transaction costs and multiple risky assets, *Journal of Finance* 59, 289–338.
Liu, W.F., 2002, Savings and portfolio decision: Observable implications of Knightian uncertainty, working paper, University of Washington.
Longstaff, F., J. Liu, and J. Pan, 2003, Dynamic asset allocation with event risk, *Journal of Finance* 58, 231–259.
Lynch, A., and S. Tan, 2009, Multiple risky assets, transaction costs and return predictability: Allocation rules and implications for U.S. investors, *Journal of Financial and Quantitative Analysis* forthcoming.
Maenhout, P.J., 2004, Robust portfolio rules and asset pricing, *Review of Financial Studies* 17, 951–983.
Maenhout, P.J., 2006, Robust portfolio rules and detection-error probabilities for a mean-reverting risk premium, *Journal of Economic Theory* 128, 136–163.
Markowitz, H.M., 1952, Portfolio selection, *Journal of Finance* 7, 77–91.
Marx, D.L., and R.R. Hocking, 1977, Moments of certain functions of elements in the inverse wishart matrix, working paper, Texas A&M University.
Merton, R.C., 1969, Lifetime portfolio selection under uncertainty: The continuous time case, *Review of Economics and Statistics* 51, 247–257.
Merton, R.C., 1971, Optimum consumption and portfolio rules in a continuous-time model, *Journal of Economic Theory* 3, 373–413.
Merton, R.C., 1973, An intertemporal capital asset pricing model, *Econometrica* 41, 867–887.
Merton, R.C., 1975, Theory of finance from the perspective of continuous time, *Journal of Financial and Quantitative Analysis* 7, 1851–1872.
Michaud, R.O., 1989, The markowitz optimization enigma: Is optimized optimal?, *Financial Analyst Journal* 45, 31–42.
Nielsen, L.T., and M. Vassalou, 2006, The instantaneous capital market line, *Economic Theory* 28, 651–664.
Nigmatullin, E., 2003, Bayesian model averaging for moment conditions models, working paper, University of Wisconsin-Madison.
Pastor, L., 2000, Portfolio selection and asset pricing models, *Journal of Finance* 50, 179–223.
Pastor, L., and R.F. Stambaugh, 2000, Comparing asset pricing models: An investment perspective, *Journal of Financial Economics* 56, 335–381.

Pastor, L., and R.F. Stambaugh, 2002, Investing in equity mutual funds, *Journal of Financial Economics* 63, 351–380.
Perold, A., and W. Sharpe, 1988, Dynamic strategies for asset allocation, *Financial Analyst Journal* 44, 16–27.
Powell, J.L., J.H. Stock, and T.M. Stoker, 1989, Semiparametric estimation of index coefficients, *Econometrica* 57, 1403–1430.
Quiggin, J.C., 1982, A theory of anticipated utility, *Journal of Economic Behavior and Organization* 3, 323–343.
Roy, A., 1952, Safety first and the holding of assets, *Econometrica* 20, 431–439.
Samuelson, P.A., 1969, Lifetime portfolio selection by dynamic stochastic programming, *Review of Economics and Statistics* 51, 239–246.
Samuelson, P.A., 1989, A case at last for age-phased reduction in equity, *Proceedings of the National Academy of Sciences* 86, 9048–9051.
Schroder, M., and C. Skiadas, 1999, Optimal consumption and portfolio selection with stochastic differential utility, *Journal of Economic Theory* 89, 68–126.
Schroder, M., and C. Skiadas, 2002, An isomorphism between asset pricing models with and without linear habit formation, *Review of Financial Studies* 15, 1189–1221.
Scowcroft, A., and J. Sefton, 2003, Enhanced indexation, in S. Satchell, and A. Scowcroft, ed.: *Advances in portfolio construction and implementation*. pp. 95–124 (Butterworth-Henemann: New York, NY).
Sharpe, W., 1963, A simplified model for portfolio analysis, *Management Science* 9, 277–293.
Shefrin, H., and M. Statman, 2000, Behavioral portfolio theory, *Journal of Financial and Quantitative Analysis* 35, 127–151.
Shimko, D.C., 1999, *Finance in Continuous Time: A Primer* (Blackwell: Malden, MA).
Simaan, Y., 1993, Portfolio selection and asset pricing three parameter framework, *Management Science* 5, 568–577.
Steele, J.M., 2001, *Stochastic Calculus and Financial Applications* (Springer Verlag: New York, NY).
Telser, L.G., 1956, Saftey first and hedging, *Review of Economic Studies* 23, 1–16.
Tepla, L., 2001, Optimal investment with minimum performance constraints, *Journal of Economic Dynamics and Control* 25, 1629–1645.
Theil, H., and A. Goldberger, 1961, On pure and mixed estimation in economics, *International Economic Review* 2, 65–78.
Tu, J., and G. Zhou, 2004, Data-generating process uncertainty: What difference does it make in portfolio decisions? *Journal of Financial Economics* 72, 385–421.
Viceira, L.M., 2001, Optimal portfolio choice for long-horizon investors with nontradable labor income, *Journal of Finance* 56, 433–470.
Wachter, J.A., 2002, Portfolio and consumption decisions under mean-reverting returns: An exact solution for complete markets, *Journal of Financial and Quantitative Analysis* 37, 63–91.
Weil, P., 1989, The equity premium puzzle and the risk-free rate puzzle, *Journal of Monetary Economics* 24, 401–421.
Yao, R., and H.H. Zhang, 2005, Optimal consumption and portfolio choices with risky housing and borrowing constraints, *Review of Financial Studies* 18, 197–239.
Zellner, Z.A., and V.K. Chetty, 1965, Prediction and decision problems in regression models from the Bayesian point of view, *Journal of the American Statistical Association* 60, 608–615.

CHAPTER 6

Heterogeneity and Portfolio Choice: Theory and Evidence

Stephanie Curcuru*, John Heaton, Deborah Lucas***,** *and* **Damien Moore******

*Federal Reserve Board of Governors, Washington, DC
**Booth School of Business, University of Chicago, Chicago, IL
NBER, Cambridge, MA
***Northwestern University Kellogg School of Management, Evanston, IL
NBER, Cambridge, MA
****Congressional Budget Office, Washington, DC

Contents

Abstract

In this chapter, we summarize and add to the evidence on the large and systematic differences in portfolio composition across individuals with varying characteristics and evaluate some of the theories that have been proposed in terms of their ability to account for these differences. Variation in background risk exposure – from sources such as labor and entrepreneurial income or real estate holdings and from factors such as transaction costs, borrowing constraints, restricted pension investments, and life-cycle considerations – can explain some but not all aspects of the observed cross-sectional variation in portfolio holdings in a traditional utility maximizing framework. In particular, fixed costs and life-cycle considerations appear necessary to explain the lack of stock market participation by young and less affluent households. Remaining challenges for quantitative theories include the apparent lack of diversification in some unconstrained individual portfolios and nonparticipation in the stock market by some households with significant financial wealth.

Keywords: portfolio allocation; investor heterogeneity; non-tradable risk; business risk; labor income risk; household allocations

1. INTRODUCTION

Data on financial behavior of households points to considerable heterogeneity in portfolio allocations. A large fraction of households holds neither common stock nor other risky financial securities. Others invest in stocks almost exclusively. The extent to which risky asset holdings are diversified also varies greatly, ranging from exclusive reliance on diversified index funds to holdings concentrated in a few individual stocks. Employees often have significant holdings in the stock of their employers. To make sense of these observations, it is useful to look for empirical regularities in the way that households with different characteristics invest their savings and to interpret these regularities using theories of portfolio choice that allow heterogeneity among investors. In this chapter, we summarize and add to the evidence on the large and systematic differences in portfolio composition across individuals with varying characteristics and evaluate some of the theories that have been proposed in terms of their ability to account for these differences.

If heterogeneity in portfolio allocations is to be explained in a traditional utility maximizing framework, it must be accounted for by heterogeneity in preferences, heterogeneity in circumstances, or a combination of the two. The recent literature on portfolio choice has emphasized both of these possibilities. Heterogeneity in circumstances encompasses a wide range of potential explanatory factors including the presence of nondiversifiable background risks, demographics, information asymmetries, and transaction costs. Potential sources of nondiversifiable background risks include labor income and proprietary business income (or more broadly human capital), restricted pension investments, and owner-occupied real estate. Demographic factors include age, occupation, inherited wealth, and education. Transaction costs include taxes, the fixed and variable costs of trading in securities markets, and also the time or psychic costs of learning about asset markets.

To provide context for the empirical findings, we briefly review some of the extensive theoretical literature on portfolio choice, with an emphasis on calibrated models explicitly designed to quantitatively explain heterogeneity. Early papers by Mossin (1968), Merton (1969), and Samuelson (1970, 1969) were the first to address the dynamic portfolio choice problem in preference-based theories. Friend and Blume (1975) found that, consistent with average asset holdings, calibrated versions of these theoretical portfolio share rules imply a fairly even division of wealth between stocks and bonds, assuming moderate risk aversion. For the next several decades, portfolio choice was thought to be a largely solved problem. Recently, however, there has been renewed interest in this area. This can be attributed to the greater availability of data that reveals apparent idiosyncrasies in individual behavior and also to the increasing interest in the implications of incomplete markets. Both naturally lead to an examination of optimal portfolio behavior in the presence of market frictions that can affect portfolio allocation rules.[1]

Apart from explaining data, understanding portfolio choice can shed light on a variety of broader issues. For one, asset pricing models presume a theory of portfolio choice. Unresolved issues in the asset pricing literature, such as the equity premium puzzle (Mehra and Prescott, 1985), are related to unsettled questions in the portfolio choice literature, such as explaining nonparticipation in the stock market, or that many portfolios are skewed toward safe assets. For instance, without the existence of a significant differential between the average return on stocks and that on short-term risk-free bonds (the equity premium), it would be quite easy to account for low stock market participation by appealing to moderate transaction costs or background risk using conventional models. Research on portfolio choice may help explain the behavior of return differentials and asset prices by suggesting the characteristics of the "marginal investor" in asset markets or by pointing toward a direction in which to modify our models of preferences or beliefs. Second, public policy questions, such as whether investing social security contributions in the stock market would be welfare improving or whether current tax laws favoring investments in own company stock should be changed, are also informed by a clearer understanding of the reasons for current asset allocations. Finally, investment advisers need to understand the causes and implications of investor heterogeneity to provide their clients with sound advice.

The remainder of the chapter is organized as follows. Section 2 presents summary statistics on heterogeneity in portfolio choice and some of the factors that suggest partial explanations for the cross-sectional variation. Section 3 briefly surveys the theoretical literature on portfolio choice. Section 4 reviews the results of many of the calibrated theoretical models that have been proposed to explain portfolio choice in the presence of market frictions and with uninsurable background risks, and it discusses model predictions are often ambiguous. Section 5 reviews the statistical evidence on background income risk and its effect on portfolio allocations and the some unresolved measurement issues. Section 6 concludes.

[1]The issue of background risk generally does not arise in the earlier work on portfolio theory which implicitly assumed that all income is capitalized into wealth. The allocation of wealth between risky stocks and risk-free bonds is therefore unaffected by the statistical properties of background risk.

2. SUMMARY STATISTICS ON STOCK MARKET PARTICIPATION AND PORTFOLIO CHOICE

There is much heterogeneity in portfolio composition to be explained, as documented for the United States in a number of papers including Bertaut (1994), Blume and Zeldes (1994), Friend and Blume (1975), Heaton and Lucas (2000b), and Poterba (1993). We begin by presenting statistics on portfolio allocations that are consistent with these studies and that incorporate more recent data. These summary statistics are primarily based on tabulations from the Survey of Consumer Finances (SCF). The SCF is a leading source of information on household portfolio choice in the United States and includes detail on the various components of wealth (see e.g., Aizcorbe et al., 2003, and references therein). It oversamples the wealthy, but inferences can be drawn about the overall population using the provided survey weights. Because the SCF lacks a time series dimension, researchers interested in life-cycle effects often turn to the Panel Survey of Income Dynamics (PSID). Although the PSID tracks households over time, it provides less financial detail than the SCF, and it surveys a much smaller sample of the wealthy households that own a disproportionate share of total financial assets.

Although much of the portfolio choice literature restricts attention to wealth in the form of stocks, bonds, and cash (liquid assets),[2] several other types of financial assets comprise a significant portion of wealth as do nonfinancial assets such as human capital. This raises the question of what measure of wealth to use in the denominator when reporting percentage portfolio allocations. In this chapter, we use a measure of "total financial wealth," which includes liquid assets plus real estate and privately held businesses. We emphasize this measure because of the quantitative importance of these assets and because these components of financial wealth represent potentially important risk factors that may influence the composition of liquid asset holdings. Table 6.1 shows the breakdown of financial wealth from the 2001 SCF. Averaging across households using the survey weights, total financial wealth consists of stocks (15.8%), bonds (7.6%), cash (24.4%), housing (41.3%), other real estate (4.8%), and the market value of private businesses (4.2%). Stocks and bonds in various types of accounts (e.g., retirement accounts, mutual funds, and brokerage accounts) are aggregated in these statistics. Other miscellaneous assets such as pensions or trusts that cannot be allocated to an asset class total 1.9%. Notice that liquid assets only average 47.8% of total financial assets. Notice also that leverage, which for many households is in the form of a home mortgage, is not reflected in these statistics. Although household debt management can be thought of as an aspect of household portfolio choice broadly defined, we do not emphasize it here (see, e.g., Gross and Souleles, 2002; Laibson, 1997).

[2]We use the term liquid assets to refer to cash, bonds, and stocks, even though some components of these holdings are not readily tradable, such as funds held in pension plans. The measure of cash in the SCF is not comprehensive because it excludes currency, but this is unlikely to be significant for the relatively wealthy households that are the main focus of analyses of portfolio choice.

Table 6.1 The composition of financial wealth

	Percent
Asset class	
Cash	24.4
Bonds	7.6
Stocks	15.8
Subtotal liquid assets	47.8
Housing	41.3
Other real estate	4.8
Private businesses	4.2
Other	1.9
Total	100

Tabulations are from 2001 SCF using survey weights. Percent of asset classes in aggregate household wealth. Aggregate value of each class calculated by averaging across households using survey weights.

A significant portion of financial wealth is held in dedicated retirement accounts. Discussions of pension investing often abstract from the broader context of portfolio choice. Conversely, the portfolio choice literature generally ignores the institutional features of pension plans that may help explain important aspects of portfolio choice. In this chapter, we emphasize the connections between these literatures. The Investment Company Institute (ICI) estimates that in 2003, the value of the retirement market stood at \$10.2 trillion in 2002. Defined contribution (DC) plans (including individual retirement accounts, employer-sponsored DCs, and federal government DCs) have grown from 35% of the market in 1990 to about 45% of the total market in 2002. Over the same period, defined benefit (DB) plans, which can be thought of as providing workers with a partially indexed bond, have shrunk from 52 to 44% in 2002. The remaining share is attributable to annuities. Interestingly, over 28% of the retirement market is provided by local, state, and federal governments to their employees. Purcell (2002) provides statistics from the U.S. Department of Labor that show DB coverage in terms of numbers of participants shrunk over the 1990 to 1998 period, whereas DC plan coverage almost doubled so that there are now more than twice as many participants in DC plans than in DB plans (50 million participants versus 22 million participants, respectively). Estimates from the 2001 SCF suggest that 52% of households participate in some form of DC tax-deferred retirement account (21% held employer-sponsored DC plans, 18% held IRAs, and 13% held both). These retirement account assets comprise 13.4% of the financial assets of U.S. households. The median retirement account balance for households who held them was \$29,000.

One aspect of portfolio choice that receives considerable attention is the decision by many households to opt out of the stock market entirely, despite the increasing participation rates seen in recent years. As emphasized by many authors (e.g., Bertaut and Haliassos, 1995; Mankiw and Zeldes, 1991; Saito, 1995), the phenomenon of stock market non-participation poses a challenge to portfolio theory, as well as to representative consumer asset pricing theory. To illustrate the trend in stock market participation rates over the last decade, Table 6.2 presents summary statistics on the distribution of the share of stocks in financial wealth in each SCF survey from 1989 to 2001. These statistics include all households with positive net worth, adjusted by the survey weights. Consistent with the relative growth of the stock market, mean stockholdings as a percentage of wealth have increased over this period. Participation rates in the stock market increased in the 1990s, although the percentage of nonparticipants remains strikingly high. Before 2001, stockholdings as a fraction of financial wealth were virtually zero in the 50th percentile. In the 75th percentile, this share increases from only 4.7% in 1989 to 26% in 2001. The increase in standard deviation and sharp decrease in skewness over the 12 years further indicate the increasingly wide, but still concentrated, distribution of stockholdings.

These statistics are consistent with the findings in earlier studies. Poterba (1998) reports approximately 69.3 million shareholders in the United States in 1995, compared with 61.4 million in 1992 and 52.3 million in 1989. There is also some evidence that people start buying stocks at a younger age than in the past. For example, Poterba and Samwick (1997) argue that baby boomers are participating more heavily in the stock market. Further Ameriks and Zeldes (2002) show that there may be important cohort effects explaining trends in participation.

The trend of increasing participation is consistent with a number of possible explanations including a fall in the costs of participation over time, for instance because of changes in risk attitudes or expected returns or reductions in background risk. It also coincides with the growth of low-cost mutual funds and employer-sponsored DC pension plans. The latter can significantly lower the cost of participation through employer

Table 6.2 Cross-sectional variation of share of stock in financial assets

Year	25%	50%	75%	Mean	Standard deviation	Skewness
1989	0	0	0.047	0.058	0.133	3.560
1992	0	0	0.077	0.077	0.158	3.005
1995	0	0	0.110	0.099	0.188	2.587
1998	0	0.021	0.217	0.140	0.210	1.800
2001	0	0.042	0.260	0.162	0.229	1.598

Tabulations are from the SCF, various years, using survey weights. Columns 2, 3, and 4 report averages across households of the share of stock in household wealth for households in the 25th, 50th, and 75th percentiles of the cross-sectional share of stock in financial assets.

contributions or matches, virtually no direct transaction costs, and relatively easy access to information. Based on the survey data from the Investment Company Institute (2002), 48% of U.S. households owning stock in January 2002 initially bought equities inside employer plans. In fact, the same study finds that the majority of equity investors own equities in employer-sponsored retirement plans in 2002. Data from the SCF, summarized in Table 6.3, confirms the importance of DC pensions and of mutual funds as the vehicles for increased participation.

Despite increases in participation, wealth and stockholdings in the United States remain highly concentrated in dollar terms. For example, in 1989, the top 10% of the wealth distribution held 84% of the stock. This dropped slightly to 83% in 1995 and further to 76.6% in 2001.

In fact, households with stock in their portfolio look considerably different than nonstockholders in many dimensions. In tabulations from the SCF that summarize some of these differences, we include only those households with positive net worth and adjust the results by the survey weights. We designate as "nonstockholders" those households with less than $500 in stock and as "stockholders" those households with at least $500 in stock. We set this cutoff above zero to avoid classifying households with economically insignificant holdings as stockholders, but the results are not very sensitive to this choice. Based on this classification, Table 6.4 reports the mean and median of total financial wealth, housing wealth, mortgage debt, other real estate wealth, business wealth, labor income, age, education, self-reported risk tolerance, and the number of households, both in 1992 and in 2001, for each group. Not surprisingly, the data reveals that stockholders are considerably wealthier, with larger holdings in all asset categories, are better educated, and describe themselves as less risk-averse (risk tolerance of 1 = willing to take substantial financial risks, 4 = not willing to take financial risks). These differences are all greater in 2001 than in 1992.

The very limited wealth of many nonparticipants suggests that they may have little incentive to optimize their portfolios or that they may be discouraged from doing so by

Table 6.3 How stocks are held (% of population)

Year	Directly owns mutual fund	Only owns equity in pension fund	Only owns direct equity	Owns equity (all account types)
1989	6.0	11.2	12.6	31.8
1992	8.4	14.9	11.1	36.7
1995	11.3	17.6	10.5	40.4
1998	15.2	20.2	10.4	48.9
2001	16.7	21.2	9.8	51.9

Tabulations are from the SCF, various years, and based on survey weights. Proportion of households with equity ownership through a mutual fund, a pension fund, or directly.

Table 6.4 Characteristics of stockholders and nonstockholders (2001 dollars)

	Nonstockholders		Stockholders	
	Mean	**Median**	**Mean**	**Median**
1992				
Total financial wealth	171,687	74,799	525,880	207,092
Owner-occupied RE wealth	78,489	51,969	143,474	107,651
Mortgage	22,854	0	47,815	18,560
Net other RE wealth	21,132	0	54,494	0
Business wealth	32,810	0	99,689	0
Labor income	35,590	25,985	79,759	56,919
Age	52.1	50	49.8	48.0
Education	12.3	12.0	14.3	15.0
Risk tolerance	3.5	4.0	3.0	3.0
Number of households	43,058,522		35,571,987	
2001				
Total financial wealth	167,729	77,885	794,817	290,850
Owner-occupied RE wealth	80,458	60,000	198,482	135,000
Mortgage	23,080	0	66,929	37,000
Net other RE wealth	20,065	0	62,980	0
Business wealth	28,315	0	140,125	0
Labor income	35,659	25,000	107,120	65,000
Age	55.3	54.0	49.0	47.0
Education	12.1	12.0	14.3	15.0
Risk tolerance	3.5	4.0	2.8	3.0
Number of households	39,937,214		49,606,571	

Tabulations are from the 1992 and 2001 SCF using survey weights. Households are limited to those with positive net worth. Nonstockholders are those with less than $500 in stock, and stockholders are those with at least $500 in stock. Mean and median characteristics across households in each group. "RE" denotes "real estate." Risk tolerance is "1" if the household reports, they are willing to take substantial risk to achieve higher returns, "2" if willing to take above average risk, "3" if willing to take average risk, and "4" if unwilling to take risk.

fairly small fixed costs. Calibrated theoretical papers that investigate this are discussed in Section 4.

Among stockholders, there is considerable heterogeneity in the share of wealth held in stocks. Conditioning on those households who have more than $500 in stock, Table 6.5 illustrates that for this group, in the 2001 SCF, the average stock share in financial wealth is 26.9% and ranges from 7.0% at the 25th percentile to 40.5% at the 75th percentile. These statistics suggest that heterogeneity is important, but not necessarily that any of these investors are making mistakes when differences in preferences and circumstances are accounted for.

Table 6.5 Cross-sectional distribution of share of stock in financial assets (stockholders only)

25%	50%	75%	Mean	Standard deviation	Skewness
0.070	0.200	0.405	0.269	0.242	1.048

Tabulations are from the 2001 SCF using survey weights. Stockholders are defined as those households with more than $500 in stock. Share of stock in financial assets calculated for each household. Statistics for the distribution of this share across households.

Some of the variation in portfolio share appears to be related to age and net worth, although these two factors only explain a small portion of the cross-sectional variance. Table 6.6 shows the relative shares of various assets in financial wealth across age and net worth brackets, where net worth is defined as financial wealth net of all personal debt, based on the 2001 SCF. Within each demographic category, there is also significant variation, and holdings are often highly skewed in individual portfolios. Owner-occupied housing is the largest component of wealth for all but the wealthiest households, and private business wealth is an important component for the wealthy, particularly those under 45.

Earlier studies on stockholding over the life cycle are largely consistent with the findings in Table 6.6. King and Leape (1987) emphasize the increase in stockholdings until retirement and attribute it to the increase over time in knowledge when financial information is costly. Others emphasize the decline in stockholdings among the very old. Poterba and Samwick (1997) analyze the relationship between age and portfolio structure, with a focus on distinguishing between age effects and cohort effects. They find evidence of both age and cohort effects. Heaton and Lucas (2000b) suggest that the age effect on stockholding is sensitive to whether wealth is broadly or narrowly defined, with a smaller negative effect of age when wealth is broadly defined.

The relation between stock market participation and portfolio shares and various household characteristics can be summarized using regression analysis. Tables 6.7 and 6.8 show the results of probit and ordinary least squares regressions of stock ownership on household characteristics using the 2001 SCF, with an emphasis on how various measures of housing affect these choices. Households with a net worth greater than $10,000 are included, and the survey weights are used.[3] Table 6.7 shows that, controlling for wealth, the probability of stock ownership is decreasing with age and home equity/net worth, and home value and mortgage scaled by total financial wealth.[4] Participation in a DB plan slightly decreases the probability of stock market participation, whereas participation

[3] We use a positive threshold for net worth because it is used to normalize real estate holdings, but the results are not sensitive to the exact cutoff.

[4] In Table 6.7 the dependent variable = 1 if the stockholdings are greater than $500.

Table 6.6 Shares of financial assets by age and net worth (mean/median)

Age	<35	35–44	45–54	55–64	65–74	75+
Panel A: \$10K < net worth < \$100K						
Stocks	16.2/5.8	16.2/3.7	11.2/0.9	9.2/0.0	0.6/0.0	1.7/0.0
Bonds	7.0/0.3	8.3/0.6	7.8/0.0	5.2/0.0	4.2/0.0	4.9/0.0
Cash	12.9/3.2	9.2/3.1	9.8/3.1	9.6/2.0	15.8/4.8	29.8/9.1
Owner-occupied housing	52.4/70.9	57.6/72.3	64.6/81.4	68.6/85.1	72.7/89.2	60.1/85.1
Other real estate	3.7/0.0	4.5/0.0	3.2/0.0	3.4/0.0	4.5/0.0	2.2/0.0
Business	2.9/0.0	2.4/0.0	1.9/0.0	2.8/0.0	1.2/0.0	0.0/0.0
Income (\$1000)	51.6/50.0	52.4/46.0	46.4/42.0	32.3/29.0	25.6/20.0	19.8/15.0
Panel B: \$100K < net worth < \$1M						
Stocks	19.7/12.1	21.2/15.9	21.4/15.7	21.2/15.0	16.8/3.1	13.3/0.0
Bonds	3.4/0.3	6.8/1.0	7.1/1.3	8.6/0.7	7.5/0.0	5.5/0.0
Cash	7.8/3.4	6.2/3.2	8.2/3.5	8.7/3.4	16.5/9.1	21.1/12.0
Owner-occupied housing	50.4/51.6	51.1/51.6	47.9/45.6	48.0/44.1	47.7/46.5	52.1/51.0
Other real estate	5.8/0.0	5.7/0.0	6.5/0.0	7.2/0.0	6.3/0.0	5.8/0.0
Business	10.7/0.0	7.4/0.0	6.8/0.0	4.9/0.0	3.4/0.0	0.7/0.0
Income (\$1000)	84.5/78.0	93.3/77.0	87.2/75.0	64.9/58.0	47.0/37.0	34.3/28.0
Panel C: net worth > \$1M						
Stocks	20.4/6.1	23.8/20.2	29.4/23.1	33.9/33.4	31.5/30.1	37.3/37.8
Bonds	9.0/0.1	5.0/0.5	8.5/3.3	12.3/4.7	11.4/5.9	18.0/12.1
Cash	4.2/1.3	4.9/2.1	5.6/2.3	6.1/2.4	9.9/3.6	7.0/3.8
Owner-occupied housing	10.6/4.3	24.7/22.7	22.9/19.1	17.7/16.1	16.5/16.0	20.1/17.6
Other real estate	6.4/0.0	8.3/0.7	11.5/1.8	12.6/2.6	18.2/8.7	9.3/0.8
Business	41.7/28.6	31.9/27.3	19.8/3.2	14.8/0.0	11.2/0.0	7.1/0.0
Income (\$1000)	317.5/130.0	413.6/235.0	443.2/200.0	365.6/168.0	222.5/120.0	144.4/97.0

Tabulations are from the 2001 SCF using survey weights. Mean and median across households of relative shares of assets in wealth. Reported as mean/median in each cell. Households are limited to those within stated age and net worth categories. Net worth is financial wealth net of personal debt. Panel A is for households with net worth between \$10,000 and \$100,000. Panel B is for households with net worth between \$100,000 and \$1 million. Panel C is for households with net worth greater than \$1 million.

Table 6.7 Probit regressions on stock ownership

	1		2		3		4		5		6	
Intercept	−4.40	(13.78)	−5.47	(15.92)	−4.96	(16.25)	−5.88	(17.93)	−4.22	(13.01)	−5.24	(15.04)
Age	−0.02	(8.46)	−0.01	(3.00)	−0.02	(9.04)	−0.01	(3.87)	−0.02	(8.45)	−0.01	(2.93)
Log(income)	0.14	(5.01)	0.08	(2.60)	0.15	(5.53)	0.09	(3.01)	0.14	(4.89)	0.08	(2.43)
Log(assets)	0.26	(10.63)	0.32	(11.93)	0.28	(11.78)	0.33	(12.75)	0.25	(10.34)	0.31	(11.59)
Number of children	−0.02	(0.77)	−0.05	(1.77)	−0.03	(1.16)	−0.06	(1.82)	−0.01	(0.49)	−0.04	(1.43)
Married (yes = 1)	0.14	(2.09)	0.10	(1.40)	0.12	(1.76)	0.09	(1.27)	0.15	(2.22)	0.11	(1.53)
Years of education	0.09	(8.41)	0.09	(7.62)	0.10	(9.13)	0.10	(8.23)	0.09	(8.36)	0.09	(7.45)
Real estate equity/ net worth	0.005	(6.34)	0.004	(5.54)								
Mortgage/financial wealth					0.003	(2.30)	−0.01	(3.46)				
House/financial wealth									−0.01	(7.43)	−0.01	(6.93)
In defined benefit plan			−0.05	(0.59)			−0.06	(0.77)			−0.03	(0.33)
In defined contribution plan			1.34	(17.23)			1.38	(17.69)			1.34	(17.37)
Pseudo-R^2	0.28		0.35		0.27		0.35		0.28		0.36	

Estimated probit coefficients for stock ownership using the 2001 SCF. A household is defined as a stockholder if the household owns more than $500 in stock. Only households with net worth > $10K are included. T-statistics are in parenthesis.

Table 6.8 OLS regressions on stock as a share of liquid financial assets – stockholders only

	1		2		3	
Intercept	37.98	(4.65)	29.08	(3.62)	37.23	(4.52)
Age	−0.19	(−4.07)	−0.19	(−3.98)	−0.19	(−4.24)
Log(income)	−1.31	(−1.48)	−1.06	(−1.19)	−1.27	(−1.44)
Log(financial assets)	3.23	(5.00)	3.51	(5.41)	3.30	(5.11)
Number of children	1.13	(2.20)	0.92	(1.78)	1.18	(2.28)
Married (yes = 1)	−0.86	(−0.62)	−1.44	(−1.03)	−0.86	(−0.62)
Years of education	0.51	(2.04)	0.58	(2.32)	0.53	(2.13)
Real estate equity/net worth	−0.07	(−4.31)				
Mortgage/Financial wealth			−0.02	(−0.64)		
House/financial wealth					−0.07	(−3.66)
Adj.-R^2	0.03		0.03		0.03	

Estimated coefficients from regressions using the 2001 SCF using survey weights. Stock/liquid financial assets (stocks + bonds + cash) are the dependent variable in all regressions. All households with positive stockholdings and net worth > $10K and stockholding greater than $000 are included in these regressions. T-statistics are in parenthesis.

in a DC plan (which usually includes stock) significantly increases the probability. The fraction of liquid financial assets[5] invested in stock has a similar relationship with these real estate measures, as shown in Table 6.8. The negative relation between stockholdings and real estate is consistent with a substitution effect – for a given level of wealth, households that choose to spend more on housing have less to invest in other assets. If fixed costs are associated with stock investments, this would imply lower participation rates. The negative relation could also result from a reduced willingness to take on stock market risk when leveraged real estate represents a significant background risk.

Perhaps the aspect of data on portfolio choice that is most challenging to traditional theories is the apparent lack of diversification in the stockholdings of a significant number of households. Table 6.9 presents tabulations from the SCF, indicating the prevalence of investments in individual stocks and also of investments in own company stock. Although the SCF does not allow a precise measure of diversification (for instance, the number of stocks in DC pension accounts are not reported), we define undiversified households as those with more than 50% of their equity holdings in brokerage accounts with fewer than 10 stocks and implicitly treat all other holdings as diversified. By this measure, diversification has increased since the early 1990s, when more than 30% of households with equity fell into this category. In 2001, this percentage had fallen to 13.7%. Undiversified households were older by about 5 years, but wealth differences varied over the 5 surveys with diversified households slightly wealthier on average in 2001. Diversified and undiversified households hold similar average shares of real estate and private businesses.

[5] Liquid financial assets are defined as the sum of stocks, bonds, and cash.

Table 6.9 Evidence on the diversification of stockholdings

	1989	1992	1995	1998	2001
Panel A: all households					
Mean percent of equity held in					
Brokerage accounts	36.4	38.4	21.4	20.0	19.3
Mutual funds	8.9	11.6	15.3	15.7	14.6
Rusts and managed accounts	4.2	3.3	2.6	4.2	4.8
Defined contribution pensions	50.4	56.7	60.7	60.2	61.3
Mean percent own company stock/total	12.3	8.9	6.4	5.2	5.3
Panel B: undiversified households					
Percent of total equity reported	21.0	18.3	13.6	11.3	12.0
Percent of households with equity	32.5	23.7	17.8	14.8	13.7
Mean percent own company stock/total	35.0	31.5	30.5	25.2	29.2
Mean age	50.9	51.0	53.9	51.7	50.3
Mean equity/net worth	16.7	18.3	23.6	29.1	28.4
Mean business/net worth	7.6	8.3	5.5	5.3	5.2
Mean real estate/net worth	51.8	48.0	47.9	49.7	50.0
Real net worth	461,327	413,194	392,998	429,649	517,481
Panel C: diversified households					
Mean percent own company stock/total	1.4	1.9	1.2	1.7	1.5
Mean age	47.0	47.6	46.0	47.2	47.1
Mean equity/net worth	20.0	26.5	31.4	35.7	36.2
Mean business/net worth	5.6	6.1	4.3	5.7	5.8
Mean real estate/net worth	53.8	49.5	50.1	42.9	45.2
Real net worth	466,896	360,744	341,218	433,978	549,104

Tabulations are from the 2001 SCF, using survey weights. Average across households of shares, levels of investments, and household characteristics. Households with positive stockholdings greater than $500 are included. Panel A is for all such households. Panel B is for undiversified households defined as those households with more than 50% of their equity positions in a brokerage account that has fewer than 10 stocks. Panel C is for all other households with stockholding greater than $500.

For undiversified households, own company stock is a significant factor in all survey years, comprising 35.0% of total stock in 1989 and 28.4% in 2001. Holdings of own company stock are particularly difficult to explain from a diversification perspective because returns are correlated with labor income risk. Undiversified households invested in own company stock and households invested in other stocks appear to be quite distinct groups (less than 20% of undiversified households held both own company stock and other stocks in all years).

Despite the apparent fall in undiversified households directly invested into single securities captured by the SCF, over the same period own company stock investments have grown rapidly in retirement accounts. Some of the increase in own company stockholding may be the result of a corporate shift away from stock option, bonus, and purchase plans toward stock-based compensation in more tax-favored retirement plans. According to the Investment Company Institute (2003), 8.8 million households owned individual stock inside employer-sponsored retirement plans, with 51% owning exclusively employer stock. The role of employer incentives to hold own company stock in DC pension plans via Employee Stock Ownership Plans (ESOPs), as discussed in Section 3.4, is likely one reason for this phenomenon. Further evidence on the role of employer stock is discussed in Section 5.3.

3. THEORIES OF PORTFOLIO CHOICE

This section provides a brief overview of the main strands of the traditional literature on portfolio choice, which has been surveyed more extensively elsewhere.[6] A common feature of many of the earlier theories is that wealth from all income sources is implicitly assumed to be capitalized and to be held in financial assets that can be freely traded. One can think of these theories as implicitly applying to a complete markets setting. We also survey the more recent theoretical literature that relaxes the assumption that all income is capitalized, complicating the portfolio choice problem but potentially explaining some of the heterogeneity observed in the data.

3.1. Basic Analytic Framework

Much of the theoretical literature shares a basic analytic framework, a representative version of which is developed here. We assume that period utility is of the constant relative risk aversion (CRRA) form because it is the most commonly used specification and it allows the derivation of some closed form results.

Assume that an investor maximizes expected utility over a horizon T:

$$U_t = E_t\left[\sum_{x=0}^{T}\left(C_{t+x}^{1-\gamma} - 1\right)/(1-\gamma)\right] \tag{3.1}$$

The agent chooses to invest s_{t+1} in stocks and b_{t+1} in bonds and consumes c_t at time t. The consumption and saving choice is subject to the flow wealth constraint:

$$c_t + s_{t+1} + b_{t+1} \leq s_t\left(1 + r_t^s\right) + b_t\left(1 + r_t^b\right) + y_t, \tag{3.2}$$

[6]See, e.g., Heaton and Lucas (2000a).

where r_t^s is the return on stocks at time t, r_t^b is the return on bonds at time t, and y_t is risky nontradable income.

For an unconstrained investor j, the resulting Euler equation is

$$E_t\left\{\left(\frac{c_{t+1}^j}{c_t^j}\right)^{-\gamma}\left(r_{t+1}^s - r_{t+1}^b\right) = 0\right\}. \tag{3.3}$$

Under the assumption that consumption growth and returns are lognormally distributed conditional on information at time t, (3.3) can be written as

$$\mu_t^s = \mu_t^b - \frac{1}{2}\mathrm{var}_t\left(r_{t+1}^s\right) + \gamma\mathrm{cov}_t\left[\log\left(c_{t+1}^j/c_t^j\right), r_{t+1}^s\right] \tag{3.4}$$

where μ denotes a mean return. Relation (3.4) implies a joint restriction on individual consumption growth and investment returns.

With assumed dynamics for returns and nontradable income, this setting yields implications for savings and the proportion of wealth invested in each security. Early and enduring contributions include Merton (1969, 1971) and Samuelson (1969). Merton (1969, 1971) develops conditions for optimal portfolio shares under a variety of assumptions about the returns process and utility specification using dynamic programming. Closed-form solutions are obtained when returns are generated by a Brownian motion process, and for HARA utility functions, a class with CRRA and constant absolute risk aversion (CARA) is included.

One important result that emerges from Merton's analysis is a two-fund separation theorem where there is no risk in nontradable income. The separation theorem states that given n assets with lognormally distributed prices, there exists a unique pair of "mutual funds" consisting of a linear combination of the assets such that independent of preferences, wealth distribution, or time horizon; investors will be indifferent between choosing from a linear combination of these two funds or a linear combination of the original n assets. This reduces the analysis of many assets to a two-asset case as assumed in (3.2).

When there is no nontradable income ($y_t \equiv 0$) and the conditional distribution of asset returns is constant over time, Merton shows that the portfolio share of risky assets in wealth, ω, is constant and is given by

$$\omega = \frac{\mu^s - \mu^b}{\mathrm{var}(r^s)\gamma} \tag{3.5}$$

3.2. Time Variation in Returns

Barberis (2000), Campbell and Viceira (1999), Kandel and Stambaugh (1996), Nielsen and Vassalou (2002), Wachter (2002), and Xia (2001), among others, study dynamic models of optimal portfolio choice in the face of time variation in the distribution of asset returns. Typically, expected returns are assumed to move with aggregate information such as price-dividend ratios and interest rates. Calibrations of these models predict considerable variation in portfolios shares because variation in expected returns is assumed not to be simultaneously accompanied by changes in risk.

Campbell and Viceira (2001, 2002) tackle the application of time variation in real and nominal interest rates in a model with a long-lived agent motivated by the desire to smooth their stream of real consumption. They show that the relative magnitude of real and inflationary components of interest rate volatility drives the demand for short- and long-term bonds. In low inflation regimes, nominal bonds are an adequate substitute for inflation indexed bonds and thus provide an effective hedge against real interest rate movements. Hence, a policy of inflation stabilization would appear to provide a motive for long horizon investors to hold long-term nominal bonds. Brennan and Xia (2001) provide closed form results on inflation hedging with long and short nominal bonds.

Campbell and Viceira (2002) and Lynch (2001) use a partial equilibrium analysis to show that the cost of ignoring return predictability through lost market timing opportunities can be significant. Because the variation in investment opportunities considered in these papers is due to aggregate information, these analyses cannot address the heterogeneity in portfolio holdings that is the subject of this chapter. A further issue is that in equilibrium, the average investors cannot arbitrarily adjust their portfolio shares. For this reason, these decision theoretic analyses are unable to address the fundamental question of whether the time variation reflects changes in preferences or other risk factors that diminish the apparent advantages of market timing.

3.3. Uninsurable Background Risk

When some income (e.g., labor or private business income) cannot be capitalized, investors must evaluate their financial investments taking into account this background risk. Undiversified investments in risky assets such as housing also generate background risk. The earlier analyses relevant to these types of complications consider the effect of constraints on portfolio weights (e.g., Anderson and Danthine, 1981; Cvitani'c and Karatzas, 1992; Mayers, 1973). In these analyses, it is assumed that a subset of risky assets must be held in fixed amounts. Under fairly standard assumptions, this produces an additional hedging term that depends on the covariance between the constrained asset and the freely traded assets but not on risk preferences. Notice that these analyses imply that heterogeneity resulting from uninsurable risk invalidates the convenient two-fund separation theorems of Merton (1971). If background risks vary across individuals in their co-variation with individual stocks, holding a combination of a diversified market portfolio and risk-free securities no longer is optimal. Rather, portfolio optimization requires underweighting or shorting stocks that hedge the nontraded component of income risk.

More recently, a number of authors have derived some analytical results on portfolio choice in the present background risk (quantitative results from related calibrated theories are discussed in detail in Section 4). For example, Cuoco (1997), Duffie et al. (1997), He and Pagès (1993), Svensson and Werner (1993), and Vila and Zariphopoulou (1997) present existence results and some characteristics of the solution to the continuous-time portfolio choice problem with nontradable stochastic labor income and borrowing constraints. Gollier (2001) provides slightly more general results (in terms of the utility and distributional assumptions required) on portfolio choices with background risk in the context of two-period and discrete time models.

Notice that in the absence of borrowing or short-sales constraints, (3.3) and (3.4) hold not only when all income comes from financial investments but also for investors with a nontraded income stream y_t. This income could come from a variety of sources, including wages, restricted pension holdings, housing rents, and private businesses. The background income process does affect portfolio composition, but only indirectly, through its effect on the variability of consumption and its correlation with financial returns.

The theoretical literature establishes that nontradable background risk can affect the desired level and composition of liquid asset holdings. When combined with fixed participation costs, it is also possible to justify nonparticipation in the stock market by households with low wealth levels or short horizons. Unfortunately, a number of theoretical complications make it difficult, if not impossible, to tease out sharp empirical predictions from these models. These caveats may help explain the mixed success of empirical attempts to explain cross-sectional variation in portfolio holdings with variation in background risk and moderate participation costs, which are surveyed in Section 4.

Intuitively, one might expect theory to predict that the fraction of investments held in risky stocks would be inversely related to the correlation between the stock returns and the background risk source because positive correlation magnifies total consumption risk. Further, one might expect that all else equal, people exposed to higher variance background risk would be expected to hold less wealth in stocks because they would have a reduced tolerance for risk. Theoretically it is easy to construct counterexamples to this intuition due to the following considerations:

1. Only utility functions exhibiting "proper risk aversion" [like the CRRA utility function of (3.1)] have the property that increased background risk, which induces higher effective risk aversion.
2. More importantly, the addition of a risky income stream that is bounded below can reduce overall consumption risk, increasing effective risk tolerance even with proper risk aversion.
3. Portfolio composition and savings decisions are intertwined. With CRRA preferences, this interaction can result in stock market participation rates that rise with the assumed coefficient of risk aversion.

Pratt and Zeckhauser (1987) characterize utility functions with "proper risk aversion," which is defined by the property that an undesirable lottery can never be made desirable by the presence of an independent, undesirable lottery. They show that this is a feature of exponential, power, and logarithmic utility functions, so it holds for all of the most commonly used utility specifications. Kimball (1993) and Gollier and Pratt (1996) further examine the relation between utility functions and background risk.

A number of papers (e.g., Bertaut and Haliassos, 1997; Cocco et al., 1998; Heaton and Lucas, 1997, 2000b; Koo, 1995; Campbell and Viceira, 2002) demonstrate that adding a risky income stream that cannot be capitalized (i.e., labor income) may actually increase tolerance for stock market risk. The reason is that any assumed floor level of exogenous income effectively is a risk-free asset, which is a perfect substitute for risk-free bond holdings. Although nontradable income is risky, it limits bad outcomes relative to investment income, which significantly reduces effective risk aversion. For this reason, including background income risk can make it more difficult to explain nonparticipation in the stock market or low levels of stockholdings. More generally, these models suggest that quantitative predictions of calibrated models are highly sensitive to the assumed stochastic processes, an implication explored further in Section 5.

3.4. Trading Frictions

A number of authors maintain the assumption that all wealth is held in financial assets but incorporate some type of trading friction. Examples of theoretical models with exclusively financial assets and trading frictions include He and Pearson (1991), Karatzas et al. (1991), and Xu and Shreve (1992). These authors analytically examine the case where the payoffs to financial securities do not span all the uncertainty in the economy, and there are short-sales restrictions.

Constantinides (1986) and Davis and Norman (1990) consider the effect of proportional transaction costs on trades of risky securities. In these papers, the only reason to trade is to rebalance one's portfolio between the risk-free and risky assets. Constantinides (1986) finds that such transaction costs do not discourage stockholding – target portfolio allocations are similar to those in a frictionless environment. Rather the effect of the costs is to discourage frequent trading so that portfolio shares fluctuate more than in a frictionless environment. Interestingly, this finding contrasts with the implications of calibrated models with risky labor income, where the primary reason to trade is consumption smoothing rather than portfolio rebalancing, and the demand for trading is relatively inelastic. In that case, Heaton and Lucas (1997) find that transaction costs can influence portfolio shares, causing agents to tilt their portfolio toward assets with lower trading costs. More generally, trading frictions are often incorporated into models with nontradable income risk and nonparticipation, but a detailed discussion of their effects in more complicated environments is discussed in Section 4.

Some types of taxes, such as those levied on capital gains, are theoretically analogous to proportional transaction costs. These taxes, by analogy, can be expected to discourage portfolio rebalancing but to have less effect on consumption smoothing. Relative taxes on different sources of capital income may also affect portfolio allocations. For instance, Black (1980) and Tepper (1981) and more recently Shoven and Sialm (2003) and Dammon et al. (2004) consider the optimal division of portfolio holdings between tax favored and taxable accounts. These studies generally reach the intuitive conclusion that placing relatively highly taxed investments in tax protected accounts is optimal. Empirical evidence, however, suggests that many people ignore this logic, holding highly taxed investments in taxable accounts. Amromin (2002) summarizes this evidence and suggests that liquidity considerations may partially explain this behavior.

The tax treatment and regulations governing DC pension plans are another friction with potentially important implications for portfolio choice. Specifically, the interaction between tax law and pension regulations may help account for the prevalence of concentrated investments in employer stock, despite the diversification losses for employees. Where employer stock is provided via employer contributions, it is common to provide it through an Employee Stock Ownership Plan (ESOP), a type of retirement plan often coupled with an employer sponsored DC plans. From an employer perspective, an ESOP is an effective vehicle for compensating employees with employer stock because it offers several tax advantages.[7] To qualify for these tax advantages, an ESOP must comply with many of the regulatory requirements of a 401(k) plan, including the rules that mandate nondiscrimination and that limit the share of benefits going to highly compensated employees. This may be a reason for companies providing stocks to lower paid workers; even if in the absence of tax incentives and regulations, they would choose to target stock distributions more narrowly.

Because employees are restricted from diversifying ESOP holdings, they are a source of background risk that can be expected to affect other aspects of portfolio choice. Interestingly, ESOP participants have a legal right to partially diversify their ESOP holdings once they have attained age 55 and have 10 years of service with the firm (the employer may impose less stringent rules). Under these rules, each participant may diversify up to 25% of their ESOP shares in the five years following eligibility and this fraction increases to 50% in the sixth year after becoming eligible. The remaining balance of shares is held in the ESOP until the employee leaves the firm. These rules create natural experiments to determine the extent that employees voluntarily maintain large exposures to the idiosyncratic risk of their company.

[7] ESOPs have also been attractive to companies attempting to fend off unwelcome merger overtures by placing the firm's equity in friendly employee hands. Additionally, they have been used as part of corporate restructurings where employees take a long-term equity stake in exchange for lower wages.

3.5. Life-Cycle Effects

Agents generally accumulate more wealth when a nontradable income source is considered than in similar models with only financial assets because a "buffer stock" of savings is used to partially self-insure against the risk from nontradable income. In finite horizon versions of the model, the life-cycle pattern of background income often creates an additional retirement motive for saving starting in middle age. A bequest motive also can influence the level of and allocation of savings.

An important question for portfolio theory is whether the share of savings invested in risky assets should vary with age? A well-known, if unintuitive, result due to Samuelson (1969) is that under normally assumed preference specifications, there is no age variation in portfolio shares when capital income is a person's only source of income. This contradicts the common view of many financial advisors (Bodie and Crane, 1997), who counsel that older people should reduce the share held in stocks. Bodie et al. (1992) provide some theoretical underpinnings for the popular view. They show that if the ability to smooth income shocks by adjusting labor supply is greater for younger workers, then older people should hold less stock in their portfolios. Jagannathan and Kocherlakota (1996), Cocco et al. (1998), Benzoni et al. (2007), and Farhi and Panageas (2007) also discuss reasons for changing portfolio investments over the life cycle.

3.6. Nonparticipation

There are two, not necessarily mutually exclusive, ways to motivate stock market nonparticipation in standard models. One is that some people are limited by a short-sales constraint. The second is that fixed costs discourage participation. This fixed cost could be tangible, such as brokerage fees or the cost of becoming informed about investing in stocks. Alternatively the cost could be some type of psychic cost of putting savings at risk that is not captured by the standard preference assumptions. Because of the difficulty of obtaining closed form solutions when these factors are considered, there are few analytical results, although an exception is Basak and Cuoco (1998). (See Section 4.4 for a discussion of calibrated theories of nonparticipation.)

An interesting but indirect implication of analyses with uninsurable background risk is that nonparticipation in the stock market cannot be explained by background risk alone – other market frictions such as short-sales constraints or fixed costs of market participation must also be present. The reason is that although background risk changes the target ratio of stocks to other liquid assets, and may even motivate a short position when stock returns are highly correlated with large background risks, the probability that the demand for stocks is exactly zero is negligible. This fact, together with the observation that many households hold no stock, is one motivation for routinely imposing short-sales constraints in these analyses.

It is often assumed that investors can borrow at most a limited amount in the bond market and cannot go short in stocks. When a short-sales constraint is binding, the equality in (3.3) is replaced by an inequality, and the constant share rule (3.5) need not hold. Perhaps the most important implication of these constraints is for asset pricing theory because they imply that the marginal investor might not have a consumption pattern proportional to aggregate consumption.

Where the agent does not participate in either the stock or the bond market and is thus against both the borrowing and short-sale constraints requires that the following inequalities are satisfied:

$$\beta E_t\left[\left(y_{t+1}/y_t\right)^{-\gamma}\left(1+r^s_{t+1}\right)\right] \leq 1 \tag{3.6}$$

and

$$\beta E_t\left[\left(y_{t+1}/y_t\right)^{-\gamma}\left(1+r^b_{t+1}\right)\right] \leq 1 \tag{3.7}$$

An empirical difficulty with this formulation, as emphasized by Heaton and Lucas (1997), is finding plausible parameters where people choose to hold risk-free assets but do not hold stocks; where (3.6) holds but (3.7) does not. For instance, when background income risk is uncorrelated with the market, and even assuming an equity premium significantly below its historical average, standard parameterizations of this model counterfactually predict that agents with low levels of wealth will put all their savings in stocks. Only at higher levels of financial wealth does the risk of stocks start to dominate the attraction of the equity premium, leading to limited investment in stocks. When stock returns are strongly positively correlated with shocks to nontraded income, the model can generate policy rules that include risk-free securities at lower wealth levels. Alternatively, a fixed cost of stock market participation can discourage stockholdings at low wealth levels.

3.7. Generalized Preferences

Recent results in the asset pricing literature emphasize the importance of relaxing the restrictive assumptions of time-separable CRRA utility. In models with habit persistence, current consumption is evaluated relative to a weighted average of past consumption. Works by Constantinides (1990), Campbell and Cochrane (1999), Heaton (1995), and others demonstrate that this modification to the representative consumer model can help explain the equity premium puzzle along with observed time variation in expected returns. Another successful class of models builds on the recursive utility specification of Kreps and Porteus (1978) and allows for separate parameters governing the elasticity of intertemporal substitution and risk aversion. This added flexibility has proven useful in simultaneously understanding observed risk premia and risk-free rates (see, e.g., Epstein and Zin, 1989; Weil, 1990).

Evaluation of decision theoretic models with these alternative preference assumptions opens additional avenues for understanding portfolio choice. First, the predicted level of savings is altered, especially under standard models of habit persistence. The first-order effect is to increase savings in reaction to an increased aversion to variation in consumption over time (Heaton and Lucas, 1997). Second, under both habit persistence and recursive utility models that build on the Kreps–Porteus specification, the individual investor chooses portfolios to hedge against variation in future consumption. This additional hedging demand can be significant, especially in the context of time varying investment opportunities as considered by Campbell and Viceira (1999) and Skiadas and Schroder (1999), for example. Even without time varying investment opportunities, there can be important variation in the optimal investment in risky assets when an investor is faced with variation in nontraded risks, again especially in models with habit persistence. This occurs because of the variation in risk aversion induced by the model. The result is substantial trading that may be counterfactual (Heaton and Lucas, 1997). The predicted dynamics of trading does allow the model's predictions to be compared to observed trading patterns, however.

The confounding effect of higher risk aversion on stock market participation in the presence of fixed participation costs is due to the connection between the risk aversion and the precautionary motive for savings under CRRA utility. In models with CRRA utility, the precautionary demand for savings depends on the assumed dynamics of income and investment opportunities. When the model assumptions induce a precautionary motive, increasing risk aversion with other parameters held fixed typically results in increased savings. Because the importance of the equity premium relative to the fixed participation cost increases with the level of savings, more risk-averse agents are therefore more likely to participate in the stock market. This mechanism is explored by Gakidis (1997) and Gomes and Michaelides (2003). They consider general settings that also allow for the separation between the risk aversion and the intertemporal elasticity of substitution. In these models, savings are also determined by the deterministic component of income along with the assumed value of the intertemporal elasticity of substitution. These types of analyses suggest that separating the coefficient of relative risk aversion from the elasticity of intertemporal substitution improves the capability to generate predictions consistent with intuition and observed behavior.

4. QUANTITATIVE ANALYSES

The cross-sectional data presented in Section 2 suggests that many households manage their financial wealth in a way that is inconsistent with frictionless markets. Once the assumptions of frictionless markets and a representative agent are relaxed, however, there are many possible avenues to explore. We begin by describing the results of several of the first studies to reinterpret traditional theories to take into account heterogeneity and its empirical implications. We then turn to calibrated theories exploring heterogeneity arising from uninsurable background risks – from sources such as labor income, private business or employer stockholdings, restrictions on pension investments, and concentrated real estate holdings – which can create considerable heterogeneity in optimal portfolio allocations. Recall that the reason for the effect on portfolio choice is that these risks affect the consumption process and hence the tolerance for tradable financial risks. Researchers have concentrated on these particular background risks because of their quantitative importance for many households (see Table 6.4) and the apparent difficulty of avoiding or insuring against them. These analyses provide some support for the idea that differential background risk systematically influences portfolio choice but overall account for only a limited amount of the observed cross-sectional variation.

4.1. The Consumption of Stockholders and Nonstockholders

A counterfactual empirical implication of calibrating (3.3) with aggregate consumption data, the historical equity premium, and standard values of the risk aversion coefficient is that the representative consumer would invest all wealth in the stock market or even takes a levered position in stocks. This is because aggregate consumption is neither very risky nor highly correlated with the stock market and because of the high equity premium. The difficulty of explaining low or even moderate levels of stockholdings in a model calibrated with aggregate consumption is the partial equilibrium counterpart of the equity premium puzzle proposed by Mehra and Prescott (1985).

The simplest way to incorporate heterogeneity as a potential solution to this empirical failure to predict portfolio shares with aggregate consumption is to calibrate (3.3) using consumption data for individuals who actually hold stocks. If markets are relatively complete for stock market participants, then the covariance of stock returns with total stockholder consumption, not aggregate consumption, is the relevant predictor of risky asset holdings.

Mankiw and Zeldes (1991) were the first to propose and test this idea, using data on food consumption in the PSID. They find that the consumption of stockholders has a higher variance and is more highly correlated with stock returns. A number of studies have repeated this type of analysis using broader measures of consumption from the Consumer Expenditure Survey (see e.g., Brav et al., 1999; Parker, 2001; Vissing-Jorgensen, 2002a,b) and the U.K. Family Expenditure Survey (Attanasio et al., 2002). Similar to the results of Mankiw and Zeldes (1991), these studies report that the consumption of identified stockholders is more consistent with the predictions of (3.3) for moderate levels of risk aversion than that of nonstockholders. In addition, Ait-Sahalia et al. (2004) find that the consumption of wealthy individuals, as represented by the consumption of luxury goods, covaries more highly with stock returns than does aggregate consumptions. To the extent that wealthier individuals are stockholders, this is also consistent with the idea that stockholders hold riskier consumption bundles.

Collectively, these studies show that model performance is improved by focusing on the consumption of market participants. Assuming moderate risk aversion, these models still predict far larger investments in stocks than observed in practice. However, these studies continue to impose significant aggregation by imposing that all stockholders experience the same consumption growth process. The models described in the rest of this section take heterogeneity further, by assuming that even stockholders have limited opportunities for consumption smoothing.

4.2. Calibrated Models with Background Risk

In the last decade, a number of authors have used numerical methods to examine the quantitative implications of background risk for portfolio choice in theoretical models. Many of these studies also assume other types of trading frictions, such as borrowing and short-sale constraints or fixed or variable trading costs. For convenience, we classify these analyses under the broad heading of background risk, even though the trading frictions are often essential elements of the story.

4.2.1. Labor Income

Labor income, because of its importance for most households and the difficulty of insuring it, is a natural source of background risk to consider. Koo (1995) studies a decision-theoretic model of portfolio choice in which infinitely lived investors with time and state separable preferences face uninsurable labor income risk. Heaton and Lucas (1997) consider a similar structure that also allows for transaction costs and habit formation. Bertaut and Haliassos (1997), Cocco et al. (1998), and Campbell and Viceira (2002) analyze similar environments with finitely lived agents.

All analyses using infinite horizon models and standard preferences find that despite high levels of assumed background risk, savings are held mostly or entirely in the stock market. In fact, for reasonable parameter values, agents often want to take a leveraged position in stocks. This is because the assumed floor on labor income tends to reduce overall risk exposure, thereby increasing risk tolerance. Further, labor income has a low correlation with stock returns, at least over the annual horizons that most of these studies focus on. These factors, in combination with a sizable equity premium, imply that stockholdings tend to dominate bond holdings.

The counterfactual prediction of portfolios concentrated in stocks has led researchers to look for alternative specifications that generate a demand for risk-free assets. It is possible, for instance, to increase the predicted share invested in risk-free bonds under alternative preferences. Assuming habit formation, Heaton and Lucas (1997) report positive bond holdings when effective risk aversion is high but income is low. Habit formation, however, has the undesirable property that portfolio composition is unrealistically volatile, varying sharply with the habit stock.

In general, life-cycle models appear to be more successful than infinite horizon models in explaining many aspects of observed portfolio choices and their interaction with labor income. Age can affect portfolio choice in a variety of ways. For instance, risk tolerance may vary with time horizon, earning potential or health status; and the age-earnings profile, and timing of bequests, affects savings behavior in the presence of borrowing constraints. Life-cycle models, in combination with time nonseparability in preferences, have been particularly successful at matching certain features of the data. Gakidis (1997) considers a finite horizon model with nontime-separable preferences where the coefficient of relative risk aversion can be separated from the elasticity of intertemporal substitution. He finds that it is possible to get positive bond holdings for the elderly, by assuming a higher elasticity of intertemporal substitution than with standard preferences. More recently, Gomes and Michaelides (2003) show that in a life-cycle model with steeply sloping age income profiles for young workers, it is relatively easy to explain nonparticipation. Young people want to consume, not save, because they anticipate higher income in the future, and they are constrained by borrowing and short-sales constraints. Even a relatively small fixed cost of stock market participation is large relative to the gains from investing their limited savings. It is also easier to explain positive bond holdings, even using standard preferences, for older people, who have primarily financial wealth rather than human capital.

4.2.2. Business Income

The higher volatility and higher correlation of business income with stock returns, as well as its prevalence in wealthy households, motivates its consideration as a potentially important background risk. It can be incorporated into models that are theoretically identical to those with nontradable labor income under the assumption that any direct effect of business ownership on utility is additively separable. Then, the main effect of including private business income is to change the stochastic process associated with background risk. As for labor income, when business income puts a floor on income, including them can make it more difficult to explain the low level of stockholdings by many households.

Heaton and Lucas (2000a) show that a background risk process that reflects proprietary business income, in combination with somewhat higher risk aversion than assumed in their earlier analysis, is sufficient to generate considerable variation in predicted portfolio shares, although it does not explain stock market nonparticipation. Polkovnichenko (2007) also considers income generated from privately held businesses or "entrepreneurial income." In part due to its higher correlation with stock market returns, he finds that the predicted demand for stocks is lower than in models that focus on labor income but still higher than what is commonly observed.

4.2.3. Housing

The largest financial investment of a typical household is owner-occupied housing. Its salient features for portfolio choice are that it is undiversified, highly leveraged and costly to adjust. These factors suggest its potential to influence portfolio choice, but there are offsetting considerations. The accompanying leverage and limitations on diversification suggest it might induce lower stockholdings, but the low correlation of housing returns with the stock market suggests it has diversification advantages that could encourage greater stockholding.

Housing is incorporated into portfolio choice models in a variety of ways. In some cases, authors posit a direct effect on utility that is separate from other types of consumption. In other models, it is treated as a lumpy investment with adjustment costs that provides a stream of consumption or income that is not distinguished in the utility function. In either case, analyzing the risk and return to housing is complicated by the unobservable consumption stream that it generates.

Henderson and Ioannides (1983) introduce the constraint that housing investment is at least as large as housing consumption. In a theoretical model, Brueckner (1997) shows that when this constraint is binding, there is a distortion in both housing and nonhousing assets and the portfolio is inefficient in a mean-variance sense. Flavin and Yamashita (2002), also abstracting from labor income, posit that the consumption demand for housing is likely to create a highly levered position in real estate for younger households. This levered position in a risky asset should affect their tolerance for stock market risk relative to older households who have paid down their mortgage. Flavin and Yamashita simulate what optimal portfolio shares should be in theory, calibrating the model with estimates of the correlation between housing and other investments. Because the return to housing has a low correlation with the return to stocks, housing improves the mean-variance efficient investment frontier. In their framework, using reasonable risk parameters, the optimal stock to net worth ratio is 9% for the youngest households and 60% for the oldest. In addition, it is optimal for each home to be fully mortgaged at all ages. These predictions differ from empirical evidence on stockholding by age in Table 6.6 and evidence on mortgage use in Curcuru (2005). Curcuru finds that only 66% of all households, and 26.4% of seniors, had a mortgage on their primary residence in the 2001 SCF.

The large transaction costs of adjusting real estate decrease housing returns and have other portfolio implications as well. Grossman and Laroque (1990) develop a theoretical model with a single illiquid durable consumption, which incurs a large transaction cost when sold. They show that it is optimal to adjust consumption of the durable only after a large wealth change, and that with CRRA utility the transaction cost reduces the optimal amount of risky asset investment. In a continuous-time framework,

Cauley et al. (2003) show that the inability to freely adjust housing investment substantially alters target holdings of financial assets. In particular, this constraint results in significantly decreased stockholdings for households with large house value to net worth ratios. Additionally when there is a rental market for housing, the relationship between rental prices and stock returns produces another source or risk when investors consider jointly housing and stockholding (see Sinai and Souleles, 2005).

As with models of portfolio choice incorporating labor income, the effect of illiquid housing also plays a larger role in a life-cycle setting. Cocco (2004) and Holden and Hu (2001) present similar models in which housing provides consumption and investment services and where the frictions in the housing market influence portfolio choice differently at different ages. For households saving to meet a down-payment constraint, there is a potential tension between the higher average returns on stocks that reduce the expected time to purchase, and greater risk that could delay purchase. In these analyses, young households anticipating a house purchase or with a highly levered position in housing are predicted to hold a smaller fraction of liquid assets in stocks than in the absence of a housing decision.

4.3. Restricted Pension Investments

As discussed earlier, a DC retirement account with investment choice allows an individual to accumulate wealth for retirement in a variety of assets free from annual taxation. When an optimizing agent has access to a retirement account, their choice set is enriched: in addition to conventional saving and portfolio choices on a taxable basis, there are saving and portfolio choices on a tax-deferred basis. Section 3.3 discussed the tax efficiency arguments for holding high-taxed assets in tax-deferred retirement accounts. However, in a precautionary life-cycle model with exogenous stochastic labor income, Amromin (2002) shows there will be situations where bonds are voluntarily held both inside and outside of the retirement habitat.

Restrictions on pension investments, such as limitations on diversifying out of ESOP investments, variations in 401(k) employer matching contributions, and pre-retirement withdrawal rules, also are expected to influence portfolio choice. Moore (2007) explores the effects of typical pension plan restrictions on life-cycle portfolio choice behavior. In the model, an employee can freely allocate his retirement contributions to stocks and bonds as well as his outside portfolio, the employer makes matching contributions, and withdrawals or loans are available for emergency consumption. Calibrations suggest that the majority of wealth should be accumulated through retirement account contributions and only a small stock of wealth should be maintained outside of the retirement account to buffer income fluctuations. When employers match retirement contributions using employer stock with long holding requirements, the pension account is less attractive, and the remaining portfolio choices become more conservative. Heterogeneity in plan rules can create significant differences in optimal plan participation and asset allocations.

Counterfactually, however, the model predicts that the outside portfolio will be more aggressively invested in stocks than the retirement portfolio, a manifestation of the tax efficiency argument presented in Section 3.3.

4.4. Explaining Nonparticipation

There have been a number of attempts to calibrate the size of the fixed costs necessary to discourage stock market participation. One of the earliest analyses is by Saito (1995), who calibrates a model in which all wealth is held in the form of stocks or bonds, and calculates how large a fixed cost would be required at time 0 to result in some agents holding only bonds. He finds costs ranging from 3 to 54% of wealth, depending on the assumed risk aversion and size of equity premium. These numbers are high for the same reason that agents are predicted to put all their wealth into stocks in the calibrated models discussed above – it is costly to forego the high equity premium.[8] Polkovnichenko (2007) finds that in a model with heterogeneous risk aversion and heterogeneous idiosyncratic income risk, the fixed cost required to generate nonparticipation is potentially much lower.

Because stockholdings are highly skewed toward households with high net worth, any convincing explanation of heterogeneity in portfolio holdings must also be consistent with this fact. Explanations emphasizing fixed costs are consistent with this observation because such costs are especially onerous for people with low wealth. Building on the work by Luttmer (1999), Paiella (2001) uses the Consumer Expenditure Survey and estimates the necessary fixed costs to preclude stock market participation when controlling for wealth and demographic variation at the household level. She finds that the fixed costs needed to explain nonparticipation might not be large. Vissing-Jorgensen (2002a,b) finds that an annual fixed participation cost of only \$50 can explain 50% of nonparticipants, whereas \$260 explains 75%.

4.5. Exploiting the Covariance of Background and Market Risks

The models discussed in Section 3.4 establish that holding stocks in the form of a diversified market portfolio need not be optimal in the presence of nontradable background risk. Most calibration exercises to date, however, abstract from the possibility of exploiting the correlation structure between tradable and nontraded risks and continue to treat a maximally diversified market portfolio as the benchmark risky asset. A partial exception is Davis and Willen (2000a,b), who measure the correlation between market returns and labor income for households with different levels of education, broad occupation group, and by sex, and they suggest that there are significant differences between groups in the effective risk of stock market investments. They do not, however, consider whether optimized portfolios could improve the ability to hedge nontradable risks. This question is addressed by Massa and Simonov (2004), using a unique panel of Swedish data with

[8]Basak and Cuoco (1998) and Vissing-Jorgensen (1997) also explore these issues.

detailed time series information on portfolio composition and income. They examine whether people use individual stocks to hedge nonfinancial income risk and find little evidence for hedging. Rather, they find a tendency to invest in stocks that are familiar in terms of geography or professional proximity. Further, exploration of these issues is likely a fruitful area for future research.

5. EMPIRICAL EVIDENCE AND ISSUES

The predictions of calibrated models, such as those outlined in Section 4, depend critically on the assumed statistical properties of background risks and their correlations with financial assets. In Section 5.1, we illustrate this issue with a stylized example. Aggregate statistics can be a starting point for many measurements of background risks. Summary statistics based on aggregate measures of background risks and their correlations with financial returns are presented in Section 5.2. Although these aggregate measures are suggestive about which risks might be important, panel data, when it is available, is arguably more informative about the individual risks that are most relevant to explaining cross-sectional differences in household portfolio choices. Section 5.3 summarizes the growing body of evidence based on panel data and attempts to link it to cross-sectional differences in portfolio choice. Although some studies find that various background risks influence portfolio choice, data limitations and statistical difficulties suggest that these results must be interpreted with caution.

5.1. An Illustrative Example

To illustrate the importance of the measurement issue, we review an example from Heaton and Lucas (2000a). At time t, the investor is assumed to maximize the utility function given by (3.1) with $T = \infty$ and subject to the budget equation given by (3.2). Further, there is a strict restriction against borrowing and short positions in the stock. To characterize the dynamics for stock returns and nontraded income, let

$$\boldsymbol{X}_t' = \left[\log\left(y_t/y_{t-1}\right) \log\left(1 + r_t^s\right)\right] \tag{5.1}$$

The vector $\boldsymbol{X}_t$ is assumed to follow a first-order autoregressive process:

$$\boldsymbol{X}_t = \mu + AX_{t-1} + B\varepsilon_t, \tag{5.2}$$

where the parameters are chosen to match several alternative assumptions about nontraded income. In Sections 5.2 and 5.3, we discuss evidence that can be used to calibrate the process (5.2).

In the "low background risk case," the mean and standard deviation of nontraded income growth are assumed to be 1 and 15%, respectively. This level of variability is consistent with studies that examine labor income risk faced by individuals. We also consider a "high background risk case" where the standard deviation of nontraded income is assumed to be 29%. As in Deaton (1991) and other studies, we assume that nontraded income growth is negatively correlated over time. This induces a precautionary demand for savings. For this example, we assume that the first-order autocorrelation of income is −0.4, which is consistent with the estimates of MaCurdy (1982).

Stock returns are assumed to have a mean of 7.75% and a standard deviation of 15.7% but are unpredictable over time. To capture the potential for hedging, we allow for correlation between the innovations in nontraded income and stock returns. The model is solved numerically using the methods described in Heaton and Lucas (1997). Table 6.10 reports summary statistics from simulations of the model under several alternative assumptions. In the table, "Corr" denotes the correlation between stock returns and nontraded income. In all cases, the discount factor β is assumed to be 0.9. This low value is needed to prevent the model from producing large levels of savings. In this way, the model can mimic some features of a life-cycle model where the individuals do not save early in life because of predictable increases in income. Because nontraded income is

Table 6.10 Model predictions of average stock and bond holdings

	Corr = −0.1	**Corr = 0**	**Corr = 0.1**	**Corr = 0.2**
	A. $\gamma = 5$, low background risk case			
Average bond holdings	0.03	0.05	0.07	0.11
Average stockholdings	1.12	1.14	1.15	1.15
Average proportion stock	0.98	0.97	0.96	0.93
	B. $\gamma = 8$, low background risk case			
Average bond holdings	0.46	0.52	0.68	0.83
Average stockholdings	0.98	0.95	0.83	0.70
Average proportion stock	0.72	0.68	0.58	0.48
	C. $\gamma = 5$, high background risk case			
Average bond holdings	0.18	0.24	0.39	0.46
Average stockholdings	1.11	1.08	0.96	0.92
Average proportion stock	0.89	0.85	0.74	0.70
	D. $\gamma = 8$, high background risk case			
Average bond holdings	0.75	0.79	0.89	0.97
Average stockholdings	0.67	0.64	0.55	0.48
Average proportion stock	0.50	0.46	0.39	0.34

Model predicted holdings. Averages across simulations. "Corr" is the assumed correlation between stock returns and labor income growth.

assumed to grow over time, the level of savings in each security is normalized by current income.

As we discussed in Section 4, this type of model has a difficult time producing reasonable levels of stock and bond holdings simultaneously, unless relatively extreme assumptions are imposed. In particular, at low levels of the risk-aversion parameter γ and for any correlation in the assumed range, there is little savings in bonds. For example, when $\gamma = 5$ and Corr $= 0$, 97% of savings is held in the form of stock in the low background risk case. Only with very high risk aversion and high levels of background risk are there significant bond holdings. If we use the more extreme parameters (panel D) as a basis for experimentation, notice that relatively small variation in the correlation between stock returns and nontraded income causes relatively large changes in the average stock position in savings. These results imply that measurement of the characteristics of background risk is critically important.

5.2. Aggregate Income Statistics

Summary statistics on the major income components and their aggregate properties in the United States are reported in Table 6.11. Wage income is "real wages and salaries," and business income is real "nonfarm proprietary income," from the national income and

Table 6.11 Aggregate income statistics – 1947–2003

	2003 values from NIPA ($ billions)		
		Percentage of total	
Wage income	5,100.2	59.9	
Business income	673.2	7.9	
Dividend income	431.0	5.1	
Interest income	583.2	6.9	
Rental income	176.3	2.1	
Housing services	1,544.9	18.2	
Total	8,508.8		
	Annual real log growth rate 1947–2003		
	Mean	**Standard deviation**	**Correlation with stock returns**
Wage income	3.14%	2.06%	0.06
Business income	1.94%	4.52%	0.11
Housing	1.96%	2.21%	0.051
Value-weighted stock	6.80%	16.71%	1

Income, housing services, and tax data is from NIPA tables. The value-weighted stock returns are from CRSP. Housing returns are from Piazessi et al. (2007).

product accounts, 1947 to 2003. Aggregate wage income, which makes up over 62% of total income, has a low contemporaneous correlation with the stock market and is not very risky. The results of Table 6.10 illustrate that models calibrated using aggregate wage income predict a counterfactually high demand for stocks. As discussed earlier, housing can be considered another source of nontraded or background risk. In the aggregate, the correlation between housing and stock returns is low at only 5.1%, and housing has a very low real return and standard deviation. This increases the difficulty of explaining low stockholdings in models calibrated with aggregate data because in aggregate housing is essentially a risk-free asset. Aggregate proprietary income is both riskier and more correlated with stock returns than is labor or housing income, suggesting it could be a slightly greater deterrent to stockholding than labor income risk. Notice, however, that at the aggregate level, this risk is still relatively small. For this reason, empirically more successful models are calibrated using measurements from individual data.

5.3. Evidence on Background Risk

5.3.1. Labor Income

Econometric analysis of panel data suggests that individual labor income is considerably more volatile than aggregate labor income. Individual labor income shocks appear to have a permanent and a transitory component, although estimates of the relative magnitude of each component vary depending on the types of heterogeneity considered and the statistical model used. For instance, Carroll and Samwick (1997) find that average individual labor income risk is roughly double aggregate risk, whereas Meghir and Pistaferri (2004) find that the risks are of the same magnitude but that aggregate risk is 2 to 3 times more persistent. There is evidence of significant heterogeneity in labor income risk. Using the PSID, Hubbard et al. (1995) find that labor income risk for individuals with only a household diploma is double that for individuals with a college degree. Gourinchas and Parker (2002) also find related differences across occupations. Managers and highly skilled professionals have about two-thirds the labor income risk of laborers or administrative staff.

Estimating the correlation between individual labor income and stock returns is complicated by the lack of data on portfolio composition that has both time series and panel dimension and by the difficulty of identifying unanticipated income shocks for individual households. These problems also make it difficult to detect a statistically significant relation between individual income processes and portfolio decisions. Nevertheless, several authors have tried to estimate these effects. Heaton and Lucas (2000a) examine income and imputed asset holdings from the 1979–1990 panel of individual tax returns. They find extensive heterogeneity in both the variability of individual income and the correlation of this income with stock returns. Using U.S. data from the PSID, Gakidis (1997) finds that households with a larger probability of realizing extremely low wage income are less likely to participate in the stock market. He finds that for those who are participating, the probability of very low wages reduces the portion invested in stocks. Heaton and Lucas (2000b) find weak evidence supporting the idea that background income risk exerts a downward influence on risky financial asset holdings. Campbell et al. (2001) and Davis and Willen (2000b) find that the correlation between labor income shocks and aggregate equity returns rises with education. However, Davis and Willen (2000a) find little evidence that occupation-level income innovations are correlated with aggregate equity returns. However, they find that for some occupations, the returns on portfolios formed on market capitalization are correlated with occupation-level income innovations.

Although much of the evidence presented in this chapter is based on U.S. data, there is a growing body of international evidence on the effect of background risk on portfolio choice. The results are also mixed. Guiso et al. (1996) find that in Italian household data, background risk has a small effect on portfolio choice. Hochguertel (1997) finds that in the Netherlands, households who report more risky income streams hold safer investment portfolios.

5.3.2. Business Ownership

Gentry and Hubbard (1998) examine the savings and investment decisions of entrepreneurs and conclude that this group accumulates more wealth than nonentrepreneurs, perhaps due to a precautionary demand for financing. Using SCF data, Heaton and Lucas (2000b) find that for those investors who hold a significant fraction of their wealth in stocks, proprietary business income is a large and more correlated background risk factor than labor income. Further, their cross-sectional regressions indicate that households with more private business wealth hold fewer stocks relative to other liquid assets.

The importance of private business ownership for households with significant stockholdings is confirmed by data in the 2001 SCF, as summarized in Table 6.12. All households with net worth above $10,000 are included, and the survey weights are used. Business owners include households who report a businesses value of more than $500. The average net worth of business owners is about four times greater than nonowners, and on average, their business accounts for 32.5% of their wealth. Consistent with higher average risk tolerance, business owners have 55.8% of their liquid financial wealth invested in stocks, whereas nonowners have 47.8%. Polkovnichenko (2007) also finds that entrepreneurs appear to be less risk-averse than average, using a variable from the SCF that polls people about their risk tolerance.

5.3.3. Employer Stock

Employers' stock is another source of concentrated risk for a significant number of households. To the extent that these holdings are voluntary, they cannot properly be considered uninsurable background risk. If, on the other hand, there are restrictions on

Table 6.12 Mean portfolio characteristics of business owners versus nonowners

	Owners	Nonowners
Liquid financial assets/total assets	24.9	37.9
Stocks/liquid financial assets	55.8	47.8
Bonds/liquid financial assets	18.2	20.3
Cash/liquid financial assets	26.1	31.9
Owner-occupied housing/total assets	34.3	54.2
Other real estate/total assets	6.8	5.7
Business/total assets	32.5	–
Age	49.1	52.0
Education (years)	14.4	13.5
Risk tolerance*	2.8	3.0
Income	$169,693	$69,533
Net worth	$1,298,065	$323,255

Tabulations are from the 2001 SCF and based on survey weights. Averages across households of share of household asset classes in total assets or liquid financial assets. Liquid assets are stocks, bonds, and cash. Averages household characteristics also reported. Risk tolerance is "1" if the household reports, they are willing to take substantial risk to achieve higher returns, "2" if willing to take above average risk, "3" if willing to take average risk, and "4" if unwilling to take risk.

pension holdings, as discussed below, they represent a source of background risk that may influence portfolio choices. Consistent with the idea that the concentrated risk that is assumed by holding employer's stock discourages investment in other risky stocks, Heaton and Lucas (2000b) report regression results indicating that the more of the employer's stock held, the lower is the share of other stocks in liquid assets.

Some evidence is available on the rising historical incidence of employer stockholding, both within and outside the retirement market. For top management, employer's stocks (and stock options) are used extensively as motivation (see Murphy, 1998, for a review). Simple information theoretic models are able to predict qualitatively some of the observed differences in executive compensation across firms, particularly the degree of pay-performance sensitivity. There is a trade off, however, between overcoming such agency costs through performance contingent payments and the cost to shareholders and lost diversification of risk-averse managers. Hall and Murphy (2002) examine the diversification cost of executive options in a certainty equivalent framework and review relevant literature. Aggarwal and Samwick (1999) support the idea that diversification costs matter, finding empirically that pay performance sensitivities appear to vary with the volatility of the firm's equity so that executives in the most volatile firms have the least dollar exposure to the company's equity.

There is an extensive empirical literature on employer stock held in retirement accounts. The National Center for Employee Ownership cites increasingly prevalent employee ownership patterns over time. According to their estimates, as of 2003, there were about 700 private and public companies that were majority owned by their ESOPs and about 500 of the top 2000 public companies offer broad-based employee ownership plans in some form (such as 401(k) plans, ESOP plans, option or stock purchase plans). They also report steady growth in ESOP coverage from around 250,000 participants in 1975 to over 8 million in 2001. In terms of asset values, total 401(k) holdings of company stock are estimated at around $400 billion and there is an estimated additional $120 billion held by ESOPs.

Mitchell and Utkus (2002) provide a review of the recent evidence on the extent of employer stockholdings in DC plans. Estimates from the 1998 U.S. Department of Labor data suggest that roughly 16% of all plan assets are held in company stock. Not all 401(k) plans offer company stock as an investment option, but among plans that do offer company stock, it is estimated from the Employee Benefit Research Institute (EBRI)/ICI 401(k) database that 29% of balances are invested in company stock. Similarly, Benartzi (2001) reports that about 1/3 of the assets in large companies' retirement savings plans is invested in own company stock. Plans offering company stock as a 401(k) option are estimated to cover 42% of all plan participants and 59% of all plan assets.

Mitchell and Utkus also report a great deal of diversity in the concentration of employer stockholding across plans. Of the plans offering company stock, roughly half held less than 20% of the plan balance in company stock. At the other end of the spectrum, more than 25% of plans held at least 60% of the plan balance in company stock. Although a large quantity of this stock appears to be voluntarily held by participants, a significant portion is contributed by the company and cannot be diversified. This is common in large listed firms using the previously discussed ESOP/401(k) combination arrangements. For example, Brown et al. (2006) study a sample of firms that match employee contributions with company stock finding that on average 28% of new contributions to a 401(k) plan are required to be held in company stock and an additional 17.1% is voluntarily directed to company stock. They also suggest that firms with high dividend payout are more likely to offer matches in company stock due to the tax deductibility of dividends paid under ESOP arrangements. However, they do not find evidence that factors usually associated with agency costs in studies of executive compensation have any impact on the provision of company stock in retirement plans.

Using the EBRI/ICI 401(k) database of participant level data, VanDerhei (2002) provides evidence on portfolio allocation in 401(k) plans and on the employee reaction to employer mandated company stockholding. The average share of retirement assets voluntarily allocated to equities across participants is lower in plans that match in company stock than plans that match in cash. However, employees enrolled in plans offering employer stock as an investment option are more likely to hold the employer's stock instead of more diversified forms of equity if the company matches in stock (a finding consistent with Brown et al.). Furthermore, at least 15% of participants in every age cohort voluntarily hold nearly all their 401(k) balance in employer stock. Choi et al. (2004b) support this evidence and also report that employer securities are voluntarily held by participants for a significant amount of time (usually a large number of years) due to the overall passivity in trading their accounts, as discussed further under Pension Investments. Bernartzi (2001), Purcell (2002), and Huberman and Sengmueller (2002), studying data at the plan (rather than participant) level, find that plans that match in company stock and plans whose stock outperformed the S&P 500 index in recent years are the ones most likely to be heavily invested in company stock.

A Vanguard report by Utkus and Waggoner (2003) surveys sponsor and participant attitudes to employer stock in 401(k) plans. Plan sponsors appear to be divided into two camps on the basis of whether the employer's match is directed to employer stock or made in cash. Those who direct in stock emphasize the role of incentives and retaining control in friendly employee hands and are less worried about employee diversification and fiduciary risks (consistent with this, Brown et al., 2004, find that low-risk firms are more likely to provide the employer match in company stock). The opposite appears to be the case for those that match in cash. Sales restrictions go hand in hand with matching employee contributions in stock.

The Vanguard survey also examines 401(k) participants' understanding of their investment in employer securities. Participants are found to have good recall of past performance of the employer's stock, but poor recall of the value of their stake and a poor understanding of risk and return concepts, with many believing their employer's stock to be as safe as or safer than a diversified equity portfolio. This is partially attributed to past performance of the employer's stock: those believing their employer's stock to be safe having experienced good past investment returns. If offered a choice between cash and stock sold to the employee at a discount that cannot be sold until age 50, 40% of respondents required a discount of less than 10% (many required no discount at all).

5.3.4. Pension Investments

An emerging strand of literature is that devoted to documenting empirical patterns in retirement plan participation rates, contribution levels, and portfolio choices. A recent review is Choi et al. (2004a). As in the closely related literature on employer stockholdings in pension plans discussed above, much of this research focuses on whether observed household retirement saving and portfolios appear to be more consistent with irrational psychological impulses than rational forward looking motives. Because most of these studies rely on data capturing only a portion of financial assets, however, it is often hard to infer the reason for the observed behavior.

Holden and VanDerhei (2003) provide estimates for the year 2002 of aggregate 401(k) asset allocation using the EBRI/ICI 401(k) database. The breakdown of asset allocation across all plans in their database is 45% to equity funds (including mutual funds and brokerage accounts), 23% to bond and money market funds, 16% to guaranteed investment contracts (GICs), and 16% to stock of the employer. However, there is a great deal of cross-sectional variation in these allocations across both plans and individuals. Some plans do not offer employer stock or GICs, and some plans choose the asset allocation of both employee and employer matching contributions. Holden and VanDerhei also show that asset allocation is more conservative for older participants and participants with lower salaries. There is also some evidence that asset allocation is more aggressive in 401(k) plans when the individual (or their family) participates in a DB plan, a relatively safe asset (see Uccello, 2000).

Papke (2004) looks at the impact individual free choice in 401(k) asset allocation has on contribution activity. She estimates that participants in a plan with investment choice are more likely to make contributions, make larger contributions, invest more aggressively in risky securities, and have larger plan balances. Iyengar and Jiang (2003), in contrast with Papke, actually find that too much choice can be a bad thing. Increasing the number of plan options (such as the number of mutual funds on offer) is associated with lower participation rates and contribution levels and more conservative portfolio choices. This is related to findings of Benartzi and Thaler (2001), who suggest participants apply naïve diversification strategies where they apportion funds equally among the available choices despite differences in the risk. Benartzi and Thaler (2002) argue that most individuals would prefer to have their investment allocation selected by a financial adviser than make the choice themselves.

An important finding about 401(k) participant behavior is the apparent inertia in plan choices (see e.g., Choi et al., 2004a; Madrian and Shea, 2001). Low tenure participants often opt into the default level of salary deferrals and asset allocation decisions rather than make an active decision. Furthermore, it often takes a period of several years before the participant deviates from these default choices. Thus, otherwise similar participants at different firms can end up with quite different retirement account balances and asset allocation just because of differences in the default choices. Such observations are consistent with participants being uninformed about their retirement plans. Using survey evidence, Gustman and Steinmeier (2001) find ignorance about retirement plans is widespread, but that individuals who are most reliant on their retirement plan as a source of retirement income are more likely to be well informed about their plan.

Other studies (e.g., Holden and VanDerhei, 2003) are more optimistic about the role of DC pension plans in fostering diversification and participation in equity markets. As discussed in Section 2, much of the growth in mutual fund participation has been through DC plans, and the prevalence of apparently diversified holdings in these plans and overall has increased over time (see Table 6.3).

5.3.5. Housing

PSID estimates of the idiosyncratic variance in housing returns are much higher than the aggregate risk. Flavin and Yamashita (2002) estimate idiosyncratic housing risk of 14.2%, using the PSID. The idea that housing affects portfolio choice has found empirical support from a variety of data sources. Using the 1983 SCF, Brueckner (1997) shows that when a housing investment constraint is binding (households are overinvested in housing because of consumption demands), nonhousing assets are different than they would be if housing allocation was optimal from an investment view.

Although all studies agree that housing affects portfolio choice, the effect of home ownership and mortgage debt on asset allocation is not yet clear. Existing research varies widely in its approach to this difficult problem, and the results are seemingly contradictory. Examination of this relationship is complicated by heterogeneity simultaneously affecting portfolio allocations and housing choices. Fratantoni (1998) finds that households with higher mortgage payment to income ratios have lower risky asset holdings in the 1989 SCF. Chetty and Szeidl (2004) find that a $1 increase in mortgage debt results in a portfolio shift of $0.50 from stocks to bonds. In their dynamic consumption model, Yao and Zhang (2001) posit that in the presence of labor income risk, home owners increase the proportion of stocks in liquid assets because of the diversification benefit and find some empirical support in the 1998 SCF. Decreases in the house value to net worth ratio as household age correspond to increases in stock to net worth ratio with age. Similarly, Flavin and Yamashita (2002) find evidence that the housing constraint induces a life-cycle pattern in holdings of stocks and bonds in the 1984 and 1989 PSID, with households holding more stock as they age and reduce the amount of mortgage debt. de Roon et al. (2002) use quarterly data for five major United States cities through 1997 and find that in each region home ownership had no impact on the relative holdings of stocks and bonds but significantly decreased the total assets allocated to stocks and bonds. Using the 1984–1999 PSID, Kullman and Siegel (2002) find that homeowners are more likely to participate in the stock market than renters, but contrary to these other results, as the amount of home equity increases, households increase the share of risk-free assets in their financial asset portfolio.

The evidence from international data also is mixed. Pelizzon and Weber (2008) perform an analysis similar to that of Flavin and Yamashita (2002) for Italian households and find that household portfolios are not conditionally efficient given housing investment. However, le Blanc and Lagarenne (2004) perform this analysis on French households, and they find that the portfolios of French households are efficient conditional on housing and observe the life-cycle pattern of risky asset holdings predicted by Flavin and Yamashita (2002).

6. CONCLUSIONS

There is substantial heterogeneity in the portfolio allocations of households. Although the majority of investors with significant net worth appear to hold diversified portfolios, a large number of households still hold no position in risky securities, whereas others take significant undiversified positions in stocks. This lack of diversification sometimes is in the form of large holdings in an employer's stock. Understanding the choices made by investors will shed light on the important factors explaining the pricing of risk in financial markets. Also many public policy choices have an impact on the portfolio allocations of households. Examples include the privatization of social security and the taxation of capital income. The potential effects of these policies greatly depend on the predicted impact on the savings and portfolio choices of households.

We presented evidence that the typical household is becoming more diversified over time and is participating more in financial markets. These changes likely reflect the evolution of institutions that make diversification easier and increases in financial education. A better understanding of the interaction between this institutional change and household behavior should be a focus of future work. For example, we presented evidence that stockholders often take undiversified positions in businesses and real estate. There have been significant changes in the marketability of real estate through real estate investment trusts and other securities. Further, there have been, and continue to be, significant changes in the way that entrepreneurial activity is financed. These changes undoubtedly will change the structure of the "background" risk faced by investors leading to significant changes in household portfolios. This will ultimately lead to an evolution in the pricing of risk in financial markets. A better understanding of the interaction of these markets for difficult to diversify assets and "standard" financial markets will be fundamental.

We reviewed several of the theoretical attempts to understand portfolio allocations in the context of important nondiversifiable income. The goal of these models is to fit the stylized facts demonstrating that human capital, privately held businesses, and the like have an important impact both on whether households participate in financial markets and the positions they choose in those markets. The current theoretical models often provide predictions inconsistent with the substantial cross-sectional heterogeneity in household portfolio choice. The models do, however, point to theoretical insights that will be important for future models to consider. These features include frictions such as trading costs, alternative preferences that separate risk aversion and intertemporal preferences for consumption, and the lumpiness in consumption such as housing.

An inability to contract on assets such as private business can be explained by informational frictions that result in moral hazard or adverse selection in markets. Actively chosen undiversified positions in a small number of stocks or an employer's stock cannot easily be explained by this economic mechanism. Institutional frictions, such as costs of trading, restrictions on pension investments, costs of setting up brokerage accounts, costs of education, and so on, are more consistent with this observed lack of diversification. In fact, both participation in financial markets and the level of diversification of households have increased with the rise of mutual funds and DC funds. The fall in real or perceived costs of investing due to these institutional changes is an important determinant of the increased stock market participation and diversification of households. Understanding the impact on household portfolio choice of past and predicted institutional changes remains a fruitful area of investigation.

ACKNOWLEDGMENTS

We thank Lars Hansen, Jonathan Parker, and two anonymous referees for helpful suggestions. Heaton thanks the Center for Research in Securities Prices at the Booth School for financial support.

REFERENCES

Aggarwal, R., and A. Samwick (1999). "The Other Side of the Trade-Off: The Impact of Risk on Executive Compensation," *Journal of Political Economy*, 107(1), 64–105.

Ait-Sahalia, Y., J. A. Parker, and M. Yogo (2004). "Luxury Goods and the Equity Premium," *Journal of Finance*, 59(6), 2959–3004.

Aizcorbe, A. M., A. B. Kennickell, and K. B. Moore (2003). "Recent Changes in U.S. Family Finance: Evidence from the 1998 and 2001 Survey of Consumer Finance," *Federal Reserve Bulletin*, 89, 1–32.

Ameriks, J., and S. Zeldes (2002). "How Do Household Portfolio Shares Vary with Age?" Working Paper, Columbia University.

Amromin, G. (2002). "Portfolio Allocation Choices in Taxable and Tax-Deferred Accounts: An Empirical Analysis of Tax-efficiency," Working Paper, Federal Reserve Board of Governors.

Anderson, R.W., and J.-P. Danthine (1981). "Cross Hedging," *Journal of Political Economy*, 89(6), 1182–1196.

Attanasio, O., J. Banks, and S. Tanner (2002). "Asset Holding and Consumption Volatility," *Journal of Political Economy*, 110(4), 771–792.

Barberis, N. (2000). "Investing for the Long Run when Returns are Predictable," *Journal of Finance*, LV, 225–264.

Basak, S., and D. Cuoco (1998). "An Equilibrium Model with Restricted Stock Market Participation," *Review of Financial Studies*, 11, 309–341.

Benartzi, S. (2001). "Excessive Extrapolation and the Allocation of 401(k) Accounts to Company Stock," *Journal of Finance*, 56, 1747–1764.

Benartzi, S., and R. Thaler (2001). "Naive Diversification Strategies in Defined Contribution Savings Plans," *American Economic Review*, 91(1), 79–98.

Benartzi, S., and R. Thaler (2002). "How Much is Investor Autonomy Worth?" *Journal of Finance*, 57(4), 1593–1616.

Benzoni, J., P. Collin-Dupresne, and R. Goldstein (2007). "Portfolio Choice over the Life-Cycle when the Stock and Labor Markets are Cointegrated," Working Paper, Federal Reserve Bank of Chicago.

Bertaut, C. (1994). "Who Holds Stocks in the U.S.? An Empirical Investigation," Manuscript, Board of Governors of the Federal Reserve System.

Bertaut, C., and M. Haliassos (1995). "Why Do So Few Hold Stocks?" *Economic Journal*, 105, 1110–1129.

Bertaut, C., and M. Haliassos (1997). "Precautionary Portfolio Behavior from a Life-Cycle Perspective," *Journal of Economic Dynamics and Control*, 21, 1511–1542.

Black, F. (1980). "The Tax Consequences of Long-run Pension Policy," *Financial Analysts Journal*, 36, 21–28.

le Blanc, D., and C. Lagarenne (2004). "Owner-Occupied Housing and the Composition of the Household Portfolio: The Case of France," *The Journal of Real Estate Finance and Economics*, 29(3), 259–275.

Blume, M., and S. Zeldes (1993). "The Structure of Stockownership in the U.S.," Working Paper, Wharton.

Blume, M., and S. Zeldes (1994). "Household Stockownership Patterns and Aggregate Asset Pricing Theories," Working Paper, University of Pennsylvania.

Bodie, Z., and D. Crane (1997). "Personal Investing: Advice, Theory, and Evidence," *Financial Analysts Journal*, 53, 13–33.

Bodie, Z., R. Merton, and W. Samuelson (1992). "Labor Supply Flexibility and Portfolio Choice in a Life-Cycle Model," *Journal of Economic Dynamics and Control*, 15, 427–450.

Brav, A., G. M. Constantinides, and C. Gezcy (1999). "Asset Pricing with Heterogeneous Consumers and Limited Participation: Empirical Evidence," Working Paper, University of Chicago.

Brown, J. R., N. Liang, and S. Weisbenner (2006). "401(k) Matching Contributions in Company Stock: Costs and Benefits for Firms and Workers," *Journal of Public Economics*, 90, 1315–1346.

Brueckner, J. (1997). "Consumption and Investment Motives and the Portfolio Choices of Homeowners," *Journal of Real Estate Finance and Economics*, 15, 159–180.

Campbell, J. Y., and J. Cochrane (1999). "By Force of Habit," *Journal of Political Economy*, 107, 205–251.

Campbell, J. Y., J. F. Cocco, F. J. Gomes, and P. J. Maenhout (2001). "Investing Retirement Wealth: A Life cycle Model," In: J. Y. Campbell and M. Feldstein (eds.), *Risk Aspects of Social Security Reform*, Chicago, IL: University of Chicago Press.

Campbell, J., and L. Viceira (1999). "Consumption and Portfolio Decisions when Expected Returns are Time Varying," *Quarterly Journal of Economics*, 114, 433–495.

Campbell, J., and L. Viceira (2001). "Who Should Buy Long Term Bonds?" *American Economic Review*, 87, 181–191.

Campbell, J., and L. Viceira (2002). Strategic Asset Allocation, Oxford University Press.

Carroll, C., and A. Samwick (1997). "The Nature of Precautionary Wealth," *Journal of Monetary Economics*, 40(1), 41–71.

Cauley, S. D., D. P. Andrey, and S. S. Eduardo (2003). "Homeownership as a Constraint on Asset Allocation," Working Paper, The Anderson School at UCLA.

Chetty, R., and A. Szeidl (2004). "Consumption Commitments and Asset Prices," Working Paper, Harvard University.

Choi, J., D. Laibson, and B. Madrian (2004a). "Plan Design and 401(k) Savings Outcomes," Working Paper 10486, NBER.

Choi, J. J., D. Laibson, B. C. Madrian, and A. Metrick (2004b). "Employees' Investment Decisions about Company Stock," Working Paper 10228, NBER.

Cocco, J. (2004). "Portfolio Choice in the Presence of Housing," Working Paper 410, IFA.

Cocco, J., F. Gomes, and P. Maenhout (1998). "Consumption and Portfolio Choice Over the Life-Cycle," Manuscript, Harvard University.
Constantinides, G. (1986). "Capital Market Equilibrium with Transactions Costs," *Journal of Political Economy*, 94, 842–862.
Constantinides, G. (1990). "Habit Formation: A Resolution of the Equity Premium Puzzle," *Journal of Political Economy*, 98, 519–543.
Cuoco, D. (1997). "Optimal Consumption and Equilibrium Prices with Portfolio Cone Constraints and Stochastic Labor Income," *Journal of Economic Theory*, 72, 33–73.
Curcuru, S. (2005). "Evidence and Implications of the Changing Asset Holdings of Seniors," Working Paper, University of Chicago.
Cvitani'c, J., and I. Karatzas (1992). "Convex Duality in Constrained Portfolio Optimization," *Annuals of Applied Probability*, 2, 767–818.
Dammon, R., C. Spatt, and H. Zhang (2004). "Optimal Asset Allocation with Taxable and Tax-deferred Investing," *Journal of Finance*, 59, 999–1037.
Davis, M., and A. Norman (1990). "Portfolio Selection with Transactions Costs," *Mathematics of Operations Research*, 15, 676–713.
Davis, S. J., and P. Willen (2000a). "Occupation-Level Income Shocks and Asset Returns: Their Covariance and Implications for Portfolio Choice," Working Paper 7905, NBER: Cambridge, MA.
Davis, S., and P. Willen (2000b). "Using financial assets to hedge labor income risks: Estimating the benefits," Working Paper, University of Chicago.
de Roon, F., P. Eichholtz, and K. Koedijk (2002). "The Portfolio Implications of Home Ownership," Discussion Paper No. 3501, CEPR.
Deaton, A. (1991). "Savings and Liquidity Constraints," *Econometrica*, 59, 1221–1248.
Duffie, D., W. Fleming, H. Soner, and T. Zariphopoulou (1997). "Hedging in Incomplete Markets with HARA Utility," *Journal of Economic Dynamics and Control*, 21, 753–782.
Epstein, L., and S. Zin (1989). "Substitution, Risk Aversion and the Temporal Behavior of Consumption and Asset Returns: A Theoretical Framework," *Econometrica*, 57, 937–969.
Farhi, E., and S. Panageas (2007). "Saving and Investing for Early Retirement: A Theoretical Analysis," *Journal of Financial Economics*, 83(1), 87–122.
Flavin, M., and T. Yamashita (2002). "Owner-Occupied Housing and the Composition of the Household Portfolio Over the Life Cycle," *American Economic Review*, 92(1), 345–362.
Fratantoni, M.C. (1998). "Homeownership and Investment in Risky Assets," *Journal of Urban Economics*, 44, 27042.
Friend, I., and M. Blume (1975). "The Demand for Risky Assets," *American Economic Review*, 65, 900–922.
Gakidis, H. (1997). "Stocks for the Old? Earnings Uncertainty and Life-Cycle Portfolio Choice," Manuscript, MIT.
Gentry, W., and R.G. Hubbard (1998). "Why Do the Wealthy Save So Much Saving and Investment Decisions of Entrepreneurs?" Working Paper, Columbia University.
Gollier, C., and R. J. Zeckhauser (1996). "Horizon Length and Portfolio Risk," Technical Working Paper 216, NBER.
Gollier, C. (2001). "The Economics of Risk and Time," Cambridge, MA: The MIT Press.

Gollier, C., and J. W. Pratt (1996). "Risk Vulnerability and the Tempering Effect of Background Risk," *Econometrica*, 64(5), 1109–1123.

Gomes, F., and A. Michaelides (2003). "Optimal Life-Cycle Asset Allocation: Understanding the Empirical Evidence," Working Paper, London School of Economics.

Gourinchas, P., and J. Parker (2002). "Consumption Over the Life-Cycle," *Econometrica*, 71(1), 47–89.

Gross, D., and N. Souleles (2002). "Do Liquidity Constraints and Interest Rates Matter for Consumer Behavior? Evidence from Credit Card Data," *The Quarterly Journal of Economics*, 117(1), 149–185.

Grossman, S. J., and G. Laroque (1990). "Asset Pricing and Optimal Portfolio Choice in the Presence of Illiquid Durable Consumption Goods," *Econometrica*, 58(1), 25–51.

Guiso, L., T. Jappelli, and D. Terlizzese (1996). "Income Risk, Borrowing Constraints and Portfolio Choice," *American Economic Review*, 86, 158–172.

Gustman, A. L., and T. L. Steinmeier (2001). "Imperfect Knowledge, Retirement and Saving," Working Paper 8406, NBER.

Hall, B. J., and K. J. Murphy (2002). "Stock Options for Undiversified Executives," *Journal of Accounting & Economics*, 33(2), 3–42.

He, H., and H. Pagès (1993). "Labor Income, Borrowing Constraints, and Equilibrium Asset Prices: A Duality Approach," *Economic Theory*, 3, 663–696.

He, H., and N. Pearson (1991). "Optimal Consumption and Portfolio Polices with an Infinite Horizon: the Infinite Dimensional Case," *Journal of Economic Theory*, 55, 259–304.

Heaton, J. (1995). "An Empirical Investigation of Asset Pricing with Temporally Dependent Preference Specifications," *Econometrica*, 63, 681–717.

Heaton, J., and D. Lucas (1997). "Market Frictions, Savings Behavior, and Portfolio Choice," *Macroeconomic Dynamics*, 1, 76–101.

Heaton, J., and D. Lucas (2000a). "Portfolio Choice in the Presence of Background Risk," *Economic Journal*, 110(460), 1–26.

Heaton, J., and D. Lucas (2000b). "Asset Pricing and Portfolio Choice: The Importance of Entrepreneurial Risk," *Journal of Finance*, 55(3), 1163–1198.

Henderson, J.V., and Y. M. Ioannides (1983). "A Model of Housing Tenure Choice," *American Economic Review* 73, 98–113.

Hochguertel, S. (1997). "Precautionary Motives and Portfolio Decisions," Manuscript, Tilburg University.

Holden, S., and J. VanDerhei (2003). "401(k) Plan Asset Allocation, Account Balances, and Loan Activity in 2001," EBRI Issue Brief, No. 255, March 2003.

Holden, S., and Hu, X. (2001). "Portfolio Choice for Homeowners," Working Paper, University of Illinois at Chicago.

Hubbard, R.G., J. Skinner, and S. Zeldes (1995). "Precautionary Saving and Social Insurance," *Journal of Political Economy*, 103, 360–399.

Huberman, G., and P. Sengmueller (2002). "Company Stock in 401k Plans," EFA 2003 Annual Conference Paper No. 659.

Investment Company Institute and Securities Industry Association (2002). Equity Ownership in America.

Iyengar, S.S., and W. Jiang (2003). "Choosing Not to Choose: The Effect of More Choices on Retirement Savings Decisions," Columbia University Working Paper, Columbia University: New York.

Jagannathan, R., and N. Kocherlakota (1996). "Why Should Older People Invest Less in Stocks Than Younger People?" *Quarterly Review, Minneapolis Federal Reserve Bank*, 20(3), 11–23.

Kandel, S., and R. Stambaugh (1996). "On the Predictability of Stock Returns: An Asset Allocation Perspective" *Journal of Finance*, 51, 385–424.

Karatzas, I., J. Lehoczky, S. Shreve, and G. Xu (1991). "Martingale and Duality Methods for Utility Maximization in an Incomplete Market," *SIAM J. Control and Optimization*, 29(3), 702–730.

Kimball, M.S. (1993). "Standard Risk Aversion," *Econometrica*, 61(3), 589–611.

King, M., and J. Leape (1987). "Asset Accumulation, Information, and the Life Cycle," Working Paper 2392, NBER.

Koo, H.-K. (1995). "Consumption and Portfolio Selection with Labor Income I: Evaluation of Human Capital," Working Paper, Washington University.

Kreps, D.M., and E.L. Porteus (1978). "Temporal Resolution of Uncertainty and Dynamic Choice Theory," *Econometrica*, 32, 82–100.

Kullman, C., and S. Siegel (2002). "Real Estate and its Role in Asset Allocation," Working Paper, The University of British Columbia.

Laibson, D. (1997). "Golden Eggs and Hyperbolic Discounting," *Quarterly Journal of Economics*, 112(2), 443–477.

Luttmer, E. (1999). "What Level of Fixed Costs Can Reconcile Consumption and Stock Returns?" *Journal of Political Economy*, 10(3), 969–1033.

Lynch, A.W. (2001). "Portfolio Choice and Equity Characteristics: Characterizing the Hedging Demands Induced by Return Predictability," *Journal of Financial Economics*, 62, 67–130.

MaCurdy, T. (1982). "The Use of Time Series Processes to Model the Error Structure of Earnings in Longitudinal Data Analysis," *Journal of Econometrics*, 18, 83–114.

Madrian, B.C., and D.F. Shea (2001). "The Power of Suggestion: Inertia in 401(k) Participation and Savings Behavior," *Quarterly Journal of Economics*, 116(4), 1149–1525.

Mankiw, N.G., and S. Zeldes (1991). "The Consumption of Stockholders and Non-Stockholders," *Journal of Financial Economics*, 29, 97–112.

Massa, M., and A. Simonov (2004). "Hedging, Familiarity and Portfolio Choice," Working Paper, Stockholm School of Economics.

Mayers, D. (1973). "Nonmarketable Assets and the Determination of Capital Asset Prices in the Absence of Riskless Asset," *Journal of Business*, 46(2), 258–267.

Meghir, C., and L. Pistaferri (2004). "Income Variance Dynamics and Heterogeneity," *Econometrica*, 72(1), 1–32.

Mehra, R., and E. Prescott (1985). "The Equity Premium: A Puzzle," *Journal of Monetary Economics*, 15, 145–161.

Merton, R. (1969). "Lifetime Portfolio Selection Under Uncertainty: The Continuous-Time Case," *Review of Economics and Statistic*, 51, 247–257.

Merton, R. (1971). "Optimum Consumption and Portfolio Rules in a Continuous-Time Model," *Journal of Economic Theory*, 3, 373–413.

Mitchell, O., and S. Utkus (2002). "Company Stock and Retirement Plan Diversification," Working Paper 2002–4, Pension Research Council.

Moore (2007). "Essays on Household Finance," Manuscript, Northwestern University.
Mossin, J. (1968). "Optimal Multiperiod Portfolio Policies," *Journal of Business*, 41(2), 215–229.
Murphy, K. J. (1998). "Executive Compensaition," In: O. Ashenfelter and D. Card (eds.), Handbook of Labor Economics, Amsterdam: North Holland.
Nielsen, L. T., and M. Vassalou (2002). "Portfolio Selection with Randomly Time-Varying Moments: The Role of the Instantaneous Capital Market Line," Working Paper, Columbia University.
Paiella, M. (2001). "Limited Financial Market Participation: A Transaction Cost-Based Explanation," IFS Working Papers W01/06, Institute for Fiscal Studies.
Papke, L.E. (2004). "Individual Financial Decisions in Retirement Saving Plans: The Role of Participant-Direction," *Journal of Public Economics*, 88(1–2), 39–61.
Parker, J. (2001). "The Consumption Risk of the Stock Market," *Brookings Papers on Economic Activity*, Economic Studies Program, The Brookins Institution, 32, 279–348.
Pelizzon, L., and G. Weber (2008). "Are Household Portfolios Efficient, An Analysis Conditional on Housing," *Journal of Financial and Quantitative Analysis*, 43(02), 401–431.
Piazessi, M., M. Schneider, and S. Tuzel (2007). "Housing, Consumption, and Asset Pricing," *Journal of Financial Economics*, 83(3), 531–569.
Poterba, J. (1993). "Who Owns Corporate Stock?: A Report to the New York Stock Exchange," Manuscript, MIT.
Poterba, J. (1998). "Population Age Structure and Asset Returns: An Empirical Approach," NBER Working Paper W6774.
Poterba, J., and A. Samwick (1997). "Household Portfolio Allocation Over the Life Cycle," Working Paper 6185, NBER.
Polkovnichenko, V. (2007). "Life Cycle Consumption and Portfolio Choice with Additive Habit Formation Preferences and Uninsurable Labor Income Risk," *Review of Financial Studies*, 20(1), 83–124.
Pratt, J.W., and R. Zeckhauser (1987). "Proper Risk Aversion," *Econometrica*, 55, 143–154.
Purcell, P. (2002). "Employer Stock in Retirement Plans: Investment Risk and Retirement Security," CRS Report for Congress, Congressional Research Service, Library of Congress, Order Code RL30922.
Saito, M. (1995). "Limited Market Participation and Asset Pricing," Manuscript, University of British Columbia, Dept. of Economics.
Samuelson, P. (1970). "The Fundamental Approximation Theorem of Portfolio Analysis in Terms of Means, Variances and Higher Moments," *The Review of Economic Studies*, 37, 537–542.
Samuelson, P.A. (1969). "Lifetime Portfolio Selection by Dynamic Stochastic Programming," *Review of Economics and Statistics*, 51, 239–246.
Shoven, J., and C. Sialm (2003). "Asset Location in Tax-Deferred and Conventional Savings Accounts," *Journal of Public Economics*, 88, 23–38.
Sinai, T., and N. Souleles (2005). "Owner-Occupied Housing as a Hedge against Rent Risk," *The Quarterly Journal of Economics*, 120, 763–789.
Skiadas, C., and M. Schroder (1999). "Optimal Consumption and Portfolio Selection with Stochastic Differential Utility," *Journal of Economic Theory*, 89, 68–126.
Svensson, L., and I. Werner (1993). "Nontraded Assets in Incomplete Markets," *European Economic Review*, 37, 1149–1168.

Tepper, I. (1981). "Taxation and Corporate Pension Policy," *Journal of Finance*, 36, 1–13.
Uccello, C.E. (2000). "401(k) Investment Decisions and Social Security Reform," Working Paper.
Utkus, S., and J. Waggoner (2003). "Employer and Employee Attitudes Toward Company Stock in 401(k) Plans," Vanguard Center For Retirement Research.
VanDerhei, J. (2002). "The Role of Company Stock in 401(k) Plans," *Risk Management and Insurance Review*, 5(1), 1–20.
Vila, J.-L., and T. Zariphopoulou (1997). "Optimal Consumption and Portfolio Choice with Borrowing Constraints," *Journal of Economic Theory*, 77, 402–431.
Vissing-Jorgensen, A. (2002a). "Limited Asset Market Participation and the Elasticity of Intertemporal Substitution," *Journal of Political Economy*, 110(4), 825–853.
Vissing-Jorgensen, A. (2002b). "Towards an Explanation of Household Portfolio Choice Heterogeneity: Nonfinancial Income and Participation Cost Structures," Manuscript, Northwestern University.
Wachter, J. (2002). "Portfolio and Consumption Decisions Under Mean Reverting Returns: An Exact Solution for Complete Markets," *Journal of Financial and Quantitative Analysis*, 37, 63–92.
Weil, P. (1990). "Nonexpected Utility in Macroeconomics," *Quarterly Journal of Economics*, 105, 29–42.
Xia, Y. (2001). "Learning about Predictability: The Effects of parameter Uncertainty on Dynamic Asset Allocation," *Journal of Finance*, 56, 205–246.
Xu, G.-L., and S. Shreve (1992). "A Duality Method for Optimal Consumption and Investment Under Short-Selling Probition II. General Market Coefficients," *Annals of Applied Probability*, 2, 87–112.
Yao, R., and H. H. Zhang (2001). "Optimal Consumption and Portfolio Choices with Risky Housing and Stochastic Labor Income," Working Paper.

CHAPTER 7

Analysis of High-Frequency Data

Jeffrey R. Russell* *and* **Robert F. Engle****

*Booth School of Business, University of Chicago, Chicago, IL

**Stern School of Business, New York University, New York, NY

Contents

Abstract

Classic asset pricing research assumes only that prices eventually reach their equilibrium value, the route taken and speed of achieving equilibrium are not specified. The introduction of widely available ultra high frequency data sets over the past decade has spurred interest in empirical market microstructure. The black box determining equilibrium prices in financial markets has been opened up. Intraday transaction by transaction dynamics of asset prices, volume, and spreads are available for analysis. These vast data sets present new and interesting challenges to econometricians. We first discuss models for the timing of events when the arrival rate may be time varying. Models for the marks are also discussed. Finally, while artificially discretizing the time intervals at which prices (or other marks) is a common practice in the literature, it does not come without cost. Different discretizing schemes trade of bias associated with temporally aggregating with variance. Averaging reduces the variability but blurs the timing of events. We also show, in a stylized model, that causal relationships can be artificially induced by discretizing the data.

Keywords: market microstructure; temporal spacing, point processes, Discrete prices

1. INTRODUCTION

From a passing airplane one can see the rush hour traffic snaking home far below. For some, it is enough to know that the residents will all get home at some point. Alternatively, from a tall building in the center of the city one can observe individuals in transit from work to home. Why one road is moving more quickly than another can be observed. Roads near the coastal waters might be immersed in a thick blanket of fog forcing the cars to travel slowly due to poor visibility while roads in the highlands, above the fog, move quickly. Traffic slows as it gets funneled through a narrow pass while other roads with alternate routes make good time. If a critical bridge is washed out by rain then some travelers may not make it home at all that night.

Like the view from the airplane above, classic asset pricing research assumes only that prices eventually reach their equilibrium value, the route taken and speed of achieving equilibrium is not specified. How does the price actually adjust from one level to another? How long will it take? Will the equilibrium be reached at all? How do market characteristics such as transparency, the ability of traders to view others actions, or the presence of several markets trading the same asset affect the answers to these questions? Market microstructure studies the mechanism by which prices adjust to reflect new information.

Answers to these questions require studying the details of price adjustment. From the passing plane in the sky, the resolution is insufficient. With high-frequency financial data we stand atop the tall building, poised to empirically address such questions.

1.1. Data Characteristics

With these new data sets come new challenges associated with their analysis. Modern data sets may contain tens of thousands of transactions or posted quotes in a single day time stamped to the nearest second. The analysis of these data are complicated by irregular temporal spacing, diurnal patterns, price discreteness, and complex often very long lived dependence.

1.1.1. Irregular Temporal Spacing

Perhaps most important is that virtually all transactions data are inherently irregularly spaced in time. Figure 7.1 plots 2 h of transaction prices for an arbitrary day in March 2001. The stock used is the U.S. stock Airgas, which will be the subject of several examples throughout the chapter. The horizontal axis is the time of day, and the vertical axis is the price. Each diamond denotes a transaction. The irregular spacing of the data is immediately evident as some transactions appear to occur only seconds apart while others, for example between 10:30 and 11:00 may be 5 or 10 min apart.

Because most econometric models are specified for fixed intervals this poses an immediate complication. A choice must be made regarding the time intervals over which to analyze the data. If fixed intervals are chosen, then some sort of interpolation rule must

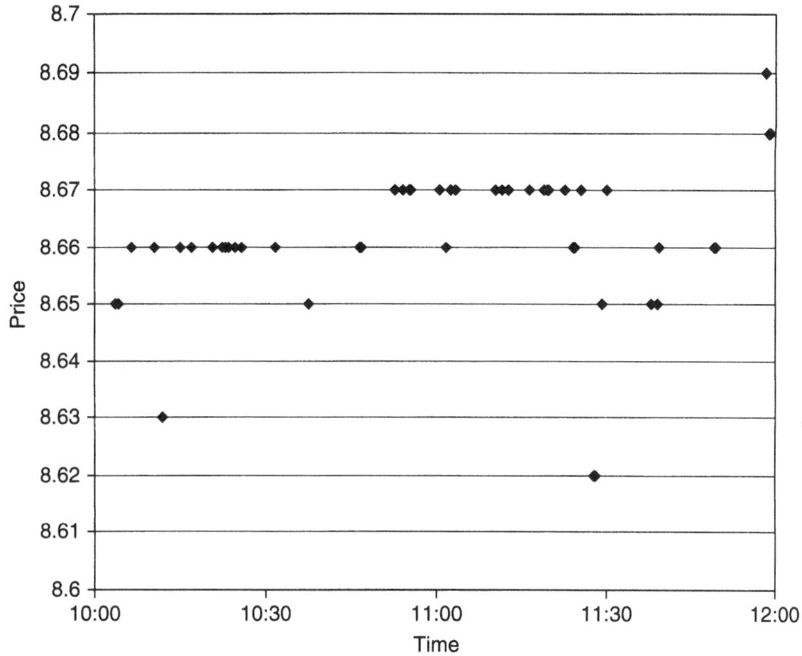

Figure 7.1 Plot of a small sample of transaction prices for the Airgas stock.

be used when no transaction occurs exactly at the end of the interval. Alternatively if stochastic intervals are used, then the spacing of the data will likely need to be taken into account. The irregular spacing of the data becomes even more complex when dealing with multiple series each with its own transaction rate. Here, interpolation can introduce spurious correlations due to nonsyncronous trading.

1.1.2. Discreteness

All economic data is discrete. When viewed over long time horizons the variance of the process is usually quite large relative to the magnitude of the minimum movement. For transaction by transaction data, however, this is not the case and for many data sets the transaction price changes take only a handful of values called ticks. Institutional rules restrict prices to fall on a prespecified set of values. Price changes must fall on multiples of the smallest allowable price change called a tick. In a market for an actively traded stock it is generally not common for the price to move a large number of ticks from one transaction to another. In open outcry markets the small price changes are indirectly imposed by discouraging the specialist from making radical price changes from one transaction to the next and for other markets, such as the Taiwan stock exchange, these price restrictions are directly imposed in the form of price change limits from one transaction to the next (say two ticks). The result is that price changes often fall on a very small number of possible outcomes.

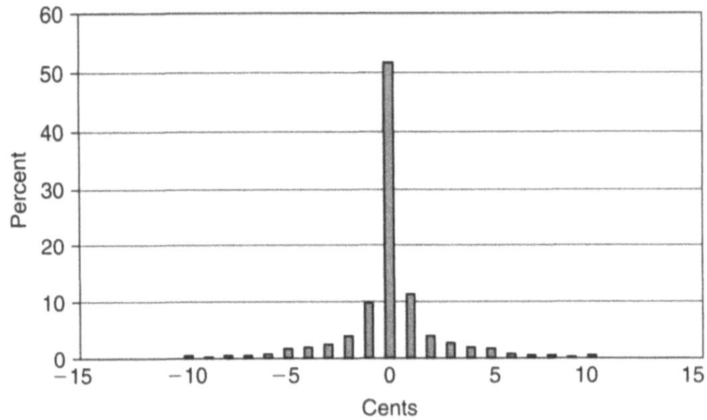

Figure 7.2 Histogram of transaction price changes for Airgas stock.

U.S. stocks have recently undergone a transition from trading in one-eighth of a dollar to decimalization. This transition was initially tested for seven NYSE stocks in August of 2000 and was completed for the NYSE listed stocks on January 29, 2001. NASDAQ began testing with 14 stocks on March 12, 2001 and completed the transition on April 9, 2001. In June of 97 NYSE permitted 1/16th prices.

As an example, Fig. 7.2 presents a histogram of the Airgas data transaction price changes after deleting the overnight and opening transactions. The sample used here contains 10 months of data spanning from March 1, 2001 through December 31, 2001. The horizontal axis is measured in cents. Fifty two percent of the transaction prices are unchanged from the previous price. Over 70% of the transaction prices fall on one of three values; no change, up one cent or down one cent. Over 90% of the values lie between −5 and +5 cents. Because the bid and ask prices are also restricted to the same minimum adjustment, the bid, ask, and the midpoint of the bid ask prices will exhibit similar discreteness. Of course data prior to decimalization is even more extreme. For these data sets it is not uncommon to find over 98% of the data taking just one of five values. This discreteness will have an impact on measuring volatility, dependence, or any characteristic of prices that is small relative to the tick size.

This discreteness also induces a high degree of kurtosis in the data. For example, for the Airgas data the sample kurtosis is 66. Such large kurtosis is typical of high frequency data.

1.1.3. Diurnal Patterns

Intraday financial data typically contain very strong diurnal or periodic patterns. For most stock markets volatility, the frequency of trades, volume, and spreads all typically exhibit a U-shaped pattern over the course of the day. For an early reference, see McInish and Wood (1992). Volatility is systematically higher near the open and generally just prior to the close. Volume and spreads have a similar pattern. The time between trades, or

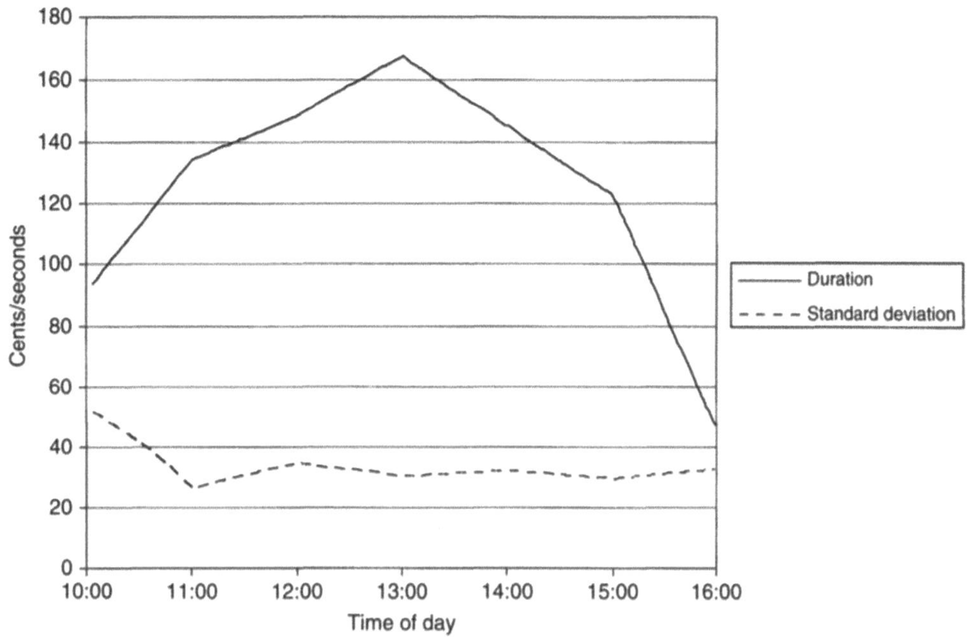

Figure 7.3 Diurnal pattern for durations and standard deviation of mid-quote price changes.

durations, tend to be shortest near the open and just prior to the close. This was first documented in Engle and Russell (1998).

Figure 7.3 presents the diurnal patterns estimated for the ARG data. The diurnal patterns were estimated by fitting a piecewise linear spline to the duration between trades and the squared midquote price changes. The vertical axis is measured in seconds for the duration and (to get the two plots on the same scale) one-tenth of a cent for the standard deviation of price changes.

Diurnal patterns are also typically present in the foreign exchange market, although here there is no opening and closing of the market. These markets operate 24 h a day, 7 days a week. Here the pattern is typically driven by "active" periods of the day. See Andersen and Bollerslev (1997) and Dacorogna et al. (2001) and for patterns in foreign exchange volatility. For example, prior to the induction of the Euro, U.S. dollar exchange rates with European countries typically exhibit the highest volatility during the overlap of time that both the U.S. markets and the European markets were active. This occurred in the late afternoon GMT when it is morning in the United States and late afternoon in Europe.

1.1.4. Temporal Dependence

Unlike their lower frequency counterparts, high-frequency financial returns data typically display strong dependence. The dependence is largely the result of price discreteness and the fact that there is often a spread between the price paid by buyer and seller initiated trades. This is typically referred to as bid-ask bounce and is responsible for the large

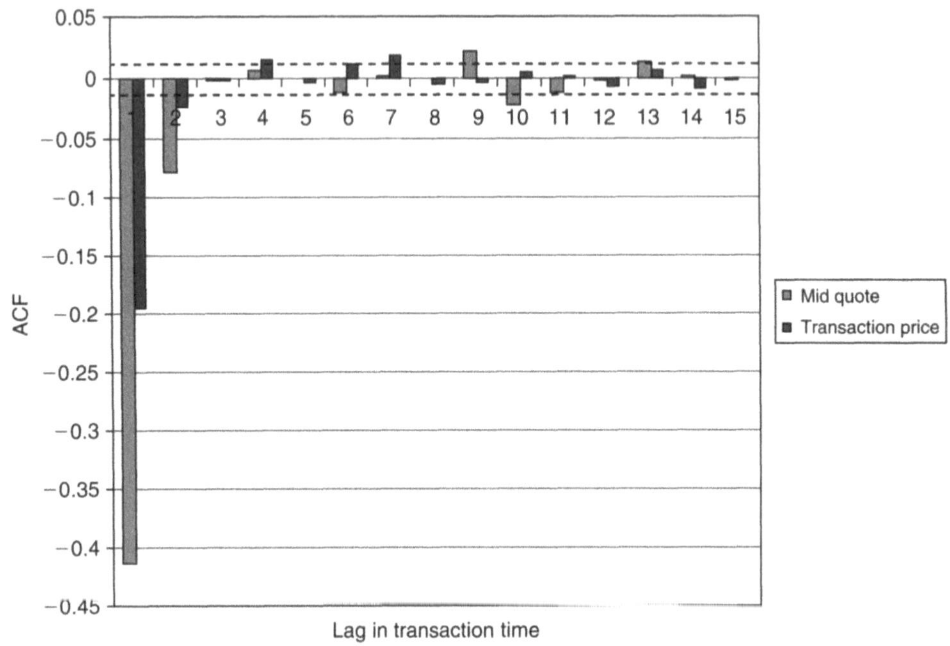

Figure 7.4 Autocorrelation function for the mid quote and transaction price changes.

first-order negative autocorrelation. Bid-ask bounce will be discussed in more detail in Section 2.3. Other factors leading to dependence in price changes include traders breaking large orders up into a sequence of smaller orders in hopes of transacting at a better price overall. These sequences of buys or sells can lead to a sequence of transactions that move the price in the same direction. Hence at longer horizons we sometimes find positive autocorrelations. Figure 7.4 contains a plot of the autocorrelation, function for changes in the transaction, and midpoint prices from one transaction to the next for the Airgas stock using the 10 months of data. Again, overnight price changes have been deleted.

Similar to lower frequency returns, high-frequency data tends to exhibit volatility clustering. Large price changes tend to follow large price changes and vice-versa. The ACF for the absolute value of the transaction price change for ARG is shown in Fig. 7.5. Because the diurnal pattern will likely influence the autocorrelation function, it is first removed by dividing the price change by the square root of its variance by time of day. The variance by time of day was estimated with linear splines. The usual long set of positive autocorrelations is present.

The transaction rates also exhibit strong temporal dependence. Figure 7.6 presents a plot of the autocorrelations for the durations between trades after removing the deterministic component discussed earlier. Figure 7.7 presents the autocorrelations for the log of volume. Both series exhibit long sets of positive autocorrelation spanning

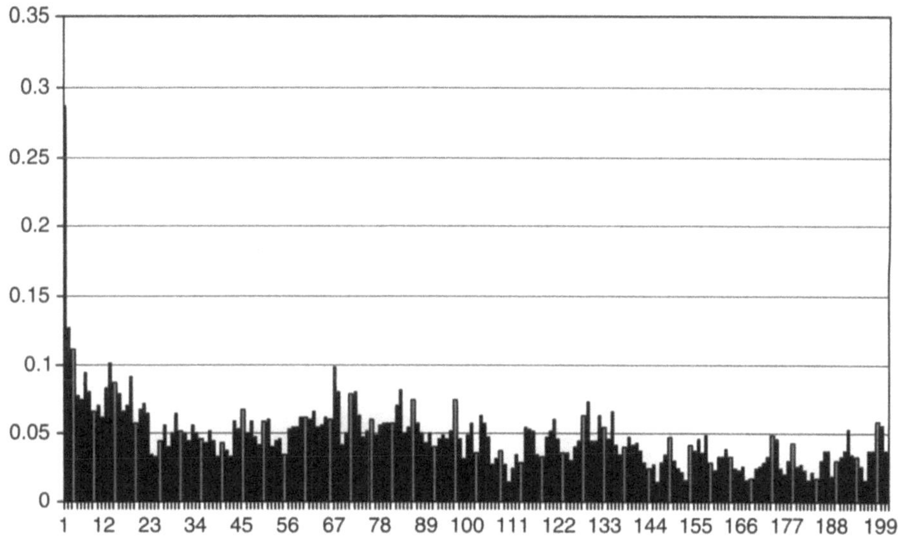

Figure 7.5 Autocorrelations for the squared midquote price changes.

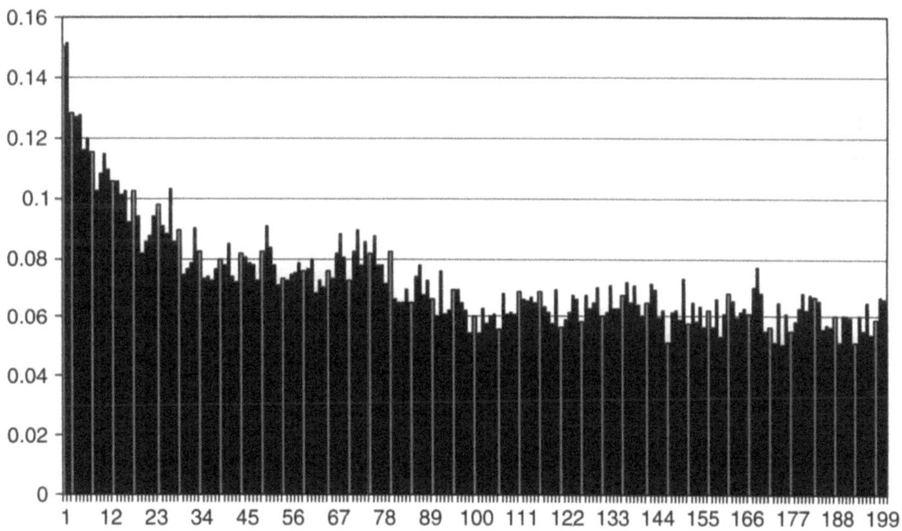

Figure 7.6 Autocorrelations for durations.

many transactions. These autocorrelations indicate clustering of durations and volume, respectively.

Under temporal aggregation the dependence in the price changes tends to decrease. However, even at intervals of a half hour or longer negative first-order autocorrelation often remains.

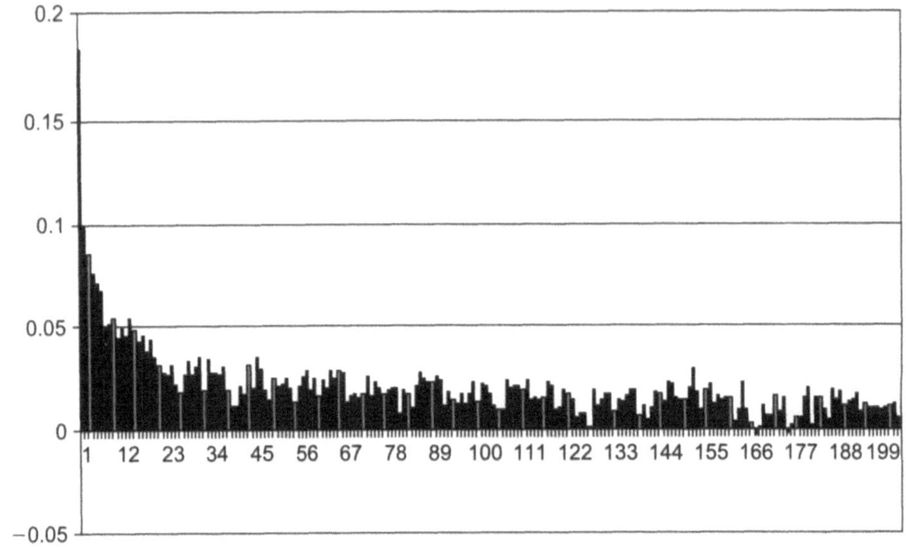

Figure 7.7 Autocorrelations for the log of volume.

1.2. Types of Economic Data

We begin this section with a general discussion of the types of high-frequency data currently available. With the advancement and integration of computers in financial markets, data sets containing detailed information about market transactions are now commonplace. High-frequency data generally refers to data that is collected at a very rapid rate. The highest rate at which data can be collected is every time that new information arrives and is referred to as ultrafrequency data. The information that arrives can take different forms in different data sets and different markets. The most fundamental data must be prices and quantities, however, there might be more than one type of price and more than one type of quantity that can be reported. Many data sets report transaction prices that are the price paid for in a given trade and the quantity (number of shares) transacted. These are usually referred to as transaction prices and trade size. A second type of price and quantity data is the limit order book. The limit order book is a historical reference to the physical books that the specialist on the NYSE would use to keep track of orders that had been placed to buy or sell fixed quantities once the price reached a designated price level. The limit order book refers to a set of prices and quantities available for sale (on the ask side of the market) and buy (on the bid side of the market). New information arrival might correspond to a change in any of these prices or quantities.

In most markets, trades or updates to the limit order book do not occur at regularly spaced intervals, but rather at the pace of the market. Some periods might be active with many trades or updates to the limit order book occurring over short periods of time and other periods have little information occurring. Most data sets contain one observation each time that a new piece of information arrives and a time stamp indicating a recorded time at which the transaction or change took place.

Markets can be centralized (a common point through which all trades occur) or decentralized (trades occur bilaterally between parties). The NYSE and the Paris Bourse are two such markets commonly analyzed. These centralized markets might be order-driven (such as NASDAQ or the Paris Bourse) where a computer algorithm matches to market participant orders or they might be open outcry where there is a centralized trading floor that market participants must trade through (like the Chicago Mercantile Exchange or the Chicago Board Options Exchange). In either case, the data sets constructed from these markets typically contain detailed information about the transactions and quotes for each asset traded on the market. The exact time of a transaction usually down to the second, and the price and quantity transacted are common data. Similarly, the bid and ask quotes are also generally available along with a time stamp for when the quotes became active. The trades and quotes (TAQ) data set distributed by the NYSE is the leading example of this type of data for US equities.

The currency exchange market is a commonly analyzed decentralized market. Here the market participants are banks that communicate and arrange transactions on a one-on-one basis with no central recording institution. Quotes are typically fed through Reuters for customers with a Reuters account to view continuous updates of quotes. Olsen and Associates has been downloading and storing this quote data and made it available for academic research. The most comprehensive data sets contain all quotes that pass through the Reuters screens and an associated time stamp. As the transactions do not pass through a centralized system there is no comprehensive source for transaction data.

The definition of the quote can vary across markets with important implications. Foreign exchange quotes are not binding. Quotes from the NYSE are valid for a fixed (typically small) quantity or depth. Quotes in electronic markets can come in various forms. For example, quotes for the Paris bourse are derived from the limit order book and represent the best ask and bid prices in the book. The depth here is determined by the quantity of volume at the best prices. Alternatively, the Taiwan stock exchange, which is an electronic batch auction market, posts a "reference price" derived from the past transaction and is only a benchmark from which to gauge where the next transaction price may fall. These difference are important not only from an economic perspective but also determine the reliability of the data. Nonbinding quotes are much more likely to contain large errors than binding ones.

Many empirical studies have focused on the stock and currency exchange high-frequency data. However, data also exists for other markets, most notably the options and futures markets. These data sets treat each contract as a separate asset reporting time quotes and transactions just as for the stocks. The Berkeley Options data base is a common source for options data. New high-frequency data sets have been created for fixed income as well. GovPX now offers tick-by-tick U.S. treasury prices and volume.

Other specialized data sets are available that contain much more detailed information. The TORQ data set, put together by Joel Hasbrouck and the NYSE, was one of the first such data sets widely distributed. This data set is not very comprehensive in that it contains only 144 stocks traded on U.S. markets covering 3 months in the early 1990s. However, it contains detailed information regarding the nature of the transactions including the order type (limit order, market order, etc.) as well as detailed information about the submission of orders. The limit order information provides a widow into the limit order book of the specialist, although it cannot be exactly replicated. The Paris Bourse data typically contain detailed information about the limit order book near the current price.

1.3. Economic Questions

Market microstructure economics focuses on how prices adjust to new information and how the trading mechanism affects asset prices. In a perfect world, new information would be immediately disseminated and interpreted by all market participants. In this full information setting prices would immediately adjust to a new equilibrium value determined by the agents preferences and the content of the information. This immediate adjustment, however, is not likely to hold in practice. Not all relevant information is known by all market participants at the same time. Furthermore, information that becomes available is not processed at the same speed by all market participants implying variable lag time between a news announcement and the agents realization of price implications. Much of modern microstructure theory is therefore driven by models of asymmetric information and the relationship between traded prices and the fair market value of the asset.

In the simplest form, there is a subset of the agents that are endowed with superior knowledge regarding the value of an asset. These agents are referred to as privately informed or simply informed agents. Agents without superior information are referred to as noise or liquidity traders and are assumed to be indistinguishable from the informed agents. Questions regarding the means by which the asset price transitions to reflect the information of the privately informed agents can be couched in this context. Early theoretical papers utilizing this framework include Glosten and Milgrom (1985), Easley and O'Hara (1992), Copeland and Galai (1983), and Kyle (1985). A very comprehensive review of this literature can be found by O'Hara (1995).

The premise of these models is that market makers optimally update bid and ask prices to reflect all public information and remaining uncertainty. For the NYSE it was historically the specialist who plays the role of market maker. Even in markets without a designated specialist bid and ask quotes are generally inferred either explicitly or implicitly from the buy and sell limit orders closest to the current price. Informed and uniformed traders are assumed to be indistinguishable when arriving to trade so the difference between the bid and the ask prices can be viewed as compensation for the risk associated with trading against potentially better informed agents. Informed traders will make profitable transactions at the expense of the uninformed.

In this asymmetric information setting, two types of prices can be defined. Prices that trades occur at and a notional fair market value that reflects both public and private information. We call the prices that trades occur at a "transaction price," although it could be a posted bid, ask, or midpoint of the bid and ask prices. Following the microstructure literature, we will call the notional fair market value an "efficient price" in the sense that it reflects all information, both public and private. If the two prices do not coincide then trades occur away from their efficient values so there is a gain to one party and a loss to another in a transaction. Natural questions arise. The larger these deviations, the larger the loss to one party. Measures of market quality can be constructed to reflect the size of these deviations. The simplest example would be half the bid-ask spread. If prices occur at the bid or the ask price and the midpoint of the bid and ask quotes are on average equal to the efficient price, then this distance reflects the average loss to trader executing a market order and the gain to the trader executing the limit order. How do the rules of trade affect market quality? How is market quality affected by the amount of asymmetric information? How does market quality vary across stocks with different characteristics such as volatility or daily volume?

In a rational expectations setting market makers learn about private information by observing the actions of traders. Informed traders only transact when they have private information and would like to trade larger quantities to capitalize on their information before it becomes public. The practical implications is that characteristics of transactions carry information. An overview of the predictions of these models is that prices adjust more quickly to reflect private information when the proportion of uninformed traders is higher. Volume is higher, transaction rates are higher when the proportion of uninformed traders is higher. The bid ask spread is therefore predicted to be increasing in volume and transaction rates. This learning process is central in the study of market microstructure data and is often referred to as price discovery. Specific examples include price impact studies where the impact of an event such as a trade on future prices is studied. Related questions involve multivariate studies of the prices of a single asset traded in multiple markets. Here questions regarding the origin of price discovery are relevant. For example, does price discovery tend to occur in the options derivative market or in the underlying. Similar questions can be asked in regional markets when one asset is traded, say in a U.S. market and a European market.

A related issue is market quality. In an ideal market, a trader should be able to transact large quantities at a price very close to the fair value of the asset, over a short period of time. In reality, the rules of the market, including the algorithms used to match buyers with sellers, who trades first (priority issues), and the cost or incentive structure for posting limit orders all play a role in the overall quality of the market. Accurate measurement of market quality is another central area in market microstructure. These measures are as simple as bid ask spreads but can also be modeled with more sophisticated techniques.

Empirical market microstructure plays a role in two larger areas. First, an ideal market would have transaction prices that accurately reflect all information. That is, the efficient price and the transaction prices would coincide. In absence of this perfect world, the deviation would be as small as possible. Because the rules of trade, that is the market structure, play a role in this relationship, market designers play a large role in determining market quality with the rules imposed. This can be a natural objective or imposed by government regulations. A more complete understanding about market features across different trading rules and platforms aides in market design.

Recently, a second role of microstructure has emerged. Market participants may prefer assets traded in more desirable, higher quality markets. In this case, market quality may have an effect on how traders value an asset and therefore potentially reflect their equilibrium value. Following the analogy in the introduction, a house with a sole access road that is occasionally impassable due to flooding might reduce the value of the home. The price path towards the equilibrium actually affects the equilibrium value.

Clearly assessing the market microstructure effects requires studying data at an intraday, high frequency. Data aggregated over the course of a day will not contain the detailed information of price adjustment discussed in this section. Implementing the econometric analysis, however, is complicated by the data features discussed in the previous section. This chapter provides a review of the techniques and issues encountered in the analysis of high-frequency data.

2. ECONOMETRIC FRAMEWORK

Empirical answers to the economic questions posed in the previous section require econometric models for high frequency, intraday data. In this section, we begin with a fundamental description of the data that accounts for the irregular spacing of the data. As such, all models considered in this review can be viewed through a single lens. The goal of this section is to specify this structure from a purely econometric perspective. Later sections will present specific models that are useful for addressing specific questions.

In the statistics literature, models for irregularly spaced data have been referred to as a point process and a large body of literature has been produced studying and applying models of point processes. Examples of applications include the study of firing of neurons or the study of earthquake occurrences. More formally, let $t_1, t_2, \ldots, t_i, \ldots$ denote a sequence of strictly increasing random variables corresponding to event arrival times such as transactions. Jointly, these arrival times are referred to as a point process. It is convenient to introduce the counting function $N(t)$, which is simply the number of event arrivals that have occurred at or prior to time t. This will be a step function with unit increments at each arrival time.

Often, there will be additional information associated with the arrival times. In the study of earthquake occurrences, there might be additional information about the magnitude of the earthquake associated with each arrival time. Similarly, for the financial transactions data there is often a plethora of information associated with the transaction arrival times including price, volume, bid and ask quotes, depth, and more. If there is additional information associated with the arrival times then the process is referred to as a marked point process. Hence, if the marks associated with the ith arrival time are denoted by an M-dimensional vector y_i then the information associated with the ith event is summarized by its arrival time and the value of the marks $[t_i, y_i]$.

Depending on the economic question at hand, either the arrival time, the marks, or both may be of interest. Often models for how the market learns in an asymmetric information setting operate in transaction time with calendar time playing little if any role. In such cases, it may be sufficient to simply examine the sequence of prices and trade characteristics without reference to the trade times. Clearly, if a model is formulated in transaction time, and a forecast in calendar time (say 5 min) is required then it is necessary to consider the trade times. Alternatively, the distribution of prices might depend on the temporal spacing of the data, again requiring a model that accounts for the spacing of the data.

We denote the filtration of arrival times and marks at the time of the ith event arrival by $\widehat{t_i} = \{t_i, t_{i-1}, \ldots, t_0\}$ and $\widehat{y_i} = \{y_i, y_{i-1}, \ldots, y_0\}$, respectively. The probability structure for the dynamics associated with a stationary, marked point process can be completely characterized and conveniently expressed as the joint distribution of marks and arrival times given the filtration of past arrival times and marks:

$$f\left(t_{N(t)+1}, y_{N(t)+1} | \widehat{t}_{N(t)}, \widehat{y}_{N(t)}\right). \tag{2.1}$$

Although this distribution provides a complete description of the dynamics of a marked point process, it is rarely specified in practice. Often the question of economic interest can be expressed in one of four ways. When will the next event happen? What value should we expect for the mark at the next arrival time? What value should we expect for the mark after a fixed time interval? Or, how long should we expect to wait for a particular type of event to occur?

The answers to the first two questions are immediately obtained from (2.1). If the contemporaneous relationship between y_i and t_i is not of interest, then the analysis may be greatly simplified by restricting focus to the marginalized distributions provided that the marks and arrival times are weakly exogenous. If the waiting time until the next event regardless of the value of the marks at termination is of interest, then the marginalized distribution given by

$$f_t\left(t_{N(t)+1} | \widehat{t}_{N(t)}, \widehat{y}_{N(t)}\right) = \int f\left(t_{N(t)+1}, y | \widehat{t}_{N(t)}, \widehat{y}_{N(t)}\right) dy \tag{2.2}$$

may be analyze. This is simply a point process where the arrival times may depend on the past arrival times and the past marks. We will refer to this as a model for the event arrival times, or simply a point process. Examples here include models for the arrival of traders.

More elaborate economic questions regard the dynamic of the marks such as prices. The distribution of the mark conditional on when the next trade occurs can be obtained from (2.1). In this case, one may be interested in modeling or forecasting the value for the next mark, regardless of when it occurs, given the filtration of the joint process. This is given by

$$f_y\left(y_{N(t)+1} \mid \widehat{t}_{N(t)}, \widehat{y}_{N(t)}\right) = \int f\left(t, y_{N(t)+1} \mid \widehat{t}_{N(t)}, \widehat{y}_{N(t)}\right) dt. \tag{2.3}$$

Here, the information set is updated at each event arrival time and we refer to such models as event time or tick time models of the marks. Of course, multiple step forecasts from (2.2) would require, in general, a model for the marks and multiple step forecasts for the mark in (2.3) would generally require a model for the durations.

Yet another alternative approach is to model the value of the mark to be at some future time $t + \tau$ $(\tau > 0)$ given the filtration at time t. That is

$$g\left(y_{N(t+\tau)} \mid \widehat{t}_{N(t)}, \widehat{y}_{N(t)}\right). \tag{2.4}$$

Here the conditional distribution associated with the mark over a fixed time interval is the object of interest. Theoretically, specification of (2.1) implies a distribution for (2.4), only in very special cases, however, will this exist in closed form. Because the distribution of the mark is specified over discrete fixed calendar time intervals, we refer to this type of analysis as fixed interval analysis. A final approach taken in the literature is to study the distribution of the length of time it will take for a particular type of event, defined by the mark, to occur. For example, one might want to know how long will it take for the price to move by more than a specified amount, or how long will it take for a set amount of volume to be transacted. This can be expressed as the conditional distribution

$$g\left(t + \tau_{\min} \mid \widehat{t}_{N(t)}, \widehat{y}_{N(t)}\right), \tag{2.5}$$

where if E_t defines some event associated with the marks, then $\tau_{\min} = \min_{\tau>0} y_{N(t+\tau)} \in E_t$. Again, only in special cases can this distribution be derived analytically from (2.1). $t_{\min}$ is called the hitting time in the stochastic process literature. Because the marks are associated with arrival times, the first crossing times will simply be a subset of the original set of arrival times. In the point process literature the subset of points is called a thinned point process.

This section proceeds to discuss each of the above approaches. We begin with a discussion and examples of point processes. Next, we consider tick time models. We then consider fixed interval analysis by first discussing methods of converting to fixed time intervals and then give examples of various approaches used in the literature.

2.1. Examples of Point Processes

It is convenient to begin this section with a discussion of point processes with no marks. A point process is referred to as a *simple point process* if, as a time interval goes to zero, the probability of multiple events occurring over that time interval can be made an arbitrarily small fraction of the probability of a single event occurring. In this case, characterization of the instantaneous probability of a single event dictates the global behavior of the process. A convenient way of characterizing a simple point process, therefore is by the instantaneous arrival rate of the intensity function given by:

$$\lambda(t) = \lim_{\Delta t \to 0} \frac{\Pr(N(t+\Delta t) > N(t))}{\Delta t}. \tag{2.6}$$

Perhaps the most well-known simple point process is the homogenous Poisson process. For a homogeneous Poisson process the probability of an event arrival is constant. A homogenous Poisson process can therefore be described by a single parameter where $\lambda(t) = \lambda$. For many types of point process the assumption of a constant arrival rate is not likely realistic. Indeed, for financial data we tend to observe bursts of trading activity followed by lulls. This feature becomes apparent when looking at the series of the time between transactions and durations. Figure 7.6 presents the autocorrelations associated with the intertrade durations of Airgas. The plot indicates strong temporal dependence in the durations between transaction events. Clearly the homogenous Poisson model is not suitable for such data.

For a point process with no marks, Snyder and Miller (1991) conveniently classify point processes into two categories, those that evolve with *after-effects* and those that do not. A point process on $[t_0, \infty]$ is said to evolve without after-effects if for any $t > t_0$ the realization of events on $[t, \infty)$ does not depend on the sequence of events in the interval $[t_0, t)$. A point process is said to be *conditionally orderly* at time $t \geq t_0$ if for a sufficiently short interval of time and conditional on any event P defined by the realization of the process on $[t_0, t)$ the probability of two or more events occurring is infinitessimal relative to the probability of one event occurring. Our discussion here focuses on point processes that evolve with after-effects and are conditionally orderly. A point process that evolves with after-effects can be conveniently described using the *conditional intensity function*, which specifies the instantaneous probability of an event arrival conditional upon filtration of event arrival times. That is, the conditional intensity is given by

$$\lambda(t|N(t), t_{i-1}, t_{i-2}, \ldots, t_0) = \lim_{\Delta t \to 0} \frac{P\big(N(t+\Delta t) > N(t)|N(t), t_{N(t)}, t_{N(t)-1}, \ldots, t_0\big)}{\Delta t}. \tag{2.7}$$

The conditional intensity function associated with any single waiting time has traditionally been called a hazard function in the econometrics literature. Here, however, the intensity function is defined as a function of t across multiple events, unlike much of the literature in macroeconomics that tends to focus on large cross-sections with a single spell. In addition, because the intensity function is defined conditional on past event arrival times, Eq. (2.7) is referred to as a self-exciting point process. It was originally proposed by Hawkes (1971) and by Rubin (1972) and are sometimes called Hawkes self-exciting processes. Numerous parameterizations have been proposed in the statistics literature.

Perhaps the simplest example of a point process that evolves with after effects is a first-order homogeneous point process where

$$\lambda\big(t|N(t), t_{N(t)-1}, t_{N(t)-2}, \ldots, t_0\big) = \lambda\big(t|N(t), t_{N(t)}\big), \tag{2.8}$$

and the durations between events $x_i = t_i - t_{i-1}$ form a sequence of independent random variables. If in addition, the durations are identically distributed then the process is referred to as a renewal process. More generally, for an mth order self-exciting point process the conditional intensity depends on $N(t)$ and the m most recent event arrivals.

As discussed by Snyder and Miller (1975), for example, the conditional intensity function, the conditional survivor function, and the durations or "waiting times" between events each completely describe a conditionally orderly point process. Letting p_i be a family of conditional probability density functions for arrival time t_i, the log likelihood can be expressed in terms of the conditional density or intensity as

$$L = \sum_{i=1}^{N(T)} \log p_i(t_i|t_0, \ldots, t_{i-1}), \tag{2.9}$$

$$L = \sum_{i=1} \log \lambda(t_i|i-1, t_0, \ldots, t_{i-1}) - \int_{t_0}^{T} \lambda\big(u|N(u), t_0, \ldots, t_{N(u)-1}\big)du \tag{2.10}$$

We now turn to some specific modeling strategies for the conditional intensity function that are particularly well suited for the analysis of financial event arrival times.

2.1.1. The ACD Model

Engle and Russell (1998) propose the Autoregressive Conditional Duration (ACD), which is particularly well suited for high-frequency financial data. This parameterization is most easily expressed in terms of the waiting times (or durations) between events, x_i. The distribution of the durations is directly specified in terms of the past durations. The ACD model is then defined by two conditions. Let ψ_i be the expectation of the duration given, the past arrival time is given by

$$E(x_i|x_{i-1}, x_{i-2}, \ldots, x_1) = \psi_i\,(x_{i-1}, x_{i-2}, \ldots, x_1) = \psi_i. \tag{2.11}$$

Furthermore, let

$$x_i = \psi_i \varepsilon_i, \tag{2.12}$$

where ε_i~ i.i.d. with density $p(\epsilon;\phi)$ with nonnegative support, and θ and ϕ are variation free. The baseline intensity, or baseline hazard, is given by

$$\lambda_0 = \frac{p(\epsilon;\phi)}{S(\epsilon;\phi)}, \tag{2.13}$$

where $S(\epsilon;\phi) = \int_\epsilon^\infty p(u;\phi)du$ is the survivor function. The intensity function for an ACD model is then given by

$$\lambda(t|N(t), t_{i-1}, t_{i-2}, \ldots, t_0) = \lambda_0\left(\frac{t - t_{N(t)-1}}{\psi_{N(t)}}\right)\frac{1}{\psi_{N(t)}}. \tag{2.14}$$

Because ψ_i enters the baseline hazard, this type of model is referred to as an accelerated failure time model in the duration literature. The rate at which time progresses through the hazard function is dependent upon ψ_i, and therefore it can be viewed in the context of time deformation models. During some periods the pace of the market is more rapid than other periods.

The flexibility of the ACD model stems from the variety of choices for parameterizations of the conditional mean in (2.11) and the i.i.d. density $p(\epsilon;\phi)$. Engle and Russell (1998) suggest and apply linear parameterizations for the expectation given by

$$\psi_i = \omega + \sum_{j=1}^{p}\alpha_j x_{i-j} + \sum_{j=1}^{q}\beta_j\psi_{i-j}. \tag{2.15}$$

Because the conditional expectation of the duration depends on p lags of the duration and q lags of the expected duration, this is termed an ACD(p, q) model. Popular choices for the density $p(\epsilon;\phi)$ include the exponential and the Weibull distributions suggested in Engle and Russell (1998). These models are termed the exponential ACD (EACD) and Weibull ACD (WACD) models, respectively. The exponential distribution has the property that the baseline hazard is monotonic. The Weibull distribution relaxes this assumption and allows for a hump-shaped baseline intensity. An appropriate choice of the distribution, and hence the baseline intensity will depend on the characteristics of the data at hand. Other choices include the Gamma distribution suggested by Lunde (1998) and Zhang et al. (2001) or the Burr distribution suggested by Grammig and Maurer (2000). These distributions allow for even greater flexibility in the baseline hazard. Given a choice for (2.11) and $p(\epsilon;\phi)$ the likelihood function is constructed from (2.9).

For each choice of $p(\epsilon;\phi)$ from (2.13) and (2.14) there is an implied intensity function. Because the exponential distribution implies a constant hazard, the intensity function takes a particularly simple form given by

$$\lambda(t|N(t), t_{i-1}, t_{i-2}, \ldots, t_0) = \frac{1}{\psi_{N(t)}} \tag{2.16}$$

and for the Weibull distribution the intensity is slightly more complicated

$$\lambda(t|N(t), t_{i-1}, t_{i-2}, \ldots, t_0) = \gamma\left(\frac{\Gamma\left(1+\frac{1}{\gamma}\right)}{\psi_{N(t)}}\right)^{\gamma}\left(t - t_{N(t)}\right)^{\gamma-1}, \tag{2.17}$$

which reduces to (2.16) when $\gamma = 1$.

The ACD(p, q) specification in (2.15) appears very similar to a ARCH(p, q) models of Engle (1982) and Bollerslev (1986) and indeed the two models share many of the same properties. From (2.12) and (2.15) it follows that the durations x_i follow an ARMA(max $(p, q), q)$. Let $\eta_i \equiv x_i - \psi_i$, which is a martingale difference by construction then

$$x_i = \omega + \sum_{j=1}^{\max(p,q)} \alpha_j x_{i-j} + \sum_{j=1}^{q} \beta_j \eta_{i-j} + \eta_i.$$

If $\alpha(L)$ and $\beta(L)$ denote polynomials in the lag operator of orders p and q, respectively, then the persistence of the model can be measured by $\alpha(1) + \beta(1)$. For most duration data this sum is very close to (but less than) one indicating strong persistence but stationarity. It also becomes clear from this representation that restrictions must be placed on parameter values to ensure nonnegative durations. These restrictions impose that the infinite AR representation implied by inverting the MA component must contain nonnegative coefficients for all lags. These conditions are identical to the conditions derived in Nelson and Cao (1992) to ensure nonnegativity of GARCH models. For example, for the ACD(1,1) model this reduces to $\omega \geq 0$, $\alpha \geq 0$, $\beta \geq 0$.

Similarly, the most basic application of the ACD model to financial transactions data is to model the arrival times of trades. In this case, t_i denotes the arrival of the ith transaction and x_i denotes the time between the ith and $(i-1)$th transactions. Engle and Russell (1998) propose using an ACD(2,2) model with Weibull errors to model the arrival times of IBM transactions. Like volatility, the arrival rate of transactions on the NYSE can have a strong diurnal (intraday) pattern. Volatility tends to be relatively high just after the open and just prior to the close; that is, they have volatility for stocks tends to exhibit a U-shaped diurnal pattern. Similarly, Engle and Russell (1998) document that the durations between trades have a diurnal pattern with high activity just after the open and just prior to the close; that is, the durations exhibit an inverse U-shaped diurnal pattern. Let $\phi_{N(t)+1} = E\left(x_{N(t)+1}|t_{N(t)}\right)$ denote the expectation of the duration given time of day alone. Engle and Russell (1998) suggest including an additional term on the right-hand side of (2.12) to account for a diurnal pattern so that the ith duration is given by:

$$x_i = \phi_i \psi_i \varepsilon_i. \tag{2.18}$$

Now, ψ_i is the expectation of the duration after partialing out the deterministic pattern and is interpreted as the fraction above or below the average value for that time of day.

The expected (nonstandardized) duration is now given by $\phi_i \psi_i$. It is natural to refer to ϕ_i as the deterministic component and ψ_i as the stochastic component. Engle and Russell (1998) suggest using cubic splines to model the deterministic pattern.

The parameters of the two components as well as any parameters associated with ε_i can be estimated jointly by maximizing (2.9) or, a two-step procedure can be implemented in which first the terms of the deterministic pattern are estimated and in a second stage the remaining parameters are estimated. The two-step procedure can be implemented by first running an OLS regression of durations on a cubic spline. Let $\widehat{\phi}_i$ denote the prediction for the ith duration obtained from the OLS regression. Then let $\widetilde{x}_i = \frac{x_i}{\phi_i}$ denote the normalized duration. This standardized series should be free of any diurnal pattern and should have a mean near unity. An ACD model can then be estimated by MLE using the normalized durations $\widetilde{x}_i$ in place of x_i in (2.9). Although this is not efficient, the two-step procedure will provide consistent estimates under correct specification. Figure 7.3 presents a plot of the estimated diurnal pattern for ARG. This plot was constructed by regressing the duration on a linear spline for the time of day at the start of the duration. We find the typical inverted U-shaped pattern with durations longest in the middle of the day and shortest near the open and close.

The similarity between the ACD model and GARCH model is greater than the dynamic specification. Engle and Russell (1998) provide the following corollary.

Corollary 1 *QMLE results for the EACD(1,1) model*

If

1. $E_{i-1}(x_i) = \psi_i = \omega + \alpha x_{i-1} + \beta \psi_{i-1}$,
2. $\epsilon_i = \frac{x_i}{\psi_i}$ is
   - **i.** strictly stationary
   - **ii.** nondegenerate
   - **iii.** has bounded conditional second moments
   - **iv.** $\sup_i E_{i-1}\left[\ln\left(\beta + \alpha \epsilon_i\right)\right] < 0$
3. $\theta_0 \equiv (\omega, \alpha, \beta)$ is in the interior of Θ
4. $L(\theta) = -\sum_{i=1}^{N(T)} \left(\log\left(\psi_i\right) + \frac{x_i}{\psi_i}\right)$

Then the maximizer of L will be consistent and asymptotically normal with a covariance matrix given by the familiar robust standard errors from Lee and Hansen (1994).

This result is a direct corollary from the Lee and Hansen (1994) and Lumsdaine (1996) proofs for the class of GARCH(1,1) models. The theorem is powerful because under the conditions of the theorem we can estimate an ACD model assuming an exponential distribution, and even if the assumption is false, we still obtain consistent estimates although the standard errors need to be adjusted as in White (1982). Furthermore, the corollary establishes that we can use standard GARCH software to perform QML estimation of ACD models. This is accomplished by setting the dependent variable equal to the square root of the duration and imposing a conditional mean equation of zero. The resulting parameter values provide consistent estimates of the parameters used to forecast the expected duration.

In addition, an estimate of the conditional distribution can be obtained nonparametrically by considering the residuals $\widehat{\epsilon}_i = \frac{x_i}{\widehat{\psi}_i}$, where $\widehat{\psi}_i = E_{i-1}\left(x_i|\widehat{\theta}\right)$. Under correct specification the standardized durations $\widehat{\epsilon}_i$ should be i.i.d. and the distribution can be estimated using nonparametric methods such as kernel smoothing. Alternatively, it is often more informative to consider the baseline hazard. Given an estimate of the density the baseline hazard is obtained from (2.13). Engle and Russell (1998), therefore, propose a semiparametric estimation procedure where in the first step QMLE is performed using the exponential distribution and in a second step the density of ϵ is estimated nonparametrically. This is referred to as a semiparametric ACD model.

ACD Model Diagnostics The properties of the standardized duration also provide a means to assess the goodness of fit of the estimated model. For example, the correlation structure or other types of dependence can be tested. Engle and Russell (1998) suggest simply examining the Ljung-Box statistic, although other types of nonlinear dependence can be examined.

Engle and Russell (1998) suggest examining autocorrelations associated with nonlinear transformations of the residuals $\widehat{\epsilon}_i$, for example, squares or square roots. An alternative test of nonlinearity advocated in Engle and Russell (1998) is to divide the diurnally adjusted durations into bins. Then regress $\widehat{\epsilon}_i$ on a constant and indicators for the magnitude of the previous duration. One indicator must be omitted to avoid perfect multicollinearity. If the $\widehat{\epsilon}_i$ are indeed i.i.d., then there should be no predictability implied from this regression. Often these tests suggests that the linear specification tends to over predict the duration following extremely short or extremely long durations. This suggests that a model where the expectation is more sensitive following short durations and less sensitive following long durations may work well.

Tests of the distributional assumptions of ϵ can also be examined. A general test is based on the fact that the integrated intensity over the duration

$$u_i = \int\limits_{s=t_{i-1}}^{t_i} \lambda(s|N(s), t_{i-1}, t_{i-2}, \ldots, t_0)ds, \tag{2.19}$$

will be distributed as a unit exponential as discussed in Russell (1999). Often this takes a very simple form. For example, substituting the exponential intensity (2.16) into (2.19) simply yields the residual $\widehat{u}_i = \widehat{\epsilon}_i = \frac{x_i}{\widehat{\phi}_i\widehat{\psi}_i}$. Similarly, for the substituting the Weibull intensity (2.17) into (2.16) yields $\widehat{u}_i = \left(\frac{\Gamma\left(1+\frac{1}{\gamma}\right)x_i}{\widehat{\phi_i\psi_i}}\right)^{\gamma}$. The variance of u_i should be unity leading Engle and Russell (1998) to suggest the test statistic

$$\sqrt{N(T)}\frac{(\widehat{\sigma}_u - 1)}{\sqrt{8}}, \tag{2.20}$$

which should have a limiting standard normal distribution. This is a formal test for remaining excess dispersion often observed in duration data. Furthermore, because the survivor function for an exponential random variable U is simply $\exp(-u)$, a plot of the the negative of the log of the empirical survivor function should be linearly related to u_i with a slope of unity hence providing a graphical measure of fit.

Nonlinear ACD Models The tests for nonlinearity discussed earlier often suggest nonlinearity. Zhang et al. (2000) propose a nonlinear threshold ACD model with this feature in mind. Here the dynamics of the conditional mean are given by

$$\psi_i = \begin{cases} \omega^1 + \alpha^1 x_{i-1} + \beta^1 \psi_{i-1} & \text{if } x_{i-1} \le a_1 \\ \omega^2 + \alpha^2 x_{i-1} + \beta^2 \psi_{i-1} & \text{if } a_1 < x_{i-1} \le a_2, \\ \omega^3 + \alpha^3 x_{i-1} + \beta^3 \psi_{i-1} & \text{if } a_2 < x_{i-1} \end{cases}$$

where a_1 and a_2 are parameters to be estimated. Hence, the dynamics of the expected duration depend on the magnitude of the previous duration. Indeed, using the same IBM data as analyzed in Engle and Russell (1998) they find $\alpha^1 > \alpha^2 > \alpha^3$ as expected from the nonlinear test results. Estimation is performed using a combination of a grid search across a_1 and a_2 and maximum likelihood for all pairs of a_1 and a_2. The MLE is the pair of a_1 and a_2 and the corresponding parameters of the ACD model for each regime that produces the highest maximized likelihood.

Another nonlinear ACD model applied in Engle and Lunde (2003), Russell and Engle (2008) is the Nelson Form ACD model. The properties of the Nelson form ACD are developed by Bauwens and Giot (2000) and for further discussion see Bauwens and Giot (2001). We refer to this as the Nelson form ACD model because it is in the spirit of Nelson (1991) EGARCH model and we want to minimize confusion with the version of the ACD model that uses the exponential distribution for ε. Here the log of the expected duration follows a linear specification.

$$\ln(\psi_i) = \omega + \sum_{j=1}^{p} \alpha_j \epsilon_{i-j} + \sum_{j=1}^{q} \beta_j \ln(\psi_{i-j}).$$

This formulation is particularly convenient when other market variables are included in the ACD model because nonnegativity of the expected duration is directly imposed.

An interesting approach to nonlinearity is taken by Fernandes and Grammig (2006) who propose a class of nonlinear ACD models. The parametrization is constructed using the Box Cox transformation of the expected duration and a flexible nonlinear function of ϵ_{i-j} that allows the expected duration to respond in a distinct manner to small and large shocks. The model nests many of the common ACD models and is shown to work well for a variety of duration data sets. Another interesting nonlinear model is proposed by Bauwens and Giot (2003) who propose a model where the dynamics of the duration model depend on the most recent price move.

ACD Example Appendix (A) contains parameter estimates for an EACD(3,2) model estimated using the GARCH module of EVIEWS. The durations were first adjusted by dividing by the time of day effect estimated by linear splines in Fig. 7.3. The sum of the α and β coefficients is in excess of 0.999 but less than one indicating strong persistence but the impact of shocks dies off after a sufficient period of time. A plot of the autocorrelations of the residuals is presented in Fig. 7.8. The autocorrelations are no longer all positive and appear insignificant. A formal test for the null that the first 15 autocorrelations are zero yields a 12.15 with a p-value of 67%.

A test for remaining excess dispersion in (2.20) yields a test statistic of $\frac{\sqrt{32365}(1.41-1)}{\sqrt{8}} = 26.07$. There is evidence of excess dispersion indicating that it is unlikely that ε is exponential. However, under the conditions of the corollary the parameter estimates can be viewed as QML estimates. A plot of the nonparametric hazard is given in Fig. 7.9. The

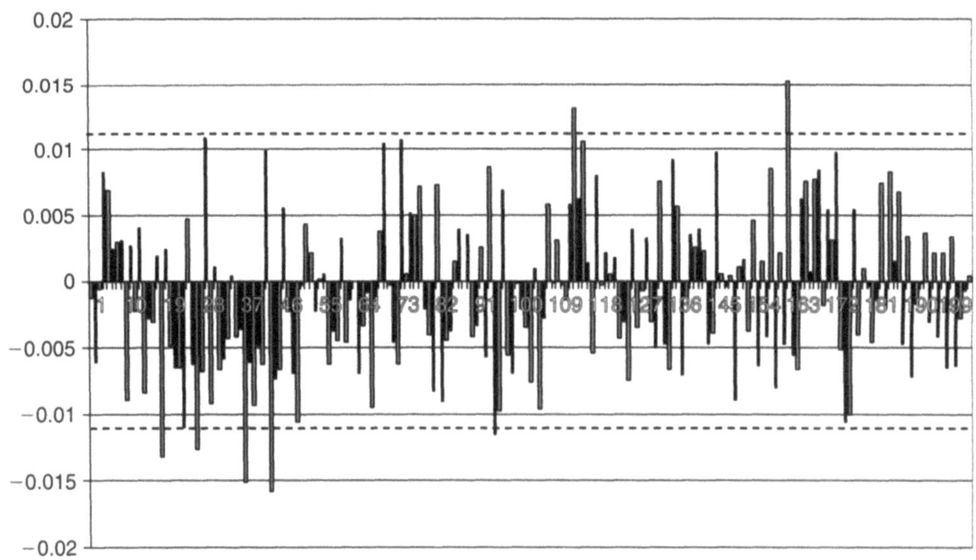

Figure 7.8 Autocorrelations for ACD duration residuals $\hat{\epsilon}_i = \frac{x_i}{\psi_i}$.

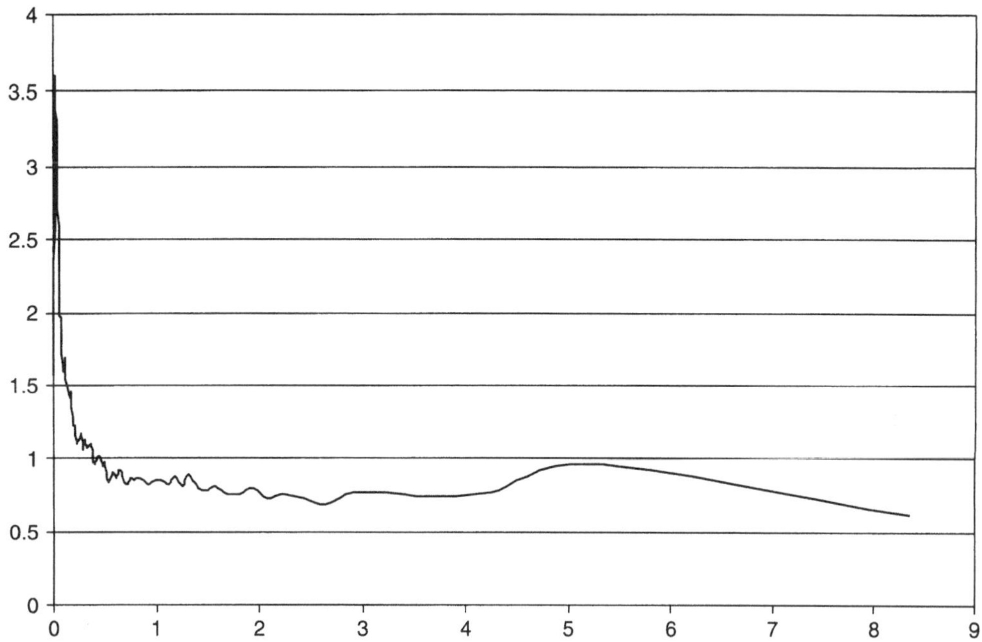

Figure 7.9 Nonparametric estimate of baseline intensity.

estimate was obtained using a nearest neighbor estimator. The hazard is nearly monotonically decreasing indicating that the longer it has been since the last transaction the less likely it is for a transaction to occur in the next instant. This is a common finding for transactions data.

2.1.2. Thinning Point Processes

Models for regularly spaced data explain dynamics per unit time. When the spacing is irregular, an alternative approach is available that may be more natural. Instead of modeling the change in the mark per unit time, one could model the time until the mark changes by some threshold value. The result is a model for the time between unit changes in the mark as opposed to the change per unit time in standard models. For example, when foreign exchange data are examined many of the posted quotes appear to be simply noisy repeats of the previous posted quotes. Alternatively, for stock data, often times many transactions are recorded with the exact same transaction price. Another example might be the time until a set amount of volume has been transacted – a measure related to liquidity. Models of this type focus on the distribution of $\tau_{\min}$ in (2.5). The sequence of arrival times corresponding to the times at which the marks take special values is called a thinned point process because the new set of arrival times will contain fewer events than the original series.

Engle and Russell (1998) refer to the series of durations between events constructed by thinning the events with respect to price and volume as price-based and volume-based durations. They suggest that the ACD model might be a good candidate for modeling for these thinned series. In Engle and Russell (1997), a Weibull ACD model is applied to a thinned series of quotes arrival times for the Dollar Deutchemark exchange rate series. More formally if t_i denotes the arrival times of the original series of quotes then let $\tau_0 = t_0$ Next, let $N^*(t)$ denote the counting function for the thinned process defined by $t_{N^*(t)+1} = t + \tau_{N^*(t)+1}$ where $\tau_{N^*(t)+1} = \min_{\tau>0} \left| p_{N(t+\tau)} - p_{N^*(t)} \right| > c$ and $N(t_0) = N^*(t_0) = 0$. So, the sequence of durations τ_i corresponds to the price durations defined by price movements greater than a threshold value c. An ACD Weibull model appears to provide a nice fit for the thinned series.

The authors suggest that this provides a convenient way of characterizing volatility when the data are irregularly spaced. The intuition is that instead of modeling the price change per unit time, as is typically done for volatility models constructed using regularly spaced data, the model for price durations models the time per unit price change. In fact, assuming that the price process locally follows a geometric Brownian motion leads to implied measures of volatility using first crossing time theory.

Engle and Lange (2001) combine the use of price durations discussed earlier with the cumulative signed volume transacted over the price duration to measure liquidity. For each of the U.S. stocks analyzed, the volume quantity associated with each transaction is given a positive sign if it is buyer initiated and negative sign if it is seller initiated using the rule proposed by Lee and Ready (1991). This signed volume is then cumulated for each price duration. The cumulative signed volume, referred to as VNET, is the total net volume that can be transacted before inducing a price move hence providing a time varying measure of the depth of the market. For each price duration several other measures are also constructed including the cumulative (unsigned) volume and number of transactions. Regressing VNET on these market variables suggest that market depth is lower following periods high transaction rates and high volatility. While VNET increases with past volume it does so less than proportionally indicating that order imbalance as a fraction of overall (unsigned) volume decreases with overall volume. Jointly these results suggest that market depth tends to be lower during periods of high transaction rates, high volatility, and high volume. In an asymmetric information environment this is indicative of informed trading transpiring during period of high transaction rates and high volume.

2.2. Modeling in Tick Time – the Marks

Often, economic hypothesis of interest are cast in terms of the marks associated with the arrival times. For example, many hypothesis in the asymmetric information literature focusing on the mechanism by which private information becomes impounded asset prices. In a rational expectations environment, the specialist will learn about a traders private information from the characteristics of their transactions. Hence, many asymmetric information models of financial participants have implications about how price adjustments should depend on the characteristics of trades such as volume or frequency of transactions. By the very nature of market micro structure field, these theories often need to be examined at the transaction by transaction frequency. This section of this chapter examines transaction by transaction analysis of the marks. We refer to this approach generally as tick time analysis.

2.2.1. VAR Models for Prices and Trades in Tick Time

Various approaches to tick time modeling of the marks have been considered in the literature. The approaches are primarily driven by the economic question at hand as well as assumptions about the role of the timing of trades. Many times the hypothesis of interest can be expressed as how the prices adjust given characteristics of past order flow. In this case, it is not necessary to analyze the joint distribution in (2.1) but only the marginal distribution of the mark given in (2.3).

Perhaps the simplest approach in application is to assume that timing of past of transactions has no impact on the distribution of the marks, that is $f_y\left(y_{i+1}|\widehat{t_i}, \widehat{y_i}\right) = f_y\left(y_{i+1}|, \widehat{y_i}\right)$. This is the approach taken in Hasbrouck (1991) where the price impact of a trade on future transaction prices is examined. Hasbrouck focuses on the midpoint of the bid and ask quotes as a measure of the price of the asset. We refer to this as the midprice and would appear to be a good approximation to the value of the asset given the information available. Hasbrouck is interested in testing and identifying how buyer and seller initiated trades differ in their impact on the expectation of the future price.

Let Δm_i denote the change in the midprice from the $(i-1)$th to the ith transactions or $m_i - m_{i-1}$. The bid and ask prices used to construct the midprice are those prevailing just prior to the transaction time t_i. Let w_i denote the signed volume of a transaction taking a positive value if the ith trade is buyer initiated and a negative value if it is seller initiated. The direction of trade is inferred using the Lee and Ready rule. Hasbrouck persuasively argues that market frictions induce temporal correlations in both the price and volume series. Regulations require the specialist to operate an "orderly" market meaning that the price should not fluctuate dramatically from one trade to the next. Hence, in the face of a large price move, the specialist will have to take intervening transactions at intermediate prices to smooth the price transition. Volume might also be autocorrelated as a result of the common practice of breaking up large orders into multiple small orders to achieve at a better overall price than had the order been executed in one large transaction. Finally, because neither price nor direction of trades can be viewed as exogenous the series must be analyzed jointly to get a full picture of the series dynamics. Hasbrouck analyzes the bivariate system using the following VAR:

$$\begin{aligned} \Delta m_i &= \sum_{j=1}^{J} a_j \Delta m_{i-j} + \sum_{j=0}^{J} b_j w_{i-j} + v_{1i} \\ w_i &= \sum_{j=1}^{J} c_j \Delta m_{i-j} + \sum_{j=1}^{J} d_j w_{i-j} + v_{2i}. \end{aligned} \tag{2.21}$$

Notice that the signed volume appears contemporaneously on the right-hand side of the quote update equation. The quote revision equation is therefore specified conditional on the contemporaneous trade. In reality, it is likely that the contemporaneous quote revision will influence the decision to transact as the marginal trader might be enticed to transact when a new limit order arrives improving the price. In fact, our application suggests some evidence that this may be the case for the Airgas stock. We estimate a VAR for price changes and a trade direction indicator variable taking the value 1 if the trade is deemed buyer initiated and -1 if the trade is deemed seller initiated using the Lee and Ready rule. Volume effects are not considered here. As expected, the b_j coefficients tend to be positive meaning that buys tend to lead to increasing quote revisions and sells tend to lead to decreasing quote revisions. The market frictions suggest that the full impact of a trade may not be instantaneous, but rather occur over a longer period of time. To gauge this effect the VAR can be expressed as an infinite vector moving average model. The coefficients then form the impulse response function.

The cummulants of the impulse response functions then provide a measure of the total price impact of a trade. Because the model operates in transaction time, these price impacts are therefore also measured in transaction time. The asymptote associated with the cumulative impulse response function is then defined as the total price impact of a trade. Because the data are indexed in tick time, the price impact is measured in units of transactions. The results indicate that it can take several transactions before the full price impact of a transaction is realized. Figure 7.10 presents a price impact plot for the stock Airgas. Similar to Hasbrouck's findings using the earlier data sets, we find that the price impact can take many periods to be fully realized and that the function is concave. The price impact is in the expected direction – buys increase the price and sells decreased the priced. Looking at a cross-section of stocks, Hasbrouck constructs measures for the information asymmetry by taking the ratio of the price impact of a 90th percentile volume trade over the average price. This measure is decreasing with market capitalization suggesting that firms with smaller market capitalization have larger information asymmetries.

Engle and Dufour also analyze the price impact of trades, but relax the assumption that the timing of trades has no impact on the marginal distribution of price changes. Easley and O'Hara (1992) propose a model with informed and uninformed traders. On any

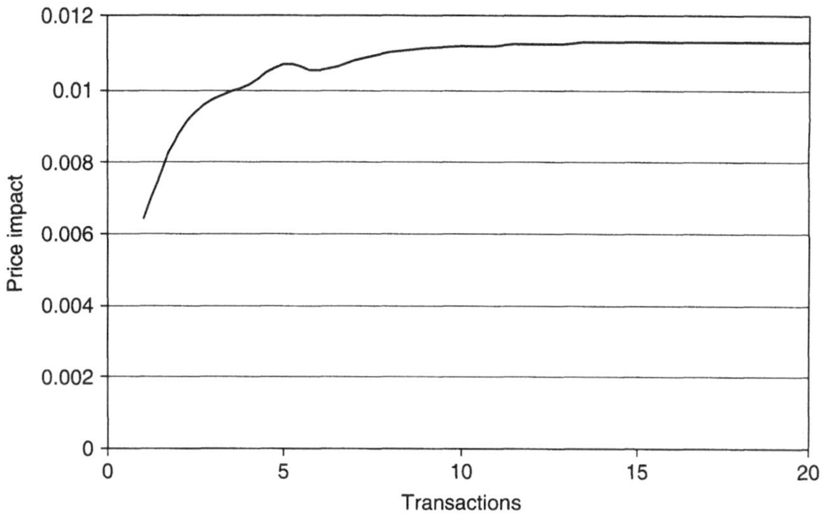

Figure 7.10 Cummulative price impact of an unexpected buy.

given day private information may or may not exist. Informed and uninformed traders are assumed to arrive in a random fashion. Informed traders only transact when private information is present, so on days with no private information, all transactions are by the uninformed. Days with high transaction rates are therefore viewed as days with more informed trading. Admati and Pfleiderer (1988) suggest that in the presence of short sales constraints the timing of trades should also carry information. Here, long durations imply bad news and suggest falling prices. The important thread here is that the timing of trades should carry information. This leads Dufour and Engle (2000) to consider expanding Hasbrouck's VAR structure to allow the durations to impact price updates. The duration between trades is treated as a predetermined variable that influences the informativeness of past trades on future quote revisions. This is done with by allowing the b_j parameters in (2.21) to be time varying parameters. In particular,

$$b_j = \gamma_j + \sum_{k=1}^{K} \delta_k D_{k,i-j} + \eta_j \ln\left(x_{i-j}\right),$$

where $D_{k,i-j}$ are dummy variables for the time of day and x_i is the duration. Because the b_j dictate the impact of past trades on quote revisions, it is clear that these effects will be time varying whenever the coefficients δ_k or η_j are nonzero. The model therefore extends the basic VAR of Hasbrouck by allowing the impact of trades to depend on the time of day as well the trading frequency as measured by the elapsed time between trades. A similar adjustment is made to the coefficients d_j in the trade equation.

The modified VAR is specified conditional on the durations and may therefore be estimated directly. Impulse response function, however, will require complete specification of the trivariate system of trades quotes and arrival times. Dufour and Engle propose using the ACD model for the arrival times.

Parameters are estimated for 18 stocks. As in the simple Hasbrouck VAR the impact of past transactions on quote revisions tends to be positive meaning that buys tend to lead to increasing quote revisions and sells lead to decreasing quote revisions. The magnitude of the d_k indicate some degree of time of day effects in the impact of trades. Trades near the open tend to be more informative, or have a larger price impact than trades at other times during the day although this effect is not uniform across all 18 stocks. The coefficients on the durations tend to be negative indicating that the longer it has been since the last trade, the smaller the price impact will be. The cumulative impulse response from an unanticipated order can be examined only now these functions will depend on the state of the market as dictated by transaction rates measured by the durations. The result is that the price impact curves will shift up when the transaction occurs with a short duration and shift down when transactions occur with long durations.

The VAR approach to modeling tick data is particularly appealing because of its ease of use. Furthermore, information about the spacing of the data can be included in these models as suggested by Dufour and Engle (2000). These VAR models can, of course, be expanded to include other variables such as the bid ask spread or measures of volatility.

2.2.2. Volatility Models in Tick Time

The VARs of the previous section proved useful in quantifying the price impact of trades. As such, they focus on the predictable change in the quotes given characteristics of a transaction. Alternatively, we might want to ask how characteristics of a transaction affect our uncertainty about the quote updates. Volatility models provide a means of quantifying our uncertainty.

The class of GARCH models by Engle (1982) and Bollerslev (1986) have proven to be a trusted work horse in modeling financial data at the daily frequency. Irregular spacing of transaction by transaction data seems particularly important for volatility modeling of transaction by transaction data because volatility is generally measured over fixed time intervals. Furthermore, it is very unlikely that, all else equal, the volatility of the asset price over a 1 h intertrade duration should be the same as the volatility over a 5 s intertrade duration. Early work on time deformation models linked the volatility over a fixed time interval to measures of market activity like trading volume. This includes work by Mandelbrot and Taylor (1967), Clark (1973) and Tauchen and Pitts (1983). Engle (2000) takes a different approach and proposes adapting the GARCH model for direct application to irregularly spaced transaction by transaction data.

Let the return from the $i-1$th to the ith transaction be denoted by r_i. Define the conditional variance per transaction as

$$V_{i-1}\left(r_i | x_i\right) = h_i, \tag{2.22}$$

where this variance is defined conditional on the contemporaneous duration as well as past price changes. The variance of interest, however, is the variance per unit time. This is related to the variance per transaction as

$$V_{i-1}\left(\frac{r_i}{\sqrt{x_i}}|x_i\right) = \sigma_i^2, \tag{2.23}$$

so that the relationship between the two variances is $h_i = x_i\sigma_i^2$.

The volatility per unit time is then modeled as a GARCH process. Engle proposes an ARMA(1,1) model for the series $\frac{r_i}{\sqrt{x_i}}$. Let e_i denote the innovation to this series. If the durations are not informative about the variance per unit time then the GARCH(1,1) model for irregularly spaced data is simply

$$\sigma_i^2 = \dot{\omega} + \dot{\alpha}e_{i-1}^2 + \dot{\beta}\sigma_{i-1}^2, \tag{2.24}$$

where we have placed dots above the GARCH parameters to differentiate these from the parameters of the ACD model with similar notation. Engle terms this model the UHF-GARCH model or ultra high-frequency GARCH model.

A more general model is inspired by the theoretical models of Easley and O'Hara (1992) and Admati and Pfleiderer (1985) discussed in Section 2.2.1 earlier. These models suggest that the timing of transactions is related to the likelihood of asymmetric trading and hence more uncertainty. Engle therefore proposes augmenting the GARCH(1,1) models with additional information about the contemporaneous duration and perhaps other characteristics of the market that might be thought to carry information about uncertainty such as spreads and past volume.

Although the model specifies the volatility per unit time, it is still operates in transaction time updating the volatility on a time scale determined by transaction arrivals. If calendar time forecasts of volatility are of interest then a model for the arrival times must be specified and estimated. Toward this end, Engle proposes using an ACD model for the arrival times. If the arrival times are deemed exogenous, then the ACD model and the GARCH model can be estimated separately although this estimation may be inefficient. In particular, under the exogeneity assumption, the ACD model could be estimated first and then the volatility model could be specified conditional on the contemporaneous duration and expected duration in a second step using canned GARCH software that admits additional explanatory variables. This is the approach taken in Engle (2000) where estimation is performed via (Q)MLE. Engle considers the following specification

$$\sigma_i^2 = \dot{\omega} + \dot{\alpha}e_{i-1}^2 + \dot{\beta}\sigma_{i-1}^2 + \gamma_1 x_i^{-1} + \gamma_2\frac{x_i}{\psi_i} + \gamma_3\psi_i^{-1} + \gamma_4\xi_{i-1},$$

where ψ_i is the expected duration obtained from an ACD model, and ξ_{i-1} characterizes the long run volatility via exponential smoothing of the squared return per unit time.

An alternative approach to modeling volatility of irregularly spaced data was simultaneously and independently developed by Ghysels and Jasiak (1998). Here the authors suggest using temporal aggregation to handle the spacing of the data. GARCH models are not closed under temporal aggregation so the authors propose working with the weak GARCH class of models proposed by Drost and Nijman (1993). For the weak GARCH class of models Drost and Nijman derive the implied low-frequency weak GARCH model implied by a higher frequency weak GARCH model. Ghysels and Jasiak propose a GARCH model with time varying parameters driven by the expected spacing of the data. This approach is complicated, however, by the fact that the temporal aggregation results apply to aggregation from one fixed interval to another, exogenously specified, fixed interval. The spacing of the transactions data is not fixed, and it is unlikely that transaction arrival times are exogenous. Nevertheless, the authors show that the proposed model is an exact discretization of a time deformed diffusion with ACD as the directing process. The authors propose using GMM to estimate the model.

2.3. Models for Discrete Prices

Discrete prices in financial markets pose an additional complication in the analysis of financial data. For the U.S. markets the graduation to decimalization is now complete, but we still find price changes clustering on just a handful of values. This discreteness can have an important influence on analysis of prices. Early analysis of discrete prices focused on the notion of a "true" or efficient price. The efficient price is defined as the expected value of the asset given all currently available public information. The focus of these early studies, therefore, was on the relationship between the efficient price and observed discrete prices. In particular, much emphasis was placed on how inference about the efficient price is influenced by measurement errors induced by discreteness.

Let P_t denote the observed price at time t and let P_t^e denote the efficient or "true" price of the asset at time t. Early models for discrete prices can generally be described in the following setting:

$$\begin{aligned} P_t^e &= P_{t-1}^e + v_t \\ P_t &= \text{round}\left(P_t^e + c_t Q_t, d\right), \\ v_t &\sim N\left(0, \sigma_t^2\right) \end{aligned} \tag{2.25}$$

where $d \geq 0$ is the tick size and *round* is a function rounding the argument to the nearest tick. Q_t is an unobserved i.i.d. indicator for whether the trade was buyer or seller initiated taking the value 1 for buyer initiated and -1 for seller initiated trades and probability given by 1/2. The parameter $c_t \geq 0$ denotes the cost of market making. It includes both tangible costs of market making as well as compensation for risk.

With $c = 0$ and $\sigma_t^2 = \sigma^2$, we obtain the model of Gottlieb and Kalay (1985)[1]. When $d = 0$ (no rounding) we obtain the model of Roll (1984). Harris (1990) considers the full model in (2.25). In this case, we can write

$$\Delta P_t = c(Q_t - Q_{t-1}) + \eta_t - \eta_{t-1} + \nu_t, \tag{2.26}$$

where $\eta_t = P_t^e - P_t$ is the rounding error. The variance of the observed price series is therefore given by

$$E(\Delta P_t)^2 = \sigma^2 + 2c^2 + E(\eta_{t+1} - \eta_t)^2. \tag{2.27}$$

Hence, the variance of the observed transaction price will exceed the variance by an amount that depends on the cost of market making and the discrete rounding errors. Furthermore, the first-order serial correlation is given by

$$E(\Delta P_t \Delta P_{t-1}) = -c^2 + E(\eta_{t+1} - \eta_t)(\eta_t - \eta_{t-1}), \tag{2.28}$$

which is shown to be negative by Harris (1990). The first-order serial correlation will be larger in absolute value when the cost of market making is larger and depends on the discreteness rounding errors. The Harris model goes a long way in describing key features of price discreteness and the implications regarding inference on the efficient price dynamics, but it is still very simplistic in several dimensions because it assumes that both the volatility of the efficient price and the cost of market making is constant. As new information hits the market the volatility of the efficient price will change. Because part of the cost of making market is the risk of holding the asset, the cost of making market will also be time varying.

Hasbrouck (1999a) builds on the previous discrete price literature by relaxing these two assumptions – both the volatility of the efficient price and the cost of making market are time varying. He also proposes working with bid and ask prices as opposed to the transaction prices circumventing the need to sign trades as buyer or seller initiated. P_t of Eq. (2.25) is therefore replaced by two prices, P_t^a and P_t^b, the bid and ask prices, respectively, where

$$\begin{aligned} P_t^a &= \text{ceiling}\left(P_t^e + c_t^a, d\right) \\ P_t^b &= \text{floor}\left(P_t^e - c_t^b, d\right) \end{aligned}, \tag{2.29}$$

$c_t^a > 0$ and $c_t^b > 0$ are the cost of exposure on the ask and bid side, respectively. These costs are the economic cost to the specialist including both the fixed cost of operation and the expected cost incurred as a result of the obligation to trade a fixed quantity at these

[1] For simplicity we have neglected a drift term in the efficient price equation and the possibility of dividend payments considered in Gottlieb and Kalay (1985).

prices with potentially better informed traders. The ceiling function rounds up to the nearest discrete tick and the floor function rounds down to the nearest tick recognizing the market maker would not set quotes that would fail to cover the cost.

The dynamics of this model are not suited for the type of analysis presented by Harris because of it's more complex dynamic structure. Instead, Hasbrouck focuses on characterizing the dynamics of the both cost of exposure and, second, estimating models for the volatility of the efficient price given only observations of the perturbed discrete bid and ask prices. Hasbrouck proposes using a GARCH model for the dynamics of the efficient price volatility σ_t^2. The dynamics of the cost of exposure is assumed to be of an autoregressive form.

$$\begin{aligned} \ln\left(c_t^a\right) &= \mu_t + \alpha\left(\ln\left(c_t^a\right) - \mu_{t-1}\right) + \nu_t^\alpha \\ \ln\left(c_t^b\right) &= \mu_t + \alpha\left(\ln\left(c_t^b\right) - \mu_{t-1}\right) + \nu_t^\beta, \end{aligned} \tag{2.30}$$

where μ_t is a common deterministic function of time of day and α is the common autoregressive parameter. ν_t^α and ν_t^β are assumed to be i.i.d. and independent of the efficient price innovation ν_t.

Estimation of the model is complicated by the fact that the efficient price is inherently unobserved – only the discrete bid and ask quotes are observed. Hasbrouck (1999a) proposes using a non-Gaussian, nonlinear state space of Kitagawa (1987) and Hasbrouck (1999b), and Manrique and Shephard (1997) propose using MCMC methods that treat the price at any given date as an unknown parameter. We refer the reader to this literature for further details on the estimation.

The early work with no time varying parameters focused on the impact of discrete rounding errors on inference regarding the efficient price. Hasbrouck also treats the object of interest as the dynamics of the efficient price and demonstrates a methodology to study the second moment dynamics of the efficient price while accounting for the discrete rounding errors. In addition, the model allows for asymmetric cost of exposure. In some states of the world the specialist may set quotes more conservatively on one side of the market than the other.

More recently, Zhang et al. (2008) appeal to the asymmetric information microstructure theory that suggests that transaction characteristics should influence the market makers perception of the exposure risk. They include in the cost of exposure dynamics (2.30) measures of the order imbalance and overall volume and find that the cost of exposure is affected by order imbalance. In particular, unexpectedly large buyer initiated volume tends to increase the cost of exposure on the ask side and decrease the cost of exposure on the bid side with analogous results for unexpected seller initiated volume. These effects are mitigated, however, the larger the total volume transacted.

If the structural parameters are not of primary interest, then an alternative is to directly model transaction prices with a reduced form model for discrete valued random variables.

This is the approach taken in Hausman Lo and MacKinlay (1992). They propose modeling the transaction by transaction price changes with an ordered Probit model. In doing so, the structural models linking the unobserved efficient price to the observed transaction price is replaced by a reduced form Probit link. The model is applied to transaction by transaction price dynamics. Let k denote the number of discrete values that the price changes can take which is assumed to be finite. Let s_i denote a vector of length k with values given by the jth column of the kxk identity matrix, if the jth state occurs on the ith transaction. Let π_i denote a k-dimensional vector with jth, where $\pi_i = E\left(s_i|I_{i-1}\right)$ and I_i is the information set associated with the ith transaction. Clearly, the jth element of x_i denotes the conditional probability of the jth state occurring. At the heart of the Probit model lies the assumption that the observed discrete transaction price changes can be represented as a transformation of a continuous latent price given by $\Delta P_i^{*\sim} N\left(\mu_i, \sigma_i^2\right)$, where μ_i and σ_i^2 are the mean and variance of the latent price given I_{i-1}. The Hausman Lo and MacKinlay model assumes that the jth element of π_i is given by

$$\pi_i^j F_{P_i^*}\left(c_{j-1}\right) - F_{P_i^*}\left(c_j\right), \tag{2.31}$$

where $F_{P_i^*}$ is the cdf associated with the price changes ΔP_i^* and $c_j, j = 1, k-1$ are time invariant parameters.

Because bid-ask bounce induces dependence in the price changes, it is natural to allow the conditional mean of price changes to depend on past price changes. Hausman Lo and Mackinlay are particularly interested in testing asymmetric information theories regarding the information content in a sequence of trades. In particular, they study how transaction prices respond to a sequence of buyer initiated trades versus a sequence of seller initiated trades. By conditioning on recent buys and sells the authors find evidence that persistent selling predicts falling prices and persistent buying predicts rising prices. The authors also suggest that the conditional variance may depend on the contemporaneous duration so that the variance associated with a price change over a long duration may not be the same as the variance of a price change associated with a relatively short duration. Indeed, they find that long durations lead to higher variance per transaction.

Russell and Engle (2002) are also interested in reduced form models for discrete prices that explicitly account for the irregular spacing of the data. They propose joint modeling the arrival times and the price changes as a marked point process. The joint likelihood for the arrival times and the price changes is decomposed into the product of the conditional distribution of the price change given the duration and the marginal distribution of the arrival times that are assumed to be given by an ACD model. More specifically if x_i denotes the ith intertransaction duration and $\widehat{z}_i = (z_i, z_{i-1}, z_{i-2} \ldots)$ then

$$f\left(x_{i+1}, \Delta p_{i+1} | \widehat{x}_i, \widehat{\Delta p_i}\right) = \varphi\left(\Delta p_{i+1} | \widehat{x}_{i+1}, \widehat{\Delta p_i}\right) \chi\left(x_{i+1} | \widehat{x}_i, \widehat{\Delta p_i}\right),$$

where φ denotes the distribution of price changes given the past price changes and durations as well as the contemporaneous duration. χ denotes the distribution of price changes given the past price changes and durations. Russell and Engle propose using the ACD model for the durations and the autoregressive conditional multinomial (ACM) model for the conditional distribution of the discrete price changes. A simple model for the price dynamics might assume a VARMA model for the state vector s_i. Because the state vector is simply a vector of ones and zeros, its expectation should be bounded between zero and one. Russell and Engle use the logistic transformation to directly impose this condition. Using the logistic link function the VARMA model is expressed in terms of the log odds. Let h_j denote a $k-1$ vector with jth element given by $\ln(\pi^j/\pi^k)$. Let $\tilde{s}_i$ and $\tilde{\pi}_i$ denote $k-1$ dimensional vectors consisting of the first $k-1$ elements of s_i and π_i. Hence, the kth element has been omitted and is referred to as the base state. Then the ACM(u, v) model with duration dependence is given by:

$$h_i = c + \sum_{m=1}^{u} A_m(\tilde{s}_{i-m} - \tilde{\pi}_i) + \sum_{m=1}^{v} B_m h_{i-m} + \sum_{m=1}^{w} \chi_m \ln(x_{i-m+1}), \tag{2.32}$$

where A_m and B_m are $(k-1)\,x\,(k-1)$ parameter matrices and ω and χ_m are $k-1$ parameter vector. Given the linear structure of the log odds VARMA the choice of the base state is arbitrary. The first $k-1$ probabilities are obtained by applying the logistic link function

$$\pi_i = \frac{1}{1 + \iota' \exp(h_i)} \exp(h_i), \tag{2.33}$$

where ι' is a $k-1$ vector of ones and $\exp(h_i)$ should be interpreted as applying the exponential function element by element. The omitted state is obtained by imposing the condition that the probabilities sum to 1. The ACD(p, q) specification for the durations allows feedback from the price dynamics into the duration dynamics as follows:

$$\ln(\psi_i) = \omega + \sum_{m=1}^{p} \alpha_m \frac{x_{i-m}}{\psi_{i-m}} + \sum_{m=1}^{q} \beta_m \ln(\psi_{i-m}) + \sum_{m=1}^{r} \left(\rho_m \Delta p_{i-m} + \zeta_m \Delta p_{i-m}^2\right).$$

For the stocks analyzed, the longer the contemporaneous duration the lower the expected price change and large price changes tend to be followed by short durations.

Another reduced form model for discrete prices is proposed by Rydberg and Shephard (2002). The model decomposes the discrete price changes into the trivariate process $\Delta P_i = Z_i D_i M_i$, where Z_i is an indicator for the ith transaction price change being nonzero and is referred to as activity. Conditional on a price move $(Z_i \neq 0)$, D_i takes the value of 1 or -1 denoting an upward or downward price change, respectively. Given a nonzero price change and its direction, M_i is the magnitude of the price change given it is nonzero and the direction. The authors suggest decomposing the distribution of price changes given an information set I_i $\Pr(\Delta P_i|I_{i-1}) = \Pr(Z_i|I_{i-1}) \Pr(D_i|Z_i, I_{i-1}) \Pr(M_i|Z_i, D_i, I_{i-1})$. The authors propose modeling the binary variables Z_i and D_i following an autoregressive logistic process first proposed by Cox (1958). A simple version for the activity variable is given by:

$$\ln\left(\frac{\Pr(Z_i = 1)}{1 - \Pr(Z_i = 1)}\right) = c + \sum_{m=1}^{u} Z_{i-m}. \tag{2.34}$$

The direction indicator variable is modeled in a similar fashion. Finally, the magnitude of the price change is modeled by a distribution for count data. Hence, it is positively valued over integers. The integers here are measured in units of ticks, or the smallest possible price change.

The Russell–Engle ACM approach and the Rydberg–Shephard components model are very similar in spirit both implementing an autoregressive structure. While this decomposition breaks the estimation down into a sequence of simpler problems it comes with a cost. To estimate the model sequentially the first model for the activity cannot be a function of lagged values of $\Pr(D_i|I_{i-1})$ or $\Pr(M_i|I_{i-1})$. Similarly the model for the direction cannot depend on the past probability associated with the magnitude. The importance of this restriction surely depends on the application at hand. A second advantage of the Rydberg–Shephard model easily accounts for a large number of states (possibly infinite).

2.4. Calendar Time Conversion

Most financial econometric analyses are carried out in fixed time units. These time intervals for many years were months, weeks, or days, but now time intervals of hours, five minutes, or seconds are being used for econometric model building. Once the data are converted from their natural irregular spacing to regular spaced observations, econometric analysis typically proceeds without considering the original form of the data. Models are constructed for volatility, price impact, correlation, extreme values, and many other financial constructs. In this section, we discuss the most common approaches used to convert irregularly spaced data to equally spaced observations, and in the next sections we will examine the implications of this conversion.

Suppose the data on prices arrive at times $\{t_i; i = 1, \ldots, N(T)\}$ so that there are N observations occurring over time $(0, T)$. These times could be times at which transactions occur and the price could be either the transaction price or the prevailing midquote at that time. An alternative formulation would have these times as the times at which quotes are posted and then the prices are naturally considered to be midquotes. Let the log of the price at time t_i be denoted p_i^*.

The task is to construct data on prices at each fixed interval of time. Denoting the discrete time intervals by integers of $t = 1, \ldots, T$, a task is to estimate p_t. The most common specification is to use the most recent price at the end of the time interval as the observation for the interval. Thus:

$$p_t = p_i^* \text{ where } t_i \le t < t_{i+1}. \tag{2.35}$$

For example, Huang and Stoll (1994) use this scheme where p is the prevailing midquote at the time of the last trade. Andersen et al. (2001) use the last trade price.

Various alternative schemes have been used. One could interpolate the price path from some or all of the p^* observations and then record the value at time t. For example, smoothing splines could be fit through all the data points. A particularly simple example of this uses the weighted average of the last price in one interval and the first price in the next interval:

$$\widetilde{p}_t = \left(\lambda p_i^* + (1-\lambda)\, p_{i+1}^*\right) \text{ where } t_i \leq t < t_{i+1}, \text{ and } \lambda = \frac{t - t_i}{t_{i+1} - t_i}. \tag{2.36}$$

Andersen et al. (2001, 2002) use this procedure with the natural log of the midpoints of the quotes to get 5 and 30 min calendar time data. The advantage of this formulation is supposed to be its reduced sensitivity to measurement error in prices. Clearly this comes at a cost of using future information. The merits of such a scheme must be evaluated in the context of a particular data generating process and statistical question.

A third possibility is adopted by Hasbrouck (2002). Because the time of a trade is recorded only to the nearest second, then if t is measured in seconds, there is at most one observation per time period. The calendar price is either set to this price or it is set to the previous period price. This version follows Eq. 2.35 but does not represent an approximation in the same sense.

Returns are defined as the first difference of the series.

$$y_i^* = p_i^* - p_{i-1}^*, \; y_t = p_t - p_{t-1}, \text{ and } \widetilde{y}_i = \widetilde{p}_i - \widetilde{p}_{i-1}, \tag{2.37}$$

Thus, y^* defines returns over irregular intervals while y defines returns over calendar intervals. In the case of small calendar intervals, there will be many zero returns in y. In this case, there are some simplifications. Means and variances are preserved if there never is more than one trade per calendar interval

$$\sum_{i=1}^{N(T)} y_i^* = \sum_{t=1}^{T} y_t \text{ and } \sum_{i=1}^{N(T)} \left(y_i^*\right)^2 = \sum_{t=1}^{T} y_t^2. \tag{2.38}$$

If the calendar time intervals are larger, then means will still be preserved but not variances as there may be more than one price in a calendar interval.

$$\sum_{i=1}^{N(T)} y_i^* = \sum_{t=1}^{T} y_t \text{ and } \sum_{i=1}^{N(T)} \left(\sum_{\substack{\text{multiple} \\ \text{trades}}} y_i^* \right)^2 = \sum_{t=1}^{T} y_t^2. \tag{2.39}$$

However, if the prices are Martingales, then the expectation of the cross products is zero and the expected value and probability limit of the calendar time and event time variances is the same. The Martingale assumption will be (nearly) satisfied for returns constructed over longer time horizons but is unlikely to hold for returns constructed over short-time horizons. Over short-time horizons, market microstructure effects induce autocorrelation in the return series as shown in Fig. 7.4.

When prices are interpolated, these relations no longer hold. In this scheme, there would be many cases of multiple observations in a calendar interval. The mean will approximately be the same in both sets of returns; however, the variances will not. The sum of squared transformed returns is given by:

$$\sum_{i=1}^{N(T)} [\widetilde{y}_i]^2 = \sum_{i=1}^{N(T)} \left[\lambda_i p_i^* + (1-\lambda_i)\, p_{i-1}^* - \lambda_j p_j^* - \left(1-\lambda_j\right) p_{j-1}^*\right]^2$$

$$= \sum_{i=1}^{N(T)} \left[\lambda_i\left(p_i^* - p_{i-1}^*\right) + \left(p_i^* - p_j^*\right) + \left(1-\lambda_j\right)\left(p_j^* - p_{j-1}^*\right)\right]^2. \quad (2.40)$$

where i and j are the events just after the end points of the calendar intervals. In the right-hand side of expression 2.40, the returns will all be uncorrelated if the y^* are Martingale differences, hence the expected variance and the probability limit of the variance estimators will be less than the variance of the process. Furthermore, the returns will be positively autocorrelated because they are formulated in terms of future prices. This is easily seen in Eq. 2.40 because the change in price around the interval endpoints is included in both adjacent returns.

2.4.1. Bivariate Relationships

A different question that could be considered is how irregular spacing of the data impacts bivariate analysis. Several papers have studied the nonsynchronous trading of more than one asset effects regression estimates to calculate market betas. Early work includes Fisher (1966), Dimson (1979), and the more explicit models of Scholes and Williams (1977), Cohen et al. (1978), Dimson (1979), and Lo and MacKinlay (1990). The early papers focus on empirical applications of the CAPM and Arbitrage Pricing theory with non-synchronous daily returns. We consider a different structure that is more compatible with high-frequency data. Our setup closely mirrors the setup of Lo and MacKinlay (1990) but our goal differs in that we are concerned with high-frequency bivariate regression coefficients while Lo and MacKinlay are concerned with autocorrelation structure. Our setup considers two correlated assets with Martingale prices. One of these asset prices is only observed at random time periods while the other is continuously observable. In this case the stochastic process of the infrequently observed process is defined on times $\{t_i; i = 1, \ldots, N(T)\}$. Let the log price of the second asset be q_t, and let its return, measured respectively in the first asset trade time and in calendar time, be:

$$z_{t_i}^* \equiv z_i^* = q_{t_i} - q_{t_{i-1}}, z_t = q_t - q_{t-1}.$$

The return on the first asset is given by

$$y_i^* = \beta z_i^* + \epsilon_i^*, \tag{2.41}$$

where the innovation is a Martingale difference sequence, independent of z, with potential heteroskedasticity because each observation may have a different time span. Because this model is formulated in transaction time, it is natural to estimate the unknown parameter beta with transaction time data. It is straightforward to show that least squares will be consistent.

Calendar time data on y can be constructed from (2.41) and (2.37). Consider the most disaggregated calendar time interval and let d_t be a dummy variable for the time periods in which a price is observed on the first asset. Then a useful expression for y_t is

$$y_t = d_t \begin{pmatrix} (\beta z_t + \epsilon_t) + (1 - d_{t-1})(\beta z_{t-1} + \epsilon_{t-1}) \\ + (1 - d_{t-2})(\beta z_{t-2} + \epsilon_{t-2}) + \cdots \end{pmatrix}. \tag{2.42}$$

With this data and the comparable calendar data on z, we are in a position to estimate beta by ordinary least squares in calendar time. The estimator is simply

$$\widehat{\beta} = \frac{\sum_{t=1}^{T} z_t y_t}{\sum_{t=1}^{T} z_t^2}, \tag{2.43}$$

which has an interesting probability limit under simplifying assumptions.

Theorem 1 *If*

a) (z_t, ϵ_t) *are independent Martingale difference sequences with finite variance*
b) d_t ˜ *independent Bernoulli with parameter* π

Then

$$\text{plim}\widehat{\beta} = \pi\beta \tag{2.44}$$

Proof Substituting and taking probability limits:

$$\text{plim}\widehat{\beta} = \frac{1}{\sigma_z^2} E\left[z_t d_t((\beta z_t + \epsilon_t) + (1 - d_{t-1})(\beta z_{t-1} + \epsilon_{t-1}) + \cdots)\right]. \tag{2.45}$$

Writing the expectation of independent variables as the product of their expectation gives

$$\text{plim}\widehat{\beta} = \frac{1}{\sigma_z^2} \begin{bmatrix} E(d_t)E\left(\beta z_t^2 + z_t\epsilon_t\right) + \\ E(d_t)E(z_t)E(1 - d_{t-1})E(\beta z_{t-1} + z\epsilon_{t-1}) + \cdots \end{bmatrix} = \beta\pi.$$

QED

The strking result is that the regression coefficient is heavily downward biased purely because of the nontrading bias. If trading is infrequent, then the regression coefficient will be close to zero. In this setting, researchers will often regress y on many lags of z. Suppose the regression includes k lags of z.

$$y_t = \beta_0 z_t + \beta_1 z_{t-1} + \cdots + \beta_k z_{t-k} + \epsilon_t. \tag{2.46}$$

The result is given by Theorem 2.

Theorem 2 *Under the assumptions of Theorem 1 the regression in (2.46) has a probability limit*

$$\text{plim}\widehat{\beta}_K = \pi\,(1-\pi)^{j-1}\beta,$$

and the sum of these coefficients approaches β as k gets large.

Proof Because z is a Martingale difference sequence, the matrix of regressors approaches a diagonal matrix with the variance of z on the diagonals. Each row of the $z'y$ matrix has dummy variables $d_t\,(1-d_{t-1})\,(1-d_{t-2})\ldots\left(1-d_{t-j}\right)$ multiplying the square of z. The result follows from independence.

QED

The regression coefficients decline from the contemporaneous one but ultimately summing up to the total impact of asset one on two. The result is, however, misleading because it appears that the price movements in asset two predict future movements in asset one. There appears to be causality orprice discovery between these assets merely because of the random trade times.

Similar results can be found in more general contexts including dynamic structure in the price observations and dependence with the z's. Continuing research will investigate the extent of the dependence and how results change with the economic structure.

3. CONCLUSION

The introduction of widely available ultra high-frequency data sets over the past decade has spurred interest in empirical market microstructure. The black box determining equilibrium prices in financial markets has been opened up. Intraday transaction by transaction dynamics of asset prices, volume, and spreads are available for analysis. These vast data sets present new and interesting challenges to econometricians.

Because transactions data are inherently irregularly spaced we view the process as a marked point process. The arrival times form the points and the characteristics of the trades form the marks. We first discuss models for the timing of events when the arrival rate may be time varying. Since the introduction of the ACD model of Engle and Russell

(1998), numerous other models for the timing of event arrivals have been proposed and applied to financial data. The models have been applicable to transaction arrival times or, if some arrival times are thought to be more informative than others the point process can be "thinned" to contain only those arrival times with special information. Examples include volume-based durations that correspond to the time it takes for a specified amount of volume to be transacted. Another example is price durations that correspond to the time it takes for the price to move a specified amount. These models can be thought of as models of volatility where the volatility is intuitively the inverse of our usual measures of volatility – namely the time it takes for the price to move a specified amount.

Models for the marks are also discussed. Often the focus is on the transaction price dynamics or joint modeling of transaction prices and volume. If the spacing of the data is ignored then the modeling problem can be reduced to standard econometric modeling procedures of VARs, simple linear regression, or GARCH models. Models that address the inherent discreteness in transaction by transaction prices are also discussed.

Alternatively, if the spacing of the data is thought to carry information then the simple approaches may be mispecified. Choices then include conditioning the marks on the arrival times as in Hausman Lo and Mackinlay, or, if forecasting is of interest joint modeling of the arrival times. The latter approach is considered in Engle (2000), Russell and Engle (2005), Rydberg and Shephard (2002), or Ghysels (1999) among others.

Finally, although artificially discretizing the time intervals at which prices (or other marks) is a common practice in the literature, it does not come without cost. Different discretizing schemes trade of bias associated with temporally aggregating with variance. Averaging reduces the variability but blurs the timing of events. We also show, in a stylized model, that causal relationships can be artificially induced by discretizing the data. Care should be taken in interpreting results from this type of analysis.

An exciting direction of microstructure research lies at the intersection of asset pricing and microstructure. This literature is still getting off the ground but promising directions can be found in the summary by O'Hara (2003). This literature seeks to demonstrate that microstructure has importance beyond market design questions. The path taken to a new equilibrium price may have an impact on the equilibrium value. A second exciting new area is the intersection between volatility estimators and microstructure affects. Recently proposed volatility estimators use the sum of very high frequency squared returns to approximate the daily variance the return. When sampled at very high frequency, the squared returns are dominated by microstructure effects. When sampled over longer horizons the return is dominated by changes in the efficient price. Bandi and Russell (2008) survey this literature. Optimal execution is another area of practical and growing interest. Empirical microstructure models of price impact are used to optimally break up a large order into smaller pieces and trade over a time interval rather than all at once. The implications of these strategies are a reduction in expected trade cost but an increase in risk as shares executed at the end of the trading period will occur at a price potentially very different from trades completed at the beginning of the trading period, see Engle and Ferstenberg (2007) for a theoretical discussion and Engle et al. (2008) for applications.

APPENDIX A: EACD(3,3) PARAMETER ESTIMATES USING EVIEWS GARCH MODULE

	Coefficient	*Robust std. err.*
ω	0.004244	0.000855
α_1	0.070261	0.007157
α_2	0.038710	0.012901
α_3	−0.055966	0.008640
β_1	0.835806	0.125428
β_2	0.107894	0.118311

where $\psi_i = \omega + \sum_{j=1}^{3} \alpha_j x_{i-j} + \sum_{j=1}^{2} \beta_j \psi_{i-j}$

Model diagnostics

APPENDIX B: VAR PARAMETER ESTIMATES

Variable	*Price equation Coefficient*	*Std. error*	*Trade equation Coefficient*	*Std. error*
c	−0.006553	0.000284	0.509648	0.004785
w_i	0.014230	0.000430		
w_{i-1}	0.000891	0.000493	0.298146	0.005557
w_{i-2}	−0.000175	0.000493	0.059228	0.005797
w_{i-3}	−0.000533	0.000493	0.036385	0.005803
w_{i-4}	0.000176	0.000493	0.026645	0.005798
w_{i-5}	−0.001295	0.000425	0.035205	0.005558
Δm_{i-1}	−0.262310	0.005734	0.250909	0.071635
Δm_{i-2}	−0.121951	0.005934	0.108735	0.081696
Δm_{i-3}	−0.054038	0.005968	−0.000260	0.084009
Δm_{i-4}	−0.026460	0.005934	−0.022889	0.081695
Δm_{i-5}	−0.011011	0.005734	−0.220448	0.071634

REFERENCES

Admati, A.R. and P. Pfleiderer, 1988, A Theory of Intraday Patterns: Volume and Price Variability, The Review of Financial Studies 1, 3–40.

Andersen, T. and T. Bollerslev, 1997, Heterogeneous Information Arrivals and Return Volatility Dynamics: Uncovering the Long-Run in High Frequency Returns, The Journal of Finance, 52, 975–1005.

Andersen, T., T. Bollerslev, F.X. Diebold and H. Ebens, 2001, The Distribution of Realized Stock Return Volatility, Journal of Financial Economics, 61, 43–76.

Andersen, T., T. Bollerslev, F.X. Diebold and P. Labys, 2003, Modeling and Forecasting Realized Volatility, Econometrica, 71, 579–625.

Bandi, F. and J. Russell, 2008, Volatility, Financial Engineering, North-Holland.

Bauwens, L. and P. Giot, 2000, The Logarithmic ACD Model: An Application to the Bid-Ask Quotes Process of Three NYSE Stocks, Annales d'conomie et de Statistique, 60, 117–149.

Bauwens, L. and P. Giot, 2001, Econometric Modeling of Stock Market Intraday Activity, Kluwer Academic Publishers.

Bauwens, L. and P. Giot, 2003, Asymmetric ACD Models: Introducing Price Information in ACD Models, Empirical Economics, 28, 709–731.

Bollerslev, T., 1986, Generalized Autoregressive Conditional Heteroskedasticity, Journal of Econometrics, 31, 307–327.

Clark, P.K., 1973, A Subordinated Stochastic Process Model with Finite Variance for Speculative Prices, Econometrica, 41, 135–156.

Copeland, T. and Galai, D., 1983, Information Effects and the Bid-Ask Spread, Journal of Finance, 38, 1457–1469.

Dacorogna, M., R. Gencay, U. Muller, R. Olsen and O. Pictet, 2001, An Introduction to High Frequency Finance, Academic Press.

Dimson, E., 1979, Risk Measurement When Shares are Subject to Infrequent Trading, Journal of Financial Economics, 7, 197–226.

Drost, F. C. and T. E. Nijman, 1993, Temporal Aggregation of GARCH Processes, Econometrica, 61, 909–927.

Easley, D. and O'Hara, M., 1992, Time and the Process of Security Price Adjustment, The Journal of Finance, 19, 69–90.

Engle, R., 1982, Autoregressive Conditional Heteroskedasticity with Estimates of the Variance of U.K. Inflation, Econometrica, 50, 987–1008.

Engle, R., 2000, The Econometrics of Ultra-High Frequency Data, Econometrica, 68, 1, 1–22.

Engle, R. and Dufour, A., 2000, Time and the Price Impact of a Trade, Journal of Finance, 55, 2467–2498.

Engle, R. and R. Ferstenberg, 2007, Execution Risk, Journal of Portfolio Management, 33, 34–45.

Engle, R., R. Ferstenberg, and Russell 2008, Measuring and Modeling Execution Cost and Risk, Working Paper, University of Chicago, Booth School of Business.

Engle, R. and J. Lange, 2001, Predicting VNET; A Model of the Dynamics of Market Depth, Journal of Financial Markets, 4, 2, 113–142.

Engle, R. and A. Lunde, 2003, Trades and Quotes a Bivariate Process, Journal of Financial Econometrics, 1, 159–188.

Engle, R. and J. Russell, 1995, Autoregressive Conditional Duration: A New Model for Irregularly Spaced Data, University of California, San Diego, Unpublished Manuscript.

Engle, R. and J. Russell, 1997, Forecasting the Frequency of Changes in Quoted Foreign Exchange Prices with the Autoregressive Conditional Duration Model, Journal of Empirical Finance, 4, 187–212.

Engle, R. and J. Russell, 1998, Autoregressive Conditional Duration: A New Model for Irregularly Spaced Data, Econometrica, 66, 5, 1127–1162.

Fernandes, M. and J. Grammig, 2006, A Family of Autoregressive Conditional Duration Models, Journal of Econometrics, 130, 1–23.

Glosten, L. R. and Milgrom P., 1985, Bid Ask and Transaction Prices in a Specialist Market with Heterogeneously Informed Agents, Journal of Financial Economics, 14, 71–100.

Ghysels, E. and J. Jasiak, 1998, GARCH for Irregularly Spaced Data: The ACD-GARCH Model, Studies in Nonlinear Dynamics and Econometrics, 2, 4, 133–49.

Gottlieb, G. and A. Kalay, 1985, Implications of the Discreteness of Observed Stock Price, The Journal of Finance, 40, 1, 135–153.

Grammig, J. and K.-O. Maurer, 2000, Non-Monotonic Hazard Functions and the Autoregressive Conditional Duration Model. The Econometrics Journal, 3, 16–38.

Harris, L., 1990, Estimation of Stock Price Variances and Serial Covariances from Discrete Observations, Journal of Financial and Quantitative Analysis, 25, 291–306.

Hasbrouck, J., 1991, Measuring the Information Content of Stock Trades, The Journal of Finance, 66, 1, 179–207.

Hasbrouck, J., 1999a, Security Bid/Ask Dynamics with Discreteness and Clustering, Journal of Financial Markets, 2, 1, 1–28.

Hasbrouck, J., 1999b, The Dynamics of Discrete Bid and Ask Quotes, Journal of Finance, 54, 6, 2109–2142.

Hausman, J., A. Lo and C. MacKinlay, 1992, An Ordered Probit Analysis of Transaction Stock Prices, Journal of Financial Economics, 31, 319–379.

Hawkes, A. G., 1971, Spectra of Some Self-Exciting and Mutually Exciting Point Process, Biometrika, 58, 83–90.

Huang, R. D. and H. R. Stoll, 1994, Market Microstructure and Stock Return Predictions, The Review of Financial Studies, 7, 1, 179–213.

Kitagawa, G., 1987, Non-Gaussian State-Space Modeling of Nonstationary Time Series, Journal of American Statistical Association, 82, 1032–1041.

Lee, S. and B. Hansen, 1994, Asymptotic Theory for the GARCH(1,1) Quasi-Maximum Likelihood Estimator, Econometric Theory, 10, 29–52.

Lee, C. and M. Ready, 1991, Inferring Trade Direction from Intraday Data, The Journal of Finance, 46, 2, 733–746.

Lo, A. and C. MacKinlay, 1990, An Econometric Analysis of Nonsynchronous Trading, Journal of Econometrics, 45, 181–211.

Lumsdaine, R., 1996, Consistency and Asymptotic Normality of the Quasi-Maximum Likelihood Estimator in IGARCH(1,1) and Covariance Stationary GARCH(1,1) Models, Econometrica, 64, 575–596.

Lunde, A., 1998, A Generalized Gamma Autoregressive Conditional Duration Model, Working Paper, Department of Economics, University of Aarhus.

Mandelbrot, B. and M. Taylor, 1967, On the Distribution of Stock Price Differences, Operations Research, 15, 1057–1062.
Manrique, A. and N. Shephard, 1997, Likelihood Analysis of a Discrete Bid/Ask Price Model for a Common Stock, Working Paper, Nuffield College, Oxford University.
Nelson, D., 1991, Conditional Heteroskedasticity in Asset Returns: A New Approach, Econometrica, 59, 347–370.
Nelson, D. and C. Cao, 1992, Inequality Constraints in the GARCH(1,1) Model, Journal of Business and Economic Statistics, 10, 229–235.
O'Hara, M., 1995, Market Microstructure Theory, Blackwell Publishers
Roll, R., 1984, A Simple Implicit Measure of the Effective Bid-Ask Spread in an Efficient Market, Journal of Finance, 39, 1127–1139.
Rubin, I., 1972, Regular Point Processes and Their Detection, IEEE Transactions on Information Theory, ITT-18, 547–557.
Russell, J., 1999, Econometric Analysis of Multivariate Irregularly Spaced Transactions Data, Working Paper, University of Chicago, Booth School of Business.
Russell, J. and R. Engle, 2005, A Discrete-State Continuous Time Model for Transaction Prices and Times: The ACM-ACD Model, Journal of Business Economics and Statistics, 23, 166–180.
Rydberg, T. H. and N. Shephard, 2002, Dynamics of Trade-by-Trade Price Movements: Decomposition and Models, Journal of Financial Econometrics, 1, 2–25.
Scholes, M. and J. Williams, 1977, Estimating Betas from Nonsynchronous Data, Journal of Financial Economics, 5, 309–327.
Snyder, D. and M. Miller, 1991, Random Point Processes in Time and Space, Springer Verlag.
Tauchen, G. and M. Pitts, 1983, The Price Variability Volume Relationship on Speculative Markets, Econometrica, 51, 485–505.
White, H., 1982, Maximum Likelihood Estimation in Mispecified Models, Econometrica, 50, 1–25.
Zhang, M., J. Russell and R. Tsay, 2001, A Nonlinear Conditional Autoregressive Duration Model with Applications to Financial Transactions Data, Journal of Econometrics, 104, 179–207.
Zhang, M., J. Russell and R. Tsay, 2008, Information Determinants of Bid and Ask Quotes: Implications for Market Liquidity and Volatility, Journal of Empricial Finance, 15, 4, 656–678.

CHAPTER 8

Simulated Score Methods and Indirect Inference for Continuous-time Models

A. Ronald Gallant* *and* **George Tauchen****

*The Fuqua School of Business, Duke University, Durham, NC

**Department of Economics, Duke University, Durham, NC

Contents

Abstract

We describe a simulated method of moments estimator that is implemented by choosing the vector-valued moment function to be the expectation under the structural model of the score function of an auxiliary model, where the parameters of the auxiliary model are eliminated by replacing them with their quasi-maximum likelihood estimates. This leaves a moment vector depending only on the parameters of the structural model. Structural parameter estimates are those parameter values that put the moment vector as closely to zero as possible in a suitable generalized method of moments (GMM) metric. This methodology can also be interpreted as a practical computational strategy for implementing indirect inference. We argue that considerations from statistical science dictate that the auxiliary model should approximate the true data-generating process as closely as possible and show that using the seminonparametric (SNP) model is one means to this end. When the view of close approximation is accepted in implementation, the methodology described here is usually referred to as Efficient Method of Moments (EMM) in the literature because (i) the estimator is asymptotically as efficient as maximum likelihood under correct specification and (ii) the detection of model error is assured under incorrect specification. There are alternative views toward the desirability of close approximation to the data, which we discuss.

Keywords: efficient method; of moments indirect; inference simulated method of moments.

1. INTRODUCTION AND OVERVIEW

In both empirical work (Bansal et al., 1993, 1995) and theoretical work (Gallant and Long, 1997; Gallant and Tauchen, 1996), we have developed a systematic strategy for choosing the moments for generalized method of moments (GMM) estimation of a structural model. The idea is relatively straightforward: use the expectation with respect to the structural model of the score function of an auxiliary model as the vector of moment conditions for GMM estimation.

The score function is the derivative of the logarithm of the density of the auxiliary model with respect to the parameters of the auxiliary model. The moment conditions obtained by taking the expectation of the score depend directly upon the parameters of the auxiliary model and indirectly upon the parameters of the structural model through the dependence of expectation operator on the parameters of the structural model. The parameters of the auxiliary model are eliminated from the moment conditions by replacing them with their quasi-maximum likelihood estimates, which are obtained by maximizing the likelihood of the auxiliary model. This leaves a random vector of moment conditions that depends only on the parameters of the structural model; the randomness is due to the random fluctuations of the quasi-maximum likelihood estimates of the parameters of the auxiliary model. When this vector of moment conditions is evaluated at the true values of the structural parameters, it tends to zero as sample size increases, presuming that the structural model is correctly specified. The parameters of the structural model may therefore be estimated by minimizing the magnitude of the vector of moment conditions as measured by the appropriate GMM metric.

This estimation method, which is the main topic of this chapter, is particularly useful in a simulation-based estimation context, where the structural model is readily simulated but the likelihood function of the structural model is intractable. This context applies to many continuous-time estimation problems. In implementation, the expectation of the score with respect to the structural model is computed by simulating the structural model and averaging the score function over the simulations. When the structural model is strictly stationary, one may average the scores over a single, very long simulated realization (case 2 of Gallant and Tauchen, 1996), while in the presence of exogenous covariates, one simulates and averages the scores at each data point conditional on the covariates and then sums across data points (case 3 of Gallant and Tauchen, 1996).

The estimator is closely related to the indirect inference estimator due to Smith (1990, 1993) and Gourieroux et al. (1993). A referee suggests that statistical methods that use an auxiliary model as an adjunct be called indirect inference. In this chapter and elsewhere, we adopt a different terminology. We refer to the score-based method as efficient method of moments and the binding function method as indirect inference. However, ideas matter and names do not. Readers can call these methods whatever they please. The main difference between score-based methods and those that use a binding function is computational. Score-based methods are computationally tractable. Methods that use a binding function can be a computational nightmare. The innovative computational methods proposed by Chernozukov and Hong (2003) appear to have further increased this computational advantage. We discuss the Chernozukov and Hong method in Section 7.

We illustrate this point regarding computations in Section 2.1.2 using what is sometimes called the Wald variant of the indirect inference estimator. It is a minimum distance estimator that entails minimizing, in a suitable metric, the difference between the parameters of the auxiliary model obtained by quasi-maximum likelihood and those predicted by the structural model. The predicted parameter values are given by the binding function, which in practice is computed by reestimating the auxiliary model on simulations from the structural model. The binding function computation is trivial for linear auxiliary models, as initially suggested by Smith (1990, 1993) but is very demanding and possible infeasible for more complicated nonlinear auxiliary models. The score-based approach discussed here circumvents the need to evaluate the binding function, which is why it is more computationally tractable. Nonetheless, for any given auxiliary model, the score-based estimator and indirect inference have the same asymptotic distribution. Thus, as just mentioned, some interpret and view the score-based estimator as a practical way to implement indirect inference in a simulation-based context. Either way, there are strong parallels to the classical simultaneous equations literature, with the auxiliary model playing the role of the reduced form and we recognize that there may be different, but asymptotically equivalent ways to work back from the reduced-form parameter estimates to obtain structural parameter estimates.

The practical implication of working from the score function is that the auxiliary model only needs to be estimated once, namely on the observed data. This added flexibility makes it possible to implement the score-based estimator using either very simple or very complicated and sophisticated auxiliary models. Complicated auxiliary models would be appropriate if the observed data exhibit important nonlinearities, and the researcher wants the structural model to confront these nonlinearities. Regardless of the score generator actually used, the estimator is consistent and asymptotically normal, subject only to mild identification conditions. Thus, there is potentially great latitude for choosing the auxiliary model.

We have consistently argued for resolving this choice by making the auxiliary model be a good statistical description of the data. That is, it should be a bona fide reduced-form model. As we shall see, by doing so the researcher can ensure that the estimator can achieve the full efficiency of maximum likelihood estimation if the structural model is correct. Furthermore, and more important, it assures the researcher of detecting misspecification if the structural model is wrong. In view of these capabilities, we ascribe the term *Efficient Method of Moments* (EMM) to the estimator.

There are three basic steps to EMM. The first, termed the *projection step*, entails summarizing the data by projecting it onto the reduced-form auxiliary model, which we frequently term the *score generator*. If one knows of a good statistical model for the data, then it should be used in the projection step. That is rarely the case, however, and we have proposed the SNP models of Gallant and Tauchen (1989) as a general purpose score generator. The second step is termed the *estimation step*, where the parameters are obtained by GMM (minimum chi-squared) using an appropriate weighting matrix. If, in the projection step, care is taken to obtain a good auxiliary model, then the weighting matrix takes a particularly simple form. The estimation step produces an omnibus test of specification along with useful diagnostic t statistics. The third step is termed the *reprojection step*, which entails postestimation analysis of simulations for the purposes of prediction, filtering, and model assessment.

Section 2 discusses and contrasts simulated score methods and indirect inference. Thereafter, the discussion is combined with a focus on the EMM estimator. As will be seen, these estimators are so closely related that, after the preliminary discussion of the differences, a unified discussion under the projection, estimation, reprojection paradigm described above is warranted.

Section 3 gives general guidelines for selecting the auxiliary model for the projection step. Section 4 gives 3 formal analysis of the efficiency theory and develops the SNP model as a general purpose score generator. Section 5 gives an intuitive over of reprojection followed by a more formal description of the theory underlying it. Section 6 reviews in detail two selected applications of EMM for estimation of continuous time models. Section 7 discusses software, practical issues, and some interesting capabilities using parallelization.

This chapter is focused on applications to continuous-time processes. But one should be aware that indirect inference, EMM, and simulated method of moments methods have far greater applicability. They apply to cross sectional data, panel data, data with fixed covariates, and spatial data. For details see Gourieroux et al. (1993), Gallant and Tauchen (1996), Pagan (1999), and Genton and de Luna (2000).

2. ESTIMATION AND MODEL EVALUATION

The simulated score estimation method was proposed and applied in Bansal et al. (1993) where it was used to estimate and evaluate a representative agent specification of a two-country general equilibrium model. The theory was developed in Gallant and Tauchen (1996) and extended to non-Markovian data with latent variables in Gallant and Long (1997).

Indirect inference was proposed and developed by Smith (1990, 1993) and Gourieroux et al. (1993). These ideas overlap with the simulated method of moments estimators proposed by Ingram and Lee (1991), Duffie and Singleton (1993), and Pakes and Pollard (1989).

Here, we shall sketch the main ideas of simulated score estimation and indirect inference in a few paragraphs at a modest technical level and then present a more detailed review of the EMM methodology.

2.1. Overview

2.1.1. Simulated Score Estimation

Suppose that $f(y_t|x_{t-1},\theta)$ is a reduced-form model for the observed data, where x_{t-1} is the state vector of the observable process at time $t-1$ and y_t is the observable process. An example of such a reduced-form model is a GARCH(1,1). If this reduced-form model, which we shall call a score generator, is fitted by maximum likelihood to get an estimate $\tilde{\theta}_n$, then the average of the score over the data $\left\{\tilde{y}_t,\tilde{x}_{t-1}\right\}_{t=1}^{n}$ satisfies

$$\frac{1}{n}\sum_{t=1}^{n}\frac{\partial}{\partial\theta}\log f(\tilde{y}_t|\tilde{x}_{t-1},\tilde{\theta}_n)=0 \tag{2.1}$$

because Eq. (2.1) is the first-order condition of the optimization problem. Throughout, as in (2.1), we shall use a tilde to denote observed values and statistics computed from observed values.

Now suppose we have a structural model that we wish to estimate. We express the structural model as the transition density $p(y_t|x_{t-1},\rho)$, where ρ is the parameter vector. In relatively simple models, $p(y_t|x_{t-1},\rho)$ is available in a convenient closed-form expression, and one can estimate ρ directly by classical maximum likelihood. However, for more complicated nonlinear models, $p(y_t|x_{t-1},\rho)$ is often not available and direct maximum likelihood is infeasible.

But at the same time, it can be relatively easy to simulate the structural model. That is, for each candidate value ρ, one can generate a simulated trajectory on $\left\{\hat{y}_t\right\}_{t=1}^{N}$ and the corresponding lagged state vector $\left\{\hat{x}_{t-1}\right\}_{t=1}^{N}$. This situation, of course, is the basic setup of simulated method of moments (Duffie and Singleton, 1993; Ingram and Lee, 1991). It arises naturally in continuous-time models because the implied discrete time density is rarely available in closed form (Lo, 1988), but-continuous time models are often quite easy to simulate. The situation also arise in other areas of economics and finance as well as discussed in Tauchen (1997).

If the structural model is correct and the parameters ρ are set to their true values ρ^o, then there should not be much difference between the data $\{\tilde{y}_t\}_{t=1}^n$ and a simulation $\{\hat{y}_t\}_{t=1}^N$. Therefore, if the first-order conditions (2.1) of the reduced form were computed by averaging over a simulation instead of the sample, viz.,

$$m(\rho, \theta) = \frac{1}{N} \sum_{t=1}^{N} \frac{\partial}{\partial \theta} \log f(\hat{y}_t | \hat{x}_{t-1}, \theta),$$

one would expect that

$$m(\rho^o, \tilde{\theta}_n) = 0,$$

at least approximately. This condition will hold exactly in the limit as N and n tend to infinity under the standard regularity conditions of quasi-maximum likelihood. One can try to solve $m(\rho, \tilde{\theta}_n) = 0$ to get an estimate $\hat{\rho}_n$ of the parameter vector of the structural model. In most applications, this cannot be done because the dimension of θ is larger than the dimension of ρ. To compensate for this, one estimates ρ by $\hat{\rho}_n$ that minimizes the GMM criterion

$$m'(\rho, \tilde{\theta}_n) \, (\tilde{\mathcal{I}}_n)^{-1} \, m(\rho, \tilde{\theta}_n)$$

with weighting matrix

$$\tilde{\mathcal{I}}_n = \frac{1}{n} \sum_{t=1}^{n} \left[\frac{\partial}{\partial \theta} \log f(\tilde{y}_t | \tilde{x}_{t-1}, \tilde{\theta}_n) \right] \left[\frac{\partial}{\partial \theta} \log f(\tilde{y}_t | \tilde{x}_{t-1}, \tilde{\theta}_n) \right]'.$$

This choice of weighting matrix presupposes that the score generator fits the data well. If not, then a more complicated weighting matrix, described below, should be considered. The estimator $\hat{\rho}_n$ is asymptotically normal.

If the structural model is correctly specified, then the statistic

$$L_0 = n \, m'(\hat{\rho}_n, \tilde{\theta}_n) \, (\tilde{\mathcal{I}}_n)^{-1} \, m(\hat{\rho}_n, \tilde{\theta}_n)$$

has the chi-squared distribution on $\dim(\theta) - \dim(\rho)$ degrees of freedom. This is the familiar test of overidentifying restrictions in GMM nomenclature and is used to test model adequacy. A chi-squared is asymptotically normally distributed as degrees of freedom increase. Therefore, for ease of interpretation, the statistic L_0 is often redundantly reported as a z-statistic, as we do later in our tables.

The vector $m(\hat{\rho}_n, \tilde{\theta}_n)$ can be normalized by its standard error to get a vector of t-statistics. These t-statistics can be interpreted much as normalized regression residuals. They are often very informative but are subject to the same risk as the interpretation of regression residuals, namely, a failure to fit one characteristic of the data can show up not at the score of the parameters that describe that characteristic but elsewhere due to correlation (colinearity) (Tauchen, 1985). Nonetheless, as with regression residuals, inspecting normalized $m(\hat{\rho}_n, \tilde{\theta}_n)$ is usually the most informative diagnostic available. To protect oneself from misinterpreting these t-statistics, one should confirm all conclusions by means of the test of model adequacy L_0 above.

If the score generator is a poor fit to the data or the chi-squared test of model adequacy L_0 is not passed, then the analysis must be viewed as a calibration exercise rather than classical statistical inference. One might, for instance, deliberately choose a score generator that represents only some characteristics of the data to study the ability of a structural model to represent only those characteristics. We do this below but, as Gallant and McCulloch (2009) illustrate, it should be done with care because it is quite possible to be seriously mislead. One might also use a rejected model to price options, arguing that it is the best available even though it was rejected. The use of EMM for calibration is discussed in Gallant et al. (1999).

The score generator can be viewed as a summary of the data. It is accomplished by, in effect, projecting the data onto a reduced-form model and is therefore called the projection step of an EMM investigation. Extraction of structural parameters from the summary by minimizing the chi-squared criterion is called the estimation step. In a later section, we shall describe a third step, reprojection, that often accompanies an EMM investigation.

2.1.2. Indirect Inference Estimation

There are variants on the indirect inference scheme, some of which we discuss at the end of this section. We first describe what is sometimes called the Wald variant. The score-based method described in Section 2.1.1 is sometimes called the Lagrange multiplier variant in this vernacular.

The indirect inference estimator is based on the binding function, which is defined as

$$b(\rho) = \underset{\theta \in \Theta}{\operatorname{argmax}} \int\int \log f(y|x,\theta)\, p(y|x,\rho)\mathrm{d}y\mathrm{d}x,$$

where $f(y|x,\theta)$ and $p(y|x,\rho)$ are the transition densities of the auxiliary model and structural model, respectively, as described above. The binding function can also be defined as the function that satisfies $m[\rho, b(\rho)] = 0$ (where, implicitly, $N = \infty$). According to the asymptotics of quasi-maximum likelihood,

$$\sqrt{n}[\tilde{\theta}_n - b(\rho)] \xrightarrow{\mathcal{L}} N\left(0, \mathcal{J}^{-1}\mathcal{I}\mathcal{J}^{-1}\right),$$

where $\tilde{\theta}_n$ is as above and

$$\mathcal{I} = \iint \left\{ \frac{1}{\sqrt{n}} \sum_{t=1}^{n} \frac{\partial}{\partial\theta} \log f[y|x, b(\rho)] \right\}^2 p(y|x, \rho)\, dydx,$$

$$\mathcal{J} = \iint \left\{ \frac{\partial^2}{\partial\theta\partial\theta'} \log f[y|x, b(\rho)] \right\} p(y|x, \rho) dydx.$$

The matrix $\mathcal{I}$ will likely have to be estimated by a heteroskedastic autocovariance consistent (HAC) variance estimator as described below because, for reasons mentioned below, the auxiliary model is not apt to be a good approximation to the structural model in most indirect inference applications. A plug-in estimator can be used to estimate $\mathcal{J}$; numerical differentiation or Chernozukov–Hong method (Chernozukov and Hong, 2003) may be required to get the second derivatives. If the auxiliary model is an accurate approximation to the true data-generating process, then $\mathcal{I} \doteq \mathcal{J}$ and one can compute whichever is more convenient. Without being specific as to the method used, let $\tilde{\mathcal{I}}_n$ and $\tilde{\mathcal{J}}_n$ denote estimates of $\mathcal{I}$ and $\mathcal{J}$.

The indirect inference estimator is

$$\hat{\rho}_n = \underset{\rho \in R}{\operatorname{argmin}}\, [\tilde{\theta}_n - b(\rho)]' \left(\tilde{\mathcal{J}}^{-1} \tilde{\mathcal{I}} \tilde{\mathcal{J}}^{-} \right)^{-1} [\tilde{\theta}_n - b(\rho)],$$

where R is the parameter space of the structural model.

Herein lies the computational difficulty with the indirect inference estimator: one must have an expression for $b(\rho)$ to compute the estimator. The expression

$$b(\rho) = \underset{\theta \in \Theta}{\operatorname{argmax}} \iint \log f(y|x, \theta)\, p(y|x, \rho) dydx,$$

can be computed numerically, with the integral computed by simulation as discussed above and $b(\rho)$ computed by numerical optimization for given ρ. This embeds one numerical optimization, that for $b(\rho)$, inside another, that for $\hat{\rho}_n$, which poses two problems: the first is cost and the second is stability. That this computation will be costly is obvious. The stability issue is that a numerical optimizer can only compute the inner optimization, that for $b(\rho)$, to within a tolerance, at best. This will cause jitter which will cause the outer optimization problem to be nonsmooth. Nonsmooth optimization problems are very difficult and costly to solve because good curvature information is not available. The Chernozukov–Hong method could lessen some of the problems caused by jitter but would, unfortunately, further increase cost. If the inner problem has local minima, the situation becomes nearly hopeless. For this reason, most practitioners convert a problem formulated as an indirect inference problem to simulated score estimation problem prior to computation so as to eliminate $b(\rho)$ and $\mathcal{J}$ from consideration; see, for instance, Pastorello et al. (2000). A verification of the equivalence of the indirect inference and simulated score formulations is in Gourieroux et al. (1993). Of course, if the auxiliary model is sufficiently simple, then analytic expressions for $b(\rho)$ and $\mathcal{J}$ become available and the computation

$$\hat{\rho}_n = \underset{\rho \in R}{\operatorname{argmin}} \, [\tilde{\theta}_n - b(\rho)]' \left(\tilde{\mathcal{J}}^{-1} \tilde{\mathcal{I}} \tilde{\mathcal{J}}^{-}\right)^{-1} [\tilde{\theta}_n - b(\rho)]$$

becomes feasible as posed.

As mentioned earlier, there are variants on the scheme outlined above. Other statistical objective functions can be substituted for the likelihood. Another variant is as follows: once the binding function has been computed from a simulation for given θ, the likelihood of the auxiliary model can be evaluated at the data and the value of the binding function at that θ and used as if it were the likelihood for purposes of inference. This is one way to implement a Bayesian variant of indirect inference as is outlined in Gallant and McCulloch (2009). They develop numerical methods to mitigate against the effects of the jitter in computing the binding function, which can be effective in a Bayesian context. Software to implement their method is http://econ.duke.edu/webfiles/arg/gsm. Del Negro and Schorfheide (2004) describe another Bayesian approach that makes use of an auxiliary model. In their approach, the structural model is used to build a hierarchical likelihood that contains both parameters from the structural and auxiliary models both of which are estimated simultaneously.

The indirect inference formulation of the estimation problem can be useful device for modifying the estimator to achieve semiparametric or robustness properties. Space does not permit an exploration of those ideas here. For a discussion of seminonparametric properties achieved through indirect inference, see Dridi and Renault (1998) and the references therein. For a discussion of robustness properties achieved through indirect inference, see Genton and de Luna (2002).

2.2. Details

We now discuss the ideas above in more detail. We consider nonlinear systems that have the features of the models described in Section 1. Specifically, (i) for a parameter vector ρ in a parameter space R, the random variables determined by the system have a stationary density

$$p(y_{-L}, \ldots, y_{-1}, y_0 | \rho), \tag{2.2}$$

for every stretch $(y_{t-L}, \ldots y_t)$; and (ii) for $\rho \in R$, the system is easily simulated so that expectations

$$\mathcal{E}_\rho(g) = \int \cdots \int g(y_{-L}, \ldots, y_0) p(y_{-L}, \ldots, y_0 | \rho) dy_{-L} \cdots dy_0 \tag{2.3}$$

can be approximated as accurately as desired by averaging over a long simulation

$$\mathcal{E}_\rho(g) \doteq \frac{1}{N}\sum_{t=1}^{N} g(\hat{y}_{t-L}, \ldots, \hat{y}_{t-1}, \hat{y}_t). \tag{2.4}$$

As conventions, we use $\{y_t\}$ to denote the stochastic process determined by the system, $\{\hat{y}_t\}_{t=1}^{N}$ to denote a simulation from the system, $\{\tilde{y}_t\}_{t=1}^{n}$ to denote data presumed to have been generated by the system, and $(y_{-L}, \ldots, y_{-1}, y_0)$ to denote function arguments and dummy variables of integration. The true value of the parameter vector of the system (2.2) is denoted by ρ^o.

We presume that the data have been summarized in the projection step, as described in Section 3, and that a score generator of the form

$$\frac{\partial}{\partial\theta}\log f(y|x, \tilde{\theta}_n),$$

and a weighting matrix

$$\tilde{\mathcal{I}}_n = \frac{1}{n}\sum_{t=1}^{n}\left[\frac{\partial}{\partial\theta}\log f(\tilde{y}_t|\tilde{x}_{t-1}, \tilde{\theta}_n)\right]\left[\frac{\partial}{\partial\theta}\log f(\tilde{y}_t|\tilde{x}_{t-1}, \tilde{\theta}_n)\right]'$$

are available from the projection step. This formula assumes that $f(y|x, \tilde{\theta}_n)$ closely approximates $p(y|x, \rho^o)$. If the SNP density $f_K(y|x, \theta)$ is used as the auxiliary model with tuning parameters selected by Bayes information criterion (BIC) (Schwarz, 1978), $\tilde{\mathcal{I}}_n$ as above will be adequate (Coppejans and Gallant, 2000; Gallant and Long, 1997; Gallant and Tauchen, 1999). If the approximation is not adequate, then a HAC weighting matrix (Andrews, 1991) must be used. A common choice of HAC matrix is

$$\tilde{\mathcal{I}}_n = \sum_{\tau=-\lceil n^{1/5}\rceil}^{\lceil n^{1/5}\rceil} w\left(\frac{\tau}{\lceil n^{1/5}\rceil}\right)\tilde{\mathcal{I}}_{n\tau}, \tag{2.5}$$

where

$$w(u) = \begin{cases} 1 - 6|u|^2 + 6|u|^3 & \text{if} \quad 0 < u < \frac{1}{2} \\ 2(1 - |u|)^3 & \text{if} \quad \frac{1}{2} \leq u < 1, \end{cases}$$

and

$$\tilde{\mathcal{I}}_{n\tau} = \begin{cases} \frac{1}{n}\sum\limits_{t=1+\tau}^{n}\left[\frac{\partial}{\partial\theta}\log f(\tilde{y}_t|\tilde{x}_{t-1}, \tilde{\theta}_n)\right]\left[\frac{\partial}{\partial\theta}\log f(\tilde{y}_{t-\tau}|\tilde{x}_{t-1-\tau}, \tilde{\theta}_n)\right]' & \text{if} \quad \tau \geq 0 \\ \tilde{\mathcal{I}}_{n,-\tau} & \text{if} \quad \tau < 0 \end{cases}$$

(Gallant and White, 1987).

Recall that the moment equations are

$$m(\rho,\theta) = \mathcal{E}_\rho \frac{\partial}{\partial\theta} \log f(y|x,\theta),$$

which can be computed by averaging over a long simulation

$$m(\rho,\tilde{\theta}_n) \doteq \frac{1}{N}\sum_{t=1}^{N} \frac{\partial}{\partial\theta} \log f\left(\hat{y}_t|\hat{x}_{t-1},\tilde{\theta}_n\right).$$

The EMM estimator is

$$\hat{\rho}_n = \underset{\rho\in R}{\operatorname{argmin}}\, m'\left(\rho,\tilde{\theta}_n\right)\left(\tilde{\mathcal{I}}_n\right)^{-1} m\left(\rho,\tilde{\theta}_n\right).$$

The asymptotics of the estimator are as follows. If ρ^o denotes the true value of ρ and θ^o is an isolated solution of the moment equations $m(\rho^o,\theta) = 0$, then under regularity conditions that include holding the parameterization of the structural and auxiliary model fixed (Gallant and Tauchen, 1996)

$$\begin{gathered}
\lim_{n\to\infty} \hat{\rho}_n = \rho^o \quad \text{a.s.} \\
\sqrt{n}\left(\hat{\rho}_n - \rho^o\right) \xrightarrow{\mathcal{L}} N\left\{0, \left[\left(M^o\right)'\left(\mathcal{I}^o\right)^{-1}\left(M^o\right)\right]^{-1}\right\} \\
\lim_{n\to\infty} \hat{M}_n = M^o \quad \text{a.s.} \\
\lim_{n\to\infty} \tilde{\mathcal{I}}_n = \mathcal{I}^o \quad \text{a.s.,}
\end{gathered} \tag{2.6}$$

where $\hat{M}_n = M(\hat{\rho}_n,\tilde{\theta}_n)$, $M^o = M(\rho^o,\theta^o)$, $M(\rho,\theta) = (\partial/\partial\rho')m(\rho,\theta)$, and

$$\mathcal{I}^o = \mathcal{E}_{\rho^o}\left[\frac{\partial}{\partial\theta}\log f\left(y_0|x_{-1},\theta^o\right)\right]\left[\frac{\partial}{\partial\theta}\log f\left(y_0|x_{-1},\theta^o\right)\right]',$$

if $f(y|x,\theta)$ encompass the data-generating process, or

$$\mathcal{I}^o = \sum_{\tau=-\infty}^{\infty} \mathcal{E}_{\rho^o}\left[\frac{\partial}{\partial\theta}\log f\left(y_0|x_{-1},\theta^o\right)\right]\left[\frac{\partial}{\partial\theta}\log f\left(y_{-\tau}|x_{-1-\tau},\theta^o\right)\right]',$$

if not. Under the null hypothesis that $p(y_{-L},\ldots,y_0|\rho)$ is the correct model,

$$L_0 = nm'\left(\hat{\rho}_n,\tilde{\theta}_n\right)\left(\tilde{\mathcal{I}}_n\right)^{-1} m\left(\hat{\rho}_n,\tilde{\theta}_n\right) \tag{2.7}$$

is asymptotically chi-squared on $p_\theta - p_\rho$ degrees of freedom. Under the null hypothesis that $h(\rho^o) = 0$, where h maps R into $\Re^q$,

$$L_h = n\left[m'(\hat{\hat{\rho}}_n, \tilde{\theta}_n)(\tilde{\mathcal{I}}_n)^{-1}m(\hat{\hat{\rho}}_n, \tilde{\theta}_n) - m'(\hat{\rho}_n, \tilde{\theta}_n)(\tilde{\mathcal{I}}_n)^{-1}m(\hat{\rho}_n, \tilde{\theta}_n)\right] \tag{2.8}$$

is asymptotically chi-squared on q degrees of freedom, where

$$\hat{\hat{\rho}}_n = \underset{h(\rho)=0}{\text{argmin}}\, m'(\rho, \tilde{\theta}_n)\,(\tilde{\mathcal{I}}_n)^{-1}m(\rho, \tilde{\theta}_n).$$

A Wald confidence interval on an element ρ_i of ρ can by constructed in the usual way from an asymptotic standard error $\sqrt{\hat{\sigma}_{ii}}$. A standard error may be obtained by computing the Jacobian $M_n(\rho, \theta)$ numerically and taking the estimated asymptotic variance $\hat{\sigma}_{ii}$ to be the ith diagonal element of $\hat{\Sigma} = (1/n)\left[(\hat{M}_n)'(\tilde{\mathcal{I}}_n)^{-1}(\hat{M}_n)\right]^{-1}$. These intervals, which are symmetric, are somewhat misleading because they do not reflect the rapid increase in the EMM objective function $s_n(\rho) = m'(\rho, \tilde{\theta}_n)(\tilde{\mathcal{I}}_n)^{-1}m(\rho, \tilde{\theta}_n)$ when ρ_i approaches a value for which the system under consideration is explosive. Confidence intervals obtained by inverting the criterion difference test L_h do reflect this phenomenon and are therefore more useful. To invert the test, one puts in the interval those ρ_i^* for which L_h for the hypothesis $\rho_i^o = \rho_i^*$ is less than the critical point of a chi-squared on one degree of freedom. To avoid reoptimization, one may use the approximation

$$\hat{\hat{\rho}}_n = \hat{\rho}_n + \frac{\rho_i^* - \hat{\rho}_{in}}{\hat{\sigma}_{ii}}\hat{\Sigma}_{(i)}$$

in the formula for L_h, where $\hat{\Sigma}_{(i)}$ is the ith column of $\hat{\Sigma}$.

The above remarks should only be taken to imply that confidence intervals obtained by inverting the criterion difference test have more desirable structural characteristics than those obtained by inverting the Wald test and not that they have more accurate coverage probabilities.

When L_0 exceeds the chi-squared critical point, diagnostics that suggest improvements to the system are desirable. Because

$$\sqrt{n}\, m(\hat{\rho}_n, \tilde{\theta}_n) \xrightarrow{\mathcal{L}} N\left\{0, \mathcal{I}^o - (M^o)[(M^o)'(\mathcal{I}^o)^{-1}(M^o)]^{-1}(M^o)'\right\},$$

inspection of the t-ratios

$$T_n = S_n^{-1}\sqrt{n}\, m(\hat{\rho}_n, \tilde{\theta}_n), \tag{2.9}$$

where $S_n = \left(\text{diag}\{\tilde{\mathcal{I}}_n - (\hat{M}_n)[(\hat{M}_n)'(\tilde{\mathcal{I}}_n)^{-1}(\hat{M}_n)]^{-1}(\hat{M}_n)'\}\right)^{1/2}$ can suggest reasons for failure. Different elements of the score correspond to different characteristics of the data and large t-ratios reveal those characteristics that are not well approximated.

In practice, one would usually prefer to inspect $\sqrt{n}\, m(\hat{\rho}_n, \tilde{\theta}_n)$, which are underestimates of the t-ratios, to avoid having to determine the matrix $\hat{M}_n$ numerically and to avoid any potential inaccuracies that numerical differentiation can introduce. Because the statistic L_0 provides an overall test of significance, it is not necessary to have exactly correct values of the t-ratios. That is, one is only relying on the t-ratios for suggestions as to where a structural model fails to fit and one is not relying on them for statistical inference.

3. PROJECTION: GENERAL GUIDELINES ON THE SCORE GENERATOR

A sensible question is how to determine the reduced-form density $f(y_t|x_{t-1}, \theta)$ that defines the score generator for EMM. Interestingly, there are two natural principles that lead to different strategies. The first principle is data-based: choose $f(y_t|x_{t-1}, \theta)$ to be good approximation to the dynamics of the data, i.e., to $\text{pdf}(y_t|x_{t-1})$, whatever that might be. In other words, $f(y_t|x_{t-1}, \theta)$ should emerge from a carefully conducted effort to model the data $\{\tilde{y}_t\}_{t=1}^n$ without much regard to the structural model. A flexible parameterization should be used if the dynamics of the data are not well understood *a priori*. The second principle is model-based: choose $f(y_t|x_{t-1}, \theta)$ to be a close approximation to the $p(y_t|x_{t-1}, \rho)$ implied by the structural model so that the moment function $(\partial/\partial\theta)\log[f(y_t|x_{t-1}, \theta)]$ for EMM should look very much like moment function $(\partial/\partial\rho)\log[p(y_t|x_{t-1}, \rho)]$ of maximum likelihood estimation. Implementing this strategy entails using detailed knowledge of the characteristics of the structural model to build up the score generator.

We initially set forth the arguments for the data-based strategy in Bansal et al. (1993, 1995) and we have consistently argued for it over the model-based strategy ever since. The issue is controversial. Dridi and Renault (1998) argue for a more model-based strategy and Hansen (2002) outlines some of the issues. The gist of our argument is that the data-based strategy will be nearly fully efficient if the structural model is correctly specified, and it will reveal the inadequacy of the structural model if it is misspecified. On the other hand, the model-based strategy is fine if the structural model is correct, but it could be potentially very misleading if the structural model is wrong. See Gallant and McCulloch (2009) for an illustration. Rarely do we know for sure that our models are indeed correct.

We now look at some of these considerations in more detail.

3.1. An Initial Look at Efficiency

Let $\mathcal{V}_f$ denote the asymptotic covariance matrix of EMM if the score generator is $f(y_t|x_{t-1}, \theta)$. In Section 2, we saw that $\sqrt{n}(\hat{\rho} - \rho) \xrightarrow{\mathcal{L}} N(0, \mathcal{V}_f)$, where from (2.2), $\mathcal{V}_f$ is given by

$$\mathcal{V}_f = [(M^o)'(\mathcal{I}^o)^{-1}(M^o)]^{-1}.$$

Let $\mathcal{V}_{\mathrm{ML}}$ denote the asymptotic distribution of the maximum likelihood estimator, which is given by

$$\mathcal{V}_{\mathrm{ML}} = \left[\mathcal{E}\left(s_t s_t'\right)\right]^{-1} = \mathcal{I}^{-1},$$

where

$$s_t = \frac{\partial}{\partial \rho} \log\left[p\left(y_t | x_{t-1}, \rho^o\right)\right]$$

is the score function of the underlying probability model, presumed correct here. From basic maximum likelihood theory, we have that

$$\mathcal{V}_{\mathrm{ML}} \leq \mathcal{V}_f.$$

Tauchen (1997) considers the i.i.d. case, $p(y_t|\rho)$, and shows that $\mathcal{V}_f$ and $\mathcal{V}_{\mathrm{ML}}$ are connected as follows. Let

$$\Omega = \mathrm{var}\left(s_t - B s_{ft}\right),$$

where $s_{ft} = (\partial/\partial\theta) \log[f(y_t|\theta^o)]$ is the score of the reduced-form model and B is the coefficient matrix from a linear projection of $s_t = (\partial/\partial\rho)\log[f(y_t|\rho^o)]$ onto s_{ft}. Then,

$$\mathcal{V}_{\mathrm{ML}} = \left(\mathcal{V}_f^{-1} + \Omega\right)^{-1} \leq \mathcal{V}_f \tag{3.1}$$

with equality if $\Omega = 0$. Hence, the better the score of f comes to spanning the score of p, then the smaller is Ω and the closer is EMM to full efficiency. Tauchen (1997) also provides some intuition as to how this result would carry over to the dynamic case. Gallant and Long (1997) handle the dynamic case and prove that

$$\lim_{K\to\infty} \mathcal{V}_{f_K} = \mathcal{V}_{\mathrm{ML}},$$

where f_K represents the Kth term in the SNP series expansion as described in Section 4 below.

The upshot is that the better the score generator approximates structural model, then the closer is $\mathcal{V}_f$ to $\mathcal{V}_{\mathrm{ML}}$. Since the structural model is presumed to be correct, the data-based approach has to produce a score function, that is, a close approximation to the true score function. If one knows of a good model for the data, then that model should be used as the auxiliary model. If not, as is often the case, then Gallant and Long's (1997) results provide a systematic strategy based on SNP modeling for getting a close approximation.

3.2. Misspecification

Suppose the structural model is itself is misspecified. Will this be detected by the EMM objective function? The issue was first formally considered in Tauchen (1997) and examined in much more detail by Aguirre-Torres (2001) and Aguirre-Torres and

Gallant (2001). The answer is essentially yes if one uses the data-based strategy to determine the score generator but no if one follows the model-based strategy for determining the score generator for EMM.

Define the densities

	conditional	joint
true model:	$\xi(y\|x)$	$\xi(x, y)$
structural model:	$p(y\|x, \rho)$	$p(x, y, \rho)$
auxiliary model:	$f(y\|x, \theta)$	$f(x, y\|\theta)$

where for simplicity, we drop the time subscripts. The pseudo-true values of θ and ρ are

$$\theta^o = \underset{\theta}{\operatorname{argmax}} \iint \log[f(y|x,\theta)]\xi(x,y)\mathrm{d}y\mathrm{d}x$$

$$\rho^o = \underset{\rho}{\operatorname{argmax}}\ m'(\rho, \theta^o)\left(\mathcal{I}^o\right)^{-1} m\left(\rho, \theta^o\right),$$

where

$$m(\rho, \theta) = \iint \frac{\partial}{\partial \theta} \log[f(y|x,\theta)]\, p(x, y, \rho)\mathrm{d}y\mathrm{d}x.$$

Note that $\mathcal{I}^o$ is the limiting pseudo-information matrix computed under $\xi(x, y)$. Following, Geweke (1983) define the approximate slope functional

$$S(f, p, \xi) = m'(\rho^o, \theta^o)\left(\mathcal{I}^o\right)^{-1} m\left(\rho^o, \theta^o\right).$$

The value of $S(f, p, \xi)$ is the limiting normalized value of the noncentrality parameter of the test of the overidentifying restrictions.

For fixed f and p, it is reasonably easy to come with plausible alternative models ξ such that

$$S(f, p, \xi) = 0.$$

In other words, given f, there is no power to detect $p \neq \xi$. It is easy to construct such examples. The danger is fitting a misspecified p-model to the scores of a misspecified f-model, and thinking everything is fine, when, in fact, $p \neq \xi$.

The problem is with leaving f fixed. If one chooses f nonparametrically, say by SNP, then the preliminary analysis of Tauchen (1997) and detailed calculations of Aguirre-Torres (2001) indicate that whenever $p \neq \xi$, then

$$\liminf_{K\to\infty} S(f_K, p, \xi) > 0,$$

so the misspecification is detected with probability one asymptotically. As the editor has pointed out, these computations are not uniform in (n, K) but rather allow n to tend to infinity first and K to tend to infinity second.

The message, again, is to think nonparametrically when choosing the auxiliary model.

3.3. Nonnested Models

Another argument in favor of the data-based strategy has emerged after some years of experience with EMM. Frequently, one considers families of nonnested structural models and one faces a model selection problem. EMM using a data-based score generator forces all structural models to confront the same set of moment conditions, and therefore, meaningful comparisons of objective values across models are available. For example, Dai and Singleton (2000) use the EMM objective function to guide model selection within and across the nonnested branches of the affine family of term structure models, as do Bansal and Zhou (2002) for regime-switching affine term structure models.

3.4. Dynamic Stability

The EMM objective function is

$$Q(\rho) = m'(\rho, \tilde{\theta})\tilde{\mathcal{I}}^{-1}m(\rho, \tilde{\theta})$$

and

$$\hat{\rho} = \underset{\rho \in \mathcal{R}}{\text{argmin}}\ Q(\rho).$$

Simulated trajectories $\{\hat{y}_t\}_{t=1}^{N}$ are used to compute the expectation that defines $m(\rho, \theta)$. Since the underlying structural model typically has a nonlinear dynamic autoregressive structure, it is natural to consider potential problems if ρ lies in the explosive region of the parameter space and $|\hat{y}_t| \to \infty$.

Tauchen (1998) examines the issue of dynamic stability of the structural model (p) and the score generator (f). The upshot is that one really need not worry about imposing dynamic stability on the structural model itself. Dynamic stability is self-enforcing. If the optimizer wanders into the region of the parameter space where the underlying structural model is unstable, then the data simulator generates a wildly explosive simulated realization that induces a large value of the objective function. The time-series properties of this explosive realization are very much unlike the time-series properties of the observed data set to which the auxiliary model has been fitted, so the objective function attains an exceedingly high value. The situation is actually a bit more subtle because automatic stability is ensured only if the auxiliary model itself is dynamically stable. The use of a dynamically unstable auxiliary model can be expected to define a GMM objective function with very poor numerical properties in both the stable and unstable regions of the parameter space.

Dynamic stability is of practical importance. Andersen and Lund (1997) carefully examine a class of GARCH and E-GARCH auxiliary models for the short-term interest rate. They find the former typically unstable, and therefore unusable as auxiliary models, while the latter are stable. Gallant and Tauchen (1998) likewise use model stability as part of the selection criterion. We now incorporate into the SNP code (Gallant and Tauchen, 2001c) nonlinear transformations of the state vector x_{t-1} that attenuate large movements and help enforce stability, but we still recommend checking long simulations to ensure that the score generator is a stable model.

As the editor has pointed out, it is possible for explosive, nonlinear dynamic processes to linger for extended periods in a strongly dependent state before they become explosive. This sort of behavior on the part of a structural model might not be detected.

4. A GENERAL PURPOSE SCORE GENERATOR

4.1. Efficiency Comparisons

In Section 2, we defined the EMM estimator as

$$\hat{\rho}_n = \underset{\rho \in R}{\operatorname{argmin}}\, m'(\rho)\left(\tilde{\mathcal{I}}_n\right)^{-1} m(\rho).$$

It is essentially a simulated method of moments estimator based on the moment function

$$m(\rho) = \mathcal{E}_\rho \tilde{\psi},$$

where

$$\tilde{\psi} = \frac{\partial}{\partial \theta} \log f\left(y|x, \tilde{\theta}\right),$$

and for now, we shall suppress the second argument of $m(\rho, \theta)$.

In Section 3.1, we noted that the closer f comes to approximating the condition density implied by the structural model, then the closer will be the asymptotic variance of the EMM estimator to that of maximum likelihood. In fact, a spanning argument can be used to show that the efficiency of EMM can be made asymptotically negligible.

But the same spanning argument applies to estimation using more traditional moments such as means, variances, etc., which we shall call the classical method of moments. Thus, an open question is whether the moment function of EMM, which entails the extra effort of estimating the score generator, defines a better set of moments, other things equal.

The question is considered and answered affirmatively by Gallant and Tauchen (1999), which we now summarize. They examine the simpler case where the random variables defined by the system (2.2) generate univariate i.i.d. random variables $\{y_t\}$ with density $p(y|\rho)$. The ideas for the general case of a multivariate, non-Markovian, stationary system are the same, but the algebra is far more complicated (Gallant and Long, 1997). Nothing essential is lost by considering the simplest case.

Consider three moment functions $\tilde{\psi}_{c,n}$, $\tilde{\psi}_{p,n}$, and $\tilde{\psi}_{f,n}$ that correspond to classical method of moments, maximum likelihood, and EMM, respectively, defined as follows:

$$\tilde{\psi}_{c,n}(y) = \begin{pmatrix} y - \frac{1}{n}\sum_{i=1}^{n} \tilde{y}_i \\ y^2 - \frac{1}{n}\sum_{i=1}^{n} (\tilde{y}_i)^2 \\ \vdots \\ y^K - \frac{1}{n}\sum_{i=1}^{n} (\tilde{y}_i)^K \end{pmatrix},$$

$$\tilde{\psi}_{p,n}(y) = \frac{\partial}{\partial \rho} \log p(y|\tilde{\rho}_n),$$

$$\tilde{\psi}_{f,n}(y) = \frac{\partial}{\partial \theta} \log f(y|\tilde{\theta}_n),$$

where the exponent K that appears in $\tilde{\psi}_{c,n}(y)$ is the degree of the largest moment used in a method of moments application, the function $f(y|\theta)$ that appears in $\tilde{\psi}_{f,n}(y)$ is a density that closely approximates the true data-generating process in a sense made precise later, and the statistics $\tilde{\rho}_n$ and $\tilde{\theta}_n$ that appear in $\tilde{\psi}_{p,n}(y)$ and $\tilde{\psi}_{f,n}(y)$ are

$$\tilde{\rho}_n = \underset{\rho}{\operatorname{argmax}} \frac{1}{n}\sum_{i=1}^{n} \log p(\tilde{y}_i|\rho),$$

$$\tilde{\theta}_n = \underset{\theta}{\operatorname{argmax}} \frac{1}{n}\sum_{i=1}^{n} \log f(\tilde{y}_i|\theta);$$

ρ is of length p_ρ and θ of length $p_\theta \geq p_\rho$.

Note that each of the moment functions $\tilde{\psi}_{p,n}$, $\tilde{\psi}_{c,n}$, and $\tilde{\psi}_{f,n}$ is in the null space of the expectation operator corresponding to the empirical distribution of the data, denoted as $\mathcal{E}_{\tilde{F}_n}$. That is, $\mathcal{E}_{\tilde{F}_n}\tilde{\psi}_{p,n} = \mathcal{E}_{\tilde{F}_n}\tilde{\psi}_{c,n} = \mathcal{E}_{\tilde{F}_n}\tilde{\psi}_{f,n} = 0$. Method of moments is basically an attempt to do the same for the model $p(y|\rho)$. That is, method of moments attempts to find a ρ that puts one of these moment functions, denoted generically as $\tilde{\psi}_n$, in the null space of the expectation operator $\mathcal{E}_\rho$ corresponding to $p(y|\rho)$.

In addition to computing $\tilde{\psi}_n$, one computes

$$\tilde{\mathcal{I}}_n = \mathcal{E}_{\tilde{F}_n}(\tilde{\psi}_n)(\tilde{\psi}_n)'.$$

Once $\tilde{\psi}_n$ and $\tilde{\mathcal{I}}_n$ have been computed, the data have been summarized, and what we refer to as "the projection step" is finished.

For estimation, define

$$m_n(\rho) = \mathcal{E}_\rho \tilde{\psi}_n.$$

If the dimensions of ρ and $\tilde{\psi}_n(y)$ are the same, then usually the equations $m_n(\rho) = 0$ can be solved to obtain an estimator $\hat{\rho}_n$. For $\tilde{\psi}_{p,n}$, the solution is the maximum likelihood estimator (Fisher, 1912; Gauss, 1816). For $\tilde{\psi}_{c,n}$ with $K = p_\rho$, it is the classical method of moments estimator (Pearson, 1894). For $\tilde{\psi}_{c,n}$ with $K > p_\rho$, no solution exists and the moment functions $\tilde{\psi}_{c,n}$ are those of minimum chi-squared or GMM (Hansen, 1982; Neyman and Pearson, 1928) as customarily implemented.

As just noted, when $K > p_\rho$, then $\tilde{\psi}_n$ cannot be placed in the null space of the operator $\mathcal{E}_\rho$ for any ρ because the equations $m_n(\rho) = 0$ have no solution. In this case, the minimum chi-squared estimator relies on the fact that, under standard regularity conditions (Gallant and Tauchen, 1996) and choices of $\tilde{\psi}_n$ similar to the above, there is a function ψ^o such that

$$\lim_{n\to\infty} \tilde{\psi}_n(y) = \psi^o(y) \quad \text{a.s.}$$

$$\lim_{n\to\infty} \tilde{\mathcal{I}}_n = \mathcal{E}_{\rho^o}(\psi^o)(\psi^o)' \quad \text{a.s.}$$

$$\sqrt{n}\, m_n(\rho^o) \xrightarrow{\mathcal{L}} N\left[0, \mathcal{E}_{\rho^o}(\psi^o)(\psi^o)'\right],$$

where $\mathcal{E}_{\rho^o}$ denotes expectation taken with respect to $p(y|\rho^o)$. For the three choices $\tilde{\psi}_{p,n}$, $\tilde{\psi}_{c,n}$, and $\tilde{\psi}_{f,n}$ of $\psi_n(y)$ above, the functions ψ_p^o, ψ_c^o, and ψ_f^o given by this result are

$$\psi_c^o(y) = \begin{pmatrix} y - \mathcal{E}_{\rho^o}(y) \\ y^2 - \mathcal{E}_{\rho^o}(y^2) \\ \vdots \\ y^K - \mathcal{E}_{\rho^o}(y^K) \end{pmatrix},$$

$$\psi_p^o(y) = \frac{\partial}{\partial \rho} \log p(y|\rho^o),$$

and

$$\psi_f^o(y) = \frac{\partial}{\partial \theta} \log f(y|\theta^o),$$

where

$$\theta^o = \underset{\theta}{\operatorname{argmax}}\, \mathcal{E}_{\rho^o} \log f(\cdot|\theta).$$

With these results in hand, ρ may be estimated by minimum chi-squared, viz.,

$$\hat{\rho}_n = \underset{\rho}{\operatorname{argmin}}\, m_n'(\rho)\,(\tilde{\mathcal{I}}_n)^{-1} m_n(\rho)$$

and

$$\sqrt{n}\,(\hat{\rho}_n - \rho^o) \xrightarrow{\mathcal{L}} N\left[0,\ (C^o)^{-1}\right],$$

where

$$C^o = \left[\mathcal{E}_{\rho^o}(\psi_p^o)(\psi^o)'\right]\left[\mathcal{E}_{\rho^o}(\psi^o)(\psi^o)'\right]^{-1}\left[\mathcal{E}_{\rho^o}(\psi^o)(\psi_p^o)'\right].$$

Note that for any nonzero $a \in \mathcal{R}^{p_\rho}$,

$$\min_b \mathcal{E}_{\rho^o}\left[a'\psi_p^o - (\psi^o)'b\right]^2 = \mathcal{E}_{\rho^o}\left(a'\psi_p^o\right)^2 - a'C^o a \geq 0. \tag{4.1}$$

Expression (4.1) implies that $a'C^o a$ cannot exceed $\mathcal{E}_{\rho^o}(a'\psi_p^o)^2 = a'\left[\mathcal{E}_{\rho^o}(\psi_p^o)(\psi_p^o)'\right]a$, and therefore, the best achievable asymptotic variance of the estimator $\hat{\rho}_n$ is $\left(\mathcal{I}_p^o\right)^{-1} = \left[\mathcal{E}_{\rho^o}(\psi_p^o)(\psi_p^o)'\right]^{-1}$, which is the variance of the maximum likelihood estimator of ρ. It is also apparent from (4.1) that if $\{\psi_i^o\}_{i=1}^{\infty}$ spans the $L_{2,p}$ probability space $L_{2,p} = \{g : \mathcal{E}_{\rho^o} g^2 < \infty\}$ and $\psi^o = (\psi_1^o, \ldots, \psi_K^o)$, then $\hat{\rho}_n$ has good efficiency relative to the maximum likelihood estimator for large K. The polynomials span $L_{2,p}$ if $p(y|\rho)$ has a moment-generating function (Gallant, 1980). Therefore, one might expect good asymptotic efficiency from $\tilde{\psi}_{c,n}$ for large K.

Rather than just spanning $L_{2,p}$, EMM requires, in addition, that the moment functions actually be the score vector $\psi_{f,n}(y)$ of some density $f(y|\tilde{\theta}_n)$ that closely approximates $p(y|\rho^o)$. Possible choices of $f(y|\tilde{\theta}_n)$ are discussed in Gallant and Tauchen (1996). Of them, one commonly used in applications is the SNP density, which was proposed by Gallant and Nychka (1987) in a form suited to cross-sectional applications and by Gallant and Tauchen (1989) in a form suited to time-series applications.

The SNP density is obtained by expanding the square root of an innovation density $h(z)$ in a Hermite expansion

$$\sqrt{h(z)} = \sum_{i=0}^{\infty} \theta_i z^i \sqrt{\phi(z)},$$

where $\phi(z)$ denotes the standard normal density function. Because the Hermite functions are dense in L_2 (Lebesque) and $\sqrt{h(z)}$ is an L_2 function, this expansion must exist. The truncated density is

$$h_K(z) = \frac{\mathcal{P}_K^2(z)\phi(z)}{\int \mathcal{P}_K^2(u)\phi(u)\mathrm{d}u},$$

where

$$\mathcal{P}_K(z) = \sum_{i=0}^{K} \theta_i z^i$$

and the renormalization is necessary so that the density $h_K(z)$ integrates to one. The location-scale transformation $y = \sigma z + \mu$ completes the definition of the SNP density

$$f_K(y|\theta) = \frac{1}{\sigma} h_K\left(\frac{y-\mu}{\sigma}\right), \tag{4.2}$$

with $\theta = (\mu, \sigma, \theta_0, \ldots, \theta_K)$. Gallant and Long (1997) have shown that

$$\psi_f^o(y) = \frac{\partial}{\partial\theta} \log f_K(y|\theta^o),$$

with

$$\theta^o = \underset{\theta}{\operatorname{argmax}}\, \mathcal{E}_{p^o} \log f_K(\cdot|\theta)$$

spans $L_{2,p}$.

Although a spanning argument can be used to show that high efficiency obtains for large K, it gives no indication as to what might be the best choice of moment functions with which to span $L_{2,p}$. Moreover, if ψ_p is in the span of ψ^o for some finite K, then full efficiency obtains at once (Gallant and Tauchen, 1996). For instance, the score of the normal density is in the span of both $\tilde{\psi}_{c,n}$ and $\tilde{\psi}_{f,n}$ for $K \geq 2$. These considerations seem to rule out any hope of general results showing that one moment function should be better than another.

With general results unattainable, the best one can do is compare efficiencies over a class of densities designed to stress-test an estimator and over some densities thought to be representative of situations likely to be encountered in practice to see if any conclusions seem to be indicated. Comparisons using Monte Carlo methods are reported by Andersen et al. (1999), Chumacero (1997), Ng and Michaelides (2000), Van der Sluis (1999), and Zhou (2001). Overall, their work supports the conjecture that EMM is more efficient than CMM in representative applications at typical sample sizes.

Analytical comparisons are possible for the i.i.d. case and are reported in Gallant and Tauchen (1999). Their measure of efficiency is the volume of a confidence region on the parameters of the density $p(y|\rho)$ computed using the asymptotic distribution of $\hat{\rho}_n$. This region has the form $\{\rho : (\rho - \rho^o)'(C^o)^{-1}(\rho - \rho^o) \leq \mathcal{X}_d^2/n\}$ with volume

$$\frac{2\pi^{d/2}(\mathcal{X}_d^2/n)^d}{d\Gamma(d/2)\det(C^o)},$$

where $\mathcal{X}_d^2$ denotes a critical value of the chi-squared distribution on d degrees of freedom. As small volumes are to be preferred, and the region $\{\rho : (\rho - \rho^o)'\mathcal{I}_p^o(\rho - \rho^o) \leq \mathcal{X}_d^2/n\}$ has the smallest achievable volume,

$$\mathrm{RE} = \frac{\det(C^o)}{\det(\mathcal{I}_p^o)}$$

is a measure of relative efficiency. Over a large collection of densities thought to represent typical applications, their computations support the conclusion that EMM dominates CMM. Moreover, their computations indicate that once $f_K(\cdot|\theta^o)$ begins to approximate $p(\cdot|\rho^o)$ accurately, the efficiency of the EMM estimator begins to increase rapidly. A representative illustration is provided by Fig. 8.1, which shows the relative efficiency comparison for a trimodal density $p(y|\rho)$ taken from the Marron–Wand test suite (Marron and Wand, 1992). As seen in Fig. 8.1, once $f_K(\cdot|\theta^o)$ has detected the third mode of the trimodal density, EMM efficiency increases rapidly.

The second question to address is how many moments to include in the moment function ψ_f. As the computations in Gallant and Tauchen (1999) and Fig. 8.1 suggest, the answer is as many as is required for f to well approximate p. The natural conclusion is that one should use standard statistical model selection criteria to determine f as we discuss later. This approach has a distinct advantage over the use of ψ_c, in that there seems to be no objective statistical criterion for determining the number of moments to include in ψ_c.

As the editor has pointed out, the Gallant and Long (1997) results that justify extending these ideas to non-Markovian situations rely on several high-level assumptions and it is not clear what low-level primitives will justify them, especially in continuous-time applications. The most serious of these high-level assumptions is their assumption 4, which requires that the asymptotic variance of the maximum likelihood estimator can be accurately approximated by the variance of the maximum likelihood estimator with lags past some large value neglected. It is an important open problem to determine which classes of models will satisfy this assumption.

4.2. SNP: A General Purpose Score Generator

As indicated in Section 4.1, the best choice of a moment function ψ to implement simulated method of moments is the score of a auxiliary model that closely approximates the density of the data. We have also seen that the SNP density is a useful, general purpose

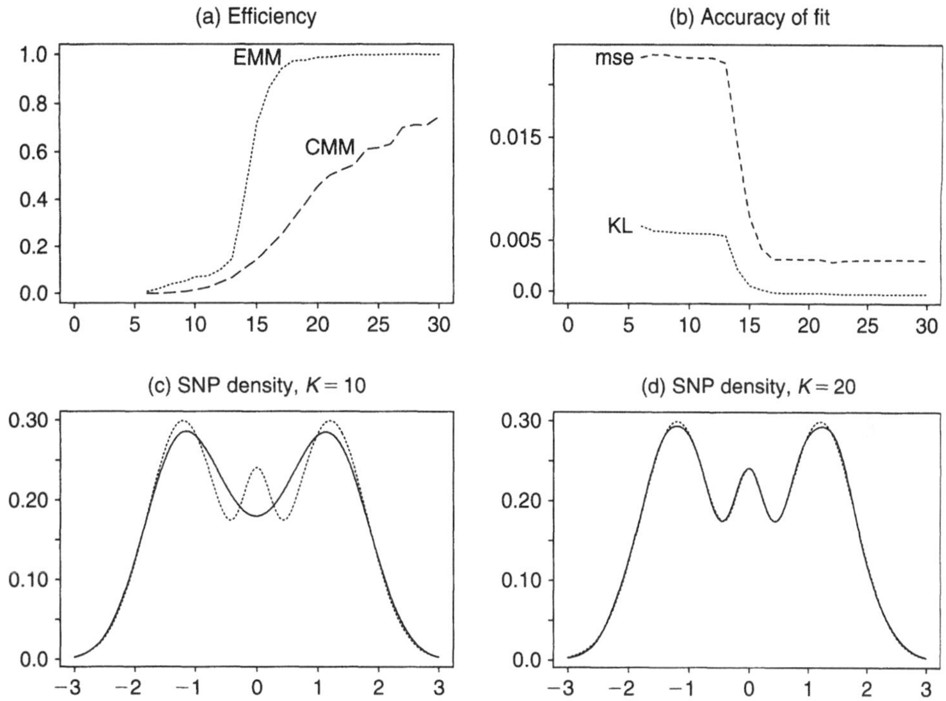

Figure 8.1 Relative Efficiency for the Trimodal Density. Panel (a) plots the relative efficiency of the EMM and CMM estimators against degree K, for the trimodal density of the Marron–Wand test suite. As seen, the effciency of the EMM estimator increases rapidly when the degree K of the SNP auxiliary model is between 10 and 20. Panel (b) plots the root mean squared error and Kullback–Leibler divergence of the SNP approximation to the trimodal density against K, labeled mse and KL, respectively. As seen, the region $10 \leq K \leq 20$ is the region where the error in the SNP approximation to the trimodal density decreases rapidly. Panel (c) plots the SNP approximation at $K = 10$, shown as a solid line, to the trimodal density, shown as a dotted line. As seen, at $K = 10$, the SNP density approximates a trimodal density by a bimodal density. Panel (d) is the same at $K = 20$. As seen, at $K = 20$, the SNP density has correctly determined the number of modes.

auxiliary model. In this section, we shall extend the SNP density to a general purpose auxiliary model suited to dynamic models. Here, y_t is multivariate, specifically a column vector of length M, and we write x_{t-1} for the lagged state vector, which typically is comprised of lags y_{t-j}. For simplicity, we often suppress the time subscript and write y and x for the contemporaneous value and lagged state vector, respectively. With these conventions, the stationary density (2.2) of the dynamic system under consideration can be written $p(x, y|\rho)$ and its transition density as

$$p(y|x, \rho) = \frac{p(x, y|\rho)}{\int p(x, y|\rho)\, \mathrm{d}x}. \tag{4.3}$$

If one expands $\sqrt{p(x, y|\rho^o)}$ in a Hermite series and derives the transition density of the truncated expansion, then one obtains a transition density $f_K(y_t|x_{t-1})$ that has the form of a location-scale transform

$$y_t = Rz_t + \mu_{x_{t-1}}$$

of an innovation z_t (Gallant et al., 1991). The density function of this innovation is

$$h_K(z|x) = \frac{[\mathcal{P}(z, x)]^2 \phi(z)}{\int [\mathcal{P}(u, x)]^2 \phi(u) du}, \tag{4.4}$$

where $\mathcal{P}(z, x)$ is a polynomial in (z, x) of degree K and $\phi(z)$ denotes the multivariate normal density function with dimension M, mean vector zero, and variance–covariance matrix equal to the identity.

It proves convenient to express the polynomial $\mathcal{P}(z, x)$ in a rectangular expansion

$$\mathcal{P}(z, x) = \sum_{\alpha=0}^{K_z} \left(\sum_{\beta=0}^{K_x} a_{\beta\alpha} x^\beta \right) z^\alpha, \tag{4.5}$$

where α and β are multiindexes of maximal degrees K_z and K_x, respectively, and $K = K_z + K_x$. Because $[\mathcal{P}(z, x)]^2 / \int [\mathcal{P}(u, x)]^2 \phi(u) du$ is a homogeneous function of the coefficients of the polynomial $\mathcal{P}(z, x)$, $\mathcal{P}(z, x)$ can only be determined to within a scalar multiple. To achieve a unique representation, the constant term a_{00} of the polynomial $\mathcal{P}(z, x)$ is put to one. With this normalization, $h_K(z|x)$ has the interpretation of a series expansion whose leading term is the normal density $\phi(z)$ and whose higher order terms induce departures from normality.

The location function is linear,

$$\mu_x = b_0 + Bx_{t-1}, \tag{4.6}$$

where b_0 is a vector and B is a matrix.

It proves advantageous in applications to allow the scale R of the location-scale transformation $y = Rz + \mu_x$ to depend on x because it reduces the degree K_x required to achieve an adequate approximation to the transition density $p(y|x, \rho^o)$. With this, the location-scale transformation becomes

$$y = R_x z + \mu_x, \tag{4.7}$$

where R_x is an upper triangular matrix that depends on x. The two choices of R_x that have given good results in applications are an ARCH-like moving average specification and a GARCH-like ARMA specification, which we describe next.

For an ARCH specification, let $R_{x_{t-1}}$ be a linear function of the absolute values of the elements of the vectors $y_{t-L_r} - \mu_{x_{t-1-L_r}}$ through $y_{t-1} - \mu_{x_{t-2}}$, viz.,

$$\text{vech}(R_{x_{t-1}}) = \rho_0 + \sum_{i=1}^{L_r} P_{(i)} |y_{t-1-L_r+i} - \mu_{x_{t-2-L_r+i}}|,$$

where vech(R) denotes a vector of length $M(M+1)/2$ containing the elements of the upper triangle of R, ρ_0 is a vector of length $M(M+1)/2$, $P_{(1)}$ through $P_{(L_r)}$ are $M(M+1)/2$ by M matrices, and $|y - \mu|$ denotes a vector containing the absolute values of $y - \mu$. The classical ARCH (Engle, 1982) has

$$\Sigma_{x_{t-1}} = R_{x_{t-1}} R'_{x_{t-1}}$$

depending on a linear function of squared lagged residuals. The SNP version of ARCH is more akin to the suggestions of Nelson (1991) and Davidian and Carroll (1987).

Because the absolute value function is not differentiable, $|u|$ is approximated in the formula for R_x above by the twice continuously differentiable function

$$a(u) = \begin{cases} (|100u| - \pi/2 + 1)/100 & |100u| \geq \pi/2 \\ (1 - \cos(100u))/100 & |100u| < \pi/2. \end{cases}$$

The scale factor 100 above represents a compromise. Small values, such as 3, improve the stability of the computations but then $a(\cdot)$ does not approximate $|\cdot|$ well.

For a GARCH specification, let

$$\begin{aligned} \text{vech}(R_{x_{t-1}}) = \rho_0 &+ \sum_{i=1}^{L_r} P_{(i)} |y_{t-1-L_r+i} - \mu_{x_{t-2-L_r+i}}| \\ &+ \sum_{i=1}^{L_g} \text{diag}(G_{(i)}) R_{x_{t-2-L_g+i}}, \end{aligned}$$

where $G_{(1)}$ through $G_{(L_g)}$ are vectors of length $M(M+1)/2$.

The classical GARCH (Bollerslev, 1986) has $\Sigma_{x_{t-1}}$ expressed in terms of squared lagged residuals and lagged values of $\Sigma_{x_{t-1}}$. As with the SNP variant of ARCH, the SNP version of GARCH, called R-GARCH, is expressed in terms of the absolute value of lagged residuals and standard deviations.

Note that when $L_g > 0$, the SNP model is not Markovian and that one must know both x_{t-1} and $R_{x_{t-2-L_g}}$ through $R_{x_{t-2}}$ to move forward to the value for y_t. Thus, x_{t-1} and $R_{x_{t-2-L_g}}$ through $R_{x_{t-2}}$ represent the state of the system at time $t-1$ and must be retained to evaluate the SNP conditional density of y_t or to iterate the SNP model forward by simulation. If one wants to compute the derivatives of the SNP density with respect to model parameters, one must retain the derivatives of $R_{x_{t-2-L_g}}$ through $R_{x_{t-2}}$ with respect to model parameters as well.

The change of variable formula applied to the location-scale transform (4.7) and innovation density (4.4) yields the SNP density

$$f_K(y|x,\theta) = \frac{h_K\left[R_x^{-1}(y-\mu_x)|x\right]}{\det(R_x)}. \tag{4.8}$$

Hereafter, we shall distinguish among the lag lengths appearing in the various components of the expansion. The number of lags in μ_x is denoted L_u; the number of lags in R_x is $L_u + L_r$ and the number of lags in the x part of the polynomial, $\mathcal{P}(z,x)$, is L_p. We set $L = \max(L_u, L_u + L_r, L_p)$.

Large values of M can generate a large number of interactions (cross product terms) for even modest settings of degree K_z; similarly, for $M \cdot L_p$ and K_x. Accordingly, we introduce two additional tuning parameters, I_z and I_x, to represent filtering out of these high-order interactions. $I_z = 0$ means no interactions are suppressed, $I_z = 1$ means the highest order interactions are suppressed, namely those of degree K_z. In general, a positive I_z means all interactions of order larger than $K_z - I_z$ are suppressed; similarly for $K_x - I_x$.

In summary, $L_u, L_g,$ and L_r determine the location-scale transformation $y = R_x z_t + \mu_x$ and hence determine the nature of the leading term of the expansion. The number of lags in the location function μ_x is L_u and the number of lags in the scale function R_x is $L_u + L_r$. The number of lags that go into the x part of the polynomial $\mathcal{P}(z,x)$ is L_p. The parameters K_z, K_x, I_z, and I_x determine the degree of $\mathcal{P}(z,x)$, and hence the nature of the innovation process $\{z_t\}$. Putting certain of the tuning parameters to zero implies sharp restrictions on the process $\{y_t\}$, the more interesting of which are displayed in Table 8.1.

The empirical work described in this article uses the R-GARCH form of the conditional variance matrix. In 2004, the SNP Fortran code was reimplemented in C++ and a BEKK variance matrix (Engle and Kroner, 1995) modified to add leverage and level effects was substituted for the R-GARCH. It is

$$\begin{aligned}
\Sigma_{x_{t-1}} = {} & R_0 R_0' + \sum_{i=1}^{L_g} Q_i \Sigma_{x_{t-1-i}} Q_i' + \sum_{i=1}^{L_r} P_i (y_{t-i} - \mu_{x_{t-1-i}})(y_{t-i} - \mu_{x_{t-1-i}})' P_i' \\
& + \sum_{i=1}^{L_v} \max[0, V_i(y_{t-i} - \mu_{x_{t-1-i}})] \max[0, V_i(y_{t-i} - \mu_{x_{t-1-i}})]' \\
& + \sum_{i=1}^{L_w} W_i x_{(1),t-i} x_{(1),t-i}' W_i'.
\end{aligned}$$

Table 8.1 Restrictions implied by settings of the tuning parameters

Parameter setting	Characterization of $\{y_t\}$
$L_u = 0, L_g = 0, L_r = 0, L_p \geq 0, K_z = 0, K_x = 0$	i.i.d. Gaussian
$L_u > 0, L_g = 0, L_r = 0, L_p \geq 0, K_z = 0, K_x = 0$	Gaussian VAR
$L_u > 0, L_g = 0, L_r = 0, L_p \geq 0, K_z > 0, K_x = 0$	semiparametric VAR
$L_u \geq 0, L_g = 0, L_r > 0, L_p \geq 0, K_z = 0, K_x = 0$	Gaussian ARCH
$L_u \geq 0, L_g = 0, L_r > 0, L_p \geq 0, K_z > 0, K_x = 0$	semiparametric ARCH
$L_u \geq 0, L_g > 0, L_r > 0, L_p \geq 0, K_z = 0, K_x = 0$	Gaussian GARCH
$L_u \geq 0, L_g > 0, L_r > 0, L_p \geq 0, K_z > 0, K_x = 0$	semiparametric GARCH
$L_u \geq 0, L_g \geq 0, L_r \geq 0, L_p > 0, K_z > 0, K_x > 0$	nonlinear nonparametric

L_u is the lag length of the location function. L_g is the lag length of the GARCH (autoregressive) part of the scale function. L_r is the lag length of the ARCH (moving average) part of the scale function. L_p is the lag length of the polynomials in x that determine the coeffcients of the Hermite expansion of the innovation density. K_z is the degree of the Hermite expansion of the innovation density. K_x is the degree of polynomials in x that determine the coeffcients of the Hermite expansion of the innovation density.

Above, R_0 is an upper triangular matrix. The matrices P_i, Q_i, V_i, and W_i can be scalar, diagonal, or full M by M matrices. The notation $x_{(1),t-i}$ indicates that only the first column of x_{t-i} enters the computation. The $\max(0, x)$ function is applied elementwise. Because $\Sigma_{x_{t-1}}$ must be differentiable with respect to the parameters of $\mu_{x_{t-2-i}}$, the $\max(0, x)$ function actually applied is a twice continuously differentiable cubic spline approximation that agrees with the $\max(0, x)$ function except over the interval $(0, 0.1)$ over which it lies slightly above the $\max(0, x)$ function.

5. REPROJECTION: ANALYSIS OF POSTESTIMATION SIMULATIONS

5.1. Simple Illustration of Volatility Extraction

We start with an illustration that gives the main idea of reprojection. In Gallant and Tauchen (2001a), we estimated through EMM the vector SDE with two stochastic volatility factors:

$$\begin{aligned} dU_{1t} &= \alpha_{10}dt + \exp(\beta_{10} + \beta_{12}U_{2t} + \beta_{13}U_{3t})\, dW_{1t} \\ dU_{2t} &= \alpha_{22}U_{2t}dt + dW_{2t} \\ dU_{3t} &= \alpha_{33}U_{3t}dt + dW_{3t}, \end{aligned} \tag{5.1}$$

using daily data on Microsoft (MSFT), 1986–2001. Here, U_{1t} is the log-price process and

$$y_t = 100 * (U_{1t} - U_{1,t-1})$$

at integer t is the observation equation for the geometric daily return expressed as a percent. U_{2t} and U_{3t} are stochastic volatility factors. We find that the stochastic volatility model cleanly separate into two distinct factors: a very persistent factor, U_{2t}, which displays very little mean reversion, and a very strongly mean-reverting factor, U_{3t}.

Thus, from the observed data set $\{\tilde{y}_t\}_1^n$, we generated through EMM the parameter estimate $\hat{\rho}$ for each model under consideration. We now summarize how to proceed backwards to infer the unobserved state vector from the observed process as implied by a particular model. The approach follows the reprojection method proposed by Gallant and Tauchen (1998), which is a numerically intensive, simulation-based, nonlinear Kalman filtering technique.

The idea is relatively straightforward. As a by-product of the estimation, we have a long simulated realization of the state vector $\{\hat{U}_t\}_{t=1}^N$ and the corresponding $\{\hat{y}_t\}_{t=1}^N$ for $\rho = \hat{\rho}$. Working within the simulation, we can calibrate the functional form of the conditional distribution of functions of $\hat{U}_t$ given $\{\hat{y}_\tau\}_{\tau=1}^t$. Given the calibrated functions determined within the simulation, we simply evaluate them on the observed data. More generally, we can determine within the simulation the conditional distribution of functions of $\hat{U}_t$ given $\{\hat{y}_\tau\}_{\iota=1}^t$ and then evaluate the result on observed data $\{\tilde{y}_t\}_{t-1}^n$.

In the application, we work with the conditional mean functions of the volatility factors. Our targets are

$$\mathcal{E}(U_{it} | \{y_\tau\}_{\tau=1}^t), \quad i = 2, 3 \tag{5.2}$$

To begin, we generated simulations $\{\hat{U}_t\}_{t=1}^N, \{\hat{y}_t\}_{t=1}^N$, at the estimated $\tilde{\rho}$ and $N = 100,000$. Keep in mind that, to generate predictions of U_{2t} and U_{3t} through filtering y_t, we are allowed to use very general functions of $\{y_\tau\}_{\tau=1}^t$ and that we have a huge data set work with. After some experimentation, we found the following strategy, which seems to work quite well. We estimate an SNP-GARCH model on the $\hat{y}_t$ because the SNP-GARCH model provides a convenient representation of the one-step ahead conditional variance $\hat{\sigma}_t^2$ of $\hat{y}_{t+1}$ given $\{\hat{y}_\tau\}_{\tau=1}^t$. We then run regressions of $\hat{U}_{it}$ on $\hat{\sigma}_t^2$, $\hat{y}_t$, and $|\hat{y}_\tau|$ and lags of these series, with lag lengths generously long (Keep in mind the huge size of the simulated data set; these regressions are essentially analytic projections). At this point, we have calibrated, inside the simulations, functions that give predicted values of U_{2t} and U_{3t} given $\{y_\tau\}_{\tau=1}^t$. Finally, we evaluate these functions on the observed data series $\{\tilde{y}_\tau\}_{\tau=1}^t$, which gives reprojected values $\tilde{U}_{2t}$ and $\tilde{U}_{3t}$ for the volatility factors at the data points.

The figures in Gallant and Tauchen (2001a) indicate that $\tilde{U}_{2t}$ is slowly moving while $\tilde{U}_{3t}$ is quite choppy. Interestingly, the crash of 1987 is attributed to a large realization of the strongly mean-reverting factor, U_{3t}. This result suggests that the volatility increase surround the 87 crash was rather temporary, which appears consistent with raw data plots. Also, the reprojected volatility factor from a model with only one stochastic volatility factor misses much of the crash of 1987, which reflects further on the shortcomings of single-factor stochastic volatility models.

5.2. General Theory of Reprojection

Having the EMM estimate of system parameters $\hat{\rho}_n$ in hand, we should like to elicit the dynamics of the implied conditional density for observables

$$\hat{p}(y_0|x_{-1}) = p(y_0|x_{-1}, \hat{\rho}_n). \tag{5.3}$$

Recall that x_{-1} represents the lagged state vector, and so in the Markov case, (5.3) is an abbreviated notation for

$$\hat{p}(y_0|y_{-L}, \dots, y_{-1}) = p(y_0|y_{-L}, \dots, y_{-1}, \hat{\rho}_n).$$

Although analytic expressions are not available, an unconditional expectation

$$\mathcal{E}_{\hat{\rho}_n}(g) = \int \cdots \int g(y_{-L}, \dots, y_0)\, p(y_{-L}, \dots, y_0|\hat{\rho}_n)\, \mathrm{d}y_{-L} \cdots \mathrm{d}y_0$$

can be computed by generating a simulation $\{\hat{y}_t\}_{t=-L}^{N}$ from the system with parameters set to $\hat{\rho}_n$ and using

$$\mathcal{E}_{\hat{\rho}_n}(g) = \frac{1}{N} \sum_{t=0}^{N} g(\hat{y}_{t-L}, \dots, \hat{y}_t).$$

With respect to unconditional expectation so computed, define

$$\hat{\theta}_K = \underset{\theta \in \Re^{pK}}{\operatorname{argmax}}\ \mathcal{E}_{\hat{\rho}_n} \log f_K(y_0|x_{-1}, \theta),$$

where $f_K(y_0|x_{-1}, \theta)$ is the SNP density given by (4.8). Let

$$\hat{f}_K(y_0|x_{-1}) = f_K(y_0|x_{-1}, \hat{\theta}_K). \tag{5.4}$$

Theorem 1 of Gallant and Long (1997) states that

$$\lim_{K \to \infty} \hat{f}_K(y_0|x_{-1}) = \hat{p}(y_0|x_{-1}).$$

Convergence is with respect to a weighted Sobolev norm that they describe. Of relevance here is that convergence in their norm implies that $\hat{f}_K$ as well as its partial derivatives in $(y_{-L}, \dots, y_{-1}, y_0)$ converge uniformly over $\Re^{\ell}$, $\ell = M(L+1)$, to those of $\hat{p}$. We propose to study the dynamics of $\hat{p}$ by using $\hat{f}_K$ as an approximation. This result provides the justification for our approach.

To approximate $\hat{p}$ by $\hat{f}_K$ values of $(L_u, L_r, L_p, K_z, I_z, K_x, I_x)$ must be chosen. It seems natural to reuse the values of the projection that determined $\hat{\rho}_n$ because, among other things, that choice facilitates a comparison of the constrained dynamics determined by the estimated system with the unconstrained dynamics determined by the data. However, if the estimated nonlinear system is to be sampled at a different frequency than was the data, then it will be necessary to redetermine $(L_u, L_r, L_p, K_z, I_z, K_x, I_x)$ by the methods described in Section 2.2. We anticipate that the dynamics at a different sampling frequency will not often be of interest and we shall presume in what follows that the sampling frequency is the same as the data. The modifications required when it differs are mentioned as they occur.

Of immediate interest in eliciting the dynamics of observables are the first two one-step-ahead conditional moments

$$\mathcal{E}(y_0|x_{-1}) = \int y_0 f_K(y_0|x_{-1}, \hat{\theta}_K)\mathrm{d}y_0$$

$$\mathrm{Var}(y_0|x_{-1}) = \int [y_0 - \mathcal{E}(y_0|x_{-1})]\,[y_0 - \mathcal{E}(y_0|x_{-1})]' f_K(y_0|x_{-1}, \hat{\theta}_K)\mathrm{d}y_0,$$

where $x_{-1} = (y_{-L}, \ldots, y_{-1})$. Owing to the form of a Hermite expansion, expressions for these integrals as linear combinations of high-order moments of the normal distribution are available (Gallant and Tauchen, 1992). The moments themselves may be obtained from standard recursions for the moments of the normal (Johnson and Kotz, 1970).

Filtered volatility is the one-step-ahead conditional standard deviation evaluated at data values; viz.,

$$\sqrt{\mathrm{Var}(y_{k0}|x_{-1})}\Big|_{x_{-1}=(\tilde{y}_{t-L},\ldots,\tilde{y}_{t-1})} \qquad t = 0, \ldots, n. \tag{5.5}$$

In (5.5), $\tilde{y}_t$ denotes data and y_{k0} denotes the kth element of the vector y_0, $k = 1, \ldots, M$. Because filtered volatility is a data-dependent concept, the dynamic system must be sampled at the same frequency as the data to determine $\hat{f}_K$. It has been claimed that filtered volatility could not be recovered from method of moments estimates of a nonlinear dynamic system with partially observed state and that this has been a criticism of such estimates. However, as just seen, filtered volatility is easily computed using the reprojection notion.

We are using the term *filtered volatility* with a purely ARCH-type meaning as in the nonlinear impulse-response literature. Another usage of filtering, perhaps the predominant one, involves estimating an unobserved state variable conditional upon all past and present observables. Filtering according to this notion (for L lags rather than back to the first observation) can be accomplished through reprojection. This may be seen by noting that one can repeat the derivation with y taken to be a contemporaneous unobserved variable and x taken to be contemporaneous and lagged observed variables. Denote y

and x thus modified by y^* and x^*, respectively. The result is a density $f_K(y^*|x^*, \theta)$ of the same form as 4.8 but with altered dimensions. One can simulate $\{y_t^*, x_t^*\}$ from the structural modal and perform the reprojection step to get $\hat{f}_K(y^*|x^*)$ as described above. The proof of Gallant and Long (1997) can be altered to justify these modifications. How one uses $\hat{f}_K(y^*|x^*)$ will be application-specific. For instance, one might wish obtain an estimate of

$$y_t^* = \int_t^{t+T} \exp(\beta_{10} + \beta_{12}U_{2t} + \beta_{13}U_{3t})\mathrm{d}t$$

in a system such as (5.1) for the purpose of pricing an option. In this instance, $x_t^* = (U_{1,t-L}, \ldots, U_{1t})$ and $\hat{y}_t^*(x^*) = \int y^* \hat{f}_K(y^*|x^*)\, \mathrm{d}y^*$. To avoid any confusion, we shall refer to (5.5) as reprojected volatility hereafter. We now return to the main discussion.

One-step-ahead dynamics may be studied by means of plots of (the elements of) $\mathcal{E}(y_0|y_{-L}, \ldots, y_{-1} + \Delta)$, $\mathrm{Var}(y_0|y_{-L}, \ldots, y_{-1} + \Delta)$, or other conditional moments against δ, where Δ is an M-vector with δ in the ith element and zeroes elsewhere. More general perturbation strategies may be considered such as $\Delta = \delta\tilde{y}_\tau$, where $\tilde{y}_\tau$ is a point chosen from the data such that perturbations in the direction $\delta\tilde{y}_\tau$ take contemporaneous correlations among the components of y_t into account. Perturbations to a single element of y_{-1} in a multivariate setting may represent a movement that is improbable according to the dynamics of the system. Some thought must be given to the perturbation scheme in multivariate applications if plots of conditional moments against δ are to be informative. This issue is discussed in Gallant et al. (1993).

Two methods for choosing $(y_{-L}, \ldots, y_{-1})$ for these plots suggest themselves. The first is to put $y_{-L}, \ldots, y_{-1}$ to the sample mean, i.e., put $(y_{-L}, \ldots, y_{-1}) = (\bar{y}, \ldots, \bar{y})$, where $\bar{y} = (1/n)\sum_{t=0}^{n} \tilde{y}_t$, and plot, for instance,

$$\mathrm{Var}(y_0|\bar{y}, \ldots, \bar{y} + \Delta) \tag{5.6}$$

against δ. The second is to average over the data and plot, for instance,

$$(1/n)\sum_{t=0}^{n} \mathrm{Var}(y_t|\tilde{y}_{t-L}, \ldots, \tilde{y}_{t-1} + \Delta) \tag{5.7}$$

against δ. If the estimated system is sampled at a different frequency than the data, then one plots the average $(1/N)\sum_{t=0}^{n}\mathrm{Var}(y_t|\hat{y}_{t-L}, \ldots, \hat{y}_{t-1} + \Delta)$ over a simulation $\{\hat{y}_t\}_{t=-L}^{N}$ at the correct frequency instead.

In an economic system, the graphics just described are interpreted as representing the consequences of a shock to the system that comes as a surprise to the economic agents involved, and similar interpretations hold in other contexts. If one wants to consider the consequences of forcing the system to a different equilibrium, the graphic obtained by plotting $\text{Var}(y_0|y_{-L}+\Delta,\ldots,y_{-1}+\Delta)$ against δ is relevant. They can be quite different.

Multistep-ahead dynamics may be studied by considering plots of the trajectories

$$\mathcal{E}\big[g(y_{j-L},\ldots,y_{j-1})|y_{-L},\ldots,y_{-1}+\Delta\big],\quad j=0,1,\ldots,J, \tag{5.8}$$

where $g(y_{-L},\ldots,y_{-1})$ is a time invariant function whose choice is discussed immediately below. As discussed in Gallant et al. (1993), if one sets the initial condition to $(y_{-L},\ldots,y_{-1}+\Delta)=(\bar{y},\ldots,\bar{y}+\Delta)$, it is helpful to net out transients by plotting either

$$\mathcal{E}\big[g(y_{j-L},\ldots,y_{j-1})|\bar{y},\ldots,\bar{y}+\Delta\big]-\mathcal{E}\big[g(y_{j-L},\ldots,y_{j-1})|\bar{y},\ldots,\bar{y}\big] \tag{5.9}$$

or

$$\frac{1}{n}\sum_{t=0}^{n}\mathcal{E}\big[g(y_{t+j-L},\ldots,y_{t+j-1})|\tilde{y}_{t-L},\ldots,\tilde{y}_{t-1}+\Delta\big] \tag{5.10}$$

against $j=0,1,\ldots,J$ instead of 5.8. Although 5.10 is conceptually superior, because it recognizes the fact that a sequence exactly equal to the stationary mean for L periods can never happen, in the examples considered by Gallant et al. (1993), plots of 5.9 had nearly the same appearance and are much cheaper to compute.

To compute 5.8, one exploits the fact that there are efficient algorithms for sampling the density $\hat{f}_K(y_0|y_{-L},\ldots,y_{-1}+\Delta)$ recursively to obtain R simulated futures

$$\big\{\hat{y}_{0,i},\ldots,\hat{y}_{J,i}\big\},\quad i=1,\ldots,R,$$

each conditional upon $y_{-L},\ldots,y_{-1}+\Delta$ (Gallant and Tauchen, 1992). Prepend $\{y_{-L},\ldots,y_{-1}+\Delta\}$ to each future to obtain the sequences

$$\big\{\hat{y}_{-L,i},\ldots,\hat{y}_{-1,i},\hat{y}_{0,i},\ldots,\hat{y}_{J,i}\big\},\quad i=1,\ldots,R.$$

$\mathcal{E}[g(y_{j-L},\ldots,y_{j-1})|y_{-L},\ldots,y_{-1}+\Delta]$ can then be computed as

$$\mathcal{E}[g(y_{j-L},\ldots,y_{j-1})|y_{-L},\ldots,y_{-1}+\Delta]=\frac{1}{R}\sum_{i=1}^{R}g(\hat{y}_{j-L,i},\ldots,\hat{y}_{j-1,i}).$$

A general discussion of appropriate choice of $g(y_{-L},\ldots,y_{-1})$ for nonlinear impulse-response analysis, the analysis of turning points, etc., is in Gallant et al. (1993). Of these, the more routinely useful are the conditional mean profiles

$$\begin{aligned}&\mu_j(y_{-L},\ldots,y_{-1}+\Delta)\\&=\mathcal{E}\big[\mathcal{E}(y_{k,j}|y_{j-L},\ldots,y_{j-1})|y_{-L},\ldots,y_{-1}+\Delta\big],\quad j=-1,\ldots,J\end{aligned}$$

for the components $k = 1, \ldots, M$ of y, which extend the impulse-response profiles of Sims (1980) to nonlinear systems, and conditional volatility profiles

$$\begin{aligned}&\sigma_j^2(y_{-L}, \ldots, y_{-1} + \Delta)\\ &= \mathcal{E}\big[\operatorname{Var}(y_{k,j} | y_{j-L}, \ldots, y_{j-1}) | y_{-L}, \ldots, y_{-1} + \Delta\big], \quad j = 0, \ldots, J,\end{aligned}$$

which extend the volatility impulse-response profiles of Engle et al. (1990) and Bollerslev and Engle (1993) to nonlinear systems. Plots of the conditional mean profile reveal the future dynamic response of system forecasts to a contemporaneous shock to the system. These will, in general, be nonlinear and can differ markedly when the sign of δ changes. Similarly for volatility.

Persistence can be studied by inspection of profile bundles, which are overplots for $t = 0, \ldots, n$ of the profiles

$$\{\mu_j(\tilde{y}_{t-L}, \ldots, \tilde{y}_{t-1}), j = -1, \ldots, J\}. \tag{5.11}$$

That is, one overplots profiles conditional on each observed datum. If the thickness of the profile bundle tends to collapse to zero rapidly, then the process is mean reverting. If the thickness tends to retain its width, then the process is persistent. Similarly, the profile bundles

$$\left\{\left\{\sqrt{\sigma_j^2}(\tilde{y}_{t-L}, \ldots, \tilde{y}_{t-1}), j = 0, \ldots, J\right\}, t = 0, \ldots, n\right\} \tag{5.12}$$

can be used to examine volatility for persistence. These are extensions to nonlinear systems of notions of persistence due to Bollerslev and Engle (1993). Rather than comparing plots, one can instead compare half-lives. A half-life $\hat{j}$ can be obtained by computing the range R_j at each ordinate $j = 0, \ldots, J$ of either 5.11 or 5.12, regressing $\log R_j$ on $j\beta$, and using $(-\log 2)/\hat{\beta}$ as an estimate of half-life.

Extensive examples of the use of the methods described here for elucidating the joint dynamics of stock prices and volume are in Gallant et al. (1993).

6. APPLICATIONS

There are now several applications of EMM to substantive problems in continuous-time estimation and economics more broadly. For reasons of space, we can only review in detail a few applications. At the end of this section, we give a short overview of the other applications of which we are currently aware. Simulation methods for continuous-time models are discussed in Kloeden and Platen (1992) in general. The papers that we discuss contain within them the details on the way these methods were adapted to the particular problem.

6.1. Multifactor Stochastic Volatility Models for Stock Returns

6.1.1. Jump Diffusions

We start with the application of Andersen et al. (2002). They consider the familiar stochastic volatility diffusion for an observed stock price S_t given by

$$\frac{dS_t}{S_t} = (\mu + cV_t)dt + \sqrt{V_t}dW_{1t}, \tag{6.1}$$

where the unobserved volatility process V_t is either log linear

$$\text{Log linear:} \quad d\log(V_t) = [\alpha - \beta\log(V_t)] + \eta dW_{2t} \tag{6.2}$$

or square root (affine)

$$\text{Square root:} \quad dV_t = (\alpha - \beta V_t) + \eta\sqrt{V_t}dW_{2t}. \tag{6.3}$$

Here, W_{1t} and W_{2t} are standard Brownian motions that are correlated with $\text{corr}(dW_{1t}, dW2_t) = \rho$. The notation is self-explanatory taking note that the term cV_t reflects possible GARCH in mean effects. The version with the log-linear volatility dynamics has attracted substantial attention in the econometrics literature, while the version with square-root volatility dynamics has attracted attention in the finance literature because of the availability of closed-form solutions for options prices.

Andersen, Benzoni, and Lund use EMM to estimate both versions of the stochastic volatility model with daily S&P 500 Stock Index data, January 2, 1953–December 31, 1996. Their auxiliary model is an E-GARCH model (Nelson, 1991) with an SNP-like Hermite series representation for the error density. They report that the EMM chi-square test statistic (2.7) sharply rejects both versions; likewise, the EMM t-ratio diagnostics (2.9) indicate that these models have difficulty accommodating the tail behavior of the data.

These authors also consider a more general jump diffusion stochastic volatility models

$$\frac{dS_t}{S_t} = (\mu + cV_t - \lambda_t\bar{\kappa})dt + \sqrt{V_t}dW_{1t} + \kappa_t dq_t \tag{6.4}$$

with jump intensity given by

$$\lambda_t = \lambda_0 + \lambda_1 V_t \tag{6.5}$$

and jump size κ_t given by

$$\log(1 + \kappa_t) \sim N[\log(1 + \bar{\kappa}) - 0.5\delta^2, \delta^2).$$

The jump diffusion models pass the EMM chi-squared test of fit and the EMM diagnostic t-ratio tests, which suggests an adequate fit. Once jumps are included in the model, the test statistics reveal no substantive difference between the log-linear and square-root specifications for volatility. Also, their estimates suggest little evidence for state-dependent jumps in (6.5). They go on to compute hypothetical option prices under various assumptions about the risk premiums on volatility and jump risks. They illustrate the role of stochastic volatility and jumps in generating anomalies such as volatility smiles and smirks.

6.1.2. Alternative Models

The fact that adding a jump component to a basic stochastic volatility model improves the fit so much reflects two familiar characteristics of financial price movements: thick non-Gaussian tails and persistent time-varying volatility. A model with a single stochastic volatility factor can accommodate either of these characteristics separately, but not both together. The addition of the jump factor accounts for the thick tails. Doing so complicates the estimation, however, because a direct simulation of a jump diffusion entails a discontinuous path and thereby a discontinuous objective function. Andersen, Benzoni, and Lund need to implement a simulation strategy that smooths out the sample path across a jump boundary.

An alternative to adding the jump component is to add another stochastic volatility factor. This step is undertaken through EMM in Gallant et al. (1999), with some encouraging initial results. A more extensive investigation is undertaken in the next paper we review.

6.1.3. Volatility Index Models

Chernov et al. (2003) consider a four-factor model of the form

$$\begin{aligned} \frac{\mathrm{d}P_t}{P_t} &= (\alpha_{10} + \alpha_{12}U_{2t})\mathrm{d}t + \sigma(U_{3t}, U_{4t})(\mathrm{d}W_{1t} + \psi_{13}\mathrm{d}W_{3t} + \psi_{14}\mathrm{d}W_{4t}) \\ \mathrm{d}U_{2t} &= (\alpha_{20} + \alpha_{22})\mathrm{d}t + \beta_{20}\mathrm{d}W_{2t} \end{aligned} \tag{6.6}$$

In the above, P_t represents the financial price series evolving in continuous time; U_{2t} is a stochastic drift factor; U_{3t} and U_{4t} are stochastic volatility factors that affect price evolution through the volatility index function $\sigma(U_{3t}, U_{4t})$.

These authors consider two broad classes of setups for the volatility index functions and factor dynamics: an affine setup, where the index function and volatility dynamics are

$$\begin{aligned} \sigma(U_{3t}, U_{4t}) &= \sqrt{\beta_{10} + \beta_{13}U_{3t} + \beta_{14}U_{4t}} \\ \mathrm{d}U_{it} &= (\alpha_{i0} + \alpha_{ii}U_{it})\mathrm{d}t + \sqrt{\beta_{i0} + \beta_{ii}U_{it}}\mathrm{d}W_{it} \quad i = 3, 4. \end{aligned} \tag{6.7}$$

and a logarithmic setup, where

$$\begin{aligned} \sigma(U_{3t}, U_{4t}) &= \exp(\beta_{10} + \beta_{13}U_{3t} + \beta_{14}U_{4t}) \\ \mathrm{d}U_{it} &= (\alpha_{i0} + \alpha_{ii}U_{i})\mathrm{d}t + (\beta_{i0} + \beta_{ii}U_{it})\mathrm{d}W_{it} \quad i = 3, 4. \end{aligned} \tag{6.8}$$

The simpler stochastic volatility models with only one volatility factor, (6.1) above, are subsumed in this setup by taking $\beta_{14} = 0$.

Chernov et al.(2003) apply EMM to estimate the above models along with affine jump diffusion models, using daily data on the DOW Index, January 2, 1953–July 16, 1999. They find that models with two volatility factors, U_{3t} and U_{4t}, do much better on the EMM chi-squared specification test than do models with only a single volatility factor. They also find that the logarithmic two-volatility factor models (6.8) outperform affine jump diffusions and basically provide an acceptable fit to the data. One of the volatility factors is extremely persistent and the other strongly mean reverting. Interestingly, the volatility feedback parameter, β_{ii}, is positive and very important for finding an acceptable fit. This parameter permits the local variability of the volatility factors to be high when the factors themselves are high, a characteristic of volatility that has been noted by others. The strongly mean-reverting factor with the volatility feedback acts much like a jump factor in the return process itself.

At this point, it is not clear whether jump diffusions or multiple-factor models with appropriate factor dynamics are the right models for equity prices. The former, with jumps entered directly into the price process, are intuitively appealing models for financial prices. But the jumps generate complications for the simulations and estimation. On the other hand, the multifactor models are far easier to simulate and estimate and might prove more adaptable to derivative computations since all sample paths are continuous and standard hedging arguments and the Ito calculus apply.

6.2. Term Structure of Interest Rates

6.2.1. Affine Term Structure Models

Dai and Singleton (2000) apply EMM for estimation of an affine term structure model. In the affine setting, the vector of underlying state variables, Y_t, follows affine dynamics

$$dY_t = \bar{\mathcal{K}}[\bar{\theta} - Y_t]dt + \Sigma\sqrt{S_t}d\tilde{W}_t, \tag{6.9}$$

where S_t is a diagonal matrix with entries $S_{ii,t} = \beta_{i0} + \beta_i' Y_t$. The short rate of interest follows

$$r_t = \delta_0 + \delta_y' Y_t.$$

On these assumptions for the risk neutral dynamics, the pure-discount bond prices are given by

$$P_t(\tau) = e^{A(\tau) - B(\tau)' Y_t},$$

where $A(\tau)$ and $B(\tau)$ are given by the solutions to ordinary differential equations.

Dai and Singleton use Eurodollar swap rates, and the observation equation is a bit more complicated than in other applications due to the nature of swaps. The no-arbitrage swap rate, $r_{s\tau t}$, on a fixed for variable swap at times $t + k\tau_0$, $k = 1, 2, \ldots, K$, $\tau = K\tau_0$, is

$$r_{s\tau t} = \frac{1 - P_t(K\tau_0)}{\sum_{k=1}^{K} P_t(k\tau_0)}.$$

They estimate ATSMs using three observed variables $y_t = (y_{1t}\ y_{2t}\ y_{3t})'$:

y_{1t}	$-0.50 \log[P_t(0.50)]$	Six-month LIBOR
y_{2t}	r_{s2t}	Two-year swap rate
y_{3t}	r_{s10t}	Ten-year swap rate

This selection defines the observation function

$$y_t = \phi(Y_t, \rho),$$

where ρ contains all the parameters of the affine term structure model (ATSM) to be estimated and tested.

Dai and Singleton focus on two stochastic volatility models for the term structure. One is due to Balduzzi et al. (1996), abbreviated (BDFS) and the other is due to Chen (1996). Each lies in a separate branch of the family of ATSMs. Dai and Singleton find that neither model fits the data, in sense that the overall goodness-of-fit chi-squared tests are very large relative to degrees of freedom and the diagnostic t-ratios are well above 2.0 in magnitude. However, if each model is expanded outwards to the maximal identified ATSM within its particular branch, then the chi-squared tests for both models become acceptable at conventional significance. To choose an overall preferred model, Dai and Singleton undertake additional analysis of postestimation simulations, much in the spirit of reprojection analysis described in Section 5 above, to select the extended version of the BDFS model as their preferred model.

6.2.2. Regime-Switching Affine Term Structure Models

Bansal and Zhou (2002) examine a class affine models with stochastic regime switching. In their class of models, factor dynamics are constant-parameter affine within each regime, but the economy shifts stochastically between regimes. They deduce appropriate closed-form bond pricing functions that properly account for the regime switching. The use of regime switching models is intuitively appealing in view of potential effects on fixed income markets of various monetary regimes. Bansal and Zhou use monthly data, 1964–1995, on yields of six months and five-year maturities for estimation. They use an ARCH-type model with an SNP error density as the auxiliary model. They find that a two-factor regime-switching model passes the EMM test of specification while every model in broad class of two- and three-factor constant regime affine models is sharply rejected. They also find that the estimated regime-switching model does pricing in pricing the cross section of bond prices beyond the two basis yields used in estimation.

6.2.3. Nonaffine Models

Ahn et al. (2002a) use EMM to examine the class of quadratic term structure models (QTSMs) for two monthly data sets, January 1952 to February 1991 and November 1971 to December 1999. They find that the QTSM models generally outperform affine models on the EMM diagnostic test, but no QTSM is capable of explaining the data. Ahn et al. (2002b) use EMM to estimate hybrid models where some underlying factors follow affine dynamics and the others quadratic. They find that hybrid models do better than either class separately but are still rejected on the EMM chi-squared test of fit.

An interesting and promising line of research would be to combine the findings Bansal and Zhou (2001), who report favorable evidence for regime-switching models, with those of Ahn et al. (2002a) who find encouraging evidence for QTSMs.

6.3. Exchange Rates

Chung and Tauchen (2001) use EMM to test various target zone models of exchange rates. They consider the basic model where the fundamental k_t evolves as

$$\mathrm{d}k_t = \mu \mathrm{d}t + \sigma \mathrm{d}w_t \tag{6.10}$$

and more general models with mean reversion

$$\mathrm{d}k_t = -\gamma(k_t - k_0) + \sigma \mathrm{d}w_t. \tag{6.11}$$

The central bank is assumed to follow policy actions to keep the fundamental with the band $[\underline{k}, \overline{k}]$. Letting s_t denote the exchange rate, then the target zone model generates the observation equation

$$s_t = G(k_t, \rho), \tag{6.12}$$

where the functional form of G is determined by the asset pricing equation that connects the dynamics of the exchange rate to the fundamental process k_t and by the boundary and smooth pasting conditions. Above, ρ represents the parameters. See Delgado and Dumas (1991) for details on specification and solution of target zone models. Evidently, it is relatively simple to simulate exchange rate data from a target zone model and thereby implement EMM.

Chung and Tauchen (2001) apply the procedure to weekly French franc-Deutsche mark exchange rates, 1987–1993. Their findings, in brief, are as follows. Consistent with previous empirical work, their specification tests reject all target zone models considered when bounds, $\underline{k}$ and $\overline{k}$, are determined directly from officially announced bands. However, they find that a very acceptable fit is given by a target zone model with implicit bands, i.e., where $\underline{k}$ and $\overline{k}$ are free parameters, and the fundamental process is with mean reversion (6.11). Their results indicate that the central banks were operating within an implicit band inside the announced official bands. Interestingly, their results are consistent with theoretical predictions for a bilateral analysis of exchange rates determined in a multilateral system (Pedroni, 2001). Finally, Chung and Tauchen present rather dramatic graphical evidence on the much better fit to the data provided by the preferred target zone model over a conventional stochastic volatility model for exchange rates.

A recent exchange rate application that uses the C++ MCMC implementation of EMM is Danielsson and Penaranda (2007). They estimate the parameters of a coordination game of market instability, which focuses on the endogenous reaction of agents to fundamentals and liquidity. They apply the model to the potential for financial turmoil caused by carry trades using data for various subperiods that bracket the yen-dollar market in 1998. They find that the strategic behavior of agents is required to account for the turmoil in that market rather than just market fundamentals and liquidity.

6.4. General Equilibrium Models

Gennotte and Marsh (1993) is an early effort to estimate a general equilibrium asset pricing model by simulated method of moments. In Bansal et al. (1993, 1995), we use EMM to estimate small-scale general equilibrium model of international currency markets. More recently, Valderrama (2001) has implemented EMM for estimation of a small-scale real business cycle model and Bansal et al. (2007) contrast the implications of the habit and long run risk models.

Estimation of completely specified equilibrium models, i.e., starting from tastes and technology, faces a computational bottleneck. For candidate values of the parameter, the users need to solve for the equilibrium along the simulated trajectory. This computational requirement is generally more demanding than that required to estimate an SDE, as described in many of the preceding examples. However, recent sharp increases in computational power, in the form of faster processors linked by parallization software, indicate that it will soon be feasible to investigate more extensively through EMM such fully articulated models. In an initial effort, we are exploring the feasibility of confronting the models of and Bansal and Yaron (2004). These models entail complicated state and time nonseparable specifications for the stochastic discount factor and elaborate multifactor model dynamics for cash flow dynamics, and thereby present serious challenges for estimation.

6.5. Additional Applications

Below we give a short summary of additional applications of which we are currently aware. Many of these applications preceded and motivated those described above. We apologize in advance for omissions and would be interested in knowing of applications we might have inadvertently left out; send an e-mail with the citation to either george.tauchen@duke.edu or ron.gallant@duke.edu.

Discrete time stochastic volatility models are well suited for EMM estimation. Van der Sluis (1997, 1999) implements the method and provides C/C+ code under Ox for discrete time univariate stochastic volatility models. Gallant et al. (1997) use it to examine an extensive list of discrete time stochastic volatility models and document a set of empirical shortcomings.

Applications to estimation of continuous-time stochastic volatility models include Engle and Lee (1996), Gallant and Tauchen (1997), and Gallant and Long (1997). Mixon (1998) generalizes the log-linear Gaussian continuous-time model to include a feedback effect in volatility. Gallant et al. (1999) also find this feedback effect to be important as well a second volatility factor in their investigation of daily returns and range data. Chernov et al. (1999) use the technique to explore stochastic volatility and state-dependent jump models.

A recent application to options pricing is Chernov and Ghysels (2000), who use the technique for joint estimation of the risk neutral and objective probability distributions using a panel of options data. Another options pricing application is Jiang and van der Sluis (2000). Pastorello et al. (2000) use it to deal with the estimation of continuous-time stochastic volatility models of option pricing.

Early applications to interest rate modeling include Pagan et al. (1996), who apply the technique for estimating a variety of factor models of the term structure, and Andersen and Lund (1997), who use the technique to estimate a stochastic volatility model of the short rate. Some evidence from EMM diagnostics on the shortcomings of a one factor model is set forth in Tauchen (1997) and in McManus and Watt (1999). An extensive analysis of multifactor models of short-rate dynamics is in Gallant and Tauchen (1998). Other term structure applications include Martin and Pagan (2000) along with Dungey et al. (2000), who undertake a factor analysis of bond yield spreads.

Some interesting recent applications to microeconometric problems include Nagypal (2007), who uses the method to estimate and compare various models of learning by doing. Her scores are not SNP scores, which, indeed, would be inappropriate in her application. The referee argues that her auxiliary model may not approximate the true data-generating process closely enough for a claim of efficiency. Austin and Katzman (2001) apply the method to estimate and test new models of multistep auctions using tobacco auction data.

7. SOFTWARE AND PRACTICAL ISSUES

7.1. Code

In this section, we first describe methods that are appropriate when a high-quality implementation of the BFGS algorithm is used. The BFGS algorithm (Fletcher, 1987) works best when analytical first derivatives of the objective function can be supplied, which is the case with EMM when using an SNP auxiliary model. The BFGS algorithm uses a rank two update scheme to compute a "Hessian" matrix, which is needed to get quadratic convergence. Therefore, second derivatives are not required. Next, we discuss the MCMC algorithm proposed by Chernozukov and Hong (2003). Its advantages are that it is not as dependent on start values for success, computing sandwich variance matrices becomes feasible, and it can cope with the jitter inherent in estimating jump diffusion models. Its disadvantage is that it can be more computationally intensive.

A Fortran program that implements the BFGS algorithm is available at http://econ.duke.edu/webfiles/get/emm. A C++ program implementing the Chernozukov–Hong method is available at http://econ.duke.edu/webfiles/arg/emm. A User's Guide (Gallant and Tauchen, 2001b) is included with the code as well as the SNP code and an SNP User's Guide. The C++ code is distributed in both a serial version and a parallel version that runs under message passing interface (MPI) (Foster, 1995). The C++ program is actually a general purpose implementation of the Chernozukov–Hong method that can be used with maximum likelihood estimation or other statistical objective functions. It can also be used for Bayesian inference and we remark in passing that the EMM objective function can be used for Bayesian inference in place of a likelihood (Gallant and Hong, 2007).

As supplied, the code presumes a CASE 2 structural model in the nomenclature of Gallant and Tauchen (1996). That is the case that we shall describe here. The setup subsumes a wide variety of situations in macroeconomics and finance. The SNP model is the score generator. The code can easily be modified to accommodate other score generators and to accommodate covariates, as in Case 1 or Case 3 of Gallant and Tauchen (1996). Although we do our work in Unix (Linix or Mac OS), EMM will run under Microsoft Windows. Running under different operating systems is discussed in the Guides.

7.2. Troubleshooting, Numerical Stability, and Convergence Problems

On the whole, the EMM package is useful and practical. An early version was used for estimating asset pricing models (Bansal et al., 1995). Recent versions of the Fortran package have been used in several applications including, among others, Chernov et al. (2003) and Gallant and Tauchen (2001a) for stochastic volatility, Gallant and Long (1997), Chung and Tauchen (2001) for exchange-rate modeling, and Dai and Singleton (2000), Ahn et al. (2002a), and Tauchen (1997) for interest rates.

Things can go awry, however. Sometimes, the program may stop prematurely, and there are some key issues of dynamic and numerical stability that the user must be attentive to. These issues affect the speed of the computations and relate to convergence problems in the nonlinear optimization. The following discussion pertains to these issues.

7.2.1. Start Value Problems and Scaling

Sometimes it is hard to get decent start values. We suggest intensive use of randomly perturbed start values. The nonlinear optimizer works best if it sees all parameters as roughly the same order of magnitude. We adopt a scaling so that all parameters as seen by the optimizer lie in the interval $(-1, 1)$. Since this scaling may not be the natural scaling for the data generator, one might want to adapt the user-supplied portion of the code so that the rescaling is done automatically, as in the log-linear example distributed with the Fortran EMM code. We find that the proper scaling mitigates many problems and accelerates convergence.

7.2.2. Enforcing Dynamic Stability

As noted in Section 3, the score generator should be dynamically stable. The SNP package incorporates a spline and/or logistic transformation feature that directly enforces dynamic stability on the score generator. This feature is discussed at length in the SNP User's Guide (Gallant and Tauchen, 2001c). The transformations only affect the conditioning variable x_{t-1} in the conditional density $f(y_t|x_{t-1}, \theta)$; it has no effect on y_t and it is not a prefiltering of the data. All it does is force a very gentle sort mean reversion so that $(\partial/\partial\theta) \log[f(\hat{y}_\tau|\hat{x}_{\tau-1}, \theta)]$ remains well defined should the optimizer happen to pass back a parameter vector ρ such that the simulation $\{\hat{y}_\tau(\rho), \hat{x}_{\tau-1}(\rho)\}$ is explosive. For series that are very persistent, such as interest rates, we find the spline transformation the best while for series that are nearly i.i.d., e.g., stock returns series, we recommend using the logistic transformation instead of the spline transformation. As explained in the SNP User's Manual, the logistic really serves a different purpose than the spline. The logistic prevents large elements of x_{t-1} from unduly influencing the conditional variance computation.

7.2.3. Bulletproofing the Data Generating Process

Recall the basic structure of EMM as outlined in Section 2.2. The core component of the distributed EMM package is the user-supplied simulator that takes as input a candidate vector ρ and generates a simulated realization. This component computes the mapping $\rho \rightarrow \{\hat{y}_t\}_{t=1}^{N}$. The EMM package evaluates the objective function

$$s_n(\rho) = m_n'(\rho, \tilde{\theta}_n)(\tilde{\mathcal{I}}_n)^{-1} m_n(\rho, \tilde{\theta}_n)$$

and optimizes it with respect to ρ.

The optimizer should see $s_n(\rho)$ as a smooth surface and care should be taken in writing the data generating process (DGP) code to ensure that small perturbations of ρ lead to small perturbations of $s_n(\rho)$. The most common source of a rough surfaces is the failure to control Monte Carlo jitter. One must ensure that when ρ changes, the random numbers used to compute $\{\hat{y}_t\}_{t=1}^{N}$ do not change. Usually, taking care that the seeds passed to random number generators do not change when ρ changes is an adequate precaution. However, as mentioned in connection with the discussion of Andersen et al. (2002), additional precautions may be necessary when adding jumps or other discrete elements to simulated paths. Large values for N also contribute to smoothness.

Our experience is that the optimizer sometimes tries outlandishly extreme values of ρ, especially in the initial phase of the optimization when it's acquiring information on functional form of the objective function. These outlandish values of ρ could entail taking the logs or square roots of negative numbers, dividing by zero, or undertaking other operations that generate numerical exceptions, within the user's simulator, within SNP (which evaluates to scores), or even within the optimizer itself. Our experience is that things proceed most smoothly when the user-supplied simulator can generate some kind of sensible simulated realization regardless of ρ and be able to compute something for $\rho \to \{\hat{y}_t\}_{t=1}^N$ given arbitrary ρ. We call this "bulletproofing" the code.

However, sometimes it extremely difficult to bulletproof completely the simulator (especially for diffusion models) and numerical exceptions occur that generate **NaN**'s. On a Unix workstation, the Fortran compiler usually has produced an executable that can appropriately propagate the **NaN**'s and the EMM objective function evaluates to either **Inf** or **NaN**. Typically, the optimizer distributed with the code can recover, as it realizes that the particular value of ρ that led to the disaster is very unpromising and it tries another. The cost of this is that the program slows down considerably while handling the numerical exceptions along a very long simulated realization.

7.3. The Chernozukov–Hong Method

The computational methods discussed here and implemented by the C++ implementation of the EMM package apply to any discrepancy function $s_n(\rho)$ that produces asymptotically normal estimates; i.e., any discrepancy function for which there exist $\rho^o, \mathcal{I}$, and $\mathcal{J}$ such that

$$\mathcal{J}\sqrt{n}(\hat{\rho}_n - \rho^o) = \sqrt{n}\frac{\partial}{\partial\rho}s_n(\rho) + o_p(1) \text{ and } \sqrt{n}\frac{\partial}{\partial\rho}s_n(\rho) \xrightarrow{\mathcal{L}} N(0,\mathcal{I}). \tag{7.1}$$

The $\mathcal{I}$ matrix discussed in this section pertains to $\hat{\rho}_n$ and is not the $\tilde{\mathcal{I}}_n$ weighting matrix of the EMM auxiliary model.

Quasi-maximum likelihood estimation requires the computation of the estimator itself, $\hat{\rho}_n = \underset{\rho}{\operatorname{argmin}}\ s_n(\rho)$, an estimate of the Hessian

$$\mathcal{J} = \frac{\partial}{\partial\rho\partial\rho'}\, s^o(\rho^o),$$

where $s^o(\rho) = \lim_{n\to\infty} s_n(\rho)$, and an estimate of Fisher's information

$$\mathcal{I} = \mathrm{Var}\left[\frac{\partial}{\partial\rho'}\sqrt{n}\, s_n(\rho^o)\right] = \mathcal{E}\left[\frac{\partial}{\partial\rho'}\sqrt{n}\, s_n(\rho^o)\right]\left[\frac{\partial}{\partial\rho'}\sqrt{n}\, s_n(\rho^o)\right]'.$$

The variance of $\sqrt{n}(\hat{\rho}_n - \rho^o)$ is then of the sandwich form

$$V_n = \mathrm{Var}\left[\sqrt{n}(\hat{\rho}_n - \rho^o)\right] = \mathcal{J}^{-1}\mathcal{I}\mathcal{J}^{-1}.$$

Put $\ell(\rho) = e^{-n\, s_n(\rho)}$. Apply Bayesian MCMC methods with $\ell(\rho)$ as the likelihood. From the resulting MCMC chain $\{\rho_i\}_{i=1}^{R}$, put

$$\hat{\rho}_n = \bar{\rho}_R = \frac{1}{R}\sum_{t=1}^{R} \rho_i \quad \text{and} \quad \hat{\mathcal{J}}^{-1} = \left(\frac{n}{R}\right)\sum_{t=1}^{R} (\rho_i - \bar{\rho}_R)\,(\rho_i - \bar{\rho}_R)'.$$

Alternatively, and definitely for EMM, use the mode of $\ell(\rho)$ as the estimator $\hat{\rho}_n$. The EMM package computes and reports both the mean and the mode.

Actually, the mode is the better choice of an estimator in most applications because the parameter values in the mode actually have generated a simulation. The parameter values in the mean vector may not even satisfy the support conditions of the structural model.

The strategy used to estimate $\mathcal{I}$ is the following. For ρ set to the mode, simulate the model, and generate I approximately independent of bootstrap data sets $\{\hat{y}_{t,i}\}_{t=1}^{n}$, $i = 1, \ldots, I$, each of exactly the same sample size n as the original data. Keeping the size to exactly n and using model simulations makes the estimator below a HAC estimator. Keeping the size to exactly n does not imply that the simulation size N should be set to n when using the program. The simulation size N should be set much larger than n in most instances. One way to get a bootstrap sample is to split this long simulation into blocks of size n. With this approach, the estimate of $\mathcal{I}$ would be a parametric bootstrap estimate. Alternatively, stationary bootstrap or some other method could be used to construct the blocks. The bootstrap-generating mechanism is coded by the user.

Let $\hat{s}_{n,i}(\rho)$ denote the criterion function corresponding to the ith bootstrap data set $\{\hat{y}_{t,i}\}_{t=1}^{n}$ and let $\hat{\rho}_n$ denote mode of $\ell(\rho)$. Compute $\frac{\partial}{\partial\rho'}\sqrt{n}\,\hat{s}_{n,i}(\hat{\rho}_n)$ numerically. An estimate of the information matrix is the average

$$\hat{\mathcal{I}} = \frac{1}{I}\sum_{i=1}^{I}\left[\frac{\partial}{\partial\rho'}\sqrt{n}\,\hat{s}_{n,i}(\hat{\rho}_n)\right]\left[\frac{\partial}{\partial\rho'}\sqrt{n}\,\hat{s}_{n,i}(\hat{\rho}_n)\right]'. \tag{7.2}$$

Note that for the EMM estimator, one must compute the likelihood of the auxiliary model from the ith bootstrap sample and optimize it to get the ith EMM objective function $\hat{s}_{n,i}(\rho)$. This is done using the BFGS method. This is the step that makes computing an accurate numerical derivative accurately both difficult and costly for EMM. The code attempts to detect failure of the optimizer and failure to compute an accurate derivative and discard those instances. An objective function such as maximum likelihood or GMM that does not rely on a preliminary optimization is not as much of a challenge to differentiate numerically. With these, one can have more confidence that the code provides the correct answer.

If the SNP model is a good approximation to the true data-generating process, the computation of $\hat{\mathcal{I}}$ is not necessary because $\mathcal{I} = \mathcal{J}$. This issue has been discussed extensively above. The same is true for maximum likelihood if the model is correctly specified.

The code provides the option of putting the parameter ρ on a grid. This increases speed by allowing $s_n(\rho)$ and related variables to be obtained by table lookup, thus avoiding recomputation for a value of ρ that has already been visited in the MCMC chain. This is a useful feature when the objective function $s_n(\rho)$ is costly to compute.

Note that $S_n(\rho) = \tau s_n(\rho)$ is also a valid criterion according to the theory. This gives one a temperature parameter τ to use for tuning the chain. This feature is implemented in the package.

A random walk, single move, normal proposal is the workhorse of the C++ EMM package. When parameters are put on a grid, a discrete proposal density is used instead that has probabilities assigned to grid points proportionally to this normal. Group moves are also supported. It is easy to substitute an alternative proposal density.

Another advantage of putting parameters on a grid is that it allows the statistical objective function to be computed less accurately because the accept–reject decision is still likely to be correct when parameter values are well separated, despite an inaccurately computed objective function, within reason. This helps mitigate against the effects of jitter discussed above. Also, it will allow smaller values of the simulation size N than hill climbers require. For small values of N, one should probably multiply variance estimates by the correction factor (1+n/N) discussed in Gourieroux et al. (1993).

Simulated method of moments is exactly the same as the foregoing but with a GMM criterion replacing $s_n(\rho)$. As with EMM, if the correct weight function is used with the GMM criterion function, then $\mathcal{I} = \mathcal{J}$ so that $\mathcal{I}$ need not be computed and there is no need for any numerical differentiation. But often, the effectiveness of the GMM weighting function is doubtful and it can cloud the interpretation of results. One may prefer sandwich standard errors regardless. With GMM, there is usually no numerical optimization to compute moments as with EMM, so better accuracy can be expected.

The MCMC method described here makes the imposition of support restrictions, inequality restrictions, and informative prior information exceptionally convenient. These restrictions and prior information can be imposed on model parameters or on (nonlinear) functionals of the model that can only be known through simulation. This feature is implemented in the EMM package. As mentioned above, when the EMM criterion function is used in connection with a prior, the results can be given a Bayesian interpretation (Gallant and Hong, 2007).

Obviously, these ideas are not restricted to simulation estimators. The EMM package is a general purpose implementation of the Chernozhukov–Hong estimator. An illustration of how the code may be used to implement maximum likelihood is included with the package and described in the User's Guide. The application used for this illustration is a translog consumer demand system for electricity by time of day with demand shares distributed as the logistic normal that is taken from

Gallant (1987). It shows off the Chernozhukov–Hong estimator to good advantage because a vexing problem with hill climbers is trying to keep model parameters in the region where predicted shares are positive for every observed price/expenditure vector. This is nearly impossible to achieve when using conventional derivative-based hill-climbing algorithms but is trivially easy to achieve using the the Chernozhukov–Hong estimator.

8. CONCLUSION

We described a simulated score method of moments estimator based on the following idea: use the expectation with respect to the structural model of the score function of an auxiliary model as the vector of moment conditions for GMM estimation. Making the procedure operational requires an estimate of the parameters of the auxiliary model and computation of the expectation through simulation. Strategies for doing this were set forth, considerations regarding choice of the auxiliary model were discussed, and the SNP density, which is a sieve, was described as a general purpose auxiliary model. When the auxiliary model is chosen to closely approximate the characteristics of the observed data, the estimation method is termed EMM. The SNP density provides a systematic method to achieve a close approximation, though, depending on the nature of the data, other auxiliary models might provide a more convenient way to achieve adequate approximation for EMM.

These ideas were related to indirect inference, which is an asymptotically equivalent methodology, and mention made of the fact that the indirect inference view of the method can be used to facilitate the choice of an auxiliary model that confers semi-nonparametric or robustness properties on the estimator. Also mentioned was that, as a practical matter, indirect inference will often have to be reformulated as a simulated score method to make it computationally feasible.

There are three steps to EMM. The first, termed the *projection step*, entails summarizing the data by projecting it onto the auxiliary model. The second is termed the *estimation step*, where the parameters are obtained by GMM. The estimation step produces an omnibus test of specification along with useful diagnostic t statistics. The third step is termed the *reprojection step*, which entails postestimation analysis of simulations for the purposes of prediction, filtering, and model assessment. It was argued that the last two steps, assessment of model adequacy and postestimation evaluation, are the real strengths of the methodology in building scientifically valid models.

There have been many applications of the EMM methodology in the literature and several of these were discussed in detail. Code is available, its use was broadly discussed with attention given to various pitfalls that need to be avoided. The code is available for both serial and parallel architectures.

REFERENCES

Aguirre-Torres, V. (2001) "Local behavior of the efficient method of moments in iid models," Technical Report DE-C01.3, Division Academica de Actuaria, Estadistica Matematicas, Instituto Tecnologico Autonomo de Mexico (ITAM), Rio Hondo #1, Mexico DF 01000, Mexico.

Aguirre-Torres, V., and A. R. Gallant (2001) "Local behavior of the efficient method of moments in dynamic models," Technical Report DE-C01.6, Division Academica de Actuaria, Estadistica Matematicas, Instituto Tecnologico Autonomo de Mexico (ITAM), Rio Hondo #1, Mexico DF 01000, Mexico.

Ahn, D.-H., R. F. Dittmar, and A. R. Gallant (2002a) "Quadratic term structure models: theory and evidence," *The Review of Financial Studies*, 15, 243–288.

Ahn, D.-H, R. F. Dittmar, A. R. Gallant, and B. Gao (2002b) "Purebred or hybrid?: reproducing the volatility in term structure dynamics," *Journal of Econometrics*, 116, 147–180.

Andersen, T. G., L. Benzoni, and J. Lund (2002) "Towards an empirical foundation for continuous-time equity return models," *Journal of Finance*, 57, 1239–1284.

Andersen, T. G., H.-J. Chung, and B. E. Sorensen (1999) "Efficient method of moments estimation of a stochastic volatility model: a Monte Carlo study," *Journal of Econometrics*, 91, 61–87.

Andersen, T. G., and J. Lund (1997) "Estimating continuous time stochastic volatility models of the short term interest rate," *Journal of Econometrics*, 77, 343–378.

Andrews, D. W. K. (1991) "Heteroskedasticity and autocorrelation consistent covariance matrix estimation," *Econometrica*, 59, 307–346.

Austin, A., and B. Katzman (2001) "Testing a model of multi-unit bidder demands using auction data," Working Paper, University of Miami.

Balduzzi, P., S. R. Das, S. Foresi, and R. K. Sundaram (1996) "A simple approach to three factor affine term structure models," *Journal of Fixed Income*, 6, 43–53.

Bansal, R., A. R. Gallant, R. Hussey, and G. Tauchen (1993) "Computational aspects of nonparametric simulation estimation," in D. A. Belsley (ed.), *Computational Techniques for Econometrics and Economic Analysis*. Boston: Kluwer Academic Publishers, 3–22.

Bansal, R., A. R. Gallant, R. Hussey, and G. Tauchen (1995) "Nonparametric estimation of structural models for high-frequency currency market data," *Journal of Econometrics*, 66, 251–287.

Bansal, R., A. R. Gallant, and G. Tauchen (2007) "Rational pessimism, rational exuberance, and asset pricing models," *Review of Economic Studies*, 74, 1005–1033.

Bansal, R., and A. Yaron (2004) "Risks for the long run: a potential resolution of asset pricing puzzles," *Journal of Finance*, 59, 1481–1509.

Bansal, R., and H. Zhou (2002) "Term structure of interest rates with regime shifts," *Journal of Finance*, 57, 1997–2043.

Bollerslev, T., (1986) "Generalized autoregressive conditional heteroskedasticity," *Journal of Econometrics*, 31, 307–327.

Bollerslev, T., and R. F. Engle (1993) "Common persistence in conditional variances," *Econometrica*, 61, 167–186.

Chen, L. (1996) *Stochastic Mean and Stochastic Volatility: A Three Factor Model of the Term Structure of Interest Rates*. Oxford, UK: Blackwell Publishers.

Chernov, M., A. R. Gallant, E. Ghysels, and G. Tauchen (1999) "A new class of stochastic volatility models with jumps: theory and estimation," Working Paper, University of North Carolina-Chapel Hill.

Chernov, M., A. R. Gallant, E. Ghysels, and G. Tauchen (2003) "Alternative models for stock price dynamics," *Journal of Econometrics*, 116, 225–257.
Chernov, M., and E. Ghysels (2000) "A study towards a unified approach to the joint estimation of objective and risk neutral measures for the purpose of options valuation," *Journal of Financial Economics*, 56, 407–458.
Chernozhukov, V., and H. Hong (2003) "An MCMC approach to classical estimation," *Journal of Econometrics*, 115, 293–346.
Chumacero, R. (1997) "Finite sample properties of the efficient method of moments," *Studies in Nonlinear Dynamics and Econometrics*, 2, 35–51.
Chung, C.-C., and G. Tauchen (2001) "Testing target zone models using efficient method of moments," *Journal of Business and Economic Statistics*, 19, 255–269.
Coppejans, M., and A. R. Gallant (2000) "Cross validated SNP density estimates," *Journal of Econometrics*, 110, 27–65.
Dai, Q., and K. J. Singleton (2000) "Specification analysis of affine term structure models," *Journal of Finance* LV (5), 1943–1978.
Danielsson, J., and F. Penaranda (2007) "On the impact of fundamentals, liquidity, and coordination on market stability," Working Paper, London School of Economics Available at http://www.riskresearch.org.
Davidian, M., and R. J. Carroll (1987) "Variance function estimation," *Journal of the American Statistical Association*, 82, 1079–1091.
Dridi, R., and E. Renault (1998) "Semiparametric indirect inference," Manuscript, Department of Economics, University of North Carolina.
Del Negro, M., and F. Schorfheide (2004), "Priors from general equilibrium models for VARS," *International Economic Review*, 45, 643–673.
Delgado, F., and B. Dumas (1991) "Target zones, broad and narrow," in P. Krugman and M. Miller (eds.), *Exchange Rate Targets and Currency Bands*. Cambridge: Cambridge University Press, 108–135.
Duffie, D., and K. J. Singleton (1993) "Simulated moments estimation of Markov models of asset prices," *Econometrica*, 61, 929–952.
Dungey, M., V. L. Martin, and A. R. Pagan (2000) "A multivariate latent factor decomposition of international bond yield spreads," *Journal of Applied Econometrics*, 15, 697–715.
Engle, R. F. (1982) "Autoregressive conditional heteroskedasticity with estimates of the variance of United Kingdom inflation," *Econometrica*, 50, 987–1007.
Engle, R. F., T. Ito, and W. -L. Lin (1990) "Meteor showers or heat waves? Heteroskedastic intra-daily volatility in the foreign exchange market," *Econometrica*, 58, 525–542.
Engle, R. F., and K. F. Kroner (1995) "Multivariate simultaneous generalized ARCH," *Econometric Theory*, 11, 122–150.
Engle, R. F., and G. G. J. Lee (1996) "Estimating diffusion models of stochastic volatility," in P. E. Rossi (ed.), *Modeling Stock Market Volatility: Bridging the Gap to Continuous Time*. New York: Academic Press, 333–384.
Fisher, R. A. (1912) "On an absolute criterion for fitting frequency curves," *Messages of Mathematics*, 41, 155–157.
Fletcher, R. (1987) *Practical Methods of Optimization (second edition)*. New York: Wiley.
Foster, I. (1995) *Designing Parallel Programs*. Boston: Addison-Wesley. Available at http://www.mcs.anl.gov/dbpp.

Gallant, A. R. (1980) "Explicit estimators of parametric functions in nonlinear regression," *Journal of the American Statistical Association*, 75, 182–193.

Gallant, A. R. (1987) *Nonlinear Statistical Models.* New York: John Wiley and Sons.

Gallant, A. R., and H. Hong (2007) "A statistical inquiry into the plausibility of recursive utility," *Journal of Financial Econometrics*, 5, 523–590.

Gallant, A. R., D. A. Hsieh, and G. Tauchen (1991) "On fitting a recalcitrant series: the Pound/Dollar exchange rate, 1974–83," in W. A. Barnett, J. Powell, and G. E. Tauchen (eds.), *Nonparametric and Semiparametric Methods in Econometrics and Statistics, Proceedings of the Fifth International Symposium in Economic Theory and Econometrics.* Cambridge: Cambridge University Press, Chapter 8, 199–240.

Gallant, A. R., D. A. Hsieh, and G. Tauchen (1997) "Estimation of stochastic volatility models with diagnostics," *Journal of Econometrics*, 81, 159–192.

Gallant, A. R., C.-T. Hsu, and G. Tauchen (1999) "Using daily range data to calibrate volatility diffusions and extract the forward integrated variance," *The Review of Economics and Statistics*, 81(4), 617–631.

Gallant, A. R., and J. Long (1997) "Estimating stochastic differential equations efficiently by minimum chi-squared," *Biometrika*, 84, 125–141.

Gallant, A. R., and R. E. McCulloch (2009) "On the determination of general statistical models with application to asset pricing," *Journal of the American Statistical Association*, 104, 117–131.

Gallant, A. R., and D. W. Nychka (1987) "Semi-nonparametric maximum likelihood estimation," *Econometrica*, 55, 363–390.

Gallant, A. R., P. E. Rossi, and G. Tauchen (1993) "Nonlinear dynamic structures," *Econometrica*, 61, 871–907.

Gallant, A. R., and G. Tauchen (1989) "Semi-nonparametric estimation of conditionally constrained heterogeneous processes: asset pricing applications," *Econometrica*, 57, 1091–1120.

Gallant, A. R., and G. Tauchen (1992) "A nonparametric approach to nonlinear time series analysis: estimation and simulation," in E. Parzen, D. Brillinger, M. Rosenblatt, M. Taqqu, J. Geweke, and P. Caines (eds.), *New Dimensions in Time Series Analysis.* New York: Springer-Verlag, 71–92.

Gallant, A. R., and G. Tauchen (1996) "Which moments to match?," *Econometric Theory*, 12, 657–681.

Gallant, A. R., and G. Tauchen (1997) "Estimation of continuous time models for stock returns and interest rates," *Macroeconomic Dynamics*, 1, 135–168.

Gallant, A. R., and G. Tauchen (1998) "Reprojecting partially observed systems with application to interest rate diffusions," *Journal of the American Statistical Association*, 93, 10–24.

Gallant, A. R., and G. Tauchen (1999) "The relative efficiency of method of moments estimators," *Journal of Econometrics*, 92, 149–172.

Gallant, A. R., and G. Tauchen (2001a) "Efficient method of moments," Manuscript, Duke University. Available at http://econ.duke.edu/webfiles/arg/papers/ee.pdf.

Gallant, A. R., and G. Tauchen (2001b) "EMM: a Program for efficient method of moments estimation, a user's guide," Manuscript, Duke University. Available at http://econ.duke.edu/webfiles/arg/emm.

Gallant, A. R., and G. Tauchen (2001c) "SNP: a program for nonparametric time series analysis, a user's guide," Manuscript, University of North Carolina. Available at http://econ.duke.edu/webfiles/arg/snp.

Gallant, A. R., and H. White (1987) *A Unified Theory of Estimation and Inference for Nonlinear Dynamic Models*. Oxford, UK: Basil Blackwell Ltd.

Gauss, C. F. (1816) "Bestimmung der genauigkeit der beobachtungen," *Zeitschrift für Astronomie und verwandte Wissenschaften*, 1, 185–196.

Gennotte, G., and T. A. Marsh (1993) "Variations in economic uncertainty and risk premiums on capital assets," *European Economic Review*, 37, 1021–1041.

Genton, M. G., and X. de Luna (2000) "Robust simulation-based estimation," *Statistics & Probability Letter*, 48, 253–259.

Genton, M. G., and X. de Luna (2002), "Simulation-based inference for simultaneous processes on regular lattices," *Statistics and Computing*, 12, 125–134.

Geweke, J. (1983) "The approximate slope of econometric tests," *Econometrica*, 49, 1427–1442.

Gourieroux, C., A. Monfort, and E. Renault (1993) "Indirect inference," *Journal of Applied Econometrics*, 8, S85–S118.

Hansen, L. P. (1982) "Large sample properties of generalized method of moments estimators," *Econometrica*, 50, 1029–1054.

Ingram, B. F., and B. S. Lee (1991) "Simulation estimation of time series models," *Journal of Econometrics*, 47, 197–250.

Jiang, G. J., and P. J. van der Sluis (2000) "Option pricing with the efficient method of moments," in Y. S. Abu-Mostafa, B. LeBaron, A. W. Lo, and A. S. Weigend (eds.), *Computational Finance*. Cambridge, MA: MIT Press.

Johnson, N. L., and S. Kotz (1970) *Distributions in Statistics: Continuous Univariate Distributions-1*. New York: Wiley.

Kloeden, P. E., and E. Platen (1992) *Numerical Solution of Stochastic Differential Equations*. New York: Springer-Verlag.

Lo, A. W. (1988) "Maximum likelihood estimation of generalized Ito process with discretely sampled data," *Econometric Theory*, 4, 231–247.

Marron, J. S., and M. P. Wand (1992) "Exact mean integrated squared error," *The Annals of Statistics*, 20, 712–736.

Martin, V. L., and A. R. Pagan (2000) "Simulation based estimation of some factor models in econometrics," in R. Mariano and T. Schuermann (eds.), *Simulation Based Estimation in Econometrics*. Cambridge: Cambridge University Press, 235–254.

McManus D., and D. Watt (1999) "Estimating one factor models of short-term interest rates," Working Paper 99-18, Bank of Canada, Ottawa, Canada.

Mixon, O. S. (1998) "Essays on financial market volatility," Ph.D. Thesis, Duke University.

Nagypal, E. (2007) "Learning-by-doing versus selection: can we tell them apart?," *Review of Economic Studies*, 74, 537–566.

Nelson, D. (1991) "Conditional heteroskedasticity in asset returns: a new approach," *Econometrica*, 59, 347–370.

Neyman, J., and E. S. Pearson (1928) "On the use and interpretation of certain test criteria for purposes of statistical inference," *Biometrika* 20A, 175–240, 263–294.

Ng, S., and A. Michaelides (2000) "Estimating the rational expectations model of speculative storage: a Monte Carlo comparison of three simulation estimators," *Journal of Econometrics*, 96, 231–266.

Pagan, A. (1999) "Some uses of simulation in econometrics," *Mathematics and Computers in Simulation*, 48, 341–349.

Pagan, A. R., A. D. Hall, and V. L. Martin (1996) "Modeling the term structure," in G.S. Maddala and C.R. Rao (eds.), *Statistical Methods in Finance, Handbook of Statistics*, Amsterdam: North-Holland, vol. 13, 91–118.

Pakes, A., and D. Pollard (1989) "Simulation and the asymptotics of optimization estimators," *Econometrica*, 57, 1027–1058.

Pastorello, S., E. Renault, and N. Touzi (2000) "Statistical inference for random variance option pricing," *Journal of Business and Economic Statistics*, 18, 358–367.

Pearson, K. (1894) "Contributions to the mathematical theory of evolution," *Philosophical Transactions of the Royal Society of London, Series A*, 185, 71–78.

Pedroni, P. (2001) "Comment on Chung and Tauchen," *Journal of Business and Economic Statistics*, 19, 271–273.

Schwarz, G. (1978) "Estimating the dimension of a model," *The Annals of Statistics*, 6, 461–464.

Sims, C. A. (1980) "Macroeconomics and reality," *Econometrica*, 48, 1–48.

Smith, A. A. (1990) "Three essays on the solution and estimation of dynamic macroeconomic models," Ph.D. Dissertation, Duke University, Durham, NC.

Smith, A. A. (1993) "Estimating nonlinear time series models using simulated vector autoregressions," *The Journal of Applied Econometrics*, 8, S63–S84.

Tauchen, G. (1985) "Diagnostic testing and evaluation of maximum likelihood models," *Journal of Econometrics*, 30, 415–443.

Tauchen, G. (1997) "New minimum chi-square methods in empirical finance," in D. Kreps and K. Wallis (eds.), *Advances in Econometrics, Seventh World Congress*. Cambridge, UK: Cambridge University Press, 279–317.

Tauchen, G. (1998) "The objective function of simulation estimators near the boundary of the unstable region of the parameter space," *Review of Economics and Statistics*, 80, 389–398.

Valderrama, D. (2001) "Can a standard real business cycle model explain the nonlinearities in U.S. national accounts data?," Ph.D. Thesis Document, Department of Economics, Duke University.

Van der Sluis, P. J. (1997) "EmmPack 1.01: C/C++ code for use with Ox for estimation of univariate stochastic volatility models with the efficient method of moments," *Nonlinear Dynamics and Econometrics*, 2, 77–94.

Van der Sluis, P. J. (1999) "Estimation and inference with the efficient method of moments: with application to stochastic volatility models and option pricing," Manuscript, Tinbergen Institute, Amsterdam, Research Series Paper No. 204.

Zhou, H. (2001) "Finite sample properties of EMM, GMM, QMLE, and MLE for a square-root interest rate diffusion model," *Journal of Computational Finance*, 5, 89–122.

CHAPTER 9

The Econometrics of Option Pricing

René Garcia*, Eric Ghysels,** *and* **Eric Renault*****

* Edhec Business School, Nice, France

** Department of Finance, Kenan-Flagler Business School and Department of Economics, University of North Carolina, Chapel Hill, NC

*** Department of Economics, University of North Carolina, Chapel Hill, NC

Contents

Abstract

Our survey will explore possible explanations for the divergence between the objective and the risk-neutral distributions. Modeling of the dynamics of the underlying asset price is an important part of the puzzle, while another essential element is the existence of time-varying risk premia. The last issue stresses the potentially explicit role to be played by preferences in the pricing of options, a departure from the central tenet of the preference-free paradigm. An important issue for option pricing is whether or not the models deliver closed-form solutions. We will therefore discuss if and when there exists a trade-off between obtaining a good empirical fit or a closed-form option pricing formula. The price of a derivative security is determined by the risk factors affecting the dynamic process of the underlying asset. We start the survey with discrete time models based on the key notion of stochastic discount factor. The analysis in Section 2 allows us to discuss many issues, both theoretical and empirical in a relatively simple and transparent setting. Sections 3 and 4 deal with continuous time processes. Section 3 is devoted to the subject of modeling the so-called objective probability measure, and Section 4 discusses how to recover risk-neutral probability densities in a parametric continuous time setting. Nonparametric approaches to pricing, hedging and recovering state price densities are reviewed in Section 5.

Keywords: stock price dynamics; multivariate jump-diffusion models; latent variables; stochastic volatility; objective and risk-neutral distributions; nonparametric option pricing; discrete-time option pricing models; risk-neutral valuation; preference-free option pricing.

1. INTRODUCTION AND OVERVIEW

To delimit the focus of this survey, we will put emphasis on the more recent contributions because there are already a number of surveys that cover the earlier literature. For example, Bates (1996b) wrote an excellent review, discussing many issues involved in testing option pricing models. Ghysels et al. (1996) and Shephard (1996) provide a detailed analysis of stochastic volatility (SV) modeling, whereas Renault (1997) explores the econometric modeling of option pricing errors. More recently, Sundaresan (2000) surveys the performance of continuous-time methods for option valuation. The material we cover obviously has many seminal contributions that predate the most recent work. Needless to say that due credit will be given to the seminal contributions related to the general topic of estimating and testing option pricing models. A last introductory word of caution: our survey deals almost exclusively with studies that have considered modeling the return process for equity indices and determining the price of European options written on this index.

One of the main advances that marked the econometrics of option pricing in the last 10 years has been the use of price data on both the underlying asset and options to jointly estimate the parameters of the process for the underlying and the risk premia associated with the various sources of risk. Even if important progress has been made regarding econometric procedures, the lesson that can be drawn from the numerous investigations, both parametric and nonparametric, in continuous time or in discrete time, is that the empirical performance still leaves much room for improvement. The empirical option pricing literature has revealed a considerable divergence between the risk-neutral distributions estimated from option prices after the 1987 crash and conditional distributions estimated from time series of returns on the underlying index. Three facts clearly stand out. First, the implied volatility extracted from at-the-money options differs substantially from the realized volatility over the lifetime of the option. Second, risk-neutral distributions feature substantial negative skewness, which is revealed by the asymmetric implied volatility curves when plotted against moneyness. Third, the shape of these volatility curves changes over time and maturities; in other words, the skewness and the convexity are time-varying and maturity-dependent. Our survey will therefore explore possible explanations for the divergence between the objective and the risk-neutral distributions. Modeling of the dynamics of the underlying asset price is an important part of the puzzle, while another essential element is the existence of time-varying risk premia. The last issue stresses the potentially explicit role to be played by preferences in the pricing of options, a departure from the central tenet of the preference-free paradigm.

The main approach to modeling stock returns at the time prior surveys were written was a continuous-time SV diffusion process possibly augmented with an independent jump process in returns. Heston (1993) proposed a SV diffusion model for which one could derive analytically an option pricing formula. Soon thereafter, see, e.g., Duffie and Kan (1996), it was realized that Heston's model belonged to a rich class of affine jump-diffusion (AJD) processes for which one could obtain similar results. Duffie et al. (2000) discuss equity and fixed income derivatives pricing for the general class of AJD. The evidence regarding the empirical fit of the affine class of processes is mixed, see, e.g., Dai and Singleton (2000), Chernov et al. (2003), and Ghysels and Ng (1998) for further discussion. There is a consensus that single volatility factor models, affine (like Heston, 1993) or nonaffine (like Hull and White, 1987 or Wiggins, 1987), do not fit the data (see Andersen et al., 2010; Benzoni, 1998; Chernov et al., 2003; Pan, 2002, among others). How to expand single volatility factor diffusions to mimic the data generating process remains unsettled. Several authors augmented affine SV diffusions with jumps (see Andersen et al., 2001; Bates, 1996a; Chernov et al., 2003; Eraker et al., 2003; Pan, 2002, among others). Bakshi et al. (1997), Bates (2000), Chernov et al. (2003), and Pan (2002) show, however, that SV models with jumps in returns are not able to capture all the empirical features of observed option prices and returns. Bates (2000) and Pan (2002) argue that the specification of the volatility process should include jumps, possibly correlated with the jumps in returns. Chernov et al. (2003) maintain that a two-factor nonaffine logarithmic SV diffusion model without jumps yields a superior empirical fit compared with affine one-factor or two-factor SV processes or SV diffusions with jumps. Alternative models were also proposed: they include volatility models of the Ornstein–Uhlenbeck type but with Lévy innovations (Barndorff-Nielsen and Shephard, 2001) and SV models with long memory in volatility (Breidt et al., 1998; Comte and Renault, 1998).

The statistical fit of the underlying process and the econometric complexities associated with it should not be the only concern, however. An important issue for option pricing is whether or not the models deliver closed-form solutions. We will therefore discuss if and when there exists a trade-off between obtaining a good empirical fit or a closed-form option pricing formula. The dynamics of the underlying fundamental asset cannot be related to option prices without additional assumptions or information. One possibility is to assume that the risks associated with SV or jumps are idiosyncratic and not priced by the market. There is a long tradition of this, but more recent empirical work clearly indicates there are prices for volatility and jump risk (see, e.g., Andersen et al., 2010; Chernov and Ghysels, 2000; Jones, 2003; Pan, 2002, among others). One can simply set values for these premia and use the objective parameters to derive implications for option prices as in Andersen et al. (2001). A more informative exercise is to use option prices to calibrate the parameters under the risk-neutral process given some version of a nonlinear least-squares procedure as in Bakshi et al. (1997) and Bates (2000). An even more ambitious program is to use both the time series data on stock returns and the panel data on option prices to characterize the dynamics of returns with SV and with or without jumps as in Chernov and Ghysels (2000), Pan (2002), Poteshman (2000), and Garcia et al. (2009).

Whether one estimates the objective probability distribution, the risk neutral, or both, there are many challenges in estimating the parameters of diffusions. The presence of latent volatility factors makes maximum likelihood estimation computationally infeasible. This is the area where probably the most progress has been made in the last few years. Several methods have been designed for the estimation of continuous-time dynamic state-variable models with the pricing of options as a major application. Simulation-based methods have been most successful in terms of empirical implementations, which will be reviewed in this chapter.

Nonparametric methods have also been used extensively. Several studies aimed at recovering the risk-neutral probabilities or state-price densities implicit in option or stock prices. For instance, Rubinstein (1996) proposed an implied binomial tree methodology to recover risk-neutral probabilities, which are consistent with a cross-section of option prices. An important issue with the model-free nonparametric approaches is that the recovered risk-neutral probabilities are not always positive and one may consider adding constraints on the pricing function or the state-price densities.

Bates (2000), among others, shows that risk-neutral distributions recovered from option prices before and after the crash of 1987 are fundamentally different, whereas the objective distributions do not show such structural changes. Before the crash, both the risk-neutral and the actual distributions look roughly lognormal. After the crash, the risk-neutral distribution is left skewed and leptokurtic. A possible explanation for the difference is a large change in the risk aversion of the average investor. Because risk aversion can be recovered empirically from the risk-neutral and the actual distributions, Aït-Sahalia and Lo (2000), Jackwerth (2000), and Rosenberg and Engle (2002) estimate preferences for the representative investor using simultaneously S&P500 returns and options prices for contracts on the index. Preferences are recovered based on distance criteria between the model risk-neutral distribution and the risk-neutral distribution implied by option price data.

Another approach of recovering preferences is to set up a representative agent model and estimate the preference parameters from the first-order conditions using a generalized method of moments (GMM) approach. Although this has been extensively done with stock and Treasury bill return data (see Epstein and Zin, 1991; Hansen and Singleton, 1982, among others), it is only more recently that Garcia et al. (2003) estimated preference parameters in a recursive utility framework using option prices. In this survey, we will discuss under which statistical framework option pricing formulas are preference-free and risk-neutral valuation relationships (RNVRs) (Brennan, 1979) hold in a general stochastic discount factor (SDF) framework (Hansen and Richard, 1987). When these statistical restrictions do not hold, it will be shown that preferences play a role. Bates (2007) argues that the overall industrial organization of the stock index option markets is not compatible with the idealized construct of a representative agent. He therefore proposes an equilibrium analysis with investor heterogeneity.

Apart from statistical model fitting, there are a host of other issues pertaining to the implementation of models in practice. A survey by Bates (2003) provides an overview of the issues involved in empirical option pricing, especially the questions surrounding data selection, estimation or calibration of the model, and presentation of results.

The price of a derivative security is determined by the risk factors affecting the dynamic process of the underlying asset. We start the survey with discrete time models based on the key notion of SDF. The analysis in Section 2 allows us to discuss many issues, both theoretical and empirical in a relatively simple and transparent setting. Sections 3 and 4 deal with continuous-time processes. Section 3 is devoted to the subject of modeling the so-called objective probability measure, and Section 4 discusses how to recover risk-neutral probability densities in a parametric continuous-time setting. Nonparametric approaches to pricing, hedging, and recovering state price densities are reviewed in Section 5.

2. PRICING KERNELS, RISK-NEUTRAL PROBABILITIES, AND OPTION PRICING

The widespread acceptance among academics and investment professionals of the Black–Scholes (BS) option pricing formula as a benchmark is undoubtedly due to its usefulness for pricing and hedging options, irrespective of the unrealistic assumptions of the initial model. The purpose of econometrics of option pricing is not really to check the empirical validity of this model. It has been widely documented that by contrast with maintained assumptions of Black and Scholes geometric Brownian motion model, stock return exhibits both stochastic volatility and jumps. Thus, the interesting issue is not the validity of the model itself. In this section, we will rather set the focus on the assessment of the possible errors of the BS option pricing formula and on empirically successful strategies to alleviate them. After all, we can get the right pricing and hedging formula with a wrong model. This is the reason why the largest part of this section is focused on econometric modeling and inference about empirically valid extensions of the BS option pricing formula.

However, it is worth stressing even more generally the econometric content of arbitrage pricing. As first emphasized by Cox et al. (1979), there is a message of the Black and Scholes approach which goes beyond any particular specification of the underlying stochastic processes. Arbitrage-free pricing models generally allow to interpret derivative prices as expectations of discounted payoffs, when expectations are computed with respect to an equivalent martingale measure. It is worth stressing in this respect a nice correspondence between the theory of arbitrage pricing and econometrics of option pricing. Although option contracts are useful to complete the markets and so to get an unique equivalent martingale measure, the statistical observation of option prices is generally informative about the underlying equivalent martingale measure. Although only the historical probability distribution can be estimated from return data on the underlying asset, option prices data allow the econometrician to perform some statistical inference about the relevant martingale measure. This will be the main focus of interest of this chapter. For sake of expositional simplicity, as in Black and Scholes (1972) first empirical tests of their option pricing approach, the option contracts considered in this chapter will be mainly European calls written on stocks. Of course, in the same way, BS option pricing methodology has since been generalized to pricing of many other derivative securities, the econometric approaches sketched below can be extended accordingly.

2.1. Equivalent Martingale Measure and Volatility Smile

Assume that all stochastic processes of interest are adapted in a filtered probability space $(\Omega, (\mathcal{F}_t), P)$. Under standard regularity conditions, the absence of arbitrage is equivalent to the existence of an equivalent martingale measure Q. Without loss of generality, we will consider throughout that the payoffs of options of interest are attainable (see, e.g., Föllmer and Schied, 2004). Then, the arbitrage-free price of these options is defined without ambiguity as expectation under the probability measure Q of the discounted value of their payoff. Moreover, for an European call with maturity T, we will rather characterize its arbitrage price at time $t < T$ as the discounted value at time t of its expectation under the time t forward measure $Q_{t,T}$ for time T. By Bayes rule, $Q_{t,T}$ is straightforwardly defined as equivalent to the restriction of Q on $\mathcal{F}_t$. The density function $dQ_{t,T}/dQ$ is $[B(t,T)]^{-1}(B_t/B_T)$, where B_t stands for the value at time t of a bank account, whereas $B(t,T)$ is the time t price of a pure discount bond (with unit face value) maturing at time T. If K and S_t denote, respectively, the strike price and the price a time t of the underlying stock, the option price C_t a time t is

$$C_t = B(t,T)E^{Q_{t,T}}\mathrm{Max}[0, S_T - K]. \tag{2.1}$$

A formula such (2.1) provides a decomposition of the option price into two components:

$$C_t = S_t \Delta_{1t} - K\Delta_{2t}, \tag{2.2}$$

where

$$\Delta_{2t} = B(t, T) Q_{t,T}[S_T \geq K] \tag{2.3}$$

and

$$\Delta_{1t} = \Delta_{2t} E^{Q_{t,T}}\left[\frac{S_T}{S_t} \mid S_T \geq K\right] \tag{2.4}$$

It follows immediately (see Huang and Litzenberger, 1998, pp. 140, 169) that

$$\Delta_{2t} = -\frac{\partial C_t}{\partial K} \tag{2.5}$$

In other words, a cross-section at time t of European call option prices all maturing at time T, but with different strike prices, K is informative about the pricing probability measure $Q_{t,T}$. In the limit, a continuous observation of the function $K \longrightarrow C_t$ (or of its partial derivative $\partial C_t / \partial K$) would completely characterize the cumulative distribution function of the underlying asset return (S_T/S_t) under $Q_{t,T}$. Let us rather consider it through the probability distribution of the continuously compounded net return on the period $[t, T]$:

$$r_S(t, T) = \log\left[\frac{S_T B(t, T)}{S_t}\right]$$

With (log-forward) moneyness of the option measured by

$$x_t = \log\left[\frac{KB(t, T)}{S_t}\right],$$

the probability distribution under $Q_{t,T}$ of the net return on the stock $r_S(t, T)$ is characterized by its survival function deduced from (2.3) and (2.5) as

$$G_{t,T}(x_t) = -\exp(-x_t)\frac{\partial C_t}{\partial x_t}, \tag{2.6}$$

where

$$C_t(x_t) = \frac{C_t}{S_t} = E^{Q_{t,T}}\{\text{Max}[0, \exp(r_S(t, T)) - \exp(x_t)]\}. \tag{2.7}$$

For the purpose of easy assessment of suitably normalized orders of magnitude, practitioners often prefer to plot as a function of moneyness x_t the BS-implied volatility $\sigma_{t,T}^{\text{imp}}(x_t)$ rather than the option price $C_t(x_t)$ itself. The key reason that makes this sensible is that in the Black and Scholes model, the pricing distribution is indexed by a single volatility parameter σ. Under BS' assumptions, the probability distribution of the net return $r_S(t,T)$ under $Q_{t,T}$ is the normal with mean $(-1/2)(T-t)\sigma^2$ and variance $(T-t)\sigma^2$. Let us denote $\aleph_{t,T}(\sigma)$ this distribution.

Then, the BS-implied volatility $\sigma_{T-t}^{\text{imp}}(x_t)$ is defined as the value of the volatility parameter σ^2, which would generate the observed option price $C(x_t)$ as if the distribution of net return under $Q_{t,T}$ was the normal $\aleph_{t,T}(\sigma)$. In other words, $\sigma_{T-t}^{\text{imp}}(x_t)$ is characterized as solution of the equation:

$$C_t(x_t) = BS_h[x_t, \sigma_h^{\text{imp}}(x_t)] \tag{2.8}$$

where $h = T - t$ and

$$BS_h[x, \sigma] = N[d_1(x, \sigma, h)] - \exp(x)N[d_2(x, \sigma, h)], \tag{2.9}$$

where N is the cumulative distribution function of the standardized normal and

$$d_1(x, \sigma, h) = \frac{-x}{\sigma\sqrt{h}} + \frac{1}{2}h\sigma^2$$

$$d_2(x, \sigma, h) = \frac{-x}{\sigma\sqrt{h}} - \frac{1}{2}h\sigma^2.$$

It is worth reminding that the common use of the BS-implied volatility $\sigma_h^{\text{imp}}(x_t)$ by no mean implies that people think that the BS model is well specified. By (2.8), $\sigma_h^{\text{imp}}(x_t)$ is nothing but a known strictly increasing function of the observed option price $C_t(x_t)$. When plotting the volatility smile as a function $x_t \longrightarrow \sigma_h^{\text{imp}}(x_t)$ rather than $x_t \longrightarrow C_t(x_t)$, people simply consider a convenient rescaling of the characterization (2.6) of the pricing distribution. However, this rescaling depends on x_t and, by definition, produces a flat volatility smile whenever the BS pricing formula is valid in cross-section (for all moneynesses at a given maturity) for some specific value of the volatility parameter. Note that the validity of the BS model itself is only a sufficient but not necessary condition for that.

2.2. How to Graph the Smile?

When the volatility smile is not flat, its pattern obviously depends whether implied volatility $\sigma_h^{\text{imp}}(x_t)$ is plot against strike K, moneyness (K/S_t), forward moneyness $(KB(t,T)/S_t) = \exp(x_t)$, log-forward moneyness x_t, etc. The optimal variable choice of course depends on what kind of information people expect to be revealed immediately when plotting implied volatilities. The common terminology "volatility smile" seems to suggest that people had initially in mind a kind of U-shaped pattern, whereas words like "smirk" or "frown" suggest that the focus is set on frequently observed asymmetries with respect to a symmetric benchmark. Even more explicitly, because the volatility smile is supposed to reveal the underlying pricing probability measure $Q_{t,T}$, a common wisdom is that asymmetries observed in the volatility smile reveal a corresponding skewness in the distribution of (log) return under $Q_{t,T}$. Note in particular that as mentioned above, a flat volatility smile at level σ characterizes a normal distribution with mean $(-\sigma^2/2)$ and variance σ^2.

Beyond the flat case, the common belief of a tight connection between smile asymmetries and risk-neutral skewness requires further qualification. First, the choice of variable must of course matter for discussion of smile asymmetries. We will argue below that log-forward moneyness x_t is the right choice, i.e., the smile asymmetry issue must be understood as a violation of the identity

$$\sigma_h^{\text{imp}}(x_t) = \sigma_h^{\text{imp}}(-x_t). \tag{2.10}$$

This identity is actually necessary and sufficient to deduce from (2.8) that the general option pricing formula (2.7) fulfills the same kind of symmetry property than the Black and Scholes one:

$$C_t(x) = 1 - \exp(x) + \exp(x)C_t(-x). \tag{2.11}$$

Although (2.11) is automatically fulfilled when $C_t(x) = BS_h[x, \sigma]$ [by the symmetry property of the normal distribution: $N(-d) = 1 - N(d)$], it characterizes the symmetry property of the forward measure that corresponds to volatility smile symmetry. It actually mimics the symmetry property of the normal distribution with mean $(-\sigma^2/2)$ and variance σ^2, which would prevail in case of validity of the Black and Scholes model. By differentiation of (2.11) and comparison with (2.6), it can be easily checked that *the volatility smile is symmetric in the sense of (2.10) if and only if, when $f_{t,T}$ stands for the probability density function of the log-return $r_S(t, T)$ under the forward measure $Q_{t,T}$, $\exp(x/2)f_{t,T}(x)$ is an even function of x.*

In conclusion, the relevant concept of symmetry amounts to consider pairs of moneynesses that are symmetric of each other in the following sense:

$$x_{1t} = \log\left[\frac{K_1 B(t, T)}{S_t}\right] = -x_{2t} = \log\left[\frac{S_t}{K_2 B(t, T)}\right].$$

In other words, the geometric mean of the two discounted strike prices coincides with the current stock price:

$$\sqrt{K_1 B(t, T)}\sqrt{K_2 B(t, T)} = S_t.$$

To conclude, it is worth noting that graphing the smile as a function of the log-moneyness x_t is even more relevant when one maintains the natural assumption that option prices are homogeneous functions of degree one with respect to the pair (S_t, K). Merton (1973) had advocated this homogeneity property to preclude any "perverse local concavity" of the option price with respect to the stock price. It is obvious from (2.7) that a sufficient condition for homogeneity is that as in the Black and Scholes case, the pricing probability distribution $Q_{t,T}$ does not depend on the level S_t of the stock price. This is the reason why, as discussed by Garcia and Renault (1998a), homogeneity holds with standard SV option pricing models and does not hold for GARCH option pricing.

For our purpose, the big advantage of the homogeneity assumption is that it allows to compare volatility smiles (for a given time to maturity) at different dates since then the implied volatility $\sigma_h^{\text{imp}}(x_t)$ depends only on moneyness x_t and not directly on the level S_t of the underlying stock price. Moreover, from the Euler characterization of homogeneity:

$$C_t = S_t \frac{\partial C_t}{\partial S_t} + K \frac{\partial C_t}{\partial K}$$

we deduce [by comparing (2.2) and (2.5)] that

$$\Delta_{1t} = \frac{\partial C_t}{\partial S_t} \tag{2.12}$$

is the standard delta-hedging ratio. Note that a common practice is to compute a proxy of Δ_{1t} by plugging $\sigma_h^{\text{imp}}(x_t)$ in the BS delta ratio. Unfortunately, this approximation suffers from a Jensen bias when the correct option price is a mixture of BS prices (see Section 2.5) according to some probability distribution of the volatility parameter. It is shown in Renault and Touzi (1996) and Renault (1997) that the BS delta ratio [computed with $\sigma_h^{\text{imp}}(x_t)$] underestimates (resp. overestimates) the correct ratio Δ_{1t} when the option is in the money (resp. out of the money), i.e., when $x_t < 0$ (resp. $x_t > 0$).

2.3. Stochastic Discount Factors and Pricing Kernels

Since Harrison and Kreps (1979), the so-called "fundamental theorem of asset pricing" relates the absence of arbitrage opportunity on financial markets to the existence of equivalent martingale measures.

The market model is arbitrage-free if and only if the set of all equivalent martingale measures is nonempty. It is a mild version of the old "efficient market hypothesis" that states that discounted prices should obey the fair game rule, i.e., to behave as martingales. Although Lucas (1978) had clearly shown that efficiency should not preclude risk-compensation, the notion of equivalent martingale measures reconciles the points of view. The martingale property and associated "risk-neutral pricing" is recovered for some distortion of the historical probability measure that encapsulates risk compensation. This distortion preserves "equivalence" by ensuring the existence of a strictly positive probability density function.

For the purpose of econometric inference, the concept of risk-neutral pricing may be less well suited because the characterization of a valid equivalent martingale measure depends in a complicated way of the time-span, the frequency of transactions, the filtration of information, and the list of primitive assets involved in self-financing strategies. Following Lucas (1978) and more generally the rational expectations literature, the econometrician rather sets the focus on investors' decisions at every given date, presuming that they know the true probability distributions over states of the world. In general, investors' information will be limited so that the true state of the world is not revealed to them at any point of time. Econometrician's information is even more limited and will always be viewed as a subset of investors' information. This is the reason why Hansen and Richard (1987) have revisited Harrison and Kreps (1979) Hilbert space methods to allow flexible conditioning on well-suited information sets. In a way, the change of probability measure is then introduced for a given date of investment and a given horizon, similarly to the forward equivalent measure.

The equivalent martingale measure approach allows to show the existence at any given date t and for any maturity date $T > t$ of an equivalent forward measure $Q_{t,T}$ such that the price π_t at time t of a future payoff g_T available at time T is

$$\pi_t = B(t, T)E^{Q_{t,T}}[g_T \mid (F_t)]. \tag{2.13}$$

Similarly, Hansen and Richard (1987) directly prove the existence of a strictly positive random variable $M_{t,T}$ such that

$$\pi_t = E_t[M_{t,T}g_T], \tag{2.14}$$

where the generic notation $E_t\{.\}$ is used to denote the historical conditional expectation, given a market-wide information set about which we do not want to be specific. Up to this degree of freedom, there is basically no difference between pricing equations (2.13) and (2.14). First note that (2.14), valid for any payoff, determines in particular the price $B(t, T)$ of a pure discount bond that delivers \$1 at time T:

$$B(t, T) = E_t[M_{t,T}]. \tag{2.15}$$

The discount factor in (2.13), equal to $B(t, T)$, is also the conditional expectation at time t of any variable $M_{t,T}$ conformable to (2.14). Such a variable is called a SDF. Thus, $\frac{M_{t,T}}{B(t,T)}$ is a probability density function that directly defines a forward measure from the historical measure. By contrast, a forward measure is usually defined in mathematical finance from its density with respect to an equivalent martingale measure. The latter involves the specification of the locally risk free spot rate. However, it is not surprising to observe that the issue of market incompleteness which is detrimental in mathematical finance due to the nonuniqueness of an equivalent martingale measure will also affect the econometric methodology of SDF pricing.

In the rest of this section, we discuss the properties of the SDF while overlooking the issue of its lack of uniqueness. It is first worth reminding the economic interpretation of the SDF. With obvious notations, plugging (2.15) into (2.14) allows to rewrite the latter as

$$B(t, T)E_t(R_{t,T}) = 1 - \text{cov}_t\left[R_{t,T}, M_{t,T}\right], \tag{2.16}$$

where $R_{t,T} = \frac{g_T}{\pi_t}$ denotes the return over the period $[t, T]$ on the risky asset with terminal payoff g_T. In other words, the random features of the discounted risky return $B(t, T)R_{t,T}$ allow a positive risk premium (a discounted expected return larger than 1) in proportion of its covariance with the opposite of the SDF.

In the same way, the Bayes rule leads to see risk-neutral densities as multiplicative functionals over aggregated consecutive periods, and we must see the SDF as produced by the relative increments of an underlying pricing kernel process. Let $\tau < T$ be an intermediate trading date between dates t and T. The time T payoff g_T could be purchased at date t, or it could be purchased at date τ with a prior date t purchase of a claim to the date τ purchase price. The "law of one price" guarantees that these two ways to acquire the payoff g_T must have the same initial cost. This recursion argument implies a multiplicative structure on consecutive SDFs. There exists an adapted positive stochastic process m_t called the pricing kernel process such that

$$M_{t,T} = \frac{m_T}{m_t}. \tag{2.17}$$

Following Lucas (1978), a popular example of pricing kernel is based on the consumption process of a representative investor. Under suitable assumptions for preferences and endowment shocks, it is well known that market completeness allows us to introduce a representative investor with utility function U. Assuming that he or she can consume C_t at date t and C_T at the fixed future date T and that he or she receives a given portfolio of financial assets as endowment at date t, the representative investor adjusts the dollar amount invested in each component of the portfolio at each intermediary date to maximize the expected utility of his or her terminal consumption at time T. In equilibrium, the investor optimally invests all his or her wealth in the given portfolio and then consumes its terminal value C_T. Thus, the Euler first-order condition for optimality imposes that the price π_t at time t of any contingent claim that delivers the dollar amount g_T at time t is such that

$$\pi_t = E_t\left[\beta^{T-t}\frac{U'(C_T)}{U'(C_t)}g_T\right], \tag{2.18}$$

where β is the subjective discount parameter of the investor. For instance, with a constant relative risk aversion (CRRA) specification of the utility function, $U'(C) = C^{-a}$ where $a \geq 0$ is the Arrow-Pratt measure of relative risk aversion, and we have the consumption-based pricing-kernel process:

$$m_t = \beta^t C_t^{-a}. \tag{2.19}$$

2.4. Black–Scholes-Implied Volatility as a Calibrated Parameter

It is convenient to rewrite the call pricing equation (2.1) in terms of pricing kernel:

$$C_t = E_t\left[\frac{m_T}{m_t}\text{Max}[0, S_T - K]\right]. \tag{2.20}$$

It is then easy to check that the call pricing formula collapses into the BS one when the two following conditions are fulfilled:

- The conditional distribution given $\mathcal{F}_t$ of the log-return $\log\left[\frac{S_T}{S_t}\right]$ is normal with constant variance σ and
- The log-pricing kernel $\log(\frac{m_T}{m_t})$ is perfectly correlated to the log-return on the stock.

An important example of such a perfect correlation is the consumption-based pricing kernel described above when the investor's initial endowment is only one share of the stock such that he or she consumes the terminal value $S_T = C_T$ of the stock. Then,

$$\log\left[\frac{m_T}{m_t}\right] = -a\log\left[\frac{S_T}{S_t}\right] + (T-t)\log(\beta). \tag{2.21}$$

We will get a first interesting generalization of the BS formula by considering now that the log-return $\log[\frac{S_T}{S_t}]$ and the log-pricing kernel $\log(m_{t,T})$ may be jointly normally distributed given $\mathcal{F}_t$, with conditional moments possibly depending on the conditional information at time t. Interestingly enough, it can be shown that the call price computed from formula (2.20) with this joint conditional lognormal distribution will depend explicitly on the conditional moments only through the conditional stock volatility:

$$(T-t)\sigma_{t,T}^2 = \text{Var}_t\left[\log\left(\frac{S_T}{S_t}\right)\right]$$

More precisely, we get the following option pricing formula:

$$C_t = S_t BS_{T-t}[x_t, \sigma_{t,T-t}]. \tag{2.22}$$

The formula (2.22) is actually a generalization of the RNVR put forward by Brennan (1979) in the particular case (2.19). With joint lognormality of return and pricing kernel, we are back to a Black and Scholes functional form due to the Cameron–Martin formula (a static version of Girsanov's theorem), which tells us that when X and Y are jointly normal:

$$E\{\exp(X)g(Y)\} = E[\exp(X)]E\{g[Y + \text{cov}(X, Y)]\}$$

Although the term $E[\exp(X)]$ will give $B(t, T)$ [with $X = \log(m_{t,T})$], the term $\text{cov}(X, Y)$ (with $Y = \log[S_T/S_t]$) will make the risk-neutralization because $E\{\exp(X)\exp(Y)\}$ must be one as it equals $E[\exp(X)]E\{\exp[Y + \text{cov}(X, Y)]\}$.

From an econometric viewpoint, the interest of (2.22), when compared with (2.8), is to deliver a flat volatility smile but with an implied volatility level which may be time varying and corresponds to the conditional variance of the conditionally lognormal stock return. In other words, the time-varying volatility of the stock becomes observable as calibrated from option prices:

$$\sigma_{t,T} = \sigma_{T-t}^{\text{imp}}(x_t), \quad \forall x_t$$

The weakness of this approach is its lack of robustness with respect to temporal aggregation. In the GARCH-type literature, stock returns may be conditionally lognormal when they are considered on the elementary period of the discrete time setting ($T = t + 1$), whereas implied time-aggregated dynamics are more complicated. This is the reason why the GARCH-option pricing literature (Duan, 1995 and Heston and Nandi, 2000) maintains the formula (2.22) only for $T = t + 1$. Nonflat volatility smiles may be observed with longer times to maturity. Kallsen and Taqqu (1998) provide a continuous-time interpretation of such GARCH option pricing.

2.5. Black–Scholes-Implied Volatility as an Expected Average Volatility

To account for excess kurtosis and skewness in stock log-returns, a fast empirical approach amounts to consider that the option price a time t is given by a weighted average:

$$\alpha_t S_t BS_h[x_t, \sigma_{1t}] + (1 - \alpha_t) S_t BS_h[x_t, \sigma_{2t}]. \qquad (2.23)$$

The rationale for (2.23) is to consider that a mixture of two normal distributions with standard errors σ_{1t} and σ_{2t} and weights α_t and $(1 - \alpha_t)$, respectively, may account for both skewness and excess kurtosis in stock log-return. The problem with this naive approach is that it does not take into account any risk premium associated to the mixture component. More precisely, if we want to accommodate a mixture of normal distributions with a mixing variable $U_{t,T}$, we can rewrite (2.20) as

$$C_t = E^P\{E^P[M_{t,T}\text{Max}[0, S_T - K] \mid \mathcal{F}_t, U_{t,T}] \mid \mathcal{F}_t\}, \qquad (2.24)$$

where, for each possible value $u_{t,T}$ of $U_{t,T}$, a BS formula like (2.22) is valid to compute

$$E^P\left[M_{t,T}\mathrm{Max}[0, S_T - K] \mid \mathcal{F}_t, U_{t,T} = u_{t,T}\right].$$

In other words, it is true that as in (2.23), the conditional expectation operator [given (F_t)] in (2.24) displays the option price as a weighted average of different BS prices with the weights corresponding to the probabilities of the possible values $u_{t,T}$ of the mixing variable $U_{t,T}$. However, the naive approach (2.23) is applied in a wrong way when forgetting that the additional conditioning information $U_{t,T}$ should lead to modify some key inputs in the BS option pricing formula. Suppose that investors are told that the mixing variable $U_{t,T}$ will take the value $u_{t,T}$. Then, the current stock price would no longer be

$$S_t = E^P\left[M_{t,T}S_T \mid \mathcal{F}_t\right]$$

but instead

$$S_t^*(u_{t,T}) = E^P\left[M_{t,T}S_T \mid \mathcal{F}_t, U_{t,T} = u_{t,T}\right]. \tag{2.25}$$

For the same reason, the pure discount bond that delivers \$1 at time T will no longer be priced at time t as

$$B(t, T) = E^P\left[M_{t,T} \mid \mathcal{F}_t\right]$$

but rather

$$B^*(t, T)(u_{t,T}) = E^P\left[M_{t,T} \mid \mathcal{F}_t, U_{t,T} = u_{t,T}\right]. \tag{2.26}$$

Hence, various BS option prices that are averaged in a mixture approach like (2.23) must be computed, no longer with actual values $B(t, T)$ and S_t of the current bond and stock prices but with values $B^*(t, T)(u_{t,T})$ and $S_t^*(u_{t,T})$ not directly observed but computed from (2.26) and (2.25). In particular, the key inputs, underlying stock price and interest rate, should be different in various applications of the BS formulas like $BS_h[x, \sigma_1]$ and $BS_h[x, \sigma_2]$ in (2.23). This remark is crucial for the conditional Monte Carlo approach, as developed for instance in Willard (1997) in the context of option pricing with SV. Revisiting a formula initially derived by Romano and Touzi (1997), Willard (1997) notes that the variance reduction technique, known as conditional Monte Carlo, can be applied even when the conditioning factor (the SV process) is instantaneously correlated with the stock return as it is the case when leverage effect is present. He stresses that "by conditioning on the entire path of the noise element in the volatility (instead of just the average volatility), we can still write the option's price as an expectation over Black-Scholes prices by appropriately adjusting the arguments to the Black-Scholes formula". Willard's (1997) "appropriate adjustment" of the stock price is actually akin to (2.25). Moreover, he does not explicitly adjust the interest rate according to (2.26) and works with a fixed risk-neutral distribution. The Generalized Black–Scholes (GBS) option pricing below makes the required adjustments explicit.

2.6. Generalized Black–Scholes Option Pricing Formula

Let us specify the continuous-time dynamics of a pricing kernel $M_{t,T}$ as the relative increment of a pricing kernel process m_t according to (2.17). The key idea of the mixture model is then to define a conditioning variable $U_{t,T}$ such that the pricing kernel process and the stock price process jointly follow a bivariate geometric Brownian motion under the historical conditional probability distribution given $U_{t,T}$. The mixing variable $U_{t,T}$ will typically show up as a function of a state variable path $(X_\tau)_{t\leq\tau\leq T}$. More precisely, we specify the jump-diffusion model

$$d(\log S_t) = \mu(X_t)dt + \alpha(X_t)dW_{1t} + \beta(X_t)dW_{2t} + \gamma_t dN_t \tag{2.27}$$

$$d(\log m_t) = h(X_t)dt + a(X_t)dW_{1t} + b(X_t)dW_{2t} + c_t dN_t, \tag{2.28}$$

where (W_{1t}, W_{2t}) is a two-dimensional standard Brownian motion, N_t is a Poisson process with intensity $\lambda(X_t)$ depending on the state variable X_t, and the jump sizes c_t and γ_t are i.i.d. independent normal variables independent of the state variable process (X_t). The Brownian motion (W_{1t}) is assumed to be part of the state variable vector (X_t) to capture the possible instantaneous correlation between ex-jump volatility of the stock [as measured by $V_t = \alpha^2(X_t) + \beta^2(X_t)$] and its Brownian innovation. More precisely, the correlation coefficient $\rho(X_t) = \frac{\alpha(X_t)}{\sqrt{V_t}}$ measures the so-called leverage effect.

The jump-diffusion model [(2.27) and (2.28)] is devised such that given the state variables path $(X_\tau)_{t\leq\tau\leq T}$ as well as the number $(N_T - N_t)$ of jumps between times t and T, the joint normality of $(\log S_T, \log m_T)$ is maintained. This remark allows us to derive a GBS option pricing formula by application of (2.24) and (2.22):

$$C_t = S_t E^P\left[\xi_{t,T} BS_{T-t}(x_t^*, \sigma_{t,T}) \mid \mathcal{F}_t\right], \tag{2.29}$$

where

$$\sigma_{t,T}^2 = \int_t^T \left[1 - \rho^2(X_\tau)\right] V_\tau d\tau + (N_T - N_t)\mathrm{Var}(\gamma_t) \tag{2.30}$$

and

$$x_t^* = \log\left[\frac{KB^*(t,T)}{S_t \xi_{t,T}}\right],$$

where $S_t\xi_{t,T}$ and $B^*(t,T)$ correspond, respectively, to $S_t^*(u_{t,T})$ and $B^*(t,T)(u_{t,T})$ defined in (2.25) and (2.26). General computations of these quantities in the context of a jump-diffusion model can be found in Yoon (2008). Let us exemplify these formulas when there is no jump. Then, we can define a short-term interest rate as

$$r(X_t) = -h(X_t) - \frac{1}{2}\left[a^2(X_t) + b^2(X_t)\right]$$

and then

$$B^*(t,T) = \exp\left[-\int_t^T r(X_\tau)\mathrm{d}\tau\right]\exp\left[\int_t^T a(X_\tau)\mathrm{d}W_{1\tau} - \frac{1}{2}\int_t^T a^2(X_\tau)\mathrm{d}\tau\right] \tag{2.31}$$

and

$$\xi_{t,T} = \exp\left[\int_t^T [a(X_\tau) + \alpha(X_\tau)]\mathrm{d}W_{1\tau} - \frac{1}{2}\int_t^T [a(X_\tau) + \alpha(X_\tau)]^2\mathrm{d}\tau\right]. \tag{2.32}$$

It may be easily checked in particular that

$$B(t,T) = E^P\left[B^*(t,T) \mid \mathcal{F}_t\right]$$

and

$$S_t = E^P\left[S_t\xi_{t,T} \mid \mathcal{F}_t\right].$$

Let us neglect for the moment the difference between $S_t\xi_{t,T}$ and $B^*(t,T)$ and their respective expectations S_t and $B(t,T)$. It is then clear that the GBS formula warrants the interpretation of the BS-implied volatility $\sigma_{T-t}^{\text{imp}}(x_t)$ as approximatively an expected average volatility. Up to Jensen effects (nonlinearity of the BS formula with respect to volatility), the GBS formula would actually give

$$\left[\sigma_{T-t}^{\text{imp}}(x_t)\right]^2 = E^P\left[\sigma_{t,T}^2 \mid \mathcal{F}_t\right]. \tag{2.33}$$

The likely impact of the difference between $S_t\xi_{t,T}$ and $B^*(t,T)$ and their respective expectations S_t and $B(t,T)$ is twofold. First, a nonzero function $a(X_\tau)$ must be understood as a risk premium on the volatility risk. In other words, the above interpretation of $\sigma_{T-t}^{\text{imp}}(x_t)$ as approximatively an expected average volatility can be maintained by using risk-neutral expectations. Considering the BS-implied volatility as a predictor of volatility over the lifetime of the option is tantamount to neglect the volatility risk premium. Beyond this risk premium effect, the leverage effect $\rho(X_t)$ will distort this interpretation through its joint impact on $\sigma_{t,T}^2$ and on $\xi_{t,T}$ as well (through $\alpha(X_t) = \rho(X_t)\sqrt{V_t}$).

Although Renault and Touzi (1996) have shown that we will get a symmetric volatility smile in case of zero-leverage, Renault (1997) explains that with nonzero leverage, the implied distortion of the stock price by the factor $\xi_{t,T}$ will produce asymmetric volatility smirks. Yoon (2008) characterizes more precisely the cumulated impact of the two effects of leverage and shows that they compensate each other almost exactly for at the money options, confirming the empirical evidence documented by Chernov (2007). Finally, Comte and Renault (1998) long-memory volatility model explains that in spite of the time averaging in (2.30), (2.33) the volatility smile does not become flat even for long-term options.

It is worth stressing that the fact that $S_t\xi_{t,T}$ and $B^*(t, T)$ may not coincide with their respective expectations S_t and $B(t, T)$ implies that, by contrast with the standard BS option pricing, the GBS formula is not preference free. Although in preference-free option pricing, the preference parameters are hidden within the observed value of the bond price and the stock price, and the explicit impact of the volatility risk premium function $a(X_t)$ in the formulas (2.32) and (2.31) for $\xi_{t,T}$ and $B^*(t, T)$ is likely to result in an explicit occurrence of preference parameters within the option pricing formula (see Garcia et al., 2005, and references therein for a general discussion). Although Garcia and Renault (1988b) characterize the respective impacts of risk aversion and elasticity of intertemporal substitution on option prices, Garcia et al. (2003) set the focus on the converse property. Because the impact of preference parameters on option prices should be beyond their role in bond and stock prices, option price data are likely to be even more informative about preference parameters. This hypothesis is strikingly confirmed by their econometric estimation of preference parameters.

Although properly taking into account the difference between historical and risk-neutral expectations, the tight connection [(2.30) and (2.33)] between BS-implied volatility and the underlying volatility process ($\sqrt{V_t}$) has inspired a strand of literature on estimating volatility dynamics from option prices data. Pastorello et al. (2000) consider directly $[\sigma_{T-t}^{\text{imp}}(x_t)]^2$ as a proxy for squared spot volatility V_t and correct the resulting approximation bias in estimating volatility dynamics by indirect inference. The "implied-states approach" described in Section 4 uses more efficiently the exact relationship between $\sigma_{T-t}^{\text{imp}}(x_t)$ and V_t, as given by (2.29), (2.30) for a given spot volatility model, to estimate the volatility parameters by maximum likelihood or GMM.

3. MODELING ASSET PRICE DYNAMICS VIA DIFFUSIONS FOR THE PURPOSE OF OPTION PRICING

Because the seminal papers by Black and Scholes (1973) and Merton (1973), the greater part of option pricing models have been based on parametric continuous-time models for the underlying asset. The overwhelming rejection of the constant variance geometric Brownian motion lead to a new class of SV models introduced by Hull and White (1987) and reviewed in Ghysels et al. (1996). Although the models in the SV class are by now well established, there are still a number of unresolved issues about their empirical performance.

The work by Heston (1993), who proposed a SV diffusion with an analytical option pricing formula, was generalized by Duffie and Kan (1996) and Duffie et al. (2000) to a rich class of AJD. This class will be reviewed in a first subsection. Alternative models, mostly nonaffine, will be covered in the second subsection. A final subsection discusses option pricing without estimated prices of risk.

3.1. The Affine Jump-Diffusion Class of Models

The general class of AJD models examined in detail by Duffie et al. (2000) includes as special cases many option pricing models that have been the object of much econometric analysis in the past few years. To describe the class of processes, consider the following return dynamics, where $\mathrm{d}\log S_t = \mathrm{d}U_{1t}$ with U_{1t} is the first element of a vector process N-dimensional U_t, which represents the continuous path diffusion component of the return process, and the second term $\exp \Delta X_t - \iota$ represents discrete jumps, where X_t is a N-dimensional Lévy process and ι is a vector of ones. The process U_t is governed by the following equations:

$$\mathrm{d}U_t = \mu(U_t, t)\mathrm{d}t + \sigma(U_t, t)\mathrm{d}W_t + \exp \Delta X_t - \iota, \tag{3.1}$$

where the process U_t is Markovian and takes values in an open subset D of $\mathbf{R}^N$, $\mu(y) = \Theta + \mathcal{K}y$ with $\mu : D \to \mathbf{R}^N$ and $\sigma(y)\sigma(y)' = h + \sum_{j=1}^{N} y_j H^{(j)}$ where $\sigma : D \to \mathbf{R}^{N\times N}$. Moreover, the vector Θ is $N \times 1$, the matrix $\mathcal{K}$ is $N \times N$, whereas h and H are all symmetric $N \times N$ matrices. The process W_t is a standard Brownian motion in $\mathbf{R}^N$. Although the first component of the U_t process relates to returns, the other components U_{it} for $i = 2, \ldots, N$ govern either the stochastic drift or volatility of returns.[1] This setup is a general affine structure that allows for jumps in returns (affecting the first component U_{1t}) and the less common situation of jumps in volatility factors (affecting the components U_{it} that determine volatility factors). Empirical models for equity have at most $N = 4$, where the U_{2t} affects the drift of U_{1t} and U_{3t} and U_{4t} affect either the volatility or jump intensity (see, e.g., Chernov et al., 2000, 2003). We will start with single volatility factor models, followed by a discussion of jump diffusions and models with multiple volatility factors.

3.1.1. Models with a Single Volatility Factor

The class is defined as the following system of stochastic differential equations:

$$\begin{pmatrix} \mathrm{d}Y_t \\ \mathrm{d}V_t \end{pmatrix} = \begin{pmatrix} \mu \\ \kappa(\theta - V_t) \end{pmatrix}\mathrm{d}t + \sqrt{V_t}\begin{pmatrix} 1 & 0 \\ \rho\sigma_v & \sqrt{(1-\rho^2)}\sigma_v \end{pmatrix}\mathrm{d}W_t + \xi \mathrm{d}N_t, \tag{3.2}$$

[1] All further details regarding the regularity conditions pertaining to the U_t are discussed by Duffie et al. (2000) and therefore omitted.

where Y_t is the logarithm of the asset price S_t, $W_t = (W_{1t}, W_{2t})'$ is a vector of independent standard Brownian motions, $N_t = (N_t^y, N_t^v)'$ is a vector of Poisson processes with constant arrival intensities λ_y and λ_v, and $\xi = (\xi^y, \xi^v)'$ is a vector of jump sizes for returns and volatility, respectively.[2] We adopt the mnemonics used by Duffie et al. and Eraker et al. (2003): SV for SV models with no jumps in returns nor volatility $(\lambda_y = \lambda_v = 0)$, SVJ for SV models with jumps in returns only $(\lambda_y > 0, \lambda_v = 0)$, and SVJJ for SV models with jumps in returns and volatility $(\lambda_y > 0, \lambda_v > 0)$. In SVJ, the jump size is distributed normally, $\xi^y \sim \mathcal{N}(\mu_y, \sigma_y^2)$. The SVJJ can be split into the SVIJ model [with independent jump arrivals in returns and volatility and independent jump sizes $\xi^y \sim \mathcal{N}(\mu_y, \sigma_y^2)$ and $\xi^v \sim \exp(\mu_v)$] and the SVCJ model [with contemporaneous Poisson jump arrivals in returns and volatility, $N_t^y = N_t^v$ with arrival rate λ_y and correlated sizes $\xi^v \sim \exp(\mu_v)$ and $\xi^y|\xi^v \sim \mathcal{N}(\mu_y + \rho_J \xi^v, \sigma_y^2)$].

A number of papers have investigated the Heston (1993) SV model. Most papers (Andersen et al., 2010; Benzoni, 1998; Eraker et al., 2003) conclude that the SV model provides a much better fit of stock return than standard one-factor diffusions. In particular, the strong negative correlation around -0.4 found between the volatility shocks and the underlying stock return shocks captures well the negative skewness observed in stock returns. However, the model is rejected because it is unable to accommodate the excess kurtosis observed in the stock returns.[3] Basically, it cannot fit the large changes in stock prices occurring during crash-like events. In the SV model, there is a strong volatility persistence (the estimated value for the mean reversion parameter κ is in the order of 0.02).

Adding jumps in returns appears therefore natural because the continuous path SV accommodates the clustered random changes in the returns volatility, whereas the discrete Poisson jump captures the large infrequent price movements. However, jump components are difficult to estimate and complicate the extraction of the volatility process.[4] Eraker et al. (2003) propose a likelihood-based methodology using Markov Chain Monte Carlo methods (see also Jones, 2003). Their estimation results for the period 1980–1999 show that the introduction of jumps in returns in the SVJ model has an important downward impact on the parameters of the volatility process. The parameters for average volatility, the volatility of volatility, and the speed of mean reversion all fall dramatically. This is somewhat consistent with the results of Andersen et al. (2010) when they estimate the models from 1980 till 1996 but with less magnitude. However, in the latter study,

[2]A specification with βV_t in the drift of the returns equation was considered by Eraker et al. (2003). This additional term was found to be insignificant, in accordance with the findings of Andersen et al. (2001) and Pan (2002).

[3]Both Andersen et al. (2001) and Benzoni (1998) estimate a nonaffine specification with the log variance. The model fits slightly better than the affine SV model, but it is still strongly rejected by the data. Jones (2003) estimates a SV model with CEV volatility dynamics, but it generates too many extreme observations.

[4]For a discussion of the different types of volatility filters, see Ghysels et al. (1996) and the chapter of Gallant and Tauchen (2010) in this Handbook.

parameters associated with volatility change much less when the models are estimated over a longer period (1953 to 1996). The difference between the two latter studies is to be found in the estimates of the jump process. In Eraker et al. (2003), jumps arrive relatively infrequently, about 1.5 jumps per year, and are typically large. The jump mean is −2.6%, and the volatility is just over 4%. The large sizes of jumps are in contrast with the smaller estimates (μ_y of zero and σ_y less than 2%) obtained by Andersen et al. (2010) and Chernov et al. (2003). The introduction of jumps lowers the negative correlation between the innovations in returns and the innovations in volatility. In all studies, the SVJ model appears to be less misspecified than the SV model.

All econometric complexities put aside, other issues remain. Adding jumps resolve the misfit of the kurtosis on the *marginal* distribution of returns, but one may suspect that the dynamic patterns of extreme events are not particularly well captured by an independent Poisson process. The stochastic structure of a one-factor SV model augmented with a Poisson jump process implies that the day after a stock market crash another crash is equally likely as the day before. In addition, the occurrence of jumps is independent of volatility. Clearly, the independent Poisson process has unappealing properties, and therefore, some alternative models for jumps, i.e., alternative Lévy specifications, have been suggested. Bates (2000) estimated a class of jump-diffusions with random intensity for the jump process, more specifically where the intensity is an affine function of the SV component. Duffie et al. (2000) generalize this class, and Chernov et al. (2000), Eraker et al. (2003), and Pan (2002) estimate multifactor jump-diffusion models with affine stochastic jump intensity. The models considered by Duffie et al. are

$$\lambda(U_t) = \lambda_0(t) + \lambda_1(t)U_t, \tag{3.3}$$

where the process U_t is of the affine class as V_t specified in (3.2). These structures may not be entirely suitable either to accommodate some stylized facts. Suppose one ties the intensity to the volatility factor V_t in (3.2), meaning that high volatilities imply high probability of a jump. This feature does not take into account an asymmetry one observes with extreme events. For instance, the day before the 1987 stock market crash the volatility measured by the squared return on the S&P 500 index was roughly the same as the day after the crash. Therefore, in this case making, the intensity of a crash a linear affine function of volatility would result in the probability of a crash the day after Black Monday being the same as the trading day before the crash. Obviously, one could assign a factor specific to the jump intensity and governed by an affine diffusion. Hence, one adds a separate factor U_t that may be correlated with the volatility factor V_t. Pan (2002) examines such processes and provides empirical estimates. Chernov et al. (2000) and Eraker et al. (2003) consider also a slightly more general class of processes:

$$\lambda(x, U) = \lambda_0(x, t) + \lambda_1(x, t)U_t, \tag{3.4}$$

where for instance $\lambda_i(x,t) = \lambda_i(t)\exp(G(x))$. This specification yields a class of jump Lévy measures which combines the features of jump intensities depending on, say volatility, as well as the size of the previous jump. The virtue of the alternative more complex specifications is that the jump process is no longer independent of the volatility process, and extreme events are more likely during volatile market conditions. There is, however, an obvious drawback to the introduction of more complex Lévy measures, as they involve a much more complex parametric structure. Take, e.g., the case where the jump intensity in (3.3) is a function of a separate stochastic factor U_t correlated with the volatility process V_t. Such a specification may involve up to six additional parameters to determine the jump intensity, without specifying the size distribution of jump. Chernov et al. (2000) endeavor into the estimation of various complex jump processes using more than a 100 years of daily Dow Jones data and find that it is not possible to estimate rich parametric specifications for jumps eve with such long data sets.[5]

Despite all these reservations about jump processes, one has to note that various papers have not only examined the econometric estimation but also the derivative security pricing with such processes. In particular, Bakshi and Madan (2000) and Duffie et al. (2000) provide very elegant general discussions of the class of AJDs with SV, which yield analytic solutions to derivative security pricing. One has nevertheless to bear in mind the empirical issues that are involved. A good example is the affine diffusion with jumps. In such a model, there is a price of jump risk and a price of risk for jump size, in addition to the continuous path volatility factor risk price and return risk. Hence, there are many risk prices to be specified in such models. Moreover, complex specifications of the jump process with state-dependent jump intensity result in an even larger number of prices of risk.

3.1.2. Multiple Volatility Factors

Affine diffusion models are characterized by drift and variance functions, which are linear functions of the factors. Instead of considering additional factors that govern jump intensities, one might think of adding more continuous path volatility factors. Dai and Singleton (2000) discuss the most general specification of such models including the identification and admissibility conditions. Let us reconsider the specification of V_t in (3.2) and add a stochastic factor to the drift of returns, namely

$$\begin{aligned}
\mathrm{d}Y_t &= (\alpha_{10} + \alpha_{12}U_{1t})\mathrm{d}t + \sqrt{\beta_{10} + \beta_{12}U_{2t} + \beta_{13}U_{3t}}(\mathrm{d}W_{1t} + \psi_{12}\mathrm{d}W_{2t} + \psi_{13}\mathrm{d}W_{3t})\\
\mathrm{d}U_{1t} &= (\alpha_{20} + \alpha_{22}U_{1t})\mathrm{d}t + \beta_{20}\mathrm{d}W_{2t} \qquad (3.5)\\
\mathrm{d}U_{it} &= (\alpha_{i0} + \alpha_{ii}U_{it})\mathrm{d}t + \sqrt{\beta_{i0} + \beta_{ii}U_{it}}\mathrm{d}W_{it}, \quad i = 2, 3.
\end{aligned}$$

[5] Chernov et al. (2000) also examine nonaffine Lévy processes, which will be covered in the next subsection.

The volatility factors enter additively into the diffusion component specification. Hence, they could be interpreted as short- and long-memory components as in Engle and Lee (1999). The long-memory (persistent) component should be responsible for the main part of the returns distribution, whereas the short-memory component will accommodate the extreme observations. This specification allows feedback, in the sense that the volatilities of the volatility factors can be high via the terms $\beta_{ii}U_{it}$ when the volatility factors themselves are high. Adding a second volatility factor helps fitting the kurtosis, using arguments similar to those that explain why jumps help fitting the tails. The extra freedom to fit tails provided by an extra volatility factor has its limitations, however, as noted by Chernov et al. (2003). In fact, their best model, which does fit the data at conventional levels, is not an affine model (see next subsection).

Bates (2000) and Pan (2002) argue that the specification of the volatility process should include jumps, possibly correlated with the jumps in returns. This is an alternative to expanding the number of volatility factors. It has the advantage that one can fit the persistence in volatility through a regular affine specification of V_t and have extreme shocks to volatility as well through the jumps, hence capturing in a single volatility process enough rich features that simultaneously fit the clustering of volatility and the tails of returns. The drawback is that one has to identify jumps in volatility, a task certainly not easier than identifying jumps in returns.

3.2. Other Continuous-Time Processes

By other continuous-time processes, we mean a large class of processes that are either nonaffine or affine but do not involve the usual jump-diffusion processes but more general Lévy processes or fractional Brownian motions. Three subsections describe the various models that have been suggested.

3.2.1. Nonaffine Index Models

Another way to capture the small and large movements in returns is to specify SV models with two factors as in Chernov et al. (2003). They propose to replace the affine setup (3.5) by some general volatility index function $\sigma(U_{2t}, U_{3t})$ able to disentangle the effects of U_{2t} and U_{3t} separately and therefore have a different effect of short- and long-memory volatility components. In particular, they consider

$$\sigma(U_{2t}, U_{3t}) = \exp(\beta_{10} + \beta_{12}U_{2t} + \beta_{13}U_{3t}) \tag{3.6}$$

$$dU_{it} = (\alpha_{i0} + \alpha_{ii}U_{it})\,dt + (\beta_{i0} + \beta_{ii}U_{it})\,dW_{it}, \quad i = 2, 3 \tag{3.7}$$

Chernov et al. (2003) study two different flavors of the logarithmic models, depending on the value of the coefficients β_{ii}. When $\beta_{ii} = 0$, the volatility factors are described by Ornstein–Uhlenbeck processes. In this case, the drift and variance of these factors are linear functions, and hence, the model can be described as logarithmic or log-affine.

Whenever, $\beta_{ii} \neq 0$ either for $i = 2$ or for $i = 3$, there is feedback, a feature found to be important in Gallant et al. (1999) and Jones (2003). The exponential specification in (3.6) is of course not the only index function one can consider.

Chernov et al. (2003) show that the exponential specification with two volatility factors (without jumps) yields a remarkably good empirical fit, i.e., the model is not rejected at conventional significance levels unlike the jump-diffusion and affine two-factor models discussed in the previous section. Others have also found that such processes fit very well, see for instance Alizadeh et al. (2002), Chacko and Viceira (1999), Gallant et al. (1999), and the two-factor GARCH model of Engle and Lee (1999). The fact that logarithmic volatility factors are used, instead of the affine specification, adds the flexibility of state-dependent volatility as noted by Jones (2003). In addition, an appealing feature of the logarithmic specification is the multiplicative effect of volatility factors on returns. One volatility factor takes care of long memory, whereas the second factor is fast mean-reverting (but not a spike like a jump). This property of logarithmic models facilitates mimicking the very short-lived but erratic extreme event behavior through the second volatility factor. Neither one volatility factor models with jumps nor affine two-factor specifications are well equipped to handle such patterns typically found during financial crises.

It should also be noted that the two-factor logarithmic specification avoids several econometric issues. We noted that the presence of jumps also considerably complicates the extraction of the latent volatility and jump components because traditional filters no longer apply. In contrast, the continuous path two-factor logarithmic SV process does not pose any difficulties for filtering via reprojection methods as shown by Chernov et al. (2003). There is another appealing property to the two-factor logarithmic SV model: the model has a smaller number of risk factors compared to many of the alternative specifications, specifically those involving complex jump process features. The major drawback of this class of processes, however, is the lack of an explicit option pricing formula: simulation-based option pricing is the only approach available.

3.2.2. Lévy Processes and Time Deformation

It was noted before that one could easily relax normality in discrete time models through the introduction of mixture distributions. Likewise, in the context of continuous-time models, it was noted that one can replace Brownian motions by so-called Lévy processes. The typical setup is through subordination, also referred to as time deformation, an approach suggested first in the context of asset pricing by Clark (1973) and used subsequently in various settings. The idea to use a Lévy process to change time scales and thus random changes in volatility can be interpreted as a clock ticking at the speed of information arrival in the market. For further discussion, see, e.g., Barndorff-Nielsen and Shephard (2001), Clark (1973), Ghysels et al. (1997), Madan and Seneta (1990), and Tauchen and Pitts (1983), among many others.

The purpose of this section is to survey the option pricing implications of assuming the broader class of time deformed Lévy processes. Various authors have studied option pricing with this class of processes, including Carr et al. (2003), Carr and Wu (2004), and Nicolato and Venardos (2003). The latter follow closely the setup of Barndorff-Nielsen and Shephard, which we adopt here as well. We already introduced in Eq. (3.1) the class of affine jump-diffusion processes. Nicolato and Venardos consider a different class, namely

$$\mathrm{d}Y_t = (\mu + \beta\sigma_t^2)\mathrm{d}t + \sigma_t \mathrm{d}W_t + \rho \mathrm{d}Z_{\lambda t} \tag{3.8}$$

$$\mathrm{d}\sigma_t = -\delta\sigma_t^2 \mathrm{d}t + \mathrm{d}Z_{\delta t} \tag{3.9}$$

with $\delta > 0$ and $\rho \leq 0$. The process $Z = (Z_{\delta t})$ is subordinator, independent of the Brownian motion W_t, assumed to be a Lévy process with positive increments, and called by Barndorff-Nielsen and Shephard (2001) the background driving Lévy process. It is assumed that Z has no deterministic drift and its Lévy measure has a density λ. Note that the solution to (3.9) can be written as

$$\sigma_t^2 = \exp -\delta t \sigma_0^2 + \int_0^t \exp t - s \mathrm{d}Z_{\delta s}. \tag{3.10}$$

The resulting dynamics of the stock price process are

$$\begin{aligned} \mathrm{d}S_t &= S_{t-}(b_t \mathrm{d}t + \sigma_t + \mathrm{d}M_t) \\ \mathrm{d}b_t &= \mu + \delta\kappa(\rho) +] \left(\beta + \frac{1}{2}\right)\sigma_t^2 \\ M_t &= \sum_{0<s\leq t} (\exp \rho\Delta Z_{\delta s} - 1) - \delta\kappa(\rho)t, \end{aligned} \tag{3.11}$$

where $\kappa(x)$ is the cumulant transform, i.e., $\kappa(x) = \log E[\exp xZ_1]$. To build models of time deformation, one exploits the property (see, e.g., Sato, 1999) that for any self-decomposable probability distribution $\mathcal{L}$ there exists a Lévy process Z such that the a OU process driven by Z has $\mathcal{L}$ as marginal. Examples of self-decomposable distributions are the inverse Gaussian and Gamma distributions. Therefore, two popular models to specify the variance process are the so-called $IG - OU$ and $\Gamma - OU$ processes studied, respectively, by Barndorff-Nielsen and Shephard (2001) and Madan and Seneta (1990).

The characteristic functions for the log of price can be derived in all the aforementioned cases and can be used to obtain option prices via the Fast Fourier transform. Equivalent martingale representations are obtained through measure changes within the class of OU process driven by Z. One interesting case that we would like to highlight is obtained by Nicolato and Venardos (2003), who express the call price of a European option as conditional expectation of the BS formula using so-called *effective* log-stock prices, namely

$$\pi_t^h = E^{Q^*}\left[BS(Y_{\text{eff}}, V_{\text{eff}})|Y_t, \sigma_t^2\right] \tag{3.12}$$

similar to an expression of Hull and White (1987) and similar to the GSB discussed earlier, except that here (as in Hull and White) the expectation is taken under the risk-neutral expectation. The *effective* log-price process X_{eff} is the original process X_t modified by the path of the future subordinator ($Z_{\delta T} - Z_{\delta t}$ where T is the maturity date of the contract) and V_{eff} is the (re-scaled) future realized volatility between t and T. Because of the processes involved, this formula applies to a wide variety of nonaffine diffusions with leverage as well as jump-diffusions. To compute actual option prices, Nicolato and Venardos (2003) suggest to simulate the pair $(Y_{\text{eff}}, V_{\text{eff}})$ and provide the relevant references to do so.

The observation that asset prices actually display many small jumps on a fine time scale has led to the development of more general jump structures, which permit an infinite number of jumps to occur within any finite time interval. Examples of infinite activity jump models include the inverse Gaussian model of Barndorff-Nielsen (1998, 2001), the generalized hyperbolic class of Eberlein et al. (1998), the variance gamma (VG) model of Madan and Milne (1991), the generalization of VG in Carr et al. (2003), and the finite moment log-stable model of Carr and Wu (2003). Empirical work by these authors is generally supportive of the use of infinite-activity processes as a way to model returns in a parsimonious way. The recognition that volatility is stochastic has led to further extensions of infinite activity Lévy models by Barndorff-Nielsen and Shephard (2001) and by Carr et al. (2003). However, these models often assume that changes in volatility are independent of asset returns and consider the leverage effect only under special cases. Carr and Wu (2004) use time-changed Lévy processes which generalize the affine Poisson jump-diffusions by relaxing the affine structure and by allowing more general specifications of the jump structure. Since the pioneering work by Heston (1993), the literature has used the characteristic function for deriving option prices. Accordingly, Carr and Wu focus on developing analytic expressions for the characteristic function of a time-changed Lévy process. Carr et al. (2003) construct option prices differently, following a method developed in Carr and Madan (1998) using a generalized Fourier transforms and parameters calibrated with cross-sections of option contracts.

To conclude, it should be noted that much has been written on testing for jumps in the context of high-frequency financial data, see for instance Andersen et al. (2010) in this Handbook as well as the survey by Brockwell (2009) and Eberlein (2009).

3.2.3. Long-Memory in Continuous Time

In Section 2, we noted that numerous distorted smiles in the shapes of smirks or frowns are often inferred from market data since 1987 and provide an explanation in terms of SV and its instantaneous correlation with the return of the underlying asset. However, as pointed out by Sundaresan (2000) in his survey of the performance of continuous-time methods for option valuation, the remaining puzzle is the so-called term structure of volatility smiles, i.e., the fact that the volatility smile effect appears to be dependent, in a systematic way, on the maturity structure of options. Sundaresan (2000) first observes that the volatility smile appears to be stronger in short-term options than in long-term ones, which is consistent with the SV interpretation. When volatility is stochastic, the option price appears to be an expectation of the BS price with respect to the probability distribution of the so-called integrated volatility $(1/h)\int_t^{t+h}\sigma^2(u)\mathrm{d}u$ over the lifetime of the option (see Renault and Touzi, 1996, in the context of the Hull and White, 1987, model) or of a fraction of it in case of leverage effect (see Romano and Touzi, 1997, in the context of the Heston, 1993, model). Then, by a simple application of the law of large numbers to time averages of the volatility process (assumed to be stationary and ergodic), one realizes that the effects of the randomness of the volatility should vanish when the time to maturity of the option increases and therefore the volatility smile should be erased.

Nevertheless, as Sundaresan (2000) emphasizes, the term structure of implied volatilities still appears to have short-term and long-term patterns that cannot be so easily reconciled. Introducing long memory in the SV process appears to be useful in this respect. To see this, it is worth revisiting the common claim that the convexity of the volatility smile is produced by the unconditional excess kurtosis of log returns. For notational simplicity, we consider that the log price has a zero deterministic drift and that there is no leverage effect, i.e., using the notations of Subsection 2.7; the two Wiener processes W^S and W^X are independent, and the log return over the period $[t, t+h]$ can be written:

$$R_t(h) = \log\frac{S_{t+h}}{S_t} = \int_t^{t+h} \sigma_u \mathrm{d}w W_u^s,$$

where the two stochastic processes σ and w^s are independent. Hence, given the volatility path, the log return is normal and we can write

$$E\left[R_t^2(h)/\sigma\right] = \int_t^{t+h} \sigma_u^2 \mathrm{d}u$$

and

$$E\left[R_t^4(h)/\sigma\right] = 3\left[\int_t^{t+h} \sigma_u^2 \mathrm{d}u\right]^2.$$

The unconditional kurtosis of the return over the period $[t, t+h]$ is therefore given by

$$k(h) = \frac{E\left[R_t^4(h)\right]}{\left(E\left[R_t^2(h)\right]\right)^2} = 3\left[1 + \frac{\mathrm{Var}\left[\frac{1}{h}\int_t^{t+h}\sigma_u^2\mathrm{d}u\right]}{\left(E(\sigma^2)\right)^2}\right]. \tag{3.13}$$

Then, to address the issue of consistency between short-term and long-term patterns, it is worth considering the limit cases of infinitely short time to maturity ($h \to 0$) and infinitely long time to maturity ($h \to \infty$). First, because $\frac{1}{h}\int_t^{t+h} \sigma_u^2 du$ converges in mean-square toward σ_t^2 when h tends to zero:

$$\lim_{h \to 0} k(h) = 3\left[1 + \frac{\mathrm{Var}(\sigma^2)}{\left(E(\sigma^2)\right)^2}\right]. \tag{3.14}$$

Equation (3.14) is a specialization to very short-term intervals of a well-known result since Clark (1973): the excess kurtosis is equal to three times the squared coefficient of variation of the stochastic variance. This excess kurtosis effect persists in the very short term even though the volatility smile evaporates and the conditional variance $V_t\left[\frac{1}{h}\int_t^{t+h} \sigma_u^2 du\right]$ tends to zero. This is a counterexample to the claim that convexity of the volatility smile is simply produced by unconditional excess kurtosis. As already previously noted, observed violations of BS pricing for very short-term options cannot be captured within the one-factor SV framework without introducing a huge volatility risk premium, which would become explosive in longer term options. This explains why jumps, multiple volatility factors, or other nonlinearities have been introduced.

The focus of interest here is the remaining puzzle that SV still appears to be significant for very long maturity options as documented by Bollerslev and Mikkelsen (1999). The implied level of volatility persistence to account for deep volatility smiles in long-term options is large in the framework of standard (short memory) models of volatility dynamics, even with a model of permanent and transitory component as in Engle and Lee (1999). Moreover, this cannot be easily reconciled with the stylized fact that the sample autocorrelogram of squared asset returns generally decreases quite abruptly in the short term, whereas it appears to converge slowly to zero in the long term. To address this issue, Comte and Renault (1998) proposed a continuous-time SV model with long memory. Long memory in volatility dynamics is a well-documented empirical fact (see, e.g., Ding et al., 1993), which has given rise to various long-memory GARCH models (Baillie et al., 1996; Bollerslev and Mikkelsen, 1996; Robinson, 1991) and long-memory discrete time SV models (Breidt et al., 1998; Harvey, 1998).

To get a long-memory continuous-time SV model, the basic idea of Comte and Renault (1998) was to extend the lognormal SV model to fractional Brownian motion. The log-volatility process follows Ornstein–Uhlenbeck dynamics but with the standard Brownian motion replaced by a fractional one. Because the main strand of the volatility literature is now more oriented toward affine models, we rather present here an overview of the affine fractional SV of Comte et al. (2001). The results are qualitatively similar to Comte and Renault (1998), but the affine setting provides closed form formulas useful for interpretation and option pricing applications as well. Starting from a CIR SV model as in Heston (1993), $d\tilde{\sigma}^2(t) = k\left(\tilde{\theta} - \tilde{\sigma}^2(t)\right) dt + \gamma\tilde{\sigma}(t)dW^X(t)$, Comte et al. consider the centered process $X(t) = \tilde{\sigma}^2(t) - \tilde{\theta}$ and a fractional integration of it:

$$X^{(d)}(t) = \int_{-\infty}^{t} \frac{(t-s)^{d-1}}{\Gamma(d)} X(s)ds, \quad 0 \leq d \leq 1. \tag{3.15}$$

To facilitate the interpretation, it is worth noting that a formal integration by part on (3.15) implies that under some convergence conditions, one can rewrite $X^{(d)}(t)$ as

$$X^{(d)}(t) = \int_{-\infty}^{t} \frac{(t-s)^{d}}{\Gamma(d+1)} dX(s). \tag{3.16}$$

It can be seen from (3.16) that $X^{(0)}(t) = X(t)$, and $X^{(1)}(t)$ corresponds to standard integration of $X(t)$ as in (3.15). It can be shown that for $0 \leq d < 1/2$, the process $X^{(d)}(t)$ is mean-square stationary centered at zero. Then, up to positivity restrictions (see Comte et al. for a discussion), the volatility process is defined by $\sigma_t^2 = X^{(d)}(t) + \theta$ for some positive parameter θ. For $d = 0, \sigma_t^2$ is a standard affine volatility process:

$$d\sigma_t^2 = k\left(\theta - \sigma_t^2\right) dt + \gamma\sqrt{\sigma_t^2 + \tilde{\theta} - \theta}\, dW^X(t).$$

Although $\mathrm{Var}\left(\sigma_t^2\right) = \tilde{\theta}\gamma^2/2k$ and the autocorrelation function of σ_t^2 has an exponential rate of decay, $\rho\left[\sigma_{t+h}^2, \sigma_t^2\right] = e^{-k|h|}$.

In contrast, for $0 < d < 1/2$, the volatility process is still mean-reverting, yet it will feature some long range dependence. Moreover,

$$\mathrm{Var}\left(\sigma_t^2\right) = \frac{\tilde{\theta}\gamma^2}{k^{2d+1}} \frac{\Gamma(1-2d)\Gamma(2d)}{\Gamma(1-d)\Gamma(d)}, \tag{3.17}$$

and the autocorrelation function of σ_t^2 has only an hyperbolic rate of decay for large lags: $\rho\left[\sigma_{t+h}^2, \sigma_t^2\right] \sim (kh)^{2d-1}/\Gamma(2d)$ when h tends to infinity. In other words, a positive value of d allows to introduce much more volatility persistence, not only, as usual, through a small mean reversion parameter k, but also, even more importantly, through a rate of decay, which is hyperbolic instead of exponential.

This long-memory model of volatility accommodates much better the volatility smile puzzle for long-term options. Indeed, it can be shown that for $0 \leq d < 1/2$,

$$\mathrm{Var}_t\left[\frac{1}{h}\int_t^{t+h} \sigma_s^2 ds\right] \sim \frac{\gamma^2\tilde{\theta}}{k^{2d+1}} \frac{(hk)^{2d-1}}{(d+1)\Gamma(d+1)^2}$$

when h tends to infinity. Hence, we can clearly disentangle two effects in the explanation of the volatility smile: (i) the first one, independent of the maturity is simply produced by the stochastic feature of volatility and is proportional to its unconditional variance through the term $\left(\gamma^2\tilde{\theta}/k^{2d+1}\right)$ and (ii) the second one captures the erosion of the volatility smile when the time to maturity increases. It is given by the term $(hk)^{2d-1}$ where, for a given long-memory parameter d, the time to maturity h is scaled by the mean reversion parameter k.

The second effect is important to understand the phenomenon that long-term options still feature deep volatility smiles. For instance, a moderate level of long memory in the volatility process, $d = 1/4$ say, would imply that the conditional variance would be divided by a factor of ten when the time to maturity h of the option contract is multiplied by 100. In contrast, the same factor 100 would divide the variance in the short-memory case ($d = 0$).

Finally, note that the kurtosis coefficient $k(h)$ will converge toward its Gaussian limit 3 at the some speed h^{2d-1} as the conditional variance goes to zero. In other words and by contrast with the short-term case, the volatility smile and the excess kurtosis vanish at the same speed when time to maturity increases to infinity. Of course, long memory may produce cumbersome statistics because the past information is very slowly forgotten. However, a convenient feature of the affine fractional SV model is that integrated volatility $\int_t^{t+h} \sigma_s^2 ds$ over the lifetime of the option and BS-implied volatilities are fractionally cointegrated. Moreover, the conditional probability distribution of $\int_t^{t+h} \sigma_s^2 ds - E_t\left[\int_t^{t+h} \sigma_s^2 ds\right]$ given information available at time t only depends on the current value of the state variable $X(t)$.

In other words, all the long-memory features relevant for option pricing are encapsulated in the expected integrated volatility and can be captured by BS-implied volatilities. Note in particular that the fractional cointegration relationship justifies the widely used predicting regressions of realized volatilities on BS-implied volatilities. See Bandi and Perron (2003) for an empirical illustration of fractional cointegration in this context. Indeed, it can even be shown that there is a deterministic relationship between expected integrated volatility and BS-implied volatilities for very long-term options. Beyond that, all the residual variations of BS-implied volatilities across moneyness (volatility smile) and across maturities (volatility term structure) are well described by the short-memory dynamics of the state variables.

3.3. Pricing Options Based on Objective Parameters

A number of papers such as Andersen et al. (2010) and Eraker et al. (2003) have derived the option pricing implications of jump-diffusion models relying only on returns data for the underlying asset. This exercise aims at evaluating the economic significance of statistical differences across models. Understanding how the various factors such as SV, jumps in returns, or jumps in volatility determine the conditional distribution as a function of time to maturity and level of volatility is equivalent to understanding how option prices change with respect to these factors. Indeed, options with different strike prices and times to maturity are affected by different attributes of the conditional distribution of returns. However, to price options in an arbitrage-free framework, one needs to specify a candidate state price density (SPD) or to characterize the transformation from the objective measure to the risk-neutral measure. In the presence of jump and SV risks, appropriate risk compensation must be incorporated in the risk-neutral dynamics. As already noted, there are potentially risk premia associated with SV, mean jump sizes, volatility of jump sizes, and jump timing. Separating the various risk premia is not an easy task. Assumptions have to be made. The crudest assumption consists in setting at zero all risk premia associated with SV and jumps. Under this assumption, the change from the objective measure to the risk-neutral measure affects only the drift of the stock index returns, which is equal to the interest rate minus the dividend yield. Andersen et al. (2001) and Eraker et al. (2003) make such an assumption and study the impact of SV and jumps on the levels of implied volatility as well as on the shapes of the implied volatility curves.

Jumps in returns affect mainly the tails of the conditional distribution and induce excess kurtosis. As shown by Das and Sundaram (1999) among others, this effect is strongest for short maturity options because the degree of excess kurtosis in a jump model decreases with maturity. With jump processes, the implied volatility smile flattens out very quickly. Unlike jumps, SV affects the conditional distribution the most at longer horizons. For typical parameterizations such as a slow-moving mean reverting volatility, the term structure of kurtosis is increasing over a reasonable horizon. Eraker et al. (2003) produce a figure of implied volatility curves for the models SV, SVJ, SVIJ, and SVCJ for four different times to maturity (2 weeks, 2 months, 6 months, and 1 year). The results indicate that there are differences both in the levels of implied volatility and in the shapes of the implied volatility curves. Regarding the volatility level, the main difference between the models comes from the estimates of the spot volatility. The spot volatility estimates for the S&P 500 are 15.10, 14.32, 15.18, and 15.51% for SV, SVJ, SVCJ, and SVIJ, respectively. This translates into a level difference of almost 2% points in the implied volatility for at-the-money options with 1 year to maturity. There are a number of noteworthy results for the shapes of the volatility curves. First, the implied volatility curves produced by the SV model are flat. Second, adding jumps in returns steepens the implied volatility curves at all maturities. With a sizable negative mean jump estimate for all the models, the implied volatility curves are downward sloping to the right and not U-shaped. Third, the addition of jumps in volatility fattens further the tails of the conditional distributions and makes the implied volatility curves steeper. Therefore, even without any risk premia, jumps and especially jumps in volatility have an important impact on option prices, which translates into term structures and cross-sections of implied volatility more consistent with data. These results are in contrast with Andersen et al. (2001) who need to add risk premia to generate steep-implied volatility curves. This is mainly due to the fact that their estimates for the jump parameters are small compared with Eraker et al. (2003). However, all studies concur in finding a flattening out of the implied volatility curves as maturity increases for all the models. Indeed, the skewness and kurtosis of the conditional distribution at longer horizons are due mainly to the volatility process and not to the jump processes.

To assess the actual quantitative importance of risk premia for option pricing, one needs to estimate these risk premia along with the parameters of the model. The option market provides us with prices which can be used, along with stock returns, to estimate these risk premia. However, to achieve this, one needs additional assumptions to characterize the form of these risk premia as well as an econometric model of option pricing errors.

4. IMPLIED RISK-NEUTRAL PROBABILITIES

The concept of pricing kernel or SPD is central to the dynamic asset pricing theory, in particular to the pricing of derivatives. The price at time t of a claim paying an $\mathcal{F}_T$−measurable random variable V at time T is given by

$$\pi_t = \frac{1}{\theta_t} E[V\theta_T \mid \mathcal{F}_T]. \tag{4.1}$$

In the context of the jump-diffusion model described in the previous section, markets are incomplete and this SPD is not unique. For a SVJ model, Pan (2002) proposes a candidate SPD of the following form:

$$\theta_t = \exp\left(-\int_0^t r_\tau \mathrm{d}\tau\right) \exp\left(-\int_0^t \zeta_\tau \mathrm{d}W_\tau - \frac{1}{2}\int_0^t \zeta'_\tau \zeta_\tau \mathrm{d}\tau\right) \exp\left(\sum_{i,\tau_i \leq t} \xi_i^\pi\right), \tag{4.2}$$

where ζ represents a vector of the market prices of risk for the price and volatility shocks and ξ_i^π is the market price of jump risk. The market prices of risk are defined by

$$\zeta_t^{(1)} = \eta^s \sqrt{V_t}, \quad \zeta_t^{(2)} = -\frac{1}{\sqrt{1-\rho^2}}\left(\rho\eta^s \frac{\eta^v}{\sigma^v}\right)\sqrt{V_t}. \tag{4.3}$$

This specification of the market prices of risk makes the risk premia for the diffusive price shock and the volatility shock proportional to V_t and equal to $\eta^s V_t$ and $\eta^v V_t$, respectively. These forms of the risk premia have been suggested by Bates (1996a, 2000) based on a log utility model for the representative investor.

The jump risks are priced by the jump components ξ_i^π in the SPD, assumed to be i.i.d. and normally distributed with mean μ_π and variance σ_π^2 and independent of W. The random jump sizes ξ_i^π and ξ_i^y are allowed to be correlated with a constant correlation ρ_π but are independent at different jump times.

It is more common to transform the model to write it under a risk-neutral measure Q^*, which is defined from a density $\theta_t \exp\left(\int_0^t r_\tau \mathrm{d}\tau\right)$. The SVJ model will be then written as

$$\begin{pmatrix} \frac{\mathrm{d}S_t}{S_t} \\ \mathrm{d}V_t \end{pmatrix} = \begin{pmatrix} r_t - \eta^s V_t - \lambda_y^* \mu_y^* \\ \kappa(\alpha - V_t) + \eta^v V_t \end{pmatrix} \mathrm{d}t + \sqrt{V_t} \begin{pmatrix} 1 & 0 \\ \rho\sigma_v & \sqrt{(1-\rho^2)}\sigma_v \end{pmatrix} \mathrm{d}W_t^* + \begin{pmatrix} \xi^y \mathrm{d}N_t^{Qy^*} \\ 0 \end{pmatrix} \quad (4.4)$$

The risk-neutral dynamics differs from the dynamics under the objective measure by the drift terms, which incorporate the risk premia and by replacing $W_t = (W_{1t}, W_{2t})'$ by $W_t^* = (W_{1t}^*, W_{2t}^*)'$, a vector of independent standard Brownian motions under Q^* defined by

$$W_t^* = W_t + \int_0^t \zeta_s \mathrm{d}s, \quad 0 \le t \le T. \quad (4.5)$$

The jump process N^{Q^*y} has the same distribution under Q^* than under Q except that $\xi^y \sim \mathcal{N}(\mu_y^*, \sigma_y^2)$, where $\mu_y^* = \mu_y + \sigma_y \sigma_\pi \rho_\pi$. It means that the model allows for a jump-size risk. It can also allow for a jump-timing risk because the λ_y^* can be different from $\lambda_y : \lambda_y^* = \lambda_y \exp(\mu_\pi + \sigma_\pi^2/2)$. In Bates (2000) and Pan (2002), the jump-size intensity is made volatility dependent with one and two factors in volatility.

The price of a European option expiring at T with a strike price of K is given by

$$\pi_t = \frac{1}{\theta_t} E_t\left[\theta_T (S_T - K)^+\right]. \quad (4.6)$$

A Fourier transform-based approach is adopted to calculate this expectation, as in Heston (1993), Bates (1996, 2000), Bakshi et al. (1997), Bakshi and Madan (2000), and Duffie et al. (2000). The explicit formula is given in these papers. For our purpose, let us characterize the solution as a function f:

$$\pi_t = S_t f(V_t, \vartheta, r_t, T - t, K/S_t), \quad (4.7)$$

where $\vartheta = (\kappa, \alpha, \sigma_v, \rho, \eta^s, \eta^v, \lambda_y, \lambda_y^*, \mu_y, \sigma_y, \mu_y^*)$ is the vector of model parameters. We will detail in the next subsection the various issues raised by the estimation of such a model.

4.1. Econometric Model of Option Pricing Errors

Typically, such a theoretical asset pricing model explains an observed stationary process Y_t of n asset "prices" as a known function of the current value X_t of K latent state variables and p unknown parameters θ:

$$Y_t = \{h_i [X_t, \theta]\}_{1 \le i \le n} . \tag{4.8}$$

Note that when one loosely says asset "prices", one should rather understand "yields" in the case of bonds or "option premium by unit of spot price" in case of options on equity or any other transformation well suited to build a n-dimensional stationary time series Y_t from the observation of time series of asset prices, likely to be nonstationary. In the context of options on equity, one may also replace (see, e.g., Chernov and Ghysels, 2000; Pastorello et al., 2000; Renault and Touzi, 1996) option prices by the corresponding BS-implied volatilities.

With respect to the most general formulation of empirical asset pricing models presented in Section 2, we focus here on a more specific approach that is more common in the arbitrage-free asset pricing literature. First, the pricing kernel is not explicitly included in the list of latent state variables. Instead, it is defined as a known function of a collection X_t of relevant risk factors as instantaneous risk free rate, diffusive return shocks, volatility shocks, and jump events as well as a collection of risk premium parameters θ_2 that define the compensation for the various risk factors. Then, the dynamics of the latent risk factors X_t only identify a set θ_1 of unknown "statistical" parameters while the risk premium parameters θ_2 must be added to define the complete vector θ of structural parameters of interest for asset pricing $\theta = [\theta_1', \theta_2']'$.

For empirical option pricing on equity, the above approach is typically the one followed by Heston (1993), Bates (2000), Chernov and Ghysels (2000), and Pan (2002) among others. For term structure modeling, this approach is particularly well suited to capture through K explanatory latent factors of the yield curve the relationships between n observed yields in cross-section. A large strand of literature, initiated in particular by Chen and Scott (1993), Pearson and Sun (1994), and Duan (1995), uses this indirect empirical modeling of bond yields through underlying latent factors. In contrast, explicit dynamic modeling of the joint stochastic process of asset returns and pricing kernel can be found in the consumption-based equilibrium asset pricing literature (see, e.g., Aït-Sahalia and Lo, 2000; Jackwerth, 2000; Rosenberg and Engle, 2002, for applications to option pricing) or in an even more general way in Constantinides (1992) and Garcia et al. (2003).

Of course, the simplest approach to estimating a K factors model is to select $n = K$ asset prices in the cross-section and to exploit the one-to-one relationship between prices and factors to get either the exact likelihood (Chen and Scott, 1993; Pearson and Sun, 1994; Duan, 1995) or an expansion of it (Aït-Sahalia and Kimmel, 2002) or implied moments (Pan, 2002, or a simulated score, Dai and Singleton, 2000). This approach leads unmistakably to neglect the potentially useful information conveyed by a number of observed related prices in the cross-section. For instance, Pan (2002) estimates a stochastic volatility model for option pricing on the S&P 500 index from the joint time series of the index and one near-the-money short dated option on it. One option price is sufficient to get a one-to-one relationship with the volatility factor, yet (see, e.g., Dumas et al., 1998), by taking into account the various possible moneynesses and maturities, the number of fairly liquid option prices on S&P 500 that can be observed at any given date may be about 10 or even more. Similarly, although common models of the yield curve involve $K = 1, 2$, or 3 factors, the number n of available maturities in the cross-section is about 30 or even more.

However, as emphasized by Renault (1997), when the number n of observed asset prices is larger than the number K of latent state variables, this produces some stochastic singularity and statistical estimation theory becomes irrelevant. If one takes the asset pricing model seriously, some parameters can be computed exactly. For example, in the BS case of no latent state variable, observing the price of one option will be enough to compute exactly the volatility of the process. In the case of SV models, one can recover the exact value of the current state of the variance process by matching observed prices with the pricing formulas after elimination of unknown parameters. But different option prices would imply different values for the current state of the variance process. This fundamental inconsistency can be resolved either by increasing ad infinitum the number of state variables and match perfectly the observed paths or cross-sections of option prices (this nonparametric approach is in the spirit of Rubinstein (1994) implied binomial tree methodology described in Section 5) or by admitting that these formulas are approximative and that the observed price is the price given by the formula plus an error term. The presence of this error term is not difficult to justify by simply recognizing that any model is intrinsically misspecified whether it is in its assumptions about the stochastic process followed by the underlying or in its simplistic description of market structure abstracting from microstructure effects and market frictions.

Therefore, the retained empirical specification of the asset pricing model (4.8) will be

$$\begin{aligned} Z_t &= (Y_{it})_{1\le i\le K} = h[X_t,\theta] = [h_i(X_t,\theta)]_{1\le i\le K} \\ V_t &= (Y_{it})_{K+1\le i\le n} = e[X_t,\theta] + u_t = [h_i(X_t,\theta)]_{K+1\le i\le n} + [u_{it}]_{K+1\le i\le n}. \end{aligned} \tag{4.9}$$

Note that we consider at this stage that the n assets prices have been relabeled to get zero pricing errors for the K first ones, whereas the $(n-K)$ other ones differ from their theoretical values by error terms u_{it}. Hence, we do not really maintain the arbitrary assumption that exactly K prices coincide with their theoretical values, whereas error terms may be added to the other ones. We just say that because the structural model already involves K latent factors, there is no reason to introduce more than $(n-K)$ error terms, while at least K independent linear combinations should be observed without error. Of course, such a specification needs to know a priori what are the K prices (or the K linear combinations of prices) that are observed without error. This is mainly an empirical question.

Let us first set the stage for inference on (4.9) in the context of maximum likelihood-based inference strategies. A maintained assumption will be that the error terms u_{it} have a zero unconditional mean and that the first K equations provide a one-to-one relationship between the vector Z_t of the K prices observed without error and the vector X_t of structural state variables:

$$Z_t = (Y_{it})_{1 \leq i \leq K} = h[X_t, \theta] \Leftrightarrow X_t = h^{-1}[Z_t, \theta]. \tag{4.10}$$

4.2. Maximum Likelihood-Based Inference

To present a variety of likelihood-based inference strategies, we follow here the presentation of implied-state maximum likelihood as first proposed by Renault and Touzi (1996) and Renault (1997). Pastorello et al. (2003) encompass a larger set of implied-state methodologies under the name of implied-state backfitting.

The conditional likelihood associated to a data set $\{Y_t, t = 1, \ldots, T\}$ (and an initial conditioning value Y_0) must be derived, through the Jacobian formula, from the latent one associated with the "latent data" set $\left\{Y_t^*, t = 1, \ldots, T\right\}$ produced by the latent realizations of a Markov process Y^* one-to-one function of Y:

$$Y_t = g[Y_t^*, \theta] \Leftrightarrow Y_t^* = g^{-1}[Y_t, \theta]. \tag{4.11}$$

Typically, (4.11) must be defined by n equations, thanks to $(n - K)$ equations that complete the K equations (4.10). A natural idea would be to define the state vector Y_t^* by augmenting the vector X_t of K structural factors with the vector u_t of $(n - K)$ error terms. However, an alternative approach is better suited for two reasons. First, the parameters η that would define the probability distribution of the error term u_t are not the focus of interest. Of course, their consistent estimation may be useful for improving the accuracy of the estimation of the parameters of interest θ. We do want to ensure, however, that even if η is not consistently estimated, we obtain a consistent estimator of θ. Typically, in case of Gaussian errors, the vector of nuisance parameters η consists of the unconditional covariance matrix Ω of the $(n - K)$ error terms u_t and possibly the parameters defining the conditional mean and variance dynamics. The mere fact that these error terms are added ex post and not rationalized within a structural asset pricing model with additional state variables implies that we have no structural information about their dynamics. Because from (4.9) we note that the estimation of the dynamics of the error terms may contaminate the estimation of the dynamics of the structural factors, it is important to define a procedure that focuses only on the structural parameters θ and not on the augmented vector (θ, η).

Second, the implied-state identification condition for θ would be problematic if we defined the latent state vector Y_t^* as $Y_t^* = (X_t, u_t)$. The empirical asset pricing model (4.9) provides a one-to-one relationship between observed prices Y_t and latent variables (X_t, u_t), but the risk premium parameters θ_2 are identified only by the relationship itself and not by the probability distribution of the latent process (X_t, u_t). However, the philosophy of the implied-state methodology is precisely to assume that the latent model (the transition equation of the state variables) carries more information about the unknown parameters of interest than their occurrence in the measurement equation. To remain true to this philosophy, a better strategy is to define the latent vector Y_t^* and the associated function $g[Y_t^*, \theta]$ in the following way:

$$\begin{aligned} Y_t^* &= [X_t', V_t']',\ Y_t = [Z_t', V_t']' \\ Y_t &= g[X_t, V_t, \theta] = [h'(X_t, \theta), V_t']'. \end{aligned} \tag{4.12}$$

Note that $(n - K)$ among the n, so-called latent variables Y_t^* are actually observed, but this is not a reason for not applying the general implied-state methodology. In this context, the transition density function of the Markov process Y_t^*:

$$l[Y_t^* \mid Y_{t-1}^*] = l[X_t \mid Y_{t-1}^*]\, l[V_t \mid X_t, Y_{t-1}^*] \tag{4.13}$$

will be specified under the maintained common assumption that error terms do not cause structural factors, neither in the Granger sense nor instantaneously. This assumption is natural because, if one imagines its violation, one implicitly endows the error terms with some structural interpretation. Then, by the no-Granger causality assumption,

$$l[X_t \mid Y_{t-1}^*] = l[X_t \mid X_{t-1}] = l[X_t \mid X_{t-1}, \theta_1], \tag{4.14}$$

where the last expression stresses the fact that this density function depends on the value of the unknown parameters only through θ_1. By the no instantaneous causality assumption, $l[V_t \mid X_t, Y_{t-1}^*]$ is simply obtained by a translation of size $e[X_t, \theta]$ applied to the conditional probability distribution $l[u_t \mid Y_{t-1}^*, \eta]$ of the error terms given the past. This probability density function depends on the value of the unknown parameters only through the nuisance parameters η.

Because we maintain the assumption that all the structural content of the model is captured by the factors X_t, we do not really want to specify the dynamics of the error terms and we will carry out inference about structural parameters through a latent quasi-likelihood, written as the likelihood of a latent model where the error terms would be i.i.d. Gaussian with a covariance matrix specified as a function $\Omega(\eta)$:

$$l[u_t \mid Y_{t-1}^*, \eta] = l[u_t \mid \eta] = (2\pi)^{-(n-K)/2}[\det\Omega(\eta)]^{-1/2} \exp\left[-\frac{1}{2} u_t' \Omega^{-1}(\eta) u_t\right] \tag{4.15}$$

Several remarks are in order about the use of this quasi-likelihood. First, it is well suited only if the scale Y_t used to measure asset prices is consistent with conditional normality like for instance log-returns or log-implied volatilities. Second, we should not forget that the quasi-likelihood may differ from the true likelihood and that we just want to get a consistent estimator of the structural parameters of interest θ. The nuisance parameters η are likely to be poorly defined and not consistently estimated. However, a general specification of the covariance matrix $\Omega(\eta)$ should at least allow us to take into account the obvious strong cross-sectional patterns of correlation and heteroskedasticity among error terms (see Renault, 1997, for a general discussion).

Starting from an estimator η_T of the nuisance parameters and a corresponding estimator $\Omega_T = \Omega(\eta_T)$, we first plug it into (4.13) to define the latent criterion for extremum estimation of the structural parameters θ:

$$Q_T^*(\theta) = \Sigma_{t=2}^T \log l[X_t | X_{t-1}, \theta_1] - \frac{1}{2}\Sigma_{t=1}^T [V_t - e(X_t, \theta)]' \Omega_T^{-1} [V_t - e(X_t, \theta)]. \tag{4.16}$$

Up to recursive refinements, the backfitting (or iterative implied-state) methodology amounts to defining a sequence $\theta^{(p)}$ of estimators in the following way:

- Start from an estimator $\theta^{(1)}$ provided by a quick procedure.
- For $\theta^{(p)}$ given, replace in (4.16) the unknown factor values X_t by $X_t\big(\theta^{(p)}\big) = h^{-1}\big[Z_t, \theta^{(p)}\big]$. This defines a sample-based criterion $Q_T\big(\theta, \theta^{(p)}\big)$.
- Compute the estimator $\theta^{(p+1)}$ as $\arg\max_\theta Q_T\big(\theta, \theta^{(p)}\big)$.

Because the nuisance parameters η have been introduced in a way that preserves adaptivity, the resulting asymptotic probability distribution of the backfitting estimator of θ will only depend on the probability limit of Ω_T and not on its accuracy as estimator of the (pseudo) true unknown value of $\Omega(\eta)$. However, at least in case where the conditional distribution of the error terms would be well specified, the most accurate backfitting estimator would be obtained when Ω_T is a consistent estimator of the true value of $\Omega(\eta)$. This is the reason why it is natural to think to a "quasi-generalized" version of backfitting in the following way.

Start from an arbitrary Ω_T (e.g., the identity matrix) and compute the corresponding backfitting estimator θ_T of θ. Then, use it to compute "estimated error terms" $u_t(\theta_T) = V_t - e[X_t(\theta_T), \theta_T]$ and to derive a consistent estimator $\eta(\theta_T)$ of the pseudo true value of η and in turn, a consistent estimator $\Omega_T^* = \Omega[\eta(\theta_T)]$ of the pseudo true value of Ω. Then, perform a second backfitting estimation of θ based on the criterion (4.16) where Ω_T has been replaced by W_T^*. Of course, such a procedure is costly because it implies several backfitting estimations. Fortunately, there exists a much faster procedure, i.e., in terms of estimation of θ, asymptotically equivalent to quasi-generalized backfitting, but in terms of computing time, equivalent to a simple backfitting.

This procedure that we term "extended backfitting" amounts to using each step $\theta^{(p)}$ of the backfitting iteration to compute a new estimator $\Omega[\eta(\theta^{(p)})]$ of the matrix Ω and to plug it into (4.16) in place of Ω_T to derive the next step estimator $\theta^{(p+1)}$ of θ. At first sight, extended backfitting is similar to standard backfitting applied to the augmented vector (θ, η) of unknown parameters. However, we do not refer to a general backfitting theory (in terms of an augmented vector of parameters) to justify this procedure. There is little hope to get a sequence that is contracting with respect to the nuisance parameters η, and this is the reason why the relevant convergence criterion of the approximation sequence for applications will only be based on the norm $||\theta^{(p+1)} - \theta^{(p)}||$.

The relevant argument is the following. Irrespective of the choice of the weighting matrix Ω_T in (4.16), the backfitting estimator is a consistent estimator of the true unknown value of θ. Therefore, it is clear that the limit of the sequence $\theta^{(p)}$ produced by the extended backfitting algorithm also provides a consistent estimator of θ, and in turn, the limit of the sequence $\Omega[\eta(\theta^{(p)})]$ provides a consistent estimator of the true unknown value of $\Omega[\eta]$. Because the asymptotic probability distribution of the backfitting estimator of θ only depends on the probability limit of Ω_T, it is then clear that we get an estimator asymptotically equivalent to the quasi-generalized backfitting. Let us briefly sketch a comparison with the maximum likelihood based competitors also well suited for inference on such empirical asset pricing models with latent factors.

A first competitor is the Kalman filter-based quasi-maximum likelihood. The most popular strategy is to introduce n error terms instead of $(n - K)$. This has been first proposed in the context of affine models of the yield curve by Duan and Simonato (1999) and systematically developed by De Jong (2000). Of course, severe nonlinearities or nonnormality of the structural model are likely to alter the validity of the Kalman filter. Generally speaking, the Kalman filter should not be used for highly nonlinear models and the backfitting filtering strategy should be much better suited. However, in the context of return dynamics that are not too far to be linear as in the case of affine models of the yield curve, the two approaches may be competitors. Roughly speaking, the Kalman filtering approach can be seen as a quick and dirty procedure to check the validity of our possibly more accurate but also more risky approach. Typically, the backfitting approach seeks to get more efficient estimators and filters by taking the risk to specify exact nonlinear relationships between prices and factors with K zero error terms.

Another quasi-maximum likelihood approach for factor models of the yield curve has been applied by Fisher and Gilles (1996) and Duffee (2002). Their idea is quite simple. Even though the latent model is conceived to be simpler than the observable one, the hard part of the latent log-likelihood (4.16) is the transition density function of the structural factors X_t. This function is in general produced by a continuous-time model and may be hard to compute or simply unknown. However, consistent (albeit inefficient) estimates can still be obtained if we substitute the true theoretical transition density with a Gaussian one, provided that the first two conditional moments of X_t are correctly specified. Besides its potential inefficiency, this alternative QML approach also suffers from a risk of misspecification bias in case of a nonlinear mapping g between the latent variables and the observables. In such a case, the Jacobian formula applied to a latent Gaussian quasi-likelihood may not yield a correct quasi-likelihood for observables. This drawback is not detrimental in the case of affine (Fisher and Gilles, 1996) or essentially affine (Duffee, 2002) term structure models but would be an issue in the case of option prices on equity with SV.

Moreover, as neatly put forward by Duffee (2002),"another advantage of QML (which it shares with maximum likelihood and related techniques) is that $(\cdots)$ a model estimated with QML will guarantee that the time-t state vector implied by time-t yields is in the state vector's admissible space (to avoid a likelihood zero). By contrast, $(\cdots)$ techniques such as efficient method of moments (EMM) $(\cdots)$ do not require that the estimated term structure model be sufficiently flexible to reproduce the term structure shapes in the data. The parameters of the model in Dai and Singleton (2000), which were estimated with EMM, illustrate this point." This point is actually an important motivation to prefer implied-state-based likelihood rather than simulation-based minimum chi-square competitors like indirect inference or EMM.

As far as efficiency is concerned, several remarks are in order. First, contrary to common belief, the fact that can invert any vector of n asset prices into the n state variables and use the implied-state variables in the estimation does not mean that one can do as if the state variables were directly observable. The crucial point is that the one-to-one relationship (4.12) between latent variables Y^* and observable variables Y does depend on the unknown parameters θ. Therefore, nobody knows whether the Cramer-Rao bound $\left(I^*\right)^{-1}$ for efficient estimation associated with the hypothetical observation of Y^* would be smaller or larger than the Cramer-Rao bound $(I)^{-1}$ associated with the actual observation Y. The backfitting strategy described above must not give the fallacious feeling that the Cramer-Rao bound associated with the maximization of the log-likelihood $\sum_{t=1}^{T} \log L\left[Y_t^* \mid Y_{t-1}^*, \theta\right]$ has been reached. This maximization is actually infeasible, and the backfitting iterative scheme is based on the sequence:

$$\theta^{(p+1)} = \operatorname{Arg}\max_{\theta} \sum_{t=1}^{T} \log L\left[g^{-1}\left(Y_t, \theta^{(p)}\right) \mid g^{-1}\left(Y_{t-1}, \theta^{(p)}\right), \theta\right].$$

As shown in Pastorello et al. (2003), the cost of this necessary iteration is to multiply the Cramer-Rao bound $\left(I^*\right)^{-1}$ by a matrix-form factor, which is all the less detrimental than the mapping $\theta^{(p)} \to \theta^{(p+1)}$ is more strongly contracting. This theory is based on a well-defined choice of the number $p(T)$ of iterations (as a function of the sample size T) to define a backfitting estimator $\theta^{p(T)+1}$. Of course, if one wants to avoid such iterations and directly maximize the actual log-likelihood to reach the Cramer-Rao bound I^{-1}, one should not maximize

$$\sum_{t=1}^{T} \log L\left[g^{-1}(Y_t, \theta) \mid g^{-1}(Y_{t-1}, \theta), \theta\right] \tag{4.17}$$

but rather

$$\sum_{t=1}^{T} \log L\left[g^{-1}(Y_t, \theta) \mid g^{-1}(Y_{t-1}, \theta), \theta\right] + \sum_{t=1}^{T} \log |Jg^{-1}(Y_t, \theta)|, \tag{4.18}$$

where $|Jg^{-1}(Y_t, \theta)|$ denote the absolute value of the Jacobian of the transformation g. This can be done in some cases but will often be involved for several reasons. First, the function g is provided by the asset pricing model. It is in general highly nonlinear and even not available in a closed form formula. Computing the Jacobian matrix can then be cumbersome.

Second, and even more importantly, the direct maximization of (4.18) will lead to look for a maximizer θ, which should simultaneously meet two requirements. On the one hand, it has to give a large value to the latent likelihood, as it is natural to require. But, on the other hand, θ will tend to be chosen to select the most likely implied-state values $g^{-1}(Y_t, \theta)$. In many circumstances, such a selection appears to be a fairly risky strategy. For instance, Pastorello et al. (2003) observe that in the case of application of Aït-Sahalia (2003) likelihood expansions for affine-type diffusion processes, this will perversely push $g^{-1}(Y_{t-1}, \theta)$ toward the frontier of the domain where the likelihood (as provided by its expansion) is infinite. This is the reason why one may prefer to perform the backfitting strategy of likelihood maximization rather than directly maximizing the possibly unpalatable log-likelihood (4.18).

Indirect inference and EMM are often presented as appealing alternatives to maximum likelihood, precisely when the likelihood function becomes unpalatable due to some unobserved state variables. Because the chapter by Gallant and Tauchen in this Handbook is devoted to these techniques, we just sketch here some specific applications for option pricing.

Pastorello et al. (2000) propose to avoid the backfitting iteration by simply using BS-implied volatilities as proxies of implied states in a one-factor SV model. Thanks to the matching of estimated parameter or fitted-score vectors on simulated data, the indirect inference principle (see Gouriéroux et al., 1993) will correct for the misspecification bias due to the use of BS-implied volatilities as proxies of actual spot volatilities which are unobserved. The main drawback of this approach is that although a fully parametric model is needed for the purpose of simulation, nobody knows the efficiency loss due to the use of an auxiliary model (here, the model on BS-implied volatilities) to simplify the likelihood.

By matching a seminonparametric (SNP) score generator, EMM aims at correcting for this efficiency loss. The EMM procedure allows estimating the model parameters under both objective and risk-neutral probability measures if one uses implied volatilities and the underlying asset data jointly. Time series of the underlying asset provide estimators under the objective probability measure, whereas risk-neutral parameters can be retrieved from options. Chernov and Ghysels (2000) adopt the Heston model, which has a closed-form option pricing formula, and compare univariate and multivariate models in terms of pricing and hedging performance. An extension of the SNP/EMM methodology introduced in Gallant and Tauchen (1998) allows one to filter spot volatilities via reprojection, i.e., to compute the expected value of the latent volatility process using a SNP density conditioned on the observable processes such as returns and/or options data. The results in Chernov and Ghysels (2000) show that the univariate approach only involving options by and large dominates. A by-product of this finding is that they uncover a remarkably simple volatility extraction filter based on a polynomial lag structure of implied volatilities. The bivariate approach appears useful when the information from the cash market provides support via the conditional kurtosis to price options. This is the case for some long-term options. Another solution to the efficiency problem may be provided by Markov Chain Monte Carlo techniques as described by Johannes and Polson (2010) in this handbook.

4.3. Implied-State GMM

Taking advantage of the explicitly known moment-generating function of return and volatility in an affine model, Pan (2003) also advocates an implied-state methodology to focus directly on the joint dynamics of the state variables rather than the market observables, which could be highly nonlinear functions of state variables. In this respect, the approach still belongs to the general class of backfitting methodologies as studied by Pastorello et al. (2003), but the convenience of the GMM setting introduces some additional simplifications. The basic idea is to start from conditional moment restrictions which would provide a feasible GMM if the latent variable Y^* were observed:

$$E\left[\Psi\left(Y_t^*,\theta\right) \mid Y_{t-1}^*\right]=0 \tag{4.19}$$

Following Hansen (1985), Pan (2003) uses the optimal instrument matrix provided by

$$M_{t-1}(\theta)=E\left[\frac{\partial\Psi'}{\partial\theta}\left(Y_t^*,\theta\right) \mid Y_{t-1}^*\right]\left(\operatorname{Var}\left[\Psi\left(Y_t^*,\theta\right) \mid Y_{t-1}^*\right]\right)^{-1}.$$

Then, one would like to work with the just identified unconditional moment restrictions:

$$E\left[M_{t-1}(\theta)\Psi\left(Y_t^*,\theta\right)\right]=0$$

and to look for the estimator $\hat{\theta}_T$ solution of

$$\frac{1}{T}\sum_{t=1}^{T}M_{t-1}\left(\hat{\theta}_T\right)\Psi\left(Y_t^*,\hat{\theta}_T\right)=0 \tag{4.20}$$

Of course, this estimator is infeasible because Y_t^* is not observed. Then, two strategies may be imagined. The implied-state backfitting of Pastorello et al. (2003) still amounts to replace every occurrence of Y^* in $M_{t-1}(\theta)$ and $\Psi\left(Y_t^*,\theta\right)$ by $g^{-1}\left(Y_t,\theta^{(p)}\right)$ where $\theta^{(p)}$ comes from a previous step estimation. Insofar as such iterations converge, they will converge toward Pan's (2003) IS-GMM estimator, which is actually the second strategy: directly solve (4.20) when Y_t^* is replaced by $g^{-1}(Y_t,\theta)$. Then, the unknown θ appears not only in the occurrences of θ in $M_{t-1}(\theta)$ and $\Psi\left(Y_t^*,\theta\right)$ but also inside any occurrence of $Y_t^*=g^{-1}(Y_t,\theta)$.

By contrast, Pastorello et al. (2003) define a number $p(T)$ of iterations (as a function of the number T of observations) such that the backfitting estimator $\theta^{p(T)+1}$ is asymptotically equivalent to the Pan (2003) IS-GMM estimator. Then, the choice between the two strategies is just a matter of computational convenience, depending whether one consider that the backfitting iterations simplify or not the solution of the IS-GMM fixed point problem.

Moreover, as stressed by Pan (2003) in her discussion of Pastorello et al. (2003), there is a case where IS-GMM may work while IS-backfitting does not work. This is the case where θ would not be fully identified from state variables dynamics Y^*, for instance due to some risk premium parameters which do not appear in the factor dynamics. Even in such a case, one may hope that IS-GMM still identifies θ. It is however worth reminding that when as in Subsection 4.2 there are more observed prices than latent state variables, same error terms are added and the vector Y^* includes same observed asset prices which do identify the risk premium parameters. Then, implied-state backfitting works. In any case, as in the implied-state likelihood methodology of Subsection 4.2, efficiency is not guaranteed by this kind of implied-state approaches. In the context of (4.19), semiparametric efficiency would involve the computation of optimal instruments for the conditional moment restrictions:

$$E\left[\Psi\left(g^{-1}\left(Y_t,\theta\right),\theta\right)\mid Y_{t-1}\right]=0. \tag{4.21}$$

Then, the Jacobian matrix of the moment conditions needed for computing optimal instruments involves differentiation with respect to the two occurrences of θ in (4.21) and not only the second one – as acknowledged by Pan (2003), we sacrifice efficiency and gain analytical tractability by ignoring the dependence of Y_t^* on θ. As already mentioned in the likelihood case, it may indeed be challenging to look simultaneously for the "optimal" value of the implied states and for the best fit in the latent model. However, although backfitting was really needed in the likelihood case because, otherwise, forgetting the Jacobian term may imply inconsistency of the estimator, there is no such consistency problem with GMM. The only consequence of not taking into account the complete Jacobian term is that the efficiency of the optimal instrument scheme may be "limited", as acknowledged by Pan (2003). Indeed, because the two estimators IS-GMM and IS-backfitting are asymptotically equivalent, this limit to efficiency is tightly related to the contracting feature of the backfitting correspondence. More contracting it is, smaller is the efficiency loss.

4.4. Joint Estimation of Risk-Neutral and Objective Distributions

The area of joint estimation of risk-neutral and objective measures is probably where most of the progress took place over the last five years. The stage was set in the early 1990s with the considerable advances made regarding estimation of diffusion processes. Exploiting the EMM estimation procedure of Gallant and Tauchen (1996) for the estimation of diffusions, Chernov and Ghysels (2000) propose a generic procedure for estimating and pricing options using simultaneously the fundamental price S_t and a set of option contracts $[(\sigma_{it}^I)_{i=1,m}]$ where $m \geq 1$ and σ_{it}^I is the BS-implied volatility. The procedure consists of two steps. The first one fits a SNP density of $[S_t, (\sigma_{it}^I)_{i=1,m}]$ conditional on its own past $[S_\tau, (\sigma_{i\tau}^I)_{i=1,m}]$ for $\tau < t$. Second, one simulates the fundamental price and option prices and calibrates the parameters of the diffusion and its associated option pricing model to fit the conditional density of the market data dynamics. The EMM procedure allows estimating the model parameters under both objective and risk-neutral probability measures if one uses implied volatilities and the underlying asset data jointly. Time series of the underlying asset provide estimators under the objective probability measure, whereas risk-neutral parameters can be retrieved from options. Chernov and Ghysels (2000) adopt the Heston model, which has a closed-form option pricing formula, and compare univariate and multivariate models in terms of pricing and hedging performance.

Computing the prices of risk involves parameters of the objective measure, the risk-neutral measure, and the latent volatility process. The univariate specifications consist of models only using the fundamental (i.e., the usual setup) and models using only options data. It should be noted, however, that the knowledge of the estimated model parameters is not sufficient to compute an option price or a hedge ratio. We have to know the latent spot volatility as well. Because the option price is a one-to-one function of the current value of the volatility process (Renault and Touzi, 1996), one can recover it via an inversion of the option pricing formula. However, this procedure is computationally cumbersome, except if one relies on approximations by series expansions (Garcia et al., 2009; Lewis, 2000).

Another possible strategy is to use an extension of the SNP/EMM methodology introduced in Gallant and Tauchen (1998), which allows one to filter spot volatilities via reprojection, i.e., compute the expected value of the latent volatility process using a SNP density conditioned on the observable processes such as returns and/or options data. The results in Chernov and Ghysels (2000) show that the univariate approach only involving options by and large dominates. A by-product of this finding is that they uncover a remarkably simple volatility extraction filter based on a polynomial lag structure of implied volatilities. The bivariate approach appears useful when the information from the cash market provides support via the conditional kurtosis to price options. This is the case for some long-term options.

Pan (2002) examines also a joint time series model of the S&P 500 index and near-the-money short-term option prices in the context of the jump-diffusion model described at the beginning of this section. She uses an implied-state GMM approach to estimate the model. For a given set of model parameters ϑ, she replaces the unobserved volatility V_t by an option-implied volatility V_t^{ϑ} inverted numerically from the spot price S_t and a near-the-money short-term option price π_t based on the option pricing formula implied by the jump-diffusion model.[6] The interest of such a method is to take advantage of the analytical tractability of the state variables S and V compared with the complicated joint dynamics of the pair S and π, given the nonlinear nature of the option pricing function. The usual GMM procedure can be applied to the moments of the pair of state variables S_t and V_t^{ϑ}, but now one of the state variables is parameter-dependent. The closer ϑ is to the true model parameter vector ϑ_0, the more accurate is the corresponding option-implied volatility V_t^{ϑ}.

Garcia et al. (2009) propose an estimation procedure that uses both option prices and high-frequency spot price feeds to estimate jointly the objective and risk-neutral parameters of SV models. This procedure is based on series expansions of option prices and implied volatilities and on a method-of-moment estimation that uses analytical expressions for the moments of the integrated volatility. In a SV model, with or without correlation, the option pricing formula involves the computation of a conditional expectation of a highly nonlinear integral function of the volatility process. To simplify this computation, the authors propose to use an expansion of the option pricing formula in the neighborhood of $\sigma_V = 0$, as in Lewis (2000), which corresponds to the BS deterministic volatility case. The coefficients of this expansion are well-defined functions of the conditional moments of the joint distribution of the underlying asset returns and integrated volatilities, which are also derived analytically. These analytical expansions allow to compute very quickly implied volatilities, which are functions of the parameters of the processes and of the risk premia. A two-step GMM approach using intraday returns for computing approximate integrated volatilities (the objective part of the estimation)

[6]The numerical procedure to compute the model-based implied volatility is described in Appendix B of Pan (2002).

and option prices for computing implied volatilities (the risk-neutral part of the estimation) allows to recover the volatility risk premia λ. The main attractive feature of this method is its simplicity once analytical expressions for the various conditional moments of interest are available. The great advantage of the affine diffusion model is precisely to allow an analytical treatment of the conditional moments of interest. Eraker (2004) applies a Markov chain Monte Carlo-based approach to joint time-series data on spot and options also for a jump-diffusion model.

5. NONPARAMETRIC APPROACHES

The financial theoretical models of the previous sections are based on parametric dynamic processes for stock returns. Despite the great deal of complexity put into these processes to capture the features of the data, they remain usually misspecified. Therefore, nonparametric methods, which are so-called model-free and make minimal assumptions about the underlying asset price process, appear as a promising tool to apply in the context of derivative pricing. Moreover, these methods are well adapted to the financial problems at hand because the quantities of interest are functions, whether it is the risk-neutral distribution or SPD, the distribution function for hedging or else the value-at-risk quantile function of the conditional distribution of returns.

Nonparametric methods have been applied to all the above-mentioned financial problems of interest. We will discuss in this section how nonparametric methods can be used to recover a pricing function, a hedging ratio and a risk-neutral distribution. As a way to make the transition between the parametric and nonparametric approaches, we will first consider a semiparametric approach proposed by Aït-Sahalia and Lo (1998) and Gouriéroux et al. (1994). The main idea is to recover risk-neutral distribution using a nonparametric deterministic volatility function while maintaining that the derivative pricing function is given by the parametric BS formula. Next, we will see a maximum entropy approach initiated by Buchen and Kelly (1996) and Stutzer (1996) to recover a risk-neutral distribution from a set of option and stock prices, as well as the implied binomial tree method of Derman and Kani (1994), Dupire (1994), or Rubinstein (1994). Third, we will survey the purely nonparametric approaches such as kerned-based techniques or learning networks used to estimate an option pricing function and recover the other quantities of interest with option price data. We will underline several potential problems associated with these purely nonparametric approaches such as negative risk-neutral probabilities and argue following Garcia and Gençay (2000) and Aït-Sahalia and Duarte (2003) that imposing weak constraints on the shape and properties of the pricing function can improve the performance of the statistical model in several dimensions.[7]

[7] See also Yatchew and Härdle (2005), Birke and Pilz (2009), and Fan and Mancini (2008).

Last, we will describe how to recover preferences from the estimates of the SPD as proposed by Jackwerth (2000), Aït-Sahalia and Lo (2000), Rosenberg and Engle (2002), and Chabi-Yo et al. (2008).

Most empirical studies of option pricing focus on European contracts. In contrast, American options while actively traded and very liquid in some cases (such as the S&P 100-based contracts) have been avoided to circumvent early exercise premia and boundaries. It is worth noting that nonparametric methods are particularly suited to handle American-type options. Broadie et al. (2000a,b) use nonparametric techniques to estimate pricing functions as well as early exercise boundaries for American options.

5.1. Semiparametric Approaches to Derivative Pricing

One of the reasons why option price data do not conform to the BS model is that volatility is not constant. One can still maintain the assumption of a one-factor diffusion process but make the diffusion coefficient a deterministic function of the available information such as the exercise price, the underlying price, and the time to maturity. Although Shimko (1993) proposed a polynomial function of these variables for the volatility, Aït-Sahalia and Lo (1998) modeled the volatility function using kernel methods. The strategy is to construct a nonparametric estimator of the expectation of volatility given the information available on the underlying stock price S_t (or the futures price $F_{t,\tau_i} = S_t e^{(r_{t,\tau}-\delta_{t,\tau})\tau}$, with r and δ the interest rate and the dividend rate), the exercise price X_i, and the time to maturity τ_i associated with n traded options:

$$\widehat{\sigma}(F_{t,\tau}, X, \tau) = \frac{\sum_{i=1}^{n} k_F\left(\frac{F_{t,\tau}-F_{t,\tau_i}}{h_F}\right) k_X\left(\frac{X-X_i}{h_X}\right) k_\tau\left(\frac{\tau-\tau_i}{h_\tau}\right) \sigma_i}{\sum_{i=1}^{n} k_F\left(\frac{F_{t,\tau}-F_{t,\tau_i}}{h_F}\right) k_X\left(\frac{X-X_i}{h_X}\right) k_\tau\left(\frac{\tau-\tau_i}{h_\tau}\right)}, \tag{5.1}$$

where the multivariate kernel is formed as a product of three univariate kernels k_F, k_X, and k_τ, each with their own bandwidth value, with respect to the three variables of interest, and where $_i$ is the BS volatility implied by the observed price of option i. A call pricing function can then be estimated as

$$\widehat{\pi}(S_t, X, \tau, r_{t,\tau}, \delta_{t,\tau}) = \pi_{BS}(F_{t,\tau}, X, \tau, r_{t,\tau}, \widehat{\sigma}(F_{t,\tau}, X, \tau)). \tag{5.2}$$

From this function, one can also obtain estimators for the option's delta and the SPD by taking the appropriate partial derivatives according to (2.6) and (2.12):

$$\widehat{\Delta}_t = \frac{\partial \widehat{\pi}(S_t, X, \tau, r_{t,\tau}, \delta_{t,\tau})}{\partial S_t} \tag{5.3}$$

$$\widehat{f}_t^*(S_T) = e^{r_{t,\tau}\tau} \left[\frac{\partial^2 \widehat{\pi}(S_t, X, \tau, r_{t,\tau}, \delta_{t,\tau})}{\partial X^2}\right]_{|X=S_T}. \tag{5.4}$$

Of course, in nonparametric methods, higher order derivatives are estimated at a slower rate of convergence. This is known as the curse of differentiation. However, in a simulation framework based on a BS model, Aït-Sahalia and Lo (1998) show that the estimation errors for all nonparametric quantities (option price, option delta, and SPD) remain within 1% of their theoretical counterparts. Aït-Sahalia and Lo (1998) apply their method to the estimation of these quantities for S&P 500 European option price data. Their sample period is January 4, 1993 to December 31, 1993. Their nonparametric estimator of volatility $\widehat{\sigma}(F_{t,\tau}, X, \tau)$ generates a strongly asymmetric volatility smile with respect to moneyness, confirming several sources of evidence according to which out-of-money put prices have been consistently bid up since the crash of 1987. The shape of the smile changes as time to maturity increases. The one-month smile is the steepest: volatility curves are flatter for longer times to maturity. Strong skewness and kurtosis effects are present in the semiparametrically estimated SPDs. The (negative) skewness in returns diminishes as the maturity increases, whereas the contrary is obtained for the positive kurtosis.

A somewhat less ambitious approach has been advocated by Erikkson et al. (2009) and Ghysels and Wang (2009). They suggest to use the normal inverse Gaussian (NIG) family to approximate an unknown distribution risk-neutral density. The appeal of the NIG family of distributions is that they are characterized by the first four moments: mean, variance, skewness, and kurtosis. These are the moments we care about in many applications – including derivative pricing. The unknown density function is approximated by matching the cumulants. The latter are obtained from the cross-section of option prices using methods proposed by Bakshi et al. (2003). One strength of their approach is that they link the pricing of individual derivatives to the moments of the risk-neutral distribution, which has an intuitive appeal in terms of how volatility, skewness, and kurtosis of the risk-neutral distribution can explain the behavior of the derivative prices. Erikkson et al. (2009) show that the approximation errors are minor when compared to several option pricing models that have known densities. Another approach, advocated by Figlewski (2009), consists of estimating the central part of the distribution only with options and extrapolating the tails via extreme value distributions.

5.2. Canonical Valuation and Implied Binomial Trees

The semiparametric approach we just described still depends on the assumptions that there is just one state variable and that it is governed by an Itô process.[8] But, as we have extensively documented in the previous sections, there is evidence of jumps and SV in the underlying stock index process. Therefore, we need procedures that extract the asset probability distribution directly from observed prices either on the asset itself or on

[8]In fact, the semiparametric approach could also be valid for i.i.d. jump processes as in Merton (1976) or Bates (1991)

options written on the asset. We will describe first a procedure based on the maximum entropy principle, which has been proposed by Buchen and Kelly (1996) and by Stutzer (1996) and contrast it with the binomial tree approach of Rubinstein (1994). Both the former procedure, called canonical valuation by Stutzer (1996), and the latter assume that a set of financial instruments are priced correctly and can be used to recover the asset distribution from an expectation pricing model. As we will see, the differences between the two approaches lie in the choice of objective function.

5.2.1. Canonical Valuation

We want to estimate the payoff distribution of the underlying asset at expiration of the option from a set of available asset and option prices. To illustrate the method, we will take the simplest case of one underlying asset that does not pay dividends, which will be used to price derivative securities expiring T periods from now. Following Stutzer (1996), we start using only returns on the underlying asset, then we will add price information coming from options. The method involves three steps. First, starting with the current price S and a historical time series $S(t)$, $t = -1, -2, \ldots, -H$, one can construct a rolling historical time series of T-period gross returns:

$$R(-h) = \frac{S(-h)}{S(-h-T)}, \quad h = 1, 2, \ldots, H-T. \tag{5.5}$$

Then, the asset's price T-periods from now is

$$S^h = SR(-h), \quad h = 1, 2, \ldots, H-T. \tag{5.6}$$

In other words, the past realized returns are used to construct possible prices at T for the underlying asset, each with estimated objective (actual) probability $\widehat{p}(h) = \frac{1}{H-T}$. The problem is to find the risk-neutral probabilities p^*, which are the closest to the empirical probabilities $\widehat{p}$ in the Kullback–Leibler Information Criterion (KLIC) distance:

$$\widehat{p}^* = \arg \min_{p^*(h)>0 \ \sum_h p^*(h)=1} I(p^*, \widehat{p}) = \sum_{h=1}^{H-T} p^*(h) \log \frac{p^*(h)}{\widehat{p}(h)} \tag{5.7}$$

and which obey the nonarbitrage economic constraint (assuming a constant interest rate):

$$\sum_{h=1}^{H-T} \frac{R(-h)}{r^T} \frac{p^*(h)}{\widehat{p}(h)} \widehat{p}(h) = 1. \tag{5.8}$$

The solution to this problem is

$$\widehat{p}^*(h) = \frac{\exp\left[\gamma^* \frac{R(-h)}{r^T}\right]}{\sum_h \exp\left[\gamma^* \frac{R(-h)}{r^T}\right]}, \quad h = 1, 2, \ldots, H-T, \tag{5.9}$$

where γ^* is found as the arg min of $\sum_h \exp\left[\gamma\left(\frac{R(-h)}{r^T} - 1\right)\right]$. The last step is of course to use the $p^*(h)$ to value say a call option with exercise price X expiring at T by

$$C = \sum_h \frac{\max[SR(-h) - X, 0]}{r^T} \widehat{p}^*(h). \tag{5.10}$$

The methodology is easily extendable to compute risk-neutral probabilities based on more than one underlying asset. One can also ensure that a subset of derivative securities is correctly priced at a particular date. For example, if we wanted to ensure the correct pricing of a particular call option expiring at date T with exercise price X and market price C, we would need to find a vector γ^* of two elements (γ_1^*, γ_2^*) such that

$$[\gamma_1^*, \gamma_2^*] = \arg\min_{\gamma} \sum_h \exp\left[\gamma_1\left(\frac{R(-h)}{r^T} - 1\right) + \gamma_2\left(\frac{\max[SR(-h) - X, 0]}{r^T} - C\right)\right] \tag{5.11}$$

These values would then be used to compute the estimated risk-neutral probabilities as

$$\widehat{p}^*(h) = \frac{\exp\left[\gamma_1^*\left(\frac{R(-h)}{r^T}\right) + \gamma_2^*\left(\frac{\max[SR(-h)-X,0]}{r^T}\right)\right]}{\sum_h \exp\left[\gamma_1^*\left(\frac{R(-h)}{r^T}\right) + \gamma_2^*\left(\frac{\max[SR(-h)-X,0]}{r^T}\right)\right]}, h = 1, 2, \ldots, H - T. \tag{5.12}$$

Stutzer (1996) uses this methodology to evaluate the impact of the 1987 crash on the risk-neutral probabilities first using only S&P 500 returns. As many other papers, he finds that the left-hand tail of the canonical distribution estimated with data including the crash extends further than the tail of the distribution without crash data. A useful diagnostic test is the skewness premium proposed by Bates (1991). It is the percentage difference of the price of a call that is x percent (> 0) out-of-the-money (relative to the current forward index value for delivery at the option's expiration) to the price of a put that is also x percent out-of-the-money. The canonical valuation passes this diagnostic test for options in the 3 to 6 month range for $x > 0.02$ using only the historical data on S&P 500 returns starting in 1987 and without incorporating market option prices in the valuation process.[9]

5.2.2. Implied Binomial Trees

The implied binomial tree methodology proposed by Rubinstein (1994) aims also at recovering the risk-neutral probabilities that will come closest to pricing correctly a set of derivative securities at a given date. The idea is to start with a prior guess for the

[9] Gray and Norman (2005) apply canonical valuation of options in the presence of SV. Haley and Walker (2007) propose alternative tilts (or probability distortions) based on the Cressie-Read divergence family.

risk-neutral probabilities say $\widetilde{p}_j^*$ and find the risk-neutral probabilities p_j^* associated with the binomial terminal stock price S_T that are the closest to $\widetilde{p}_j^*$ but price correctly an existing set of options and the underlying stock. The risk-neutral probabilities p_j^* are solutions to the following program:

$$\min_{p_j^*} \sum_j \left(p_j^* - \widetilde{p}_j^*\right)^2 \text{ subject to} \tag{5.13}$$

$$\sum_j p_j^* = 1 \text{ and } p_j^* \geq 0 \text{ for } j = 0, \ldots, n$$

$$S^b \leq S \leq S^a \text{ where } S = \left(\sum_j p_j^* S_j\right) \Big/ r^\tau$$

$$C_i^b \leq C_i \leq C_i^a \text{ where } C_i = \left(\sum_j p_j^* \max[0, S_j - K_i]\right) \Big/ r^\tau \text{ for } i = 1, \ldots, m,$$

where j indexes the ending binomial nodes from lowest to highest, S_j is the underlying asset prices (supposing no dividends) at the end of a standard binomial tree, S^b and S^a are the current observed bid and ask underlying asset price, C_i^a and C_i^b are the current observed bid and ask call option prices with striking price K_i, r is the observed annualized riskless return, and τ is the time to expiration.

The two methods are therefore very similar, the main difference being the distance criterion used.[10] Although the maximum entropy criterion appears the best one from a theoretical point of view, because it selects the posterior that has the highest probability of being correct given the prior, there does not seem to be a statistical criterion behind the quadratic distance. A goodness of fit criterion given by $\min_{p_j^*} \sum_j (p_j^* - \widetilde{p}_j^*)^2 / \widetilde{p}_j^*$ seems more natural and is closer to the criterion used by Hansen and Jagannathan (1997) (see Subsection 5.2.3). The goodness of fit criterion places greater weight on states with lower probabilities. Another criterion used is to maximize smoothness by minimizing $\sum_j (p_{j-1}^* - 2p_j^* + p_{j+1}^*)^2$, as in Jackwerth and Rubinstein (1996) to avoid the overfitting associated with exactly pricing the options. With the smoothness criterion, there is a trade-off between smoothing the risk-neutral distribution and explaining the option prices. All these approaches will produce risk-neutral distributions that have much more weight in the lower left tail than the lognormal case after the 1987 crash, but they will distribute the probability differently in the tail.

[10] Cont and Tankov (2004) use a relative entropy criterion with respect to a chosen prior model to find a risk-neutral exponential Lévy model that reproduces observed option prices.

5.2.3. A SDF Alternative to Implied Binomial Trees

One might also measure closeness as the distance between pricing kernels and not between risk-neutral probabilities by looking for the SDF m^*_{t+1} defined by

$$m^*_{i,t+1} = B(t, t+1)\left(\frac{p^*_{it}}{p_{it}}\right), \quad i = 0, 1, \ldots, I+1$$

which is closest to a prior SDF

$$\tilde{m}^*_{i,t+1} = B(t, t+1)\left(\frac{\tilde{p}^*_{it}}{p_{it}}\right).$$

For instance, according to Hansen and Jagannathan (1997), one can choose the L^2-distance between SDFs:

$$E_t\left[m^*_{t+1} - \tilde{m}^*_{t+1}\right]^2 = B^2(t, t+1)\sum_{i=0}^{I+1}\frac{1}{p_{it}}\left(p^*_{it} - \tilde{p}^*_{it}\right)^2. \tag{5.14}$$

Therefore, the Hansen and Jagannathan (1997) measure of closeness (5.14) between SDFs and the goodness of fit criterion between probabilities $\sum_{i=0}^{I+1}(1/\tilde{p}^*_{it})\left(p^*_{it} - \tilde{p}^*_{it}\right)^2$ will lead to similar conclusions if and only if the prior risk-neutral probabilities p^*_{it} are close to the objective probability distribution p_{it}. However, risk-neutral probabilities may include agents anticipations about rare risks, which are not apparent in a historical estimation of objective probabilities. This is the well-documented peso problem, which has been discussed in the context of option pricing by Eraker (2004).

This discussion makes clear the potential drawback of the Euclidian distance (5.13) between probabilities. It does not put a sufficient weight on extreme events with small probabilities. This may lead to severe pricing errors because these small probabilities appear at the denominator of SDFs and therefore, have a large weight in the effective computation of derivative asset prices. Almeida and Garcia (2008) generalize the quadratic Hansen and Jagannathan (1997) measure of closeness by choosing the Cressie-Read family of discrepancy measures. Because this family includes the KLIC and the empirical likelihood divergence criteria, this extension makes clear the links between all the nonparametric approaches adopted to recover risk-neutral probabilities or pricing kernels to price options.

All of the methodologies we have described in this section are geared toward extracting conditional risk-neutral distributions in the sense that they fit cross-sections of option prices and in that sense have to be opposed to the unconditional approach of the previous section. In the next section, we summarize the advantages and disadvantages of both methods.

5.3. Comparing the Unconditional and Conditional Methodologies for Extracting Risk-Neutral Distributions

Because the canonical valuation or the implied tree methodologies aim at obtaining risk-neutral probabilities that come closest to pricing correctly the existing options at a single point in time, the risk-neutral distribution will change over time. On the contrary, a nonparametric kernel estimator aims at estimating the risk-neutral distribution as a fixed function of variables such as the current stock price, the exercise price, the riskless rate, and other variables of interest. The functional form of the estimated risk-neutral distribution should be relatively stable over time. Because we cannot really say that one approach is better than the other, we can only sketch the advantages and disadvantages of both methods following Aït-Sahalia and Lo (1998).

We will compare the implied binomial tree method of Rubinstein (1994) to the semiparametric estimate of the risk-neutral distribution of Aït-Sahalia and Lo (1998). The first method produces a distribution that is completely consistent with all option prices at each date, but it is not necessarily consistent across time. The second may fit poorly for a cross-section of option prices at some date but is consistent across time. However, being a fixed function of the relevant variables, the variation in the probabilities has to be captured by the variation in these variables. Another consideration is the intertemporal dependency in the risk-neutral distributions. The first method ignores it totally, whereas the second exploits the dependencies in the data around a given date. Implied binomial trees are less data-intensive, whereas the kernel method requires many cross-sections. Finally, smoothness has to be imposed for the first method, whereas the second method delivers a smooth function by construction. The stability of the risk-neutral distribution obtained with the kernel-based estimate should lower the out-of-sample forecasting errors at the expense of deteriorating the in-sample fit. Aït-Sahalia and Lo (1998) compare the out-of-sample forecasting performance of their semiparametric method with the implied tree method of Jackwerth and Rubinstein (1996) and conclude that at short horizons (up to 5 days) the implied tree forecasting errors are lower but that at horizons of 10 days and longer, the kernel method performance is better.

Aït-Sahalia and Duarte (2003) proposed a nonparametric method to estimate the risk neutral density from a cross-section of option prices. This might appear surprising given that we know that nonparametric methods require a large quantity of data. Their nonparametric method is based on locally polynomial estimators that impose shape restrictions on the option pricing function. From the absence of arbitrage, we know that the price of a call option must be a decreasing and convex function of the strike price. The method consists therefore in two steps, first a constrained least square regression to impose monotonicity and convexity, followed by a locally polynomial kernel smoothing that preserves the constraints imposed in the first step. In a Monte Carlo analysis,

Aït-Sahalia and Duarte (2003) show these constrained nonparametric estimates are feasible in the small samples encountered in a typical daily cross section of option prices.

In an application to S&P 500 call option data with about 2 months to maturity on a day in 1999, they compare several estimators (unconstrained Nadaraya–Watson, unconstrained locally linear, quadratic and cubic, shape-constrained locally linear) in terms of price function, first derivative with respect to the strike price and SPD (second derivative). The comparison emphasizes that the price function is well estimated near the money but that for high values of the strike, the locally quadratic and cubic estimators are highly variable, whereas the unconstrained Nadaraya–Watson estimator violates the convexity constraint on prices for low values of the strike. These poor properties show even more in the first and the second derivatives. For the first derivative, all estimators except the constrained and unconstrained locally linear violate the first derivative constraint, whereas for the SPD (the second derivative), all the unconstrained estimators violate the positivity constraint in the left tail of the density or are too flat at the globally optimal bandwidth. This nonparametric approach with shape restrictions appears therefore promising, but more evidence and comparisons are needed.

In the next subsections, we will revisit these constrained and unconstrained approaches in the SNP context. A first way to enforce the shape restrictions is to use a parametric model for the SDF while remaining nonparametric for the historical distribution. It is the main motivation of the Extended Method of Moments (XMM). A second strategy is to directly fit a SNP model for the option pricing function. Then sieve estimators and especially neural networks are well suited to take into account shape restrictions.

5.4. Extended Method of Moments

The GMM was introduced by Hansen (1982) and Hansen and Singleton (1982) to estimate a structural parameter θ identified by Euler conditions:

$$p_{i,t} = E_t\left[M_{t,t+1}(\theta)p_{i,t+1}\right], \quad i = 1, \ldots, n, \ \forall t, \tag{5.15}$$

where $p_{i,t}, i = 1, \ldots, n$, are the observed prices of n financial assets, E_t denotes the expectation conditional on the available information at date t, and $M_{t,t+1}(\theta)$ is the stochastic discount factor. Model (5.15) is semiparametric. The GMM estimates parameter θ regardless of the conditional distribution of the state variables. This conditional distribution however becomes relevant when the Euler conditions (5.15) are used for pricing derivative assets. Indeed, when the derivative payoff is written on $p_{i,t+1}$ and its current price is not observed on the market, the derivative pricing requires the joint estimation of parameter θ and the conditional distribution of the state variables.

The XMM estimator of Gagliardini et al. (2008) extends the standard GMM to accommodate a more general set of moment restrictions. The standard GMM is based on uniform conditional moment restrictions such as (5.15), which are valid for any value of the conditioning variables. The XMM can handle uniform moment restrictions, as well as local moment restrictions, that are only valid for a given value of the conditioning variables. This leads to a new field of application to derivative pricing, as the XMM can be used for reconstructing the pricing operator on a given day, by using the information in a cross section of observed traded derivative prices and a time series of underlying asset returns. To illustrate the principle of XMM, consider an investor at date t_0 is interested in estimating the price $c_{t_0}(h,k)$ of a call option with time-to-maturity h and moneyness strike k that is currently not (actively) traded on the market. She has data on a time series of T daily returns of the S&P 500 index, as well as on a small cross section of current option prices $c_{t_0}(h_j,k_j)$, $j=1,\ldots,n$, of n highly traded derivatives. The XMM approach provides the estimated prices $\hat{c}_{t_0}(h,k)$ for different values of moneyness strike k and time-to-maturity h, which interpolate the observed prices of highly traded derivatives and satisfy the hypothesis of absence of arbitrage opportunities. These estimated prices are consistent for a large number of dates T, but a fixed, even small, number of observed derivative prices n.

We are interested in estimating the pricing operator at a given date t_0, i.e., the mapping that associates any European call option payoff $\varphi_{t_0}(h,k)=\left(\exp R_{t_0,h}-k\right)^+$ with its price $c_{t_0}(h,k)$ at time t_0, for any time-to-maturity h and any moneyness strike k. We denote by r_t the logarithmic return of the underlying asset between dates $t-1$ and t. We assume that the information available to the investors at date t is generated by the random vector X_t of state variables with dimension d, including the return r_t as the first component, and that X_t is also observable by the econometrician. The process (X_t) on $\mathcal{X}\subset\mathbf{R}^d$ is supposed to be strictly stationary and Markov under the historical probability with transition density $f(x_t|x_{t-1})$. Besides the cross section of option prices $c_{t_0}(h_j,k_j)$, $j=1,\ldots,n$ the available data consist in T serial observations of the state variables X_t corresponding to the current and previous days $t=t_0-T+1,\ldots,t_0$. The no-arbitrage assumption implies two sets of moment restrictions for the observed asset prices. The constraints concerning the observed derivative prices at t_0 are given by

$$c_{t_0}(h_j,k_j)=E\left[M_{t,t+h_j}(\theta)(\exp R_{t,h_j}-k_j)^+|X_t=x_{t_0}\right],\quad j=1,\ldots,n. \tag{5.16}$$

The constraints concerning the risk free asset and the underlying asset are

$$\begin{cases} E[M_{t,t+1}(\theta)|\ X_t=x]=B(t,t+1), & \forall x\in\mathcal{X}, \\ E[M_{t,t+1}(\theta)\exp r_{t+1}|\ X_t=x]=1, & \forall x\in\mathcal{X}, \end{cases} \tag{5.17}$$

respectively, where $B(t,t+1)$ denotes the price at time t of the short-term risk free bond. The conditional moment restrictions (5.16) are local because they hold for a single value of the conditioning variable only, namely the value x_{t_0} of the state variable at time t_0. This is because we consider only observations of the derivative prices $c_{t_0}(h_j,k_j)$ at date t_0.

Conversely, the prices of the underlying asset and the risk free bond are observed for all trading days. Therefore, the conditional moment restrictions (5.17) hold for all values of the state variables. They are called the uniform moment restrictions. The distinction between the uniform and local moment restrictions is a consequence of the differences between the trading activities of the underlying asset and its derivatives. Technically, it is the essential feature of the XMM that distinguishes this method from its predecessor GMM.

The XMM estimator presented in this section is related to the literature on the information-based GMM (e.g., Imbens et al., 1998; Kitamura and Stutzer, 1997). It provides estimators of both the SDF parameter θ and the historical transition density $f(y|x)$. By using the parameterized SDF, the information-based estimator of the historical transition density defines the estimated SPD for pricing derivatives.

The XMM approach involves a consistent nonparametric estimator of the historical transition density $f(y|x)$, such as the kernel density estimator:

$$\hat{f}(y|x) = \frac{1}{h_T^{\tilde{d}}} \sum_{t=1}^{T} \tilde{K}\left(\frac{y_t - y}{h_T}\right) K\left(\frac{x_t - x}{h_T}\right) \Big/ \sum_{t=1}^{T} K\left(\frac{x_t - x}{h_T}\right), \tag{5.18}$$

where K (resp. $\tilde{K}$) is the d-dimensional (resp. $\tilde{d}$-dimensional) kernel, h_T is the bandwidth, and (x_t, y_t), $t = 1, \ldots, T$, are the historical sample data.[11] Next, this kernel density estimator is improved by selecting the conditional pdf that is the closest to $\widehat{f}(y|x)$ and satisfies the moment restrictions as defined below.

The XMM estimator $\left(\hat{f}^* (\cdot|x_0), \hat{f}^* (\cdot|x_1), \ldots, \hat{f}^* (\cdot|x_T), \widehat{\theta}\right)$ consists of the functions $f_0, f_1, \ldots, f_T$ defined on $Y \subset R^{\tilde{d}}$, and the parameter value θ that minimize the objective function:

$$L_T = \frac{1}{T} \sum_{t=1}^{T} \int \frac{\left[\widehat{f}(y|x_t) - f_t(y)\right]^2}{\widehat{f}(y|x_t)} dy + h_T^d \int \log\left[\frac{f_0(y)}{\widehat{f}(y|x_0)}\right] f_0(y) dy,$$

subject to the constraints:

$$\int f_t(y) dy = 1, \quad t = 1, \ldots, T, \qquad \int f_0(y) dy = 1,$$

$$\int g(y; \theta) f_t(y) dy = 0, \quad t = 1, \ldots, T, \qquad \int g_2(y; \theta) f_0(y) dy = 0. \tag{5.19}$$

[11] For expository purpose, the dates previous to t_0, at which data on (X, Y) are available, have been reindexed as $t = 1, \ldots, T$ and accordingly the asymptotics in T correspond to a long history before t_0.

The objective function L_T has two components. The first component involves the chi-square distance between the density f_t and the kernel density estimator $\widehat{f}(.|x_t)$ at any sample point x_t, $t = 1, \ldots, T$. The second component corresponds to the KLIC between the density f_0 and the kernel estimator $\widehat{f}(.|x_0)$ at the given value x_0. In addition to the unit mass restrictions for the density functions, the constraints include the uniform moment restrictions written for all sample points and the whole set of local moment restrictions. The combination of two types of discrepancy measures is motivated by computational and financial reasons. The chi-square criterion evaluated at the sample points allows for closed form solutions $f_1(\theta), \ldots, f_T(\theta)$ for a given θ. Therefore, the objective function can be easily concentrated with respect to functions $f_1, \ldots, f_T$, which reduces the dimension of the optimization problem. The KLIC criterion evaluated at x_0 ensures that the minimizer f_0 satisfies the positivity restriction (see, e.g., Kitamura and Stutzer, 1997; Stutzer, 1996). The positivity of the associated SPD at t_0 guarantees the absence of arbitrage opportunities in the estimated derivative prices. The estimator of $\hat{\theta}$ minimizes the concentrated objective function:

$$\mathcal{L}_T^c(\theta) = \frac{1}{T}\sum_{t=1}^{T} \widehat{E}\big(g(\theta)|x_t\big)' \,\widehat{V}\big(g(\theta)|x_t\big)^{-1} \widehat{E}\,\big(g(\theta)|x_t\big) - h_T^d \log \widehat{E}\big(\exp\big(\lambda(\theta)' g_2(\theta)\big)\,|x_0\big), \quad (5.20)$$

where the Lagrange multiplier $\lambda(\theta) \in \mathbf{R}^{n+2}$ is such that

$$\widehat{E}\left[g_2(\theta) \exp\left(\lambda\,(\theta)'\, g_2(\theta)\right) |x_0\right] = 0, \quad (5.21)$$

for all θ, and $\widehat{E}\,\big(g(\theta)|x_t\big)$ and $\widehat{V}\,\big(g(\theta)|x_t\big)$ denote the expectation and variance of $g(Y;\theta)$, respectively, w.r.t. the kernel estimator $\widehat{f}(y|x_t)$. The first part of the concentrated objective function (5.20) is reminiscent from the conditional version of the continuously updated GMM (Ai and Chen, 2003; Antoine et al., 2007). The estimator of $f(y|x_0)$ is given by

$$\widehat{f}^*(y|x_0) = \frac{\exp\left(\lambda\left(\hat{\theta}\right)' g_2(y;\hat{\theta})\right)}{\widehat{E}\left[\exp\left(\lambda\left(\hat{\theta}\right)' g_2(\hat{\theta})\right)|x_0\right]} \widehat{f}(y|x_0), \; y \in \mathcal{Y}. \quad (5.22)$$

This conditional density is used to estimate the pricing operator at time t_0.

The XMM estimator of the derivative price $c_{t_0}(h, k)$ is

$$\hat{c}_{t_0}(h, k) = \int M_{t_0,t_0+h}(\hat{\theta}) \left(\exp R_{t_0,h} - k\right)^+ \hat{f}^* \left(y|x_0\right) dy, \quad (5.23)$$

for any time-to-maturity $h \leq \bar{h}$ and any moneyness strike k. The constraints (5.19) imply that the estimator $\hat{c}_{t_0}(h,k)$ is equal to the observed option price $c_{t_0}(h_j,k_j)$ when $h = h_j$ and $k = k_j, j = 1,\ldots,n$.

The large sample properties of estimators $\hat{\theta}$ and $\hat{c}_{t_0}(h,k)$ are examined in Gagliardini et al. (2008). These estimators are consistent and asymptotically normal for large samples T of the time series of underlying asset returns, but a fixed number n of observed derivative prices at t_0. The linear combinations of θ that are identifiable from uniform moment restrictions on the risk free asset and the underlying asset only are estimated at the standard parametric rate $\sqrt{T}$. Any other direction η_2^* in the parameter space and the derivative prices as well are estimated at the rate $\sqrt{Th_T^d}$ corresponding to nonparametric estimation of conditional expectations given $X = x_0$. The estimators of derivative prices are (nonparametrically) asymptotically efficient.

5.5. Other SNP Estimators

In the SNP approach, the nonlinear relationship f between the price of an option π and the various variables that affect its price, say Z, is approximated by a set of basis functions g:

$$f(Z,.) = \sum_{n=1}^{\infty} \alpha_n g_n(Z,.). \tag{5.24}$$

The term SNP is explained by the fact that the basis functions are parametric, yet the parameters are not the object of interest because we need an infinity of them to estimate the function in the usual nonparametric sense. The methods vary according to the basis functions chosen. Hutchinson et al. (1994) propose various types of learning networks, Gouriéroux and Monfort (2001) consider approximations of the pricing kernel through splines, whereas Abadir and Rockinger (1998) investigate hypergeometric functions. In what follows, we will develop the neural network approach and see how one can choose the basis to obtain a valid SPD function. The basis chosen for neural networks will be

$$g_n(Z,\alpha_n) = \frac{1}{1+\exp(-\alpha_n Z)}, \tag{5.25}$$

which is a very flexible sigmoid function. Then, the function can be written as

$$f(Z,\theta) = \beta_0 + \sum_{i=1}^{d} \beta_i \frac{1}{1+\exp(\gamma_{i,0} - \gamma_{i,1} Z)}, \tag{5.26}$$

where the vector of parameters $\theta = (\beta, \gamma)$ and the number d of units remains to be determined as the bandwidth in kernel methods. In neural network terminology, this is called a single hidden-layer feedforward network. Many authors have investigated the universal approximation properties of neural networks (see in particular Gallant and White, 1988, 1992). Using a wide variety of proof strategies, all have demonstrated that under general regularity conditions, a sufficiently complex single hidden-layer feedforward network can approximate a large class of functions and their derivatives to any desired degree of accuracy where the complexity of a single hidden layer feedforward network is measured by the number of hidden units in the hidden layer. One of the requirements for this universal approximation property is that the activation function has to be a sigmoidal such as the logistic function presented above.

One nice property of this basis function is that the derivatives can be expressed in closed form. If we denote $h(Z) = \frac{1}{1+e^Z}$, then

$$h'(Z) = h(Z).(1 - h(Z))$$
$$h''(Z) = h(Z).(1 - h(Z)).(1 - 2h(Z)).$$

Therefore, once the parameters of the pricing function are estimated for a given number of units, we can compute the hedge ratio or the risk-neutral distribution. Hutchinson et al. (1994) show using simulations that such an approach can learn the BS formula. To reduce the number of inputs, Hutchinson et al. (1994) divide the function and its arguments by X and write the pricing function as a function of moneyness (S/X) and time-to-maturity (τ):

$$\frac{\pi_t}{X} = f\left(\frac{S_t}{X}, 1, \tau\right). \tag{5.27}$$

Although they kept the number of units fixed, it is usually necessary as with any non-parametric method to choose it in some optimal way. The familiar trade-off is at play. Increasing the number of units d given a sample of data will lead to overfit the function in sample and cause a loss of predictive power out of sample. A way to choose the number of units is to use a cross-validation type of method on a validation period as proposed in Garcia and Gençay (2000).[12] Although it is not mentioned in Hutchinson et al. (1994), even if we estimate well the pricing function, large errors are committed for the derivatives of the function, and most notably, negative probabilities are obtained. This is consistent with what Aït-Sahalia and Duarte (2003) have found with local polynomial estimators based on a small sample of data, except that these bad properties are also present in large samples used for estimating the function over a long-time period.

A partial and imperfect way to better estimate the hedge ratio and the risk-neutral distribution is to use a network that will capture the homogeneity of the pricing function as in Garcia and Gençay (2000). The form in (5.27) assumes the homogeneity of degree

[12] Gençay and Qi (2001) studied the effectiveness of cross-validation, Bayesian regularization, early stopping, and bagging to mitigate overfitting and improving generalization for pricing and hedging derivative securities.

one in the asset price and the strike price of the pricing function f. Another technical reason for dividing by the strike price is that the process S_t is nonstationary, whereas the variable S_t/X is stationary as strike prices bracket the underlying asset price process. This point is emphasized in Ghysels et al. (1996). From a theoretical point of view, the homogeneity property is obtained under unconditional or conditional independence of the distribution of returns from the level of the asset price (see Merton, 1973, or Garcia and Renault, 1998b). Garcia and Gençay (2000) estimate a network of the form

$$\frac{C_t}{X} = \beta_0 + \sum_{i=1}^{d} \beta_i^1 h\left(\gamma_{i,0}^1 + \gamma_{i,1}^1 \frac{S_t}{X} + \gamma_{i,2}^1 \tau\right) \tag{5.28}$$

$$- \mathrm{e}^{-\alpha\tau} \sum_{i=1}^{d} \beta_i^2 h\left(\gamma_{i,0}^2 + \gamma_{i,1}^2 \frac{S_t}{X} + \gamma_{i,2}^2 \tau\right) \tag{5.29}$$

with $h(Z) = \left(1 + \mathrm{e}^Z\right)^{-1}$. This has a similar structure than the BS formula (which is itself homogeneous), except that the distribution function of the normal is replaced by neural network functions.[13] Garcia and Gençay (2000) show that this structure improves the pricing performance compared to an unconstrained network, but that it does not improve the hedging performance. In fact, this network suffers (albeit slightly less) from the same deficiencies in terms of derivatives. To impose monotonicity and convexity on the function and ensuring that the resulting risk-neutral distribution is a proper density function as in Aït-Sahalia and Duarte (2003), we need to choose an appropriate structure for the network. The following basis function proposed in Dugas et al. (2001)

$$\xi(Z) = \log(1 + \mathrm{e}^Z) \tag{5.30}$$

is always positive and has its minimum at zero. Its first derivative

$$\xi'(Z) = \frac{\mathrm{e}^Z}{1 + \mathrm{e}^Z} = h(Z) \tag{5.31}$$

is always positive and between 0 and 1 and therefore qualifies for a distribution function. Finally, its second derivative

$$\xi''(Z) = h'(Z) = h(Z).(1 - h(Z)) \tag{5.32}$$

is always positive, becomes 0 when $h \to 0$ $(Z \to -\infty)$ or when $h \to 1$ $(Z \to +\infty)$, and has its maximum at $h = 1/2$ $(Z = 0)$. These properties qualify for a density function.

[13]This is what distinguishes this SNP approach from the semiparametric approach of Aït-Sahalia and Lo (2000), who use the BS formula with a nonparametric estimator of volatility.

Abadir and Rockinger (1998) with hypergeometric functions, Gottschling et al. (2000) with neural networks, and Gouriéroux and Monfort (2001) with splines on the log-pricing kernel are three other ways to make sure that the estimated option pricing function always lead to a valid density, i.e., nonnegative everywhere and integrating to one. Härdle and Yatchew (2001) also use nonparametric least squares to impose a variety of constraints on the option pricing function and its derivatives. Their estimator uses least squares over sets of functions bounded in Sobolev norm, which offers a simple way of imposing smoothness on derivatives. Birke and Pilz (2009) propose a completely kernel-based estimate of the call price function, which fulfills all constraints given by the no-arbitrage principle. Fan and Mancini (2008) propose a new nonparametric method for pricing options based on a nonparametric correction of pricing errors induced by a given model.

There is a need for a comparison of these methods, which impose constraints on the estimation. Bondarenko (2003) proposes a new nonparametric method called positive convolution approximation, which chooses among a rich set of admissible (smooth and well behaved) densities the one that provides the best fit to the option prices. He conducts a Monte Carlo experiment to compare this method to seven other methods, parametric and nonparametric, which recover risk-neutral densities. Daglish (2003) also provides a comparison between parametric and nonparametric methods for American options.

5.6. An Economic Application of Nonparametric Methods: Extraction of Preferences

Because, in a continuum of states, the SPD or risk-neutral density corresponds to the Arrow–Debreu prices, it contains valuable information about the preferences of the representative investor. Indeed, the ratio of the SPD to the conditional objective probability density is proportional to the marginal rate of substitution of the representative investor, implying that preferences can be recovered given estimates of the SPD and the conditional objective distribution. A measure of relative risk aversion is given by

$$\rho_t(S_T) = S_T\left(\frac{f_t'(S_T)}{f_t(S_T)} - \frac{f_t^{*\prime}(S_T)}{f_t^*(S_T)}\right), \tag{5.33}$$

where $f_t(S_T)$ and $f_t^*(S_T)$ denote, respectively, the conditional objective probability density and the SPD. This measure assumes that S_T, the value of the index at the maturity of the option, approximates aggregate consumption, the payoff on the market portfolio.

Several researchers have extracted risk aversion functions or preference parameters from observed asset prices. Aït-Sahalia and Lo (2000) and Jackwerth (2000) have proposed nonparametric approaches to recover risk aversion functions across wealth states from observed stock and option prices. Rosenberg and Engle (2002), Garcia et al. (2003), and Bliss and Panigirtzoglou (2004) have estimated preference parameters based on parametric asset pricing models with several specifications of the utility function.

These efforts to exploit prices of financial assets to recover fundamental economic parameters have produced puzzling results. Aït-Sahalia and Lo (2000) find that the non-parametrically implied function of relative risk aversion varies significantly across the range of S&P 500 index values, from 1 to 60, and is U-shaped. Jackwerth (2000) finds also that the implied absolute risk aversion function is U-shaped around the current forward price but even that it can become negative. Parametric empirical estimates of the coefficient of relative risk aversion also show considerable variation. Rosenberg and Engle (2002) report values ranging from 2.36 to 12.55 for a power utility pricing kernel across time, whereas Bliss and Panigirtzoglou (2004) estimate average values between 2.33 and 11.14 for the same S&P 500 index for several option maturities.[14] Garcia et al. (2003) estimate a consumption-based asset pricing model with regime-switching fundamentals and Epstein and Zin (1989) preferences. The estimated parameters for risk aversion and intertemporal substitution are reasonable with average values of 0.6838 and 0.8532, respectively, over the 1991–1995 period.[15]

As noticed by Rosenberg and Engle (2002), the interpretation of the risk aversion function is debatable because the estimation technique of the implied binomial tree is based on time-aggregated data. This is the reason why Rosenberg and Engle (2002) propose to estimate the pricing kernel as a function of contemporaneously observed asset prices and a predicted asset payoff density based on an asymmetric GARCH model. The price to pay for this generality is the need to refer to a parametric model for the SDF. They propose

$$m^*_{t+1} = E_t\left[\frac{m_{t+1}}{g_{t+1}}\right] = \theta_{0t}(g_{t+1})^{-\theta_{1t}}. \tag{5.34}$$

The parameters of interest θ_{0t} and θ_{1t} are then estimated at each date t to minimize the sum of squared pricing errors, i.e., differences between observed derivative prices (in a cross section of derivatives all written on the same payoff g_{t+1}) and prices computed with the model SDF (5.34). As in the multinomial example, there is some arbitrariness created by the choice of this particular quadratic measure of closeness. First, as discussed in Renault (1997), one may imagine that the pricing errors are severely heteroskedastic and mutually correlated. A GMM distance should get rid of this better than the uniform weighting. However, as stressed by Hansen and Jagannathan (1997), the GMM distance

[14] Rosenberg and Engle (2002) also estimate an orthogonal polynomial pricing kernel and find that it exhibits some of the risk-aversion characteristics noted by Jackwerth (2000), with a region of negative absolute risk aversion over the range from 4 to 2% for returns and an increasing absolute risk aversion for returns greater than 4%.

[15] The authors also estimate a CCRA-expected utility model and find a similar variability of the estimates as in the related studies. The average value is 7.2 over the 1991–1995 period with a standard deviation of 4.83.

is probably not optimal to rank various misspecified SDFs because it gives an unfair advantage to the most volatile SDFs.

As explained above, Hansen and Jagannathan (1997) propose to consider directly a L^2 distance between SDFs. They show that it leads to a weighting matrix for pricing errors, which is only defined by the covariance matrix of the net returns of interest and not by the product of returns with the SDF as in efficient GMM. Indeed, Buraschi and Jackwerth (2001) observe that the δ-metric of Hansen and Jagannathan (1997) has to be preferred to the GMM metric to select the best option pricing model because it is model independent, whereas the optimal GMM weighting matrix is model dependent and asymptotic chi-square, tests typically reward models that generate highly volatile pricing errors.

Irrespective of the choice of a particular measure of closeness, the interpretation of parameters θ_{0t} and θ_{1t} which have been estimated from (5.34) may be questionable, except if a very specific model is postulated for the agent preferences. To illustrate this point, let us consider the general family of SDFs provided by the Epstein and Zin (1989) model of recursive utility:

$$m_{t+1} = \beta \left[\frac{C_{t+1}}{C_t}\right]^{\gamma(\rho-1)} \left[\frac{W_{t+1}}{(W_t - C_t)}\right]^{\gamma-1}, \tag{5.35}$$

where $\rho = 1 - 1/\sigma$ with σ the elasticity of intertemporal substitution, $\gamma = \alpha/\rho$, and $a = 1 - \alpha$ the index of comparative relative risk aversion. The variables C_t and W_t denote, respectively, the optimal consumption and wealth paths of the representative agent. They obey the following relationship:

$$\left[\frac{C_t}{W_t}\right] = [A(J_t)]^{1-\sigma},$$

where $V_t = A(J_t) \cdot W_t$ denotes the value at time t of the maximized recursive utility function. This value V_t is proportional to the wealth W_t available at time t for consumption and investment (homothetic preferences), and the coefficient of proportionality generally depends on the information J_t available at time t. Therefore,

$$m_{t+1} = \beta \left[\frac{W_{t+1}}{W_t}\right]^{-a} \left[\frac{A(J_{t+1})}{A(J_t)}\right]^{1-a} \left[1 - A(J_t)^{1-\sigma}\right]^{\gamma-1}. \tag{5.36}$$

Let us imagine, following Rosenberg and Engle (2002), that the agent wealth is proportional to the underlying asset payoff. Then,

$$m^*_{t+1} = E_t[m_{t+1} | g_{t+1}] = E_t[m_{t+1} | W_{t+1}]$$

will depend in general in a complicated way on the forecast of the value function $A(J_{t+1})$ as a function of W_{t+1}. For instance, we see that

$$E_t[\log m_{t+1}|g_{t+1}] = B(J_t) - a\log\left[\frac{W_{t+1}}{W_t}\right] + (1-a)E_t[\log A(J_{t+1})|W_{t+1}].$$

This illustrates that except in the particular case $a = 1$ (logarithmic utility) or in a case where $A(J_{t+1})$ would not be correlated with W_{t+1} given J_t, the parameter θ_{1t} cannot be interpreted as risk aversion parameter and is not constant insofar as conditional heteroskedasticity will lead to time varying regression coefficients in $E_t[\log A(J_{t+1})|W_{t+1}]$. In other words, the intertemporal features of preferences that lead the agent to a nonmyopic behavior prevent one to conclude that the risk aversion parameter is time-varying simply because one finds that the parameter θ_{1t} is time-varying. More generally, this analysis carries over to any missing factor in the parametric SDF model.

The general conclusion is that empirical pricing kernels that are computed without a precise account of the state variables and enter into the value function $A(J_t)$ cannot provide valuable insights on intertemporal preferences. For example, Chabi-Yo et al. (2008) show that in an economy with regime changes either in fundamentals or in preferences, an application of the nonparametric methodology used by Jackwerth (2000) to recover the absolute risk aversion will lead to similar negative estimates of the risk aversion function in some states of wealth even though the risk aversion functions are consistent with economic theory within each regime.

Of course, one can also question the representative agent framework. For example, Bates (2007) points out that the industrial organization of the stock index options market does not seem to be compatible with the representative agent construct and proposes a general equilibrium model in which crash-tolerant market makers insure crash-averse investors.

6. CONCLUSION

We have tried in this survey to offer a unifying framework to the prolific literature aimed at extracting useful and sometimes profitable economic information from derivatives markets. The SDF methodology is by now the central tool in finance to price assets and provides a natural framework to integrate contributions in discrete and continuous time. Because most models are written in continuous time in option pricing, we have established the link between these models and the discrete time approaches trying to emphasize the fundamental unity underlying both methodologies. To capture the empirical features of the stock market returns, which is the main underlying empirically studied in the option pricing literature, models have gained in complexity from the standard geometric Brownian motion of the seminal Black and Scholes (1973) model. Jump-diffusion models with various correlation effects have become increasingly complex to estimate. A main difficulty is the interplay of the latent variables, which are everywhere present in the models and the inherent complex nonlinearities of the pricing formulas. This is the main aspect of the estimation methods on which we put some emphasis because the estimation of continuous-time models is the object of another chapter in this Handbook.

Another major thread that underlies the survey is the interplay between preferences and option pricing. Even though the preference-free nature of the early formulas was often cited as a major advantage, it was not clear where this feature was coming from. We have made a special effort to specify the statistical assumptions that are needed to obtain this feature and to characterize the covariance or leverage effects which reintroduce preferences. In an equilibrium framework, the role of preferences appears clearly. In approaches based on the absence of arbitrage, these preferences are hidden in risk premia and it is harder to account for the links they impose between the risk premia of the numerous sources of risk. Researchers often treat these risk premia as free parameters and manage to capture some empirical facts, but a deeper economic explanation is lacking. The extraction of preferences from option prices using nonparametric methods is even more problematic. The puzzles associated with this literature often come from the fact that state variables have been omitted in the analysis.

Despite the length of the survey, there are a host of issues that we left unattended, especially issues pertaining to the implementation of models in practice. First, it is often difficult to obtain synchronized price data for derivatives and underlying fundamentals. This leads researchers to use theoretical relationships such as the put-call parity theorem to infer forward prices for the index. The same theorem is sometimes also used to infer prices for some far in-the-money options for which the reliability of the reported price is questionable because of staleness or illiquidity. Other types of filters such as taking out close-to-maturity options or options with close-to-zero prices are also imposed. All these data transformations have certainly an effect on model estimation and testing. A second issue concerns the final objective of the modeling exercise. Is the model intended to forecast future prices (or equivalently the moneyness and term structure of volatilities), to compute hedge ratios (or other greeks), or to recover risk-neutral probabilities for a certain horizon to price other derivatives on the same underlying asset? This is important both for estimation and for testing of the model. Estimating a model according to a statistical criterion or to a financial objective leads to different estimates and performance in case of specification errors. Third, is the model taken at face value or do we recognize that it is fundamentally misspecified? Often, AJD models are reestimated every day or week, and parameters can vary considerably from one cross section to the other. Is it better to assume some latent structure instead of letting parameters vary from one period to the next. When agents make their financial decisions do they know the parameters or do they have to learn them? Is parameter uncertainty important? Do they try to make robust decisions? Finally, instead of exploiting fully specified models, are the prices or bounds obtained by imposing weak economic restrictions useful? A retrospective by Bates (2003) addresses some of these issues.

ACKNOWLEDGMENTS

The first and the last authors gratefully acknowledge financial support from the Fonds de la Formation de Chercheurs et l'Aide à la Recherche du Québec (FCAR), the Social Sciences and Humanities Research Council of Canada (SSHRC), the Network of Centres of Excellence MITACS, and the Institut de Finance Mathématique de Montréal (IFM2). The second author thanks CIRANO for financial support. We would like to thank Lars Hansen for invaluable comments on a previous draft of this chapter.

REFERENCES

Abadir, K.M. and M. Rockinger (1998) Density-Embedding Functions, Working Paper, University of York and Groupe HEC.

Ai, C. and X. Chen (2003) Efficient Estimation of Models with Conditional Moment Restrictions Containing Unknown Functions, *Econometrica*, 71, 1795–1843.

Aït-Sahalia, Y. (2003) Telling From Discrete Data Whether the Underlying Continuous-Time Model is a Diffusion, *Journal of Finance*, 57, 2075–2112.

Aït-Sahalia, Y. and J. Duarte (2003) Nonparametric Option Pricing Under Shape Restrictions, *Journal of Econometrics*, 116, 9–47.

Aït-Sahalia, Y. and R. Kimmel (2007) Maximum Likelihood of Stochastic Volatility Models, *Journal of Financial Economics*, 83, 413–452.

Aït-Sahalia, Y. and A.W. Lo (1998) Nonparametric Estimation of State-Price Densities Implicit in Financial Asset Prices, *Journal of Finance*, 53, 499–547.

Aït-Sahalia, Y. and A.W. Lo (2000) Nonparametric Risk Management and Implied Risk Aversion, *Journal of Econometrics*, 94, 9–51.

Aït-Sahalia, Y., L.P. Hansen and J. Scheinkman (2010) Operator Methods for Continuous-Time Markov Processes, in Y. Aït Sahalia and L.P. Hansen (eds.), *Handbook of Financial Econometrics*, Amsterdam: North-Holland. In press.

Almeida, C. and R. Garcia (2008) Assessing Misspecified Asset Pricing Models with Empirical Likelihood Estimators, mimeo, FGV (Rio de Janeiro) and Edhec Business School.

Antoine, B., H. Bonnal and E. Renault (2007) On the Efficient Use of the Informational Content of Estimating Equations: Implied Probabilities and Euclidean Empirical Likelihood, *Journal of Econometrics*, 138, 461–487.

Alizadeh, S., M. Brandt and F.X. Diebold (2002) Range-based Estimation of Stochastic Volatility Models, *Journal of Finance*, 57, 1047–1091.

Amin, K.I. and R. Jarrow (1992) Pricing Options in a Stochastic Interest Rate Economy, *Mathematical Finance*, 3, 1–21.

Amin, K.I. and V.K. Ng (1993) Option Valuation with Systematic Stochastic Volatility, *Journal of Finance*, 48, 881–910.

Andersen, T.G., L. Benzoni and J. Lund (2001) Towards an Empirical Foundation of Continuous-Time Equity Return Models, *Journal of Finance*, 57, 1239–1284.

Andersen, T.G., T. Bollerslev and F.X. Diebold (2010) Parametric and Nonparametric Volatility Measurement, in Y. Aït Sahalia and L. Hansen (eds.), *Handbook of Financial Econometrics*, Amsterdam: North-Holland. In press.

Baillie, R.T., T. Bollerslev and H.O. Mikkelsen (1996) Fractionally Integrated Generalized Autoregressive Conditional Heteroskedasticity, *Journal of Econometrics*, 74, 3–30.

Bakshi, G. and D.B. Madan (1999) Crash Discovery in Stock and Options Markets, Working Paper, University of Maryland.

Bakshi, G. and D. Madan (2000) Spanning and Derivative-Security Valuation, *Journal of Financial Economics*, 55, 205–238.

Bakshi, G., C. Cao and Z. Chen (1997) Empirical Performance of Alternative Option Pricing Models, *Journal of Finance*, 94, 1–2, 277–318.

Bakshi, G., N. Kapadia and D. Madan (2003) Stock Return Characteristics, Skew Laws, and the Differential Pricing of Individual Equity Options, *Review of Financial Studies*, 16, 101–143.

Bandi, F. and B. Perron (2006) Long Memory and the Relation Between Implied and Realized Volatility, *Journal of Financial Econometrics*, 4, 636–670.

Bansal, R. and S. Viswanathan (1993) No Arbitrage and Arbitrage Pricing: A New Approach, *Journal of Finance*, 4, 1231–1262.

Banz, R. and M. Miller (1978) Prices for State-Contingent Claims: Some Estimates and Applications, *Journal of Business*, 51, 653–672.

Barndorff-Nielsen, O.E. (1998) Processes of Normal Inverse Gaussian Type, *Finance and Stochastics*, 2, 41–68.

Barndorff-Nielsen, O.E. (2001) Superposition of Ornstein-Uhlenbeck Type Processes, *Theory of Probability and Its Applications*, 45(2), 175–194.

Barndorff-Nielsen, O.E. and N. Shephard (2001) Non-Gaussian Ornstein-Uhlenbeck-based models and some of their uses in financial economics (with discussion), *Journal of the Royal Statistical Society – Series B*, 63, 167–241.

Bates, D. (1991) The Crash of '87: Was it Expected? *Journal of Finance*, 46, 1009–1044.

Bates, D. (1996a) Jumps and Stochastic Volatility: Exchange Rate Processes Implicit in Deutsche Mark Options, *Review of Financial Studies*, 9, 69–107.

Bates, D. (1996b) Testing Option Pricing Models, in G.S. Maddala and C.R. Rao (eds.), *Statistical Methods in Finance (Handbook of Statistics, vol. 14)*, Amsterdam: Elsevier.

Bates, D. (2000) Post-'87 Crash Fears in the S&P 500 Futures Option, *Journal of Econometrics*, 94, 181–238.

Bates, D. (2003) Empirical Option Pricing: A Retrospection, *Journal of Econometrics*, 116, 387–404.

Bates, D. (2007) The Market for Crash Risk, *Journal of Economic Dynamics and Control*, 32, 2291–2321.

Benzoni, L. (1998) Pricing Options Under Stochastic Volatility: An Econometric Analysis, Unpublished Manuscript, Kellog Graduate School of Management.

Bertsimas, D., L. Kogan and A. Lo (2000) When is Time Continuous? *Journal of Financial Economics*, 55, 173–204.

Birke, M. and K. Pilz (2009) Nonparametric Option Pricing with No-Arbitrage Constraints, *Journal of Financial Econometrics*, 7, 53–76.

Black, F. (1976) Studies of Stock Price Volatility Changes, Proceedings of the 1976 Meetings of the American Statistical Association, Business and Economics Statistics Section, 177–181.

Black, F. and M. Scholes (1972) The Valuation of Option Contracts and a Test of Market Efficiency, *Journal of Finance*, 27, 399–417.

Black, F. and M. Scholes (1973) The Pricing of Options and Corporate Liabilities, *Journal of Political Economy*, 81, 637–659.

Bliss, R.R. and N. Panigirtzoglou (2004) Option-implied Risk Aversion Estimates, *Journal of Finance*, 59, 407–446.

Bollerslev, T. and H.O. Mikkelsen (1996) Modelling and Pricing Long Memory in Stock Market Volatility, *Journal of Econometrics*, 73, 151–184.

Bollerslev, T. and H.O. Mikkelsen (1999) Long-Term Equity Anticipation Securities and Stock Market Volatility Dynamics, *Journal of Econometrics*, 92, 75–99.

Bondarenko, O. (2003) Estimation of Risk-neutral Densities Using Positive Convolution Approximation, *Journal of Econometrics*, 116, 85–112.

Boyle, P.P. (1988) A Lattice Framework for Option Pricing with Two State Variables, *Journal of Financial and Quantitative Analysis*, 23, 1–12.

Breeden, D. and R. Litzenberger (1978) Prices of State Contingent Claims Implicit in Option Prices, *Journal of Business*, 51, 621–651.

Breidt, J., N. Crato and P. de Lima (1998) On the Detection and Estimation of Long Memory in Stochastic Volatility, *Journal of Econometrics*, 73, 325–334.

Brennan, M.J. (1979) The Pricing of Contingent Claims in Discrete-Time Models, *Journal of Finance*, 34, 53–68.

Broadie, M. and Ö. Kaya (2006) Exact Simulation of Stochastic Volatility and Other Affine Jump Diffusion Processes, *Operations Research*, 54, 217–231.

Broadie, M., J. Detemple, E. Ghysels and O. Torrès (2000a) American Options with Stochastic Dividends and Volatility: A Nonparametric Investigation, *Journal of Econometrics*, 94, 53–92.

Broadie, M., J. Detemple, E. Ghysels and O. Torrès (2000b) Nonparametric Estimation of American Options Exercise Boundaries and Call Prices, *Journal of Economic Dynamics and Control*, 24, 1829–1857.

Brockwell, P. (2009) Lévy-Driven Continuous-Time ARMA Processes, in Andersen et al. (eds.), *Handbook of Financial Time Series*, Springer Verlag, 457–479.

Buchen, P.W. and M. Kelly (1996) The Maximum Entropy Distribution of an Asset Inferred from Option Prices, *Journal of Financial and Quantitative Analysis*, 31, 143–159.

Buraschi, A. and J. Jackwerth (2001) The Price of a Smile: Hedging and Spanning in Option Markets, *Review of Financial Studies*, 14, 495–527.

Campa, J.M. and P.H.K. Chang (1995) Testing the Expectations Hypothesis of the Term Structure of Volatilities in Foreign Exchange Options, *Journal of Finance*, 50, 529–547.

Carmona, P. and L. Coutin (1999) Stochastic Integrated with Respect to Fractional Brownian Motion, Preprint.

Carr, P. and D. Madan (1999) Option Pricing and the Fast Fourier Transform, *Journal of Computational Finance*, 2(4), 61–73.

Carr, P. and L. Wu (2004) Time-changed Lévy Processes and Option Pricing, *Journal of Financial Economics*, 71, 113–142.

Carr, P., H. Geman, D.B. Madan and M. Yor (2003) Stochastic Volatility for Lévy Processes, *Mathematical Finance*, 13(3), 345–382.

Chabi-Yo, F., R. Garcia and E. Renault (2008) State Dependence Can Explain the Risk Aversion Puzzle, *Review of Financial Studies*, 21, 973–1011.

Chacko, G. and L. Viceira (1999) Spectral GMM Estimation of Continuous-Time Processes, Working Paper, Graduate School of Business, Harvard University.

Chamberlain, G. and M. Rothschild (1983) Arbitrage, Factor Structure, and Mean-Variance Analysis on Large Asset Markets, *Econometrica*, 51, 1281–1304.

Chen, R-R. and L. Scott (1992) Pricing Interest-Rate Options in a Two Factor Cox–Ingersoll–Ross Model of the Term Structure, *Review of Financial Studies*, 5, 613–636.

Chernov, M. (2007) On the Role of Risk Premia in Volatility Forecasting, *Journal of Business and Economic Statistics*, 25, 411–426.

Chernov, M. and E. Ghysels (2000) A Study Towards a Unified Approach to the Joint Estimation of Objective and Risk Neutral Measures for the Purpose of Options Valuation, *Journal of Financial Economics*, 56, 407–458.

Chernov, M., R. Gallant, E. Ghysels and G. Tauchen (2000) A New Class of Stochastic Volatility Models with Jumps: Theory and Estimation, Discussion Paper.

Chernov, M., R. Gallant, E. Ghysels and G. Tauchen (2003) Alternative Models for Stock Price Dynamics, *Journal of Econometrics*, 116, 225–257.

Chourdakis, K. and E. Tzavalis (2001) Option Pricing Under Discrete-Time Regime Shifts in Stock Returns, Working Paper, Department of Economics, Queen Mary, University of London.

Clark, P.K. (1973) A Subordinated Stochastic Process Model with Finite Variance for Speculative Prices, *Econometrica*, 41, 135–156.

Cochrane, J. (2001) *Asset Pricing*, Princeton, NJ: Princeton University Press.

Comte, F. and E. Renault (1996) Non-Causality in Continuous Time Models, *Econometric Theory*, 12, 215–256.

Comte, F. and E. Renault (1998) Long Memory Continuous Time Stochastic Volatility Models, *Mathematical Finance*, 8, 291–323.

Comte, F., L. Coutin and E. Renault (2001) Affine Fractional Volatility Models, Discussion Paper, Université de Montréal.

Constantinides, G. (1992) A Theory of Nominal Term Structure of Interest Rates, *Review of Financial Studies*, 5, 531–552.

Cont, R. and P. Tankov (2004) Non-parametric Calibration of Jump-Diffusion Option Pricing Models, *Journal of Computational Finance*, 7, 1–49.

Cox, J.C., S.A. Ross and M. Rubinstein (1979) Option Pricing: A Simplified Approach, *Journal of Financial Economics*, 7, 229–263.

Daglish, T. (2003) A Pricing and Hedging Comparison of Parametric and Nonparametric Approaches for American Index Options, *Journal of Financial Econometrics*, 1, 327–364.

Dai, Q. and K. Singleton (2000) Specification Analysis of Affine Term Structure Models, *Journal of Finance*, 55, 1943–1978.

Das, S.R. and R.K. Sundaram (1999) Of Smiles and Smirks: A Term Structure Perspective, *Journal of Financial and Quantitative Analysis*, 34, 211–239.

David, A. and P. Veronesi (2002) Option Prices with Uncertain Fundamentals: Theory and Evidence on the Dynamics of Implied Volatilities, Working Paper, Graduate School of Business, University of Chicago.

De Jong, F. (2000) Time Series and Cross Section Information in Affine Term Structure Models, *Journal of Business and Economic Statistics*, 18(3), 300–314.

Derman, E. and I. Kani (1994) Riding on the Smile, *Risk*, 7, 32–39.

Ding, Z., C.W.J. Granger and R.F. Engle (1993) A Long Memory Property of Stock Market Returns and a New Model, *Journal of Empirical Finance*, 1, 83–106.

Duan, J.C. (1995) The GARCH Option Pricing Model, *Mathematical Finance*, 5, 13–32.

Duan, J.C. (2001) Risk Premium of Derivatives in Complete Markets, Discussion Paper, Rotman School of Management, University of Toronto.

Duan, J.C. and J.G. Simonato (1999) Estimating and Testing Exponential-Affine Term Structure Models by Kalman Filter, *Review of Quantitative Finance and Accounting*, 13, 111–135.

Duffie, D. (2001) *Dynamics Asset Pricing*, Princeton, NJ: Princeton University Press.

Duffie, D. and R. Kan (1996) A Yield-Factor Model of Interest Rates, *Mathematical Finance*, 6, 379–406.

Duffie, D., J. Pan and K. Singleton (2000) Transform Analysis and Asset Pricing for Affine Jump-Diffusions, *Econometrica*, 68, 1343–1376.

Dugas, C., Y. Bengio, F. Belisle, C. Nadeau and R. Garcia (2001) Incorporating Second-Order Functional Knowledge for Better Option Pricing, *Advances in Neural Information Processing Systems*, 13.

Dumas, B., J. Fleming and R.E. Whaley (1998) Implied Volatility Functions: Empirical Tests, *Journal of Finance*, 53(6), 2059–2106.

Dupire, B. (1994) Pricing with a Smile, *Risk*, 7, 18–20.

Eberlein, E. (2009) Jump-Type Lévy Processes, in Andersen et al. (eds.), *Handbook of Financial Time Series*, Springer Verlag, 439–454.

Eberlein, E., U. Keller and K. Prause (1998) New Insights into Smile, Mispricing, and Value at Risk: The Hyperbolic Model, *The Journal of Business*, 71, 371–405.

Engle, R.F. and G.G.J. Lee (1999) A Permanent and Transitory Component Model of Stock Retrun Volatility, in R.F. Engle and H. White (eds.), *Cointegration, Causality, and Forecasting: A Festschrift in Honour of Clive W.J. Granger*, 475–497. Oxford, UK: Oxford University Press.

Epstein, L. and S. Zin (1989) Substitution, Risk Aversion, and the Temporal Behavior of Consumption and Asset Returns: A Theoretical Framework, *Econometrica*, 57, 937–969.

Epstein, L. and S. Zin (1991) Substitution, Risk Aversion, and the Temporal Behavior of Consumption and Asset Returns I: An Empirical Analysis, *Journal of Political Economy*, 99, 263–286.

Eraker, B. (2004) Do Stock Prices and Volatility Jump? Reconciling Evidence from Spot and Option Prices, *Journal of Finance*, 58, 1367–1403.

Eraker, B., M.S. Johannes and N.G. Polson (2003) The Impact of Jumps in Returns and Volatility, *Journal of Finance*, 53, 1269–1300.

Erikkson, A., E. Ghysels and F. Wang (2009) Normal Inverse Gaussian Risk Neutral Probability Measures and the Pricing of Derivatives, *Journal of Derivatives*, 16, 23–37.

Fan, J. and L. Mancini (2008) Option Pricing with Model-guided Nonparametric Methods, Working Paper, Bendheim Center for Finance, Princeton University.

Figlewski, S. (2009) Estimating the Implied Risk Neutral Density for the U.S. Market Portfolio, in T. Bollerslev, J. Russell and M. Watson (eds.), *Volatility and Time Series Econometrics: Essays in Honor of Robert F. Engle*, Oxford, UK: Oxford University Press.

Föllmer, H. and A. Schied (2004) *Stochastic Finance: An Introduction in Discrete Time*, Berlin and New York: Walter de Gruyter.

Fouque, J.-P., G. Papanicolaou and K.R. Sircar (2000) *Derivatives in Financial Markets with Stochastic Volatility*, Princeton University Press.

Gagliardini P., C. Gouriéroux and E. Renault (2008) Efficient Derivative Pricing and the Extended Method of Moments, Mimeo.

Gallant, A.R. and G. Tauchen (1996) Which Moments to Match? *Econometric Theory*, 12, 657–681.

Gallant, A.R. and G. Tauchen (1998) Reprojecting Partially Observed Systems with Applications to Interest Rate Diffusions, *Journal of the American Statistical Association*, 93, 10–24.

Gallant, A.R. and G. Tauchen (2010) Simulated Score Methods and Indirect Inference for Continuous-Time Models, in Aït Sahalia and L. Hansen (eds.), *Handbook of Financial Econometrics*, Amsterdam: North-Holland. In press.

Gallant, A.R. and H. White (1988) There Exists a Neural Network that does not Make Avoidable Mistakes, Proceedings of the Second Annual IEEE Conference on Neural Networks, San Diego, CA, I.657-I.664, New York: IEEE Press.

Gallant, A.R. and H. White (1992) On Learning the Derivatives of an Unknown Mapping with Multilayer Feedforward Networks, *Neural Networks*, 5, 129–138.

Gallant, A.R., C. Hsu and G. Tauchen (1999) Using Daily Range Data to Calibrate Volatility Diffusions and Extract the Forward Integrated Variance, *The Review of Economics and Statistics*, 81, 617–631.

Garcia, R. and E. Renault (1998a) A Note on GARCH Option Pricing and Hedging, *Mathematical Finance*, 8(2), 153–161.

Garcia, R. and E. Renault (1998b) Risk Aversion, Intertemporal Substitution and Option Pricing, Working Paper 98s-02, CIRANO.

Garcia, R. and E. Renault (2001) State Variables Models for Stochastic Discount Factors, in J. Cvitanic, E. Jouini and M. Musiela (eds.), *Handbooks of Mathematical Finance*: Topics in Option Pricing, Interest Rates and Risk Management, Cambridge University Press.

Garcia, R. and R. Gençay (2000) Pricing and Hedging Derivative Securities with Neural Networks and a Homogeneity Hint, *Journal of Econometrics*, 94, 93–115.

Garcia, R., M.A. Lewis, S. Pastorello and E. Renault (2009) Estimation of Objective and Risk-Neutral Distributions Based on Moments of Integrated Volatility, *Journal of Econometrics* (Forthcoming).

Garcia, R., R. Luger and E. Renault (2003) Empirical Assessment of an Intertemporal Option Pricing Model with Latent Variables, *Journal of Econometrics*, 116, 49–83.

Garcia, R., R. Luger and E. Renault (2005) Viewpoint: Option Prices, Preferences and State Variables, *Canadian Journal of Economics*, 38, 1–27.

Gençay, R. and M. Qi (2001) Pricing and Hedging Derivative Securities with Neural Networks: Bayesian Regularization, Early Stopping, and Bagging, *IEEE Transactions on Neural Networks*, 12, 726–734.

Ghysels, E. and F. Wang (2009) Some Useful Densities for Risk Management and their Properties, Discussion Paper, UNC.

Ghysels, E. and S. Ng (1998) A Semi-Parametric Factor Model of Interest Rates and Tests of the Affine Term Structure, *Review of Economics and Statistics*, 80, 535–548.

Ghysels, E., A. Harvey and E. Renault (1996) Stochastic Volatility, in G.S. Maddala (eds.), *Statistical Methods in Finance (Handbook of Statistics, vol. 14)*, Amsterdam: North-Holland, 119–191.

Ghysels, E., C. Gouriéroux and J. Jasiak (1997) Market Time and Asset Price Movements: Theory and Estimation, in D. Hand and S. Jacka (eds.), *Statistics in Finance*, Chapter 15, 307–332. London: Edward Arnold.

Ghysels, E., V. Patilea, E. Renault and O. Torrès (1996) Nonparametric Methods and Option Pricing, in D. Hand and S. Jacka (eds.), *Statistics in Finance*, 261–282. London: Edward Arnold.

Gottschling, A., C. Haefke and H. White (2000) Closed Form Integration of Artificial Neural Networks with Some Applications to Finance, Working Paper, University of California, San Diego.

Gouriéroux, C., A. Monfort and C. Tenreiro (1994) Kernel M-Estimators: Nonparametric Diagnostics for Structural Models, Working Paper 9405, CEPREMAP, Paris.

Gouriéroux, C., A. Monfort and E. Renault (1993) Indirect Inference, *Journal of Applied Econometrics*, 8, S85–S118.

Gouriéroux, C. and A. Monfort (2001) Pricing with Splines, Working Paper, Crest-Insee (Paris).

Gray, P. and S. Newman (2005) Canonical Valuation of Options in the Presence of Stochastic Volatility, *The Journal of Futures Markets*, 25, 1–19.

Haley, R. and T. Walker (2007) Alternative Tilts for Nonparametric Option Pricing, mimeo, Department of Economics, Indiana University.

Hamilton, J.D. (1989) A New Approach to the Economic Analysis of Nonstationary Time Series and the Business Cycle, *Econometrica*, 57, 357–84.

Hansen, L. (1982) Large Sample Properties of Generalized Method of Moments Estimators, *Econometrica*, 50, 1029–1054.

Hansen, L.P. and R. Jagannathan (1997) Assessing Specification Errors in Stochastic Discount Factor Models, *Journal of Finance*, 52, 557–590.

Hansen, L.P. and S. Richard (1987) The role of Conditioning Information in Deducing Testable Restrictions Implied by Dynamic Asset Pricing Models, *Econometrica*, 55, 587–613.

Hansen, L.P. and J. Scheinkman (2009) Long Term Risk: An Operator Approach, *Econometrica*, 77, 177–234.

Hansen, L. and K. Singleton (1982) Generalized Instrumental Variables Estimation of Nonlinear Rational Expectations Models, *Econometrica*, 50, 1269–1285.

Härdle, W. and A. Yatchew (2001) Dynamic Nonparametric State Price Density Estimation, Working Paper, University of Toronto.

Harvey, A.C. (1998) Long Memory in Stochastic Volatility, in J. Knight and J. Satchell (eds.), *Forecasting Volatility in Financial Markets*. London, UK: Butterworth-Heinemann.

Harrison, J.M. and D. Kreps (1979) Martingales and Arbitrage in Multiperiod Securities Markets, *Journal of Economic Theory*, 20, 381–408.

Heston, S. (1993) A Closed Form Solution for Options with Stochastic Volatility with Applications to Bond and Currency Options, *The Review of Financial Studies*, 6, 327–343.

Heston, S. and S. Nandi (2000) A Closed-Form GARCH Option Valuation Model, *Review of Financial Studies*, 13, 585–625.

Huang, C. and R.H. Litzenberger (1998) *Foundations for Financial Economics*, Amsterdam: North-Holland.

Hull, J. (2005) *Options, Futures and Other Derivatives*, 6th Edition, Prentice Hall.

Hull, J. and A. White (1987) The Pricing of Options on Assets with Stochastic Volatilities, *Journal of Finance*, 42, 281–300.

Hutchinson, J.M., A.W. Lo and T. Poggio (1994) A Nonparametric Approach to Pricing and Hedging Derivative Securities via Learning Networks, *Journal of Finance*, 3, 851–889.

Imbens, G., R. Spady and P. Johnson (1998) Information Theoretic Approaches to Inference in Moment Conditions Models, *Econometrica*, 66, 333–357.

Jackwerth, J. (2000) Recovering Risk Aversion from Option Prices and Realized Returns, *Review of Financial Studies*, 13, 433–451.
Jackwerth, J. and M. Rubinstein (1996) Recovering Probabilities Distributions from Option Prices, *Journal of Finance*, 51, 1611–1631.
Johannes and Polson (2010) MCMC Methods for Continuous-Time Financial Econometrics, in Y. Aït Sahalia and L. Hansen (eds.), *Handbook of Financial Econometrics*, Amsterdam: North-Holland. In press.
Jones, C. (2003) The Dynamics of Stochastic Volatility: Evidence From Underlying and Options Markets, *Journal of Econometrics*, 116, 181–224.
Kallsen, J. and M.S. Taqqu (1998) Option Pricing in ARCH-type Models, *Mathematical Finance*, 8, 13–26.
Kamrad, B. and P. Ritchken (1991) Multinomial Approximating Models for Options with *k* State Variables, *Management Science*, 37, 1640–1652.
Kitamura, Y. (2007) Empirical Likelihood Methods in Econometrics: Theory and Practice, in R. Blundell, W. Newey and T. Persson (eds.), Advances in Economics and Econometrics, Theory and Applications: Ninth World Congress of the Econometric Society, Vol. 3, Econometric Society Monograph Series, 174–237. Cambridge University Press.
Kitamura, Y. and M. Stutzer (1997) An Information Theoretic Alternative to Generalized Method of Moments Estimation, *Econometrica*, 65, 861–874.
Kitamura, Y., G. Tripathi and H. Ahn (2004) Empirical Likelihood Based Inference in Conditional Moment Restriction Models, *Econometrica*, 72, 1667–1714.
Lewis, A. (2000) *Option Valuation Under Stochastic Volatility with Mathematica Code*, Finance Press.
Longstaff, F.A. (1995) Option Pricing and the Martingale Restriction, *Review of Financial Studies*, 8, 1091–1124.
Madan, D.B. and E. Seneta (1990) The Variance Gamma (VG) Model for Share Market Returns, *Journal of Business*, 63, 511–524.
Madan, D.B. and F. Milne (1991) Option Pricing with VG Martingale Components, *Mathematical Finance*, 1, 39–56.
Manaster, S. and R.J. Rendleman, Jr. (1982) Option Prices as Predictors of Equilibrium Stock Prices, *Journal of Finance*, 37, 1043–1057.
Merton, R.C. (1973) Theory of Rational Option Pricing, *Bell Journal of Economics and Management Science*, 4, 141–183.
Merton, R.C. (1992) *Continuous-Time Finance*, Cambridge: Basil Blackwell.
Nicolato, E. and E. Venardos (2003) Option Pricing in Stochastic volatility Models of the Ornstein-Uhlenbeck Type, *Mathematical Finance*, 13, 445–466.
Pan, J. (2002) The Jump-Risk Premia Implicit in Options: Evidence from an Integrated Time-Series Study, *Journal of Financial Economics*, 63, 3–50.
Pastorello, S., E. Renault and N. Touzi (2000) Statistical Inference for Random Variance Option Pricing, *Journal of Business and Economics Statistics*, 18, 358–367.
Pastorello, S., V. Patilea and E. Renault (2003) Iterative and Recursive Estimation of Structural Non Adaptive Models, *Journal of Business and Economic Statistics*, 21, 449–509.
Pliska, S. (1997) *Introduction to Mathematical Finance: Discrete Time Models*, Basil Blackwell.
Poteshman, A.M. (2000) Estimating a General Stochastic Variance Model from Option Prices, Working Paper, University of Illinois at Urbana-Champaign.

Renault, E. (1997) Econometric Models of Option Pricing Errors, in D. Kreps and K. Wallis (eds.), Advances in *Economics and Econometrics: Theory and Applications*, Vol. 3, Cambridge University Press.
Renault, E. and N. Touzi (1996) Option Hedging and Implied Volatilities in a Stochastic Volatility Model, *Mathematical Finance*, 6, 279–302.
Robinson, P.M. (1991) Testing for Strong Serial Correlation and Dynamic Conditional Heteroskedasticity in Multiple Regression, *Journal of Econometrics*, 47, 67–84.
Rogers, L.C.G. (1997) Arbitrage with Fractional Brownian Motion, *Mathematical Finance*, 7, 95–105.
Romano, M. and N. Touzi (1997) Contingent Claims and Market Completeness in a Stochastic Volatility Model, *Mathematical Finance*, 7, 399–412.
Ross, S.A. (1976) The Arbitrage Theory of Capital Asset Pricing, *Journal of Economic Theory*, 13, 341–360.
Rosenberg, J.V. (2000) Asset Pricing Puzzles: Evidence from Option Markets, Working Paper, NYU Stern School of Business.
Rosenberg, J.V. and R.F. Engle (2002) Empirical Pricing Kernels, *Journal of Financial Economics*, 64, 341–372.
Rubinstein, M. (1994) Implied Binomial Trees, *Journal of Finance*, 44, 771–818.
Rubinstein, M. (1996) The Valuation of Uncertain Income Streams and the Pricing of Options, *Bell Journal of Economics and Management Science*, 7, 407–425.
Sato, K. (1999) *Lévy Processes and Infinite Divisibility*, Cambridge: Cambridge University Press.
Shephard, N. (1996) Statistical Aspects of ARCH and Stochastic Volatility, in D.R. Cox, D.V. Hinkley and O.E. Barndorff-Nielson (eds.), *Time Series Models in Econometrics, Finance and Other Fields*, 1–67. London: Chapman & Hall.
Shimko, D. (1993) Bounds on Probability, *Risk*, 6, 33–37.
Stutzer, M. (1996) A Simple Nonparametric Approach to Derivative Security Valuation, *Journal of Finance*, 51, 1633–1652.
Sundaresan, S. (2000) Continuous-Time Methods in Finance: A Review and an Assessment, *Journal of Finance*, 55, 1569–1622.
Tauchen, G. and M. Pitts (1983) The Price Variability-Volume Relationship on Speculative Markets, *Econometrica*, 51, 485–505.
Taylor, S.J. (1986) *Modeling Financial Time Series*. Chichester: John Wiley.
Tenreiro, C. (1995) Estimation fonctionnelle: Applications Aux Tests d'équation et de paramètre Constant, Ph.D. Thesis, University of Paris VI.
Turnbull, S. and F. Milne (1991) A Simple Approach to Interest-Rate Option Pricing, *Review of Financial Studies*, 4, 87–121.
Wiggins, J. (1987) Option Values Under Stochastic Volatility, *Journal of Financial Economics*, 19, 351–372.
Willard, G.A. (1997) Calculating Prices and Sensitivities for Path-independent Derivative Securities in Multifactor Models, *The Journal of Derivatives*, 45–61.
Yatchew, A. and W. Härdle (2005) Nonparametric State Price Density Estimation Using Constrained Least Squares and the Bootstrap, *Journal of Econometrics*, 133, 579–599.
Yoon, J. (2008) Option Pricing with Stochastic Volatility Models, PhD Thesis, UNC at Chapel Hill.

CHAPTER 10

Value at Risk

Christian Gourieroux* *and* **Joann Jasiak****
*Department of Economics, University of Toronto, ON, Canada
**Department of Economics, York University, Toronto, ON, Canada

Contents

Abstract

We study the risk to portfolios posed by liquid assets. Next, we examine portfolios of liquid assets to which derviatives have been added. The last subject is credit risk. Each section on a specific VaR presents the methods of VaR computation that exist in the literature and point out their advantages and limitations. Among the presented methods are those presented by the Basel Committee. The methods are not necessarily the most efficient or robust, but are quite straightforward and easy to implement. This is because the Basel Committee is also committed to enhancing the level of technological expertise of the banking sector. Indeed, the recommendations and computational tools to be recommended by the Basel Committee in the future are intended to become gradually more and more sophisticated. The chapter concludes with comments on interesting directions of research on the VaR.

Keywords: value-at-risk; market risk; credit risk; liquidity risk; model risk; estimation risk

1. INTRODUCTION

This chapter is a survey of literature on the management, supervision, and measurement of extreme and infrequent risks in Finance. Extreme risks are the risks of very large losses per dollar invested. As losses associated to extreme risks occur infrequently, investors tend to become less alert to these risk over time. In the 1990s, a series of bank failures, due to mismanaged portfolios of corporate loans, real estate, and complex derivatives, was a painful reminder of the existence of extreme risks. It prompted new regulations and research on new instruments of risk protection.

In 1995, the governors of Central Banks gathered in Basle (Switzerland) adopted a mandatory risk measure called the Value at Risk (VaR) to be calculated by all banks for each line of their balance sheets. Since then, banks have been required to report the VaR to the regulators and update it daily and hold a sufficient amount of capital (the so-called **required capital** (RC)) as a hedge against extreme risks.

In the late 1990s, a number of banks and financial institutions did not possess the adequate databases, know-how and technology to satisfy those requirements. Consequently, a permanent committee, called the Basle Committee, was established to coordinate the technological development of the banking sector.

The implementation of the common guidelines for risk supervision was a very ambitious initiative designed to address a variety of risks. These risks can be divided into the following three categories:

(i) **market risk** is due to asset price uncertainty when assets are traded on competitive markets. It is often neglected by investors when asset prices keep rising for a long period of time. Then, investors tend to increase their investments in risky assets and buy options to benefit from the price increase while exposing their portfolios to the risk of a speculative bubble.

(ii) credit risk or **risk of default** is specific to loans and is due to the probability of future payment defaults.

There exist various types of loans. For example, loans can be classified with respect to the type of borrowers or lenders. The borrower can be a consumer, a firm, a local government, or the Treasury. The loans can be granted directly by a credit institution [over the counter (OTC), also called retail loan] or acquired indirectly by purchasing a bond issued by a firm, local government, or the Treasury.

The risk of default is often underestimated by lenders. More specifically, if a credit institution increases the credit limit on a credit line of its customer, it exposes itself to higher risk of default if the new credit limit entails higher monthly payments. Another example is the belief held by many investors on corporate bond markets that bond with triple A ratings are risk-free. In fact, any company, even a highly rated one, can be downrated at some point in time, and eventually defaulted.

(iii) liquidity risk or **risk of counterparty** arises if it becomes difficult to trade quickly a large amount of assets at reasonable prices. Any company or bank that evaluates the assets on its balance sheet at the market price per share [the so-called mark-to-market] is exposed to this risk. The market price is usually valid for a small traded quantity. It is much higher than a price the firm is paid when it attemps to sell quickly a large volume of assets. This explains why, in the cases of corporate or bank failures, assets are sold below their values listed on the balance sheets.

(iv) A number of financial strategies rely on the estimation of dynamic models of asset returns. A typical example is the Black–Scholes model which assumes the geometric Brownian motion of asset prices and is used for derivative/option pricing. Obviously, any theoretical model is necessarily misspecified to some extent and does not provide an exact representation of the reality.[1] Moreover, a theoretical model involves unknown parameters that need to be estimated. The two types of errors due to misspecification and parameter estimation determine the so-called model risk and estimation risk, respectively. Although the Basle Committee recommended the assessment of model risk, such a task is conceptually infeasible as the true model that could serve as a benchmark of comparison is unknown.

The primary intention of the Basle Committee was mandatory computation of the VaR and minimum capital reserve to cover all the aforementioned notions of risk. This objective was supposed to be accomplished in several steps. More specifically, the Basle

[1]"I sometimes wonder why people still use the Black–Scholes formula since it is based on such simple assumptions, unrealistically simple assumptions. Yet that weakness is also its greatest strength. People like the model because they can easily understand its assumptions" (F. Black). "There are two sources of uncertainty in the prediction made by the trader or the econometrician. The first is parameter estimation and the second is model error" (Jacquier and Jarrow). See Merton (1974) for a list of assumptions underlying the Black–Scholes model.

Committee has launched a long-term project of implementing the VaR measures for various risk categories in the following order:

1. VaR for market risk on portfolios of basic liquid assets, such as stocks included in market indexes, Treasury bonds, and foreign currencies.
2. VaR for market risk on portfolios that contain basic liquid assets and liquid derivatives such as options on interest rates, foreign currencies, and market indexes.
3. VaR on portfolios of loans with default risk, called the CreditVaR. It concerns two types of loans: bonds for which market prices are available, and retail loans for which the bank has insider information about the individual credit histories of borrowers.
4. The **back-testing** procedures for assessing the goodness of fit of internal models and for examining the model-based predictions under extreme scenarios of price evolution (also called stress testing). *Steps 1 and 2 (3 and 4) are outlined in Basle 1 (Basle 2) Accords, respectively.*

Our discussion proceeds in the same order. First, we study the risk on portfolios of liquid assets. Next, we examine portfolios of liquid assets to which derivatives are added. The last topic is credit risk. Each section on a specific VaR presents the methods of VaR computation that exist in the literature and points out their advantages and limitations. Among the presented methods are those recommended by the Basle Committee. These methods are not necessarily the most efficient or robust but are quite straightforward and easy to implement. This is becasuse the Basle Committee is also committed to enhance the level of technological expertise of the banking sector.[2] Indeed, the definitions and computational tools to be recommended by the Basle Committee in the future are intended to become gradually more and more sophisticated. The chapter concludes with the comments on interesting directions of research on the VaR. This survey was written in 2001. The updates that were added prior to publication in 2009 are given in italics.

2. VALUE AT RISK

The aim of this section is to define and compare various notions of the VaR for portfolios of assets traded on competitive markets. It is assumed that assets can be traded at any time, and the price per share does not depend on the traded volume or on whether the transaction is a buy or sell. Hence, the traded asset price is equal to the quoted ask

[2] In a survey conducted in Australia by Gizycki and Hereford in 1998, a number of portfolios of stocks, bonds, foreign currencies, and derivatives of different types were sent to all Australian banks with a request to compute the daily VaR for each of these portfolios according to each bank's own method. Out of all Australian banks, only 22 have responded. Out of these, only two banks were able to calculate the VaR for all portfolios.

and bid prices since these are identical. To ensure that this condition is approximately satisfied in practice, the Basle Committee recommended to compute the VaR from daily data on market closure prices. Indeed, on some stock markets, such as Paris and Toronto, the market closure prices are determined by a market closing auction that yields a single equilibrium price for each asset.

2.1. Definition

Let us consider a portfolio of n assets, with fixed allocations $a = (a_1, \ldots, a_n)'$ between t and $t + h$ (say), which represent the quantities of assets and not their monetary values. At date t, the investor has endowment $W_t(a) = a'p_t$ that can be used to purchase this portfolio plus an additional amount R_t (say), called the reserve. R_t is supposed to compensate for potential adverse changes in the market price (market risk); it has to be put aside and cannot be invested on the market. The investor chooses the amount of R_t such that the global position (that is the portfolio value plus the reserve) corresponds to a loss with a predetermined small probability α at date $t + h$. Probability α measures the risk level. This condition can be written as

$$P_t[W_{t+h}(a) + R_t < 0] = \alpha, \tag{2.1}$$

where P_t is the conditional distribution of future prices given information I_t used by the investor to predict future prices. Thus, $-R_t$ is the α-quantile of the conditional distribution of future portfolio value, called the profit and loss [P&L] distribution.

The **required capital** at time t is the sum of the initial endowment plus the reserve. Theoretically, it is equal to the VaR denoted by

$$\text{VaR}_t = W_t(a) + R_t, \tag{2.2}$$

and is characterized by the condition

$$P_t[W_{t+h}(a) - W_t(a) + \text{VaR}_t < 0] = \alpha. \tag{2.3}$$

It depends on (1) information I_t available at time t, (2) horizon h, (3) the set of assets considered, (4) portfolio allocation, and (5) loss probability α. These arguments can be introduced directly into the VaR formula

$$\text{VaR}_t = \text{VaR}(I_t, a, h, \alpha). \tag{2.4}$$

Since condition (2.3) is equivalent to

$$P_t[a'(p_{t+h} - p_t) < -\text{VaR}_t] = \alpha, \tag{2.5}$$

the VaR equals the α-quantile of the conditional distribution of the change of portfolio value.

Note that

$$\begin{aligned} a'(p_{t+h} - p_t) &= \sum_{i=1}^{n} a_i(p_{i,t+h} - p_{i,t}) \\ &= \sum_{i=1}^{n} a_i p_{i,t}[(p_{i,t+h} - p_{i,t})/p_{i,t}] \\ &= \sum_{i=1}^{n} a^*_{i,t} r_{i,t,t+h}, \end{aligned}$$

where $a^*_{i,t}$, $i = 1, \ldots, n$ is the portfolio allocation measured in dollars and $r_{i,t,t+h}$, $i = 1, \ldots, n$ are the asset returns. Therefore, the VaR analysis can be based on either asset returns or price changes.[3]

The VaR has two objectives (1) to measure the risk and (2) to determine the capital reserve. The VaR is a better measure of risk than the asset volatility and has the same applications. More specifically, it can be used for portfolio management, audit, risk hedging and so forth [see, e.g., Arzac and Bawa (1997); Foellmer and Leukert (1999); Jansen et al. (2000); Levy and Sarnat (1972)]. To provide a comprehensive assessment of risk, several VaR measures can be computed, for a set of different risk levels such as $\alpha = 1\%, 5\%$, etc., and a set of different horizons, such as $h = 1, 10, 20$ days. As mentioned earlier in the text, the VaR is also used by the supervisors to fix the level of capital reserve. Even though the theoretical value of the required capital is equal to the VaR, the Basle Committee has fixed the regulatory required capital RC_t at a different level, defined as follows. The banks are required to report daily estimates of the Value at Risk $\widehat{\text{VaR}}_t$ at a horizon of 10 business days (i.e., two weeks) and to compute the required capital defined by

$$RC_t = \text{Max}\left[\widehat{\text{VaR}}_t, 3(\text{trigger}/8)\frac{1}{60}\sum_{h=1}^{60}\widehat{\text{VaR}}_{t-h}\right]. \tag{2.6}$$

This complicated formula is used for the following reasons: (a) to alleviate the effect of potential underestimation of the VaR by fixing the multiplicative factor at a value larger than 3, (b) to create a positive incentive for a bank to perform the best possible evaluation of risk by introducing an adjustable trigger that depends on the ex-post accuracy of the VaR (trigger between 8 and 25), (c) to avoid erratic changes in the level of required capital

[3] For the VaR, returns should not be computed as log-price differences.

by averaging its lagged values, and (d) to allow for quick updating in case of unexpected market changes.

Formula (2.6) was criticized during the financial crisis of 2008. Indeed, the return on real estate entailed systemic risk for all banks, and formula (2.6) became $RC_t = \text{VaR}_t$ *for the majority of banks. All banks had to increase their reserves with cash or investment graded bonds. Thus, formula (2.6) amplified the liquidity crisis.*

2.2. Examples

A closed-form expression of the VaR can be found for specific distributions of price changes (or returns). In this section, we derive the VaR for a conditional Gaussian distribution and compare the VaR formulas for distributions with different types of tails. Next, we discuss the dependence of the VaR on the holding time, i.e., the computational horizon h.

2.2.1. The Gaussian VaR

For convenience, we assume that the time horizon is equal to one unit of time $h = 1$. We also suppose that the price changes are conditionally Gaussian with mean $\mu_t = E[p_{t+1} - p_t | I_t]$ and variance–covariance matrix $\Omega_t = V(p_{t+1} - p_t | I_t)$. We get

$$
\begin{aligned}
&P_t[a'(p_{t+1} - p_t) < -\text{VaR}_t] = \alpha \\
&\Leftrightarrow P_t\left[\frac{a'(p_{t+1} - p_t) - a'\mu_t}{[a'\Omega_t a]^{1/2}} < \frac{-\text{VaR}_t - a'\mu_t}{[a'\Omega_t a]^{1/2}}\right] = \alpha \\
&\Leftrightarrow -\text{VaR}_t - a'\mu_t = \Phi^{-1}(\alpha)(a'\Omega_t a)^{1/2} \\
&\Leftrightarrow \text{VaR}_t = -a'\mu_t + \Phi^{-1}(1-\alpha)(a'\Omega_t a)^{1/2},
\end{aligned}
\tag{2.7}
$$

where Φ denotes the cumulative distribution function (c.d.f.) of the standard normal distribution. In practice, the predetermined probability of loss is small. Thus, the VaR is an increasing function of the volatility of portfolio value and a decreasing function of the expected change of portfolio value and loss probability α. As this approach relies on the two first conditional moments only, it is called the method of the variance–covariance matrix.

The required amount of reserve is nonnegative if and only if

$$
\frac{a'(\mu_t + p_t)}{[a'\Omega_t a]^{1/2}} < \Phi^{-1}(1-\alpha),
$$

i.e., when the portfolio's Sharpe performance measure is small. Otherwise, the reserve is negative and the investor has a possibility of additional borrowing while satisfying the VaR constraint.

2.2.2. Comparison of Tails

Let us consider two portfolios of identical assets, with different allocations a and a^* (say). We assume that their values at date t are equal $a'p_t = a^{*'}p_t$, and let F_t (resp. F_t^*) denote the conditional c.d.f. of the change of portfolio value $y_{t+1} = a'(p_{t+1} - p_t)$ [resp. $y_{t+1}^* = a^{*'}(p_{t+1} - p_t)$]. At risk level α, the VaRs for these portfolios are given by

$$\text{VaR}_t(\alpha, a) = -F_t^{-1}(\alpha), \quad \text{VaR}_t(\alpha, a^*) = -(F_t^*)^{-1}(\alpha). \tag{2.8}$$

Intuitively, portfolio a^* is more risky than portfolio a if , for any small α, portfolio a^* requires a larger reserve than portfolio a. This condition is equivalent to

$$-\left(F_t^*\right)^{-1}(\alpha) > -F_t^{-1}(\alpha), \quad \text{for any small } \alpha,$$
$$\Leftrightarrow F_t^*(y) > F_t(y), \quad \text{for any small } y.$$

Thus, the reserve for portfolio allocation a^* is larger than that for a if and only if the left tail of the conditional distribution of changes of portfolio value is fatter for allocation a^* than for allocation a. If the portfolio is invested in a single risky asset, the change of portfolio value is $a(p_{t+1} - p_t)$. If $a > 0$, the left tail of the distribution of changes of portfolio value corresponds to the left tail of the distribution of asset price changes. Otherwise, it corresponds to the right tail. An investor who holds a positive amount of that single asset is averse to the risk of a price decrease. An investor is averse to the risk of a price increase if his/her position is short, that is when he/she holds a negative quantity of that asset. In a multiasset framework, the situation is more complicated due to the fact that some asset prices are positively and some are negatively correlated with one another.

One can compare the extreme risks on two portfolios by considering the limiting left tails of either their c.d.fs (y tends to minus infinity) or their quantile functions (α tends to zero). For example, the left tails of univariate distributions are often classified as follows:

(i) Distribution F has a Gaussian left tail if and only if $\exists m, \sigma > 0, a > 0 : F(y) \approx a\Phi\left(\frac{y-m}{\sigma}\right)$, when $y \to -\infty$.

(ii) Distribution F has an exponential left tail if and only if $\exists \lambda > 0, a > 0 : F(y) \approx a \exp \lambda y$, when $y \to \infty$. λ is called the tail index of an exponential tail.

(iii) Distribution F has a Pareto (hyperbolic) left tail if and only if $\exists \lambda > 0, a > 0 : F(y) \approx a(-y)^{-\lambda}$ when $y \to -\infty$. λ is called the tail index of a Pareto tail.

Asymptotically, Pareto tails are fatter than exponential tails which, in turn, are fatter than Gaussian tails. Alternatively, the size of the tails can be assessed in terms of the quantile function or in terms of the VaR. For a distribution with an exponential left tail, the VaR is a logarithmic function of risk level α: $\text{VaR}(\alpha) \approx -\frac{1}{\lambda}\log\left(\frac{\alpha}{a}\right)$ for α small. For a distribution with a Pareto left tail, the VaR is a hyperbolic function of α: $\text{VaR}(\alpha) \approx (\alpha/a)^{-1/\lambda}$, for small α. Thus, the rate at which the tails taper off is linked directly to the rate of the VaR increase when α tends to zero.

Examples of distributions with exponential left tails are

the double exponential (Laplace) distribution with c.d.f.:

$$F(y) = \frac{1}{2} \exp \lambda(y-m), \quad \text{if } y \leq m, \qquad (2.9)$$

$$1 - \frac{1}{2} \exp -\lambda(y-m), \quad \text{if } y \geq m;$$

the logistic distribution with c.d.f.:

$$F(y) = \left[1 + \exp - \left(\frac{y-m}{\eta}\right)\right]^{-1}.$$

Examples of distributions with Pareto tails are

the Cauchy distribution with c.d.f.:

$$F(y) = \frac{1}{\pi} \arctan\left(\frac{y-m}{\sigma}\right) + \frac{1}{2};$$

the double Pareto distribution with c.d.f.:

$$F(y) = \frac{1}{2}(\mu - y)^{-\lambda}, \quad \text{if } y \leq \mu - 1,$$

$$1 - \frac{1}{2}(y - \mu)^{-\lambda}, \quad \text{if } y \geq \mu - 1.$$

The thickness of tails and estimation of tail indexes have been widely discussed in the statistical and probabilistic literatures [see, e.g., Embrechts et al. (1999)]. However, any asymptotic comparison of tails has to be carried out with caution as in Finance the interest is in small, but fixed risks levels, such as $\alpha = 1$ or 5%. To illustrate this point, let us consider a logistic distribution with c.d.f. $F(y) = (1 + \exp y)^{-1}$ and a normal distribution with the same mean and variance as the logistic distribution, that are mean 0 and variance $\sigma^2 = \pi^2/3$. The VaR computed from the $N(0, \pi^2/3)$ is given by

$$\text{VaR}_N(\alpha) = \pi/\sqrt{3}\Phi^{-1}(1-\alpha),$$

while the VaR computed from the logistic distribution is

$$\text{VaR}_L(\alpha) = \ln\left(\frac{1-\alpha}{\alpha}\right).$$

The normal and logistic VaRs are ploted in Fig. 10.1 as functions of α.

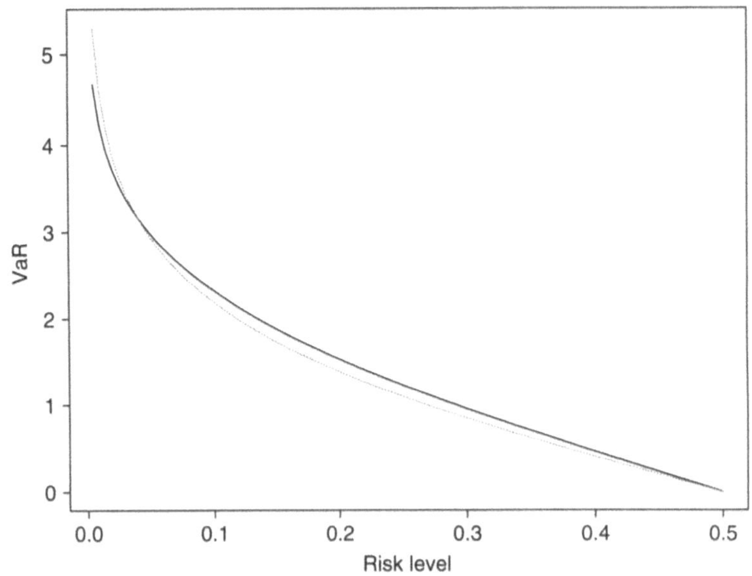

Figure 10.1 Comparison of normal and logistic VaR.

Once the mean and variance effects are eliminated, we observe that the VaR curves are very close except for very small risk levels. Moreover, the two curves intercept at $\alpha = 4\%$. At $\alpha = 5\%$, the Gaussian VaR is 2.98 and is larger than the logistic VaR equal to 2.94. At $\alpha = 1\%$, the Gaussian VaR is 4.22 and is less than the logistic VaR equal to 4.59, although they are quite close. In brief, we find that (1) a thicker (asymptotic) tail does not necessarily imply a larger VaR for some small fixed values of α; (2) the tail comparison is conclusive after eliminating the differences in mean and variance in a preliminary step.

2.2.3. Term Structure of the VaR

After examining the dependence of the VaR on risk level α, we focus on the dependence of the VaR on horizon h. More precisely, we investigate whether the VaR can be considered as a simple function of α and h, and written as VaR(α, h). Some results are easy to derive for i.i.d. variables y_t, $t = 1, \ldots, T$. For instance, it is easy to show that

$$\mathrm{VaR}(\alpha, h) = h^{1/a} b(\alpha), \forall \alpha, \qquad (2.10)$$

where a is a scalar and b is a function if and only if the characteristic function of y_t is of the type

$$\Psi(u) = E(\exp -iuy_t) = \exp(-c|u|^a).$$

This restriction on the characteristic function is satisfied by a zero mean normal distribution with $a = 2$. In this special case, the term structure of the VaR is such that $\text{VaR}_N(\alpha, h) = \sqrt{h}b(\alpha)$. The restriction is also satisfied for Cauchy-distributed y_ts with $a = 1$. Then, the term structure of the VaR is such that $\text{VaR}_C(\alpha, h) = hb^*(\alpha)$. According to this VaR formula for Cauchy-distributed y_ts, the larger the tails, the greater the impact of the holding time on the value of the VaR.

Note that the Basle Committee (1995, p. 8) suggested to calculate the 10-day VaR from the one-day VaR by multiplying it by the square root $\sqrt{h} = \sqrt{10} = 3.16$. This suggestion assumes implicitly the independence and normality of price changes.

2.3. Conditional and Marginal VaR

We know that the VaR depends on the information set used for forecasting the future values of a portfolio. The content of that information set may differ, depending on the approach. For the calculation of the conditional VaR, the information set can consist of either the lagged values of prices of all assets in the portfolio (I_t^1) or the lagged values of the entire portfolio (I_t^2). The outcomes of computations conditioned on either (I_t^1) or (I_t^2) are generally not identical. It is also possible to disregard all information on the past asset prices and portfolio values, i.e., use an empty information set and compute the marginal VaR defined by

$$P[W_{t+h}(a) - W_t(a) + \text{VaR}_t < 0] = \alpha, \tag{2.11}$$

where P denotes the marginal probability distribution. When the price changes $(p_t - p_{t-1})$, $\forall t$, are stationary, the marginal VaR is time independent and its time index can be suppressed. On the contrary, the conditional VaR varies in time due to the changes in market conditions. For example, if the price changes follow a Gaussian vector autoregressive (VAR) process of order 1: $\Delta p_t = p_t - p_{t-1} = A\Delta p_{t-1} + \epsilon_t$[4], where $\epsilon_t \sim IIN(0, \Omega)$, A is the $n \times n$ matrix of autoregressive coefficients, and Ω the $n \times n$ variance–covariance matrix of the error term, then the conditional distribution of Δp_t given $\Delta p_{t-1}, \Delta p_{t-2} \ldots$ is Gaussian $N(A\Delta p_{t-1}, \Omega)$. Therefore, the conditional VaR is given by: $\text{VaR}_t(a, \alpha) = a' A\Delta p_{t-1} + \Phi^{-1}(1-\alpha)(a'\Omega a)^{1/2}$. Moreover, we know that the marginal distribution of Δp_t is also Gaussian $N(0, \Sigma)$, where $\Sigma = V(\Delta p_t)$ satisfies the equation $\Sigma = A\Sigma A' + \Omega = \sum_{h=0}^{\infty} A^h \Omega A'^h$. Therefore, the marginal VaR is

$$\text{VaR}(a, \alpha) = \Phi^{-1}(1-\alpha)(a'\Sigma a)^{1/2}.$$

Since the marginal mean and variance are such that $E\Delta p_t = 0$ and $\Sigma = V(\Delta p_t) \gg \Omega$, the marginal VaR is larger than the conditional VaR, on average.

[4]The terminology is confusing. Note the difference between the VaR and VAR.

2.4. Sensitivity of the VaR

Let us consider the VaR at horizon 1 defined by

$$P_t[a'\Delta p_{t+1} < -\text{VaR}_t(a,\alpha)] = \alpha.$$

The VaR depends on the vector of portfolio allocations. In practice, a portfolio manager has to update the portfolio frequently, and his/her major concern is the impact of the updating on risk (or on the capital reserve). Hence, the manager is concerned more about the effect of portfolio allocation on the VaR than about the value of the VaR.

The analytical expressions of the first- and second-order derivatives of the VaR with respect to portfolio allocation were derived in Gourieroux et al. (2000):

$$\text{i)} \quad \frac{\partial \text{VaR}_t(a,\alpha)}{\partial a} = -E_t[\Delta p_{t+1} | a'\Delta p_{t+1} = -\text{VaR}_t(a,\alpha)]. \tag{2.12}$$

$$\text{ii)} \quad \frac{\partial^2 \text{VaR}_t(a,\alpha)}{\partial a \partial a'} = \frac{\partial \log g_{a,t}}{\partial z}[-\text{VaR}_t(a,\alpha)] V_t[\Delta p_{t+1} | a'\Delta p_{t+1} = -\text{VaR}_t(a,\alpha)] \tag{2.13}$$

$$+ \left\{ \frac{\partial}{\partial z} V_t[\Delta p_{t+1} | a'\Delta p_{t+1} = z] \right\}_{z=-\text{VaR}_t(a,\alpha)}, \tag{2.14}$$

where $g_{a,t}$ denotes the conditional probability distribution function (p.d.f.) of $a'\Delta p_{t+1}$.

The first- and second-order derivatives of the VaR can be written in terms of the first- and second-order conditional moments of price changes in a neighbourhood of the condition $a'\Delta p_{t+1} = -\text{VaR}_t(a,\alpha)$.

The sensitivity of the VaR can be examined directly for normally distributed price changes [see, e.g., Garman (1996, 1997)]. Let us denote by μ_t, Ω_t the conditional mean and variance of Δp_{t+1}, respectively. The VaR is given by

$$\text{VaR}_t(a,\alpha) = -a'\mu_t + \Phi^{-1}(1-\alpha)(a'\Omega_t a)^{1/2}.$$

For example, we get

$$\begin{aligned} \frac{\partial \text{VaR}_t(a,\alpha)}{\partial a} &= -\mu_t + \frac{\Omega_t a}{(a'\Omega_t a)^{1/2}} \Phi^{-1}(1-\alpha) \\ &= -\mu_t + \frac{\Omega_t a}{a'\Omega_t a}[\text{VaR}_t(a,\alpha) + a'\mu_t] \\ &= -E_t[\Delta p_{t+1} | a'\Delta p_{t+1} = -\text{VaR}_t(a,\alpha)]. \end{aligned}$$

The closed-form formulas of VaR sensitivities are used for granularity adjustments of large portfolios of credits [see, e.g., section 7.4 and Wilde (2001)].

3. ESTIMATION OF THE MARGINAL VaR

In this section, we discuss the estimation of the marginal VaR from historical data on the changes of portfolio value. We denote by $y_t = a'(p_t - p_{t-1})$ the change of portfolio value and consider the marginal VaR at risk level α. For notational convenience, we drop the arguments a and α from the VaR function, and fix the horizon h equal to one.

The marginal VaR is given by

$$P[y_t < -\text{VaR}] = \alpha. \tag{3.1}$$

It means that the opposite of the marginal VaR is equal to the α-quantile of the marginal distribution of y_t and can be characterized in the two following ways:

First, the VaR can be defined from the marginal cumulative distribution function (c.d.f.) of y_t, denoted by F:

$$F(-\text{VaR}) = \alpha \Leftrightarrow \text{VaR} = -F^{-1}(\alpha). \tag{3.2}$$

Second, the VaR can be defined as a solution to the minimization of the following objective function

$$-\text{VaR} = \underset{\theta}{\text{Argmin}}\, E[\alpha(y_t - \theta)^+ + (1 - \alpha)(y_t - \theta)^-], \tag{3.3}$$

where $(y_t - \theta)^+ = \text{Max}(y - \theta, 0), (y_t - \theta)^- = \text{Max}(\theta - y, 0)$. It is easy to show that the first-order condition to the above minimization leads to equation (3.1).

In the sequel, these two characterizations are used to define the parametric, semi-parametric, and nonparametric VaR estimators. The properties of estimators are first described for i.i.d. changes of portfolio values $y_t, t = 1, \ldots, T$, for which the marginal VaR and the conditional VaR are equal (see Section 2.2). The properties of estimators when the i.i.d. assumption is relaxed are given in Section 4.

3.1. Historical Simulation

VaR estimators that do not rely on any assumptions about the marginal distribution of y_t are obtained from the empirical counterparts of expressions (3.3) and (3.2):

$$\widehat{\text{VaR}} = \underset{\theta}{\text{Argmin}}\, \frac{1}{T}\sum_{t=1}^{T}[\alpha(y_t - \theta)^+ + (1 - \alpha)(y_t - \theta)^-], \tag{3.4}$$

and

$$\widehat{\text{VaR}} = \underset{\theta}{\text{Argmin}}[\hat{F}(-\theta) - \alpha]^2, \tag{3.5}$$

where $\hat{F}(y) = \frac{1}{T}\sum_{t=1}^{T} 1_{y_t<y}$ denotes the sample c.d.f., and $1_{y_t<y} = 1$, when $y_t < y$ and 0, otherwise, is the indicator function.

Under this approach, the theoretical α-quantile is approximated by a sample α-quantile. The minimizations in (3.4) and (3.5) are equivalent. However, their solutions are generally not unique. Since the sample distribution is discrete, and the sample c.d.f. is not continuous, we obtain an interval of solutions, called the empirical α-quantile interval.

In practice, the solution is easily obtained as follows. Let us assume that $T = 200$ and $\alpha = 1\%$. The observations $y_t, t = 1, \ldots, 200$ can be ranked in an ascending order $y_{(1)} = \mathrm{Min}_t y_t < y_{(2)} \cdots < y_{(T)} = \mathrm{Max}_t y_t$. Then, the 1%-quantile interval is $[y_{(2)}, y_{(3)}]$. Its lower bound is equal to the second smallest observation since $2/200 = 1/100$, and the upper bound is equal to the next smallest observation.

The asymptotic properties of the sample quantiles were derived by Basset and Koenker (1978) [see also Gourieroux and Monfort (1998), section 8.5] for i.i.d. data.

When T tends to infinity and the risk level α is fixed

(i) the length of the empirical α-quantile interval tends to zero;
(ii) any value in the empirical α-quantile interval is a consistent and asymptotically normal estimator:

$$\sqrt{T}(\widehat{\mathrm{VaR}} - \mathrm{VaR}) \sim N\left[\mathrm{VaR}, \frac{F(-\mathrm{VaR})[1 - F(-\mathrm{VaR})]}{f^2(-\mathrm{VaR})}\right], \tag{3.6}$$

where f denotes the marginal p.d.f. of y_t.

For small α, the asymptotic variance of the VaR estimator depends on the risk level and the size of the left tail of the marginal distribution of y_t. The estimator is less accurate when either α diminishes or the left tail increases. To illustrate this point, let us consider a distribution with hyperbolic tails [called the Pareto tails]. If $F(y) \sim c(-y)^{-\beta}$, for small α, the asymptotic variance,

$$V_{as}[\sqrt{T}(\widehat{\mathrm{VaR}} - \mathrm{VaR})] \approx \frac{F(-\mathrm{VaR})}{f^2(-\mathrm{VaR})} \approx \frac{1}{\beta^2 c}(-\mathrm{VaR})^{\beta+2},$$

is an increasing function of tail parameter β.

The asymptotic results given above are intended to clarify the accuracy of the sample quantile estimator. They do not hold when T tends to infinity and α tends to zero, which is a situation encountered in Finance where, in many applications, T is large and α is small. To give more insights on this problem, let us consider a sample of $T = 100$ for which the sample 1%-quantile is $Z = y_{(1)} = \mathrm{Min}_t y_t$. The finite-sample distribution of $y_{(1)}$ is easy to find. Indeed, we have $P[Z > z] = P[\mathrm{Min}_t y_t > z] = P[y_t > z, t = 1, \ldots 100] = [1 - F(z)]^{100}$. Then the median $z_{0.5}$ of the 1%-quantile Z is given by

$$[1 - F(z_{0.5})]^{100} \Leftrightarrow z_{0.5} = F^{-1}[1 - (0.5)^{1/100}] \tag{3.7}$$

$$\Leftrightarrow 1 - F(z_{0.5}) = (0.5)^{1/100} \Leftrightarrow z_{0.5} \approx F^{-1}\left[-\frac{ln 0.5}{100}\right] = F^{-1}\left[\frac{0.7}{100}\right]. \tag{3.8}$$

For example, when the marginal distribution is a Cauchy distribution with c.d.f. $F(y) = \frac{1}{\pi}\text{Arctan}\, y + \frac{1}{2}$, the theoretical 1%-quantile is equal to −31.8. The median of the distribution of sample quantile Z is −45.5 and the 90% confidence interval is [−636.6, −10.5]. It is clear that the finite-sample distribution of the sample quantile is skewed and its median is very different from the true value. This evidence indicates that the sample quantile is not asymptotically normally distributed.

The finite-sample properties of sample quantile estimators can be revealed by Monte Carlo experiments. Let us consider $T = 200$ observations and risk levels $\alpha = 1$ and 5%. Figure 10.2 shows the finite-sample distribution of $y_{(1)}, y_{(2)}, y_{(3)}$ associated with $\alpha = 1\%$ when the true distribution F is N(0,1), two-sided exponential, and Cauchy, respectively. The true values of the 1%-quantile are −2.33, −3.91, −31.82, respectively.

We observe that the sample quantile $y_{(3)}$ of the Gaussian and of the two-sided exponential distribution is less biased than the sample quantile $y_{(2)}$. Moreover, for the Cauchy, the left tail of the distribution of the sample quantile is very heavy and the accuracy of that estimator is poor.

Figure 10.3 shows similar results for $y_{(9)}, y_{(10)}, y_{(11)}$, and the level $\alpha = 5\%$. The true values of the 5%-quantile are −1.64, −2.30, −6.31, respectively.

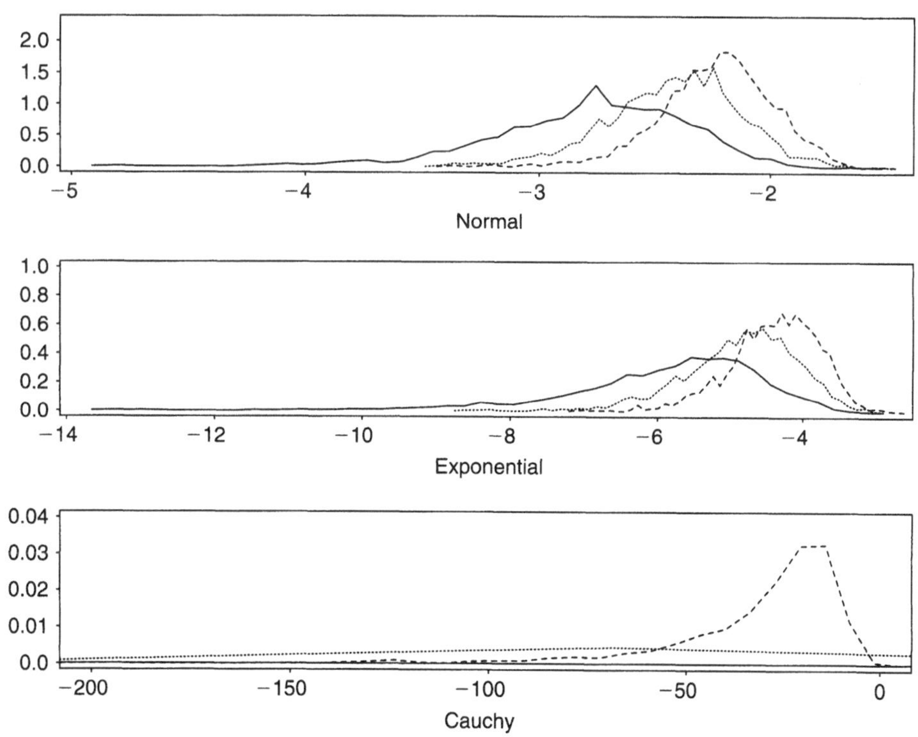

Figure 10.2 Finite-sample distributions of the 1%-empirical quantile.

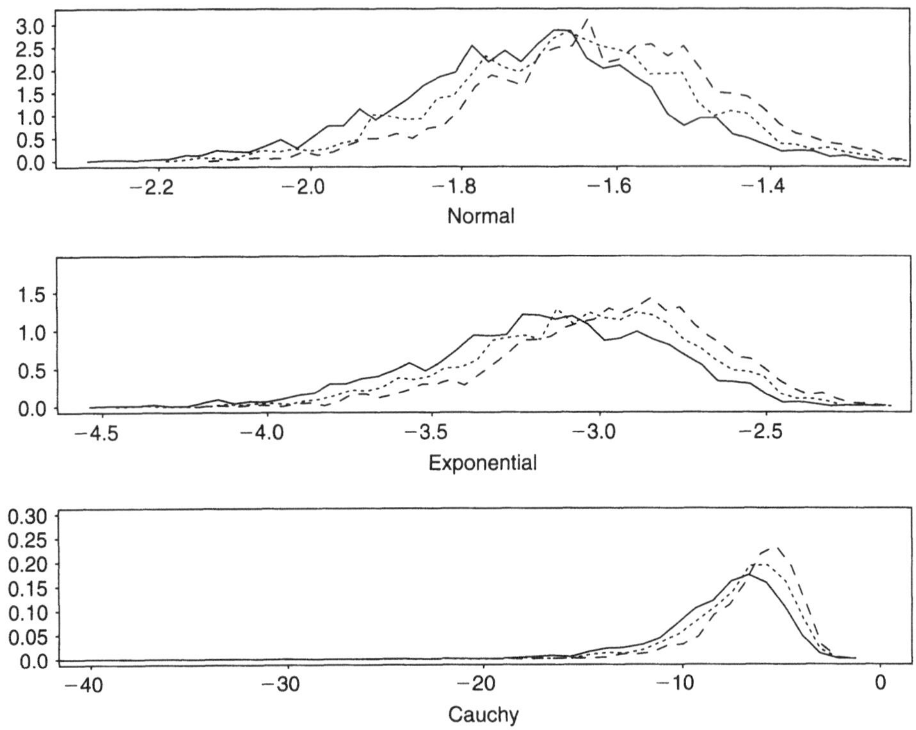

Figure 10.3 Finite-sample distributions of the 5%-empirical quantile.

In conclusion, the estimation of the theoretical α-quantile from its empirical counterpart is an appealing method of VaR estimation. However, it may lead to very inaccurate and unstable estimates, especially for small risk levels. *In some sense, the estimated* VaR *is risky itself.*

Finally, let us point out another limitation of the sample quantile approach. In practice, it is common to compute this estimate for different risk levels and different portfolio allocations, from the same set of asset price changes. Although the true underlying VaR is a continuously differentiable function of arguments α and a, its estimator $\widehat{\text{VaR}}$ is not. Due to the discreteness, a small change in a portfolio allocation can trigger a jump in the value of the estimated VaR while the true underlying VaR changes continuously. This drawback can be partly eliminated by smoothing the estimator. This can be done by using a kernel K and bandwidth h; a VaR estimator smoothed with respect to α and a is the solution of

$$\frac{1}{T}\sum_{t=1}^{T} K\left[\frac{-a'(p_t - p_{t-1}) - \widehat{\text{VaR}}(a,\alpha)}{h}\right] = \alpha, \tag{3.9}$$

and depends on α and a. The asymptotic properties of this estimator are identical to the asymptotic properties of the sample α-quantile, when α is fixed, T tends to infinity, and the bandwidth h tends to zero at an appropriate rate [Falk (1985); Horowitz (1992)].

In fact, one should be interested in estimating the functional parameter $(a, \alpha) \to \text{VaR}(a, \alpha)$ rather than in finding a specific value of that function. Then, it would be possible to impose on the functional estimator $(a, \alpha) \to \widehat{\text{VaR}}(a, \alpha)$ the same regularity conditions as those satisfied by the theoretical VaR function.

3.2. Parametric Methods

Let us assume that the price changes $\Delta p_t = p_t - p_{t-1}$ have a common distribution from a parametric family with p.d.f. g_θ that depends on parameter θ. Parameter θ can be estimated by the maximum likelihood

$$\hat{\theta}_T = \operatorname*{Argmax}_{\theta} \sum_{t=1}^{T} \ln g_\theta(\Delta p_t).$$

The VaR can be approximated by

$$\widehat{\text{VaR}} = -F^{-1}_{a,\hat{\theta}_T}(\alpha),$$

where $F_{a,\theta}$ is the c.d.f. of $\Delta W_t(a) = a' \Delta p_t$, when Δp_t has density g_θ.

For Gaussian price changes $\Delta p_t \sim N(\mu, \Omega)$, the VaR is simply estimated by

$$\widehat{\text{VaR}} = -a'\hat{\mu} + \Phi^{-1}(1-\alpha)(a'\hat{\Omega}a)^{1/2}, \tag{3.10}$$

where $\hat{\mu}$ and $\hat{\Omega}$ are the sample mean and variance–covariance matrix computed from the observations on $\Delta p_1, \ldots, \Delta p_T$. Since under the normality, the finite-sample distribution of $(a'\hat{\mu}, a'\hat{\Omega}a)$ is known, we can also find the distribution of the VaR estimator and build the confidence interval. The practitioners should be aware that the estimated measure of risk is random, and therefore is risky (the so-called estimation risk).

3.3. Semiparametric Analysis

The nonparametric and parametric estimation methods discussed in the previous sections have some drawbacks. Under the nonparametric approach, the sample quantile at a small risk level α may be inaccurate, as it is estimated from a limited number of extreme observations. Under the parametric approach, there is a possibility that the model is misspecified and the VaR estimator biased. To circumvent both difficulties, one can find the sample quantiles at some relatively large αs (say) and derive the VaR of interest using a parametric model of the tail. In practice, the parametric tail model can be Pareto, exponential, or a mixture of two normals [Longerstay (1996); Venkataraman (1997)].

This approach is called the **model building** method. Let us assume, for instance, a Pareto-type model for the left tail where we have approximately

$$F(y) \sim c(-y)^{-\beta},$$

where c and β are positive tail parameters. The following paragraphs describe two alternative methods of estimation of parameters c and β and the derivation of the VaR estimator.

3.3.1. Estimation from Sample Quantiles

Let us consider two relatively low risk levels, such as $\alpha_0 = 10\%, \alpha_1 = 5\%$. For such risk levels, the sample quantiles, denoted $\widehat{\text{VaR}}_e(\alpha_0)$ and $\widehat{\text{VaR}}_e(\alpha_1)$ are quite accurate estimators of the true quantiles and we get the approximate moment conditions:

$$\begin{cases} \alpha_0 & \sim & c[\widehat{\text{VaR}}_e(\alpha_0)]^{-\beta} \\ \alpha_1 & \sim & c[\widehat{\text{VaR}}_e(\alpha_1)]^{-\beta}. \end{cases}$$

By solving the system of equations with respect to c and β, we obtain consistent estimators of the tail parameters:

$$\begin{cases} \alpha_0 & \sim & \hat{c}[\widehat{\text{VaR}}_e(\alpha_0)]^{-\hat{\beta}} \\ \alpha_1 & \sim & \hat{c}[\widehat{\text{VaR}}_e(\alpha_1)]^{-\hat{\beta}}. \end{cases}$$

Then the VaR at any high risk level α ($\alpha = 1\%$, say) can be estimated by

$$\alpha = \hat{c}[\widehat{\text{VaR}}_e(\alpha_1)]^{-\hat{\beta}}. \tag{3.11}$$

The logarithms of the last two systems of equations are linear in $\hat{\beta}$ and $\log \hat{c}$.

$$\begin{cases} \log \alpha_0 & = & \log \hat{c} - \hat{\beta} \log \widehat{\text{VaR}}_e(\alpha_0), \\ \log \alpha_1 & = & \log \hat{c} - \hat{\beta} \log \widehat{\text{VaR}}_e(\alpha_1) \\ \log \alpha & = & \log \hat{c} - \hat{\beta} \log \widehat{\text{VaR}}(\alpha). \end{cases}$$

Therefore, the estimated $\widehat{\text{VaR}}(\alpha)$ is related to the sample quantiles $\widehat{\text{VaR}}_e(\alpha_0)$ and $\widehat{\text{VaR}}_e(\alpha_1)$:

$$\det \begin{pmatrix} \log \alpha_0 & 1 & \log \widehat{\text{VaR}}_e(\alpha_0) \\ \log \alpha_1 & 1 & \log \widehat{\text{VaR}}_e(\alpha_1) \\ \log \alpha & 1 & \log \widehat{\text{VaR}}(\alpha) \end{pmatrix} = 0,$$

or equivalently

$$\widehat{\text{VaR}}(\alpha) = [\widehat{\text{VaR}}_e(\alpha_1)]^A [\widehat{\text{VaR}}_e(\alpha_0)]^B, \tag{3.12}$$

where $A = \frac{\log\alpha - \log\alpha_0}{\log\alpha_1 - \log\alpha_0}$ and $B = \frac{\log\alpha_1 - \log\alpha}{\log\alpha_1 - \log\alpha_0}$.

This formula allows extrapolation of the values $\widehat{\text{VaR}}(\alpha)$, for any small α, from two sample quantiles at larger αs. We find that the Pareto-type tail model considered above implies geometric extrapolation.

3.3.2. The Use of the Hill Estimator

When the left tail of a distribution is exactly Pareto, then

$$F(y) = c(-y)^{-\beta}, \quad \text{for } y < \underline{y}, \tag{3.13}$$

where $\underline{y}$ is a given tail cutoff point. Then, the right-truncated observations y_t such that $y_t < \underline{y}$[5] can be used to estimate the tail parameter β by the maximum likelihood. The c.d.f. of the truncated Pareto distribution is

$$F_{\underline{y}}(y) = \frac{F(y)}{F(\underline{y})} = \left(\frac{y}{\underline{y}}\right)^{-\beta},$$

and depends only on parameter β. The truncated ML estimator of β is

$$\hat{\beta} = \underset{\beta}{\text{Argmax}} \sum_{t=1}^{T} 1_{y_t<\underline{y}}[\log\beta - (\beta+1)(\log y_t - \log \underline{y})].$$

The first-order condition yields

$$1/\hat{\beta} = \sum_{t=1}^{T} 1_{y_t<\underline{y}}(\log y_t - \log \underline{y}). \tag{3.14}$$

This estimator was first proposed by Hill (1975), and is therefore called the Hill estimator.

The Hill estimator can be used jointly with an empirical quantile estimator to recover the VaR along the following lines [see, e.g., Danielsson and de Vries (1997, 1998)]. Let risk level α_0 be relatively large ($\alpha_0 = 10\%$, say). We consider the sample quantile $\widehat{\text{VaR}}_e(\alpha_0)$ and the Hill estimator associated with $\underline{y} = -\widehat{\text{VaR}}_e(\alpha_0)$.

[5] The use of the maximum likelihood approach restricted to tails has been recommended by Embrecht et al. (1998) to estimate the VaR.

The relation

$$\alpha_0 \approx c[-\widehat{\text{VaR}}_e(\alpha_0)]^{-\hat{\beta}}$$

is used to obtain a consistent estimator of c,

$$\hat{c} = \alpha_0[-\widehat{\text{VaR}}_e(\alpha_0)]^{\hat{\beta}}.$$

Then the VaR at any small risk level α is approximated by $\widehat{\text{VaR}}(\alpha)$ such that

$$\alpha = \hat{c}[-\widehat{\text{VaR}}(\alpha)]^{-\hat{\beta}}$$
$$\Leftrightarrow \widehat{\text{VaR}}(\alpha) = \widehat{\text{VaR}}_e(\alpha_0)\left(\frac{\alpha_0}{\alpha}\right)^{1/\hat{\beta}}.$$

The sample quantile $\widehat{\text{VaR}}_e(\alpha_0)$ is multiplied by a scale factor, which is a power function of α_0/α. When β increases, the tail of the Pareto distribution decreases and so does the VaR.

3.4. The i.i.d. Assumption

Since the marginal and conditional VaRs are equal for i.i.d. price changes, it seems natural to present the statistical properties of the VaR estimators in the i.i.d. framework. In practice, however the i.i.d. assumption is not satisfied. This is known from the empirical evidence on serial correlation of price changes, conditional heteroskedasticity, and volatility persistence. Moreover, for theoretical reasons, the i.i.d. assumption cannot be satisfied by both price changes Δp_t and returns $r_t = \Delta p_t/p_{t-1}$. But, even if the price changes (or returns) were i.i.d. at horizon 1, they could not remain i.i.d. at higher horizons h: $\Delta^h p_t = p_t - p_{t-h}$. This is because intervals $\{t-h, t\}$ and $\{t-1-h, t-1\}$ overlap, which implies correlation between $\Delta^h p_{t-1}$ and $\Delta^h p_t$.

In practice, the i.i.d. assumption does not hold, e.g., when (i) the returns are serially independent and nonstationary. Then, the conditional and marginal distributions are identical, but are both time varying. If their time variation is smooth, at close dates, these distribution may be hard to distinguish. (ii) the price change process is serially correlated and stationary. In that case, the marginal and conditional distributions are different. The conditional distributions at different dates can resemble one another if the price histories prior to those dates are similar.

The marginal VaR in application to data that violate the i.i.d. condition is misspecified. In the case of a nonstationary process without serial dependence, misspecification arises because the true time-varying marginal VaR is approximated by a constant time invariant VaR. Then, a constant, VaR estimator is not consistent. In the case of a stationary process with serial dependence, a marginal VaR estimator is consistent, but its estimated variance is different from the variance evaluated under the i.i.d. assumption.

The guidelines of the Basle Committee are set out as if the marginal distributions of price changes (returns) were varying smoothly over time. Therefore, to diminish the bias in VaR estimation, the Committee recommended rolling estimation of the marginal VaR. More precisely, it is proposed to select a window of T_0 observations (equivalent to at least one year, i.e., $T_0 > 200$). At date t, the estimation is performed from the T_0 most recent observations: $y_t, y_{t-1}, \ldots, y_{t-T_0+1}$. At time $t+1$, the newly arrived observation y_{t+1}, is added to the sample, while the oldest one y_{t-T_0+1} is deleted. The rolling procedure provides time-varying estimates of the VaR. It can be improved by introducing exponentially weighted moving averages [Phelan (1995)].

To illustrate the use of rolling estimators, we perform a Monte Carlo experiment, in which the changes of portfolio value are i.i.d. and the marginal VaR is estimated by rolling from a window of 200 observations. Two estimators were considered: the rolling sample quantile and the rolling Gaussian VaR at 1%. Moreover, we consider three sets of i.i.d. simulated price changes with Gaussian, double exponential and Cauchy distributions, respectively. The simulation results are displayed in Figs. 10.4–10.6.

We observe that the evolution of the rolling sample quantile in time is a stepwise function. This is easy to explain by considering for example the 1% sample quantile. The value

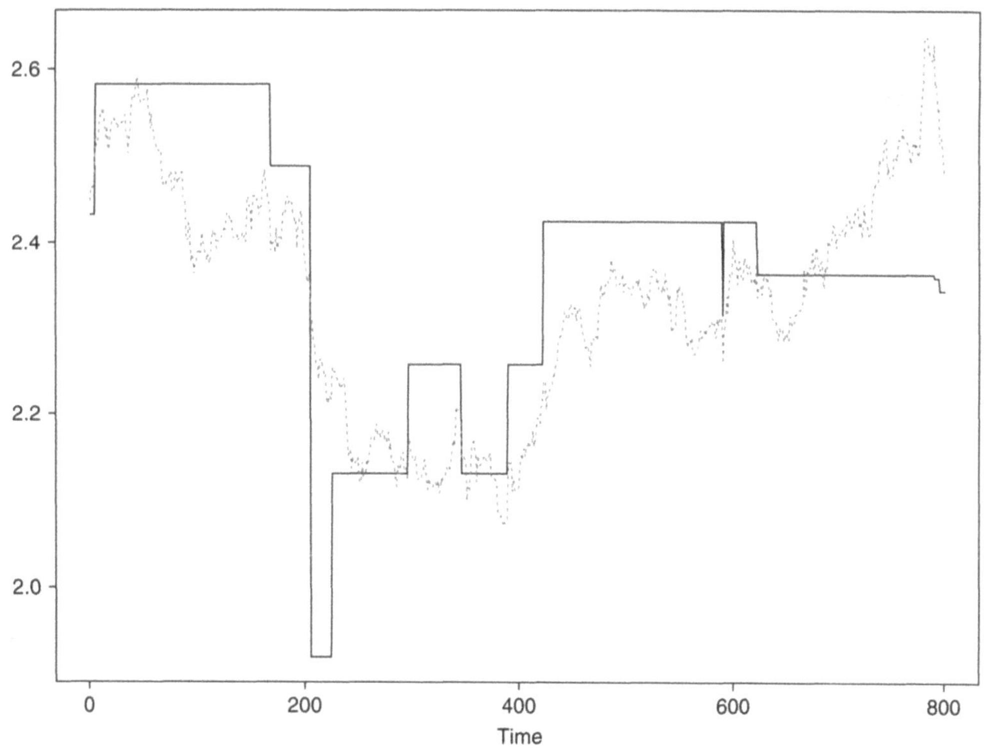

Figure 10.4 i.i.d. Gaussian price changes.

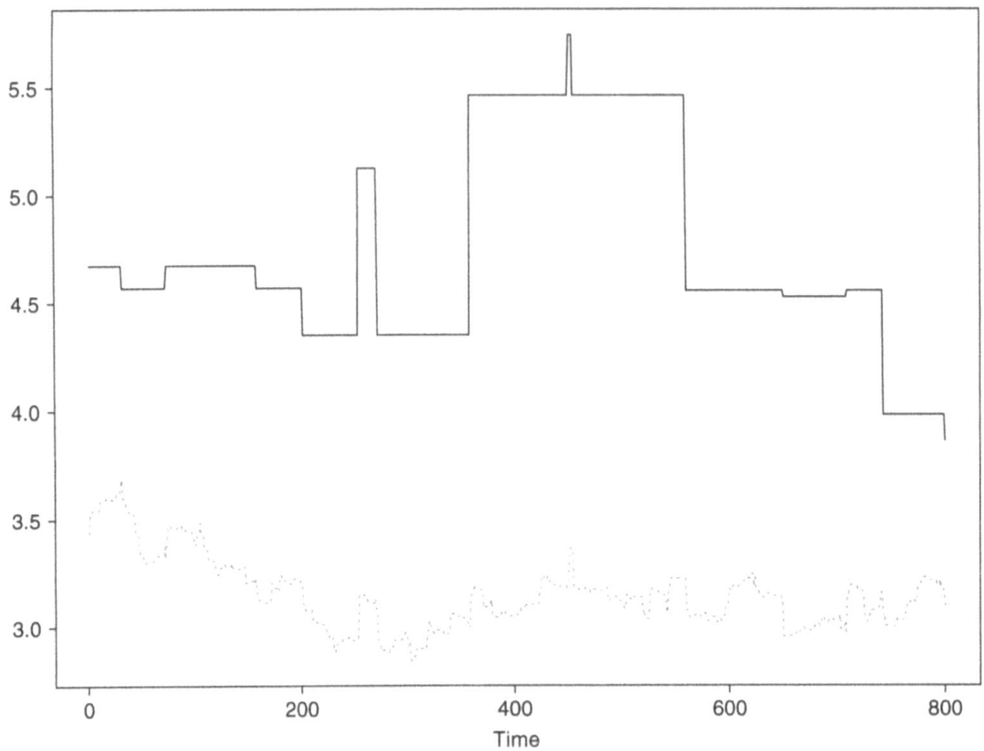

Figure 10.5 i.i.d. double exponential price changes.

of the sample quantile between dates t and $t+1$ changes only if the new and the deleted observations are neither greater nor smaller than the value of the quantile estimated at t. This occurs with probability $1-(1\%)^2-(99\%)^2=0.0198$. Therefore, the value of the sample quantile remains constant for a random time, which has a geometric distribution with parameter equal to $(1\%)^2+(99\%)^2=0.980$. The corresponding average duration is approximately 50.[6]

The outcomes of the rolling sample quantile and Gaussian VaR estimations are close for Gaussian price changes, whereas the Gaussian VaR is smaller than the sample quantile for exponentially distributed price changes. This is because the Gaussian VaR estimation formula underestimates the exponential tail. A converse effect is observed when the VaR estimators from Gaussian data are compared to those from Cauchy distributed data. The first- and second-order moments of the Cauchy distribution do not exist. Moreover, the sample mean and variance of Cauchy variables do not converge

[6] To avoid the stepwise effect, it has been proposed by Hull to compute a weighted empirical quantile, solution of $\widehat{\text{VaR}}_t = \text{Argmin}_\theta \sum_{\tau=t-T_0+1}^{t} \rho^{t-\tau}[\alpha(y_\tau-\theta)^+ + (1-\alpha)(y_\tau-\theta)^-]$.

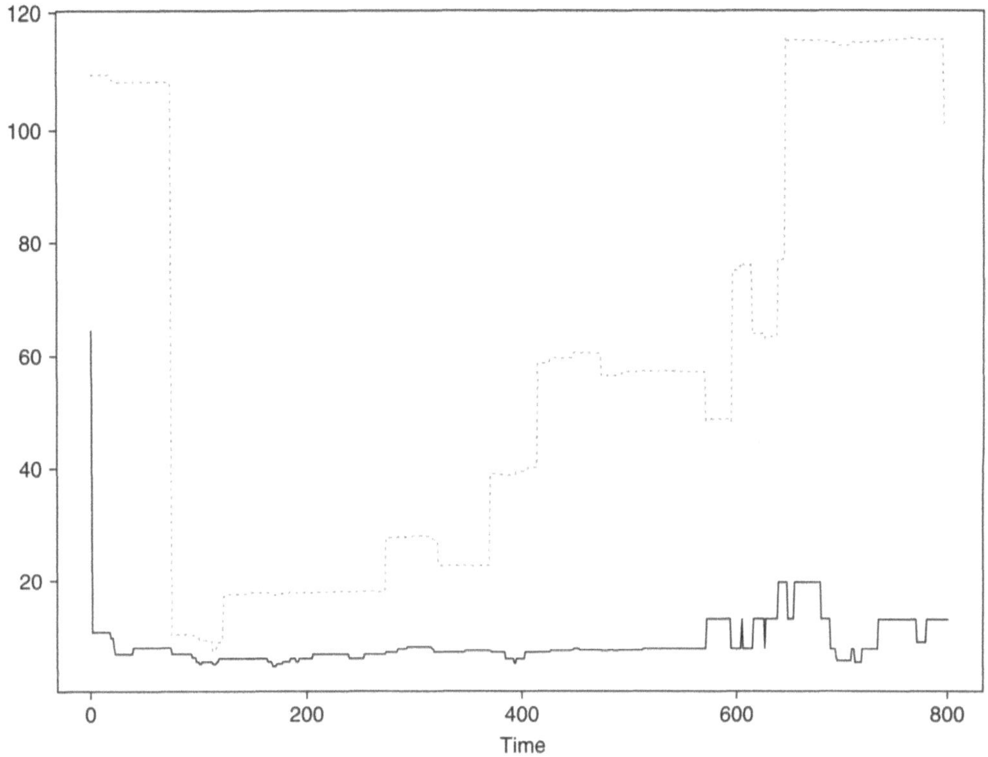

Figure 10.6 i.i.d. Cauchy price changes.

and have fat-tailed asymptotic distributions.[7] We also observe that rolling can induce a spurious trend effect in the estimated VaRs.

4. ESTIMATION OF THE CONDITIONAL VaR

As mentioned in Section 2.3, two types of conditional VaR can be considered depending on the selected information set, which may contain either the lagged price changes of each asset in the portfolio $\left(I_t^1\right)$ or the lagged portfolio values $\left(I_t^2\right)$. The estimation methods can be parametric, semiparametric, and nonparametric.

4.1. Conditionally Heteroskedastic Autoregressive Models

A widely used dynamic model of price change dynamics (or returns) is the conditionally heteroskedastic autoregressive model.

[7] For example, the empirical average of independent Cauchy variables also admits a Cauchy distribution.

When the conditioning information set is $\left(I_t^1\right)$, the model is multivariate:

$$\Delta p_t = \mu(\underline{\Delta p_{t-1}}) + B(\underline{\Delta p_{t-1}})u_t, \tag{4.1}$$

where $(\underline{\Delta p_{t-1}}) = (\Delta p_{t-1}, \Delta p_{t-2}, \ldots)$ denotes the set of lagged values of price changes, μ is a n-dimensional vector of conditional location parameters, B is a $n \times n$ matrix of conditional scale parameters, and u_t, $t = 1, \ldots, T$ is a sequence of i.i.d. random vectors, with common distribution with p.d.f. g.

When the information set is $\left(I_t^2\right)$, the model is univariate:

$$y_t = m(\underline{y_{t-1}}) + \sigma(\underline{y_{t-1}})v_t, \tag{4.2}$$

where m and σ are scalar functions and v_t, $t = 1, \ldots, T$, is a sequence of i.i.d. variables. The basic models, in the family of ARCH (GARCH) models are the ARCH(1) [see Engle (1982)],

$$y_t = (\theta_0 + \theta_1 y_{t-1})^2 v_t,$$

and IGARCH models,

$$y_t = \left[(1-\theta)\sum_{j=1}^{\infty}\theta^{j-1}y_{t-j}^2\right]^{1/2} v_t.$$

The link between specifications (4.1) and (4.2) needs to be examined with caution. For illustration, let us consider the linear VAR of order one of asset price changes:

$$\Delta p_t = A\Delta p_{t-1} + \Omega^{1/2}u_t,$$

where u_t is $IIN(0, Id)$, and Id denotes the identity matrix. We know that the conditional distribution of $y_t = \Delta W_t(a) = a'\Delta p_t$, given I_t^1, is Gaussian $N[a'A\Delta p_{t-1}, a'\Omega a]$, and the conditional distribution of $\Delta W_t(a)$ given the lagged portfolio values $\left(I_t^2\right)$ is of the type $N\left[\sum_{j=1}^{\infty}\alpha_j a'\Delta p_{t-j}, \sigma^2\right]$. Thus, the use of information set $\left(I_t^2\right)$ leads to a univariate model $y_t = m(\underline{y_{t-1}}) + \sigma v_t, v_t \sim IIN(0,1)$ of an infinite autoregressive order, which differs from the univariate specification of y_t conditional on the full information set $\left(I_t^1\right)$. The situation is even more complex in nonlinear and nongaussian frameworks. Indeed, if the location and scale parameters in (4.1) are nonlinear and if u_t is nongaussian, it is always possible to compute numerically the univariate conditional distribution of $y_t = \Delta W_t(a)$ given its own past. However, that conditional distribution may not be compatible with any univariate nonlinear models such as (4.2).

So far, we assumed that the allocation vector a is fixed. It can also be shown that a set of nonlinear autoregressive models (4.2) specified for a set of portfolios with different allocations may be incompatible.[8] For example, let us consider a Gaussian ARCH(1) model

$$\Delta W_t(a) = \left[\theta_0(a) + \theta_1(a)\Delta W_{t-1}(a)^2\right]^{1/2} v_t(a),\ \forall a,$$

where $v_t(a)$ is $IIN(0,1)$. The models for $\Delta W_t(a), \forall a$, are compatible only if $\theta_1(a) = 0, \forall a$, that is in the absence of conditional heteroskedasticity. This lack of coherency needs to be emphasized because of the following method introduced by J.P. Morgan (1995) and endorsed by the Basle Committee. The Committee recommended to use systematically (that is for any set of assets and any portfolio allocation) the Gaussian IGARCH model defined by

$$\Delta W_t(a) = \sigma_t v_t,$$

where

$$\begin{aligned}\sigma_t^2 &= \theta\sigma_{t-1}^2 + (1-\theta)\Delta W_{t-1}(a)^2 \\ &= (1-\theta)\sum_{j=1}^{\infty}\theta^{j-1}\Delta W_{t-j}(a)^2 \\ &= (1-\theta)\sum_{j=1}^{\infty}\theta^{j-1}y_{t-j}^2,\end{aligned}$$

with $\theta = 0.95$. This model can be valid for some allocations, but it cannot fit equally well the data for all possible allocations *a*s.

4.1.1. Estimation Given the Information on Portfolio Value

The estimation of the VaR conditional on I_t^2 is quite straightforward when the location and scale functions m and σ are parametric:

$$y_t = m(\underline{y_{t-1}};\theta) + \sigma(\underline{y_{t-1}};\theta)v_t. \tag{4.3}$$

Parameter θ can be consistently estimated by the quasi(pseudo)-maximum likelihood and its estimator $\hat{\theta}_T$ is given by

$$\hat{\theta}_T = \underset{\theta}{\text{Argmax}} -\frac{1}{2}\sum_{t=1}^{T}\log\sigma^2(\underline{y_{t-1}};\theta) - \frac{1}{2}\sum_{t=1}^{T}\frac{(y_t - m(\underline{y_{t-1}};\theta))^2}{\sigma^2(\underline{y_{t-1}};\theta)}. \tag{4.4}$$

[8] It cannot be derived from the same dynamic specification (4.1) of the vector of asset returns.

Given this estimator, we can find the approximations of the conditional drift and volatility, $\hat{m}_t = m(\underline{y_{t-1}}; \hat{\theta}_T)$, $\hat{\sigma}_t = \sigma((\underline{y_{t-1}}; \hat{\theta}_T)$, and the standardized residuals,

$$\hat{v}_t = \sum_{t=1}^{T} \frac{y_t - m(\underline{y_{t-1}}; \hat{\theta}_T)}{\sigma(\underline{y_{t-1}}; \hat{\theta}_T)}, \tag{4.5}$$

that are approximations of the true errors v_t. Then , the computation of the conditional VaR at horizon 1 can be accomplished by calculating a marginal VaR at horizon 1 from the i.i.d. errors. Indeed, at horizon 1, we get

$$\begin{aligned} &P_t[y_{t+1} < \mathrm{VaR}_t(a, \alpha, 1)] = \alpha \\ &\Leftrightarrow P_t\Big[m(\underline{y_{t-1}}; \theta) + \sigma(\underline{y_{t-1}}; \theta)v_t < -\mathrm{VaR}_t(a, \alpha, 1)\Big] = \alpha \\ &\Leftrightarrow P_t\left[v_t < -\frac{\mathrm{VaR}_t(a, \alpha, 1) - m(\underline{y_{t-1}}; \theta)}{\sigma(\underline{y_{t-1}}; \theta)}\right] = \alpha. \end{aligned}$$

Therefore $-[\mathrm{VaR}_t(a, \alpha, 1) - m(\underline{y_{t-1}}; \theta)]/\sigma(\underline{y_{t-1}}; \theta)$ is the α-quantile of the distribution of the standardized errors v_t. Since errors $v_t, t = 1, \dots, T$, (resp. the residuals) are i.i.d. (resp. approximately i.i.d.), we can estimate the α-quantile of the v distribution, using, for example, a parametric method. When the distribution of the error is assumed Gaussian, the conditional VaR estimator is

$$\widehat{\mathrm{VaR}}_t(a, \alpha, 1) = -\hat{m}_t + \hat{\sigma}_t \Phi^{-1}(1 - \alpha).$$

However, empirical evidence indicates that the distributions of residuals are often fat-tailed. Therefore, parametric models with t-student or α-stable distributions of the error term were proposed in the literature.

Alternatively, a semiparametric approach can be followed, which relies on the empirical distribution of residuals $\hat{v}_1, \dots, \hat{v}_T$. Given the α-quantile $\hat{Q}(\alpha)$ evaluated from the residuals, the VaR estimate is

$$\widehat{\mathrm{VaR}}_t(a, \alpha, 1) = -m(\underline{y_{t-1}}; \hat{\theta}_T) - \sigma(\underline{y_{t-1}}; \hat{\theta})\hat{Q}(\alpha). \tag{4.6}$$

An analytical formula of the VaR estimator exists only for holding horizon 1. Typically, under a parametric approach where (y_t) follow a conditionally Gaussian ARCH model, the conditional distribution at horizon 2 is no longer Gaussian and is very complicated. Hence, the VaR estimator for holding horizons greater than one has to be derived by Monte Carlo methods. The simulation can be based on a nonlinear conditional autoregressive model. For ease of exposition, let us assume the autoregressive order equal to one:

$$y_{t+1} = m(y_t; \theta) + \sigma(y_t; \theta)v_{t+1}$$

and

$$y_{t+2} = m(y_{t+1};\theta) + \sigma(y_{t+1};\theta)v_{t+2}.$$

y_{t+2} can be approximately simulated from the conditional distribution of y_{t+2} given y_t along the following lines.[9] For two independent drawings v^s_{t+1}, v^s_{t+2} in the sample distribution of residuals, a simulated value of y_{t+2} given the currently observed $y_t = y$ is

$$y^s_{t+2} = m\left(y^s_{t+1};\hat{\theta}_T\right) + \sigma\left(y^s_{t+1};\hat{\theta}_T\right) v^s_{t+2},$$

where

$$y^s_{t+1} = m\left(y^s_t;\hat{\theta}_T\right) + \sigma\left(y^s_t;\hat{\theta}_T\right) v^s_{t+1}.$$

By replicating this procedure S times, we obtain a set of values $y^s_{t+2}, s = 1, \ldots, S$, approximately independently drawn in the conditional distribution of y_{t+2} given the currently observed $y_t = y$. An estimator of $\mathrm{VaR}(a, \alpha, 2)$ is the empirical quantile of the simulated sample $y^s_{t+2}, s = 1, \ldots, S$. Note that the number of replications S should be large.

4.1.2. Estimation Given the Full Information

A similar approach is available when the information set I^1_t contains asset price changes, and the location and scale functions are parametric, i.e., $\mu(\underline{\Delta p_{t-1}};\theta)$ and $\Omega(\underline{\Delta p_{t-1}};\theta)$, respectively. Parameter θ is estimated by the quasi(pseudo)-maximum likelihood:

$$\begin{aligned}\hat{\theta}_T = \underset{\theta}{\mathrm{Argmax}} & -\frac{1}{2}\log\det\Omega(\underline{\Delta p_{t-1}};\theta) \\ & -\frac{1}{2}[\Delta p_t - \mu(\underline{\Delta p_{t-1}};\theta)]'\Omega(\underline{\Delta p_{t-1}};\theta)^{-1}[\Delta p_t - \mu(\underline{\Delta p_{t-1}};\theta)].\end{aligned}$$

The residuals are

$$\hat{u}_t = \Omega(\underline{\Delta p_{t-1}};\hat{\theta}_T)^{-1/2}[\Delta p_t - \mu(\underline{\Delta p_{t-1}};\hat{\theta}_T)].$$

Next, the multivariate distribution of u_t is approximated by the sample distribution of residuals.

In the multivariate framework, the VaR has to be approximated by simulation even at horizon 1. In general, the conditional distribution of $a'\Delta p_t$ given $\underline{\Delta p_{t-1}}$ is complicated,

[9] This simulation is approximate because the true parameter θ is replaced by $\hat{\theta}_T$ and the true distribution of errors by the sample distribution of residuals.

even if the multivariate distribution of u_t is as simple as a multivariate Student, for example.

4.2. Nonparametric Methods

Let us now consider the conditional distribution of price changes (or changes in portfolio values) as completely unspecified. Due to the curse of dimensionality, a nonparametric approach can be applied only if the price changes have short memory, that is when the autoregressive order is small. For this reason, we assume that process (y_t) is stationary and Markov of order 1, and describes the estimation of the conditional distribution of y_t given y_{t-1}, or equivalently the joint distribution of (y_{t-1}, y_t).

It is known that the joint c.d.f. of (y_{t-1}, y_t) can be written as a product of the marginal distribution and a term that represents serial dependence. More precisely, we have [Sklar (1959)]

$$\begin{aligned} F_2(y_t, y_{t-1}) &= P[Y_t < y_t, Y_{t-1} < y_{t-1}] \\ &= P[F(Y_t) < F(y_t), F(Y_{t-1}) < F(y_{t-1})], \end{aligned}$$

where F denotes the marginal c.d.f. of y_t. Since $F(Y_t)$ follows a uniform distribution on [0,1], we find that

$$F_2(y_t, y_{t-1}) = C[F(y_t), F(y_{t-1})], \tag{4.7}$$

where C is the joint c.d.f. of theoretical ranks $U_t = F(Y_t)$, $U_{t-1} = F(Y_{t-1})$. Function C is called a copula c.d.f.

The VaR at horizon 1 can be expressed in terms of marginal distribution F and copula C. Indeed, we have

$$\begin{aligned} &P[Y_t < \mathrm{VaR}_t | Y_{t-1} = y_{t-1}] \\ &= P[F(Y_t) < F(-\mathrm{VaR}_t) | F(Y_{t-1}) = F(y_{t-1})] \\ &= P[U_t < F(-\mathrm{VaR}_t) | U_{t-1} = F(y_{t-1})] \\ &= \frac{\partial C}{\partial u_{t-1}}[F(-\mathrm{VaR}_t), F(y_{t-1})]. \end{aligned}$$

Thus, the VaR is the solution of

$$\frac{\partial C}{\partial u_{t-1}}[F(-\mathrm{VaR}_t), F(y_{t-1})] = \alpha. \tag{4.8}$$

It seems natural to estimate nonparametrically functions F and C from their (kernel smoothed) empirical counterparts and solve Eq. (4.8) after replacing functions F and

C by these counterparts. However, the difficulty encountered in estimating the sample quantile described in Section (3.1) arises also in the bidimensional framework and results in inaccurate VaR estimates. Indeed, the rate of convergence of these estimators depends on the dimension of the distribution.

To circumvent this problem, nonparametric constraints on the copula can be imposed. For example, we can consider an Archimedean copula defined by

$$C(u, v) = \Psi^{-1}[\Psi(u) + \Psi(v)], \tag{4.9}$$

where Ψ is a real function.[10] In an Archimedean copula, the serial dependence is captured by univariate function Ψ (instead of the bidimensional function C in the unconstrained case and of the scalar autoregressive parameter ρ in the Gaussian case). It is easy to check that

$$P[C(U_t, U_{t-1}) < s] = s - \Psi(s)/\frac{\mathrm{d}\Psi}{\mathrm{d}s}(s), \ \forall s. \tag{4.10}$$

This equality can be used to obtain a consistent functional estimator of function Ψ. The estimation method consists of the following three steps.

(i) First step: The data on $y_t, t = 1, \ldots, T$ are used to find approximations of ranks $U_t = F(Y_t)$ as follows. First, the observations are ranked in an ascending order $y_{(1)} < \cdots < y_{(T)}$. Next, we assign to each $y_t, t = 1, \ldots, T$ its rank divided by T. The rank divided by T is called $\hat{u}_t$. It is equal to the value of $\hat{F}(y_t)$, where $\hat{F}$ is the sample c.d.f. A similar approach is applied to the lagged values $y_t, t = 0, \ldots, T-1$ to derive approximations $\tilde{u}_{t-1}$ of u_{t-1}.

(ii) Second step: The copula cumulative function evaluated at $\hat{u}_t, \tilde{u}_{t-1}$ can now be approximated from its empirical counterpart

$$\hat{C}(\hat{u}_t, \tilde{u}_{t-1}) = \frac{1}{T}\sum_{\tau=1}^{T} 1_{\hat{u}_\tau < \hat{u}_t, \tilde{u}_{\tau-1} < \tilde{u}_{t-1}}.$$

(iii) Third step: By applying formula (4.23), we find a smoothed estimator of function $A(s) = \Psi(s)/\frac{\partial\Psi}{\mathrm{d}s}(s)$ by

$$\hat{A}(s) = \frac{1}{T}\sum_{t=1}^{T} \Phi\left[\frac{\hat{C}(\hat{u}_t, \tilde{u}_{t-1}) - s}{h}\right],$$

[10] Ψ has to be the Laplace transform (moment generating function) of a positive random variable [see Joe (1997)].

where Φ is the c.d.f. of the standard normal used for smoothing and h is the bandwidth. Next, the estimator of function Ψ is derived by integration

$$\hat{\Psi}(u) = \exp\left[\int^{u} \frac{1}{s - \hat{A}(s)} ds\right].$$

4.3. Miscellaneous

In this section, we review other methods of VaR computation that exist in the literature. They are based on dynamic models other than those considered so far, or arise as extensions of methods described in Section 3.

4.3.1. Switching Regimes

The idea is to extend the basic Gaussian model by allowing for endogeneous regime switching. Conditional on a given regime, the distribution of price changes is multivariate normal. However, when the endogeneous regimes are integrated out, it becomes a mixture of Gaussian distributions. This approach accommodates heavy tails, persistence, and nonlinear dynamics. More precisely, let $k = 1, \ldots, K$ denote the admissible regimes and Z_t with values in $\{1, \ldots, K\}$ denote the market regime at date t. It is assumed that

(a) (Z_t) is a Markov chain with transition matrix Q.

(b) The distribution of price changes Δp_t conditional on $Z_t = k, \underline{\Delta p_t}, \underline{Z_t}$ is multivariate normal $N[\mu_k, \Omega_k]$.

Then the conditional distribution of price changes is

$$l(\Delta p_t | \underline{\Delta p_{t-1}}) = \sum_{k=1}^{K} p_k(\underline{\Delta p_{t-1}}) N(\mu_k, \Omega_k), \tag{4.11}$$

where $p_k(\underline{\Delta p_{t-1}}) = P[Z_t = k | \underline{\Delta p_{t-1}}]$.

Probabilities p_k can be computed numerically and parameters $\mu_k, \Omega_k, \forall k$, and Q can be estimated by means of the Kitagawa's algorithm [see, e.g., Hamilton (1989)]. Then, the conditional VaR is estimated from drawings in the mixture distribution (4.11), after replacing p_k, μ_k, Ω_k by their estimates [see Billio and Pelizzon (2000) for an application]. This approach is different from the mixture of normal distributions proposed by J.P. Morgan as a new methodology of VaR computation [Longerstay (1996)]. Under the J.P. Morgan approach, the regime indicators (Z_t) are assumed time independent.

4.3.2. Conditional Autoregressive VaR

The conditional Autoregressive VaR (CaViaR) model proposed by Engle and Manganelli (2004) is a univariate model that represents the dynamics of the VaR for a single portfolio with a given vector of allocations:

$$\begin{aligned}\mathrm{VaR}_t &= \beta_0 + \beta_1 \mathrm{VaR}_{t-1} + \beta_2 |y_{t-1}| \\ &= \gamma_0(\beta) + \sum_{j=1}^{\infty} \gamma_j(\beta)|y_{t-j}|, \text{ say,}\end{aligned}$$

where $\gamma_0(\beta), \gamma_j(\beta), j$ varying are functions of $\beta_0, \beta_1, \beta_2$. Parameter β is estimated by the quantile regression [Basset and Koenker (1978)], that is,

$$\begin{aligned}\hat{\beta} = \underset{\beta_0,\beta_1,\beta_2}{\mathrm{Argmin}} \sum_{t=1}^{T} \Big\{ \alpha\Big[y_t - \gamma_0(\beta) - \sum_j \gamma_j(\beta)|y_{t-j}|\Big]^+ \\ + (1-\alpha)\Big[y_t - \gamma_0(\beta) - \sum_j \gamma_j(\beta)|y_{t-j}|\Big]^- \Big\}.\end{aligned}$$

The VaR estimator is

$$\widehat{\mathrm{VaR}} = \gamma_0(\hat{\beta}) + \sum_{j=1}^{\infty} \gamma_j(\hat{\beta})|y_{t-j}|.$$

This approach is easy to implement but has two limitations. First, the CAViaR models for portfolios with different allocations can be incompatible [see remark in Section 4.1]. Second, the CAViaR models have to be specified separately for each different risk level α. This leads to VaR estimates

$$\widehat{\mathrm{VaR}}(\alpha_0) = \gamma_0(\hat{\beta}_{\alpha_0}) + \sum_{j=1}^{\infty} \gamma_j(\hat{\beta}_{\alpha_0})|y_{t-j}| \quad \text{and}$$
$$\widehat{\mathrm{VaR}}(\alpha_1) = \gamma_0(\hat{\beta}_{\alpha_1}) + \sum_{j=1}^{\infty} \gamma_j(\hat{\beta}_{\alpha_1})|y_{t-j}|,$$

that do not necessarily satisfy the monotonicity property

$$\widehat{\mathrm{VaR}}(\alpha_0) > \widehat{\mathrm{VaR}}(\alpha_1), \quad \text{if } \alpha_o < \alpha_1.$$

4.3.3. Dynamic Quantile Models

This family of VaR *models, introduced by Gourieroux and Jasiak (2009), satisfies the condition of monotonicity with respect to the risk level. The conditional quantile function of y_t given y_{t-1} is written as a sum of baseline quantile functions with path-dependent coefficients. The basic model is*

$$\mathrm{VaR}_t(\alpha) = a_0(y_{t-1},\theta) + a_1(y_{t-1},\theta)Q_1(\alpha,\beta) + a_2(y_{t-1},\theta)Q_2(\alpha,\beta),$$

where β is the parameter of baseline quantile functions Q_1 and Q_2, and θ parametrize the path-dependent positive coefficients a_0, a_1, a_2.

4.3.4. Local Maximum Likelihood

Let us assume that the process (y_t) of changes in portfolio values is a Markov process of order 1. Gourieroux and Jasiak (2000) approximate locally the tail of the true conditional density $l(y_{t+1}|y_t = y)$, say, by a parametric distribution such as a Gaussian distribution. The procedure consists of the following steps:

First step: Compute the 1%-empirical quantile from the sample $y_1, \dots, y_T$ and denote it by $\hat{q}$.

Second step: Compute the mean and variance in a neighborhood of $y_{t+1} = \hat{q}$ and $y_t = y$. For a kernel K and bandwidth h, the approximate mean and variance are

$$\hat{m}(\hat{q}, y) = \sum_{\tau=1}^{T} K\left(\frac{y_\tau - \hat{q}}{h}\right) K\left(\frac{y_{\tau-1} - y}{h}\right) y_\tau \Big/ \sum_{\tau=1}^{T} K\left(\frac{y_\tau - \hat{q}}{h}\right) K\left(\frac{y_{\tau-1} - y}{h}\right) \quad \text{and}$$

$$\hat{\sigma}^2(\hat{q}, y) = \sum_{\tau=1}^{T} K\left(\frac{y_\tau - \hat{q}}{h}\right) K\left(\frac{y_{\tau-1} - y}{h}\right) y_\tau^2 \Big/ \sum_{\tau=1}^{T} K\left(\frac{y_\tau - \hat{q}}{h}\right) K\left(\frac{y_{\tau-1} - y}{h}\right) - \hat{m}^2(\hat{q}, y).$$

Third step: Apply the Gaussian VaR formula with mean and variance $\hat{m}(\hat{q}, y_T)$, $\hat{\sigma}^2(\hat{q}, y_T)$ to get

$$\widehat{\text{VaR}}_T = -\hat{m}(\hat{q}, y_T) + \Phi^{-1}(1-\alpha)\hat{\sigma}(\hat{q}, y_T).$$

5. VaR FOR PORTFOLIOS WITH DERIVATIVES

In the financial theory, a considerable attention is given to derivative pricing and hedging, especially for derivatives such as European call options. Let us recall that a European call with maturity T and strike K pays $(S_T - K)^+ = \text{Max}(S_T - K, 0)$ at date T, where S_T is the price at T of the underlying asset. Since the payoffs of derivatives with any strike, written on the same asset, depend on the same benchmark S_T and are defined by nonlinear payoff functions, people tend to believe that prices of such derivatives are strongly and nonlinearly dependent.[11] Various theories supporting this belief lead to two types of derivative pricing formulas. Under the complete market hypothesis, the price at t of a European call with strike K and maturity T can be written as

$$C_t(K, T) = C(S_t, r_t, K, T - t), \tag{5.1}$$

[11] In reality, they also depend on other factors that influence the demand and supply of derivative assets, especially since they are illiquid.

where r_t is the interest rate and C is a deterministic function that depends on the (risk-neutral) dynamics of the underlying asset price. An example of this approach is the Black–Scholes model [Black and Scholes (1973)].

Under the incomplete market hypothesis, the price depends also on other factors Z_t:

$$C_t(K, T) = C(S_t, Z_t, r_t, K, T - t). \tag{5.2}$$

An example of this approach is the Hull–White model [Hull and White (1987)], in which the additional factor is stochastic volatility.

The option pricing under the complete- and incomplete-market hypotheses relies on restrictive assumptions. In particular, both approaches assume[12] that a) all assets, including the derivatives are liquid, b) all assets including the derivatives can be traded at any time, c) the derivative prices are functions of state variables (S_t, r_t) or (S_t, Z_t, r_t) only, d) the state variables are Markov processes. In practice, however, these assumptions are not satisfied. For example, index derivatives are written on market indexes, which are not traded directly on the markets.[13] The derivative securities are generally not liquid and their prices may depend on the demand and supply effects.

Since the derivative trading can potentially cause financial losses, it is natural to introduce a VaR measure for portfolios that include derivatives. Because of the lack of liquidity of such complex assets, it is difficult to come up with a VaR measure based on the lagged observed derivative prices, like historical simulation. In this section, we use the theoretical pricing formulas derived under the liquidity assumption to derive model-based approximations of the VaR for portfolios with derivatives. The accuracy of such approximations depends on the model used by a bank for derivative pricing (called the internal model, henceforth). Therefore, it is necessary to examine the sensitivity of the VaR with respect to potential misspecification of the internal model.

5.1. Parametric Monte Carlo Method

For ease of exposition, let us consider a portfolio of European calls, all written on the same asset. This portfolio is defined by the set of associated strikes and maturities: $(K_i, T_i), i = 1, \ldots, n$. If one of the strikes is zero, then the portfolio contains the underlying asset too. On a complete market, the change of portfolio value is

$$y_{t+1} = \Delta W_{t+1}(a) = \sum_{i=1}^{n} a_i[C(S_{t+1}, r_{t+1}; K_i, T_i - t - 1) - C(S_t, r_t; K_i, T_i - t)]. \tag{5.3}$$

[12] See Merton (1974) for a complete list of assumptions for the Black–Scholes model.

[13] Some index mimicking portfolios can actually be traded, such as the Standard and Poor Depository Receipts (SPDR) that mimicks the S&P 500. However, the nonlinear dynamic properties of the S&P 500 and of the SPDR are significantly different, especially for extreme values.

It is a known function of the current and future interest rates and asset prices. Moreover, it depends on the unknown parameter θ that characterizes the (risk-neutral) dynamics of price S_t. Let us denote the function in (5.3) by

$$y_{t+1} = w_t(S_t, S_{t+1}, r_t, r_{t+1}; \theta). \tag{5.4}$$

The conditional distribution of y_{t+1} has generally no closed-form expression and has to be approximated by Monte Carlo experiments. Under the assumption of a deterministic interest rate, the procedure is implemented as follows[14]:

(i) First step: Estimation of parameter θ

The dynamics of (S_t) are summarized by the conditional historical distribution of S_t given S_{t-1}: $l(S_t | S_{t-1}; \theta)$, (say).[15] Parameter θ can be estimated from the historical data on (S_t) by the maximum likelihood, for example (the so-called historical approach). The estimator is denoted by $\hat{\theta}_T$.

(ii) Second step: Simulation of future values of S

For a given value of S_t, simulated values $S^s_{t+1}, s = 1, \dots, S$ are drawn in the conditional distribution $l(S_{t+1} | S_t; \hat{\theta}_T)$.

(iii) Third step: Simulation of y_{t+1}

We simulate the values[16] of y_{t+1} as

$$y^s_{t+1} = w_t\left(S_t, S^s_{t+1}, r_t, r_{t+1}; \hat{\theta}_T\right), \quad s = 1, \dots, S.$$

(iv) Fourth step: Estimation of the VaR

Finally, the conditional VaR estimate can be obtained directly from the empirical quantile of the simulated sample $y^s_{t+1}, s = 1, \dots, S$.

It is interesting to discuss this approach in the context of the Black–Scholes model, in which the asset price follows a geometric Brownian motion

$$\mathrm{d}S_t = \mu S_t \mathrm{d}t + \sigma S_t \mathrm{d}W_t,$$

where (W_t) is a standard Brownian motion. The asset price dynamics depends on two parameters $\theta = (\mu, \sigma)$, whereas the option price depends on volatility σ only. Both parameters μ and σ have to be estimated prior to the VaR estimation. Indeed, while the derivative price depends on σ only, its conditional distribution depends on both volatility σ and drift μ. This explains why it is necessary to use the historical

[14] If the interest rate is stochastic, it is also necessary to estimate the dynamics of the rate and to simulate the future interest rates.

[15] We assume that the risk-neutral parameter is a component of the historical parameter as in the Black–Scholes.

[16] In the formula below, we assume analytical expressions of the derivative prices. Otherwise, they have also to be approximated by Monte Carlo [see Gourieroux and Jasiak (2001a), chapter 11].

data $S_t, t = 1, \ldots, T$ to recover μ, instead of using only the data on derivative prices (cross sectional or implied volatility approach) since the derivative prices allow only for estimation of volatility σ.

The method outlined above can be extended to incomplete markets by considering the distribution of all state variables, including factor Z for estimation and simulation.

5.2. Taylor Expansion of Nonlinear Portfolios

As the simulation of the VaR is computationally demanding, the financial sector has proposed some approximate closed-form expressions of the VaR. These VaR estimation methods are straightforward but can produce misleading outcomes.

5.2.1. The Delta Method

Under the complete market hypothesis, it is possible to build an instantaneously riskless portfolio that contains a European call and the underlying asset. The allocation of the riskless portfolio is -1 unit of the European call and $\delta_t(K, T) = \frac{\partial C}{\partial S}(S_t, r_t, K, T - t)$ units of the underlying asset. δ_t is called the delta of the derivative security. In this framework, the European call is equivalent to a portfolio that contains the underlying asset and a risk-free asset with allocations $\delta_t(K, T)$ and $\alpha_t(K, T)$, say, respectively.

This result can be used for the computation of the VaR as follows. Let us consider a portfolio of European calls. This portfolio is equivalent to a portfolio of $\sum_{i=1}^n a_i\delta_t(K_i, T_i)$ units of the underlying asset and $\sum_{i=1}^n a_i\alpha_t(K_i, T_i)$ units of the riskless asset. The conditional VaR is computed as outlined in Section 4 for a portfolio linear in S. This simple method of VaR computation differs from the suggestion of the Basle Committee. According to the Basle Committee, the VaR has to be computed for a portfolio with fixed allocations (called a crystallized portfolio) and should disregard any portfolio updating during the holding period. In contrast, the δ-method assumes continuous updating of the allocations performed in an optimal way (provided that the internal model is well specified). As a consequence, the δ-based VaR is smaller than the VaR with constant allocations and underestimates the true VaR. In an extreme case, the internal model views as risk-free a portfolio with -1 units of the derivative and δ_t units of the underlying asset. Thus, this method is not robust. A slight misspecification of the internal model suffices to perceive an extremely risky portfolio as risk-free.

5.2.2. The Delta–Gamma Method

The approach described above can be extended by considering a second-order Taylor expansion of the derivative price with respect to the price of the underlying asset

$$\Delta C(S_t, r_t, K, T - t) \approx \alpha_t + \delta_t \Delta S_{t+1} + \frac{1}{2}\gamma_t(\Delta S_{t+1})^2, \tag{5.5}$$

where the second-order derivative γ_t is the so-called gamma of the option. This expansion includes a nonlinear quadratic function of ΔS. Several authors [see, e.g., Jorion (1997) p. 144] proposed to apply the method of the variance–covariance matrix (see 2.2 i) under the conditional normality of ΔS_{t+1}. The derivative portfolio is such that

$$\Delta W_t(a) \approx \sum_{i=1}^{n} a_i \alpha_t^i + \left(\sum_{i=1}^{n} a_i \delta_t^i\right) \Delta S_{t+1} + \frac{1}{2}\left(\sum_{i=1}^{n} a_i \gamma_t^i\right) \Delta S_{t+1}^2. \tag{5.6}$$

We get

$$E_t[\Delta W_{t+1}(a)] \approx \sum_{i=1}^{n} a_i \alpha_t^i + \left(\sum_{i=1}^{n} a_i \delta_t^i\right) E_t(\Delta S_{t+1}) + \frac{1}{2}\left(\sum_{i=1}^{n} a_i \gamma_t^i\right) [V_t(\Delta S_{t+1}) + (E_t \Delta S_{t+1})^2];$$

$$\begin{aligned} V_t[\Delta W_{t+1}(a)] &\approx \left(\sum_{i=1}^{n} a_i \delta_t^i\right)^2 V_t(\Delta S_{t+1}) + \left(\frac{1}{2}\sum_{i=1}^{n} a_i \gamma_t^i\right)^2 V_t[(\Delta S_{t+1})^2] \\ &\quad + \left(\sum_{i=1}^{n} a_i \delta_t^i\right)\left(\sum_{i=1}^{n} a_i \gamma_t^i\right) \mathrm{Cov}_t(\Delta S_{t+1}, \Delta S_{t+1}^2) \\ &\approx \left(\sum_{i=1}^{n} a_i \delta_t^i\right)^2 V_t(\Delta S_{t+1}) + \frac{1}{2}\left(\sum_{i=1}^{n} a_i \gamma_t^i\right)^2 [V_t(\Delta S_{t+1})]^2, \end{aligned}$$

since $\mathrm{Cov}[\Delta S, (\Delta S)^2] = 0$ and $V[(\Delta S)^2] = 2[V(\Delta S)]^2$ for a Gaussian variable. Therefore the first- and second-order conditional moments of $\Delta W_{t+1}(a)$ are easily computed from the first- and second-order conditional moments of ΔS_{t+1}. The drawbacks of this common approach are as follows. First, the expansions are valid when the derivative price is differentiable with respect to S and are not valid at dates close to the maturity of the option. Second, the mean–variance approach assumes implicitly the approximate normality of the change in portfolio value. Even if ΔS_{t+1} is conditionally normal, the normality of the change of portfolio value is no longer satisfied due to the presence of a quadratic term. Finally, the second-order Taylor expansion given above disregards the time-varying features of a European call, as explained below.

5.2.3. Linearization of Nonlinear Portfolios

The characteristics of a European call change in time. In particular, the residual maturity decreases while the interest rate varies. Therefore, a correct first-order expansion of the derivative price is

$$
\begin{aligned}
&C(S_{t+1}, r_{t+1}, K, T - t - 1) - C(S_t, r_t, K, T - t) \\
&= \frac{\partial C}{\partial S}(S_t, r_t, K, T - t)\Delta S_{t+1} + \frac{\partial C}{\partial r}(S_t, r_t, K, T - t)\Delta r_{t+1} - \frac{\partial C}{\partial T}(S_t, r_t, K, T - t).
\end{aligned}
$$

It differs from the expansion considered in the previous section by the presence of the first-order derivatives with respect to the interest rate and the residual maturity. The same remark is true for the second-order Taylor expansion as well.

The expansion can be extended to include time-varying parameters. For example, it is common to use the Black–Scholes model with time–varying volatility σ_t, say. In that case, the expansion could also be written with respect to the volatility (or the log-volatility) and would involve the associated derivative of the price, i.e., the vega of the option. That expansion is easy to use under the assumption of joint normality of the conditional distribution of $\Delta S_{t+1}, \Delta r_{t+1}, \Delta \log \sigma_{t+1}$. This approach was suggested by the RiskMetrics Group [see, e.g., Malz (2000)], who report the variance–covariance matrices, as well as the returns on implied volatilities. However, the normality assumption is very unrealistic and the observed implied volatility returns are generally leptokurtic and skewed.

5.2.4. The Normality Assumption in the Case of Option Prices

The motivation for using the first-order expansion is to extend the normality assumption on the price change of the underlying asset to the change in derivative prices. The argument is that the normality is satisfied by "sufficiently large portfolios of independent options," to which the central limit theorem can be applied [Finger (1997)]. However, this argument is not valid since the prices of derivatives on the same asset are highly correlated and the fit of the normal approximation to the tails of an empirical distribution is poor. In general, the conditional distributions of derivative prices are nongaussian. They often have several modes, and feature skewness and fat tails [see, e.g., Gourieroux and Jasiak (2001a) chapter 12].

Despite the aforementioned limitations, the use of delta or delta–gamma methods is recommended by the Capital Adequacy Directive (1993) and by the Banking Supervision Proposal (1995) of the Basle Committee. A survey of the Group of Thirty (1993) showed that 98% of 125 respondents were using delta or delta-gamma methods.

6. CREDIT RISK

As mentioned earlier in the text, the most common losses incurred by banks are losses on corporate loans and mortgages. The credit risk is essentially the risk of a default of payment,[17] which depends on the evolution in time of the solvency of a borrower. Factors that influence the credit risk are (1) the heterogeneity of borrowers and loans, and (2) the lack of liquidity as only a fraction of loans can be traded on secondary markets. More specifically, market prices are generally available only for corporate bonds and mortgage-backed securities. Among risky credits with no market prices are mortgages, consumption loans, revolving credit (credit cards), OTC corporate loans, and cash advances, known as retail credits.

This section is organized as follows. The first part clarifies the link between the distribution of default and the actuarial value (resp. market price) of an OTC loan (resp. bond). The second part shows the assessment of default rates from the data on (i) individual borrowers, (ii) bonds, (iii) equity prices. The third part describes the credit migration approach, and the last part presents the profit and loss distributions for portfolios of bonds and retail loans.

6.1. Spread of Interest Rates

Let us consider a consumer loan of initial amount B_0 with fixed contractual interest rate r to be repaid in H units of time by equal monthly payments of amount m. If the borrower has zero probability of default, then the following actuarial relationship is satisfied,

$$B_0 = \frac{m}{1+r} + \frac{m}{(1+r)^2} + \cdots + \frac{m}{(1+r)^H}, \tag{6.1}$$

which equates the initial balance to the sum of discounted cash-flows. This relation can be used to find initial balance B_0 for given m, r, H, or to find interest rate r for given B_0, m, H.

The actuarial formula (6.1) needs to be modified when the probability of default is different from zero. Let Y denote the time to default (with time origin $Y = 0$ assigned to the date when credit is granted). Suppose that after time Y, the borrower will not repay, even a fraction of the outstanding balance (i.e., the recovery rate is equal to zero).[18] Then, the actuarial formula implies

$$\begin{aligned} B_0^* &= \frac{m^*}{1+r^*} P[Y \geq 1] + \cdots + \frac{m^*}{(1+r^*)^H} P[Y \geq H] \\ &= m^* \left[\frac{S(1)}{1+r^*} + \cdots + \frac{S(H)}{(1+r^*)^H} \right], \end{aligned} \tag{6.2}$$

[17] And of the risk of prepayment, which is not discussed in this section.

[18] The size and timing of the recovery should also be taken into account. For ease of exposition, we assume a zero recovery rate. Even though this assumption is unrealistic, it is important to note that it is used to recover the implied probability of default from bond prices. Moreover, when the recovery is assumed independent of default, the actuarial prices are simply inferred from the proposed ones by multiplying them by the expected recovery rate. This approach is recommended by the Basle Committee.

where S denotes the survivor function for time to default. Formulas (6.1) and (6.2) can be compared in two different ways.

(i) If interest rates $r^* = r$ and monthly payment $m^* = m$ are given, we get different actuarial values of the loan depending on the possibility of default. The loan value computed without default risk, that is $B_0 = \sum_{h=1}^{H} \frac{m}{(1+r)^h}$, is strictly larger than the value $B_0^* = \sum_{h=1}^{H} \frac{mS(h)}{(1+r)^h}$. The omission of default risk leads to overvaluation of credit.

(ii) If loan value $B_0^* = B_0$ and monthly payment $m^* = m$ are given, we find that different interest rates satisfy the actuarial formulae (6.1) and (6.2). It is easy to check that interest rate r is strictly higher than interest rate r^* to compensate for default risk. The difference $s = r - r^*$ is called the spread of interest rate.

As an illustration, let us assume an exponentially distributed time to default Y with default intensity λ. We get $S(h) = \exp(-\lambda h)$ and,

$$\begin{aligned} B_0 &= m\left[\frac{S(1)}{1+r^*} + \cdots + \frac{S(H)}{(1+r^*)^H}\right] \\ &= m\left[\frac{\exp -\lambda}{1+r^*} + \cdots + \frac{\exp -\lambda H}{(1+r^*)^H}\right] \\ &= m\left[\frac{\exp -\lambda}{1+r^*} + \cdots + \left[\frac{\exp -\lambda}{1+r^*}\right]^H\right]. \end{aligned}$$

We find that

$$\begin{aligned} &1 + r = (1 + r^*) \exp \lambda \\ &\Leftrightarrow s = r - r^* = (1 + r^*)[\exp \lambda - 1]. \end{aligned}$$

The spread is an increasing function of default intensity λ.

So far, we assumed a constant rate of interest and a flat term structure. The approach can be easily extended to any type of fixed income bonds (or retail loans without indexed payments) and to a varying term structure of interest rates. Let us consider a bond with known future payments F_τ (say) at dates τ, and let $B(t, t+h)$ denote the price at t of the zero coupon bond that pays 1 \$ at date $t+h$. Without default risk, the price of this bond at date t is

$$P_t(F) = \sum_{h=1}^{\infty} F_{t+h} B(t, t+h). \tag{6.3}$$

The bond price is derived by treating a fixed income bond as a portfolio of zero coupon bonds and by applying the arbitrage free condition. In the presence of default risk, the bond price will decrease. If default probability is independent of the evolution of the risk-free interest rate, the price of a bond with default possibility that a risk neutral investor is willing to pay is

$$P_t(F,S) = \sum_{h=1}^{\infty} F_{t+h} B(t,t+h) S_t(t,t+h), \tag{6.4}$$

where $S_t(t,t+h) = P_t[Y \geq t+h | Y \geq t]$ and the time to default is the time elapsed after the bond was issued. The conditioning on the time to default Y is necessary because the bond can only be priced while it is still alive, and the information set used to predict Y increases with t.

Formulas (6.3) and (6.4) involve two term structures of interest rates: the term structure without default risk is characterized by the set $B(t,t+h), h = 1, \ldots, H$; the term structure with default risk is characterized by $B^*(t,t+h) = B(t,t+h)S_t(t,t+h), h = 1, \ldots, H$, and depends on the distribution of time to default. $S_t(t,t+h), h = 1, \ldots, H$, defines the term structure of spread that is the mapping $h \to s_{t,t+h} = r_{t,t+h} - r^*_{t,t+1} = \frac{1}{h} \log \frac{B(t,t+h)}{B^*(t,t+h)} = -\frac{1}{h} \log S_t(t,t+h)$.[19]

6.2. Assessment of Default Rates

There are two sources of randomness in the future price of a bond or retail loan, which need to be predicted: the future risk-free term structure of interest rates and the future probability of default. Since these are generally considered independent, we first focus on the estimation of default probability $S_t(t,t+h)$. The existing methods differ with respect to the assumption on the existence of a secondary market for loans.

There is an important difference between the corporate bonds and consumer loans. On the bond markets, bonds are offered for sale by a large number of issuers. The bond issuings are organized and the lenders possess information on the credit ratings of borrowers. In contrast, retail loans such as consumer loans and mortgages may be provided to several thousands borrowers by a single bank. In general, these loans are small and very heterogeneous with respect to the initial balance, maturity, interest rate, monthly payments, and characteristics of individual borrowers.

6.2.1. Recovering Default Rates from Market Prices of Bonds

Let us consider firm j that issues bonds $l = 1, \ldots, L_{jt}$, which are traded on the market at date t. At date t, these bonds differ with respect to their cash-flows F^{jl}_{t+h} and prices

[19] Similarly, when the recovery rates are taken into account, there exists a term structure of recovery rates.

$P_t^{jl}(F,S)$, which are related as follows:

$$P_t^{jl}(F,S) = \sum_{h=1}^{\infty} F_{t+h}^{jl} B(t,t+h) S_t^j(t,t+h), l = 1,\ldots,L_{jt}, \tag{6.5}$$

where the conditional survivor function depends only on borrower j and not on the bond.

Let us assume that number L_{jt} of traded bonds is large and their cash-flows are very diversified. To recover the term structure of yields on these corporate bonds, we can apply the regression method or a smoothing method by local polynomials or splines, where the last two methods are used for recovering the term structure of Treasury bonds. These procedures yield the approximated term structure of yields on bond j:

$$\hat{B}^{*j}(t,t+h) \approx B(t,t+h) S_t^j(t,t+h), \text{ for any } t,h.$$

Next, by using the T-bond prices, one can estimate the term structure of interest on a risk-free asset $\hat{B}(t,t+h)$, $\forall t,h$, and find the estimators of individual default probabilities[20]:

$$\hat{S}_t^{*j}(t,t+h) = \hat{B}^{*j}(t,t+h)/\hat{B}(t,t+h). \tag{6.6}$$

This approach requires only the knowledge of prices of bonds traded on the market. Therefore, it can be used by banks that do not possess the data on individual credit histories of corporate borrowers. In practice, however, the market information is rather poor and leads to biased estimators of default rates. This is because for a given issuer j, the number of corporate bonds issued by that firm that are actively traded on the market at a given date is rather limited. For this reason, the quoted prices can be quite different from their theoretical values and methods such as regression or smoothing are not reliable. To circumvent this difficulty, bond issuers can be divided into homogenous categories $k = 1,\ldots,K$, with respect to their actual Standard and Poor's (resp. Moody's) credit ratings with the top rating AAA (resp. Aaa), and the lowest rating CCC (resp. Caa).[21] Then, the term structure of bond yield spread is assumed identical for all issuers in the same rating category. This allows for the use of a larger number of traded bonds for recovering the rates of default. This pragmatic approach is discussed in detail in Section 6.3.

[20] Called the implied survivor probability.

[21] The complete list of ratings assigns one of the following 10 symbols:
Moody's (Aaa, Aa, A, Baa, Ba, B, Caa, Ca, C, D) and Standard and Poor (AAA, AA, A, BBB, BB, B, CCC, CC, C, D).

6.2.2. Recovering Default Rates from Equity Prices

The Merton's model [Crosbie (1998); Janosi et al. (2003); Merton (1974)] can be used to recover default probabilities from data on equity value. More precisely, let us consider firm j with the equity value, asset value, and liabilities denoted by $V_{E,t}$, $V_{A,t}$ and L_t, respectively. The equity can be considered as a call option on future value $V_{A,t+1}$ with strike L_{t+1}. If the liabilities are predetermined and the asset values follow a Black–Scholes model, then value $V_{E,t}$ can be derived from the Black–Scholes option pricing formula as a function of $V_{A,t}$ and volatility σ_A of the asset value. Moreover, under the Black–Scholes model, the equity and asset volatilities are related by

$$\sigma_E V_{E,t} = V_{A,t}\sigma_A\delta_t,$$

where δ_t is the delta of the call option. Therefore, given the data on equity value and equity volatility, we can find σ_A and $V_{A,t}$ by using the last equality and the Black–Scholes option pricing formula. The results allow for further computation of the conditional probability of default at $t+h$:

$$S_t(t, t+h) = P[V_{A,t+h} < L_{t+h}, V_{A,t+h-1} > L_{t+h-1}, \ldots, V_{A,t+1} > L_{t+1} | V_{A,t}].$$

This approach was recommended to the practitioners by the KMV corporation. It can be criticized for disregarding the information contained in bond prices and for assuming that future liabilities are known, which is equivalent to disregarding the possibility of future borrowing and debt renegotiation. The method is valid, provided that the assumptions of the continuous-time model of asset value are satisfied.

6.2.3. Recovering Default Rates from Individual Credit Histories

Let us now consider the retail loans. To reduce market incompleteness due to the heterogeneity of individual loans(contracts), we can aggregate the data as follows. In the first step, we define homogenous categories of loan contracts (with identical initial balance, term, interest rate, and monthly payments) granted to similar borrowers. These categories of loans, indexed by k, $k = 1, \ldots, K$, are next partitioned with respect to the generation of loans, leading to a set of cohorts doubly indexed by k, τ, where k is the category index and τ is the beginning of a loan agreement. If the number of contracts in each cohort is sufficiently large (greater than 200–300), the market incompleteness is reduced by computing the averages of homogenous loans. Under this approach, the individual data is replaced by the aggregate data on default rates (prepayment rates, recovery rates) cohort by cohort.[22]

[22] As mentioned earlier, we focus on default and do not consider potential prepayments or partial recoveries.

For illustration, let us show an example of data aggregation. The time unit is set equal to one semester. In each cohort, we observe default rates over all semesters from the beginning of a loan agreement until the current date. Let $D_k(\tau; h)$ denote the default rate in cohort k, τ in semester $\tau + h$; h denotes the age of a loan, i.e., the time elapsed since the loan agreement was signed. For each category k, we get a double entry table, which may contain various pairs of entries, such as the generation and current date, the generation and age, or the current date and age. Tables 10.1–10.3 below display the data on two-year loans (i.e., that need to be repaid in four semesters). The dates are given in a "year.semester" format. Cohort category indexes are suppressed for clarity. The last

Table 10.1 Default rate by generation and current date

Current date generation	97.1	97.2	98.1	98.2	99.1	99.2
97.1	$D(97.1;1)$	$D(97.1;2)$	$D(97.1;3)$	$D(97.1;4)$		
97.2		$D(97.2;1)$	$D(97.2;2)$	$D(97.2;3)$	$D(97.2;4)$	
98.1			$D(98.1;1)$	$D(98.1;2)$	$D(98.1;3)$	$D(98.1;4)$
98.2				$D(98.2;1)$	$D(98.2;2)$	$D(98.2;3)$
99.1					$D(99.1;1)$	$D(97.1;2)$
99.2						$D(99.2;1)$

Table 10.2 Default rate by generation and age

Age generation	1	2	3	4
97.1	$D(97.1;1)$	$D(97.1;2)$	$D(97.1;3)$	$D(97.1;4)$
97.2	$D(97.2;1)$	$D(97.2;2)$	$D(97.2;3)$	$D(97.2;4)$
98.1	$D(98.1;1)$	$D(98.1;2)$	$D(98.1;3)$	$D(98.1;4)$
98.2	$D(98.2;1)$	$D(98.2;2)$	$D(98.2;3)$	
99.1	$D(99.1;1)$	$D(99.1;2)$		
99.2	$D(99.2;1)$			

Table 10.3 Default rate by age and current date

Current date age	97.1	97.2	98.1	98.2	99.1	99.2
1	$D(97.1;1)$	$D(97.2;1)$	$D(98.1;1)$	$D(98.2;1)$	$D(99.1;1)$	$D(99.2;1)$
2		$D(97.1;2)$	$D(97.2;2)$	$D(98.1;2)$	$D(98.2;2)$	$D(99.1;2)$
3			$D(97.1;3)$	$D(97.2;3)$	$D(98.1;3)$	$D(98.2;3)$
4				$D(97.1;4)$	$D(97.2;4)$	$D(98.1;4)$

semester observed is (the end of) 99.2. Note that, Tables 10.2 and 10.3 are easier to read and require less memory for computer storage.[23]

6.3. The Credit Migration Approach

Let us consider again the corporate loans. Because of the heterogeneity of bond issuers, discussed in Section 6.2.1, we distinguish the conditional distributions of time to default for each credit rating category. The objective of the credit migration approach is to analyze the joint dynamics of credit rating and default.

6.3.1. The Model

The model was initially conceived as a continuous-time model by Jarrow (1997). Below, we present an extended and time-discretized version of that model. The key assumption is the existence of a finite number of states $k = 1, \dots, K$ that represent credit quality. At each date, a borrower occupies one state, in which it can stay or migrate to another state at a future date. Let (Z_t) denote the qualitative process formed by the sequence of states occupied by a borrower. It is assumed that this process is a Markov chain with transition matrix $Q = (q_{kl})$, with elements $q_{kl} = P[Z_t = k | Z_{t-1} = l]$.

The knowledge of recent state history is assumed to be sufficient information to define the term structure of credit spread. More precisely, if a borrower has spent h periods of time in state k, after moving into state k from state l, the credit spread is determined by the value of survivor function $S_{kl}(h)$. Thus, the model is parametrized by transition matrix Q and the set of survivor functions $S_{kl}, \forall\, k, l$. To illustrate the zero coupon price dynamics, let consider a credit-rating history. The term structures of zero coupon price with and without default risk are given in Table 10.4.

Table 10.4 The term structures of zero coupon price

date t	Z_t	$B(0,t)$	$B^*(0,t)$
1	1	$B(0,1)$	.
2	3	$B(0,2)$	$B(0,2)S_{31}(1)$
3	3	$B(0,3)$	$B(0,3)S_{31}(2)$
4	3	$B(0,4)$	$B(0,4)S_{31}(3)$
5	1	$B(0,5)$	$B(0,5)S_{13}(1)$
6	2	$B(0,6)$	$B(0,6)S_{21}(1)$
7	2	$B(0,7)$	$B(0,7)S_{21}(2)$
8	3	$B(0,8)$	$B(0,8)S_{32}(1)$
9	3	$B(0,9)$	$B(0,9)S_{32}(2)$
10	3	$B(0,10)$	$B(0,10)S_{32}(3)$

[23] Similar tables can be designed for the recovery rates.

Several versions of the model under simplified assumptions can be found in the financial literature. For example, Jarrow (1997) assumed that the credit spread is a constant function of the current state only: $S_{kl}(h) = \exp(-\lambda_k h)$. Longstaff and Schwartz (1995), Duffie and Kan (1996), and Lando (1998) allowed for more complicated term structure patterns but maintained the dependence on the current state. Intuitively, it is clear that the past state contains information about future default. Loosely speaking, we do not expect to observe the same term structure of spread for a borrower with credit rating AA who was AAA before as for a borrower with the same current rating AA, who was rated A before.

6.3.2. Statistical Inference when the State is Observable

Let us assume independent risk dynamics of different borrowers. When the state histories are observed, the transition matrix is easily estimated from its empirical counterpart. Then, one can consider all the observed histories that end in state k after a transition from l, and estimate the survivor function S_{kl} from the observed bond prices of firms in state k.

This approach is followed by market practitioners with admissible states defined as credit ratings AAA, AA, A, BBB, BB, B, CCC by the Standard and Poor.[24] For this purpose, the rating agencies report regularly the estimated transition matrix and the term structures of bond yield spread at horizon one year that depend on the current state k only (see Tables 10.5 and 10.6).

We observe that the spread is not constant. In this example, it increases with the term, except for low ratings. Indeed, the long-term spread takes into account the fact that a bond is still alive, which is a very positive signal about an a priori risky borrower.

6.3.3. Unobservable States

The approach outlined in the previous section is easy to implement and accommodates the joint dynamics of rating and default. However, it identifies the credit quality with a

Table 10.5 Estimated transition matrix

Rating	AAA	AA	A	BBB	B	BB	CCC	Default
AAA	90.81	8.33	0.68	0.06	0.12	0	0	0
AA	0.70	90.65	7.79	0.64	0.06	0.14	0.02	0
A	0.09	2.27	91.05	5.52	0.74	0.26	0.01	0.06
BBB	0.02	0.33	5.95	86.93	5.30	1.17	0.12	0.18
BB	0.03	0.14	0.67	7.73	80.53	8.84	1.00	1.06
B	0	0.11	0.24	0.43	6.48	83.46	4.07	5.20
CCC	0.21	0	0.22	1.30	2.38	11.24	64.86	19.79

[24]Note that the Standard and Poor rating and the Moody's rating are not completely compatible, especially for dates close to a change of rating, that is to a sudden change of risk level [see, e.g., the discussion in Kliger and Sarig (2000)].

Table 10.6 The spread curve

Category	Year 1	Year 2	Year 3	Year 4
AAA	3.60	4.17	4.73	5.12
AA	3.65	4.22	4.78	5.17
A	3.72	4.32	4.93	5.32
BBB	4.10	4.67	5.25	5.63
BB	5.55	6.02	6.78	7.27
B	6.05	7.02	8.03	8.52
CCC	15.05	15.02	14.03	13.52

rating assigned by a private rating agency, whose rating strategy may vary over time. For example, the transition matrices reported by Moody's are clearly time varying and seem to reflect a tendency for toughening the rules over time.

Moreover, even though the details on the Moody's rating system are not publicly known for confidentiality reason, one can expect that the ratings depend not only on the structure of the balance sheet of a firm and its dynamics but also on the market price history. This dependence is not compatible with the assumption that Z_t is as a Markov chain, and that the current rating depends on the last rating only.

When the state is considered unobservable, the model becomes a complicated Hidden Markov model, which requires simulation-based methods for parameter estimation and for recovering the unobserved state histories.

6.4. VaR for Credit Portfolio

The analysis of profit and loss distributions for VaR computation can be carried out in various ways. Below, we describe two methods. The first method is based on the credit migration approach and is suitable for corporate bonds. The second method assumes that the heterogeneity of loans is exogenous, and is suitable for retail consumer loans. Later in the text, we address the correlation of default.

6.4.1. The Future Portfolio Value

To determine the VaR, we need to define precisely the future value of a portfolio of bonds. Each bond is characterized by a time-varying cash-flow pattern and coupon payments that occur during the holding period. To simplify the discussion, let us consider a single bond with a cash-flow sequence $F_\tau, \tau = t+1, t+2, \ldots$. Without the risk of default, its price at t is

$$W_t = P_t(F) = \sum_{h=1}^{\infty} F_{t+h} B(t, t+h). \tag{6.7}$$

With the risk of default, its price becomes

$$W_t = P_t(F, S) = \sum_{h=1}^{\infty} F_{t+h} B(t, t+h) S_t(t, t+h). \tag{6.8}$$

Its future value at $t+2$, say, depends on the coupons, which will be paid at dates $t+1$ and $t+2$, and on the value at $t+2$ of the residual bond with cash-flows $F_\tau, \tau \geq t+3$. Before aggregating these components, we need to explain how the cashed-in coupons are reinvested. For ease of exposition, we assume that they are invested in the risk-free asset.

Without the risk of default, the future bond price is

$$W_{t+2} = F_{t+1}[B(t+1, t+2)]^{-1} + F_{t+2} + \sum_{h=1}^{\infty} F_{t+2+h} B(t+2, t+2+h).$$

With the risk of default, the future bond price can be

$W_{t+2} = 0$, if there is default at $t+1$;

$W_{t+2} = F_{t+1}[B(t+1, t+2)]^{-1}$, if there is default at $t+2$;

$W_{t+2} = F_{t+1}[B(t+1, t+2)]^{-1} + F_{t+2} + \sum_{h=1}^{\infty} F_{t+2+h} B(t+2, t+2+h) S_{t+2}$ $(t+2, t+2+h)$, otherwise.

At date t, the future bond price is stochastic since (i) we don't know if the bond will still be alive at dates $t+1$ and $t+2$. (ii) the future term structure is unknown, (iii) the conditional survivor probabilities have to be updated.

6.4.2. The Credit Migration Approach

The credit migration model is suitable for approximating the profit and loss distribution by simulations. Suppose that the portfolio contains bonds of n issuers $i = 1, \ldots, n$, where each issuer i is characterized by its state history $\underline{Z}_{i,t} = (Z_{i,t}, Z_{i,t-1}, \ldots,)$. Different bonds of the same issuer i in the portfolio can be aggregated leading to a sequence of aggregated cash-flows $F_{i,\tau}, \tau = t+1, t+2, \ldots$. Let $P_{i,t}(\underline{Z}_{i,t})$ denote the price at t of this sequence of cash-flows and $P_{i,t+h}(\underline{Z}_{i,t+h})$ denote the price at $t+h$ of the residual sequence $F_{i,\tau}, \tau \geq t+h+1$. These prices include the cost of the risk of default and depend on individual state histories, which influence the default probabilities.

The current value of the portfolio of bonds is

$$W_t = \sum_{i=1}^{n} W_{i,t} = \sum_{i=1}^{n} P_{i,t}(\underline{Z}_{i,t}),$$

where $W_{i,t}$ denotes the total value of all bonds of issuer i in the portfolio. The future value is

$$W_{t+h} = \sum_{i=1}^{n} W_{i,t+h}.$$

The conditional distribution of this future value can be approximated by the sample distribution of

$$W_{t+h}^s = \sum_{i=1}^{n} W_{i,t+h}^s, \quad s = 1, \dots, S, \tag{6.9}$$

where the simulated values for each issuer $W_{i,t+h}^s$, $\forall i$, are drawn independently. Let us now describe the drawing of the issuer-specific value at horizon 2. At date t, after a transition from state l_t, the issuer i stays in state $Z_t = k_t$ for time H_t.

First step: Drawing of the future state Z_{t+1}
The future state Z_{t+1}^s is drawn in the conditional distribution of Z_{t+1} given $Z_t = k_t$ by using the estimated transition matrix.

Second step: Simulation of survival at date $t+1$
Two cases have to be distinguished depending on whether $Z_{t+1}^s = Z_t$.
If $Z_{t+1}^s = Z_t = k_t$, there is default at $t+1$ with probability $1 - S_{k_t,l_t}(H_t + 1)/S_{k_t,l_t}(H_t)$ and no default otherwise.
If $Z_{t+1}^s = k_{t+1} \neq k_t$, there is default at $t+1$ with probability $1 - S_{k_{t+1},k_t}(1)$ and no default otherwise.
These distributions are used to simulate the potential default at date $t+1$.

Third step: Drawing of the future state Z_{t+2}
This step is reached, provided that the contract is not terminated. The state is drawn in the conditional distribution of Z_{t+2} given $Z_{t+1}^s = k_{t+1}$, where k_{t+1} is the state drawn in step 1.

Fourth step: Simulation of time to default at $t+2$
Three cases have to be distinguished. They are described below along with the associated conditional probabilities of default.
case 1: $Z_{t+2}^s = Z_{t+1}^s = Z_t = k_t$
probability of default: $1 - S_{k_t,l_t}(H_t + 2)/S_{k_t,l_t}(H_t + 1)$;
case 2: $Z_{t+2}^s = Z_{t+1}^s = k_{t+1} \neq Z_t = k_t$
probability of default: $1 - S_{k_{t+1},k_t}(2)/S_{k_{t+1},k_t}(1)$;
case 3: $Z_{t+2}^s = k_{t+2} \neq Z_{t+1}^s = k_{t+1}$
probability of default: $1 - S_{k_{t+2},k_{t+1}}(1)$.
The simulated time to default is denoted by Y^s.

Fifth step: The simulated issuer-specific portfolio value is computed from

$$W^s_{i,t+2} = F_{i,t+1}[B(t,t+1,t+2)]^{-1} 1_{Y^s_i>t+1} + F_{i,t+2} 1_{Y^s_i>t+2} + 1_{Y^s_i>t+2} P_{i,t+2}(\underline{Z}^s_{i,t+2}),$$

where $\underline{Z}^s_{i,t+2} = (Z^s_{i,t+2}, Z^s_{i,t+1}, \underline{Z}_{i,t})$ and $1_{Y^s_i>t+1} = 1$ if $Y^s_i > t+1$, 0 otherwise, denotes the indicator function.

This approach assumes that the future term structure of interest on the risk-free asset is known and so is the price $P_{i,t}(\underline{Z}_{i,t})$ for a given price history. Let us focus on the risk of default and disregard the risk on the T-bond interest rate. The prices $P_{i,t}(\underline{Z}_{i,t})$ [or $P_{i,t+2}(\underline{Z}^s_{i,t+2})$] are functions of default probabilities. These probabilities are unknown and can be approximated by simulations that take into account the future credit rating migration.[25] Let us replace the prices in the last expression by their approximations $\hat{P}$, say. The change in portfolio value becomes

$$\begin{aligned}\Delta W^s_{t+2} = \sum_{i=1}^{n} \{ & F_{i,t+1}[B(t+1,t+2)]^{-1} 1_{Y^s_i>t+2} \\ & + 1_{Y^s_i>t+2} \hat{P}_{i,t+2}(\underline{Z}^s_{i,t+2}) - \hat{P}_{i,t}(\underline{Z}_{i,t}) \} \; s = 1, \ldots, S. \end{aligned} \tag{6.10}$$

The VaR is the empirical α-quantile of the distribution of ΔW^s_{t+2}, $s = 1, \ldots, S$.

The estimated diagonal elements of transition matrices are generally close to 90% (see Table 10.5). The CreditMetrics, among others, suggested to eliminate the Monte Carlo computation of prices $P_{i,t}(\underline{Z}_{i,t})$ [resp. $P_{i,t+2}(Z^s_{i,t+2})$] by assuming that after t [resp. after $t+2$], no migration between credit rating categories will take place. This rough approximation simplifies the determination of the VaR but can induce a significant bias. To see that, consider the most risky category CCC. The computation of the bond price, as if the CCC issuer were to stay in the same rating category CCC, disregards the high probability of default and the possibility of a zero future price of its bond.

6.4.3. The Cohort Approach

Let us now consider the retail loans and introduce a dynamic model for data on default rates aggregated by cohorts, which is easy to estimate and simulate. This model includes some autoregressive effects of lagged default and macroeconomic factors and accounts for unobserved time heterogeneity. Because of the autoregressive component, the specification for the first semester of a loan agreement of any term is different from the specification for the next semester and the following ones. In the first semester of the loan, there is no information on past default history of the cohort. The initial credit

[25] It is natural to approximate these prices by simulations because they can be viewed as prices of American options.

quality of that cohort can be approximated by using the basic credit score of the credit granting institution. Let $S_{k,\tau}$ and $\sigma^2_{S,k,\tau}$ denote the average initial score and its dispersion in cohort k, τ. In semester $h = 1$, we use the following logistic model:

$$l[D_k(\tau; 1)] = a_1 + b_1 l(S_{k,\tau}) + c_1 \sigma^2_{S,k,\tau} + d_1' X_{\tau+1} + \alpha_1 l[D_k(\tau - 1; 1)] + \varepsilon_k(\tau; 1), \qquad (6.11)$$

where the components of X are macroeconomic variables, $\varepsilon_k(\tau; 1)$ is an error term, and $l(x) = \log[x/(1-x)]$ denotes the logit transformation. For the following semesters of the loan, we introduce an additional autoregressive effect of the same cohort (τ, k) and a lagged effect of the previous cohort $(\tau - 1, k)$:

$$\begin{aligned} l[D_k(\tau; h)] &= a_h + b_h l(S_{k,\tau}) + c_h \sigma^2_{S,k,\tau} + d_h' X_{\tau+h} + \alpha_h l[D_k(\tau - 1; h)] \\ &\quad + \beta_h l[D_k(\tau, h-1)] + \varepsilon_k(\tau, h), h \geq 2. \end{aligned} \qquad (6.12)$$

The joint model [(6.11) and (6.12)] is a spatial regression model. It is completed by specifying the distribution of error term $\varepsilon_k(\tau, h)$, for any k, τ, h. Let us assume the independence between cohorts and allow for correlation between semesters. More precisely, we assume

$[\varepsilon_k(\tau, h), h = 1, \ldots, H], \tau, k$ varying, are independent, normally distributed, with mean zero and variance–covariance matrix Σ.

Parameters $a_h, b_h, \ldots, \beta_h, h = 1, \ldots, H$ and Σ can be estimated by the ordinary least squares. Even though the number of parameters is large, in each semester h, the number of available observations is too large and equal to the number of cohorts times the number of loans with different terms.

The estimated models can be used for prediction making. In particular, the following columns of Table 10.3 can be found by simulations. For example, for the future date 00.1 (first calendar semester of year 2000), error $\epsilon^s(00.1; 1)$ is drawn and the simulated default rate $D^s(00.1; 1)$ is determined by model (6.11) from $D(99.2; 1)$ and the simulated error. For the second row of that column, we simulate error $\epsilon^s(99.2; 2)$ and use $D^s(99.2; 2)$ determined by model (6.12), $D(99.2; 1)$, $D(99.1; 1)$ and $\epsilon^s(99.2; 2)$, and so forth. Note the difficulty in predicting the future values of macroeconomic variables X. A solution consists in considering several scenarios of their future evolution to assess the default rate.

6.4.4. Default Correlation

The procedures outlined in the previous sections assumed the independence of risks of various borrowers and disregarded the possibility of simultaneous bankruptcies. Under the migration approach, simultaneous bankruptcies can be examined by considering more complicated transition matrices that represent, e.g., the probabilities of joint migration of two issuers, rated BB and A, say. Simultaneous bankruptcies can be incorporated into the cohort-based approach by introducing the correlation between error terms of two different cohorts or credit ratings. These extensions to the model are difficult to implement, as they involve complicated multivariate distributions. The challenge consists of finding a constrained multivariate distribution that would provide good fit to the data and be relatively easy for prediction making. Recently, various factor models have been introduced in the literature to capture systemic risks, such as the so-called stochastic migration models [see, e.g., Feng et al. (2008); Gourieroux and Gagliardini (2002); Schonbucher (2000)].

7. FUTURE DIRECTIONS FOR RESEARCH AND DEVELOPMENT

In the previous sections, we described various methods that exist in the academic and professional literatures for determining the VaR. They can be applied to portfolios of liquid financial assets, portfolios of derivatives, and can take into account the risk of default. However, the work in this field is far from completion. The aim of this chapter is to provide some insights on various promising directions for future research.

7.1. Coherent Risk Measures

The VaR defined as a conditional quantile differs from risk measures used in the insurance sector. The reason is that the VaR disregards the size of a loss. To improve the risk measurement in this respect, Artzner et al. (1997) proposed a method of computing the required capital in a two-period framework. They introduced four axioms given below.

Let $R_t(W)$ denote the required capital for the future portfolio of value W. The axioms concern the properties of monotonicity, invariance with respect to drift, homogeneity, and subadditivity.

(i) Monotonicity

If W^* is prefered to W^* in terms of stochastic dominance at order 1 (that is if the c.d.f. of W^* is larger than the c.d.f. of W), then

$$R_t(W) \geq R_t(W^*).$$

(ii) Invariance with respect to drift

$$R_t(W + c) = R_t(W) - c,$$

for any W and any deterministic amount c.

(iii) Homogeneity

$$R_t(\lambda W) = \lambda R_t(W), \quad \forall \lambda \geq 0, \forall W.$$

(iv) Subadditivity

$$R_t(W + W^*) \leq R_t(W) + R_t(W^*), \quad \forall W, W^*.$$

The homogeneity and subadditivity properties imply the convexity of function R_t. It is easy to check that the conditional quantile does not satisfy the convexity condition. Artzner et al. (1997) described all functions R_t that satisy the four axioms and called them coherent risk measures. They also provided their interpretations in terms of expected utility. In particular, they showed that the expected shortfall or Tail VaR,

$$\text{TVaR}(a, \alpha) = E_t[W_{t+1}(a) | W_{t+1}(a) - W_t(a) + \text{VaR}_t(a, \alpha) < 0], \tag{7.1}$$

is a coherent risk measure. TVaR measures the expected value of a portfolio conditional on loss probability α. It can be considered as the (historical) price of a reinsurance contract and the required capital can be viewed as a self-reinsurance.

The axiomatic approach is useful for risk measurement as it emphasizes the importance of the size of a loss, in addition to the occurrence. However, it can be criticized for the following reasons.

(i) Even if the (conditional) quantile function does not satisfy the convexity property for any portfolio value, in practice, the convexity holds for the conditional distribution of returns and portfolio allocations [see, e.g., Gourieroux et al. (2000)].

(ii) The homogeneity and subadditivity axioms are clearly not satisfied in practice. The price per share depends on the traded quantity of shares. For example, when the shares are sold, their individual prices decrease with the quantity. This stylized fact is not compatible with axioms (iii) and (iv), which assume that risk can be diminished by increasing the size of a portfolio.

If the VaR was replaced by a coherent risk measure by the regulators, banks would be motivated to merge to diminish the amount of required capital [axioms (iii) and (iv)]. Clearly, such an incentive to merge may create noncompetitive effects and increase the risk.

Another axiomatic approach was introduced by Wang and Young (1998) for derivative assets. Wang considered a distortion risk measure, which is a weighted average of the VaR,

$$\text{DRM} = \int_0^1 \text{VaR}(u) \mathrm{d}H(u),$$

where the distortion probability measure is such that c.d.f. H is increasing and convex. It includes as a special case the Tail VaR, which corresponds to a distortion measure that is uniformly distributed on $[0, \alpha]$.

It is insightful to examine the conditions that a risk measure should satisfy. For example, any risk measure should help reduce the risk. This condition is not satisfied by the VaR defined as a conditional quantile. A portfolio manager has an incentive to change the standard mean–variance strategy and select a portfolio allocation that minimizes the VaR under the constraint on the expected value of the portfolio [see, e.g., Foellmer and Leukert (1998); Gourieroux et al. (2000)]. If that portfolio contains derivatives, such a strategy implies much riskier positions in derivatives than the standard mean–variance strategy. This is because to diminish the loss probability, which is the only constraint, the portfolio manager increases the size of a loss. Such a strategy is prevented under the variance-based measures of risk. In general, such risky strategies can be eliminated by imposing multiple constraints, such as joint constraints on the VaR and the Tail VaR. However, the definition of the required capital as a function of the VaR and Tail VaR does not exist in the literature.

7.2. Infrequent Extreme Risks and Utility Functions

To define coherent risk measures, it is necessary to specify the risks to be covered and describe the aversions of investors to these risks. Intuitively, we wish to study extreme risks that induce large losses, but are infrequent. Gourieroux and Monfort (1998) proposed the following model of infrequent risks. A sample of excess returns Y features infrequent extreme risks if the distribution of Y is a mixture of Gaussian distributions:

$$Y \sim \alpha N\left[m, \frac{1}{\alpha}\Omega_1\right] + (1-\alpha) N\left[m, \frac{1}{1-\alpha}\Omega_2\right].$$

The mean and variance of Y are $EY = m$ and $VY = \Omega_1 + \Omega_2$, respectively. When α tends to zero, the effect of the first distribution in the mixture diminishes while the variance–covariance matrix $\frac{1}{\alpha}\Omega_1$ tends to infinity, creating extreme risk. The commonly used utility functions such as the exponential [Constant Absolute Risk Aversion (CARA)] utility function can not be used in the presence of infrequent extreme risks because investors who maximize an expected CARA utility function, e.g., have zero demand for risky assets. As a consequence, these assets are not traded at the equilibrium.

Gourieroux and Monfort (2000) characterized the class of utility functions for which the demand for risky assets is different from zero. These utility functions may be written as

$$U(w) = -\int (w-x)^{-} \mathrm{d}G(x) + cw, \tag{7.2}$$

where G is a c.d.f. and c a nonnegative scalar. They are called Left Integrable (absolute) Risk Aversion (LIRA).

The associated expected utility has a simple expression. Indeed, we get for $c = 0$,

$$E_w U(w) = -E_w E_x (w - x)^-,$$

where E_w and E_x denote the expectations with respect to the distribution of the portfolio value and to distribution G, respectively. By commuting the expectations, we get

$$E_w U(w) = -E_x E_w (w - x)^- = -E_x P[x], \tag{7.3}$$

where $P[x]$ is the price of a European put written on W with strike X (computed under the historical probability). The expected utility is equal to the average price of puts, (the strike average) with the minus sign. This is an interesting interpretation of expected utility since it links the extreme risk to the price of puts with some specific strikes.

7.3. The Dynamics of Infrequent Extreme Risks

Infrequent extreme risks can be analyzed in a dynamic framework. Loosely speaking, extreme risks arise from infrequent jumps in the return trajectory of a single asset that are caused by large negative returns (or large positive returns if the quantity of assets in the portfolio is negative). The following questions concerning the dynamic models of returns were addressed in the literature.

(i) How to construct a dynamic model of returns with infrequent extreme risks, which is compatible with the stylized facts, such as extreme risks clustering and differences between standard and extreme risks dynamics?

Gourieroux and Jasiak (2001a,c) assumed that the conditional distribution of returns are in the family of Levy distributions that involve four parameters of location, scale, skewness, and tail. These four parameters were modeled as dynamic stochastic factors. Distinct dynamics of standard and extreme risks were generated by specifying different serial dependence of the scale and tail parameters. The clustering of extreme risks was observed when the stochastic tail parameter followed a unit root process.

(ii) Another important question concerns the misspecification (also called model risk in the VaR literature). What are the consequences of omitting infrequent extreme risks in the model? It has been shown that such a misspecification induces spurious long memory effects [see, e.g., Diebold and Inoue (2001); Gourieroux and Jasiak (2001b); Gourieroux and Robert (2006); Lobato and Savin (1997)]. In some sense, it is good news that the omission of extreme risks induces serial smoothing of the VaR, which was proposed by the regulators and implemented in the definition of the required capital.

7.4. Large Portfolio

Risks on large portfolios of assets are difficult to examine. To see that, consider the standard mean–variance approach and assume that the conditional distribution of returns is multivariate normal $Y \sim N[m, \Sigma]$. The allocation of a mean–variance efficient portfolio is proportional to $a = \Sigma^{-1}(m - r_f e)$, where r_f is the risk-free rate and $e = (1, \ldots, 1)'$ [see, e.g., Gourieroux and Jasiak (2001a), Section 3.4]. The joint dependence between the n assets is summarized by volatility matrix Σ and its spectral decomposition. Let us consider the eigenvalues of Σ ranked in a descending order $\lambda_1 > \ldots > \lambda_n$ and the corresponding eigenvectors $a_1, \ldots, a_n$, say. a_1 [resp. a_n] represents the portfolio allocation with the largest [resp. smallest] return volatility. Moreover, if $m = 0$ (the efficient market hypothesis), we see from Eq. (2.7) that a_1 [resp. a_n] maximizes [resp. minimizes] the gaussian VaR; this result is valid for any risk level α.

When n is large, the smallest eigenvalue λ_n is close to zero. This gives a spurious impression of perfect arbitrage opportunity. Moreover, the estimates of Σ^{-1} and of the optimal allocation are not accurate. A number of methods in the mean–variance framework were proposed to improve the robustness of these estimators.

Analogous methods for improving the robustness of estimators in the presence of fat tails of conditional return distributions have not yet been developed. Below are some questions that concern the modeling of fat-tailed distributions and need to be answered:

(i) How to model the tails that depend on portfolio allocations, that is, are Gaussian for some allocations and Pareto for other?

(ii) Are the VaR minimizing (resp. maximizing) allocations independent of risk level α? Otherwise, what is the α dependence?

(iii) In the mean–variance framework, can the structure of dependence be simplified by imposing, for instance, an equicorrelation constraint? How to define the notion of equidependence in a nongaussian framework?

This question has recently been addressed in a number of scientific articles that distinguish the systemic risk, which creates joint dependence from the residual effects of the asset specific risks. It is related to the theory of granularity introduced by Gordy (2004) [see also Gordy et al. (2007)].

7.5. Extreme Value Theory

The analysis of stochastic properties of extremes is an important field of the probabilistic and statistical literatures [see, e.g., Embrecht et al. (1998) for a survey oriented toward applications to insurance and finance]. The extreme value theory (EVT) was initially concentrated on applications other than Finance. Recently, EVT has been used to study extreme risks on large portfolios of individual contracts and to predict the occurrence and size of extreme losses.

The results that exist in the EVT literature concern the following issues in the univariate framework:

(i) the definition end estimation of tail magnitude;
(ii) the asymptotic behavior of the sample mean $\frac{1}{T}\sum_{t=1}^{T} y_t$, with respect to the law of large numbers and large deviations;
(iii) the asymptotic behavior of sample maximum: $M_T = \max_{t\in\{1,\dots,T\}} y_t$;
(iv) the distributional properties of the count process of dates when process (y_t) exceeds a given threshold y_T, function of T.

The EVT concerns mainly i.i.d. observations or processes with simple forms of temporal dependence. Only a limited number of results are available for complicated nonlinear dynamic processes encountered in Finance [see, e.g., Hsing (1991); Resnick and Starica (1995) for estimation of a tail index, Robert (2000) for determination of the tail parameter in an α-ARCH model or Gourieroux and Robert (2006) for complete analysis of stochastic unit root models].

Let us briefly comment on how the results from research on (i)–(iv) can be applied to Finance and used for computing the VaR.

(i) Magnitude of tail

EVT provides a classification of tails, which was exploited in Section 2.2.2. Moreover, the EVT literature offers various estimators of the tail index and their asymptotic properties. A tail index estimator, called the Hill estimator, appeared in the model building approach is discussed in Section 3.3.

The accuracy of the Hill estimator and its extensions is rather poor, as it is difficult to estimate the probability of infrequent events. Another problem is that the Hill-type estimators depend on the number of observations in a very erratic way. Their properties have been established in the i.i.d. framework (i.e., without serial dependence that characterizes Financial data) and under the assumption that risk level α tends to zero when the number of observations tends to infinity (while α is small, but fixed, according to the regulators).

(ii) Asymptotic behavior of the sample mean

The results on sample mean $\frac{1}{h}(y_t + y_{t+1} + \cdots + y_{t+h})$ can be used to study the dependence of the term structure of the VaR on serial dependence and the tails of the conditional distribution. An illustration is given in Section 2.2.3 for a simple case of i.i.d. α-stable distributed returns to show that the term structure depends on $h^{1/a}$, where a is the stability coefficient.

(iii) Asymptotic behavior of the maximum

These results seem not very useful for the determination of the VaR as the maximum operator is not involved in the computation of the portfolio value (except for derivatives written on the maximum of returns over a contractual period). These theoretical results are rather applicable to insurance against catastrophic events. As such they can be interesting for defining the required capital for operational risk due to events such as fire or earth quakes that could bring the trading markets to a halt.

(iv) The count process of large events

This stream of research is applicable to Finance, as it can explain how the distribution of a count process of large events depends on the nonlinear serial dependence of returns and the tail of their conditional distribution [see, e.g., Gourieroux and Robert (2001) for a detailed illustration of this relation]. The count process of exceedances can be used for (a) predicting the date (and size) of future losses, and (b) the internal VaR monitoring by the banks.

Recent literature points out that the count of exceedances may be misleading as an instrument of VaR control. Alternative methods were proposed by Giacomini and White (2005) and Gourieroux and Jasiak (2009). These authors explain how a coherent supervision criterion has to be used for fixing the optimal level of capital reserve and controlling the quality of the method ex-post.

8. CONCLUDING REMARKS

The review of literature on the VaR given in this chapter emphasizes the variety of risks on financial assets that need to be measured and controlled. Among risky assets are the assets and derivatives traded on organized financial markets and OTC. There exist several methods for computing the VaR for portfolios of those assets. Their common feature is that they rely on some internal models of asset return dynamics, derivative pricing, and default probabilities.

The Basle Committee has acknowledged that the internal models require strict monitoring. In this respect, it has explored two types of regulation, that are common standards for the internal models used by banks and mandatory VaR sensitivity analysis with respect to various departures from the assumptions of the internal models.

ACKNOWLEDGMENTS

The authors gratefully acknowledge financial support of the Natural Sciences and Engineering Council of Canada (NSERC) and Chair AXA.

REFERENCES

Ait-Sahalia, Y., and A.W., Lo: "Nonparametric Risk Management and Implied Risk Aversion," Journal of Econometrics, 94, 9–51.

Artzner, P., and F., Delbaen (1992): "Credit Risk and Repayment Option," ASTIN Bulletin, 22, 81–96.

Artzner, P., F., Delbaen, J., Eber, and D., Heath (1997): "Thinking Coherently," Risk, 10, 68–71.

Arzac, E., and V., Bawa (1977): "Portfolio Choice and Equilibrium in Capital Markets with Safety First Investors," Journal of Financial Economics, 4, 277–288.

Barone-Adesi, G., and K., Giannopoulos (1996): "A Simplified Approach to the Conditional Estimation of VaR," Futures and Options World, 68–72.

Barone-Adesi, G., and K., Giannopoulos (1999a): "The Case for Nonparametric Market Risk Measures," Risk Professional, 1, 18–20.

Barone-Adesi, G., K., Giannopoulos, and L., Vosper (1999b): "VaR without Correlations for Nonlinear Portfolios," Journal of Futures Markets, 19, 583–602.

Basle Committee on Banking Supervision (1995): "An Internal Model-Based Approach to Market Risk Capital Requirements," Basle, Switzerland.

Basle Committee on Banking Supervision (1996a): "Supervisory Framework for the Use of Backtesting in Conjunction with the Internal Approach to Market Risk Capital Requirement," Basle, Switzerland.

Basle Committee on Banking Supervision (1996b): "Overview of the Amendment to the Capital Accord to Incorporate Market Risk," Basle, Switzerland.

Basle Committee on Banking Supervision (1996c): "Amendment to the Capital Accord to Incorporate Market Risk," Basle, Switzerland.

Basle Committee on Bankin'g Supervision (2000): "Principles for the Management of Credit Risk," Basle, Switzerland.

Basset, G., and R., Koenker (1978): "Regression Quantiles," Econometrica, 46, 33–50.

Bassi, F., P., Embrechts, and M., Kafetzaki (1997): "Risk Management and Quantile Estimation," In: Adler, R., R., Feldman, and M., Taqqu (eds.), Practical Guide to Heavy Tails, Birkhauser, Boston.

Beder, T. (1995): "VaR : Seductive, but Dangerous," Financial Analyst Journal, 12–21.

Bielecki, T., and M., Rutkowski (2000): "Credit Risk: Modelling, Valuation and Hedging," Springer-Verlag, New York (Inpress).

Billio, M., and L., Pelizzon (2000): "Value-at-Risk: A Multivariate Switching Regime Approach," Journal of Empirical Finance, 7, 531–554.

Black, F., and M., Scholes (1973): "The Pricing of Options and Corporate Liabilities," Journal of Political Economy, 81, 637–659.

Boos, D. (1984): "Using Extreme Value Theory to Estimate Large Percentiles," Technometrics, 26, 33–39.

Chernozhukov, V., and L., Umantsev (2001): "Conditional Value-at-Risk: Aspects of Modeling and Estimation," Empirical Economics, 26, 271–292.

Coles, S. (2001): "An Introduction to Statistical Modelling of Extreme Value," Springer Series in Statistics, Springer-Verlag, London.

Crosbie, P. (1998): "Modeling Default Risk," Document 999.0000.031, KMV Corporation.

Crouhy, M., D., Galai, and R., Mark (2000): "A Comparative Analysis of Current Credit Risk Models," Journal of Banking and Finance, 24, 59–117.

Danielsson, J., and C., de Vries (1997): "Tail Index and Quantile Estimation with Very High Frequency Data," Journal of Empirical Finance, **4**, 241–257.

Danielsson, J., and C., de Vries (1998): "Beyond the Sample: Extreme Quantile and Probability Estimation," London School of Economics, Discussion Paper 298.

Davidson, A., and R., Smith (1990): "Model for Exceedances over High Threshold," Journal of the Royal Statistical Society, 52, 393–442.

Dekkers, A., J., Einmahl, and L., De Haan (1989): "A Moment Estimator for the Index of an Extreme Value Distribution," Annals of Statistics, 17, 1833–1855.
De Haan, L., D., Janses, K., Koedjik, and C., de Vries (1994): "Safety First Portfolio Selection, Extreme Value Theory and Long Run Asset Risk," In: Extreme Value Theory and Applications, Galambos (ed.) Kluwer, 471–487.
Diebold, F., and A., Inoue (2001): "Long Memory and Regime Switching," Journal of Econometrics, 105, 131–160.
Dowd, K. (1998): "Beyond Value at Risk. The New Science of Risk Management," Wiley and Sons, London.
Duffie, D., and R., Kan (1996): "A Yield Factor Model of Interest Rates," Mathematical Finance, 6, 379–406.
Duffie, D., and J., Pan (1997): "An Overview of Value-at-Risk," Journal of Derivatives, 4, 7–49.
El Jahel, L., W., Perraudin, and P., Sellin (1998): "Value-at-Risk for Derivatives," Journal of Derivatives, 7–26.
Embrechts, P., G., Kluppelberg, and T., Mikosch (1997): "Modelling Extremal Events," Springer, Applications of Mathematics.
Embrechts, P., A., Mc Neil, D., Straumann, and R., Kaufmann (1999): "Modeling Extremal Events for Insurance and Finance," 15th International Summer School of the Swiss Association of Actuaries.
Embrechts, P., S., Resnick, and G., Samorodnitsky (1998): "Living on the Edge," Risk, 11, 96–100.
Engle, R. (1982): "Autoregressive Conditional Heteroskedasticity with Estimates of the Variance of U.K. Inflation," Econometrica, 50, 987–1008.
Engle, R., and S., Manganelli (2004): "CaViaR: Conditional Autoregressive Value-at-Risk by Regression Quantiles," Journal of Business and Economic Statistics, 2(4).
Estrella, A. (1996): "Taylor, Black and Scholes: Series Approximations and Risk Management Pitfalls," In: Risk Measurement and Systematic Risk, Proceedings of the Joint Central Bank Research Conference, Board of Governors of the Federal Reserve System (ed.), Washington D.C. 359–379.
Falk, M. (1985): "Asymptotic Normality of the Kernel Quantile Estimator," The Annals of Statistics, 13, 428–433.
Feng, D., C., Gourieroux, and J. Jasiak (2008): "The Ordered Qualitative Model for Credit Rating Transitions," Journal of Empirical Finance, 15, 111–130.
Finger, C. (1997): "When is a Portfolio of Options Normally Distributed," Quarterly Risk-Metrics Monitor, Third Quarter, 33–41.
Foellmer, H., and P., Leukert (1999): "Quantile Hedging," Finance and Stochastics, 3, 251–273.
Fons, J. (1994): "Using Default Rates to Model the Term Structure of Credit Risk," Financial Analyst Journal, 25–32.
Gagliardini, P., and C., Gourieroux (2005): "Migration Correlation: Definition and Consistent Estimation," Journal of Banking and Finance, 29, 865–891.
Gagliardini, P., and C., Gourieroux (2005): "Stochastic Migration Models with Applications to Corporate Risk," Journal of Financial Econometrics, 3, 188–226.
Garman, M. (1996): "Improving on VaR," Risk, 9, 61–63.
Garman, M. (1997): "Taking VaR to Pieces," Risk, 10, 70–71.
Genest, C., and L., Rivest (1993): "Statistical Inference Procedures for Bivariate Archimedean Copulas," Journal of the American Statistical Association, 88, 1034–1043.

Giacomini, P., and H., White (2005): "Test of Conditional Predictive Ability," Econometrica, 74, 1545–1578.
Gizycki, M., and N., Hereford (1998): "Assessing the Dispersion in Banks Estimates of Market Risk: The Results of a Value-at-Risk Survey," Discussion Paper, October, Australian Prudential Regulation Authority.
Golub, B., and L., Tilman (1997): "Measuring Yield Curve Risk Using Principal Component Analysis, Value at Risk and Key Durations," The Journal of Portfolio Management, 23, 72–84.
Gordy, M. (2004): "Granularity Adjustment in Portfolio Risk Management," In: Risk Measures for the 21st Century, Szego, G. (ed.), Wiley.
Gordy, M., and E., Luthebohmert (2007): "Granularity Adjustment for Basel II," Deutsche Bank, Discussion Paper 01/2007.
Gourieroux, C., and J., Jasiak (1999b): "Nonlinear Impulse Response Function," Annales d'Economie et de Statistique, 78, 1–33.
Gourieroux, C., and J., Jasiak (2000): "Local Likelihood Density Estimation and Value at Risk," CREST DP.
Gourieroux, C., and J., Jasiak (2001a): "Econometrics of Finance," Princeton University Press, Princeton.
Gourieroux, C., and J., Jasiak (2001b): "Memory and Infrequent Breaks," Economics Letters, 70, 29–41.
Gourieroux, C., and J., Jasiak (2001c): "Dynamic Factor Models," Econometric Reviews, 20(4), 385–424.
Gourieroux, C., and J., Jasiak (2008): "Dynamic Quantile Models," Journal of Econometrics, 147, 198–205.
Gourieroux, C., and W., Liu (2009): "Control and Out-of-Sample Validation of Dependent Risk," Journal of Risk and Insurance (Inpress).
Gourieroux, C., J.P., Laurent, and O., Scaillet (2000): "Sensitivity Analysis of Values at Risk," Journal of Empirical Finance, 7, 225–247.
Gourieroux, C., and A., Monfort (1998): "Statistics and Econometric Models," Vol I, Cambridge University Press.
Gourieroux, C., and A., Monfort (2004): "Infrequent Extreme Risks," Geneva Papers on the Risk and Insurance Theory, 29, 5–12.
Gourieroux, C., and C., Robert (2006): "Stochastic Unit Root Models," Econometric Theory, 22, 1052–1090.
Group of Thirty (1993): "Derivatives: Practices and Principles," Global Derivatives Study Group, G30, Report, July.
Hamilton, J. (1989): "A New Approach to the Economic Analysis of Nonstationary Time Series and the Business Cycle," Econometrica, 57, 357–384.
Hill, D. (1975): "A Simple Approach to Inference About the Tail of a Distribution," The Annals of Statistics, 13, 331–341.
Horowitz, J. (1992): "A Smoothed Maximum Score Estimator for the Binary Response Model," Econometrica, 60, 505–531.
Hsing, T. (1991): "On Tail Index Estimation Using Dependent Data," Annals of Statistics, 19, 1547–1569.
Huisman, R., (1997): "VaR+: Fat Tails in Financial Risk Managament," Journal of Risk, 1, 47–61.

Hull, J., and A., White (1987): "The Pricing of Options on Assets with Stochastic Volatilities," Journal of Finance, 42, 281–300.
Hull, J., and A., White (1992): "The Price of Default," Risk, 5, 101–103.
Hull, J., and A., White (1998a): "Incorporating Volatility Updating into the Historical Simulation Method for Calculating Value at Risk," Journal of Risk, 1.
Hull, J., and A., White (1998b): "Value at Risk when Daily Changes in Market Variables are not Normally Distributed," Journal of Derivatives, 5, 9–19.
Hull, J., and A., White (2001): "Valuing Credit Default Swaps II : Modelling Default Correlations," Journal of Derivatives, 8, 12–23.
Jackson, P., D., Mande, and W., Perraudin (1997): "Bank Capital and Value at Risk," Journal of Derivatives, 73–89.
Jamshidian, F., and Y., Zhu (1997): "Scenario Simulations: Theory and Methodology," Finance and Stochastics, 1, 43–67.
Janosi, T., R., Jarrow, and Y., Yildirim (2003): "Estimating Default Probabilities in Equity Prices," Journal of Investment Management, 1, First Quarter.
Jansen, D., K., Koedijk, and C., de Vries (2000): "Portfolio Selection with Limited Downside Risk," Journal of Empirical Finance, 7, 247–269.
Jarrow, R. (2001): "Default Parameter Estimation Using Market Prices," Fiancial Analyst Journal, 57, 75–92
Jarrow, R., D., Lando, and S., Turnbull (1997): "A Markov Model for the Term Structure of Credit Risk Spreads," Review of Financial Studies, 10, 481–523.
Jarrow, R., D., Lando, and F., Yu (2005): "Default Risk and Diversification: Theory and Applications," Mathematical Finance, 15, 1–26.
Jarrow, R., and S., Turnbull (2000): "The Intersection of Market and Credit Risk," Journal of Banking and Finance, 24, 271–299.
Joe, H. (1997): "Multivariate Models and Dependence Concepts," Chapman and Hall.
Jorion, P. (1997): "Value-at-Risk: The New Benchmark for Controlling Market Risk," McGraw-Hill, Chicago.
Kliger, D., and O., Sarig, (2000): "The Information Value of Bond Ratings," Journal of Finance, 55, 2879–2902.
Kotz, S., and S., Nadarajah (2000): "Extreme Value Distributions," Imperial College Press, London.
Lando, D. (1997): "Modelling Bonds and Derivatives with Default Risk," In: Dempster, M., and S., Pliska (ed.), Mathematics of Derivative Securities, Cambridge University Press, 369–393.
Lando, D. (1998): "On Cox Processes and Credit Risky Securities," Review of Derivatives Research, 2, 99–120.
Lando, D. (2000): "Some Elements of Rating Based Credit Risk Modeling" In: Jegadeesh, N., and B., Tuckman (ed.), Advanced Fixed Income Valuation Tools, Wiley, 193–215.
Lando, D., and T., Skoderberg (2002): "Analysing Rating Transition and Rating Drift with Continuous Observations," The Journal of Banking and Finance, 26, 423–444.
Levy, H., and M., Sarnat (1972): "Safety First. An Expected Utility Principle," Journal of Financial and Quantitative Analysis, 7, 1829–1834.
Lobato, I., and N., Savin (1997): "Real and Spurious Long Memory Properties of Stock Market Data," Journal of Business and Economic Statistics, 16, 261–283.

Longerstay, J. (1996): "An Improved Methodology for Measuring VaR," RiskMetrics Monitor, Second Quarter, J.P. Morgan.

Longin, F. (2000): "From Value at Risk to Stress Testing: The Extreme Value Approach," Journal of Banking and Finance, 7, 1097–1130.

Longin, F. (2001): "Beyond the VaR," Journal of Derivatives, 8, 36–48.

Longstaff, F., and E., Schwartz (1995): "A Simple Approach to the Valuing Risky Fixed and Floating Rate Debt," Journal of Finance, 50, 789–819.

Malz, A. (2000): "Vega Risk and the Smile," Working Paper, The RiskMetrics Group.

Mandelbrot, B. (1963): "The Variation of Certain Speculative Prices," Journal of Business, 36, 394–419.

Marshall, C., and M., Siegel (1997): "Value at Risk: Implementing a Risk Measurement Standard," The Journal of Derivatives, 4, 91–110.

Merton, R. (1974): "On the Pricing of Corporate Debt: The Risk Structure of Interest Rates," The Journal of Finance, 29, 449–470.

Mina, J., and A., Ulmer (1999): "Delta-Gamma Four Ways," Working Paper, the RiskMetrics Group.

Minnich, M. (1998): "A Primer on Value at Risk," In: Fabozzi, F. J. (ed.), Perspectives on Interest Rate Risk Management for Money Managers and Traders, chapter 3, 39–50.

Moody's Investors Service (1997): "Moody's Rating Migration and Credit Quality Correlation, 1920 -1996," July.

Morgan Guaranty Trust Company (1996): "RiskMetrics Technical Document," 4th ed.

Nielsen, L., J., Saa-Requejo, and P., Santa-Clara (1993): "Default Risk and Interest Rate Risk: The Term Structure of Default Spreads," INSEAD.

Oda, N., and J., Muranoga (1997): "A New Framework for Measuring the Credit Risk of a Portfolio - Ex-VaR Model," Discussion Paper, Institute of Monetary and Economic Studies, Bank of Japan, 97, 1–45.

Phelan, M. (1995): "Probability and Statistics Applied to the Practice of Financial Risk Management: The Case of J.P. Morgan's RiskMetrics," Working Paper, Wharton School of Management.

Pickands, J. (1975): "Statistical Inference Using Order Statistics," Annals of Statistics, 3, 119–131.

Pritsker, M. (1997): "Evaluating Value at Risk Methodologies: Accuracy versus Computational Time," Journal of Financial Services Research, 201–241.

Resnick, S. (1987): "Extreme Values, Regular Variation and Point Processes," Springer, New-York.

Resnick, S., and C., Starica (1995): "Consistency of Hill's Estimator for Dependent Data," Journal of Applied Probability, 32, 139–167.

Ridder, T. (1997): "Basics of Statistical VaR- Estimation," SGZ-Bank, Frankfurt, Karlsruhe.

Robert, C. (2000): "Extremes of α-ARCH Models," In: Franke, Hardle, and Stahl (ed.), Measuring Risk in Complex Stochastic Systems, vol 147, Lecture Notes in Statistics, Springer.

Schachter, B., and J., Butler (1998): "Estimating Value at Risk with a Precision Measured by Combining Kernel Estimation with Historical Simulation," Review of Derivatives Research, 1, 371–390.

Schonbucher, P. (2000): "Factor Models for Portfolio of Credit Risk," Bonn Univ. DP.

Sklar, A. (1959): "Fonctions de répartition à *n* dimensions et leurs marges," Publications de, Institut de Statistique de Universite de Paris, 8, 229–231.
Smith, R. (1989): "Extreme Value Analysis of Environmental Time Series: An Application to Trend Detection in Ground Level Ozone," Statistical Science, 4, 367–393.
Smithson, C. (1996a): "Value at Risk ," Risk, 9, 25–27.
Smithson, C. (1996b): "Value at Risk (2)," Risk, 9, 38–39.
Tasche, D. (2002): "Expected Shortfall and Beyond," Journal of Banking and Finance, 26, 1519–1533.
Venkataraman, S. (1997): "Value at Risk for a Mixture of Normal Distributions. The Use of Quasi Bayesian Estimation Techniques," Economic Perspectives, Federal Reserve Bank of Chicago, 21, 2–13.
Wang, S., and V., Young (1998): "Ordering Risk: Expected Utility Theory versus Yaari's Dual Theory of Risk," Insurance: Methematics and Economics, 22, 1445–161.
Wilde, T. (2001): "Probing Granularity," Risk Magazine, 14, 103–106.
Wilson, T. (1996): "Calculating Risk Capital," In: Alexander, C. (ed.), The Handbook of Risk Management and Analysis, Wiley, Chichester, 193–232.
Zangari, P. (1996): "An Improved Methodology for Measuring VaR," Quarterly RiskMetrics Monitor, Second Quarter, 7–25.

CHAPTER 11

Measuring and Modeling Variation in the Risk-Return Trade-off

Martin Lettau* *and* **Sydney C. Ludvigson****

*Haas School of Business, University of California at Berkeley, Berkeley, CA

**Department of Economics, New York University, New York, NY

Contents

Abstract

This chapter reviews what is known about the time-series evolution of the risk-return trade-off for stock market investment and presents some new empirical evidence. We emphasize several aspects of U.S. stock market data.

1. It is difficult to reconcile the historical behavior of the U.S. stock market without admitting some degree of predictability in excess returns. We conclude that the conditional expected excess return on the U.S. stock market is an important contributor to volatility in the Sharpe ratio.
2. The evidence for changing stock market risk is not confined to high-frequency data; stock market volatility is forecastable over horizons ranging from one quarter to six years.
3. The empirical risk-return relation cannot be understood without distinguishing the conditional from unconditional correlation between the expected excess stock return and its expected volatility. We find a positive conditional correlation that is strongly statistically significant, whereas the unconditional correlation is weakly negative and statistically insignificant.

4. The Sharpe ratio for the U.S. aggregate stock market is countercyclical and highly volatile, and its dynamic behavior is not well captured by leading consumption-based asset pricing models that can rationalize a time-varying price of risk. Thus, the data imply is a "Sharpe ratio variability puzzle" that remains to be explained.

Keywords: Sharpe ratio; risk-return; predictability; stock market volatility; expected returns

1. INTRODUCTION

Financial markets are often hard to understand. Stock prices are highly volatile and difficult to predict, requiring that market participants and researchers devote significant resources to understanding the behavior of expected returns relative to the risk of stock market investment. Does the expected return to stock market investment change over time and, if so, at what horizons and with which economic indicators? Can predictable movements in the excess return be explained by changes in stock market volatility? How does the mean return per unit risk change over time? For academic researchers, the progression of empirical evidence on these questions has presented a continuing challenge to asset pricing theory and an important road map for future inquiry. For investment professionals, finding practical answers to these questions is the fundamental purpose of financial economics, as well as its principal reward.

Despite both the theoretical and practical importance of these questions, relatively little is known about how the risk-return trade-off varies over the business cycle or with key macroeconomic indicators. This chapter reviews the state of knowledge on such variation for stock market investment and discusses some new empirical evidences based on information contained in macroeconomic indicators. We define the risk-return trade-off as the conditional expected excess return on a broad stock market index divided by its conditional standard deviation, a quantity we refer to hereafter as the *Sharpe ratio*. The focus of this chapter is not on the unconditional value of this ratio but rather on its evolution through time.

Understanding the time-series properties of the Sharpe ratio is crucial to the development of theoretical models capable of explaining observed patterns of stock market predictability and volatility. For example, Hansen and Jagannathan (1991) showed that the maximum value of the Sharpe ratio places restrictions on the volatility of the set of discount factors that can be used to price returns. The same reasoning implies that the pattern of time-series variation in the Sharpe ratio places restrictions on the dynamic behavior of discount factors capable of pricing equity returns. In addition, the behavior of the Sharpe ratio over time is fundamental for assessing whether stocks are safer in the long run than they are in the short run, as increasingly advocated by popular guides to investment strategy (e.g., Siegel, 1998). Only if the Sharpe ratio grows more quickly than the square root of the horizon – so that the standard deviation of the return grows more slowly than its mean – stocks are safer investments in the long run than they are in the short run. Such a dynamic pattern is not possible if stock returns are unpredictable, i.i.d. random variables. Thus, understanding the time-series behavior of the Sharpe ratio not only provides a benchmark for theoretical progress but also it has profound implications for investment professionals concerned with strategic asset allocation.

In this chapter, we are concerned with the risk-return trade-off for a broad stock market return, R_{st}, as measured by the asset's conditional Sharpe ratio, denoted SR_t and defined

$$\mathrm{SR}_t \equiv \frac{E_t(R_{st+1}) - R_{ft}}{E_t V_{t+1}}, \tag{1.1}$$

where $E_t(R_{st+1})$ is the mean net return from period t to period $t+1$, conditional on information available at time t; R_{ft} is a short-term interest rate paying a return from t to $t+1$, known as of time t. $E_t V_{t+1}$ is a measure of the standard deviation of the excess return, conditional on information available at time t. The Sharpe ratio is an intuitively appealing characterization of the price of stock market risk: it measures how much return an investor can get per unit of volatility in the asset.

The two components of the risk-return relation are the conditional mean excess stock return, in the numerator of the Sharpe ratio, and the conditional standard deviation of the excess return, in the denominator. We focus here on empirically measuring and statistically modeling each of these components separately, a process that can be unified to reveal an estimate of the conditional Sharpe ratio or *price* of stock market risk. We argue below that the preponderance of evidence implies that excess returns on broad stock market indexes are predictable over long horizons, implying that the reward for bearing risk varies over time.

One possible explanation for time variation in the equity risk premium is time variation in stock market volatility. In classic asset pricing models such as the capital asset pricing model (CAPM) of Sharpe (1964) and Lintner (1965), the equity risk premium varies proportionally with stock market volatility. These models require that periods of high excess stock returns coincide with periods of high stock market volatility, implying a constant price of risk. It follows that variation in the equity risk premium must be perfectly positively correlated with variation in stock market volatility.

An important empirical question is whether a positive correlation between the mean and volatility of returns exists, implying a Sharpe ratio that is less variable than the mean or even constant. The body of empirical evidence on the risk-return relation is mixed and inconclusive. Some evidence supports the theoretical prediction of a positive risk-return trade-off, but other evidence suggests a strong negative relation. Yet a third strand of the literature finds that the relation is unstable and varies substantially through time. Bollerslev et al. (1988), Harvey (1989), Harrison and Zhang (1999), Ghysels et al. (2005), and Ludvigson and Ng (2007) find a positive relation, while Campbell (1987), Breen et al. (1989), Pagan and Hong (1991), Glosten et al. (1993), Whitelaw (1994), and Brandt and Kang (2004) find a negative relation. French et al. (1987) and Campbell and Hentschel (1992) find a negative relation between ex-post returns and the unpredictable component of volatility, a phenomenon often referred to as the "volatility feedback effect." This could be indirect evidence of a positive relation between volatility and ex-ante (expected) returns if ex-post and ex-ante returns are negatively related, or it could indicate a negative correlation between shocks to stock prices and shocks to volatility because negative shocks to stock prices raise financial or operating leverage (e.g., Black, 1976).

We argue that the disagreement in the empirical literature on the risk-return relation is likely to be attributable, in large part, to the relatively small amount of conditioning information that is typically used to model the conditional mean and conditional volatility of excess stock market returns. To the extent that financial market participants have information not reflected in the chosen conditioning variables, measures of conditional mean and conditional volatility – and ultimately the risk-return relation itself – will be misspecified and possibly misleading. Moreover, the estimated risk-return relation is likely to be highly dependent on the particular conditioning variables analyzed in any given empirical study.

Following the application in Ludvigson and Ng (2007), we discuss one potential remedy to this problem based on the methodology of dynamic factor analysis for large data sets, whereby a large amount of economic information can be summarized by a few estimated factors. The estimated factors can be used to augment empirical specifications for estimating conditional mean and conditional volatility. This procedure eliminates the arbitrary reliance on a small number of exogenous predictors to model conditional moments and allows the researcher to condition on far richer information sets than what is possible using conventional econometric procedures. In practice, estimated common factors appear to contain important information about the conditional moments of stock market returns that is not already contained in commonly used predictor variables. For example, factor-augmented specifications for the conditional mean return are found to predict an unusual 16–20% of the one-quarter ahead variation in excess stock market returns, with much of this predictability attributable to the estimated factors.

In addition to reviewing existing evidence, this chapter presents some updated evidence on the risk-return relationship, building off insights from earlier studies. As a summary assessment of this evidence, we emphasize four aspects of U.S. stock market behavior.

First, despite complexities with statistical inference in return predictability regressions, it is difficult to reconcile the historical behavior of the U.S. stock market without admitting some degree of predictability in excess returns. Even after accounting for various potential statistical biases, there is evidence of stock return predictability both in-sample and out-of-sample, albeit accompanied by some evidence of instability in the predictive relations. We conclude that the conditional expected excess return on the U.S. stock market varies over long horizons and is an important contributor to volatility in the Sharpe ratio.

Second, the evidence for changing stock market risk is not confined to high frequency data; instead, stock market volatility is forecastable over horizons ranging from one quarter to six years. In addition, we find that a proxy for the log consumption-aggregate wealth ratio, cay_t, a variable shown elsewhere to predict excess returns and constructed using information on aggregate consumption and aggregate labor income (Lettau and Ludvigson, 2001a), is also a strong predictor of stock market volatility. These findings differ from some existing evidence because they reveal the presence of at least one observable conditioning variable that strongly forecasts both the mean and volatility of returns.

Third, the empirical risk-return relation is characterized by important lead-lag interactions. In particular, evidence suggests that distinguishing between the *conditional* correlation (conditional on lagged mean and lagged volatility) and *unconditional* correlation between the expected excess stock return and its expected volatility is crucial for understanding the empirical risk-return relation. We find a positive conditional correlation that is strongly statistically significant, whereas the unconditional correlation is weakly negative and statistically insignificant.

Fourth, the Sharpe ratio for the U.S. aggregate stock market is countercyclical and highly volatile. Thus, predictability of excess stock returns cannot be fully explained by changes in stock market volatility. This evidence weighs against many time-honored asset pricing models that specify a constant price of risk (e.g., the static CAPM of Sharpe, 1964 and Lintner, 1965) and toward more recent paradigms capable of rationalizing a time-varying price of risk. Yet despite evidence that the Sharpe ratio varies countercyclically, we find that its dynamic behavior for the U.S. stock market is not well captured by leading consumption-based asset pricing models capable of rationalizing a countercyclical price of risk. As an illustration, we compare our empirically estimated Sharpe ratio over time with that implied by the habit-based asset pricing model of Campbell and Cochrane (1999), in which the price of risk varies with time-varying risk aversion. Under the benchmark calibration of this model, the magnitude of volatility in the Sharpe ratio is almost one-fifth the size of that for the U.S. stock market.

Even if stock market volatility were constant, predictable variation in excess stock returns might be explained by time variation in *consumption* volatility. In a wide range of equilibrium asset pricing models, more risky consumption streams require asset markets that, in equilibrium, deliver a higher mean return per unit risk. Thus, we consider two models with time-varying consumption risk: a standard power utility model, as well as the the generalization of this model based on recursive utility and stochastic consumption volatility considered in Bansal and Yaron (2004). Some variation in aggregate consumption volatility is evident in the data, as we document here. However, this variation is small and its dynamic behavior is such that models with time-varying consumption risk have Sharpe ratios that are *negatively* correlated with the Sharpe ratio for the U.S. stock market. This evidence suggests that changes in consumption risk are insufficiently important empirically to explain the dynamic behavior of the Sharpe ratio observed in U.S. aggregate stock market data. Thus, the data imply is a "Sharpe ratio variability puzzle" that remains to be explained.

The rest of this chapter is organized as follows. Section 2 discusses empirical evidence on time variation in the conditional mean excess return for the U.S. stock market. In this section, we evaluate the statistical evidence for stock return predictability and review the range of indicators with which such predictability has been associated. Section 3 discusses empirical evidence on time variation in conditional volatility of the U.S. stock market and its dynamic relation with estimates of the conditional mean. Section 4 ties together the evidence on the conditional mean of excess returns with that on the conditional variance to derive implications for the time-series behavior of the conditional Sharpe ratio. Section 5 provides a summary and concluding remarks.

2. THE CONDITIONAL MEAN OF STOCK RETURNS

If excess stock market returns are predictable, the conditional mean of excess returns moves over time. The early empirical literature on predictability generally concluded that stock returns were unforecastable, but research in the last 20 years has found evidence of predictability in stock returns. In addition, an active area of recent theoretical research has shown that such predictability is not necessarily inconsistent with market efficiency: forecastability of equity returns can be generated by time variation in the rate at which rational, utility maximizing investors discount expected future income from risky assets. Prominent theoretical examples in this tradition include models with time-varying risk aversion (e.g., Campbell and Cochrane, 1999) and models with idiosyncratic labor income risk (e.g., Constantinides and Duffie, 1996).

2.1. Origins of Predictability Evidence

The evidence for predictability of stock returns and time-varying risk premia has its origins in two empirical literatures: the literature on permanent and transitory components of stock prices, and the literature on stock market volatility.

In the literature on permanent and transitory components of stock prices, Fama and French (1988b) examined autocorrelations of stock returns for several holding periods. In a univariate setting, negative autocorrelations in stock prices signify mean reversion in stock returns, implying that stock returns have a transitory component and are predictable. Fama and French (1988b) found large negative autocorrelations in stock market prices for return horizons beyond a year, consistent with the hypothesis that mean-reverting price components are important in the variation of returns. They report that such predictable variation accounts for about 40% of three- to five-year return variance for small-firm portfolios, and about 25% for portfolios of large firms.

In the literature on stock market volatility, LeRoy and Porter (1981) and Shiller (1981) argued that stock returns were too volatile to be accounted for by variation in expected future dividend growth, discounted at a constant rate. Such an empirical finding, often referred to as "excess volatility," is indirect evidence of stock return forecastability. This point may be understood by examining an approximate present-value relation for stock market returns.

Let d_t and p_t be the log dividend and log price, respectively, of the stock market portfolio, and let the log return be denoted $r_{s,t} \equiv \log(1 + R_{s,t})$, where $R_{s,t}$ is the simple net return on stock market investment. Similarly, denote the log return on a one-period riskless bond $r_{t,t} \equiv \log(1 + R_{f,t})$, where $R_{f,t}$ is the simple net return on a risk-free investment whose return is know with certainty at time $t - 1$. Let the sample size be denoted T and let variables $\overline{x}_t$ with "bars" over them denote sample means. Throughout this chapter we use lowercase letters to denote log variables, e.g., $\log D_t \equiv d_t$.

Campbell and Shiller (1989) show that an approximate expression for the log dividend-price ratio may be written as

$$p_t - d_t \approx \kappa + E_t \sum_{j=1}^{\infty} \rho_s^j \Delta d_{t+j} - E_t \sum_{j=1}^{\infty} \rho_s^j r_{s,t+j}, \tag{2.1}$$

where E_t is the expectation operator conditional on information at time t, $\rho_s \equiv 1/(1 + \exp(\overline{d_t - p_t}))$, and κ is a constant that plays no role in our analysis. This equation is often referred to as the "dynamic dividend growth model" and is derived by taking a first-order Taylor approximation of the equation defining the log stock return, $r_{st} = \log(P_t + D_t) - \log(P_t)$, applying a transversality condition (that rules out rational bubbles), and taking expectations.

Equation (2.1) states that, when the price-dividend ratio is high, agents must be expecting either low returns on assets in the future or high-dividend growth rates. Thus, stock prices are high relative to dividends when dividends are expected to grow rapidly or when they are discounted at a lower rate. If discount rates are constant, the last term on the right-hand side of (2.1) is absorbed in κ, and variation in the price-dividend ratio can only be generated by variation in expected future dividend growth. Note that this result does not require one to accurately measure expectations since (2.1) is derived from an identity and therefore holds *ex-post* as well as *ex-ante*. Multiplying both sides of (2.1) by

$(p_t - d_t) - E(p_t - d_t)$ and taking unconditional expectations, a formula for the variance of the log price-dividend ratio is obtained:

$$\begin{aligned}\operatorname{Var}\left(p_t - d_t\right) = \operatorname{Cov}\left((p_t - d_t), \sum_{j=0}^{\infty} \rho^j \Delta d_{t+1+j}\right) \\ - \operatorname{Cov}\left((p_t - d_t), \sum_{j=0}^{\infty} \rho^j r_{s,t+1+j}\right).\end{aligned} \tag{2.2}$$

The variance of the price-dividend ratio can be decomposed into two covariance terms: one for the covariance of $p_t - d_t$ with future dividend growth and one for the covariance of $p_t - d_t$ with future returns. An implicit assumption in (2.2) is that expectations are rational.

Campbell (1991) and Cochrane (1991a) use (2.2) to quantify the relative importance of dividend and return predictability in the variability of the price-dividend ratio. For example, Cochrane (1991a) truncates the infinite sums above at 15 years to compute the covariances on the right-hand side. Cochrane (2005) updates these computations using annual data for the value-weighted NYSE stocks and finds

$$\frac{100 \times \operatorname{Cov}\left(p_t - d_t, \sum_{j=0}^{15} \rho^j \Delta d_{t+1+j}\right)}{\operatorname{Var}\left(p_t - d_t\right)} = -34$$

$$\frac{-100 \times \operatorname{Cov}\left(p_t - d_t, \sum_{j=0}^{15} \rho^j r_{s,t+1+j}\right)}{\operatorname{Var}\left(p_t - d_t\right)} = 138$$

Notice that nothing in the computation of these numbers constrains them to sum to unity, to be less than 100, or to be positive. As it turns out, the data imply that numbers above approximately sum to 100 and that a high price-dividend ratio forecasts *lower* dividend growth. Thus, the first term is negative and return forecastability, therefore, accounts for more than 100% of the variability in the price-dividend ratio. Results of this form lead Campbell (1991) and Cochrane (1991a) to conclude that nearly all the variation in $p_t - d_t$ is attributable to changing forecasts of excess returns rather than to variation in expected future dividend growth.

Equation (2.1) also demonstrates an important statistical property that is useful for understanding the possibility of predictability in asset returns. Under the maintained hypothesis that dividend growth and returns follow covariance stationary processes, Eq. (2.1) says that the price-dividend ratio on the left-hand side must also be covariance stationary, implying that dividends and prices are cointegrated. Thus, prices and dividends cannot wonder arbitrarily far from one another so that deviations of $p_t - d_t$

from its unconditional mean must eventually be eliminated by a subsequent movement in dividend growth, a subsequent movement in returns, or some combination of the two. The hypothesis of cointegration implies that, if the price-dividend ratio varies at all, it must forecast either future returns to equity or future dividend growth, or both. We discuss this property of cointegrated variables further below.

Note that the equity return $r_{s,t+1}$ in (2.2) can trivially be expressed as the sum of the excess return over a risk-free rate plus the risk-free rate $r_{s,t+1} = \left(r_{s,t+1} - r_{f,t+1}\right) + r_{f,t+1}$. In principle, variation in the price-dividend ratio could be entirely attributable to variability in the expected risk-free rate, even if expected dividend growth rates and risk premia are constant. Such a scenario does not appear to be consistent with empirical evidence. Campbell et al. (1997), Chapter 8, show that variation in expected real interest rates is too small to account for the volatility of price-dividend ratios on aggregate stock market indexes. Instead, variation in price-dividend ratios is dominated by forecastable movements in the excess stock market return, $\left(r_{s,t+1} - r_{f,t+1}\right)$, that is by variation in the reward for bearing risk.

2.2. Linking the Macroeconomy to Conditional Mean Excess Returns

There is evidence that expected excess returns on common stocks vary countercyclically, implying that risk premia are higher in recessions than they are in expansions. Fama and French (1989) and Ferson and Harvey (1991) plot fitted values of the expected risk premium on the aggregate stock market and find that it increases during economic contractions and peaks near business cycle troughs. Harrison and Zhang (1999) form nonparametric estimates of the conditional mean excess return and correlate these estimates with proxies for the business cycle, in each case finding that the expected return is countercyclical. More recently, Campbell and Diebold (2009) use the Livingston business conditions survey data to directly explore the linkages between expected business conditions and expected excess stock returns. They find that expected business conditions, as measured by this survey, are predictors of excess stock market returns. In addition, their findings reinforce the conclusion that risk premia are countercyclical: depressed expected business conditions are associated with high-expected excess returns.

If such cyclical variation in the market risk premium is present, we would expect to find evidence of it from forecasting regressions of excess returns on macroeconomic variables over business cycle horizons. Yet the most widely investigated predictive variables have not been macroeconomic variables but instead financial indicators such as equity-valuation ratios that have forecasting power concentrated over horizons longer than the typical business cycle. Over horizons spanning the length of a typical business cycle, stock returns are commonly found to be only weakly forecastable by these variables. Exceptions are the term spread and short-term interest rates, both of which have been found to have predictive power for stock returns at business cycle frequencies. But even this evidence is based on purely financial indicators and begs the question of why predictable variation in excess returns cannot be linked to macroeconomic fundamentals.

One approach to investigating the linkages between the macroeconomy and financial markets is considered in Lettau and Ludvigson (2001a), who study the forecasting power for stock returns not of financial valuation ratios such as the dividend-price ratio, but of a proxy for the log consumption-aggregate wealth ratio, denoted cay_t. This variable is an estimated cointegrating residual for log consumption, c_t, log asset wealth, a_t, and log labor income, y_t, and has been found to have strong forecasting power for excess stock market returns. We describe the motivation behind this variable next.

2.2.1. Consumption, Aggregate Wealth, and Expected Stock Market Returns

Consider a representative agent economy in which all wealth, including human capital, is tradable. Let W_t be beginning of period t *aggregate* wealth (defined as the sum of human capital, H_t, and nonhuman, or asset wealth, A_t) and let $R_{w,t+1}$ be the net return on aggregate wealth. For expositional convenience, we consider a simple accumulation equation for aggregate wealth, written

$$W_{t+1} = (1 + R_{w,t+1})(W_t - C_t), \tag{2.3}$$

where C_t is per capita aggregate consumption. Labor income Y_t does not appear explicitly in this equation because of the assumption that the market value of tradable human capital is included in aggregate wealth.[1]

Defining $r \equiv \log(1 + R)$, Campbell and Mankiw (1989) derive an expression for the log consumption-aggregate wealth ratio by taking a first-order Taylor expansion of (2.3), solving the resulting difference equation for log wealth forward, imposing a transversality condition, and taking expectations. The resulting expression is

$$c_t - w_t = E_t \sum_{i=1}^{\infty} \rho_w^i (r_{w,t+i} - \Delta c_{t+i}), \tag{2.4}$$

where $\rho_w \equiv 1 - \exp(\overline{c_t - w_t})$. The consumption-wealth ratio embodies rational forecasts of returns and consumption growth. The Eq. (2.4) generally contains a constant, which has been suppressed since it plays no role in the analysis below. We omit unimportant linearization constants in the equations throughout the chapter. Under the maintained assumption that returns to aggregate wealth and consumption growth are covariance stationary random variables, (2.4) implies that log consumption and log aggregate wealth are cointegrated.

[1] None of the derivations below are dependent on this assumption. In particular, Eq. (2.12), below, can be derived from the analogous budget constraint in which human capital is nontradable: $A_{t+1} = (1 + R_{a,t+1})(A_t + Y_t - C_t)$, where $H_t = E_t \sum_{j=0}^{\infty} \prod_{i=0}^{j} (1 + R_{a,t+i})^{-i} Y_{t+j}$.

Equation (2.4) states that the log consumption-wealth ratio will be high when returns are expected to be higher in the future or when consumption is expected to grow less quickly. Although this expression is intuitively appealing, it is of little use in empirical work because aggregate wealth w_t includes human capital, which is not observable. Lettau and Ludvigson (2001a) address this problem by reformulating the bivariate cointegrating relation between c_t and w_t as a trivariate cointegrating relation involving three observable variables, namely c_t, a_t, and labor income y_t.

To understand this reformulation, denote the net return to nonhuman capital $R_{a,t}$ and the net return to human capital $R_{h,t}$, and assume that human capital takes the form, $H_t = E_t \sum_{j=0}^{\infty} \prod_{i=0}^{j} (1 + R_{h,t+i})^{-i} Y_{t+j}$. Following Campbell and Shiller (1989), a log-linear approximation of H_t yields

$$h_t \approx \kappa + y_t + v_t, \tag{2.5}$$

where κ is a constant, v_t is a mean zero, stationary random variable given by

$$v_t = E_t \sum_{j=1}^{\infty} \rho_h^j (\Delta y_{t+j} - r_{h,t+j})$$

and $\rho_h \equiv 1/(1 + \exp(\overline{y - h})$. Under these assumptions, labor income y_t defines the trend in human wealth, h_t.

Assume that $\rho_h = \rho_w$ (the equations below can easily be extended to relax this assumption with the cost of considerably more cumbersome notation). Following Campbell (1996), we assume that the return on aggregate wealth is a portfolio weighted average of the return on asset wealth and the return on human capital, and has log approximation given by

$$r_{w,t} \approx (1 - \nu) r_{a,t} + \nu r_{y,t}, \tag{2.6}$$

where $(1 - \nu)$ is the mean asset wealth share A/W. Similarly, the log of aggregate wealth is approximated as a function of its component elements,

$$w_t \approx (1 - \nu) a_t + \nu h_t. \tag{2.7}$$

This requires an assumption that the wealth shares are stationary and have well-defined means given by $(1 - \nu)$ and ν. Lettau and Ludvigson (2001a) plug (2.5)–(2.7) into (2.4) to obtain an approximate expression linking log consumption, log asset wealth, and log labor income to expected future returns to asset wealth, consumption growth, and labor income:

$$c_t - (1 - \nu)\, a_t - \nu y_t \approx E_t \sum_{i=1}^{\infty} \rho_w^i \big((1 - \nu) r_{a,t+i} - \Delta c_{t+i} + \nu \Delta y_{t+1+i} \big). \tag{2.8}$$

Several points about Eq. (2.8) deserve emphasis. First, if log labor income follows a random walk and the expected return to human capital is constant, $c_t - (1-\nu)\, a_t - \nu y_t$ is proportional to the log consumption-wealth ratio, $c_t - w_t$. To see this, note that, in this case, terms in (2.8) involving expected future income growth drop out and (2.8) becomes

$$c_t - (1-\nu)\, a_t - \nu y_t \approx E_t \sum_{i=1}^{\infty} \rho_w^i \big((1-\nu) r_{a,t+i} - \Delta c_{t+i}\big). \tag{2.9}$$

A constant expected return for human capital implies $E_t r_{w,t+1} \approx (1-\nu) E_t r_{a,t+1}$ so that the log consumption-wealth ratio (2.4) becomes

$$c_t - w_t = E_t \sum_{i=1}^{\infty} \rho_w^i ((1-\nu)\, r_{a,t+i} - \Delta c_{t+i}). \tag{2.10}$$

Thus, under these assumptions, (2.9) and the log consumption-wealth ratio are proportional to one another. We therefore refer loosely to $c_t - (1-\nu)\, a_t - \nu y_t$ as a proxy for the log consumption-wealth ratio.

Second, under the maintained hypothesis that $r_{w,t}$, Δc_t, and Δy_t are stationary, the budget constraint identity implies that log consumption, c_t, log labor income, y_t, and log nonhuman (asset) wealth, a_t, share a common long-run trend (they are cointegrated) and $c_t - (1-\nu)\, a_t - \nu y_t$ is a cointegrating residual.

Third, the expression (2.8) implies that the cointegrating coefficients $(1-\nu)$ and ν should sum to unity. In practice, we find that estimates of these coefficients sum to a number around 0.9. To understand why the estimated coefficients could sum to a number less than one, observe that the theoretical consumption measure, c_t, in (2.8) refers to total consumption. In empirical practice, nondurables and services expenditures are used to proxy for c_t (Blinder and Deaton, 1985). Total consumption is unobservable since it includes the *service flow* from the stock of all consumer durables, a quantity that is not measured even though durables *expenditures* are measured. Denote nondurables and services expenditures as c_t^{NDS}. Measured nondurables and services expenditures are one piece of unobservable total consumption, c_t.

Now suppose that the ratio of total consumption to nondurables and services expenditures has a very pronounced low-frequency component that – over our sample – appears as a secular decline in the share of nondurables and services consumption in total consumption (or a secular increase in the ratio of total consumption to nondurable and services consumption). Such a secular change can be captured empirically by assuming that the log of unobservable real total consumption is a multiple, $\lambda > 1$, of the log nondurables and services expenditures, c_t^{NDS}, possibly plus a stationary, mean zero-independent component, u_t:

$$c_t = \lambda c_t^{\text{NDS}} + u_t. \tag{2.11}$$

In this case, the average growth in the ratio of total consumption C_t to nondurables and services consumption C_t^{NDS} is given by

$$E_T\left[\Delta \log\left(\frac{C_t}{C_t^{\mathrm{NDS}}}\right)\right] = (\lambda - 1)\, E_T\left[\Delta \log\left(C_t^{\mathrm{NDS}}\right)\right],$$

where E_T denotes the sample mean. A secular increase in the ratio of total consumption to nondurable and services consumption over the sample means that the average growth rate on the left-hand side is positive, which will be true as long as $\lambda > 1$ and $E\left[\Delta \log\left(C_t^{\mathrm{NDS}}\right)\right] > 0$. Plugging (2.11) into (2.8), we now obtain an approximate expression linking the log of nondurables and services expenditures, log asset wealth, and log labor income to expected future returns to asset wealth, consumption growth, and labor income:

$$\mathrm{cay}_t \equiv c_t^{\mathrm{NDS}} - \alpha_a a_t - \alpha_y y_t \approx E_t \sum_{i=1}^{\infty} \rho_w^i \left((1-\nu) r_{a,t+i} - \Delta c_{t+i} + \nu \Delta y_{t+1+i}\right) - u_t, \qquad (2.12)$$

where $\alpha_a = -(1/\lambda)(1-\nu)$ and $\alpha_y = -(1/\lambda)\nu$. Again, under the maintained hypothesis that r_{wt}, Δc_t, and Δy_t are stationary, (2.12) implies that the log of nondurables and services consumption, c_t^{NDS}, the log labor income, y_t, and the log nonhuman (asset) wealth, a_t, are cointegrated) and $c_t^{\mathrm{NDS}} - \alpha_a a_t - \alpha_y y_t$ is a cointegrating residual, denoted cay_t for short. Notice that the estimated cointegrating vector for c_t^{NDS}, a_t, and y_t is given by $[1, -(1/\lambda)(1-\nu), -(1/\lambda)\nu]$, with

$$(1/\lambda)(1-\nu) + (1/\lambda)\nu = 1/\lambda < 1,$$

as long as $\lambda > 1$. Thus, the cointegrating parameters in (2.12) sum to a number less than one, and $\alpha_a + \alpha_y$ identifies $1/\lambda$.

Given the unobservability of total consumption, c_t, it is impossible to know whether the ratio nondurables and services consumption to total consumption has declined over our sample. There is, however, a pronounced secular decline in the share of *expenditures* on nondurables and services over the postwar period, which is suggestive (see Yogo, 2006). Many models assume that expenditures on durable goods are proportional to the service flow from those goods, in which case we would expect a secular decline in the ratio of nondurables and services consumption to total consumption based on the observed behavior of the expenditure shares. Whether these ratios are actually nonstationary is another matter. Many bivariate ratios of macroeconomic time series, including the "great ratios" presumed to be stationary in virtually all general equilibrium macroeconomic models, display a pronounced low-frequency component in the samples currently available so that a unit root cannot be rejected in formal tests of stationarity. This could mean that these ratios are in fact nonstationary, at odds with balanced growth, or more likely that the ratios are stationary and we need many more decades of data to statistically reject the hypothesis that they contain a stochastic trend.

Note that stock returns, $r_{s,t}$, are but one component of the return to asset wealth, $r_{a,t}$. Stock returns, in turn, are the sum of excess stock returns and the real interest rate. Therefore, Eq. (2.12) says that cay_t embodies rational forecasts of either excess stock returns, interest rates, consumption growth, labor income growth, or some combination of all four. Below we discuss evidence on the forecastability of excess stock market returns using cay_t as a predictor variable.

The cointegrating residual cay_t contains cointegrating parameters α_a and α_y that must be estimated, a task that is straightforward using procedures developed by Johansen (1988) or Stock and Watson (1993).[2] Lettau and Ludvigson (2001a) describe these procedures in more detail and apply them to data on aggregate consumption, labor income, and asset wealth to obtain an estimate of cay_t. We denote the estimate of cay_t as $\widehat{\text{cay}}_t$.

Lettau and Ludvigson (2001a) find evidence of a single cointegrating vector among c_t, a_t and y_t. Note, however, that the budget-constraint model discussed above has two wealth components, a_t and h_t. If these wealth components were themselves cointegrated, and if labor income y_t defines the trend in human wealth, as argued above, we would expect to find evidence of a second linearly independent cointegrating relationship between a_t and y_t. It is difficult to find evidence of a second cointegrating relation, however, because there is a pronounced low-frequency component in the log ratio of asset wealth to labor income. This should not be interpreted as evidence that a_t and y_t are not cointegrated – finding no evidence in favor of cointegration is not the same as finding evidence against cointegration. An equally valid interpretation of the data is that the log ratio of asset wealth to labor income, while stationary, is sufficiently persistent that it is not possible to reject a unit root null in our sample.

Regardless of whether there are one or two linearly independent cointegrating relations among the variables c_t, a_t, and y_t, Eq. (2.12) is a valid description of a trivariate cointegrating relation among c_t, a_t, and y_t. The number of cointegrating relations matters only for how the cointegrating vector(s) is (are) estimated and only for the interpretation of the cointegrating coefficients. If there is a single cointegrating relation, the cointegrating coefficients can be consistently estimated from a single-equation dynamic least squares regression. If there are two cointegrating relations, they must be estimated jointly

[2]Notice that theory implies an additional restriction, namely that the consumption-wealth ratio should be covariance stationary (not merely trend stationary) so that it contains no deterministic trends in a long-run equilibrium or steady state. If this restriction was not satisfied, the theory would imply that either per capita consumption or per capita wealth must eventually become a negligible fraction of the other. The requirement that the consumption-wealth ratio be covariance stationary corresponds to the concept of deterministic cointegration emphasized by Ogaki and Park (1997). When theory suggests the presence of deterministic cointegration, it is important to impose the restrictions implied by deterministic cointegration and exclude a time trend in the static or dynamic ordinary least squares (OLS) regression used to estimate the cointegrating vector. Simulation evidence (available from the authors upon request) shows that, in finite samples, the distribution of the coefficient on the time trend in such a regression is highly nonstandard and its inclusion in the static or dynamic regression is likely to bias estimates of the cointegrating coefficient away from their true values under the null of deterministic cointegration.

from a system of equations. If there are two cointegrating relations and the researcher erroneously uses a single equation to estimate the cointegrating parameters, the resulting parameter estimates will typically be a linear combination of the cointegrating coefficients in the two relations, but the budget constraint analysis above still implies that the trivariate relation so estimated should be related to expectations of future asset returns, consumption growth, or labor income growth, or to some combination of all three.

Since the data provide no evidence of a second bivariate cointegrating relation among c_t, a_t, and y_t, we follow the advice of Campbell and Perron (1991) and empirically model only the single, trivariate cointegrating relation for which we find direct statistical evidence in our sample. This means that we use a single-equation methodology to estimate the cointegrating coefficients in cay_t. Suppose that a series is stationary, but is sufficiently persistent that one cannot reject the hypothesis of nonstationarity in a finite sample. Simulation evidence in Campbell and Perron suggests that treating the data in accordance with the stationarity properties inferred from unit root/cointegration tests can result in better finite-sample approximations of test statistics than treating the data according to its stationary asymptotic distribution that is true in population. Thus, a near-integrated stationary data-generating process may be better modeled in a finite sample as a unit root variable, even though the asymptotically correct distribution is the standard one appropriate for stationary variables. Accordingly, we treat the bivariate relation between a_t and y_t as a unit root variable, even though it could be stationary in population.

In the more recent data available at the time of this writing, we find evidence of a single cointegrating relation between c_t, a_t, and y_t. Here, we update our estimate of cay_t. The log of asset wealth, a_t, is a measure of real, per capita household net worth, which includes all financial wealth, housing wealth, and consumer durables. The variable y_t is a measure of the log of after-tax labor income. Observe that durable goods expenditures are included in nonhuman wealth, A_t, a component of aggregate wealth, W_t, and so should not be included in consumption or treated purely as an expenditure.[3] The budget constraint applies to the flow of consumption, C_t; durables expenditures are excluded in this definition because they represent replacements and additions to a capital stock (investment) rather than a service flow from the existing stock. All variables are measured in real, per capita terms. Appendix contains a detailed description of the data used in to obtain these values. Using a sample spanning the fourth quarter of 1952 to the first quarter of 2001, we estimate $\widehat{\text{cay}}_t = c_t^{\text{NDS}} - 0.61 - 0.30a_t - 0.60y_t$ using dynamic least squares, as described in Lettau and Ludvigson (2001a).

The principal of cointegration is as important for understanding (2.12) as it is for understanding (2.1). In direct analogy to (2.1), (2.12) implies that if cay_t varies at all, it

[3]Treating durables purchases purely as an expenditure (by, e.g., removing them from A_t and including them in C_t) is also improper because it ignores the evolution of the asset over time, which must be accounted for by multiplying the stock by a gross return. In the case of many durable goods, this gross return would be less than one and consist primarily of depreciation.

must forecast future returns, future consumption growth, future labor income growth, or some combination of these. Thus, cay_t is a possible forecasting variable for stock returns, consumption growth, and labor income growth for the same reasons the price-dividend ratio is a possible forecasting variable for stock returns and dividend growth. In the next section, we review empirical evidence on how well these variables and other popular predictors actually forecast U.S. stock returns.

2.3. Popular Predictor Variables for Excess Stock Returns

The early literature on stock market volatility concluded that price-dividend ratios were too volatile to be accounted for by variation in future dividend growth or interest rates alone. Such a finding provides indirect evidence that expected excess stock returns must vary. A more direct way of testing whether expected returns are time-varying is to explicitly forecast excess returns with predetermined conditioning variables. The empirical asset pricing literature has produced many such variables that have been shown, in one subsample of the data or another, to contain statistically significant predictive power for excess stock returns. A summary of the most commonly used of these predictor variables is as follows.

- *Price-dividend and price-earnings ratios.* Fama and French (1988a), Campbell and Shiller (1989), Campbell (1991), and Hodrick (1992) find that the ratios of price to dividends or earnings have predictive power for excess returns. In more recent data, Ang and Bekaert (2007) find that the dividend-price ratio for the aggregate stock market predicts returns over short horizons when a short-term interest rate is included in the predictive regression. Harvey (1991) finds that similar financial ratios predict stock returns in many different countries.[4]
- *The dividend-payout ratio.* Lamont (1998) argues that the ratio of dividends to earnings should be a predictor of excess returns because high dividends typically forecast high returns, whereas high earnings typically forecast low returns.
- *Short-term interest rates.* Fama and Schwert (1977), Campbell (1991), Hodrick (1992), and Ang and Bekaert (2007) find that short-term interest rates, often measured as a "relative T-bill rate" (e.g., the 30-day Treasury-bill rate minus its 12-month moving average) predicts returns. In what follows, we denote the relative T-bill rate $RREL_t$.
- *Term spreads and default spreads.* Fama and French (1988a) study the forecasting power of the 10-year Treasury bond yield minus the one-year Treasury bond yield (a measure of the term spread) and the BAA corporate bond yield minus the AAA corporate bond yield (a measure of the default spread). We denote the term spread, TRM_t, and the default spread DEF_t.

[4] Boudoukh et al. (2004) construct an adjustment to the dividend-price ratio where the numerator includes repurchases, as well as cash dividends. They refer to this variable as the payout yield. Below, we find that this variable has little forecasting power for future returns in our sample.

- *Book-market ratios.* Lewellen (1999) and Vuolteenaho (2000) forecast returns with an aggregate book-market ratio.
- *Proxies for the consumption-wealth ratio*, cay_t. As discussed above, Lettau and Ludvigson (2001a,b) use a log-linear approximation of a representative investor's consumption-wealth ratio to show that deviations from a cointegrating relation for log consumption, c_t, log asset wealth, a_t, and log labor income, y_t (abbreviated as cay_t), is a potential predictor of excess stock market returns. Lettau and Ludvigson (2001a,b) find evidence that this variable predicts quarterly stock returns both at the stock market level and at the portfolio level.
- *Latent common factors from large data sets of financial indicators.* As additional predictors, we include the "volatility" and "risk-premium" common factors estimated by Ludvigson and Ng (2007) from a quarterly data set of 172 financial indictors, denoted $\widehat{F}_{1t}$ and $\widehat{F}_{2t}$, respectively. We discuss the economic interpretation of these factors in Section 3.

2.4. The Forecastability of Stock Market Returns: Empirical Evidence

We now have a number of variables, based on both financial and macroeconomic indicators, that have been documented, in one study or another, to predict excess stock market returns. To summarize the empirical findings of this literature, Table 11.1 presents the results of in-sample predictive regressions of quarterly excess returns on the value-weighted stock market index from the Center for Research in Securities Prices (CRSP), in excess of the return on a three-month Treasury bill rate. Let $r_{s,t}$ denote the log real return of the CRSP value-weighted index and $r_{f,t}$ the log real return on the three-month Treasury bill (the risk-free rate). Log price, p_t, is the natural logarithm of the CRSP-VW index. Log dividends, d, are the natural logarithm of the sum of the past four quarters of dividends per share. We call $d_t - p_t$ the dividend yield. Denote the log excess return and level excess return as

$$r^e_{t+1} \equiv r_{s,t+1} - r_{f,t+1} \quad \text{and} \quad R^e_{s,t+1} \equiv R_{s,t+1} - R_{f,t+1},$$

respectively. Table 11.1 reports the results of forecasting regressions of the level of excess returns

$$R^e_{s,t+1} = \gamma' Z_t + \varepsilon_{t+1},$$

and of the log of excess returns

$$r^e_{s,t+1} = \beta' Z_t + \epsilon_{t+1},$$

where Z_t is a vector of predictor variables.

Here, we compare the forecasting power of $\widehat{\text{cay}}_t$, $d_t - p_t$, RREL_t, TRM_t, and DEF_t. As additional predictors, we include the "volatility" and "risk-premium" common factors estimated by Ludvigson and Ng (2007) from a quarterly data set of 172 financial

Table 11.1 Forecasting quarterly stock returns, 1952:4–2000:4

No	Constant (t-stat)	lag (t-stat)	$\widehat{cay}_t$ (t-stat)	$d_t - p_t$ (t-stat)	$RREL_t$ (t-stat)	TRM_t (t-stat)	DEF_t (t-stat)	$\widehat{F}_{1t}$ (t-stat)	$\widehat{F}_{2t}$	$\overline{R}^2$
				Panel A: excess returns; 1952:4–2000:4						
1	0.02	0.07								0.00
	(3.66)	(1.07)								
2	−1.18		2.00							0.10
	(−3.66)		(4.37)							
3	−1.18	0.09	2.05							0.10
	(−4.28)	(1.45)	(4.47)							
4	0.12			0.03						0.01
	(1.89)			(1.60)						
5	−1.23		2.06	−0.00						0.09
	(−4.20)		(4.69)	(−0.24)						
6	−1.17	0.03	1.95	−0.00	−2.35	−0.32	0.00			0.13
	(−3.69)	(0.47)	(4.41)	(−0.12)	(−2.83)	(−0.43)	(0.05)			
7	−1.43	0.03	2.21	−0.03	−1.70	−0.08	0.01	0.01	0.02	0.20
	(−3.89)	(0.41)	(4.35)	(−1.17)	(−1.81)	(−0.10)	(0.26)	(3.16)	(2.90)	
				Panel B: log excess returns; 1952:4–2000:4						
8	0.02	0.06								−0.00
	(2.93)	(0.93)								
9	−1.18		1.99							0.09
	(−4.35)		(4.43)							
10	−1.21	0.09	2.03							0.10
	(−4.43)	(1.36)	(4.51)							
11	0.11			0.03						0.01
	(1.85)			(1.61)						
12	−1.24		2.05	−0.01						0.09
	(−4.25)		(4.69)	(−0.29)						
13	−1.14	0.03	1.92	−0.01	−2.24	−0.19	−0.00			0.13
	(−3.69)	(0.45)	(1.37)	(−0.08)	(−2.67)	(−0.25)	(−0.25)			
14	−1.41	0.04	2.18	−0.03	−1.57	0.02	0.00	0.01	0.02	0.19
	(−3.81)	(0.57)	(4.18)	(−1.14)	(−1.56)	(0.03)	(0.17)	(3.25)	(2.61)	

The table reports estimates from OLS regressions of stock returns on lagged variables named at the head of a column. The dependent variable is the excess level or log of the return on the CRSP value-weighted stock market index. The regressors are as follows: lag denotes a one-period lag of the dependent variable, $\widehat{cay}_t \equiv c_t - \widehat{\beta}_a a_t - \widehat{\beta}_y y_t$, where c_t is consumption, a_t is asset wealth, y_t is labor income, and $d_t - p_t$ is the log dividend-price ratio; $RREL_t$ is the relative bill rate; TRM_t is the term spread, the difference between the 10-year Treasury bond yield and the three-month Treasury bond yield, DEF_t is the BAA Corporate Bond rate minus the AAA Corporate Bond rate, and $\widehat{F}_1$ and $\widehat{F}_2$ are the principle component factor constructed in Ludvigson and Ng (2007). Newey–West corrected t-statistics appear in parentheses below the coefficient estimate. Significant coefficients at the 5% level are highlighted in bold face. Regressions use data from the fourth quarter of 1952 to the fourth quarter of 2000.

indicators, denoted $\widehat{F}_{1t}$ and $\widehat{F}_{2t}$, respectively. Ludvigson and Ng (2007) find that $\widehat{F}_{1t}$ and $\widehat{F}_{2t}$ have strong forecasting power for quarterly excess stock market returns, above and beyond that contained in other popular forecasting variables such as the dividend-yield, $\widehat{\text{cay}}_t$ and short-term interest rates (we discuss the motivation behind these factors in Section 3). Table 11.1 reports the regression coefficient, heteroskedasticity-and-autocorrelation-consistent t statistic, and adjusted R^2 statistic for each regression. Notice that although the error term in these regressions is serially uncorrelated under the null of no predictability, it may be serially correlated under plausible alternatives. It is therefore important to correct the standard errors of the estimated coefficients for potential serial correlation in the residuals. The top panel reports results for excess stock market returns in levels; the bottom panel reports results for log excess returns.

At a one-quarter horizon, the $\widehat{\text{cay}}_t$, the relative-bill rate, RREL_t, and the two common factors $\widehat{F}_{1t}$ and $\widehat{F}_{2t}$ have statistically significant marginal predictive power for excess returns. The first row of each panel of Table 11.1 shows that a regression of returns on one lag of the dependent variable displays no forecastability. Adding last quarter's value of $\widehat{\text{cay}}_t$ to the model allows the regression to predict 9% of the variation in next quarter's excess return. The relative bill rate, while statistically significant, adds less than 2% to the adjusted R^2. The dividend-price ratio, the term spread and default spreads have little forecasting power for quarterly excess returns in this sample.

Ludvigson and Ng (2007) find that the volatility and risk-premium factors $\widehat{F}_{1t}$ and $\widehat{F}_{2t}$ alone explain 9% of next quarter's excess return, and they retain their marginal predictive power no matter what other commonly used predictor variables are included in the regression. In particular, the information in these two factors is largely independent of that in the consumption-wealth variable cay_t. The last row of Table 11.1 shows that when $\widehat{F}_{1t}$ and $\widehat{F}_{2t}$ are included as predictors along with cay_t, the result is largely cumulative: the regression model now explains 19% of one-quarter ahead excess stock market returns.

The theory behind (2.1) and (2.12) makes clear that both the dividend-price ratio and the consumption-wealth ratio should track longer term tendencies in asset markets rather than provide accurate short-term forecasts of booms or crashes. To assess whether these predetermined variables forecast returns over longer horizons, Table 11.2, Panel A, presents the results of long-horizon forecasting regressions of excess returns on the CRSP-VW index, on some combination of $\widehat{\text{cay}}_t$, $d_t - p_t$, and RREL_t. (Results using TRM_t, and DEF_t as predictive variables indicated that these variables displayed no forecasting power at any horizon in our sample. Those regressions are therefore omitted from the table to conserve space.) The dependent variable is the H-quarter continuously compounded log excess return on the CRSP-VW index, equal to

$$r^e_{s,t+H,H} = r_{s,t+1} - r_{f,t+1} + \cdots + r_{s,t+H} - r_{f,t+H}.$$

Table 11.2 reports regressions of the form

$$r^e_{t+H,H} = b' Z_t + \varepsilon_{t+H,H}, \tag{2.13}$$

where, as above, Z_t is a set of predictor variables. For each regression, the table reports the estimated coefficient on the included explanatory variables, the adjusted R^2 statistic, and the Newey–West corrected t-statistic for the hypothesis that the coefficient is zero.

Table 11.2 Forecasting stock market returns

Row	Regressors	Forecast horizon H in quarters							
		1	2	4	6	8	12	16	24
1	$\widehat{cay}_t$	1.95	3.79	6.23	8.45	9.82	12.28	12.91	17.31
		(4.58)	(3.99)	(3.05)	(3.42)	(3.98)	(5.37)	(5.47)	(4.58)
		[0.08]	[0.14]	[0.20]	[0.26]	[0.28]	[0.34]	[0.33]	[0.33]
2	$d_t - p_t$	0.02	0.04	0.07	0.11	0.12	0.13	0.15	0.59
		(1.24)	(1.26)	(0.94)	(0.84)	(0.68)	(0.54)	(0.55)	(1.59)
		[0.00]	[0.01]	[0.01]	[0.02]	[0.02]	[0.01]	[0.01]	[0.15]
3	$RREL_t$	−2.58	−4.15	−6.83	−6.28	−3.16	−1.97	−2.81	−4.80
		(−3.89)	(−3.22)	(−2.79)	(−2.56)	(−1.38)	(−0.79)	(−0.84)	(−1.23)
		[0.05]	[0.06]	[0.10]	[0.06]	[0.01]	[0.00]	[0.00]	[0.01]
4	$\widehat{cay}_t$	1.91	3.73	5.94	8.05	9.60	12.12	12.66	14.92
		(4.50)	(4.17)	(3.87)	(4.34)	(4.65)	(4.83)	(4.32)	(3.07)
	$d_t - p_t$	−0.01	−0.01	−0.01	0.01	0.01	0.05	0.06	0.37
		(−0.49)	(−0.36)	(−0.08)	(0.09)	(0.10)	(0.28)	(0.32)	(1.22)
		−2.21	−3.47	−5.92	−5.19	−1.70	0.04	−0.70	−2.23
	$RREL_t$	(−3.49)	(−3.52)	(−3.48)	(−3.68)	(−1.42)	(0.01)	(−0.24)	(−0.70)
		[0.11]	[0.19]	[0.27]	[0.29]	[0.28]	[0.34]	[0.33]	[0.37]
5	$\widehat{cay}_t$	2.16	4.06	6.21	8.49	10.45	14.05	14.60	18.11
		(4.53)	(4.63)	(3.84)	(4.28)	(4.86)	(6.50)	(5.97)	(3.70)
	$d_t - p_t$	−0.03	−0.06	−0.08	−0.11	−0.15	−0.16	−0.13	0.05
		(−1.62)	(−1.50)	(−1.21)	(−1.09)	(−1.23)	(−1.14)	(−0.70)	(0.18)
	$RREL_t$	−1.77	−2.66	−4.98	−4.27	−0.96	0.59	−1.48	−2.61
		(−3.02)	(−2.26)	(−2.48)	(−2.48)	(−0.71)	(0.23)	(−0.48)	(−0.80)
	$\widehat{F}_{1t}$	0.01	0.02	0.01	0.02	0.02	0.01	−0.01	0.01
		(3.37)	(4.45)	(2.08)	(2.16)	(3.00)	(1.19)	(−0.57)	(0.37)
	$\widehat{F}_{2t}$	0.02	0.02	0.02	0.02	0.02	0.01	0.00	0.03
		(3.06)	(1.91)	(1.64)	(1.40)	(0.98)	(0.94)	(0.29)	(0.97)
		[0.16]	[0.23]	[0.28]	[0.31]	[0.34]	[0.46]	[0.42]	[0.40]

The table reports results from long-horizon regressions of excess returns on lagged variables. H denotes the return horizon in quarters. The regressors are as follows: lag, which denotes a one-period lag of the dependent variables, one-period lagged values of the deviations from trend $\widehat{cay}_t = c_t - \widehat{\beta}_a a_t - \widehat{\beta}_y y_t$, the log dividend yield $d_t - p_t$, the dividend earnings ratio $d_t - e_t$, the detrended short-term interest rate $RREL_t$, and Ludvigson and Ng (2007)'s factors $\widehat{F}_1$ and $\widehat{F}_2$. For each regression, the table reports OLS estimates of the regressors, Newey–West corrected t-statistics in parentheses, and adjusted R^2 statistics in square brackets. Significant coefficients at the 5% level are highlighted in bold. The sample period is fourth quarter of 1952 to fourth quarter of 2000.

The first row of Table 11.2 shows that $\widehat{\text{cay}}_t$ has significant forecasting power for future excess returns at horizons ranging from 1 to 24 quarters. The t-statistics are above 3 for all horizons. The predictive power of $\widehat{\text{cay}}_t$ is hump-shaped and peaks around three years in this sample; using this single variable alone the regression model is capable of predicting 34% of the variability in the three-year excess return. Similar findings are reported using U.K. data to construct a measure of $\widehat{\text{cay}}$ (Fernandez-Corugedo et al., 2002), using Australian data (Fisher and Voss, 2004; Tan and Voss, 2004), and using German data (Xu, 2005). These results suggest that the conditional mean of excess stock returns varies over horizons of several years.

The remaining rows of Panel A give an indication of the predictive power of other variables for long-horizon excess returns. Row 2 reports long-horizon regressions using the dividend-yield as the sole forecasting variable. Because we use more recent data, these results are quite different than those obtained elsewhere (e.g., Fama and French, 1988a; Lamont, 1998; Campbell et al., 1997). The dividend-price ratio has no ability to forecast excess stock returns at horizons ranging from 1 to 24 quarters when data after 1995 are included. The last half of the 1990s saw an extraordinary surge in stock prices relative to dividends, weakening the tight link between the dividend-yield and future returns that has been documented in previous samples. The forecasting power of $\widehat{\text{cay}}_t$ seems to have been less affected by this episode. Lettau et al. (2008) provide a partial explanation for this finding based on a fall in macroeconomic risk or the volatility of the aggregate economy. Because of the existence of leverage, their explanation also implies that the consumption-wealth ratio should be less affected by changes in macroeconomic risk than the dividend-price ratio. This may explain why the predictive power of the consumption-wealth variable is less affected by the 1990s than the financial variables investigated here.

Consistent with the findings of Ang and Bekaert (2007), row 3 of Panel A shows that RREL_t has forecasting power that is concentrated at short horizons, displaying its highest long-horizon R^2 for forecasting three-quarter returns. Also consistent with their findings, the dividend yield does not univariately predict excess returns at any horizon in this sample. Ang and Bekaert (2007) find instead that the predictive ability of the dividend yield is enhanced at short horizons in a bivariate regression with a short-term interest rate. Row 4 of Table 11.2 suggests that the dividend-yield is driven out of the predictive regression by $\widehat{\text{cay}}_t$ even when included with a short-term interest rate. The coefficient estimates are strongly statistically significant, with t-statistics in excess of 3 at one and two quarter horizons, but the variable explains a smaller fraction of the variability in future returns than does $\widehat{\text{cay}}_t$. Row 4 of Table 11.2 presents the results of forecasting excess returns using a multivariate regression with $\widehat{\text{cay}}_t$, RREL_t, $d_t - p_t$, and the estimated factors $\widehat{F}_{1t}$ and $\widehat{F}_{2t}$ as predictive variables. The results suggest that excess returns are predictable by several variables for return horizons from 1 to 24 quarters.

2.5. Statistical Issues with Forecasting Returns

The results presented above indicate that excess equity returns are forecastable, suggesting that the equity risk-premium varies with time and that fluctuations in the conditional mean excess return are an important contributor to the fluctuations in the Sharpe ratio. There are, however, a number of potential statistical pitfalls that arise in interpreting these forecasting tests. We discuss these next.

2.5.1. Problems with Overlapping Data

One potential difficulty for statistical inference with return predictability arises as a result of using overlapping data in direct long-horizon regressions, as in (2.13). Recall that, in the long-horizon regressions discussed above, the dependent variable is the H-quarter log excess return, equal to $r_{s,t+1} - r_{f,t+1} + r_{s,t+2} - r_{f,t+2} + \cdots + r_{s,t+H} - r_{f,t+H}$. Notice that at time $t+2$, this return is equal to $r_{s,t+2} - r_{f,t+2} + \cdots + r_{s,t+H} - r_{f,t+H} + r_{s,t+H+1} - r_{f,t+H+1}$. Thus, by construction, the continuously compounded H-period return contains data that overlaps with $H-1$ lags of itself. It follows that, even if one-period returns are i.i.d., the fitted residuals in a regression of long-horizon returns on a constant are serially correlated and a rolling summation of such series will behave asymptotically as a stochastically trending variable. This creates statistical problems when the return horizon H is large relative to the sample size T. Valkanov (2003) shows that the finite-sample distributions of R^2 statistics from direct long-horizon regressions do not converge to their population values, and also that t-statistics do not converge to well-defined distributions whenever long-horizon returns are formed by summing over a nontrivial fraction of the sample.

One way to avoid problems with the use of overlapping data in long-horizon regressions is to use vector autoregressions (VARs) to impute the long-horizon R^2 statistics rather than estimating them directly from long-horizon returns. The approach assumes that the dynamics of the data may be well described by a VAR of a particular lag order, implying that conditional forecasts over long horizons follow directly from the VAR model. The insight here is that long-horizon linear predictions can be obtained by iterating one-step ahead linear projections from a VAR, without requiring the use of any long-horizon return data.

Consider the vector

$$Q_t \equiv \left[r^e_{s,t} - E\left(r^e_{s,t}\right), x_{1t} - E(x_{1t}), x_{2t} - E(x_{2t})\right]',$$

where r^e_t are excess returns, x_{1t} is a predictor variable for returns, and x_{2t} another variable about whose dynamics the researcher may be concerned. (In general, x_{2t} could be a vector of variables.) We assume the variables in Q_t are demeaned. Suppose we describe the vector time series as a VAR(1)[5]:

$$Q_{t+1} = AQ_t + u_{t+1},$$

where A is a $(q+2) \times (q+2)$ matrix. In general, enough lags should be included in the VAR so that the error process is unpredictable, implying that

$$E_t Q_{t+j} = A^j Q_t. \tag{2.14}$$

It is straightforward to use (2.14) to impute the statistics for regressions of long-horizon returns on predictor variables x_{1t}. For example, consider the slope coefficient $\beta_{H,1}$ from a univariate regression of H-period continuously compounded returns on x_{1t}:

$$r^e_{s,t+1} + \cdots + r^e_{s,t+H} = \alpha_H + \beta_{H,1} x_{1t} + u_{t+H,H}. \tag{2.15}$$

Let $e1 = (1,0,0)'$, $e2 = (0,1,0)'$, $C(j) = \mathrm{Cov}(Z_t, Z_{t-j})$, and $V_H = \mathrm{Var}\left(\sum_{j=1}^{H} Q_{t+j}\right)$. Then the estimator of $\beta_{H,1}$ implied by the VAR is

$$\frac{\mathrm{Cov}\left(r^e_{s,t+1} + \cdots + r^e_{s,t+H}, x_{1t}\right)}{\mathrm{Var}(x_{1t})} \equiv \beta_{H,1} = \frac{e1' \left[C(1) + \cdots + C(H)\right] e2}{e2' C(0) e2},$$

and the implied long-horizon R^2 statistic for the regression (2.15) is

$$R^2_H = \left(\frac{\overbrace{\beta^2_{H,1} e2' C(0) e2}^{\text{explained var. of sum of } H \text{ returns}}}{\underbrace{e1' V_H e1}_{\text{var. of sum of } H \text{ returns}}} \right).$$

This methodology for measuring long-horizon statistics by estimating a VAR has been covered by Campbell and Shiller (1989), Campbell (1991), Hodrick (1992), and Kandel and Stambaugh (1989), and we refer the reader to those articles for further details.

Notice that the approach requires no use of overlapping data (since the long-horizon returns are imputed from the VAR); hence it is immune to statistical problems that arise from the use of overlapping data. In a simulation study, Hodrick (1992) finds the VAR methodology for imputing long-horizon statistics has good finite-sample properties

[5] Higher-order systems can be handled in the same way as the first-order system that is described, by stacking the VAR(p) into the companion form.

Table 11.3 VAR long-horizon R^2

Row	z_t	Implied R^2 for forecast horizon H in quarters							
		1	2	4	6	8	12	16	24
1	$\widehat{\text{cay}}_t$	0.09	0.16	0.23	0.26	0.26	0.24	0.21	0.16
2	RREL_t	0.06	0.07	0.07	0.05	0.04	0.03	0.02	0.01
3	$\widehat{\text{cay}}_t, \text{RREL}_t$	0.13	0.20	0.27	0.28	0.27	0.24	0.21	0.15
4	$\widehat{\text{cay}}_t, \text{RREL}_t, \widehat{F}_{1t}, \widehat{F}_{2t}$	0.18	0.23	0.27	0.28	0.27	0.23	0.20	0.15

The table reports implied R^2 statistics for H-period stock market returns from VARs for $r_t - r_{f,t}$ and forecasting variables z_t. The implied R^2 statistics for stock market returns for horizon H are calculated from the estimated parameters of the VAR and the estimated covariance matrix of VAR residuals. The sample period is fourth quarter of 1952 to fourth quarter of 2000.

that produce unbiased measurements of the long-horizon R^2 statistics and regressor coefficients, conditional on the VAR being correctly specified.

We present the results of using this methodology in Table 11.3, which investigates the long-horizon predictive power of the multiple predictors in Table 11.2. All results use a first-order VAR. We calculate an implied R^2 statistic using the coefficient estimates of the VAR and the estimated covariance matrix of the VAR residuals. The first row presents results for predicting returns with $\widehat{\text{cay}}_t$, the second row present result for predicting returns with RREL_t, the third row with both $\widehat{\text{cay}}_t$ and RREL_t, and the final row reports the results of using these variables along with $\widehat{F}_{1t}$ and $\widehat{F}_{2t}$ to predict returns. We do not include the dividend-price ratio in these calculations because the point estimate of the autoregressive root for $d_t - p_t$ in this sample is explosive, invalidating the VAR procedures described above.

The results in Table 11.3 show that the pattern of the implied R^2 statistics obtained from the VAR methodology is very similar to that obtained from the direct long-horizon regressions in Table 11.2. For example, for predicting returns over the next six quarters using $\widehat{\text{cay}}_t$ as the single predictor variable, the implied R^2 statistic from the VAR is 0.26, the same as the actual R^2 from the direct long-horizon regression. Similarly, for predicting returns over the next six quarters using $\widehat{\text{cay}}_t$, RREL_t, $\widehat{F}_{1t}$, and $\widehat{F}_{2t}$ as predictors, the implied R^2 statistic from the VAR is 0.28, whereas the actual R^2 from the direct long-horizon regression is 0.29. This suggests that evidence favoring predictability in Table 11.2 cannot be attributed to spurious inference arising from problems with the use of overlapping data.

Valkanov (2003) proposes an alternative approach to addressing the problem that t-statistics do not converge to well-defined distributions when long-horizon returns are formed by summing over a nontrivial fraction of the sample. Instead of using the standard t-statistic, he proposes a renormalized t-statistic, $t/\sqrt{T}$, for testing long-horizon predictability. The limiting distribution of this statistic is nonstandard and depends on two nuisance parameters. Once those nuisance parameters have been estimated, Valkanov provides a look-up table for comparing the rescaled t-statistic with the appropriate distribution. Lettau and Ludvigson (2005) use this rescaled t-statistic and Valkanov's critical values to determine statistical significance and find that the predictive power of $\widehat{\text{cay}}_t$ for future returns remains statistically significant at better than the 5% level. At most horizons, the variables are statistically significant predictors at the 1% level. As for the VAR analysis, these findings imply that the predictive power of $\widehat{\text{cay}}_t$ is unlikely to be an artifact of biases associated with the use of overlapping data in direct long-horizon regressions.

2.5.2. Problems with Persistent, Predetermined Regressors

A second and distinct possible statistical pitfall with return forecasting regressions arises when returns are regressed on a persistent, predetermined regressor. Stambaugh (1999) considered a common return forecasting environment taking the form

$$r_{s,t+1} = \alpha + \beta x_t + \eta_{t+1} \tag{2.16}$$

$$x_{t+1} = \theta + \phi x_t + \xi_{t+1}, \tag{2.17}$$

where x_t is the persistent regressor, assumed to follow the first-order autoregressive process given in (2.17).[6] Recall the result from classical OLS that the coefficient β will not be unbiased unless η_{t+1} is uncorrelated with x_t at all leads and lags. For most forecasting applications in finance, x_t is a variable like the dividend-price ratio, which is positively serially correlated and whose innovation ξ_{t+1} is correlated with the innovation η_{t+1} in returns.

Observe that if x_t is the dividend-price ratio, ξ_{t+1} is mechanically negatively correlated with the innovation η_{t+1} in returns. This occurs because dividends are smoother than stock prices. Thus, an increase in stock prices is typically accompanied by a less than proportional increase in dividends so that an increase in stock prices drives down the dividend-price ratio while at the same time driving up the current-period stock return, thereby generating a negative correlation between ξ_{t+1} and η_{t+1}. A negative correlation between ξ_{t+1} and η_{t+1}, when it is accompanied by positive serial correlation in x_t (i.e., $\phi > 0$), implies that x_t is correlated with past values of η_t, even though it is uncorrelated with contemporaneous or future values. It follows that forecasting variables such as the dividend-price ratio are merely predetermined and not exogenous.

Stambaugh (1999) points out that, under these circumstances, the predictor coefficient β will be biased upward in finite samples, with the degree of bias increasing in the persistence, ϕ, of the forecasting variable. To derive the exact finite-sample distribution of

[6] Mankiw and Shapiro (1986) studied the econometric problems posed by (2.16) and (2.17) for general x_t in a simulation study. Elliott and Stock (1994) studied statistical inference for such a system when the autoregressive root of x_t is close to unity.

β, Stambaugh assumes that the vector $(\eta_{t+1}, \xi_{t+1})'$ is normally distributed, independently across t, with mean zero and constant covariance matrix.

These results suggest that regression coefficients of the type reported in Table 11.2 maybe biased up in finite samples as long as the return innovation covaries with the innovation in the forecasting variable. Indeed, using the dividend-price ratio as a predictive variable, Stambaugh finds that the exact finite-sample distribution of the estimates implies a one-sided p-value of 0.15 for β when NYSE returns are regressed on the lagged dividend-price ratio from 1952–1996. Other researchers have also conducted explicit finite sample tests and concluded that evidence of predictability using the dividend-price ratio may be weaker than previously thought. Nelson and Kim (1993) use bootstrap and randomization simulations for finite-sample inference. Ferson et al. (2003) show that, when expected returns are very persistent, a particular regressor can spuriously forecast returns if that regressor is also very persistent.

Nevertheless, other researchers have directly addressed these problems and find that evidence of long-horizon predictability remains. For example, Lewellen (2004) shows that the evidence favoring predictability by the dividend-yield (and other financial ratios) increases dramatically if one explicitly accounts for the persistence of the dividend yield. In particular, Lewellen finds evidence of return predictability by financial ratios if one is willing to rule out an explosive root in the ratios. Campbell and Yogo (2002) use the results from near-unit root econometrics to develop a test of return predictability that is asymptotically valid under general assumptions on the dynamics of the predictor variable (i.e., a finite-order autoregression with the largest root less than, equal to, or greater than one) and on the distribution of the innovations (i.e., homo or heteroskedastic). Using this test that is robust to the persistence problem, they find that the earnings-price ratio reliably predicts returns at all frequencies in the sample period 1926–2002 and the dividend-price ratio predicts returns at annual frequency.

The forecasting power of variables other than the dividend-earnings ratio and the dividend-price ratio also appears robust to alternative procedures designed to address the difficulties with using persistent, predetermined regressors. Lettau and Ludvigson (2001a, 2005) test return forecastability by $\widehat{cay}_t$ using a bootstrap procedure to assess the sampling variability of key forecasting statistics in samples of the size currently available. The methodology is based on bootstrap simulations carried out under the null of no predictability of excess returns. Artificial sequences of excess returns are generated by drawing randomly (with replacement) from the sample residual pairs. The results of these tests show that the estimated regression coefficient and R^2 statistics lie outside of the 95% confidence interval based on the empirical distribution. In most cases, they lie outside of the 99% confidence interval. Ludvigson and Ng (2007) conduct a similar small-sample bootstrap excercise for $\widehat{F}_{1t}$ and $\widehat{F}_{2t}$. The statistical relation of these factors to future returns is strong, even accounting for the small-sample distribution of standard test statistics.

A potential concern with such bootstrap procedures arises when the predictor variable is so highly persistent that local-to-unity asymptotics must be applied to assess the sampling variability of estimated regression coefficients and R^2 statistics. Stock and Watson (1996) show that, in this case, the standard bootstrap is asymptotically invalid. This will occur when the predictor variable exhibits sufficiently "small" deviations from an exact unit root. For practical applications, these results raise the question of how small is small?[7] There are several reasons to think that at least some predictor variables commonly used deviate sufficiently from a unit root to avoid these complications. For example, $\widehat{cay}_t$ (with an AR coefficient around 0.85) and the relative t-bill rate are less persistent and less correlated with innovations to returns than valuation ratios such as the price-dividend ratio. Ferson et al. (2003) find that regressors with autocorrelation coefficients on the order of 0.85 generally have well-behaved t-statistics and R^2 statistics. Moreover, other simulation studies suggest that even financial variables far more persistent than these may be stationary enough to validate standard bootstrap procedures. Clark and West (2006, 2007) conduct Monte Carlo simulations of simple bivariate data-generating processes to evaluate the finite-sample size and power of out-of-sample forecasting procedures that compare prediction mean square error (PMSE) across models. One data-generating process they study is designed to reflect asset pricing applications and is calibrated to monthly excess returns on the S&P 500 and the dividend-price ratio. The dividend-price ratio is modeled as having a first-order autoregressive coefficient of 0.95, and its correlation with return innovations is calibrated to match the data. These studies find that tests of equal forecast accuracy based on a comparison of PMSEs are roughly correctly sized, suggesting that the bootstrap is quite reliable in samples of the size currently encountered, even for regressions involving very persistent (but stationary) financial predictor variables.

2.5.3. Problems with Interpreting Long-Horizon Forecasts

The evidence on long-horizon return predictability in Table 11.2 above suggests that returns become more forecastable as the horizon extends. In response to such evidence, Boudoukh et al. (2008) point out that, even under the null of no return predictability, long-horizon R^2 statistics and coefficients from direct long-horizon regressions will rise monotonically with the horizon, as long as the predictor variable has some persistence. These findings imply that long-horizon returns could, in principle, appear more forecastable than short-horizon returns even if they are no more forecastable.

In principle, this phenomenon is attributable both to the small sample bias emphasized by Stambaugh (1999), as well as to the use of overlapping return data emphasized by

[7] Campbell and Yogo (2002) address this question by developing a pretest based on the confidence interval for the largest autoregressive root of the predictor variable. If the confidence interval indicates that the predictor variable is sufficiently stationary, then for a given level of correlation between the innovations to returns and the predictor variable, they show that one can proceed with inference based on the conventional t-test with conventional critical values rather than basing inference on local-to-unity asymptotics.

Valkanov (2003). In practice, however, Boudoukh et al. (2008) find that, for plausible data-generating processes, most of the observed monotonicity is attributable not to small sample biases but rather to the use of overlapping return data interacting with persistence of regressor. As noted above, problems with overlapping return data can be avoided by using VARs to impute long-horizon statistics rather than using overlapping return data directly. Recalling the results reported in Table 11.3, we observe that the implied long-horizon R^2 statistics and regression coefficients from the VAR methodology rise with the return forecast horizon in a manner similar to that found when overlapping return data is directly utilized. Thus, the VAR evidence lends support to the hypothesis that long-horizon returns really are more predictable than short-horizon returns despite the ambiguity on this question that arises in direct long-horizon regressions.

2.6. Conceptual Issues with Forecasting Returns

This section discusses several conceptual issues that arise when evaluating the evidence for time variation in expected excess stock returns.

2.6.1. Expected Returns versus Average Realized Returns

The literature discussed above measures movements in ex-ante expected returns as forecastable variation in excess returns, with variables such as the dividend-price ratio, short-term interest rates, term spreads, and cay_t as forecasting variables. For example, the dynamic Gordon growth model (2.1) motivates the use of the dividend-price ratio as a forecasting variable for future returns, and therefore as a measure of ex-ante expected returns. Although we have emphasized this approach as a motivation for estimating time variation in conditional expected returns over horizons ranging from quarterly to several years, other researchers have used the framework to estimate the very long-run-expected market return, which converges to an unconditional expected market return (e.g., Fama and French, 2002). To estimate the unconditional expected market return, it is commonplace to use the sample average ex-post return on a broad portfolio of stocks. But as Fama and French (2002) point out, this procedure can be misleading when expected returns (as measured, e.g., by the dividend-price ratio) are declining for an extended period of time. In this scenario, declining expected returns lead to persistently lower dividend-price ratios, but the sample average ex-post returns over the same period are necessarily high as a result of rising stock prices. In this case, the sample average return can be higher than usual even though expected future return is declining. Fama and French use the Gordon growth model to argue that the period since 1950 is one such episode. Campello et al. (2005) make a similar point for firm-specific measures of expected equity returns. These papers underscore the need to distinguish between average realized returns and ex-ante expected returns when estimating very long-run-expected market returns.

2.6.2. Cointegration and Return Forecasting

Consider using the log dividend-price ratio as a predictor of excess returns. Studies that conduct such an analysis typically assume, either explicitly or implicitly, that the ratio of prices to dividends, P_t/D_t, is covariance stationary. This assumption implies that the log price-dividend ratio, $p_t - d_t$, is also covariance stationary and that p_t and d_t are cointegrated with cointegrating vector $(1, -1)'$.

Some researchers object to the description of the price-dividend ratio as covariance stationary because the statistical behavior of the variable over our sample appears subject to structural change. Indeed, there is evidence of a structural break in the mean price-dividend ratio (e.g., Lettau et al., 2008; Lettau and Van Nieuwerburgh, 2007). Whether statistical evidence of structural change implies that a series is nonstationary is unclear. The issue of identifying structural breaks in cointegrated relationships with finite samples is a subtle and tricky one. Long data spans are often required to obtain consistent estimates of cointegrating coefficients, yet instability tests require those parameters to be estimated by splitting an already finite sample into even smaller subsamples. This requirement has led to a well-known criticism of the entire structural break approach, namely that the data-driven specification searches inherent in the methodology can bias inferences dramatically toward finding breaks where none exist (Leamer, 1978; Lo and MacKinlay, 1990). Thus, a very persistent covariance-stationary series can appear, in a finite sample, as one subject to multiple structural breaks. We discuss structural change further below.

Whether or not structural breaks are evidence of nonstationarity, it seems reasonable to rule out at least one form of nonstationarity, namely the nonstationarity exhibited by prices that wander arbitrarily far from measures of fundamental value. Valuation ratios should not be explosive. For the purposes of this subsection, we discuss conceptual issues that arise when dividends and prices are cointegrated, and the price-dividend ratio is nonexplosive and covariance stationary.

Cointegration implies that movements in $p_t - d_t$ must forecast future dividend growth, future returns, or some combination of the two. Notice that this statement is not conditional on the accuracy of the approximation in (2.1). Instead, it follows on purely statistical grounds from the presumption of cointegration. An important cointegration theorem is the *Granger representation theorem* (GRT). This theorem states that if a system of variables is cointegrated in a given sample, the growth rates in at least one of the variables involved in the cointegrated system must be forecastable by the cointegrating residual, in this case $p_t - d_t$. That is, an error-correction representation exists. It follows that the Granger representation theorem states that variation in $p_t - d_t$ must be related to variation in future dividend growth, future returns, or both.[8]

[8] If dividends and prices are cointegrated with cointegrating vector $(1, -1)$, the GRT states that $d_t - p_t$ must forecast either Δp_t, or Δd_t, the log difference of dividend growth. Using the approximation, $r_{st} \approx \Delta p_t$, it follows that $d_t - p_t$ must forecast either Δd_t or r_{st} up to a first-order approximation.

These considerations imply that expected returns cannot be constant if the price-dividend ratio varies unless expected dividend growth rates vary. In the data, the dividend-price ratio is volatile, having a quarterly standard deviation of 0.34. Thus, evidence that expected returns are constant requires not merely that returns be *unforecastable* by $d_t - p_t$ but also that dividend growth be strongly *forecastable* by $d_t - p_t$, forecastable enough to account for the observed variability in $d_t - p_t$. Although some statistical tests suggest that $d_t - p_t$ is a weak and/or unstable predictor of returns, the evidence that $d_t - p_t$ predicts dividend growth in postwar U.S. data is even weaker (Campbell, 1991; Campbell and Shiller, 2001; Cochrane, 1991b, 1994, 1997). Cochrane (2008) formalizes this intuition and shows that the absence of dividend growth predictability in the data provides much stronger evidence of return predictability than do the results from an unrestricted regression of returns on lagged values of the dividend-price ratio. These findings suggest that returns are forecastable by the dividend-price ratio, even though some statistical tests fail to confirm that forecastability.

It is possible that expected dividend growth and expected returns are *both* time-varying, and that a positive correlation between the two makes it difficult to identify variation in either using the dividend-price ratio. Equation (2.1) shows that movements in expected dividend growth that are positively correlated with movements in expected returns should have offsetting affects on the dividend-price ratio. Such movements will not necessarily have offsetting affects on cay_t because it is not a function of both expected returns and expected dividend growth. Lettau and Ludvigson (2005) investigate this possibility using data on aggregate consumption and dividend payments from aggregate (human and nonhuman) wealth. Using either cay_t or a proxy for the log consumption-dividend ratio, denoted cdy_t, they find that stock market dividend growth is strongly predictable and that the dividend forecasts are positively related to changing forecasts of excess stock returns. An implication of these findings is that both expected returns and expected dividend growth vary more than what can be revealed using the dividend-price ratio alone.

The reasoning on cointegration applied above to the dividend-price ratio also applies to the consumption-wealth variable, cay_t. Since c, a, and y are cointegrated, it follows that the cointegrating residual must forecast future consumption growth, future returns to asset wealth (wealth growth), or future labor income growth. Lettau and Ludvigson (2001a, 2004) find no evidence that $\widehat{\text{cay}}_t$ has any forecasting power for consumption growth or labor income growth, at any future horizon. Since there is no evidence that consumption or labor income growth are forecastable by $\widehat{\text{cay}}_t$, $\widehat{\text{cay}}_t$ must forecast some component of the growth in a_t, and indeed the empirical evidence is strongly supportive of this hypothesis. The forecastable component is found to be the excess return on the aggregate stock market; $\widehat{\text{cay}}_t$ has no forecasting power for the growth in nonstock wealth (Lettau and Ludvigson, 2004). Since the growth in total asset wealth, Δa_t, is highly correlated with the return on the aggregate stock market (displaying a correlation with the return on the CRSP value-weighted index of over 88% in quarterly data), it is not hard to understand why $\widehat{cay}_t$ forecasts stock returns.

When parameters of a common long-run trend must be estimated, as for $\widehat{cay}_t$, long samples of data may be required to estimate them consistently. How long such samples must be will depend on the data-generating process, something that can be assessed in a particular application with Monte Carlo analysis. However, once a sufficiently large span of data is available, the cointegrating parameters may be treated as known in subsequent estimation because they converge at a rate proportional to the sample size T rather than the usual $\sqrt{T}$ rate. Moreover, cointegration theory implies that once we know the cointegrating parameters, the resulting cointegrating residual must forecast at least one of the growth rates of the variables in the cointegrated system.

2.6.3. Use of Macroeconomic Data in Empirical Asset Pricing

A separate set of conceptual issues arises in using macroeconomic variables, such as $\widehat{cay}_t$, to forecast returns. Unlike financial data, macroeconomic data are not available in real time. When thinking about this issue, it is essential to distinguish two questions about return forecastability. The first question – the question of concern in this paper – is "are expected excess returns time-varying?" The second question, of interest to practitioners, is "can the predictability of returns be statistically detected in real time?"

All macroeconomic data undergo revisions. For example, data from the national income and product accounts (NIPA) are released three times, first as an initial estimate, then as a preliminary estimate, and last as a "final" estimate. We put quotes around the word final because even this last estimate is subsequently revised. Every year in July or August, there are revisions made to the entire NIPA account, and there are periodic benchmark revisions that occur on an irregular schedule. These subsequent revisions are likely to be far less significant that the initial two, however.

Delays in data release and data revision are not a reason to ignore macroeconomic data but instead are a reason to apply macroeconomic data to research questions for which historical data are relevant. Data revisions can be a concern if the goal is to assess predictability in real time but are not a concern for explaining and interpreting the historical data.[9] For example, in the theoretical framework of Lettau and Ludvigson (2001a) discussed above, if expected returns vary over time (for any reason), the logic of a budget constraint implies that $\widehat{cay}_t$ should forecast returns, consumption growth, or labor income growth, or some combination of all three. In a full insurance equilibrium where individual consumptions are proportional, agents not only know their own consumption, wealth and income (and their wealth shares), they also know their aggregate

[9]Issues of data release and data revision are obviously less of a issue for forecasting long-horizon returns than they are for forecasting short-horizon returns.

counterparts, even though the econometrician does not. In this case, evaluation of the model implications should use the fully revised, historical data series, since those series come closest to matching what the representative agent observes.

2.6.4. When Is "Look-Ahead Bias" a Concern?

One question that arises in assessing the predictive power of macroeconomic variables such as $\widehat{\mathrm{cay}}_t$ is whether estimating the cointegrating coefficients over the full sample in a first-stage regression induces a "look ahead bias" into the forecasting regressions. In thinking about this question, it is important to keep in mind that when samples are sufficiently long, cointegrating coefficients can be estimated superconsistently and treated as known in subsequent estimation. Thus, there can be no look-ahead bias when a sufficiently long sample of data is available to estimate the parameters of a cointegrating relation.

A Monte Carlo study can be used to assess the rate at which cointegrating parameter estimates converge to their true values. Our own Monte Carlo analyses suggest that samples of the size currently available are large enough to obtain consistent estimates of the cointegrating parameters in $\widehat{\mathrm{cay}}_t$. In a cointegrated setting, the question of look-ahead bias is therefore one of data availability.

Look-ahead bias could be a concern if the primary research goal is to ask whether a practitioner, operating in early part of our sample without access to the data sample currently available, could have exploited the forecasting power of an estimated cointegrating residual such as $\widehat{\mathrm{cay}}_t$. Out-of-sample or subsample analysis is often used to assess questions of this nature. A difficulty with these procedures, however, is that the subsample analysis inherent in out-of-sample forecasting tests entails a loss of information, making out-of-sample tests substantially less powerful than in-sample forecasting tests (Inoue and Kilian, 2004). This loss of power means that out-of-sample (and subsample) analyses can fail to reveal true forecasting power that even a practitioner could have had in real time.

With these considerations in mind, Lettau and Ludvigson (2005) provide an alternative approach to assessing the forecasting power of $\widehat{\mathrm{cay}}_t$. The approach eliminates the need to estimate cointegration parameters using the full sample in a first-stage regression but at the same time avoids the power problems inherent in out-of-sample and subsample analyses.

Consider single-equation, multivariate regressions taking the form

$$z_{t+H,H} = a + b_1 c_t + b_2 a_t + b_3 y_t + u_{t+H,H}, \tag{2.18}$$

where $a, b_1, b_2,$ and b_3 are regression coefficients to be estimated. The dependent variable $z_{t+h,h}$ is either the H period excess return on the CRSP value-weighted index or, in Lettau and Ludvigson (2005), the H period dividend growth rate on the CRSP value-weighted index. Rather than estimating the cointegration relation among $c_t, a_t,$ and y_t in a first-stage regression and then using the cointegration residual as the single right-hand side variable, the regression (2.18) uses the multiple variables involved in the cointegration relation as regressors directly. If there is a relation between the left-hand side variable to be forecast and some stationary linear combination of the regressors c_t, a_t, and y_t, the regression can freely estimate the nonzero coefficients b_1, b_2, and b_3, which generate such a relation. If we maintain the hypothesis that the left-side variable is stationary while the right-hand side variables are $I(1)$, then under the null hypothesis that $(c_t, a_t, y_t)'$ has a single cointegration relation, it is straightforward to show that the limiting distributions for b_1, b_2, and b_3 will be standard, implying that the forecasting regression (2.18) will produce valid R^2 and t-statistics.[10] Because this procedure does not require any first-stage estimation of cointegration parameters, it is clear that the forecasting regression (2.18), in particular its coefficients and R^2 statistics, cannot be influenced by any look-ahead bias.

Lettau and Ludvigson (2005) report regression results for excess returns and dividend growth from an estimation of (2.18). The results are similar to those obtained using $\widehat{\text{cay}}_t$ as forecasting variables. The individual coefficients on each regressor are strongly statistically significant as predictive variables for excess returns and dividend growth, and the R^2 statistics indicate that the regressors jointly explain about the same fraction of variation in future returns and future dividend growth explained by the individual regressor $\widehat{\text{cay}}_t$. For example, in the data of Lettau and Ludvigson (2005), the multivariate regression with c_t, a_t, and y_t explains about 26% of one year ahead excess returns, whereas $\widehat{\text{cay}}_t$ explains 25%. These results do not support the conclusion that $\widehat{\text{cay}}_t$ has forecasting power merely because the cointegrating coefficients have been obtained in a preestimation using data from the whole sample period.

Another approach to the issue of look-ahead bias is to mimic the estimation strategy of the real-time practitioner by performing an out-of-sample investigation. In such an investigation, the parameters in $\widehat{\text{cay}}_t$ are reestimated every period using only information that would have been available at the time of the forecast, as in section V of Lettau and Ludvigson (2001a). We should expect to find the statistical predictive power of $\widehat{\text{cay}}_t$ to be weakened by such a recursive procedure since a large number of observations required to obtain consistent estimates of the cointegrating parameters must be discarded

[10] Inference on b_1, b_2, and b_3 can be accomplished by rewriting (2.18) so that the hypotheses to be tested are written as a restrictions on $I(0)$ variables (Sims et al., 1990). For example, the hypothesis $b_1 = 0$ can be tested by rewriting (2.18) as

$$\begin{aligned} z_{t+H,H} &= a + b_1 \left[c_t - \omega a_t - (1-\omega)\, y_t\right] + \left[b_2 + b_1 \omega\right] a_t + \left[b_3 + b_1 (1-\omega)\right] y_t + u_{t+H,H} \\ &= a + b_1 \left[\text{cay}_t\right] + \left[b_2 + b_1 \omega\right] a_t + \left[b_3 + b_1 (1-\omega)\right] y_t + u_{t+H,H}. \end{aligned}$$

It follows that the OLS estimate of b_1 has a limiting distribution given by

$$\sqrt{T}\left(\widehat{b}_1 - b_1\right) \longrightarrow N\left(0, \frac{\sigma_u^2}{T \sum_{t=1}^{T} \left(\text{cay}_t - \overline{\text{cay}}\right)^2}\right),$$

where σ_u^2 denotes the variance of $u_{t+H,H}$, and $\overline{\text{cay}}$ is the sample mean of cay_t. These may be evaluated by using the full sample estimates, $\widehat{\text{cay}}_t$. A similar rearrangement can be used to test hypotheses about b_2 and b_3. Note that the full sample estimates of the cointegration coefficients are only required to do inference about the forecasting excercise, they do not affect the forecasting excercise itself.

in the process. Nevertheless, the results of such an excercise will take into account the noisiness in these estimates over short subsamples, and, we hope, tell us something about whether a practitioner operating over our sample could have detected predictability in real time. Both Lettau and Ludvigson (2001a) and Guo (2006) find evidence of stock return predictability in out-of-sample tests, using cay and/or cay and stock market volatility as predictive variables. We discuss out-of-sample forecasts further below.

2.6.5. Structural Change

A related issue is that there may be long-run "permanent" shifts in the mean of the dividend-price ratio, or in the cointegrating coefficients or in the mean of $\widehat{\text{cay}}_t$. Lettau et al. (2008) and Lettau and Van Nieuwerburgh (2007) document evidence of a structural break in the mean of the dividend-price ratio for the aggregate stock market, which exhibits a marked shift to a lower value in the mid-1990s. Note, however, that any hypothesis about structural change in the parameters of the common trend among c, a, and y must be reconciled with the evidence that these variables appear cointegrated over the full postwar sample.

Even if there were little evidence of structural change in current data, it is possible that future data will exhibit structural change. Structural change could be caused by persistent shifts in tastes or technology that coincide with forward looking behavior. If infrequent regime shifts are present, agents in the model may be required to learn about underlying parameters, a phenomenon that can, by itself, have an important impact on the equilibrium risk-return relation (Hansen, 2007; Lettau et al., 2008). If there are such breaks in the data, altering the framework discussed above to explicitly model the underlying probability structure governing any changing parameters may allow the researcher to do even better at predicting returns since estimates of the cointegrating residual could then be made conditional on the regime.

An important challenge in developing ideas about structural change, however, will be to derive an economic model of changes in regime that are caused by factors other than the raw data we are currently trying to understand. Such a model is necessary to both explain any past regime shifts and to predict potential future regime shifts. Unfortunately, such an endeavor is far from trivial since we are likely to observe, at most, only a handful of regimes in a given sample. Moreover, it is not interesting merely to document breaks *ex-post* using change-point methods since such methods assume these shifts are deterministic and provide no guidance about when they might occur in the future. Finally, one also has to grapple with the well-known criticism of the entire structural break approach, namely that the data-driven specification searches inherent in these methodologies can bias inferences dramatically toward finding breaks where none exist (see Leamer, 1978; Lo and MacKinlay, 1990).

This last critique may be particularly relevant today, only a short time after the most extraordinary bull market in U.S. stock market history. This period might represent a regime shift, or it could simply be a very unusual period, perhaps the most unusual ever. The most recent data available suggests that at least a part of this period was simply unusual: the market eventually retreated, and the correction in asset values largely restored $\widehat{cay}_t$ returned to its long-run mean subsequent to the market declines in 2000 (see Lettau and Ludvigson, 2004).

But note that questions about the stability of cointegrating coefficients cannot be addressed by performing rolling regressions, recursive regressions, subsample analysis, or any other methodology in which the cointegrating parameters are estimated over short samples of data. Again, this follows because a large span of data may be required to estimate the parameters of a common trend consistently. Without consistent estimates, the estimated cointegrating residual cannot be expected to forecast returns or the growth rates of any of the other variables in the system since such forecastability is predicated on identification of the true cointegrating parameters. This observation shows both a blessing and a curse of econometric forecasts based on estimates of common stochastic trends. On the one hand, these methodologies offer a blessing by providing predictor variables that can be treated as known in subsequent forecasting analysis when samples are sufficiently long. On the other hand, longer samples of data may be more prone to regime changes, which, if present, may add considerably to the sampling uncertainty in the predictive relationship between the estimated cointegrating residual and future financial indicators. Such a trade-off must be weighed on a case-by-case basis, pending a careful examination of the data-generating process.

2.7. In-Sample versus Out-of-Sample Prediction

So far, we have been discussing evidence on time-varying expected returns in the context of in-sample predictability. A common perception in applied work is that out-of-sample prediction is more reliable than in-sample prediction, and that in-sample tests are more prone to uncovering spurious predictability than are out-of-sample tests. Goyal and Welch (2007), e.g., investigate a large number of predictor variables for stock market returns and conclude that many of them perform poorly in out-of sample tests. They recommend that practitioners abandon attempts to forecast returns and instead use the historical mean as a benchmark.

These conclusions raise several important questions. First, is there any evidence that popular indicators that have displayed in-sample predictive power have statistically significant out-of-sample predictive power? Second, why might an in-sample test show evidence of predictability while an out-of-sample test does not? Third, what is the motivation for undertaking out-of-sample tests, given evidence for in-sample predictability? We address each question in turn.

Are stock returns predictable out-of-sample? The results in Goyal and Welch (2007) suggest that many popular forecasting variables have little ability to predict stock returns out-of-sample. They show that the out-of-sample mean-square prediction error is higher when using many predictor variables than when using the historical mean to forecast excess returns. Yet even the results in Goyal and Welch (2007) show that these conclusions do not apply to all forecasting variables, return horizons, or forecast subsamples. On the contrary, many economic indicators have displayed out-of-sample forecasting power for excess stock market returns across a range of studies. For example, Goyal and Welch (2007) find that, relative to forecasts based on the historical mean, reductions in root-mean-square forecast error are obtained in out-of-sample forecasts of stock returns by a measure of $\widehat{\text{cay}}_t$, a measure of the investment-capital ratio, and a measure of corporate issuance activity. Campbell and Thompson (2005) find similar results in out-of-sample forecasts by these variables as well as for the earnings-price ratio, a Treasury bill rate, a term-spread, and a measure of inflation. Lettau and Ludvigson (2001a) and Guo (2006) find that $\widehat{\text{cay}}_t$ predicts stock returns out-of-sample even when the parameters in $\widehat{\text{cay}}_t$ are reestimated every period using only information that would have been available at the time of the forecast. Similar findings are reported in Rapach and Wohar (2002). Eliasz (2005) uses the best median unbiased estimator in the presence of nearly-integrated regressors and finds that the dividend-price ratio forecasts excess stock returns out-of-sample even in recent data. Finally, Ludvigson and Ng (2007) show that the risk premium and volatility factors $\widehat{F}_{1t}$ and $\widehat{F}_{2t}$, examined above, exhibit remarkably stable and strongly statistically significant out-of-sample forecasting power for quarterly excess stock market returns.

Thus, in answer to the first question raised above, stock returns do appear to be predictable out-of-sample. But the evidence for out-of-sample predictive power depends on the choice of predictor variable, the sample period, the forecast subsample, and the return horizon. The sensitivity of the results to these factors naturally leads to the second question posed above, namely why in-sample results can differ from out-of-sample results.

Why do in-sample results sometimes differ from out-of-sample results? One possible reason for this discrepancy is the bias-variance trade-off emphasized by Inoue and Kilian (2004), Campbell and Thompson (2005), and Cochrane (2008). To fix ideas, consider the case where returns are predictable in a linear regression by some variable x_t so that the predictive regression,

$$r_{s,t+1} = \mu + \beta x_t + u_{t+1}, \tag{2.19}$$

holds with $\beta \neq 0$. In this case, the historical mean μ is a biased predictor of returns. This bias contributes to a higher mean-square prediction error for forecasts based solely on the historical mean relative to a forecast that exploits information on x_t. But estimation error in β tends to increase the variance of the return forecast, which contributes to a greater mean-square forecast error for predictive regressions that use x_t relative to predictions based solely on the historical mean. Thus, the historical mean forecast is biased but has lower variance, while forecasts based on x_t are unbiased but have greater variance. Whether the overall forecast error from estimating (2.19) is higher or lower than that generated by the historical mean forecast depends on how large the reduction in bias is relative to the increase in variance.

Note that whatever the level of bias in the historical mean forecast, the variance of the forecast error is greater for an out-of-sample forecast than for an in-sample forecast. Since an in-sample forecast uses all available information in the given sample, it should produce lower estimation error in β and less variance in the return forecast relative to an out-of-sample procedure where β is estimated over subsamples of the data, and information is discarded. It follows that a powerful in-sample test could correctly detect $\beta \neq 0$, even though an out-of-sample test indicates the historical mean forecast is superior. This reasoning shows that poor out-of-sample results *per se* cannot be taken as evidence against predictability. But they do imply that there may be too little information in small samples to accurately estimate β and improve the return forecast. Examples of this form can be found in simulation studies by Campbell and Thompson (2005) and Cochrane (2008).

A formalization of this intuition is provided in recent theoretical work by Inoue and Kilian (2004), where both environments subject to data mining and environments free of data mining are considered. They demonstrate that in-sample and out-of-sample tests of predictability are asymptotically equally reliable under the null of no predictability.[11] Given that in-sample tests display no greater size distortions than do out-of-sample tests, the choice between in-sample and out-of-sample prediction is reduced to the question of which test is more powerful. Any out-of-sample analysis based on sample splitting involves a loss of information and hence lower power in small samples. Inoue and Kilian find that for most out-of-sample design choices, in-sample tests are more powerful than out-of-sample tests even asymptotically. They conclude that, in many cases, an out-of-sample test may fail to detect predictability that exists in population, whereas the in-sample test correctly will detect it.

One way of addressing the power problems of out-of-sample tests is to develop more powerful statistics for assessing out-of-sample predictability. McCracken (1999) and Clark and McCracken (2001) develop several out-of-sample test statistics that are almost as powerful as in-sample test statistics.

Campbell and Thompson (2005) show that poor out-of-sample performance can also come from bad luck in a particular sample. Suppose that $\beta \neq 0$ is known so that there is no estimation error contributing to the forecast variance. Returns are forecastable and the forecasting relation is known with certainty. Campbell and Thompson show that, in a large number of such cases, the historical mean can display lower mean forecast error

[11] A test is defined to be unreliable if its effective size exceeds its nominal size.

in out-of-sample tests than a model that exploits information on x_t (with known β), simply because of sampling uncertainty. Even if stock returns are genuinely predictable by some variable x_t, it can be associated with poor out-of-sample forecasts in a finite sample.

What is the motivation for undertaking out-of-sample tests? These findings bring us to the third question posed above, namely what is the motivation for undertaking out-of-sample tests, given evidence for in-sample predictability? As we have seen, poor out-of-sample performance is not necessarily evidence against predictability. This suggests that if one is interested only in whether $\beta \neq 0$, the researcher should use the most powerful test available, typically an in-sample regression. In this chapter, we are concerned with the historical behavior of the risk-return relation. For this purpose, there is no reason to throw away information when constructing estimates of the conditional mean and conditional variance of stock returns, as required by out-of-sample forecasts.

So why are researchers motivated to conduct out-of-sample tests? Several possible reasons appear in the extant literature, given either implicitly or explicitly.

1. *To mimic the behavior of a real-world investor.* It is often argued that recursive or rolling out-of-sample forecasts mimic the behavior of a practitioner in real time. Although this argument may at first appear axiomatic, upon closer inspection, it is clear that much hinges on the researcher's view of how practitioners actually behave. For example, Campbell and Thompson (2005) argue that real-world investors would not naively run the unrestricted forecasting regressions that form the basis of out-of-sample tests conducted in the literature. Instead, they would impose restrictions on the regression coefficient β to require nonnegative estimates of the risk premium. They show that when such restrictions are imposed, the evidence for out-of-sample predictability is significantly stronger than when they are not imposed. These findings underscore the important role of behavioral assumptions in the outcome of out-of-sample forecast tests.
2. *As protection against overfitting/data mining.* Researchers often use the terms "overfitting" and "data mining" synonymously. Moreover, it is commonly presumed that out-of-sample tests can provide better protection against data mining than in-sample tests. Whether this presumption is valid, however, depends on how the tests are implemented. In much current practice, out-of-sample tests are routinely implemented upon the completion of a statistically significant in-sample finding. In this case, out-of-sample procedures offer no more protection from data mining than do in-sample procedures. The problem is that once the out-of-sample exercise is completed, the researcher knows exactly the out-of-sample performance of the forecasting variable and is free to experiment with alternative predictors until she finds one that reduces the mean-square forecast error. The irony here is that the stated motivation for routinely implementing out-of-sample tests along-side in-sample tests is the desire to guard

against data mining. Yet these observations suggest that if data mining is a concern, we should be equally skeptical of in-sample and out-of-sample tests.

3. *To detect structural change or model instability.* It is sometimes argued that out-of-sample tests provide one way of assessing whether there has been structural change in a forecasting relation. For example, this argument motivates the investigation of Goyal and Welch (2007), who write that out-of-sample tests "help determine whether a model is stable and well specified, or changing over time, either suddenly or gradually." Indeed, Clark and McCracken (2005) study the effects of structural breaks on the power of predictability tests and find that if predictability holds in part of the sample, but is subject to structural change, out-of-sample tests may suggest no predictability, while in-sample tests reject the null of no predictability. Similarly, Lettau and Van Nieuwerburgh (2007) study the behavior of financial ratios such as the price-dividend ratio and conclude that structural breaks in the mean of these ratios can account for the discrepancy between in-sample and out-of-sample forecasting results where these ratios are used as predictor variables. If model stability is the primary concern, however, a simple subsample analysis using in-sample techniques can often address these concerns. Moreover, in the presence of structural change, there are often more powerful ways to do inference than the use of out-of-sample forecasting procedures. Rossi (2005) develops a test of the joint null of no predictability and no parameter instability and shows that it is locally asymptotically more powerful than rolling or recursive out-of-sample tests.

We conclude this section on return predictability with the following summary. There are many statistical issues that make inference about predictability of stock returns challenging. Among these, variables that predict stock returns tend to be highly persistent, only predetermined rather than exogenous, and in some cases subject to structural breaks in their mean values. Moreover, given the persistence of these variables, samples of the size currently available are short, making asymptotic approximations less useful.

Despite these statistical concerns, the preponderance of evidence suggests that stock returns are modestly predictable over longer horizons. Not only is the evidence for predictability in excess stock returns much stronger than that of dividend growth, the volatility of equity market valuation ratios cannot be explained by variation in expected cash-flow measures alone, requiring forecastable variation in returns. Moreover, even the most rigorous statistical tests suggest that stock returns are predictable both in-sample and out-of-sample by some variables over some forecast horizons. At the same time, there is some evidence of instability in the predictive relations. An important question for future research is determining whether and how such forecastability changes over time, and why. For now, we conclude that the numerator in the Sharpe ratio varies and is likely to continue to be an important contributor to volatility in the risk-return trade-off.

3. THE CONDITIONAL VOLATILITY OF STOCK RETURNS AND ITS RELATION TO THE CONDITIONAL MEAN

The denominator of the Sharpe ratio is the conditional standard deviation of excess returns. Although several papers have investigated the empirical determinants of stock market volatility, few have found real macroeconomic conditions to have a quantitatively important impact on conditional volatility. In a classic paper, Schwert (1989) finds that stock market volatility is higher during recessions than at other times, but he also finds that this recession factor plays a small role in explaining the behavior of stock market volatility over time. Thus, existing evidence that stock market risk is related to the real economy is at best mixed. There is even more disagreement among studies that seek to determine the empirical relation between the conditional mean and conditional volatility of stock market returns. We argue below that this disagreement is likely to be attributable, in part, to the relatively small amount of conditioning information typically used in empirical studies.

Empirical studies of the relation between the conditional mean and volatility of stock returns have been based on a variety of estimation methodologies. A popular empirical specification relates conditional means to conditional volatility in regressions taking the form

$$E[R_{s,t+1} - R_{f,t+1} \mid Z_t] = \alpha + \beta \operatorname{Var}(R_{s,t+1} - R_{f,t+1} \mid Z_t), \tag{3.1}$$

where Z_t denotes the information set of investors. With $\alpha = 0$, this empirical specification is a valid representation of the risk-return trade-off in the CAPM.

A common empirical approach for modeling the conditional expectations underlying the conditional mean on the left-hand side of (3.1) is to use projections of excess stock market returns on to predetermined conditioning variables.[12] Empirical studies differ according to what conditioning information is used in projections of excess returns. We discuss this further below.

Conditional volatility may also be measured by a projection onto predetermined conditioning variables, taking the fitted value from this projection as a measure of conditional variance or conditional standard deviation. The dynamic relation between conditional volatility and conditional mean may then be assessed by evaluating the correlation between fitted mean and fitted volatility obtained from these separate projections.

Within the set of papers that measure conditional volatility by a projection onto predetermined conditioning variables, two approaches are common. One is to take the squared residuals from a regression of excess returns onto a predetermined set of conditioning

[12] A less common approach is to infer the conditional expected return from a model. Pastor et al. (2008) use a measure of the implied cost of capital to infer the conditional expected stock return, an approach that delivers a positive risk-return relation in seven countries.

variables and regress them on to the same set of conditioning variables, using the fitted values from this regression as a measure of conditional variance. Notice that while the residuals themselves are uncorrelated by construction with these conditioning variables, the squared residuals need not be. This approach is taken by Campbell (1987) and Breen et al. (1989). These authors find that when short-term nominal interest rates are high, the conditional volatility of stock returns is high while the conditional mean of stock returns is low, implying a negative risk-return trade-off.

Alternatively, volatility can be estimated using high-frequency (e.g., daily) return data to compute the sample standard deviation of returns for longer holding periods. We call such sample standard deviations constructed from high-frequency data a measure *realized volatility*. The realized (ex-post) volatility computed from daily returns is then projected onto time t information variables to obtain a consistent estimate of the conditional variance (or conditional standard deviation) of returns. This approach is taken in French et al. (1987), Schwert (1989), Whitelaw (1994), Ludvigson and Ng (2007). A variation on this procedure is used by Ghysels et al. (2005) who forecast monthly variance computed from daily returns with past daily squared returns.

Yet a third set of papers estimates conditional volatility of excess stock market returns by specifying a parametric conditional volatility model, such as generalized autoregressive conditional heteroskedasticity (GARCH), GARCH-M, exponential GARCH (EGARCH), or stochastic volatility. Examples include French et al. (1987), Bollerslev et al. (1988), Glosten et al. (1993). A variation on this approach is taken by Brandt and Kang (2004), who use a latent vector autoregressive for log mean and log volatility to estimating the relation between the conditional mean and conditional volatility.

The methodologies described above estimate the conditional mean and conditional volatility by presuming particular functional forms for fitted mean and fitted volatility. Instead, the entire conditional distribution of asset returns could be estimated nonparametrically, using a flexible parametric form for the conditional joint density of a vector of asset returns. This approach is taken in Gallant et al. (1990), who use the seminonparametric (SNP) methodology developed in Gallant and Tauchen (1989) to estimate the conditional distribution of a vector of asset payoffs. The conditional mean and conditional volatility can then be inferred from the estimated conditional distributions. The authors use this methodology to compute conditional volatility bounds for stochastic discount factor models. Harrison and Zhang (1999) use the SNP methodology to estimate how the risk-return relation varies over different holding periods.

The advantage of the SNP methodology relative to the reduced-form approach taken here is that it is potentially more efficient because it uses information on the entire conditional distribution of asset returns. A potential disadvantage is that it requires nonparametric estimation of the entire likelihood function, the dimensionality of which can become large, especially as the desired number of return or conditioning series increases. As an alternative, one could estimate the conditional moments themselves using a nonparametric sieve estimator (e.g., Chen and Ludvigson, 2004, 2007). A rigorous comparison of these methodologies and their implications for the dynamic risk-return relation is beyond the scope of this chapter, but is a promising area for future research.

3.1. Updated Evidence on Risk and Return

Following much of the literature above, in this section, we provide summary evidence on the dynamic relationship between the conditional mean excess return and conditional volatility, using fitted values for mean and volatility from reduced-form forecasting regressions. The fitted values provide one way of forming an empirical proxy for the conditional mean and conditional volatility of stock returns and thereby investigating the time-series behavior of their ratio over time. Most applications of this procedure, however, are subject to a number of important criticisms that relate to the relatively small amount of conditioning information that is typically used to model the conditional mean and conditional volatility of excess stock market returns. Indeed, we argue that the disagreement in the empirical literature on the risk-return relation is likely to be attributable, in large part, to the relatively small amount of conditioning information typically used. We make this argument for several reasons.

First, the conditional expectations underlying the conditional mean and conditional volatility are typically measured as projections onto predetermined conditioning variables. But as Harvey (2001) points out, the decision of *which* predetermined conditioning variables to be used in the econometric analysis can influence the estimated risk-return relation. In practice, researchers are forced to choose among a few conditioning variables because conventional statistical analyses are quickly overwhelmed by degrees-of-freedom problems as the number rises. Such practical constraints introduce an element of arbitrariness into the econometric modeling of expectations and may lead to omitted-information estimation bias since a small number of conditioning variables is unlikely to span the information sets of financial market participants. If investors have information not reflected in the chosen conditioning variables used to model market expectations, measures of conditional mean and conditional volatility will be misspecified and possibly highly misleading.

Second, the estimated relation between the conditional mean and conditional volatility of excess returns often depends on the parametric model of volatility, e.g., GARCH, GARCH-M, EGARCH, stochastic volatility, or kernel density estimation (Harvey, 2001). Many of these approaches implicitly use a relatively small amount of information to model conditional volatility.

Third, the reliance on a small number of conditioning variables exposes existing analyses to problems of temporal instability in the underlying forecasting relations being modeled. For example, it is commonplace to model market expectations of future stock returns using the fitted values from a forecasting regression of returns on to a measure of the market-wide dividend-price ratio. A difficulty with this approach is that the predictive power of the dividend-price ratio for excess stock market returns is unstable and exhibits statistical evidence of a structural break in the mid-1990s (Lettau et al., 2008; Lettau and Van Nieuwerburgh, 2007).

In this chapter, we discuss one potential remedy to these problems using the methodology of dynamic factor analysis for large data sets. The discussion follows the application found in Ludvigson and Ng (2007).

Recent research on dynamic factor models finds that the information in a large number of economic time series can be effectively summarized by a relatively small number of estimated factors, affording the opportunity to exploit a much richer information base than what has been possible in prior empirical study of the risk-return relation. In this methodology, "a large number" can mean hundreds or, perhaps, even more than one thousand economic time series. By summarizing the information from a large number of series in a few estimated factors, the researcher can eliminate the arbitrary reliance on a small number of exogenous predictors to estimate the conditional mean and conditional volatility of stock returns, and make feasible the use of a vast set of economic variables that are more likely to span the unobservable information sets of financial market participants. An added benefit of this approach is that the use of common factors can provide robustness against the structural instability that plagues low-dimensional forecasting regressions since such instabilities in individual series often "average out" in the construction of common factors (Stock and Watson, 2002). In the analysis of this chapter, we include two estimated factors in the construction of fitted mean found by Ludvigson and Ng (2007) to be particularly important for forecasting quarterly excess returns on the aggregate stock market.

One study that does not rely on predetermined conditioning variables in the construction of fitted moments is Brandt and Kang (2004) who model the conditional mean and conditional volatility as latent state variables identified only from the history of return data. An important advantage of this approach is that it eliminates the reliance on a few arbitrary conditioning variables in forming estimates of conditional moments. A corresponding disadvantage is that potentially useful information is discarded. Moreover, in practice, latent variables must be modeled as following low-order, linear time-series representations of known probability distribution. For example, Brandt and Kang assume that the conditional mean and conditional volatility evolve according to first-order Gaussian vector autoregressive processes. If the true representation is of higher order, nonlinear, or non-Gaussian, we again face an omitted information problem.

In this chapter, we use realized volatility to model return volatility, motivated by recent findings in the volatility modeling literature. Andersen et al. (2002) and Andersen et al. (2003) argue that nonparametric volatility measures such as realized volatility benefit from being free of tightly parametric functional form assumptions and provide a consistent estimate of ex-post return variability. Realized volatility, in turn, permits the use of traditional time-series methods for modeling and forecasting, making possible the use of estimated common factors from large data sets to measure conditional, or expected, volatility.

To obtain a measure of realized volatility for the excess return on the CRSP-VW index, we use the time-series variation of daily returns:

$$V_t = \sqrt{\sum_{k \in t} (R_{sk} - \overline{R}_s)^2}, \tag{3.2}$$

where V_t is the sample volatility of the market return in period t, R_{sk} is the daily CRSP-VW return minus the implied daily yield on the three-month Treasury bill rate, $\overline{R}_s$ is the mean of R_{sk} over the whole sample, k represents a day, and t is a quarter.

3.1.1. Econometric Framework

As above, for $t = 1, \ldots T$, let $r^e_{s,t+1}$ denote log excess returns in period $t+1$ and let V_{t+1} be an estimate of their volatility. In what follows, we will model returns and volatility both in levels and logs. The objective is to estimate $E_t r^e_{s,t+1}$, the conditional mean of $r^e_{s,t+1}$, and conditional volatility $E_t V_{t+1}$, using information up to time t. We confine ourselves to estimation of $E_t r^e_{s,t+1}$ and $E_t V_{t+1}$ using linear parametric models.

First, consider estimation of the conditional mean $E_t r^e_{s,t+1}$. A standard approach is to select a set of K predetermined conditioning variables at time t, given by the $K \times 1$ vector Z_t, and then estimate

$$r^e_{s,t+1} = \beta' Z_t + \epsilon_{t+1} \tag{3.3}$$

by least squares. The estimated conditional mean is then the fitted value from this regression, $\widehat{r}_{s,t+1|t} = \widehat{\beta}' Z_t$. An important question is whether we can go beyond (3.3) to make use of the substantially more information that is available to market participants. That is, suppose we observe a $T \times N$ panel of data with elements x_{it}, $i = 1, \ldots N, t = 1, \ldots, T$, where the cross-sectional dimension, N, is large, and possibly larger than the number of time periods, T. Observe that there are potentially 2^N possible combinations of predictor variables to consider; letting x_t denote the $N \times 1$ vector of panel observations at time t, estimates from the regression

$$r^e_{s,t+1} = \gamma' x_t + \beta' Z_t + \epsilon_{t+1}$$

quickly run into degrees-of-freedom problems as the dimension of x_t increases, and estimation is not even feasible when $N + K > T$.

To address this problem, Ludvigson and Ng (2007) posit that x_{it} has a factor structure taking the form

$$x_{it} = \lambda_i' f_t + e_{it}, \tag{3.4}$$

where f_t is a $r \times 1$ vector of latent common factors, λ_i is a corresponding $r \times 1$ vector of latent factor loadings, and e_{it} is a vector of idiosyncratic errors. The crucial point here is that $r << N$ so that substantial dimension reduction can be achieved by considering the regression

$$r^e_{s,t+1} = \alpha' \widehat{F}_t + \beta' Z_t + \epsilon_{t+1}, \tag{3.5}$$

where $\widehat{F}_t \subset \widehat{f}_t$, and "hats" denote estimated values. In practice, f_t are estimated by principal components analysis (PCA).[13,14]

Here we estimate regressions of the form (3.5), where the vector $\widehat{F}_t$ contains the "volatility" and "risk-premium" factors formed by Ludvigson and Ng (2007) from a quarterly data set of 172 financial indictors, and the vector Z_t contains a range of predictor variables used in other studies to forecast excess stock returns.

What economic interpretation can be given to these factors? The "volatility factor," denoted $\widehat{F}_{1t}$, is the square of the first common factor of the data set comprised of financial indicators. This factor explains almost 80% of the contemporaneous variation in squared stock market returns; therefore, we consider it a volatility factor. The "risk-premium" factor, denoted $\widehat{F}_{2t}$, is the third common factor from this data set and is highly correlated with a linear combination of three state variables widely used in the empirical asset pricing literature to explain cross-sectional variation in risk premia: the Fama-French factors SMB_t, HML_t, and the market return (Fama and French, 1993). We include these factors here because $\widehat{F}_{1t}$ and $\widehat{F}_{2t}$ have strong forecasting power for quarterly excess stock market returns, above and beyond that contained in other popular forecasting variables such as the dividend-yield, $\widehat{cay}_t$ and short-term interest rates, consistent with findings in Ludvigson and Ng (2007) (see Tables 11.1 and 11.2).

In what follows, we denote the fitted conditional mean

$$\mu_t \equiv \widehat{r}^e_{s,t+1|t} = \widehat{\alpha}' \widehat{F}_t + \widehat{\beta}' Z_t, \tag{3.6}$$

where μ_t is an estimate of either the conditional mean of log excess returns, $E_t(r^e_{s,t+1})$, or the conditional mean of level excess returns $E_t(R^e_{s,t+1})$. In the tables below, we report results for both cases.

[13] To be precise, the $T \times r$ matrix $\widehat{f}$ is $\sqrt{T}$ times the r eigenvectors corresponding to the r largest eigenvalues of the $T \times T$ matrix $xx'/(TN)$ in decreasing order. Let Λ be the $N \times r$ matrix of factor loadings $(\lambda'_1, \ldots, \lambda'_N)'$. Λ and f are not separately identifiable, so the normalization $f'f/T = I_r$ is imposed, where I_r is the r-dimensional identity matrix. With this normalization, we can additionally obtain $\widehat{\Lambda} = x'\widehat{f}/T$, and $\widehat{\chi}_{it} = \widehat{\lambda}'_i \widehat{f}_t$ denotes the estimated common component in series i at time t. The number of common factors, r, is determined by the panel information criteria developed in Bai and Ng (2002).

[14] Under the assumption that $N, T \to \infty$ with $\sqrt{T}/N \to 0$, Bai and Ng (2006) showed that (i) $(\widehat{\alpha}, \widehat{\beta})$ obtained from least squares estimation of (3.5) are $\sqrt{T}$ consistent and asymptotically normal, and the asymptotic variance is such that inference can proceed as though f_t is observed, (ii) the estimated conditional mean, $\mu_t = \widehat{F}'_t \widehat{\alpha} + Z'_t \widehat{\beta}$ is $\min[\sqrt{N}, \sqrt{T}]$ consistent and asymptotically normal, and (iii) the h period forecast error $m_{t+h} - m_{t+h|t}$ from (3.5) is dominated in large samples by the variance of the error term, just as if f_t is observed. The importance of a large N must be stressed, however, as without it, the factor space cannot be consistently estimated however large T becomes.

Given a measure of the volatility of excess returns at time t, estimation of conditional volatility is carried out in the same way as estimation of the conditional mean, and the same asymptotic results for conducting inference apply. That is, we estimate a final model for volatility based on

$$V_{t+1} = b'Z_t + u_{t+1}. \tag{3.7}$$

In principal, factors could be included as additional regressors in (3.7); we omit them here because Ludvigson and Ng (2007) found that much of the information in estimated factors for future volatility was subsumed by conventional predictor variables. In what follows, we denote the fitted conditional volatility

$$\sigma_t \equiv \widehat{V}_{t+1|t} = \widehat{b}'Z_t, \tag{3.8}$$

and use it as a measure of the conditional volatility of excess returns, $E_t V_{t+1}$. For the CRSP-VW index, the quarterly mean excess return is 0.019; the quarterly standard deviation is 0.0817.

A related estimator of the conditional variance is explored in a recent paper by Ghysels et al. (2005). They use a mixed data sampling approach, which they call MIDAS, that forecasts the monthly variance with a weighted average of lagged daily squared returns. The MIDAS estimator explains about 40% of the variation of realized variance in the subsequent month because the estimated weights on the lagged daily squared returns decay slowly, thereby capturing the persistence in the conditional variance. The lagged daily squared returns can be thought of as elements of Z_t in (3.7). They find that the MIDAS estimator of conditional variance is positively related to and explains about 2% of the variation of next month's stock market returns (and 5% in the period since 1964). Since expected returns are modeled as a function of time-t volatility, they find a positive relation between conditional expected returns and conditional volatility.

The final aspect of our econometric framework is a reduced-form linear equation for the conditional mean as a function of the contemporaneous conditional volatility and lags of the two:

$$\mu_t = \delta + \beta_1\sigma_t + \beta_2\sigma_{t-1} + \alpha\mu_{t-1} + \varepsilon_t. \tag{3.9}$$

This is a generalization of the more common *volatility-in-mean* model that relates the conditional mean to the conditional volatility of returns. Here, we follow Whitelaw (1994), Brandt and Kang (2004), and Ludvigson and Ng (2007) and include lags of μ_t and σ_t in modeling the risk-return relation. These studies all find important lead-lag interactions between conditional mean and conditional volatility. The coefficient β_1 measures the volatility-in-mean effect; the coefficient β_2 measures the *lag-volatility-in-mean* effect.[15] We refer to the estimated relation between μ_t and σ_t when lags of μ_t and σ_t are included in the risk-return regression as the *conditional* risk-return relation.

In what follows, we also consider specifications in which lagged values of mean and volatility are omitted as regressors in estimating the risk-return relation:

$$\mu_t = \delta + \beta\sigma_t + \varepsilon_t. \quad (3.10)$$

We refer to the estimated relation between μ_t and σ_t from the empirical specification (3.10) as the *unconditional* risk-return relation.

3.1.2. Forecasts of Volatility

When constructing volatility forecasts, a question arises as to whether the volatility of returns should be forecast in logs or in levels. One reason to take logs is that variances cannot be negative. Another is that the realized volatility measures using daily returns give a lot of weight to relatively rare, high-volatility periods (Engle and Patton, 2000). However, the risk-return relation and the conditional Sharpe ratio are a function of the level of volatility rather than its log value. We discuss this issue further below. Here, we present forecasts for volatility both in levels and in logs.

Table 11.4 presents long-horizon regressions of volatility, V_{t+h}, for several horizons, $t+1, .. h$, on a variety of predictive variables. Table 11.4A presents results for the level of volatility; Table 11.4B presents results for the log of volatility. Each table reports the regression coefficient, heteroskedasticity and autocorrelation consistent t statistic, and adjusted R^2 statistic. There is substantial autocorrelation in measured volatility, thus we include two lags of volatility in our forecasting equations for V_t. The results of estimating a purely autoregressive specification are reported in row 1 of each table. Past volatility is a statistically significant predictor of future volatility up to four quarters ahead, with adjusted R^2 statistics monotonically declining from 22% at a one-quarter horizon. At a horizon of six quarters, past volatility has little explanatory power for future volatility.

The second and third rows of Table 11.4A display the forecasting power of the consumption-wealth ratio proxy, $\widehat{cay}_t$, for future volatility using quarterly data. Two aspects of these findings stand out. First, the signs of the significant coefficients in these regressions are all negative. Recalling that high values of $\widehat{cay}_t$ predict high excess returns (Table 11.1), this result implies that conditional expected excess returns are *negatively*

[15] Ludvigson and Ng (2007) have also studied an analogous mean-in-volatility equation taking the form

$$\sigma_t = \delta + \alpha_1\mu_t + \alpha_2\mu_{t-1} + \beta\sigma_{t-1} + \xi_{t+1}.$$

The empirical results lead to the same conclusions about the risk-return relation as the volatility-in-mean equation (3.9). We therefore omit those results to conserve space.

Table 11.4A Levels: Forecasting stock market volatility

Row	Regressors	Forecast horizon H in quarters							
		1	2	4	6	8	12	16	24
1	V_t	0.35	0.43	0.34	0.21	0.04	−0.08	−0.08	−0.03
		(5.45)	(4.48)	(2.31)	(1.48)	(0.41)	(−0.69)	(−0.51)	(−0.15)
	V_{t-1}	0.22	0.07	−0.06	−0.12	−0.07	−0.08	0.04	0.26
		(3.18)	(0.89)	(−0.63)	(−0.88)	(−0.61)	(−0.41)	(0.23)	(1.10)
		[0.22]	[0.20]	[0.10]	[0.04]	[0.00]	[0.00]	[0.00]	[0.03]
2	$\widehat{\text{cay}}_t$	−0.71	−1.09	−1.60	−1.87	−1.97	−1.41	−0.59	−0.41
		(−2.88)	(−3.25)	(−3.72)	(−3.78)	(−3.67)	(−2.55)	(−0.83)	(−0.59)
		[0.10]	[0.14]	[0.19]	[0.20]	[0.19]	[0.08]	[0.01]	[0.00]
3	V_t	0.34	0.38	0.32	0.15	0.04	−0.03	−0.04	0.05
		(4.88)	(4.26)	(2.25)	(1.56)	(0.38)	(−0.20)	(−0.21)	(0.21)
	V_{t-1}	0.17	0.05	−0.09	−0.04	0.10	0.11	0.11	0.31
		(2.84)	(0.78)	(−0.94)	(−0.28)	(0.76)	(0.41)	(0.55)	(1.28)
	$\widehat{\text{cay}}_t$	−0.55	−0.91	−1.48	−1.79	−2.11	−1.57	−0.75	−1.07
		(−3.69)	(−4.26)	(−4.15)	(−3.98)	(−3.97)	(−2.44)	(−0.92)	(−1.39)
		[0.27]	[0.29]	[0.27]	[0.21]	[0.19]	[0.07]	[0.01]	[0.05]
4	V_t	0.35	0.40	0.37	0.22	0.09	−0.02	−0.06	−0.09
		(4.72)	(4.49)	(2.40)	(1.76)	(0.84)	(−0.16)	(−0.43)	(−0.44)
	V_{t-1}	0.19	0.09	−0.07	−0.08	0.00	0.00	0.05	0.25
		(2.53)	(1.14)	(−0.69)	(−0.58)	(−0.03)	(0.00)	(0.24)	(1.07)
	$d_t - p_t$	−0.01	−0.02	−0.03	−0.04	−0.04	−0.03	−0.01	0.05
		(−2.39)	(−2.52)	(−2.12)	(−1.58)	(−1.25)	(−0.70)	(−0.17)	(1.20)
		[0.24]	[0.23]	[0.16]	[0.09]	[0.04]	[0.01]	[−0.01]	[0.05]
5	V_t	0.34	0.38	0.32	0.17	0.06	0.01	−0.03	0.00
		(4.74)	(4.23)	(2.29)	(1.68)	(0.64)	(0.11)	(−0.16)	(0.00)
	V_{t-1}	0.17	0.06	−0.09	−0.02	0.13	0.12	0.11	0.32
		(2.68)	(0.78)	(−0.89)	(−0.19)	(1.04)	(0.42)	(0.55)	(1.34)
	$\widehat{\text{cay}}_t$	−0.49	−0.81	−1.33	−1.64	−1.96	−1.51	−0.74	−1.30
		(−3.80)	(−4.59)	(−3.90)	(−3.72)	(−3.76)	(−2.44)	(−0.93)	(−1.46)
	$d_t - p_t$	−0.01	−0.01	−0.01	−0.02	−0.02	−0.02	−0.01	0.06
		(−1.29)	(−1.27)	(−1.06)	(−0.76)	(−0.74)	(−0.52)	(−0.15)	(1.34)
		[0.27]	[0.29]	[0.27]	[0.22]	[0.20]	[0.08]	[0.00]	[0.09]
6‡	V_t	0.21	0.23	0.15	−0.03	−0.15	−0.16	−0.25	−0.21
		(3.14)	(2.59)	(1.07)	(−0.30)	(−1.15)	(−1.23)	(−1.66)	(−1.23)
	V_{t-1}	0.12	0.01	−0.14	−0.01	0.17	0.11	0.02	0.10
		(2.08)	(0.07)	(−1.38)	(−0.07)	(1.61)	(0.47)	(0.12)	(0.66)

Table 11.4A Levels: Forecasting stock market volatility

Row	Regressors	Panel A: Forecast horizon H in quarters							
		1	2	4	6	8	12	16	24
6‡	$\widehat{\mathrm{cay}}_t$	−0.44	−0.75	−1.26	−1.57	−1.88	−1.27	−0.22	0.22
		(−3.30)	(−3.47)	(−3.93)	(−4.14)	(−4.46)	(−2.63)	(−0.31)	(0.34)
	$d_t - p_t$	−0.01	−0.02	−0.03	−0.04	−0.05	−0.06	−0.05	−0.09
		(−2.49)	(−2.30)	(−2.15)	(−1.74)	(−1.60)	(−1.31)	(−1.12)	(−1.65)
	DEF_t	0.00	0.00	0.01	0.01	0.02	0.01	0.02	0.05
		(0.47)	(0.34)	(0.54)	(0.52)	(0.75)	(0.63)	(0.81)	(2.28)
	CP_t	1.68	2.30	2.52	3.01	3.87	2.19	1.25	1.03
		(3.29)	(3.04)	(3.23)	(3.33)	(3.75)	(2.04)	(0.95)	(0.68)
	$\mathrm{TB1Y}_t$	0.13	0.20	0.31	0.37	0.39	0.65	0.75	0.93
		(2.06)	(1.84)	(1.66)	(1.64)	(1.47)	(2.59)	(2.11)	(2.64)
		[0.33]	[0.37]	[0.37]	[0.35]	[0.37]	[0.28]	[0.24]	[0.38]

Table 11.4B Logs: Forecasting stock market volatility

Row	Regressors	Forecast horizon H in quarters							
		1	2	4	6	8	12	16	24
1	$\log(V_t)$	0.44	0.51	0.44	0.25	0.06	−0.06	−0.05	0.01
		(8.88)	(6.90)	(3.28)	(2.05)	(0.57)	(−0.46)	(−0.34)	(0.04)
	$\log(V_{t-1})$	0.23	0.08	−0.11	−0.12	−0.05	−0.08	0.03	0.18
		(3.45)	(0.97)	(−1.05)	(−0.90)	(−0.34)	(−0.39)	(0.15)	(0.80)
		[0.34]	[0.29]	[0.16]	[0.05]	[−0.01]	[0.00]	[−0.01]	[0.01]
2	$\widehat{\mathrm{cay}}_t$	−9.43	−10.49	−11.15	−10.57	−9.75	−6.10	−2.38	−1.54
		(−2.62)	(−3.21)	(−3.70)	(−3.74)	(−3.70)	(−2.53)	(−0.85)	(−0.67)
		[0.08]	[0.13]	[0.17]	[0.17]	[0.15]	[0.07]	[0.01]	[0.00]
3	$\log(V_t)$	0.43	0.45	0.42	0.19	0.04	−0.01	−0.02	0.10
		(7.51)	(7.08)	(3.10)	(1.97)	(0.40)	(−0.09)	(−0.09)	(0.40)
	$\log(V_{t-1})$	0.19	0.07	−0.16	−0.06	0.13	0.12	0.10	0.23
		(2.78)	(0.88)	(−1.42)	(−0.40)	(0.81)	(0.47)	(0.48)	(1.00)
	$\widehat{\mathrm{cay}}_t$	−6.60	−8.12	−9.93	−9.81	−10.73	−7.01	−2.99	−3.72
		(−4.11)	(−4.26)	(−4.18)	(−3.89)	(−4.09)	(−2.49)	(−0.97)	(−1.41)
		[0.37]	[0.35]	[0.30]	[0.19]	[0.16]	[0.07]	[0.00]	[0.04]
4	$\log(V_t)$	0.44	0.47	0.47	0.27	0.10	−0.01	−0.06	−0.06
		(8.28)	(6.90)	(3.37)	(2.29)	(0.92)	(−0.08)	(−0.38)	(−0.29)
	$\log(V_{t-1})$	0.21	0.11	−0.13	−0.09	0.01	0.00	0.03	0.18
		(3.07)	(1.25)	(−1.14)	(−0.67)	(0.09)	(0.00)	(0.14)	(0.79)

(Continued)

Table 11.4B *(Continued)*

Row	Regressors	Panel B: Forecast horizon H in quarters							
		1	2	4	6	8	12	16	24
4	$d_t - p_t$	−0.13	−0.17	−0.20	−0.18	−0.18	−0.08	0.01	0.17
		(−2.28)	(−2.30)	(−1.76)	(−1.18)	(−0.90)	(−0.40)	(0.08)	(1.20)
		[0.34]	[0.30]	[0.21]	[0.08]	[0.02]	[−0.01]	[−0.01]	[0.03]
5	$\log(V_t)$	0.43	0.45	0.43	0.20	0.06	0.01	−0.02	0.04
		(7.49)	(6.74)	(3.14)	(2.02)	(0.54)	(0.06)	(−0.14)	(0.17)
	$\log(V_{t-1})$	0.18	0.07	−0.15	−0.05	0.14	0.13	0.09	0.24
		(2.78)	(0.87)	(−1.38)	(−0.35)	(1.01)	(0.47)	(0.45)	(1.08)
	$\widehat{cay}_t$	−6.12	−7.55	−9.35	−9.35	−10.29	−6.89	−2.99	−4.45
		(−3.89)	(−4.06)	(−3.82)	(−3.51)	(−3.69)	(−2.46)	(−0.96)	(−1.42)
	$d_t - p_t$	−0.04	−0.05	−0.05	−0.05	−0.08	−0.06	0.02	0.21
		(−0.68)	(−0.70)	(−0.54)	(−0.36)	(−0.40)	(−0.25)	(0.08)	(1.31)
		[0.37]	[0.35]	[0.30]	[0.19]	[0.16]	[0.07]	[0.00]	[0.08]
6‡	$\log(V_t)$	0.33	0.33	0.26	−0.01	−0.17	−0.16	−0.23	−0.17
		(6.54)	(4.59)	(2.07)	(−0.08)	(−1.22)	(−1.08)	(−1.47)	(−1.03)
	$\log(V_{t-1})$	0.14	0.04	−0.20	−0.03	0.19	0.13	0.02	0.05
		(2.12)	(0.46)	(−1.78)	(−0.18)	(1.59)	(0.59)	(0.10)	(0.34)
	$\widehat{cay}_t$	−5.57	−7.03	−8.95	−9.07	−10.02	−5.98	−1.09	0.44
		(−3.39)	(−3.57)	(−3.94)	(−3.90)	(−4.49)	(−2.79)	(−0.41)	(0.19)
	$d_t - p_t$	−0.13	−0.14	−0.17	−0.18	−0.21	−0.20	−0.14	−0.29
		(−2.01)	(−1.77)	(−1.63)	(−1.21)	(−1.16)	(−1.00)	(−0.82)	(−1.50)
	DEF_t	0.02	0.00	0.06	0.06	0.09	0.05	0.08	0.15
		(0.30)	(0.02)	(0.47)	(0.44)	(0.72)	(0.56)	(0.76)	(2.17)
	CP_t	17.61	17.47	15.40	18.73	22.95	11.53	6.24	3.48
		(3.09)	(2.96)	(2.85)	(3.50)	(3.68)	(2.38)	(1.21)	(0.70)
	$TB1Y_t$	2.06	2.49	2.81	2.73	2.38	3.11	3.01	3.13
		(2.35)	(2.25)	(2.03)	(1.91)	(1.66)	(2.71)	(2.22)	(2.82)
		[0.41]	[0.41]	[0.40]	[0.33]	[0.37]	[0.29]	[0.25]	[0.36]

The table presents results from long-horizon regressions of stock market volatility on lagged variables using quarterly data from 1952:4–2000:4, OLS estimation. The dependent variable at each forecast horizon H is the H-step ahead volatility, equal to

$$v_{t+1,t+H} = [\Sigma_{s \in t+1,\ldots,t+h}(r_s - \bar{r})^2]^{1/2},$$

where v denotes the standard deviation of the CRSP value-weighted index estimated from daily returns. The H-period volatilities are regressed on one-period lagged values of the log dividend yield, $d_t - p_t$, the consumption-wealth ratio proxy $\widehat{cay}_t = c_t - \widehat{\beta}_a a_t - \widehat{\beta}_y y_t$, the BAA Corporate Bond rate minus the AAA Corporate Bond rate, DEF_t, the difference between the yield on six-month commercial paper and the three-month Treasury bill yield, CP_t, the one-year Treasury yield, $TB1Y_t$, and their own first and second lagged values, denoted V_t and V_{t-1}. For each regression, the table reports OLS estimates of the regressors, Newey–West corrected t-statistics in parentheses, and adjusted R^2 statistics in square brackets. The sample period is the fourth quarter of 1952 to the fourth quarter of 2000 for quarterly forecasts, except for regression 6 (marked with a ‡), which uses a sample running from the second quarter of 1953 to the fourth quarter of 2000, the largest common sample for which all the data are available.

related to conditional volatility forecasts based on prediction by $\widehat{cay}_t$. The finding suggests that stock market volatility by itself is a poor proxy for variation in the equity risk premium since high risk-premia cannot be explained by high stock market volatility and vice versa. Second, the regression results indicate that $\widehat{cay}_t$ is both a statistically significant and economically important determinant of future stock market volatility. When $\widehat{cay}_t$ is the sole predictive variable (row 2), it is statistically significant at the 5% level, over horizons ranging from 1 to 12 quarters, with R^2 statistics starting at 12% for a one-quarter horizon and rising to a peak of 19% six quarters ahead. The marginal predictive power of $\widehat{cay}_t$ survives when past volatility is controlled for (row 3). These results demonstrate that volatility is predictable by at least some of the same variables that predict excess returns, contrary to perception that this is not the case (e.g., Cochrane, 2005, p. 396.).

The fourth row of Table 11.4A uses the dividend-price ratio to forecast volatility. The coefficient on this variable, like that on $\widehat{cay}_t$, is negative, and it is statistically significant up to three quarters ahead, although the predictive power of the dividend-yield is driven out by $\widehat{cay}_t$ (row 5).

The sixth row adds three additional regressors to the set of forecasting variables for volatility: DEF_t, a commercial paper-Treasury spread, CP_t, and the one-year Treasury yield, $\mathrm{TB1Y}_t$. The last three predictive variables are those used by Whitelaw (1994) to forecast volatility at monthly and quarterly horizons. In this multivariate regression, all variables have marginal predictive power at one horizon or another, with $\widehat{cay}_t$, $d_t - p_t$, and CP_t displaying forecasting power at horizons less than six quarters, and $\mathrm{TB1Y}_t$ displaying forecasting power at horizons in excess of three years; the default spread only has forecasting power at a 24-quarter horizon.

The same results are presented in Table 11.4B for log volatility. The results are very similar to those obtained when the level of V_t is forecast. The log specification is found to explain a larger fraction of future log volatility than the level specification explains of the future level of volatility.

A noteworthy aspect of the results in Tables 11.4A and 11.4B is the finding that quarterly conditional volatility varies: although there is a vast literature documenting time variation in stock market volatility at high frequencies, it is often thought that volatility is not strongly forecastable at frequencies as low as a quarter (e.g., Campbell, 2003; Christoffersen and Diebold, 2000). The evidence presented here, along with more recent evidence in Brandt and Jones (2005), shows that conditional volatility varies over horizons ranging from a quarter to several years.

Figure 11.1 plots an estimate over time of the conditional volatility of the excess return on the CRSP-VW index. The figure plots the fitted values from the regression specification given in row 3 of Table 11.4A, which includes $\widehat{cay}_t$ and two lags of volatility as predictors of quarterly volatility. NBER dated recessions are indicated with shaded bars. The figure suggests that conditional volatility is high in recessions but falls through the course of the recession when expected returns are rising. By contrast, conditional volatility

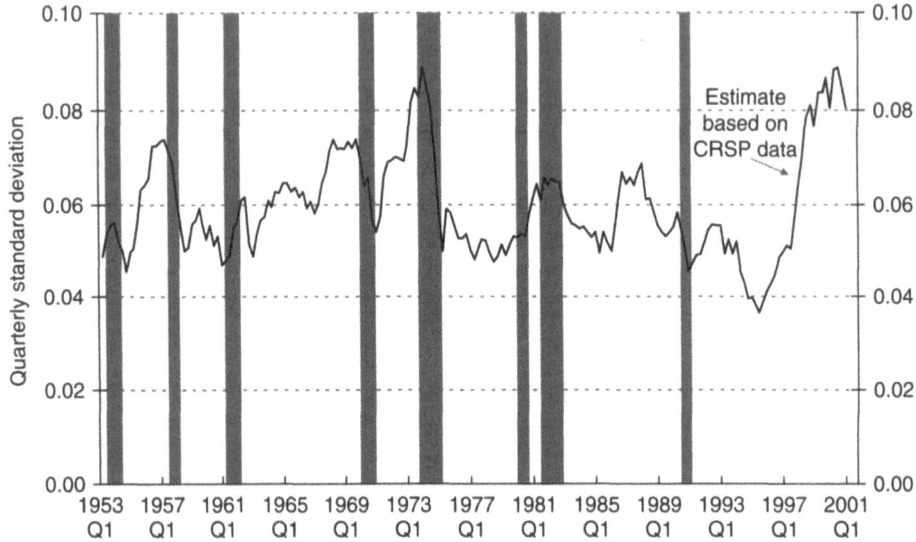

Figure 11.1 Conditional volatility for the CRSP-VW Index.
Note: Shading denotes quarters designated recession by the NBER.
Source: Authors' calculations.

tends to rise over the course of an expansion when conditional expected returns are falling.

The estimates above rely on realized volatility as a measure of the variance of stock returns. There are many other possible measures of volatility available to the researcher. Among these are variants of the standard GARCH and EGARCH models developed by Bollerslev (1986) and Nelson (1991). Harvey (2001) considers a range of possibilities for modeling volatility including modeling conditional volatility using nonparametric density estimation, GARCH or EGARCH estimation, or forming a variance estimator based on the squared residuals from a regression of returns on conditioning variables. Engle (2001) explores a wide range of potential estimators based on GARCH type models that can be used for any type of nonnegative time-series such as volatility. He proposes a multiplicative error model that specifies the forecast error of the nonnegative series to be multiplied by its conditional mean. Engle shows that this model can be estimated with GARCH software by taking the square root of the realized variance as the dependent variable, specifying it to have zero mean, and an error process assumed normal GARCH(p, q) with possible exogenous variables.

3.1.3. Empirical Results on Risk and Return

We now turn to estimates of (3.9), the generalized volatility-in-mean model that relates the conditional mean to the conditional volatility of returns. Table 11.5 reports results

Table 11.5 Risk-return Trade-off

Row	Constant	σ_t	σ_{t-1}	μ_{t-1}	R^2
			Levels		
		$z_t^r = (\text{cay}_{t-1}), z_t^v = (V_{t-1}, V_{t-2}, \text{cay}_{t-1})$			
1	0.08	−1.02			0.36
	(6.03)	(−4.46)			
2	0.02	−1.02	0.76	0.03	0.71
	(2.26)	(−0.96)	(13.45)	(0.13)	
		$z_t^r = (\text{cay}_{t-1}, \widehat{F}_{1t-1}, \widehat{F}_{2t-1}, \text{RREL}_{t-1}), z_t^v = (V_{t-1}, V_{t-2}, \text{cay}_{t-1})$			
3	0.04	−0.33			0.02
	(1.90)	(−1.00)			
4	0.02	0.75	0.55	−1.03	0.35
	(2.52)	(2.24)	(8.36)	(−3.69)	
			Logs		
		$z_t^r = (\text{cay}_{t-1}), z_t^v = (V_{t-1}, V_{t-2}, \text{cay}_{t-1})$			
5	−0.13	−0.05			0.23
	(2.84)	(−3.18)			
6	−0.02	−0.00	0.80	−0.01	0.70
	(−1.34)	(−0.05)	(17.92)	(−0.89)	
		$z_t^r = (\text{cay}_{t-1}, \widehat{F}_{1-1}, \widehat{F}_{2t-1}, \text{RREL}_{t-1}), z_t^v = (V_{t-1}, V_{t-2}, \text{cay}_{t-1})$			
7	0.00	−0.00			0.00
	(0.04)	(−0.16)			
8	−0.02	0.05	0.59	−0.06	0.34
	(−0.52)	(2.78)	(9.42)	(−3.65)	

This table reports results from the regressions of conditional expected excess returns on conditional volatility:

$$\widehat{\mu}_t = \alpha_0 + \alpha_1 \widehat{v}_t + \alpha_2 \widehat{v}_{t-1} + \alpha_3 \widehat{\mu}_{t-1} + e_t,$$

where fitted conditional moments are constructed from linear regressions

$$\widehat{\mu}_t = \widehat{\boldsymbol{\beta}}_r \boldsymbol{z}_t^r \text{ and } \widehat{v}_t = \widehat{\boldsymbol{\beta}}_v \boldsymbol{z}_t^v$$

$$r_t - r_t^f = \boldsymbol{\beta}_r \boldsymbol{z}_{t-1}^r + e_{rt} \text{ and } v_t = \boldsymbol{\beta}_v \boldsymbol{z}_{t-1}^v + e_{rt}.$$

The top panel reports results for conditional excess return and conditional standard deviations while the bottom panel reports results for conditional log excess returns and conditional log standard deviations. The sample runs from the first quarter of 1953 to the first quarter of 2001.

from estimating (3.9). The top panel displays results relating the conditional excess return to the conditional standard deviation (in levels) of returns; the bottom panel presents the results using the conditional log excess return and the conditional log standard deviation of returns. In each case, fitted volatility (3.8) is constructed using $Z_t = \left(\widehat{\text{cay}}_t, V_t, V_{t-1}\right)'$.

Fitted mean, (3.6), is constructed using one of two sets of conditioning information: $Z_t = \widehat{\text{cay}}_t$ alone, or $Z_t = \left(\widehat{\text{cay}}_t, \text{RREL}_t\right)'$, and $\widehat{F} = \left(\widehat{F}_{1t}, \widehat{F}_{2t}\right)'$. Based on the evidence presented in Tables 11.1 and 11.2, each of $\widehat{\text{cay}}_t$, $\widehat{F}_{1t}$, $\widehat{F}_{2t}$, and RREL_t are found to have marginal predictive power for excess returns, and so are included in the information set used to construct fitted mean (3.6).

Several results in Table 11.5 deserve emphasis. First, when lags of μ_t and σ_t are omitted from the risk-return regression, as when estimating specification (3.10), the estimated relation between fitted mean and fitted volatility is negative, although it is not statistically significant when $\widehat{F} = \left(\widehat{F}_{1t}, \widehat{F}_{2t}\right)'$ are included as conditioning variables in the construction of fitted mean. Thus, the unconditional risk-return relation is negative but not statistically different from zero. Graham and Harvey (2008) use multiyear surveys of Chief Financial Officers of U.S. corporations and find that the conditional expected excess return at a one-year horizon is negatively correlated with ex-ante measures of volatility. Such a negative correlation between conditional mean and conditional volatility is inconsistent with leading equilibrium asset pricing models that are capable of generating a countercyclical price of risk (e.g., Barberis et al., 2001; Campbell and Cochrane, 1999). These models predict a positive correlation between the conditional mean and conditional volatility, and generate a countercyclical Sharpe ratio only because there is more variation in the mean than in conditional volatility.[16]

Second, in all cases, the lagged values of mean and volatility are a statistically important feature of the empirical risk-return relation; these variables are strongly statistically significant and add considerably to overall fit of the regression, consistent with the findings of Whitelaw (1994) and Brandt and Kang (2004). Thus, the *conditional* risk-return relation (3.9) fits the data far better than the *unconditional* risk-return relation (3.10).

Third, the results in Table 11.5 show that distinguishing between the conditional risk-return relation (conditional on lagged mean and lagged volatility) and unconditional relation is important for understanding the empirical risk-return relation, but depends on the conditioning information used to construct fitted mean, μ_t. The conditional correlation between the fitted mean and fitted volatility is positive whenever information on the volatility and risk-premium factors $\widehat{F} = \left(\widehat{F}_{1t}, \widehat{F}_{2t}\right)'$ are used in the construction of fitted mean. In this case, the volatility-in-mean effect β_1 in (3.9) is positive and strongly statistically significant (rows 2 and 4). In this case, the sign of the conditional risk-return relation is opposite of the sign of the unconditional relation. On the other hand, when information on $\widehat{F} = \left(\widehat{F}_{1t}, \widehat{F}_{2t}\right)'$ is omitted in the construction of μ_t, as, e.g., when $\widehat{\text{cay}}_t$ is

[16]One theoretical framework that can generate a negative correlation between the conditional first and second moments of returns is the model considered in Whitelaw (2000). Whitelaw, building off work by Abel (1988) and Backus and Gregory (1993), assumes that consumption growth follows a Markov regime-switching process with time-varying transitory probabilities and shows that such a structure can generate a negative correlation between stock market volatility and expected returns. An important difficulty with this Markov regime-switching framework, however, is that it does not deliver persistent price-dividend ratios nor does it generate long-horizon forecastability of excess returns by the consumption-wealth ratio.

the only conditioning information, the conditional risk-return relationship has the same sign as the unconditional relationship, which is negative (rows 1 and 3).

Initially, these results might seem to suggest that the estimated risk-return relation can depend on the conditioning variables used in the construction of fitted moments. It is important to bear in mind, however, that the fitted moments constructed here use factors $\widehat{F} = (\widehat{F}_{1t}, \widehat{F}_{2t})'$, which already summarize a large amount of economic information upon which expectations may be based, and are included because statistical criteria for choosing parsimonious models of relevant factors and conditioning variables found these variables to be important for forecasting excess returns.[17] Thus, the inclusion of $\widehat{F}_{1t}$ and $\widehat{F}_{2t}$ makes our analysis less dependent than previous applications on only a handful of predetermined conditioning variables. In addition, results in Ludvigson and Ng (2007) indicate that the conclusions reached here about the estimated risk-return relation are robust to using a variety of statistically relevant factors and conditioning variables in the modeling of fitted moments, as long as the two financial factors (volatility and risk-premium) $\widehat{F}_{1t}$ and $\widehat{F}_{2t}$ are included when estimating the conditional mean. This is important because statistical criteria considered in Ludvigson and Ng (2007) indicate that these factors have marginal forecasting power for future returns that should not be omitted when modeling the conditional mean.

The finding that the sign of the estimated risk-return relation depends on whether lagged mean and lagged volatility are included in the risk-return regression (3.9) is consistent with that of Brandt and Kang (2004) who argue that the distinction may explain the disagreement in the literature about the contemporaneous correlation between risk and return. In contrast to Brandt and Kang (2004), however, the results here and in Ludvigson and Ng (2007) imply a positive conditional correlation between risk and return (conditional on lagged mean and lagged volatility) that is strongly statistically significant, whereas the unconditional correlation is weakly negative and statistically insignificant whenever the information in $\widehat{F}_{1t}$ and $\widehat{F}_{2t}$ is used in the construction of fitted mean. Brandt and Kang (2004) report a negative conditional correlation and a positive unconditional correlation.

There are a number of possible reasons why the results here differ from those of Brandt and Kang. First, the econometric methodologies differ. Brandt and Kang use a latent VAR approach to model the conditional mean and conditional volatility, assuming that these variables follow first-order, linear Gaussian processes. This approach relies on the history of returns to infer μ_t and σ_t and does not condition upon the vast set of exogenous information variables used to construct the latent factors $\widehat{F}_{1t}$ and $\widehat{F}_{2t}$. Second,

[17] See Ludvigson and Ng (2007). Ludvigson and Ng also considered factors constructed from a large data set of macroeconomic indicators. The information in these factors for future mean returns was subsumed by information in the financial factors used here. They did find one factor estimated from a large data set of macroeconomic indicators to have predictive power for realized stock return volatility. We omit this variable here in our construction of fitted volatility because doing so does not change the main results of the risk-return regression (3.9).

Brandt and Kang model the log moments, whereas we follow the bulk of the literature and model the relation between the mean and volatility in levels.[18] Third, our sample size and data frequency differ: Brandt and Kang studied monthly data from January 1946 through December 1998, while the construction of factors follows Ludvigson and Ng (2007) and uses quarterly data from the first quarter of 1960 to the second quarter of 2003. Several variables that are important for predicting returns and volatility (e.g., cay_t) are only available at quarterly frequency and the predictable dynamics may vary from monthly to quarterly horizons.

4. THE CONDITIONAL SHARPE RATIO

In this section, we investigate the time-series behavior of the conditional Sharpe ratio using our estimates of fitted mean and fitted volatility from the previous sections.

Above, we computed estimates of conditional volatility by forecasting both the level and the log of the volatility of returns. The conditional Sharpe ratio, however, is a function of the level of volatility rather than its log value. In practice, we find that our estimate of fitted volatility in levels is never negative in our sample (see Fig. 11.1). At the same time, some of the estimated coefficients in the fitted volatility regressions are negative (Table 11.4A), suggesting that the positive forecasts of volatility could break down out of sample.

If we assume that the log of volatility is normally distributed, then a Jensen's adjustment to the conditional forecast of the log of the variance delivers an estimate of the conditional forecast of the level. Thus, estimates of the conditional expectation of the log of volatility could be used to obtain estimates of the conditional expectation of the level of volatility that are identically positive. Without a detailed investigation into whether this normality assumption is plausible for our quarterly data set or how best to model the Jensen's adjustment,[19] for the purposes of this chapter, we adopt the approach of simply computing the conditional Sharpe ratio using the fitted values from our regressions in levels. Thus, we report estimates of

$$\text{SR}_t^{\text{VW}} = \frac{E_t(R_{s,t+1} - R_{f,t})}{\sigma_t\left(R_{s,t+1} - R_{f,t}\right)} = \frac{\mu_t}{\sigma_t},$$

where SR_t^{VW} denotes the quarterly Sharpe ratio on the CRSP-VW stock market index, and the numerator and denominators are computed as fitted values for mean and volatility, as discussed above. With these fitted values in hand, an estimated value of SR_t^{VW} is plotted

[18] Brandt and Kang use their assumption that the log moments are bivariate normally distributed to infer the relation between the level moments.

[19] The Jensen's adjustment requires an estimate of the conditional volatility of volatility, or the conditional fourth moment of returns.

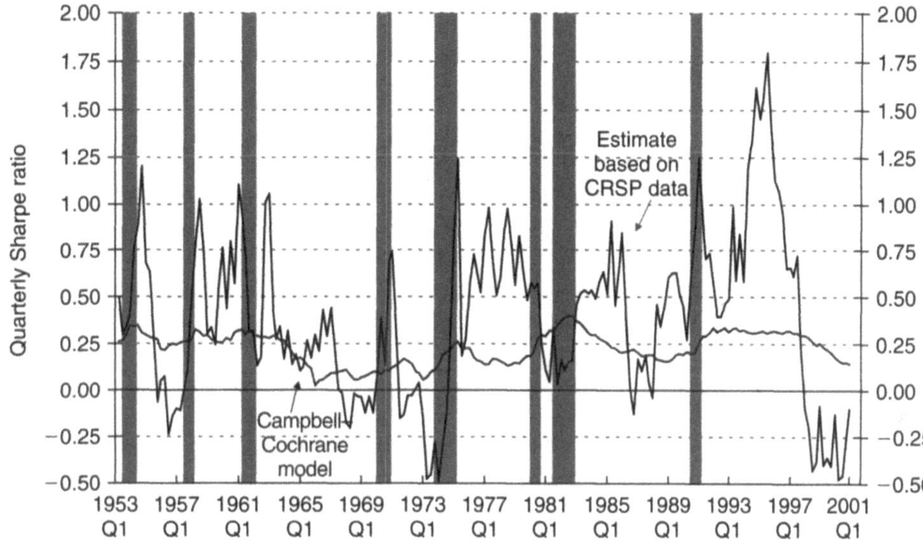

Figure 11.2 Conditional Sharpe ratio.
Note: Shading denotes quarters designated recession by the NBER.
Source: Authors' calculations, Campbell and Cochrane (1999).

over time in Fig. 11.2. For this plot, we forecast $R_{st+1} - R_{ft+1}$ using the log consumption-wealth ratio proxy, $\widehat{\text{cay}}_t$; and we forecast V_t using cay_t and two lags of V_t. The figure is similar if we include other conditioning variables discussed above.

Figure 11.2 shows that the Sharpe ratio, plotted on a quarterly basis, is strongly countercyclical, falling over the course of an expansion and rising at the beginning of recessions, consistent with the evidence in Harvey (2001). There are a few periods during which the conditional Sharpe ratio is estimated to be negative. This occurs because our estimate of conditional expected returns – the fitted values from a regression of excess returns on lagged variables – are occasionally negative, a result attributable to the linear regression specification underlying our identification of expected returns. The result is not unique to the use of any particular forecasting variable. Nevertheless, its worth noting that an occasional negative risk premium on stock market wealth is not necessarily inconsistent with equilibrium asset pricing models in which the covariance of consumption growth with the stochastic discount factor varies over time (Boudoukh et al., 1997; Whitelaw, 2000).

How well do economic models explain the time-series behavior of the Sharpe ratio displayed in Fig. 11.2? To address this question, it is instructive to first derive the formula for the conditional Sharpe ratio in any economic model with stochastic discount factor (pricing kernel) M_{t+1}. In the models considered here, M_{t+1} is the intertemporal marginal rate of substitution in consumption, or pricing kernel. The asset pricing model comes from the first-order conditions for optimal consumption choice, which imply that, for any traded asset indexed by i, the following equation holds:

$$E_t\left[M_{t+1}\left(1 + R_{i,t+1}\right)\right] = 1. \tag{4.1}$$

Equation (4.1) shows that the intertemporal marginal rate of substitution in consumption, Π_t, is the stochastic discount factor, or pricing kernel. Applying a covariance decomposition to (4.1), and using $R_{ft} = 1/E_t(M_{t+1})$, the risk premium on stocks is given by

$$\begin{aligned} E_t(R_{s,t+1}) - R_{f,t+1} &= -R_{f,t+1}\text{cov}_t(M_{t+1}, R_{s,t+1}) \\ &= -R_{f,t+1}\sigma_t\left(M_{t+1}\right)\sigma_t\left(R_{s,t+1}\right)\rho_t\left(M_{t+1}, R_{st+1}\right), \end{aligned}$$

where $\sigma_t(x)$ denotes the standard deviation of x conditional on time t information, and $\rho_t(x, y)$ denotes the correlation between x and y conditional on time t information. Thus, the conditional Sharpe ratio for any model with pricing kernel M_{t+1} is given by

$$\frac{E_t(R_{s,t+1}) - R_{f,t+1}}{\sigma_t\left(R_{s,t+1}\right)} = -R_{f,t+1}\sigma_t\left(M_{t+1}\right)\rho_t\left(M_{t+1}, R_{s,t+1}\right).$$

The conditional Sharpe ratio can vary if either the risk-free rate $R_{f,t+1}$ varies if the pricing kernel is conditionally heteroskedastic so that $\sigma_t(M_{t+1})$ varies, or if the conditional correlation $\rho_t(M_{t+1}, R_{s,t+1})$ varies.

We argue here that many consumption-based asset pricing models are unlikely to explain the dynamic behavior of the empirically estimated Sharpe ratio displayed in Fig. 11.2. As an illustration of the existing theoretical gap, we consider the implied conditional Sharpe ratios from three models and compare their behavior to that of the empirical Sharpe ratio plotted in Fig. 11.2. These models are

- The habit model explored in Campbell and Cochrane (1999). This model has been uniquely successful at rationalizing a range of asset pricing phenomena in a single framework, including the predictability of excess stock returns, the average value of the equity risk premium, the low mean and volatility of interest rates, and variability in the conditional Sharpe ratio.
- The standard time-separable, constant relative risk aversion model with power utility $u(C_t) = \frac{(C_t)^{1-\gamma}}{1-\gamma}$ and time-varying consumption volatility referred to hereafter as the *consumption-volatility model*. In this model, the Sharpe ratio moves over time because of time-varying consumption volatility, which generates conditional heteroskedasticity in the pricing kernel, or movements in $\sigma_t(M_{t+1})$.
- The generalization of the standard power utility model based on Epstein and Zin (1989, 1991) and Weil (1989) (EZW) considered in Bansal and Yaron (2004), with stochastic consumption volatility. This model also generates conditional heteroskedasticity

in the pricing kernel, or movements in $\sigma_t(M_{t+1})$ as a result of time-varying consumption volatility. We refer to this as the BY-EZW *model* with stochastic consumption volatility.

The Campbell–Cochrane model is a habit persistence framework in which utility takes the form $u(C_t, X_t) = \frac{(C_t - X_t)^{1-\gamma}}{1-\gamma}$, where X_t is the external consumption habit. The Sharpe ratio predicted by the Campbell–Cochrane model, which we denote $\mathrm{SR}_t^{\mathrm{CC}}$, is a nonlinear function of consumption growth and takes the form

$$\mathrm{SR}_t^{\mathrm{CC}} = \{e^{\gamma^2\sigma^2[1+\lambda(s_t)]^2} - 1\}^{1/2} \approx \gamma\sigma[1 + \lambda(s_t)], \tag{4.2}$$

where s_t is the log of the surplus consumption ratio, defined $S_t \equiv \frac{C_t - X_t}{C_t}$, and $\lambda(s_t)$ is the sensitivity function specified in Campbell and Cochrane. The log surplus consumption ratio evolves as a heteroskedastic, first-order autoregressive process:

$$s_{t+1} = (1 - \phi)\bar{s} + \phi s_t + \lambda(s_t)(\Delta c_{t+1} - g), \tag{4.3}$$

where g is the mean rate of consumption growth and ϕ is the persistence of the habit stock. It is straightforward to compute the implied Sharpe ratio of the Campbell–Cochrane model by combining (4.2) and (4.3) with data on aggregate consumption.[20]

In the consumption-volatility model, investors have constant relative risk aversion utility taking the form $u(C_t) = \frac{(C_t)^{1-\gamma}}{1-\gamma}$, with $u(c_t) = \log(c_t)$ in the limit as $\gamma \to 1$. In this case, the investor's first-order condition for optimal consumption choice is an Euler equation relating excess stock returns to the marginal rate of substitution in consumption:

$$1 = \beta E_t\left(R_{st+1}\frac{c_{t+1}^{-\gamma}}{c_t^{-\gamma}}\right), \tag{4.4}$$

where β is the subjective rate of time preference, R_{st+1} is the net return on stocks, and $\Pi_{t+1} \equiv \beta\frac{c_{t+1}^{-\gamma}}{c_t^{-\gamma}}$ is the marginal rate of substitution in consumption. If we assume that consumption growth is lognormally distributed, we obtain the following approximate expression for the conditional Sharpe ratio in this model:

$$\frac{E_t R_{st+1} - R_{ft}}{\sigma_t(R_{st+1})} \approx \gamma\sigma_t(\Delta c_{t+1})\rho_t(\Delta c_{t+1}, R_{st+1}). \tag{4.5}$$

This expression says that the conditional Sharpe ratio is proportional to γ, the coefficient of relative risk aversion. Movements in the Sharpe ratio can be generated by movements in consumption volatility, $\sigma_t(\Delta c_{t+1})$, or movements in $\rho_t(\Delta c_{t+1}, R_{st+1})$.

[20] We use the value of $\bar{s}$ calibrated in Campbell and Cochrane (1999).

In the BY-EZW model, variation in the Sharpe ratio is also driven by time-varying stochastic consumption volatility. Bansal and Yaron (2004) show that an approximate relation for the maximum Sharpe ratio (where $\rho_t(\Pi_{t+1}, R_{st+1}) = -1$) is

$$\left(\frac{E_t R_{st+1} - R_{ft}}{\sigma_t(R_{st+1})}\right)^{\text{MAX}} \approx a + b\sigma_t(\Delta c_{t+1}), \tag{4.6}$$

where $\left(\frac{E_t R_{st+1} - R_{ft}}{\sigma_t(R_{st+1})}\right)^{\text{MAX}}$ denotes the maximum Sharpe ratio, and where the constants a and b depend on model parameters. Notice that the maximum Sharpe ratio in (4.6) is therefore closely related to the maximum Sharpe ratio for the consumption-volatility model, which takes the form

$$\left(\frac{E_t R_{st+1} - R_{ft}}{\sigma_t(R_{st+1})}\right)^{\text{MAX}} \approx b\sigma_t(\Delta c_{t+1}),$$

where $b = \gamma$. The constant term a in (4.6) appears as a result of the stochastic volatility specification in Bansal and Yaron (2004). Stochastic volatility allows for shocks to volatility that are uncorrelated with the consumption innovations.

The Sharpe ratio for the Campbell–Cochrane model is plotted in Fig. 11.3 along with our estimate of the Sharpe ratio over time. Although Campbell and Cochrane (1999) show that the model they study does a reasonable job of matching variation in the first moment of excess returns, Fig. 11.3 suggests that the model produces an unrealistically small amount of countercyclical variation in the Sharpe ratio. The estimated Sharpe ratio for excess returns on the CRSP-VW index, SR_t^{VW}, ranges from −0.45–1.76 on a quarterly basis. By contrast, SR_t^{CC} ranges from 0–0.4.

For the consumption-volatility model, we assume that the conditional correlation, $\rho_t(\Delta c_{t+1}, R_{s,t+1})$, is −1, and choose risk aversion, γ, to match the mean Sharpe ratio. We discuss the possible role of time-varying correlations below. Any portfolio that is sufficiently diversified (a mean–variance efficient portfolio) will have $\rho_t(M_{t+1}, R_{s,t+1}) = -1$, which in this model implies $\rho_t(\Delta c_{t+1}, R_{st+1}) = -1$. Although a broad stock market return may not be an efficient portfolio, setting this correlation to one provides a reasonable benchmark because many asset pricing studies implicitly assume that such an asset is highly correlated with an efficient portfolio and set this correlation to 1 in undertaking calibration exercises.[21] In addition, this approach allows us to isolate the contribution of consumption risk in explaining the pattern of variability in the risk-return trade-off. Thus, the Sharpe ratio we measure for the consumption model in (4.5) is simply γ

[21] Campbell (2003) and Cochrane (2005) emphasize that this correlation is hard to measure accurately because estimates are sensitive to data definition, measurement error, the length of the horizon, and data aggregation.

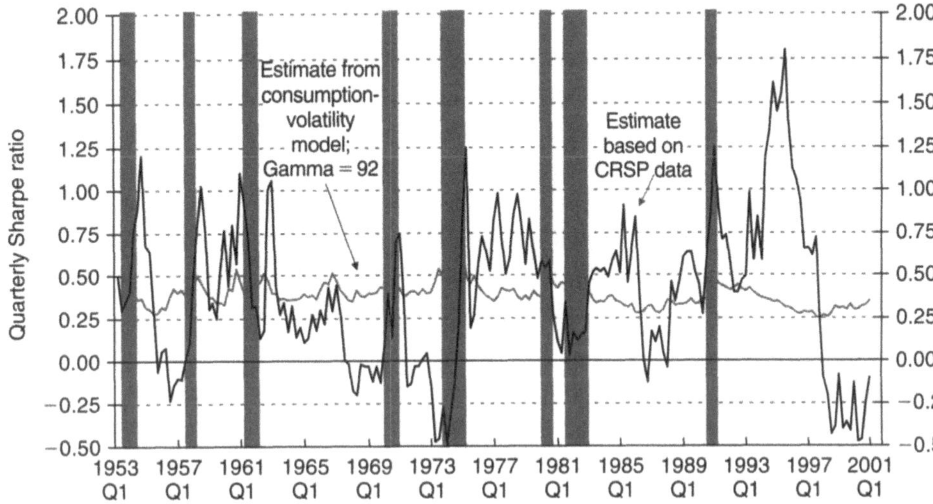

Figure 11.3 Estimates of the Sharpe ratio from the consumption-volatility model and from the CRSP-VW Index.

Note: Shading denotes quarters designated recession by the NBER. Gamma refers to the risk aversion scale factor in the consumption volatility model. Gamma = 92 is the constant coefficient of risk aversion.

Source: Authors' calculations.

$\widehat{\sigma}_t(\Delta c_{t+1})$, where $\widehat{\sigma}_t(\Delta c_{t+1})$ denotes an estimate of consumption volatility. We denote the Sharpe ratio implied by this model as

$$\mathrm{SR}_t^{\mathrm{CV}} \equiv \gamma \widehat{\sigma}_t(\Delta c_{t+1}).$$

Within the confines of this chapter, it is not possible to investigate the range of possible econometric techniques for modeling changing volatility in consumption growth. Here, we make a first-pass at addressing this question by modeling the volatility of consumption growth as a GARCH process (Bollerslev, 1987). With these estimates of $\sigma_t(\Delta c_{t+1})$ in hand, we then move on to ask whether the framework in (4.5) is helpful in explaining the pattern of variability in the Sharpe ratio that we document here.

To ensure that estimates of the conditional variance of consumption growth are non-negative, we estimate an EGARCH model through maximum likelihood for the volatility of the innovation of quarterly consumption growth. The EGARCH model takes the form

$$\Delta c_t = \alpha_0 + \sum_{i=1}^{3} \alpha_i \Delta c_{t-1} + \epsilon_t$$

$$\log(\sigma_t^2) = \delta_0 + \delta_1 \log(\sigma_{t-1}^2) + \delta_2 \left| \frac{\epsilon_{t-1}}{\sigma_{t-1}} \right| + \delta_3 \left(\frac{\epsilon_{t-1}}{\sigma_{t-1}} \right) + \delta_4' \mathbf{X}_{t-1},$$

where σ_t^2 is the conditional variance of ϵ_t, and $\mathbf{X}_{t-1}$ is a vector of predetermined conditioning variables that may influence the volatility of consumption growth. Table 11.6 reports estimates of the parameters α_i and δ_i for four specifications: one with no conditioning variables (column 1); one in which $\mathbf{X}_{t-1} = \widehat{\text{cay}}_{t-1}$ (column 2); one in which $\mathbf{X}_{t-1} = r_{s,t-1} - r_{f,t-1}$ (column 3); and one in which $\mathbf{X}_{t-1} = (\widehat{\text{cay}}_{t-1}, r_{s,t-1} - r_{f,t-1})'$ (column 4). The results suggests that the volatility of consumption growth is not constant over time; e.g., the coefficient on the GARCH term, δ_2, is much larger than its standard deviation. This result is the same as that found by Piazzesi (2002). We take the exponential of fitted values of $\log\left(\sigma_t^2\right)$ from the fourth column as our estimate $\widehat{\sigma}_t^2(\Delta c_{t+1})$. The square root of these fitted values, $\sqrt{\widehat{\sigma}_t^2}$, is our estimate of the conditional standard deviation, $\widehat{\sigma}_t(\Delta c_{t+1})$, used to compute SR_t^{CV}.

The value of relative risk aversion, γ, that matches the mean Sharpe ratio in our sample is 92, a large number that illustrates the equity premium puzzle emphasized by Mehra and Prescott (1985) and Hansen and Jagannathan (1991).[22] The focus of this chapter is not on this unconditional puzzle but on the pattern of variability in the conditional Sharpe ratio. Nevertheless, the high value for risk aversion required to match the mean Sharpe ratio underscores an important point, namely that modeling the variance of consumption growth as time-varying does not by itself help resolve the equity premium puzzle. Although the results in Table 11.6 imply that there may be some variation in the volatility of consumption growth, it is quantitatively minuscule when compared to the variability of SR_t^{VW}. This is evident in Fig. 11.3, which plots the volatility of SR_t^{CV} along with that of SR_t^{VW}.

For the BY-EZW model, the constants a and b can be chosen freely to match the mean and volatility of the Sharpe ratio estimated in the data. Given the estimate $\widehat{\sigma}_t(\Delta c_{t+1})$, an estimate of an unrestricted version of this model's implied Sharpe ratio is obtained as

$$\text{SR}_t^{\text{BY-EZW}} = a + b\widehat{\sigma}_t(\Delta c_{t+1}).$$

In the BY-EZW model, the parameters are restricted by the calibration in their model. By choosing a and b freely, we ensure that the BY-EZW model fits the first two moments of the Sharpe ratio and ask how well it then fits the dynamics of the empirical Sharpe ratio. This model, like the consumption-volatility model, does not match the dynamic behavior of the empirical Sharpe ratio for the CRSP stock market return.

[22] The mean Sharpe ratio in our sample is 0.78 on an annual basis, somewhat larger than that typically reported (e.g., Campbell and Cochrane (1999) report a Sharpe ratio for log returns of 0.43 in postwar data). As a result, the value for γ needed to match this Sharpe ratio is also somewhat larger than that typically required of the consumption-based model considered above. The reason is that we compute volatility, in the denominator, from daily returns and then convert to a quarterly rate. Because daily returns are positively serially correlated, this number is smaller than the volatility of quarterly or monthly returns. Computing volatility from either of the latter delivers a value for γ that is closer to 50 rather than the 92 we report above.

Table 11.6 Maximum likelihood estimates of EGARCH(1,1) model for consumption growth

	1	2	3	4
		Mean equation		
Constant	0.002	0.002	0.003	0.003
(SE)	(0.001)	(0.001)	(0.001)	(0.001)
Δc_{t-1}	0.319	0.252	0.292	0.295
(SE)	(0.076)	(0.070)	(0.070)	(0.071)
Δc_{t-2}	0.029	0.064	0.042	0.040
(SE)	(0.082)	(0.065)	(0.078)	(0.078)
Δc_{t-3}	0.201	0.172	0.181	0.190
(SE)	(0.069)	(0.068)	(0.071)	(0.071)
		Variance equation		
Constant	−1.007	−1.487	−1.562	−0.828
(SE)	(0.098)	(1.153)	(0.984)	(2.534)
$\left\lvert\frac{\epsilon_{t-1}}{\sigma_{t-1}}\right\rvert$	0.173	−0.036	0.167	0.168
(SE)	(0.079)	(0.057)	(0.092)	(0.112)
$\frac{\epsilon_{t-1}}{\sigma_{t-1}}$	−0.057	0.021	−0.035	−0.043
(SE)	(0.089)	(0.064)	(0.086)	(0.086)
σ^2_{t-1}	0.920	1.007	0.866	0.881
(SE)	(0.087)	(0.026)	(0.088)	(0.098)
$\widehat{\text{cay}}_{t-1}$		−2.301		−0.948
(SE)		(2.1364)		(2.751)
$r_{t-1} - r_{f,t-1}$			−1.85	−1.675
(SE)			(1.269)	(1.527)

This table reports estimates from the EGARCH(1,1) model:

$$\Delta c_t = \alpha_0 + \alpha_1 \Delta c_{t-1} + \alpha_2 \Delta c_{t-2} + \alpha_3 \Delta c_{t-3} + \epsilon_t$$
$$\log(\sigma_t^2) = \delta_0 + \delta_1 \log(\sigma^2_{t-1}) + \delta_2 \left|\frac{\epsilon_{t-1}}{\sigma_{t-1}}\right| + \delta_3 \frac{\epsilon_{t-1}}{\sigma_{t-1}} + \delta_4 X_{t-1},$$

where σ_t^2 is the conditional variance of ϵ_t. The regressors in X_{t-1} are as follows: Δc_t is consumption growth, $\widehat{\text{cay}}_{t-1} \equiv c_{t-1} - \widehat{\beta}_a a_{t-1} - \widehat{\beta}_y y_{t-1}$, and $r_{t-1} - r_{f,t-1}$ is lagged excess returns for the CRSP-VW index. Bollerslev–Wooldridge robust standard errors appear in parentheses beneath the coefficient estimates. The sample runs from the first quarter of 1953 to the first quarter of 2001.

This can be seen in Table 11.7, which presents summary statistics for the empirical Sharpe ratio estimated from the data, SR_t^{VW}, the Campbell–Cochrane Sharpe ratio, SR_t^{CC}, the consumption-volatility Sharpe ratio, SR_t^{CV}, and the BY-EZW model, $\text{SR}_t^{\text{BY-EZW}}$. The table illustrates several aspects of the Sharpe ratio on the U.S. stock market that these models have difficulty explaining. First, the standard deviation of SR_t^{VW}

Table 11.7 Summary statistics for sharpe ratios

	SR_t^{VW}	SR_t^{CC}	SR_t^{CV}	$SR_t^{BY\text{-}EZW}$
		Correlation matrix		
SR_t^{VW}	1.00	0.39	0.03	0.03
SR_t^{CC}	0.39	1.00	−0.03	−0.03
SR_t^{CV}	0.03	−0.03	1.00	1.00
$SR_t^{BY\text{-}EZW}$	0.03	−0.03	1.00	1.00
		Univariate summary statistics		
Mean	0.39	0.23	0.39	0.39
Standard deviation	0.47	0.09	0.08	0.47
Autocorrelation	0.85	0.97	0.86	0.86

SR_t^{VW} is the Sharpe ratio estimated from the CRSP-VW index using conditional mean of the level of the standard deviation of returns. SR_t^{CC} is the Sharpe ratio implied by Campbell and Cochrane (1999); SR_t^{CV} is the Sharpe ratio implied by the consumption volatility model where the conditional correlation of consumption growth and stock returns is set to unity:

$$SR_t^{CV} = \frac{E_t(R_{t+1}) - R_t^f}{\sigma_t(R_{t+1})} = \gamma\, \sigma_t(\Delta c_{t+1}),$$

where γ is the constant coefficient of risk aversion and is set equal to 92. $SR_t^{BY\text{-}EZW}$ is calculated as

$$SR_t^{BY\text{-}EZW} = \frac{E_t(R_{t+1}) - R_t^f}{\sigma_t(R_{t+1})} = a + b\, \sigma_t(\Delta c_{t+1}),$$

where a and b are chosen to match the mean and volatility of $SR_t^{BY\text{-}EZW}$ to the estimated Sharpe ratio SR_t^{VW}. The statistics are computed for the largest common set of available data for all the variables, which spans the fourth quarter of 1953 to the fourth quarter of 2000.

is over five times as large as that of either SR_t^{CC} or SR_t^{CV}, reinforcing the notion that consumption-based models fail to replicate the magnitude of volatility in the risk-return trade-off. Second, the Campbell–Cochrane Sharpe ratio is too autocorrelated, whereas the consumption-volatility model produces about the right autocorrelation. Third, SR_t^{CC} is positively correlated with SR_t^{VW} with this correlation equal to about 0.4. By contrast, the consumption-volatility model fails miserably along this dimension, displaying a *negative* correlation, equal to −0.3 with SR_t^{VW}. By construction, $SR_t^{BY\text{-}EZW}$ matches the mean and volatility of SR_t^{VW} but has the same negative correlation with SR_t^{VW} that the consumption-volatility model has. That's because both models are linear functions of consumption volatility, which itself is negatively correlated with the Sharpe ratio for the U.S. stock market. This negative correlation is evident in Fig. 11.3, which plots SR_t^{VW} and SR_t^{CV} over time. These results suggest that time variation in consumption volatility is unhelpful in explaining observed variability in the risk-return trade-off on broad stock returns. Consistent with this conclusion, Kandel and Stambaugh (1990) report that fitted mean and fitted volatility for five-year returns are both higher in recessions than in booms, a finding at odds with their estimates of the dynamic behavior of consumption volatility.

The conclusions so far have been based on calculations in which the conditional correlation, $\rho_t(\Delta c_{t+1}, R_{st+1})$, is fixed at unity. It is reasonable to ask whether this approach may be overly restrictive, in that allowing for time variation in the conditional correlation might help explain the pattern of variability in the Sharpe ratio we observe. In Whitelaw (2000), e.g., time variation in the Sharpe ratio is generated by time variation in the conditional correlation, $\rho_t(\Delta c_{t+1}, R_{st+1})$. But a recent empirical study by Duffee (2002) suggests that times of higher expected excess returns and higher Sharpe ratios on the U.S. stock market coincide with times of *lower* correlations of consumption with returns, not higher as required by (4.5).

Other models of the pricing kernel could produce different results. Barberis et al. (2001) study an economy in which investors derive utility from consumption and wealth, and show that this model can replicate persistent time variation in conditional excess returns. Like the Campbell–Cochrane model, however, the Sharpe ratio they report ranges from about 0.20 to 0.40 on a quarterly basis, far less than that documented in Fig. 11.2.[23] Alternatively, the pricing kernel could be a function of durable goods consumption if households have nonseparable utility across durable and nondurable consumption. Yogo (2006) finds some evidence for conditional heteroskedasticity in the consumption of durable goods, which could impart empirically relevant conditional heteroskedasticity into the pricing kernel. An important question for future research is whether the dynamic behavior of durable goods volatility can help explain the dynamic behavior of the Sharpe ratio on the U.S. stock market.

The shortcomings of existing equilibrium models documented here are distinct from those underlying the "equity premium puzzle" of Mehra and Prescott (1985) and Hansen and Jagannathan (1991). These studies show that standard asset pricing theory fails to account for the high mean value of the Sharpe ratio. Although those papers focused on the average value of the Sharpe ratio, we concentrate here on its variation through time. The evidence presented in this chapter suggests that even our best fitting asset pricing models have difficulty replicating the observed pattern of variation in the price of stock market risk and leave a "Sharpe ratio variability puzzle" that remains to be explained.

5. CONCLUSION

There is now a large and growing body of empirical evidence that finds forecastability of excess equity returns and measures of their volatility. Recent theoretical work in financial

[23]These statements are based on the numbers reported in Figure 6 of Barberis et al. (2001).

economics has demonstrated that such forecastability is not necessarily inconsistent with market efficiency. In particular, stock market predictability can be generated by time variation in the rate at which rational, utility maximizing investors discount expected future cash-flows from risky assets. These theoretical advances hold out hope that a unified framework for rationalizing variation in the risk-return trade-off can be developed.

This chapter reviews what is known about the risk-return relation in the U.S. stock market. We examine the empirical procedures and results of a large number of studies that canvass the subject of predictability in stock returns and stock return volatility, and we assess whether the current state of theoretical knowledge can account for such predictability. We also present updated empirical evidence on the risk-return relation by forecasting both the mean and volatility of excess stock market returns.

We draw several conclusions. First, after an extensive review of the statistical issues in return predictability regressions, we conclude that the historical behavior of the U.S. stock market cannot be understood without admitting some degree of predictability in excess returns. The conditional expected excess return on the U.S. stock market varies over long horizons and is an important contributor to volatility in the Sharpe ratio. Second, the evidence for changing stock market risk is not confined to high-frequency data; instead, stock market volatility is forecastable over horizons ranging from one quarter to six years. Third, distinguishing between the *conditional* correlation (conditional on lagged mean and lagged volatility) and *unconditional* correlation between the conditional expected excess stock return and its conditional volatility is crucial for understanding the empirical risk-return relation. In our most general empirical specification, we find a positive conditional correlation that is strongly statistically significant, whereas the unconditional correlation is weakly negative and statistically insignificant. Fourth, the Sharpe ratio for the U.S. aggregate stock market is both countercyclical and highly volatile, and its dynamic behavior is not well captured by leading consumption-based asset pricing models, including habit-based models and models based on time-varying or stochastic consumption volatility. More theoretical work is needed to explain the sheer magnitude of volatility in the Sharpe ratio, as well as its pattern of dynamic behavior with the macroeconomy.

APPENDIX: DATA DESCRIPTION

Consumption, C_t

Consumption is measured as expenditure on nondurables and services, excluding shoes and clothing. The quarterly data are seasonally adjusted at annual rates, in billions of chain-weighted 1996 dollars. The components are chain-weighted together, and this series is scaled up so that the sample mean matches the sample mean of total personal consumption expenditures. Our source is the U.S. Department of Commerce, Bureau of Economic Analysis.

After-Tax Labor Income, Y_t

Labor income is defined as wages and salaries + transfer payments + other labor income − personal contributions for social insurance − taxes. Taxes are defined as [wages and salaries/(wages and salaries + proprietors' income with IVA and Ccadj + rental income + personal dividends + personal interest income)] times personal tax and nontax payments, where IVA is inventory valuation and Ccadj is capital consumption adjustments. The quarterly data are in current dollars. A real per capita series is created by dividing by a measure of the population and the price deflator listed below. Our source is the Bureau of Economic Analysis.

Population

A measure of population is created by dividing real total disposable income by real per capita disposable income. Our source is the Bureau of Economic Analysis.

Wealth, A_t

Total wealth is household net worth in billions of current dollars, measured at the end of the period. Stock market wealth includes direct household holdings, mutual fund holdings, holdings of private and public pension plans, personal trusts, and insurance companies. Nonstock wealth includes tangible/real estate wealth, nonstock financial assets (all deposits, open-market paper, U.S. Treasuries and Agency securities, municipal securities, corporate and foreign bonds, and mortgages), and also includes ownership of privately traded companies in noncorporate equity and other. Subtracted off are liabilities, including mortgage loans and loans made under home equity lines of credit and secured by junior liens, installment consumer debt, and other. Our source is the Board of Governors of the Federal Reserve System. A complete description of these data may be found at http://www.federalreserve.gov/releases/Z1/Current/.

Price Deflator

The nominal after-tax labor income and wealth data are deflated by the personal consumption expenditure chain-type deflator (1996 = 100), seasonally adjusted. In principle, one would like a measure of the price deflator for total flow consumption here. Since this variable is unobservable, we use the total expenditure deflator as a proxy. Our source is the Bureau of Economic Analysis.

Excess Returns, $r_{t+1} - r_{ft}$

Excess returns are returns to the CRSP value-weighted stock index, less than the 3-month treasury bill yield. Our sources are the Center for Research in Securities Prices and the Board of Governors of the Federal Reserve System.

CRSP Dividend-Price Ratio, $d_t - p_t$

The CRSP dividend-ratio is calculated as the log ratio of CRSP dividends to the price level of the CRSP value-weighted stock index (imputed from CRSP-VW returns, including dividends). Our source is the CRSP.

Default Spread, DEF_t

The default spread is the difference between the BAA corporate bond rate and the AAA corporate bond rate. Our source is the Moody's Corporate Bond Indices.

Relative Bill Rate, $RREL_t$

The relative bill rate is the three-month treasury bill yield less its four-quarter moving average. Our source is the Board of Governors of the Federal Reserve System.

Term Spread, TRM_t

The term spread is the difference between the 10-year treasury bond yield and the three-month treasury bill yield. Our source is the Board of Governors of the Federal Reserve System.

Commercial Paper Spread, CP_t

The commercial paper spread is the difference between the yield on six-month commercial paper and the three-month treasury bill yield. Our source is the Board of Governors of the Federal Reserve System.

One-Year Treasury Bill Yield, $TB1Y_t$

Our source for the one-year treasury bill yield is the Board of Governors of the Federal Reserve System.

ACKNOWLEDGMENTS

We acknowledge financial support from the National Science Foundation (Lettau and Ludvigson) and the Alfred P. Sloan Foundation (Ludvigson). We are grateful to Michael Brandt, Rob Engle, Stijn Van Nieuwerburgh, and Jessica Wachter for helpful comments. Nathan Barczi and Adam Kolasinski provided excellent research assistance.

REFERENCES

Abel, A. B. (1988) "Stock Prices Under Time-Varying Dividend Risk," *Journal of Monetary Economics*, 22, 375–393.

Andersen, T. G., T. Bollerslev, and F. X. Diebold (2002) "Parametric and Nonparametric Volatility Measurement," Unpublished paper, University of Pennsylvania.

Andersen, T. G., T. Bollerslev, F. X. Diebold, and P. Labys (2003) "Modeling and Forecasting Realized Volatility," *Econometrica*, 71, 579–626.

Ang, A., and G. Bekaert (2007) "Stock Return Predictability: Is it There?," *Review of Financial Studies*, 20(3), 651–707.

Backus, D. K., and A. W. Gregory (1993) "Theoretical Relations between Risk Premiums and Conditional Variances," *Journal of Business and Economic Statistics*, 11(2), 177–185.

Bai, J., and S. Ng (2002) "Determining the Number of Factors in Approximate Factor Models," *Econometrica*, 70(1), 191–221.

Bai, J., and S. Ng (2006) "Confidence Intervals for Diffusion Index Forecasts and Inference for Factor-Augmented Regressions," *Econometrica*, 74(4), 1133–1150.

Bansal, R., and A. Yaron (2004) "Risks for the Long-Run: A Potential Resolution of Asset Pricing Puzzles," *Journal of Finance*, 59(4), 1481–1509.

Barberis, N., M. Huang, and T. Santos (2001) "Prospect Theory and Asset Prices," *Quarterly Journal of Economics*, 116(1), 1–53.

Black, F. (1976) "Studies of Stock Price Volatility Changes," *Proceedings of teh 1976 Meetings of the Business and Economics Statistics Section (American Statistical Association)*, pp. 177–181.

Blinder, A. S., and A. Deaton (1985) "The Time Series Consumption Function Revisited," *Brookings Papers on Economic Activity*, 2, 465–511.

Bollerslev, T. (1986) "Generalized Autoregressive Conditional Heteroskedasticity," *Journal of Econometrics*, 31, 307–327.

Bollerslev, T. (1987) "A Conditionally Heteroskedastic Time Series Model for Speculative Prices and Rates of Return," *Review of Economics and Statistics*, 69(3), 542–547.

Bollerslev, T., R. Engle, and J. Wooldridge (1988) "A Capital Asset Pricing Model with Time-Varying Covariances," *Journal of Political Economy*, 96, 116–131.

Boudoukh, J., M. Richardson, and R.F. Whitelaw (1997) "Nonlinearities in the Relation between the Equity Risk Premium and the Term Structure," *Management Science*, 43(3), 371–385.

Boudoukh, J., M. Richardson, and R. F. Whitelaw (2004) "On the Importance of Measuring Payout Yield: Implications for Empirical Asset Pricing," NBER Working Paper No. 10651.

Boudoukh, J., M. Richardson, and R. Whitelaw (2008) "The Myth of Long-Horizon Predictability," *Review of Financial Studies*, 21(4), 1577–1605.

Brandt, M. W., and C. S. Jones (2005) "Bayesian Range-Based Estimation of Stochastic Volatility Models," *Finance Research Letters*, 2, 201–209.

Brandt, M. W., and Q. Kang (2004) "On the Relation Between the Conditional Mean and Volatility of Stock Returns: A Latent VAR Approach," *Journal of Financial Economics*, 72, 217–257.

Breen, W., L. R. Glosten, and R. Jagannathan (1989) "Economic Significance of Predictable Variations in Stock Index Returns," *Journal of Finance*, 44(5), 1177–1189.

Campbell, J. Y. (1987) "Stock Returns and the Term Structure," *Journal of Financial Economics*, 18, 373–399.

Campbell, J. Y. (1991) "A Variance Decomposition for Stock Returns," *Economic Journal*, 101, 157–179.

Campbell, J. Y. (1996) "Understanding Risk and Return," *Journal of Political Economy*, 104(2), 298–345.

Campbell, J. Y. (2003) "Consumption-Based Asset Pricing," In G. Constantinides, M. Harris, and R. Stulz (eds.), *Handbook of the Economics of Finance Vol. I-B*, pp. 803–887. Amsterdam: North-Holland.

Campbell, J. Y., and J. H. Cochrane (1999) "By Force of Habit: A Consumption-Based Explanation of Aggregate Stock Market Behavior," *Journal of Political Economy*, 107, 205–251.

Campbell, J. Y., and L. Hentschel (1992) "An Asymmetric Model of Changing Volatility in Stock Returns," *Journal of Financial Economics*, 31, 281–318.
Campbell, J. Y., A. W. Lo, and C. MacKinlay (1997) *The Econometrics of Financial Markets*. Princeton, NJ: Princeton University Press.
Campbell, J. Y., and G. Mankiw (1989) "Consumption, Income, and Interest Rates: Reinterpreting the Time Series Evidence," In: O. Blanchard, and S. Fischer (eds.), *NBER Macroeconomics Annual: 1989*, pp. 185–216. Cambridge, MA: MIT Press.
Campbell, J. Y., and P. Perron (1991) "Pitfalls and Opportunities: What Macroeconomists Should Know About Unit Roots," In: O. J. Blanchard, and S. Fischer (eds.). *NBER Macroeconomics Annual: 1991*, pp. 141–201. Cambridge, MA: MIT Press.
Campbell, J. Y., and R. J. Shiller (1989) "The Dividend-Price Ratio and Expectations of Future Dividends and Discount Factors," *Review of Financial Studies*, 1(3), 195–228.
Campbell, J. Y., and R. J. Shiller (2001) "Valuation Ratios and the Long-Run Stock Market Outlook: An Update," NBER Working Paper No. 8221.
Campbell, J. Y., and S. Thompson (2005) "Predicting the Equity Premium Out of Sample: Can Anything Beat the Historical Average?," NBER Working Paper No. 11468.
Campbell, J. Y., and M. Yogo (2002) "Efficient Tests of Stock Return Predictability," Unpublished paper, Harvard University.
Campbell, S. D., and F. X. Diebold (2009) "Stock Returns and Expected Business Conditions: Half a Century of Direct Evidence," *Journal of Business and Economic Statistics*, 27, 266–278.
Campello, M., L. Chen, and L. Zhang (2005) "Expected Returns, Yield Spreads, And Asset Pricing Tests," NBER Working Paper No. 12555.
Chen, X., and S. C. Ludvigson (2004) "Land of Addicts? An Empirical Investigation of Habit-Based Asset Pricing Models," Unpublished paper, New York University.
Chen, X., and S. C. Ludvigson (2007) "An Estimation of Economic Models with Recursive Preferences," Unpublished paper, New York University.
Christoffersen, P. F., and F. X. Diebold (2000) "How Relevant is Volatility Forecasting for Financial Risk Management?," *The Review of Economics and Statistics*, 82, 12–23.
Clark, T., and M. McCracken (2001) "Tests of Equal Forecast Accuracy and Encompassing for Nested Models," *Journal of Econometrics*, 105, 85–110.
Clark, T., and M. McCracken (2005) "The Power of Tests of Predictive Ability in the Presence of Structural Breaks," *Journal of Econometrics*, 124(1), 1–31.
Clark, T., and K. D. West (2006) "Using Out-of-Sample Mean Squared Prediction Errors to Test the Martingale Difference Hypothesis," *Journal of Econometrics*, 135, 155–186.
Clark, T., and K. D. West (2007) "Approximately Normal Tests For Equal Predictive Accuracy in Nested Models," *Journal of Econometrics*, 138, 291–311.
Cochrane, J. H. (1991a) "Explaining the Variance of Price-Dividend Ratios," *Review of Financial Studies*, 5(2), 243–280.
Cochrane, J. H. (1991b) "Volatility Tests and Efficient Markets: A Review Essay," *Journal of Monetary Economics*, 127, 463–485.
Cochrane, J. H. (1994) "Permanent and Transitory Components of GDP and Stock Prices," *Quarterly Journal of Economics*, 109, 241–265.
Cochrane, J. H. (1997) "Where is the Market Going? Uncertain Facts and Novel Theories," *Economic Perspectives, Federal Reserve Bank of Chicago*, 11, 1–37.

Cochrane, J. H. (2005) *Asset Pricing, Revised ed.* Princeton, NJ: Princeton University Press.

Cochrane, J. H. (2008) "The Dog That Did Not Bark: A Defense of Return Predictability," *Review of Financial Studies*, 21(4), 1533–1575.

Constantinides, G. M., and D. Duffie (1996) "Asset Pricing With Heterogeneous Consumers," *Journal of Political Economy*, 104, 219–240.

Duffee, G. R. (2002) "Term Premia and Interest Rate Forecasts in Affine Models," *Journal of Finance*, 57, 405–443.

Eliasz, P. (2005) "Optimal Median Unbiased Estimation of Coefficients on highly Persistent Regressors," Unpublished paper, Princeton University.

Elliott, G., and J. H. Stock (1994) "Inference In Time Series Regression When the Order of Integration of a Regressor is Unknown," *Econometric Theory*, 10, 672–700.

Engle, R. F. (2001) "New Frontiers for Arch Models," Unpublished paper, Stern School of Business, New York University.

Engle, R. F., and A. J. Patton (2000) "What Good is A Volatility Model?," Unpublished paper, Stern School of Business, New York University.

Epstein, L., and S. Zin (1989) "Substitution Risk Aversion and the Temporal Behavior of Consumption and Asset Returns: A Theoretical Framework," *Econometrica*, 57, 937–968.

Epstein, L., and S. Zin (1991) "Substitution, Risk Aversion, and the Temporal Behavior of Consumption and Asset Returns: An Empirical Investigation," *Journal of Political Economy*, 99, 555–576.

Fama, E. F., and K. R. French (1988a) "Dividend Yields and Expected Stock Returns," *Journal of Financial Economics*, 22, 3–27.

Fama, E. F., and K. R. French (1988b) "Permanent and Temporary Components of Stock Prices," *Journal of Political Economy*, 96(2), 246–273.

Fama, E. F., and K. R. French (1989) "Business Conditions and Expected Returns on Stocks and Bonds," *Journal of Financial Economics*, 25, 23–49.

Fama, E. F., and K. R. French (1993) "Common Risk Factors in the Returns on Stocks and Bonds," *Journal of Financial Economics*, 33, 3–56.

Fama, E. F., and K. R. French (2002) "The Equity Premium," *Journal of Finance*, 57(2), 637–659.

Fama, E. F., and G. W. Schwert (1977) "Human Capital and Capital Market Equilibrium," *Journal of Financial Economics*, 4, 115–146.

Fernandez-Corugedo, E., S. Price, and A. Blake (2002) "The Dynamics of Consumer Expenditure: The UK Consumption ECM Redux," Bank of England Working Paper.

Ferson, W. E., and C. R. Harvey (1991) "The Variation of Economic Risk Premiums," *Journal of Political Economy*, 99, 385–415.

Ferson, W. E., S. Sarkissian, and T. T. Simin (2003) "Spurious Regressions in Financial Economics?," *Journal of Finance*, 58(4), 1393–1413.

Fisher, L., and G. Voss (2004) "Consumption, Wealth, and Expected Stock Returns in Australia," *The Economic Record*, 80, 359–372.

French, K., G. W. Schwert, and R. F. Stambaugh (1987) "Expected Stock Returns and Volatility," *Journal of Financial Economics*, 19, 3–30.

Gallant, A. R., L. P. Hansen, and G. Tauchen (1990) "Using Conditional Moments of Asset Payoffs to Infer the Volatility of Intertemporal Marginal Rates of Subsitution," *Journal of Econometrics*, 45(2), 141–179.

Gallant, A. R., and G. Tauchen (1989) "Seminonparametric Estimation of Conditionally Constrained Heterogeneous Processes: Asset Pricing Applications," *Econometrica*, 57(5), 1091–1120. Ghysels et al.

Ghysels, E., P. Santa-Clara, and R. Valkanov (2005) "There is a Risk-Return Tradeoff After All!," *Journal of Financial Economics*, 76, 509–548.

Glosten, L. R., R. Jagannathan, and D. E. Runkle (1993) "On the Relation Between the Expected Value and the Volatility of the Nominal Excess Return on Stocks," *Journal of Finance*, 48(5), 1779–1801.

Goyal, A., and I. Welch (2007) "A Comprehensive Look at the Empirical Performance of Equity Premium Prediction," *Review of Financial Studies* (forthcoming).

Graham, J. R., and C. R. Harvey (2008) "Expectations of Equity Risk Premia, Volatility, and Asymmetry from a Corporate Finance Perspective," *Review of Financial Studies*, 21(4), 1455–1508.

Guo, H. (2006) "On the Out-of-Sample Predictability of Stock Market Returns," *Journal of Business*, 79(2), 645–670.

Hansen, L. P. (2007) "Beliefs, Doubts and Learning: Valuing Macroeconomic Risk," *American Economic Association Papers and Proceedings Richard T. Ely Lecture*, 97(2), 1–30.

Hansen, L. P., and R. Jagannathan (1991) "Restrictions on Intertemporal Marginal Rates of Substitution Implied by Asset Returns," *Journal of Political Economy*, 99, 225–262.

Harrison, P., and H. H. Zhang (1999) "An Investigation of the Risk and Return Relation at Long Horizons," *Review of Economics and Statistics*, 81(3), 399–408.

Harvey, C. R. (1989) "Time-Varying Conditional Covariances in Tests of Asset Pricing Models," *Journal of Financial Economics*, 24, 289–371.

Harvey, C. R. (1991) "The World Price of Covariance Risk," *Journal of Finance*, 46, 111–117.

Harvey, C. R. (2001) "The Specification of Conditional Expectations," *Journal of Empirical Finance*, 8(5), 573–638.

Hodrick, R. (1992) "Dividend Yields and Expected Stock Returns: Alternative Procedures for Inference and Measurement," *Review of Financial Studies*, 5, 357–386.

Inoue, A., and L. Kilian (2004) "In-Sample or Out-of-Sample Tests of Predictability: Which One Should We Use?," *Econometric Reviews*, 23(4), 371–402.

Johansen, S. (1988) "Statistical Analysis of Cointegrating Vectors," *Journal of Economic Dynamics and Control*, 12, 231–254.

Kandel, S., and R. F. Stambaugh (1989) "Modeling Expected Stock Returns for Long and Short Horizons," Unpublished Paper, Rodney L. White Center, Wharton School, University of Pennsylvania.

Kandel, S., and R. F. Stambaugh (1990) "Expectations and Volatility of Consumption and Asset Returns," *Review of Financial Studies*, 3, 207–232.

Lamont, O. (1998) "Earnings and Expected Returns," *Journal of Finance*, 53, 1563–1587.

Leamer, E. (1978) *Specification Searches*. New York, NY: John Wiley and Sons.

LeRoy, S., and R. Porter (1981) "The Present Value Relation: Tests Based on Variance Bounds," *Econometrica*, 49, 555–557.

Lettau, M., and S. C. Ludvigson (2001a) "Consumption, Aggregate Wealth and Expected Stock Returns," *Journal of Finance*, 56(3), 815–849.

Lettau, M., and S. C. Ludvigson (2001b) "Resurrecting the (C)CAPM: A Cross-Sectional Test When Risk Premia are Time-Varying," *Journal of Political Economy*, 109(6), 1238–1287.

Lettau, M., and S. C. Ludvigson (2004) "Understanding Trend and Cycle in Asset Values: Reevaluating the Wealth Effect on Consumption," *American Economic Review*, 94(1), 276–299.

Lettau, M., and S. C. Ludvigson (2005) "Expected Returns and Expected Dividend Growth," *Journal of Financial Economics*, 76, 583–626.

Lettau, M., S. C. Ludvigson, and J. A. Wachter (2008) "The Declining Equity Premium: What Role Does Macroeconomic Risk Play?," *Review of Financial Studies*, 21(4), 1653–1687.

Lettau, M., and S. Van Nieuwerburgh (2007) "Reconciling the Return Predictability Evidence: In-Sample Forecasts, Out-of-Sample Forecasts, and Parameter Instability," *Review of Financial Studies*, 21(4), 1607–1652.

Lewellen, J. W. (1999) "The Time Series Relations Among Expected Return, Risk, and Book-to-Market," *Journal of Financial Economics*, 54, 5–53.

Lewellen, J. W. (2004) "Predicting Returns With Financial Ratios," *Journal of Financial Economics*, 74, 209–235.

Lintner, J. (1965) "Security Prices, Risk and Maximal Gains from Diversification," *Journal of Finance*, 20, 587–615.

Lo, A., and A. C. MacKinlay (1990) "Data Snooping Biases in Test of Financial Models," *Review of Financial Studies*, 3, 175–208.

Ludvigson, S. C., and S. Ng (2007) "The Empirical Risk-Return Relation: A Factor Analysis Approach," *Journal of Financial Economics*, 83, 171–222.

Mankiw, N. G., and M. D. Shapiro (1986) "Do We Reject Too Often? Small Sample Bias in Tests of Rational Expectations Models," *Economic Letters*, 20, 139–145.

McCracken, M. (1999) "Asymptotics for Out-of-Sample Tests of Causality," Unpublished manuscript, Louisiana State University.

Mehra, R., and E. C. Prescott (1985) "The Equity Premium Puzzle," *Journal of Monetary Economics*, 15, 145–161.

Nelson, C. C., and M. J. Kim (1993) "Predictable Stock Returns: The Role of Small Sample Bias," *Journal of Finance*, 43, 641–661.

Nelson, D. B. (1991) "Conditional Heteroskedasticity in Asset Returns: A New Approach," *Econometrica*, 59(2), 347–370.

Ogaki, M., and J.Y. Park (1997) "A Cointegration Approach to Estimating Preference Parameters," *Journal of Econometrics*, 82(1), 107–134.

Pagan, A. R., and Y. S. Hong (1991) "Nonparametric Estimation and the Risk Premium," In: W. A. Barnett, J. A. Powell, and G. E. Tauchen (eds.), *Nonparametric Models in Econometrics and Statistics: Proceedings of the Fifth International in Economic Theory and Econometrics*, pp. 51–75. Cambridge, New York and Melbourne: Cambridge University Press.

Pastor, L., M. Sinha, and B. Swaminathan (2008) "Estimating the Intertemporal Risk-Return Tradeoff Using the Implied Cost of Capital," *Journal of Finance*, 63, 2859–2897.

Piazzesi, M. (2002) "Comment on Gabaix and Laibson, 'The 6D Bias and the Equity Premium Puzzle'," In: B. S. Bernanke, and K. Rogoff (eds.), *NBER Macroeconomics Annual: 2001*, vol. 16, pp. 317–329. Cambridge and London: MIT Press.

Rapach, D. E., and M. E. Wohar (2002) "In-Sample vs. Out-of-Sample Tests of Stock Return Predictability in the Context of Data Mining'," Unpublished paper, Department of Economics, University of Nebraska at Omaha.

Rossi, B. (2005) "Optimal Tests for Nested Model Selection with Underlying Parameter Instability," *Econometric Theory*, 21(5), 962–990.

Schwert, G. W. (1989) "Why Does Stock Market Volatility Change over Time," *Journal of Finance*, 44(5), 1115–1153.
Sharpe, W. (1964) "Capital Asset Prices: A Theory of Market Equilibrium under Conditions of Risk," *Journal of Finance*, 19, 425–444.
Shiller, R. J. (1981) "Do Stock Prices Move Too Much to be Justified by Subsequent Changes in Dividends?," *American Economic Review*, 71, 421–436.
Siegel, J. J. (1998) *Stocks for the Long Run: The Definitive Guide to Financial Market Returns and Long-term Investment Strategies, Seconded*. New York, NY: McGraw Hill.
Sims, C. A., J. H. Stock, and M. W. Watson (1990) "Inference in Linear Time-Series Models with Some Unit Roots," *Econometrica*, 58(1), 113–144.
Stambaugh, R. F. (1999) "Predictive Regressions," *Journal of Financial Economics*, 54, 375–421.
Stock, J. H., and M. W. Watson (1993) "A Simple Estimator of Cointegrating Vectors in Higher Order Integrated Systems," *Econometrica*, 61, 783–820.
Stock, J. H., and M. W. Watson (1996) "Confidence Sets In Regressions With Highly Serially Correlated Regressors," Unpublished paper, Princeton University.
Stock, J. H., and M. W. Watson (2002) "Forecasting Using Principal Components From a Large Number of Predictors," *Journal of the American Statistical Association*, 97(460), 1167–1179.
Tan, A., and G. Voss (2004) "Consumption and Wealth in Australia," *The Economic Record*, 79, 39–56.
Valkanov, R. (2003) "Long-Horizon Regressions: Theoretical Results and Applications," *Journal of Financial Economics*, 68, 201–232.
Vuolteenaho, T. (2000) "Understanding the Aggregate Book-Market Ratio and its Implications to Current Equity-Premium Expectations," Unpublished paper, Harvard University.
Weil, P. (1989) "The Equity Premium Puzzle and the Risk-Free Rate Puzzle," *Journal of Monetary Economics*, 24(3), 401–421.
Whitelaw, R. F. (1994) "Time Variations and Covariations in the Expectation and Volatility of Stock Market Returns," *The Journal of Finance*, 49(2), 515–541.
Whitelaw, R. F. (2000) "Stock Market Risk and Return: An Equilibrium Approach," *Review of Financial Studies*, 13(3), 521–547.
Xu, F. (2005) "Does Consumption-Wealth Ratio Signal Stock Returns?–VECM Results for Germany," *Economics Bulletin*, 3(30), 1–13.
Yogo, M. (2006) "A Consumption-Based Explanation of the Cross Section of Expected Stock Returns," *Journal of Finance*, 61(2), 539–580.

CHAPTER 12

Affine Term Structure Models

Monika Piazzesi
Department of Economics, Stanford University, Stanford, CA

Contents

Abstract

This chapter reports some recent successes in the study of affine term structure models. After explaining the importance of understanding bond yields and the need for cross-equation restrictions, the paper describes the general technique of pricing bonds in continuous time. Section 3 explains how to specify the short rate, the dynamics of the state vector, and the risk premia in an affine model. Section 4 links them to the fundamentals of an economy, and Section 5 examines some famous affine models. Section 6 explains how to estimate affine models, and Section 7 discusses the empirical performance of affine models.

Keywords: bond yields; affine term structure models; term structure models

1. INTRODUCTION

1.1. Overview

The quest for understanding what moves bond yields has produced an enormous literature with its own journals and graduate courses. Those who want to join the quest are faced with considerable obstacles. The literature has evolved mostly in continuous time, where stochastic calculus reigns and partial differential equations (PDEs) spit fire. The knights in this literature are fighting for different goals, which makes it often difficult to comprehend why the quest is moving in certain directions. But the quest is moving fast, and dragons are being defeated. This chapter wants to report some of these victories made by those working on *affine term structure models*.

Bond yield movements over time can be captured by simple vector autoregressions (VARs) in yields and maybe other macroeconomic variables. Several aspects of bond yields, however, set them apart from other variables typically used in VAR studies. One aspect is that bonds are assets, and that bonds with many different maturities are traded at the same time. Bonds with long maturities are risky when held over short horizons, and risk-averse investors demand compensation for bearing such risk. Arbitrage opportunities in these markets exist unless long yields are risk-adjusted expectations of average future short rates. Movements in the cross section of yields are therefore closely tied together. These ties show up as *cross-equation restrictions* in a yield-VAR. Another aspect of yields is that they are not normally distributed, at least not until recently. This makes it difficult to compute the risk-adjusted expected value of future short rates.

Term structure models capture exactly these aspects of bond yields. They impose the cross-equation restrictions implied by no-arbitrage and allow yields to be nonnormal. The word "affine term structure model" is often used in different ways. I will use the word to describe any arbitrage-free model in which bond yields are affine (constant-plus-linear) functions of some state vector x.[1] Affine models are thus a special class of term structure models, which write the yield $y^{(\tau)}$ of a τ-period bond as

$$y^{(\tau)} = A(\tau) + B(\tau)^{\top} x$$

for coefficients $A(\tau)$ and $B(\tau)$ that depend on maturity τ. The functions $A(\tau)$ and $B(\tau)$ make these yield equations consistent with each other for different values of τ. The functions also make the yield equations consistent with the state dynamics.

The main advantage of affine models is tractability. Having tractable solutions for bond yields is useful because otherwise yields need to be computed with Monte Carlo methods or solution methods for PDEs. Both approaches are computationally costly, especially when model parameters are estimated using panel data on bond yields. The literature on bond pricing starting with Vasicek (1977) and Cox et al. (1985), therefore has focused on closed-form solutions. The riskless rate in these early setups was the only state variable in the economy so that all bond yields were perfectly correlated. A number of extensions of these setups followed both in terms of the number of state variables and the data-generating processes for these variables. Duffie and Kan (1996) finally provided a more complete characterization of models with affine bond yields.[2]

Tractability has to be paid with restrictive assumptions. The functional form of bond yields is obtained from computing risk-adjusted expectations of future short rates. Therefore, restrictive assumptions have to be made on the risk-adjusted dynamics of the state vector. More concretely, the risk-adjusted process for the state vector needs to be an affine diffusion, a process with affine instantaneous mean and variance. (There are no functional form assumptions on the data-generating process for the state vector.) The question is whether this assumption leads to counterfactual data-generating processes for yields. The answer seems to be "yes" when risk premia are specified in ways that imply either constant or time-varying but strictly positive expected excess returns. Recent research, however, has made more flexible assumptions on risk premia. The answer now seems to be "maybe not." A lot more research is needed before the answer is clear–exciting times lie ahead!

The rest of this chapter is organized as follows. The remainder of this introduction argues the importance of understanding bond yields in Subsection 1.2 and the need for cross-equation restrictions in Subsection 1.3. Section 2 explains the general technique of how to price bonds in continuous time. Section 3 explains how to specify the short

[1] New terms such as completely affine, essentially affine, semiaffine, and generalized affine have appeared in the literature. The use of "affine" in this chapter refers to the way yields depend on the state variables, not on the data-generating process of the state variables themselves.

[2] Recently, Gourieroux and Sufana (2004) and Cheridito et al. (2004) have presented affine diffusion models that do not fit into the Duffie–Kan framework.

rate, the dynamics of the state vector, and the risk premia in an affine model. Section 4 links them to the fundamentals of an economy. Section 6 explains how to estimate affine models. Section 7 discusses the empirical performance of affine models.

1.2. Why Care About Bond Yields?

Understanding what moves bond yields is important for at least four reasons. One of these reasons is forecasting. Yields on long-maturity bonds are expected values of average future short yields, at least after an adjustment for risk. This means that the current yield curve contains information about the future path of the economy. Yield spreads have indeed been useful for forecasting not only future short yields (Campbell and Shiller, 1991; Cochrane and Piazzesi, 2005; Fama and Bliss, 1987) but also real activity (Ang et al., 2006; Estrella and Hardouvelis, 1991; Hamilton and Kim, 2002; Harvey, 1988) and inflation (Fama, 1990; Mishkin, 1990), even though these forecasting relationships may be unstable (Stock and Watson, 2003). These forecasts provide a basis for investment decisions of firms, savings decisions of consumers, and policy decisions.

Monetary policy is a second reason for studying the yield curve. In most industrialized countries, the central bank seems to be able to move the short end of the yield curve. What matters for "aggregate demand," however, are long-term yields. For example, U.S. households base their decision on whether to buy or rent a house on long-term mortgage rates and not on the rate in the federal funds market which seems to be controlled by the Federal Reserve Bank. For a given state of the economy, a model of the yield curve helps to understand how movements at the short end translate into longer-term yields. This involves understanding both how the central bank conducts policy and how the transmission mechanism works. The expectations hypothesis (EH) is at work in most papers in this area (e.g., Balduzzi et al., 1996). Little work has been done with more flexible risk premia (Evans and Marshall, 1998, 2001; Piazzesi, 2001).

Debt policy constitutes a third reason. When issuing new debt, governments need to decide about the maturity of the new bonds. For example, the Kennedy administration actively managed the maturity structure of public debt in the early 1960s in what is known as "operation twist." The treasury at the time was trying to flatten or invert the yield curve by selling short maturity debt and buying long maturity notes. The outcome of such operations depends crucially on how bond yields depend on the supply of bonds with different maturities. Real yields in models with nondistortionary taxation and perfect markets are independent of the maturity structure of public debt. The reason is that Modigliani–Miller in these models applies to how the government finances its budget deficit. Cochrane (2001) characterizes the dependence of the nominal term structure on debt policy in a frictionless economy. Missale (1997) considers distortionary taxation, whereas Angeletos (2002) assumes that markets are incomplete.

Derivative pricing and hedging provide a fourth reason. For example, coupon bonds are priced as baskets of coupon payments weighted by the price of a zero-coupon bond that matures on the coupon date. Even the price of more complicated securities, such as swaps, caps and floors, futures, and options on interest rates, is computed from a given model of the yield curve (see the references in Duffie et al., 2000). Banks need to manage the risk of paying short-term interest rates on deposits while receiving long-term interest rates on loans. Hedging strategies involve contracts that are contingent on future short rates, such as swap contracts. To compute these strategies, banks need to know how the price of these derivative securities depends on the state of the economy.

1.3. Why Care About Cross-Equation Restrictions?

Some of the issues just mentioned, such as forecasting and the impact of Fed interventions on long-term yields, may be addressed without imposing the cross-equation restrictions implied by no-arbitrage. I can add measurement error $\varepsilon^{(\tau)}$ to each yield equation

$$y_t^{(\tau)} = A(\tau) + B(\tau)^\top x_t + \varepsilon_t^{(\tau)},$$

select specific variables for x, and then run an *unrestricted* regression of yields $y^{(\tau)}$ on x for each maturity τ separately. Least squares is easy, is fast, and delivers consistent estimates of parameters, at least conditional on the linear structure. For example, Fama and Bliss (1987) forecast changes in short rates without imposing the cross-equation restrictions implied by the absence of arbitrage. Evans and Marshall (1998) estimate the impact of policy shocks on long-term bonds outside of a yield-curve model.

More patience is required to estimate a system of yield equations in a way that ensures no-arbitrage. The cross-equation restrictions have to be derived from parameters that describe the state dynamics and risk premia. Although the model is affine in the state vector x, the functions $A(\tau)$ and $B(\tau)$ are nonlinear functions of the underlying parameters. Using ordinary least squares (OLS) is thus no longer possible. Maximum likelihood is not feasible either because the density of yields is not available in closed form. There are a few exceptions for which the density is known, such as normal densities for yields, but they are easily rejected by the data. New econometric methods have been produced to solve these estimation problems, and this Handbook shows some of these exciting developments. The implementation of these methods, however, requires substantial coding and computation time. Before rolling up the sleeves and getting into the work of implementing cross-equation restrictions when distributions are nonnormal, I would therefore like to spend some time explaining why we actually need them.

Cross-equation restrictions have many advantages. First, these restrictions ensure that the yield dynamics are consistent. $A(\tau)$ and $B(\tau)$ make yield equations consistent with each other in the cross section and the time series. Most bond markets are extremely liquid, and arbitrage opportunities are traded away immediately by large investment banks. The assumption of no-arbitrage thus seems natural for bond yields.

Second, term structure models allow us to separate risk premia from expectations about future short rates. These models are therefore key to understanding to what extent investors think of long bonds as safe investments. Sargent (1979) and Hansen and Sargent (1991) are early papers that explore the EH under which expected excess bond returns are zero. Modified versions of the EH have been tested under which expected excess returns are constant. These tests compare, e.g., the ratio of the likelihood function with and without restrictions implied by the EH (for references, see Bekaert and Hodrick, 2001). The evidence suggests that expected returns on long bonds are on average higher than on short bonds and that they are time-varying. Cross-equation restrictions are then needed to model these risk premia.

Third, unrestricted regressions imply that the number of variables needed to describe the yield curve equals the number of yields in the regression. Lower-dimensional systems have been shown to work well in approximating true yield dynamics. Factor decompositions of the variance-covariance matrix of yield changes show that over 97% of the variance is attributable to just three principal components. Litterman and Scheinkman (1991) named these three principal components level, slope, and curvature according to how shocks to these factors affect the yield curve. This interpretation of the driving forces of yields seems to be stable across model specifications, estimation samples, and types of interest rates. Measurement errors arising from the data construction methods, data entry errors, and asynchronous data sampling [of London Interbank offered rate (LIBOR) and swap yields, for example] are responsible for at least some of the remaining variance of yields.

Fourth, the number of estimated parameters in unrestricted regressions is usually large. Imposing the cross-equation restrictions from no-arbitrage improves the efficiency of these estimates. Ang and Piazzesi (2003) show that this helps out-of-sample forecasting of yields.

Finally, "missing bond yields" can be recovered from a small set of other yields in a way that is consistent with no-arbitrage. Certain multifactor models predict yields that were not included in the estimation within a couple of basis points. This property of yield-curve models is important for studies of emerging markets where bonds with only few maturities are traded at any given point in time. Alvarez and Neumeyer (1999), e.g., apply interpolation methods to construct yields for Argentina. The same issue arises in the context of the construction of zero-coupon bond yields. Nelson and Siegel (1987), Fama and Bliss (1987), and McCulloch and Kwon (1993) propose interpolation methods to infer these yields from observed prices of traded coupon bonds or interest-rate derivatives. These interpolation methods ignore that bond yields need to be consistent with risk-adjusted expectations of interpolated future short rates. These methods thereby admit arbitrage opportunities, which can be avoided with a term structure model.

2. BASICS

2.1. Bond Pricing in Continuous Time

Term structure modeling determines the price of zero-coupon bonds. These bonds pay a terminal payoff, usually normalized to 1 unit, without risk of default and without paying any intermediate coupons. A zero-coupon bond that matures τ periods from now trades at price $P^{(\tau)}$. Buying this bond at time t and reselling it at that time $t+n$ generates a log holding period return of

$$\text{hpr}_{t\to t+n}^{(\tau)} = \log P_{t+n}^{(\tau-n)} - \log P_t^{(\tau)}. \tag{2.1}$$

The holding period n cannot exceed time to maturity τ, so we have $n \leq \tau$. The holding period return is usually random because it depends on the resale value of the bond $P_{t+n}^{(\tau-n)}$, which is generally not known at time t. The resale value is equal to its payoff when the bond matures so that holding the bond until maturity ($n = \tau$) generates a return which is known at time t. The per-period holding period return in this case is the *yield-to-maturity*:

$$y_t^{(\tau)} = \frac{\text{hpr}_{t\to t+\tau}^{(\tau)}}{\tau} = -\frac{\log P_t^{(\tau)}}{\tau}.$$

The short rate is the limit of yields as maturity approaches, $r_t = \lim_{\tau\downarrow 0} y_t^{(\tau)}$. Excess holding period returns $\text{hprx}_{t\to t+n}^{(\tau)} = \text{hpr}_{t\to t+n}^{(\tau)} - \text{hpr}_{t\to t+n}^{(n)}$ are returns made in excess of the riskless return over the holding period.

Bonds are usually priced with the help of a so-called "risk-neutral probability measure" Q^*. Just like the name of this artificial measure suggests, risk-neutral pricing applies under Q^*. In other words, asset prices are the expected values of their future payoffs discounted at the riskless rate, where the expectation is computed using the probability measure Q^*. When agents are risk-neutral, this pricing result applies under the data-generating measure Q. In general, the risk-neutral probability measure Q^* will be different from Q. The payoff of zero-coupon bonds is 1 unit at maturity, so their price is

$$P_t^{(\tau)} = E_t^*\left[\exp\left(-\int_t^{t+\tau} r_u \, du\right)\right]. \tag{2.2}$$

where E^* denotes expectation under Q^*. Standard results show that if there exists a risk-neutral probability measure Q^*, a system of asset prices is arbitrage free. The converse is also true under reasonable restrictions on trading strategies. Moreover, the uniqueness of Q^* is equivalent to markets being complete. Details and references for these powerful results can be found, e.g., in Duffie (2001).

Under the risk-neutral measure, expected excess returns on bonds are zero. Put differently, the expected rate of return on a long bond equals the riskfree rate. I think the gain in intuition justifies the following abuse in notation:

$$E_t^*\left[\frac{dP_t^{(\tau)}}{P_t^{(\tau)}}\right] = r_t dt. \tag{2.3}$$

This is abuse because $dP_t^{(\tau)}$ is not even a random variable.

The pricing relation (2.2) shows that any *yield-curve model* consists of two ingredients:

(i) the change of measure from Q to Q^* and
(ii) the dynamics of the short rate r under Q^*.

In so-called *factor models* of the yield curve, (ii) is replaced by the following assumption:

(ii)$'$ the short rate r is a function $R(x)$ of x and
$x \in \mathbb{R}^N$ is a time-homogeneous Markov process under Q^*.

This means that x is the relevant state vector, a vector of *factors*. This modified (ii)$'$ assumption implies that the conditional expectation in (2.2) is some function F of time-to-maturity τ and the state x_t at time t, or

$$P_t^{(\tau)} = F(x_t, \tau).$$

To capture certain features of yield data (e.g., seasonalities around macroeconomic news releases), I will later consider functions R that also depend on time t and time-inhomogeneous Markov processes x, in which case $P_t^{(\tau)} = F(x_t, t, \tau)$ separately depends on t and τ (in addition to x_t).

The big advantage of pricing bonds (or any other assets) in continuous time is Ito's Lemma. The lemma says that smooth functions F of some Ito process x and time t are again Ito processes (see Duffie, 2001, Chapter 5 for details). The lemma thus preserves the Ito property even if F is nonlinear. Ito's Lemma allows me to turn the problem of solving the conditional expectation in (2.2) into the problem of solving a PDE for the bond price $F(x, \tau)$. The trick of computing (2.2) by solving a PDE is called the Feynman–Kac approach. I will first explain the local expectations hypothesis (LEH) in Section 2.2 and then use it to derive the PDE for bond prices in Section 2.3. Section 2.4 derives the PDE without LEH.

2.2. Local Expectations Hypothesis

The LEH states that the pricing relation (2.2) holds under the data-generating measure Q. Bond yields are thus given by

$$\text{LEH}: \quad y_t^{(\tau)} = -\log E_t \left[\exp(-S)\right] / \tau, \tag{2.4}$$

where $S = \int_t^{t+\tau} r_u du$. The LEH therefore amounts to risk-neutral pricing: the data-generating measure Q and the risk-neutral measure Q^* coincide. This means that expected excess returns on long bonds are zero.

The LEH is not the same as the more prominent EH, which states that bond yields $y_t^{(\tau)}$ are expected values of average future short rates, or

$$\text{EH}: \quad y_t^{(\tau)} = E_t[S] / \tau. \tag{2.5}$$

The difference between the two hypotheses (2.4) and (2.5) is due to Jensen's inequality. For example, suppose that the short rate is Gaussian under $Q = Q^*$, which implies that

S is also Gaussian (as the sum of Gaussians). With this normality assumption, Eq. (2.4) becomes

$$y_t^{(\tau)} = E_t[S]/\tau - \frac{1}{2}\text{var}_t[S]/\tau,$$

which differs from (2.5) because of the variance term.

For example, suppose that the short rate is a random walk with normally distributed shocks. More concretely, the short rate r solves the stochastic differential equation (SDE)

$$\mathrm{d}r_t = \sigma_r \mathrm{d}z_t,$$

where z is a standard Brownian motion (under the data-generating measure) and σ_r is some constant. The shocks $\mathrm{d}z_t$ are, loosely speaking, independently normally distributed with mean 0 and variance $\mathrm{d}t$. I can solve for the short rate explicitly as

$$r_t = r_0 + \int_0^t \sigma_r \mathrm{d}z_u = r_0 + \sigma_r z_t$$

because the Brownian motion z_0 starts at 0 with probability 1. The EH predicts a flat yield curve in this case,

$$y_t^{(\tau)} = E_t[S]/\tau = E_t\left[\int_t^{t+\tau} r_t + \sigma_r(z_u - z_t)\ \mathrm{d}u\right]/\tau = r_t$$

because $E_t(z_u - z_t) = 0$ for all $u \geq t$. The LEH predicts a downward-sloping yield curve because[3]

$$y_t^{(\tau)} = r_t - \frac{\text{var}_t[S]}{2\tau} = r_t - \frac{\sigma_r^2\tau^2}{6}.$$

Cox et al. (1981) argue that the EH is not consistent with no-arbitrage. Counterexamples to this argument exist for some special economies (e.g., Fisher and Gilles, 1998). Longstaff (2000a) argues that market incompleteness may make it impossible to actually exploit such arbitrage opportunities. Campbell (1986) finds that the Jensen's inequality terms tend to be small in the data, except in periods of high volatility such as the end of the 1970s and for bonds with long maturities.

[3]The variance can be computed as

$$\text{var}_t\left[\int_t^{t+\tau} z_u - z_t\,\mathrm{d}u\right] = \text{var}\left[\int_0^{\tau} z_u\,\mathrm{d}u\right] = \int_0^{\tau}\int_0^{\tau} \text{cov}(z_u, z_s)\,\mathrm{d}u\,\mathrm{d}s$$

$$= \int_0^{\tau}\int_0^{\tau} \min\{s, u\}\,\mathrm{d}u\,\mathrm{d}s = \frac{\tau^3}{3}.$$

2.3. Partial Differential Equation for Bond Prices with LEH

For now, I assume that the LEH holds. An advantage of the LEH is that there is no need to know how to change the probability measure in step (i). Another advantage is that we have some intuition about the parameters that determine the dynamics of the short rate under the data-generating measure, whereas we do not have such intuition about the parameters under the risk-neutral measure. The LEH is therefore a useful starting point. I will discuss the change of measure in the next subsection.

In continuous time, a Markov process x lives in some state space $D \subset \mathbb{R}^N$ and solves the SDE

$$dx_t = \mu_x(x_t)\, dt + \sigma_x(x_t)\, dz_t, \tag{2.6}$$

where z is an N-dimensional standard Brownian motion under Q, $\mu_x : D \to \mathbb{R}^N$ is the drift of x, and $\sigma_x : D \to \mathbb{R}^{N\times N}$ is its volatility. Gaussian processes have an affine drift $\mu_x(x)$, and their volatility $\sigma_x(x)$ is constant. Fat tails in the distribution of the state vector can be modeled by specifying an appropriate state-dependence for the volatility $\sigma_x(x)$. Another way to depart from Gaussianity is to model "large moves" in the process x, which I will add in Section 3.5. The Markov process solving (2.6) is time-homogenous because the functions μ_x and σ_x do not depend on time. The extension to time-inhomogeneous Markov processes is straightforward.

Bond prices can now be solved using the Feynman–Kac approach. The idea is to view the conditional expected value (2.2) as the solution of the PDE for the bond price $F(x, \tau)$. The PDE can be obtained in four steps. First, the pricing Eq. (2.2) implies that the price of the bond at maturity is equal to its payoff (here the bond price is taken to be *cum-dividend*). This means that $F(x, 0) = 1$ for all $x \in D$. Second, the pricing equation also shows that the bond price is the expected value of an exponential function, so $F(x, \tau)$ is strictly positive (which makes it possible to divide by F). Third, Ito's Lemma implies that $F(x, \tau)$ itself is an Ito process

$$\frac{dF(x_t, \tau)}{F(x_t, \tau)} = \mu_F(x_t, \tau)\, dt + \sigma_F(x_t, \tau)\, dz_t \tag{2.7}$$

with instantaneous expected bond return

$$\mu_F(x, \tau) = -\frac{F_\tau(x, \tau)}{F(x, \tau)} + \frac{F_x(x, \tau)^\top}{F(x, \tau)} \mu_x(x) + \frac{1}{2} tr \left[\sigma_x(x)\sigma_x(x)^\top \frac{F_{xx}(x, \tau)}{F(x, \tau)} \right], \tag{2.8}$$

where F_τ, F_x, and F_{xx} are partial derivatives of F and tr denotes trace. Finally, the LEH implies that the expected return $\mu_F(x, \tau)$ is equal to the short rate $r = R(x)$. The following *Cauchy problem* summarizes these steps:

$$\mu_F(x, \tau) = R(x) \tag{2.9}$$

$$F(x, 0) = 1$$

for all $x \in D$ and $\tau > 0$. A number of regularity conditions are needed for the Feynman–Kac approach to work. For example, $F(x, \tau)$ needs to be smooth enough for Ito's Lemma. These conditions are stated in Duffie (2001, Appendix E).

Bond prices can now be computed in different ways. The conditional expected value in (2.2) can be computed using Monte–Carlo methods. The PDE in (2.9) can be solved numerically. For small dimensional systems ($N \leq 3$), solving the PDE is precise and relatively fast. For larger dimensional systems ($N \geq 3$), Monte–Carlo methods tend to be more attractive. The alternative is to make strong functional form assumptions on the coefficients $\mu(x)$ and $\sigma(x)$ and the short-rate function $R(x)$ so that the PDE has a closed form solution. The broad class of exponential-affine solutions for $F(x, \tau)$ is called affine term structure models. The requirements on the coefficients and the short-rate function are laid out next.

2.4. Without LEH

The last step in the derivation of the PDE (2.9) for the bond price invoked the LEH to conclude that the expected return on long-term bonds $\mu_F(x, \tau)$ is equal to the riskless rate $R(x)$. I will now derive the PDE for the (empirically relevant) case where *the LEH does not hold.* The key is to realize that expected returns are always equal to the riskless rate under the risk-neutral measure Q^*, or

$$\mu_F^*(x, \tau) = R(x).$$

Instead of the state-dynamics (2.6) under the data-generating measure, the state vector x solves

$$\mathrm{d}x_t = \mu_x^*(x_t)\,\mathrm{d}t + \sigma_x^*(x_t)\,\mathrm{d}z_t^* \tag{2.10}$$

for a Brownian motion z^* under the risk-neutral measure Q^*. To get some intuition about risk-neutral coefficients, consider the case of a single state variable equal to the riskless rate, $x = r$. Risk-neutral pricing then applies after appropriately adjusting the distribution of the short rate. For example, the conditional density of the short rate may need to be shifted right, toward higher values of r. This would make the risk-neutral mean of the short rate higher than its actual mean. In this case, yields are roughly equal to the expected values of average future short rates r, but the expectation is computed using a twisted distribution, a distribution with a higher mean. A unique feature of the continuous-time setting is that the volatility turns out to stay the same under both probability measures: $\sigma_x^* = \sigma_x$. In other words, changes of probability measure do not affect the variance of innovations to x, unless we allow for jumps.

Now I can derive the PDE for bond prices by relying on risk-neutral coefficients and then later link the risk-neutral dynamics of the state vector to its data-generating process. The SDE for the bond price is the "starred" version of Eq. (2.7)

$$\frac{\mathrm{d}F(x_t, \tau)}{F(x_t, \tau)} = \mu_F^*(x_t, \tau)\,\mathrm{d}t + \sigma_F^*(x_t, \tau)\,\mathrm{d}z_t^*,$$

where z^* is a Brownian motion under Q^* and the formula for the expected rate of return $\mu_F^*(x,\tau)$ is analogous to (2.8)

$$\mu_F^*(x,\tau) = -\frac{F_\tau(x,\tau)}{F(x,\tau)} + \frac{F_x(x,\tau)^\top}{F(x,\tau)}\,\mu_x^*(x) + \frac{1}{2}tr\left[\sigma_x^*(x)\sigma_x^*(x)^\top \frac{F_{xx}(x,\tau)}{F(x,\tau)}\right],$$

with the difference of being based on the drift $\mu_x^*(x)$ and the volatility $\sigma_x^*(x)$ of x under Q^*.

The easiest way to write down a pricing model is to start with a process x under Q^* and to then link Q^* to the data-generating measure Q. These two ingredients imply a data-generating process for x, which can be estimated. The change of measure captures risk adjustment. The change involves the *density* ξ, which is a strictly positive martingale (so that Q and Q^* agree on probability zero events) and starts at $\xi_0 = 1$ (so that Q^* is a probability measure). The SDE is

$$\frac{d\xi_t}{\xi_t} = -\sigma_\xi(x_t)\,dz_t, \tag{2.11}$$

where $\sigma_\xi : D \to \mathbb{R}^{1\times N}$. Novikov's condition makes ξ a martingale.[4] Now consider the process z^* defined by

$$dz_t^* = dz_t + \sigma_\xi(x_t)^\top\,dt.$$

Girsanov's theorem (Duffie, 2001, Appendix D) implies that z^* is a Brownian motion under Q^*.

By inserting the definition of z^* into the SDE (2.10)

$$dx_t = \left(\mu_x^*(x_t) - \sigma_x^*(x_t)\,\sigma_\xi(x_t)^\top\right)dt + \sigma_x^*(x_t)\,dz_t,$$

it becomes clear that the volatility of the state vector is the same under both measures

$$\sigma_x(x) = \sigma_x^*(x).$$

This is often called *diffusion invariance principle*. Only the drift changes:

$$\mu_x(x) = \mu_x^*(x) - \sigma_x(x)\,\sigma_\xi(x)^\top. \tag{2.12}$$

[4]The solution to (2.11) is $\xi_t = \exp\left(\int_0^t \sigma_\xi(x_u)\,dz_u - \frac{1}{2}\int_0^t \sigma_\xi(x_u)\,\sigma_\xi(x_u)^\top\,du\right)$. The process ξ is a martingale if Novikov's condition is satisfied:

$$E\left[\exp\left(\frac{1}{2}\int_0^T \sigma_\xi(x_u)\,\sigma_\xi(x_u)^\top\,du\right)\right] < \infty.$$

For more details, see Appendix D in Duffie (2001).

3. AFFINE MODELS

Affine term structure models make functional-form assumptions in step (ii)′ of yield-curve modeling, which lead to tractable pricing formulas. The functional-form assumptions are on the short-rate function $R(x)$ and the process x for the state vector under the risk-neutral measure. The functional form is affine in both cases:

- $R(x)$ is affine
- x is an affine diffusion under Q^*:
  - the drift $\mu_x^*(x)$ is affine
  - the variance matrix $\sigma_x^*(x)\sigma_x^*(x)^\top$ is affine.

These functional forms are for coefficients under the risk-neutral measure. In particular, the drift $\mu_x(x)$ is affine under the data-generating measure only when $\sigma_x(x)\,\sigma_\xi(x)^\top$ is affine, which can be seen from (2.12). The next sections make these assumptions more precise and show that bond prices $F(x,\tau)$ are exponential-affine in x. In this setting, yields are thus affine in x which explains the name of this class of models.[5]

3.1. Affine Short Rate

The functional form of the short rate is made precise in the following assumption.

Assumption 1 *The short rate is given by*

$$r = R(x) = \delta_0 + \delta_1^\top x$$

for $\delta_0 \in \mathbb{R}$ *and* $\delta_1 \in \mathbb{R}^N$.

The choice of short-rate parameters δ_0 and δ_1 depends on the number of factors in the model. The short rate usually is the factor in one-factor models, which means $\delta_0 = 0$ and $\delta_1 = 1$. The short rate in one-factor models is Markov. In N-factor models, the short rate alone is not Markov, but the short rate together with $N-1$ yields is typically Markov. The short rate often serves as one of the factors in multidimensional models. In this case, we still have $\delta_0 = 0$ and $\delta_1 = (1, 0_{N-1})^\top$. Long yields still depend on the other factors because the expected future path of the short rate depends on the current state x in (2.2), when the short rate covaries with these other factors under the risk-neutral measure.

3.2. Affine Diffusions

Again, I will start by imposing the LEH, which means that risk-neutral pricing applies under the data-generating probability measure. I will therefore assume that the state

[5]Discrete-time analogous to affine diffusions is defined in Darolles et al. (2001) and applied to term structure modeling in Gouriéroux et al. (2002). For an introduction into discrete-time affine models, see Backus et al. (1998).

vector is an affine diffusion under Q, which is more restrictive than necessary to get affine solutions for yields. The more general case of an affine diffusion under Q^* with flexible risk premia will appear in the next subsection. These risk premia may introduce nonlinearities in the data-generating process for x. I start with the following two assumptions:

Assumption 2 *The process x is an affine diffusion. This means that x solves*

$$dx_t = \mu_x(x_t)\,dt + \sigma_x(x_t)dz_t,$$

with coefficients

$$\mu_x(x) = \kappa(\overline{x} - x)$$
$$\sigma_x(x) = \Sigma s(x),$$

where $s(x)$ is a diagonal $N \times N$ matrix with ith diagonal element $s_i(x) = \sqrt{s_{0i} + s_{1i}^\top x}$, and where $s_{0i} \in \mathbb{R}, \overline{x}, s_{1i} \in \mathbb{R}^N$, and $\Sigma, \kappa \in \mathbb{R}^{N\times N}$ are constants.

Some intuition about affine diffusions is easy to get in the univariate case. The affine drift $\mu(x_t)$ makes sure that if the current state x_t is above its mean $\overline{x}$, the change dx_t is likely to be negative as long as $\kappa > 0$. If the current state x_t is instead below its mean $\overline{x}$, the change is likely to be positive. In both cases, the process x_t is likely to be pulled back to its mean. The speed of this adjustment is determined by κ. If the speed is zero, $\kappa = 0$, the process is nonstationary. The autoregressive coefficient of discretely sampled observations is $\exp(-\kappa h)$, where h is the interval length between two observations. Time is usually measured in years so that $h = 1$ is 1 year. Monthly and weekly observation intervals then simply mean that $h = \frac{1}{12}$ and $h = \frac{1}{52}$, respectively. For daily data, the choice of h is less obvious. Most papers shorten the year to an average number of 250 business days so that $h = \frac{1}{250}$. Few papers take weekends and holidays seriously and set $h = \frac{1}{365}$.

Shocks dz_t disturb x_t from moving back to its mean. These shocks are normally distributed with mean zero and variance dt. The effect of these shocks on x_t is determined by the volatility $\sigma_x(x_t)$. With constant volatility, the normally distributed shocks dz_t translate into a conditional normal distribution for changes dx_t. More generally, shocks dz_t may translate more into dx_t during times of high volatility $\sigma_x(x_t)$ and less in times of low volatility. This state-dependent amplification effect introduces conditional heteroskedasticity. In bond-yield data, the pattern of this heteroskedasticity seems to positively depend on the level of yields. The half-life H of shocks solves $\exp(-H\kappa) = 0.5$. For example, with $\kappa = 5$, the half-life is $H = -\log 0.5/\kappa = 0.1386$ years, about 7 weeks.

Gaussian processes and square-root processes are the best known examples of affine diffusions. The two classes differ with respect to their assumptions about the variance matrix $\sigma_x(x)\sigma_x(x)^\top$. *Gaussian processes* have a constant variance matrix, which requires that $s_{1i} = 0$ for $i = 1, \ldots, N$. Without loss of generality, I can set $s(x)$ equal to the identity matrix ($s_{0i} = 1$) because the variance parameters Σ are free. The SDE (2.6) then becomes a so-called linear SDE (Karatzas and Shreve, 1988, Chapter 5.6)

$$dx_t = \kappa(\bar{x} - x_t)dt + \Sigma dz_t.$$

Existence and uniqueness of solutions to linear SDEs are not problematic. The solution x is Gaussian and thus can take on negative values with positive probability.

Square-root processes introduce conditional heteroskedasticity by allowing $\sigma_x(x)$ to depend on the state. Now additional restrictions are needed to ensure that the variance matrix $\sigma_x(x)\sigma_x(x)^\top$ is positive definite. A univariate square-root process solves

$$dx_t = \kappa(\bar{x} - x_t)\,dt + \Sigma\sqrt{x_t}dz_t,$$

where $\kappa, \bar{x}, \Sigma$ are now all scalars. For arbitrary parameter values $(\kappa, \bar{x}, \Sigma)$, the conditional variance $\Sigma^2 x_t$ may not be positive. The Feller condition $\kappa\bar{x} > \frac{1}{2}\Sigma^2$ makes zero an entrance boundary. In other words, this condition makes sure that zero is never reached. This is important because once the process hits zero, its conditional variance $\Sigma^2 x_t$ collapses to zero as well. Intuitively, the parameter restriction ensures that the drift term is strong enough to always pull the process x away from the zero boundary. Note that the parameter restrictions rule out unit roots ($\kappa = 0$). The solution of the last SDE only takes on positive values (which makes it possible to compute $\sqrt{x}$). The conditional variance of square-root processes is thus proportional to the level of the process. The larger x, the higher its variance. For multidimensional but independent square-root processes, the Feller condition can be imposed equation-by-equation.

More generally, the coefficients $\mu_x(x)$ and $\sigma_x(x)$ need to satisfy regularity requirements to guarantee the existence of a unique solution to the SDE (2.6). These solutions x are called strong solutions, which means that any other Ito process that solves (2.6) is equal to x almost everywhere. The regularity requirements make sure that the solution does not explode (*growth conditions*) and is unique (*Lipschitz conditions*).[6] Although these conditions may sound like technical details, they severely restrict the correlation structure of affine diffusions. Moreover, they are not satisfied in even simple cases like square-root diffusions. (The volatility $\Sigma\sqrt{x}$ does not satisfy the Lipschitz condition, which is why we need the Feller condition.) The following two standard examples are not affine, but they illustrate that these conditions are natural in the context of deterministic differential equations ($\sigma_x(x) \equiv 0$). The first example is $\mu_x(x) = x^2$ and $x_0 = 1$, which does not satisfy the growth condition. The unique solution is $x_t = \frac{1}{1-t}, 0 \leq t \leq 1$, which explodes

[6] A measurable function f satisfies Lipschitz and growth conditions in x if there exist constants c and k such that

$$||f(x) - f(y)|| \leq c||x - y||$$

$$||f(x)||^2 \leq k(1 + ||x||^2)$$

for all $x, y \in \mathbb{R}^N$. The norm on matrices used here is $|A| = \text{tr}(AA^\top)^{1/2}$ where tr denotes trace.

for $t \to 1$. The second example is $\mu_x(x) = 3x_t^{2/3}$ and $x_0 = 0$, which does not satisfy the Lipschitz condition at $x = 0$. The equation has many solutions, which are indexed by a scalar $a > 0 : x_t = 0$ for $t \le a$ and $x_t = (t - a)^3$ for $t > a$.

Duffie and Kan (1996) provide a multidimensional extension of the Feller condition. Their condition handles general correlated affine diffusions. The condition ensures that only positive factors enter the volatility $\sigma_x(x)$. This involves restrictions on the correlations between state variables, which prevent a potentially negative variable from pulling a variable that enters $s(x)$ into the negative orthant. The condition is sufficient for the existence of a unique solution to the SDE (2.6). For necessary and sufficient conditions, see Theorem 2.7 in Duffie et al. (2003).

Condition A (sufficient for the existence of a solution to the SDE):

1. *For all x such that $s_i(x) = 0$, $s_{1i}^\top \kappa(\bar{x} - x) > \frac{1}{2} s_{1i}^\top \Sigma \Sigma^\top s_{1i}$.*
2. *For all j, if $\left(s_{1i}^\top \Sigma\right)_j \neq 0$, then $s_i(x)$ and $s_j(x)$ are proportional.*

The following examples illustrate how Condition A restricts the admissible cross-correlations between state variables.[7]

Example 1 *$x = (x_1, x_2)$ with $s_{01} = 1$, $s_{11} = \begin{pmatrix} 0 & 0 \end{pmatrix}^\top$ for x_1, and $s_{02} = 0, s_{12} = \begin{pmatrix} 0 & 1 \end{pmatrix}^\top$ for x_2. Suppose first that Σ is diagonal and κ is unrestricted. In particular, $\kappa_{21} \neq 0$ where κ_{21} is the $(2, 1)$-th element in κ, which means that the drift of x_2 (which enters the volatility) depends on x_1. For Condition A.1. to be satisfied, we need that $\kappa_{21}(\bar{x}_1 - x_1) + \kappa_{22}\bar{x}_2 > \frac{1}{2}\Sigma_{22}^2$. This inequality cannot hold for all $x_1 \in R$ (which is a direction in which $s_2(x) = 0$) so that the drift of x_1 is not allowed to depend on x_2 or $\kappa_{21} = 0$. Suppose now that κ is diagonal and Σ is unrestricted. In particular, $\Sigma_{21} \neq 0$. For the process to satisfy A.2., we need that $s_1(x)$ and $s_2(x)$ are proportional, which is not true. This implies that it must be that $\Sigma_{21} = 0$. Analogous considerations for x_2 show that it is possible to have $\kappa_{12} \neq 0$ and $\Sigma_{12} \neq 0$.*

Example 2 *$x = (x_1, x_2)$ with $s_{01} = 0, s_{11} = \begin{pmatrix} 1 & 0 \end{pmatrix}^\top$ for x_1, and s_{02}, s_{12} as in Example 1, Σ is diagonal. Suppose κ is unrestricted with $\kappa_{21} \neq 0$. Again, Condition A.1. requires $\kappa_{21}(\bar{x}_1 - x_1) + \kappa_{12}\bar{x}_2 > \frac{1}{2}\Sigma_{22}^2$ for all directions in which $s_2(x) = 0$. The difference to Example 1 is that x_1 can only take on positive values. If $\kappa_{21} < 0$, it is now possible to choose parameters such that A.1. is satisfied for all $x_1 \in \mathbb{R}_+$. Condition A.2. rules out any off-diagonal terms in Σ.*

The examples show that the main restriction coming from Condition A is on the dependence of variables entering the volatility $s(x)$ on other variables. These volatility-determining variables may not be correlated through κ with other variables that do not enter $s(x)$ (as shown in Example 1). Volatility-determining variables may, however,

[7]Alternatively, we can replace the strong inequality in the first part of the condition with a weak inequality and work with weak solutions. Longstaff (1992) discusses this issue in the context of CIR.

be correlated with each other through κ, provided this correlation is *positive* ($\kappa_{12} < 0$ and $\kappa_{21} < 0$ in Example 2). Variables in $s(x)$ cannot be conditionally correlated through Σ with any variable (Examples 1 and 2). Other variables (that do not determine the volatility) are free to be correlated with variables in $s(x)$.

3.2.1. Mean

For the univariate case, we can rewrite the SDE (2.6) for affine diffusions as

$$x_t = \bar{x} + \exp\{-\kappa(t-s)\}\,[x_s - \bar{x}] + \int_s^t \exp\{-\kappa(t-u)\}\,\Sigma s(x_u)\,\mathrm{d}z_u \tag{3.1}$$

for any value x_u, $0 \leq s \leq t$. The same formula applies to the multivariate case, where $\mathrm{e}^{-\kappa(t-s)}$ is a matrix exponential. These are coded in MATLAB as "expm". The conditional expected value can be computed immediately

$$E_s[x_t] = \bar{x} + \exp\{-\kappa(t-s)\}\,(x_s - \bar{x})\,. \tag{3.2}$$

The unconditional expected value $E\,[x_t]$ solves

$$E[x_t] = \bar{x} + \exp\{-\kappa(t-s)\}\,(E\,[x_t] - \bar{x})$$

for stationary processes, which implies that $E\,[x_t] = \bar{x}$. Again, these are matrix exponentials.

3.2.2. Variance

The conditional variance of affine diffusions is

$$\mathrm{var}_s(x_t) = \int_s^t \exp\{-\kappa(t-u)\}\,\Sigma s(E_s\,[x_u])\,s(E_s\,[x_u])^\top\,\Sigma^\top \exp\left\{-\kappa^\top\,(t-u)\right\}\mathrm{d}u. \tag{3.3}$$

For Gaussian processes, the conditional variance is

$$\mathrm{var}_s(x_t) = \int_s^t \exp\{-\kappa(t-u)\}\,\Sigma\Sigma^\top \exp\left\{-\kappa^\top(t-u)\right\}\mathrm{d}u.$$

For univariate Gaussians, this reduces to

$$\mathrm{var}_s(x_t) = \Sigma^2 \frac{(1 - \exp\{-2\kappa(t-s)\})}{2\kappa}. \tag{3.4}$$

For univariate square root processes, the conditional variance boils down to

$$\mathrm{var}_s(x_t) = \bar{x}\Sigma^2 \frac{(1 - \exp\{-\kappa(t-s)\})^2}{2\kappa} + x_t\Sigma^2 \frac{(\exp\{-\kappa(t-s)\} - \exp\{-2\kappa(t-s)\})}{\kappa}. \tag{3.5}$$

3.3. Affine Bond Pricing with LEH

To compute bond prices, I now add the assumption of risk-neutral pricing under Q.

Assumption 3 *The LEH holds.*

Under the Assumptions 1, 2, and 3 (and additional integrability conditions on the SDE coefficients for the Feynman–Kac approach to work stated in Duffie et al., 2003, Section 11), Duffie and Kan (1996) guess a solution $F(x, \tau)$ for the PDE (2.9) of the form

$$F(x, \tau) = \exp\Big(a(\tau) + b(\tau)^\top x\Big), \tag{3.6}$$

where the coefficients $a(\tau) \in \mathbb{R}$ and $b(\tau) \in \mathbb{R}^N$ solve the ODEs

$$a'(\tau) = -\delta_0 + b(\tau)^\top \kappa\bar{x} + \frac{1}{2}\sum_{i=1}^{N}\Big[b(\tau)^\top \Sigma\Big]_i^2 s_{0i} \tag{3.7}$$

$$b'(\tau) = -\delta_1 - \kappa^\top b(\tau) + \frac{1}{2}\sum_{i=1}^{N}\Big[b(\tau)^\top \Sigma\Big]_i^2 s_{1i}$$

starting at $a(0) = 0$ and $b(0) = 0$. This guess can be verified as follows. Given the exponential affine form (3.6), the instantaneous bond return for Eq. (2.8) is

$$\mu_F(x, \tau) = -a'(\tau) - b'(\tau)^\top x + b(\tau)^\top \mu_x(x) + \frac{1}{2} b(\tau)^\top \sigma_x(x)\sigma_x(x)^\top b(\tau). \tag{3.8}$$

The PDEs in (2.9) and therefore Eq. (3.8) hold for all x in an open set D so that the method of undetermined coefficients leads to the system of ODEs above.

The coefficients $a(\tau)$ and $b(\tau)$ can be computed in closed form only for a few cases. For example, the coefficients for a one-factor model based on a square-root process are in Cox et al. (1985), p. 393. The coefficients for the two-factor case with independent square-root processes are in Chen and Scott (1992), p. 616. The coefficients for a one-factor model based on a Gaussian process are in Vasicek (1977), p. 186. More generally, the system of ODEs (3.7) can be solved fast and efficiently numerically using Runge–Kutta methods. The MATLAB command "ode45" performs the computation.

The bond-price equation (3.6) shows that the LEH together with a short rate which is affine in an affine diffusion (Assumptions 1–3) implies that yields are given by

$$y_t^{(\tau)} = -\frac{\log F(x_t, \tau)}{\tau} = A(\tau) + B(\tau)^\top x_t \tag{3.9}$$

for coefficients $A(\tau) = -a(\tau)/\tau$ and $B(\tau) = -b(\tau)/\tau$.

3.4. Without LEH

I will now drop Assumption 3 and modify Assumption 2 in the following way.

Assumption 2′ *The process x solves*

$$dx_t = \mu_x^*(x_t)\,dt + \sigma_x^*(x_t)\,dz_t^*$$

for a Brownian motion z^* under Q^* and coefficients

$$\mu_x^*(x) = \kappa^*\left(\overline{x}^* - x\right)$$
$$\sigma_x^*(x) = \Sigma^* s^*(x),$$

where $s^*(x)$ is a diagonal $N \times N$ matrix with ith diagonal element $s_i^*(x) = \sqrt{s_{0i}^* + s_{1i}^{*\top} x}$, and where $s_{0i}^* \in \mathbb{R}, \overline{x}^*, s_{1i}^* \in \mathbb{R}^N$, and $\Sigma^*, \kappa^* \in \mathbb{R}^{N\times N}$ are constants.

To obtain exponential-affine bond-price solutions, the risk-neutral drift $\mu_x^*(x)$ and variance-covariance matrix $\sigma_x^*(x)\sigma_x^*(x)^\top$ need to be affine. Because of diffusion invariance, the variance-covariance matrix $\sigma_x(x)\sigma_x(x)^\top$ under the data-generating measure needs to be affine as well. But the data-generating drift

$$\mu_x(x) = \mu_x^*(x) - \sigma_x(x)\,\sigma_\xi(x)^\top$$

may be nonlinear, depending on the functional form of $\sigma_\xi(x)$. The data-generating drift is only affine if the product $\sigma_x(x)\sigma_\xi(x)^\top$ is affine. Many examples of affine yield-curve models in the literature described in Section 5 take the drift to be affine under both measures.

Assumptions 1 and 2′ (and again integrability conditions from Duffie et al., 2003, Section 11) then imply that the ODEs for the bond-price coefficients become

$$a'(\tau) = -\delta_0 + b(\tau)^\top \kappa^* \overline{x}^* + \frac{1}{2}\sum_{i=1}^{N}\left[b(\tau)^\top \Sigma\right]_i^2 s_{0i} \tag{3.10}$$

$$b'(\tau) = -\delta_1 - \kappa^{*\top} b(\tau) + \frac{1}{2}\sum_{i=1}^{N}\left[b(\tau)^\top \Sigma\right]_i^2 s_{1i},$$

where the risk-neutral parameters κ^* and $\overline{x}^*$ replace κ and $\overline{x}$ in (3.7). Finally, the drift-equation (3.8) has to be starred as well to hold under Q^*.

3.5. Jumps

Up to now, the state vector has been an affine diffusion under the risk-neutral probability measure. Diffusions evolve continuously through time. Large movements in yields, however, happen around macroeconomic news releases, and Federal Reserve policy moves at discrete points in time. These large movements can be modeled as discontinuous moves, or *jumps*, in the state vector. These jumps occur at arrival times $t_1, \ldots, t_n$ as in Fig. 12.1. These arrival times are either stochastic or deterministic. Counting processes start at 0 and then record the number of jumps as illustrated in the lower graph in Fig. 12.1. The value of the state vector x "right before" a jump at time t is the left limit $x_{t-} = \lim_{s\uparrow t} x_s$. The jump in x at t is $\Delta x_t = x_t - x_{t-}$. The process x is right-continuous as in the upper graph in Fig. 12.1.

In principle, the conditional probability $\lambda_t dt$ of a jump during the interval $[t, t + dt]$ and the distribution of the jump size Δx_t conditional on a jump at time t may both depend on the state x_{t-}. In affine models, however, it turns out that there is a *dichotomy* under the risk-neutral measure between specifying the jump timing to be state dependent and specifying the jump size distribution to be state dependent. The two cannot be mixed together without giving up on tractability, so one of them has to be state independent. Either the conditional jump distribution depends on the state, but then the jump timing

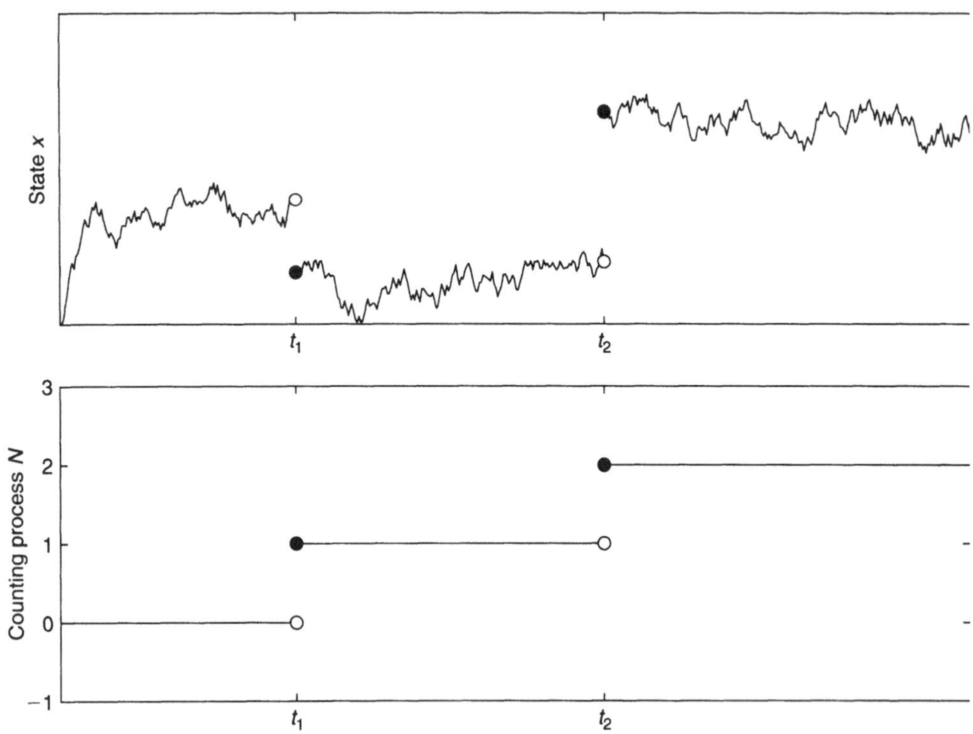

Figure 12.1 The upper graph illustrates jumps in the state variable x at jump arrival times t_1 and t_2. The lower graph illustrates the corresponding counting process N.

has to be deterministic, or the conditional probability of a jump depends on the state, but then the size distribution needs to be state independent. Taken together, these two types of jumps can be used to accommodate release calendars, central bank meetings, and surprising events such as the Gulf war. Jumps at stochastic jump times have been introduced by Duffie and Kan (1996, Section 11), whereas jumps at deterministic jump times have been introduced by Piazzesi (2001).

Formally, jump-diffusions x solve

$$dx_t = \mu_x(x_{t-})dt + \sigma_x(x_{t-})dz_t + dJ_t,$$

where J is a pure jump process and the other terms are as before in (2.6). The jump process J can be activated in two possible ways. First, jumps may be caused by a Poisson process N^P with stochastic intensity λ (see Brémaud, 1981). Heuristically, $\lambda_t dt$ is the conditional probability of a jump in the interval $[t, t + dt]$. For tiny intervals, we can therefore intuitively think of a Poisson process as a 0-1 coin flip with conditional probability $\lambda_t dt$ of observing 1 and probability $1 - \lambda_t dt$ of observing 0. We may observe more than one jump during longer intervals. Second, jumps may happen at deterministic points in time. These jump times are recorded by a deterministic counting process N^D. The processes N^P and N^D each start at 0 and count up in increments of 1. I use one jump process of each type to save on notation. The extension to multiple jump processes is immediate (it only involves summing up different jump processes in the formulas below).

Affine jump-diffusions make the same functional form assumptions on the coefficient $\mu_x(x)$ and the volatility $\sigma_x(x)$ as in the case without jumps. In addition, functional-form assumptions are needed for the jump intensities and the distribution of jump sizes conditional on information "right before" the jump. These assumptions are stated next.

Assumption 4

1. *(Stochastic intensity). The stochastic intensity λ of the Poisson process is affine*

$$\lambda(x) = \lambda_0 + \lambda_1^\top x$$

for $\lambda_0 \in \mathbb{R}$ and $\lambda_1 \in \mathbb{R}^N$.

2. *(Conditional jump distribution). Given a Poisson jump at a stopping time t, the distribution of the jump size Δx_t is independent of x_{t-}. Given a deterministic jump at t counted by the deterministic counting process, the distribution of the jump size Δx_t conditional on x_{t-} has an exponential-affine Laplace transform. More precisely, for any given $\alpha \in \mathbb{R}$ and $\beta \in \mathbb{R}^N$, there exist coefficients $a(\alpha) \in \mathbb{R}$ and $b(\beta) \in \mathbb{R}^N$ such that*

$$E_{t-}\left[\exp(\alpha + \beta \Delta x_t)\right] = \exp\Big(a(\alpha) + b(\beta)^\top x_{t-}\Big).$$

3.5.1. Calendar Time Does Not Matter

Consider first the case without deterministic jump counter N^D. Let M be the compensated Poisson process $\mathrm{d}M_t = \mathrm{d}N_t^P - \lambda_t \mathrm{d}t$. Intuitively, the compensated Poisson process is a demeaned version of the Poisson process because we are taking out the conditional mean change $\lambda_t \mathrm{d}t$. This leaves us with a mean 0 shock process $\mathrm{d}M$, similar to Brownian shocks $\mathrm{d}z$. Then we can rewrite

$$\mathrm{d}x_t = \overline{\mu}_x(x_{t-})\mathrm{d}t + \sigma_x(x_{t-})\mathrm{d}z_t + \Delta x_t \,\mathrm{d}M_t,$$

where the drift of x is now

$$\begin{aligned}\overline{\mu}_x(x) &= \mu_x(x) + \lambda(x)E[\Delta x] \\ &= \kappa(\overline{x} - x) + \left(\lambda_0 + \lambda_1^\top x\right) E\left[\Delta x\right].\end{aligned}$$

The new term in the drift is the expected jump in x, which is simply the probability $\lambda(x)\mathrm{d}t$ of a jump in the interval $[t, t + \mathrm{d}t]$ times the expected jump size $E\left[\Delta x\right]$ conditional on a jump. The expectation has no subscript because the distribution of the jump size Δx is state-independent by Assumption 4.2. Because $E\left[\Delta x\right]$ is a constant and $\mu_x(x)$ and $\lambda(x)$ are both affine in x, the drift $\overline{\mu}_x$ in the case of Poisson jumps is again affine.

Now suppose again that the LEH holds. Ito's Lemma for the case with Poisson jumps (Duffie, 2001, Appendix F) implies that the bond price is itself an Ito process

$$\frac{\mathrm{d}F(x_t, \tau)}{F(x_{t-}, \tau)} = \overline{\mu}_F(x_{t-}, \tau)\mathrm{d}t + \sigma_F(x_{t-}, \tau)\mathrm{d}z + J_F^P(\Delta x_t, \tau)\mathrm{d}M_t, \tag{3.11}$$

and the size of the jump in bond returns is

$$J_F^P(\Delta x_t, \tau) = \frac{F(x_t, \tau) - F(x_{t-}, \tau)}{F(x_{t-}, \tau)}.$$

The jump size J_F^P is a function of the jump Δx in the state vector and the time-to-maturity τ of the bond. The instantaneous expected bond return now is

$$\overline{\mu}_F(x, \tau) = \mu_F(x, \tau) + \lambda(x)E[J_F^P(\Delta x, \tau)],$$

where $\mu_F(x, \tau)$ is the return in the case without jumps given by (2.8). The additional term reflects that bond returns now also compensate for jumps in the state vector. The compensation is equal to the probability $\lambda(x)\mathrm{d}t$ of a jump in the interval $[t, t + \mathrm{d}t]$ times the expected return $E[J_F^P(\Delta x, \tau)]$ conditional on a jump. Again, the expectation has no subscript because the distribution of the jump size Δx is state-independent by Assumption 4.2.

The guess for the bond price is again of the exponential-affine form (3.6). This means that the jump in returns is

$$J_F^P(\Delta x, \tau) = \exp\Big(b(\tau)^\top \Delta x\Big) - 1.$$

The bond-price coefficients solve the ODEs:

$$a'(\tau) = -\delta_0 + b(\tau)^\top \kappa\bar{x} + \frac{1}{2}\sum_{i=1}^{N}\Big[b(\tau)^\top\Sigma\Big]_i^2 s_{0i} + \lambda_0 E\big[J_F^P(\Delta x, \tau)\big] \tag{3.12}$$

$$b'(\tau) = -\delta_1 - \kappa^\top b(\tau) + \frac{1}{2}\sum_{i=1}^{N}\Big[b(\tau)^\top\Sigma\Big]_i^2 s_{1i} + \lambda_1 E\big[J_F^P(\Delta x, \tau)\big]$$

starting at $a(\tau) = 0$ and $b(\tau) = 0$. When $\lambda_0 = 0$ and $\lambda_1 = 0_N$, these equations collapse to the ODEs for the case without jumps (3.7). For some special cases, the ODEs can be computed by pencil and paper. Das and Foresi (1996) compute coefficients for two such cases. The first case has jumps in a mean-reverting short rate with constant volatility. The sign of the jump size is chosen by a coin flip, and the absolute value of the jump size is exponentially distributed. In the second case, the short rate reverts to a stochastic mean, which is a random walk with i.i.d. jumps.

3.5.2. Calendar Time Matters

Bond yields are nonstationary when there are deterministic jump arrival times counted by N^D. Thus, calendar time now matters. I therefore change the notation for the bond price in this subsection: $P_t^{(T)}$ now denotes the price of a bond at time t for a bond that *matures* at time T. The price will be given by $P_t^{(T)} = F(x, t, T)$. The guess for the bond price is now

$$F(x, t, \tau) = \exp\big(a(t, T) + b(t, T)^\top x\big).$$

The computation of $a(t, T)$ and $b(t, T)$ proceeds recursively, starting at the time of maturity with boundary condition $a(T, T) = 0$ and $b(T, T) = 0$. The recursive procedure applies two main results from Piazzesi (2001, Appendix B). Result 1 computes the coefficients at a deterministic jump time, whereas result 2 computes the coefficients for the interim period between two deterministic jump times. More concretely, result 1 says that if the bond price at the next deterministic jump date t is exponential-affine in the state vector $\exp\big(\alpha + \beta^\top x_t\big)$ for coefficients $\alpha \in \mathbb{R}$ and $\beta \in \mathbb{R}^N$, then the price $P_{t-}^{(T)}$ of a bond just before the jump date is of the same form. The proof of this result relies on Assumption 4.2. Result 2 states that if the bond price just before the next deterministic jump date t_{i+1} is exponential-affine $\exp\big(\alpha + \beta^\top x_t\big)$ for some coefficients $\alpha \in \mathbb{R}, \beta \in \mathbb{R}^N$, and $t = t_{i+1}-$, then the price during the entire interim period $[t_i, t_{i+1})$ between two deterministic jump dates is given by $\exp\big(a(s, t) + b(s, t)^\top x_s\big)$ with coefficients $a(s, t)$ and $b(s, t)$ for which $\widehat{a}(t - s) := a(s, t)$ and $\widehat{b}(t - s) := b(s, t)$ solve the ODEs (3.12) with terminal conditions $\widehat{a}(0) = \alpha$ and $\widehat{b}(0) = \beta$. Together, the two results guarantee that for every t, the price $P^{(\tau)}$ is exponential affine.

3.5.3. Risk Adjustment with Jumps

Changes of measure with jumps have generally effects on the jump intensity and jump size distribution. Intuitively, risk-neutral pricing applies under a probability measure under which jumps counted by N^P tend to occur more often and are on average larger in size once they occur. Jumps at deterministic times counted by N^D have the same timing under both measures, only their size distribution changes. Technically, the risk-adjustment involves a density ξ as in the case with diffusions, but now the density may jump as well. The density solves

$$\frac{d\xi_t}{\xi_{t-}} = \sigma_\xi(x_{t-})dz_t + J_\xi^D(\Delta x_t)dN_t^D + J_\xi^P(\Delta x_t)dM_t,$$

starting at $\xi_0 = 1$. For notational simplicity, the jump sizes J_ξ^D and J_ξ^P only depend on the jump size Δx_t. The extension to dependence $J_\xi^D(\Delta x_t, x_{t-})$ and $J_\xi^P(\Delta x_t, x_{t-})$ on the current state x_{t-} is immediate. Assumptions on the coefficients (in addition to Novikov) are needed for ξ to be a strictly positive martingale. First, both jump sizes J_ξ^D and J_ξ^P need to be greater than -1 for ξ to stay positive because the jump size $\Delta\xi_t$ at the deterministic jump time t is given by $\xi_{t-}J_\xi^D(\Delta x_t)$. The same argument holds for Poisson jump times. Second, the conditional expected value of the jump size at deterministic jump times must be zero for ξ to be a martingale. For a deterministic jump time t, the following equalities show why

$$\begin{aligned} E_{t-}[\xi_t] &= E_{t-}\left[\xi_{t-}\left(1 + J_\xi^D(\Delta x_t)\right)\right] \\ &= \xi_{t-}\left(1 + E_{t-}\left[J_\xi^D(\Delta x_t)\right]\right) \\ &= \xi_{t-}. \end{aligned}$$

Example 3 *Suppose there is only one deterministic jump time t. The jump in the state is $\Delta x_t = \mu + \sigma\varepsilon$ where $\varepsilon \sim N(0,1)$ is a random variable known at time t, and $J_\xi^D(\Delta x_t) = \exp\left(-\overline{\sigma}\varepsilon - \frac{1}{2}\overline{\sigma}^2\right) - 1$ for some constant $\overline{\sigma}$. This jump size assumption for ξ satisfies $J_\xi^D > -1$. Also, $E_{t-}\left[J_\xi^D(\Delta x_t)\right] = 0$. Under the risk-neutral measure Q^*, the random variable ε is distributed $N(-\overline{\sigma}, 1)$, which implies that $\Delta x_t \sim N\left(\mu - \sigma\overline{\sigma}, \sigma^2\right)$ under Q^*.*

The jump intensity λ^* under the risk-neutral measure is given by

$$\lambda_t^* = \lambda_t E_{t-}\left(1 + J_\xi^P(\Delta x_t)\right),$$

which is well defined because $J_\xi^P > -1$. Unlike at deterministic jump times, the expected jump size in ξ does not have to be zero at Poisson jump times.

Example 4 *Suppose that the intensity λ is affine under the data-generating measure, $\lambda(x) = \lambda_0 + \lambda_1^\top x$. Also, suppose that $E_{t-}\left(J_\xi^P(\Delta x_t)\right) = v$ for some constant $v > 0$. Then the jump intensity λ^* under the risk-neutral measure is again affine but with coefficients $\lambda_0^* = \lambda_0(1+v)$ and $\lambda_1^* = \lambda_1(1+v)$.*

To see where the form of this intensity comes from, consider M^* that solves

$$\begin{aligned} dM_t^* &= dN_t^P - \lambda_t^* dt \\ &= dM_t + \left(\lambda_t - \lambda_t^*\right)dt. \end{aligned}$$

I want to choose λ^* to make M^* the compensated Poisson process under Q^* and thus a martingale under Q^*. For M^* to be a Q^*-martingale, the product ξM^* needs to be a Q-martingale. This can be seen from the following sequence of equations:

$$E_t^*\left[M_s^*\right] = \frac{E_t\left[\xi_s M_s^*\right]}{\xi_t} = \frac{\xi_t M_t^*}{\xi_t} = M_t^*.$$

Using Ito's lemma (see Duffie, 2001, Appendix E), the product can be written as

$$\begin{aligned} d\left(\xi M^*\right) &= M_{t-}^* d\xi_t + \xi_{t-} dM_t^* + \Delta\xi_t \Delta M_t^* \\ &= M_{t-}^* d\xi_t + \xi_{t-} dM_t + \xi_{t-}\left(\lambda_t - \lambda_t^*\right) dt + \xi_{t-} J_\xi^P(\Delta x_t) dN_t^P. \end{aligned}$$

Both ξ and M are Q-martingales, so $\int M^* d\xi$ and $\int \xi dM$ are Q-martingales. Now if $\lambda^* = \lambda E\left(1 + J_\xi^P\right)$, then the last two terms are

$$\xi_{t-}\left(\lambda_t - \lambda_t^*\right)dt + \xi_{t-} J_\xi^P(\Delta x_t)\, dN_t^P = \xi_{t-} J_\xi^P(\Delta x_t) dM_t,$$

which gives another Q-martingale.

At deterministic jump times, the risk-neutral jump-size distributions satisfy

$$E_{t-}^*\left[\Delta x_t\right] = E_{t-}\left[\frac{\Delta x_t \xi_t}{\xi_{t-}}\right] = E_{t-}\left[\frac{\Delta x_t\left(\xi_{t-} + \Delta\xi_t\right)}{\xi_{t-}}\right] = E_{t-}\left[\Delta x_t\left(1 + J_\xi^D(\Delta x_t)\right)\right].$$

At Poisson jump times, the risk-neutral distributions satisfy

$$E_{t-}^*\left[\Delta x_t\right] = E_{t-}\left[\frac{\Delta x_t\left(1 + J_\xi^P(\Delta x_t)\right)}{E_{t-}\left[1 + J_\xi^P(\Delta x_t)\right]}\right]$$

Because the expected jump in ξ at deterministic jump times is zero, $E_{t-}\left[J_\xi^D\right] = 0$, we can see that the last two equations are very similar.

Example 5 *Suppose that the jump size Δx at Poisson jumps, the Poisson intensity λ, and J_ξ^P are all constant. Then the risk-neutral jump size is unchanged Δx, only the jump intensity under the risk-neutral measure is different:* $\lambda^* = \lambda\left(1 + J_\xi^P\right)$.

3.6. Negative Short Rates and Jump Intensities

Affine models do not constrain the short rate and jump intensities to be positive in general. Assumption 1 specifies the short rate to be affine in the state x, which itself may take on negative values. Assumption 4.1 specifies jump intensities to be affine in x. Negative nominal short rates are undesirable because they lead to arbitrage opportunities in economies with money. Negative intensities (just like negative probabilities) do not make sense by definition. Within affine models, there are only two ways out of this problem. The first way is to only include square-root processes in the state vector. Condition A allows these square-root processes to be positively correlated but not negatively (see Section 3.1). Thus, the correlation structure in the model is severely restricted. For example, jump intensities of different Poisson processes can then only be positively correlated. But negative correlation in Poisson arrival rates is useful in various contexts. For example, up and down moves in a central bank's policy rate come with conditional probabilities that depend on the business cycle and are therefore negatively correlated.

The second way is to view the affine term structure model as a tool to approximate true bond prices. The true short rate and the true intensity are nonlinear,

$$r_t^{\text{true}} = \max\{r_t, 0\} = \max\left\{\delta_0 + \delta_1^\top x, 0\right\}$$

$$\lambda_t^{\text{true}} = \max\{\lambda_t, 0\} = \max\left\{\lambda_0 + \lambda_1^\top x, 0\right\},$$

whereas r and λ are affine in the state x and enter the (now approximate) pricing Eq. (2.2). The approximating model for bond prices ignores the truncation induced by the max-operators and is therefore affine. To be clear, the approximating affine model may still allow arbitrage opportunities. For example, in states of the word where r takes on negative values, long-term bond yields from the approximating model may be negative as well, again giving rise to arbitrage strategies involving money. The approximation is good provided that the probability $\Pr\{r < 0\}$ that r takes on negative values is small. Similarly, $\Pr\{\lambda < 0\}$ needs to be small for the approximating model to work well. The accuracy of this approximation at a given parameter vector can be checked, e.g., by computing true bond yields based on r^{true} and λ^{true}. This computation involves either Monte–Carlo methods applied to (2.2) or numerically solving the PDE (2.8). I am not aware of any study of nominal bond yields that performs such a check regarding short rates. Some estimated affine models imply negative short rates on average, which suggests that such a check would be useful. Piazzesi (2001) performs this check for negative intensities.

Leaving the affine setup is another alternative. This does not necessarily mean giving up on closed-form solutions for yields. For example, the short rate is quadratic in Constantinides (1992), El Karoui et al. (1993), and Ahn et al. (2002). Both the short rate and jump arrival intensities are quadratic in Piazzesi (2001).

3.7. Expected Returns

Expected returns in excess of the riskfree rate in affine models can be computed as follows. Ito's lemma implies that the volatility of bond returns is

$$\sigma_F(x_t,\tau) = b(\tau)^\top \sigma_x(x_t).$$

I insert the definition of the Brownian motion $dz_t^* = dz_t - \sigma_\xi^\top(x_t)dt$ and compensated Poisson process

$$dM_t^* = dM_t - \lambda_t E_{t-}\left(J_\xi^P\right)dt$$

under Q^* into the SDE for the bond price (3.11). This leads to a capital asset pricing model (CAPM)-type equation linking expected bond returns under the two measures, $\mu_F(x,\tau)$ and $\mu_F^*(x,\tau) = R(x)$, between any two deterministic jump dates:

$$\mu_F(x,\tau) - R(x) = -b(\tau)^\top \sigma_x(x)\sigma_\xi(x)^\top - \lambda(x)E\left[J_\xi^P(\Delta x)J_F^P(\Delta x,\tau)\right]. \tag{3.13}$$

Without Poisson jumps ($\lambda(x) \equiv 0$), expected excess returns are determined by their covariance with the density ξ, which in continuous time is just the product of the volatilities. The volatility of bond returns is the factor loading $b(\tau)$ times the volatility of the factor $\sigma_x(x)$. The volatility $\sigma_\xi(x)$ of the density contains the *market prices of risk for each Brownian motion.* These risk prices have the usual mean-variance trade-off interpretation: the ith market price of risk measures the percentage change in expected return that compensates an investor for a 1% increase in return volatility attributable to the ith Brownian motion. Typically, $b(\tau)$ contains negative numbers (at least in one-factor models) so that $b(\tau)^\top\sigma_x(x)$ is negative. Investors thus want more expected excess returns in compensation for holding extra risk, measured as $-b(\tau)^\top\,\sigma_x(x)$. The next section will show that Lucas models with a representative agent imply that ξ is high in recessions (when aggregate consumption growth is low). A high covariance between bond returns and the density means that bonds pay out in recessions, which makes bonds valuable. Low excess returns are therefore required to compensate the agent to hold the bond.

With Poisson jumps, expected excess returns also compensate for jump risk. The compensation is the probability of a jump times the expected jump in returns J_F^P weighted with the *market price of Poisson jump risk* J_ξ^P. Again, because $b(\tau)$ usually contains negative numbers, J_F^P is negative.

At deterministic jump times, expected returns under the risk-neutral measure are zero

$$E^*_{t-}\left[J_F^D(\Delta x_t, \tau)\right] = 0.$$

To understand why, remember that expected excess returns under the risk-neutral measure are equal to the short rate. In the instant of a jump, the short rate is zero, and expected excess returns under Q* must be therefore zero. Intuitively, the instant of a jump is too short for there to be a positive short rate. This implies that expected returns under Q satisfy an analogous condition to the one for Poisson jumps:

$$E_{t-}\left[J_F^D(\Delta x_t, \tau)\right] = -E_{t-}\left[J_\xi^D(\Delta x_t, x) J_F^D(\Delta x_t, \tau)\right].$$

Intuitively, expected returns are again the probability of a jump, which is equal to 1 for deterministic jump times, multiplied with the expected return weighted with the *market price of jump risk for deterministic jump arrival times.*

4. AFFINE GENERAL EQUILIBRIUM MODELS

The pricing equations derived so far did not link fundamentals to the yield curve. Moreover, the transition from the data-generating measure Q to the risk-neutral measure Q* was specified exogenously and was not tied to preference parameters. For real bonds, this link to fundamentals can be achieved within a representative agent endowment economy along the lines of Exercise 10.3 in Duffie (2001). Suppose the representative agent has a time-separable utility function

$$U(c) = \int_0^\infty e^{-\delta t} u(c_t, \eta_t) dt \quad \text{with} \quad u(c_t, \eta_t) = \frac{(c_t - \eta_t)^{1-\alpha}}{1-\alpha},$$

where δ is the rate of time preference, α is some power, and η is an exogenous preference shock process. The agent eats an endowment process and receives preference shocks such that

$$c_t - \eta_t = \exp\left(\gamma^\top x_t\right),$$

where the state vector x is a diffusion. The coefficient of relative risk aversion

$$-\frac{c_t u_{cc}(c_t, \eta_t)}{u_c(c_t, \eta_t)} = \frac{\alpha c_t}{c_t - \eta_t}$$

is time-varying. In the absence of preference shocks ($\eta \equiv 0$), the coefficient of relative risk aversion is the constant α, the aggregate endowment is $c_t = \exp\left(\gamma^\top x_t\right)$, the instantaneous expected endowment growth rate equals $\gamma^\top \mu_x(x) + \frac{1}{2}\gamma^\top \sigma_x(x)\sigma_x(x)^\top \gamma$, and the volatility of endowment growth is $\gamma^\top \sigma_x(x)$.

The time-t price of a bond paying 1 unit of consumption at time $t+\tau$ is the conditional expected value of the marginal rate of substitution between t and $t+\tau$,

$$P_t^{(\tau)} = E_t\left[\frac{m_{t+\tau}}{m_t}\right],$$

where marginal utility is given by

$$m_t = \exp(-\delta t)u_c(c_t, \eta_t) = \exp\left(-\delta t - \alpha\gamma^\top x_t\right).$$

Ito's Lemma now implies that m is given by

$$\frac{\mathrm{d}m_t}{m_t} = \mu_m(x)\mathrm{d}t + \sigma_m(x)\mathrm{d}z_t$$

with drift and volatility

$$\mu_m(x) = -\delta - \alpha\gamma^\top \mu_x(x) + \frac{1}{2}\alpha^2\gamma^\top\sigma_x(x)\sigma_x(x)^\top\gamma, \tag{4.1}$$

$$\sigma_m(x) = -\alpha\gamma^\top\sigma_x(x).$$

No-arbitrage is a necessary condition for an equilibrium to exist, and from Section 2.1, no-arbitrage is also equivalent to risk-neutral pricing. The marginal utility process m thus provides the link between the data-generating probability Q and the risk-neutral probability Q*. The following equations hold:

$$P_t^{(\tau)} = E_t\left[\frac{m_{t+\tau}}{m_t}\right] = E_t\left[\frac{\xi_{t+\tau}}{\xi_t}\exp\left(-\int_t^{t+\tau} r(u)\mathrm{d}u\right)\right] = E_t^*\left[\exp\left(-\int_t^{t+\tau} r(u)\mathrm{d}u\right)\right],$$

where

$$\xi_t = \frac{m_t}{m_0}\exp\left(\int_0^t r(u)\mathrm{d}u\right) \tag{4.2}$$

is the density of Q* with respect to Q (a concept defined in Section 2.4).

Because the process ξ is a martingale, an application of Ito's Lemma to Eq. (4.2) implies that

$$\mu_m(x) = -r = -R(x).$$

Equation (4.1) therefore describes minus the short rate. The usual comparative statics arguments apply to this short-rate equation, at least in the case without preference shocks. A higher rate of time preference δ makes the agent want to save less so that the real rate must be higher to compensate the agent for saving as much as before. Higher future expected endowment growth makes the agent want to consume more today. The real rate must therefore be higher to prevent him from borrowing. Higher endowment volatility activates a precautionary savings motive so that the real rate must be lower to prevent the agent from saving.

The short-rate map $R(x)$ is affine if the drift $\mu_x(x)$ and variance-covariance matrix $\sigma_x(x)\sigma_x(x)^\top$ are affine. In other words, the data-generating process for x has to be an affine diffusion for Assumption 1 to be satisfied. Equations (4.1) and (4.2) imply that market prices of risk are given by $\sigma_m(x) = -\alpha\gamma^\top\sigma_x(x)$. In the absence of preference shocks, market prices of risk are thus given by minus the coefficient of relative risk aversion times the volatility of consumption growth $\gamma^\top\sigma_x(x)$. A higher volatility of consumption growth makes recessions worse and therefore makes bonds, which pay out in these bad times even more attractive. The drift of x under Q^* satisfies

$$\mu_x^*(x) = \mu_x(x) - \alpha\sigma_x(x)\sigma_x(x)^\top\gamma,$$

which is automatically affine.

To summarize, the real yield curve is affine if the state x is an affine diffusion under Q in this model.[8] Campbell (1996) computes bond and stock prices in a discrete-time version of this economy in which consumption growth is a univariate ARMA process of any order. Cox et al. (1981) discuss the specification of higher-order autoregressive processes in continuous time. Bekaert and Grenadier (2000) relax the homoskedasticity assumption on the state vector in a discrete-time setting. Campbell (1996) and Bekaert and Grenadier (2000) allow for preference shocks to increase risk premia.[9] Campbell et al. (1997) specify consumption growth as an AR(1) plus noise, which amounts to an ARMA(1,1). This specification differs from the one in Campbell because the number of shocks matters, e.g., for determining the spanning number of assets. Wachter (2006) combines an ARMA(1,1) for consumption growth with a "surplus ratio" $(c - \eta)/c = \exp(x_1)$, where x_1 is a square-root process in discrete time as in Campbell and Cochrane (1999). The continuous-time analog of the aggregate endowment in her economy is $c = \exp(x_2)$, where $x_2(t) = x_2(0) + \int_0^t x_3(s)\mathrm{d}s + z_2(t)$, and x_3 is a Gaussian autoregressive process. The expected instantaneous endowment growth rate is x_3 plus a constant. In terms of the general specification outlined above, this amounts to choosing $\gamma^\top x = x_1 + x_2$.

Even though there is no role for money in this economy, nominal bonds can still be priced by specifying an *exogenous* price process p_t. Cox et al. (1985) do this in their Section 7. To be concrete, the dollar-price $PN_t^{(\tau)}$ of a bond that pays out one dollar at τ periods from now is

$$PN_t^{(\tau)} = E_t\left[\frac{m_{t+\tau}}{m_t}\frac{p_t}{p_{t+\tau}}\right].$$

[8] For stock pricing in affine economies, see Bakshi and Chen (1997), Bekaert and Grenadier (2001), Mamaysky (2002), and Longstaff and Piazzesi (2004).

[9] Alternatively, Telmer and Zin (1996) investigate the real term structure in an incomplete (nonaffine) setting, which also implies higher premia for long-term bonds.

Cox et al. (1985), Gibbons and Ramaswamy (1993), Pearson and Sun (1994), and Heston (1991) assume that $m_{t+\tau}$ and $1/p_{t+\tau}$ are independent. This assumption leads to

$$PN_t^{(\tau)} = P_t^{(\tau)} E_t\left[\frac{p_t}{p_{t+\tau}}\right],$$

which is the nominal price $P_t^{(\tau)} p_t$ of a bond that pays one consumption good at time $t+\tau$ multiplied with how much one dollar at $t+\tau$ is expected to be worth in terms of the consumption good $E_t[1/p_{t+\tau}]$. In this setting, the nominal yield is equal to the real yield plus expected inflation (plus a Jensen's inequality term). This is not true in general

$$PN_t^{(\tau)} = P_t^{(\tau)} E_t\left[\frac{p_t}{p_{t+\tau}}\right] + \operatorname{cov}_t\left(\frac{m_{t+\tau}}{m_t}, \frac{p_t}{p_{t+\tau}}\right)$$

due to the covariance of the pricing kernel and the inverted inflation rate. Pennacchi (1991) and Sun (1992) allow their exogenous inflation process to be correlated with real variables.

The real value of a dollar at $t+\tau$ can be computed conveniently if the price level p and expected inflation π are specified as in (Cox et al., 1985, Section 7):

$$\frac{\mathrm{d}p_t}{p_t} = \pi_t \mathrm{d}t + \sigma_p \sqrt{\pi_t}\mathrm{d}z_t^p,$$
$$\mathrm{d}\pi_t = \kappa_\pi\left(\overline{\pi} - \pi_t\right)\mathrm{d}t + \sigma_\pi \sqrt{\pi_t}\mathrm{d}z_t^\pi$$

for constants σ_p, $\kappa_\pi, \overline{\pi}, \sigma_\pi$ and independent Brownian motions z^p, z^π. Here, expected inflation is always positive. This specification boils down to evaluating

$$E_t\left[\frac{p_t}{p_{t+\tau}}\right] = E_t\left[\exp\left(-\int_t^{t+\tau}\left(1 - \frac{1}{2}\sigma_p^2\right)\pi_u \mathrm{d}u - \int_t^{t+\tau}\sigma_p\sqrt{\pi_u}\mathrm{d}z_u^p\right)\right].$$

Because the conditional expected value of the second integral is zero, this expression has a closed form solution. More generally, any price process $p_t = \exp\left(\rho^\top x_t\right)$ would work.

An *endogenous* price process can be derived, e.g., in models with a cash-in-advance constraint. The motive for holding money in these models is that good purchases need to be made with money so that the agent maximizes utility subject to a budget constraint and the cash-in-advance constraint

$$p_t c_t \leq M^d.$$

This constraint binds as long as the nominal interest rate is positive. This is a serious restriction within the class of affine yield-curve models because many affine specifications allow nominal rates to become negative (Section 3.6 discusses how to maybe deal with this problem). The model also specifies an exogenous money-supply process M^s, and equilibrium requires the money market to clear so that $M^d = M^s$. Together with good-market clearing, the price process in this economy is implied by the quantity equation $p_t c_t = M^s$. Rebelo and Xie (1999) and Bakshi and Chen (1996) include money in the utility function. Taxation of nominal capital makes money nonneutral in the money-in-the-utility setup of Buraschi and Jiltsov (2005). Wu (2006) computes an affine model by linearizing a model with sticky prices.

5. SOME FAMOUS AFFINE MODELS

First-generation affine models were based on one of the two basic diffusions.

1. Vasicek-type models: x is Gaussian.
2. Cox–Ingersoll–Ross (CIR)-type models: x consists of independent square-root processes.
3. Mixture models: x consists of possibly correlated affine processes.

These early models were one-factor models. The factor was called "short rate." The key features of the Vasicek model are

$$\begin{aligned} R(x) &= x \\ \sigma_x(x) &= \Sigma \\ \sigma_\xi(x) &= q \end{aligned} \tag{5.1}$$

for constants Σ and q. Inserting these coefficients into Eq. (2.12) shows that the speed of mean reversion $\kappa = \kappa^*$ in x (and therefore the short rate) is the same under both probability measures, only the long run mean differs, because $\bar{x}^* = x - \kappa^{-1}\Sigma q$. The market price of risk q is usually estimated to be negative. Intuitively, this means that yields are expected values of average future short rates (apart from a Jensen's inequality term), which are on average higher $\bar{r}^* > \bar{r}$ than their historical average. This is therefore an implicit form of risk adjustment.

The CIR model sets

$$\begin{aligned} R(x) &= x \\ \sigma_x(x) &= \Sigma\sqrt{x} \\ \sigma_\xi(x) &= q\sqrt{x} \end{aligned} \tag{5.2}$$

for constants Σ and q. Here, the change of measure affects not only the long-run mean but also the speed of mean reversion. A negative q implies that under the risk-neutral measure x mean reverts more slowly ($\kappa > \kappa^*$) to a higher mean ($\bar{x} > \bar{x}^*$). The Vasicek and CIR model share the feature that the state is an affine diffusion under both the risk-neutral and the data-generating probability measure. Vasicek (1977) only contains the one-factor version of the model, which was later extended to the multifactor case by Langetieg (1980). Cox et al. (1985) already contains the multifactor case in Section 6.

Duffie and Kan (1996) paved the way for a second generation of mixture models. Mixture models are built from the two basic building blocks. Duffie and Kan completely characterize the general class of multifactor affine models. To classify these mixture models, Dai and Singleton (2000) count the number m of processes that enter the volatility $s(x)$. More precisely, $m = \text{rank}(s_1)$ where $s_1 = [s_{11} \cdots s_{1N}]$. In their notation, $A_m(N)$ denotes a model with a total of N state variables, of which m enter the volatility. For example, the one-factor Vasicek model is $A_0(1)$, the N-factor Vasicek model is $A_0(N)$, and the multifactor CIR model is $A_N(N)$. The classification of models does not depend on how the risk adjustment is specified (because of diffusion invariance).

Factor models need to specify what their factors stand for. Duffie and Kan (1996) propose to explain yields with *latent* factors. This means that the econometrician does not get to observe x directly but may be able to infer x from yields. In other words, the state x can in this case be thought of as consisting of yields. Most papers with latent factors still try to give their variables intuitive labels. There are two broad types of labels. The first type refers to statistical properties of the short rate, whereas the second type refers to fundamentals of an underlying general equilibrium model.

5.1. Labels Based on Moments of the Short Rate

To be able to identify latent variables as moments of the short rate, these models feature one state variable which is called the short rate r. The linear map $R(x)$ in these models thus picks just one component of the state vector, say the first, by setting $\delta_0 = 0$ and $\delta_1 = [1, 0, \ldots]^\top$. The one-factor Vasicek and CIR models are special cases with $\delta_1 = 1$. Multifactor models with this feature have a short rate which is not Markov under the risk-neutral probability measure so that other variables (in addition to r_t) help in forecasting the short rate and thus to compute bond yields.

Stochastic mean models take $x = (r, \theta)$, where the short rate r reverts quickly to a time-varying mean θ, which reverts slowly to its long-run (unconditional) mean $\overline{\theta}$. The relevant SDEs are

$$\begin{aligned} \mathrm{d}r_t &= \kappa_r(\theta_t - r_t)\mathrm{d}t + \sigma_r \mathrm{d}z_t^r \\ \mathrm{d}\theta_t &= \kappa_\theta\left(\overline{\theta} - \theta_t\right)\mathrm{d}t + \sigma_\theta(\theta_t)\,\mathrm{d}z_t^\theta, \end{aligned} \tag{5.3}$$

where $\kappa_r, \kappa_\theta, \sigma_r$, and $\overline{\theta}$ are scalars, with $\kappa_r > \kappa_\theta$ for θ to be interpreted as stochastic mean. The Brownian motions z_r and z_θ are independent. Balduzzi et al. (1998) assume that $\sigma_\theta(\theta_t)$ does not depend on θ_t, which makes the stochastic mean normally distributed. This model is a $A_0(2)$-model. Market prices of risk σ_ξ are constant in these models.

Chen (1996) assumes that θ is a square-root process so that $\sigma_\theta(\theta_t) = \nu\sqrt{\theta_t}$ for some constant ν. This leads to $z = (z_r, z_\theta)^\top$, and

$$\sigma_x(x) = s(x) = \begin{pmatrix} \sigma_r & 0 \\ 0 & \nu\sqrt{\theta} \end{pmatrix},$$
$$\sigma_\xi(x) = q^\top s(x),$$

which constitutes an $A_1(2)$-model for some $q \in \mathbb{R}^2$. Here, the matrix Σ in the volatility $\sigma_x(x) = \Sigma s(x)$ is a 2×2 identity matrix I.

Stochastic volatility models take $x = (r, v)^\top$, where v is interpreted as the volatility v of the short rate. To keep volatility positive, it is specified to be a square-root process:

$$\begin{aligned} dr_t &= \kappa_r(\bar{r} - r_t)dt + \sqrt{v_t}dz_t^r \\ dv_t &= \kappa_v(\bar{v} - v_t)dt + \sigma_v\sqrt{v_t}dz_t^v \end{aligned} \tag{5.4}$$

for constants $\kappa_r, \bar{r}, \kappa_v, \bar{v}, \sigma_v$ and independent Brownian motions z^r, z^v. This leads to $z = (z^r, z^v)^\top$ and

$$\sigma_x(x) = s(x) = \begin{pmatrix} \sqrt{v} & 0 \\ 0 & \sigma_v\sqrt{v} \end{pmatrix},$$
$$\sigma_\xi(x) = q^\top s(x).$$

Again, $q \in \mathbb{R}^2$ and $\Sigma = I$. Longstaff and Schwartz (1992) interpret their $A_1(2)$-model in this way.

Combinations of these labels can be found in many three-factor models where the state $x = (r, \theta, v)$ consists of the short rate, a stochastic mean, and stochastic volatility. Examples are the $A_1(3)$ model of Balduzzi et al. (1996) and the $A_2(3)$ model of Chen (1996). Dai and Singleton (2000) write down the most flexible $A_1(3)$ and $A_2(3)$ models in which all parameters are just identified. Their model has the general form:

$$\begin{aligned} \sigma_x(x) &= \Sigma s(x) \\ \sigma_\xi(x) &= q^\top s(x) \end{aligned} \tag{5.5}$$

for a constant vector $q \in \mathbb{R}^N$. Under this assumption, the state is an *affine diffusion under both measures*. The drift parameters κ and $\bar{x}$ under Q are related to those under Q^* in the following way:

$$\begin{aligned} \kappa &= \kappa^* - \Sigma\Phi \\ \bar{x} &= \kappa^{-1}\left(\kappa^*\bar{x}^* + \Sigma\psi\right), \end{aligned} \tag{5.6}$$

where the ith row of $\Phi \in \mathbb{R}^{N\times N}$ is given by $q_i s_{1i}^{\top}$ and the ith row of $\psi \in \mathbb{R}^N$ is given by $q_i s_{0i}$. This shows that both the speed of mean reversion κ and the long-run mean $\overline{x}$ may be different under the data-generating measure than under the risk-neutral measure, where κ^* and $\overline{x}^*$ are responsible for determining the drift of the process x.

5.2. Labels Based on Fundamentals

Yield curves in general equilibrium models depend on state variables that have natural interpretations in terms of fundamentals. In principle, the model can then be estimated using observations on both macro variables and yields. This is, however, not what is usually done. The reason is that for "reasonable" coefficients of relative risk aversion, representative agent models can match neither average excess returns on long bonds nor their time series properties when calibrated to aggregate quantities such as consumption. This "bond premium puzzle" is documented for real bonds in Backus et al. (1989) and Chapman (1997). Den Haan (1995) documents the puzzle for nominal bonds.

When the same models are estimated using asset prices alone, the model implies dynamics for the macro variables that have little to do with their historical behavior. In this sense, labels from fundamentals are often empty labels. For example, Pearson and Sun (1994) use the model mentioned by Cox et al. (1985) in Section 7 with exogenously specified "expected inflation." Their estimation does not use any data on inflation, however, only data on yields. Similarly, "consumption growth" in Buraschi and Jilsov (2005), "expected aggregate consumption growth" in Wachter (2006), and "labor income" in Dai (2001) are labels for latent variables. Sometimes data from outside the bond market is combined with many, often more than 5, yields. The key in these applications is that yields far outnumber the macro series, and Kalman filtering tends to match only moments of yields. In this case, again, the filtered variables usually have little to do with their names.

6. ESTIMATION METHODS FOR AFFINE MODELS

To estimate affine models, various choices have to be made regarding measurement errors and estimation methods. This section is long because these choices are not obvious. In thinking about these choices, it is useful to view affine models as *state space systems* with an observation equation which links observable yields to the state vector and a state equation which describes the dynamics of the state:

$$y_t^{(\tau)} = A(\tau) + B(\tau)^{\top} x_t + \varepsilon_t^{(\tau)} \tag{6.1}$$
$$\mathrm{d}x_t = \mu(x_t)\mathrm{d}t + \sigma(x_t)\mathrm{d}z_t.$$

The system (3.7) of ODEs provides the cross-equation restrictions for this system. Empirical applications start with a choice of how to add "measurement errors" $\varepsilon^{(\tau)}$, which I discuss in Section 6.1. I explain moment-based estimation methods in Section 6.3

and likelihood-based methods in Section 6.2. Identification of parameters is tricky as in any state space model and is discussed in Section 6.4.

6.1. Stochastic Singularity

Affine models rely on a low-dimensional state vector to describe what drives the yield curve. Data on N different yields can therefore be used to back out N state variables. The N yields $y^{(\tau_1)}, \ldots, y^{(\tau_N)}$ can be used to invert equations (3.9) for $\tau = \tau_1, \ldots, \tau_N$ to obtain the model-implied state vector x. Any additional yield is predicted by the model with an R^2 of 1. The model can therefore be rejected with a single observation on $y^{(\tau_{N+1})}$. Put differently, the variance-covariance matrix of $N + 1$ yields in the model is singular, a feature called stochastic singularity.

Stochastic singularity is a problem because we have lots of cross-sectional yield data (many different τs) and want to use models with few state variables. Adding measurement error $\varepsilon^{(\tau)}$ to the yield equation, as done in (6.1), breaks this singularity. Now different assumptions can be made on the properties of these measurement errors. Either all the yields are observed with error or only a subset of yields is observed with error. The variance of the measurement error $\varepsilon^{(\tau)}$ is nonzero for all τ according to the first assumption, whereas some of the $\text{var}(\varepsilon^{(\tau)})$ may be zero according to the second assumption.

The assumption that all yields are observed with error seems plausible. Data entry mistakes and interpolation methods for constructing zero-coupon yields are among the obvious sources for such errors. When all yields have errors, we cannot invert the yield coefficients in (6.1) to compute the state vector. Kalman filtering is useful here, especially when the state vector is normally distributed (Campbell and Viceira, 2001; Gong and Remolona, 1996; Pennacchi, 1991), but also in more general setups (Collin-Dufresne et al., 2009).

The alternative assumption is that data on N yields is flawless where N also happens to be the number of factors in the model. This assumption is clearly arbitrary. The econometrician is even supposed to know which N yields in his dataset are flawless. All other yields are observed with error so that the model cannot be easily rejected. Some estimations include the yields with error in the estimation to exploit all available data (Chen and Scott, 1993). Other applications leave the contaminated yields out and then use them for an out-of-sample check of the model. To be clear, the check is "out-of-sample" only in the cross section, because these are yields not included in the estimation, not in the time-series sense (e.g., Dai and Singleton, 2000; Pearson and Sun, 1994; Piazzesi, 2005).

The measurement errors recovered using any of these approaches are typically highly autocorrelated. This autocorrelation may be due to the interpolation method used to construct zero-coupon yields. This does not seem very plausible, however, because one would expect data construction methods to generate measurement errors that are correlated with each other in the cross section and not necessarily over time. Moreover, swap yields are not interpolated and their measurement errors are still highly autocorrelated

(Duffie and Singleton, 1997). Autocorrelation in measurement errors is worrisome because it suggests that these errors might have in fact nothing to do with measurement issues but with omitted state variables or functional form assumptions. For example, Table IV in Dai and Singleton (2000) computes average measurement errors for their three-factor affine model over periods with upward or downward sloping swap curve. Their preferred $A_1(3)$ model makes larger errors when the yield curve is upward sloping. Nonlinearities may account for such a pattern. Model misspecification is not handled by the estimation methods and the computation of standard errors. Much more research is needed in this direction.

6.2. Likelihood-Based Methods

Maximizing the likelihood function relies on being able to compute the density $f(x_{t+1}|x_t)$ of the state vector x_{t+1} given x_t. The conditional density of an N-dimensional vector of observed yields Y can be obtained by a change of variable. The density of Y is the product of the conditional density of x and the determinant of the Jacobian

$$f_y(Y_{t+1}|Y_t) = f(x_{t+1}|x_t)\left|\frac{dx_{t+1}}{dY_{t+1}}\right|.$$

The log-likelihood function of observed yields $\{Y_t\}_{t=1}^T$ is then constructed as the usual sum of log densities $\log f_y(Y_{t+1}|Y_t)$ over the sample. To maximize the log-likelihood, the state x_{t+1} is backed out from Y_{t+1} for any given parameter vector. This method works both with linear zero-coupon yields or invertible nonlinear functions of the state x, such as coupon-bond prices, because the nonlinearity is absorbed by the Jacobian term.

6.2.1. Closed Form Densities

The density $f(x_{t+1}|x_t)$ is known in closed form for only a few affine processes. For Gaussian processes, f is multivariate normal. Zero-coupon yields are affine in x and therefore also Gaussian. Their likelihood function is therefore particularly easy to compute. To implement the procedure, we only need the conditional expected value (3.2) and variance (3.3). For independent Gaussians, the conditional variance is (3.4).

For independent square-root processes, f is the product of noncentral chi-square densities. The formula for the densities is based on the modified Bessel function of the first kind of order q (see Cox et al., 1985, pp. 391–2). The command "besseli" computes the function in MATLAB. The conditional mean is given again by (3.2), but now the conditional variance is (3.5).

6.2.2. Quasi-Maximum Likelihood

For general affine diffusions, f cannot be computed in closed form. The temptation is then to discretize the SDE and apply maximum likelihood to the density of the discretized process. The discretization assumes that the data is generated from the stochastic difference equation

$$\Delta x_{t+h} = \mu(x_t)h + \sigma(x_t)\varepsilon_{t+h}\sqrt{h}, \tag{6.2}$$

where ε_{t+h} has an N-dimensional standard normal distribution and h is the length of the observation interval. The density of the discretized process x_{t+h} conditional on x_t is normal with mean $\mu(x_t)h$ and conditional variance $\sigma(x_t)\sigma(x_t)^\top h$. The conditional distribution of the discretization (6.2) converges to the one of the SDE (2.6) when h tends to 0. The estimator that maximizes the likelihood function of the discretization is, however, not consistent for any given h. Lo (1988) shows this for explicit examples. The reason for this inconsistency is that the discretized process has conditional moments $\mu(x_t)h$ and $\sigma(x_t)\sigma(x_t)^\top h$, whereas the true process has discrete-time first and second moments given by Eqs. (3.2) and (3.3). However, quasi-maximum likelihood estimation based on the *correct* discrete-time first and second moments in (3.2) and (3.3) and a normal density, however, is consistent (Fisher and Gilles, 1996). This works only if the process is linear under the data-generating measure Q.

6.2.3. Fourier Inversion of the Characteristic Function

The density f of affine diffusions can be computed by Fourier inversion of the characteristic function. The characteristic function $\phi_t(u)$ is defined as the Fourier transform of the density of $x_{t+1} \in D$ conditional on x_t,

$$\phi_t(u) = E_t\left[\exp\left(iu^\top x_{t+1}\right)\right] = \int_D f(x_{t+1}|x_t)\exp\left(iu^\top x_{t+1}\right) \mathrm{d}x_{t+1}$$

for some $u \in \mathbb{R}^N$ and the imaginary number $i = \sqrt{-1}$. Duffie et al. (2000) show that the characteristic function $\phi_t(u)$ can be computed in closed form for affine diffusions. The idea is to apply the Feynman–Kac approach to the conditional expected value

$$\phi_t(u) = \exp\left(\alpha(1) + \beta(1)^\top x_t\right) \tag{6.3}$$

with coefficients $\alpha(\tau)$ and $\beta(\tau)$ that start at $\alpha(0) = 0$ and $\beta(0) = iu$ and solve the complex-valued ODEs

$$\alpha'(\tau) = \beta(\tau)^\top \kappa\bar{x} + \frac{1}{2}\sum_{i=1}^{N}\left[\beta(\tau)^\top\Sigma\right]_i^2 s_{0i}$$

$$b'(\tau) = \kappa^\top\beta(\tau) + \frac{1}{2}\sum_{i=1}^{N}\left[\beta(\tau)^\top\Sigma\right]_i^2 s_{1i}$$

For more details, see Duffie (2001), Appendix H.

Knowing the characteristic function $\phi_t(u)$ of an affine diffusion means that its conditional density f can be computed by Fourier inversion

$$f(x_{t+1}|x_t) = \frac{1}{\pi^N} \int\limits_{\mathbb{R}^N} \mathrm{Re}\left\{\exp\left(-iu^\top x_{t+1}\right) \phi_t(u)\right\} du, \tag{6.4}$$

where Re denotes the real part of complex numbers. Maximum likelihood by Fourier inversion has been implemented in the univariate case. Singleton (2001) estimates a one-factor CIR model by maximizing the likelihood function obtained with this method. The conditional density (6.4) is computed using Gauss–Legendre quadrature. For higher-dimensional state spaces, this computation becomes costly. The number of grid points used for the quadrature grows from d for $N = 1$ to d^N for general N. The MATLAB command "quad" performs these computations.

For general diffusions, not necessarily affine, the density can be computed by numerically solving a PDE, simulation, or Hermite expansions. Of these three methods, only simulation has been applied to the case of many factors so far.

6.2.4. Solving the PDE for the Density

The PDE for the conditional density f is given by the usual forward Kolmogorov equation (see, e.g., Lo, 1988). The PDE can be solved numerically. The curse of dimensionality applies here as well, see Lo (1988) and Jensen and Poulsen (1999).

6.2.5. Simulated Maximum Likelihood

Pedersen (1995) and Santa–Clara (1995) propose to simulate the likelihood function. Simulations of general diffusions cannot be based on their true density f, which is unknown. Instead, the simulations use the Euler scheme (6.2). Starting with the observed value x_t at time t, the sth simulated path of the state vector $\widehat{x}^{x_t}[s]$ is taken from (6.2) using independent draws $\widehat{\varepsilon}[s]$ from an N-dimensional standard normal distribution. The MATLAB command "randn" takes these draws. The idea is to write the density of x_{t+1} conditional on the last observation x_t, using Bayes' Rule and the Markov property of x, as

$$f(x_{t+1}|x_t) = \int\limits_D f(x_{t+1}|x_{t+1-h}) f(x_{t+1-h}|x_t) dx_{t+1-h} \tag{6.5}$$

for any time interval h. The density $f(x_{t+1}|x_{t+1-h})$ is now approximated with the density $\widehat{f}$ of the discretized process (6.2) for small h. This density is normal with mean $x_{t+1-h} + \mu(x_{t+1-h})h$ and standard deviation $\sigma(x_{t+1-h})\sqrt{h}$. The integral in (6.5) can then be computed using Monte Carlo

$$f(x_{t+1}|x_t) \approx \frac{1}{S} \sum_{s=1}^{S} \widehat{f}\left(x_{t+1}|\widehat{x}^{x_t}_{t+1-h}[s]\right),$$

where the summation is over a total of S simulated paths of the state that start at the last observation x_t at time t. The computer only needs to store the terminal simulated value $\widehat{x}^{x_t}_{t+1-h}[s]$ for each simulation s, not the entire simulated path. Standard variance reduction techniques, such as antithetic sampling, can be used to improve the efficiency of Monte Carlo integration (for a survey, see Geweke, 1996). Brandt and Santa-Clara (2002) use this simulated maximum likelihood (SML) method to estimate a multifactor diffusion model. Piazzesi (2005) extends SML to the case of jumps with time-varying jump intensities. Honoré (1998) conducts a Monte Carlo to compare the accuracy of the SML estimator for different discretization intervals h and numbers of simulations S. His findings suggest that even coarse discretizations and small simulated samples improve considerably over quasi-maximum likelihood (which amounts to $h = 1$). Durham and Gallant (2002) investigate importance-sampling techniques to improve the accuracy of this method.

6.2.6. Hermite Expansions

Aït-Sahalia (2001) approximates $f(x_{t+1}|x_t)$ for univariate diffusions x by constructing a standardized version $\widetilde{x}$ of the process x and then approximating the density of $\widetilde{x}$ by Hermite expansions. The reason for the standardization is that convergence results for Hermite expansions only apply to densities that are "close to normal," not for densities of general diffusions. The standardized version is a diffusion with unity volatility: $\widetilde{x} = \int^x 1/\sigma(w)\, dw$. For every $x \in \mathbb{R}^N$, Hermite polynomials are given by

$$H_j(x) = \exp\left(0.5x^2\right) \frac{\partial^j}{\partial x^j} \exp\left(-0.5x^2\right), \quad j = 0, 1, \ldots, J$$

For large J, the conditional density f of x can be written in terms of the density $f_{\widetilde{x}}$ of $\widetilde{x}$ which can be approximated with Hermite expansions

$$\begin{aligned} f(x_{t+1}|x_t) &\approx \frac{1}{\sigma(\widetilde{x}_{t+1})} f_{\widetilde{x}}(\widetilde{x}_{t+1}|\widetilde{x}_t) \\ &\approx \frac{1}{\sigma(\widetilde{x}_{t+1})} \exp\left(-0.5(\widetilde{x}_{t+1} - \widetilde{x}_t)^2\right) \sum_{j=0}^{J} \eta^{(j)}(\widetilde{x}_t) H_j(\widetilde{x}_{t+1} - \widetilde{x}_t) \end{aligned}$$

with coefficients

$$\eta^{(j)}(\widetilde{x}_t) = \frac{1}{j!} E\left[H_j(\widetilde{x}_{t+1} - \widetilde{x}_t) \,|\, \widetilde{x}_t\right]$$

which are conditional moments of functions of $\widetilde{x}$. Aït-Sahalia (2008) computes closed-form expressions for these coefficients using Taylor approximations. Jensen and Poulsen (1999) compare the accuracy of Hermite expansions with other methods for the case of a univariate square-root process. Aït-Sahalia (2008) extends the method to multivariate diffusions.

6.3. Matching Moments

The computation of moments for Hansen's (1982) generalized method of moments (GMM) depends on whether the yield equation is affine and on whether the data-generating process of the state vector is an affine diffusion. Moments of affine diffusions can be computed in closed form using the characteristic function. But this result is only useful for matching moments of zero-coupon yields, not for nonlinear yield formulas (e.g., which arise with coupon bonds and swaps) To avoid nonlinear yield formulas, zero-coupon yields can be constructed by interpolating swap data or be other "nonlinear" yield data. For nonaffine dynamics under the data-generating measure and nonlinear yield formulas, moments can either be simulated using the methods explained in Gallant and Tauchen (2010) or be computed using operator-methods explained in Aït-Sahalia et al. (2010).

Higher-order moments of affine diffusions can be conveniently computed from the characteristic function. First and second moments were already computed in Section 3.2. Conditional cross-moments of the ith and jth component of x are given by

$$
\begin{aligned}
E_t\left(x_{i,t+1}^m x_{j,t+1}^n\right) &= i^{m+n}\frac{\partial^m}{\partial u_i^m}\frac{\partial^n}{\partial u_j^n}\phi_t(u)\mid_{u=0} \\
&= i^{m+n}\frac{\partial^m}{\partial u_i^m}\frac{\partial^n}{\partial u_j^n}\exp\left(\alpha(1)+\beta(1)^\top x_t\right)\mid_{u=0}
\end{aligned}
$$

for $1 \leq i,j \leq N$. This computation is particularly convenient if the coefficients $\alpha(1)$ and $\beta(1)$ can be computed with paper and pencil. For an early estimation of a CIR model with GMM, see Gibbons and Ramaswamy (1993).

Another set of moments is computed in Singleton (2001) and Chacko and Viceira (2003). In these papers, the characteristic function is used to set up moment conditions

$$
E_t\left[\exp\left(iu^\top x_{t+s}\right) - \phi_t(u)\right] = 0.
$$

Each such complex-valued moment condition implies two real-valued moment conditions based on the real and the imaginary part of the expression. Singleton (2001) shows that GMM is efficient in this case when the number of grid points u goes to infinity. Carrasco et al. (2001) demonstrate how to actually implement this efficiency result.

6.4. Identification

Just like in a state-space system with latent state dynamics, the conditions ensuring identification of parameters are tricky. Ideally, we would not have to care about these conditions because identification should be an invertibility condition on the information matrix. In practice, this invertibility condition is not useful for checking whether parameters are identified. The likelihood function would have to be maximized for many different trial-parametrization to find out which of the parameters are not identified. Moreover, numerical gradient-methods for computing the information matrix are imprecise, especially when the likelihood function is computed numerically or simulated. The information matrix may turn out to be numerically invertible, even in cases where parameters are not identified. Theoretical results are therefore important. Dai and Singleton (2000) provide such results.

7. EMPIRICAL EVIDENCE ON AFFINE MODELS

Empirical studies of term structure models usually pick a set of stylized facts about yields and tailor their model to match these. There is no benchmark for evaluating the performance of different models because different sets of facts are being matched, and there is no consensus about the relative importance of these facts. I therefore organize the discussion of the empirical findings of affine models around these stylized facts and, in particular, around the moments of yields that are being matched. After discussing data issues in Section 7.1, I focus on factor interpretation in Section 7.2, cross-sectional fitting errors in Section 7.3, unconditional and conditional first moments in Sections 7.4 and 7.5, unconditional and conditional second moments in Section 7.6 and 7.7, higher-order moments in Section 7.8, seasonalities in Section 7.9, and zoom back in on fitting the short end in Section 7.10. Then, I discuss joint systems of yields with macroeconomic variables in Section 8.

7.1. Data Issues

The choice of suitable data to estimate yield-curve models needs to balance concerns about measurement errors, sample length, observation frequency, nonlinearities in pricing formulas, and even the documentation quality of different data sets. In this chapter, I use monthly Fama CRSP zero-coupon bond tapes from 1964:1 to 2003:12. CRSP provides detailed documentation for this data set. The data set is problematic because these yields are interpolated from traded Treasuries, which introduces measurement error. Moreover, the 1-month T-bill from the dataset looks strange when compared with the other short rates in the same dataset. For example, the persistence of the 1-month rate decreases after 1985, whereas the persistence of all other short rates increases. Watson (1999) documents an increase in persistence in the (overnight) Fed funds rate after 1985, which means that the behavior of the 1-month rate does not seem to be a special feature of very short rates. I also omit data from 1952:1 to 1963:12 like Fama and Bliss (1987). The data over this early period behaves much different from the rest in terms of, e.g., predictability regressions. Then, there are data entry errors: September 1987 shows a 0% yield for the

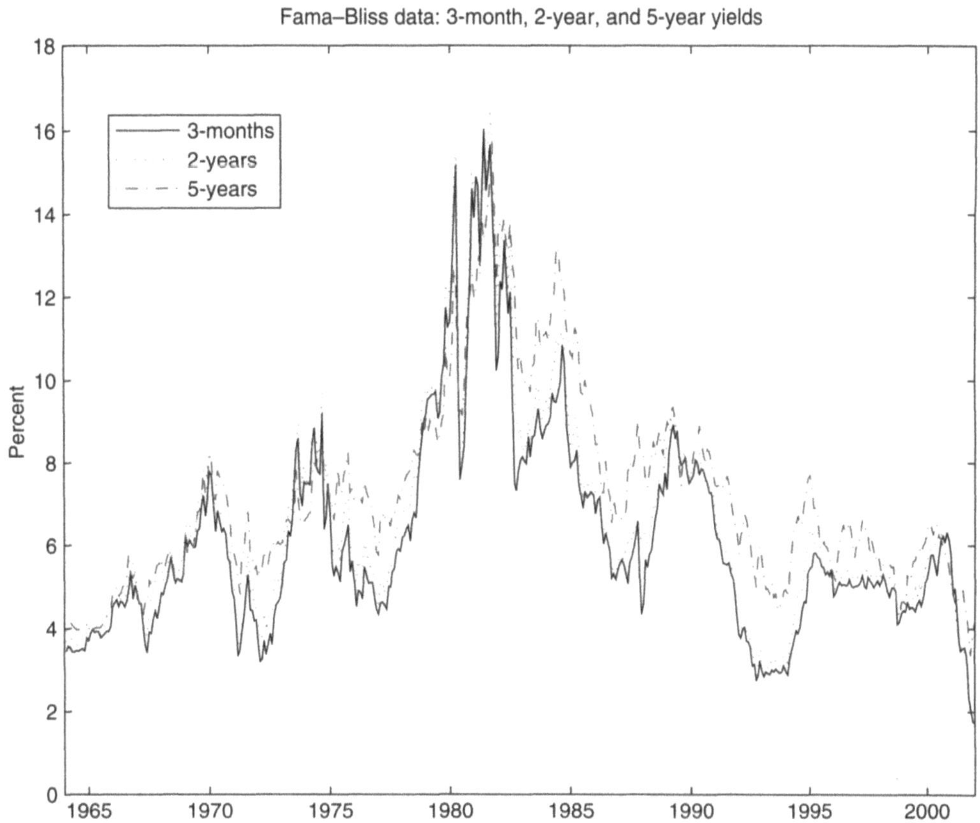

Figure 12.2 Monthly Fama–Bliss data for 3 month, 2-year, and 5 year yields, 1964:1–2003:12.

6-month T-bill in the CRSP file for short maturity T-bills. I therefore interpolate that datapoint. Like ants, errors usually come in company, and this company may be less obvious.[10] Figure 12.2 plots some of the Fama–Bliss yields used in this chapter.

7.1.1. Short Yields

Short-maturity yields are often used as proxies for the short rate. Seasonality in measurement error is a worry in this context. For example, overnight rates (like fed funds in Hamilton, 1996; repo in Piazzesi, 2005), other short-term rates (like term fed funds in Balduzzi et al., 1996; 7-day Eurodollar in Durham, 2001), and even yields with maturities of a few months (like the 3-month T-bill in Durham, 2001, 6-month LIBOR in Piazzesi, 2001) have been shown to be affected by the 2-week reserve maintenance period of

[10] An example for a less obvious data entry error is the Federal Reserve target-rate change that happened on February 4, 1994. Datastream assigns this Fed move to February 3.

banks. These 2-week periods start on a Thursday and ending on the so-called "settlement Wednesday." During this period, banks must hold required reserves in accounts at the Federal Reserve. These reserves are associated with opportunity costs for banks because the Fed does not pay any interest on these accounts. Until July 30, 1998, the Fed used a contemporaneous reserve maintenance system. In this system, the reserve computation period, the period over which required reserves are actually computed, overlapped with the reserve maintenance period. This overlap implied that the exact amount of reserves that banks were required to hold was not known until the very end of the maintenance period. To avoid the opportunity costs of excess reserve holdings, banks used to hold few reserves until they knew the required amount and then started borrowing on the day before the settlement Wednesday. The increased demands for funds at the end of reserve maintenance periods lead to huge seasonal spikes in interest rates in this contemporaneous reserve system. This seasonality has weakened since 1998, when the Fed adopted a lagged reserve maintenance system. According to the new rules, the reserve computation period ends 30 days before the maintenance period so that banks know the required amount before they start holding reserves. Settlement Wednesdays and other day-of-the-week effects, such as FOMC meetings, introduce seasonalities in interest rates which may bias, e.g., estimates of mean-reversion parameters (more on this in Section 7.9). Piazzesi (2005) and He (2001) therefore argue to use the target rate set by the Federal Reserve as "cleaner" measure of the short rate. Chapman et al. (1999) argue that short T-bill rates are good short-rate proxies, at least when used in one-factor affine models. Duffee (1996), however, points out that very short T-bill rates behave differently from other short rates. More concretely, T-bills with maturities less than 3 months do not share much variation with other short-term yields such as Eurodollar rates or Fed funds rates.

7.1.2. Long Yields of Zero-Coupon Bonds

Zero-coupon bonds have the advantage that the yield equation is easy to invert for x. True zero-coupon bonds are, however, not easy to come by. These bonds are supposed to be default-free, which may apply to government securities in the United States but certainly not to those in many other countries such as Italy and Spain (Favero et al., 1997) or Russia (Duffie et al., 2003). U.S. Treasury bills are zero-coupon bonds with maturities up to 1 year. Duffee (1996) documents that T-bills with maturities less than 3 months seem to be disconnected from longer term Treasuries. Treasury notes have longer maturities (from 2 to 30 years), but they do pay semiannual coupons. The principal and coupons of these notes can be stripped and traded as separate securities since 1985. This means that data on prices of some long zero-coupon bonds exists (Grinblatt and Longstaff, 2000; Jordan et al., 2000). Various authors have developed interpolation methods to construct long-time series of zero-coupon bond yields. Of course, these data-construction methods introduce measurement error. The "McCulloch–Kwon" data until 1991 is available on the Website of J. Huston McCulloch at Ohio. Bliss (1999) updates this data set until the end of 1998. The "Fama–Bliss" data set is updated each year and available from the Fama CRSP zero-coupon bond tapes. Both data sets consist of monthly observations over the whole postwar period. Estimations of affine models with zero-coupon bonds include Balduzzi et al. (1996), Duffee (2002), Ang and Piazzesi (2003), Wu (2006), and Buraschi and Jilsov (2005).

7.1.3. Long Yields of Treasuries

The U.S. Treasury interpolates the yields of traded securities when computing constant-maturity Treasury yield data which is released by the Federal Reserve Board in its H.15 release. Daily data since 1962 on these yields is posted on the Federal Reserve's Web site (which also has the short-term Treasury bill data). Treasuries pay semiannual coupons. Their yields can be computed as par bond rates $yc^{(\tau)}$ from

$$1 = \sum_{j=1}^{2\tau} P_t^{(0.5j)} \frac{yc_t^{(\tau)}}{2} + P_t^{(\tau)}.$$

Solving this equation for $yc_t^{(\tau)}$ gives

$$yc_t^{(\tau)} = \frac{2\left(1 - P_t^{(\tau)}\right)}{\sum_{j=1}^{2\tau} P_t^{(0.5j)}}. \tag{7.1}$$

The inversion of observed yields for the unobserved state x can no longer be accomplished by hand with coupon-yields because the pricing map (7.1) is nonlinear. Instead, the map needs to be inverted numerically for each observation t in the sample. The speed of this loop can be increased considerably by supplying the analytical gradient $\partial yc_t^{(\tau)}/\partial x_t$ to the gradient-based method that inverts the pricing map. For example, Pearson and Sun (1994) use prices of traded Treasuries in their estimation.

7.1.4. Long Yields for Swaps

Swap rates are truly constant maturity yields which makes interpolation unnecessary. Swaps are agreements to exchange fixed and floating rates semiannually for a time of τ years. The τ-year swap rate is the fixed coupon rate in this contract, whereas the floating side is usually specified to be the 3-month or 6-month London Interbank offered rate (LIBOR). Under the assumption that swap rates can be valued as par bond rates, the Formula (7.1) also applies to swap rates. Without default risk, the formula follows from the absence of arbitrage. With default risk, the formula applies if the credit quality in LIBOR and swap markets is the same. The assumption is somewhat problematic because of the institutional features of swap markets. For example, netting features imply that swap rates are minimally affected by credit risk apart from being tied to LIBOR rates (Collin-Dufresne and Solink, 2001; Duffie and Huang, 1996). Swaps have only started trading at the end of the 1980s, which means that swap data is silent about periods of high volatility such as the monetary experiment in the early 1980s in Fig. 12.2. Daily data on both swap rates and LIBOR can be obtained from Datastream, which only supplies poor documentation of this data. Moreover, the data is asynchronous because LIBOR data is recorded at 11 A.M. London time, whereas swap data is recorded at the end of the business day in London. Estimations of affine models usually ignore this issue. See, e.g., Duffie and Singleton (1997), Dai and Singleton (2000), Piazzesi (2001), He (2001), Collin–Dufresne et al. (2009), and Liu et al. (2002).

7.1.5. Other Data

Term structure models can, of course, also be estimated with data on futures, caps, floors, and other derivative securities. For example, Jegadeesh and Pennacchi (1996) use Eurodollar futures. Jagannathan et al. (2001) include data on caps and swaptions. Data on all these contracts can be found in Datastream.

7.2. Level, Slope, and Curvature

Traditional factor analysis already delivers much of the intuition for what drives yields. Principal components can be computed from levels and changes in yields, I will do both. Suppose the econometrician has data on K different yields that are contained in the vector Y_t at time t. The variance-covariance matrix of Y_t can be written as

$$\mathrm{var}(Y_t) = \Omega \Lambda \Omega^\top,$$

where Λ is a diagonal matrix of eigenvalues of the matrix $\mathrm{var}(Y_t)$ and Ω is an orthogonal matrix (which means it satisfies $\Omega^\top = \Omega^{-1}$) whose columns are standardized eigenvectors. Principal components pc are then defined by

$$pc_t = \Omega^\top \left(Y_t - \overline{Y}\right), \tag{7.2}$$

where $\overline{Y} \in \mathbb{R}^K$ is the sample mean of the yields. The variance of the kth principal component is just equal to Λ_k, the kth eigenvalue of $\mathrm{var}(Y_t)$. It is also true that the total variation in yields $\mathrm{tr}(\mathrm{var}(Y_t))$ is equal to the total variation of principal components $\mathrm{tr}(\Lambda)$, where tr denotes trace. Details can be found, e,g., in Mardia et al. (1979). The same procedure can be repeated for yield changes by replacing Y_t with ΔY_t and $\overline{Y}$ with 0 in the above formulas.

Looking at principal components of yield changes reveals that much of the variance in yield changes is explained by the first few principal components. I use $K=11$ Fama and Bliss yields from Center for Research in Security Prices (CRSP) with maturities $1, 2, 3,$

Table 12.1 % variation in yield changes and levels explained by the first k principal components

k	1	2	3	4	5
% explained in ΔY_t	79.2	91.4	96.4	97.5	98.3
% explained in Y_t	96.6	99.6	99.8	99.9	100

The total variation in yields is given by $\text{tr}(\Lambda)$, where Λ is the diagonal matrix of eigenvalues of $\text{var}(\Delta Y_t) = \Omega\Lambda\Omega^\top$ in the first row and $\text{var}(Y_t) = \Omega\Lambda\Omega^\top$ in the second row. The numbers in the table are the percentage variation in yield changes (yield levels) explained by the first k principal components computed as

$$100 \times \frac{\sum_{i=1}^{k} \Lambda_i}{\text{tr}(\Lambda)}$$

The yields are from the Fama tapes of CRSP. The maturities are 1, 2, 3, 4, 5, and 6 months and 1, 2, 3, 4, and 5 years. The sample is 1964:1-2003:12.

4, 5, and 6 months and 1, 2, 3, 4, and 5 years for the months 1964:1–2003:12. Table 12.1 computes the cumulative percentage in the variation of yield changes and levels explained by the first k principal components. The table shows that for the postwar period, the first $k = 3$ principal components already explain over 96% of the total variation in yield changes. This number is similar for weekly (Chapman and Pearson, 2001; Litterman and Scheinkman, 1991) and even daily yields (Hull, 2000, Chapter 14.10). In the case of yield levels, the numbers are higher.

To use only $k \leq K$ principal components, I define the $K \times k$ matrix $\widetilde{\Omega}$ by

$$\widetilde{\Omega}_{i,j} = \begin{cases} \Omega_{i,j} & \text{for } j \leq k \\ 0 & \text{otherwise} \end{cases}$$

and compute the k principal components of yield levels as

$$pc_t = \widetilde{\Omega}^\top (Y_t - \overline{Y}).$$

The k principal components are linear combinations of $K = 11$ yields. Figure 12.3 plots the coefficients of these linear combinations (or loadings), which are the $k = 3$ columns of $\widetilde{\Omega}$, as function of the maturity of the yields in months. Figure 12.3 looks very similar for the loadings of principal components of yield changes, so I do not include them here. The loadings of the first principal component are horizontal. This pattern means that changes in the first principal component correspond to parallel shifts in the yield curve. This principal component is therefore called the *level factor.* The loading of the second principal component is downward sloping. Changes in the second principal component thus rotate the yield curve. This means the second component is a *slope factor.* The loading

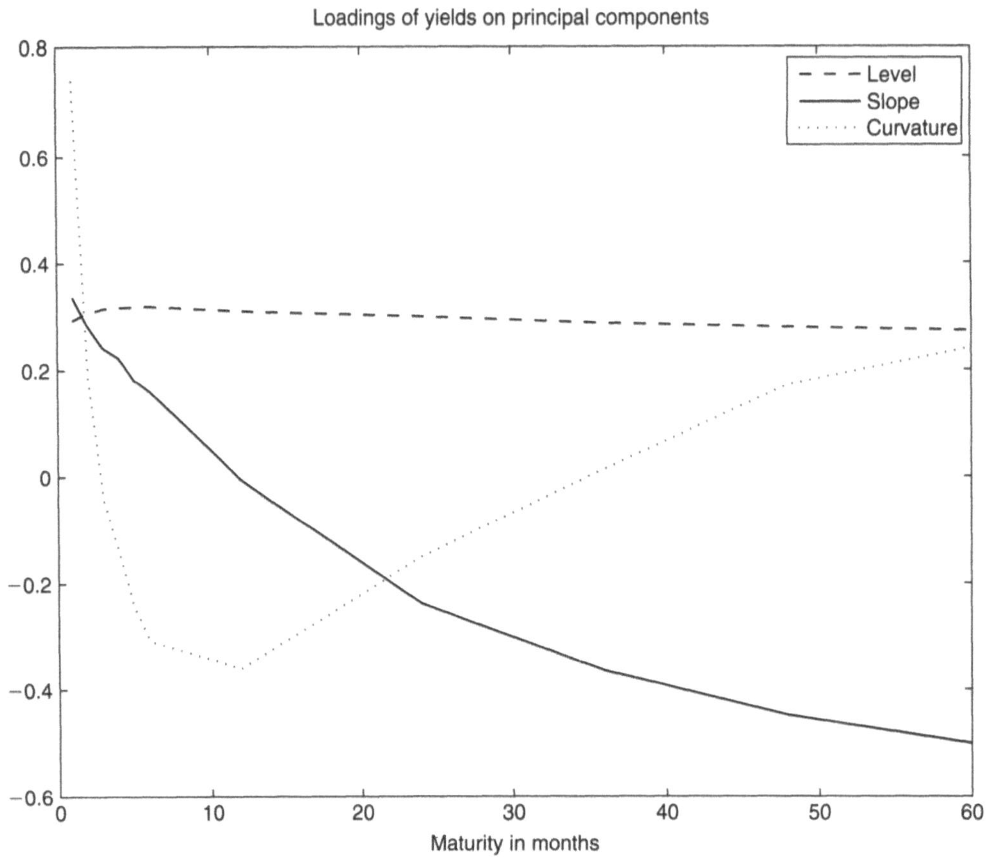

Figure 12.3 Principal components are linear combinations of yields in the data set. The coefficients of these linear combinations are the columns of $\tilde{\Omega}$. The coefficients of each of the three principal components are plotted as a function of the maturity of the yields.

of the third principal component is hump shaped. The hump occurs at intermediate maturities. The third principal component therefore affects the curvature of the yield curve, which is why it is called the *curvature factor*. These three principal components can be ordered according to their persistence. The level factor is very persistent with a monthly autocorrelation of 0.98. The slope factor is less persistent with an autocorrelation of 0.92. The curvature factor is the least persistent with an autocorrelation of 0.50.

The interpretation of these principal components in terms of level, slope, and curvature goes back to Litterman and Scheinkman (1991). These labels have turned out to be extremely useful in thinking about the driving forces of the yield curve until today. The *latent factors* implied by estimated affine models typically behave like principal components. This empirical finding applies to different sample periods, data sets, and model specifications. More concretely, the coefficients from estimated yield equations (3.9) show the same general patterns as in Fig. 12.3 for the case of $N = 3$ state variables. This applies to models with only square-root processes as in Chen and Scott (1993), only Gaussian processes as in Gong and Remolona (1996) and Ang and Piazzesi (2003), or mixture models as in Balduzzi et al. (1996) and Dai and Singleton (2000). There is no one-to-one mapping between labels such as stochastic mean and stochastic volatility and the Litterman–Scheinkman labels. For example, stochastic volatility behaves like a curvature factor in some estimated models, but it turns out to be so persistent that it becomes the level factor in others. Lower dimensional models with $N < 3$ feature state variables with yield coefficients that correspond to the first N principal components. In other words, models with only two state variables find a level and a slope factor. Again, this empirical finding is robust across specifications. In particular, it holds for stochastic mean models (5.3) and stochastic volatility models (5.4) alike. The square-root case for $N = 2$ is in Chen and Scott (1993), and the Gaussian case is in Balduzzi et al. (1998). Models with only one state variable (namely the short rate r) have one persistent level factor.

7.3. Cross-Sectional Performance

Affine models predict yields of any maturity τ with an R^2 of 1. Once we fix a time series of factors, the yields are just linear functions of these factors. Traditional factor models provide a natural benchmark for the cross-sectional fit. Factor models based on k principal components predict all K yields in the cross section as

$$\widehat{Y}_t = \overline{Y} + \widetilde{\Omega} pc_t, \tag{7.3}$$

where pc_t is given by (7.2). The yield coefficients in this prediction do not impose the cross-equation restrictions from no-arbitrage. Unlike in a term structure model, there is no link between the data-generating process of the factors pc and the way yields depend on pc. The model implies *fitting errors* for yields, which are defined as the difference between actual yields Y_t and model-predicted yields $\widehat{Y}_t$. Table 12.2 computes the mean, standard deviation, and maximum of the absolute value of these fitting errors for $k = 3$ principal components. The mean absolute fitting errors are less than 11 basis points for all yields in the data set. This suggests that this low-dimensional factor model not only explains much of the variance in yields by construction but also performs extremely well according to this additional metric.

The fitting errors in Table 12.2 turn out to be hard to beat in practice with an affine model. In other words, the difference between the yields predicted by an affine model at the estimated parameter values and the actual yield data can be substantial. Affine models do not deal with measurement errors explicitly. Such errors are usually tagged onto yields by the econometrician. But they are usually larger in absolute value than those in

Table 12.2 Absolute value of fitting errors for yields

Maturity	1 month	3 months	6 months	1 year	2 years	3 years	4 years	5 years
Mean	0.10	0.08	0.06	0.11	0.09	0.05	0.05	0.08
Standard deviation	0.09	0.09	0.06	0.11	0.07	0.05	0.05	0.06
Maximum	0.68	0.78	0.73	1.11	0.52	0.48	0.41	0.52

The table shows the mean, standard deviation, and maximum of absolute fitting errors $|Y_t - \widehat{Y}_t|$, where $\widehat{Y}_t$ is computed as in Eq. (7.3) with $k = 3$ principal components of yield levels. The yield data is from the Fama tapes of CRSP for 1964:1–2003:12.

Table 12.2. Moreover, these errors are usually highly autocorrelated. Affine models with many Gaussian factors tend to do relatively better in the cross section than models with many square-root factors. For example, the fitting errors from the $A_2(3)$ model in Table IV of Dai and Singleton (2000) are larger than the errors from the $A_1(3)$ model. The fitting errors from the three-factor jump model without the Gaussian 'inertia factor' in Table 2 of Piazzesi (2001) are larger than the errors from the three-factor jump model with stochastic volatility.

7.4. Unconditional First Moments (Positive Slope)

Yields of bonds with longer maturities are on average higher than those of bonds with shorter maturities. This means that the yield curve is on average upward sloping. Figure 12.4 shows this stylized fact by plotting the sample average of the Fama and Bliss yields as a function of maturity. The solid line of point estimates is shown together with dotted approximate 95% confidence bounds (two times Newey–West standard errors using six lags). The plot suggests that the shortest yield is significantly lower than the longest yield on average.

An upward sloping yield curve is easy to generate with an affine model. To do this, the risk-neutral long-run mean of the short rate must be higher than its true long-run mean

$$\bar{r}^* > \bar{r}.$$

From the short-rate equation in Assumption 1, these parameters are linked to the long-run mean of the state vector x under Q^* and Q as follows:

$$\delta_0 + \delta_1^\top \bar{x}^* > \delta_0 + \delta_1^\top \bar{x}.$$

The parameters $\bar{x}^*$ and $\bar{x}$ differ only when market prices of risk differ from zero. For example, constant market prices of risk together with constant factor volatility do the

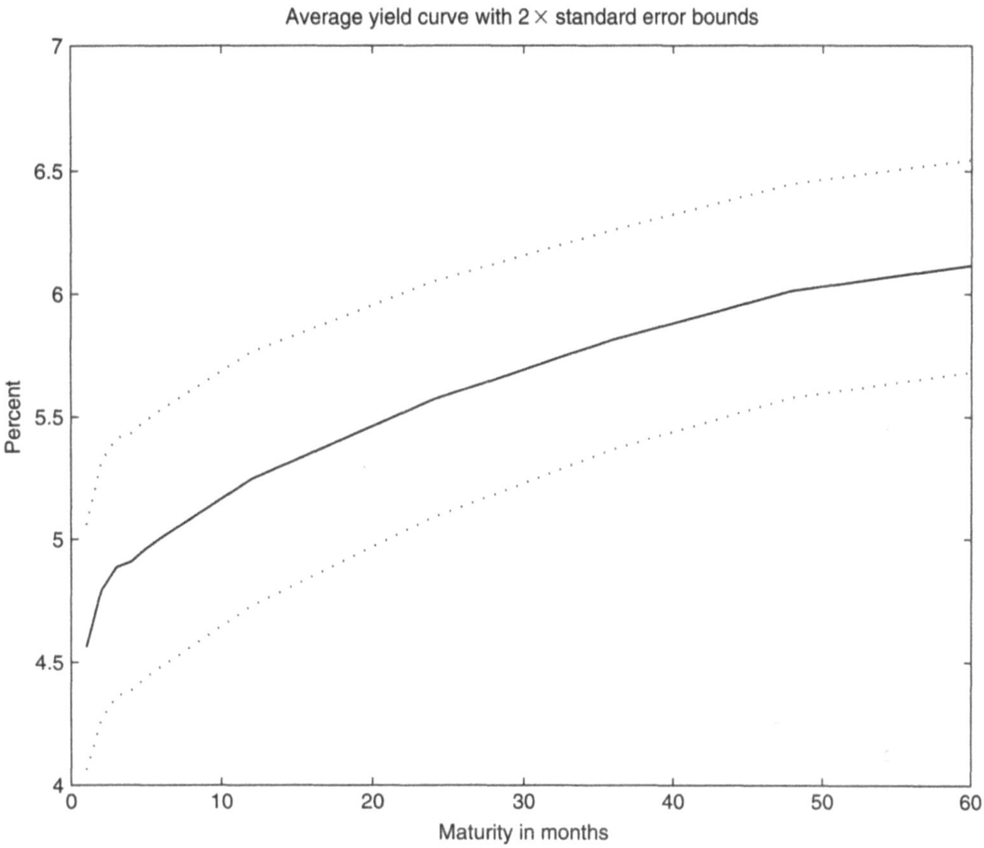

Figure 12.4 The average yield curve is computed using the Fama and Bliss yields with maturities 1, 2, 3, 4, 5, and 6 months and 1, 2, 3, 4, and 5 years. The sample period is 1964:1–2003:12. The dotted lines are two times Newey–West standard error bounds computed using six lags.

job. From Eq. (2.12), this assumption gives

$$\sigma_\xi(x) = q^\top$$
$$\sigma_x(x) = \Sigma$$
$$\overline{x}^* = \overline{x} - \kappa^{-1}\Sigma q.$$

When $R(x) = x$, the risk-neutral mean $\overline{x}^*$ is larger than $\overline{x}$ as long as the market price of risk $q < 0$. The CAPM-type equation (3.13) shows that expected excess returns on bonds are *constant and positive* in this example. The Vasicek model makes these assumptions [see Eq. (5.1)].

7.5. Conditional First Moments (Persistence, Predictability, Nonlinearity)

7.5.1. Persistence

Yields are highly autocorrelated. Table 12.3 shows the autocorrelations of Fama–Bliss yields together with standard errors around the autocorrelation estimates (which are not corrected for small-sample bias). The monthly autocorrelation coefficient of the 5-year yield implies that shocks to this yield have a half-life of $\log(0.5)/\log(0.987) \approx 53$ months, over 4 years. This persistence in yield levels is behind the large standard errors around the mean estimates in Fig. 12.4. Longer yields tend to be more persistent than short yields, at least judging from the point estimates.

There is some evidence that persistence in short rates has increased over time, again according to the point estimates. For example, the autocorrelation of the 3-month yield in the Fama–Bliss file goes from 0.969 before 1985 to 0.993 after 1985. The evidence is not strong, through. Watson (1999) is unable to detect a change in persistence using a Chow test for structural break based on distributions that take into account small sample bias. There is strong evidence that persistence in short rates has increased since the creation of the Federal Reserve in 1914. Mankiw and Miron (1986) document higher predictability of short-rate changes for quarterly data from 1880 to 1914 than after 1914.

Affine models describe yields as affine in the factors. This implies that persistence of yields must come from persistent factors. In fact, all estimations of affine models find a level factor, which is very persistent. This fact was already mentioned in the context of principal component models (Section 7.2).

Persistence contributes to the practical problems associated with the estimation of affine models. Consider the simple example of estimating the parameters of an AR(1), $x_t = \mu + \rho x_{t-1} + \varepsilon_t$, with Gaussian errors ε_t using maximum likelihood. When the autoregressive coefficient ρ is close to one, gradient-based optimization methods typically converge very slowly. They take tiny steps around reasonable values of ρ while still being far from reasonable values of μ. The reason is that the likelihood function is essentially flat in μ but very steep in ρ. There is a simple solution to this problem in the univariate case. Fixing a value for ρ close to one while optimizing over μ typically delivers a great starting

Table 12.3 Autocorrelations of yields

Maturity	1	3	6	12	24	36	48	60
Autocorrelation	0.962	0.983	0.984	0.983	0.986	0.987	0.986	0.987
Standard errors	0.017	0.013	0.013	0.012	0.011	0.011	0.011	0.010

The maturity of yields is in months. Standard errors (in brackets) are computed with six Newey–West lags. The yield data is from the Fama tapes of CRSP for 1964:1–2003:12.

value for μ that can be used in the optimization over both parameters. With multidimensional AR(1) systems, the same strategy can be applied but often becomes more tricky.

7.5.2. Predictability of Excess Returns

Fama and Bliss (1987) investigate whether excess holding period returns on bonds are predictable using the forward-spot spread. The regressions involve holding periods of 1 year. For this horizon, the 1-year rate $y^{(1)}$ is the riskless rate. Holding period returns are the difference in log prices $\text{hpr}_{t\to t+1}^{(\tau)} = p_{t+1}^{(\tau-1)} - p_t^{(\tau)}$, where $t \leq t+1 \leq t+\tau$. Fama and Bliss regress excess holding period returns on the forward-spot spread $f_t^{(n-1\to n)} - y_t^{(1)}$, where the forward rate is $f_t^{(n-1\to n)} = p_t^{(n-1)} - p_t^{(n)}$. Table 12.4 reports the R^2 from these predictability regressions. R^2s are substantial, 14% for bonds with maturities from 2 to 4 years. Excess returns on 5-year bonds are less predictable, with an R^2 of 6%. Expected excess returns are thus not constant over time.

Cochrane and Piazzesi (2005) show that this R^2 more than doubles when all forward rates $f_t^{(1\to 2)}, f_t^{(2\to 3)}, f_t^{(3\to 4)}$, and $f_t^{(4\to 5)}$ are included on the right-hand side of this regression. Moreover, they find that the predictability is mostly due to a single factor. This "return-predicting" factor turns out to be only weakly related to level, slope, and curvature. Also, monthly VARs with one lag in the yields with maturities 1–5 years do not find the return-predicting factor.

This evidence against the EH is of course based on a rather small sample. Bekaert et al. (1997) and Bekaert and Hodrick (2001) stress the importance of taking into account the small sample distributions of these R^2s and other standard tests of the EH. Tests based on small sample distributions tend to make a weaker case against the EH. Cochrane and Piazzesi (2005) construct 95% confidence intervals for R^2 for the predictability regressions. Confidence intervals for R^2 in the Fama–Bliss regressions indeed include 0. Confidence intervals for R^2 from the regression on all forward rates are far away from 0, however, even if the EH is imposed on the bootstrap. The cross-country evidence about the EH is more mixed. In some countries like Germany, the EH seems to hold

Table 12.4 R^2 from predictability regressions

n	2	3	4	5
FB (1987)	0.14	0.14	0.15	0.06
CP (2001)	0.34	0.34	0.37	0.34

The table reports R^2 from two predictability regressions. Fama–Bliss (1987) regress $\text{hpr}_{t\to t+1}^{(n)} - y_t^{(1)}$ on a constant and $f_t^{(n-1\to n)} - y_t^{(1)}$. Cochrane–Piazzesi (2004) regress the same variable on a constant and $y_t^{(1)}, f_t^{(1\to 2)}, f_t^{(2\to 3)}, f_t^{(3\to 4)}$, and $f_t^{(4\to 5)}$. The sample is 1964:1–2001:12.

up better than in the United States (Bekaert et al., 1997, 2007; Gerlach and Smets, 1997; Hardouvelis, 1994). Finally, the very short end of the yield curve seems to conform better with the EH (Longstaff, 2000b).

Figure 12.5 shows the fitted values from the predictability regressions in Table 12.4 for $n = 3$. Excess returns on long-term bonds are small and on average positive. For Fama–Bliss yields, average excess returns are 0.42, 0.65, 0.79, and 0.72% for $n = 2, 3, 4$, and 5. This stylized fact can be generated even in the simple one-factor Vasicek model. Inserting coefficients (5.1) into the CAPM equation (3.13) gives expected excess returns $-b(\tau)^{\top}\Sigma q$, where $b(\tau) > 0$ because the short-rate coefficient δ_1 is equal to 1. Expected excess returns are positive provided that $q < 0$.

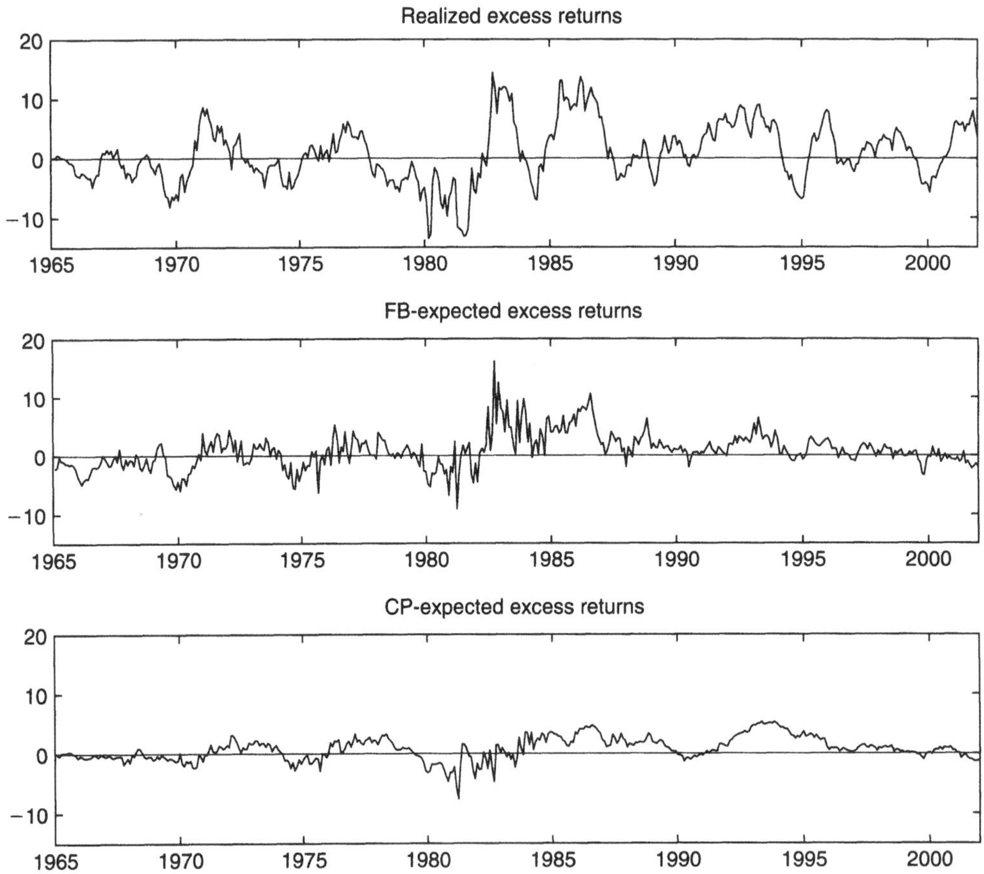

Figure 12.5 Realized excess returns are $\mathrm{hpr}_t^{(3)} - y_t^{(1)}$. FB-expected excess returns are the fitted values of the Fama and Bliss (1987) regression in Table 12.3 for $n = 3$. CP-expected excess returns are the fitted values of the Cochrane and Piazzesi (2001) regression for $n = 3$. Returns expected for t are plotted together with returns at t.

However, expected excess returns in the Vasicek model are constant. According to Fig. 12.5 expected excess returns seem to vary through time. In particular, they switch signs over time. In other words, expected excess returns are not always positive but also sometimes negative. They tend to be positive when the term structure is upward sloping and negative when the term structure is downward sloping. Time-variation alone is easy to generate within an affine model, but many popular affine models are unable to generate the switching signs. The modeling key to this stylized fact is either in the market prices of risk $\sigma_\xi(x)$ or in the factors loadings $b(\tau)$. I will discuss this in detail next.

7.5.3. Affine Diffusions Under Both Measures

Examples of models with time-varying expected excess returns that are not able to switch signs are the CIR and Dai and Singleton (2000) models. From the CAPM equation (3.13), expected excess returns in the CIR model are $-b(\tau)^\top \Sigma r_t q$, where $b(\tau) > 0$ because $\delta_1 = 1$. The time variation in expected excess returns thus comes through the short rate r_t, which is a square-root process and therefore always positive. This implies that expected excess returns are either always positive or always negative–they cannot switch signs. The same mechanism is at work in Dai and Singleton (2000). The coefficients (5.5) imply expected excess returns $-b(\tau)^\top \Sigma s(x)s(x)^\top q$. Condition A allows only square-root processes to enter the volatility $s(x)$. Together with the assumption that $\delta_1 = (1, 0, \ldots, 0)$, the model cannot generate expected excess returns that switch signs.

Recent affine models have attacked this problem in different ways. Backus et al. (2001) make the following assumptions:

$$R(x) = x_1 - x_2$$

$$\sigma_x(x) = \begin{pmatrix} \sqrt{x_1} & 0 \\ 0 & \sqrt{x_2} \end{pmatrix}$$

$$\sigma_\xi(x) = q^\top \sigma_x(x).$$

Both factors x_1 and x_2 are square-root processes, and the short rate is the difference between the two. The CAPM-equation (3.13) shows that the coefficients $b(\tau)$ generate the switch in expected excess returns in this "negative CIR model." This can be seen from the fact that yield coefficients $B(\tau) = -b(\tau)/\tau$ go to $\begin{bmatrix} 1 & -1 \end{bmatrix}$ as maturity τ goes to 0.

Market prices of risk had so far always the form $\sigma_\xi(x) = q^\top \sigma_x(x)$. A number of papers obtain switching signs in expected excess returns with other functional forms for $\sigma_\xi(x)$. El Karoui et al. (1992) and Ahn et al. (2002) propose a setting with Gaussian x, an affine market prices of risk, and a linear-quadratic short rate r. When the short rate is constrained to be affine in x (no quadratic terms), this framework collapses to the affine model[11]

$$\begin{aligned} R(x) &= \delta_0 + \delta_1^\top x \\ \sigma_x(x) &= \Sigma \\ \sigma_\xi(x) &= q_0^\top + x^\top q_1, \end{aligned}$$

where $q_0 \in \mathbb{R}^N$ and $q_1 \in \mathbb{R}^{N\times N}$. This is the model considered in Fisher (1998) and Dai and Singleton (2002). Ang and Piazzesi (2003) specify a discrete-time version of the model. In this setup, again, the process x is Gaussian under both measures as in Vasicek (1977), but now both the long-run mean and the speed of mean reversion differ under the two measures (unlike in the Vasicek model before, where only the long-run mean was different). In particular, expected excess returns switch signs because of q_1. The setup is a special case of Duffee (2002) who considers

$$\begin{aligned} \sigma_x(x) &= \Sigma s(x) \\ \sigma_\xi(x) &= q_1^\top s(x) + x^\top q_2 s(x)^- \end{aligned}$$

with $q_1 \in \mathbb{R}^N$, $q_2 \in \mathbb{R}^{N\times N}$, and

$$s_{ii}(x_t)^- = \begin{cases} \left(s_{0i} + s_{1i}^\top x_t\right)^{-1/2} & \text{if } \inf\left(s_{0i} + s_{1i}^\top x_t\right) > 0; \\ 0 & \text{otherwise.} \end{cases}$$

This definition ensures that $s(x)^-$ does not explode, as diagonal elements in $s(x)$ go to zero. Suppose x is Gaussian so that $s_{0i} = 1$ and $s_{1i} = 0$, then $\sigma_\xi(x)$ is affine in x.

7.5.4. Risk-Neutral Affine Diffusions with Nonlinear Data-Generating Process

In all setups considered so far, x is an affine diffusion under both probability measures Q and Q*. As noted before, there is no reason for x to be an affine diffusion under Q, at least not for pricing bonds. Duarte (2004) considers this case by specifying

$$\begin{aligned} \sigma_\xi(x) &= q_0 + q_1^\top s(x) \\ \sigma_x(x) &= s(x) = \mathrm{diag}\left(\sqrt{x}\right) \end{aligned}$$

$q_0 \in \mathbb{R}$ and $q_1 \in \mathbb{R}^N$, and a vector x of square-root processes under Q*. The data-generating process for x is no longer affine because the drift under Q depends on $\sqrt{x}$ and x. Again, switching signs in expected returns are generated through the matrix q_1.

[11] Constantinides (1992) is an early solution to the problem of switching signs within a quadratic term structure model. In his model, the short rate is quadratic in Gaussian state variables x. The model does not collapse to an affine model because the drift of $r = x^2$ depends on both $\sqrt{r}$ and r.

7.5.5. More on Nonlinearities

The statistical discussion about nonlinearities in the term structure literature has much to do with the macroeconomic discussion about the policy rule of the Federal Reserve. I postpone policy rules to Section 8.1 and regime switching models to Section 7.8 and discuss the purely statistical evidence here. Aït-Sahalia (1996), Stanton (1997), and Conley et al. (1997) present considerable evidence against affine conditional first moments of short-term interest rates for univariate settings. Ghysels and Ng (1998) and Boudoukh et al. (1999) also find such evidence for two-factor models. The main empirical pattern found in these papers is that the speed of mean reversion seems to be higher when the short rate is far away from its mean. The pattern may, however, be due to small sample biases. Chapman and Pearson (2000) argue that empirical evidence about what happens in the tails of the distribution, far away from the mean, is necessarily based on few data points. Moreover, they simulate short-rate data under the null of an affine conditional mean and find nonlinearities in the mean using the nonparametric estimators of Aït-Sahalia (1996) and Stanton (1997). Some of these observations may also be due to seasonal measurement error. Large spikes in short rates occur on certain calendar days, such as at the end of calendar years. The verdict is still out on whether there are nonlinearities in conditional means and, more importantly, whether they matter for long-term bond yields.

7.6. Unconditional Second Moments (Vol Curve)

The volatility curve or "vol curve" is the standard deviation of yield changes ΔY_t. Figure 12.6 plots the volatility curve for the Fama–Bliss data during the Greenspan era (1987:8–now). During this time period, the curve is "snake-shaped": high for short maturities (< 6 months), low at 6 months, then increasing with a peak at intermediate maturities around 2–4 years, and then again decreasing. The "back" of the snake, or hump, in volatility for intermediate maturities can also be found in swap data or Treasury yield data over this period. The "head" of the snake in Fig. 12.6 comes from the 1- and 2-month yields from the Fama tapes which may not be reliable. Data on the federal funds rate, short-term repo, and LIBOR rates, however, confirms the overall picture. The snake is documented in Piazzesi (2001). Over different time periods, the volatility curve looks different. Although the volatility of short-term interest rates is always high, the hump at 2–4 years disappears, e.g., during the monetary experiment of the early 1980s.

The modeling key to the back of the snake, the hump in volatility, is correlation between factors. For example, the multifactor CIR model based on independent square-root processes is unable to generate the hump in volatility. A stochastic mean model can generate the hump. Intuitively, the shocks to the stochastic mean do not affect the short rate directly and therefore only affect the volatility of longer-term yields. To match the hump quantitatively, negative correlation between the Brownian motion of the short-rate and the stochastic mean seems to be needed. Dai and Singleton (2000) document this

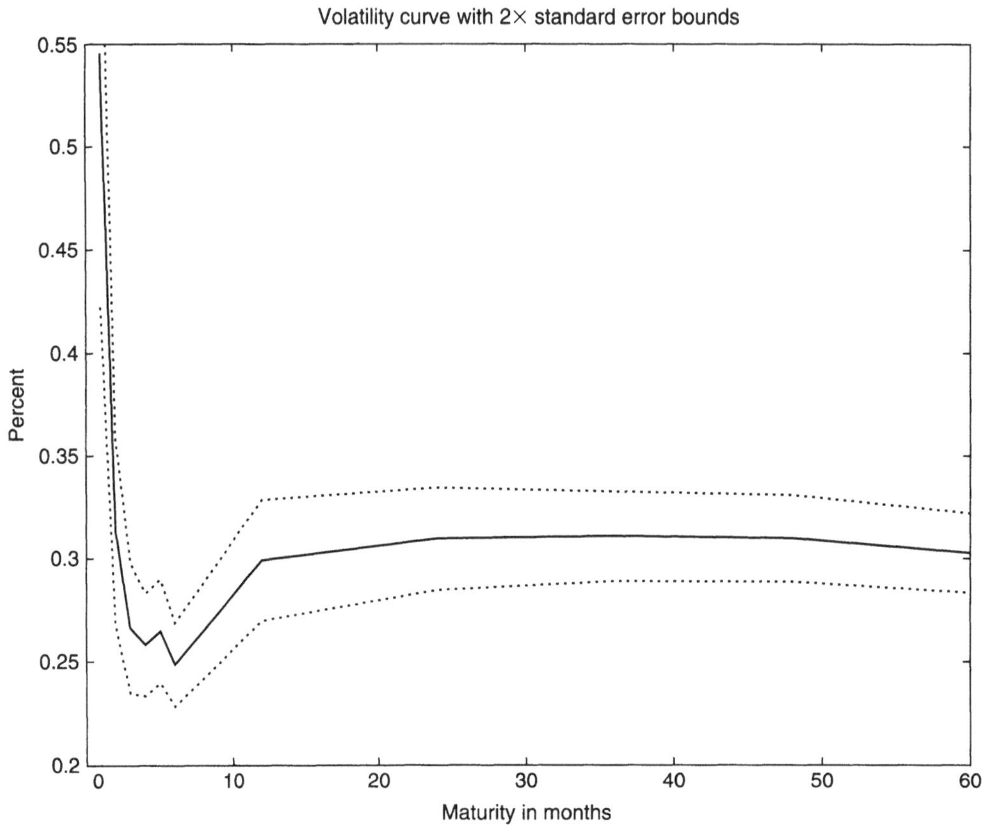

Figure 12.6 The volatility curve is the standard deviation of yield changes. Yields are from the Fama tapes, 1987:8–2003:12.

finding within their three-factor setup. More evidence on the importance of negative correlation between factors is given in Duffie and Singleton (1997). In their two-factor CIR model, the two model-implied factors turn out to be negatively correlated. The correlation coefficient of the factors is -0.5 when they are inverted from yield data. The correlation is thus far from zero, which is what the theoretical model assumes.

The back of the snake can be linked to *policy inertia* by the Federal Reserve, defined as positive autocorrelation in target-rate changes. This positive autocorrelation is induced by the Fed's tendency to moves its policy rate, the Fed funds target rate, in a series of small steps. Piazzesi (2001) builds an affine model with interest-rate targeting by the Fed in which policy inertia generates the back of the snake for the period after 1994. The different look of the snake over different subperiods may be explained by the varying degree of policy inertia under different Fed chairmen. The head of the snake is money market noise: short-lived deviations of the short rate from the target rate.

7.7. Conditional Second Moments (Stochastic Vol)

To gather some evidence about conditional second moments of yields, I estimate a VAR of all 11 Fama–Bliss yields (with maturities of 1–6 months and 1–5 years) and compute the squared residuals from this VAR. Figure 12.7 plots the time series of these squared VAR-residuals for the 1-year yield (together with the 1-year yield itself). Several stylized facts about volatility become clear from this figure. First, volatility varies over time. In particular, time-varying volatility is really about two episodes: the oil price shock in 1974 and the monetary experiment in 1979–1982. Any volatility study therefore has to decide first on how to treat these two episodes. The choice already starts with the data set. For example, studies with swap yields are completely silent about these episodes because swaps only started trading at the end of the 1980s. Stationary $A_0(N)$-models of the Vasicek-type are obviously unable to match the volatility experience of the entire sample, but Fig. 12.7 suggests that a model with two regimes–high volatility and low volatility–may be enough. Another possibility is that the world is not stationary, and these "regimes" are really structural breaks. To just describe the experience of the most recent years, constant volatility models may then be enough. More evidence on this "return to normality" is given in the next section in terms of higher-order moments.

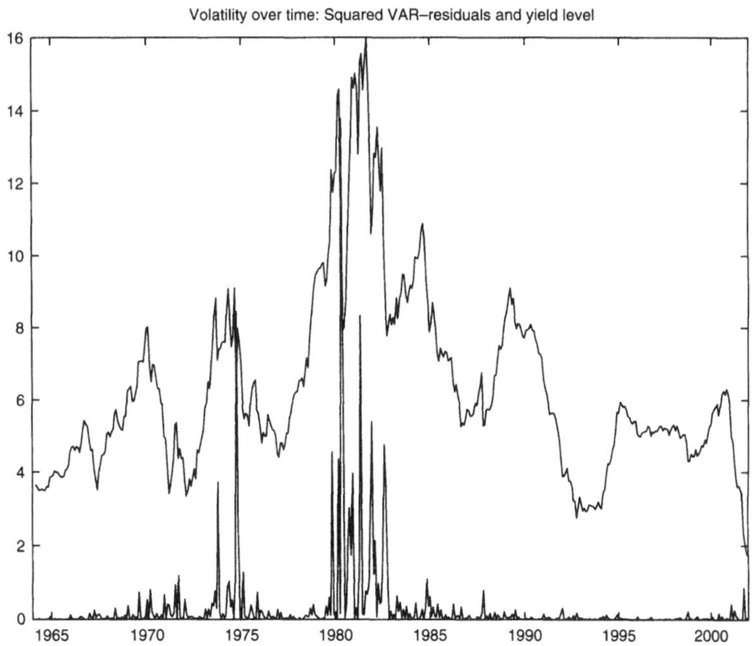

Figure 12.7 The figure plots the 1-year Fama–Bliss yield together with the squared residuals for the 1 year yield estimated from a VAR with all 11 Fama–Bliss yields (with maturities 1–6 months and 1–5 years). The squared residuals are on the bottom of the graph.

Table 12.5 Properties of squared VAR-residuals

Maturity	1	3	6	12	24	36	48	60
Regression of squared residuals on yield level								
Slope	0.17	0.15	0.15	0.13	0.09	0.07	0.05	0.05
Standard errors	0.03	0.02	0.02	0.02	0.01	0.01	0.01	0.01
R^2	0.10	0.12	0.15	0.14	0.12	0.11	0.11	0.11
Autocorrelations of squared residuals								
Autocorrelation	0.27	0.37	0.40	0.27	0.25	0.15	0.16	0.12
Standard errors	0.05	0.10	0.12	0.10	0.10	0.07	0.07	0.07

Squared residuals come form a VAR with one lag using all 11 Fama–Bliss yields (1–6 months, 1–5 years). Slope is the slope coefficient from the regression of squared VAR-residuals for yield i on a constant and the level of yield i. Standard errors for the slope coefficients are standard OLS standard errors. R^2 is the R^2 from this regression. Autocorrelation is the first-order autocorrelation of squaredVAR-residuals together with Newey–West standard errors computed with six lags. All these standard errors ignore sampling noise from the VAR. The yield data is from the Fama tapes of CRSP for 1964:1–2001:12.

Second, volatility is positively correlated with the level of interest rates. This becomes clear from eyeballing the years 1974 and 1979–1982 in Fig. 12.7. More precise evidence is given in the "slope"-row of Table 12.5, which computes the slope coefficient of regressing the VAR-squared residuals of any given yield on the level of the same yield. The slope coefficient is positive for all squared residuals and significant for most (at least judging from OLS-standard errors which are not adjusted for the two-step estimation procedure). The positive correlation between volatility and yield levels motivated the square-root specification for the short rate in the CIR model and later multifactor models such as the model by Longstaff and Schwartz (1992) or Chen (1996), which feature volatility as one of their factors. The residuals from the regression of the squared residuals in Fig. 12.7 on all Fama–Bliss yields still show spikes in 1974 and 1979–1982. In other words, yield levels only explain some of the time-variation in volatility. This can also be seen from the R^2 in Table 12.5, which range from 10 to 15%.

Third, volatility is autocorrelated. Table 12.5 computes the autocorrelation of the squared VAR-residuals for all maturities. The autocorrelation is positive and significant for all maturities but the 5-year yield (again, standard errors ignore the VAR-step of the estimation).

Stochastic volatility is a feature of the data that standard affine models may have problems to match. The problem arises because volatility plays two roles in affine models. One role is to match the time-series properties of the short rate. Volatility can in fact be computed from the second moment of some short-rate proxy. For example, Chan et al. (1992) do this. Another role of volatility is to match the cross section of yields. Volatility can be inverted from affine yield equations. Brown and Dybvig (1986) and Brown and Schaefer (1994) take this route. There is a natural tension between these two roles in any affine model, and panel data studies of affine models need to deal with this tension.

In practice, the tension arises when the inversion of affine yield-equations leads to negative values for volatility. These negative values make some estimation procedures choke, such as maximum-likelihood, and tricks have to be used to avoid them. For example, Duffie and Singleton (1997) find that it helps to add a constant to the short rate equation in a two-factor CIR model. Other estimation methods are more robust to negative volatility. Efficient method of moments is an example because volatility is only simulated to evaluate the EMM objective function, not inverted from yields. The problem remains, however, of how to interpret parameter estimates that lead to negative model-implied volatility in-sample.

More evidence on this tension is documented by Collin–Dufresne et al. (2009) who estimate $A_1(3)$ models with swap data. Ideally, the stochastic volatility factor in these models should be highly correlated with conditional second moments of the short rate implied by the model. Collin-Dufresne et al. proxy the conditional second moment with a Garch model estimated with the time series of the model-implied short rate. Garch-volatility turns out to be *negatively* correlated with the volatility factor from the affine model.

A way out of this tension is to construct models in which bond markets are incomplete in a way that volatility cannot be inverted from the cross section of bond yields. This is the idea behind the "string models" proposed by Santa-Clara and Sornette (2001), "random field models" by Goldstein (2000) and Kimmel (2001), and "unspanned volatility models" by Collin-Dufresne and Goldstein (2002). Useful results on how affine models are related to such more flexible models of volatility are in De Jong and Santa-Clara (1999) and Collin-Dufresne and Goldstein (2002). Empirical support for these models is given in Longstaff et al. (2001) who compare option prices computed from standard affine models with those from string models and find that affine models underprice options. Also, Collin-Dufresne and Goldstein (2002) regress returns on straddles on swap yield changes for different countries and find low R^2s, whereas affine models would predict R^2s of 1. Straddles are portfolios of caps and floors, which are particularly sensitive to volatility.

When volatility is not invertible from the cross section of bond yields, it is truly latent when only information about bond yields is used in the estimation. Collin–Dufresne et al. (2009) therefore use Bayesian methods to estimate their model. Brandt and Sasta-clara (1999) make volatility an observable factor by using data on at-the-money options.

7.8. Higher-Order Moments (Jumps and Regimes)

Yields are not normally distributed over the sample 1964:1–2001:12. If they were, then yield changes would have to be normally distributed as well. Table 12.6 computes the

Table 12.6 Higher-order moments of yield changes

Maturity	1	3	6	12	24	36	48	60
				Skewness				
Full sample	−1.00	−1.35	−1.51	−1.01	−0.68	−0.11	−0.16	−0.26
Standard error	(0.80)	(0.61)	(0.80)	(0.69)	(0.57)	(0.39)	(0.31)	(0.30)
1990s	−0.18	−0.88	−0.60	−0.05	0.05	0.19	0.19	0.13
Standard error	(0.39)	(0.32)	(0.29)	(0.26)	(0.18)	(0.16)	(0.16)	(0.17)
				Kurtosis				
Full sample	14.34	13.92	16.93	15.38	11.90	9.16	7.07	6.84
Standard error	(4.48)	(3.10)	(5.24)	(4.78)	(3.15)	(2.71)	(1.22)	(1.25)
1990s	5.31	5.47	4.56	3.59	2.73	2.64	2.68	2.72
Standard error	(0.72)	(1.08)	(0.74)	(0.37)	(0.24)	(0.23)	(0.26)	(0.26)

Skewness is $m_3/m_2^{3/2}$ and kurtosis is m_4/m_2^2, where m_i is the ith central moment of yield changes. Full sample computes the statistic over the entire sample 1964:1–2001:12, whereas 1990s uses the subsample 1990:1–2001:12. Standard errors (in brackets) are computed using GMM with six Newey–West lags. The yield data is from the Fama tapes of CRSP for 1964:1–2001:12. Maturities are in months.

skewness and kurtosis of yield changes. Benchmark normal distributions are symmetric around the mean so that their skewness is 0. Their kurtosis is 3, anything beyond that is called excess kurtosis. The distribution of yield changes shows negative skewness. This means that the distribution of yield changes is skewed to the left. (The distribution has a long thin left tail, whereas most of the probability mass is around and above the mean.) The evidence for skewness is weak, however, because GMM-standard errors around the estimates are large. The distribution of yield changes shows clear excess kurtosis, however, which means that its tails are heavier compared to the normal distribution.

Recently, yields seem to have become "more Gaussian." Table 12.6 also computes the skewness and kurtosis of yield changes for the subsample 1990:1–2001:12. The difference is striking. There seems to be only weak evidence against normality during the last 10 years. The squared residuals in Fig. 12.7 during this period are, in fact, barely visible to the eye. Have yields "returned to normal"?

Affine models offer two ways to capture fat tails: stochastic volatility and jumps. Das (2002) and Johannes (2004) estimate short-rate models with jumps. The nonparametric method by Johannes implies jump arrival rates in-sample that place high probability on jumps occurring at scheduled macroeconomic news releases (which are discussed in the next subsection).

Regime switching models also generate nonnormal distributions and are consistent with evidence on nonlinearities in conditional first moments. In general, these models are outside the affine class (Ang and Bekaert, 2002; Bansal and Zhou, 2002;

Gray, 1996; Hamilton, 1994, Chapter 22; Veronesi and Yared, 2000). For some special cases, affine solutions can be still be obtained (Ang and Bekaert, 2008; Landen, 2000). Estimated regime switching models tend to find two regimes: a high-persistence low-volatility regime and a low-persistence high-volatility regime. This finding is intuitive from Fig. 12.7, which suggests that we are in the high-persistence low-volatility regime most of the time, with the exception of the oil price shock and the monetary policy experiment.

7.9. Seasonalities (Settlement Wednesdays and Macro Releases)

Fleming and Remolona (1997), Furfine (2001), and Johannes (2004) go back to see whether the largest yield-movements over a given time period coincide with certain events. Fleming and Remolona (1999) and Furfine (2001) use 5-minute price changes in the 5-year Treasury note, whereas Johannes (2004) uses daily data on the 3-month T-Bill rate. Table 12.7 summarizes the findings of these three studies. The results show that most large yield-movements happen around employment releases and Federal Reserve policy rate moves. The bulk of these events is scheduled announcements. Only few happen at random times, such as the outbreak of the Gulf war which coincides with one of the 10 largest yield movements in the Johannes sample. More evidence on seasonalities around macroeconomic news releases is documented in Jones et al. (1996), Fleming and Remolona (1997), Balduzzi et al. (2001), and Li and Engle (2000).

When large yield movements at macroeconomic news releases are modeled as jumps, the timing of these jumps is deterministic. Piazzesi (2001) builds an affine model with deterministic jump times and state-dependent jump size distributions to be able to impose the release calendar on the estimation.

Another type of seasonality is documented in Hamilton (1996). Large spikes in the federal funds rate occur on so-called "settlement Wednesdays," which mark the end of the biweekly reserve maintenance period. Less pronounced spikes on these days can also be found in other short-term interest rates, such as overnight LIBOR or repos (Piazzesi, 2001). An estimation with data on these very short rates therefore needs to carefully take into account these seasonalities. High-frequency studies of the effects of monetary policy are especially affected by these seasonalities because most target moves happen around settlement Wednesdays.

7.10. Fitting Errors at the Short End

When affine models are estimated with panel data, the fit at the very short end of the yield curve often turns out to bad. One of the reasons is that estimations typically do not use any data on extremely short yields. Indeed, seasonalities and other microstructure noise would make such an estimation difficult, as mentioned in the previous section. Piazzesi (2001) and He (2001) argue that the Federal Reserve target rate can serve as a "clean" short rate that helps in fitting the short end. These papers use the target rate

Table 12.7 Largest moves in bond yields

Daily data on 3-month T-Bill, January 1991–December 1993		
1.	January 2, 1992	Fed policy rate
2.	December 20, 1991	Fed policy rate
3.	September 4, 1992	Employment
4.	April 9, 1992	Large Japanese market decline
5.	February 1, 1991	Employment, Fed policy rate
5-minute data on 5-year T-note, August 1993–August 1994		
1.	August 5, 1994	Employment
2.	May 6, 1994	Employment
3.	July 8, 1994	Employment
4.	April 1, 1994	Employment
5.	July 29, 1994	GDP
5-minute data on 5-year T-note, January 1999–December 1999		
1.	June 30, 1999	Fed policy rate
2.	May 5, 1999	Employment
3.	September 3, 1999	Employment
4.	May 14, 1999	Consumer price index
5.	August 6, 1999	Employment

The three panels show the five largest bond-yield moves in their subsample. The first column indicates the rank of the move, the second column gives the date of the move, and the third column indicates what happened during the move. The amount of the move is not available for the top panel, so it is not included here. The top panel combines information from Table 4 and Figure 5 in Johannes (2004). The middle panel is from Table 3 in Fleming and Remolona (1999). The lower panel is from Table 1 in Furfine (2001).

to pin down the short end of the swap curve. Another reason for the poor fit is that it seems like more than three factors are needed to capture the short end of the yield curve. Evidence of the need of a fourth factor is in Knez et al. (1994), Longstaff et al. (2001), and Piazzesi (2001).

8. JOINT SYSTEM WITH OTHER MACROECONOMIC VARIABLES

Macroeconomics often views the Federal Reserve as setting the short end of the nominal yield curve. Many issues that are being debated in the term structure literature–such as persistence, predictability, nonlinearities, and structural breaks in short yields–are therefore also being debated in monetary economics. Section 8.1 links some of these discussion points. Yields have much to do with other macroeconomic variables. Inflation in Section 8.2 and the other macro variables in Section 8.3 may teach us something about yields.

8.1. Monetary Policy

Most central banks in industrialized countries target some overnight interbank lending rate. The Federal Reserve does so by fixing a target rate for the funds rate, which is implemented by the New York Fed using open market operations. The way the Fed sets the target is usually described with policy rules, which are maps from macro variables to the target. According to the Taylor rule, e.g., the Fed sets the target in response to inflation and the output gap. Policy rules are structural equations, which can be identified in several ways (for a survey, see Christiano et al., 1999). The identification scheme proposed by Christiano et al. boils down to taking conditional expectations. The literature on structural breaks in policy rules and interest-rate smoothing by the Fed is thus intimately related to the statistical discussion about short-rate dynamics. Monetary policy regimes are usually associated with Fed chairmen. An example is the 1979–1982 monetary experiment under Paul Volcker. During this time period, the Fed stopped targeting short-term interest rates and started targeting nonborrowed reserves instead. The economy underwent two recessions during this 3-year experiment, but eventually inflation was under control. When policy rules are estimated over different regimes, coefficient estimates are very different. Cogley and Sargent (2001, 2002) address this issue with a random-coefficients model. Sims (1999) and Sims and Zha (2002) argue that what looks like nonlinearities and structural breaks in policy rules may be due to time-varying second moments.

Knowledge about the operations procedures of the Fed can be used for yield-curve modeling. The model proposed by Piazzesi (2001) explicitly uses the meeting calendar of the Fed to determine the short end of the yield curve. The Fed meets eight times per year and changes its target-short rate mostly at meetings since 1994. The market short rate fluctuates around the target. Between meetings, the short rate is thus likely to stay close to the old target level. The target is constant for long periods of time, which can be captured with counting processes for up and down moves. The yield-curve model predicts, e.g., the reaction of yields to monetary policy surprises, defined as the difference between the actual target and the Fed's policy rule. The reaction of yields to these surprises turns out to be large. Cochrane and Piazzesi (2005) confirm this finding in a setting that does not impose no-arbitrage. Traditional studies in which the Fed only reacts to macroeconomic variables tend to find small reactions of yields to policy shocks (Evans and Marshall, 1998, 2001). In fact, the policy rule estimated with the yield-curve model captures Fed behavior better compared to traditional rules based exclusively on macro variables. The estimated rule features both interest rate smoothing (autocorrelation in levels) and policy inertia (autocorrelation in changes).

Mankiw and Miron (1986) find that short-rate movements have become much less predictable since the creation of the Fed in 1914. The reason is that the Fed smoothes short rates (increases their autocorrelation in levels), which makes changes in the short rate unpredictable. Mankiw and Miron conclude that rejections of the EH may be due to the Fed-induced random walk character of interest rates. This idea can be used to construct a term structure model by estimating the short rate and then computing long yields with the EH (Balduzzi et al., 1996). This explanation may be consistent with the fact that the persistence of short rates seems to have increased in the 1990s (Watson, 1999), a decade during which the EH has failed spectacularly.

Yield-curve models that incorporate interest-rate targeting by the Fed can be used to learn about policy rules. For example, the reaction of yields to macroeconomic surprises, such as nonfarm payroll numbers, seems to be hump-shaped with peaks around 2–3 years. This evidence is not consistent with a yield-curve model in which the Federal Reserve reacts to current macro variables (Piazzesi, 2001). The reason is that macroeconomic release surprises, measured as the difference between actual released number and analyst forecasts, do not seem to forecast future macroeconomic variables. Because future employment numbers are unaffected by the surprise, the Fed is likely not move the short rate in the future. This implies that long yields should not be reacting to release surprises–but they do. The Fed thus seems to react to some moving average of past release surprises instead of current macro variables.

Central banks in other countries use different operational procedures. For example, the Bundesbank used to make its policy decisions at bi-weekly meetings without announcing an official target. Yield-curve models can then be used to learn about the latent target (Piazzesi, 2002).

8.2. Inflation

Central banks need to decompose nominal yields into expected inflation, risk premia, and real yields (which are yields on real bonds, see Section 4 for definitions). The policy response to high expected inflation is much different from the response to high real yields, while both situations are characterized by high nominal yields. Holders of nominal bonds worry about future inflation because that is what determines the real value of the principal payment at the maturity date. This implies that expected inflation should matter for at least the determination of nominal yields. Expected inflation may also matter for real yields in a world in which money is not neutral.

Fama (1990) documents that the correlation between expected inflation and state variables that drive the real yield curve is negative, at least for horizons up to 1 year. More precisely, he defines the real rate as the difference between the nominal 1-year yield and actual inflation over 1 year. The negative correlation is between the expected real short rate and the expected inflation. Expected values are measured by the fitted values from regressions of actual inflation and the real short rate on a particular yield spread, the difference between the 5-year and the 1-year yield. The finding is that regression coefficients have opposite signs so that high yield spreads forecast higher inflation and lower real rates. For horizons up to 1 year, the signs of these forecasts cancel each other such that the yield spread does not forecast changes in the nominal rate. The R^2 from these forecasts are around 20% for inflation and about half that for the real rate. For horizons beyond 1 year, the yield spread only predicts inflation and not the real short rate. The R^2 from the real-rate forecasts decrease fast with horizon, whereas the R^2 from the inflation forecasts stay high for several years. This means that yield spreads are able to predict changes in the nominal short rate for longer horizons.

Barr and Campbell (1997) and Campbell and Viceira (2001) also find negative correlation using affine two-factor models. Expected inflation and the actual real short rate are Gaussian, and market prices of risk are constant. Expected excess returns on all bonds, real and nominal, are therefore constant. The model for the real yield curve is a one-factor Vasicek model, whereas the nominal yield-curve is a two-factor Vasicek model. Nominal yields in this model can thus become negative with positive probability. Expected inflation and the real rate are inherently latent variables, which are estimated using Kalman filtering with McCulloch–Kwon zero-coupon yield data and CPI inflation. All yields are assumed to be observed with error. Buraschi and Jilsov (2005) also find negative correlation with a three-factor model. Finally, Barr and Campbell (1997) and Campbell and Shiller (1991) find the same result with U.K. data on indexed bonds.

During the monetary experiment, inflation was high and the Fed under Volcker increased nominal short rates dramatically. This fight against inflation was successful in the sense that the estimated yield-curve model by Campbell and Viceira (2001) shows that expected inflation has been much less variable since 1983. Real rates, however, have become more variable. This is also reflected in the persistence of these variables since 1983. Although expected inflation appears to have a unit root over the whole postwar period and shocks to the real short rate have a half-life of five quarters, these results are almost reversed for the subperiod after 1983. Expected inflation has become much less persistent, with shocks to expected inflation having half-life of only five quarters. Shocks to the real short rate now have a half-life of 12 years!

8.3. Other Macroeconomic Variables

Ang and Piazzesi (2003) address whether macro variables add to our understanding of yields by looking at out-of-sample forecasts of yields. The forecasts are computed using a discrete-time Gaussian yield-curve model with macro variables as observable factors. Discrete time makes it easy to incorporate higher-order autoregressive lags that are often needed to capture the dynamics of macroeconomic variables. Longer lags can be incoporated simply by expanding the state space. Hansen and Sargent (1991) discuss how to do this in continuous time. Market prices of risk in the model are affine in the Gaussian state variables. The estimation uses data on various inflation measures and real activity measures. The authors find that yield-curve models with macro variables turn out to do better in out-of-sample forecasting. Ang et al. (2006) estimate a three-factor model based on a short rate, term spread, and GDP growth. Their model completely characterizes the predictive regressions of GDP growth over different horizons and different term spreads on the right-hand side. Their model recommends the use of the short rate instead of any term spread for forecasting growth. This finding is in contrast to unrestricted OLS regressions and is confirmed in out-of-sample forecasts. Intuitively, arbitrage-free pricing imposes restrictions that improve the efficiency of parameter estimates. This gain in efficiency leads to vastly different point estimates in the case of forecasting GDP growth, even though the yield-curve parameters are well within confidence bounds of the corresponding OLS regression. A lot more research is needed in this area.

ACKNOWLEDGMENTS

I am indebted to Pedro Santa-Clara and Martin Schneider for many helpful discussions. I would also like to thank participants at the "Handbook of Financial Econometrics Conference" in November 2001 at Princeton and David Chapman, Pierre Collin-Dufresne, Mike Johannes, Bob Kimmel, Luis-Fernando Mejia, Antonio Mele, Bruno Miranda, Juha Seppala, Selale Tuzel, and two anonymous referees for helpful comments.

REFERENCES

Ahn, Dong-Hyun, Robert Dittmar, and Gallant A. Ronald (2002) "Quadratic term structure models: Theory and evidence." *Review of Financial Studies* 15, 243–288.

Aït-Sahalia, Yacine (1996) "Testing continuous-time models of the spot interest rate." *Review of Financial Studies* 9, 385–426.

Aït-Sahalia, Yacine (2001) "Maximum likelihood estimation of discretely sampled diffusions: A closed form approximation approach." *Econometrica* 70, 223–262.

Aït-Sahalia, Yacine (2008) "Closed-form likelihood expansions for multivariate diffusions." *Annals of Statistics* 36, 906–937.

Aït-Sahalia, Yacine, Lars Peter Hansen, and Jose A. Scheinkman (2010) "Discretely sampled diffusions." In: Yacine Aït Sahalia and Lars Peter Hansen, eds. *Handbook of Financial Econometrics*, Amsterdam: North-Holland (forthcoming).

Alvarez, Fernando and Pablo Andres Neumeyer (1999) "Constructing historical time and maturity dependent yield spreads for emerging country sovereign debt." Working Paper, University of Chicago.

Ang, Andrew and Geert Bekaert (2002) "Regime switches in interest rates." *Journal of Business and Economic Statistics* 20, 163–182.

Ang, Andrew, Geert Bekaert, and Min Wei (2008) "The term structure of real rates and expected inflation." *Journal of Finance* 63, 797–849.

Ang, Andrew and Monika Piazzesi (2003) "A no-arbitrage vector autoregression of term structure dynamics with macroeconomic and latent variables." *Journal of Monetary Economics* 50, 745–787.

Ang, Andrew, Monika Piazzesi, and Min Wei (2006) "What does the yield curve tell us about GDP growth?" *Journal of Econometrics* 131, 359–403.

Angeletos, George-Marios (2002) "Fiscal policy with non-contingent debt and the optimal maturity structure." *Quarterly Journal of Economics* 117, 1105–1131.

Backus, David, Silverio Foresi, Abon Mozumdar, and Liuren Wu (2001) "Predictable changes in yields and forward rates." *Journal of Financial Economics* 59, 281–311.

Backus, David, Silverio Foresi, and Chris Telmer (2000) "Discrete-time models of bond pricing." In: Narasimhan Jegadeesh and Bruce Tuckman, eds. *Advanced Fixed Income Valuation Tools,* New York: Wiley.

Backus, David, Allan W. Gregory, and Stan E. Zin (1989) "Risk premiums in the term structure: Evidence from artificial economies." *Journal of Monetary Economics* 24, 371–399.

Balduzzi, Pierluigi, Giuseppe Bertola and Silverio Foresi (1996) "A model of target changes and the term structure of interest rates." *Journal of Monetary Economics* 39, 223–249.

Balduzzi, Pierluigi, Sanjiv R. Das, and Silverio Foresi (1998) "The central tendency: A second factor in bond yields." *Review of Economics and Statistics* 80, 62–72.

Balduzzi, Pierluigi, Sanjiv R. Das, Silverio Foresi, and Rangarajan K. Sundaram (1996) "A simple approach to three factor affine term structure models." *Journal of Fixed Income* 6, 43–53.

Balduzzi, Pierluigi, Edwin J. Elton, and Green T. Clifton (2001) "Economic news and the yield curve: Evidence from the U.S. Treasury market." *Journal of Financial and Quantitative Analysis* 36, 523–543.

Bakshi, Gurdip S. and Zhiwu Chen (1996) "Inflation, asset prices, and the term structure of interest rates in monetary economies." *Review of Financial Studies* 9, 241–275.

Bakshi, Gurdip S. and Zhiwu Chen (1997) "An alternative valuation model for contingent claims." *Journal of Financial Economics* 44, 123–165.

Bansal, Ravi and Hui Zhou (2002) "Term structure of interest rates with regime shifts." *Journal of Finance* 57, 1997–2043.

Barr, David G. and John Y. Campbell (1997) "Inflation, real interest rates, and the bond market: A study of UK nominal and index-linked government bond prices." *Journal of Monetary Economics* 39, 361–383.

Bekaert, Geert and Steven R. Grenadier (2000) "Stock and bond pricing in an affine economy." Working Paper, Columbia Business School.

Bekaert, Geert and Robert Hodrick (2001) "Expectations hypothesis tests." *Journal of Finance* 56, 115–138.

Bekaert, Geert, Robert Hodrick, and David Marshall (1997) "On biases in tests of the expectations hypothesis of the term structure of interest rates." *Journal of Financial Economics* 44, 309–348.

Bekaert, Geert, Min Wei, and Yuhang Xing (2007) "Uncovered interest rate parity and the term structure." *Journal of International Money and Finance*, 26, 1038–1069.

Bliss, Robert (1999) "Fitting term structures to bond prices." Working Paper, Chicago Fed.

Boudoukh, Jacob, Matthew Richardson, Richard Stanton, and Robert Whitelaw (1999) "The stochastic behavior of interest rates: Implications from a nonlinear continuous-time model." Working Paper, NYU Stern and UC Berkeley.

Brandt, Michael W. and Pedro Santa-Clara (2002) "Simulated likelihood estimation of diffusions with an application to exchange rates dynamics in incomplete markets." *Journal of Financial Economics* 63, 161–210.

Brown, Stephen J. and Philip H. Dybvig (1986) "The empirical implications of the Cox, Ingersoll, and Ross theory of the term structure of interest rates." *Journal of Finance* 41, 617–632.

Brown, Roger H. and Stephen Schaefer (1994) "The term structure of real interest rates and the Cox, Ingersoll, and Ross Model." *Journal of Financial Economics* 35, 3–42.

Buraschi, Andrea and Alexei Jiltsov (2005) "Inflation risk premia and the expectations hypothesis: Taylor monetary policy rules and the Treasury yield curve." *Journal of Financial Economics* 75, 429–490.

Brémaud, Pierre (1981) "*Point processes and queues: Martingale dynamics.*" New York: Springer.

Campbell, John Y. (1986) "A defense of the traditional hypotheses about the term structure of interest rates." *Journal of Finance* 41, 183–193.

Campbell, John Y. and John H. Cochrane (1999) "By force of habit: A consumption-based explanation of aggregate stock market behavior." *Journal of Political Economy* 107, 205–251.

Campbell, John Y., Andrew W. Lo, and MacKinlay A. Craig (1997) "*The Econometrics of Financial Markets.*" Princeton: Princeton University Press.

Campbell, John Y. and Robert Shiller (1991) "Yield spreads and interest rates: A bird's eye view." *Review of Economic Studies* 58, 495–514.

Campbell, John Y. and Luis Viceira (2001) "Who should buy long term bonds?" *American Economic Review* 91, 99–127.

Carrasco, Marine, Mikhail Chernov, Jean-Pierre Florens, and Eric Ghysels (2001) "Estimation of jump-diffusions with a continuum of moment conditions." Working Paper, University of Rochester.

Chacko, George and Luis Viceira (2003) "Spectral GMM estimation of continuous-time processes." *Journal of Econometrics* 116, 259–292.

Chan, K, Andrew Karolyi, Francis Longstaff, and Anthony Sanders (1992) "The volatility of the short-term interest rates: An empirical comparison of alternative models of the term structure of interest rates." *Journal of Finance* 68, 1209–1227.

Chapman, David, John Long, and Neil D. Pearson (1999) "Using proxies for the short rate: When are three months like an instant?" *Review of Financial Studies* 12, 763–806.

Chapman, David (1997) "The cyclical properties of consumption growth and the real term structure." *Journal of Monetary Economics* 39, 145–172.

Chapman, David and Neil D. Pearson (2000) "Is the short rate drift actually nonlinear?" *Journal of Finance* 55, 355–388.

Chapman, David and Neil D. Pearson (2001) "Recent advances in estimating term-structure models." *Financial Analysts Journal*, July/August, 77–95.

Chen, Lin (1996) "*Stochastic Mean and Stochastic Volatility - A Three-factor Model of the Term Structure of Interest Rates and its Application to the Pricing of Interest Rate Derivatives.*" Oxford, UK: Blackwell Publishers.

Chen, Ren-Raw and Louis Scott (1992) "Pricing interest-rate options in a two-factor Cox-Ingersoll-Ross model of the term structure." *Review of Financial Studies* 5, 613–636.

Chen, Ren-Raw and Louis Scott (1993) "Maximum likelihood estimation for a multifactor equilibrium model of the term structure of interest rates." *Journal of Fixed Income* 3, 14–31.

Cheridito, Patrick, Damir Filipovic, and Robert Kimmel (2004) "A note on the canonical representation of affine diffusion processes." Working Paper, Princeton University.

Christiano, Lawrence, Martin Eichenbaum, and Charles Evans (1999) "Monetary policy shocks: What have we learned and to what end?" In: Michael Woodford and John B. Taylor, eds. *Handbook of Macroeconomics*. Amsterdam: North Holland.

Cochrane, John H. (2001) "Long term debt and optimal policy in the fiscal theory of the price level." *Econometrica* 69, 69–116.

Cochrane, John H. and Monika Piazzesi (2002) "The fed and interest rates: A high-frequency identification." *American Economic Review* 92, 90–95.

Cochrane, John H. and Monika Piazzesi (2005) "Bond risk premia." *American Economic Review* 95, 138–160.

Cogley, Timothy and Thomas J. Sargent (2001) "Evolving post-world war II U.S. inflation dynamics." *NBER Macroannual 2001* (forthcoming).

Cogley, Timothy and Thomas J. Sargent (2002) "Drifts and volatilities: Monetary policies and outcomes in the post WWII U.S." Working Paper, Stanford University.

Collin-Dufresne, Pierre and Robert Goldstein (2002) "Do bonds span the fixed-income markets? Theory and evidence for unspanned stochastic volatility." *The Journal of Finance* 57, 1685–1730.

Collin-Dufresne, Pierre, Robert Goldstein, and Christopher Jones (2009) "Can interest rate volatility be extracted from the cross section of bond yields? An investigation of unspanned stochastic volatility." *Journal of Financial Economics* (forthcoming).

Collin-Dufresne, Pierre and Bruno Solnik (2001) "On the term structure of default premia in the swap and LIBOR markets." *Journal of Finance* 56, 1095–1015.

Conley, Tim G., Lars Peter Hansen, Erzo G.J. Luttmer, and Jose A. Scheinkman (1997) "Short-term interest rates as subordinated diffusions." *Review of Financial Studies* 10, 525–577.

Constantinides, George (1992) "A theory of the nominal term structure of interest rates." *Review of Financial Studies* 5, 531–552.

Cox, John C., Jonathan E. Ingersoll, and Stephen A. Ross (1981) "A reexamination of traditional hypotheses about the term structure of interest rates." *Journal of Finance* 36, 321–346.

Cox, John C., Jonathan E. Ingersoll, and Stephen A. Ross (1985) "A theory of the term structure of interest rates." *Econometrica* 53, 385–407.

Dai, Qiang and Kenneth Singleton (2000) "Specification analysis of affine term structure models." *Journal of Finance* 55, 1943–1978.

Dai, Qiang and Kenneth Singleton (2002) "Expectation puzzles, time-varying risk premia, and affine models of the term structure." *Journal of Financial Economics* 63, 415–441.

Darolles, Serge, Christian Gouriéroux, and Joann Jasiak (2001) "Compound autoregressive models." Working Paper, CREST, Paris.

Das, Sanjiv (2002) "The surprise element: Jumps in interest rates." *Journal of Econometrics* 106, 27–65.

Das, Sanjiv and Silverio Foresi (1996) "Exact solutions for bond and option prices with systematic jump risk." *Review of Derivatives Research* 1, 7–24.

De Jong, Frank and Pedro Santa-Clara (1999) "The dynamics of the forward interest rate: A formulation with state variables." *Journal of Financial and Quantitative Analysis* 34, 131–157.

Den Haan, Wouter (1995) "The term structure of interest rates in real and monetary economies." *Journal of Economic Dynamics and Control* 19, 909–940.

Duarte, Jefferson (2004) "Evaluating an alternative risk preference in affine term structure models." *Review of Financial Studies* 17, 370–404.

Duffee, Gregory (1996) "Idiosyncratic variation of Treasury bill yields." *Journal of Finance* 51, 527–552.

Duffee, Gregory (2002) "Term premia and interest rate forecasts in affine models." *Journal of Finance* 57, 405–443.

Duffie, Darrell (2001) "*Dynamic asset pricing theory.*" Third ed. Princeton: Princeton University Press.

Duffie, Darrell, Damir Filipovic, and Walter Schachermayer (2003) "Affine processes and applications in finance." *Annals of Applied Probability* 13, 984–1053.

Duffie, Darrell and Ming Huang (1996) "Swap rates and credit quality." *Journal of Finance* 51, 921–949.

Duffie, Darrell and Rui Kan (1996) "A yield-factor model of interest rates." *Mathematical Finance* 6, 379–406.

Duffie, Darrell, Jun Pan, and Kenneth Singleton (2000) "Transform analysis and asset pricing for affine jump-diffusions." *Econometrica* 68, 1343–1376.

Duffie, Darrell, Lasse Pedersen, and Kenneth Singleton (2003) "Modeling sovereign yield spreads: A case study of Russian debt." *Journal of Finance* 58, 119–159.

Duffie, Darrell and Kenneth Singleton (1997) "An econometric model of the term structure of interest rate swap yields." *Journal of Finance* 52, 1287–1323.

Durham, Garland B. and A. Ronald Gallant (2002) "Numerical techniques for maximum likelihood estimation of continuous time diffusion processes." *Journal of Business and Economic Statistics* (forthcoming).

El Karoui, Nicole, R. Myneni, and R. Viswanathan (1993) "Arbitrage pricing and hedging of interest rate claims with state variables." Working Paper, Université de Paris VI, Laboratoire de Probabilité.

Estrella, Arturo and Gikas A. Hardouvelis (1991) "The term structure as a predictor of real economic activity." *Journal of Finance* 46, 555–576.

Evans, Chales L. and David Marshall (1998) "Monetary policy and the term structure of nominal interest rates: Evidence and theory." *Carnegie-Rochester Conference Series on Public Policy* 49, 53–111.

Evans, Charles L. and David Marshall (2001) "Economic determinants of the term structure of nominal interest rates." Working Paper, Chicago Fed.

Fama, Eugene F. (1990) "Term-structure forecasts of interest rates, inflation, and real returns." *Journal of Monetary Economics* 25, 59–76.

Fama, Eugene F. and Robert R. Bliss (1987) "The information in long-maturity forward rates." *American Economic Review* 77, 680–692.

Farnsworth, Heber and Richard Bass (2001) "The term structure with credible and semi-credible targeting." Working Paper, Washington University in St. Louis.

Favero, Carlo, Francesco Giavazzi, and Luigi Spaventa (1997) "High yields: The spread on German interest rates." *Economic Journal* 107, 663.

Fisher, Mark (1998) "A simple model of the failure of the expectations hypothesis." Working Paper, Federal Reserve Atlanta.

Fisher, Mark and Christian Gilles (1996) "Estimating exponential-affine models of the term structure." Working Paper, Federal Reserve Atlanta.

Fisher, Mark and Christian Gilles (1998) "Around and around: The expectations hypothesis." *Journal of Finance* 53, 365–383.

Fleming, J. Michael and Eli M. Remolona (1997) "What moves the bond market?" *FRBNY Economic Policy Review* December, 31–50.

Fleming, J. Michael and Eli M. Remolona (1999) "The term structure of announcement effects." Working Paper, Federal Reserve Bank of New York.

Furfine, Craig (2001) "Do macroeconomic announcements still drive the Treasury market?" *BIS Quarterly Review*, 49–57.

Gallant, A. Ronald and George Tauchen (2010) "Simulated score methods and indirect inference for continuous-time models." In: Yacine Aït-Sahalia and Lars Peter Hansen, eds. *Handbook of Financial Econometrics*. Amsterdam: North-Holland (forthcoming).

Gerlach, Stefan and Frank Smets (1997) "The term structure of euro-rates: some evidence in support of the expectations hypothesis." *Journal of International Money and Finance* 16, 305–321.

Geweke, John (1996) "Monte Carlo simulation and numerical integration." In: H.M. Amman, D.A. Kendrick and J. Rust, eds. *Handbook of Computational Economics* 13. North-Holland, Amsterdam: Elsevier Science.

Ghysels, Eric and Serena Ng (1998) "A semi-parametric factor model of interest rates and tests of the affine term structure." *Review of Economics and Statistics* 80, 535–548.

Gibbons, Michael R. and Krishna Ramaswamy (1993) "A test of the Cox, Ingersoll and Ross model of the term structure." *Review of Financial Studies* 6, 619–658.

Goldstein, Robert (2000) "The term structure of interest rates as a random field." *Review of Financial Studies* 13, 365–384.

Gong, Frank F. and Eli M. Remolona (1996) "A three-factor econometric model of the U.S. term structure." Working Paper, Federal Reserve Bank of New York.

Gouriéroux, Christian, Alain Monfort, and Vassilis Polimenis (2002) "Affine term structure models." Working Paper, CREST, Paris.

Gouriéroux, Christian and R. Sufana (2004) "A classification of two factor affine diffusion term structure models." Technical report, University of Toronto.

Grinblatt, Mark and Francis Longstaff (2000) "Financial innovation and the role of derivative securities: An empirical analysis of the treasury STRIPS program." *Journal of Finance* 55, 1415–1436.

Hamilton, James D. (1996) "The daily market for federal funds." *Journal of Political Economy* 104, 26–56.

Hamilton, James D. (1994) "*Time Series Analysis*." Princeton, New Jersey: Princeton University Press.

Hamilton, James D. and Dong Kim (2002) "A re-examination of the predictability of the yield spread for real economic activity." *Journal of Money, Credit, and Banking* 34, 340–360.

Hansen, Lars Peter (1982) "Large sample properties of generalized method of moments estimators." *Econometrica* 50, 1029–1054.

Hansen, Lars Peter and Thomas J. Sargent (1991) "Exact linear rational expectations models: Specification and estimation." *Rational Expectations Econometrics*. Oxford: Westview Press.

Hardouvelis, Gikas (1994) "The term structure spread and future changes in long and short rates in the G7 countries: Is there a puzzle?" *Journal of Monetary Economics* 33, 255–283.

Harvey, Campbell R. (1988) "The real term structure and consumption growth." *Journal of Financial Economics* 22, 305–333.

He, Hua (2001) "Modeling term structures of swap spreads." Working Paper, Yale School of Management.

Heston, Steven L. (1991) "Testing continuous time models of the term structure of interest rates." Working Paper, Yale University.

Honoré, Peter (1998) "Maximum likelihood estimation of non-linear continuous-time term-structure models." Working Paper, Aarhus School of Business, Denmark.

Hull, John (2000) "*Options, Futures, and Other Derivatives*," fourth ed. Englewood Cliffs, NJ: Prentice Hall.

Jagannathan, Ravi, Andrew Kaplin, and Steve Guoqiang Sun (2001) "An evaluation of multi-factor CIR models using LIBOR, swap rates, and cap and swaption prices." *NBER Working Paper* 8682.

Jegadeesh, Narasimhan and George G. Pennacchi (1996) "The behavior of interest rates implied by the term structure of Eurodollar futures." *Journal of Money, Credit and Banking* 28, 420–446.

Jensen, Bjarke and Rolf Poulsen (1999) "A comparison of approximation techniques for transition densities of diffusion processes." Working Paper, Aarhus University.

Johannes, Michael (2004) "The economic and statistical role of jumps to interest rates" *Journal of Finance* 59, 227–260.

Jones, Charles M., Owen Lamont, and Robin Lumsdaine (1996) "Macroeconomic news and bond market volatility." *Journal of Financial Economics* 47, 315–337.

Jordan, Bradford D., Randy. D. Jorgensen, and David R. Kuipers (2000) "The relative pricing of U.S. Treasury STRIPS: Empirical evidence." *Journal of Financial Economics* 56, 89–123.

Karatzas, Ioannis and Steven E. Shreve (1988) "*Brownian Motion and Stochastic Calculus.*" Heidelberg: Springer Verlag.

Kimmel, Robert (2001) "Modeling the term structure of interest rates: A new approach." Working Paper, Princeton University.

Knez, Peter, Robert Litterman, and José Scheinkman (1994) "Explorations into factors explaining money market returns." *Journal of Finance* 49, 1861–1882.

Landen, Camilla (2000) "Bond pricing in a hidden Markov model of the short rate." *Finance and Stochastics* 4, 371–389.

Langetieg, Terence C. (1980) "A multivariate model of the term structure." *Journal of Finance* 25, 71–97.

Li, Li and Robert F. Engle (1998) "Macroeconomic announcements and volatility of treasury futures." Working Paper No. 98-27, UC San Diego.

Litterman, Robert and José Scheinkman (1991) "Common factors affecting bond returns." *Journal of Fixed Income* 1, 54–61.

Liu, Jun, Francis Longstaff, and Ravit Mandell (2002) "The market price of credit risk: An empirical analysis of interest rate swap spreads." Working Paper, UCLA.

Lo, Andrew W. (1988) "Maximum likelihood estimation of generalized Ito processes with discretely-sampled data." *Econometric Theory* 4, 231–247.

Longstaff, Francis (1992) "Multiple equilibria and term structure models." *Journal of Financial Economics* 32, 333–344.

Longstaff, Francis (2000a). "Arbitrage and the expectations hypothesis." *Journal of Finance* 55, 989–994.

Longstaff, Francis (2000b). "The term stucture of very short term rates: New evidence for the expectations hypothesis." *Journal of Financial Economics* 58, 397–396.

Longstaff, Francis, Pedro Santa-Clara, and Eduardo Schwartz (2001) "The relative valuation of caps and swaptions: Theory and empirical evidence." *Journal of Finance* 56, 2067–2109.

Longstaff, Francis and Eduardo Schwartz (1992) "Interest rate volatility and the term structure: A two-factor general equilibrium model." *Journal of Finance* 47, 1259–1282.

Longstaff, Francis and Monika Piazzesi (2004) "Corporate earnings and the equity premium." *Journal of Financial Economics* 74, 401–421.

Mamaysky, Harry (2002) "A model for pricing stock and bonds." Working Paper, Yale University.

Mankiw, Gregory N. and Jeffrey A. Miron (1986) "The changing behavior of the term structure of interest rates." *Quarterly Journal of Economics* CI(2), 211–228.

Mardia, Kani V., John T. Kent, and John M. Bibby (1979) "*Multivariate Analysis.*" San Diego: Academic Press.

McCulloch, J. Huston and Heon-Chul Kwon (1993) "U.S. Term structure data, 1947–1991." Working Paper, Ohio State University.

Mishkin, Frederik S. (1990) "What does the term structure tell us about future inflation?" *Journal of Monetary Economics* 25, 77–95.

Missale, Alessandro (1997) "Managing the public debt: The optimal taxation approach." *Journal of Economic Surveys* 11, 235–265.

Naik, Vasant and Moon Hoe Lee (1997) "Yield curve dynamics with discrete shifts in economic regimes: Theory and Estimation." Working Paper, University of British Columbia, Canada.

Nelson, Charles R. and Andrew F. Siegel (1987) "Parsimonious modelling of yield curves." *Journal of Business* 60, 473–489.

Pearson, Neil D. and Tong-Sheng Sun (1994) "Exploiting the conditional density in estimating the term structure: An application to the Cox, Ingersoll and Ross model." *Journal of Finance* 49, 1279–1304.

Pedersen, Asger Roer (1995) "A new approach to maximum likelihood estimation for stochastic differential equations based on discrete observations." *Scandinavian Journal of Statistics* 22, 55–71.

Pennacchi, George G. (1991) "Identifying the dynamics of real interest rates and inflation: Evidence using survey data." *Review of Financial Studies* 4, 53–86.

Piazzesi, Monika (2005) "Bond yields and the Federal Reserve." *Journal of Political Economy* 113, 311–344.

Piazzesi, Monika (2001) "An econometric model of the yield curve with macroeconomic jump effects." *NBER Working Paper* 8246.

Rebelo, Sergio and Danyang Xie (1999) "On the optimality of interest-rate smoothing." *Journal of Monetary Economics* 43, 263–282.

Santa-Clara, Pedro (1995) "Simulated likelihood estimation of diffusions with an application to the short term interest rate." Ph.D. Dissertation, Insead, France.

Santa-Clara, Pedro and Didier Sornette (2001) "The dynamics of the forward interest rate curve with stochastic string shocks." *Review of Financial Studies* 14, 149–185.

Sargent, Thomas J. (1979) "A note on maximum likelihood estimation of the rational expectations model of the term structure." *Journal of Monetary Economics* 5, 133–143.

Sims, Christopher (1999) "Drifts and breaks in monetary policy." Working Paper, Princeton University.

Sims, Christopher and Tao Zha (2002) "Macroeconomic switching." Working Paper, Princeton University.

Stanton, Richard (1997) "A nonparametric model of term structure dynamics and the market price of interest rate risk." *Journal of Finance* 52, 1973–2002.
Singleton, Kenneth (2001) "Estimation of affine asset pricing models using the empirical characteristic function." *Journal of Econometrics* 102, 111–141.
Stock, James and Mark Watson (2003) "Forecasting output and inflation: The role of asset prices." *Journal of Economic Literature* 16, 788–829.
Sun, Tong-Sheng (1992) "Real and nominal interest rates: A discrete-time model and its continuous time limit." *Review of Financial Studies* 5, 581–611.
Telmer Chris and Stan E. Zin (1996) "The yield curve: The terms of endearment or terms of endowment." Working Paper, Carnegie-Mellon University.
Wachter, Jessica (2006) "A consumption-based model of the term structure of interest rates." *Journal of Financial Economics* 79, 365–399.
Watson, Mark (1999) "Explaining the increased variability in long term interest rates." Working Paper, Princeton University.
Wu, Tao (2006) "Macro factors and the affine term structure of interest rates." *Journal of Money, Credit, and Banking* 38(7), 1847–1875.
Vasicek, Oldrich A. (1977) "An equilibrium characterization of the term structure." *Journal of Financial Economics* 5, 177–188.
Veronesi, Pietro and Francis Yared (2000) "Short and long horizon term and inflation risk premia in the U.S. term structure: Evidence from an integrated model for nominal and real bond prices under regime shifts." Working Paper, Chicago GSB.

INDEX

Note: The "(1)" or "(2)" indicates volume number.

E

N

S

T

Kolibri 360 GmbH
Ferdinand-Jühlke-Straße 7
99095 Erfurt, Deutschland
produktsicherheit@kolibri360.de